HANDBOOK OF CONSTRUCTIONIST RESEARCH

Handbook of
CONSTRUCTIONIST
RESEARCH

edited by
James A. Holstein
Jaber F. Gubrium

THE GUILFORD PRESS
New York   London

© 2008 The Guilford Press
A Division of Guilford Publications, Inc.
72 Spring Street, New York, NY 10012
www.guilford.com

Printed in the United States of America

This book is printed on acid-free paper.

Last digit is print number: 9 8 7 6 5 4 3 2 1

Library of Congress Cataloging-in-Publication Data
Handbook of constructionist research / edited by James A. Holstein, Jaber F. Gubrium.
  p. cm.
  Includes bibliographical references and index.
  ISBN-13: 978-1-59385-305-1 (hardcover)
  ISBN-10: 1-59385-305-X (hardcover)
  1. Social psychology—Research. 2. Subjectivity—Research. 3. Social sciences—Philosophy—
Research. 4. Human information processing—Research. I. Holstein, James A. II. Gubrium,
Jaber F.
  HM251.H2233 2008
  302.01—dc22

                                                          2007015395

*The editors chose a work by Wassily Kandinsky for the book's cover. His art was influenced
by the Russian constructivist movement in painting, and they thought the image telling.
As the constructionist mosaic does, the profile sparkles many directions, befitting the themes
and variations of its endeavors.*

Preface

Constructionist research in the early 21st century finds itself both riding high and under assault. To be sure, there is no shortage of constructionist work being published in the social sciences. Indeed, sometimes it seems that everyone is a social constructionist. As philosopher Ian Hacking wryly notes in his widely read 1999 book, *The Social Construction of What?*, it is nearly impossible to find something that has not been called a social construction. The recent proclivity for such pronouncements has thrust constructionism squarely into the science and culture "wars." The outcomes have not always been pretty. Many have reviled constructionism for its rampant relativism and faddishness. If the approach is currently popular, it also has plenty of impassioned detractors.

The *Handbook of Constructionist Research* enters the cacophony surrounding the approach from a decidedly more affirmative position than Hacking's detached critique. We have chosen the term *mosaic* to characterize the diversity of the constructionist enterprise and also to suggest that it is possible to find meaningful coherence in the variety. We have called on some of the very best and brightest of constructionist researchers across a variety of disciplines to make the case.

The authors in this volume represent the empirical forefront of the constructionist movement in the social sciences. More important, perhaps, they have fashioned their research self-consciously, considering the epistemological, ontological, methodological, and disciplinary grounds and implications of their work. They have remained mindful of the space their empirical work occupies in the more abstract, conceptual arena of constructionist dialogue. Indeed, many of the contributors have been at the center of constructionist debates for decades. Their commentary on the constructionist mosaic is assuredly state of the art.

The *Handbook* is a scholarly reference book; its intended audience includes academics, practicing researchers, and graduate students who are interested in how, and to what ends, research is conducted in a constructionist vein. In addition, the volume is explicitly thematic, with a clear emphasis on the variety of conceptual stances within constructionism and their relationships to methodological choices and technical applications. Many in the audience for this book are college and university instructors. Time and again, they are faced with the need to present the broad parameters of a topic, and they often have to dredge through endless texts and countless journals. This handbook solves this problem by presenting, under one cover, the general contours of constructionism as an empirical enterprise. It offers a compendium of substantive information, with particular chapters presenting overviews of the state of knowledge in their particular areas. But it also offers conceptual and methodological commentary, providing instructors and readers alike with the intellectual scaffolding on which to hang this information.

The *Handbook* also serves graduate students with pedagogical and intellectual needs of their own. The editors and contributors recognize that researchers are trained and develop skills primarily in graduate seminars and through concrete empirical exercises. Accordingly, the volume keeps this contingent of the audience in view. Each chapter strives not only to deal with its particular topic but also to cover related conceptual, empirical, and methodological waterfronts in the process. Each of the chapters sets the scene, as it were, before it delves into research particulars, providing those in training with the broader context of the issues under consideration.

Doctoral dissertations typically contain the obligatory chapters in which the writer demonstrates his or her command of the methodological and conceptual underpinnings of the research being pursued. The *Handbook* will be a valuable resource to dissertation writers for parsing the distinctions, procedural nuances, and overall sources of agreement and debate in the area.

Finally, the volume addresses the working researcher who may or may not practice his or her craft in colleges or universities. This part of the audience includes applied researchers and grant writers. Literature reviews and citation practices in this quarter require useful knowledge and the demonstration of up-to-the-minute expertise. Grant writers especially need ready access to issues and information in the areas in which they are seeking funds. This volume provides this expert informational content, featuring the primary debates and controversies as they play out in historical and contemporary research contexts.

*   *   *

We have many individuals to acknowledge for the help and the support we have received in assembling this handbook. First, of course, we thank the contributors for their superb work in crafting insightful and informative chapters. We also thank members of our International Advisory Board and the many colleagues who reviewed and commented on drafts of chapters. Finally, we offer a very warm thanks to the staff at The Guilford Press and, especially, to our editor, C. Deborah Laughton. It is the greatest pleasure to work with Ms. Laughton, whose consummate professionalism, unflagging enthusiasm, and tireless support make our partnership a real joy.

Contents

Part VI. Continuing Challenges

INTRODUCTION

CHAPTER 1

The Constructionist Mosaic

● **Jaber F. Gubrium**
  James A. Holstein

The term *constructionism* has reverberated across the social sciences since the 1960s. From the start, constructionist research has highlighted both the dynamic contours of social reality and the processes by which social reality is put together and assigned meaning. The leading idea always has been that the world we live in and our place in it are not simply and evidently "there" for participants. Rather, participants actively construct the world of everyday life and its constituent elements. Grounded on this principle, constructionism has become an intellectual movement whose empirical insights are widely recognized.

As promising and vibrant as the movement might be, it is also under fire on several fronts. Heated debates have erupted on nearly every disciplinary terrain. Con-structionism has been called radical and conservative; liberating, managerial, and oppressive; relativist, revisionist, and neo-objectivist; cancerous, pernicious, and pandemic; protean, faddish, trendy, and dull. It has been a major combatant in the "science wars" and "culture wars" of the 1990s and 2000s. (See Hacking, 1999; Holstein & Miller, 1993; Lynch, 2001. Also see Best, Chapter 3; Lynch, Chapter 37; and Restivo & Croissant, Chapter 11, this volume.) Ian Hacking's widely noted collection of philosophical essays, *The Social Construction of What?* (1999) is an exception in this regard. It offers a dispassionate, even amiable critique of both constructionism and the controversy surrounding it. Although Hacking is decidedly ambivalent about constructionism's contributions, his own empirical work

3

and his philosophical ruminations bring considerable nuance to the discussion of what constructionism has to offer.

This *Handbook* does not aspire to resolve these debates. Instead, it works from the presumption that constructionism as embodied in the social sciences offers a useful empirical perspective that has proven remarkably fruitful over the past four decades. The volume offers a forum for an array of constructionist adherents to present and respond to the issues. The aim of the *Handbook* is to explore the conceptual and empirical developments that have produced a broad and deep corpus of constructionist research across the social sciences. If the volume speaks to the debates at all, it is by way of ample and compelling demonstrations of the ideas, methods, and findings that constitute the constructionist enterprise.

The Constructionist Project

One of the earliest and most influential statements of constructionist sentiments was Peter Berger's and Thomas Luckmann's *The Social Construction of Reality* (1966). The book took the social sciences by storm, encouraging empirical attention to the ordinary, taken-for-granted reality-constructing processes of everyday life. It rendered problematic the most common understanding, the "facts" of experience that heretofore were treated as matters to be straightforwardly discovered, recorded, and analyzed. Berger and Luckmann (1966) accepted Emile Durkheim (1961, 1964) at his word in presenting a framework for viewing how social facts become matters in categories of their own, *sui generis*, separate from the actions of those who seek to know them. The constructionist perspective implicated everyone, from those to whose lives the ostensible facts referred, to those who studied them through scientific investigation.

Forty years later, the term *constructionism* has become a prominent label, prefacing or

attached to myriad accounts of the organization of experience. From the social construction of mind (Coulter, 1979) and self (Wiley, 1994) to the social construction of social problems (Spector & Kitsuse, 1977), wife abuse (Loseke, 1992), and pregnancy (Gardner, 1994), constructionism has flourished as a frame of understanding and a vocabulary for conducting empirical research. It has arrived with considerable fanfare on many fronts, a source of inspiration to some postmodernist projects and, curiously enough, also enthusiastically applied by some who adopt critical perspectives. Constructionism now belongs to everyone and to no one—a highly variegated mosaic of itself. Indeed, the rush to jump on the constructionist bandwagon prompted Hacking (1999) to caution his audience about its wholesale acceptance across the disciplines. His book prods us to consider the scope of the "realities" that are constructed, encouraging us to take stock of what constructionism has become and can or cannot be in its analytic and empirical ambitions.

Rationale for the Volume

We have assembled this *Handbook of Constructionist Research* because the time is right to critically but appreciatively take stock of where constructionist research has been, what it has become, and where it is likely to go in the future. Despite the controversies, constructionist research is increasingly popular across the disciplines, and there are no signs that it will lose momentum. Indeed, Hacking's book, if cautionary, is also generous in its recognition of constructionist achievements and possible growth areas. Yet, beyond Hacking's commentary, there has been no comprehensive review of constructionist research across the social and behavioral sciences and associated disciplines. Research along constructionist lines continues apace without considered attention to the diversity within the enterprise and without a judicious examination of the analytic implications and issues of the constructionist project.

In editing the *Handbook of Constructionist Research*, our aim is to be both general and specific in addressing theoretical, methodological, and technical issues in the context of empirical research. The volume is not simply philosophical and abstract, dealing with the various assumptions of the research enterprise (see, e.g., Holstein & Miller, 1993). Instead, the *Handbook* turns to insiders—constructionist researchers themselves—for reflections on and assessments and critiques of what has been done and what can be accomplished within this framework. Constructionist researchers from across the disciplines—including psychology, anthropology, sociology, political science, education, management, communications, and related fields—address the enterprise from the bottom up. From the history of constructionist thinking to alternative analytic frameworks, strategies for empirical work, and techniques of constructionist data collection, the chapters provide a comprehensive overview of the foundations and the practice of constructionist research. The *Handbook* addresses the particular issues and concerns that distinctly arise in and from constructionist work, from the contours of various forms of constructionist understanding to diverse research programs to distinctive forms of empirical outcomes.

Theme of the *Handbook*

Just as constructionism belongs to no one and to everyone, the term *constructionism* has come to virtually mean both everything and nothing at the same time. Michael Lynch (2001) calls constructionism "remarkably protean," too diverse and diffuse to define, let alone assess. This volume seeks to address, if not counter, this accusation by providing a forum highlighting the variety as well as the common elements of constructionist empirical work. In doing so, it presents explanations and rationales for how and why research is distinctively constructionist. The theme of the *Handbook* is that constructionism is not spun out of whole cloth but rather is a rubric for a mosaic of research efforts with diverse—but shared—theoretical, methodological, and empirical groundings and significance. As readers will note, despite the remarkably varied involvement of disciplines and research topics, constructionist social science has more or less common motivations and aspirations.

Popular and comprehensive analytic rubrics are often thoughtlessly adopted and carelessly applied. Recently, we have witnessed the tendency for researchers and writers to claim glibly to be working from a constructionist stance (see Berbrier, Chapter 29, this volume). Too often, they display in their work either a profound ignorance of or a disregard for the epistemological, ontological, methodological, and practical foundations of constructionism that distinguish it from other approaches. Doing constructionist research is not a synonym for qualitative inquiry. Nor is constructionism fully congruent with symbolic interactionism, social phenomenology, or ethnomethodology, even though they share an abiding interest in social interaction. Instead it is a distinctive way of seeing and questioning the social world—a vocabulary, an idiom, a language of interpretation (see Gubrium & Holstein, 1997). One's analytic vocabulary virtually specifies the parameters and contours of the empirical horizons explored by the research approach. An analytic stance and vocabulary cannot be casually taken on board.

There are distinctive empirical implications, methodological concerns, and technical challenges that flow directly from constructionism's analytic vocabulary. Constructionist research typically deals with practical workings of *what* is constructed and *how* the construction process unfolds. The constructionist vocabulary does not lend itself easily to dealing with the *why* questions that predominate in more positivistically oriented inquiry, even though some *Handbook* contributors do not view this as an impediment. The *Handbook* focuses on the relation between the foundations of constructionism and how the perspective is put into practice in theoretically and conceptually viable, empirically productive ways.

Constructionism's analytic vocabulary points researchers in distinctive directions, virtually demanding answers to particular questions. At the same time, other questions would seem less appropriate. For example, constructionists offer major contributions by describing the complex contours of meaning associated with social forms that are interactionally and/or discursively produced, dealing with questions such as, what are mental illness and child abuse as social constructions? They can outline the historical and contextual development of social forms, such as how homelessness emerged as a recognizable phenomenon in the 1970s. They specify the processes and practices whereby social forms are brought into meaningful existence, such as how family troubles or emotional disturbance are "talked into being" in the course of everyday life.

For some, constructionism is less viable, theoretically and empirically, when researchers attempt to establish the "reality" of one social construction over another. Constructionism is narrowly partisan or analytically compromised when it becomes a "debunking" enterprise that invidiously compares or challenges the everyday life constructions by which people live (see Best, Chapter 3, this volume). In general, the perspective is more empirically robust when it is implemented as a broad framework or analytics for appreciating, not critiquing, everyday reality-constructing practices in general.

The Variety of Constructionisms

The considerable variety in constructionist research can be viewed as distributed along two fronts. One is the kind of question the researcher asks. Most constructionist investigations address the question of *how* social reality is assembled. But the *what* questions

regarding the working—often hidden—elements and organization of constructed realities are similarly important. Researchers who stress the *hows* of experience and the social world target the everyday methods, rules, and strategies by which reality is put together, setting aside concern with substantive matters while they pursue this interest. Others focus more on making visible important features of otherwise unknown experiences or social worlds, in which case the *hows* of the matter take a back seat to the goal of describing the unrecognized realities of everyday life. Still other constructionists take both *how* and *what* interests on board, working back and forth between them.

The leading concerns of the *how* and the *what* approaches parallel the differences between the so-called strong and weak programs in the sociology of science (see Restivo & Croissant, Chapter 11, this volume), as well as between so-called strict and contextual constructionisms in the study of social problems (see Best, Chapter 3, and Ibarra, Chapter 18, this volume). Perhaps the most extreme variants adopt postmodern approaches to the *hows*, concentrating on representational practices to the extent that they abandon most conventionally empirical concerns and direct their attention to researchers' textual practices in the construction of reality (see Clifford & Marcus, 1986; Holstein & Gubrium, Chapter 19, this volume).

On another front, constructionist research also may be viewed as varying in terms of the "scope," "level," or "empirical register" of analysis. Like social researchers in general, constructionists carry with them favored orientations to the scale of reality. Some habitually orient to the face-to-face or microinteractional sites of the construction process (see, e.g., Marvasti, Chapter 16; Potter & Hepburn, Chapter 14; and Sparkes & Smith, Chapter 15, this volume). They bring with them a heritage of interest in talk, situated interaction, local culture, and the interaction order. This is the bailiwick, for example, of symbolic interactionists and ethnomethodologists, whose leading concern with social accomplishment has always resonated with constructionist sensibilities.

The empirical interest of other constructionists veers in a more interactionally distant direction, toward the macroscopic contexts of the construction process. This is the domain of those concerned with collective representations and constructed social forms writ large, as in the tradition of constructionism associated with Malcolm Spector's and John Kitsuse's programmatic book *Constructing Social Problems* (1977). Constructionists of this ilk commonly focus on the media-embedded discourses and discursive structures of social construction projects. For example, they deal with how social movements promote particular constructions of social reality through print and electronic media (see Lowney, Chapter 17, this volume). Foucauldian studies also reside at this level (see L. Miller, Chapter 13, this volume). This mode of research sets the analytic stage in terms of the historical/genealogical discourses that provide the institutional frameworks mediating subjectivity and everyday life. These researchers tend to work comparatively, tracing institutional and state formations as discourse relates to differences.

The theme of diversity—the constructionist mosaic—echoes throughout the *Handbook*. If it were not so awkward, it would be compelling for the volume's title to refer to the variety of *constructionisms* (plural) and their diverse contributions to the corpus of constructionist research. Accordingly, the volume does not center so much on what constructionism *is* as on what it *can be*. The various chapters present this diversity in rich detail. For example, chapters describe various approaches to constructive processes in terms of discourse analysis, interactional analysis, interview analysis, and the analysis of diverse texts, documents, and other informational media. Other chapters highlight a wide variety of disciplinary concerns. Perhaps constructionism in the social sciences is too broad and diverse to simply define. But this diversity, we would argue, is part of constructionism's strength and appeal.

The Design of the Volume

If there are discernible dimensions to constructionist research—ranging across the *hows* and *whats* of reality and representation and spanning conventionally macroscopic and microscopic levels of analysis—there also are particular concerns linked to substantive, theoretical, and procedural matters and their ongoing challenges. The volume is organized in relation to these issues.

The two chapters of Part I set the stage for the range of topics. As a start, it is important to note that, whether research deals with the physical, social, literary, artistic, or spiritual, it has philosophical bearings. Long before a stream of thinking and empirical work took the label of constructionism in the social sciences, constructionist inclinations were emanating from the basic philosophical questions commonly asked about life and the social world. What is the nature of our selves and our surroundings? How do these matters operate in time and space? What can be known about them? How should this be represented and communicated? Each of these philosophical questions has constructionist bearings.

The social sciences are hardly more than a hundred years old; philosophical discussions have gone on for centuries. Chapter 2, by Darin Weinberg, takes a trip through the philosophical literature that has most directly influenced the social sciences. Reading about the "invention of the mind" in the 17th century, a space viewed as an inner preserve categorically separate from its surroundings, we are apprised of a debate that launches a long and illustrious philosophical commentary on the relation between ordinary reality within and the world outside. An inclination to eschew a straightforward connection between interior and exterior realms moved us toward constructionist sensibilities long before social researchers took up the issues in their own right. We soon learn that the present and continuing themes and challenges of constructionist research have a preliminary and intensely controversial philosophical background.

Chapter 3, by Joel Best, deals less with philosophical matters than with the historical context of social constructionism as a research agenda. It introduces the reader to key concerns that launched a distinct stream of empirical work related to social and cultural forms. The chapter takes Berger and Luckmann's (1966) *The Social Construction of Reality* as the pioneering constructionist text in the social sciences. The chapter traces constructionist themes primarily through sociology, in which the deconstruction of deviance and social problems provided the initial inspiration. This line of inquiry presented trenchant conceptual and explanatory challenges to what previously were figured to be plainly obvious social issues such as crime, poverty, sexual deviance, alcoholism, and substance abuse.

From the newly emergent constructionist perspective, even the vocabulary of "real" social problems was challenged. The constructionist argument was that understandings of "problems" such as sexual nonconformity or domestic abuse were as much matters of rhetoric, power, and influence as they were concrete social conditions. Although few constructionists argued that social problems were just rhetoric, constructionists nonetheless were challenged for making the claim and taken to task for inconsistencies in their stance regarding the empirical realities. This led to a lengthy debate centered on ontological and rhetorical, as well as empirical, dimensions of constructionist inquiry.

Part II turns to the disciplinary contexts of constructionist research. As the chapters show, Berger and Luckmann's work resonates far and wide, if not to every corner of the social sciences. Although each discipline had early realist and positivistic commitments, each has been challenged by constructionist themes, some sooner than others. For example, anthropologists James D. Faubion and George E. Marcus argue in Chapter 4 that the representational and comparative cultural challenges of their discipline sparked constructionist ruminations almost from the start. Indeed, they ask how

the dramatic categorical differences in human nature across the globe could not be viewed as socially constructed to begin with.

As each chapter in Part II surveys distinctive disciplinary developments, constructionism's cross-cutting themes become apparent. Readers will note that often constructionist sensibilities materialize in similar ways in the various disciplines, despite their traditional boundaries. Clearly, the diverse constructionisms are of the same family, even if they are not identical siblings. At the same time, however, it is surprising the extent to which the various disciplines have developed lines of constructionist inquiry without reference to one another. It appears that the constructionist wheel has been reinvented on more than one occasion. This volume provides the opportunity for the various disciplines to benefit from advances in allied fields. The constructionist sociology of social problems, for instance, should undoubtedly consult constructionist studies of public policy, and vice versa.

The concern with disciplinary applications in Part II also raises an implied question about the varied use of the terms *constructionist* versus *constructivist*. There has been a tendency to apply the former term as a more socially centered usage, as in anthropology, sociology, and some branches of psychology. Constructivism, however, has considerable currency in science, mathematics, and technology studies, as well as in lines of inquiry concerned with inner psychological space (e.g., constructivist psychotherapy). Rather than inviting a deconstruction of the competing terms and their implied realities or provoking a debate over the utility of the distinction, we simply have asked the contributors to adopt the generic term *constructionist* whenever possible. They have taken up the distinction only in those instances in which it seems to bear importantly on empirical matters.

Part III turns to the scope of constructionist inquiry, dealing with the concerns of the various levels of analysis we broached earlier. The context here is less disciplinary than it is related to matters of empirical register and emphasis. For more macroscopic applications, the concerns are applied to historical and broadly discursive differences. Leslie Miller's chapter (Chapter 13) on Foucauldian constructionism, for example, is "macroscopic" in its discussion of Michel Foucault's historical genealogies of regimes/regimens of knowledge. The word "macroscopic" necessarily is in quotation marks because Foucault's project would readily deconstruct the macro–micro distinction itself. Foucauldian discourses implicate both the macroscopic and microscopic. The other end of the conventional scope of constructionist inquiry takes us to the narrative and interactional work that produces and assembles realities in everyday life. Here, the accent is on "work," such as the reality work whose claims and related communicative practices construct a shared sense of, and facts about, entities such as homelessness and the life course.

Part IV deals with procedural matters. The leading question here is what difference constructionist impulses make in how social researchers do their work—in particular, how they gather and analyze empirical material. Kathy Charmaz (Chapter 20), for example, challenges grounded theorists to think in constructionist terms, suggesting that they "ground" systematic participant observation in representational practices as much as in real-life circumstances. The constructionist challenge is to approach social worlds as realities assembled and sustained, not just as evidently available for documentation and analysis. Although this part of the *Handbook* is divided into chapters dealing with distinct methodological approaches, from ethnographic fieldwork to interviewing to the analysis of historical and personal documents, a comparison clearly shows that these are not straightforwardly different strategies and techniques. The division again bears on methods *in practice* as much as on conventional distinctions. Fieldworkers interview, interviewers observe, discourse analysts conduct fieldwork, and archival material is related to oral history and field observation. The list goes on, and the permutations are virtually endless. Still, the common concerns of constructionist inquiry provide a committed orientation to the field, the data, and its analysis.

The title of Part V borrows from Hacking's book by the same title. Hacking raises the question of the extent to which various kinds of reality are constructed. For example, in what sense are natural or physical realities (e.g., quarks) socially constructed as opposed to more social phenomena, such as child abuse? Although the chapters in this part do not address this issue philosophically, they do provide useful surveys of how the construction of reality has been construed at some of the leading edges of social research. From the construction of the body, emotions, and gender to the construction of race, therapy, and the nation, it is evident that, although the concerns are similar, the applications raise diverse questions and shed multifaceted light on the substantive and related mechanics of the construction process.

The final contributions, in Part VI, bring us face-to-face with the continuing challenges of, and to, constructionism. If constructionism raises serious issues regarding the nature of reality, how then can reality be politically contested and changed? Can constructionism be critical? This is a question that takes up the issue of preferred realities. Other concerns emanate from feminist, postcolonial, and cultural studies agendas, all of which, at the same time, have integral constructionist impulses. If they are critical, they also are inspired by one of constructionism's leading themes, namely, that realities that are constructed can be deconstructed and assembled otherwise. This places constructionism squarely in a political environment, something which, interestingly enough, some constructionists seek to deconstruct. As curiously juxtaposed as they are, these concerns and the challenges are integral to the constructionist project, providing both inspiration for and barriers to its ongoing development and application.

References

Berger, P., & Luckmann, T. (1966). *The social construction of reality: A treatise in the sociology of knowledge.* Garden City, NY: Doubleday.

Clifford, J., & Marcus, G. (Eds.). (1986). *Writing culture.* Berkeley: University of California Press.

Coulter, J. (1979). *The social construction of mind.* London: Macmillan.

Durkheim, E. (1961). *The elementary forms of the religious life.* New York: Collier Macmillan.

Durkheim, E. (1964). *The rules of sociological method.* New York: Free Press.

Gardner, C. B. (1994). The social construction of pregnancy and fetal development. In T. Sarbin & J. Kitsuse (Eds.), *Constructing the social* (pp. 45–64). Thousand Oaks, CA: Sage.

Gubrium, J. F., & Holstein, J. A. (1997). *The new language of qualitative method.* New York: Oxford University Press.

Hacking, I. (1999). *The social construction of what?* Cambridge, MA: Harvard University Press.

Holstein, J. A., & Miller, G. (Eds.). (1993). *Reconsidering social constructionism: Debates in social problems theory.* New York: Aldine de Gruyter.

Holstein, J. A., & Miller, G. (Eds.). (2003). *Challenges and choices: Constructionist perspectives on social problems.* Hawthorne, NY: Aldine de Gruyter.

Loseke, D. (1992). *The battered woman and shelters: The social construction of wife abuse.* Albany: State University of New York Press.

Lynch, M. (2001). The contingencies of social constructionism. *Economy and Society, 30*(2), 240–254.

Spector, M., & Kitsuse, J. (1977). *Constructing social problems.* Menlo Park, CA: Cummings.

Wiley, N. (1994). *The semiotic self.* Chicago: University of Chicago Press.

PART I

FOUNDATIONS AND HISTORICAL CONTEXT

CHAPTER 2

The Philosophical Foundations of Constructionist Research

● **Darin Weinberg**

A chapter on the philosophical foundations of constructionist research may strike some as more than just a little bit ironic. Social constructionists are usually noted not for any particular philosophical pedigree but for a steadfast refusal to philosophically privilege knowledge of any kind, including our own. It is therefore tempting to organize this chapter as a statement of social constructionism's thoroughly antiphilosophical stance and its rejection of the very idea of philosophical foundations. However, I think this temptation should be resisted. It should be resisted in the first instance because constructionist research always has been, and will very likely continue to be, heavily influenced by philosophers and philosophical debates. One routinely finds, in even the most empirically grounded social constructionist texts, citations of the work of such philosophers as Judith Butler, Jacques Derrida, John Dewey, Sandra Harding, Karl Marx, George Herbert Mead, Maurice Merleau-Ponty, Friedrich Nietzsche, Richard Rorty, Alfred Schutz, Ludwig Wittgenstein, and many others. Although some of these writers may be seen as marginal to their profession by mainstream academic philosophers, they have not, for that, ceased to be philosophers, nor have their arguments grown immune to philosophical debate.

In the second instance, the temptation to cast constructionism as a uniformly anti-foundational and/or antiphilosophical school of thought should be resisted because it is plainly wrong. Not all constructionist researchers are opposed to building their arguments on explicitly philosophical foundations.[1] We are not all opposed to the same philosophical arguments, and even when we do oppose the same arguments, we often do so for very different reasons. Thus neglecting the various philosophical commitments that inform constructionist research can only foster misunderstandings and impede productive dialogue. Deciding whether our philosophical commitments are best understood as logically necessary, empirically grounded, ethical, socially inherited, habitual, or otherwise inevitably requires philosophical reflection and debate. Moreover, it should also be noted that professional philosophers have often offered more meticulously considered and precisely articulated arguments both for and against the philosophical positions inherent in social constructionism than have we who focus primarily on empirical research. Hence, if we wish to develop our conceptual grasp of these positions, it is well worth our while to consider the philosophical arguments both for and against the various forms that constructionist research has taken. It is toward this end that this chapter has been written.

After briefly discussing some of the basic imperatives of social constructionist research itself, I begin the chapter with an overview of what I am calling the rise and implosion of philosophical foundationalism. By *philosophical foundationalism* I mean the intellectual tradition that has sought to devise logically or scientifically irrefutable ground rules for the production of all valid knowledge.[2] Because constructionists so often invoke this tradition as their philosophical antithesis, it is important to establish just what the major philosophical foundationalists have argued and the extent to which social constructionism actually is or is not consistent with these arguments. Hence in this section I trace the development of the foundationalist tradition, indicating along the way various debts that constructionist researchers owe to writers who have figured in this tradition. I finish this section by indicating some of the more serious critiques of foundationalism that have been made from within analytic philosophy itself. In the next

section I trace what I am calling the *critical theoretical tradition*. By *critical theory* I mean those post-Kantian approaches to social research explicitly dedicated not only to understanding or explaining the social world but also to critiquing it in the interest of progressive social change. I then discuss what I am calling the *hermeneutic tradition*, by which I mean those approaches to social research that are predicated on an ontological distinction between the "natural" and the "social" and that variously seek to discern the intrinsic meaning(s) to be found in social life. I conclude the chapter with a critical commentary on some of the more pressing philosophical challenges facing social constructionist research today.

Some Imperatives of (and for) Constructionist Research

As many others have observed, what actually counts as a social constructionist study is not a self-evident or uncontested matter. For the purpose of this chapter I take the very inclusive view that social constructionist studies are those that seek, at least in part, to replace fixed, universalistic, and sociohistorically invariant conceptions of things with more fluid, particularistic, and sociohistorically embedded conceptions of them. Although they often differ considerably in any number of their basic conceptual commitments, I define as social constructionists all researchers who seek to demonstrate either that or, specifically, how certain states of affairs that others have taken to be eternal and/or beyond the reach of social influence are actually products of specific sociohistorical and/or social interactional processes. By this definition, it does not matter whether the producers of these studies explicitly embrace or reject the mantle of social constructionism themselves. Rather, the only question of interest is the degree to which a study extends the reach of the social sciences into realms in which they had once been discounted (Weinberg, in press).

In his uncommonly balanced and useful philosophical discussion of social constructionism and its critics, Ian Hacking (1999) has argued that our first priority in assessing the intellectual value of social constructionist studies should not be to produce a general definition of exactly what the term *social constructionism* ought to mean but to consider the practical point in conducting a social constructionist study in any particular case. As he also notes, constructionist research has generally been concerned less with establishing the necessary and sufficient conditions needed to explain empirical events than with raising people's consciousness in a more general sense. The practical point, then, of doing constructionist studies has very often been to promote a better way of thinking and, more important, living with respect to the worlds we inhabit. Hence, considerations of the objective, essential, or universal properties of things have commonly taken a back seat to normative questions concerning how to most *valuably* or *beneficially* conceptualize them.

Indeed, many constructionists not only cast questions of objective truth as ancillary to questions of human benefit but also cast aspersions on the very idea that objective truth is a proper goal of inquiry. One of the more ubiquitous claims in the social constructionist literature is that the quest to discover objective and/or universal truths promotes the reification of things—or the unnecessary, unjustified, and often unjust conversion of mere hypotheses or observed regularities into fixed and unalterable definitions of those things. The normative upshot of this argument is unmistakable: Not only is the quest to discover universal truths less useful than research that explores how we have come by, now use, and/or might transcend our current conceptual orientations, but the quest to discover universal truths can also be downright harmful, because it encourages us to think fatalistically about the status quo and to naturalize aspects of our existence that are not inevitable and that ought to be challenged and changed.

Given this distaste for reification, it is not surprising that social constructionist movements have tended to emerge as self-consciously critical of the institutional mainstream of the various academic disciplines and subdisciplines within which they are found. Whereas mainstream scientists (including social scientists) tend to work with the general aim of building on, fortifying, and promoting the intellectual credentials of their respective disciplines, social constructionists have tended to cast themselves as gadflies, deconstructing and unmasking their colleagues' myriad sacred cows as the socially contingent and eminently provisional achievements that they are. Their critical engagement with the intellectual edifices of established academic disciplines has infused constructionists' work with a recognizable intellectual identity and hence a place at the table in academically consecrated dialogues. This critical interrogation of the pretenses and foibles of the academy (not to mention other settings wherein one finds presumptions to objectivity) is important and necessary work that should, no doubt, continue.

However, I also believe that this relatively exclusive commitment to deconstructive intellectual projects might reflect a certain philosophical immaturity. It would appear that our intellectual *raison d'être* has been primarily to deflate the knowledge claims of others rather than to explicitly justify our own claims to intellectual respectability (Calhoun, 1995; Habermas, 1987). In addition to producing studies that engage in what Theodor Adorno (1990) famously called *negative dialectics* with hegemonic ideas, I believe social constructionist researchers can benefit from a more sustained consideration of the intellectual legitimacy and/or social value of our own research as such. This will entail moving beyond the well-established fact that claims to truth or objectivity are always, in some sense, claims to power toward the development of approaches that help us to more reasonably, justly, compassionately, and systematically arbitrate between such claims. It is toward these ends that our philosophical reflections are most productively devoted.

The Rise and Implosion of Philosophical Foundationalism

The Rise and Varieties of Philosophical Foundationalism in the Modern Era

Because philosophical foundationalism is often invoked emblematically as the antithesis of social constructionism, I think it is sensible to begin a chapter like this one by first outlining the main arguments of the most influential contributors to this intellectual tradition. This will then allow us to think more clearly and carefully about exactly what social constructionist researchers do and do not oppose in this tradition and, indeed, what social constructionists have drawn from it.

Strictly speaking, the origins of philosophical foundationalism are diverse and may be traced at least as far back as Plato. However, were we to confine our attention to the writings of its constructionist critics, we might be forgiven for assuming it is a uniquely modern conceit. It is said to hail from the misguided efforts of such philosophers as René Descartes, John Locke, and Immanuel Kant to forge a universal and unassailable set of ground rules for the production of valid knowledge. We might also be forgiven for assuming that the efforts of these and other Enlightenment-era philosophers were born exclusively of the aristocratic, imperialist, racist, and sexist predilections they inherited from their socially privileged patrons. By these lights, the presumption to set the ground rules for the pursuit of truth and objectivity was never anything other than a veiled effort to exert power over those who could not so effectively claim their social and epistemological privilege. Although I do not wish to take issue with such arguments (there is more than a kernel of truth in

them), I would like to supplement them with a reminder that many Enlightenment philosophers fancied themselves as revolutionary defenders of the rights of the oppressed and their philosophical writings as resources for emancipatory social movements. Rather than in the aristocratic will to legitimate oppression, the social origins of modern philosophical foundationalism must be located first and foremost in the liberal revolutionary movements of the 17th and 18th centuries. These movements were pitted, to greater and lesser degrees, against the socially stifling authority both of the Church and of feudalism. Truth, then, in its modern philosophical sense, was invented precisely to be spoken to power.

In his magisterial deconstruction of the foundationalist philosophical tradition, Richard Rorty (1980) traces this tradition to what he calls the "invention of the mind." It is Descartes who is usually credited with initiating this invention. He did so by prescribing a total disengagement with both tradition and the evidence of our senses. Because both of these sources of information were capable of deceiving us, the achievement of genuinely valid knowledge required us to withdraw from them into a space of pure critical reflection—*res cogitans*, or the mind. If the constructionist tradition is predicated on what Jean-François Lyotard (1984) has called "incredulity toward metanarratives" (p. xxiv), then we must certainly acknowledge Descartes as a foundational figure in this tradition. Few social constructionists have ever matched the intensity of Descartes' incredulity toward the preeminent ideas of his day. Following Descartes' conceptual disengagement of the human mind from both the human body and the rest of the material world, it was Locke who produced the next major philosophical statement concerning the relation between the human mind and the world that is perceptually available to it. This statement was intimately linked to his radical politics. As Roy Porter (2003, p. 72) notes:

Locke was by far the most influential philosopher of the late seventeenth century. In his early years a conservative Oxford don, Locke was subsequently radicalized by the reactionary politics of post-Restoration years, and played a decisive role in the politics of the years following the Glorious Revolution of 1688, when he published key writings championing constitutional government, religious toleration, rational Christianity, liberal economics and currency reform. The coping stone of his oeuvre lay, however, in his vision of man.

What was this vision? It was essentially a vision of the human mind as such and its relation with the world. For Locke, humans are unique in our possession of consciousness. Unlike other animals, humans are aware of themselves as always implicated in the act of perception. This premise shared with Descartes' work a cleavage of subjective perception from the objective world perceived and, hence, a skepticism as to whether mental events correspond with anything outside the mind. But breaking with Descartes, Locke eschewed all claims to innate truths and hence declined to suggest that our self-consciousness was a source of epistemological certainty. For Locke, the human mind is at birth a *tabula rasa*, a blank slate, and it is only through the rational assessment of the information provided by our senses that we acquire knowledge. Locke looked to the scientific methods being developed by friends such as Robert Boyle and Isaac Newton for examples of what such a rational assessment might consist. Although such knowledge fell short of absolute certainty, Locke argued that it provides a sufficient probability of truth to be both adequate to the demands of human life and decisively superior to any other means of acquiring belief. This combination of a fallibilist understanding of knowledge with the exaltation of reason as the best tribunal for the interrogation of our beliefs served Locke's liberal and antiauthoritarian politics well.

His eschewal of innate knowledge was also a refusal to confer legitimacy on any argument, religious or secular, that traded in such notions. Legitimate knowledge, just as legitimate politics and genuine service to God, entails the submission of our ideas to the public and accessible tribunal of reason. His conception of human nature as the capacity for consciousness and rational reflection was also an implicit foundation both for an egalitarian and social contractarian[3] theory of government and for a critique of any government that would prevent our free exercise of these faculties. With Thomas Hobbes, Locke located the state's legitimacy in its capacity to serve the needs of the governed. However, unlike Hobbes, Locke construed these needs as extending well beyond our physical protection. Locke argued that, as conscious and rational beings, humans possess inalienable rights to life, liberty, and property. These rights, and the mental faculties that justified them, were *natural* endowments that preceded our entrance into the social contract embodied by the state and law. Thus, *naturally*, any government that failed to honor them ought not to enjoy the obedience of its people. It was precisely his foundationalist philosophy of mind that justified the obligations Locke insisted the state had to those it governed.

These ideas would prove immensely influential during the modern era, not least for the defense of democracy, freedom, and equality they embodied. Indeed, the egalitarian presupposition of a universal human capacity to rationally interrogate the evidence of our senses (and to thereby recognize our own self-interest) and of the obligations this imposes on governments (as well as on our fellow citizens) is one of the most common philosophical presuppositions to be found in social constructionist research itself. The constructionist aspiration to give "voice" to those historically denied it is based directly on these Lockean premises. However, despite their profound impact on our modern understanding of the human condition, Locke's formulations left many matters unresolved. How, for example, are our mental representations of them actually caused by the things with which our senses bring us into contact? Beyond their merely representing empirically perceptible things, how do we properly combine the ideas in our minds to synthesize meaningful perceptions into more generally valid theoretical systems? Given our equal capacities for rational reflection, on what bases should disputes between us regarding matters of fact or matters of value be adjudicated? It fell to later philosophers to try to work through these problems. The most monumental contributions in this respect were no doubt made by Immanuel Kant.

Before Kant, many secular philosophers had been working to divest nature of moral force. Initially, this was intended to isolate natural philosophy[4] from the concerns of Christian theology and to thereby minimize the threats that Church leaders saw in these new ideas (Taylor, 1989, p. 161). By these lights, natural philosophy did not threaten the Church because it was concerned only with discovering nature's laws and had nothing to say about the supernatural or morality. For these philosophers, nature was a wholly mechanistic realm ruled by eternal laws that were uniformly indifferent to human purposes and devoid of moral implications. Questions of fact were thereby divorced from those of value. However, these arguments did not prevent natural philosophers from pronouncing on the nature of human beings as readily as they pronounced on the nature of anything else.

Kant took exception to this practice because he felt that making human nature a topic of natural philosophy was to inevitably cast it as unfree. It was to cast human beings and human action as mere effects of the same kinds of fixed natural laws by which natural philosophers sought to explain the rest of the world. Insofar as human beings are free, Kant insisted that they must be seen to transcend the laws of nature. With his philosophical distinction between the transcendental domain of human freedom and the mechanistic domain of nature, Kant inaugurated an intellectual revolution in phi-

losophy and planted the seeds for one that would later occur in the social sciences, as well (cf. Levine, 1995, pp. 181–211). By articulating a voluntaristic conception of human subjectivity in specific contrast to the causally determined realm of nature, Kant set the basic philosophical foundations for all forms of modern idealism and/or subject-centered social thought. These run the gamut, including the traditions that flowed from Georg W. F. Hegel (e.g., Marxism and American pragmatism), from Wilhelm Dilthey (e.g., *Verstehen* sociology and cultural anthropology), from Friedrich Nietzsche (e.g., Michel Foucault, Jacques Derrida), and from Edmund Husserl (e.g., Martin Heidegger, Maurice Merleau-Ponty, Alfred Schutz). Obviously, his successors took exception to one or another of Kant's arguments as often as they invoked them supportively. But the fact that the philosophical origins of these various forms of subjectivist social thought are to be found in Kant's invention of the transcendental subject is undoubted. To the extent that social constructionist researchers consider meaning, interpretation, human agency, or social practice more generally as irreducible to explanations that invoke timeless causal mechanisms or natural laws, we are indebted to Kant's great influence on Western philosophy.

But Kant went beyond merely distinguishing the realms of human freedom and nature. He argued that what we know of these realms cannot be derived from empirical investigation alone. The evidence of our senses is inevitably structured by intrinsic features of the mind itself. For example, Kant accepted David Hume's argument that the relation of causality is never empirically observable but is instead projected onto empirical observations of merely correlated events (Hume, 1978). Hume presented this argument as grounds to reject the possibility of certain knowledge of causal relations, but Kant sought to rescue epistemological certainty by suggesting that this projection was not merely a contingent habit of the mind (as Hume proposed) but a functional operation universally performed by human minds to confer order on sense data that would otherwise remain meaningless. The perception of events in space and through time was likewise a universal functional operation of the mind that set basic and universal parameters for rationally interrogating the evidence of our senses. By separating the empirical ego (as those contingent aspects of ourselves that can be empirically experienced) from the transcendental ego (as that logically necessary agent that actively perceives and judges), Kant was able to argue that there are elements of the human condition that can be accessed only through the use of pure reason, or philosophy. In this way, Kant promoted the discipline of philosophy as the ultimate arbiter of what must be posited a priori, or in advance of empirical investigation, in order for us to make sense of the very availability of a meaningful empirical world to human consciousness.

This distinction between logically necessary truths and truths provisionally derived from empirical inquiry was captured with the terms *analytic* and *synthetic*. For Kant and his followers, genuinely philosophical truths are analytic, or true by definition. Though Kant did not himself accept this, many later philosophers have held up the truths of mathematics as quintessentially analytic: The proposition $2 + 2 = 4$ is true simply by virtue of the definition of its terms. Synthetic truths such as "all men are mortal," on the other hand, are true by virtue of their relationship to the empirical world. Hence it has been argued that whereas science (and empirical research more generally) trades primarily in synthetic truths, which are inevitably fallible because they can, in principle, always be disproved by new empirical evidence, philosophy trades in analytic truths, or the work of unpacking what we must necessarily accept as true to avoid logical contradiction. Since Kant, many philosophers have held that because philosophy's analytic truths are not contingent on the available empirical evidence, they can provide universally valid guidance to every manner of scientific research both as to what the basic requirements of any sound investigation will entail (e.g., rules of statistical inference) and what it is reasonable to seek to discover (e.g., laws of nature or causal mechanisms as opposed to ethical facts). It was Kant who first gave us this modernist sense of philosophy as the discipline concerned with establishing the logical foundations of all other forms of knowledge. The proposition that philosophy must guide empirical research in all its incarnations also gave rise to the widely held conviction that there must be a formal unity among the sciences and that all scientific work must seek to converge on a single coherent understanding of the cosmos. Because they appear to insist that Western philosophy and science possess a rationality and/or access to reality that is not historically or culturally specific but unsurpassable *in principle*, it is propositions such as these that have most often been singled out in social constructionist critiques of philosophical foundationalism.

Despite the resistance to it of social constructionists, this self-image was accepted by many philosophers in what came to be known in the 20th century as analytic philosophy. But its most influential 20th-century proponents were those associated with the school of logical positivism.[5] The logical positivists rejected any reasoning that entailed presumptive arguments regarding unobservables such as God, the mind, or even hypothetical physical entities. They felt that if something was neither directly observable nor logically deducible from direct observation, then it could never be rigorously analyzed. Systems of thought that included reference to such things were therefore condemned as merely speculative. Although the logical positivists rejected Kant's transcendental idealism on these grounds, they retained his distinction between analytic and synthetic truths. In place of speculation, the logical positivists sought to build a system of knowledge that relied only on analytic truths in combination with the direct testimony of the senses. This entailed: (1) purifying logic of any reliance on empirically refutable, or synthetic, claims regarding the nature of cognition and (2) producing an absolutely pure, or atheoretical, observation language with which to capture or picture immediate experiences. Though logical positivism dominated the philosophy of science in the mid-20th century, it has suffered a variety of devastating critiques not only from outside but also from within analytic philosophy itself. It is to these that I now turn.

The Implosion of Foundationalism in Analytic Philosophy

The first major critique of the logical positivists' foundationalist philosophical efforts came from Karl Popper (1992). Popper noted that even if logical positivists are successful in empirically verifying the truth of propositions describing particular immediate experiences, they will not be able to logically infer from these propositions the truth of a general theory. This is true because no finite number of observations can ever logically rule out the possible existence of an empirical case that disproves the general theory. Popper's critique of induction was a powerful indictment of the logical positivists' view that we might somehow become absolutely certain of a theory's truth and, in this, a powerful argument in support of the claim that all theoretical knowledge, including scientific knowledge, is necessarily fallible. Popper still held that, despite its fallibility, through his doctrine of falsificationism we could nonetheless distinguish the superior epistemic logic of science from the rest of culture. He thus remained, despite his critique of the logical positivists, a staunch philosophical foundationalist himself. But this was not to be the end of the story.

Ludwig Wittgenstein, who had earlier in his career been one of the logical positivists' favorite philosophical authorities, began in the 1930s to reformulate his regard for philosophy and philosophical problems. In his

first book, the *Tractatus Logico-Philosophicus*, Wittgenstein (1922) had embraced the efforts of Gottlob Frege and Bertrand Russell to completely divorce logic, as a purely analytic and universally valid system of propositions, from the contingent world of empirical facts. Once logic had been purified in this way, he thought it would be possible to distinguish meaningful from meaningless propositions by considering whether they honored the limit conditions imposed on language by logic and whether they pictured observable states of affairs in the world. In the book *Philosophical Remarks*, Wittgenstein (1975) added a verificationist principle analogous to those being developed among the logical positivists to the picture theory of meaning outlined in his first book. Here the meaning of propositions is defined by the logical procedure through which they can be verified. However, very shortly after drafting these arguments, Wittgenstein began to entertain serious doubts about the "dogma" that philosophical problems could be logically *solved* in this way. Distancing himself from the view that a concept's meaning could be decisively established or verified by means of an "ideal" logical language, he began to argue that the meaning of concepts can be established only by learning how people actually use those concepts in their "ordinary" or "natural" languages (cf. Wittgenstein, 1953). Thus rather than seeking to logically *solve* philosophical problems, Wittgenstein advised that philosophers should now seek only to *dissolve* them by demonstrating how they are nothing more than artifacts of the grammatical conventions found in natural languages.

Wittgenstein relinquished the view that language and the world must conform to a singular logical structure to remain meaningful and began to argue instead that meaning is established in practice through a multitude of different logical structures that he called "language games." This idea had revolutionary philosophical ramifications. In place of the logical concept of "identity," which entailed establishing the essential properties that all instances of a concept shared, Wittgenstein installed the concept of "family resemblance." Instead of looking for essential properties, he advised philosophers to look for the webs of similarity and relation that make it meaningful to speak of, for example, football, 20 Questions, and solitaire as each instances of the concept "game." Wittgenstein's later writings suggested that these activities share no essence that warrants use of the concept "game" but are variously linked in ways that have at one time or another merited notice. The philosophical concept of logic itself is replaced by the concepts of language games, or grammars, which are held to consist in disparate sets of rules for using language in various practical contexts. Unlike so-called analytic propositions, which are said to derive their meaning exclusively from the definition of their terms, the meanings of grammatical rules are said to inhere in their practical application. We understand the meaning of these rules only to the extent that we can be observed to apply them correctly in practice. This linkage of the perceived coherence and compulsion of logic with the worldly contexts of its use has proved attractive to social constructionist researchers primarily because it appears to negate the notion of an ahistorical and/or acultural ground for true belief and to thoroughly nest the nature of meaning and logic within particular sociocultural contexts, or what Wittgenstein called "forms of life."[6] Though Wittgenstein had a great deal to say about the logical positivists' flawed conception of logic, he was considerably less vocal on the matter of positivism—or empiricism. Harvard philosopher Willard van Orman Quine addressed this topic much more directly than did Wittgenstein and with far-reaching influence.

In his well-known essay "Two Dogmas of Empiricism," Quine (1951) cast considerable doubt on the notion that empirical evidence, or the testimony of experience, could either confirm or refute theoretical claims in isolation of one another. Quine noted that all linguistic propositions, including scientific ones, acquire meaning in relation not only to the experiences they presume to describe but also to other propositions with which they are meaningfully related. Hence the testimony of experience can never decisively confirm or refute any particular proposition because it is always possible to adjust related propositions so as to change the theoretical consequences of the experiential evidence. For Quine, then, empirical evidence cannot be set against propositions on a piecemeal basis but must be set against what he called *conceptual schemes* (sets of meaningfully related propositions) as wholes. Furthermore, conceptual schemes themselves cannot be demarcated in any way that decisively distinguishes science from nonscience. The reason is that scientific propositions are often woven together with nonscientific propositions that influence their meaning.[7] Science is thus seen as constructed not on a foundation of enduring logical truths or sense data but of commonsense cultural assumptions, all of which are potentially subject to revision.[8]

Quine also suggested that different conceptual schemes might, in principle, be equally capable of accounting for a given body of empirical evidence. This came to be known as the thesis that theory choice is "underdetermined" by the available empirical evidence, a thesis that has been taken up widely among social constructionists of various stripes. Quine's argument for meaning holism was equally fatal to the ambitions of both logical positivists and Popperian falsificationists to erect a logical partition between science and nonscience on the foundation of brute experience. It also undermined the very idea that there is a philosophically important distinction to be made between analytic and synthetic propositions. For followers of Quine, the meaning of both analytic and synthetic propositions hails simultaneously from their positions in a given conceptual scheme and the relations of that scheme to the empirical phenomena it is meant to capture. This view cannot be easily reconciled with the claim that, unlike synthetic propositions, analytic propositions are true (or false) by definition and without reference to anything in the empirical world. By Quineian lights, putatively analytic propositions can, at best, be understood as those propositions we are considerably less willing to forsake. They are not categorically distinct from synthetic propositions in any philosophically significant sense (Putnam, 2002). The collapse of the analytic–synthetic distinction, combined with the apparent loss of "experience" as a panhistorical and pancultural ground for universalistic knowledge claims, left the project of philosophical foundationalism, as it has been known since Descartes, in very serious trouble.

Although Quine claimed to reject philosophical foundationalism, or what he called "first philosophy," he held that epistemology could be preserved as a strictly scientific, rather than a philosophical, enterprise (cf. Quine, 1969). Instead of seeking to ground knowledge in principles derived from "pure reason" or logic, he argued that we should seek to "naturalize epistemology," or ground it in a scientific theory of how we come to develop our conceptual schemes of the world and of why and how they work. Quine was a staunch physical reductionist and assumed that this scientific theory must inevitably be about the nature of knowing subjects as physical beings and their relationships with their physical environments. Joseph Rouse (2002, p. 133) has persuasively argued that, far from abolishing it, Quine's presumption in this regard actually smuggles in a new candidate for first philosophy in the form of

> an implicit metaphysics of nature as the already determined object of what natural science *can* be about, and the already unified subject of knowledge in the physical bodies of individual human organisms. What physical bodies, the physical world, and their causal interactions are like is to be determined by ongoing scientific inquiry. That these are physical

bodies, interacting causally, and that the "subject" of knowledge is the individual organism to which the rest of the world is "external" have nevertheless been specified in advance as the prior conditions for epistemology having been naturalized.[9]

Quine vehemently critiqued the notion that philosophy could or should legitimate scientific research from a position external to it. Indeed, he sought to undermine the very distinction between philosophy and science itself. However, despite its being at odds with several of his own philosophical insights, Quine remained faithful that the natural sciences are epistemologically superior to the rest of culture. Although this presumption is not without its contemporary defenders, many prominent analytic philosophers have grown increasingly less convinced. Nelson Goodman (1978), in his discussion of "worldmaking," embraces a kind of relativism that appears to deny that science has any special claim to epistemological privilege. Paul Feyerabend (1978) attacked both the views that science is conducted according to a unified "method" that distinguishes it from nonscience and that science ought to enjoy a categorically privileged position vis-à-vis the rest of culture. Thomas Kuhn (1962) did perhaps more than anyone else to promote a relativist and descriptive understanding of science in place of any kind of universalistic philosophical explanation or justification of it. Each of these philosophers argued persuasively that science is not methodologically uniform, discontinuous with the rest of culture, or equipped to capture the empirical world in a manner untainted by theoretical preconceptions (see also Putnam, 1981; Rorty, 1991b). These claims have often been appropriated by social constructionists to strengthen philosophically their own claims to interpret or explain sociologically the production of knowledge and/or other types of hegemonic ideas, belief systems, or practices.

By contemporary lights, the project of defining the grounds for the production of all genuine knowledge in terms of a single, conceptually integrated, and universally valid set of *analytic* propositions has lost most, if not all, of its intellectual luster. Neither the majority of practicing philosophers themselves nor philosophically informed social scientists continue to take this project very seriously. However, this should by no means suggest that the project of philosophically grounding the production of social scientific knowledge is dead. Nor, more specifically, should it suggest that it is dead among social constructionists themselves. It means only that the philosophical traditions to which researchers now make recourse tend more often to be those I am calling, for the sake of exposition, the critical theoretical and hermeneutic philosophical traditions rather than the analytic tradition. It is important to emphasize that the writers I categorize as analytic, critical, and hermeneutic have exercised considerable influences on one another over the years. Hence, these categories should not be taken to describe completely separate philosophical movements but only certain consequential tendencies in the history of Western philosophy.

Critical Theory

Hegel's Legacy

Though he has often been described by mainstream Anglo–American philosophers as the worst kind of speculative dogmatist, Georg Wilhelm Friedrich Hegel has also inspired legions of philosophers and social scientists for his insistence that philosophy (and human consciousness more generally) be understood as inextricable from history, rather than somehow transcendent of it (cf. Habermas, 1987). In opposition to Kant's positing of a transcendental subject whose form is beyond the influence of history or nature, Hegel insisted that the mind and the world arise and develop together by way of an antagonistic *mutual* influence that came to be known as dialectic. But Hegel's historicism was by no means uncritical or rela-

tivist. He remained committed to the Enlightenment proposition that philosophy, or reason, had a critical role to play in effecting progressive social change. Hegel argued that it is precisely reason that is the driving force of human historical development. It is through the application of reason to the particular contradictions, or "diremptions," that embody its historical moment that these contradictions are overcome and human progress is achieved. A wide variety of social constructionists have built on these Hegelian ideas both to historically situate the forms of knowledge and practice they analyze and to philosophically ground their own presumptions to critique them.

The most influential heir to Hegel is, without doubt, Karl Marx. Although he adopted Hegel's teleological view of historical development and his dialectical method, Marx claimed to have completely inverted Hegel's understanding of history by prioritizing the materiality of the human condition over consciousness itself. As he famously wrote in "A Contribution to the Critique of Political Economy,"

> the mode of production of material life conditions the social, political, and intellectual process in general. It is not the consciousness of men that determines their being, but, on the contrary, their social being that determines their consciousness. (Tucker, 1978, p. 4)

Expanding on this idea, Marx suggested that those who control the mode of material production also control the mode of intellectual production such that politics, law, religion, morality, art, and culture more generally tend overwhelmingly to reflect and promote the material interests of the dominant economic class. Marx developed his concept of *ideology* to suggest how the working class could be made to suffer from a *false consciousness* that renders them complicit in their own oppression. These ideas were developed by later Marxists such as Georg Lukacs and Antonio Gramsci, whose elaborations on such concepts as *class conscious-*

ness, reification, and *hegemony* have exercised an immense influence on social constructionist research. Transforming Marx's critical concept of ideology as false consciousness into a general and noncritical concept of knowledge as such, Karl Mannheim (1936) called for the sociological analysis of all knowledge (except natural science) as socially embedded and constructed. This was, of course, a monumental precedent for social constructionist research, but it tended to undermine the possibility of critiquing knowledge claims by leveling the epistemological ground between critic and the object of critique.[10] Mannheim's sociology of knowledge was therefore looked on by his Marxist contemporaries with considerable suspicion.

In keeping with his materialism, Marx dismissed the Hegelian notion of effecting progressive social change through rational criticism and sought to identify the social structural mechanisms that would yield emancipation. This he found in the material deprivations suffered by the proletariat, or working class, under capitalism. According to Marx, the logic of capitalism would inevitably result in the unrelenting growth and immiseration of the working class such that they would eventually be faced with the dichotomous choice of death or revolution. Because Marx held this logic was governed by natural laws of history, he placed minimal importance on the role of philosophical critique, or consciousness raising. Although not completely irrelevant to the project of emancipation, ideas, for Marx, were basically epiphenomenal to the dynamics of material production and were therefore largely powerless to divert the course of historical change. Hence, the orthodox Marxist study of ideas, and/or what social constructionists have sometimes called "claimsmaking," has been predominantly concerned with explaining the acquiescence of the working class to domination. It has been less concerned with effecting or understanding political change.

After the Russian Revolution, Marx's writings on the relation between history and consciousness were given relatively vulgar, dogmatic, and antidemocratic interpretations by Soviet writers. This eventually alienated many younger Western Marxists who felt that the profound deflation of critical reason and consciousness raising as forces for social change too easily degenerated into an excuse for ideological intolerance and technocratic totalitarianism. Marxist theory ceased to appear as a merely well-supported but fallible set of empirical arguments and took on the guise of a reified naturalistic metaphysic analogous to the kind that Rouse (2002) critiqued Quine for adopting. This disillusionment with the dogmatism of Soviet Marxism, combined with the apparent failure of the working classes in Western capitalist societies to exhibit any manner of revolutionary stirrings, served to motivate a return to questions concerning the social significance of culture, reason, and consciousness among several leading Western Marxists, most notably members of the so-called Frankfurt School (cf. Horkheimer & Adorno, 1972; Jay, 1996).

The Frankfurt School is the name scholars have retrospectively given to a group of neo-Marxist social theorists, including Theodor Adorno, Walter Benjamin, Erich Fromm, Max Horkheimer, and Herbert Marcuse, who were connected to the Institute for Social Research in Frankfurt, Germany. These scholars shared a general skepticism regarding the applicability of orthodox Marxist thought to their own historical moment insofar as Marx had failed to anticipate several major historical developments that were having profound sociological effects on the 20th century. These included such things as the rise of Nazism, monopoly capitalism, the welfare state, the explosion in mass-mediated cultural fare, and Soviet socialism. They drew eclectically from Max Weber, Sigmund Freud, German idealism, and Hegel himself in an effort to reconcile Marxist theory with these 20th-century developments. Although there were certainly disagreements among members of the Frankfurt School as to the details of their various diagnoses of modern times, they shared a broad commitment to forging a comprehensive critical understanding of world historical social change and a profound dissatisfaction with both Soviet and Western conceptions of science and knowledge. It is for their combination of a comprehensive indictment of the contemporary forms that science and philosophy had taken in the 20th century and a commitment to critical reason as a force for progressive social change that the Frankfurt School is best remembered.

In the West, what they called "instrumental rationality" had run amuck, restricting the production of knowledge to the technical service of powerful political and economic actors and depriving the working classes of any opportunity to raise an emancipatory critical consciousness. In the East, coercive insistence on a Marxist orthodoxy effectively inhibited truly *critical* dialogue and paved the way for a dictatorship legitimated by reference to putatively incorrigible "laws of history." The Frankfurt School sought to reinvigorate Marxism by rethinking the role of critical discourse in fostering critical understanding and, in turn, progressive social change. They sought a form of knowledge that was capable of providing a ground from which to objectively critique the status quo but that did not thereby slip into a political or philosophical dogmatism. Though their own efforts were ultimately unsuccessful, their project was taken up in a new guise by Adorno's one-time protégé, Jurgen Habermas. Habermas inherited from the Frankfurt School a strong conviction that, to be truly critical and emancipatory, the production of knowledge must effectively navigate between the mistaken presumption of detachment and value-neutrality of ascendant models of scientific knowledge in the West and the unreflexive ideological dogmatism of ascendant

Marxist models of scientific knowledge in the East.

Habermas, Feminist Theory, and Pragmatism

For the past few decades Habermas has been refining his argument that what he calls "communicative rationality" can be a viable alternative to both positivist "instrumental rationality" and dogmatism (cf. Habermas, 1984, 1988, 1996). According to Habermas, the Enlightenment's exaltation of rationality as the basic resource for human emancipation was not entirely off the mark. The error of the classical Enlightenment philosophers was not their exaltation of rationality as such but their reduction of rationality to an essentially *instrumental* resource for strategically grasping and manipulating the environment. We have been too preoccupied with an image of rationality and knowledge that focuses attention on the individual knower as a socially isolated and self-interested observer–controller of the workings of the empirical world. Alongside this image, Habermas insists that we must add the image of *communicative rationality*, which construes the individual knower as always already intrinsically socially embedded, socially constituted, and concerned with achieving not only *instrumental mastery* over the empirical world but *mutual understanding* with his or her fellow human beings.

Through open and unfettered critical dialogue aimed at mutual understanding, social actors can ultimately come to see the force of the better argument and thereby achieve consensus among themselves. For Habermas, the legitimacy that attaches to the social critique of existing institutions and, conversely, the legitimacy that attaches to those institutions themselves is thus to be found in their observance of certain procedures for maximizing consent. In the case of critical dialogue, legitimacy is the product of uncoerced agreement. In the case of social institutions, legitimacy is secured by maximizing the extent to which what Habermas calls their "addressees" are empowered to influence their creation and reform (Habermas, 1996). Habermas defends his theory of communicative rationality as a universally valid philosophical ground on which to base critical dialogue that does not fall victim either to dogmatism or to the difficulties that have arisen with classic philosophical and scientific efforts to set epistemological foundations. There can be no doubting the theoretical sophistication and truly vast range of learning that informs this body of work. Habermas has thoroughly earned his current reputation as the world's foremost contributor to a post-Marxist critical philosophy. That said, however, his work is by no means without its incisive critics.

Chief among these criticisms is that Habermas, despite his best efforts to remain socially inclusive, inevitably excludes from the communicatively rational and deliberatively democratic process people who are at too far a remove from the basic traits of "the citizen" as construed in classical liberal political philosophy. This citizen is understood to be adult, independent, wholly rational, self-interested, self-assertive, and both morally and intellectually consistent or integrated. Deviations from these traits are regarded as either personal deficiencies that ought to be overcome or as irrelevant to the critical dialogical process. Hence, it is argued that to the extent that gender, cultural, and historical differences embody departures from this model of the social actor, Habermas is relatively incapable of taking these differences seriously (cf. Calhoun, 1995).[11] Feminist "standpoint theorists" have done more than most to highlight the limitations of the universalism and rationalism evident in critical theories such as Habermas's while remaining committed to the project of objective critique itself. It is largely they who have set the foundations for social constructionist critical theorizing.

Feminist standpoint theorists such as Sandra Harding (1986), Nancy Harstock (1983), and Dorothy Smith (1987) were some of the first scholars to borrow from Marxian writings on the maturation of working-class consciousness to develop an epistemology of women's experience and a distinctively women's knowledge. They argued that the social structural position of women in society yields a distinctively authoritative understanding of not only the specific forms of suffering and injustice that women must endure but also the broader structural dynamics that yield those forms of suffering and injustice. Conversely, the social structural position of men in society yields a distinctive form of blindness to these issues. Hence women's social structural disadvantage fosters a critical epistemological *advantage* when it comes to objectively understanding the causes, nature, and consequences of sexism. Standpoint theory provides an interesting and important contribution to the history of critical theory and epistemology by philosophically defending the notions that our sociohistorical differences may be sources of objectivity, as well as "bias," and that knowledge need not take a totalizing or universalistic form. Standpoint theorists instead defend pluralistic and situated understandings of knowledge and objectivity without thereby slipping into a full-blown and wholly uncritical relativism (Haraway, 1991).

Comparatively early into its development, defenders of standpoint theory began to recognize that their simultaneous attention to an objectivist ontology of social structural position and a more subjectivist epistemology of "learning from experience" created certain tensions in this approach. Clearly, not everyone who shares a given social structural position in society experiences it in the same way or shares a similar outlook on the causes and/or (in)justice of their occupying that position. It soon became clear that to make sense of feminist standpoint theory, the standpoint of certain more attentive and/or insightful women would have to be privileged over that of other women who remained comparatively unenlightened. Feminist scholars of color, including Patricia Hill Collins (1991) and bell hooks (cf. 1989), also noted in this literature a tendency to assume that the epistemologically privileged women were relatively affluent white feminists. It was not long before standpoint theory began to succumb to an apparent centrifugal force wherein the epistemological authority of any woman to speak about the experiences of other women came into question. As part of an effort to overcome this problem, contemporary standpoint theory tends to highlight women's experience not as an unequivocal philosophical foundation for knowledge but as a source of important, perhaps indispensable, information for constructing empirically grounded feminist theory. However, feminist theory itself must be legitimated not by experience alone nor by ontological references to specific social structural locations but in critical dialogue with other theories. This return to deliberation and debate has brought several major feminist critical theorists a good deal closer to Habermas's theory of communicative rationality (cf. Benhabib, 1992; Fraser, 1997).

Seyla Benhabib, in particular, has been at the forefront of a community of philosophers who are committed to Habermasian theory but who are seeking to better reconcile Habermasian insights with the challenge posed by postmodern social theory, feminist social theory, and multiculturalism more generally. While acknowledging the complicity of Western science and instrumental rationality in legitimating injustices, including eugenics, slavery, and much else, Benhabib criticizes the postmodern tendency to define those once regarded as modernity's "others" (e.g., so-called primitives, fools, children, and sometimes women) only in terms of their alterity to Western reason. Speaking of these groups only in terms of difference precludes contemplation of whether we share points of commonality that may serve as the basis for meaningful dialogue. This, in turn, encourages a merely abstract, disengaged, and static respect or tolerance in place of genuine social engagement, dialogue, and mutual instruction. As Benhabib (1992, p. 83) writes:

The view that all these groups of individuals represent the "other" of reason is fraught with difficulties, for in stating this, we are defining their identity only with regard to what they are not. I believe this kind of categorisation of the "others" of reason is just as imperialistic in its cognitive attitude as the instrumental reason it criticizes. For any definition of a group's identity not in terms of its own constitutive experiences but in terms of its victimization by others reduces that group's subjectivity to the terms of the dominant discourse and does not allow for an appreciation of the way in which it may challenge that discourse.

These remarks not only indict some of the more extreme versions of postmodernism but also cast aspersion on radical epistemological relativism more generally. Benhabib, among a growing host of others, insists that dignifying modernity's "others" cannot come at the cost of precluding meaningful dialogue with them. This argument is not only of ethical and political value but is also supported by the best philosophical work on the nature of language, interpretation, and communication (cf. Davidson, 1984, 2005). The claim that there might be a radical incommensurability that prevents meaningful communication across lines of cultural, racial, gender, sexual, or class differences is largely regarded among today's most philosophically sophisticated critical theorists as an academic anachronism.[12] There can be no doubting that the world certainly does remain divided by considerable differences of interest, perspective, and communicative style that seriously interfere with our efforts to build social solidarities, cooperation, and consensus, but these differences are no longer viewed as the fixed and insurmountable barriers to productive dialogue and mutual instruction that they once were.

Although pragmatist philosophical approaches are a good deal more modest than traditional critical theories in their specification of both the possibilities for progressive social change and the role that reason and critical dialogue might play in promoting it, these approaches are becoming increasingly ubiquitous resources among contemporary critical theorists, including critical social constructionists. Pragmatists have always held that the value of knowledge should be broadly assessed in terms of its wider ramifications for the good of the individual and society rather than in the more formal, rigid, and narrowly specified philosophical or scientific terms proposed by other philosophical schools of thought. Furthermore, pragmatists advise us to expect these terms of reference to be multiple and to change through time. The comparative evaluation of knowledge claims is not forsaken, but it is nested deeply within the specific sociohistorical contexts under which it must be accomplished. As both Kantian rational formalism and Marxian pretensions to a universalistic understanding of world historical change give way to the reflexivity, pluralism, and localism of feminist and multicultural critical theories, and as the radical relativism of early feminist and multicultural work gives way to a more dialogical approach to the grounding of ideas, it is beginning to seem to many critical theorists that some type of philosophical pragmatism may be the only tenable game in town.

Pragmatism embeds all *intellectual* activity firmly within the *practical* contexts within which it occurs. This means that it firmly rejects the fact–value dichotomy and the notion that philosophical or scientific inquiry should be value-neutral or disinterested. For pragmatists, such notions are absurd not least because they deprive inquiry of any purpose, and they are pernicious because they divorce philosophy and science from the pressing concerns of the wider society. Philosophy and science are viewed as systematic attempts to cope with vital human problems and decidedly not as merely scholastic games of gratifying intellectual curiosity for its own sake. Hence pragmatism shares with the critical theoretical tradition an enduring concern with the relationship between understanding the social world and actively changing

it for the better (Baert, 2005).[13] However, unlike the critical tradition up to Habermas, pragmatists such as William James, John Dewey, and George Herbert Mead were deeply suspicious of the claim that rationality, traditionally conceived, was either the motivating force governing the movement of history or the only adequate resource for promoting progressive social change.

Rational discourse is instead seen to be embedded in lived experience, which is itself understood as a prediscursive, often habitual and nonreflective, practical engagement with the worldly circumstances that confront us. This engagement is skilled and purposeful, but it is not confined to the discursive or propositional logic that we normally associate with rationality—be it instrumental or communicative. Moreover, pragmatists give us good reasons to doubt that our embodied coping skills are sufficiently determinate, sufficiently transparent to conscious self-reflection, or sufficiently self-consistent to be described as the coherent "worldviews" of singular, morally and intellectually consistent social actors. And if in the actual conduct of our practical lives we are not morally and intellectually "of one mind," in the sense presumed by the liberal philosophical tradition, then it is not clear what is to be made of the Habermasian project of consensus building (cf. Calhoun, 1995; Shalin, 1992). We may not have to forsake the prospect of using our various sensemaking capabilities (discursive or otherwise) to support collaboration on particular practical projects. It is quite evident that particular projects can be forged at national, and even global, levels of participation. But by pragmatist lights, the Habermasian dream of building a rationally self-consistent "just society" on such a foundation, with all its implications of a simultaneous and holistic discursive justification and integration of the multifarious intrapersonal, interpersonal, and social structural dimensions of our lives, seems at the very least remote and perhaps completely unimaginable.

The Hermeneutic Tradition

Dilthey's Legacy

The German philosopher and historian Wilhelm Dilthey is generally credited with expanding the scope of hermeneutics beyond the analysis of ancient texts and into a general philosophical argument against conflating the social and natural sciences. Influenced most directly by the theologian Friedrich Schleiermacher, but also drawing selectively from Kantian and Hegelian idealism, Dilthey fiercely opposed the efforts of social theorists such as John Stuart Mill, Herbert Spencer, and Auguste Comte to produce mechanistic causal analyses of society. He insisted that because it is purposeful, meaningful, and creative, social life cannot be explained by natural laws but can be grasped only through *Verstehen*, or interpretive understanding. Dilthey advocated what he called a *lebensphilosophie*, a "philosophy of life," anchored neither in sense data nor in a grand philosophical cosmology but in the variety and complexity of "lived experience" itself. He argued that philosophy, like all meaningful activity, is inevitably motivated and informed by the sociohistorical conditions under which it is accomplished (and from which it cannot be dislodged).

In his later work Dilthey argued that we do not intuit the meaning of people's thoughts, feelings, and intentions but interpretively infer them from what he called their public "expressions." These expressions can be fleeting (such as kisses) or more enduring (such as urban designs), and they may exhibit any manner of human concern. The specific expressions we consider depend on the elements of the social world we wish to understand. However, the more we know about the cultural context of an expression, the more fully equipped we are to interpret it. Dilthey portrayed the work of the human sciences as interpreting the meaning of expressions in light of their relationship to other expressions and to the wider social wholes of which they form parts. Because our understanding of each of these elements can be informed only by our understanding of the others, interpretation is inevitably trapped within the horizons set by these culturally specific forms, or what came to be known as the *hermeneutic circle.* Dilthey was eclectic about the empirical materials and topics proper to the human sciences. Research might focus on individuals (in light of their particular expressions and those others have made about them), or it might be focused on "worldviews" (in light of the more enduring expressions shared by larger social groups), but, in any case, the methodology of the human sciences was held categorically distinct from that of the natural sciences. Dilthey's ideas had direct and profound influences on two of the most important figures in 20th-century intellectual history: Max Weber and Martin Heidegger. I consider in turn these influences and the lines of philosophical development they initiated.

Weber adopted Dilthey's *Verstehen* approach but did not share his concern for articulating universal *philosophical* foundations for the human sciences. Instead, he sought to articulate the *methodological* foundations of his own empirical research (Weber, 1949). He explicitly disavowed Dilthey's claim that understanding the meaning of historical events for those who enact them precluded causal explanations of those events. However, for Weber, causal explanation need not be cast in terms of universal "laws of history" but could instead address the serial causality of particular historical events through theoretically selective comparisons with other cases (Zaret, 1980). Such comparisons can both yield and be facilitated by the formulation of what Weber called *ideal types*—not general theories in the positivist sense but merely heuristic axes of empirical comparison. To the extent that social constructionists have called on comparative historical and/or comparative ethnographic methods to explain the sociohistorical specificity of certain beliefs and practices, they owe a considerable debt to Weber.[14]

Beyond legitimating and popularizing the *Verstehen* methodology, Weber's influence on social constructionism can also be seen, albeit in a mediated form, in Alfred Schutz's adoption of the concept *ideal types*. Whereas Weber had described this concept as specific to social scientific methodology, Schutz integrated it into a general phenomenology of the human *lebenswelt*, or lifeworld, and a philosophically foundationalist defense of *Verstehen* sociology. Schutz argued that intersubjectivity is not preordained by logic, history, or human nature but is actively achieved in ongoing social interaction through use of a vast catalogue of ideal types, or "typifications," compiled into a "stock of knowledge" shared by social actors (Schutz, 1962). Because interaction requires people to interpret each other, Schutz criticized Weber and others for failing to judge the adequacy of their own scientific typifications of social action by their fidelity to those offered by social actors themselves. These ideas had an immense and valuable influence on constructionist studies primarily via their adoption by Peter Berger and Thomas Luckmann (1967) and by Harold Garfinkel (1967). However, Schutz has also come in for a rather lengthy list of valid criticisms (cf. Lynch, 1993, pp. 133–141). For the present, let us suffice to say that Schutz did not fully appreciate the importance of the facts that: (1) perception and practical action are embodied and (2) there is a deeply consequential continuity between the *lebenswelt*, science, and philosophy.

Heidegger drew on Dilthey's work on *Verstehen* to formulate his critique of Husserl's phenomenology of consciousness. Husserl, he felt, had too reverently accepted that science, or scientific philosophy, can objectively describe the nature of subjectivity and its relationship with the world. Heidegger argued that science, although an important resource, did not, and could not, attend to the phenomenological conditions of its own possibility. By its very nature, science must reify the ontological distinction between theory and world and hence can never explain how this distinction could itself emerge as a meaningful and useful picture of human life. In *Being and Time* (1962), he argued that to understand why humans distinguish theory from world, mind from body, and subject from object and, indeed, to understand how we live, it is necessary to interpret what is underneath Husserl's Cartesian reification of the mind, to draft a phenomenological ontology of human being-in-the-world. This entails acknowledging that, prior to our conscious interpretation of it, we are always already variously engaged with, and immersed in, the world in ways that inevitably shape interpretation. This engagement is practical, not theoretical; concerned, not detached; inexplicit, but sensually attentive; conceptually diffuse, but skilled; and, above all, "mindless" (Dreyfus, 1991). Coping is phenomenologically prior to theorizing or, indeed, to the conceptual identification of any "thing," including our own "self." It is precisely this pretheoretical coping that *discloses* aspects of the phenomenal world as relevant, meaningful, and either familiar or deserving of reflective consideration.

Heidegger influenced Maurice Merleau-Ponty (1962), who, in turn, revolutionized phenomenology with his fine-grained analyses of the body as a crucial medium for human being-in-the-world (see also Leder, 1990; Turner, 1992). Heidegger also inspired unprecedented concern for what Michael Polanyi (1967) has called "tacit knowledge" and the priority of everyday coping, in all its diversity of skills, to theoretical or discursive knowledge (cf. Bourdieu, 1990). Later in his career, though, Heidegger became increasingly interested in language as what he called the "house of Being."[15] This reduction of hermeneutics to a concern for the "linguisticality" of human being-in-the-world was further promoted by the influential work of Hans-Georg Gadamer (1975).[16] Although Gadamer cast much new light on the process of dialogue as a vehicle for mutual understanding, his work has also encouraged a confinement of *Verstehen* scholarship to language (or language use) and abandonment of the wider phenomenological concern with the meanings embodied in both linguistic and nonlinguistic events. Though they were by no means Saussurian structuralists, the later Heidegger and Gadamer helped to cultivate a fertile intellectual ground for the seeds of structuralism to take root. For if language is not merely an important species of meaningful social practice but the "home in which man dwells," it is hard to avoid the conclusion that language preexists and prestructures all social practices in just the sense suggested by structuralism. These ideas piqued profound interest in the kinds of "things" that language, or discourse, might be.

Poststructuralism and Postmodernism

The tendency to reduce all meaning to linguistic meaning has been even more strongly encouraged by the explicitly structuralist writings of such people as Claude Levi-Strauss and Michel Foucault. Following Ferdinand de Saussure (1983), Levi-Strauss argued that language possesses an objective identity that structures human history and experience from positions external to them. Although this was an argument that Foucault also took quite seriously in his early works, including *Madness and Civilization* (1965), *The Archaeology of Knowledge* (1972), and *The Order of Things* (1973), he disavowed it later, contributing with others, such as Jacques Lacan and Jacques Derrida, to the rise of poststructuralism. Foucault was always interested not only in the linguistic "discourses" or "epistemes" that confine meaningful thought and experience but also in the various regimes of power within which these discourses are forged and participate. As he moved from his archaeological method to Nietzschean genealogy, he grew increasingly attentive not only to discourse as a linguistic structure but also to the body as a materially incarnate site of inscription and discipline (Foucault, 1977). Moreover, Foucault rejected what he called the "search for origins" and instead recommended tracing the diffuse historical movements that shape specific fragments of the present. In his latest work on ethics and the care of the self, Foucault drifted still further away from his structuralist roots to attend much more closely to issues of individual agency and embodiment (see Foucault, 1988). Foucault in each of his various incarnations has had an incalculable influence throughout the social constructionist literature (though I fear it is his early linguistic structuralism and tendency to reify "discourse" that remains most influential).

A chapter on the philosophical foundations of social constructionism cannot possibly conclude without some mention of postmodernism. The term *postmodernism* now has many different meanings, but I think it is reasonable for the sake of the present discussion to take a minimal and literal reading. Postmodernists hold that there is value in distinguishing the present historical moment, or at least certain features of it, from the modern era. Whereas the modern era is held to have been defined by its rational secular humanism, its universalism, its liberalism, and its cosmopolitanism, the postmodern era is said to be defined in opposition to one or all of these values. Postmodernists have, for a variety of reasons, lost faith in the modernists' Promethean dream (or nightmare) of building society on the grounds cleared by a rational and disinterested grasp of the universe. In place of rational mastery, they install an irrational or aesthetic taste for the sublime; in place of universalism, perspectivism; in place of liberalism, rebellion; and in place of cosmopolitanism, localism. Not all so-called postmodernists are equally opposed to all so-called modernist values. But for many, some combination of these ideas form a heady, perhaps intoxicating, brew that appears to provide a powerful antidote to the many corruptions of the modern era.

The literary brilliance of such writers as Nietzsche, Foucault, Derrida, and Rorty has also encouraged many of us to take seriously the value of blurring genre distinctions between literature, science, and philosophy. The traditions stemming from both Dewey and Nietzsche remind us that human flourishing can be promoted by much more than rational dialogue, and it is often both affirming and progressive to appeal to our audiences' broader sense and sensibilities (cf. Nehamas, 1998; Rorty, 1998; Shusterman, 1997). Indeed, these writers have made the pretense that reason was ever so distinct from rhetoric, or that scientists were ever successful in purging rhetorical devices from their texts, extremely difficult to sustain. However, these arguments can be taken too far. As Habermas has noted, blurring the line between reasonable and beautiful argument provides fodder for demagogues. Moreover, though our criteria for judging them do certainly sometimes overlap, there remain important differences between beautifully crafted and empirically substantiated arguments. These differences are by no means grounded on timeless and universal foundations, but they are, nonetheless, extremely well grounded in our current intellectual cultures and institutions. These cultures and institutions will no doubt change in time, but those who would hope to influence the direction of their change must be rhetorically deft enough to persuade their peers of the wisdom in their suggestions. Though we may have long since been persuaded to leave aside all notions of infallibility, I am not sure many of us engaged in empirical research are ready to forsake use of the concept of "evidence" just yet.

The critical flaw in most postmodern philosophy is its failure to sufficiently heed the pragmatic and early Heideggerian point that inexplicit everyday coping is always temporally prior to and infused throughout the production and consumption of linguistic meaning. Theories, narratives, epistemes, discourses, texts, and indeed language use in general are grounded and embodied not in fixed linguistic structures that hover above,

beneath, or behind social practices but in a vast and often incongruous collection of concrete social activities in which people are practically and emotionally, not just conceptually, invested. Our lives are not only linguistically meaningful but also, more fundamentally, meaningful at the level of our embodied and prediscursive practical engagements and activities (Bourdieu, 1990; Lynch, 1993; Shusterman, 1997; Turner, 1992). Because they neglect this, too many postmodernists remain bewitched by linguistic reductionism and the specter of a truly perfect antithesis in linguistic structuralism—as if there really were, as Derrida once claimed, nothing beyond the text. They remain confined to a binary choice between the absolute reality of a stodgy structuralist dogma and the absolute unreality of a careless postmodern irony. By their lights there can be, *literally*, nothing else.

But this trap can hold us only if we accept the highly dubious claim that modernity can really be reduced to the merely symbolic interplay of explicit linguistic orderings (discourses or narratives) and their explicit linguistic antitheses (critiques, deconstructions). Only then will we read the whole of modern history, in all of its infinite variety, as comprised inevitably either in conformity with or in resistance to specific discourses or narratives. But contra both linguistic structuralism and postmodernism, there are countless social activities that are neither mere embodiments nor mere critiques of established discourses, if by *discourses* we mean relatively integrated and identifiable conceptual systems. Although these social activities may often involve using language and may sometimes implicate the relatively stable and explicit conceptual orders that some cultural sociologists like to call "codes," they are decidedly not reducible to either (cf. Bourdieu, 1991; de Certeau, 1984; Lynch, 1993; Turner, 1994). Free from the tyranny of structuralist dogma and the havoc of postmodern disorder, we are all engaged in myriad meaningful activities that, quite plainly, we care about. And it is precisely the fact that we do care about them that both animates our discussions and anchors the resolution of our disputes. There are no fixed linguistic structures grounding our common lives. But there is no need for them.

In sum, language is not the prestructured container of all social practices but simply a conceptual category we sometimes use to interpret or describe a particular subset of social practices. Furthermore, as Quine showed us, our interpretations and/or descriptions of language (or anything else) do not and cannot correspond, in the positivist sense, with the practices they are about. Instead, our interpretations, descriptions, analyses, and theories are socially constructed to do particular kinds of work. Their forms are thoroughly mediated by the interests and practical involvements for which they are devised. But, contra Descartes, these interests and practical involvements do not necessarily distort our understanding. Because no understanding of the world is disinterested or divorced from practical action, it is senseless to speak of distortion without also speaking to the specific, socially constructed standards by which distortion is measured. These standards are inevitably contestable, in science and philosophy no less than anywhere else (Habermas, 1987, pp. 408–409). Hence, if and when epistemological disputes arise, they are not, and could never be, resolved by recourse to fixed natural or logical standards. They can be resolved only by recourse to the provisional standards that we ourselves create in light of the specific practical projects we hope to fulfill. These standards embody our claims to power/knowledge and we must expect to be held accountable for them. But although our claims are certainly fallible and may be flawed, they are by no means always arbitrary. Their legitimacy resides in the practices they make possible and in our willingness to defend them in open and inclusive dialogue.

Conclusion

At the beginning of the chapter I expressed my belief that social constructionists could benefit from a more sustained and explicit consideration of the intellectual legitimacy and/or social value of our own research as such. I also suggested that this would entail getting past the well-established fact that all claims to knowledge are inevitably claims to power and developing an approach that helps us more effectively arbitrate between such claims.

One major obstacle to doing so that has haunted the constructionist literature is radical relativism. Too many of us have clung too fast to the principle that our beliefs, practices, and experiences are somehow confined by our different belief systems, conceptual schemes, cultures, discourses, epistemes, languages, paradigms, or worldviews. This has then dissuaded us from seriously considering the possibilities (and the immense value) of critical dialogue across these lines of difference. I have argued that although we are no doubt conditioned by our pasts, we are by no means *confined* by them. Despite our various predilections and biases, people can (and do) learn and constructively engage with each other across lines of considerable differences of interest, perspective, and intellectual style. This is certainly not to suggest that there are never difficulties in doing so. My point is that these difficulties are never ontological, nor are they as insurmountable as our intellectual ancestors have sometimes supposed. This goes not only for broad lines of social difference but also for the narrower lines of theoretical and/or methodological difference that sometimes separate us from our colleagues. Who we engage in dialogue should be governed only by our substantive interests and a desire to improve our understanding of the world, never by fixed philosophical partitions between cultures, between academic disciplines, or between their different branches.

A second, perhaps related, obstacle has been fixed philosophical divides that separate causal explanation and *Verstehen* understanding. As Weber suspected long ago, there is no philosophical chasm here. Social research (including constructionist research) cannot be purely nomothetic because social life is not a closed system and because it is replete with hugely consequential singular events (e.g., the French Revolution, the Industrial Revolution, the Holocaust) that cannot be understood as mere exhibits of universal laws of history. But it cannot be purely idiographic, either, because social life is impossible to understand exclusively in terms of its particularity. We cannot sustain a Diltheyian refusal to ever speak of structural causation in the social realm, because we cannot plausibly sustain the view that human history has been governed by nothing but the uncaused interplay of human intentions (whether tacit or conscious).[17] Hence there can, and must, be constructive dialogue between causal and *Verstehen* approaches to social research. Philosophy gives us no grounds to regret this. As Popper taught us, even statements of strict universal laws are conjectural and fallible. They, too, are social constructions to be valued for their practical payoffs and their resistance to critique. Moreover, there are many more modest alternatives to either strict or probabilistic covering laws that nonetheless allow us to speak meaningfully of causation in the social world (cf. Barnes, 1974; Calhoun, 1998). Although they all may be extensional, they are not necessarily incompatible with alternative explanatory or descriptive vocabularies (Rorty, 1991a). Thus there is no intrinsic threat that causal explanations commit us to any manner of foundationalism. Though constructionist research seeks to describe and/or explain how people use and have come by their conceptual orientations to things, it should not seek to do so with exclusive reference to the uncaused interplay of human intentions.

A third unnecessary philosophical impediment to maximizing open and inclusive critical dialogue pertains to the question of scale. Lyotard (1984), among many other antifoundationalists, seems to think that large-scale narratives run a higher risk of foundationalism than small-scale narratives. This is mistaken. Universalistic ontologies, theories of epochal change, Robert Merton's middle-range theories, conversation analytic theories, and theories concerning particular societies, language games, and even particular people or events are all equally capable of being cast in foundationalist or constructionist terms.[18] If we think that such things as nature, humanity, culture, men, women, capitalism, role conflict, social norms, language games, conversations, Europe, Mahatma Gandhi, or this sentence have unequivocal and discoverable essences that occur independently of the standards of evaluation in force within particular cultures of inquiry, we will fall to the foundationalist side of this dichotomy, regardless of the scale of our investigation. If we accept Quine's critiques of both positivism and the analytic–synthetic distinction, we will fall to the constructionist side of this dichotomy, once again, regardless of the scale of our investigation. By Quinean lights, regardless of its scale, anything describable as research (constructionist or not) must be meaningfully embedded in sociohistorically specific contexts of inquiry; it must be fallible in light of local standards; and it must be theoretical in the sense that it contributes to a general (and generalizing) body of wisdom. Even if we forsake nomothetic research completely to concern ourselves solely with the particularity of single case studies, our work will nonetheless inevitably be evaluated for its contributions to more general lines of inquiry. Therefore, it behooves us all to think carefully and broadly about what those more general lines of inquiry might be and to design our research accordingly.

Last, if we are to foster more fruitful and inclusive dialogue, constructionists must reconsider what distinguishes us from nonconstructionists. More specifically, we must reconsider the rather widely entrenched idea that, by confining our attention to linguistic structures or linguistic activities, we might somehow dodge the pretense of objectivism. We cannot.[19] Regardless of our topic, constructionist research cannot avoid the performative presumption to be *about* something. This is entailed in any act of research. And, if we wish to preserve some sense for the idea that our inquiries are more than mere imaginative exercises, we must commit to the provisionally objectivist claim that our research is about something *in the world* (Weinberg, 2006). We can, and certainly should, acknowledge our fallibility and selectivity and the unavoidable embeddedness of our research in particular cultures of inquiry. And we can, and should, acknowledge that our own descriptive and/or explanatory vocabularies do not necessarily preclude the validity of others with which they cannot be conflated. But these gestures do not avoid the performative presumption to be validly referring to some thing(s) in the world. Hence confining our discussion to linguistic structures and/or linguistic activities does not spare us the presumption to objectivity. It only eviscerates our understanding of these matters by artificially divorcing them from the broader, extradiscursive, practical contexts within which they participate (Bourdieu, 1991; Goodwin, 1994, 2000; Gubrium, 1993).

To my mind, constructionist research is not about evading the presumption to have validly described the world. It cannot be. Instead, constructionism is about the recognition that things could be otherwise and that we might make them so. It is about recognizing that our theories are answerable to our common lives before, during, and after their answerability to our common world. It is about recognizing that with claiming the power to have valuably and validly described the world inevitably comes the personal responsibility to defend our claims against all comers—that our legitimacy in doing so comes from nowhere else. And it is about rec-

ognizing that if it is anything, epistemology is an ethics of truth. It is about making normative claims as to how we might better, or more valuably, understand the worlds we inhabit. Researchers who present themselves as amoral or, as they might prefer, "value-free" and disembodied spectators on the workings of the social world are mistaken. The truth is that we must live in the world if we would hope to understand it.

• Notes

1. One of the most famous cases of a philosophically foundationalist social constructionism is Peter Berger and Thomas Luckman (1967) themselves, who predicate much of their argument in *The Social Construction of Reality* on Arnold Gehlen's foundationalist philosophical claims regarding the intrinsic "world-openness" of human nature and Alfred Schutz's foundationalist philosophical claims regarding the universal characteristics of the human *lebenswelt*, or lifeworld.

2. Though historically they have been very closely related, philosophical foundationalism should not be confused with analytic, or Anglo–American, philosophy more generally. Many self-described analytic philosophers are resolutely opposed to philosophical foundationalism.

3. Only if human beings actually possess the faculties to rationally recognize and pursue their own self-interests might they be held entitled to do so and genuinely equipped to freely consent to a social contract that constrains their freedoms. Like so many democratic theorists who have followed after him, Locke did not cast our possession of these faculties as a fallible empirical hypothesis but as a self-evident philosophical truth.

4. Before Kant, those we would now identify as early modern philosophers did not distinguish themselves from scientists. They identified themselves, along with such people as Galileo, Boyle, and Newton, as practitioners of natural philosophy, which was an amalgam of speculative reason and empirical investigation. Only after Kant were these pursuits seen as distinct and was the practical craft of philosophical research distinguished from that of scientific research.

5. Some of the more prominent logical

positivists were Rudolf Carnap, Carl Hempel, Ernest Nagel, Otto Neurath, and Moritz Schlick.

6. The pervasive popularity of Wittgenstein's later work among social constructionists should not suggest that there is any consensus as to its specific ramifications for social research. For a taste of the controversies surrounding this matter see David Bloor (1992, 2004), David Bogen (1999), Martin Kusch (2004), Michael Lynch (1992a, 1992b, 1993), Wes Sharrock (2004), and Peter Winch (1958).

7. Before Quine, many philosophers believed that one could formulate explicit criteria, or truth conditions, with which to validate a proposition such as "It is raining outside" by directly linking this proposition with the sense data that could confirm its truth. Quine's holism suggested that this was impossible because the terms of the proposition (i.e., *rain, outside, it, is*) derive their meaning not only from their worldly referents but also from their relation to other propositions regarding the nature of "rain" as opposed to, say, "sleet" or "fog," the nature of "outside" as opposed to, say, "elsewhere," and so forth. These related propositions often hail not only from the formalized languages of logic or science but also from the broader culture. The term *rain*, for example, may figure in meteorological propositions, but its meaning in these propositions cannot be established exclusively by its relation to other meteorological terms.

8. Quine's insight that our beliefs about the world are interdependent and fallible has led many to cite him in support of radical cultural relativism. However, as Donald Davidson (1984), Richard Rorty (1991b), and others have noted, Quine's work can actually be adapted to support a powerful critique of both philosophical foundationalism and cultural relativism. Extending Quine's (1960) work on "radical translation," Davidson (1984) has argued that, although all of our beliefs, scientific or otherwise, are indeed fallible, revisable, and interdependent, it is patently impossible to seriously consider the idea that most of our current beliefs are in error because to do so would completely immobilize us. Therefore, our revisions must be of particular beliefs (or sets of beliefs) and, if they are to occur through a process of learning, must occur so as to make our new beliefs compatible with the bulk of what we presently hold to be true. Conversely, the same principle holds true for our efforts to understand cultural others. To interpret another's beliefs and practices, we must assume that they are intelligible *by our own lights*, not only theirs. Hence, the culturally relativist idea that another culture might be radically "incommensurable" with our own can be entertained only in the abstract. It cannot be taken seriously in the actual course of cross-cultural empirical research or communication. To perceive someone as a language user at all is to perceive much of what they do as meaningful and to thereby possess resources with which to facilitate cross-cultural dialogue.

9. Social constructionist research programs as varied as David Bloor's (1991) "strong program" in the sociology of knowledge, Pierre Bourdieu's (1990) "logic of practice," Harry Collins and Steven Yearley's (1992) "social realism," and Malcolm Spector and John Kitsuse's (2001) social constructionist sociology of social problems, among others, exhibit different sociological variants on Quine's naturalized epistemology that also exhibit analogous metatheoretical commitments regarding the nature of the "social world" and its causal relationships to the knowing subject. To the extent that these commitments are cast as essentially immune to empirically grounded arguments, it is fair to consider them, along with Quine's, as philosophically foundationalist commitments.

10. Critical theorists have found the threat of relativism that they see in the work of Mannheim and other sociologists of knowledge and science anathema because they have been reluctant to let go of the distinction between epistemologically authoritative or objective *critique*, on the one hand, and merely partisan, opinionated, or subjective *complaint*, on the other. Even when they leave aside any claim to "the scientific method" to merely amplify the voices of dispossessed members of our societies, this is still done on the grounds that these voices are epistemologically authoritative (cf. Harding, 1986; Smith, 1987). They are lauded as uniquely objective insofar as they arise from the experiences of actual "eyewitnesses" at the *true* sites of human suffering and injustice. Thus although critical theorists certainly do debate the efficacy of particular techniques for achieving epistemological authority or "objectivity," rarely do they forsake the project of transcending relativism as, at least, an ultimately realizable goal (Fondacaro & Weinberg, 2002). I will return to this topic later.

11. But see, for example, Lincoln Dahlberg (2005) for a defense of Habermas on this score.

12. These theorists do not argue that it is possible to find a set metalanguage within which to arbitrate the merits of competing belief systems, nor that we might find the unequivocally optimum translation manual with which to facilitate dialogue across lines of cultural difference. Rather, the claim is that recognizing one another as language users in the first place is evidence of our possessing resources with which to begin to find each other's beliefs and practices meaningful. Through mutual engagement we learn from and about each other, and our linguistic and cultural resources expand. Therefore, we are not culturally, linguistically, or ethically isolated from one another, as radical relativists once had it. It is quite true that one cannot practice Western and Chinese medicine simultaneously. But that does not mean that Chinese doctors cannot learn Western medicine, and vice versa.

13. This has sometimes been forgotten by social scientists whose encounters with pragmatism have been mediated by the writings of Herbert Blumer (1969). Blumer, though by no means unconcerned with the solution of social problems or progressive social change, tended to present the merits of pragmatism more narrowly in terms of its superior theoretical grasp of human perception, learning, and social interaction. The normative commitments of the early pragmatist philosophers were thereby understated. But see Robert Antonio (1989), Hans Joas (1997), and Dmitri Shalin (1992) for sociological treatments that highlight the ramifications of American pragmatism for critical theory.

14. One might also argue that constructionist research has benefited considerably from Weber's deflationary redefinition of the concept "rationality" from a philosophically privileged mode of thought or argument into a mere species of social action marked by its links to institutionalized rules.

15. In his "Letter on Humanism," Heidegger writes, "Language is the house of Being. In its home man dwells. Those who think and those who create with words are the guardians of this home. Their guardianship accomplishes the manifestation of Being insofar as they bring the manifestation to language and maintain it in language through their speech" (Heidegger, 1977, p. 217). More tellingly still, in *Poetry, Language, Thought*, he writes, "Man acts as though he were the shaper and master of language, while in fact language is the mistress of man. . . . For strictly, it is language that speaks. Man first speaks when, and only when, he responds to language by listening to its appeal" (as quoted in Rorty, 1991a, p. 64).

16. Gadamer (2006, p. 48) writes, "All human knowledge of the world is linguistically mediated. . . . The linguisticality [*Sprachlichkeit*] of our being-in-the-world articulates in the end the whole realm of our experience."

17. Moreover, if one is persuaded, as I am, by philosophers such as Davidson and Rorty that the attribution of reasons to agents can be causal explanations of their actions, then idiographic analyses become just a particular species of causal explanation rather than its antithesis. Human agents, or selves, then appear alongside a multitude of other kinds of hypothetical causal mechanisms we use to proffer interpretive, explanatory, and/or predictive analyses of people's behavior (Weinberg, 1997, 2005). One need not speak of timeless universal laws to speak meaningfully, and/or scientifically, of causal explanations.

18. Nancy Fraser writes in this regard, "In general, I am not persuaded that post-structuralist suspicions of 'totality,' certainly well founded when it comes to ahistorical philosophical 'metanarratives,' tell against attempts to devise 'big' empirical theories about historically specific social formations. Rather I assume a big diagnostic picture is both epistemically possible and politically useful" (as quoted in Antonio, 1998, p. 32, n. 18). I would take this one step further to note that the ahistoricality of a philosophical metanarrative is problematic only to the extent that we forget the sociohistorically specific conditions that give it sense and value. It is not the universality of a narrative's topical scope but its presumption to "a view from nowhere" that is problematic.

19. Lynch (1998, p. 28) comments poignantly, "In many [constructionist] case studies, the accent of reality is withheld by the analyst when describing what participants in a controversy avow or presume to be true, but this does not apply to analyst's stance toward the disputes themselves. The disputes, and their relevant social contexts, are treated as actual social events to be described (and sometimes explained) with all due empirical care." See also Lawrence Hazelrigg's (1986) incisive discussion of this issue.

References

Adorno, T. W. (1990). *Negative dialectics*. London: Routledge.

Antonio, R. J. (1989). The normative foundations of emancipatory theory: Evolutionary versus pragmatic perspectives. *American Journal of Sociology, 94,* 721–748.

Antonio, R. J. (1998). Mapping postmodern social theory. In A. Sica (Ed.), *What is social theory?* (pp. 22–75). Malden, MA: Blackwell.

Baert, P. (2005). *Philosophy of the social sciences: Towards pragmatism*. Cambridge, UK: Polity.

Barnes, B. (1974). *Scientific knowledge and sociological theory*. London: Routledge.

Benhabib, S. (1992). *Situating the self*. London: Routledge.

Berger, P. L., & Luckmann, T. (1967). *The social construction of reality: A treatise in the sociology of knowledge*. New York: Anchor.

Bloor, D. (1991). *Knowledge and social imagery* (2nd ed.). Chicago: University of Chicago Press.

Bloor, D. (1992). Left and right Wittgensteinians. In A. Pickering (Ed.), *Science as practice and culture* (pp. 266–282). Chicago: University of Chicago Press.

Bloor, D. (2004). Institutions and rule skepticism: A reply to Martin Kusch. *Social Studies of Science, 34*(4), 593–601.

Blumer, H. (1969). *Symbolic interactionism*. Englewood Cliffs, NJ: Prentice Hall.

Bogen, D. (1999). *Order without rules*. Albany: State University of New York Press.

Bourdieu, P. (1990). *The logic of practice*. Stanford, CA: Stanford University Press.

Bourdieu, P. (1991). *Language and symbolic power*. Cambridge, MA: Harvard University Press.

Calhoun, C. (1995). *Critical social theory*. Cambridge, MA: Blackwell.

Calhoun, C. (1998). Explanation in historical sociology: Narrative, general theory, and historically specific theory. *American Journal of Sociology, 104*(3), 846–871.

Collins, H., & Yearley, S. (1992). Journey into space. In A. Pickering (Ed.), *Science as practice and culture* (pp. 369–389). Chicago: University of Chicago Press.

Collins, P. H. (1991). *Black feminist thought*. New York: Routledge.

Dahlberg, L. (2005). The Habermasian public sphere: Taking difference seriously? *Theory and Society, 34,* 111–136.

Davidson, D. (1984). On the very idea of a conceptual scheme. In D. Davidson, *Inquiries into truth and interpretation* (pp. 183–198). Oxford, UK: Oxford University Press.

Davidson, D. (2005). *Truth, language, and history*. Oxford, UK: Oxford University Press.

de Certeau, M. (1984). *The practice of everyday life*. Berkeley: University of California Press.

Dreyfus, H. L. (1991). *Being-in-the-world*. Cambridge, MA: MIT Press.

Feyerabend, P. (1978). *Science in a free society*. London: New Left Books.

Fondacaro, M. R., & Weinberg, D. (2002). Concepts of social justice in community psychology: Toward a social ecological epistemology. *American Journal of Community Psychology, 30*(4), 473–492.

Foucault, M. (1965). *Madness and civilization*. New York: Vintage.

Foucault, M. (1972). *The archaeology of knowledge*. New York: Pantheon.

Foucault, M. (1973). *The order of things*. New York: Vintage.

Foucault, M. (1977). Nietzsche, genealogy, history. In D. Bouchard (Ed.), *Language, counter-memory, practice* (pp. 139–164). Ithaca, NY: Cornell University Press.

Foucault, M. (1988). *The care of the self*. New York: Vintage.

Fraser, N. (1997). *Justice interruptus*. London: Routledge.

Gadamer, H.-G. (1975). *Truth and method*. London: Sheed & Ward.

Gadamer, H.-G. (2006). Classical and philosophical hermeneutics. *Theory, Culture and Society, 23*(1), 29–56.

Garfinkel, H. (1967). *Studies in ethnomethodology*. Englewood Cliffs, NJ: Prentice Hall.

Goodman, N. (1978). *Ways of worldmaking*. Indianapolis, IN: Hackett.

Goodwin, C. (1994). Professional vision. *American Anthropologist, 96*(3), 606–633.

Goodwin, C. (2000). Action and embodiment within situated human interaction. *Journal of Pragmatics, 32,* 1489–1522.

Gubrium, J. F. (1993). For a cautious naturalism. In J. A. Holstein & G. Miller (Eds.), *Reconsidering social constructionism* (pp. 89–101). New York: Aldine de Gruyter.

Habermas, J. (1984). *Theory of communicative action* (Vol. 1). Boston: Beacon Press.

Habermas, J. (1987). *The philosophical discourse of modernity*. Cambridge, MA: MIT Press.

Habermas, J. (1988). *Theory of communicative action* (Vol. 2). Boston: Beacon Press.

Habermas, J. (1996). *Between facts and norms*. Cambridge, MA: MIT Press.

Hacking, I. (1999). *The social construction of what?* Cambridge, MA: Harvard University Press.

Haraway, D. J. (1991). *Simians, cyborgs, and women*. London: Routledge.

Harding, S. (1986). *The science question in feminism*. Ithaca, NY: Cornell University Press.

Hartsock, N. (1983). The feminist standpoint: Developing the ground for a specifically feminist historical materialism. In S. Harding & M. Hintikka (Eds.), *Discovering reality* (pp. 283–310). Dordrecht, The Netherlands: Reidel.

Hazelrigg, L. E. (1986). Is there a choice between "constructionism" and "objectivism"? *Social Problems, 33*(6), S1–S13.

Heidegger, M. (1962). *Being and time*. New York: Harper & Row.

Heidegger, M. (1977). *Basic writings*. New York: Harper & Row.

hooks, b. (1989). *Talking back*. Boston: Southend.

Horkheimer, M., & Adorno, T. W. (1972). *The dialectics of enlightenment*. New York: Herder & Herder.

Hume, D. (1978). *A treatise on human nature*. Oxford, UK: Oxford University Press.

Jay, M. (1996). *The dialectical imagination*. Berkeley: University of California Press.

Joas, H. (1997). *G. H. Mead*. Boston: MIT Press.

Kuhn, T. S. (1962). *The structure of scientific revolutions*. Chicago: University of Chicago Press.

Kusch, M. (2004). Rule scepticism and the sociology of scientific knowledge: The Bloor–Lynch debate revisited. *Social Studies of Science, 34*(4), 571–591.

Leder, D. (1990). *The absent body*. Chicago: University of Chicago Press.

Levine, D. N. (1995). *Visions of the sociological tradition*. Chicago: University of Chicago Press.

Lynch, M. (1992a). Extending Wittgenstein: The pivotal move from epistemology to the sociology of science. In A. Pickering (Ed.), *Science as practice and culture* (pp. 215–265). Chicago: University of Chicago Press.

Lynch, M. (1992b). From the "will to theory" to the discursive collage: A reply to Bloor's "Left and Right Wittgensteinians." In A. Pickering (Ed.), *Science as practice and culture* (pp. 283–300). Chicago: University of Chicago Press.

Lynch, M. (1993). *Scientific practice and ordinary action*. Cambridge, UK: Cambridge University Press.

Lynch, M. (1998). Toward a constructivist genealogy of social constructivism. In I. Velody & R. Williams (Eds.), *The politics of constructionism* (pp. 13–32). London: Sage.

Lyotard, J.-F. (1984). *The postmodern condition*. Minneapolis: University of Minnesota Press.

Mannheim, K. (1936). *Ideology and utopia*. New York: Harvest.

Merleau-Ponty, M. (1962). *Phenomenology of perception*. London: Routledge.

Nehamas, A. (1998). *The art of living*. Berkeley: University of California Press.

Polanyi, M. (1967). *The tacit dimension* (2nd ed.). New York: Anchor.

Popper, K. (1992). *The logic of scientific discovery*. London: Routledge.

Porter, R. (2003). *Flesh in the age of reason*. London: Penguin.

Putnam, H. (1981). *Reason, truth, and history*. Cambridge, UK: Cambridge University Press.

Putnam, H. (2002). *The collapse of the fact value dichotomy and other essays*. Cambridge, MA: Harvard University Press.

Quine, W. van O. (1951). Two dogmas of empiricism. *Philosophical Review, 60*(1), 20–43.

Quine, W. van O. (1960). *Word and object*. Cambridge, MA: MIT Press.

Quine, W. van O. (1969). Epistemology naturalized. In W. van O. Quine, *Ontological relativity and other essays* (pp. 69–90). New York: Columbia University Press.

Rorty, R. (1980). *Philosophy and the mirror of nature*. Oxford, UK: Blackwell.

Rorty, R. (1991a). *Essays on Heidegger and others*. Cambridge, UK: Cambridge University Press.

Rorty, R. (1991b). *Objectivity, relativism, and truth*. Cambridge, UK: Cambridge University Press,

Rorty, R. (1998). *Achieving our country*. Cambridge, MA: Harvard University Press.

Rouse, J. (2002). *How scientific practices matter*. Chicago: University of Chicago Press.

Saussure, F. de. (1983). *Course in general linguistics*. Oxford, UK: Duckworth.

Schutz, A. (1962). *Collected papers* (Vol. 1). The Hague, The Netherlands: Nijhoff.

Shalin, D. N. (1992). Critical theory and the pragmatist challenge. *American Journal of Sociology, 98*, 237–279.

Sharrock, W. (2004). No case to answer: A response to Martin Kusch's "Rule scepticism and the sociology of scientific knowledge." *Social Studies of Science, 34*(4), 603–614.

Shusterman, R. (1997). *Practicing philosophy*. London: Routledge.

Smith, D. (1987). *The everyday world as problematic*. Boston: Northeastern University Press.

Spector, M., & Kitsuse, J. I. (2001). *Constructing social problems* (2nd ed.). London: Transaction.

Taylor, C. (1989). *Sources of the self: The making of the modern identity*. Cambridge, MA: Harvard University Press.

Tucker, R. C. (Ed.). (1978). *The Marx–Engels reader*. New York: Norton.

Turner, B. S. (1992). *Regulating bodies*. London: Routledge.

Turner, S. (1994). *The social theory of practices*. Chicago: University of Chicago Press.

Weber, M. (1949). *The methodology of the social sciences*. New York: Free Press.

Weinberg, D. (1997). The social construction of nonhuman agency: The case of mental disorder. *Social Problems, 44*(2), 217–234.

Weinberg, D. (2005). *Of others inside: Insanity, addiction and belonging in America*. Philadelphia: Temple University Press.

Weinberg, D. (2006). Language, dialogue, and ethnographic objectivity. In P. Drew, G. Raymond, & D. Weinberg (Eds.), *Talk and interaction in social research methods* (pp. 97–112). London: Sage.

Weinberg, D. (in press). Social constructionism. In B. Turner (Ed.), *The new Blackwell companion to social theory* (3rd ed.). Malden, MA: Blackwell.

Winch, P. (1958). *The idea of a social science and its relation to philosophy*. London: Routledge.

Wittgenstein, L. (1922). *Tractatus logico–philosophicus*. London: Routledge.

Wittgenstein, L. (1953). *Philosophical investigations*. Oxford, UK: Blackwell.

Wittgenstein, L. (1975). *Philosophical remarks*. Oxford, UK: Blackwell.

Zaret, D. (1980). From Weber to Parsons and Schutz: The eclipse of history in modern social theory. *American Journal of Sociology, 85*(5), 1180–1201.

CHAPTER 3

Historical Development and Defining Issues of Constructionist Inquiry

- Joel Best

We are all social constructionists today, almost.
—JASPER AND GOODWIN (2005, p. 3)

The term *social construction* has a surprisingly long history within American sociology. Its first appearance in the literature seems to have been in Lester F. Ward's 1905 article "Evolution of Social Structures": "A structure is something that has been constructed, and a study of social structure is the study of a process and not a product. Our task, therefore, is . . . to inquire into the methods of social construction" (p. 589). This is not inconsistent with today's usage. Although never especially common, the term continued to pop up in the literature: searches of JSTOR, a full-text database, identify more than a dozen articles in sociology journals that mention either of the terms *social construction* or *socially constructed* prior to

1966; the terms also appeared on rare occasions in other social science disciplines, such as anthropology, history, and political science.

In 1966, of course, Peter L. Berger and Thomas Luckmann brought widespread attention to the term with the publication of *The Social Construction of Reality: A Treatise in the Sociology of Knowledge*. Their book received only modest attention from reviewers (among the major sociology journals, only the *American Sociological Review* ran a review), but by 1967 it was available in an inexpensive paperback edition. Berger already had broad recognition for another short paperback (*Invitation to Sociology*; Berger, 1963), and the new book became widely

41

cited.[1] Berger and Luckmann, in short, were responsible for spreading the language of social construction not just to sociology but to other scholarly disciplines and beyond.

This chapter's focus is relatively narrow; it seeks to trace the diffusion of particular terminology, of analysts referring to the process of "social construction" and to phenomena as having been "socially constructed." A more ambitious author might try to address a much broader topic—to examine the intellectual history of the range of ideas and insights that contemporary analysts might see as in some sense constructionist or at least as congruent with constructionism (see Weinberg, Chapter 2, this volume). For example, during the 1960s and 1970s, any number of social scientific analyses were titled "the manufacture of *X*" (e.g., Szasz, 1970), "the invention of *Y*" (e.g., Platt, 1969), or "the discovery of *Z*" (e.g., Rothman, 1971); all of these terms were intended to draw attention to the social processes by which particular ideas or arrangements came into being. Our ambitious author might argue that there was some sort of shift in the broader culture, so that people were less willing to take the social order for granted, that *manufacture, invention, construction,* and so on were conceptual competitors in an intellectual marketplace, and that *constructionism* increasingly emerged as the term of choice. However, I consider the task of tracing all of these congruent ideas to be unmanageable, given the very broad range of thinkers whose ideas might be seen as overlapping the constructionist approach, and I begin my story with the people who brought the term *social construction* to what would, by the end of the 20th century, become a fairly broad audience—that is, with Berger and Luckmann.

It is important to appreciate that academia was changing at the time that Berger and Luckmann published their book. Undergraduate and graduate enrollments swelled during the 1960s, as the baby-boom cohorts reached college age and student draft deferments encouraged young men to stay in school. But enrollments would grow much less rapidly during the 1970s, causing analysts to begin worrying that graduate schools were producing too many PhDs. Young academics found themselves peddling their wares in a buyers' market, and pressures to publish began to rise. This situation fostered the emergence of new venues for the display of scholarship—new scholarly associations and new journals. In other words, Berger and Luckmann revived the idea of social construction at a time when demand was growing for fresh ideas that might guide scholarship. Social constructionism would prove to be a malleable notion, one that diffused to many disciplines.

Berger and Luckmann were fundamentally interested in ways that knowledge was shaped by social processes. They derived their perspective from the phenomenological writings of Alfred Schutz and argued that human beings inevitably use language to assign meanings to the world and that language is learned from other humans. Language acquisition is a key element in childhood socialization; young children learn words (such as *water* or *dog*), as well as the meanings of those words. That is, they learn to correctly identify instances of the category represented by the word and to distinguish that which does not belong in the category (thus that a big black hound and a small white terrier are both dogs or that water is different from milk). The particular vocabulary of any culture structures how its members think of the world, of reality.

Berger and Luckmann's focus was on how *meanings* are created through social interaction. They presumed that water and dogs exist independently of people; people do not somehow think them into existence. Because water is essential for life, and because it is found in puddles and streams and rain, we might suspect that every human culture has developed a word for water. Still, we know that the meanings assigned to water do vary—some people, for example, believe that some water is holy, and they may treat that water differently than do others who do not share that particular belief. Similarly, our modern understanding that water is composed of molecules containing two hydrogen atoms and one oxygen atom emerged relatively late in human history; traditional cultures did not understand water as having that chemical composition. Thus we can speak of the social construction of water—and everything else. Berger and Luckmann sought to extend the sociology of knowledge—traditionally focused on high-status ideological or intellectual ideas—to encompass the study of all forms of knowledge, even mundane, everyday understandings.

No doubt Berger and Luckmann intended their title to be arresting. In what sense, we might ask, is reality socially constructed? After all, isn't reality, well, just real? Doesn't it exist independent of whatever humans think about it? Although it is possible to answer this question in different ways, Berger and Luckmann's answer did not require any surprising philosophical leaps:

> We immediately disclaim any pretension to the effect that sociology has the answer to these ancient philosophical preoccupations. . . . The philosopher . . . is professionally obligated to take nothing for granted, and to obtain maximal clarity as to the ultimate status of what the man on the street believes to be "reality" and "knowledge." Put differently, the philosopher is driven to decide where the quotation marks are in order and where they may safely be omitted, that is, to differentiate between valid and invalid assertions about the world. This the sociologist cannot possibly do. (Berger & Luckmann, 1966, pp. 1–2)

In short, Berger and Luckmann viewed social construction as a concept that might inform sociological analysis, not as an idea that somehow challenged the existence of a physical universe. However, once they reintroduced the terms *social construction* and *socially constructed* into sociologists' phrase books, those terms would be adopted by all sorts of other analysts, in various disciplines, who would put them to all manner of uses.

Constructionism Spreads within Sociology

Not surprisingly given the term's origin in sociology, sociologists were the first to take to the notion of social construction. By the late 1970s, constructionist language was becoming common in sociological analyses of four topics: news, science, deviance, and social problems. Both news and science were readily recognized as forms of knowledge, so that it was a small step for sociologists studying those topics to draw on Berger and Luckmann's effort to extend the sociology of knowledge to cover knowledge developed in practical settings. Press coverage had become a contentious topic; in particular, there were disputes over the news media's treatment of the Vietnam War and the Watergate scandal. A new generation of sociologists began observing reporters and editors and framing the resulting analyses in constructionist language. The titles of new ethnographies revealed their links to Berger and Luckmann; for example, David Altheide's *Creating Reality: How TV News Distorts Events* (1976) and Gaye Tuchman's *Making News: A Study in the Construction of Reality* (1978). Studies of scientific work, such as Latour and Woolgar's *Laboratory Life: The Social Construction of Scientific Facts* (1979) and Knorr-Cetina's *The Manufacture of Knowledge: An Essay on the Constructivist and Contextual Nature of Science* (1981), also began featuring constructionist titles. Constructionist thinking has continued to inform research on both topics, although, as we shall see, constructionist analyses of science have come in for a good deal of criticism.

If the links between the sociology of knowledge and studies of news or science seem obvious, the speed with which the idea of social construction spread among sociologists of deviance was more surprising. However, when Berger and Luckmann published *The Social Construction of Reality* in 1966, the labeling perspective was near its peak. The processes by which individuals were assigned to categories of deviance could, of course, be seen as a form of constructing knowledge. Moreover, labeling wove together various theoretical strands, of which phenomenological sociology was an important thread. Prominent studies of deviance, such as those by John I. Kitsuse and Aaron Cicourel (1963) and David Sudnow (1965), adopted phenomenological or ethnomethodological frameworks. As a result, sociologists of deviance were already somewhat familiar with the theoretical tradition within which Berger and Luckmann were writing; they understood how it could be applied to research on labeling, so that some were relatively quick to adopt the terminology of social construction. Thus Jack D. Douglas's (1967) *The Social Meanings of Suicide* had a chapter titled "The Construction of Social Meanings," and Douglas (1970) later edited a collection, *Deviance and Respectability: The Social Construction of Moral Meanings*, in which 7 out of 14 chapter titles contained the words *construction* or *constructing*.

By the 1970s, the labeling approach was coming under attack from several directions; there were various critiques by conflict sociologists, feminists, identity politics advocates, and mainstream sociologists (Best, 2004). At the same time, there were efforts to develop theoretically coherent perspectives on social problems (Blumer, 1971; Mauss, 1975). This attracted the attention of John I. Kitsuse—a phenomenological thinker and prominent member of the labeling school—who, in collaboration with Malcolm Spector, began developing a theory of social problems. Spector and Kitsuse's efforts would culminate in the publication of a short book, *Constructing Social Problems* (1977), that brought a constructionist approach to the study of social problems. Some sociologists began to shift their research interests from the embattled field of deviance to the less contested terrain of social problems. Constructionism attracted already prominent figures who had been associated with the labeling perspective, such

as Kitsuse and Joseph Gusfield (1981), and many early case studies of the construction of social problems dealt with forms of deviance, such as rape (Rose, 1977).

Studying social problems offered advantages for constructionist analysts. The term *social problem* was familiar; many sociology departments already offered courses in the topic, so there was no need to invent and establish a new field of study. (In contrast, another branch of phenomenological sociology—ethnomethodology—continues, after more than four decades, to struggle to gain widespread recognition, acceptance, and integration within the discipline's curriculum.) But, more important, there was no rival theoretical school contending for control of the study of social problems. Spector and Kitsuse began *Constructing Social Problems* (1977) with the declaration: "There is no adequate definition of social problems within sociology, and there is not now and never has been a sociology of social problems" (p. 1). Social problems existed primarily as a title for undergraduate courses and for textbooks designed to be assigned in those courses. Typically, those courses and textbooks lacked intellectual coherence; they simply examined a series of topics understood to be social problems without any attempt at theoretical integration. Few sociologists had bothered to develop the concept of social problems in their research; the well-regarded journal *Social Problems* published many articles on specific topics considered to be social problems, but very little on the general topic. If constructionists wanted to study social problems, no one else was likely to object.

Constructionism also allowed analysts of social problems to adopt a variety of political stances. The conflict-theory, feminist, and identity-politics critiques of labeling theory all had political overtones; they argued that the labeling approach led sociologists to apply the wrong values to the study of the wrong topics. In contrast, constructionism proved to be adaptable. Analysts might valorize some forms of claimsmaking, such as feminist campaigns to raise awareness about rape or domestic violence. But they might use the same analytic stance to call other claims into question by speaking dismissively of "drug scares" or "moral panics." This analytic flexibility—coupled with the absence of theoretical rivals—helped constructionism emerge as the leading approach to the analysis of social problems.

Debates and Misunderstandings within Sociology

By the early 1980s, then, it had become increasingly common for sociologists to adopt constructionist language for the study of news, science, deviance, and social problems. In addition, sociologists in other specialties were beginning to write about the social construction of gender (Lorber & Farrell, 1991), race (Frankenberg, 1993), sexuality (Laws & Schwartz, 1977; Weinberg, 1983), and a host of other topics. However, even as the new terminology spread, there were growing disagreements and confusions about the meaning of social construction and how it should be used in sociological analysis. These sometimes concerned exactly the sorts of "ancient philosophical preoccupations" that Berger and Luckmann (1966, p. 1) had considered outside the sociologist's purview. That is, the nature of reality and of social construction became topics for debate.

Vulgar Constructionism

Here, we might begin with a fairly straightforward misunderstanding. As the idea of social construction spread within sociology, it often became equated with flawed knowledge, with ideas that were mistaken or self-serving or arbitrary. In its least sophisticated form, we can call this *vulgar constructionism* (Best, 1995a, p. 345). Within it, an analyst might dismiss dubious beliefs—in, say, UFO abductions—as mere social constructions and contrast them with genuine social problems, such as poverty. In this usage, to describe a belief in some phenomenon as "socially constructed" is to cast doubt upon that phenomenon's existence, to discredit the belief. Of course, vulgar constructionism strays considerably from the perspective's origins; although Berger and Luckmann would agree that the belief in UFO abductions is indeed socially constructed, so, too, in their view, is the information about chemical elements taught in college chemistry classes. Still, Berger and Luckmann (1966) would recognize that the evidence brought to bear to support the chemistry professor's claims takes very different forms than does the evidence presented by UFO advocates: Chemists can make and test all manner of hypotheses that might be disproven, we can see that their claims have predictive value, and we can therefore have considerable confidence that their description of the world is accurate. To be sure, chemistry has evolved through centuries of research; we can see this as a long process of social construction, guided by (socially constructed) principles for scientific thinking that allow chemists to develop knowledge in which we have considerable confidence. Modern chemistry is a social construction, as was Aristotle's model of a world composed of four elements, but they are not equally useful for making nylon, and Berger and Luckmann would not have understood them as having equal standing as descriptions of empirical reality.

Yet it is easy to understand how the vulgar constructionists became confused. Analysts who wanted to focus on processes of social construction had to make a case that these processes were important. To be sure, our world is filled with objects to which we assign names and meanings—water, dogs, and so on. Although it is true that members of our society must learn these names and meanings, this is a fairly mundane truth, already subsumed under such familiar concepts as culture and socialization. Justifying the study of social construction required making that process interesting, that is, making a case that it was an important, consequential, nonmundane process. Analysts naturally sought subjects for study that offered a sort of analytic leverage, cases that clearly illustrated the workings and importance of social construction.

For instance, in their quest for analytic leverage, sociologists of science tended to study instances in which scientific practice seemed to fall short of the scientific ideal—scientists who found what they hoped to find and ignored inconvenient findings, former scientific orthodoxies that fell from grace, once scorned hypotheses that later gained acceptance, and the like. Analysts tended to emphasize episodes in the history of science that could be read as parables of scientific fallibility: the initial dismissal and eventual acceptance of Wegener's model of plate tectonics; the early rejection of Barbara McClintock's genetic research, eventually validated with a Nobel Prize; advocates of cold fusion and other communities of scientists who persisted in following lines of research that their larger disciplines consider discredited; and so on (Collins, 2000; Simon, 2002). Although scientists might prefer to think of these as exceptional instances, constructionist ethnographies sought to expose the messy process by which working scientists came to conclusions; such moments revealed that science was a social process in which scientists work to construct what their colleagues will recognize as facts:

> "Reality" cannot be used to explain why a statement becomes a fact, since it is only after it has become a fact that the effect of reality is obtained. . . . Once the controversy has settled, reality is taken to be the cause of this settlement; but while the controversy is still raging, reality is the consequence of debate, following each twist and turn in the controversy as if it were the shadow of scientific endeavour. (Latour & Woolgar, 1979, pp. 180, 182)

These awkward moments—and the even more awkward cases in which scientific debates did not lead to clean resolutions—provided the analysts' analytic leverage; they

made evident the importance of the social world in shaping science.

Similarly, sociologists examining the construction of social problems found it tempting to study moral panics and drug scares, alarms raised over fanciful or at least wildly exaggerated dangers—Halloween sadism, satanic ritual abuse, snuff films, child pornography, stranger abductions of children, and so on. (In much the same way, labeling theorists had been fond of using witch crazes to illustrate societal reaction; Rains, 1975.) These were wonderful examples in that the analyst could argue that these were nonexistent—or at least very uncommon or highly exaggerated—dangers turned into prominent social problems through the means of social construction. By pointing to examples of scientific errors and moral panics, the process of social construction could be laid bare and its importance demonstrated. Of course, not all constructionist work focused on scientific errors or dubious social problems claims, but as Steve Woolgar and Dorothy Pawluch (1985b) famously argued, one could at least suspect that making an interesting constructionist argument depended on implying that there was a disjunction between claims and objective reality. Such leverage made analysts' arguments more compelling, but it did so at the cost of encouraging vulgar constructionism and other confusion.

The quest for analytic leverage leads to the use of what I have called the "apparently innocuous 'just' " (Best, 2003b, p. 138). We see this, for example, in the statement: "That's *just* a social construction." The statement seems innocent enough—it is apparently innocuous—but it invites misunderstanding. The apparently innocuous *just* is applicable to many of the more dubious claims that attracted analysts, such as those about satanic ritual abuse; thus "satanic ritual abuse is just a social construction." Regrettably, this statement invites both ambiguity and confusion. It is ambiguous in that it has two distinct—and easily confused—meanings. On the one hand, saying that satanic ritual abuse is "just" a social construction might be read as meaning that, although all language is a social construction, most words (e.g., *water*) are social constructions that denote empirical phenomena; however, *satanic ritual abuse* (like, say, *elf*) is a term that has no empirical referent—it is a social construction unanchored to empirical reality. This meaning points to the analytic leverage offered by the subject for study—in the case of satanic ritual abuse, we can see social construction clearly; because satanic ritual abuse does not actually exist, it is "just" (that is, nothing but, only) a social construction. On the other hand, saying that satanic ritual abuse is "just" a social construction can be heard as juxtaposing reality and social construction—as implying that phenomena are *either* real *or* "just" social constructions. In this meaning, *just* implies that calling something a social construction means that it is not real, that it is less than real, that it is simply an arbitrary interpretation; in other words, when used in this sense, *just* invites a vulgar constructionist interpretation. Although this second meaning is quite inconsistent with Berger and Luckmann's (1966) original use of the term *social construction*, it is simpler to understand. Many people came to misunderstand social construction in precisely this way, and vulgar constructionism was merely one product of this confusion.

Characterizing constructionism as the study of bogus ideas offers critics a quick way of dismissing the wider utility of the approach. They may acknowledge that claims about UFO abductions ought to be debunked, but they argue that calling other phenomena *social constructions* might give people the wrong idea. For instance, Hacking (1999, p. 4) worries that "the next stage in the notorious series of holocaust denials might be a book entitled *The Social Construction of the Holocaust*, a work urging that the Nazi extermination camps are exaggerated and the gas chambers [just] fictions." But Ronald J. Berger (2002) presents a constructionist interpretation of the Holocaust,

arguing that it is through routine processes of claimsmaking and policymaking that the banality of evil becomes manifest. That is, we can understand that the Holocaust was socially constructed without implying that it is "just" a fanciful social construction.

Ontological Gerrymandering and Social Problems Theory

A second, far more subtle critique targeted what Woolgar and Pawluch (1985b) termed *ontological gerrymandering*. Whereas vulgar constructionist critics try to narrowly restrict the domain of constructionist analysis to false knowledge, Woolgar and Pawluch charged that constructionists failed to adopt a sufficiently expansive vision of what their own theoretical orientation required. Their basic argument was that, just as sociologists recognize that the language and concepts of their subjects are social constructions, so too are the language and concepts used by the sociologists themselves. In their view, analysts should not—must not—privilege their own assumptions; rather, they should apply simultaneously the same sort of constructionist critique to their own ideas as to those of their subjects. Woolgar and Pawluch suggested that constructionist analysts of social problems routinely fail to meet this standard: "The successful [constructionist] social problems explanation depends on making problematic the truth status of certain states of affairs selected for analysis and explanation, while backgrounding or minimizing the possibility that the same problems apply to assumptions upon which the analysis depends" (p. 216). They called this *ontological gerrymandering*.

Woolgar and Pawluch (1985b) illustrated constructionists' analytic inconsistencies with a passage from Spector and Kitsuse's *Constructing Social Problems* (1977). While discussing changing definitions of marijuana, Spector and Kitsuse noted: "The nature of marijuana remained constant" (1977, p. 43). Woolgar and Pawluch pounced on this statement: "The key assertion is that the actual character of a substance (marijuana), condition, or behavior remained constant" (1985b, p. 217). This was a troubling critique; even Spector and Kitsuse, who repeatedly had warned analysts against making assumptions about objective conditions, made such assumptions:

> Proponents fail to live up to the programmatic relativism which they espouse in calling for a purportedly different, definitional perspective. In the course of specific, empirical case studies, the programmatic claims give way to clearly discernible lapses into realism. (Woolgar & Pawluch, 1985b, p. 224)

Abbott (2001) argues that scholarly disciplines develop through the emergence of fractal distinctions, whereby old debates are repeatedly reinvigorated. The charge of ontological gerrymandering illustrates this pattern. Constructionist studies of social problems had begun as a critique of the objectivist assumptions that characterized traditional textbook discussions of social problems That is, constructionists such as Spector and Kitsuse had criticized the theoretical naiveté of those who viewed social problems as objectively identifiable, harmful conditions; they had argued that analysts needed to recognize that social problems claims were social constructions. Then Woolgar and Pawluch (1985b) had applied essentially the same critique to constructionism by charging that Spector and Kitsuse based their own analyses on naive assumptions about the empirical world. A new fractal distinction emerged between *strict constructionism* and *contextual constructionism* (Best, 1995a).

The strict constructionist position accepted Woolgar and Pawluch's (1985a) reasoning that onotological gerrymandering posed a serious problem, that analysts were indeed obliged to avoid all objectivist assumptions about reality. Initially, some suggested that careful analysts might avoid ontological gerrymandering: Schneider (1985, p. 233), for instance, dismissed Woolgar and

Pawluch's examples as "mistakes in applying the definitional perspective, . . . instances of careless talk" and spoke of "researcher carelessness and confusion." The presumed remedy would be to take greater care to avoid those "lapses into realism," but this proved to be difficult in that researchers who sought to study real-world events, such as case studies of social problems construction, continually seemed to make these slips. When John Kitsuse, who became the most prominent advocate of the strict constructionist position, coedited a collection of empirical constructionist case studies, the book's introduction confessed: "None of the chapters in this volume is an exemplar of strict constructionism. . . . Investigators and analysts in spite of themselves cannot help but import their interests, if not their professional agendas, into their interactions with their informants" (Sarbin & Kitsuse, 1994, p. 14).

In response to this challenge, those wedded to a strict constructionist position began to warn analysts against venturing into the real world. Woolgar and Pawluch (1985a, p. 162) called for constructionists to "move beyond constructivism"[2] and refocus their analyses on the nature of sociological inquiry, although they conceded that this ""will not contribute . . . to our understanding of the world as we have traditionally conceived that pursuit." In collaboration with Peter R. Ibarra, Kitsuse recommended studying general rhetorical principles:

> Our position is that developing a general theory of social problems discourse is a much more coherent way of proceeding than, for example, the development of a series of discrete theories on the social construction of X, Y, and Z. To develop a theory about condition X when the ontological status of X is suspended results in "ontological gerrymandering" . . . which is to say flawed theory. (Ibarra & Kitsuse, 1993, p. 33)

These solutions proved to be dead ends. For one thing, it proved easy to demonstrate that Ibarra and Kitsuse (1993) had themselves engaged in ontological gerrymandering; it became evident that it was impossible for any analyst to avoid bootlegging at least some cultural assumptions into even abstract theorizing (Best, 1993). After all, analysts depend on language, and, as Berger and Luckmann (1966) had demonstrated, language inevitably causes people to construct the world in particular ways. More important, most constructionist sociologists of social problems were interested in exploring how and why particular issues came to public attention. They were not interested in the sort of introspective examination of how sociologists study the world advocated by Woolgar and Pawluch (1985a); and, although they might be willing to borrow some of the concepts Ibarra and Kitsuse devised to study social problems rhetoric, they wanted to apply those concepts to case studies of social problems construction. Strict constructionists' insistence that analysts had to choose between theoretical consistency and studying the empirical world attracted few adherents to the path of pure theory.

However, the fractal distinction created by the critique of ontological gerrymandering offered a second, less radical option—contextual constructionism. In this, analysts accepted the basic constructionist insight that people assigned categories and meanings to the empirical world, and they sought to observe and understand this process by locating claims in their larger context. They conceded that ontological gerrymandering occurred but saw it as a necessary evil, something to be aware of, to be done with caution. Woolgar and Pawluch (1985b) may have caught Spector and Kitsuse (1977) assuming that marijuana's nature had gone unchanged, but how big an analytic problem did that pose? Was there some reason to suspect that that assumption was incorrect? After all, all science requires precisely that sort of ontological gerrymandering; chemists routinely assume that the nature of oxygen and the molecular composition of water remain the same, in the absence of any good reason to assume the contrary. In fact, it is difficult to imagine a cumulative science that does not build on such assumptions.

Contextual constructionism, then, gave sociologists a sort of theoretical license to explore substantive topics, such as how and why particular issues came to public attention when they did, where they did, and in the form they did. Constructionist analysts of social problems faced a choice: They could wander cautiously down the narrow path of strict constructionism, carefully eschewing any language that hinted that they might presume to know something about the empirical world, or they could declare themselves contextual constructionists, free to explore, analyze, and interpret any of the cornucopia of contemporary claims about missing children, "frankenfoods," road rage, and Gulf War syndrome. Few found it a difficult decision:

> While strict constructionists might command the high ground as being more theoretically "principled" than their competitors, contextual constructionists took the upper hand on practical grounds. Try as one might, it is difficult to conceive of sociological analysis completely purged of social context as an explanatory factor. (Holstein & Gubrium, 2003, p. 189)

Hundreds of books, articles, and chapters examining the construction of a wide range of substantive issues continued to appear. Although a few of those analysts bravely insisted that they were following the tenets of strict constructionism, and although there were further efforts to articulate theoretically defensible grounds for incorporating context into constructionist analyses (Bogard, 2003; Holstein & Gubrium, 2003), the issue had become moot.

The Debate within the Sociology of Science

A similar pattern of fractal distinctions emerged in the sociology of science. In this area, constructionism encountered more resistance. Although never a particularly large specialty, sociological studies of science had the cachet of being associated with Robert K. Merton (1973), the leading American sociologist of the 20th century. The line of research pioneered by Merton assumed that science involved discovering the true nature of reality:

> The sociology of science . . . could be said to turn on the elucidation of the set of normative and other institutional arrangements that enable science—the asking and answering of questions about Nature—to exist and function efficiently. A crucial feature of this program of inquiry is the assumption that the ultimate answers to the question are Nature's. (Collins, 1983, p. 266)

However, a more critical stance was emerging. Kuhn's (1962) *The Structure of Scientific Revolutions* had argued that science experienced paradigm shifts when scientists' collective understanding of the world changed in fundamental ways, as with the emergence of the Copernican view of the solar system. Once Berger and Luckmann (1966) introduced the constructionist orientation, sociologists of science who had acknowledged the importance of Kuhn's work began trying to explore more deeply the social processes by which scientific knowledge emerged. Increasingly, this led them to try to avoid assumptions about truths of the scientists' conclusions:

> The sociology of scientific knowledge . . . is concerned precisely with what comes to count as scientific knowledge and how it comes to count. The crucial phrase here is "comes to count" since no knowledge of what lies beyond human scientific activity is claimed. The strongest variant of this view is often called "relativism" since it assumes neither fixed points in the physical world nor a fixed realm of logic that would compel agreements between unbiased observers or thinkers from radically different cultures. (Collins, 1983, p. 267)

Constructionists contrasted traditional sociological analyses of science—which they characterized as "rationalist" (for assuming that science was a straightforward process of accumulating ever-more-correct knowledge)—with their own "strong programme" in which "passive, contemplative accounts of the character of knowledge generation should be replaced by a more active sociological conception of the relation between knowledge producer and reality" (Woolgar, 1981, p. 366).

Whereas this constructionist turn discomfited some scientists and sociologists of science, traditional science had long been aware that scientists were only human, that they sometimes made errors, that they might become invested in particular, mistaken notions, and so on. Scientists catalogued various forms of error as pathological science (Langmuir, 1953), experimenter effects (Rosenthal, 1966), and so on, and they sought to address them. One of the principal purposes of scientific methodology is to prevent or at least uncover such problems through replication and the use of placebos, double-blind designs, and the like. To the degree that constructionist ethnographies revealed how scientists produced their results and how social arrangements shaped that process, constructionism could be viewed as not inconsistent with science or even with the Mertonian sociology of science.

But, paralleling the case of the sociology of social problems, constructionist studies of science experienced their own fractal division, in which some critics argued that the strong program was not strong enough and warned against analysts bootlegging objectivist assumptions into their research. Here again, Steve Woolgar (1981) advocated the more theoretically consistent, more purely subjectivist approach. For instance, he pointed to problems with the ways constructionists invoked the concept of interests to explain scientists' findings: "The construction of interests on the basis of actions and their subsequent use in explaining actions entailed schema in principle beset by methodological difficulties. These difficulties were backgrounded, minimized and otherwise made to seem inconsequential by the use of various rhetorical and argumentative strategies" (p. 389).

In short, Woolgar's (1981) critique paralleled his later analysis of the role of ontological gerrymandering within the study of social problems. However, whereas the debate over social problems theory was restricted to the relatively small number of sociologists concerned with developing the concept of social problems, the most radical constructionist claims about the nature of scientific inquiry attracted notice far beyond the boundaries of sociology.

Constructionism Spreads Beyond Sociology

Although Berger and Luckmann's *The Social Construction of Reality* (1966) was addressed to sociologists, the notion of social construction proved to have considerable appeal beyond the confines of that discipline. We have already noted how it came to the attention of scholars in the natural sciences through studies in the sociology of science. Other social scientists, including historians, also began to pick up the term, as did, perhaps more surprisingly, scholars in the humanities.

Constructionism and the Social Sciences

Not unexpectedly, constructionism began to spread beyond sociology to the other social and behavioral sciences, including political science, psychology, and anthropology. (History—a somewhat special case—is discussed in the next section.) Although the social sciences have probably grown less integrated over time—a product of universities' departmentalization and the separate reward structures in the various disciplines, each with its own professional associations, conferences, and journals—it remains the case that these disciplines share overlapping substantive interests, conceptual vocabularies, and

methodological approaches. Although most social scientists find it difficult to keep up with developments in other social scientific disciplines, some manage to keep a foot in at least one other social science, and they serve the vital function of "weak ties"—those individuals who link otherwise distinct social networks and serve as conduits for diffusion (Granovetter, 1973).

Political scientists, like sociologists, began focusing less on structures and more on processes during the late 20th century. It proved relatively easy to adopt a constructionist vocabulary to discuss the process that drew attention to political issues and led to public policies. Murray Edelman was probably the most prominent theorist; already the author of books describing the ways politics depended on the manipulation of symbols, he adopted constructionist language in *Constructing the Political Spectacle* (1988). By 1993, the discipline's flagship journal, the *American Political Science Review*, published an article titled "Social Constructions of Target Populations" (Schneider & Ingram, 1993). Collections of case studies of how political problems came to be defined in specific terms or how particular public policies were assembled, many featuring overtly constructionist vocabularies, also began to appear (Rochefort & Cobb, 1994; Schneider & Ingram, 2005). JSTOR allows us to trace the spread of terminology through four decades. Between 1960 and 1969, only 6 articles in the 41 political science journals catalogued in the database used either *social construction* or *socially constructed* at least once, but the rise thereafter was striking: 43 articles in 1970–1979; 91 articles in 1980–1989; and 484 articles in 1990–1999.

Unfortunately, to date JSTOR catalogues only a handful of psychology journals—too few to track the spread of constructionist ideas. Clearly, however, the language of constructionism was accepted by some psychologists, particularly those who viewed their discipline as more a "human science" than a biological science. Like the sociological specializations in social problems and the sociology of science, psychology also developed a substantial constructionist literature that generated theoretical debates about the nature of constructionist analysis (Gergen, 1994, 2001) and supported a book series, *Inquiries in Social Construction*, published by Sage. Of course, psychologists of various stripes had long tried to understand how individuals made sense of their experiences. Adopting the perspective of social constructionism allowed psychologists to draw attention to the social context within which that process occurred (de Rivera & Sarbin, 1998). Constructionist language also found its way into clinical psychology (Miller, 1997), social work, and other helping professions.

Constructionism also proved somewhat influential in anthropology. Of course, coming to terms with other cultures had always been a central concern for anthropologists. Berger and Luckmann's basic insight—that reality could be viewed only through some cultural lens—was fully familiar to a discipline that had devised all manner of analytic schema for thinking about other cultures. Although we might imagine that this familiarity might have discouraged anthropologists from adopting a constructionist vocabulary, a JSTOR search reveals a pattern that seems to parallel constructionism's spread in political science. Counting articles in the 20 anthropology journals catalogued in JSTOR that mention either *social construction* or *socially constructed*, we find: 2 articles in 1960–1969; 36 articles in 1970–1979; 161 articles in 1980–1989; and 470 articles in 1990–1999. The last decades of the 20th century marked something of a crisis within anthropology: Economic and political developments were making it increasingly difficult to gain access to ethnographic subjects in preindustrial settings, and anthropological analysts were justifying their increasingly abstract work by adopting novel theoretical stances. We can suspect that taking on a constructionist vocabulary by some analysts may have been part of this larger process.

Constructionism and History

Of course, historians specialize in tracing developments, including the rise and fall of particular ideas. In historiography, in intellectual history—in fact, in every branch of the discipline—historians assume that people's actions result from evolving meanings. That is, they take for granted one of the principal insights that sociologists gained from adopting the language of social construction. What, then, was the term's attraction for historians? For at least some historians, speaking of social construction drew attention to how particular groups within the social structure promoted and spread ideas. In their usage, the emphasis was on *social* constructionism.

The 1960s saw the emergence of the new social history under the slogan "History from the Bottom Up." Social history had long occupied a low-status, marginal place in the discipline; now it experienced a revival. In part, events of the 1960s—the civil rights movement, the war on poverty, and so on—drew historians' attention to what had been relatively neglected social issues. In part, historians began to discover how to use computers to compile and analyze massive data sets drawn from manuscript census schedules and other records left behind by ordinary people. Earlier generations of historians had concentrated on the well-documented lives of kings, generals, and other elite figures; they studied history from the top down. But the focus began to shift as historians sought to understand the places and perspectives of the poor, ethnic minorities, and others who had received less attention from their discipline.

Studying history from the bottom up required new intellectual tools, and social historians began to borrow both methodological techniques and concepts from sociologists. Social construction was one such imported concept: by the early 1970s, historians were beginning to cite Berger and Luckmann (1966). Moreover, that decade saw a new interest in women's history, and studies of the histories of race, class, and gender—and their various intersections—became increasingly common. This work challenged the basis of social stratification, and the idea that races, classes, and genders were social constructions became a way of expressing that there was nothing inevitable about social hierarchies. Historians, then, tended to invoke social construction to describe systems of social inequality, and their adoption of constructionist language outpaced that of disciplines such as political science or anthropology. A JSTOR search of 59 history journals reveals 4 articles mentioning either of the terms *social construction* and *socially constructed* during the decade 1960–1969, followed by startling growth in the number of mentions in successive decades: 28 articles in 1970–1979; 137 articles in 1980–1989; and 510 articles in 1990–1999.

Constructionism in the Humanities

The appeal of constructionism was somewhat different for scholars in the humanities. One of the principal intellectual challenges for scholars who analyze, say, literary works is to devise new, publishable insights regarding texts that have been closely examined and interpreted for decades, even centuries. This makes novel intellectual perspectives particularly attractive, and literary criticism follows closely behind most other intellectual fashions. When psychoanalysis was in vogue, literary theorists offered interpretations grounded in the works of Freud, Jung, and Adler. Various strains of Marxian thought inspired other analyses. The expansion of the post–World War II academy (and the rising expectations for scholarly publication) encouraged literary analysts to join virtually every intellectual movement in virtually any discipline; existentialism, semiotics, structuralism, poststructuralism, and postmodernism all found adherents. Not surprisingly, social constructionism gained its own cadre of devotees.

One suspects that few scholars in the humanities who professed constructionism had much grounding in the work of Berger and Luckmann or of other sociologists. They seem to have understood constructionism to involve two principles. First, like historians, they often used the term *social construction* to explain how race, class, and gender stratification served to promote some ideas. In their view, social constructions were one tool used by elites to maintain their dominance within societies. The second principle was a sense of extreme relativism: Analysts proposed that there could be many social constructions and that they were all equally valid.

One can see the attraction of this second argument within the humanities. One might argue that there are many ways to construct the meaning of some literary text—this was, after all, what generations of literary critics had demonstrated—and that no particular interpretation could be proved to be superior to any other. One might even argue that there are many ways of making art and that no particular way of making art is necessarily superior to any other, that any set of criteria for judging artistic merit is "just" a social construction, and that, in particular, elitist standards for evaluating art are a form of class-based domination. In this way, constructionist language could be conflated with postmodernism and other schools of highly relativistic thought:

> Cultural studies insisted that the political responsibility of criticism was best served by taking culture as its object rather than the work of literature. . . . [C]ertain external pressures . . . (1) the increased demand for credentialing to technical as opposed to humanistic fields; (2) the increasing demand on the literary professoriate to remediate the language skills of an ever expanding and more demographically diverse university population, effectively deemphasizing the study of literature; (3) the continued transfer of de facto acculturation functions from high culture to mass culture; and (4) the decisive shift to the Right of the po-

litical public sphere during the later seventies and eighties . . . combined to refocus the literary professoriate on questions of multiculturalism and mass culture. The effect of these externalities was not only to undermine further the status of literary study as a discourse of knowledge—which could only weaken it in the modern system of university disciplines—but also to create an opportunity for the reassertion of "cultural criticism." . . . The tendency of the social construction concept in cultural studies was ultimately . . . to equate the political and the epistemological. (Guillory, 2002, pp. 484–486)

Thus, in his book *The Social Construction of What?*, the philosopher Ian Hacking (1999) argues that scholars adopt six gradations of constructionism. The "least demanding grade" is historical: "Someone presents a history of X and argues that X has been constructed in the course of social processes" (p. 19). This is more or less what Berger and Luckmann (1966) had in mind. But, for Hacking, constructionist arguments take several other forms, through ironic constructionism and on to rebellious and then revolutionary constructionism. These latter two stances hold that X is wrong and should be eliminated. In Hacking's view, the language of constructionism often becomes a vehicle for various political claims, particularly within the humanities.

By the 1990s, then, the term *social construction* had spread widely throughout the academy, although its meaning and uses had morphed in the process. Probably many of the people using the term did not understand what sociologists meant when they spoke of social construction. It proved very easy for scholars in other disciplines to fall into the trap of vulgar constructionism (an error, after all, to which sociologists had themselves not been immune), to use *social construction* as a label for debunking ideas the analyst wished to challenge. And, having spread from the social sciences to the natural sciences and the humanities, social construction now began to attract attention in the public sphere. In particular, its new, far

more relativistic forms began to be attacked in debates over science and social policy.

Backlash: Constructionism's Critics

The landmark moment that marked constructionism's arrival in the public consciousness was the Sokal affair. Alan Sokal, a physicist, submitted a bogus manuscript that was accepted and published in 1996 in *Social Text*, a literary journal. Slathered in literary-critical (lit-crit) jargon, Sokal's hoax advanced a variety of patently ridiculous claims about the physical world. The fact that *Social Text*'s editors were willing to publish an article that they obviously could not understand exposed at least one theory-laden wing of the humanities to ridicule from physical scientists and other commentators. Often, these critiques disparaged the idea of social construction: "Sokal's relay of the term to the mass public sphere . . . irrevocably linked [it] to an extreme antirealism or skepticism about the claims of scientific knowledge" (Guillory, 2002, p. 484). For example, George Will (1996, p. A31) stated: "The lumpen Marxists and other theory-mongers begin with Nietzsche's assertion that there are no facts, only interpretations. Everything, they assert, is a 'social construction' and thus arbitrary." Similarly, Sokal characterized the book he published following the uproar over his article as an attack on "epistemic relativism . . . the idea . . . that modern science is nothing more than a 'myth,' a 'narration' or a 'social construction' . . . " (Sokal & Bricmont, 1998, p. x).

The Sokal hoax brought constructionism into the public view and, in the process, equated it with an exaggerated form of vulgar constructionism. In this interpretation, calling something a social construction was presumed to be equivalent to denying its existence—a view that could be dismissed or railed against. Thus Freeman J. Dyson notes (1999, p. 19): "Some less perceptive social analysts have attempted to show that a virus is a social construction. It is difficult to make a strong case for the unreality of a virus." George Will (who, as noted previously, had earlier weighed in on the Sokal affair) wrote two columns linking constructionism to culture wars. The first concerned a critique (Stolba, 2002) of women's studies texts: "the postmodern premise (explicitly endorsed in one of the texts) is that 'no purely factual studies exist.' That is, 'truth' is 'socially constructed,' and in the 'patriarchal,' 'phallo-centric' societies 'factual'—scare quotes are obligatory among postmodernists—assertions merely reflect power relations of male domination" (Will, 2002a, p. B7). The second column criticized Title IX: " 'gender' suggests differences that are 'socially constructed' and can be erased by sufficiently determined social engineers" (Will, 2002b, p. 82).

Meanwhile, revived coverage of the scandal over the Catholic Church's handling of sexual abuse allegations against priests led to other denunciations. Garry Wills (2002) attacked Philip Jenkins (1996) for his "analysis of 'constructed' social fears":

> In each case an "imaginary menace" is manufactured. . . . [B]y his definition all such panics are artificial. . . . He never seems to consider the possibility that the panic was not manufactured . . . [and assumes] that there was nothing to the priest-pedophile phenomenon but bad faith on the part of those "exploiting" it. (p. 10)

Meanwhile, the *New York Times* reported that Missouri legislators were offended by a professor's article about pedophilia (Mirkin, 1999) that argued "that the notion of the innocent child was a social construct"; one state senator was quoted: "taxpayers [should] not subsidize this guy's attempt to legitimize a despicable behavior and a dangerous behavior. . . . Legitimizing molestation doesn't fall under academic freedom" (Wilgoren, 2002). However useful the term might seem to academics, many popular commentators equated social construction with the dangerous denial of real problems.

In particular, denunciations of constructionist language became a cudgel wielded by conservatives in culture-war skirmishes. Searching Lexis Nexis's full-text database for popular magazine articles featuring the words *social construction* or *socially constructed* results in locating numerous pieces in *National Review* and other conservative periodicals. These references to constructionism tend to be critical, if not dismissive:

> the leftist fads that dominate and retard the human sciences—the P.C. shibboleths about sex and race being mere "social constructions," for instance. . . . (Derbyshire, 2006)
>
> Never mind the hundreds, if not thousands, of serious researchers—geneticists, endocrinologists, neuroscientists, developmental psychologists—who . . . provide compelling evidence for many innate differences and against the social construction thesis [about gender]. (Sommers, 2005)
>
> Being a wife and mother, for example, is not just about assuming a socially constructed role. It is a natural moral reality upon which culture—and law—rightly supervenes, and in so doing structures, specifies, reinforces, and protects an awesome opportunity to live a good life. (Bradley, 2004)

In these arguments, social construction stands for an irresponsible relativism, a straw figure that ignores "natural moral reality" or scientific evidence, that can be dismissed as a politically correct "shibboleth." (These critiques are not restricted to conservatives; the critique by Garry Wills cited earlier shows that commentators on the left sometimes make parallel arguments.)

At least some of its critics understand constructionism as arguing that all ideas are equally valuable and that they cannot be tested against the empirical world. Here is another political conservative:

> Sure, "the moon orbits the earth" is true in Western culture. But a tribe of aborigines may decide that the moon is a goddess who comes out at night; that is their truth. The critical point is that neither of these truths is "truer"

than the other because reality is socially constructed, not objectively discernable.

The names most often associated with this worldview—i.e., that reality is socially constructed, and that objective truth cannot be had—constitutes a glittering who's who of late 20th-century thinkers in France and America: Jacques Derrida, Michel Foucault, Jacques Lacan, Roland Barthes, Paul de Man, Jean Lyotard, Julia Kristeva, Luce Irigaray, Bruno Latour, Jean Baudrillard, Gilles Deleuze, Thomas Kuhn, Richard Rorty, and Stanley Fish. (Goldblatt, 2004)

A sociologist cannot help but be struck by this list of "constructionist" thinkers, mostly philosophers, literary critics, and other figures from the humanities; only Latour has contributed to the sociological literature. These critics in the popular media seem unaware of constructionism's sociological roots and unfamiliar with how social scientists actually make use of the concept.

Nor is the equation of constructionism with extreme relativism restricted to culture-war conservatives. The philosophy professor Paul Boghossian (2006) has published a short book titled *Fear of Knowledge: Against Relativism and Constructivism*. He begins by examining a debate over the origins of the Zuni people and quotes one archeologist as having said, "Science is just one of many ways of knowing the world. [The Zunis' worldview is] just as valid as the archeological viewpoint of what prehistory is all about" (p. 2). This leads Boghossian to articulate "the doctrine of Equal Validity: There are many radically different, yet 'equally valid' ways of knowing the world, with science being just one of them" (p. 2). Not surprisingly, during the course of his book, he is able to mount various arguments to demonstrate that this principle is deeply flawed.

To the degree that constructionism has become a subject of controversy, it has come under attack from scientists, philosophers, and political conservatives. Those attacks have largely ignored the sociological origins and uses of constructionism and have characterized the approach as advocating complete relativism, for which it can then be denounced.

On the other hand, there is evidence that a less radical—and more sociological—version of the concept of social construction has begun to penetrate the public consciousness. On some occasions the press uses constructionist language in a casual, taken-for-granted manner. For instance, a *Boston Globe* article on marketing targeted at children begins with the sentence: "The child is a gift of nature, but how the child is perceived is always a social construction" (Elkind, 2004, p. D7). A newspaper article on efforts to trace African Americans' genetic heritage quotes a black business executive: "We have to remember that race is not genetic; it is a social construction" (Dyer, 2006, p. C1). Another feature article remarks, "But all that social-construction-of-gender stuff has gotten so passe" (Pickett, 2003, p. 60). These examples suggest that, in spite of all the denunciations, the idea of social construction has established a beachhead in the larger culture.

Are We All Social Constructionists Now?

Social construction, then, has become one of those terms—like *role model*, *significant other*, or *charisma*—that originated in sociology but have diffused far beyond that discipline's boundaries and, in the process, have morphed to take on whole new meanings. Certainly sociologists have found the concept useful, but its value in other realms of thought is less clear.

For sociologists who have followed the path originally laid down by Peter Berger and Thomas Luckmann (1966), thinking about social construction as a process by which knowledge is created has drawn attention to cultural dynamics and thereby served to help redirect the discipline. American sociology in the mid-20th century seemed to emphasize social structure; a good deal of sociologists' attention went toward classifying and examining such entities as social classes, formal organizations, voluntary associations, and small groups. In contrast, we might characterize the discipline at the beginning of the new millennium as being more interested in culture and process. Obviously, the change was not stark or sudden; it involved a gradual shift in emphasis. Post–World War II sociology recognized that culture was important and that change occurred, just as today's analysts are aware of social structure; but interest in culture grew, even as the focus on social structure diminished. The growing interest in constructionist ideas was one part of this larger trend that redirected sociologists' attention toward culture and social processes.

In particular, the notion of social construction lets sociologists emphasize the contingent nature of social activity. People constantly make choices based on how they understand their alternatives, they must account for the choices they have made, and those choices and accounts then constrain what they will do next. Many of these choices are soon lost from sight, and an edifice of taken-for-granted assumptions about the world emerges and evolves. Adopting a constructionist stance makes it easier for analysts to penetrate those assumptions and to recognize and study these processes.

Here we might consider the larger cultural context within which constructionism emerged. Smith (1974) argues that social structures be characterized as more or less crystallized and claims that society experiences cycles of crystallization and decrystallization. Roles are relatively rigid during periods of high crystallization and relatively permeable during periods of low crystallization. Certainly we might characterize the second half of the 20th century as a time of low crystallization, when the nature of such well-established statuses as race and gender came under question. The point is neither that constructionism caused decrystallization nor that decrystallization caused constructionism. Rather, we can suspect that shifting intellectual currents—including social constructionism—and developments in the larger society (such as economic expansion, increased educational levels, and technological improvements) reinforced one another so that it became easier to challenge existing social structures throughout the larger society, and decrystallization resulted. These changes fostered one of the great waves in American social movement activity that included the civil rights movement, feminism, and so on.

Decrystallization has had at least two important consequences within intellectual circles. First, it provided a cultural context that supported questioning established ideas through the introduction of new theoretical frameworks. The scandals of the 1960s and 1970s—the confrontation with legalized segregation, the failure in Vietnam, Watergate, the revelations that government and industry had ignored the risks of smoking, pesticides, and unsafe automobiles, and so on—encouraged scholars, as well as activists, to question authority. Ideas that challenged orthodoxies and promoted alternative points of view were in vogue. Critical scholars warned against "privileging" some ideas over others. Constructionism, like postmodernism and other late-20th-century perspectives that could be understood as favoring more relativistic interpretations, seemed to be in harmony with the larger cultural trends. Berger and Luckmann's (1966) title appeared at a moment when reality had never seemed less solid, more malleable.

The second consequence of decrystallization for intellectuals meant that it became easier to advance and get a hearing for new ideas. The expansion of graduate education led to increased competition for positions as college teachers, which allowed employers to become more choosy and to insist that job candidates display stronger scholarly credentials. The bars for tenure and promotion rose, which in turn created an intense demand for outlets for scholarship—new professional associations, new journals, and so on. The resulting expansion of scholarly activity within sociology and other academic disciplines encouraged the fractal processes described by Abbott (2001). There were rewards for those who could distinguish their thinking from that of their colleagues, particularly if they could establish control of their own scholarly venues—separate sessions at annual conferences or even distinct organizations that could hold their own meetings; specialized journals and book series; prizes for outstanding work in an area; and the like (Best, 2003a). Decrystallized disciplines featured specialized subgroups that offered forums at which many people could speak, although usually only fellow specialists were listening. In sociology, these developments led to concerns that the discipline lacked a "core" (Cole, 2001).

This larger context of decrystallization also helps explains the diffusion of social constructionism into other sectors of the academy, including the humanities. We have already noted the humanities' appetite for new intellectual frameworks, and we might imagine that, under circumstances of decrystallization, relativistic ideas would be especially likely to find adherents. However, the constant need for new critical vocabularies within which critiques can be posed, to say nothing of the abuse heaped on lit-crit constructionism in the culture wars, makes it unlikely that constructionist language will long endure—or at least retain a prominent place—within the humanities; outside the social sciences, constructionism seems likely to prove to be an intellectual fad.

Within sociology, though, the prospects seem more promising. We have already noted that the two specialties within sociology in which constructionism has had the greatest impact are studies of social problems and of science. They present very different problems for analysts who hope to promote and extend the constructionist stance. The area of social problems is largely uncontested turf. As Spector and Kitsuse (1977) noted, prior to the emergence of constructionism, sociologists had made minimal analytic use of the concept of social problems. There were courses and textbooks ti-

tled "Social Problems," but there were few theories of social problems. Therefore, when constructionists began to develop their framework for thinking about social problems, there was no dominant rival theory to be challenged and overthrown, only a vacuum waiting to be filled.

Importantly, social problems analysts also had a readily available forum for promoting the perspective. The well-respected journal *Social Problems* had championed the rise of the labeling theory of deviance, and when Kitsuse and other labeling theorists turned to constructionism, the journal published their work. In 1981, Spector became the journal's editor—the first of several constructionists who would serve terms in that post. (Spector was well aware of the ways a journal could foster an intellectual movement; he had published an article describing how *Social Problems* promoted labeling [Spector, 1976].) By the late 1980s, there was also a constructionist book series (*Social Problems and Social Issues* from Aldine de Gruyter) that published monographs, as well as collections of empirical (Best, 1995b) and theoretical (Holstein & Miller, 1993, 2003) pieces, and an annual journal, *Perspectives on Social Problems*; both continued publication for more than 10 years.

In other words, constructionist analysts of social problems had venues in which they could publish their work. Although their initial case studies tended to sketch the construction of particular social problems, more specialized studies soon began to appear, including studies of claims-making rhetoric, social problems work, and so on. The emergence of electronic databases expanded the opportunities for research. The fact that a typical case study published around 1980 concerned how and why some social problem attracted national attention in the contemporary United States was partially a reflection of the relative ease of gathering information on such cases via printed indexes for national-level sources, such as the *New York Times Index*, the *Readers Guide to Periodical Literature*, *Television News Index and Abstracts*, and indexes of Congressional hearings, that were available in research libraries. The emergence of new electronic databases and the Internet have made it much easier to study social problems construction at the local level, in other countries, or at other times, so constructionist research on social problems could—and has—become more diverse, more than just a collection of contemporary case studies.

Sociology—like all scholarly disciplines—is prone to fads. Concepts, theories, methods, and substantive specialties come into and fall out of favor. Some novelty, for instance a new approach such as labeling theory or constructionism, emerges and attracts interest. Other scholars adopt the approach and extend it, which gives still other analysts an even broader foundation on which they can build their work. Young scholars decide that this is a promising perspective for them to pursue, and as people trained in an approach take jobs and acquire students of their own, the ideas can spread further. But this must be a constant, continuing progress. Like sharks, schools of thought need to keep moving forward in order to survive. If people have trouble framing additional questions or finding new ways to extend the approach, it will become harder to publish new work, and the approach will weaken and eventually drop from sight.

This means that constructionist scholars of social problems must continue to identify ways to extend the perspective, to demonstrate that it offers opportunities for further scholarship. Because there really is no rival school of social problems theory, the burden of finding new research topics and new angles for extending constructionism falls on the constructionists themselves. Ironically, competition among rival theoretical schools seems to spur—not discourage—intellectual activity. One reason that social movements scholarship has thrived in recent years is that there are competing theories—resource mobilization, framing, new social movements, and the like—so that scholars are encouraged to try to test the relative value of those

different approaches, to develop theoretical syntheses, and so on. Constructionism may dominate sociological discussions of social problems, but it is by no means clear that that bodes well for its future development; its prospects might be better if it had a theoretical rival to pique interest in both approaches. Similarly, debates within a school of thought are often healthy. The tussle between strict and contextual constructionism struck some constructionists as interesting, at least for a time, and this inspired some intellectual activity. However, the inability of strict constructionists to find a way out of their armchairs meant that virtually all recent work has adopted a contextual framework.

Here, the contrast with constructionist work in the sociology of science is suggestive. The sociology of science was an established research topic well before the emergence of constructionism; those sociologists who followed in Merton's footsteps studied the social structure of science and its system of stratification and social organization, although their work tended to take for granted the essential accuracy of scientific findings. In sharp contrast, the emergence of constructionist analyses focused on how scientists produced knowledge. Thus constructionist studies of science confronted a well-established, rival sociological school of thought. Moreover, as the constructionist analysis of science developed, its practitioners disagreed among themselves over just how strong their program ought to be. The result was a good deal of debate among sociologists of science. And, to make things even more complicated, the sociology of science was embedded in a long-standing rivalry with other disciplines interested in the scientific enterprise; in particular, historians of science and philosophers of science—as well as some scientists themselves—responded to the constructionists' challenge. In other words, the emergence of constructionist studies of science was treated as an important development, both within sociology and among the various other disciplines interested in science studies. Although the more radical constructionist work experienced harsh treatment at the hands of these various critics, constructionism continues to occupy a prominent place in science studies.

Within sociology, constructionist ideas have spread beyond those specializing in the study of social problems and science. Table 3.1 illustrates what has occurred; it displays the number of articles that include the words *social construction* or *socially constructed* in each of three leading general sociology journals, as well as nine leading specialized journals in sociology.[3] The pattern revealed in Table 3.1 is quite clear: In all 12 journals, mentions increased with each passing decade, from the 1970s through the 1990s. As might be expected, *Social Problems* and *Social Studies of Science* contained far more articles in which the words appeared, yet constructionist language also has spread in sociological studies of formal organizations, religion, medicine, family, law, social psychology, and education, as well as in the "big three" bastions of mainstream sociology. Jasper and

Goodwin (2005, p. 3) may exaggerate when they say "We are all social constructionists today, almost," yet the constructionist ideas do seem to have spread throughout much of sociology.

However, this spread should not be taken as evidence that there is one constructionism within sociology, let alone among the various other disciplines that have adopted some sort of constructionist perspective. Although scholars in a variety of disciplines have, during the past 40 years, developed what they call "constructionist" or "constructivist" approaches, these literatures often have little connection to one another. I have argued that most—if not all—of this work derives from Berger and Luckmann's (1966) revival of the expression *social construction*. However, we can suspect that a large share of those who have marched under one or another constructionist banner have never read *The Social Construction of Reality*. In practice, *social construction* has been taken to mean different things, not only in different disciplines but also within

---

TABLE 3.1. Number of Articles in Which the Words *Social Construction* or *Socially Constructed* Appeared in Leading General and Specialized Sociology Journals, 1970–1999

Journal	1970–1979	1980–1989	1990–1999
General journals			
American Journal of Sociology	25	34	71
American Sociological Review	31	30	73
Social Forces	11	31	67
Specialized journals			
Administrative Science Quarterly	9	37	65
Journal for the Scientific Study of Religion	11	29	30
Journal of Health and Social Behavior	6	11	18
Journal of Marriage and the Family	4	25	49
Law and Society Review	1	18	25
Social Problems	34	73	109
Social Psychology Quarterly	8	14	35
Social Studies of Science	8	106	143
Sociology of Education	2	8	27

Note. Data from JSTOR.

particular disciplines and even within specific specializations. There is no single "constructionism"; rather, there are many self-proclaimed constructionisms that make very different assumptions about the nature of reality, about the ways constructionist analysis ought to be conducted, about the sorts of answers constructionist analysis should produce, about the political implications of adopting a constructionist stance, and so on.

The decentralization that characterizes contemporary disciplines, in which different specializations operate as virtually independent social worlds, each with its own professional associations, conferences, journals, book series, prizes, and such, makes it possible for—and even encourages—scholars in one specialization to ignore work by their colleagues in the same discipline who work in different specializations (Best, 2003a). The same process fosters the disciplinary balkanization that characterizes contemporary scholarship. It is very difficult to keep track of developments in other disciplines, and there are few practical rewards for doing so.

This helps explain why modern universities feature such an array of constructionisms that may share little besides a fondness for speaking of "social construction" and roots that can be traced back to Berger and Luckmann (1966). Many constructionist sociologists probably know little about the work of their constructionist brethren in, say, political science or psychology, just as those constructionist political scientists and psychologists probably are not following developments in sociology. Typically, when a scholar does cite a work in another discipline, it is an older work, perhaps something read during graduate school, before one's own efforts became narrowly focused. All this helps ensure that, as a concept such as social construction takes on new meanings within a particular specialization, that development is likely to go unnoticed even within other specializations and almost certainly in other disciplines.

It is now some 40 years after Berger and Luckmann (1966) breathed new life into the old—but little used—idea of social construction. Although the approach has attracted broad attention, even to the point that the popular press sometimes borrows its language, constructionism's greatest impact remains within sociology and, to a lesser degree, the other social sciences. A growing number of scholars in an increasingly diverse set of sociological specialties have been adopting a constructionist vocabulary (and the publication of this reference book compiling constructionist ideas may be taken as a further sign of constructionism's well-being). Still, the future of constructionism will depend on scholars finding additional ways to extend the approach and to make contributions that their colleagues can recognize as valuable.

• Acknowledgment

Portions of this chapter are based on Best (2003b).

• Notes

1. In early 2006, a search of the Web of Science citation indexes identified nearly 4,000 sources that had cited Berger and Luckmann; this underestimates the book's influence, because citation indexes locate citations in scholarly journals but generally do not turn up citations in anthologies or other books. In comparison, Holzner's similarly titled *Reality Construction in Society* (1968) would attract much less attention—fewer than 75 Web of Science citations over the same period.

2. Sociologists seem to use *constructionist* and *constructivist* interchangeably. The latter term carries some high-culture overtones: *constructivism* was an early-20th-century school of modern art. When used by sociologists, *constructivism* may be more favored by British scholars and by sociologists of science, but there are exceptions (e.g., Joseph Gusfield, an American social problems analyst, also preferred *constructivism*). Two philosophers who have written book-length critiques also

disagree: Hacking (1999) uses *constructionism*; Boghossian (2006) uses *constructivism*.

3. These data come from a search of JSTOR, a full-text database. Because there is usually a lag of up to 5 years before a journal's contents are entered into JSTOR, the results for the 2000s are too fragmentary to be meaningful, and they have not been included. Note that the data may overestimate constructionism's impact in that a single reference to, say, *The Social Construction of Reality* would qualify an article for inclusion. Still, they provide a rough indication of usage in the professional literature; other studies have traced how the usage of various terms in the sociological literature has risen and fallen (Best, 2004; Best & Schweingruber, 2003).

• References

Abbott, A. (2001). *Chaos of disciplines*. Chicago: University of Chicago Press.

Altheide, D. L. (1976). *Creating reality: How TV news distorts events*. Beverly Hills, CA : Sage.

Berger, P. L. (1963). *Invitation to sociology*. Garden City, NY: Doubleday Anchor.

Berger, P. L., & Luckmann, T. (1966). *The social construction of reality: A treatise in the sociology of knowledge*. New York: Doubleday.

Berger, R. J. (2002). *Fathoming the Holocaust*. Hawthorne, NY: Aldine de Gruyter.

Best, J. (1993). But seriously folks: The limitations of the strict constructionist interpretation of social problems. In J. A. Holstein & G. Miller (Eds.), *Reconsidering social constructionism: Debates in social problems theory* (pp. 129–147). New York: Aldine de Gruyter.

Best, J. (1995a). Constructionism in context. In J. Best (Ed.), *Images of issues: Typifying contemporary social problems* (2nd ed., pp. 337–354). New York: Aldine de Gruyter.

Best, J. (Ed.). (1995b). *Images of issues: Typifying contemporary social problems* (2nd ed.). New York: Aldine de Gruyter.

Best, J. (2003a). Killing the messenger: The social problems of sociology. *Social Problems, 50*(1), 1–13.

Best, J. (2003b). Staying alive: Prospects for constructionist theory. In J. A. Holstein & G. Miller (Eds.), *Challenges and choices: Constructionist perspectives on social problems* (pp. 133–152). Hawthorne, NY: Aldine de Gruyter.

Best, J. (2004). *Deviance: Career of a concept*. Belmont, CA: Wadsworth.

Best, J., & Schweingruber, D. (2003). First words: Do sociologists actually use the terms in introductory textbooks' glossaries? *American Sociologist, 34*(3), 97–106.

Blumer, H. (1971). Social problems as collective behavior. *Social Problems, 18*(3), 298–306.

Bogard, C. J. (2003). Explaining social problems: Addressing the whys of social constructionism. In J. A. Holstein & G. Miller (Eds.), *Challenges and choices: Constructionist perspectives on social problems* (pp. 209–235). Hawthorne, NY: Aldine de Gruyter.

Boghossian, P. (2006). *Fear of knowledge: Against relativism and constructivism*. Oxford, UK: Clarendon.

Bradley, G. V. (2004, July 12). Stand and fight. *National Review Online*. Retrieved April 9, 2007, from *www.lexisnexis.com*

Cole, S. (Ed.). (2001). *What's wrong with sociology?* New Brunswick, NJ: Transaction.

Collins, H. M. (1983). The sociology of scientific knowledge: Studies of contemporary science. *Annual Review of Sociology, 9*, 265–285.

Collins, H. M. (2000). Surviving closure: Post-rejection adaptation and plurality in science. *American Sociological Review, 65*(6), 824–845.

de Rivera, J., & Sarbin, T. R. (Eds.). (1998). *Believed-in imaginings: The narrative construction of reality*. Washington, DC: American Psychological Association.

Derbyshire, J. (2006, January 11). Out of the corner. *National Review Online*. Retrieved April 9, 2007, from *www.lexisnexis.com*

Douglas, J. D. (1967). *The social meanings of suicide*. Princeton, NJ: Princeton University Press.

Douglas, J. D. (Ed.). (1970). *Deviance and respectability: The social construction of moral meanings*. New York: Basic Books.

Dyer, E. (2006, March 29). Tracking codes: DNA tests locate the genetic branches on African-Americans' family trees. *Pittsburgh Post-Gazette*, p. C1.

Dyson, F. J. (1999). *The sun, the genome, and the Internet: Tools of scientific revolutions*. New York: Oxford University Press.

Edelman, M. (1988). *Constructing the political spectacle*. Chicago: University of Chicago Press.

Elkind, D. (2004, September 26). Attention, smallest shoppers!: How marketing makes consumers out of kids. *Boston Globe*, p. D7.

Frankenberg, R. (1993). *White women, race matters: The social construction of whiteness*. Minneapolis: University of Minnesota Press.

Gergen, K. J. (1994). *Realities and relationships: Soundings in social constructionism*. Cambridge, MA: Harvard University Press.

Gergen, K. J. (2001). *Social constructionism in context*. Thousand Oaks, CA: Sage.

Goldblatt, M. (2004, January 15). Academic anti-Bushism. *National Review Online*. Retrieved April 9, 2007, from *www.lexisnexis.com*

Granovetter, M. S. (1973.) The strength of weak ties. *American Journal of Sociology, 78*(6), 1360–1380.

Guillory, J. (2002). The Sokal affair and the history of criticism. *Critical Inquiry, 28*(2), 470–508.

Gusfield, J. R. (1981). *The culture of public problems: Drinking–driving and the symbolic order.* Chicago: University of Chicago Press.

Hacking, I. (1999). *The social construction of what?* Cambridge, MA: Harvard University Press.

Holstein, J. A., & Gubrium, J. F. (2003). A constructionist analytics for social problems. In J. A. Holstein & G. Miller (Eds.), *Challenges and choices: Constructionist perspectives on social problems* (pp. 187–208). Hawthorne, NY: Aldine de Gruyter.

Holstein, J. A., & Miller, G. (Eds.). (1993). *Reconsidering social constructionism: Debates in social problems theory.* New York: Aldine de Gruyter.

Holstein, J. A., & Miller, G. (Eds.). (2003). *Challenges and choices: Constructionist perspectives on social problems.* Hawthorne, NY: Aldine de Gruyter.

Holzner, B. (1968). *Reality construction in society.* Cambridge, MA: Schenkman.

Ibarra, P. R., & Kitsuse, J. I. (1993). Vernacular constituents of moral discourse: An interactionist proposal for the study of social problems. In J. A. Holstein & G. Miller (Eds.), *Reconsidering social constructionism: Debates in social problems theory* (pp. 5–23). New York: Aldine de Gruyter.

Jasper, J. M., & Goodwin, J. (2005). From the editors. *Contexts, 4*(3), 3.

Jenkins, P. (1996). *Pedophiles and priests: Anatomy of a contemporary crisis.* New York: Oxford University Press.

Kitsuse, J. I., & Cicourel, A. V. (1963). A note on the uses of official statistics. *Social Problems, 11*(2), 131–139.

Knorr-Cetina, K. D. (1981). *The manufacture of knowledge: An essay on the constructivist and contextual nature of science.* New York: Pergamon.

Kuhn, T. S. (1962). *The structure of scientific revolutions.* Chicago: University of Chicago Press.

Langmuir, I. (1953, December). *Pathological science.* Paper presented at the colloquium at Knolls Research Laboratory, Niskayuna, NY.

Latour, B., & Woolgar, S. (1979). *Laboratory life: The social construction of scientific facts.* Beverly Hills, CA: Sage.

Laws, J. L., & Schwartz, P. (1977). *Sexual scripts: The social construction of female sexuality.* Hinsdale, IL: Dryden.

Lorber, J., & Farrell, S. A. (1991). *The social construction of gender.* Newbury Park, CA: Sage.

Mauss, A. L. (1975). *Social problems as social movements.* Philadelphia: Lippincott.

Merton, R. K. (1973). *The sociology of science: Theoretical and empirical investigations.* Chicago: University of Chicago Press.

Miller, G. (1997). *Becoming miracle workers: Language and meaning in brief therapy.* Hawthorne, NY: Aldine de Gruyter.

Mirkin, H. (1999). The pattern of sexual politics. *Journal of Homosexuality, 37*(2), 1–24.

Pickett, D. (2003, November 7). Sex as a weapon: Yes, you can trade lovemaking for household chores—just don't admit it. *Chicago Sun-Times*, p. 60.

Platt, A. M. (1969). *The child savers: The invention of delinquency.* Chicago: University of Chicago Press.

Rains, P. (1975). Imputations of deviance: A retrospective essay on the labeling perspective. *Social Problems, 23*(1), 1–11.

Rochefort, D. A., & Cobb, R. W. (1994). *The politics of problem definition: Shaping the policy agenda.* Lawrence: University Press of Kansas.

Rose, V. M. (1977). Rape as a social problem: A byproduct of the feminist movement. *Social Problems, 25*(1), 75–89.

Rosenthal, R. (1966). *Experimenter effects in behavioral research.* New York: Irvington.

Rothman, D. J. (1971). *The discovery of the asylum.* Boston: Little, Brown.

Sarbin, T. R., & Kitsuse, J. I. (1994). Prologue. In T. R. Sarbin & J. I. Kitsuse (Eds.), *Constructing the social* (pp. 1–18). Thousand Oaks, CA: Sage.

Schneider, A. L., & Ingram, H. M. (1993). Social constructions of target populations: Implications for politics and policy. *American Political Science Review, 87*(2), 334–347.

Schneider, A. L., & Ingram, H. M. (Eds.). (2005). *Deserving and entitled: Social constructions and public policy.* Albany: State University of New York Press.

Schneider, J. W. (1985). Defining the definitional perspective on social problems. *Social Problems, 32*(3), 232–234.

Simon, B. (2002). *Undead science: Science studies and the afterlife of cold fusion.* New Brunswick, NJ: Rutgers University Press.

Smith, T. S. (1974). Aestheticism and social structure: Style and social network in the dandy life. *American Sociological Review, 39*(5), 725–743.

Sokal, A., & Bricmont, J. (1998). *Fashionable nonsense: Postmodern intellectuals' abuse of science.* New York: Picador.

Sokal, A. D. (1996). Transgressing the boundaries: Toward a transformative hermeneutics of quantum gravity. *Social Text, 46/47,* 217–252.

Sommers, C. H. (2005, March 22). Who stole Harvard? *National Review Online.* Retrieved April 9, 2007, from *www.lexisnexis.com*

Spector, M. (1976). Labeling theory in *Social Problems*: A young journal launches a new theory. *Social Problems, 24*(1), 69–75.

Spector, M., & Kitsuse, J. I. (1977). *Constructing social problems.* Menlo Park, CA: Cummings.

Stolba, C. (2002). Lying in a room of one's own: How women's studies textbooks miseducate students. Retrieved April 9, 2007, from Independent Women's Forum, *www.iwf.orgpdf/roomononesown.pdf*

Sudnow, D. (1965). Normal crimes: Sociological features of the penal code in a public defender office. *Social Problems, 12*(3), 255–276.

Szasz, T. S. (1970). *The manufacture of madness.* New York: Harper & Row.

Tuchman, G. (1978). *Making news: A study in the construction of reality.* New York: Free Press.

Ward, L. F. (1905). Evolution of social structures. *American Journal of Sociology, 10*(5), 589–605.

Weinberg, T. S. (1983). *Gay men, gay selves: The social construction of homosexual identities.* New York: Irvington.

Wilgoren, J. (2002, April 30). Scholar's pedophilia essay stirs outrage and revenge. *New York Times,* p. 18.

Will, G. (1996, May 30). Smitten with gibberish. *Washington Post,* p. A31.

Will, G. (2002a, May 19). Feminism hijacked. *Washington Post,* p. B7.

Will, G. (2002b, May 27). A train wreck called Title IX. *Newsweek,* p. 82.

Wills, G. (2002, June 13). Priests and boys. *New York Review of Books, 49*(10), 12–13.

Woolgar, S. (1981). Interests and explanation in the social study of science. *Social Studies of Science, 11*(3), 365–394.

Woolgar, S., & Pawluch, D. (1985a). How shall we move beyond constructivism? *Social Problems, 33*(2), 159–162.

Woolgar, S, & Pawluch, D. (1985b). Ontological gerrymandering: The anatomy of social problems explanations. *Social Problems, 32*(3), 214–227.

PART II

CONSTRUCTIONISM ACROSS THE DISCIPLINES

CHAPTER 4

Constructionism in Anthropology

- **James D. Faubion**
  George E. Marcus

In anthropology, constructionism has reached something of a saturation point. It began to snowball as early as the 1960s. Especially since the interdisciplinary theory movements of the 1980s, however, it has become pervasive. Anthropology can now claim a constructionist approach to just about everything—identities, markets, institutions, diseases, technologies, and so forth. Sometimes still illuminating and still pleasing to a certain aesthetics of critique, constructionism as "one note" with few fresh variations has nevertheless begun to chafe. The symptoms are straightforward enough: on the one hand, ever more baroque efforts at "product differentiation"; on the other, searches for real alternatives (which are not easy to find).

The exhaustion with constructionist argument is, however, not limited to anthropology alone. It is currently a general predicament, common to many disciplines, in which anthropology is caught up. So, if we limited ourselves to anthropology's engagement with constructionism during the past four decades, we would be telling a story not very different from those of the several other fields in which constructionist approaches and theories have been just as dominant since the 1960s. We would tell it by appeal to most of the same sources of theory and discussion to which their stories would also appeal. This would be a story about how constructionism provided the most clear and easily assimilated theoretical and analytic perspective left standing after vigorous critiques—not just of past genres of representation but of representation itself—that so saturated the humanistic precincts of the academy throughout the 1980s and well

67

into the 1990s. Instead, we have chosen to begin much farther back in the modern history of anthropology to find the deeper and more particular roots of constructionist approaches embedded within it. By so doing, perhaps we might come up with an analysis specific to anthropology of the current situation of scholarship devoted to critical cultural inquiry. In anthropology, as in other fields, that scholarship continues to share in the critique of reigning theories and of representation itself of the 1980s. Yet precisely because it does so, it bears the burdens of a constructionist excess that remains difficult to cast off.

A Matrix of Diversity

To render the specificity we seek more precisely, we can begin by considering Peter Berger and Thomas Luckmann's *The Social Construction of Reality* (1966), surely one of the most recognized benchmarks of constructionism in all of the social sciences. No doubt, most social and cultural anthropologists today are familiar with it. A few continue to cite it. Neither today nor in the past decades, however, has it ever functioned as an icon of anthropological constructionism, much less as the centerpiece of a disciplinary canon. The source of its relative marginality does not lie in professional exclusivity; on the contrary, anthropologists tend to be opportunists who will take social and cultural theory wherever they can get it. It probably does not lie in a positivist disdain of Burger and Luckmann's antipositivism, even if many anthropologists are considerably more positivistic than they are likely to admit to being. The source of that marginality lies more securely in the historical depth of constructionist frameworks of analysis that were already well established in anthropology when *The Social Construction of Reality* appeared in print. One must nevertheless give Burger and Luckmann their due. Until the 1960s, American anthropologists pursuing the generative potential of microscalar inter-

action restricted their attention largely to practices of childrearing. They owe to Herbert Blumer and Erving Goffman, as well as to Berger and Luckmann, a significant enrichment of their analytic tool kit. Anthropologists reading even the first edition of *The Social Construction of Reality* tended already to approach their terrains of research in terms so close to Berger and Luckmann's own that they were very likely to feel themselves often on already familiar ground. Though we duly note potential signs of change on the horizon, we think it fair further to observe that most American anthropologists are similar to their colleagues in the other national traditions of anthropology (mainly British and French) in remaining true even now to most of those terms, even if they have wittingly or unwittingly found many new guises for them from one decade to the next.

Such terms exist in a multitude, but they cluster into doctrinal types that yield exemplary cases. One of these—we call it *Durkheimian* after the social theoretician who is its source—has the status of a proper analytic program or intellectual tradition, which continues from the beginning of the 20th century to the present. A second is analytically more diffuse and more difficult to associate with a single theoretical figurehead; we accordingly stress its common engagement with a particular complex of questions—a "problematic"—having to do with power and the dynamics of sociocultural reproduction. Because of the considerable analytic heritage they share, our third and fourth types belong effectively to the same cluster. The third still has enough of a national flavor that we can designate it *American* and enough of a common eye on culture that we can further designate it *culturalist*. The fourth reflects the specific methodology of cultural analysis formalized in the works of Lévi-Strauss. Their methodological differences aside, both of the latter rest analytically in what we characterize as "structuralist semiotics." That semiotics has many sources and inspirations. It has its distinguishing fingerprint, however, in the postulate that the semiotic domain is analytically independent of whatever attachment the symbols and signs of which it is constituted might have with the nonsemiotic world. Thus identified, structuralist semiotics is of such long-standing and analytic eminence that it approaches paradigmatic status.

This said, we would be remiss were we to restrict our treatment of constructionism in anthropology to those clusters alone. We must also note many outliers. We would further be remiss were we to ignore the matrix of a certain disciplinary "common sense" that informs the anthropological practices of the clustered and the outliers alike. For our purposes, any position is constructionist in anthropology that treats one or more dimensions of human experience or practice as the result of processes of socialization or enculturation. Among the various inspirations for a distinctively anthropological constructionism, we distinguish three salient domains. One domain is the social. It comprises all the relations that might obtain between any particular system of imperatives and ideals and the actions for which that system provides an essential point of orientation. Another such domain is the cultural. It comprises imperatives and ideals and the relations in which they stand to one another, as well as systems of classification and symbolization, of mood and motivation, of inscription and stylization. Especially, but not only, in the American tradition, cultures (pluralizable since the Boasians; [7], [8], [13] in Figure 4.1) have until recently been taken for granted as the largest scale of its systemic, coherent expressions. A third domain—largely anathema to the British tradition but well within the purview of the American and the French—is the psychological. It comprises cognition, perception, and affect and addresses a double subject: either the human being in his or her individuality and particularity or the human being as a species, a natural kind.

Intersecting these domains, four method-

ologies of analysis have been important to anthropologists of one or another constructionist bent. One of these is *functionalist*. Its most authoritative anthropological wellsprings are Emile Durkheim's *Division of Labor in Society* (1893/1933) and *The Elementary Forms of the Religious Life* ([3]; see Figure 4.1). It inquires into the sociological purposes or practical consequences of such collective formations as groups and institutions. Another approach is *semiological*. It targets all that has to do with the constitution of meaning and the process of communication. Theoretically and methodologically its hallmark systems are spoken languages, though since the 1970s they have been displaced in many analytic circles by written or otherwise encoded texts. A third approach, which we term *rhetoricist*, deals with the situational use of speech as an instrument to some practical end. Such an approach distinguishes what has come to be known as the ethnography of communication. Its seminal idea—from Aristotle on—is that of the effectiveness of speech, of its capacity to influence thought and feeling and (so) action; to produce, rather than merely to express, meaning. Rhetoricist analysis as it is now exercised, however, extends well beyond the act of speaking, beyond the linguistic or the discursive, to include all meaningful action. A fourth approach is *hermeneutical*. It comprises all processes of interpretation, from the solution to some practical problem, however trivial or profound, through all the ways of generating a "reading" of an action or a material or ideational artifact to the formal assignation of a word to its referent. This approach has diverse versions and variations. It also has a long lineage. It descends from the problematization of the relation between experience and meaning that rippled through the European Enlightenment in the latter half of the 18th century. It evinces the fact that anthropological constructionism is a direct heir to such skeptical empiricists as David Hume and his greatest successor, the original philosophical constructionist, Immanuel Kant.

We offer a matrix of the diverse and pervasive manifestations of constructionism in the history of anthropology from the mid-19th century on (see Figure 4.1). The matrix consists of the intersections of domains of inquiry with analytic approaches to them, yielding social–functionalist, social–semiological, social–rhetorical, social–hermeneutical, psychological–functionalist, psychological–semiological, psychological–rhetorical, psychological–hermeneutical, and so on. All these might be thought of as versions of anthropological common sense.

Figure 4.1 plots 61 texts (see the accompanying roster) that jointly reveal the central clusters and trajectories of constructionist analysis or, if one prefers, constructionist discourse of anthropological tenor in the past and into the present century. We include Karl Marx and Friedrich Engels's *German Ideology* [1] not as a work *in* anthropology but certainly a work *of* it. It also serves as a reference point for later developments that are very much in its debt. Durkheim and Marcel Mauss's *Primitive Classification* [2], Durkheim's *Elementary Forms of the Religious Life* [3], Sigmund Freud's *Totem and Taboo* [4], Max Weber's "Social Psychology of the World Religions" [5], and Bruno Latour's *We Have Never Been Modern* [55] merit inclusion for similar reasons. All of the works in the roster at least arguably deserve to be considered "major" works, if not for the scope or durability of their influence, then for the clarity and the specificity of the example of constructionism they offer. Not all of them have constructionism as an explicit thematic; all, instead, are of interest for the constructionism they include. In every case, our assignations should be understood as summary judgments. In no case do we claim to do full justice to subtlety or nuance.

Our ordering of the works reflects the date of their original publication, indicated in parentheses, and with the exception only of the first entry. The *German Ideology* was not published in full until 1932, some nine decades after it was completed as a manuscript. An effective evocation of the histori-cal breadth and depth of the intellectual ecology of anthropological constructionism demands privileging the latter date over the former. A selection of works better evokes that ecology than a selection of authors, because the same author, as with Claude Lévi-Strauss [14], [22], [23] or Clifford Geertz [33], [35], may have different constructionist emphases from one occasion to another. Or, as with Paul Rabinow [38], [61], he or she may evince a shift from one constructionist perspective to another over time. The same mode of selection also allows us to make note of the consistency of certain authors' constructionism through time. Mary Douglas [30], [46] is one such author. Pierre Bourdieu [31], [42]—anthropologist by vocation if not by station—is another.

The Durkheimian Legacy

The general distribution of the entries in Figure 4.1 indicates the attraction of synthetic or holistic doctrines over their "purer" or more strongly deterministic modalities. This is especially so as anthropology settles into its own intergenerational reproduction. It is all the more so as the conceptual and methodological boundaries among the major national traditions—British, French, and North American—begin in the 1960s to become more permeable. Falling in the upper right quadrant, the strongly deterministic works are in their greatest majority among the first 30 on the roster. More than a few of them (e.g., [1], [2], [3], [4], [7], [9], [10], [11], [22], and [23]) put forward analytic or explanatory programs of foundational stature. Most of these are in at least implicit competition with the foundational programs of other, proximate disciplines or of the anthropological establishment that precedes them.

Of special longevity is the Durkheimian program. Its regulative protoconstructionist idea is that the form and content of social organization are responsible for or determine the form and content of moral and cognitive

	soc	psy	cul	soc–psy	soc–cul	psy–cul	soc–psy–cul
f							9
s			♦ 10, 17, 27, 54		♣ 24, 37	♣ 22, 23	
r			♦				
h			♦ 26, 35, 56	♦	♦ 38, 57, 59	♦ 7, 8, 13, 15, 19, 36	5
f-s			♦ 33		♥ 2, 3, 11, 16, 30, 32, 46, 60		
f-r			♦		♠ 28, 21, 39		
f-h			♦		♠ 1, 40	12, 25	4
s-r	61		♦		♠ 53		
s-h			♦ 43		♠ 34		
r-h			♦ 41, 44		♠ 55		20
f-s-r					♠ 31, 42		
f-s-h					♠ 6, 45, 52		29, 58
f-r-h							
r-s-h					47		
f-s-r-h					18	14, 49, 51	48, 49, 50

domains	*modes*
soc: social	f: functionalist
psy: psychological	s: semiological
cul: cultural	r: rhetorical
	h: hermeneutical

Roster of texts

1. K. Marx & F. Engels, *The German ideology* (1846)
2. E. Durkheim & M. Mauss, *Primitive classification* (1903)
3. E. Durkheim, *The elementary forms of the religious life* (1912)
4. S. Freud, *Totem and taboo* (1913)
5. M. Weber, The social psychology of the world religions (1915)
6. M. Mauss, *The gift* (1927)
7. R. Benedict, *Patterns of culture* (1934)
8. M. Mead, *Coming of age in Samoa* (1934)
9. B. Malinowski, The group and the individual in functional analysis (1939)
10. B. L. Whorf, The relation of habitual thought and behavior to language (1939)
11. A. R. Radcliffe-Brown, On social structure (1940)
12. G. Roheim, *The eternal ones of the dream* (1945)
13. C. Kluckhohn & D. Leighton, *The Navaho* (1946)
14. C. Lévi-Strauss, The effectiveness of symbols (1949)
15. J. Whiting & I. Child, *Child training and personality* (1953)
16. E. E. Evans-Pritchard, *Nuer religion* (1956)
17. H. Conklin, Hanunóo color categories (1955)

(continued)

FIGURE 4.1. Domains and modes of anthropological constructionism.

18. V. Turner, *Schism and continuity in an African society* (1957)
19. A. I. Hallowell, Ojibwa ontology, behavior and worldview (1960)
20. J.-P. Sartre, *The critique of dialectical reason* (1960)
21. G. Berreman, Behind many masks (1962)
22. C. Lévi-Strauss, *The savage mind* (1962)
23. C. Lévi-Strauss, *The raw and the cooked* (1964)
24. L. Dumont, *Homo hierarchicus* (1966)
25. M. Spiro, *Burmese supernaturalism* (1967)
26. D. Schneider, *American kinship* (1968)
27. B. Berlin & P. Kay, *Basic color terms* (1969)
28. F. Barth, ed., *Ethnic groups and boundaries* (1969)
29. V. Turner, *The ritual process* (1969)
30. M. Douglas, *Natural symbols* (1970)
31. P. Bourdieu, *Outline of a theory of practice* (1972)
32. R. Needham, *Language, belief and experience* (1972)
33. C. Geertz, Thick description (1973)
34. M. de Certeau, *The practice of everyday life* (1974)
35. C. Geertz, From the native's point of view (1974)
36. A. Dundes, Projection in folklore (1976)
37. M. Sahlins, *Culture and practical reason* (1976)
38. P. Rabinow, *Reflections on fieldwork in Morocco* (1977)
39. B. Latour & S. Woolgar, *Laboratory life* (1979)
40. S. Ortner & H. Whitehead, eds., *Sexual meanings* (1981)
41. G. Marcus & D. Cushman, Ethnographies as texts (1982)
42. P. Bourdieu, *Homo academicus* (1984)
43. E. V. Daniel, *Fluid signs* (1984)
44. D. Schneider, *A critique of the study of kinship* (1984)
45. S. Tambiah, *Culture, thought and social action* (1985)
46. M. Douglas, *How institutions think* (1986)
47. J. Fernandez, *Persuasions and performances* (1986)
48. V. Turner, *The anthropology of performance* (1986)
49. S. Tyler, Post-modern ethnography (1986)
50. N. Scheper-Hughes & M. Lock, The mindful body (1987)
51. A. Kleinman, *The illness narratives* (1988)
52. M. Strathern, *The gender of the gift* (1988)
53. D. Kondo, *Crafting selves* (1990)
54. M. Marriott, *India through Hindu categories* (1990)
55. B. Latour, *We have never been modern* (1991)
56. M. Strathern, *After nature* (1992)
57. R. Rosaldo, *Culture and truth* (1993)
58. F. Héritier-Augé, *The two sisters and their mother* (1994)
59. G. Marcus, Ethnography in/of the world system (1995)
60. V. Das, Wittgenstein and anthropology (1998)
61. P. Rabinow, *Anthropos today* (2003)

FIGURE 4.1. *(continued)*

organization. The anthropological champions of that program constitute a structural–functionalist block of a single cell in Figure 4.1, marked with the sign of the heart (♥). The cell begins with Durkheim's own works and continues through A. R. Radcliffe-Brown's mechanistic appropriation of Durkheim [11] to the much more carefully tempered contributions of E. E. Evans-Pritchard [16] and his student Douglas [30], [46]. At the discursive margins of this block lie the works of Rodney Needham [32] and Veena Das [60]. Both of the latter owe to the philosopher Ludwig Wittgenstein their conviction that the determination of the meaning of any symbol or sign must always rest in an interpersonal assessment of the conditions of its actual use.

Durkheim's original idea of the social determination of "collective representations" is, as Stephen Lukes (1972) and others have pointed out, considerably ambiguous. Durkheim is probably best understood as postulating the social causation of the form and content of those ensembles of ethos, ethic, and worldview that the Boasians and their American successors would deem cultures. The British Durkheimians became fully constructionist only once they provided a processual account of how particular patterns of organized interaction give rise to particular habits of heart and mind. For the Durkheim of *The Elementary Forms of the Religious Life* (1912/1995), the cardinal principle of such an account lay with ritual interaction, for two basic reasons. First, ritual brings about in its practice the synthesis of the social, the moral, and the cognitive orders. Second, in inducing the "effervescent" experience of collective unity, ritual serves to galvanize commitment to collective representations already in place [3]. The first, synthetic function of ritual remains central to Stanley Tambiah's much more semiologically sophisticated analysis, whose career arguments came together in *Culture, Thought and Social Action* in 1985 [45]. The second of the functions of ritual frequently calls for celebrants to suspend, invert, or ecstatically escape from the mundane normative order of everyday life in the course of fulfilling their ordained roles or duties. It has held special and persistent fascination for anthropologists since Durkheim made a theoretical issue of it ([3]; cf. Durkheim, 1973). It provides the motive for Victor Turner's elaboration of the "liminal" or transformative phase of initiations and other rites of passage in *The Ritual Process* [29].

Any account of the interactive production or reproduction of the cultural order that relies exclusively on the role of ritual conduct must nevertheless struggle to assign a constructive role to mundane practice. As Durkheim was already aware, any such account would have to struggle further to make sense of sociocultural reproduction among collectivities whose members rarely if ever engage in anything resembling common, collective ritual interaction. Such collectivities are far from uncommon. Institutionally or religiously plural, they are precisely the sort of collectivities to which the vast majority of human beings now belong. Reasonably enough, Durkheim looked to the educational system to achieve in secular terms what the conduct of ritual and the religious life could no longer achieve on their own.

Power and Sociocultural Reproduction

In his long-standing inquiry into the educational system as the principal source of the reproduction of class and status stratification in modern France, Bourdieu (1984/1988; [42]) is Durkheim's most immediate heir. Yet Bourdieu's sensibility takes shape within a quite distinct atmosphere, which is charged above all with the collapse of political colonialism. Like the sensibilities of many others of his historical cohort, Bourdieu's own sensibility exhibits a skepticism toward the legally legitimated metropolitan state, along with an appreciation of the tactical and the informal as the textures of resistance. We accordingly relegate Bourdieu's work to a distinct block in Figure 4.1, abutting its Durkheimian counterpart but marked with the sign of the spade (♠). We similarly mark those cells whose works share with Bourdieu's the presumption that the analysis of social and cultural constructions must be approached through an analysis of the dynamics and distribution of material and sociocultural power. Such a presumption brings together otherwise odd bedfellows. Not least, it constitutes the common ground between *The German Ideology* (1) and Mauss's decidedly pro-Durkheimian and antieconomistic essay on reciprocity, *The Gift* (1927/1990; [6]). It brings Bourdieu himself together with one of his most trenchant critics, Michel de Certeau (1974/1984; [34]). Bourdieu, indeed, often sees the reproduction of socioeconomic domination where de Certeau sees resistance to it. De Certeau is the more enthusiastically informal of the two. Yet Bourdieu's (1972/1977; [31]) placement of all the unwritten, unspoken, but traded tricks of the pedagogue of moods and motivations on the same analytic footing as the rigid curricula of the *lycée* complicates the Durkheimian spotlight on education. At the very least, it overcomes the officiousness of Durkheim's tendency to reduce the educational system itself to the single institution of the school.

With their focus on childrearing and child training, the Boasian culturalists [7], [8], [13], [19] had in fact already identified the dynamic locus that both Bourdieu and another of his contemporaries, the properly Durkheimian Douglas [30], would subsequently make their own. In Durkheim's own works, the link between social norms and collective representations, on the one hand, and actual human actions, on the other, is always somewhat missing. Bourdieu and Douglas join the culturalists in making that link on the plane of human corporeality. The "mindful body," as Nancy Scheper-Hughes and Margaret Lock (1987; [50]) call it, is for Bourdieu the essential medium that through the course of both formal and informal education is quite literally constructed as an organized set of dispositions to think, to feel, and to act—in a word, as a *habitus*—in just such a way that it will reinforce the very education out of which it is made. So, in turn, it contributes to the reproduction of the overarching sociocultural system of which that education is a functional component. This is the classic statement of the ironic twist that characterizes so many arguments of a constructionist nature, including that at the core of Anthony Giddens's theory of structuration (Giddens, 1984).

In defining the habitus as an "organized" set of dispositions, Bourdieu in fact implies his acceptance of a postulate once widely embraced but now controversial. The postulate has its first systematic formulation in Ruth Benedict's *Patterns of Culture* (1934; [7]). In Benedict's terms, it amounts to the claim that cultures are "integrated," or, in other words, that they are cognitively and affectively consistent and coherent, even if not always congenial to every temperament. Ernest Gellner (1970) is not alone in underscoring the idea that less in the way of cultural consistency and coherence is typically more in the way of cultural congeniality and sustainability. Such qualifications aside, however, some version of the integrationist postulate in fact follows from the Durkheimian conception of society as an organized totality persisting well beyond the term of the life of any of its individual members.

Stronger versions of that postulate are typically—though not necessarily—operative in analyses that join Durkheim in deeming collective solidarity a virtue. They are operative as well in analyses that diverge from both Durkheim and dialecticians of Marxist stripe in regarding the reproduction of the same sociocultural order through time as largely inertial. Constructionisms vary accordingly. Douglas (1970; [30]), approving of solidarity if not an unmitigated apologist for it, treats integration as a common psychological quest. Each actor's striving for the aesthetic integration of his or her modes of thinking and feeling motors the constructionist process of the adaptation of a particular "upbringing" to a particular organizational context—sometimes broadly societal, sometimes institutionally specific [46]. Douglas's actors are not always fully conscious of what they are doing. They are even less conscious of what they are constructing, but their conatus for integration is constitutive of the social all the same. Bourdieu responds to the problematic of the maintenance of social solidarity with an inertial but also critical analysis of the reproduction of sociocultural stratification. He accordingly locates adjustment or adaptation less in the striving of a self-craving coherence than in the systematic misrecognition of incoherence that is the typical result of socialization itself. The constructionist thesis of *The German Ideology* (Marx & Engels, 1846/1970; [1]) is well known: The ruling ideas are the ideas that serve the maintenance of the ruling class. That thesis becomes broadly anthropological in the *Outline of a Theory of Practice* (Bourdieu, 1972/1977; [31]). The habits of heart and mind that the pupils of Bourdieu's social universe acquire are constructions that equip them to reproduce the material and social conditions—the conditions constitutive of class—into which they have been born precisely through misrecognizing that they are doing so.

Without further qualification, Bourdieu's theory of sociocultural reproduction is among the strongest constructionist programs ever proposed—and it requires (as does the central theory of *The German Ideology*) an equally strong affirmation of the possibility of a positivist liberation from illusion in order to sustain its own consistency. On what other basis, after all, can the social and cultural observer even begin to claim that his or her observations are not simply further illusions? Perhaps for this reason, there are few if any purely Marxist or purely Bourdieusian anthropologists of gender or sexuality—for whom the choice between a self-subsuming constructionism and the corrective of a happy positivism seems not to be any choice at all. Such anthropologists are well aware of the relation between misrecognition and the reproduction of the almost always asymmetrical and substantially conventional difference between the masculine and the feminine or the heterosexual and the homosexual. Their works include the early writings of Douglas (1966) through Sherry Ortner and Harriet Whitehead's pivotal *Sexual Meanings* [40] and Scheper-Hughes and Lock's (1987) "The Mindful Body" [50] to Marilyn Strathern's *Gender of the Gift* (1988; [52]) and *After Nature* (1992; [56]) and Dorrine Kondo's *Crafting Selves* (1990; [53]). Neither these works nor any others of which we are aware, however, are quite prepared to adopt a constructionism so strong as to risk rendering the social actor—not even to mention the sociocultural analyst—the eternal prisoner of (mis)constructions without any hope of enlightened escape. All accordingly endow their actors with at least some measure of epistemological and practical agency. If such actors are not sufficiently endowed to become free of all the constructions with which everyone must live, at least they are endowed enough to be able to recognize constructions as constructions. In doing so, they also begin to contract the breadth of the divide that separates the Bourdieusian practitioner from the scientist of practice.

The practitioner of the *Outline* (Bourdieu, 1972/1977) is still more distant from the considerably self-aware actors of Fredrik Barth's (1969) introduction to *Ethnic Groups and Boundaries* [28] and its cellmates, Gerald Berreman's (1962) "Behind Many Masks" [21] and Latour and Woolgar's (1979) *Laboratory Life* [39]. Barth's introduction is widely regarded as the classic constructionist account of ethnic identity formation. "Behind Many Masks" addresses the staging of the ethnographic subject's presentation of self and society to the ethnographer and its relationship to the threat of a loss of status. Both Barth and Berreman make explicit use of concepts derived from Erving Goffman's *Presentation of Self in Everyday Life* (1959). Both appear to owe to Goffman their conception of the actor as the constructor of impressions of self and world intentionally deployed to maximize (or to reduce the threat of the debasement of) his or her status. The later *Laboratory Life* [39] has many Goffmanian traces of its own. Its attention to the ad hoc further suggests ethnomethodological adaptations of Goffman's original analysis of impression management (cf. Garfinkel, 1967). It, too, ties the analysis of constructionist success to the right deployment of resources. At issue for Latour and Woolgar, however, is not the self but the scientific fact and the resources at stake in establishing the latter, which are technological and monetary rather than strictly symbolic in nature.

In *We Have Never Been Modern* [55], Latour (1991) is at pains to distinguish the constructionism with which he is associated—at the current forefront of much work in science and technology studies, as well as in the anthropology of science—from the radical epistemological and ontological relativism for which *Laboratory Life* has often been understood to stand. He insists in the later monograph that scientific facts are indeed constructions or fabrications but that they are hybrid fabrications that unite such sociocultural elements as the distribution of epistemic authority with entirely natural states and events. He is quite prepared to maintain in any case that the scientific fact is always also what in the broadest sense must be called a "political" construction. Though not always in his footsteps, all current anthropologists of the sciences follow him at least this far.

Structuralist Semiology

A strong and varied thread of interactionist approaches to the genesis of things as constructed runs through the majority of the works in the later Durkheimian tradition, as well as in the works of a more politically preoccupied tradition, Latour's included. Yet the microanalysis of communicative interaction in anthropology has remained a subspecialty at best, a second-class enterprise at worst. Berger and Luckmann are not alone in undergoing a certain anthropological marginalization as a consequence. The same trend leads from the 1960s on to the increasing self-enclosure of that ever more specialized specialization known as *sociolinguistics* (see Gumperz & Hymes, 1986; Saville-Troike, 1982). Meanwhile, what was formerly known as *symbolic anthropology* now announces itself to be an anthropology of *performance*. It still claims allegiance to Turner [18], [29], [48], but it increasingly appeals also to cultural theorist Judith Butler. Not even the current transatlantic fashion of Butler and her conception of that potentially subversive way of imitation that she calls *performativity* (1993), however, have made even this current of communicative microanalysis as central as one might expect.

Politically, the sources of such sidelining are many and scattered. They include the vigorous objections of such Oxonian empiricists as philosopher–anthropologist Gellner (1959) to the Cambridgian Wittgenstein and his thoroughgoing (constructionist) epistemological and moral conventionalism, the same functionalist conventionalism that Berger and Luckmann exhibit and that cultural anthropologists have often found to

be of intuitive appeal. They also include the early French branding of Weber as "rightist" and the great delay with which French social scientists thought it proper even to read him, much less to take his thought seriously. The Weberian phenomenologist Alfred Schutz would thus fare little better among anthropologists than Burger and Luckmann themselves. We cannot fail to mention, either, the relative dominance of French over German social and cultural theory from the later 1960s through the later 1980s.

Nothing, however, is more decisive for the apparent neglect of the microanalysis of communicative interaction, at least in anthropology, than the long dominance of a distinct semiological analytics—an abstract schematic of the categories of the semiological as such. This analytics did permit of alternatives, most notably that of the semiotics of Charles Peirce and the rhetoric of Kenneth Burke. Yet, for perhaps a half-century, it largely occluded them. It did so less because it precluded its competitors from gaining notice than because it inspired even some of its competitors' admirers to treat the very competition as perpetrating merely secondary variations of its own already secure and far more primary themes. From the 1960s onward, the semiological analytics we have in mind has been primarily associated with the Swiss (Francophone) linguist Ferdinand de Saussure (1906–1911/1959). Its sources nevertheless antedate de Saussure. They come, in the course of the later-19th-century transformation of philology into linguistics, from across Europe. Originally, they come more from Germanic than Gallic Europe to the United States. We call the analytic *structuralist*.

This ascription has the benefit of linking the American culturalist tradition, the largest grouping in Figure 4.1 and designated by the sign of the diamond (♦), with the two cells of the uppermost right quadrant, designated by the club (♣). For the former tradition, "descriptive structural linguistics" is a primary theoretical and methodological resource, from Benjamin Whorf [10] and his teacher, the Boasian and protosociolinguist Edward Sapir (see Mandlebaum, 1949), to David Schneider [26], [44]. The latter grouping—more school than tradition—should itself be known as the structuralist tradition proper. In hindsight, Durkheim and Mauss's investigation [2] of the isomorphism of social and cognitive categorization—an investigation that remains open in Durkheim's *The Elementary Forms* [3]—is a classic precedent of structuralism. "Structuralism" self-appointed as such, however, is the product of that fertile moment at which Lévi-Strauss encounters Roman Jakobson's relationalist and differentialist theory of phonological systems. It emerges full-fledged when Lévi-Strauss extrapolates from the matrix of binary oppositions (e.g., between voiced and voiceless) that appear to be constitutive of those systems a general theory of the basic apparatus of the mind's coming to meaningful terms with experience as such. The latter cells include Lévi-Strauss's programmatic works [22], [23], as well as those in which his signature structuralism is most evident [24], [37].

One might correctly speak of structuralist semiology generally, perhaps alone among programmatic directives in anthropology, as a "paradigm" in Thomas Kuhn's sense of the term (Kuhn, 1962). It is a generative program of procedure and question formation that would include any members of those cells that we mark with a diamond (♦), including those that we in fact must leave empty, as possibilities yet to be fulfilled. Three of its lemmata are of special consequence. One is that the relation between the meaning-bearing units of any semiological system and the worldly entities to which they might refer is conventional or, in de Saussure's terms, "arbitrary." The second is that the referential function of the meaning-bearing units of a semiological system never determines the meaning of those units. The third is that the formal relations among the various meaning-bearing units of a semiological system are themselves both necessary and sufficient determinations of the meaning of those units. Structural semiology, in short, resolves into the basic postulate that the semiological system as a grammatical-semantic system is analytically independent of its descriptive, referential, or other worldly functions.

For Peirce, for such empirical realists in Anglo–American philosophy as Saul Kripke (1980) and Hilary Putnam (1975), and for such contemporary linguists as Michael Silverstein (2003), the referential and especially the indexical or deictic function of language—its use to point at and pick out events and objects and states of worldly affairs—remains implicated in the semiological production of meaning. In some classes of cases, such as natural-kind terms, reference is the primary determinant of meaning. Within the structuralist ambit, however, the indexical use of language, which one familiarly exercises in English with, for example, *this* or *that, today* or *you*, is evidence precisely that reference does not generally determine meaning. (Otherwise—so the structuralist argument goes—*this* and its indexical cousins would have to mean on every occasion of their referential use what they referred to on the first or on some particular lexically authoritative occasion of their use. They do not.) The structuralist assessment of indexicals as "shifters," whose source is Jakobson (1957/1990), has bolstered constructionist doubt in many disciplines about the rigor of the attachment between language and the empirical world. In anthropology, it is only one of the intellectual motives of a broader doubt—Kantian in its general parameters—of the mind's faithful reproduction and representation of the body it informs and the world it encounters.

Refigured more positively, such doubt amounts to the thesis that the mind imposes its own categories and schemata on both affective and cognitive experience. Or, if the mind does not do so altogether automatically, then it does so with specific processes of socialization or enculturation as its catalysts. This thesis is as much a keystone for Boasian and for later American cultural anthropology as it is for structuralism in accord with Lévi-Strauss. The Boasians and their American successors through Geertz and Schneider have their primary reputation as "cultural relativists." They are also thought to be relativists whose relativism goes hand in hand with a conviction of the extreme plasticity of the human psyche, cognitively and affectively. Their reputation is, in fact, more or less deserved. American culturalism has long understood cultural difference to imply psychic plasticity. Yet the classic empiricists, favoring a theory of mind as *tabula rasa*, are themselves much more extreme plasticists than such linguistic relativists as Whorf [10] or Stephen Tyler [49]. Benedict and Sapir, the ablest of the Boasian theorists, indeed emphasized affective malleability. Yet both appealed to a very strong analogy between the integration or coherence of culture and the psychic *Gestalt*, or "patterning" of experience, in setting limits to the scope of variability that the anthropologist should expect to encounter. Benedict further joined Mead in cleaving to a psychology of the inherence of temperament that served as the precise counterpart of a relativist and constructionist theory of the culturally specific selection of the good or desirable personality. Both were thus able to indict the failure of a culture to accommodate and approve each and every one of the given types of human temperaments as the source of maladjustment and unhappiness and of the stigmatization of the unpopular as the deviant.

The psychologistic turn in American culturalism is the reason that the errant structural–functionalist Turner [29], [48] and the structuralist Lévi-Strauss both find a more congenial readership across the Atlantic than in the British Isles themselves. Psychologism nevertheless diminishes markedly in Geertz [33], who is silent on the issue of how inherent temperament is while still maintaining an integrationist understanding of culture as a mutually adjusted ensemble of systems of cognitive, ethical, and affective orientation. This hedging qualifies his emphasis on the variability of "human nature" and the scope of the cultural variation that it permits.

Whorf more than Sapir has lasting notoriety for the constructionist "hypothesis" that the grammatical categories and syntactic rules of one's native language (or one's native language family) determine not simply how one talks about the world but how one experiences it. As with Durkheimian determinism, Whorfian determinism is ambiguous. Sometimes, Whorf is cast as a radical linguistic relativist. Yet this is difficult to reconcile with his apparent trust in the truth of Einstein's theory of general relativity. Alternatively, he can be cast as a linguistic "mediationist" who holds that one's language is the interface between world and experience without quite amounting to an insuperable barrier between the two. He is in any event best known for asserting that the Hopi would have had a much easier path toward the discovery and formulation of general relativity than Einstein did himself. Einstein had to labor with and through his fluency in the "standard average European" family to which German and English both belong. According to Sapir, that family is much poorer at registering the unity of object and event and the four dimensions of Einsteinian space–time than is the Hopi language, whose speakers were hampered only by the lack of sufficient intellectual technologies and sufficiently developed scientific institutions to help them along their way.

The Sapir–Whorf hypothesis is not a hypothesis because it permits of no test. It is instead an ironic mockery of the intellectual pretensions of the standard average European in that erudite–populist style whose formulae and devices were, in the 1920s, already the American professor's mode of address to the public and whose greatest anthropological master remains Geertz. The same style has its most distinct echoes in Tyler's rejection of the descriptive and analytic functions in favor of the evocative and therapeutic functions of the ethnographic text in a chapter (Tyler, 1986) that often stands, for both its admirers and its critics, as the very quintessence of anthropological "postmodernism" [49]. Tyler's chapter can hardly be read as radically relativist in its own right. It proffers a diagnosis of contemporary life as a life of irremediable fragmentation; it proffers a portrait of the contemporary subject in therapeutic need of imaginative participation in the sort of integrated modality of life that the ethnographic text can evocatively conjure. Its diagnosis of language, and especially scientific language, as having become entirely self-referential, however, is indeed a radicalization of the more mediationist, more Whorfian structuralism of Tyler's (1969) earlier efforts as a cognitive anthropologist. Tyler shared in those efforts with such anthropological linguists as Harold Conklin (1955; [17]) and Brent Berlin and Paul Kay (1969; [27]). With Tyler and his colleagues, cognitive anthropology occupies a crossover zone that has one foot in the precultural domain of a universal psychology of the Kantian sort and the other in the squarely cultural domain of the specific grammar and semantics of one or another specific language. That zone has proven to be unstable. On the one hand, it has given way in the succeeding decades to a cognitive anthropology that has confined itself to the quest for precultural "schemata" (e.g., Boyer, 2001). On the other, under the impact of Jacques Derrida's (1974) deconstructionism and the early works of Michel Foucault (1970, 1979, 1982), it has broken the confines of a strictly linguistic relativism and led to what became the historically more sensitive and semiologically broader "discursive" relativism on which Tyler's (1986) chapter depends.

Call that relativism "postmodernist": It retains the same understanding of the constituents of meaning and of the cognitive–linguistic constitution of experience that marks the high intellectual modernism (and high academicism) of Lévi-Strauss himself. We would need to explore in far greater detail than we have space to do here the full texture of the intellectual ecology of the years

immediately preceding and immediately following the student unrest of the later 1960s to provide an adequate exegesis of the charisma of historical particularity that saturates it. In shorthand, we simply note that the universalism of the reigning apologia for imperialist colonialism and the canonicity of the Euro–American academy are especially vulnerable during the period. They are vulnerable above all to particularistic counterclaims in intellectual and moral favor of difference and diversity. Even so, the historicist "correction" of Lévi-Strauss in such iconic expressions as Derrida's "Structure, Sign and Play in the Discourse of the Human Sciences" (1978) in fact preserves Lévi-Strauss's own conclusion that between history as the train of particular events and meaning as the product of a differential matrix, the relation is enduringly antagonistic. Tending to merge indeterminacy with unintelligibility, Lévi-Strauss assigns the investigation of serial and open systems to anyone but the anthropologist. Celebrating indeterminacy, Derrida insists that the particularistic "play" of "signs" is much more the rule in semiology than the semantic determinacy of the insular and insulated semantic system. Such a divergence of opinion is genuine. The ultimate authority on which Lévi-Strauss's semiology ([22], [23]; cf. Lévi-Strauss, 1963) rests, however, and the authority on which Derrida's rests in *Of Grammatology* (1974) is the same: In both cases, it is de Saussure's unmitigatedly structuralist–semiological *Course in General Linguistics* (1906–1911/1959).

Ranging between strictly linguistic and largely psycholinguistic versions, structuralist semiology is merely nonphenomenological in the American case; it is in that case merely neutral toward the phenomenological tenet that our experience owes its intelligibility to ideas innate to the mind. It is more often antiphenomenological in the French case. In its prioritization of the cultural domain, as in its semiological antifunctionalism, it in fact has little affinity with Berger and Luckmann's "social" constructionism. The psychological functionalism that has a home in the American tradition from Benedict through Geertz to Tyler does little to increase that affinity. Geertz's programmatic works nevertheless deserve further comment, both for their influence and for their apparent incorporation of Wittgenstein. In "Thick Description" (Geertz, 1973; [33]), Wittgenstein indeed has an important place. His identification of the always interactive "language game" (or "form of life"; Wittgenstein, 1958) as the practice that yields the public criteria of correct linguistic usage and meaning provides Geertz with the premises of an argument for the empirical availability of semiological data; following Wittgenstein, Geertz can claim that meaning is visible and objective in every action that puts language to use. Yet, however pivotal to his "interpretive theory of culture" it may be, Wittgenstein's semiological functionalism does not in fact establish the prevailing bearings of Geertz's analytic orientation. In "Thick Description," the model for anthropological interpretation is medical diagnosis. In "From the Native's Point of View" [35], however, it is that of textual exegesis—a model far more characteristic of Geertz's later works than of their earlier, more socioculturally synthetic precursors. Once again, an ecological perspective would have to note that even if Geertz had completed his formal academic training well before the tumult of the 1960s, he was an intimate witness to wars of liberation and the collapse of social–scientific universalism alike. After the 1960s, Geertz's work rapidly leaves behind the functionalist and synthetic trappings of his teacher, Talcott Parsons, in favor of an increasingly textualist and contextualist and pointedly literary hermeneutics that is averse to the formalism of Lévi-Strauss and the linguists but that preserves the lemmata of structuralist semiology almost in spite of itself. Geertz is indeed a constructionist in characterizing human beings as inhabitants of the webs of significance that they themselves weave [33], but like so many of the other authors and

works that we have visited, his constructionism is better deemed to be of a "cultural" rather than of any "social" variety.

The Future of Anthropological Constructionism

If anthropological postmodernism thus turns out to share more of its constructionism with its modernist predecessors than most postmodernists or modernists are inclined to admit or even to notice, we might well wonder whether, for all its surface ripples, anthropology is not a discipline in which, after all, *plus ça change....* As we have already hinted, we think that there are indications of a decline in the dominance of structuralist semiology on the contemporary horizon. If they are not yet endowed with a manifesto, they are still too many to ignore. Elements of that decline are scattered in the works [48], [50] that accumulate in the lowest right-hand cell of Figure 4.1, though they are too eclectic to yield a discrete position of either a semiological or a constructionist sort. Scheper-Hughes and Lock's "Mindful Body" [50] is nevertheless suggestive. In its epistemologically untroubled attention to the causal dynamics of the body in pain and the body oppressed, as well as in its similarly untroubled moralism, it hints at an objectivist and perhaps neohumanist drift away from structuralist relativism. What is at issue is not, however, merely a return to or a revival of American culturalism. What is at issue is also the continuing development of the objectification of sociocultural structure and process that is a signature especially of Bourdieu's contributions to the problematic of reproduction.

Further symptomatic of the decline of structuralist semiology is the shift of constructionist perspective that distinguishes George Marcus and Dick Cushman's "Ethnographies as Texts" [41] from Marcus's "Ethnography in/of the World System" [59]. The former work is semiologically as textualist as the works of the later Geertz. The latter focuses no longer on the ethnographic text but instead on the process of fieldwork. It leaves behind the homogeneous totalism of classic ethnography and of all the leading lights of American culturalism, from Benedict and Mead through Geertz. It pursues instead the heterogeneous interconnectivity of artifacts gathered from multiple sites. It continues to acknowledge that ethnographic diagnosis or interpretation is a "construction." But now it is a construction that is "realist," not because it adopts all the conventions of literary realism but rather because, or insofar as, it succeeds in articulating the actual interconnectivity of the artifacts themselves.

No less dramatic is the perspectival divergence of Rabinow's *Reflections on Fieldwork in Morocco* [38] from his later *Anthropos Today* [61]. *Reflections on Fieldwork* is grounded in the imperfect dialectics of the always imperfect comprehension of otherness. It thus retains at least a weak version of the structuralist hiatus between mind and mind and between mind and world. At the same time, it resists the static formalism of the more structuralist versions of structuralist semiology in refusing to license the abstraction and decontextualization of the experiential knowledge that fieldwork yields. *Anthropos Today* seeks to define the primary subject of the inquiries of an "anthropology of the contemporary." It arrives heuristically at the "assemblage," whose ontology receives a concise synopsis but whose epistemological profile remains almost entirely undrawn. An anthropology of meanings thus seems on the verge of giving way to an anthropology of things. The intellectual result of fieldwork may, for its part, still be a construction. If so, it is a construction for whose methodology Rabinow offers the oblique analogy of the procedures and the productions of the none too classifiable artists Marcel Duchamp and Paul Klee.

Whatever else might be made of these programmatically still uneasy examples, they suggest jointly a relative rehabilitation of the ontological at the expense of the epistemological. They suggest that the exhaustion of and with constructionism is beginning to favor a resort to things over and against further well-tried labor on the questions of what things we know and how we know them—or do not know them, as the case may be. Whatever else, such a shift runs very much against the grain of structuralist semiology and structuralist constructionism in all their radically relativist versions. Short of the full ecological investigation required and in lieu of any definitive conclusion, we simply note that a correlative reinvestment of priorities has recently begun to develop into something of a modest snowball from its beginnings, once again in the 1960s, in the anti-Kantian and ontologically wanton philosophical writings of Gilles Deleuze (1990, 1994) and his collaborator Félix Guattari (Deleuze & Guattari, 1983, 1987) to the epistemologically cavalier and ontologically ingenuous writings of Antonio Negri and Michael Hardt (Hardt & Negri, 2000, 2004). The same ontological bullishness animates Latour and his companions in their study of sciences and technologies and the very stuff of truth. None of this points to an end to constructionism. Nor does it point to the opposite. We can consequently conclude only with a question that we cannot answer. We do not know whether we are currently witnessing the renewal of the problem of the determination of the dividing line between the constructed and the given, the cultural and the natural, nurture and nature, with which anthropology has long labored. Just as likely, or in any case not beyond possibility, we are witnessing a turning away from that problem in favor of a posthumanist vision of the human as always already an objective hybrid of the constructed and the given, the natural and the cultural, far more thoroughgoing than even the most radical of anthropologists past had dared imagine in print. We can only offer our readers the maxim by which we are ourselves compelled to abide: Stay tuned.

• References

Barth, F. (Ed.). (1969). *Ethnic groups and boundaries: The social organization of cultural difference.* London: Allen & Unwin.

Benedict, R. (1934). *Patterns of culture.* Boston: Houghton & Mifflin.

Berger, P. L., & Luckmann, T. (1966). *The social construction of reality: A treatise in the sociology of knowledge.* New York: Anchor Books.

Berlin, B., & Kay, P. (1969). *Basic color terms: Their universality and evolution.* Berkeley: University of California Press.

Berreman, G. (1962). *Behind many masks: Ethnography and impression management in a Himalayan village* (Monograph No. 4). Ithaca, NY: Society of Applied Anthropology.

Bourdieu, P. (1977). *Outline of a theory of practice* (R. Nice, Trans.). Cambridge, UK: Cambridge University Press. (Original work published 1972)

Bourdieu, P. (1988). *Homo academicus* (P. Collier, Trans.). Cambridge, UK: Polity Press. (Original work published 1984)

Boyer, P. (2001). *Religion explained: The evolutionary origins of religious thought.* New York: Basic Books.

Butler, J. (1993). *Bodies that matter: On the discursive limits of "sex."* New York: Routledge.

Conklin, H. (1955). Hanunóo color categories. *Southwestern Journal of Anthropology, 11*(4), 339–344.

Daniel, E. V. (1984). *Fluid signs: Being a person the Tamil way.* Berkeley: University of California Press.

Das, V. (1998). Wittgenstein and anthropology. *Annual Review of Anthropology, 27,* 171–195.

de Certeau, M. (1984). *The practice of everyday life* (S. Rendall, Trans.). Berkeley: University of California Press. (Original work published 1974)

Deleuze, G. (1990). *The logic of sense* (C. V. Boundas, Ed.; M. Lester with C. Stivale, Trans.). New York: Columbia University Press.

Deleuze, G. (1994). *Difference and repetition* (P. Patton, Trans.). New York: Columbia University Press.

Deleuze, G., & Guattari, F. (1983). *Capitalism and schizophrenia: Vol. 1. Anti-oedipus* (R. Hurley, M. Seem, & H. R. Lane, Trans.). Minneapolis: University of Minnesota Press.

Deleuze, G., & Guattari, F. (1987). *Capitalism and schizophrenia: Vol. 2. A thousand plateaus* (B. Massumi, Trans.). Minneapolis: University of Minnesota Press.

Derrida, J. (1974). *Of grammatology* (G. C. Spivak, Trans.). Baltimore: Johns Hopkins University Press.

Derrida, J. (1978). Structure, sign, and play in the discourse of the human sciences. In J. Derrida, *Writing and difference* (A. Bass, Trans.). Chicago: University of Chicago Press.

de Saussure, F. (1959). *Course in general linguistics* (W. Baskin, Trans.). New York: The Philosophical Library. (Original work published 1906–1911)

Douglas, M. (1966). *Purity and danger: An analysis of concepts of pollution and taboo.* London: Routledge & Kegan Paul.

Douglas, M. (1970). *Natural symbols: Explorations in cosmology.* New York: Pantheon.

Douglas, M. (1986). *How institutions think.* Syracuse, NY: University of Syracuse Press.

Dumont, L. (1970). *Homo hierarchicus: The caste system and its implications* (M. Sainsbury, Trans.). Chicago: University of Chicago Press. (Original work published 1970)

Dundes, A. (1976) Projection in folklore: A plea for psychoanalytic semiotics. *MLN, 91,* 1500–1533.

Durkheim, E. (1933). *The division of labor in society* (G. Simpson, Trans.). New York: The Free Press. (Original work published 1893)

Durkheim, E. (1973). The dualism of human nature and its social conditions. In R. E. Bellah (Ed.), *Emile Durkheim on morality and society* (pp. 149–163). Chicago: University of Chicago Press.

Durkheim, E. (1995). *The elementary forms of the religious life* (K. E. Fields, Trans.). New York: The Free Press. (Original work published 1912)

Durkheim, E., & Mauss, M. (1963). *Primitive classification* (R. Needham, Trans.). London: Cohen & West. (Original work published 1903)

Evans-Pritchard, E. E. (1956). *Nuer religion.* Oxford, UK: Clarendon Press.

Fernandez, J. (1986). *Persuasions and performances: The play of tropes in culture.* Bloomington: Indiana University Press.

Foucault, M. (1970). *The order of things: An archaeology of the human sciences* (A. Sheridan, Trans.). New York: Random House.

Foucault, M. (1979). *Discipline and punish: The birth of the prison* (A. Sheridan, Trans.). New York: Vintage Press.

Foucault, M. (1982). *The archaeology of knowledge, and the discourse on language* (A. Sheridan Smith, Trans.). New York: Pantheon.

Freud, S. (1950). Totem and taboo. In J. Strachey (Ed. & Trans.), *The standard edition of the complete psychological works of Sigmund Freud.* New York: Norton. (Original work published 1913)

Garfinkel, H. (1967). *Studies in ethnomethodology.* Englewood Cliffs, NJ: Prentice Hall.

Geertz, C. (1973). Thick description: Toward an interpretive theory of culture. In C. Geertz, *The interpretation of cultures* (pp. 3–30). New York: Basic Books.

Geertz, C. (1983). "From the native's point of view": On the nature of anthropological understanding. In C. Geertz, *Local knowledge: Further essays in interpretive anthropology* (pp. 55–70). New York: Basic Books. (Original work published 1974)

Gellner, E. (1959). *Words and things: A critical account of linguistic philosophy and a study in ideology.* Boston: Beacon Press.

Gellner, E. (1970). Concepts and society. In B. R. Wilson (Ed.), *Rationality* (pp. 18–49). London: Blackwell.

Giddens, A. (1984). *The constitution of society*. Berkeley: University of California Press.

Goffman, E. (1959). *The presentation of self in everyday life*. New York: Anchor Books.

Gumperz, J. J., & Hymes, D. (Eds.). (1986). *Directions in sociolinguistics: The ethnography of communication*. New York: Blackwell.

Hallowell, I. A. (1960). Ojibwa ontology, behavior and worldview. In S. Diamond (Ed.), *Culture in history: Essays in honor of Paul Radin* (pp. 19–52). New York: Columbia University Press.

Hardt, M., & Negri, A. (2000). *Empire*. Cambridge, MA: Harvard University Press.

Hardt, M., & Negri, A. (2004). *Multitude: War and democracy in the age of empire*. New York: Penguin Press.

Héritier-Augé, F. (2002). *The two sisters and their mother: The anthropology of incest* (J. Harman, Trans.). New York: Zone Books. (Original work published 1994)

Jakobson, R. (1990). Shifters, verbal categories, and the Russian verb. In L. Waugh & M. Monville-Burston (Eds.), *On language: Roman Jakobson* (pp. 386–392). Cambridge, MA: Harvard University Press.

Kleinman, A. (1988). *The illness narratives: Suffering, healing, and the human condition*. New York: Basic Books.

Kluckhohn, C., & Leighton, D. (1946). *The Navaho*. Cambridge, MA: Harvard University Press.

Kondo, D. (1990). *Crafting selves: Power, gender, and discourses of identity in a Japanese workplace*. Chicago: University of Chicago Press.

Kripke, S. (1980). *Naming and necessity*. Cambridge, MA: Harvard University Press.

Kuhn, T. (1962). *The structure of scientific revolutions*. Chicago: University of Chicago Press.

Latour, B. (1991). *We have never been modern* (C. Porter, Trans.). Cambridge, MA: Harvard University Press.

Latour, B., & Woolgar, S. (1979). *Laboratory life: The social construction of scientific facts*. Beverly Hills, CA: Sage.

Lévi-Strauss, C. (1963). The effectiveness of symbols. In C. Lévi-Strauss, *Structural anthropology* (C. Jacobson & B. Grundfest Scheepf, Trans.) (Vol. 1, pp. 186–205). New York: Basic Books.

Lévi-Strauss, C. (1966). *The savage mind*. Chicago: University of Chicago Press. (Original work published 1962)

Lévi-Strauss, C. (1969). *The raw and the cooked: Introduction to a science of mythology* (Vol. 1, J. Weightman & D. Weightman, Trans.). New York: Harper Torchbooks. (Original work published 1964)

Lukes, S. (1972). *Emile Durkheim: His life and work: A historical and critical study*. New York: Harper & Row.

Malinowski, B. (1939, May). The group and the individual in functional analysis. *American Journal of Sociology*, 44, 938–964.

Mandlebaum, D. (Ed.). (1949). *Selected writings of Edward Sapir in language, culture, and personality*. Berkeley: University of California Press.

Marcus, G. (1995). Ethnography in/of the world system: The emergence of multi-sited ethnography. *Annual Review of Anthropology*, 24, 95–117.

Marcus, G., & Cushman, D. (1982). Ethnographies as texts. *Annual Review of Anthropology*, 11, 25–69.

Marriott, M. (Ed.). (1990). *India through Hindu categories*. Newbury Park, CA: Sage.

Marx, K., & Engels, F. (1970). *The German ideology*. London: Lawrence & Wishart. (Original work published 1846)

Mauss, M. (1990). *The gift: The forms and reason for exchange in primitive societies* (W. D. Halls, Trans.). New York: Norton. (Original work published 1927)

Mead, M. (1934). *Coming of age in Samoa: A psychological study of primitive youth for Western civilization*. New York: Blue Ribbon Books.

Needham, R. (1972). *Language, belief and experience*. Chicago: University of Chicago Press.

Ortner, S., & Whitehead, H. (Eds.). (1981). *Sexual meanings: The cultural construction of gender and sexuality*. New York: Cambridge University Press.

Putnam, H. (1975). *Mind, language and reality: Philosophical papers* (Vol. 2). Cambridge, UK: Cambridge University Press.

Rabinow, P. (1977). *Reflections on fieldwork in Morocco*. Berkeley: University of California Press.

Rabinow, P. (2003). *Anthropos today: Reflections on modern equipment*. Princeton, NJ: Princeton University Press.

Radcliffe-Brown, A. R. (1952). On social structure. In A. R. Radcliffe-Brown, *Structure and function in primitive society* (pp. 188–204). New York: Free Press. (Original work published 1940)

Roheim, G. (1945). *The eternal ones of the dream: A psychoanalytic interpretation of Australian myth and ritual*. New York: International Universities Press.

Rosaldo, R. (1993). *Culture and truth: The remaking of social analysis*. Boston: Beacon Press.

Sahlins, M. (1976). *Culture and practical reason*. Chicago: University of Chicago Press.

Sartre, J. P. (1976). *Critique of dialectical reason: Vol. 1. Theory of practical ensembles* (J. Rice, Ed. & A. Sheridan-Smith, Trans.). Atlantic Highlands, NJ: Humanities Press. (Original work published 1960)

Sartre, J. P. (1991). *Critique of dialectical reason: Vol. 2. The intelligibility of history* (A. Elkaïm-Sartre, Ed. & Q. Hoare, Trans.). London: Verso.

Saville-Troike, M. (1982). *The ethnography of communication: An introduction*. Oxford, UK: Blackwell.

Scheper-Hughes, N., & Lock, M. (1987). The mindful body. *Medical Anthropology Quarterly*, 1(1), 6–41.

Schneider, D. (1968). *American kinship: A cultural account*. Englewood Cliffs, NJ: Prentice Hall.

Schneider, D. (1984). *A critique of the study of kinship*. Ann Arbor: University of Michigan Press.

Silverstein, M. (2003). Indexical order and the dialectics of sociolinguistic life. *Language and Communication*, 23(3–4), 193–229.

Spiro, M. (1967). *Burmese supernaturalism: A study in the*

explanation and reduction of suffering. Englewood Cliffs, NJ: Prentice Hall.

Strathern, M. (1988). *The gender of the gift: Problems with women and problems with society in Melanesia.* Berkeley: University of California Press.

Strathern, M. (1992). *After nature: English kinship in the late twentieth century.* Cambridge, UK: Cambridge University Press.

Tambiah, S. (1985). *Culture, thought and social action: An anthropological perspective.* Cambridge, MA: Harvard University Press.

Turner, V. (1957). *Schism and continuity in an African society: A study of Ndembu social life.* Manchester, UK: University of Manchester Press.

Turner, V. (1969). *The ritual process: Structure and anti-structure.* Chicago: Aldine.

Turner, V. (1986). *The anthropology of performance.* New York: PAJ.

Tyler, S. (Ed.). (1969). *Cognitive anthropology: Readings.* New York: Holt, Rinehart & Winston.

Tyler, S. (1986). Post-modern ethnography: From occult document to document of the occult. In J. Clifford & G. Marcus (Eds.), *Writing culture* (pp. 122–140). Berkeley: University of California Press.

Weber, M. (1946). The social psychology of the world religions. In H. Gerth & C. W. Mills (Eds.), *From Max Weber: Essays in sociology* (pp. 267–301). Oxford, UK: Oxford University Press. (Original work published 1915)

Whiting, J., & Child, I. (1953). *Child training and personality: A cross-cultural study.* New York: Yale University Press.

Whorf, B. L. (1956). The relation of habitual thought and behavior to language. In J. B. Carroll (Ed.), *Language, thought, and reality: Selected writings* (pp. 134–159). Cambridge, MA: MIT Press. (Original work published 1939)

Wittgenstein, L. (1958). *Philosophical investigations* (G. E. M. Anscombe, Trans.). London: Macmillan.

CHAPTER 5

Social Constructionist Perspectives in Communication Research

- **Elissa Foster**
  Arthur P. Bochner

We live in a world in which violence and oppression have become a standard political response to the expression of divergent worldviews. In light of the destructive consequences that increasing polarization and misunderstanding produce, constructionist work feels to us more like a calling than a research perspective. If we are to build strong communities and help people take positive actions, we must help them develop mutual understanding and trust; this is an ethical mandate of a constructionist standpoint. Thus we believe that constructionist research matters, that it is useful, that it contributes to social change and social justice, and that it can improve the quality of people's lives.

Our goal in writing this chapter is to inspire a conversation about the contributions of constructionist inquiry by underscoring the intimate connection between communication and the creation of social realities. As scholars who work within the field of communication, we have come to understand social science as constructionist practice writ large. Whether social scientists identify themselves as theorists, ethnographers, critics, storytellers, or practitioners, they share two basic characteristics: The chief product of their work is language, and the processes through which they work involve interactive communication. Thus the work of social scientists is inherently social and constructionist. To the degree that research makes a difference in the world, it intervenes in the world and changes it. Communication and social construction are coterminous. To think about, theorize, investigate, write, or perform the constitutive qualities of communication is to inhabit the world of social construction; to root one's work in social construction is to plant one's feet squarely in the world of interactive communication.

Peter Berger and Thomas Luckmann (1967) understood this very well. In *The Social Construction of Reality*, they emphasized how language functions as the principle vehicle of what they call the "objectivations" that fill the reality of everyday life, "a repository of vast accumulations of meaning and experience" (p. 37). For Berger and Luckmann, "[A]n understanding of language is . . . essential for any understanding of the reality of everyday life" (p. 37). Moreover, "the most important vehicle for reality-maintenance is conversation . . . [by which the individual] maintains, modifies, and reconstructs his subjective reality" (p. 152).

Considering the vast corpus of monographs and research studies identified with social construction, however, we are given pause to ask, how *social* is social construction? Too often, the social is assumed rather than investigated. Consequently, attention is diverted from the critical issue of how language and communication bring into being an idea that was not inevitable (Hacking, 1999). When this happens, the term *social construction* becomes imprecise, even obscure (Powell, 2001). One of our goals is to bring the social and the communicative into broader relief in work classified as social constructionist. Constructionist inquiry should focus not only on the consequences of the social but also on the social processes themselves.

As a discipline, communication is uniquely positioned to respond to contemporary needs for unifying discourse and social justice. As a framework for inquiry as well as action, social construction offers a paradigm that recognizes the potential that communication holds for transformation and sustainable change. Communication is an unusual discipline insofar as its research agenda extends across the spectrum of humanistic and social scientific approaches to inquiry—historical, critical, interpretive, empiricist, ethnographic, and performative. Although many different perspectives exist on *how* and *what* to study under the disciplinary umbrella of communication studies, the field now generally holds to the conviction expressed by Clifford Geertz (1980, pp. 166–167) that researchers should "become free to shape their work in terms of its necessities rather than received ideas as to what they ought or ought not be doing." It has become clearer and clearer that communication is not about quantities but about patterns (Bateson, 1981) and therefore needs to be grounded on an epistemology of interacting human beings. Thus scholars have turned increasingly to qualitative approaches to inquiry and to conceptions of communication grounded on the idea that the terms by which the world is viewed and understood are communicative productions (Bochner, 1981). It is now widely understood that communication is not merely a mode of representing but also a means of constituting reality. Communication creates the webs of belief and meaning to which human beings become attached, and these webs have far-reaching, recursive consequences. As Mark Engel (1972, p. vii) observed in the preface to Gregory Bateson's tour de force, *Steps to an Ecology of Mind*, "we create the world that we perceive, not because there is no reality outside our heads . . . but because we select and edit the reality we see to conform to our beliefs about what sort of world we live in."

Still, similar to colleagues in sociology, psychology, political science, and even anthropology, disciplines that gained legitimacy in the 20th century, social scientists in communication sought a place at the table of academic respectability, which meant that conforming to science was more important than being true to the phenomena of joint action (Shotter, 1987). The problem of legitimation has been a sticking point for the discipline because communication turns up as a topic, variable, or theme of research in virtually all of the social sciences and humanities. Even today, the lack of circumscribed boundaries demarcating communication inquiry continues to plague the field, contributing to the increasing fragmentation of communication research. In the 1940s, when communication began to emerge as a distinct and recognizable discipline-like entity, the field identified its core research mission as the investigation of the processes through which messages shape attitudes, beliefs, and values. The pioneering communication researchers pinned their hopes for distinctive achievements in research on the methodological presumptions of the received view of scientific knowledge (Delia, 1987). The hegemony of the quantitative model of social science had the effect of stifling and marginalizing alternative programs of research, especially those seeking to explore the connections between communication and culture; those emphasizing intersubjective, interpretive, and social processes; and those focusing on discourse, metaphor, symbolic action, and performativity in everyday life. Within the closed fist of objectivist methodologies, communication as a phenomenon became an object, and communication as a discipline was largely restricted to studying and describing objects.

But the influence of constructionism established that communication is not an object; nor is communication a discipline that studies objects. Communication involves patterns and sequences of interactions and the activities of studying them. In this view, the model of ordinary human interaction should be the foundation of not only how we think about communication but also how we study, write about, and/or perform it (Bochner & Waugh, 1995). This revised view entailed a paradigm shift, what Art Bochner and Joanne Waugh (1995, p. 224, emphasis added) referred to as "a transformation from description to *communication*." Communication should be not only *what* we study but also *how* we study. In contrast, objectivist models of research attempt to describe in neutral and value-free terms what is already inscribed in mind or nature. They are grounded on a theory of theory that takes what the world *causes* us to believe as a

model for writing about and describing it. However, as philosophers of history, language, and science from Thomas Kuhn to Donald Davidson (Davidson, 1984, 1986; Derrida, 1981; Kuhn, 1962, 1977; Rorty, 1979; Sellars, 1963) have emphasized, language does not give form or structure to the world, nor is it a medium of linking nature to the mind. Rather, it is a part of actions and events in the world, a matter of getting around in the world (Bochner & Waugh, 1995). The rub is that language activity mediates all attempts to represent reality. As Richard Rorty (1979) observed, the world does not exist in the shape of the sentences we write when we theorize about it. What we can say about the world involves the indistinguishable provocations of the world *and the mediations of language by which we make claims about it.*

To take the crisis of representation seriously, the discipline of communication needed to close the gap between what communication does in the world and how we study what communication does; that is, our theory, methodologies, and research practices. The interactive epistemology that evolved to meet this need appreciates the ways in which we are a part of the world we investigate. An interactive and relational conception of communication—how the practices of speaking, writing, reading, listening, and interpreting enable us to make our way through the world—displaces the transmission or depiction notion of communication in which language was viewed as nothing more than a vehicle or tool for describing or inscribing a preexisting ontological world. In a human science of communication that embraces an interactive epistemology, the objectivist ideal of a detached observer using neutral language to produce an unmediated mirroring of reality is replaced by the premise that all attempts to speak for, write about, or represent other people's lives necessarily are partial, situated, and mediated activities of creating value and inscribing meanings. The texts that we craft to represent others become, as

Laurel Richardson (1997) writes, "a site of moral responsibility" (p. 56).

A History of Constructionist Research in Communication

Our charge is to review how constructionist work evolved in the discipline of communication, as well as to discuss our vision for its future. We write this chapter knowing that some of our readers will be members of our discipline but that many will not. We try, therefore, to make a rather complicated evolution simpler than it was, compressing 30 years of work into the space we have to tell the story. Like so many of the social sciences and humanities, communication has evolved as an interdiscipline, and thus it was difficult to restrict our review to contributions that were unequivocally positioned within communication studies. Another challenge we faced was to acknowledge social constructionism in research that "invokes" (Leeds-Hurwitz, 2006) rather than explicitly defines itself as "social constructionist." In general, the emphasis in this chapter is on scholarship published by communication scholars—in communication journals, handbooks, texts, and monographs—that articulates or exemplifies constructionist principles and methods.

Berger and Luckmann's (1967) book, *The Social Construction of Reality*, is recognized as the leading inspiration for constructionist work in communication. Berger and Luckmann placed communication processes and everyday interactions at the center of inquiry into how knowledge is generated and transformed in social life. Their concepts of "objectivation" (p. 34) and "internalization" (p. 129) point to the significance of communication as the process by which the subjective realities of individuals are externalized, most often through language, and come to be shared intersubjectively between and among people. They introduce a distinction between primary and secondary socialization (p. 130) to explain the processes by which social worlds come to be internalized as taken-for-granted both within the family of origin (primary socialization) and through interaction with other social groups and institutions (secondary socialization). These concepts linked communication to the construction of social realities, established the primacy of close personal relationships, and drew attention to the circulation and consumption of cultural and institutional narratives.

The first signs that communication scholars were recognizing the heuristic potential of Berger and Luckmann's theorizing did not appear until nearly a decade after the publication of their book. In the mid-1970s, the received view of knowledge, which had functioned for three decades as the methodological paradigm for communication research, came under attack on several fronts (Bochner, 1985). Social psychologists were vigorously debating the question of whether laws of social behavior could ever be developed (Gergen, 1973), the questionable ethics of deception in social science research (Harré & Secord, 1972), and the appropriateness of applying methodologies of the natural sciences to studies of human beings (Taylor, 1977). This perceived "crisis of confidence," though centered in social psychology, inspired new conversations among communication researchers about the most appropriate models of research for communication inquiry, as well as about the sorts of questions that needed to be asked if the assumptions commonly made about interactive communication were to be taken seriously (Bochner, 1978).

By the late 1970s, the ferment in the field set the stage for new approaches and avenues of research that reflected a constructionist perspective broadly conceived and a turn, however slight, toward a more interpretive social science. First, researchers were encouraged to expand the setting for inquiry beyond the laboratory to focus on the interactions of everyday life, in which communication could be studied as a constitutive process governed by situated rules

(Cushman, 1977; Pearce, 1976, 1977; Pearce & Cronen, 1980; Sigman, 1980) rather than covering laws. Second, researchers began to focus on the relationships between interactive communication and the emergence of larger social systems, such as organizations and cultures, and to define the study of institutions as constituted through communication as a primary focus in the field. Third, scholars shifted their attention from individuals to relationships as the appropriate focus of inquiry within communication, which necessitated the adoption of interpretive modes of inquiry that encompassed intersubjectivity and reflexivity. Thus for many of the scholars whose studies we review in this chapter, a turn toward social construction represented a shift in both the conceptualization of communication research and the methodologies appropriate to such inquiry.

Everyday Interaction as the Focus of Research

Humanists in communication have had a long history of interest in rhetoric and symbolic action. Among rhetoricians in the field, social constructionist thinking was initially used to broaden the focus of rhetorical scholarship, recognizing that rhetoric was pragmatic and relevant to social life rather than merely reflective of it (e.g., Bormann, 1972; Bormann, Pratt, & Putnam, 1978; Cherwitz, 1980; Gronbeck, 1978a, 1978b). These writers saw the power of conceptually linking their respective projects to the increasing emphasis within the discipline on communication-as-practiced. For example, Ernest Bormann (1972) articulated the concepts of "symbolic convergence" and the "fantasy theme" to explain how group members adapt to one another's expressions and come to adopt specific terms, frames, metaphors, and stories as a shared reality emerges within a group.[1]

Linda Putnam (1982) pointed out that the incorporation of critical–rhetorical approaches into the study of human interaction and the processes of organizing allowed for "coherent conceptual and methodological treatments of multiple layers of symbol systems" (p. 203), wherein microlevel analyses could be connected to a larger social reality. In these early rhetorical studies, arguments supporting a social constructionist perspective in communication naturally led to a reconsideration of the appropriateness of various methodological paradigms, both rhetorical (e.g., Hikins & Zagacki, 1988) and empirical (e.g., Orr, 1978; Stewart, 1981). Some of the questions raised in these articles—for example, the importance of observing interaction in natural settings (Bormann, 1972) and the need to respond to critiques raised by objectivist and realist inquiry (Hikins & Zagacki, 1988)—persist to this day.

In 1980, Barnett Pearce and Vernon Cronen (1980) published a theory of meaning management, which was one of the first communication theories specifically inspired by social construction.[2] Derived from a communication rules perspective, "coordinated management of meaning" (CMM) was grounded on the premise that communication is a form of action through which individuals collectively create and manage their social realities. Insisting that meaning must be negotiated and coordinated and thus that it is produced transpersonally, Pearce and Cronen used this theory to model and measure the processes by which individuals embedded in interpersonal systems of both regulative and constitutive rules generated meaning together. Their theoretical perspective stood in stark contrast to the emphasis on intrapersonal management of meaning or the interpersonal management of other people's meanings (Pearce & Cronen, 1980, p. 149).[3] In subsequent applications of this theory, interpersonal and organizational perspectives have merged to generate practices related to organizational development and community dialogue, which we describe later. Pearce and Cronen urged researchers to examine communication in action and in context, to integrate theory and practice, and to recognize how social realities are shaped by language and habitual patterns of relating in everyday encounters.

Language and Interaction in Organizational Cultures

Earlier, we emphasized the importance of focusing on the social. As Berger and Luckmann (1967) observed, social construction emphasizes the processes through which language, externalized through interaction, becomes habitualized and generates institutions that are perceived as objective realities. In the 1980s, organizational communication scholars began to apply this way of understanding the emergence of social forms by construing organizations as symbolically constituted cultures rather than material entities. This cultural view of organizations highlighted the need for interpretive methods of research. Eric Eisenberg and Allen Scult's (1986) review of three books—including Linda Putnam and Michael Pacanowsky's (1983) edited volume *Meaning and Interpretation in Organizations*—illustrated the shifting view of organizational studies toward interpretation and organizational culture. They argued that organizational communication should no longer be viewed as instrumental (with an emphasis on transmission) but rather as constitutive (with an emphasis on meaning; see also Carey, 1992), and they attributed this shift to the theoretical insights of social constructionism (Berger & Luckmann, 1967) and structuration (Giddens, 1984). As the paradigm of organizational culture spread swiftly through the field, communication scholars turned increasingly to studies of organizational metaphors, stories, and the multiple, negotiated meanings that comprise organizational life (e.g., Brown, 1985; Browning, 1992; Pacanowsky & O'Donnell-Trujillo, 1983; Trujillo, 1985). Whether examining conflict at Disneyland (Smith & Eisenberg, 1987), life at a baseball park (Trujillo, 1992), or talk at a television station (Carbaugh, 1988), these studies underscored the impor-

tance of a "spoken system of symbols, symbolic forms, and meanings that constitutes and enacts a common sense of work-life" (Carbaugh, 1988, p. 216).

At about the same time, the concept of "culture" began to inform the study of interpersonal relationships on two levels; first, by appealing to the idea that relationships are embedded within the sociohistorical-cultural milieu of society and must be interpreted contextually (Bochner, 1984) and, second, by recognizing that relationships themselves constitute unique relational cultures (Baxter, 1987, 1992) with shared histories, beliefs, and practices. In 1989, a special issue of the *Journal of Applied Communication Research* was devoted to family communication (Bochner, 1989), and the social constructionist orientation to families also was incorporated into one of the first family communication textbooks (Yerby, Buerkel-Rothfuss, & Bochner, 1990). The emergence of family communication as a research area in the field signaled not only a recognition of how family patterns and cultures emerge through interactive communication (Jorgenson, 1989; Lannamann, 1989; McNamee, 1989; Rawlins, 1989; Yerby, 1989) but also the arrival of a new era of qualitative research oriented toward interpretive, reflexive, and contextualized research methods (Steier, 1989) better suited to the exploration of the emergent, lived experiences of families.

Relationships as Central to Social Life

Under the influence of Batesonian communication theory (Bateson, 1972) and the worldview of social construction, communication researchers developed a distinctly relational perspective, one that centered on what goes on between people rather than what goes on within a person; that is, individual differences or cognitive processes (Bochner, 1978, 1984). Frank Millar and L. Edna Rogers (1976) published one of the first articles exemplifying the relational approach, emphasizing that "people become aware of themselves only within the context of their social relationships" (p. 87) and identifying the relational dimension of messages as the site of relationship formation. Taking as a starting point the axiom that every message has both content and a relational dimension (Watzlawick, Beavin, & Jackson, 1967), in which the relationship dimension of a message defines the nature of the relationship system, Millar and Rogers made the dyad—rather than the individual—the unit of analysis. The express purpose of their approach was to identify patterns or rules governing interaction within the particular relationship under investigation. As with CMM theory (Pearce & Cronen, 1980), research on relational communication focused on how relationships evolve *between* specific individuals, attempting to grasp the patterns of interaction that govern these relationships (Bateson, 1972) rather than testing predictions about the behavior of individuals within the relationship (Pearce, 1976).

In the 1990s, relational communication began to incorporate dialogic approaches to inquiry (Baxter, 1992; Baxter & Montgomery, 1996; Stewart, 1978), many of which were tied directly to social construction and the relational worldview. In contrast to approaches that view relationships primarily as a product of individual cognition, intention, and strategic action, dialogic approaches emphasize how meaning is negotiated and emerges through interaction in the context of relationships. This focus shifts the attention of the researcher to the question: "What are the kinds of jointly-enacted communication events by which the social fabric is woven?" (Baxter, 1992, p. 331). The dialogic approach reflects Kenneth Gergen's (1994) articulation of social constructionism as an alternate paradigm (or intelligibility) whose relational worldview constitutes a distinctly different epistemic orientation from the individualistic framing of knowledge associated with logical empiricism. Specifically, Gergen argues that knowledge is a byproduct of "*communal* relationships" (p. 25, emphasis in the original) and not an in-

dividual possession. By recognizing that communication is the process and relationships are the context within which knowledge emerges, dialogic approaches necessarily turn attention to the quality and patterns of interaction and the ethical ideals of respecting difference while striving toward understanding.

Family communication scholars were among the first to adopt this relational, constructionist perspective as a research model for investigating complex processes of interaction within families (Jorgenson & Bochner, 2004). Drawing on a range of influences that include systems theory, structural family therapy (Minuchin, 1974), and particularly the work of Bateson (1972) and the Palo Alto group (Watzlawick, Beavin, & Jackson, 1967) on relational patterns, family communication scholars took an interest in the pragmatic and "everyday" interactions of families as constitutive of family life (Bavelas, 1984; Bochner, 1981; Bochner & Eisenberg, 1987; Sieburg, 1985). As with the interpretive movement in organizational studies, family communication scholars saw a need to adopt new research practices that would better conform to the relational worldview of systems theory and social construction (Bochner & Eisenberg, 1987).

In the 1990s, narrative inquiry began to emerge as one of the newer research practices that could accommodate the relational emphasis of communication research. Commenting on the burgeoning interest in dialogue among communication scholars and its significance for relational communication, Leslie Baxter (1992) noted that "personal narratives are likely to emerge as the distinguishing method of social approaches to personal relationships" (p. 333). Art Bochner and Carolyn Ellis's (1992, 1995) exemplary study of narrative coconstruction in a couple's epiphany and their subsequent development of the narrative and autoethnographic approach to relationship studies (Bochner, 1994, 2001, 2002; Bochner, Ellis, & Tillmann-Healy, 1997, 1998; Ellis & Bochner, 2001) illustrated the potential of narrative inquiry to capture the subjective and emotional dimensions of social life valued by social constructionists. Specifically, they showed how narrative research embraces the details of lived experience, the reflexive relationship between personal interaction and cultural contexts, and the dialogic and dialectical complexity of relationships and communities.

By the mid-1990s, the constructionist perspective had flourished sufficiently to produce a number of publications that solidified and reinforced the importance of social inquiry within communication studies; these included John Shotter's (1993) *Conversational Realities: Constructing Life Through Language,* John Stewart's (1995) *Language as Articulate Contact: Toward a Post-Semiotic Philosophy of Communication,* and Gerry Philipsen's (1992) *Speaking Culturally: Explorations in Social Communication.* These formative texts argued persuasively for communication-in-relationship as the central and essential focus for social research, thus repositioning the site of "knowledge" and "reality" construction to the everyday interactions and relationships between people—precisely the activities that occupy the communication researcher. By this time, sufficient scholars were working from a social constructionist perspective that Wendy Leeds-Hurwitz (1995) was able to assemble a series of essays from the communication discipline, *Social Approaches to Communication,*[4] which followed her *Communication in Everyday Life: A Social Interpretation* (1989). The essays in this collection confirmed the value of the social constructionist perspective within the discipline and provided an inspiration for future work.

Current Perspectives and Practices

As social construction in communication has evolved, it has increasingly emphasized engaged, performative, and interpretive research practices and employed a critical lens to examine a variety of contexts and to address important questions. Reviewing almost 40 years of social constructionist research in communication, we can identify several assumptions and characteristics shared by most social constructionist approaches to communication studies[5]:

1. Language, embedded and exchanged through communicative action and performance, is central to the construction of social worlds. We live by metaphors (Lakoff & Johnson, 1980), and our relationships evolve and are constituted through conversational interaction.
2. Many social realities exist. We live in a world of multiple and divergent rationalities (Shweder, 1986).
3. Meanings are the products of understandings negotiated in and through relational communication.
4. Contexts matter. The terms by which we understand the world are socially, historically, and culturally situated; once in place, they enable and constrain meanings and actions.
5. In the world of social inquiry, where we live within what we study, we must demonstrate a heightened awareness not only that we affect what we study but also that what we study, in turn, affects us.
6. Social constructionist inquiry is necessarily moral, ethical, critical, and political inquiry. The idea that we should preserve a complex, nuanced understanding of the social world is itself a moral and ethical stance.

These assumptions underlie the kinds of questions that we ask, the modes of inquiry in which we engage, and the overarching purposes to which we direct our research. For many, the constructionist perspective has become coterminous with communication, reflecting a turn away from objects and toward meanings, away from individuals and toward relationships, away from neutrality and toward moral reflection and social justice, away from hard and fast distinctions between researchers and participants and toward ways of expressing or representing reflexive relationships between communicative action and larger patterns that make up social life.

Notwithstanding the messiness of disciplinary typologies, as well as the looseness with which they are often applied, we have grouped current perspectives and practices into the following categories: (1) studies of discourse, (2) relational research, and (3) studies of organizational and community life. Our emphasis in this chapter is not on differences and boundaries but rather on the meaningful relationships and connections that can be identified across various social constructionist projects.

Exploring Texts and Material Realities

Discourse analysis in communication focuses on how texts construct ideologies. Recently, performance studies has evolved as a subfield of communication that unites interpretative methods with an understanding of bodily expression, textuality, and social context. The discourse-analytic projects undertaken by both rhetorical and performance studies scholars share in common an interest in how language constructs realities that preserve existing power structures and thus obliterate alternate ways of seeing and being in the world. The ways in which performance studies scholars are able to theorize the body in relation to social discourse make performance studies a uniquely powerful and evocative mode of critical inquiry that links micro and macro practices of communication.

Sexuality, race, and gender serve as sites of tension in everyday life, in which the material realities of bodies meet the discursive constructions of social interaction, and thus many notable studies of discourse focus on these struggles. Within performance studies, Elizabeth Bell's (1999, 2005) essays on sex and sexuality weave together moments of intimate and personal insight with critical analysis of social texts, demonstrating the ways that public discourse intersects with

private experience. Jeffrey Bennett (2003) analyzes "reparative therapy" discourse as articulated in the personal narratives of "exgays," noting that narratives reveal the incorporation of ideological (or, in this case, religious) convictions into performances of identity, thus problematizing the notion of "authenticity" in relation to the self. E. Patrick Johnson (2001, 2002) examines identity performances at the intersections of race and sexuality. He describes the potential of performance studies both to resist oppressive (colonizing) discourses and to produce "performances of possibility"—dialogic performances that enable identification between self and other without erasing an acknowledgement of difference. Writing of race as performance, Johnson (2003) states that "performance theory provides a critical analytic to navigate the slippage between racial and ethnic performance and performativity, material embodiment and discursivity" (p. 106).

Through its ability to theorize the body, the performance studies lens also is well suited to the analysis of health and illness. In a study of public discourse that intersects health, sexuality, and performance, Jay Baglia (2005) construes the introduction of Viagra as a historical moment in which constructions of masculinity and aging became dominated by a tangible and hegemonic discourse. Analyzing texts from news sources, print and electronic media advertising, and promotional materials distributed by the Pfizer pharmaceutical company to physicians, Baglia shows that Viagra discourse is overwhelmingly biomedical and heterocentric and is now integrated into a taken-forgranted understanding of sexuality and aging. Examples of feminist discourse analysis associated with critical health communication research include Dacia Charlesworth's (2003) study of women's identities in the early days of the AIDS crisis and Davi Johnson's (2004) study of Sarafem, a drug promoted for the alleviation of premenstrual syndrome. This work reflects the major goals of critical discourse analysis within the social constructionist paradigm: to unmask oppressive discursive practices and resist dominant constructions that obscure, silence, or marginalize lived experiences that fall outside the "mainstream."

In a self-consciously overstated characterization intended to be provocative, Pearce (2006) describes scholars who engage in critical discourse analysis as necessarily more depressed than those who study construction at the level of interaction, because they turn their attention to the constraints that public discourses impose on the agency of individuals. Even if they were depressed by the injustices produced by oppressive power—and we view their capacity to express their anger outwardly as constructive and not depressive—discourse analytic studies are a crucial component of the social constructionist landscape, because they reveal the ways that language, publicly circulated and privately consumed, generates ideological and material realities that create unnecessary suffering. Calling attention to social injustice is an affirming act that creates possibilities for transforming social action, in which hope resides in the process of moving beyond deconstruction to imagining reconstruction and the creation of inclusive and emancipatory discourses.

Dialogue, Narrative, and Everyday Life

Under the influence of social construction, communication researchers turned their attention to the everyday, ordinary, lived experiences of individuals involved in ongoing relationships with one another. Researchers now recognize that it is necessary to utilize methods and interpretive practices that are able to capture a sense of "real life" as constituted through interaction[6] and to focus on the relationship, rather than the individual, as the primary unit of analysis (Rogers & Escudero, 2004). These two qualities—an emphasis on lived experience and an interest in what emerges in "the between"—characterize a number of current approaches to relationship research in communication.

Relational dialectics is an approach to the study of close personal relationships that embraces the complexity of human interaction and emphasizes contradiction, change, praxis, and totality (Baxter & Montgomery, 1996; Montgomery & Baxter, 1998; Rawlins, 1992). The relational dialectics perspective resonates with social constructionists because it encourages researchers to retain a sense of the emergent nature of relationships through communication, recognizes that relational realities are in a state of flux, and acknowledges the tension between past and present action and between individual agency and context. Relational dialectics has been applied to the study of friendship (Rawlins, 1992), relational transitions (Conville, 1991, 1998), family life (Cissna, Cox, & Bochner, 1990; Yerby, 1995), the transition to motherhood (Foster, 2005b), community life (Adelman & Frey, 1997), and many other topics both within and beyond interpersonal relationships. In addition, dialectics has shed light on methodological assumptions within the study of relationships, specifically to demonstrate the value of interpretive and narrative approaches (Bochner et al., 1998; Van Lear, 1998).

Narrative inquiry focuses on stories and storytelling as both individual and collective practices of sensemaking. Two general forms of narrative research have emerged in studies of relationships: (1) studies of others' narratives, often generated through ethnographic interviews, and (2) personal narratives that take the reader inside the interaction. Both forms incorporate a cultural understanding of relationships and the ways that meanings are culturally framed, supported, and resisted through storytelling.

Narrative studies in which the researcher observes and analyzes stories of participants have been conducted in a variety of contexts, such as support group meetings (Arrington, 2005), medical interviews (Eggley, 2002), and family discussions (Koenig Kellas, 2006). In many cases, participants' stories have been elicited through indepth interviewing (Weigel, 2003; Wood,

2000, 2001). These studies usually address the language that participants use to describe their own experiences in relation to a particular audience. It is important to understand that when interview participants are sharing stories with a researcher, their stories are being constructed interactively, for an audience, and that the teller is expressing social meanings to make sense of his or her experience. Even when these studies do not foreground the *social*, they still tend to reflect many of the working assumptions of social construction.

Narrative inquiry within relationship studies is also evident in projects that work from inside the interaction. Specifically, personal narrative or autoethnographic research "implies a process of evocative narrative writing, systematic introspection, and theoretical reflection that is grounded in the experience of the fieldworker" (Foster, 2005a, p. 151). The autoethnographic method permits descriptions of relationships and social interactions that describe the concrete, lived experiences of the writer and simultaneously reflect on the social significance of the story. The strengths and contributions of autoethnography are discussed in detail in Chapter 23 of this *Handbook*; however, we felt it important here to underscore the important role that autoethnography has played—and is poised to play—in our discipline, communication studies.

Carolyn Ellis's (1995) *Final Negotiations* has achieved the status of a foundational text that exemplifies some of the best and most important characteristics of autoethnography. Ellis tells the story of her relationship with her partner, Gene, from the time of their meeting through the journey of illness, caregiving, and dying as Gene eventually succumbs to emphysema. *Final Negotiations* evocatively depicts unfolding relational realities as they occur through interaction between Carolyn and Gene in specific contexts. Other studies that utilize autoethnographic research and writing strategies include Carol Rambo-Ronai's (1995) story of childhood sexual abuse; Lisa Tillmann-

Healy's (2001) study of friendship, *Between Gay and Straight*; Loreen Olson's (2004) autoethnographic narrative of spousal abuse; Elissa Foster's (2007) ethnography of relationships between hospice volunteers and patients; and many of the chapters in two collections edited by Bochner and Ellis—*Composing Ethnography* (Ellis & Bochner, 1996) and *Ethnographically Speaking* (Bochner & Ellis, 2002). Many of these projects carry out what Norman Denzin (1997, p. 274) has called a "communitarian moral ethic," in which the researcher is personally engaged in voicing experiences that have been silenced and drawing attention to experiences of people who are marginalized. Autoethnography breaks away from many of the conventions of social science writing, choosing to introduce forms of discourse that are aesthetically and artistically compelling and seeking to evoke an interactive engagement with readers. The goals of accessible writing and intense engagement with readers offers an opportunity for communication scholars to use their work as a mode of intervention into the processes through which oppressive ideologies and practices are reproduced and to provide visions of the social world that may ameliorate human suffering.

Organizations and Communities

Communication scholars tend to view organizations as discursive constructions. Gail Fairhurst and Linda Putnam (2004) identify three different orientations to discourse in organizations: (1) discourse as objectivated organizational reality; (2) organizations as constructed through ongoing discourse; and (3) organizations as cultures that are grounded in discursive practices. We focus on the latter orientations—organizations as constructed through discourse and organizations as cultures that provide organizational members with both resources for action and constraints on individual agency.

Studies of organizations from a cultural perspective made a relatively early entry into the discipline, and this approach continues to provide insights into organizational life. Alexandra Murphy's (2001, 2002) studies of commercial airlines point to the "constructedness" of these organizations through the lens of performance and discourse. She describes the occupations of flight attendants, wherein mundane performances are employed to maintain a sense of normalcy during a very "nonmundane" experience (Murphy, 2002), and also the discursive regulations that discourage communication across certain boundaries, such as flight attendants talking to pilots about safety (Murphy, 2001), which can undermine the very security that other performances are intended to demonstrate. Similarly, Gary Ruud's (1995, 2000) studies of a regional symphony orchestra reveal its organization as a site of contested ideologies between business and artistic goals. In a significant variation of organizational culture studies that focuses on intervention in addition to description and criticism, Eric Eisenberg, Jay Baglia, and Joan Pynes (2006) used a narrative ethnographic process to facilitate change at a community hospital. The research team generated a narrative of organizational life based on their observations of the emergency department and employed that narrative to reveal and revise the taken-for-granted assumptions of the organizational members. The research team's efforts to address the problems of the organization succeeded where others had failed because they began by acknowledging the lived experiences and communication dynamics of the emergency department and by communicating this reality through a story that was accessible to all stakeholders in the hospital.

Although not precisely a cultural study of organizations, Kevin Barge's (2004) discussion of reflexivity and managerial practice provides an important bridge between action research in organizations and the kinds of work undertaken in community dialogue initiatives. Barge describes and analyzes training provided at the Kensington Consul-

tation Center, particularly the center's focus on managers' reflexivity. The Kensington Consultation Center's mission revolves around "the development of systemic social constructionist theory in organizations" (Barge, 2004, p. 74), and one of its approaches is to train managers in dialogic practices that mirror the kinds of reflexivity engaged in by constructionist researchers. This strategy reflects the understanding that "managers are instrumental in creating the very situations they are reading" (p. 74). One of the key assumptions underlying this work is that changing the ways that managers see and respond discursively to organizational realities will have a direct impact on those realities—an assumption that also underlies community dialogue initiatives.

Communication scholars who engage in dialogic community initiatives represent a relatively new movement in the field that is targeted at transformation. At the heart of this scholarship is a belief in the power of language and communicative action to generate positive change in situations in which seemingly intractable differences between individuals and groups undermine peaceful and productive coexistence. Scholars working in this area believe that (1) "we make our realities through social interaction and live in a world co-constructed with other people" (Littlejohn, 2004, p. 340); (2) that theory and practice are inseparable (Barge, 2004; Pearce, 1998); and (3) that it is important to promote practices that emphasize appreciation (Cooperrider & Whitney, 1999; Srivastva & Cooperrider, 1990) over "deficit discourse" (Gergen, 1994). These projects focus on dialogic practices that help people find ways to "go on together" (Gergen, McNamee, & Barrett, 2001, p. 682), and they exhibit significant overlap with social justice communication research, which also focuses on the process, context, and consequences of research (Pearce, 1998). One well-documented example of community-based research is the Cupertino Project, designed and facilitated by the Public Dialogue Consortium (Pearce & Pearce, 2000; Spano, 2001), in which a group of scholars initiated a series of dialogic interventions intended to increase civic engagement and participatory democracy in a community under stress from rapid change and racial difference. In the final section of this chapter, we discuss this project at greater length as an exemplar of possibilities for engaged, transformative, and reflexive communication research that is framed by principles of social construction.

The current research in discourse analysis, relationship development, and organizational communication shows that scholars influenced by social construction often see themselves and their work occupying the spaces between and across disciplinary lines. For example, Leslie Baxter (Baxter & Braithwaite, 2002; Baxter & Clark, 1996; Baxter & Harper, 1998) invokes a performance frame to write about ritual in marriage and family life; Patrice Buzzanell applies feminist discourse analysis to critiques of organizational policy (Buzzanell, 1995; Buzzanell & Liu, 2005); and Kristen Langellier's (1989, 1999) performance studies scholarship in the area of narrative is often cited by scholars of interpersonal relationships. In part, this cross-fertilization of ideas stems from the necessity for social constructionists to conceptualize what they study from a range of perspectives and to view the activities of "construction" as occurring between multiple levels of human life.

In the final section of this chapter, we build on the foundations of the past and present—the qualities, values, assumptions, and practices that have emerged over time— to propose a possible future for social construction research in communication. We focus particularly on the potential for communication scholars to work in the "in-between," where humanists and social scientists with varied interests could meet and apply the lessons of social construction scholarship to the challenges and struggles people face in contemporary social life.

Future Directions

In the summer of 2006 in Albuquerque, New Mexico, 60 communication scholars and practitioners gathered to address the state of social constructionism, to converse together, and to envision a more concerted and visible presence within the discipline and beyond it. The initial call for the conference described the rationale for the conference in this way:

> While many in the discipline espouse constructionist viewpoints, much of the teaching, scholarship, and practice of communication emphasize discovery, description, and transmission. Participants will explore the ways in which constructionist approaches currently occur in their work and develop specific innovations for transforming our scholarship, teaching, and practice through new applications of those perspectives. ("NCA Summer Institute," 2005, p. 1)

In addition to soliciting state-of-the-field statements from a number of scholars— Barnett Pearce (2006), Gloria Galanes (2006), John Stewart (2006), Ken Cissna (2006), Linda Putnam (2006), and Wendy Leeds-Hurwitz (2006)—the conveners of the conference, in true social constructionist fashion, established a format for the meeting that encouraged participants to spend more time in dialogue with one another than in passive listening to presentations. Although it is impossible to do justice to the rich details of the many discussions that emerged during the course of the conference, we do want to include a brief account that might express the sense of excitement about the future of social construction that many of the participants experienced. Three themes that punctuated discussions among participants at the conference included: (1) how best to articulate different levels of analysis within social constructionist research and address the "micro–macro" issue; (2) the need to integrate theory and practice with a focus on communication processes rather than products; and (3) how a shift in paradigm to a social construction[7] perspective might result in more humane and ethical communication within the discipline and at the level of national and international conversations.

Social construction research links communication practices at a micro level (e.g., observed interaction, specific language use in spoken or written text) to communication practices at a macro level of social reality. The most obvious manifestation of this distinction is between those who study texts of public discourse (macro-level analysis) and those who study interaction (micro-level analysis) (Burr, 2003). Without ignoring the differences between the macro and micro approaches, the question could be reframed from attempting to locate social construction as occurring *either* in interaction *or* in public discourse. Rather, the challenge is to acknowledge more fully the role of *context* in social construction research. Specifically, conference participants proposed that an awareness of both individual agency and meaning *and* socio-cultural-historical contexts, as well as explicit efforts to understand the relationship *between* these two, are essential to a social constructionist approach to communication.

Seeking to carve out a distinctly communicative branch of social construction, participants at the conference worked to identify concepts that focus specifically on communication processes and how these relate to meanings. The work of the Palo Alto group (Bateson, 1972; Watzlawick et al., 1967) and applied cybernetic approaches such as CMM (Pearce & Cronen, 1980) offer a vocabulary for understanding interactional patterns and the emergence of meaning through punctuation, framing, feedback, questioning, and metacommunication. These concepts not only distinguish a communication approach from other fields of inquiry and practice but also help both researchers and practitioners to focus on the details of interaction, allowing us to look *at* communication and not merely *through* it. Rather than focusing exclusively on meaning, such an orientation views communication *as* action, which helps reveal the habitual ways of relating that too often keep us locked within particular realities that we have created. As communication works toward the goals of dialogue and emancipatory discourse, we perceive that scholars will focus increasingly on *how* we communicate with one another, as well as on *what* we choose to communicate.

Another working group at the conference examined issues related to "transforming the national conversation." Recognizing that the Albuquerque conference itself was situated in a larger socio-cultural-historical context, discussion turned to the potential for social constructionist thinking and practices to influence both *what* is being talked about and *how* it is discussed. As we suggested at the beginning of this chapter, many communication researchers are deeply concerned about the propensity to frame political, social, and moral issues in the most extreme, unitary, and absolute terms, leaving no room for the coexistence of multiple realities or the emergence of new realities through dialogue. These patterns of public discourse stand in direct opposition to principles of communication grounded in social constructionist perspectives, and they are the kinds of patterns that could and should be addressed by those who study communication. The emphasis of such intervention would be on reclaiming complexity as a feature of social life and on sustaining peaceful and productive coexistence among multiple voices, with the goal of strengthening democracy and enhancing the ability of individuals and collectives to make better decisions. Those who work in public dialogue initiatives have already undertaken such projects in a number of contexts, and the challenge will be to extend the influence of this work to the national and international arenas.

Three Commitments of Social Constructionist Communication Research

The meeting at Albuquerque signaled a burgeoning interest in social constructionist research that adopts a variety of commitments in the integration of theory and practice. In presenting this series of "commitments," we do not intend to bring all constructionist research in line with a single set of qualifying descriptors—to do so would be to ignore the constructionist principle of embracing multiple perspectives and, worse, to discourage the emergent and evolving ferment that gives rise to these commitments in the first place. Rather, we offer these descriptions as touchstones or catalysts for future social constructionist research.

First, for some researchers, new constructionist research will be committed to political action, social justice, and mobilizing community engagement. The Cupertino Project (Pearce & Pearce, 2000; Spano, 2001) exemplifies the potential for such transformation through a community dialogue process. Initiated by a group of scholars and practitioners (the Public Dialogue Consortium), the Cupertino Project initially set out to apply principles of "good" communication to a sustained community project. From a series of focus group interviews and dialogue sessions, the project developed through four phases of engagement that gradually, over 4 years, turned over responsibility for sustained dialogue and action to community members in cooperation with city government. Key features of this project include: (1) providing a forum in which voices of participants can be shared and heard, (2) training community members in skills of facilitation and dialogue to ensure engagement and sustainability of the project, and (3) developing a structure for the community dialogue process that was flexible enough to respond to the emergent needs and interests of the participants. The entire project reflects a commitment to social construction that moves beyond representation to social intervention. As described by one of the key facilitators of the project, Shawn Spano (2001):

> We are not content to simply describe or criticize patterns of public communication, although we see tremendous value in these activities for the way we work. We have chosen instead to go the road of intervention, to join with citizens, government officials, and stakeholder groups to improve the quality of public decision making in communities. As a result, we find ourselves traversing the worlds of theory and practice, believing that both can be enriched by the other. (pp. 47–48)

The second commitment that we anticipate in new constructionist research is to social criticism directed toward emancipation as an outcome of the research process. The transdisciplinary performance projects of Ross Gray and Christina Sinding (Gray, Ivonoffski, & Sinding, 2002; Gray & Sinding, 2002) demonstrate how the process of research can be a healing intervention for individuals and communities. Drawing on expertise as health practitioners, performer/directors, and social scientists, the research team conducted in-depth interviews with women with metastatic breast cancer to produce the play *Handle with Care?* and with men with prostate cancer and their spouses to produce the play *No Big Deal?* The authors acknowledge that the process was "negotiated," "messy," and "not a value-free process" and that they focused on "encouraging voices often silenced by dominant discourses, including biomedicine" (Gray et al., 2002, p. 59). As described in their book, *Standing Ovation* (Gray & Sinding, 2002), each aspect of their process engaged the emancipatory potential of ethnographic performance—from eliciting the narratives to the collaborative writing process and the performances for community members, medical professionals, and men and women with cancer. These projects reveal the oppressiveness of dominant discourses and practices in a way that can unite people in a common understanding and motivate communities toward more humane ways of being and responding.[8]

Third, reflecting an emphasis on reflexivity and commitment to the research process, new constructionist research holds implications for ethical methodologies; specifically, for the kinds of relationships we have with participants and the adoption of evocative writing practices that reflect the transformational potential of research for the researcher. Elissa Foster's (2007) study of hospice began when she recognized that her own anxiety about communicating with someone at the end of life was a manifestation of a much wider cultural stigmatization of death and dying. To overcome her own fears and to discover ways to help others do the same, Foster undertook hospice volunteer training, began visiting patients, and interviewed other new volunteers during their first 18 months of volunteer work. The book about this project weaves together intimate stories of what volunteering was like, revealing insights about communicating at the end of life and the importance of "being there" for other people—without expectation or demands, with humility and compassion. Foster's project exemplifies how the research process can transform the researcher, unmasking the traditional assumptions of social scientific research and revealing the power of "being with" others in order to understand what it means to be human.

At the Albuquerque conference, participants turned reflexively to examine the social practices of the communication discipline itself, which is similar to many other disciplines. Many expressed serious reservations about the individualistic and competitive practices of research and publication that currently dominate the discipline and do not reflect the values of dialogue, collaboration, emancipation, and attention to context that social constructionists espouse. For example, the practice of blind review came under scrutiny for the hierarchical, monologic, and occasionally abusive discourse that it can generate, which could be coun-

tered with a review process modeled on mentoring. Similarly, the largely monologic format of our annual meetings can be justly criticized for failing to take advantage of the opportunity to generate emergent knowledge. To be fair, some moves have already been made by the leadership of our national association to eschew the traditional paper-presentation format. Yet such changes meet resistance because of the wider professional contexts within which these professional activities occur. Specifically, many attendees receive travel funding and/or credit toward tenure and promotion only if they present in a traditional panel format. By encouraging us to turn our attention to issues of process, principles of social construction may be able to reform academic institutions, helping them evolve toward a greater sense of communication and collaboration.

Another group at the conference specifically addressed community practice and social justice. Recognizing that communication *is* action, the group asked, "What are our commitments as a discipline to the communities in which we live and work?" At the level of our research projects, reflexivity about the relationship between the researcher and research participants is key to practices of social construction. Social constructionists are not dispassionate and objective researchers, because we recognize that we are within what we are studying, which in turn has implications for research ethics. Conference participants hope to enlarge the goals of research to include action and praxis, particularly within contexts that call out for change (V. Cronen, personal communication, August 3, 2006). This shift toward social action and practice entails a vision of research as intervention and transformation, as well as knowledge production, so that we may extend our ability to move the world in more positive and just directions.

In a related yet distinct move, a final sphere in which a social constructionist approach could develop is through viewing our research practices *as processes of social* construction, a position that emerges from a now long-standing respect for reflexivity (Steier, 1989; Stewart, 1981) and acknowledgement of our practices as inherently ideological (Lannamann, 1991). Although not all social constructionist projects align with critical perspectives, there is a growing sense that, as generators of knowledge about the human condition, researchers should be more mindful of the ways in which their research contributes to the construction of particular social realities (Foster, in press). In a political climate that is hostile to progressive ideas, social research that ignores the contexts of its own production is in danger of contributing to the marginalization of voices and experiences that are deemed to be "illegitimate" or "subversive." As Shotter (1993) argues, what we are engaged in as social constructionists is a *moral* and not a natural science; therefore, we are faced with an imperative to examine what we are *making* when we generate knowledge about the social world (see also Anderson, 1990). We face the future with the ability to make a better, more just world if we engage in our work with the reflexivity, sensitivity, and appreciation for complexity that characterizes the social constructionist sensibility.

• Notes

1. It is interesting to note that Bormann's work in the area of fantasy theme analysis subsequently became applied to the analysis of small group interaction and organizational life, in addition to rhetorical discourse, emphasizing the pragmatic emphasis of his approach (see Bormann, Pratt, & Putnam, 1978).

2. Our review in this chapter focuses on social construction, and thus we have omitted, for the most part, approaches to communication research that are decidedly individualist. In the 1980s a team of researchers at the University of Illinois, headed by Jesse Delia, developed a theory they referred to as "the constructivist approach to communication" (Delia, O'Keefe, & O'Keefe, 1982), which inspired a large body of research. Although the constructivists were instrumental in

drawing much-needed attention to the interpretive processes by which people make sense and attach meanings to experiences, they did not apply constructivism to their own research practices and thus maintained a non-self-reflexive stance toward inquiry that Steier (1991, p. 4) refers to as "first-order or naive constructivism." Despite the appeal of the constructivists' emphasis on the organization and interpretation of experience, their apparent attachment to individualism and to objectivist methodologies places their work outside the scope of interest of this chapter.

3. Despite Pearce and Cronen's (1980) work on CMM theory, many undergraduate students enter the interpersonal communication classroom with an abiding interest in intrapersonal meanings or in acquiring the ability to manage another person's meanings. Much of the subsequent work of the interpersonal communication professor is to disabuse students of these notions and invite them to embrace the understanding of communication as emergent and transacted in the "in-between."

4. This edited volume followed a special issue of *Communication Theory* (Leeds-Hurwitz, 1992) that included essays by Bochner and Ellis (1992), Carbaugh and Hastings (1992), Jorgenson (1992), and Lannamann (1992). A number of responses appeared in a subsequent issue that year, including essays by Baxter (1992), Sigman (1992), and Stewart (1992).

5. Many of the principles articulated in this chapter reflect the work of numerous scholars who attended the National Communication Association (NCA) Summer Institute on social constructionist approaches in Albuquerque, New Mexico, in August 2006. The meeting was convened under the NCA Summer Institute program and was sponsored by the Crooked Timbers Project. Reflecting the goals and interests of the organizers and participants, the conference title was "Catching Ourselves in the Act: A Collaborative Planning Session to Enrich Our Discipline through Social Constructionist Approaches."

6. This focus on "everyday" interactions has been taken up in a number of interpersonal communication textbooks by Steve Duck and Julia Wood that emphasize ordinary interaction as the proper focus of interpersonal communication research (see Duck, 1994; Wood, 2003, 2005; Wood & Duck, 2006).

7. In his keynote address, John Stewart (2006) proposed that we adopt the term *social construc-*

tion without the *-ist* or *-ism* to distinguish the emphasis on practice within the communication discipline. This term entered the discourse of the conference almost immediately, and time will tell whether it is adopted more widely and permanently.

8. Another powerful example of this type of work is Michelle Miller-Day's (2006) *HOMEwork*, an ethnographic study of a community in Harrisburg, Pennsylvania, which was adapted for performance. The performance involved community members as they presented stories about their experiences of maternal work, parenting, and growing up in the community.

• References

Adelman, M. B., & Frey, L. R. (1997). *The fragile community: Living together with AIDS*. Mahwah, NJ: Erlbaum.

Anderson, J. (1990). Preface. *Communication Yearbook, 13*, 11–15.

Arrington, M. I. (2005). "She's right behind me all the way": An analysis of prostate cancer narratives and changes in family relationships. *Journal of Family Communication, 5*, 141–162.

Baglia, J. (2005). *The Viagra ad venture*. New York: Lang.

Barge, J. K. (2004). Reflexivity and managerial practice. *Communication Monographs, 71*, 70–96.

Bateson, G. (1972). *Steps to an ecology of mind*. New York: Ballantine.

Bateson, G. (1981). Pragmatic conservatism. In C. Wilder-Mott & J. H. Weakland (Eds.), *Rigor and imagination: Essays from the legacy of Gregory Bateson* (pp. 347–355). New York: Praeger.

Bavelas, J. B. (1984). On "naturalistic" family research. *Family Process, 23*, 337–341.

Baxter, L. A. (1987). Symbols of relationship identity in relationship cultures. *Journal of Social and Personal Relationships, 7*, 187–208.

Baxter, L. A. (1992). Interpersonal communication as dialogue: A response to the "Social Approaches" forum. *Communication Theory, 2*, 330–337.

Baxter, L. A., & Braithwaite, D. O. (2002). Performing marriage: Marriage renewal rituals as cultural performance. *Southern Communication Journal, 67*, 94–109.

Baxter, L. A., & Clark, C. L. (1996). Perceptions of family communication patterns and the enactment of family rituals. *Western Journal of Communication, 60*, 254–268.

Baxter, L. A., & Harper, A. M. (1998). The role of rituals in the management of the dialectical tensions of "old" and "new" in blended families. *Communication Studies, 49*, 101–120.

Baxter, L. A., & Montgomery, B. M. (1996). *Relating: Dialogues and dialectics*. New York: Guilford Press.

Bell, E. (1999). Weddings and pornography: The cultural performance of sex. *Text and Performance Quarterly, 19*, 173–195.

Bell, E. (2005). Sex acts beyond boundaries and binaries: A feminist challenge for self care in performance studies. *Text and Performance Quarterly, 25*, 187–219.

Bennett, J. (2003). Love me gender: Normative homosexuality and "ex-gay" performativity in reparative therapy narratives. *Text and Performance Quarterly, 23*, 331–352.

Berger, P. L., & Luckmann, T. (1967). *The social construction of reality: A treatise in the sociology of knowledge*. Garden City, NY: Anchor.

Bochner, A. P. (1978). On taking ourselves seriously: An analysis of some persistent problems and promising directions in interpersonal research. *Human Communication Research, 4*, 179–191.

Bochner, A. P. (1981). Forming warm ideas. In C. Wickler-Mott & J. H. Weakland (Eds.), *Rigor and imagination: Essays from the legacy of Gregory Bateson* (pp. 65–81). New York: Praeger.

Bochner, A. P. (1984). The functions of communication in interpersonal bonding. In C. Arnold & J. Bowers (Eds.), *The handbook of rhetoric and communication* (pp. 544–621). Boston: Allyn & Bacon.

Bochner, A. P. (1985). Perspectives on inquiry: Representation, conversation, and reflection. In M. L. Knapp & G. R. Miller (Eds.), *Handbook of interpersonal communication* (pp. 27–58). Beverly Hills, CA: Sage.

Bochner, A. P. (Ed.). (1989). Applying communication theory to family process [Special issue]. *Journal of Applied Communication Research, 17*, 1–2.

Bochner, A. P. (1994). Perspectives on inquiry II: Theories and stories. In M. Knapp & G. R. Miller (Eds.), *Handbook of interpersonal communication* (2nd ed., pp. 21–41). Thousand Oaks, CA: Sage.

Bochner, A. P. (2001). Narrative's virtues. *Qualitative Inquiry, 7*, 131–157.

Bochner, A. P. (2002). Perspectives on Inquiry III: The moral of stories. In M. Knapp & J. Daley (Eds.), *Handbook of interpersonal communication* (3rd ed., pp. 73–101). Thousand Oaks, CA: Sage.

Bochner, A. P., & Eisenberg, E. (1987). Family process: Systems perspectives. In C. R. Berger & S. H. Chaffee (Eds.), *Handbook of communication science* (pp. 540–563). Beverly Hills, CA: Sage.

Bochner, A. P., & Ellis, C. (1992). Personal narrative as a social approach to interpersonal communication. *Communication Theory, 2*, 165–172.

Bochner, A. P., & Ellis, C. (1995). Telling and living: Narrative co-construction and the practices of interpersonal relationships. In W. Leeds-Hurwitz (Ed.), *Social approaches to communication* (pp. 201–213). New York: Guilford Press.

Bochner, A. P., & Ellis, C. (Eds.). (2002). *Ethnographically speaking: Autoethnography, literature, and aesthetics*. Lanham, MD: AltaMira Press.

Bochner, A. P., Ellis, C., & Tillmann-Healy, L. (1997).

Relationships as stories. In S. Duck (Ed.), *Handbook of personal relationships: Theory, research, and interventions* (pp. 307–324). Chichester, UK: Wiley.

Bochner, A. P., Ellis, C., & Tillmann-Healy, L. (1998). Mucking around looking for truth. In B. M. Montgomery & L. A. Baxter (Eds.), *Dialectical approaches to studying personal relationships* (pp. 41–62). Mahwah, NJ: Erlbaum.

Bochner, A. P., & Waugh, J. B (1995). Talking-with as a model for writing about: Implications of Rortian pragmatism for communication theory. In L. Langsdorf & A. Smith (Eds.), *Recovering pragmatism's voice: The classical tradition and the philosophy of communication* (pp. 211–234). Albany: State University of New York Press.

Bormann, E. G. (1972). Fantasy and rhetorical vision: The rhetorical criticism of social reality. *Quarterly Journal of Speech, 58,* 396–407.

Bormann, E. G., Pratt, J., & Putnam, L. (1978). Power, authority, and sex: Male responses to female leadership. *Communication Monographs, 45,* 119–155.

Brown, M. H. (1985). That reminds me of a story: Speech action in organizational socialization. *Western Journal of Speech Communication, 49,* 27–42.

Browning, L. D. (1992). Lists and stories as organizational communication. *Communication Theory, 2,* 281–302.

Burr, V. (2003). *Social constructionism* (2nd ed.). London: Routledge.

Buzzanell, P. (1995). Reframing the glass ceiling as a socially constructed process: Implications for understanding and change. *Communication Monographs, 62,* 327–354.

Buzzanell, P. M., & Liu, M. (2005). Struggling with maternity leave policies and practices: A poststructuralist feminist analysis of gendered organizing. *Journal of Applied Communication Research, 33,* 1–25.

Carbaugh, D. (1988). Cultural terms and tensions in the speech at a television station. *Western Journal of Speech Communication, 52,* 216–237.

Carbaugh, D., & Hastings, S. O. (1992). A role for communication theory in ethnography and cultural analysis. *Communication Theory, 2,* 156–164.

Carey, J. (1992). *Communication and culture: Essays on media and society.* New York: Routledge.

Charlesworth, D. (2003). Transmitters, caregivers, and flowerpots: Rhetorical constructions of women's early identities in the AIDS pandemic. *Women's Studies in Communication, 26,* 61–87.

Cherwitz, R. A. (1980). The contributory effect of rhetorical discourse: A study of language-in-use. *Quarterly Journal of Speech, 66,* 33–50.

Cissna, K. (2006, August). *Remarks from the applied communication rapporteur.* Paper presented at the National Communication Association Summer Institute, Albuquerque, NM.

Cissna, K. N., Cox, D. E., & Bochner, A. P. (1990). The dialectic of marital and parental relationships within the step family. *Communication Monographs, 57,* 44–61.

Conville, R. L. (1991). *Relational transitions.* Westport, CT: Praeger.

Conville, R. L. (1998). Telling stories: Dialectics of relational transition. In B. M. Montgomery & L. A. Baxter (Eds.), *Dialectical approaches to studying personal relationships* (pp. 17–40). Mahwah, NJ: Erlbaum.

Cooperrider, D., & Whitney, D. (1999). *Appreciative inquiry.* San Francisco: Berrett-Koeler.

Cushman, D. (1977). The rules perspective as a theoretical basis for the study of human communication. *Communication Quarterly, 25,* 30–45.

Davidson, D. (1984). *Inquiries into truth and interpretation.* Oxford, UK: Clarendon Press.

Davidson, D. (1986). A nice derangement of epitaphs. In E. LePore (Ed.), *Truth and interpretation: Perspectives on the philosophy of Donald Davidson* (pp. 433–446). Oxford, UK: Basil Blackwell.

Delia, J., O'Keefe, B., & O'Keefe, D. (1982). The constructivist approach to communication. In F. Dance (Ed.), *Human communication theory* (pp. 147–191). New York: Harper & Row.

Delia, J. G. (1987). Communication research: A history. In C. R. Berger & S. H. Chaffee (Eds.), *Handbook of communication science* (pp. 20–98). Newbury Park, CA: Sage.

Denzin, N. (1997). *Interpretive ethnography: Ethnographic practices for the 21st century.* Thousand Oaks, CA: Sage.

Derrida, J. (1981). *Positions.* Chicago: University of Chicago Press.

Duck, S. (1994). *Meaningful relationships: Talking, sense, and relating.* Thousand Oaks, CA: Sage.

Eggly, S. (2002). Physician–patient co-construction of illness narratives in the medical interview. *Health Communication, 14,* 339–360.

Eisenberg, E., Baglia, J., & Pynes, J. E. (2006). Transforming emergency medicine through narrative: Qualitative action research at a community hospital. *Health Communication, 19,* 197–208.

Eisenberg, E., & Scult, A. (1986). Meaning and interpretation in organizations. *Quarterly Journal of Speech, 72,* 88–97.

Ellis, C. (1995). *Final negotiations: A story of love, loss, and chronic illness.* Philadelphia: Temple University Press.

Ellis, C., & Bochner, A. P. (Eds.). (1996). *Composing ethnography: Alternative forms of qualitative writing.* Walnut Creek, CA: AltaMira Press.

Ellis, C., & Bochner, A. P. (2001). Writing from the periphery. In S. Cole (Ed.), *What's wrong with sociology?* (pp. 341–372). New Brunswick, NJ: Transaction.

Engel, M. (1972). Preface. In G. Bateson, *Steps to an ecology of mind* (pp. v viii). New York: Ballantine.

Fairhurst, G. T., & Putnam, L. L. (2004). Organizations as discursive constructions. *Communication Theory, 14,* 5–26.

Foster, E. (2005a). Communication at the end of life:

Volunteer–patient relationships in hospice. In S. Hornig Priest (Ed.), *Communication impact: Designing research that matters* (pp. 143–158). Boulder, CO: Rowman & Littlefield.

Foster, E. (2005b). Desiring dialectical discourse: A feminist ponders the transition to motherhood. *Women's Studies in Communication, 28*, 57–83.

Foster, E. (2007). *Communicating at the end of life: Finding magic in the mundane.* Mahwah, NJ: Erlbaum.

Foster, E. (in press). Commitment, communication, and contending with heteronormativity: An invitation to greater reflexivity in interpersonal research. *Southern Communication Journal.*

Galanes, G. (2006, August). *Social constructivist approaches: How they are taught in the discipline.* Paper presented at the National Communication Association Summer Institute, Albuquerque, NM.

Geertz, C. (1980). Blurred genres: The reconfiguration of social thought. *American Scholar, 49*, 165–179.

Gergen, K. (1973). Social psychology as history. *Journal of Personality and Social Psychology, 26*, 309–320.

Gergen, K. J. (1994). *Realities and relationships: Soundings in social construction.* Cambridge, MA: Harvard University Press.

Gergen, K. J., McNamee, S., & Barrett, F. J. (2001). Toward transformational dialogue. *International Journal of Public Administration, 24*, 679–707.

Giddens, A. (1984). *The constitution of society: Outline of the theory of structuration.* Berkeley: University of California.

Gray, R., Ivonoffski, V., & Sinding, C. (2002). Making a mess and spreading it around: Articulations of an approach to research-based theater. In A. P. Bochner & C. Ellis (Eds.), *Ethnographically speaking: Autoethnography, literature, and aesthetics* (pp. 57–75). Walnut Creek, CA: AltaMira Press.

Gray, R., & Sinding, C. (2002). *Standing ovation: Performing social science research.* Lanham, MD: AltaMira Press.

Gronbeck, B. E. (1978a). The functions of presidential campaigning. *Communication Monographs, 45*, 268–280.

Gronbeck, B. E. (1978b). The rhetoric of political corruption: Sociolinguistic, dialectical, and ceremonial processes. *Quarterly Journal of Speech, 64*, 155–172.

Hacking, I. (1999). *The social construction of what?* Cambridge, MA: Harvard University Press.

Harré, R., & Secord, P. (1972). *The explanation of social behavior.* Oxford, UK: Blackwell.

Hikins, J. W., & Zagaki, K. S. (1988). Rhetoric, philosophy, and objectivism: An attenuation of the claims of the rhetoric of inquiry. *Quarterly Journal of Speech, 74*, 201–228.

Johnson, D. (2004). Selling Sarafem: Priestly and Bardic discourses in the construction of premenstrual syndrome. *Women's Studies in Communication, 27*, 330–351.

Johnson, E. P. (2001). "Quare" studies, or (almost) everything I know about queer studies I learned from my grandmother. *Text and Performance Quarterly, 21*, 1–25.

Johnson, E. P. (2002). Performing blackness Down Under: The Café of the Gate of Salvation. *Text and Performance Quarterly, 22*, 99–119.

Johnson, E. P. (2003). Race, ethnicity, and performance. *Text and Performance Quarterly, 23*, 105–106.

Jorgenson, J. (1989). Where is the "family" in family communication?: Exploring families' self-definitions. *Journal of Applied Communication Research, 17*, 27–41.

Jorgenson, J. (1992). Communication, rapport, and the interview: A social perspective. *Communication Theory, 2*, 148–156.

Jorgenson, J., & Bochner, A. P. (2004). Imagining families through stories and rituals. In A. Vangelisti (Ed.), *Handbook of family communication* (pp. 513–538). Mahwah, NJ: Erlbaum.

Koenig Kellas, J. (2006). Finding meaning in difficult family experiences: Sense-making and interaction processes during joint family storytelling. *Journal of Family Communication, 6*, 49–76.

Kuhn, T. S. (1962). *The structure of scientific revolutions.* Chicago: University of Chicago Press.

Kuhn, T. S. (1977). *The essential tension: Selected essays in scientific tradition and change.* Chicago: University of Chicago Press.

Lakoff, G., & Johnson, M. (1980). *Metaphors we live by.* Chicago: University of Chicago Press.

Langellier, K. (1989). Personal narrative: Perspectives on theory and research. *Text and Performance Quarterly, 9*, 243–276.

Langellier, K. (1999). Personal narrative, performance, performativity: Two or three things I know for sure. *Text and Performance Quarterly, 19*, 120–139.

Lannamann, J. W. (1991). Interpersonal communication research as ideological practice. *Communication Theory, 1*, 179–203.

Lannamann, J. W. (1992). Deconstructing the person and changing the subject of interpersonal studies. *Communication Theory, 2*, 139–148.

Lannamann, M. (1989). Communication theory applied to relational change: A case study in Milan systemic family therapy. *Journal of Applied Communication Research, 17*, 71–91.

Leeds-Hurwitz, W. (1989). *Communication in everyday life: A social interpretation.* Norwood, NJ: Ablex.

Leeds-Hurwitz, W. (1992). Forum introduction: Social approaches to interpersonal communication. *Communication Theory, 2*, 131–139.

Leeds-Hurwitz, W. (Ed.). (1995). *Social approaches to communication.* New York: Guilford Press.

Leeds-Hurwitz, W. (2006, August). *Social constructionism: Moving from theory to research (and back again).* Paper presented at the National Communication Association Summer Institute, Albuquerque, NM.

Littlejohn, S. W. (2004). The transcendent communication project: Searching for a praxis of dialogue. *Conflict Resolution Quarterly, 21*, 337–359.

McNamee, S. (1989). Creating new narratives in family

therapy: An application of social constructionism. *Journal of Applied Communication Research, 17,* 92–112.

Millar, F. E., & Rogers, L. E. (1976). A relational approach to interpersonal communication. In G. R. Miller (Ed.), *Explorations in interpersonal communication* (pp. 87–104). Beverly Hills, CA: Sage.

Miller-Day, M. (2006, May). *Ethnodrama as a tool for social reform.* Paper presented at the International Congress of Qualitative Inquiry, University of Illinois, Urbana–Champaign.

Minuchin, S. (1974). *Families and family therapy.* Cambridge, MA: Harvard University Press.

Montgomery, B. M., & Baxter, L. A. (Eds.). (1998). *Dialectical approaches to studying personal relationships.* Mahwah, NJ: Erlbaum.

Murphy, A. G. (2001). The flight attendant dilemma: An analysis of communication and sense-making during in-flight emergencies. *Journal of Applied Communication Research, 29,* 30–53.

Murphy, A. G. (2002). Organizational politics of place and space: The perpetual liminoid performance of commercial flight. *Text and Performance Quarterly, 22,* 297–316.

NCA Summer Institute to be held in Albuquerque. (2005, November). *Spectra, 41*(11), 1.

Olson, L. N. (2004). The role of voice in the (re)construction of a battered woman's identity: An autoethnography of one woman's experiences of abuse. *Women's Studies in Communication, 27,* 1–33.

Orr, J. C. (1978). How shall we say: "Reality is socially constructed through communication"? *Central States Speech Journal, 29,* 263–274.

Pacanowsky, M. E., & O'Donnell-Trujillo, N. (1982). Organizational communication as cultural performance. *Communication Monographs, 50,* 126–147.

Pearce, W. B. (1976). The coordinated management of meaning: A rules-based theory of interpersonal communication. In G. R. Miller (Ed.), *Explorations in interpersonal communication* (pp. 17–35). Beverly Hills, CA: Sage.

Pearce, W. B. (1977). Preface. *Communication Quarterly, 25,* 1.

Pearce, W. B. (1998). On putting social justice in the discipline of communication and putting enriched concepts of communication in social justice research. *Journal of Applied Communication Research, 26,* 272–276.

Pearce, W. B. (2006, August). *Claiming our birthright: Social constructionism and the discipline of communication.* Paper presented at the National Communication Association Summer Institute, Albuquerque, NM.

Pearce, W. B., & Cronen, V. E. (1980). *Communication, action, and meaning: The creation of social realities.* New York: Praeger.

Pearce, W. B., & Pearce, K. A. (2000). Extending the theory of the coordinated management of meaning through a community dialogue process. *Communication Theory, 10,* 405–423.

Philipsen, G. (1992). *Speaking culturally: Explorations in social communication.* Albany: State University of New York Press.

Powell, C. (2001). What's social about social construction?: How to bridge a political schism by reaffirming an ontological divide. *Social Studies of Science, 31,* 299–307.

Putnam, L. (1982). Paradigms for organizational communication research: An overview and synthesis. *Western Journal of Communication, 46,* 192–206.

Putnam, L. (2006, August). *Exploring the role of communication in transforming conflict situations: A social constructionist view.* Paper presented at the National Communication Association Summer Institute, Albuquerque, NM.

Putnam, L., & Pacanowsky, M. E. (Eds.). (1983). *Communication and organizations: An interpretive approach.* Beverly Hills, CA: Sage.

Rambo-Ronai, C. (1995). Multiple reflections on child abuse: An argument for a layered account. *Journal of Contemporary Ethnography, 4,* 395–426.

Rawlins, W. K. (1989). Metaphorical views of interaction in family of origin and future families. *Journal of Applied Communication Research, 17,* 52–70.

Rawlins, W. K. (1992). *Friendship matters: Communication dialectics and the life course.* New York: Aldine de Gruyter.

Richardson, L. (1997). *Fields of play: Constructing an academic life.* New Brunswick, NJ: Rutgers University Press.

Rogers, L. E, & Escudero, V. (Eds.). (2004). *Relational communication: An interactional perspective to the study of process and form.* Mahwah, NJ: Erlbaum.

Rorty, R. (1979). *Philosophy and the mirror of nature.* Princeton, NJ: Princeton University Press.

Ruud, G. (1995). The symbolic construction of organizational identities and communities in a regional symphony. *Communication Studies, 46,* 201–221.

Ruud, G. (2000). The symphony: Organizational discourse and the symbolic tensions between artistic and business ideologies. *Journal of Applied Communication Research, 28,* 117–143.

Sellars, W. (1963). *Science, perception and reality.* New York: Routledge.

Shotter, J. (1987). The social construction of an "us": Problems of accountability and narratology. In P. McGee, R. Burnett, & D. Clarke (Eds.), *Accounting for relationships: Explanation, representation, and knowledge* (pp. 225–247). London: Methuen.

Shotter, J. (1993). *Conversational realities: Constructing life through language.* London: Sage.

Shweder, R. A. (1986). Divergent rationalities. In D. W. Fiske & R. A. Shweder (Eds.), *Metatheory in social science: Pluralisms and subjectivities* (pp. 163–196). Chicago: University of Chicago Press.

Sieburg, E. (1985). *Family communication: An integrated systems approach.* New York: Gardener Press.

Sigman, S. (1980). On communication rules from a social perspective. *Human Communication Research, 7,* 37–51.

Sigman, S. (1992). Do social approaches to communication constitute a contribution to communication theory? *Communication Theory, 2,* 347–356.

Smith, R., & Eisenberg, E. M. (1987). Conflict at Disneyland: A root metaphor analysis. *Communication Monographs, 54,* 367–380.

Spano, S. (2001). *Public dialogue and participatory democracy: The Cupertino Project.* Creskill, NJ: Hampton Press.

Srivastva, S., & Cooperrider, D. (1990). *Appreciative management and leadership: The power of positive thought and action in organizations.* San Francisco: Jossey-Bass.

Steier, F. (1989). A radical constructivist approach to family inquiry. *Journal of Applied Communication Research, 17,* 1–26.

Steier, F. (1991). Introduction: Research as self-reflexivity, self-reflexivity as social process. In F. Steier (Ed.), *Research and reflexivity* (pp. 1–11). London: Sage.

Stewart, J. (1978). Foundations of dialogue in communication. *Quarterly Journal of Speech, 64,* 183–201.

Stewart, J. R. (1981). Philosophy of qualitative inquiry: Hermeneutic phenomenology and communication research. *Quarterly Journal of Speech, 67,* 109–120.

Stewart, J. R. (1992). One philosophical dimension of social approaches to interpersonal communication. *Communication Theory, 2,* 337–347.

Stewart, J. R. (1995). *Language as articulate contact: Toward a post-semiotic philosophy of communication.* Albany: State University of New York Press.

Stewart, J. R. (2006, August). *Changing the dominant conception.* Paper presented at the National Communication Association Summer Institute, Albuquerque, NM.

Taylor, C. (1977). Interpretation and the sciences of man. In F. Dallmayr & T. McCarthy (Eds.), *Understanding and social inquiry* (pp. 101–131). Notre Dame, IN: University of Notre Dame Press.

Tillmann-Healy, L. M. (2001). *Between gay and straight: Understanding friendship across sexual orientation.* Lanham, MD: AltaMira Press.

Trujillo, N. (1985). Organizational communication as cultural performance: Some managerial considerations. *Southern Speech Communication Journal, 50,* 201–224.

Trujillo, N. (1992). Interpreting (the work and talk of) baseball: Perspectives on ballpark culture. *Western Journal of Communication, 56,* 350–371.

Van Lear, C. A. (1998). Dialectic empiricism: Science and relationship metaphors. In B. M. Montgomery & L. A. Baxter (Eds.), *Dialectical approaches to studying personal relationships* (pp. 109–136). Mahwah, NJ: Erlbaum.

Watzlawick, P., Beavin, J., & Jackson, D. D. (1967). *Pragmatics of human communication.* New York: Norton.

Weigel, D. J. (2003). A communication approach to the construction of commitment in the early years of marriage: A qualitative study. *Journal of Family Communication, 3,* 1–19.

Wood, J. T. (2000). "That wasn't the real him": Women's dissociation of violence from the men who enact it. *Qualitative Research Reports in Communication, 1,* 1–7.

Wood, J. T. (2001). The normalization of violence in heterosexual romantic relationships: Women's narratives of love and violence. *Journal of Social and Personal Relationships, 18,* 239–261.

Wood, J. T. (2003). *Interpersonal communication: Everyday encounters* (4th ed.). Belmont, CA: Wadsworth.

Wood, J. T. (2005). *Communication in our lives* (4th ed.). Belmont, CA: Wadsworth.

Wood, J. T., & Duck, S. (Eds.). (2006). *Composing relationships: Communication in everyday life.* Belmont, CA: Wadsworth.

Yerby, J. (1989). A conceptual framework for analyzing family metaphors. *Journal of Applied Communication Research, 17,* 42–51.

Yerby, J. (1995). Family systems theory reconsidered: Integrating social construction theory and dialectical process. *Communication Theory, 5,* 339–365.

Yerby, J., Buerkel-Rothfuss, N., & Bochner, A. P. (1990). *Understanding family communication.* Scottsdale, AZ: Gorsuch Scarisbrick.

CHAPTER 6

Educational Constructionisms

- **Stanton Wortham**
  Kara Jackson

Education is not a discipline but a phenomenon. We conceptualize education as a fuzzy set of processes that occur in events and institutions that involve both informal socialization and formal learning. Various objects are constructed in educational processes, such as the identities of teachers and learners, the subject matter learned, and the social structures produced and reproduced. These objects are constructed through mechanisms that involve various levels of organization, including psychological, interactional, cultural, and social elements. Constructionist approaches to education are important because they can help educators understand and change the highly enabling and constraining outcomes that educational processes have. Constructionist inquiries illuminate how learners' identities and competence, distinctions between valued and devalued subject matter, and the social organization of schooling are constructed, and in so doing they may help education better achieve its transformative potential.

We organize our account of educational constructionisms around the objects and mechanisms that various accounts take as basic. As Ludwig Wittgenstein (1969) argues in *On Certainty*, no matter how attuned we are to the ongoing construction of reality, we must take some things for granted.

> It might be imagined that some propositions, of the form of empirical propositions, were hardened and functioned as channels for such empirical propositions as were not hardened but fluid; and that this relation altered with time, in that fluid propositions hardened, and hard ones became more fluid. (p. 96)

In order to consider the indeterminacy that lurks within any apparent certainty, we must take other, provisional certainties for granted. In Wittgenstein's metaphor, this means that we can never consider our experience as if all is fluid without accepting some provisionally solid channels through which the fluid moves. Social constructionist accounts, then, must take some provisional certainties for granted as they analyze how other aspects of the social world are constructed. As illustrated throughout this volume and in other discussions (e.g., Gergen, 1994; Holstein & Gubrium, 2003), constructionisms vary in which certainties they implicitly or explicitly presuppose.

In our review of educational constructionisms, we attend to three dimensions along which diverse accounts make assumptions about stable aspects of the social world: (1) the object being constructed, ranging from individual identities to academic learning to institutionalized social structures; (2) the mechanism of construction, ranging from interactional construction to local practices and beliefs to more enduring social processes; (3) the timescale (Lemke, 2000; Wortham, 2006) of these objects and mechanisms, with each varying in the characteristic time interval at which relevant events happen. We summarize these dimensions in Figure 6.1, with the object of construction represented along the horizontal axis and the mechanism of construction along the vertical, and with each dimension organized (left to right and top to bottom) from shorter to longer timescales.

This figure might imply that nine discrete types of educational construction exist. As we show, some work on construction in education does focus on one cell or another in this figure—describing how one type of object is constructed through a particular mechanism. More often, however, educational constructionisms describe how multiple objects and mechanisms are involved in any process of construction. Social identification, learning, and social organization often influence each other, as people, groups, and systems use multiple resources to accomplish multiple ends. The first major section reviews accounts that focus on one cell. The second major section presents accounts that more extensively combine various objects and mechanisms.

Focused Educational Constructionisms

In order to illustrate our heuristic for organizing educational constructionisms, we be-

What is constructed (object) ▶ How (mechanism) ▼	Individual Social Identity	Individual Learning	Social Stratification
Interaction			
Local meaning systems or practices			
Enduring social organization			

FIGURE 6.1. Dimensions along which educational constructionisms make assumptions about stable aspects of the social world.

What is constructed (object) ▶ How (mechanism) ▼	Individual Social Identity	Individual Learning	Social Stratification
Interaction	Erickson & Shultz	Macbeth	
Local meaning systems or practices	Eder		
Enduring social organization			Oakes

FIGURE 6.2. Focused accounts of social construction in education.

gin with accounts that fall more neatly into one or another of the cells in Figure 6.1. No interesting account limits itself to one cell, but some accounts do focus primarily on one type of object and one type of mechanism. Figure 6.2 shows the four accounts that we discuss in this section. Our descriptions of these four cases show how each does cite more than one object and/or more than one mechanism, but we argue that these accounts nonetheless focus primarily on one cell. This section reviews these four cases, both to provide several important examples of educational constructionism and to define more precisely what we mean by the six terms in our heuristic.

Local Construction of Identities: Eder

One cluster of studies focuses on the construction of social identities in school, emphasizing local meaning systems as the primary mechanism of construction (Eder, 1995; Kinney, 1993, 1999; Perry, 2002). We use the work of Donna Eder to exemplify this cluster and to illustrate what we mean by "social identities" as an object of construction and "local meaning systems" as a mechanism. In *School Talk*, Eder (1995) describes how middle school students develop social identities and relationships. She shows how middle school students at one school use in-

formal talk such as stories and gossip to create stable ways of understanding themselves as types of people, and she focuses in particular on the construction of gendered identities. She argues, for example, that the proliferation of derogatory words for sexually active girls (*slut*, *whore*, and so on) and the relative absence of such terms for sexually active boys normalizes male sexual desire and pathologizes female sexuality. She shows how students construct homophobia through the deployment of derogatory terms such as *queer*, as well as through ritualized stories that either praise hypermasculinity and aggressive heterosexuality or insult other boys' lack of toughness. And she describes how boys construct women as objects through ritual stories of possession and conquest and through insults in which they accuse other boys of failing to conquer girls sexually.

Eder's primary objects, then, are the social identities that students construct and adopt, especially their identities as types of boys and girls. She is also concerned with the social stratification that occurs around gender roles, and she suggests that the local construction of gender through informal talk plays a role in constructing more widespread social beliefs about gender. In this way she also treats social stratification as an object. But her claims about social stratification are limited to suggestions, in her opening theoretical section, that the local construction of identities across many sites will add up to more enduring social patterns. She does not provide empirical analyses of such enduring social stratification, and she would probably argue that analysts should not stray too far from the action of locally constructed identities in search of abstract structures. Her close attention to the construction of gender identities in one school shows how children's habitual acts and beliefs about gender sometimes follow predictable patterns that one might expect from knowledge of the larger society, but she also shows how these acts and beliefs can take unexpected form as children construct alternative gender identities for themselves and others in local contexts.

The primary mechanism of construction in Eder's (1995) analysis, then, is the local meaning system—the emerging set of beliefs and practices about gender that girls and boys in this school both construct and are constrained by. She describes types of words, stories, and insults that become routine and that characterize gender talk in this setting, and she argues that this informal talk "collectively create[s] various notions of what it means to be male or female" (p. 2). Habitual ways of talking about boys and girls in this setting lead to habitual beliefs about gender. Eder also describes the creative potential of interaction as a site for construction, and thus her analysis cites interactional mechanisms of construction, as well as local ones. We argue that she is primarily concerned with local meaning systems because she does not study the details of actual interactions, in which a single event can take unexpected turns and in which the meaning of the event is often in doubt. She focuses instead on habitual ways of interacting, which sediment in a local setting such as a middle school and which thereby construct habitual senses of what it means to be male and female. Eder's account is certainly compatible with a focus on discrete interactional events,

and work on interactional mechanisms of construction would complement hers.

Interactional Construction of Learning: Macbeth

We can see the difference between local meaning systems and interactional work as mechanisms of educational construction—as well as the potential compatibility between these mechanisms—by examining an account that focuses more on interactions. In "Classrooms as Installations: Direct Instruction in the Early Grades," Douglas Macbeth (2000) describes how students' learning of academic content is accomplished through interactional work in the classroom. He describes, for example, how students come to spell the word *evaporation* over several minutes in a kindergarten spelling lesson. Although he agrees that most of the individual students would probably falter if asked to spell the word *evaporation* individually, he shows how they produce the correct spelling as a group. He analyzes how students learn not only what sounds particular letters make but also what spelling as a classroom activity entails (e.g., repetition, overlapping sounds, parsing words). Macbeth thus describes how the whole class accomplishes both the spelling of the word *evaporation* and a feeling that the correct spelling is "everyone's achievement" (p. 31). For Macbeth, academic learning is constructed by drawing on multiple resources—in this case, other students, posters on the wall, and a song they learned to help them remember how to spell the suffix *-tion*—that are brought together in a particular event and allow academic success.

Macbeth's primary object is the construction of academic learning. He is peripherally concerned with the social identities that are afforded as learning unfolds within the classroom. For example, he shows how a kindergarten child is constructed as "fluent" in Spanish through a particular sequence of teacher–student talk. Overall, however, Macbeth (2000) focuses on the production of the "local curriculum," on how academic content learned within the classroom involves an understanding both of particular subject matter and of what it means to learn that content in a classroom context.

Such academic learning is primarily constructed through interactional mechanisms, in events that unfold over seconds and minutes, in which students learn particular academic subject matter such as spelling, fractions, or Spanish. Talk is of primary importance in Macbeth's analyses, but he also includes other resources, including gestures and material objects. Like Eder, he recognizes that local meaning systems help to organize the interactions that construct particular sorts of learning. Unlike Eder, however, Macbeth (2000) focuses on how sometimes unpredictable interactions constitute local orders. Macbeth analyzes how interactional events unfold in the classroom and how the sometimes unexpected course of such events helps construct students' learning of particular content. Macbeth also acknowledges the historical location and sociocultural roots of what happens in classrooms. Teacher–student talk in classrooms is a particular sort of discourse that has evolved over decades and that has recognizable patterns. The classrooms Macbeth studied manifest such patterns, but he argues that the actual shape of any classroom event is somewhat indeterminate. The crucial work of construction happens as events that have the potential to count as various sorts of interaction—exemplary learning, failure to learn, learning of one thing but not another, and so forth—come to accomplish something recognizable. Because of this indeterminacy at the interactional level, the learning that is accomplished is, in important ways, unique to individual events.

Interactional Construction of Identities: Erickson and Shultz

Like Macbeth, Frederick Erickson and Jeffrey Shultz (1982) focus on the details of discrete interactions and the construction accomplished through interactional work. Unlike Macbeth, they study how this interactional work helps construct individual social identities. Their study explores gatekeeping encounters between junior college counselors and students from diverse economic, racial, and ethnic backgrounds—encounters in which the counselors can make evaluations or recommendations that might redirect a student's educational and career trajectory. They show how counselors and students accomplish educational sorting as they negotiate their relatively brief discussions. Central to these encounters is the question of who the student is—as a student, as a future worker, as a person. In a 10-minute interview, the counselor must form an impression of the student's motivation, abilities, character, and aspirations. Erickson and Shultz show how counselors do this only as they and the student negotiate the course of their interaction. Like all encounters, they argue, these gatekeeping events have an ecology: Various aspects of the participants' appearance, background, and actions are relevant to what occurs, along with both verbal and nonverbal signs, documents, and the layout of physical space. They trace how some of these potentially relevant components become salient to the ecology of any particular conversation, such that it becomes smooth and ends in approbation or becomes erratic and ends with disillusionment.

For their object, then, Erickson and Shultz (1982) focus on individual social identities. The junior college students become recognizable kinds of people in these gatekeeping encounters, as the counselors rely on the tone of the interaction and their emergent judgments about students' identities to recommend or impose various educational paths. Erickson and Shultz are also concerned about social stratification as an object. They argue that counselors and students often "reenact and revivify a small piece of the social and cultural order of society at large" (p. 12). They study gatekeeping encounters because these represent key moments in students' careers, in which educational institutions sort out academic successes and failures, and thus they are concerned with studying how academic success and social stratification are constructed. They nonetheless focus on individuals' identities as their primary object, arguing that social stratification exists only as it is constructed and reconstructed in individual cases.

Erickson and Shultz (1982) thus focus on interactional construction as the primary mechanism through which student identities are constructed. Counseling encounters do not have locally or institutionally determined courses. Instead, the course of any interaction emerges over seconds and minutes, as the counselor and the student negotiate positions and present themselves in sometimes unexpected ways. Erickson and Shultz's account emphasizes the creative production of relevance in interaction. Both local and broader social patterns are crucial to understanding any interaction, but these become relevant only as participants make them relevant in particular instances. If we were to focus on enduring social organization as the mechanism of construction, we would expect that socially institutionalized or culturally sedimented categories of identity would largely determine the outcome of gatekeeping encounters. But Erickson and Shultz show that demographic categories such as race, although sometimes crucial, must be made relevant, and can be made irrelevant, by the contextualized actions of individuals in interaction. They acknowledge that established cultural norms, practical constraints, and institutionalized roles and practices all limit participants' opportunities for renegotiating interactions. But they show that, nonetheless, both counselors and students must improvise in order to establish which of the many possibly relevant social categories and expectations will become salient in a given interaction. They also show how counselors and students can disrupt

habitual expectations and establish unexpected identities for themselves. Their overall findings show that situationally emergent identity is more important than demographic identity, although either can be crucial in any given event. Participants selectively reveal aspects of their identities such that interaction can yield unexpectedly relevant identities in context.

Social Organizational Construction of Social Stratification: Oakes

Eder (1995), Macbeth (2000), and Erickson and Shultz (1982) show how individual identities and academic learning can be constructed through interactional and local mechanisms. Each of these accounts also suggests that interactional and local work can contribute to more stable social stratification. (See also Marlaire and Maynard, 1990, for research that highlights the interactional construction of social organization.) But other accounts argue that social stratification is constructed more through enduring social organization than through moment-to-moment or local action. Research that focuses on institutional mechanisms of construction describes how "natural" ways of imagining and stratifying students are in fact socially constructed (e.g., Bernstein, 1977; Bowles & Gintis, 1976; Willis, 1977). These constructionist approaches show how widespread, habitual practices both reproduce and legitimate social stratification. To illustrate how these accounts take social stratification as an object of construction and enduring social organization as a mechanism, we describe Jeannie Oakes's (1985) work on ability grouping.

Oakes (1985) describes how "tracking"— the sorting of students into different academic or vocational groups—results in unequal opportunities to learn and helps construct hierarchical social relationships. Her study draws on a comprehensive data set that includes 25 junior and senior high schools from socioeconomically diverse locations. Oakes analyzes several data sources:

school district information on the tracking practices in these 25 schools, particularly in English, mathematics, and vocational education classrooms; surveys of teacher and student attitudes toward the quality of instruction and climate; and observations of the quantity of instructional time across tracked classrooms. She concludes that students in high tracks are exposed to "high status knowledge" and greater opportunities to learn, whereas students in lower tracks are provided with "low status knowledge" and fewer opportunities to learn. These differences result from differential "provision of time to learn" as well as differential "quality of instruction provided" (p. 111). High-track students spend more time in classrooms working toward learning goals (e.g., critical thinking), whereas low-track students spend more time working toward behavioral goals (e.g., listening to directions and developing study habits). Oakes's data show that students cannot easily move between tracks, and she argues that decisions regarding track placements are made arbitrarily, often based on counselors' and teachers' flawed impressions of students' potential.

Oakes (1985) takes as her object the construction of social stratification. Through tracking practices, students are given qualitatively and quantitatively unequal educational opportunities and experiences. These differences, Oakes argues, both reflect and perpetuate class- and race-based inequities in the larger society. Poor children and minority children are more likely to be placed in lower tracks than their middle-class and white counterparts, and they receive an education that limits their academic and career opportunities. Furthermore, differential classroom practices legitimate inequality in society. Students who receive minimal opportunities to learn and a focus on behavioral norms of deference maintain this sort of relationship with other institutional structures in society, whereas those who are encouraged to be independent and are given greater opportunities to learn are better prepared to occupy higher social positions. By

describing the "natural order of schools" (p. 192), Oakes thus shows how social stratification is constructed through institutionalized educational practices such as tracking.

Oakes cites enduring social organization, not interactions or local meaning systems, as the primary mechanism of educational construction. She begins with a history of the emergence of tracking as an institutionalized practice. This helps to situate tracking as a phenomenon that emerged sociohistorically. Following from the work of other social reproduction theorists (e.g., Bernstein, 1977; Bourdieu & Passeron, 1977; Bowles & Gintis, 1976; Rist, 1970; Willis, 1977), Oakes argues that the sorting of students into tracks and the divergent practices that characterize tracked classrooms organize students in ways that reproduce the hierarchical order of society. Oakes recognizes that tracking may play out differently in specific interactions and local contexts. However, unlike Eder (1995), Macbeth (2000), and Erickson and Shultz (1982), her analyses do not focus on contingent events or distinctive local settings. She focuses instead on how groups of individuals come regularly to fill institutional slots that appear to be structurally determined.

Hybrid Educational Constructionisms: Four Important Topics

Each of the four cases just described focuses on one object and one mechanism. We have used these cases to introduce our heuristic for mapping educational constructionisms and to illustrate the six objects and mechanisms represented in Figure 6.1. Even these focused cases, however, touch on several objects and mechanisms—aiming to explain how different types of objects are constructed together through one process or how a given object is constructed through a complex set of mechanisms. Most accounts of social construction in education describe more than one object and/or rely on more than one type of mechanism. This section illustrates how various combinations of object and mechanism work by focusing on four topics around which many important studies cluster: the construction of marginality, stratification, literacy, and personhood. These topics do not provide a comprehensive taxonomy of work in educational construction. They simply allow us to show how four important types of educational objects are constructed and how different accounts rely on multiple objects and multiple mechanisms in various combinations.

The Construction of Educational Marginality

As Philip Jackson (1968) observes, schools must deal with "crowds, praise and power." In order to manage the crowds, they often sort students into groups. Because schools praise students for meeting academic and behavioral standards, the resulting groups are often hierarchically organized—with some groups praised as fulfilling the mission of the institution and others criticized for failing to do so. Using their power over students, educators often marginalize the "failing" groups. Such marginalized students reside in "special education" classes, "alternative" schools, and similar places, where they are often labeled as "disabled," "disruptive," "unintelligent," or "failing." Many have studied how marginality is constructed in educational institutions and interactions, and this work has shown that educational marginalities do not generally result from inherent characteristics of individuals or groups.

Betsy Rymes (2001) studies how students in an alternative high school both adopt and resist identities as marginal students. She describes typical "dropping out" and "dropping in" autobiographical stories, through which students in the alternative school construct senses of self and reject or embrace formal education. She does not describe speakers as passively invoking habitual patterns, however. Widely circulating, recognizable stories are resources that educators and

learners use, and sometimes transform, as they construct particular identities in context. Rymes shows how students from the alternative school reproduce, contest, ridicule, and otherwise reconstrue typical dropping-out and dropping-in stories. Sometimes they even contest the distinction between students who have embraced and those who have rejected school, thereby positioning themselves in unpredictable ways with respect to linguistic, ethnic, and economic stereotypes.

Rymes (2001) takes individual social identities as the object of her analysis. She is also concerned with the social stratification that disadvantages such students as the poor minority youths she worked with, but she analyzes how such stratification is invoked and sometimes inverted as students construct their social identities. She describes how both interactional and local mechanisms facilitate this construction. Her analyses trace the sometimes unexpected ways that both marginalized and mainstream speakers interactionally position and reposition themselves with respect to more widely circulating models of identity. She also shows how, in the local setting of one alternative school, educators and students develop relatively stable practices and beliefs that become resources for subsequent interactions. Her analyses thus focus on indeterminacies and emerging identities at both the interactional and the local levels.

Like Rymes, Michelle Fine (1991) studied "dropouts" through a year-long ethnographic study at a comprehensive urban high school. Fine describes institutional practices that label and punish low-income minority adolescents who do not conform to school expectations. She documents both institutional and local practices that silence critique and mask the seriousness of the dropout problem. These practices include tracking and retention policies, as well as the school's ability to blame individuals for dropping out. In addition to documenting these exclusionary practices, Fine also describes dropouts' own stories of how they came to drop out. As with Rymes's alternative school students, many of Fine's dropouts are critical of the public schools and see their rejection of schooling as a critique of the system. They recognize the contradictions in educational rhetoric about educational attainment and economic prosperity. Fine argues that the availability of "dropout" as a category allows schools to purge these critically minded students from the system. The schools rid themselves of those who question them.

Rymes (2001) and Fine (1991), then, both take as their object the social identity of "dropout" and how this category of identity helps schools reproduce the marginalization of youths who are structurally disadvantaged in the larger society. Whereas Rymes's analysis relies on a combination of interactional and local mechanisms, however, Fine's account focuses on local meaning systems and enduring social practices that together produce both the identity of "dropout" and the processes through which this category of identity functions to preserve the status quo. (Like Fine, Signithia Fordham, 1996, and Nancy Lopez, 2003, provide accounts of how local practices and enduring structures together construct the social identities of marginalized minority youths.)

Other work on the construction of educational marginality also takes social identities as the object of construction but describes how interactional and enduring structural mechanisms can work together. Jane Mercer (1973), for instance, describes how children are assigned to the category "mentally retarded" by schools and other institutions. She finds that "schools not only labeled more persons as mentally retarded than did any other formal organization but also held the most central position in the network of formal organizations in the community dealing with mental retardation" (p. 96). Mercer argues that the criteria used to define someone as "retarded" rely tacitly on an Anglocentric norm, carried especially through IQ tests. A disproportionate number of black, Latino, and low-income children become "mentally retarded" because their knowledge and styles do not conform to the tacit norm. In addition to describing the enduring structural bias of the IQ test, Mercer also describes how individuals do interactional work to apply the IQ test in practice, and thus she begins to show how enduring structures and interactional work can function together as mechanisms of construction.

Ray McDermott (1993), Hugh Mehan (1996) and Hervé Varenne and McDermott (1998) offer more complex accounts of how interactional work constructs both marginal identities and social stratification. Mehan, for example, analyzes how educators produce the "clarity of labeled social facts" out of the "ambiguity of everyday life" (p. 255), focusing on how students come to be seen as "special education" or "disabled" students. He analyzes the routine bureaucratic work that produces opportunities for individuals to become special education students, exploring the three stages of referral, educational testing, and placement and examining the ways such texts as teacher notes and testing reports move across contexts and organize subsequent opportunities for identifying students. Similarly, McDermott and Varenne and McDermott describe how routine school practices produce categories of marginal identity that we assume some individuals must occupy, even if it takes significant work to apply the categories to diverse individuals. Mehan, Varenne, and McDermott thus focus on "disability" both as an attribute of individuals and as a social category with a history. The social category has been constructed across decades and centuries (cf. Hacking, 1990). No matter how robust, however, this category must be made relevant in particular situations, as Erickson and Shultz (1982) also argue. Construction happens within interactions, as well as across historical time, as widely circulating identities are assigned to individuals in practice.

Mehan (1996; see also Mehan, Villanueva, Hubbard, & Lintz, 1996) thus describes a complex set of mechanisms that construct both individual identities and social stratification, as individuals are identified as "disabled." Instead of proposing either interactional construction or enduring social organization as the primary factor, he cites both mechanisms. But he also moves beyond a simple combination of the two. He explores various realms that influence "disabled" and "at-risk" students' school success and failure—ranging from tendencies and actions of the student him- or herself to parents' stances and actions, habitual activities in the classroom, the organization of the school, peer group practices and attitudes, and the community's beliefs about education, as well as national educational policy and broader socioeconomic constraints. Instead of describing "micro" and "macro," either alone or together, Mehan and his colleagues describe how resources from many different spatial and temporal scales together facilitate or impede students' academic success. They give a more complex account of how "disability," "intelligence," "educational success," and other identities are constructed in practice, describing how resources from various layers of social context come together to facilitate a given student's path. The relevant mechanism is not just interaction, or local regularities, or social organization, but interactions among aspects of all three.

The Construction of Educational Stratification

As described by Jackson (1968) and others, educational institutions spend significant time sorting students into groups, often in ways that generate hierarchy. There are several ways in which educational processes contribute to and/or perpetuate social stratification. Some are institutional (e.g., grading, tracking), whereas others are more local (e.g., teachers' choosing particular students to participate more than others). In an earlier section, we reviewed Oakes's (1985) work on tracking, a widespread educational phenomenon that helps construct stratification. In this section, we review research on the construction of educational stratification that more centrally involves multiple objects and mechanisms.

Some accounts focus on the construction of social stratification as their primary object and cite a combination of two mechanisms, interactions and enduring forms of social organization. Pierre Bourdieu's research on the French education system (Bourdieu & Passeron, 1979) provides a classic model of "social reproduction," describing how educational institutions reproduce social divisions by credentialing students who come to school possessing more symbolic and economic capital. Formal education, Bourdieu argues, is a largely middle-class institution, and its practices reflect this. Children from middle- and upper-class backgrounds are more likely to succeed than their lower-class peers because the practices and dispositions developed in middle- and upper-class homes align more easily with school practices. Students who display habits associated with the middle and upper classes advance, and those who do not tend to do poorly—not because educators consciously discriminate against some students but because students with unfamiliar habits seem less intelligent and less refined.

Bourdieu's account does not rely simply on enduring social organization—on the differential allocation of capital across social classes—to explain social stratification, because of his concepts of *habitus* and improvisation. *Habitus* refers to durable, embodied dispositions that are developed mostly in primary socialization (Bourdieu & Passeron, 1977). Habitus is not deterministic. Individuals tend to act in accordance with these dispositions, but any interaction involves improvisation and the potential for uncharacteristic actions. One important example of habitus is linguistic, the tendency to speak in characteristic ways. Bourdieu and Jean-Claude Passeron (1979) show, for example, that professors in the top French schools tend to award better grades to those students who come from middle- and upper-class backgrounds in part because these students demonstrate linguistic practices (e.g., they use phonological patterns associated with middle-class French speakers) that mark those students as being "fit" for education. Students come to school with speech patterns that reflect their variable upbringings. Professors do not explicitly say (or even recognize) that they tend to prefer students who speak in particular ways. Their evaluative actions (e.g., grading) nonetheless correlate with the linguistic practices of students. Moreover, because the school conceives itself as a meritocratic institution, lower-class students then fault themselves for failing, and middle-class students believe they have succeeded because they are more intelligent. What appears to many as a natural way to classify individuals ("intelligent" vs. "dumb," "successful" vs. "unsuccessful") is actually a socially constructed phenomenon that serves to perpetuate class-based social stratification.

Annette Lareau (2000, 2003) follows Bourdieu's theoretical model in key respects. Lareau's *Home Advantage* (2000) analyzes social class and parental involvement in elementary education. Her ethnographic study of white working-class and middle-class first-grade children describes parent–child, child–teacher, and parent–teacher interactions. Lareau shows how middle-class families have access to more cultural capital and deploy this capital effectively to further their children's education. They know more educators as a function of their middle-class occupations and their own formal education, they understand formal educational practices and institutions, and they know how to request special privileges for their children. Upper-middle-class families tend to believe that both the family and the school are responsible for a child's formal education, whereas working-class families tend to believe that education is the job of schools and not families. Middle-class parents thus tend to be involved in school as teachers expect (even though teachers do not always welcome parents' demands), and their children benefit educationally.

Teachers tend to characterize working-class parents as uninvolved, even though these parents deeply care about their children's educational futures. Lareau also describes how working-class families make their children feel distant from and, at times, afraid of school, whereas middle-class families teach their children to speak up and demand individualized attention.

Lareau focuses on social stratification as her object. Like Bourdieu, she cites both interactional and social organizational mechanisms—although both Bourdieu and Lareau present enduring social organization as the more central mechanism. Lareau shows how middle-class parents accomplish educational advantage for their children by navigating interactions successfully, but she also describes how typical patterns do not always occur and how parents encourage their children to be more and less demanding of teachers in both typical and atypical ways. Lareau connects these sometimes unpredictable interactional moments to larger class-based patterns of interaction and to the enduring social organization of schooling. Her analysis thus moves between these two levels to explain the educational advantages that middle-class children tend to have over their working-class peers.

Somewhat more than Bourdieu and Lareau, Aaron Cicourel and John Kitsuse (1963) describe how the "daily transactions between school personnel and students" (p. 134) contribute to the construction of stratification, and thus they include interactional mechanisms more centrally in their analysis. Cicourel and Kitsuse focus on the distinction between "college prep" and other tracks and on the role of guidance counselors in accomplishing this stratification. They argue that educational sorting can be explained by "the patterned activities of the organization and not in the behaviors of students per se" (p. 9). Counselors classify students using relatively arbitrary criteria that have been established by the educational bureaucracy, and in most cases this enduring social organization sorts students in predictable ways. Cicourel and Kitsuse do describe instances, however, in which school personnel struggle to label a particular student, such as when a student has a low GPA but scores high on a standardized test. In such cases counselors must improvise and sometimes make unexpected judgments—claiming, for example, that there is a problem with the student rather than with the sorting system, that the student's low GPA reflects his or her "laziness" rather than a flaw in the tracking system, and that the student should be placed in a lower track. Like Oakes (1985), then, Cicourel and Kitsuse describe regular institutional practices that produce predictable hierarchies. Their account of the mechanisms by which this happens is more varied, however. Cicourel and Kitsuse focus on the relationship between day-to-day counselor–student interactions and the institutional practices that organize these interactions. This combination of mechanisms allows for cases in which the school assigns an unexpected category of identity to a student.

Bourdieu and Passeron (1977, 1979), Lareau (2000, 2003), and Cicourel and Kitsuse (1963) focus primarily on social stratification as their object. They do describe categories of identity that people use to identify individuals, but they focus on widely circulating categories and practices and do not spend much time describing how these categories are applied to individuals. Other work takes widespread social stratification as one object but also attends more closely to how categories of identity are applied to individuals at shorter timescales, across days and months in particular schools. Ray Rist (1970), Ben Rampton (2005), and Penelope Eckert (2000) fall into this group. Their work also combines mechanisms to explain the construction of individual identities and social stratification, describing how enduring social organization alone cannot explain how either the construction of individual identities or social stratification is accomplished in local and interactional contexts.

Drawing on symbolic interactionist methods, Rist (1970) followed a cohort of black inner-city students from kindergarten through second grade. He describes how the kindergarten teacher put children in reading groups that persisted for 3 years and that corresponded closely to the social-class backgrounds of the children's families. Within the first few days of kindergarten, the teacher evaluated each child as either a "fast" or a "slow" learner. The teacher made these evaluations based on her image of an "ideal" learner, which included characteristics she saw as linked to success in school and adult careers. Once she sorted the children, she spoke and acted in distinct ways with the various groups. She called on the "fast learners" more and praised them, and she ignored the "slow learners" during academic tasks and focused on correcting their behavior. Furthermore, the "fast learners" adopted the teacher's stance toward the "slow learners." Thus, Rist argues, the classroom reflected and served to reinforce broader social stratification.

Rist (1970) focuses both on individual identities and on social stratification and the interconnections between these two objects. Educators draw on widely circulating, stratifying categories of identity, which Rist argues are class-based, as they organize classrooms. When they apply these categories to individual students, both teachers and children help to reproduce the class structure of the larger society. The mechanisms of construction, for Rist, centrally include local practices and meaning systems. The local work of developing groups and routines draws on and contributes to enduring social organization. Unlike Oakes's data, Rist's data show lived instantiations and distinctive local manifestations of larger class-based norms. Like Oakes, however, Rist does not investigate how people resist social organization in particular interactions.

Rampton (2005; see also Hall, 2002) describes the "hybrid" identities that are increasingly emerging as people and media images move around the world. His work on language "crossing" in urban, multiethnic groups of adolescents illustrates a combination of objects (both identity and social stratification) and mechanisms (both interaction and enduring structures). *Crossing* is the use of words or other linguistic features from one or more other languages in the course of an utterance. Rampton studies the use of Panjabi, Carribean Creole, and Stylized Asian English by white, South Asian, and Caribbean youths in the United Kingdom. He does not argue simply that minority languages are devalued and used to stigmatize nonmainstream youths, nor that such youths use their home languages to resist such discrimination. Both of these processes, among others, do occur, but Rampton studies how various social effects are achieved in practice. Crossing is a "discursive strategy" in which diverse youths contest and create relations around race, ethnicity, and youth culture. The use of terms from a minority language does not have one or two fixed meanings—such as stigma or resistance—because particular uses involve contestation, teasing, resistance, irony, and other stances with respect to the larger social issues surrounding minority identities in Britain.

Rampton (2005) focuses on how individuals adopt and play with individual identities in practice, but he is also deeply concerned about how the cultural politics of difference can disadvantage minority youths, and he describes the larger social and political forces regimenting language, identity, and politics in the United Kingdom. He does not reduce disadvantage to predictable forms of identity politics, in which certain signs of identity routinely signal negative stereotypes, however. He shows instead how youths use language to navigate among the conflicting forms of solidarity and identity available to them in multiethnic Britain. Thus the mechanism of construction for him includes interactional work, as well as the shifting social organization of language and identity in multiethnic locations such as London.

Eckert (2000) describes how student identities can turn out in ways that we would not predict from their social positions. She studies how teenagers use phonological variants—different ways of pronouncing the "same" sound, in ways that often mark relative social status—in order to establish and sometimes transform their identities and relationships. She comes from a ("variationist") tradition that correlates different pronunciations with different social locations, and she provides systematic analyses of how boys and girls and middle- and working-class students use different pronunciations. Using data from a suburban high school, she shows how students identify each other and mark themselves by using characteristic phonological variants. But she also shows how, in practice, students often deploy variants in unpredictable ways. "I have looked away from the 'big' picture, to see how us 'little' people use variation to both find and make our way in the world, and in the process connect to, and create, the big picture" (p. xiv). Eckert takes both individual identities and social organization as objects. She studies how widely prevalent oppositions such as *jock* and *burnout* and large-scale phonological regularities that hold across regions of the United States manifest in one school. But she also studies how both predictable and unpredictable individual identities emerge through the deployment and inversion of such regularities.

Eckert (2000) thus argues that apparently stable and homogeneous social stratification is more variable than a primary focus on the mechanism of enduring social organization would lead us to believe. "Masculinity," "heterosexuality," "sluttiness," and other social categories are constructed in practice instead of being stable prior to instances of language use. Eckert does not abandon social organization as mechanism, but she explores how more widespread regularities are deployed in unexpected ways. She also shows how one school has distinctive local phonological patterns that cannot be derived from more widespread patterns and must be uncovered through ethnographic and sociolinguistic explorations of the local site. Her mechanism of construction thus includes social resources that manifest in distinctive local ways and are deployed interactionally to create distinctive identities against the background of enduring social organization.

The Construction of Literacy

The third of our topics for constructionist educational research involves the construction of literacy. Literacy has traditionally been conceived as a set of context-independent reading and writing skills (Street, 1993) and has been used as a marker to distinguish more and less "civilized" peoples (Gee, 1990/1996; Street, 1993). Constructionist research calls these assumptions into question, arguing that literacy and an individual's or group's identity as "literate" or "illiterate" are not stable and self-evident skills (see, e.g., Holstein [1983], who illustrates how evaluators of essays construct college students as competent or incompetent writers based on local, subjective knowledge, yet claim their evaluations are "objective"). Work on the construction of literacy tends to include multiple objects and mechanisms. "Literacy" as a category and a set of practices has been used to construct larger scale marginality and has thus contributed to social stratification. Accounts of literacy also describe the social construction of academic learning, as well as the construction of individual identities. Different researchers have accounted for the construction of literacy with different combinations of the three mechanisms in our heuristic.

Brian Street (1984, 1993, 2001, 2005) was one of the first to show systematically how literacy is socioculturally constructed. He argues that, contrary to popular notions, literacy is not a universal set of cognitive skills that people either acquire or do not. Rather, Street (2001) claims that "literacy is a social practice, not simply a technical and neutral skill; that it is always embedded in socially constructed epistemological principles. . . . Literacy in this sense is always contested, both its meanings and its practices, hence particular versions of it are always 'ideological', they are always rooted in a particular world-view" (pp. 7–8). Street's work has generated a subfield of literacy research called "New Literacy Studies" that explores the socially constructed nature of literacy.

The traditional model of literacy, which Street calls the "autonomous" model, has guided most formal educational practice. Following such a model, educators classify a particular way of reading and writing as literate, and individuals are classified as either literate or illiterate based on a narrow view of what counts as literacy. Street argues that, on the contrary, all literacy practices are "ideological" and that a more accurate account of literacy should take into account that there are many literacy practices. People in different social and cultural locations use text for various purposes and as part of various activities, many of which do not proceed with the sort of autonomous decoding that most schools assume. Furthermore, Street argues, the literacy practices expected and taught in schools tend to reflect the practices of those in power. Street's argument here fits with the work of Bourdieu (Bourdieu & Passeron, 1979), Shirley Brice Heath (1983) and others who show how schools expect children to enact and learn literacy practices that are associated with the dominant group. People are identified as more and less literate only against a background of "normative" literate practices. Nonmainstream ways of using text appear "deviant" against this background, even though people may accomplish their ends quite well through such alternative literacies. It appears that some progress is being made in the world of educational practice on this issue, however. Street's (2005) most recent edited collection describes several formal educational contexts that explicitly recognize the multiple literacy practices of their marginalized students and that, in doing so, allow their students both to cultivate multiple ways of using texts and to construct powerful senses of their literate selves.

Street's work spans all three objects in our heuristic—the construction of social identities, learning, and social stratification. Literacy involves individual learning, as people are taught to accomplish tasks that involve reading and writing. While learning to read and write, individuals become socially identified as more or less literate, and this identification contributes to the social stratification accomplished in and by schools. For Street, the mechanisms of construction are local and social organizational. He is interested in the local social practices associated with diverse forms of literacy and with how these more local literacies are judged against widely circulating, institutionalized ideologies about official, schooled literacy.

David Barton and Mary Hamilton (1998) describe how reading and writing are complex activities woven into local places and relationships. They show that literacy is social, local, and often "vernacular." Instead of viewing literacy as a modular set of skills that individual minds acquire, Barton and Hamilton follow Street in conceiving the basic unit of literacy as social practices. For reading and writing to occur successfully, various resources must contribute: thoughts, texts, physical settings and tools, relationships with others, and so on. Stripping away the context and focusing only on lexicon, grammar, and decoding would miss these other resources that are essential for actual literacy events to have the meaning they do. By studying literacy practices and events in one English city (Lancaster), Barton and Hamilton show how local knowledge, relationships, and activities are important to the reading and writing that people accomplish there. They show how the political writings of one person, for example, are embedded in individual and neighborhood histories. These texts could not have been written and cannot be fully understood out of this context. Barton and Hamilton also focus on "vernacular literacy practices . . . which are

not regulated by the formal rules and procedures of dominant social institutions and which have their origins in everyday life" (1998, p. 247). Vernacular literacy practices do not follow the paradigms of schooled reading and writing but nonetheless use reading and writing successfully to accomplish local aims. Sometimes, such practices allow structurally disempowered people to accomplish political aims.

In their account, then, Barton and Hamilton (1998) take both individual identities and learning as objects. They describe the literacy life stories of several individuals, tracing their experiences with various literacy practices in and out of school. They show how literacy practices have been important for these people's identities, as they became more and less "educated," "refined," and "successful." They also show how people's ability to participate in literacy events does not depend mainly on discrete cognitive skills but instead on a configuration of resources, including physical and symbolic tools, others' knowledge, and so on. Barton and Hamilton account for the construction of identity and learning primarily through local mechanisms, describing the local character of literacy practices in Lancaster, the specific relationships, histories, political agendas, and other contexts that shape how people read and write there. They also describe more enduring social organization, such as the enduring relationship between schooled literacies and social position and the corresponding devaluation of vernacular literacies, but they focus on the local.

James Collins and Richard Blot (2003) focus more on social stratification as an object and enduring social organization as a mechanism, but their account is nonetheless broadly compatible with those of Street and of Barton and Hamilton. Collins and Blot describe how literacy practices are embedded in global processes such as colonialism and neoliberalism and institutionally anchored power relations. They analyze interdependencies between local uses of literacy and larger sociohistorical movements—

describing, for instance, the hegemony of the literate standard and how this has provided cultural capital to some and disadvantaged others. They argue against the common assumption that schooled literacy will provide intellectual and economic salvation for less literate peoples in all cases, showing instead how this assumption devalues nonstandard literacies and has been used to justify exploitation.

Collins (1996) also provides a more structural account, describing the ideology of "textualism," which holds that texts and meaning are fixed and that individuals acquire discrete skills that allow them to decode these meanings. Schooling takes the textualist ideology for granted, but Collins argues that this ideology masks the social stratification accomplished through schools' assignment of more and less "literate" identities to students. Collins also describes how the typical processes of social reproduction are interrupted sometimes, as classroom interactions have unexpected results. He analyzes conversations from a low reading group, for instance, and shows how calling out can be understood as disruptive and as an indicator of less talented students. But he also shows how calling out can on other occasions be interpreted by both teacher and students as supportive, as an indication that a student understands and wants to work collaboratively with others. Collins thus analyzes the construction of both individual identities and social stratification, and he does so with reference to social organizational and interactional mechanisms.

The Construction of Educational Personhood

As Martin Packer has argued, education is not only epistemological but also ontological (Packer & Goicoecha, 2000). When students learn subject matter, they do more than change their cognitive states. They also become different kinds of people—the kinds of people who would think about the subject matter in that way, who would engage in the cognitive practices required to learn as the school teaches. Schools favor one set of cognitive practices and thus tend to produce a kind of person who, for example, favors decontextualized knowledge over knowledge embedded in craft and apprenticeship activities. Schooling is not just about cognitive development, then, but also about the construction of persons. The ontological character of education means that, when students learn things in school, both academic learning and the construction of individual identities occur. Most research on the construction of persons explores how academic learning and individual identities are constructed together, citing interactional, local, and organizational mechanisms. Some of this work also describes the construction of social stratification (e.g., Packer, 2001).

"Cultural–historical activity theory" provides a comprehensive framework for conceptualizing how both social identification and social stratification play important roles in academic learning and the cooccurring development of personhood (e.g., Cole, 1996; Engeström, 1999). This tradition, which draws on and expands Lev Vygotsky's (1934/1987) work, attends to phylogenetic, sociohistorical, cultural, and situational resources for and constraints on learning. Activity theorists study how humans have evolved to be as dependent on sociohistorical artifacts, such as symbolic tools and cultural models, as on neuropsychological capabilities. Humans differ from animals because human evolution can proceed very rapidly through socially acquired artifacts and ideas that extend our phylogenetically evolved capacities—without having to wait for genetic change to establish new ways of acting or thinking. On this account, learning necessarily involves socioculturally located artifacts. Such artifacts are differentially distributed, depending on the social location of teachers and students. As shown by Oakes and by Lareau, for example, certain ways of approaching problems are taught in high-track but not in low-track classes and in middle-class but not in lower-class homes. Learning to use these socioculturally located artifacts not only facilitates certain cognitive activity but also identifies the learner as someone who would use those sorts of tools. Approaching domestic problems in a school-based, decontextualized way, for instance, could cause tension with relatives from cultural traditions that do not favor decontextualization and efficiency. Thus individual learners are identified socially as they learn to use certain approaches and resources to solve cognitive problems.

Activity theorists take individual social identification and learning as their objects. They present local practices and meaning systems as one mechanism that plays a central role in facilitating learning and identification. Yrjö Engeström (1993), for instance, describes the use of various artifacts and resources in local workplaces as people learn to solve problems in their jobs. Activity theorists also focus on the developmental trajectories along which individuals travel as they learn to solve more complex problems. Such trajectories are composed of events, each involving an individual or group using some tools to accomplish an object, but activity theorists do not generally focus on the emergence of unpredictable patterns within events. Instead, they analyze the emergence of unpredictable developmental trajectories as individuals move across ontogenetic time. And, as activity theorists describe individuals navigating these trajectories, they show how individuals draw on social resources that are woven into more enduring social organization. Activity theory thus proposes a comprehensive set of mechanisms through which learning and identity are constructed, including all three mechanisms in our heuristic. As Michael Cole (1996) puts it, "Human cognition [is] the emergent outcome of transformations within and among several developmental domains: phylogenetic history, cultural history, ontogeny and microgenesis" (p. 147).

Dorothy Holland and Jean Lave (2001) also provide a comprehensive framework for understanding the construction of persons through educational and other activi-

ties. One chapter in their edited collection, by Steven Gregory (2001), describes how social class identities do not simply reflect preexisting categories but are instead "formed and reformed through political and cultural practices that occur at multiple sites in community life" (p. 141). Gregory describes how the social class identities of African American community activists emerged from contentious practices as they both learned and struggled with each other at church, in the neighborhood, in political organizations, and elsewhere. As they learned to participate in politics, these community activists changed who they were in some respects, and thus Gregory describes the connections between individual identity development and learning in an out-of-school context. The identities and experiences of particular individuals depended on the enduring struggles in play at a given time, but their "social class" took on particular meaning and force only in the context of the local practices and struggles relevant in the local setting. Gregory shows how a focus on enduring struggles and/or contingent events, as givens apart from the local context, would fail to capture how social identification actually happened.

Like the activity theorists, Holland and Lave (2001) propose complex mechanisms through which social identities are constructed. They describe the "mutually constitutive nature" of enduring social struggles that involve categories such as social class, together with individuals' acts in educational and other settings. Practices are sociohistorically produced, but they are not merely derived from publicly circulating models and institutional processes. Holland and Lave redescribe sociohistorical models and structures in terms of "enduring struggles" between and among people, groups, and institutions in order to emphasize how they are contested and constituted in practice. Events and actions can intervene in and transform these struggles, but such events and acts are always mediated by more widely circulating sociocultural patterns that are invoked in particular events.

Like Holland and Lave, Kevin Leander (2002) describes interconnections between learning and social identification and those between enduring organization and more contingent sites of practice. Leander, however, provides a more detailed account of how social identities "are stabilized during the course of interaction" (p. 198). Following Erickson and Shultz (1982), Mehan (1996), and others in arguing that any interaction might yield a broad range of social identities for an individual, Leander examines how more stable identities are established in practice as participants react to each other in classroom events. Leander analyzes how one African American student is socially identified and identifies herself as "ghetto" in an American studies class. He shows that her emerging identity is constructed as participants mobilize various "identity artifacts." These include "any instrument (material, tool, embodied space, text, discourse, etc.) that mediates identity-shaping activity" (p. 201). Just as there are many identities that an individual might inhabit in any interactional event, there are also many resources that could be recruited to help stabilize these emerging identities. In the case that Leander describes, classroom participants draw on a classroom banner, different descriptions of black Americans, different students' histories, and how students are spatially arranged in the classroom in order to suggest and then stabilize Latanya's identity as a "ghetto" person.

Leander thus focuses on social identities as his object. Interaction is his primary mechanism of construction, but he offers a more complicated account of how interaction works to produce stable identities. The identity artifacts that are recruited, produced, and configured in particular ways carry with them local, historical, and institutional connotations and affordances. As the activity theorists describe, the institutional location of such resources colors the people who use these resources, and Leander traces the more complex relations among widely circulating and locally emergent meanings.

Thus he describes a mechanism of construction that includes both interactional and more enduring social mechanisms.

Stanton Wortham (2006) describes how social identification and academic learning can deeply depend on each other, through both a theoretical account of the two processes and a detailed empirical analysis of how students' identities emerge and how students learn curriculum over a year in one classroom. His analysis traces the identity development of two students in a ninth-grade urban classroom, showing how they came habitually to occupy characteristic roles across an academic year. He also traces two major themes from the curriculum, showing how students came to make increasingly sophisticated arguments about them. The analysis shows in detail how social identification and academic learning became deeply interdependent in this classroom. The two students developed unexpected identities in substantial part because curricular themes provided categories that teachers and students used to identify them. And students learned about those curricular themes in part because the two students were socially identified in ways that illuminated those themes.

Wortham's (2006) analysis emphasizes local models that specify the different types of "student" one might be in this classroom, describing distinctive gendered models that emerged across several months. These local models both drew on and transformed more widely circulating models, and both students and teachers used them in sometimes unexpected ways in classroom interactions. The two focal students' identities emerged as speakers transformed more widely circulating models of race and gender into local models of appropriate and inappropriate studenthood and as they contested individual students' identities in particular interactions. Wortham thus takes social identities and academic learning (and their interrelations) as objects and describes both local and interactional mechanisms through which these objects are constructed.

Conclusion

Educational institutions and processes are in some cases powerfully restraining and in others powerfully liberating. Constructionist research in education has the potential to help practitioners make their work more liberating and less restraining in at least three ways. First, by working against essentialist notions of student identity, constructionist accounts can help students, educators, parents, and others avoid "deficit" models of students' potential and appreciate the power that education has to construct more productive identities for students. Second, by working against naturalized versions of social stratification, constructionist research can help us appreciate alternative ways that we might work to organize our educational institutions and our broader social relations in more just ways. Third, by working against essentialist notions of learning, constructionist research can help students and educators appreciate the social situatedness and the complexity of cognitive activities and the curriculum. Kenneth Gergen and Stanton Wortham (2001) describe more concretely how a social constructionist view of knowledge could guide educational enterprises along these lines, recommending several pedagogical innovations, such as "greater democracy in negotiating what counts in educational practice, the local embedding of curricula, the breaking of disciplinary boundaries, the lodgement of disciplinary discourses in societally relevant practices, educational practice in societal issues and a shift from subject and child centred modes of education to a focus on relationships" (p. 136).

Our account of educational constructionisms in this chapter has illustrated the diversity of approaches that researchers have taken toward these three ends, focusing on several objects and mechanisms of constructionism. We explicitly do not claim that our heuristic covers all potentially relevant approaches or that our review touches all important traditions. We have not, for instance, been able to discuss constructionist work on dialogic approaches to teaching and communication (e.g., Buttny, 1993) or epistemological arguments about constructivism (von Glasersfeld, 1995). We also caution against rigid use of Figure 6.1, imagining that the two dimensions exhaust all relevant distinctions or that individual cells can capture the essence of complex accounts. Despite its limitations, however, the heuristic illuminates various educational constructionisms, showing how constructionist accounts attend both to objects and to mechanisms and showing how more than one object and mechanism can be combined in a coherent account.

• References

Barton, D., & Hamilton, M. (1998). *Local literacies.* New York: Routledge.

Bernstein, B. (1977). *Class, codes and control.* London: Routledge.

Bourdieu, P., & Passeron, J.-C. (1977). *Reproduction in education, society and culture* (2nd ed.). London: Sage.

Bourdieu, P., & Passeron, J.-C. (1979). *The inheritors: French students and their relation to culture* (R. Nice, Trans.). Chicago: University of Chicago Press.

Bowles, S., & Gintis, H. (1976). *Schooling in capitalist America.* New York: Basic Books.

Buttny, R. (1993). *Social accountability in communication.* London: Sage.

Cicourel, A. V., & Kitsuse, J. I. (1963). *The educational decision-makers.* Indianapolis, IN: Bobbs-Merrill.

Cole, M. (1996). *Cultural psychology: A once and future discipline.* Cambridge, MA: Harvard University Press.

Collins, J. (1996). Socialization to text. In M. Silverstein & G. Urban (Eds.), *Natural histories of discourse* (pp. 203–228). Chicago: University of Chicago Press.

Collins, J., & Blot, R. (2003). *Literacy and literacies: Texts, power, and identity.* Cambridge, UK: Cambridge University Press.

Eckert, P. (2000). *Linguistic variation as social practice: The linguistic construction of identity in Belten High.* Malden, MA: Blackwell.

Eder, D. (1995). *School talk: Gender and adolescent culture.* New Brunswick, NJ: Rutgers University Press.

Engeström, Y. (1993). Developmental studies of work as a testbench of activity theory: The case of primary care medical practice. In S. Chaiklin & J. Lave (Eds.), *Understanding practice: Perspectives on activity and context* (pp. 64–103). Cambridge, MA: Cambridge University Press.

Engeström, Y. (1999). Activity theory and individual

and social transformation. In Y. Engeström, R. Miettinen, & R.-L. Punanaki (Eds.), *Perspectives on activity theory* (pp. 19–38). New York: Cambridge University Press.

Erickson, F., & Shultz, J. (1982). *Counselor as gatekeeper: Social interaction in interviews.* New York: Academic Press.

Fine, M. (1991). *Framing dropouts: Notes on the politics of an urban public high school.* Albany: State University of New York Press.

Fordham, S. (1996). *Blacked out: Dilemmas of race, identity, and success at Capitol High.* Chicago: University of Chicago Press.

Gee, J. (1996). *Social linguistics and literacies: Ideology in discourses.* London: Routledge. (Original work published 1990)

Gergen, K. (1994). *Realities and relationships: Soundings in social construction.* Cambridge, MA: Harvard University Press.

Gergen, K., & Wortham, S. (2001). Social construction and pedagogical practice. In K. Gergen (Ed.), *Social construction in practice* (pp. 115–136). London: Sage.

Gregory, S. (2001). Placing the politics of black class formation. In D. Holland & J. Lave (Eds.), *History in person: Enduring struggles, contentious practice, intimate identities* (pp. 137–170). Santa Fe, NM: School of American Research Press.

Hacking, I. (1990). *The taming of chance.* Cambridge, UK: Cambridge University Press.

Hall, K. D. (2002). *Lives in translation: Sikh youth as British citizens.* Philadelphia: University of Pennsylvania Press.

Heath, S. B. (1983). *Ways with words: Language, life, and work in communities and classrooms.* Cambridge, UK: Cambridge University Press.

Holland, D., & Lave, J. (Eds.). (2001). *History in person: Enduring struggles, contentious practice, intimate identities.* Santa Fe, NM: School of American Research Press.

Holstein, J. A. (1983). Grading practices: The construction and use of background knowledge in evaluative decision-making. *Human Studies, 6,* 377–392.

Holstein, J. A., & Gubrium, J. F. (2003). A constructionist analytics for social problems. In J. A. Holstein & G. Miller (Eds.), *Challenges and choices: Constructionist perspectives on social problems* (pp. 187–208). Hawthorne, NY: Aldine de Gruyter.

Jackson, P. (1968). *Life in classrooms.* New York: Holt, Rinehart & Winston.

Kinney, D. A. (1993). From nerds to normals: The recovery of identity among adolescents from middle school to high school. *Sociology of Education, 66*(1), 21–40.

Kinney, D. A. (1999). From "headbangers" to "hippies": Delineating adolescents' active attempts to form an alternative peer culture. In J. A. McLellan & M. J. V. Pugh (Eds.), *The role of peer groups in adolescent social identity: Exploring the importance of stability and change* (pp. 21–35). San Francisco: Jossey-Bass.

Lareau, A. (2000). *Home advantage: Social class and parental intervention in elementary education.* Lanham, MD: Rowman & Littlefield.

Lareau, A. (2003). *Unequal childhoods: Class, race, and family life.* Berkeley: University of California Press.

Leander, K. (2002). Locating Latanya: The situated production of identity artifacts in classroom interaction. *Research in the Teaching of English, 37,* 198–250.

Lemke, J. L. (2000). Across the scales of time: Artifacts, activities, and meanings in ecosocial systems. *Mind, Culture, and Activity, 7*(4), 273–290.

Lopez, N. (2003). *Hopeful girls, troubled boys: Race and gender disparity in urban education.* New York: Routledge.

Macbeth, D. (2000). Classrooms as installations: Direct instruction in the early grades. In S. Hester & D. Francis (Eds.), *Local educational order: Ethnomethodological studies of knowledge in action* (pp. 21–71). Amsterdam: Benjamins.

Marlaire, C. L., & Maynard, D. W. (1990). Standardized testing as an interactional phenomena. *Sociology of Education, 63,* 83–101.

McDermott, R. (1993). The acquisition of a child by a learning disability. In S. Chaiklin & J. Lave (Eds.), *Understanding practice: Perspectives on activity and context* (pp. 269–305). Cambridge, UK: Cambridge University Press.

Mehan, H. (1996). The construction of an LD student. In M. Silverstein & G. Urban (Eds.), *Natural histories of discourse* (pp. 253–276). Chicago: University of Chicago.

Mehan, H., Villanueva, I., Hubbard, L., & Lintz, A. (1996). *Constructing school success: The consequences of untracking low-achieving students.* Cambridge, UK: Cambridge University Press.

Mercer, J. (1973). *Labeling the mentally retarded: Clinical and social system perspectives on mental retardation.* Berkeley: University of California Press.

Oakes, J. (1985). *Keeping track: How schools structure inequality.* New Haven, CT: Yale University Press.

Packer, M. J. (2001). *Changing classes: School reform and the new economy.* New York: Cambridge University Press.

Packer, M. J., & Goicoecha, J. (2000). Sociocultural and constructivist theories of learning: Ontology, not just epistemology. *Educational Psychologist, 35*(4), 227–241.

Perry, P. (2002). *Shades of white: White kids and racial identities in high school.* Durham, NC: Duke University Press.

Rampton, B. (2005). *Crossing* (2nd ed.). Manchester, UK: St. Jerome.

Rist, R. (1970). Student social class and teacher expectations: The self-fulfilling prophecy in ghetto education. *Harvard Educational Review, 40*(3), 411–451.

Rymes, B. (2001). *Conversational borderlands: Language and identity in an alternative urban high school*. New York: Teachers College Press.

Street, B. V. (1984). *Literacy in theory and practice*. Cambridge, UK: Cambridge University Press.

Street, B. V. (Ed.). (1993). *Cross-cultural approaches to literacy*. Cambridge, UK: Cambridge University Press.

Street, B. V. (Ed.). (2001). *Literacy and development: Ethnographic perspectives*. London: Routledge.

Street, B. V. (Ed.). (2005). *Literacies across educational contexts: Mediating learning and teaching*. Philadelphia: Caslon.

Varenne, H., & McDermott, R. (1998). *Successful failure: The school America builds*. Boulder, CO: Westview Press.

von Glasersfeld, E. (1995). *Radical constructivism: A way of knowing and learning*. London: Falmer Press.

Vygotsky, L. (1987). *Thought and language* (A. Kozulin, Trans.). Cambridge, MA: MIT Press. (Original work published 1934)

Willis, P. (1977). *Learning to labour: How working class kids get working class jobs*. Lexington, MA: Heath.

Wittgenstein, L. (1969). *On certainty*. New York: Harper & Row.

Wortham, S. (2006). *Learning identity: The joint emergence of social identification and academic learning*. New York: Cambridge University Press.

CHAPTER 7

Social Constructionism in Management and Organization Studies

● Dalvir Samra-Fredericks

M anagement and organization studies (MM/OS) is a diverse field, which Dan Karreman and Mats Alvesson (2001, p. 60) also characterize as one in which the "dominance of the functionalist paradigm in organizational research" continues to be an "important" reason that studies of the "socially constructed nature of organizations" remain rare or marginal. Pushkala Prasad (2005, p. 289) adds that the disciplines of "industrial and organizational psychology and economics" continue to dominate the field, resulting in positivist forms of social science. In some ways, the current position is best summed up by Kenneth Gergen and Tojo Thatchenkery (2006, p. 39) who observe that whereas a "vast share of contemporary theory and practice in organizational science is still conducted within a modernist framework," a "new sensibil-

ity"—postmodernism—offers "grounds for a social constructionist vision of organizational science" (see also Alvesson, 1996; Chia, 1995, 1996, 2000; Cooper & Burrell, 1988; Parker, 1992; Prasad, 2005; Reed, 2000; Tsoukas, 2000; Willmott, 1994). Given space issues and the objectives of this chapter, the debates and issues over how, and to what extent, postmodernism overlaps or complements social constructionist thinking are set aside.[1] What can be stated, though, is that over the past two decades, scholars across these two broad philosophically informed terrains have put forth critiques of the epistemological and ontological assumptions underpinning management and organization theory. Indeed, questions about structure being elevated over agency and the ontological status of notions such as hierarchy, leadership, and "organization" have

129

arisen alongside critiques of the ways researchers' efforts to generalize findings result in smoothing over important differences (class, gender, and race) and the loss of contextual particulars, and so forth.

In this chapter, a small selection of studies signaling social constructionist thinking or ideas are discussed. Furthermore, given the crucial point that the "language used in everyday life continuously provides me with the necessary objectifications and posits the order within which these make sense and within which everyday life has meaning for me . . . [It] marks the coordinates of my life in society and fills that life with meaningful objects" (Berger & Luckmann, 1967, pp. 35–36), then attending to organizational members' language use is shown to be one important entry point for MM/OS scholars. More generally, the studies cited here have been variously influenced by the interpretive and linguistic "turns" within the social sciences, as well as displaying varying levels of sensitivity to Ludwig Wittgenstein's (1968) proposal that language gains meaning from its use (talk) in context, together with John Austin's (1962/1981) proposal that language use/talk is action. Adhering to a nonrepresentational view of language has also led to a steady growth in conferences, journal special issues, and edited books within MM/OS.[2] Complicating matters further, varieties of social constructionist research within MM/OS are influenced not only by Berger and Luckmann's (1967) seminal thesis but also by other theoretical traditions that seemingly deploy overlapping methodologies, concerns, and vocabularies, too. These are noted by Sandberg (2001, pp. 28–29) and include theories of "practice" (Bourdieu, 1990; Giddens, 1984), discourse (Potter & Wetherell, 1987), *discourse* (explained shortly; Foucault, 1972, 1980), critical theory (Habermas, 1972, 1979, 1984), institutional theory (Powell & DiMaggio, 1991), poststructuralism (Derrida, 1988), sensemaking (Weick, 1995), and, more recently, ethnomethodology (Garfinkel, 1967; Heritage, 1984) and the "institutional talk program" (e.g., Arminen, 2005; Heritage, 1997).

At the same time, Sandberg (2001, p. 34) observes that a familiar set of differences and tensions "in descriptions of the social construction of reality" thread their ways through these approaches and hence, research within MM/OS. For example: "micro versus macro levels of social construction; the role of language; and the nature of the relationship between subjectivity and objectivity" (Sandberg, 2001, p. 34). Another issue, though, concerns researchers who declare their studies to be rooted in social constructionist thinking, although the full import of the methodological implications remain unrealized. For example, in Dennis Gioia and Kumar Chittipeddi's (1991, p. 434) study of strategic change initiation, access to "rounds of negotiated social construction" is declared, but so, too, is evidence of a curious mix of methodologies in terms of assumptions or presuppositions about reality and how we can know it. For example, the authors enlisted a "detached investigator who analyses the data more objectively" (p. 436), together with efforts at "cross-check[ing] the incoming data" (p. 437). Equally, others notably within the poststructuralist "camp" do not label their work *social constructionist*, but similar ontological–epistemological tenets provide the foundations for their exploration of the discursive (social and political) construction of phenomena such as workplace identities and tasks.

As the broad field of MM/OS continues to grapple with the various forms and emphases of social constructionist thinking and ideas, useful accounts surveying various aspects are emerging. For example, within the subfield of entrepreneurship, Denise Fletcher (2006) discusses the overlap and/or emphases across social constructivism, social constructionist, and relational constructionism, and Steve Downing (1993, 2005) has sought to theoretically develop this subfield through integrating social constructionist ideas, dramatism, and narrative modes of knowing. The basis for the distinction between the three forms noted by Fletcher (2006, pp. 426–427, 431–433) revolve around the extent to which researchers address and theorize aspects of the contextual and/or situated nature of members' accounts. Given my objective here, the core distinctions can be distilled as follows: within *social constructivism* (e.g., following Vygotsky, 1981), the concern is "with how individuals mentally construct their worlds with categories," and hence it "privileges individual, subjective knowing" (Fletcher, 2006, pp. 426, 431). The social context and environment enter the analysis as "linguistic expressions" but "would be seen as the external expressions of internal cognitive processes" (p. 432).[3] In contrast, *social constructionist* efforts (following Berger & Luckmann, 1967) centralize the "interplay between agency and structure linking individual constructions of sense-making and enactment to the societal level through processes of structuration" (Fletcher, 2006, pp. 426–427). So, for example, interest in the ways members narrate, or story management–organizational processes, would also take account of the various broader contextual elements observed and thus enacted or reproduced. *Relational constructionism* is coined by Fletcher to emphasize further the "*relationality* and co-ordinations between people and their text/context" (p. 427, emphasis added). So, when we speak, a "*relationship* to the culture, society and the institutions (of capitalism, family, market economy, enterprise discourse)" (p. 434, emphasis added) is always marked in subtle and complex ways. This third form pivots on scrutinizing the "relational and communal" basis of meaning making (Fletcher, 2006, p. 437).

As noted earlier, though, it is inevitable that this chapter can offer only a fleeting overview of the ways social constructionism and relational constructionism have been taken up within MM/OS, given space constraints.[4] Equally, my particular interests, knowledge, and preferred way of seeing must inform the forthcoming selection of studies. This interest revolves around *how* human beings interactionally do (and thus constitute) everyday organizing (organization) or managing (management) or leading (leadership) turn by turn. Exposure to the ethnomethodological and conversation analytic traditions was central, as too was Berger and Luckmann's (1967) treatise, in guiding my early decision (mid-1980s) to conduct ethnographies of organizational members at talk/work. These were extended to include audio and video recordings of their all-day, every-day interactional routines. This orientation shapes the forthcoming account. However, I have curbed all temptation to push analytic possibilities further in the studies cited, even though the rich data suggest additional understandings of organizational members' social constructions of this and that.[5]

So, bearing in mind this backdrop, and given the space issue here, two practical moves have also been undertaken. First, I have selected just three particular "intellectual traditions" (Prasad, 2005) or approaches to illustrate aspects of social constructionist tenets or thinking within MM/OS. They are narrative, critical/Foucauldian perspectives, and talk-in-interaction/ethnomethodology.[6] Each of the three approaches selected demarcates itself through adoption of different conceptual and analytic vocabularies, and in this chapter referral to three or four studies under each mode must suffice given constraints on space. Second, I have narrowed the conceptual terrain to *identity*, *organizational change*, and *strategizing/leading*. As part of this narrowing, and given the (often) realized asymmetrical nature of organizing forms, power and resistance will fold into the discussion. Taken together, though, it is hoped that a sense of how particular MM/OS scholars have sought to understand the incessant human effort invested to interpret and to make meaning and to assemble, for example, subjective identity (as manager, strategist, worker, etc.) or tasks (organizational change) is conveyed, together with a glimpse of how they pull together the social–moral, political, economic, cultural, and institutional processes into recognizable phenomena or order (i.e., *organization*).

The chapter is organized as follows: a brief commentary on language, talk, discourse, and organization leads into discussion of each of the three modes, with narrative discussed first, then critical perspectives. The penultimate section moves into studies in which observation *and* recording of organizational members' interactions are pursued to also embrace, in fine-grained detail, *how* particular phenomena are socially constructed. A brief conclusion follows.

Language, Talk, Discourse, and "Organization"

As the earlier quotation drawn from Berger and Luckmann's (1967) seminal contribution indicates, *language* is a pivotal resource drawn on in situated practices (Schatzki, 2005; Schatzki, Knorr-Cetina, & von Savigny, 2000) constituting organizational worlds. Words have "constituting possibilities" (Deetz, 1992, p. 126) that organizational members seek to anchor as imparting specific meanings given their crystallizing or mosaic-like sense of what they are doing, who they are with, and where they are (i.e., task, others, and setting/context). Furthermore, given that when we observe people at work what we often see is a lot of *talk* (Mintzberg, 1973; see also Kotter, 1982; Samra-Fredericks, 1994, 1996, 1998, 2000, 2003b; Stewart, 1983; Watson, 1994, 1995), it is unsurprising that MM/OS researchers have increasingly sought to centralize the talk of various organizational members in their analyses, set against Wittgenstein's (1968) and/or Austin's (1981) foundational contributions whereby the formative and performative view of language are central presuppositions. Indeed, through attending to forms of language use (and the symbolic

domain more generally), additional understanding of the construction of workplace identities and occupations (Bruni & Gherardi, 2002; Watson, 2002), or tasks (e.g., organizational change—Heracleous & Barrett, 2001; Morgan & Sturdy, 2000) is shown to be secured. Although the ethnomethodological *talk-in-interaction* (Psathas, 1995; Sacks, 1992; Sacks, Scheloff, & Jefferson, 1974) intellectual tradition remains rare within MM/OS, more broadly, as Shotter (1993, p. 152; see also Samra-Fredericks, 1994, 1996; Watson, 1994) asserted, managing is conceptualized as a conversational process with the manager as a key "author" who "creat[es] from a set of incoherent and disorderly events a coherent 'structure' within which both current actualities and further possibilities can be given an intelligible 'place.' " It is done "not alone, but in continual conversations with all the others who are involved."

We shall see shortly the ways in which this growing interest in language, interpretation, meaning making, and the varying levels of attention to the (invoked) social, cultural, and political context is played out within the studies selected. In terms of grappling with what "discourse" entails, especially when there is a focal interest in power and the institutional elements, a useful account differentiating and organizing the various approaches and usages has been put forward by Mats Alvesson and Dan Karreman (2000). Here, they categorize the Foucauldian usage as "muscular" or "mega" discourse (hereafter italicized as *discourse*). Obvious examples are *discourses* of capitalism, enterprise, the market, or leadership, which embrace forms of talk, text, ideologies, practices, and, more generally, bodies of knowledge. This includes knowledge surrounding rules-of-use in terms of what can be said and by whom. For Tony Watson (1995, p. 816; see also 1994; and for other definitions and applications, see Hardy, Grant, Keeney, Oswick, & Phillips, 2004), a notion of discourse . . . [is] a connected set of statements, concepts, terms and expression which constitutes a way of talking about a particular issue, thus framing the way people understand and act with respect to that issue. This in part corresponds to Foucault's use of the concept (1980), but, whilst I would accept that such discourses can, in a sense, "exert power," I prefer to stress the way they function as menus of discursive resources which various social actors draw on in different ways . . . to achieve . . . particular purposes [e.g.,] interest based . . . Or . . . making sense of what is happening in the organization or what it is to "be a manager."

Yet the issue of how some organizational members can more legitimately deploy particular *discourses* is one research route evident within MM/OS, also signaling a more critical encounter. One example is David Knights and Glenn Morgan's (1991) Foucauldian-inspired theoretical account of the emergence of a *discourse* of corporate strategy. Their identification of the ways in which this *discourse* constitutes seven power "effects," such as maintaining the "prerogative of management" (pp. 262–263) to strategize, was subsequently empirically demonstrated by Samra-Fredericks (2005a).

Efforts to tie close-range studies of language use *in situ* with *discourse* or discursive formations is also claimed as crucial for advancing understanding within the social sciences. One suggestion from Alvesson and Karreman (2000, p. 1134) is that "synthesis or connections" would arise from scrutinizing speakers invoking "widely used cultural categories or resources." Put another way, what is called for is undertaking empirical studies of *linkages* between what is ostensibly deemed to be either *micro* (human interaction, talk, etc.) or *macro* (e.g., social structure, markets, etc.) (Samra-Fredericks, 2003b). Although they adopt a different theoretical framework, Robyn Thomas and Alison Linstead (2002) also empirically explore the issue of linkages in their study of middle managers' discursive practices.

Moving swiftly on to summarize what this broad set of considerations implies for the ontological status of "organization," we begin with Stephen Barley's (1983, p. 393) early proposal that "organizations are speech communities sharing socially constructed systems of meaning" (see also Mangham, 1986). However, as we shall glimpse shortly, the polyphonic aspects, together with explorations of the ways members resist ostensibly shared meaning systems, also fuels a strong stream of research. One example from a more critical perspective is Martin Parker's (1997, p. 134) contention that "organization is a contested process, a continually shifting set of claims and counter claims and there is surely no place or time from which it can be finally captured and presented as fact." Other conceptualizations include Watson's (2002, p. 114) process-relational perspective, which echoes social constructionist thinking, as organization is "patterns of understanding and relationships . . . shaped and reshaped as they [managers, individuals] exchange material and symbolic resources with . . . [various] constituencies . . . to continue into the long term."

Robert Chia's (1996) proposal for organizational analysis as "deconstructive practice" is also one in which organizations are conceptualized as "concretized networks of representational practices." He adds that as "regularized patterns of interactions," they exude an "appearance of the former as unified entities." Hence, organization is "stabilising and simple locating" (Chia, 1999, p. 224) and language is one critical constitutive "resource" that underpins this accomplishment (Samra-Fredericks, 2005b). Taking the broad narrative and dramatistic perspectives, Czarniawska (1997, p. 41) adds that within a "constructionist view," "organizations are not people. . . . They are *nets of collective action* undertaken in a effort to shape the world and human lives . . . [and] following the linguistic cue . . . cmphasiz[es] that organization is an activity and not the resulting 'object'." Indeed, as Bittner's

(1973) ethnomethodological stance urges us too, we need to examine the ways in which the concept *organization* is put to use *in situ* by members to construct social order.

When discussing theories of organizational change, Chia (1999; see also Barrett, Thomas, & Hocevar, 1995; Ford & Ford, 2003; Morgan & Sturdy, 2000) also displaces accounts that signal a "pervasive commitment to an ontology of being which privileges outcomes and end-states" (p. 215). Instead, an ontology of *becoming*, in which movement and process are emphasized, is proposed; this seemingly reflects one aspect of social constructionist thinking. Yet capturing "movement" and "becoming" remains a challenge, as is the *idea* of "organization" as no longer "out there" or a separate entity but as something ultimately "talked into being" (Heritage, 1997) with others. The studies discussed shortly in various ways either explicitly or implicitly conceive of "organization" in these broad terms—that is, as a phenomenon constituted by a complex and dynamic mix of *relationally* generated processes in which culturally and historically established meaning systems are *instantiated* as organizational members negotiate (talk) and manipulate technologies and artifacts and so forth as they endeavor to complete specific tasks and meet goals. But, as we shall see, too, some studies veer more toward subjective meaning-making processes and/or identity assembly, whereas others explore the ways in which context (social, cultural, economic, political, and institutional) is recursively and often asymmetrically evoked and constituted. So, beginning with a pervasive human activity, let me tell you a story.

Narrative/Storytelling

Kaj Skoldberg (1994) has suggested that narratives "reflexively constitute" organizations, a suggestion that François Cooren (1999) elaborates in terms of "organizational reality" being constructed through "discursive action," which is mediated through narrative. Within MM/OS, storytelling and narrative approaches are often associated with David Boje (1991, 2001), Barbara Czarniawska (1999), and Yannis Gabriel (1995, 2000), who, in turn, have taken inspiration from a variety of sources across the social sciences and humanities. Story and narrative are often used interchangeably; or, as Carl Rhodes and Andrew Brown (2005, p. 170) state, they are "conceptual neighbours," together with saga (Clark, 1972) and myth (Kaye, 1995). Rhodes and Brown (2005) continue by highlighting the range and scope of narrative research, in which there are "those who collect stories told in organizations (Martin et al., 1983), tell stories about organizations (Van Maanen, 1988), define organizations as storytelling systems (Boje, 1991; Currie & Brown, 2003), and conceptualize organization studies as a set of storytelling practices (Clegg 1993; Czarniawska, 1999; Hatch, 1996)" (p. 170).

Early studies of stories focused on their role in creating and sustaining corporate culture and hierarchical structures (Brown, 1986; Weick & Browning, 1986) or as a means to convey taken-for-granted role expectations and organizational norms (Brown, 1986; Hansen & Kahnweiler, 1993, cited in Rhodes & Brown, 2005). Stories have also been shown to be a means of learning and transmitting contextually specific knowledge for effective execution of work tasks (Orr, 1990), also reflecting the idea that knowledge takes a narrative form (Bruner, 1990; see also Fisher, 1987; Lyotard, 1979). When treating narratives as data within a social constructivist framework, then, researchers foreground subjective expressions. When particular aspects of the context are also acknowledged and theorized, then studies of members' emotional and symbolic lives within organizations (e.g., Gabriel, 1998) are embedded, and various emphases are given to that essential "relational or communal" aspect of meaning making (Fletcher, 2006, p. 437). Overall, the narrative approaches and studies cited here do shift our view of the "organization . . . Not . . . as an object of study, but seen rather to be subjectively and inter-subjectively constructed through the stories told" (Rhodes & Brown, 2005, p. 178). It is in this light that the subjective experience or meaningfulness of organizational life for participants is foregrounded here. In addition, the studies noted in this section all deal with the concepts of identity and organizational change but vary in their emphasis on the four key elements of a narrative. These are: (1) interpretations of sequential or chronological relations of events through selection of a "plot"—an essential temporal ordering (Czarniawska, 1997, 1998); (2) delineation of subject position and intentionality; (3) a drawing on *discourses* that circulate in particular epochs; and (4) identity work.

Beginning with Gabriel's (1999) suggestion that narratives provide an "effective way of analyzing how identities are continuously constructed" (p. 196), one such study of organizational restructuring and middle-manager identities was undertaken by Thomas and Linstead (2002). These authors take off from a critique of the "epistemological underpinning of much of the existing research" on middle managers, which is locked within a positivist epistemology. They add that one outcome of "functionalist and technicist roots in theorising" is an ascription of "facticity to concepts that are socially constructed" (pp. 72–73). Adopting social constructionist thinking, Thomas and Linstead highlight the "diversity and agency" in the construction of identities. Their middle managers were seemingly caught between two meta-*discourses* of management within the public sector (in the United Kingdom). One was the "discourse of the New Right and managerialism," which was deemed to "strip them of their role as the sole bearers of managing and open it up to various professionals" (p. 73). The second was a "new wave management" *discourse*, which elevated the "leadership, empowerment, and entrepreneurialism" features and which then presented them as "saviours of

the modern organization" (p. 73). By conducting a series of interviews, Thomas and Linstead ought to explore the active process of fashioning meaningfulness from the events and phenomena seemingly experienced by "particular actors, in particular places, at particular times" (Schwandt, 1998, cited in Thomas & Linstead, 2002, p. 77; see also Watson & Harris, 1999). Attending to the interviewees' talk and language use was the crucial starting point.

From analysis of managers' utterances, four forms of discourse (i.e., concerning expertise, being different, the public sector, and the price of commitment) are illustrated (Thomas & Linstead, 2002). So, for example, as a way to manage the tensions and engage in identity-construction processes, a discourse of expertise was employed to assemble a self in the face of insecurity. This process was illustrated through reproducing the voice of one such manager, who drew on a range of factors to anchor a viable self. In particular, his reference to "technical expertise" led Thomas and Linstead to propose that this was his crucial "sense-making tool" to fill the void left by the removal of the title of manager. Significantly, because the category description of "manager" was no longer legitimately available, he, like others, felt "sometimes like I'm losing the plot." What is being socially constructed (with the researchers here) is identity and members' current conceptions of an organizational world that may potentially be constituted along the same lines with particular others elsewhere as well.

In sum, Thomas and Linstead (2002) manage to convey aspects of the complex organizational world that the managers inhabit or, rather, constitute. We glimpse their evoked relational webs that are characterized by a lack of stability and solidity. Indeed, in their efforts to make meaning, the *discourses* of managerialism or entrepreneurialism were observed (invoked), constituting those effects documented by the researchers. Thomas and Linstead also stress that they were not looking for the most accurate and truthful picture of the state of middle management today but instead "*how* middle managers construct their identity" and "what discourses are drawn on in this construction process" (2002, p. 87). It is one example of how members, through telling their stories, "reflexively make *sense* of organizations and organizational life and infuse their working lives with *meaning*" (Rhodes & Brown, 2005, p. 171, emphasis added; Boje, 1991; Czarniawska, 1997, p. 28; Gabriel, 1999; Watson, 1994). More broadly, through doing so, they socially construct phenomena such as *organization, markets, managers,* and so forth.

Other phenomena, such as career (Cohen, Duberley, & Mallon, 2004) and entrepreneurship (Fletcher, 2006), have also been insightfully tackled by MM/OS scholars drawing on social constructionist thinking. Moreover, both Laurie Cohen and her colleagues and Denise Fletcher explicitly set out to demonstrate the value and contribution of social constructionist thinking to these domains of study. Cohen and colleagues (2004) drew on research that examined the relationship between women (both women with "portfolio careers" and scientists) and their social contexts through the ways their accounts were "framed by cultural norms and understandings" (Cohen et al., 2004, pp. 411–412). Yet, at the same time, the women were shown to "manoeuvre . . . between what are seen as socially legitimate and illegitimate career scripts, sometimes reinforcing, sometimes subverting, traditional 'rules' for action" (Cohen et al., 2004, p. 412). One example was that of being a good mother or worker, also indicating the "intersection" of the *discourses* of career and gender. Cohen and colleagues also cite Kenneth Gergen (1994, p. 188), stating that these career stories were shown to be "forms of social accounting or public discourse"—a social practice—that the women utilized while also varying in the ways they emphasized particular contexts (scientific, professional, personal, and societal; see also Wajcman & Martin, 2002). As part of this ef-

fort, time is inevitably employed as a central organizing concept by the members themselves (Rhodes & Brown, 2005, p. 177). As Boje (2001, p. 113, as cited in Rhodes & Brown, 2005, p. 177) observed, this is crucial because "plot requires a pre-understanding of time and temporal structures."

Recollections of the past were particularly pivotal in both Eero Vaara's (2002) and Andrew Brown and Michael Humphrey's (2002) studies. In Vaara's (2002, p. 211) case, he sought to explore organizational members' "social construction of success and failure in narratives of organizational change" through undertaking 126 "active" (Holstein & Gubrium, 1997) interviews with key senior "actors" involved in eight Finnish–Swedish mergers and acquisitions. In "recount[ing] their experiences of the integration process" (p. 222), four particular *discourses* were identified—rationalistic, cultural, role-bound, and individualistic. Unsurprisingly, the rationalistic discourse was the dominant framework; for example, one manager declared that "[w]hat was important was that we could make those changes, based on careful evaluation of potential synergy" (Vaara, 2002, p. 227). Clearly, it may not have happened in this way, but what is interesting is the ways (postevent) that people make sense and reason to consolidate a self that knew all along. Equally, in speaking in this fashion, they work to constitute a viable identity and aspects of environment.

In Brown and Humphreys's (2002) study of organizational change within a Turkish faculty of vocational education, we also see that when *collective* tales are told, an *organizational identity* crystallizes, too (Czarniawska, 1997). These authors drew upon 42 semistructured interviews to discern how members prized open a "space" arising from the "potential disjunction between the representations of official rhetoric [from elites/ leaders] and the meanings embedded in lived experience" (Brown & Humphreys, 2002, p. 142). Here, fieldwork also potentially provides an additional interpretive base from which to make sense of members making sense of their setting and themselves. One emergent analytic route was this "[focus] on the past and how they regretted its passing" (2002, p. 145). As the speakers sought to reflexively anchor sought after or claimed identities, the researchers also observed that the "college's original purpose and aims had not been relinquished but lived on in nostalgic reminiscence" (2002, p. 152). Through doing so, the members were deemed to have created "social meanings and group identities" (2002, p. 153). Furthermore, such acts of "collective self-authorship" were a "source of resistance to hegemonic influence," and, overall, this "trading in memories" was the filter through which they "processually constitute[d] the organizations they populate" (Brown & Humphreys, 2002, p. 157). What remains in the background, though, is scrutiny of this as a real-time interactional or relationally derived accomplishment among the organizational members themselves. What is being socially constructed here is the past, aspects of identity, and, integrally, accounts of resistance that presumably surface and temper their ongoing collective actions at other times, in other spaces, with others, and realizing or not effective task completion and "organization."

Today, interest in the discursive construction of organizational change continues (e.g., Grant, Michelson, Oswick, & Wailes, 2005; Heracleous & Barrett, 2001) and is summed up well by Haridimos Tsoukas (2005, p. 99), who argues that "there is hardly an organizational change which does not involve the re-definition, the re-labelling, or the re-interpretation of an institutional activity. Such acts of re-definition and re-interpretation are, partly at least, performative speech acts that help bring about what speakers pronounce." Tsoukas adds that for "discursivists" (a term that applies to many of the studies cited here) "the world appears, or is constructed through, the way people talk and use sign systems more generally" (p. 102). As part of this, the inherent shifting and complex nature of

workplace identities being claimed, rejected, or resisted crystallizes, too. (See also Prasad & Prasad's [2000] study in which employees' retrospective accounts highlighted how they *reconstituted* apparently harmless activities such as interruptions during training events as resistance.) Symon's (2005, p. 1659; see also Knights & McCabe, 1998) study of resistance is relevant, too. Here a "rhetorical perspective" is shown to yield a detailed account of how organizational members' skillful negotiations (with the researcher) also constituted a workable sense of self, other, and task/job.[7]

Organizational members' "doing" resignation, compliance, resistance, and so forth is, then, another important thread within MM/OS, with recent research moving on to explore the everyday *interactional* nature of such phenomena, too (Iedema, Rhodes, & Scheeres, 2006). This also neatly takes us to the second "mode." When multiple "voices" are vying or jostling to constitute self-identity, tasks, and settings (organization) to advantage, then this explicitly brings to our attention the politically imbued nature of our social constructions. It is where "discursive regimes within which individual and collective identities are constituted [and which] provide social actors with important symbolic resources for identity negotiation" (Read & Bartowski, 2000, p. 398, as cited in Brown & Humphreys, 2002, p. 142) are also deemed to constitute forms of advantage and disadvantage.

Critical Perspectives

Studies that explore the idea that some individuals are more able to articulate and legitimate their interpretations (Hazen, 1993, as cited in Rhodes & Brown, 2005) and thus come to constitute the organizational world to their advantage often draw on poststructuralist and critical social theory. It is where, as Dennis Mumby (1993, 1987/1995; see also Deetz, 1994) argues, narratives assume a "legitimating device" because they are "one of the principle symbolic forms through which organizational ideology and power structures are both expressed and constituted" (1995, p. 219). Prasad (2005, p. 148) also asserts that "discursive exclusion is accomplished by subtle moves to delegitimize alternative positions rather than by crude forms of visible coercion." One example is the discursive domain of environmental management, which is dominated by managerialist and corporatist voices and in which others are positioned (constituted) as "naive" (Prasad & Elmes, 2005, as cited in Prasad, 2005). Mumby's conception of narratives and Prasad's voices shift attention to the ways in which organizational members, *in situ*, invoke or observe particular *discourses* (of rationality, masculinity, capitalism, etc.) and hence exercise power, constituting a relational web that advantages some and not others (Samra-Fredericks, 2005a). Often, though, it is the lowly worker/employee, as opposed to the manager, whose stories or narratives are collected during interviews. These are then analyzed in terms of the nexus of wider social institutions as "disciplinary apparatuses"—and often utilizing a Foucauldian schema—alongside the micro-level practices giving rise to the constitution of subjectivity (e.g., Ball & Wilson, 2000; Brewis, 2001; Knights, 1992; Knights & McCabe, 1998; Knights & Willmott, 1993; see also Alvesson & Willmott's, 2002, account of the ways identity is regulated). Others have also explored this nexus but employed different theoretical traditions (see, e.g., Chreim, 2006; Kuhn, 2006; Tietze, 2005).

Another strand of research (more macroscopic) examines the ways particular discourses emerge and have become embedded or taken for granted. For example, Roy Jacques (1996) examined the emergence of the *discourse* of the employee over an extended period of time, and Knights and Morgan (1991) scrutinized the emergence of the *discourse* of strategy that gives rise to particular "power effects." In Paul Du Gay's (1996) study, it was the *discourse* of enterprise; through employing both interview and observation, this *discourse* (seemingly a macro phenomenon) and the discursive production of identities (micro) in four retail organizations (meso) was explored. Along similar lines, Joanna Brewis (2001) examined gendered *discourses* routinely employed by women and their simultaneous (re)production of gendered identities and a particular social, economic, and organizational configuration (and, inadvertently, realizing constraint)—often characterized or "glossed" as the gendered division of labor (see also Bruni & Gherardi, 2002; Wajcman & Martin, 2002).

As noted earlier, this interest in the social construction of hierarchies, or asymmetrical relations of power and allied subjective identities, often points to specific theoretical traditions, of which one is Foucauldian. One study that took Foucault's account of incarceration and the notion of the panopticon as an unobtrusive form of social control—a technology of surveillance—was undertaken by Kirstie Ball and David Wilson (2000). In this case the technology of surveillance was a computer-based performance monitoring (CBPM) system which was shown to function to *produce* particular kinds of employees. Through both observation and interviews, Ball and Wilson (2000, pp. 542–543) examined this meshing of technologies and subjectification. Citing Foucault's (1977) conception of "power"—taken as being "everywhere, produced and reproduced in localized bodies of knowledge and forms of discourses," CBPM was reconceptualized as a technology of power or a "grid of intelligibility" whereby "processes of classification . . . render a worker population knowable to management." It is a "normalized" technology with "associated practices of appraisal, evaluation, feedback and broadcasting of performance data . . . [which] enables a diffusion of disciplinary power and its mobilization in local discursive systems" (Bull & Wilson, 2000, p. 543).

Yet, although the overriding element arising from the CBPM was the generation of statistics and targets that were publicly broadcast (by the supervisors and managers) and deemed to constitute forms of disciplinary "gazes," there was also no simple rendering of the "workplace" and subjective identities as "productive worker." The subject positions that were made available and taken up *or* resisted yielded a complex and dynamic picture of workers constituting self, others, and setting/organization (although this is not the language employed by Ball and Wilson). The discursive data did highlight four types of "subject positioning": empowerment, life-in-work, legitimate authority, and power-through-experience. Although easily overlooked, the "powerful and benevolent position of the manager" was shown to be subtly evoked through workers/employees stating, for example, something so simple as managers being "prepared" to allow "having a laugh" for hard work (Ball & Wilson, 2000, p. 552). In such taken-for-granted ways, hierarchy is routinely constituted. In another example, the legitimate-authority repertoire is marked up when a worker/employee states that "its just a feeling you get inside. It's just fear of the managers and you can't talk to them . . . they're not easy going, I should say. They try to be, which is quite funny" (p. 554). Ball and Wilson (p. 555) suggest that this speaker positions managers as "they who should be feared" and, reciprocally, "those with whom I am unable to talk." It is summed up as a "troubled self position" but, importantly, also "troubles managerial positions through their ridicule" (p. 555). This latter action reasserts a "self" that judges and can resist, even if it is limited in its material effects (also echoing Symon's, 2005, study of public sector "inspectors"). The power-through-experience repertoire was also found to be mobilized to elevate forms of "tacit knowledge" that managers did not possess and was interpreted as a means of questioning "management's right to manage" (the

legitimate authority repertoire). Yet, arguably, too, its reach was materially limited.

Overall, though, a sense of the complex relational webs in which particular subjective identities could be legitimately articulated (i.e., claimed) given particular apparatuses (gazes) and simultaneously accomplishing particular "organizational forms" is conveyed in this and similar studies. Furthermore, what such critical accounts sensitize us to is that, when particular *discourses* are privileged (e.g., competition and capitalism) and others marginalized (e.g., community and collaboration)—while acknowledging them to be historically and culturally established in complex ways—then particular worldviews are reproduced (socially constructed) that favor some individuals and groups and not others. The interest remains in how particular "voices and meanings get 'closed off' while others 'gain momentum' " (Iedema, Degeling, Braithwaite, & White, 2004, p. 18), constituting particular social, cultural, economic, political, and institutionally imbued forms of organization. Indeed, it is significant that "resistant women" could not be interviewed by Ball and Wilson, given the senior managers' gatekeeping role. Yet, paradoxically, knowing that such silenced voices exist also conveys *to us* some sense of a particular (shadow) organizational "form" being recursively constituted somewhere in the background.

Accessing different spaces/sites to hear (silenced) "voices" is a challenge. So too are attempts to scrutinize the ways power is subtly and intricately exercised turn by turn and, as an integral part of this, how both *movement and becoming* "organization" or "manager" (or other socially and economically prescribed roles) are fashioned as members go about earning their "daily bread." Fine-grained studies of such processes are beginning to surface, and the next section touches on a small illustrative selection.

Researching the Everyday Fine-Grained Constitution of Phenomena

Karreman and Alvesson (2001, p. 60) rightly contend that we need to access *interaction happening* if we are to rectify the current situation in which "our understanding of reality construction in, between, and around organizations is poor." This seems to call for ethnographic–observational studies, which Michael Rosen (1991) suggests allow us "to understand how members of a social group, through their participation in social process, enact their particular realities and endow them with meaning" (p. 6).

Although not declaring explicit allegiance to social constructionist thinking, seminal ethnographic studies (Barley, 1988; Dalton, 1959; Jackall, 1988; Kondo, 1990; Kunda, 1992; Rosen, 1985; Watson, 1994; Van Maanen, 1973, 1978) of various occupations, professions, and organizational members in a range of workplace settings have conveyed the routine "doing" of work tasks and members making sense of and enacting their roles. Access to the rich tapestry of social, cultural, economic, political, and institutional facets *enacted* through the particular uses of language, *discourses*, artifacts, rituals, myths, and so forth has also varied across these studies. Yet, as Dorinne Kondo's (1990) study of a Japanese factory demonstrates, through reproducing vignettes of *interactions*, we do see *how* those (usually) reified categories (here, of race and gender) are constituted. Today, ethnographic–observational studies are also being supplemented by moves to audio-record workplace interactional routines. One early example is a study by Boje (1991) that included tape recordings of members' story performances to explore the meanings of the stories as they unfolded.

Ian Mangham's (1986, 1998) dramaturgical–symbolic interactionist study of executives at work is noteworthy not only because he put managers at center stage but also because it was one early account that captured the interactional, on-the-spot coconstruction of a social–political and emotionally imbued organizational world. He empirically substantiated a crucial issue—that not only do we perform *together* but we also create ourselves "in relation to some particular Other(s)" (Hosking & McNamee, 2006, p. 31). Mangham accessed the unfolding backstage drama that is usually inaccessible to interview-based research efforts. So, too, in Watson's (1994, 1995) ethnographic study of a telecommunications company, a rare opportunity arose enabling him to audio-record two managers' mundane conversation with each other (as opposed to a one-to-one "chat" with the ethnographer). Although at first he overlooked it, Watson (1995, p. 812) then put it "under the microscope" to highlight the intricate details of "social process[es]" constituted through "mundane organizational conversations." He showed how the managers drew upon shared "linguistic devices" or "resources" to turn-by-turn "negotiat[e] an order or [construct] a reality." For example, the ways one manager handled a "balancing act" given the contradictory *discourses* of empowerment versus downsizing through his selection of the "oxymoron 'honest con'" (Watson, 1995, p. 815). Indeed, Watson adds (p. 815) that a management that "was looking two ways at once is described with a phrase which is correspondingly two-sided." This flexible appropriation and "switching between vocabularies" (Watson, 1995, p. 818) was shown to be a routine affair that inherently (re)produced a particular organizational setting and that, over time, constituted strategic change for that community of managers and employees (detailed in Watson, 1994).

Studies of organizational members' *everyday* and *interactional* doing of work and the *tacit* procedures of talk and methods for reality construction as forwarded by ethnomethodology (EM) and conversation analysis (CA) have yet to make inroads in MM/OS. Yet, in an article titled "Re-viewing Organization," Tsoukas (2001, p. 7) perceptively noted that "the great ethnomethodological insight has been to show the implicit organization underlying the most routine and taken-for-granted aspects of social reality (Garfinkel, 1984)." As noted elsewhere, too, EM's basic principles are consistent (epistemologically and ontologically) with the tenets of social constructionism (Berger & Luckmann, 1967). For example, it is where everyday talk may "presume an objective world of facts 'out there,' " yet close analysis of the ways members "apprehend that world reveals their own collaborative social construction of those facts" (Molotch & Boden, 1985, pp. 273–274). EM's foundational bearings are concisely conveyed through the notion of "doing organization" (Bittner, 1973; Samra-Fredericks, 2004c), "doing the self" (Holstein & Gubrium, 2000), and "doing social structure" (Boden, 1994; Boden & Zimmerman, 1991).

Beyond the MM/OS field, though, studies drawing upon these traditions have examined how members constitute organizational, institutional, and professional settings (e.g., in welfare agencies and health care centers, Cicourel, 1981; classrooms, Mehan, 1991; hospital health counseling, Perakyla, 1995; job interviews, Silverman & Jones, 1973). Furthermore, as David Silverman (1997, p. 15) argued, only from recording events can we begin to "answer basic questions about *how* people are constituting that setting through their talk." This assertion is also borne out by a range of studies in the overlapping fields of sociolinguistics and professional discourse (e.g., Sarangi & Roberts, 1999); EM, the workplace, and technologies (Luff, Hindmarsh, & Heath, 2000); CA and institutional talk (Drew & Heritage, 1992; Heritage, 1997).

Within the MM/OS field, Karreman and Alvesson's (2001) study of newspaper editorial work explicitly referred to the CA perspective and argued for the need to foreground "micro events." In their case, the event is a meeting that both "mak[es] organization visible" and is a "vehicle for manifest-

ing, clarifying and solidifying identity constructions through conversations" (p. 59). Donald Andersen's (2005) study of project meetings takes this one step further by examining the turn-by-turn language used. Here, detailed analysis of the audio recordings of the interactions highlighted the ways mundane phrases such as "usually happens" or "usually said" enabled speakers to surface and shift practices as they tried out "how proposed organization changes might sound in the future" (p. 66). Indeed, through doing so, the stance was that they potentially and incrementally come to constitute a different organizational form. For example, one member—who had been asked to explain how forecasting was undertaken—conveyed the typicality of this organizational practice though quoting apparently typical statements in the present tense. Andersen (p. 70) comments that in this way his "representations of his prior utterances in team meetings temporarily stabilize[d] this kind of utterance as a genre, a momentary 'fixing' of organizational practice as a potential object for change." Another feature involved taking the "voice of a categorical person"; for example, a speaker "pretends to be a salesperson, imaging a conversation between a salesperson and a customer" (p. 73). By doing so, the speaker "works from another widely recognised assumption that people . . . will behave in ways [suggested] . . . " (pp. 73–74). Although not developed by Andersen, here we have Berger and Luckmann's (1967) notion of typifications (of roles) being invoked and put to work. Equally, although Andersen did not pursue the idea, it *is* evidently through such routinized forms of talk that "organization" relationally materializes, as too did their identities as particular "types" of organizational members (see also Samra-Fredericks, 2005a)

Attending to workplace conversations (Woodilla, 1998; see also Forray & Woodilla, 2002) and interaction happening (Fairhurst, 2004) is also central in Asa Makitalo and Roger Saljo's (2002) study of employment offices. As the employment officers and the clients (job seekers) subtly displayed their orientations, we saw how they accomplished the employment interview but also fundamentally made meaningful and tied the client to that spectacularly abstract and complex phenomenon, the labor market. Another study drawing upon an alternative theoretical terrain—discourse analysis (Iedema et al., 2004, pp. 28–29)—also grounded the ways government- or state-imposed reform within health care is enacted by those at the front line; in particular, the ways three *discourses* (clinical medicine, resource-efficiency/systematization discourse of management, and interpersonalizing discourse) were skillfully blended by an organizational member (a doctor–manager) who was positioned between those ostensibly external entities, profession and organization. This doctor–manager's talk-based interactional routines revealed, in exceptional detail, the ways he "discursively pulls off the delicate navigations" to "construe shared meanings" for others (Iedena et al., 2004, pp. 28–29). Arguably, as he "creatively fused multiple and sometimes contradictory positions" (pp. 28–29) during his turns at talk, he also kept a viable sense of "organization" going.

Others, conceptualizing leadership to be a "process of enac*ting*, organiz*ing*, explain*ing*, manag*ing*, shap*ing* collective movement/action/*ing*" (Pye, 2005, p. 35, emphasis added), have sought to access the everyday interactional doings of particular organizational members claiming the category description of "leader." Jonathon Clifton (2006) drew on CA to argue that when we link analysis of conversational turns at talk to "wider social theorizing, notably a social constructivist approach to leadership and the construction of reality," we can discern the "seen but unnoticed machinery of talk with which leadership is enacted" (p. 202) and particular organizational forms socially constructed. In this case, the specific machinery of formulations was shown to shape subsequent sensemaking efforts and, importantly, when there was a challenge to a formulation, then "reality [was] once again open to negotiation" (Clifton, 2006, p. 213). This is also acutely glimpsed in another study of a manufacturing company undertaken by Samra-Fredericks (2003b). In this case, one component of leadership processes, strategy development or strategizing, was explored through observing and audio-recording a group of senior managers' routines over a 12-month period. As it transpired, the study was able to trace their constitution of "facts" around two organizational facets, further fine-tuned into weaknesses: one concerned a lack of information technology (IT) capability and the second, a weakness in strategic thinking.

Both weaknesses were shown to be socially and culturally (Samra-Fredericks, 2003b) *and* politically and institutionally (Samra-Fredericks, 2005a) constructed in intricate, complex, and dynamic ways during the ebb and flow of human talk-based interaction over a period of time. Eventual material outcomes included decisions to invest in IT and to terminate the employment of others (in particular, one executive director). In many ways it was a study revealing the complex ways in which organizational members "construct, filter, frame, create facticity . . . and render the subjective into something more tangible" (Weick, 1995, p. 14). To glimpse *how* a strategist undertook this task and shaped the attention of others accordingly, one extract (from Samra-Fredericks, 2003b) is reproduced here. It concisely illustrates six particular features: speaking forms of knowledge; mitigation and observation of the protocols of human interaction (the moral order); question and query; displaying appropriate emotion; deploying metaphors; and putting history "to work" (Samra-Fredericks, 2003b). Knowing *when* to do this (the "right time") is, of course, a tacit form of *knowing*, which also brings into the analytic frame the relational element for effective performance and identity assembly (Deetz, 1992; Gergen, 1985; Shotter & Gergen, 1989; Shotter, 1993). (See Appendix 7.1 for simplified transcription conventions.)

Strategist A	=can I [come back to *simple* manufacturing man's
MD	[yeah
Strategist A	language and and (.) and leave
5	the intelligent stuff so we'll keep it at manufacturing level urm (.) I would query why we need another (.) analyst for two reasons number one it is one of
10	the other stated policies that you told me about (.) that the stated policy is that the *manager* and the user department will develop the expertise and
15	systems understanding necessary to identify their requirements and to be able to spell out what they need=
Strategist B	=um um
20 **Strategist A**	given that why the *hell do you need an analyst* number two (.) our bottleneck is obviously right now and it looks as though [glances at collection of papers]
25	it has been for some time and our skill shortage and our bottleneck is programming (.) so if you get another analyst all you do is increase the work on the
30	bottleneck=
MD	=um=
Strategist A	=which can't process it anyway=
MD	=yeah um
Strategist B	yeah but I think
35 **MD**	I think thats a [fair
Strategist A	[now you've got two analysts=
MD	=thats a fair point=

Although the talk here is about a seemingly trivial matter, it was shown to be transformed into an opportunity by strategist A (hereafter, SA) to draw others' attention to his perception of more significant problems or "the facts" (the weaknesses). Brief comment on *how* this was accomplished follows. We begin with his self-description as a "simple manufacturing man"; in this instance, it swiftly displaced the prior, technically informed monologue by strategist C. In terms of the six features (italicized): Reasonableness is initially linguistically conveyed through *mitigation* ("can I"). Then, through what may seem like a self-depreciating comment ("simple manufacturing man's"), he *queries* (line 7) what he has been told, and thus the *past* is mundanely invoked. On this simple basis he warrants his switch to a more assertive style and conveys both frustration and worry, leading to his more overt expression of anger (lines 20–21). This *emotional* display is further legitimated through a rational component in which it is shown that what he was told was not happening and also through articulating the belief that analysts add to the bottleneck. This contested the *typified knowledge* held by strategist B (SB; his colleague) regarding what analysts and programmers do. Then, in describing a situation in which analysts "increase the work on bottlenecks" (*metaphorical* expression) and in which inefficiencies had apparently been tolerated for some time (lines 22–23, the past again), a *moral* responsibility is also evoked. Indeed, here is the subtle everyday and usually elusive speaking about what is right (e.g., "manufacturing man's language") and wrong ("intelligent stuff") or good (solving problems) and bad (tolerating inefficiencies) management. The latter two aspects are not easily displaced, as they constitute a form of "conventional wisdom" within MM/OS. It is also just one small example of the everyday speaking of an economic sensibility informing (socially and politically constructing) strategic/management practice, which Foucauldians would term a "*discourse* of efficiency." So, too, in a taken-for-granted fashion, this *discourse* exudes a range of effects, including subjective identity (see Knights & Morgan, 1991, and Samra-Fredericks, 2005a, for empirical detail). On an everyday level, these *discourses*, as "ways of reasoning/constituting the social world" (Alvesson & Karreman, 2000, p. 1125), are linguistically invoked and put to work as glimpsed here by individuals during their efforts to make meaning with others.

Another feature touched on in the original study was the use of personal pronouns such as *I* and *you*. Although they, too, may appear to be a trivial linguistic resource, they are significant in terms of indexing and interpersonally positioning self and others, thereby constructing social and political relations (Samra-Fredericks, 1996, 2003b, 2005a). Indeed, CA studies have shown that *we* (line 5) and *our* (line 22) are fundamental resources for constituting an identity, task and setting (Drew & Sorjonen, 1997, within institutions; Malone, 1997, more generally). *I* is active and evokes responsibility, and here it also positioned *you* (SB) as failing to ensure that practice follows policy. In speaking in this way and utilizing personal pronouns, SA was shown to spatially and temporally locate SB in a specific network of relations and artifacts (here, the policy). As each of the six features were further elaborated across other extracts in the original study, a sense of how this "minor move" laminated onto the next "minor move" and so on became clear. In other words, we saw *how* SA undertook *sensemaking* and *sense giving* (influencing) and integrally assembled that *plausible story/narrative* about the past and what they needed to do to project a viable sense of organization into the future. Indeed, in this everyday interactional fashion, a self, others, and objects were made meaningful and thus constituted. Integral to this was their combining and expressing culturally derived knowledges of "typified" organizational "categories," as Berger and Luckmann (1967; see also Boden, 1994, p. 134) point out. Here, selection of lexemes, such as *policies, user department*, and *bottlenecks*, were crucial resources in constituting institution or "organization"; they are "activity bound," with rights and obligations, in turn, furnishing those constitutive elements (Hester & Eglin, 1997). In

ethnomethodological terms, these typified categories . . . allowed these strategists to sensemake, to reason and ultimately, to deploy a rhetoric to 'do' organization (Bittner, 1973; Garfinkel, 1967) . . . [and that] a Schutzian (1932/1972) principle which interested Garfinkel was where we are deemed to 'hold' knowledge in 'typified forms' but that it is incomplete and progressively clarified and expanded during interaction. (Samra-Fredericks, 2003b, p. 155)

Simply, in the preceding excerpt, this knowledge concerned what IT analysts and programmers do. In another extract, a "contest" over whose knowledge and expertise was to "count" was played out through referral to the "membership category" (Sacks, 1992) of accountants. This was set against what strategists *should* do. In speaking as he did, SA effectively constituted a "reality" in which particular "human resources were to be valued 'more than' another group" (2003b, p. 155); these evaluations were based on their "apparent contribution to organizational effectiveness and efficiencies" (2003b, p. 155) and often subtly conveyed in ways glimpsed in the extract here (see Samra-Fredericks, 2003b; and, on emotional assembly, 2004a). Overall, "through talking as they did (negotiating, contesting, evaluating, blaming, etc.), the strategists I observed and recorded constituted a specific sense of organization with which they then 'worked' (Berger & Luckmann, 1967; Bittner, 1973; also Boden, 1994; Chia, 1995, 1996, 2000)" (Samra-Fredericks, 2003b, p. 167).

This sense of organization had specific material consequences; one was the termination of another's employment. In addition, if in broad terms the contention is that it is "through discourse [that] individual subjectivity, social institutions and social processes are defined, constituted and contested" (Thomas & Linstead, 2002, p. 75), a later publication (Samra-Fredericks, 2005a) subjected the same empirical materials to a more *critical* rendering. It was in this later publication that Habermas's (1979, 1984) theory of communicative action and Foucault's (1980) notion of power discourse—in particular, the capillary image of power relations that Deetz and Mumby (e.g., 1995) have articulated so well—was deployed (see also Forester, 1992, in which analysis of 12 turns at talk between professionals highlighted the intricate ways in which speakers reproduced social and political relations and socially constructed "problems" at hand).

The social, cultural, economic, political, and institutionally imbued construction of problems and solutions that a *discourse* of strategy makes available was empirically traced in this 2005a publication. More specifically, the everyday constitution of seven *power effects* (Knights & Morgan, 1991) were empirically traced across detailed extracts of members' talk in interaction. This included the ways SA and his colleagues *relationally constituted* themselves as managerial elites and/or strategists (gendered/masculine) and the phenomena we label (and thus come to know) as "strategy documents" and other similar objects/artifacts or tasks. In sum, it was a study of *how power is intricately exercised* through analysis of the specialist vocabularies, techniques, practices, and procedures that constitute effects such as the reproduction of masculine manager identities. Equally, the earlier noted issue of "linkages," alongside countering misunderstandings about being rooted in the "micro," was addressed, too. In sum, the "social construction of what?" (Hacking, 1999) is an important question that this *Handbook* explores. In addition, some researchers, given their backgrounds, interests, and so forth, have also explicitly examined the power effects arising from our taken-for-granted social constructions of this-and-that. By drawing on social constructionist thinking and ideas, we may begin to discern, for example, the complexities whereby "power produces: it produces reality; it produces domains of objects and rituals of truth" (Foucault, 1977, p. 194). In addition, when such studies are taken into classrooms and board rooms, then others, too, can consider the ways in which our world is routinely (re)produced, whether to advantage or not (Samra-Fredericks, 2003a).

Conclusion

The three "modes," or intellectual traditions, selected here reflect aspects of social constructionist thinking and are a tiny proportion of studies within the diverse MM/OS field. It is also important to note that they are filtered through my interests, knowledge, and understandings. Nevertheless, I hope that I have conveyed a sense of the kinds of research undertaken on the complex ways organizational members go about their daily business of work, thereby constituting that world of work (organizing/managing/leading). Each mode also variously conveys allegiance to particular social constructionist tenets in terms of embracing the performative and formative view of language and the centrality of meaning-making that constitutes self-identities, together with those spectacular, apparently out-there, phenomena such as organizational weaknesses, change projects and "organization." Furthermore, as inquiry shifts from interviews to efforts to access the *interactional or relational* aspect happening at that moment among organizational members, further understandings will become available—in particular, and when allied with audio recordings, *how* organizational members intricately and *inter*actively construct, for example, "facts" and associated forms of "organization" and/or make visible those taken-for-granted reified phenomena such as leadership or strategy. In sum, as Hosking (2006, p. 57) observes, to study organizing processes requires placing at center stage the interactional or relational element to see "persons and worlds . . . [being] (re)constructed, actively maintained, and changed."

Finally, I hope this chapter also conveys my interest in continuing conversations with alternative disciplines in order to extend our understandings of what human beings "do" to legitimately claim membership in, *and* simultaneously construct (in my case) a viable notion of organization management and leadership. Equally, the act of writing this chapter is an attempt to claim membership of (and thus, also constitute) "academia." Furthermore, as Paul Atkinson (1990, p. 2) noted with regard to sociological texts, MM/OS texts are also "not matters of neutral report: the conventions of text and rhetoric are among the ways in which reality is constructed."

• Appendix 7.1. Transcription Symbols (Simplified)

MD, managing director

[signals interruption

(.) signals a brief pause

[square brackets] contain references to names of people, financial figures, products etc. *or* transcriber is unsure of exact word spoken

E::longated sound

= signals immediate latching on

italic signals emphasis

underlining signals rising intonation

• Notes

1. This also applies to debates between social constructionism and critical realism in organization studies, as a recent "call for papers" for a Summer 2009 special issue of *Organization Studies* attests to. Another "debate" usefully summarized as "point–counterpoint" is one between positivism and social constructionism and is undertaken by Donaldson (2003) and Czarniawska (2003).

2. For example, a series of conferences on organizational discourse have been held since the mid-1990s, and (more or less) the same group of organizers have been at the forefront of journal special issues and, more recently, a handbook (Grant, Hardy, Oswick, & Putman, 2004; Oswick, Kennoy, & Grant, 2000; see also Westwood & Linstead, 2001).

3. Debates over social constructivism and how it differs from social constructionism or the extent to which there is an overriding emphasis on individuals and phenomena such as mind maps or schemata in the former are necessarily set aside here.

4. Placing human beings and their doings center stage within MM/OS is ostensibly the domain of researchers often located within the subfield of organizational behavior (OB). There are, though, pockets of activity within the subfields of marketing, accounting, entrepreneurship, and information systems that also centralize human beings' doings, as well as embracing social constructionist thinking. Some explicitly draw on the "critical tradition" (see, e.g., Alvesson & Willmott, 1992, 1996). Overall, what we shall discern here is that, although some feel that social constructionist thinking still remains "largely absent . . . were it to be present—these subjects [subfields] would be significantly re-constructed" (Hosking & McNamee, 2006, p. 9), it is gaining ground. It is also finding its way into textbooks for MM/OS students (Watson, 2002; see also Tietze, Cohen, & Musson, 2003).

5. For example, in Carol Rigg's (2005, p. 63) study of "ongoing reality construction through retrospective sensemaking," the rich quotes reproduced from recorded interviews suggest three other insightful analytic routes, too: First, we could easily scrutinize the ways in which metaphor and language more generally do or do not assist the constitution of particular worldviews therein. Second, the ways in which organizational members construct workplace constraint or hierarchy (*what* is socially constructed) as we encounter their talk are also discernible. Indeed, their talk momentarily gave shape or "visibility" (Karreman & Alvesson, 2001, pp. 79–80) to such aspects of "organization." Another integral feature was members' observance of several divergent *discourses* (emphasis explained shortly). Rigg observes that one organizational member's MSc course had "introduced him to wider managerial (marketing) discourse which provoked him both to personally employ new discursive resources and to try to affect those of his organization colleagues" (Rigg, 2005, p. 72). Here a critical analysis would be a third route that could also be widened to consider the role of business and management schools in equipping students and practitioners in particular ways (Alvesson & Willmott, 1992, 1996; Grey & Willmott, 2005).

6. Other approaches set aside but that also have social constructionist tenets threaded through include dramaturgy and structurationist studies. Indeed, Giddens's (1979, 1984) theory of structuration has inspired a number of studies aiming to examine the ways ritual and routine language use (re)produce aspects of our world. In addition, a potential fourth intellectual tradition—sensemaking—also had to be set aside due to space issues. As an approach in which "to talk about sensemaking is to talk about reality as an ongoing accomplishment" (Weick, 1995, p. 15), its flipside—*sensegiving*, defined as an influencing process—may also explain why leadership studies have employed this schema (e.g., Pye, 2005). This is apparent in Sally Maitlis's (2005, p. 38) study of top managers, but it also demonstrated that when there is a *collapse* of

sensemaking, then instability or, literally, a lack of "organization" arises. In other words, organization could not be neatly (efficiently) accomplished (see also Weick, 2001; arguably, notions of efficiency, effectiveness, control, prediction, etc., are long-standing watchwords within the field of MM/OS).

7. Significantly, too, Symon (2005) comments that "cultural, organizational and situational discourses" allow possibilities for reinvention, and this echoes Alvesson and Willmott's (2002) notion of "micro-emancipation." It is, however, beyond the scope of this chapter to delve into debates concerning whether, and to what extent, efforts invested to expose the taken-for-granted socially constructed nature of our world open up possibilities for realizing more egalitarian forms of "organizing": It remains an issue within the growing critical management studies field (see Alvesson & Willmott, 1992, 1996) where, for example, Hugh Willmott (1994) contends that the potential of social constructionist research remains to be exploited in these terms (pedagogic possibilities have been tentatively proposed by Samra-Fredericks, 2003a).

• References

Alvesson, M. (1996). *Communication, power and organization*. Berlin: Walter de Gruyter.

Alvesson, M., & Karreman, D. (2000). Varieties of discourse: On the study of organizations through discourse analysis. *Human Relations, 53*(9), 1125–1149.

Alvesson, M., & Willmott, H. (Eds.). (1992). *Critical management studies*. London: Sage.

Alvesson, M., & Willmott, H. (1996). *Making sense of management: A critical introduction*. London: Sage.

Alvesson, M., & Willmott, H. (2002). Identity regulation as organizational control: Producing the appropriate individual. *Journal of Management Studies, 39*(5), 619–644.

Andersen, D. L. (2005). What you'll say is . . . : Represented voice in organization change discourse. *Journal of Organizational Change Management, 18*(1), 63–77.

Arminen, I. (2005). *Institutional interaction: Studies of talk at work*. Aldershot, UK: Ashgate.

Atkinson, P. (1990). *The ethnographic imagination*. London: Routledge.

Austin, J. L. (1981). *How to do things with words*. Oxford, UK: Clarendon Press. (Original work published 1962)

Ball, K., & Wilson, D. C. (2000). Power, control and computer-based performance monitoring: Reper-

toires, resistance and subjectivities. *Organization Studies, 21*(3), 539–565.

Barley, S. R. (1983). Semiotics and the study of occupational and organizational cultures. *Administrative Science Quarterly, 28*, 393–413.

Barley, S. R. (1988). The social construction of a machine: Ritual, superstition, magical thinking and other pragmatic responses to running a CT scanner. In M. Lock & D. Gordon (Eds.), *Knowledge and practice in medicine: Social, cultural and historical approaches* (pp. 497–540). Boston: Kluwer Academic.

Barrett, F. J., Thomas, G. F., & Hocevar, S. P. (1995). The central role of discourse in large-scale change: A social construction perspective. *Journal of Applied Behavioral Science, 31*(3), 352–372.

Berger, P., & Luckmann, T. (1967). *The social construction of reality*. London: Penguin.

Bittner, E. (1973). The concept of organization. In G. Salaman & K. Thompson (Eds.), *People and organizations*. Milton Keynes, UK: Open University Press.

Boden, D. (1994). *The business of talk*. Cambridge, UK: Polity Press.

Boden, D., & Zimmerman, D. H. (Eds.). (1991). *Talk and social structure: Studies in ethnomethodology and conversation analysis*. Cambridge, UK: Polity Press.

Boje, D. M. (1991). The story-telling organization: A study of story performance in an office supply firm. *Administraative Science Quarterly, 36*(1), 106–126.

Boje, D. M. (2001). *Narrative methods for organizational and communication research*. London: Sage.

Bourdieu, P. (1990). *The logic of practice*. Cambridge, UK: Polity Press.

Brewis, J. (2001). Telling it like it is?: Gender, language and organizational theory. In R. Westwood & S. Linstead (Eds.), *The language of organization* (pp. 283–309). London: Sage.

Brown, A. D., & Humphreys, M. (2002). Nostalgia and the narrativization of identity: A Turkish case study. *British Journal of Management, 13*, 141–159.

Brown, M. H. (1986). Sense making and narrative forms: Reality construction in organizations. In L. Thayer (Ed.), *Organizational communication: Emerging perspectives* (Vol. 1, pp. 71–84). Norwood, NJ: Ablex.

Bruner, J. (1990). *Acts of meaning*. Cambridge, MA: Harvard University Press.

Bruni, A., & Gherardi, S. (2002). Omega's story: The heterogeneous engineering of a gendered professional self. In M. Dent & S. Whitehead (Eds.), *Managing professional identities: Knowledge performativity and the "new professional."* London: Routledge.

Chia, R. (1995). From modern to postmodern organizational analysis. *Organization Studies, 16*, 579–604.

Chia, R. (1996). *Organizational analysis as deconstructive practice*. Berlin: Walter de Gruyter.

Chia, R. (1999). A "rhizomic" model of organizational change and transformation: Perspective from a metaphysics of change. *British Journal of Management, 10*, 209–229.

Chia, R. (2000). Discourse analysis as organizational analysis. *Organization, 7*(3), 513–518.

Chreim, S. (2006). Managerial frames and institutional discourses of change: Employee appropriation and resistance. *Organization Studies, 27*(9), 1261–1287.

Cicourel, A. (1981). Notes on the integration of micro- and macro-levels of analysis. In K. Knorr-Cetina & A. Cicourel (Eds.), *Advances in social theory and methodology: Towards an integration of micro- and macro-sociologies* (pp. 51–80). Boston: Routledge & Kegan Paul.

Clark, B. R. (1972). The organizational saga in higher education. *Administrative Science Quarterly, 17*, 178–184.

Clifton, J. (2006). A conversation analytical approach to business communication: The case of leadership. *Journal of Business Communication, 43*(3), 202–219.

Cohen, L., Duberley, J., & Mallon, M. (2004). Social constructionism in the study of career: Accessing the parts that other approaches cannot reach. *Journal of Vocational Behavior, 64*, 407–422.

Cooper, R., & Burrell, G. (1988). Modernism, postmodernism and organizational analysis. *Organization Studies, 9*, 91–112.

Cooren, F. (1999). Applying socio-semiotics to organizational communication: A new approach. *Management Communication Quarterly, 13*, 294–304.

Czarniawska, B. (1997). *Narrating the organization: Dramas of institutional identity.* Chicago: University of Chicago Press.

Czarniawska, B. (1998). *A narrative approach to organization studies.* Thousand Oaks, CA: Sage.

Czarniawska, B. (1999). *Writing management: Organization theory as a literary genre.* Oxford, UK: Oxford University Press.

Czarniawska, B. (2003). Social constructionism and organization studies. In R. Westwood & C. Stewart (Eds.), *Debating organization: Point-counterpoint in organization studies.* Malden, MA: Blackwell.

Dalton, M. (1959). *Men who manage: Fusions of feeling and theory in administration.* New York: Wiley.

Deetz, S. A. (1992). *Democracy in an age of corporate colonization: Developments in communication and the politics of everyday life.* Albany: State University of New York Press.

Deetz, S. A. (1994). The micro-politics of identity formation in the workplace: The case of a knowledge intensive firm. *Human Studies, 17*, 23–44.

Deetz, S. A., & Mumby, D. K. (1995). Power discourse and the workplace: Reclaiming the critical tradition. In C. Hardy (Ed.), *Power and politics in organizations.* Aldershot, UK: Dartmouth Publishing.

Derrida, J. (1988). *Limited, inc.* Chicago: Northwestern University Press.

Donaldson, L. (2003). Position statement for positivism. In R. Westwood & C. Stewart (Eds.), *Debating organization: Point-counterpoint in organization studies.* Malden, MA: Blackwell.

Downing, S. J. (1993). *The social construction of strategy: networking interaction skills amongst business owners.* Unpublished doctoral dissertation, Brunel University, West London, United Kingdom.

Downing, S. J. (2005). The social construction of entrepreneurship: Narrative and dramatistic processes in the co-production of organizations and identities. *Entrepreneurship Theory and Practice, 19*, 185–204.

Drew, P., & Heritage, J. (Eds.). (1992). *Talk at work: Interaction in institutional settings.* Cambridge, UK: Cambridge University Press.

Drew, P., & Sorjonen, M.-L. (1997). Institutional dialogue. In D. A. van Dijk (Ed.), *Discourse as social interaction* (pp. 92–118). London: Sage.

Du Gay, P. (1996). *Consumption and identity at work.* London: Sage.

Fairhurst, G. T. (2004). Textuality and agency in interaction analysis. *Organization, 11*(3), 335–353.

Fisher, W. (1987). *Human communication as narration: Toward a philosophy of reason, value and action.* Columbia: University of South Carolina Press.

Fletcher, D. (2006). Entrepreneurial processes and the social construction of opportunity. *Entrepreneirship and Regional Development, 18*, 421–440.

Ford, J. D., & Ford, L. W. (2003). Conversations and the authoring of change. In D. Holman & R. Thorpe (Eds.), *Management and language: The manager as practical author* (pp. 141–156). London: Sage.

Forester, J. (1992). Critical ethnography: On field work in a Habermasian way. In M. Alvesson & H. Willmott (Eds.), *Critical management studies* (pp. 46–65). London: Sage.

Forray, J. M., & Woodilla, J. (2002). Temporal spans in talk: Doing consistency to construct fair organization. *Organization Studies, 23*(6), 899–917.

Foucault, M. (1972). *The archeology of knowledge.* London: Routledge.

Foucault, M. (1977). *The history of sexuality.* Harmondsworth, UK: Penguin.

Foucault, M. (1980). *Power/knowledge: Selected interviews and other writings.* Brighton, UK: Harvester.

Gabriel, Y. (1995). The unmanaged organization: Stories, fantasy and subjectivity. *Organization Studies, 16*, 477–501.

Gabriel, Y. (1998). The use of stories. In G. Symon & C. Cassell (Eds.), *Qualitative methods and analysis in organizational research: A practical guide* (pp. 135–160). Thousand Oaks, CA: Sage.

Gabriel, Y. (1999). Beyond happy families: A critical re-evaluation of the control–resistance–identity triangle. *Human Relation, 52*, 179–203.

Gabriel, Y. (2000). *Storytelling in organizations: Facts, fictions and fantasies.* Oxford, UK: Oxford University Press.

Garfinkel, H. (1967). *Studies in ethnomethodology.* Englewood Cliffs, NJ: Prentice Hall.

Gergen, K. J. (1994). *Toward transformation in social knowledge.* London: Sage.

Gergen, K. J. (1985). The social constructionist movement in modern psychology. *American Psychologist, 40,* 266–275.

Gergen, K. J., & Thatchenkery, T. (2006). Organizational science and the promises of postmodernism. In D. M. Hosking & S. McNamee (Eds.), *The social construction of organization.* Ljubljana, Slovenia: Liber & Copenhagen Business School Press.

Giddens, A. (1979). *Central problems in social theory: Action, structure and contradiction in social analysis.* London: Macmillan.

Giddens, A. (1984). *The constitution of society.* Oxford, UK: Polity Press/Blackwell.

Gioia, D. A., & Chittipeddi, K. (1991). Sensemaking and sensegiving in strategic change initiation. *Strategic Management Journal, 12*(6), 433–448.

Grant, D., Hardy, C., Oswick, C., & Putman, L. (Eds.). (2004). *The Sage handbook of organizational discourse.* London: Sage.

Grant, D., Michelson, G., Oswick, C., & Wailes, N. (2005). Guest Editorial: Discourse and organizational change [Editorial]. *Journal of Organizational Change Management, 18*(1), 6–15.

Grey, C., & Willmott, H. (Eds.). (2005). *Critical management studies: A reader.* Oxford, UK: Oxford University Press.

Habermas, J. (1972). *Knowledge and human interest.* London: Heinemann.

Habermas, J. (1979). *Communication and the evolution of society* Boston: Beacon Press.

Habermas, J. (1984). *The theory of communicative action, reason and the rationalization of society* (Vol. 1). Cambridge, UK: Polity Press.

Hacking, I. (1999). *The social construction of what?* Cambridge, MA: Harvard University Press.

Hardy, C., Grant, D., Keenoy, T., Oswick, C., & Phillips, N. (Guest Eds.). (2004). Organizational Discourse [Special issue]. *Organization Studies, 25*(1).

Heracleous, L., & Barrett, M. (2001). Organizational change as discourse: Communicative actions and deep structures in the context of information technology implementation. *Academy of Management Journal, 44*(1), 755–778.

Heritage, J. (1984). *Garfinkel and ethnomethodology.* Cambridge, UK: Polity Press.

Heritage, J. (1997). Conversation analysis and institutional talk: Analyzing data. In D. Silverman (Ed.), *Qualitative research: Theory, method and practice* (pp. 161–182). London: Sage.

Hester, S., & Eglin, P. (1997). *Culture in action: Studies in membership categorization analysis.* Lanham, MD: International Institute for Ethnomethodology and University Press of America.

Holstein, J., & Gubruim, J. (1997). Active interviewing. In D. Silverman (Ed.), *Qualitative research: Theory, methods and practice* (pp. 113–129). London: Sage.

Holstein, J., & Gubrium, J. (2000). *The self we live by: Narrative identity in a postmodern world.* New York: Oxford University Press.

Hosking, D. M. (2006). Organizations, organizing, and related concepts of change. In D. M. Hosking & S. McNamee (Eds.), *The social construction of organization* (pp. 54–68). Ljubljana, Slovenia: Liber & Copenhagen Business School Press.

Hosking, D. M., & McNamee, S. (Eds.). (2006). *The social construction of organization,* Ljubljana, Slovenia: Liber & Copenhagen Business School Press.

Iedema, R., Degeling, P., Braithwaite, J., & White, L. (2004). It's an interesting conversation I'm hearing: The doctor as manager. *Organization Studies, 25*(1), 15–33.

Iedema, R., Rhodes, C., & Scheeres, H. (2006). Surveillance, resistance, observance: Exploring the teleo-affective volatility of workplace interaction. *Organization Studies, 27*(8), 1111–1130.

Jackall, R. (1988). *Moral mazes: The world of corporate managers.* New York: Oxford University Press.

Jacques, R. (1996). *Manufacturing the employee: Management knowledge from the 19th to the 21st centuries.* London: Sage.

Karreman, D., & Alvesson, M. (2001). Making newsmakers: Conversational identity at work. *Organization Studies, 22*(1), 59–89.

Kaye, M. (1995). Organizational myths as storytelling in communication management: A conceptual framework for learning an organization's culture. *Journal of the Australian and New Zealand Academy of Management, 1,* 1–13.

Knights, D. (1992). Changing spaces: The disruptive impact of a new epistemological location for the study of management. *Academy of Management Review, 17*(3), 514–536.

Knights, D., & McCabe, D. (1998). What happens when the phone goes wild? Staff, stress and spaces for escape in a BPR telephone banking work regime. *Journal of Management Studies, 35,* 163–194.

Knights, D., & Morgan, G. (1991). Corporate strategy, organizations and subjectivity: A critique. *Organization Studies, 12*(2), 251–273.

Knights, D., & Willmott, H. (1993). "It's a very foreign discipline": The genesis of expenses control in a mutual life assurance company. *British Journal of Management, 4,* 1–18.

Kondo, D. (1990). *Crafting selves: Power, gender and discourses of identity in a Japanese workplace.* Chicago: University of Chicago Press.

Kotter, J. P. (1982). *The general manager.* New York: Free Press.

Kuhn, T. (2006). A demented work ethic and a lifestyle firm: Discourse, identity and workplace time commitments. *Organization Studies, 27*(9), 1339–1358.

Kunda, G. (1992). *Engineering culture: Control and commitment in a high-tech corporation.* Philadelphia: Temple University Press

Luff, P., Hindmarsh, J., & Heath. C. (Eds.). (2000). *Workplace studies.* Cambridge, UK: Cambridge University Press.

Lyotard, J.-F. (1979). *The postmodern condition: A report*

on knowledge. Manchester, UK: Manchester University Press.

Maitlis, S. (2005). The social processes of organizational sensemaking. *Academy of Management Journal, 48*(1), 21–49.

Makitalo, A., & Saljo, R. (2002). Talk in institutional context and institutional context in talk: Categories as situated practices. *Text, 22*(1), 57–82.

Malone, M. J. (1997). *Worlds of talk: The presentation of self in everyday conversations.* Oxford, UK: Blackwell.

Mangham, I. L. (1986). *Power and performance in organizations: An exploration of executive process.* Oxford, UK: Blackwell.

Mangham, I. L. (1998). Emotional discourse in organizations. In D. Grant, T. Keenoy, & C. Oswick (Eds.), *Discourse + organization.* London: Sage.

Mehan, H. (1991). The school's work of sorting students. In D. Boden & D. Zimmerman (Eds.), *Talk and social structure: Studies in ethnomethodology and conversation analysis* (pp. 71–90). Cambridge, UK: Polity Press.

Mintzberg, H. (1973). *The nature of managerial work.* New York: Harper & Row.

Molotch, H. L., & Boden, D. (1985). Talking social structure: Discourse, domination and the Watergate hearings. *American Sociological Review, 50,* 273–288.

Morgan, G., & Sturdy, A. (2000). *Beyond organizational change: Structure, discourse and power in UK financial services.* London: Macmillan.

Mumby, D. K. (Ed.). (1993). *Narrative and social control: Critical perspectives.* Newbury Park, CA: Sage.

Mumby, D. K. (1995). The political function of narrative in organizations. In C. Hardy (Ed.), *Power and politics in organizations* (pp. 219–233). Cambridge, UK: Cambridge University Press. (Original work published 1987)

Orr, J. E. (1990). Sharing knowledge, celebrating identity: community memory in a service culture. In D. Middleton & D. Edwards (Eds.), *Collective remembering* (pp. 169–189). London: Sage.

Oswick, C., Keenoy, T., & Grant, D. (2000). Introduction. *Human Relations, 53*(9), 1115–1123.

Parker, I. (1992). *Discourse dynamics.* London: Routledge.

Parker, M. (1997). Dividing organizations and multiplying identities. In K. Hetherington & R. Munro (Eds.), *Ideas of difference* (pp. 114–138). Oxford, UK: Blackwell & The Sociological Review.

Perakyla, A. (1995). *AIDS counselling: Institutional interaction and clinical practice.* Cambridge, UK: Cambridge University Press.

Potter, J., & Wetherell, M. (1987). *Discourse and social psychology: Beyond attitudes and behaviour.* London: Sage.

Powell, W. W., & Di Maggio, P. J. (1991). *The new institutionalism in organizational analysis.* Chicago: University of Chicago Press.

Prasad, P. (2005). *Crafting qualitative research: Working in postpositivist traditions.* New York: Sharpe.

Prasad, P., & Prasad, A. (2000). Stretching the iron cage: The constitution and implications of routine workplace resistance. *Organization Science, 11,* 387–403.

Psathas, G. (1995). *Conversation analysis: The study of talk-in-interaction.* Newbury Park, CA: Sage.

Pye, A. (2005). Leadership and organizing: Sensemaking in action. *Leadership, 1*(1), 31–50.

Reed, M. (2000). The limits of discourse analysis in organizational analysis. *Organization, 7,* 524–530.

Rhodes, C., & Brown, A. D. (2005). Narrative, organizations and research. *International Journal of Management Reviews, 7*(3), 167–188.

Rigg, C. (2005). It's in the way they talk: A discourse analysis of managing in two small businesses. *International Journal of Entrepreneurial Behaviour and Research, 11*(1), 58–75.

Rosen, M. (1985). Breakfast at Spiro's: Dramaturgy and dominance. *Journal of Management, 11,* 31–48.

Rosen, M. (1991). Coming to terms with the field: Understanding and doing organizational ethnography. *Journal of Management Studies, 28,* 1–24.

Sacks, H. (1992). *Lectures on conversation* (Vols. 1 & 2, G. Jefferson, Ed.). Oxford, UK: Blackwell.

Sacks, H., Scheloff, E., & Jefferson, G. (1974). A simplest systematics for the organization of turn-taking for conversation. *Language, 50*(4), 696–735.

Samra-Fredericks, D. (1994). *Organising the past in the present as a way of beginning to construct tomorrow: Talking change and changing talk.* Paper presented at the Standing Conference on Organizational Symbolism, Calgary, Alberta, Canada.

Samra-Fredericks, D. (1996). *The interpersonal management of competing rationalities: A critical ethnography of board level competence for "doing" strategy as spoken in the "face" of change.* Unpublished doctoral thesis, Brunel University, West London, United Kingdom.

Samra-Fredericks, D. (1998). Conversation analysis. In G. Symon & C. Cassell (Eds.), *Qualitative methods and analysis in organizational research: A practical guide.* London: Sage.

Samra-Fredericks, D. (2000). Doing "boards-in-action" research: An ethnographic approach for the capture and analysis of directors' and senior managers' interactive routines. *Corporate Governance: An International Review, 8*(3), 244–257.

Samra-Fredericks, D. (2003a). A proposal for developing a critical pedagogy in management from researching organizational members' everyday practice. *Management Learning, 34*(3), 291–312.

Samra-Fredericks, D. (2003b). Strategizing as lived experience and strategists' everyday efforts to shape strategic direction. *Journal of Management Studies, 40*(1), 141–174.

Samra-Fredericks, D. (2004a). Managerial elites making rhetorical and linguistic "moves" for a moving (emotional) display. *Human Relations, 57*(9), 1103–1143.

Samra-Fredericks, D. (2004b). Talk-in-interaction/conversation analysis. In G. Symon & C. Cassell (Eds.),

The essential guide to qualitative methods in organization studies (pp. 214–227). Thousand Oaks, CA: Sage.

Samra-Frederiks, D. (2004c). Understanding the production of "strategy" and "organization" through talk amongst managerial elites. *Culture and Organization, 10*(2), 125–141.

Samra-Frederiks, D. (2005a). Strategic practice, *discourse,* and the everyday constitution of power effects. *Organization, 12*(6), 803–841.

Samra-Frederiks, D. (2005b, June). *Understanding our world as it happens.* Paper presented at the Organization Studies Summer Workshop, Myronos, Greece.

Sandberg, J. (2001). The constructions of social constructionism. In S.-E. Sjostrand, J. Sandberg, & M. Tyrstrup (Eds.), *Invisible management: The social construction of leadership* (pp. 167–187). London: Thomson.

Sarangi, S., & Roberts, C. (Eds.). (1999). *Talk, work and institutional order: Discourse in medical, mediation and management settings.* Berlin: Mouton de Gruyter.

Schatzki, T. (2005). The sites of organizations. *Organization Studies, 26*(3), 465–484.

Schatzki, T., Knorr-Cetina, K., & von Savigny, E. (2000). *The practice turn in contemporary theory.* London: Routledge.

Shotter, J. (1993). *Conversational realities: The construction of life through language.* Newbury Park, CA: Sage.

Shotter, J., & Gergen, K. (Eds.). (1989). *Texts of identity.* London: Sage.

Silverman, D. (1997). The logics of qualitative research. In G. Miller & R. Dingwall (Eds.), *Context and method in qualitative research* (pp. 12–25). London: Sage.

Silverman, D., & Jones, J. (1973). Getting in: The managed accomplishment of "correct" outcomes. In J. Child (Ed.), *Man and organization: The search for explanation and social relevance* (pp. 63–106). London: Allen & Unwin.

Skoldberg, K. (1994). Tales of change: Public administration, reform and narrative mode. *Organization Science, 5,* 219–238.

Stewart, R. (1983). Managerial behaviour: How research has changed the traditional picture. In M. J. Earl (Ed.), *Perspectives on management* (pp. 82–98). Oxford, UK: Oxford University Press.

Symon, G. (2005). Exploring resistance from a rhetorical perspective. *Organization Studies, 26*(11), 1641–1663.

Thomas, R., & Linstead, A. (2002). Losing the plot? Middle managers and identity. *Organization, 9*(1), 71–93.

Tietze, S. (2005). Discourse as strategic coping resource: Managing the interface between "home" and "work." *Journal of Organizational Change Management, 18,* 48–62.

Tietze, S., Cohen, L., & Musson, G. (2003). *Understanding organizations through language.* London: Sage.

Tsoukas, H. (2000). False dilemmas in organization theory: Realism of social constructivism. *Organization, 7*(3), 531–535.

Tsoukas, H. (2001). Re-viewing organization. *Human Relations, 54*(1), 7–12.

Tsoukas, H. (2005). Afterword: Why language matters in the analysis of organizational change. *Journal of Organizational Change Management, 18*(1), 96–104.

Vaara, E. (2002). On the discursive construction of success/failure in narrative of post-merger integration. *Organization Studies, 23*(2), 211–248.

Van Maanen, J. (1973). Observations on the making of policemen. *Human Organization, 32,* 407–418.

Van Maanen, J. (1978). The asshole. In P. K. Manning & J. Van Maanen (Eds.), *Policing* (pp. 221–238). New York: Random House.

Vygotsky, L. (1981). The genesis of higher mental functions. In J. V. Wertsch (Ed.), *The concept of activity in Soviet psychology.* Armonk, NY: Sharpe.

Wajcman, J., & Martin, B. (2002). Narratives of identity in modern management: The corrosion of gender difference? *Sociology, 36*(4), 985–1002.

Watson, T. J. (1994). *In search of management: Culture, chaos and control in managerial work.* Routledge: London.

Watson, T. J. (1995). Rhetoric, discourse and argument in organizational sense making: A reflexive tale. *Organization Studies, 16*(5), 805–821.

Watson, T. J. (2002). *Organizing and managing work.* Harlow, UK: Prentice Hall.

Watson, T. J., & Harris, P. (1999). *The emergent manager.* London: Sage.

Weick, K. E. (1995). *Sensemaking in organizations.* Thousand Oaks, CA: Sage.

Weick, K. E. (2001). *Making sense of the organization.* Oxford, UK: Blackwell.

Weick, K. E., & Browning, L. (1986). Argument and narration in organizational communication. *Journal of Management, 12,* 243–260.

Westwood, R., & Linstead, S. (Eds.). (2001). *The language of organizations.* London: Sage.

Willmott, H. (1994). Social constructionism and communication studies: Hearing the conversation but losing the dialogue. In S. A. Deetz (Ed.), *Communication yearbook.* Thousand Oaks, CA: Sage.

Wittgenstein, L. (1968). *Philosophical investigations.* Oxford, UK: Blackwell.

Woodilla, J. (1998). Workplace conversations: The text of organizing. In D. Grant, T. Keenoy, & C. Oswick (Eds.), *Discourse and organization* (pp. 31–50). London: Sage.

CHAPTER 8

Critical Constructionism in Nursing Research

● **Joanna Latimer**

V|ery little nursing research examines how nurses are implicated in the social construction of health care. Some research in nursing explores the context of nursing practice as socially constructed, particularly in terms of how nurses' practices are somehow determined by their structural location. Some nursing researchers also seem to assert that there are, in any context, multiple possibilities for interpretation and that these, particularly the subjective perspective of patients and nurses, need to be taken into account when defining what nursing is or what patients need. In order to gather evidence of how nursing is socially determined or of the ways in which phenomena can be differently viewed, nursing researchers have applied many qualitative styles, such as narrative analysis and grounded theory. But the mainstream qualitative tradition in nursing research, particu-

larly when it draws on ideas that come from phenomenology, is caught by the demand for *positive* knowledge, together with overly romantic notions about the experiencing individual (Silverman, 1989). The result can be research that is sociologically naive.

In this chapter, I review nursing research that has applied aspects of interpretive methodology. I suggest that much nursing research aims to extend understanding to the representation of multiple realities as matters of interpretation of the meaning of different phenomena. I discuss how the mainstream of qualitative nursing research is concerned with how people, such as nurses and patients, interpret, that is invest, different phenomena, such as an illness or a disease, with subjective meaning. The meanings, like the phenomena, become "matters of fact" (Raffel, 1979); of subjective rather than objective fact, but of fact nonetheless.

This tradition in nursing research is contra to constructionist understandings. Of course, in terms of Anthony Giddens's (1984/1989) understandings of how domination works, it would seem that nursing research that holds itself out as grounded in positive knowledge of phenomena will have less trouble influencing how resources are distributed, what patients need, and how staff should work. That is, it will be more visible to the dominant paradigm in health care research. The difficulty, as Davina Allen (2004b), among others, has helped to show, is that in pursuit of "positive evidence," much qualitative nursing research risks being reductive.

I go on to illuminate an emergent critical constructionist tradition in nursing research. This tradition is concerned with researching the domain of nursing in relation to how nurses are involved in the *construction of the meaning of phenomena* but in the context of a multidisciplinary domain of sometimes competing, sometimes complementary meanings and values (cf. Robinson, Avis, Latimer, & Traynor, 1999). To illuminate this emergent tradition in detail, I focus on several aspects of my own ethnography of nursing in an acute medical unit in a prestigious U.K. teaching hospital, *The Conduct of Care* (Latimer, 2000a). The study took place at a time just before the radical reforms of the U.K. National Health Service in the 1990s and, in a sense, anticipates some of the effects of these reforms. One aim of the book is an "evocation" (Tyler, 1986) of nursing life in contemporary health care services, and practicing nurses' responses to talks about the study suggest that it does indeed resonate with their experiences.

Interpretavism, Constructivism, and Nursing

In the 1960s, 1970s, and 1980s, nurse researchers and medical sociologists increasingly turned their attention to how nursing is socially constructed. The interest here derived in part from a push to realize nursing as a profession that appeared to be very difficult to accomplish, together with an increasing awareness of what has come to be known as the "theory–practice" gap.

Researchers began to apply concepts and theories, as well as methods of inquiry deriving from sociology, to help explain some of the phenomena and politics of nursing practice (e.g., Abbott & Wallace, 1990; Dingwall & Mackintosh, 1978; Salvage, 1985). For example, a proliferation of research examined nursing in relation to theories of occupational socialization (e.g., Hearn, 1982; Melia, 1987; Simpson, 1979) and the division of labor between doctors and nurses (e.g., Hughes, 1988; Stein, 1967) and how this could be understood as a specifically gendered division (e.g., Gamarnikow, 1978).

Many of these themes in research on nursing persist, particularly concerning the gender politics of nursing as a profession in general (e.g., Davies, 1995; see Porter, 1992, for a summary) and of nursing knowledge and theory in particular (e.g., Cash, 1997; Rafferty, 1996). Much of the research in this area draws on conventional sociological perspectives to explain how the world of nursing is socially organized as an effect of nurses' *structural* location, particularly as women, and the stratification of the societies in which they work and practice. In this sense, then, these studies help to illuminate how nursing is socially structured.

In the 1990s another approach to researching nursing began to emerge that claimed to draw heavily on interpretavist and phenomenological understandings in philosophy (e.g., Banonis, 1989; Benner, 1994; Benner & Wrubel, 1989; Darbyshire, 1994; Darbyshire, Diekelmann, & Diekelmann, 1999; Gullickson, 1993; Haase, 1987; Koch, 1995, 1996; Morse, Bottorff, & Hutchinson, 1994; Munhall, 1994). The adoption of the notion of multiple perspectives and, in particular, of *subjective* realities is of concern to nurses, partly because of the development of models of nursing and nursing theories that stressed that the patient in *all his or her needs* is the proper focus of nursing. Thus much of this research is directed at making visible the specificities of nursing as a *field of expertise* that is as concerned with understanding the subjective aspects of illness and its treatment as with knowing about disease processes. This research thus helps to create a knowledge base for nursing that articulates clinical work as concerned with the biophysical, psychosocial, emotional, and spiritual consequences of illness. This emphasis on a more holistic approach extended the clinical remit of nursing and resulted in nursing research that focuses more and more on what illness and its effects *mean* to patients and their families. This emphasis on subjective realities can also be understood as helping to distinguish nursing from medicine. This tradition does not stand against empiricism in any way but sets out to complement a too-restricted view of what patients need and of what nurses do. Patricia Benner (1994), for example, has attempted to make *nursing* expertise "visible" as a unique phenomenon in its own right.

Underpinning these approaches to research in nursing is an idea that research can access realities, either individual or shared, as "lived." The critical and central notion of this tradition is the idea of experience and that experience can be recaptured in such things as interviews. Frequently, interviews are deployed to elicit narratives and stories with the idea that the world of the other can be shared and understood and, critically, that nurses can see things from the perspective of their patients. Nurses and patients in this view are on the same side and, critically, are in dyadic relations with one another; the complex world of health care organization is usually not considered.

There is much debate as to whether "lived experience research" in nursing that claims to be, or that has been assumed to be, in the interpretive tradition does actually incorporate a constructionist approach. The issues at stake include the relationship between experience and reality on the one hand (e.g., Allen & Cloyes, 2005) and the question of reality itself on the other (cf. Crotty, 1996; Lawler, 1998; Paley, 1998). The problem is that much of this research perpetuates distinctions between objective and subjective realities and preserves the idea that there are indeed realities to be had. As John Paley (1998) puts it, much nursing research that adopts constructivist notions ends up as qualitative positivism. Critically, this research is privileging a methodology that lays claims to being a science that can represent meaning as if it is a thing that can be known—as a "what is." In a similar way, nursing research that draws on ever more rigid versions of grounded theory has been held to be attempting to make itself more "positive" and thereby acceptable to the world of health care funding (May, 2003).

In contrast, there is a more critical tradition of nursing research whose roots are firmly in phenomenology, but in a phenomenological tradition that posits the constitutive effects of language and the constructed nature of phenomena. This tradition includes approaches that derive from discourse analysis (e.g., Allen, 1995, 1996; Allen & Hardin, 2001; Traynor, 2006), ethnomethodology (e.g., Allen, 2004a; Bowers, 1992), and anthropology (e.g., Lawler, 1991). Although the approach to social constructionism grows out of the interpretive tradition and the idea that there are always multiple possibilities for meaning, in a sense it goes beyond this tradition. Research in this area is not attempting to simply represent reality as a thing that is socially constructed by setting out to "tell it like it is" (Melia, 1987). Yet there remains a commitment to the idea that what nursing is or what an illness or disease entity is are socially occurring phenomena, effects that may become visible from studying what it is that nurses do and how they talk, interact, and write (Allen, 2004a).

Critical Constructionism in Nursing Research

The rest of the chapter discusses ongoing developments in constructionist research in nursing. I want to call this emergent tradition *critical constructionism* because it makes issues of power explicit as at the same time its protagonists are not simply applying methodologies derived from elsewhere. Research in this field ranges across many different sites, including community nursing and health promotion (Purkis, 1993, 1999); nursing assessment of older people in acute care (Latimer, 1994, 1995, 2000a); nursing care of the dying (May, 1991, 1992); psychiatric nursing (Tilley, 1990); critical care nursing of people with burns (Rudge, 1997, 1999); nursing technology (Sandelowski, 1999, 2000); the history of nursing practice (Nelson, 2000) and nursing education (Rafferty, 1996); and the "new nursing" (Savage, 1995, 2000).[1] Authors here engage with, rather than simply apply, theory and draw together understandings deriving from many different disciplines, including anthropology, social philosophy, and literary, feminist, and psychoanalytical theory.

This emergent critical constructionist tradition treats the world of health care as a political and contested site while at the same time centralizing the importance of engaging people as persons. It is less concerned with resorting to monolithic explanations of practice as an effect of the structural location of nurses than it is with nursing and health care as meaningful and affective processes.

A key feature of this tradition, then, is to offer ways to research nursing as located in sociocultural relations at the same time as nurses, as well as researchers, are featured as persons embedded *in relations* with others. Indeed, otherness is a central concern of nursing practice. This is not to suggest that regard for the other is straightforward. Nurses' engagements with the other cannot be taken for granted; on the contrary, nurses' relations are mediated by many social and cultural influences in ways that nursing theory does not always admit to except in terms of ideas of cultural difference and "diversity." Rather, the *problem* of otherness is a central concern for clinical practice and for the development of appropriate critical methodologies for researching nursing and health care.

It is not that it does not matter whether there is a world that exists independent of those who apprehend it. Rather, what is of concern to this tradition is how, in apprehending the world, people are "making it up." And, critically, it is not that individuals make worlds up on their own; rather, what is of interest is how people construct worlds together or, indeed, against each other.

Recognizing that nursing and researching are both dynamic practices changes everything. First, it means that time, space, and context have to be taken seriously. Second, it means that we have to face up to the fact that nursing and researching are interactive. Third, it means that we will be flying in the face of a dominant research paradigm in health research that stresses the need for knowledge that helps to predict, control, and standardize.

This approach to reality as socially constructed through people's talk and action does not lessen the authenticity of experience; rather, it asserts that experience itself is an *effect*. Within this view, then, there is no one single or even multiple realities to be ascertained and represented. This is not the object of what I am calling *critical social constructionism*. Rather, social constructionism in this critical tradition of constructionist research on nursing is concerned with the matter of how people are "making things up"—for example, what is being figured as good or bad practice or as normal or abnormal bodily states or behavior—as a way of seeing how the social is being organized, what the consequences are, unintended or otherwise, and who (or what) benefits. Some specific aspects of the methodology are now explicated.

The Field: Constructing a Site

Qualitative methodologies usually engage researchers in fieldwork. This term implies an important shift of focus, from the laboratory to everyday life (Berger & Luckman, 1966/1991). It helps to suggest that qualitative research is concerned with "naturally" occurring events and practices, rather than those that are determined by the research, through either a laboratory or another kind of experiment. What is important here is not just that a field of practice is a place that people have feelings about. Rather, the idea of a field helps to remind us that it is *experienced* in very particular and specific ways. In this way the idea of studying a field of practice helps remind us that it is a *lived* space.

However, the term *field* can also be deceptive: It suggests that the field is a given, a bounded space, that can be entered and observed. In contrast, a constructionist approach acknowledges that the field is itself a construct (Turner, 1989). But critical to the way in which the field is approached is the question: What or who is doing the constructing? For example, the way the researcher "enters" the field prefigures the field in ways that affect the researcher's capacity to "represent" it (Coffey & Atkinson, 1995). So the way a field researcher answers the question of who or what is constructing the field depends on his or her methodology.

For example, our approach to the field can acknowledge that, yes, the field is lived, but the parameters that define and dissect the field lie outside the power and control of those living it. Here the field is understood as a function or effect of social structures, such as dominant gender or class relations. Here a researcher may enter the field to "get" accounts of individuals' experiences of the field or to find out more about what they do in terms of restraint, values, and norms. Researchers in this methodological tradition, while acknowledging that the field is lived, enter it as if it is *pre*constructed.

The difficulty here is that the subjects of field research may end up appearing to be cultural dopes (Garfinkel, 1967), at the mercy of those structures that define the field, so that their creativity as *social beings* is effaced. So how can we get a balance? We can understand the idea of a field differently. First, we can understand with ethnomethodologists that the field, like any socially organized space, is the accomplishment of its members (Bittner, 1965). Second, with contemporary anthropologists, such as Clifford Geertz (1993), we can understand that there is not one but many potential fields, which are constituted by the researched individuals as they interact in the course of their daily lives. Third, we can also understand that these actors, as they go about their daily lives, are not free agents. So we can seek ways to make explicit how sociocultural relations position research participants at the same time that they are themselves active participants in those relations. Fourth, we can, with the poststructuralists, understand that the field is made up of different and sometimes competing representations: that there is not one field that means the same to everyone, but multiple possible meanings and interests. If we take this approach to the field, we must pay attention to power effects and how they are accomplished.

The field, defined by the researcher's approach to it, is both a lived and a contested and political site (Silverman & Gubrium, 1989). In this critical constructionist perspective of the field, there are multiple possibilities for interpretation and conduct, which may also be in opposition to one another. In addition, a field does not "exist" but rather is constructed by the very ways in which it is "thought" by a research project. And this way of thinking connects to the very ways in which nursing and health care are being imagined—to the assumptions and taken-for-granted ideas that underpin a research study. To put it another way, a research project "thinks" the field up in ways that have distinct political effects.

The approach in my book *The Conduct of Care* (Latimer, 2000a) brings issues of identity together with those of power and knowledge. My approach was to consider the field as a site made up of the "conditions of possibility" (Foucault, 1976) under which nurses practice and that their practices help reproduce. Siobhan Nelson (1997, 2000, 2001a, 2001b), a historian of nursing practice and knowledge, shows that a critical historical approach can help illuminate how the present is a site underpinned by ideas and attitudes sedimented over time. In contrast, my approach was to do an ethnography of present practice but in what I understood to be a critical location.

As I researched nurses' conduct, I read widely in sociology, anthropology, and social theory. Soon I found I began to ask different kinds of questions from those posed by mainstream nursing research. Rather than seeing nurses as failing to live up to set ideals posited by models and theories of nursing, I asked what nurses' conduct was accomplishing, and why nurses were accomplishing these matters rather than others. That is, what are the wider sociocultural effects in which nurses are embedded? And how does their conduct help reaccomplish those effects? In asking these kinds of questions, my topic, the assessment and care of older people in an acute medical unit, began to emerge as a site of critical interest to nursing and to sociology.

In what follows I show how we can examine and understand nursing practice in all its complexity. I suggest how to situate nurses' conduct not just in relations with patients but in all their relations, both strategic and everyday. In order to do this, I suggest that we have to get *inside* nursing. This means *finding* nursing in the complex interplay between cultural materials and social practices. The approach offered is not the only approach that can be taken to study nursing, or any other domain of social life for that matter, but it is especially useful for illuminating what nurses accomplish and why.

Occasions for Nursing

If, whenever housewives were let into a room, each one, on her own, went to some same spot and started to clean it, one might conclude that the spot surely needed cleaning. On the other hand, one might conclude that there is something about the spot and about the housewives that make the encounter of one by the other an occasion for cleaning, in which case the fact of cleaning, instead of being evidence of dirt, would itself be a phenomenon. (Garfinkel & Sacks, 1986, p. 168)

Taking the assessment and care of older people as my focus, I had put my finger on something of political interest to governments, to professionals, and to older people themselves. The reason is that in the acute medical domain the status of older people *and* of nurses is precarious: For older people, their worthiness and personhood is easily effaced (Cohen, 1994), and nurses' contributions as important and effective work can remain invisible (Goffman, 1958). So my topic was certainly a focus for examining the complex politics of contemporary health care. But it was the ways in which I approached my chosen topic that helped illuminate nurses' assessment and care of older people as a "site."

My objective was not to describe nurses' behavior and then attempt to *evaluate* how older people were assessed and cared for against some preconceived notion about their medical or nursing needs. I do not think this approach is underpinned by an adequate representation of how nursing occurs: Nurses do not simply identify needs and give care or not. To think so would be to be reduce them to rational–cognitive rather than social beings. Rather, as my study proceeded, my objectives extended.

At the same time that I created "thick descriptions" (Geertz, 1983) of nurses' conduct, following Harold Garfinkel and Harvey Sacks I also began to want to understand "occasions for nursing" as *social* phenomena that have to be explained. To put it another way, as I went about my ethnographic work of creating thick descriptions of how nurses conducted occasions for nursing, I began to want to be able to *explain* why nurses conducted "occasions" for nursing in the ways in which they did. So I wanted to understand nursing as something that is not just self-evident or an effect of things that are given in the world but as "done" (Garfinkel, 1967).

For example, I wanted to understand why one staff nurse told me during a morning shift that she did not conduct her care of an elderly woman in line with procedures directed toward preserving dignity because she did not have time, whereas later in the same shift I saw her making time for the medication round. Rather than seeing the staff nurse's behavior as simply contradictory or deviant in some way, I identified a motility (Munro, 1996b, 2005; Latimer, 2007; Latimer & Munro, 2006) to how she was going along and getting along. By *motility* I mean a shifting backward and forward between different spaces of discourse and alternative possibilities for conduct—shifts that shift the world. Competence in this complex, discursive world of nursing requires the capacity to construct oneself and others in terms of different discourses and to be called to one rather than another at the right moment. This is a competence in the ethnomethodological sense and can be understood as "doing member." By "doing member" I am, with Garfinkel (1967), emphasizing how membership and belonging are ongoing accomplishments. In this particular case, motility involves a shift that, through her attachment to the medication round, aligns the nurse with one world, that of heroic, technological medicine, and her detachment from another, that of the mundane world of the old lady and her dignity. This is not to suggest that the moment of alignment to the world that the medication round brings into play completely eradicates the world of an older person's dignity; on the contrary, it remains connected, if dis-

placed, silently available and calling, but only sometimes. I return to this idea of motility later.

Let me recapitulate here. I could have gone along with the ways that many nursing theorists imagine nurses' behavior. By seeing nurses' behavior as a matter of individual choice or of group dynamics rather than considering how practice connects to nurses' socialness, theorists limit explanation of good practice or of "deviations" from good practice. Where the social in nursing research is incorporated, it is often marginalized, for example, by suggesting that nurses' behavior is merely mimetic or attributable to the effects of the structural properties of institutions, such as the dominance of medicine or class and gender divisions.

In contrast, I want to emphasize the idea of conduct rather than behavior. The term *conduct* suggests that the ways in which nurses act and speak reflect aspects of the social. Specifically, the term *conduct* helps keep in mind that what nurses do helps to organize the world, but not in any way that they please. Both Garfinkel (1967) and Foucault (1983) speak of conduct; the former asserts that the social is always a matter of moral form, and the latter asserts that what counts as moral is always being manipulated by technologies of power, or programs for conduct. So the term *conduct* reminds us that nurses are not free to do whatever they will; rather, they are, like all social beings, *conduits* through whose doing and being particular power effects are produced and reproduced.

We can "see" this aspect of conduct in the ways in which nurses, such as the staff nurse previously mentioned, privilege some kinds of patients or work over others. But we can only understand what it is that they are privileging if we attend to what these moments are made to mean. For example, what it is about the medication round and what it is about the old woman that gave the staff nurse permission to privilege the medication round over the old woman's dignity?

We need to construct a research approach that enables us to follow through such moments. But we need to be able to follow them not just to their meanings and their effects, although these are important things to understand. Crucially, we need to be able to understand how the *staff nurse* knows[2] what and whom to privilege and when. We need to be able to identify where *she* gets her permissions from. So the question arises as to how we can go about "knowing" what she knows.

The social, then, has to be understood as about *being* social. Social life is being imagined as the product of interaction rather than individual choice or cognition. But in order to *explain* nurses' conduct, the research needs to encompass all possible points of influence in nurses' work and lives. In order to find these key points of influence, the researcher needs to *get inside* nursing life.

The Priority of Membership

The approach I am featuring presumes that to understand nursing practice there is a recognized need to *go inside*. In making this stand, my own work joins other ethnographies of organization to take the mundane and the taken for granted seriously, because it is through the mundane and the taken for granted, as well as the strategic, that meanings are circulated. In doing participant research the researcher must get inside—but inside whose or what part? How does an ethnographer locate herself? There are, of course, critical issues about self and others in the context of participant observation (Savage, 2000). But I want to press further the issue of *what* we want to get inside.

My concern in this chapter is less with issues of theory and more with making explicit the methods of researching the kind of realities imagined here. Very specifically, one of the ways in which we can observe how social actors together construct reality is by examining their social practices. A crucial social practice in a Euro–American context

is the giving of accounts (Garfinkel, 1967). Giddens (1984/1989), drawing on Schutz (1967), states that in their accounts actors not only draw on "stocks of knowledge" to go on in their everyday interactions but also draw on these same stocks of knowledge to make sense of their actions (and the actions of others), to "make their accounts, offer reasons" (Giddens, 1984/1989, p. 29). "Stocks of knowledge" involve the "interpretative schemes" that are the "modes of typification" that actors use to constitute meaning (p. 29) and are implicated in the communication of meaning. Giddens suggests that although the communication of meaning in interactions is to a certain extent governed by the "structural ordering of sign-systems" (p. 30), "signs exist only *as the medium and outcome of communicative processes in interaction*" (p. 31, emphasis added).

Thus displaying knowledgeability of interpretative schemes and modes of typification is how social actors "do member" (Garfinkel, 1967), but the meanings that things have has to be produced and reproduced through their use. Members thus perform identity through their participation in those communicative processes that produce and reproduce sign systems. This means that we can begin researching social life by examining how people organize their world through modes of typification, such as the distinctions in the medical domain between "social" and "medical," "acute" and "chronic" problems. But we need to go a bit further; we need to be able to identify what it is that they make these typifications mean. As Garfinkel (1967), in his breaching experiments, demonstrates, it may take a moment of deviance to provoke a situation in which taken-for-granted or implicit meanings can come into view. But in many ordinary situations, such as for the staff nurse discussed earlier, matters are not so settled. There are always multiple possibilities, so that knowing how and when to align with one way of doing or seeing rather than another is more complex. It is this motility that gives the apparatus the appearance of stability.

Although we can begin to know what it is that people like the staff nurse know through paying attention to their social practices, such as the giving of accounts (Munro, 1996a), we need to know *how* she knows what to privilege and when. So what we need to be able to unpack is how it is that she knows what to privilege, and when, for example, a medication round over an old woman's dignity.

Getting Inside: Following Cultural Materials

I want to suggest that we can find a way to get inside by following nurses' key cultural materials. It is not enough to simply follow nurses around. Rather than shadowing the main actors, as other ethnographers have done before us (e.g., Mintzburg, 1983), we need to find another way to get inside nursing life. Sandelowski (2000) and Nelson (2000) have both in their different ways justified paying attention to the materials that nurses make and use. But what are nurses' key cultural materials? And how can we follow them? Let's turn to Clifford Geertz for inspiration here.

On arrival in a Balinese village, Geertz (1993) found that he was invisible: Despite his being the guest of the village chief, the local people looked through him as if he were dust or air. This state of affairs went on for a few weeks, and Geertz thought he never would be able to get inside the life of the Balinese village that he and his wife had come to study. One night he was intrigued by the idea of attending a cockfight, partly because cockfights were banned and partly because everywhere he went he saw Balinese men sitting around talking about and fondling their cockerels.

In the middle of the fight, there was a police raid. Geertz and his wife, despite being illustrious guests, joined the villagers and ran, heaving themselves over a wall into someone's yard. By the time the police got there, Geertz and his wife were sitting sipping tea with members of the household. When asked, they denied any knowledge of

the cockfight. The next day everyone Geertz passed in the street acknowledged him, smiling and making jokes; the strange anthropologist shifted from being invisible to being included.

From then on Geertz continued to follow not the Balinese as such but their attachment to cockerels. He followed cockerels through all the practices that the Balinese participated in around them. These practices defined cockerels' significance and included all aspects of the ways the Balinese cared for their cockerels, as well as the organization of the fights themselves.

In his analysis, the love and care of cockerels and of cockfighting emerge as a marginal space—it falls between the old orders of Balinese life and the new republican demands for civilized society, which includes restricting cockfighting to high days and holidays. But the love and care of the birds and the organization of cockfights constitutes a space in which many different layers of Balinese society intersect and interact. Even as it is highly ordered and organized, the domain that the care of cocks and cockfighting constructs reflects and helps to reproduce the organization of Balinese society. Geertz makes vivid that this space is possible only because it is engendered by and engenders extreme and ambiguous emotions. Put baldly, the practices that construct the space of cockfighting are critical because it is through them that the Balinese people perform their distinctiveness and thereby the (re)ordering of the Balinese domain. Specifically, cocks and cockfighting help the Balinese to keep in play all the ambivalence that makes them distinctive. What emerges is that very little about the Balinese is ever completely settled.

Geertz did not go to Bali expecting to make cocks and cockfighting so central: his entry was haphazard, not planned in any way. Anthropologists before him had studied much less mundane activities, such as religious rites. But his focus on cocks and on all the practices that go on around cocks and cockfighting helped Geertz to "get inside" the ambiguities and tensions that construct Balinese life, as opposed to any other kind of life.

Cockerels are key cultural materials for the performance of Balinese identities in all their heterogeneity and complexity.[3] Nurses work on, talk about, observe, and interact not with cockerels but with patients and other people also concerned with patients. Patients rather than cockerels are nurses' cultural material. Patients are nurses' key extensions. This is not to suggest that one discourse makes up the identity of a patient; the meanings patients have for nurses have to be produced through discourses and other practices of distinction. There are flesh-and-blood patients whom nurses handle, touch, serve, administer, speak with, ignore, and move around. And there is also the "virtual" patient, made up of nurses' and other's representations, composed of systems of distinction. And rather than the living, breathing patient simply defining the virtual patient, the virtual patient's identity, to some extent, constitutes how nurses conduct their interactions with the living, breathing patient.

Tracking Patients

In order, then, to get inside nursing life and understand all the points of influence on their conduct, we need to follow patients, not nurses. It is not even a matter of simply following patients; rather, there is a need to *track*[4] all the work of caring for and distinguishing patients to get inside nursing. It is through this work that nurses perform their identity and keep their world in order. But one needs to find a place from which to track patients through all of nurses' practices and through all the points of influence on these practices. In a hospital this place is the bedside.

In traveling to the patient's bedside, I was able to locate myself at the margins and intersections of many aspects of life in a hospital. Doctors, nurses, and many others all come to the bedside, encountering the patient as well as each other. In specifically focusing on the bedsides of older people, I, like Geertz, put my finger on a margin between old orders and new, and between contradictory agendas for conduct. The new included increased managerial demands for enhanced visibility and efficiency that older people in their complexity can threaten. But also within this view the bedside, as a space from which to administer and care for patients, is increasingly constituted as banal and mundane. Relatives, domestics, and care assistants are meant to operate at the bedside of care, not professional nurses. Professional nurses are supposed to perform as decision makers at the nurses' station, poring over notes and charts or staring into screens. At the same time, however, as discussed earlier, professional calls to nurses imply the potentially contradictory demand for an extended kind of health care—more patient-centered, holistic, and individualized. How do nurses settle these apparently contradictory agendas? One way is for them to go to the bedside, not with washbowls or bandages but with a new kind of technology—the nursing process, materialized in forms to be filled in and charts to be displayed.

So in my ethnographic work I travel, like an anthropologist—not to the inside of a mud hut or to a tent in the Sahara Desert but to the bedsides of patients. At the bedside I sit and wait, observing what flows to and from the patient, noting when and how it flows. This flow includes people (such as nurses and doctors) and other materials[5] (such as food, charts, forms to be filled in, chairs, drugs, and machines). What flows from the bedside are excreta and parts of patients (such as blood samples or pots of spit), as well as the *virtual patient* constituted by nurses', doctors,' and others' representations of them. I track the virtual patients through all their "translations" (Callon, 1986; Callon & Latour, 1981) in doctors' ward rounds, nursing handovers, case conferences, and nursing and medical records. Critically, I trace what and who authorizes the flow of materials to and from the bedside. It is in these accounts that one can find *what* has authority, *what* gives permission to privilege one kind of work or one kind of patient over another.

The bedside thus lies in between many facets of hospital life. Nurses, too, lie in between these different facets. The move to the bedside thus helps to make explicit what is usually implicit: that nurses do not have only one part to play. Rather, they are themselves situated in between many parts, many agendas, and many occasions. And they have to work hard to know how to settle matters.

Figuring Patients, Figuring Nursing

Patients are nurses' key materials for the performance of identity, and through these performances nurses help (re)order their world. But patients, as cultural materials, have to be made to *mean*. Their symbolic value cannot be taken for granted, and their meaning does not simply travel from one context to the next. Margaret Sandelowski (2003) suggests ways in which the researcher can understand what materials are made to mean. For example, following Mary Douglas and Baron Isherwood (1986), we can understand what materials mean through examining how they are talked about and used.

I want to press the idea that in a world in which meanings are unsettled, materials have to be *made* to mean; their meanings are not implicit and cannot be taken for granted. The meanings that materials are made to have must be continuously accomplished and sometimes, where meanings are contested, settled.

The virtual *and* the flesh-and-blood patient are key performative materials for nurses. But nurses, in order for patients to be expressive of their identity, have to construct the symbolic meanings that the figure of a patient, or the category of patient, is made to carry. A patient's distinctiveness is not given by, for example, his or her medical diagnosis.

We can identify how patients, or categories of patients, are made to mean things by examining the practices of distinction that

nurses draw on to "figure" patients (cf. Latimer, 1997a). For example:

Charge Nurse: I do tend to leave the geriatric long-term patients to really middle grade nurses with an auxiliary . . . second years, or occasionally first years, depending on the quality of students we have.

Researcher: Why, how do you make that sort of decision? What do you base that on?

Charge Nurse: Well I tend to think that even most of the junior nurses know what basic nursing care is. They tend to know how to wash people, feed people, dress and just sit and listen to the older ladies. And they, I would suspect, would probably be a bit more frightened to look after somebody who's got central lines, IVs [intravenous infusions], although they do get an opportunity to do that as well, with the staff nurse. (Latimer, 2000a, pp. 39–40)

In this account, Charge Nurse is justifying her distribution of the resources at her disposal. Here, then, we are seeing how the flow of resources is authorized. Within contemporary health care in all its managerial demands, this, the justification for the distribution of resources, is central to members' work. For Charge Nurse, the resources at her disposal include the grades of nurses, as well as the things that they do and use. She justifies the ways in which she distributes these resources by associating different kinds of work with different grades of nurse. By a process of association, washing and dressing people is made to seem less difficult than activities concerned with medical technology, such as IVs and central venous lines. In this way, materials such as those connected to washing and dressing (clothes, soap, facecloths, washbowls, baths, and showers) are all distinguished as of less importance than technical or clinical materials (such as IV infusions and central venous pressure lines). Similarly, by association, the identity of one category of patient—"long-term geriatrics"—is being figured. Long-term geriatric patients who only need bathing and washing, rather than medical technology, are downgraded. This "constituting of classes" (Latimer, 1997b, 2000a) of persons, work, and things is continuously accomplished; it is what helps to keep the medical domain in order.

The symbolic meaning of different patients and different categories of patients is accomplished through these kinds of processes of association. By association, materials, such as patients' virtual identities, are thus made to mean at the same time as they also give meaning. Nurses perform their identity not just through talk but through the materials they work with because of the meanings they make these materials have. To be simplistic for a moment, one of the ways in which nurses perform a hierarchy is through the kinds of materials they are permitted to use and work with, as we can see from the preceding quote from Charge Nurse. The kinds of patients a nurse is permitted to work with helps signify his or her identity in the hierarchy. But the meanings that patients are made to have are themselves continuously accomplished through nurses' practices of distinction, such as Charge Nurse's.

In performing these hierarchies, nurses, like Charge Nurse, are of course drawing on what is already prefigured (Strathern, 1992): the asymmetrical relation between technology and other kinds of cultural material. Drawing on this relation is what makes Charge Nurse's move effective. But in doing this, in drawing on this relation, Charge Nurse is reproducing it and helping to (re)order the world. In this instant, then, at the same time as she helps give nurses identity, she aligns[6] with, and reconstructs (see also Latour, 1986), a world in which personal care signifies the banal and mundane, whereas the technological is elevated to the heroic. Where these kinds of "move" are in circulation across many differently situated occasions, we begin to know what the staff

nurse at the beginning of the chapter knows. And we can begin to understand why she privileged the medication round over the dignity of the old woman. The old woman was a "long-term geriatric"; the procedure that the nurse cut corners with was a bath using a hoist.

Motility

I have stressed the need for research methods that get us inside nursing. What I have problematized throughout this chapter is that how we imagine social life affects the question of what it is that we want to get inside. In this penultimate section, I want to draw out more of the interconnections between social theories and the practice of research.

The approach to researching nursing in the emergent tradition I am delineating owes a lot to work such as the seminal study of medical students, *The Boys in White* (Becker, Geer, Hughes, & Strauss, 1961), and the interactionist Chicago school of social science. In making this reference, I want to connect the approach that I am offering to the interactionist perspective on how social life is produced—but only up to a certain point. For Howard Becker (1993), becoming a doctor was shown to be as much about a process of socialization as it was about coming to grips with medical knowledge and skills. Within this view of socialization, the medical students want to be seen to belong, and in order to do so they learn and follow the social rules and conventions that underpin the medical domain. Behavior is thus explained as being more about learning and following the rules and routines of social life than it is about being rational. The difficulty here is that social actors emerge as what Garfinkel (1967) calls *cultural dopes*: being social, in this view of socialization, is too rigidly conceived as about learning the conventions as somehow fixed and "out there" and "knowing" all about when to follow and when to deviate.

Although the idea of conduct is also based on a theoretical tradition that has as its starting point that persons are not free to do whatever they will, it incorporates a notion that social organization depends for its coherence on people *participating as persons*. Indeed, as Garfinkel (1967) suggests, it is the commitment and interest of people to act together, albeit tacitly, that helps accomplish the social. Although people's participation depends on their engagement and commitment to being a part or a member of something, the ways in which membership is accomplished call for creativity and responsiveness. It is persons together, through their social knowledge, who produce and reproduce reality (Berger & Luckman, 1966/ 1991); they perform their membership (Garfinkel, 1967) through their *participation*.

Participation is about much more than simply following rules or conventions that are somehow already settled. Membership is much more complex than just a matter of routine and repetition, production and reproduction. We have to locate ourselves in different identities and perform to multiple audiences. Knowing, like the staff nurse, at what moments *this* will do rather than *that*, which world to align with and which to dispose of, is all a part of being and doing the social. This is not a matter of being fluid or mobile, as other authors have stressed. Rather, I am calling this effect *motility*: the movement *between*, the processes of shifting between callings, the attachment *and* detachment that are needed to go along and get along. It is knowing how and when to be called one way rather than another that is a part of the conundrum of our unsettled times and that is particularly true for nurses. The staff nurse already mentioned acted, and accounted for her actions, in ways that privileged some kinds of work and patients over others at one moment. Critically, in the next moment, she or someone else might invert the order and privilege dignity over the medication round. This very idea of privileging suggests that there are always alterna-

tives. For example, at the same time as they want more and more to be seen as professionals rather than just as "good women," nurses also need to demonstrate their worth to managers and accountants. Nurses cannot rely on being easily identifiable; rather, their visibility is extremely difficult to accomplish.

This problematic over the precariousness of identity means that, increasingly, nurses, like other social beings, have to be persuasive. Nurses cannot just act or give an account of themselves; their accounts, to be compelling, have to be convincing. So participation is also about making *moves* (Latimer, 1997b, 2000b). In this view, nurses, like Charge Nurse cited earlier, do more than follow rules; they *draw on* discursive grounds, rules, and conventions and other materials to give authority to their performances and to legitimate what they do. But not all grounds are equal or available; not all materials will do. Knowing what will give authority, what will do and when, is all a part of "doing member" in the complex world of contemporary health care.

Conclusion

What I have highlighted in this chapter is a critical approach to studying nursing that gets away from the abstractions of theories and models of nursing, although these will of course enter into nurses' accounts as they offer reasons and justify what they or others do. The approach begins by bringing together two key constructionist traditions in qualitative social research: first, an idea that reality is produced and reproduced by participants as they go about their business, and, second, that this going about their business is connected to identity. This is not to suggest for a moment that identity is ascribed or given and that action or accounts simply flow from it. Rather, with Erving Goffman (1958), we can understand that identity has always been a precarious business. But I have stretched both the symbolic interactionist and ethnomethodological perspectives to late modern times.

The upshot of these complex ideas about social realities is that identity is becoming increasingly haphazard and problematic (Bauman, 1997). At the same time, the call for individuals to perform their distinctiveness is being intensified (Latimer, 2001). On the one hand, then, there is an intensification of the need for individuals to *perform* their identities, but on the other hand, the typifications and categories in which people participate to perform their identities are less and less fixed or settled. Part of the work of belonging is precisely to show, like the charge nurse and the staff nurse cited earlier, that you know how to settle (or unsettle) matters of identity and, critically, at what moments and on which occasions. I have called this feature of sociality and the doing of membership *motility*.

My focus, the assessment and care of older patients in an acute adult care unit, helps make the relation between motility and membership explicit. Here there is no singular reality, no grand narrative (Lyotard, 1984) to help settle matters, but multiple possibilities for interpretation and conduct. This means that as researchers we are not just looking to see how matters are already settled. That is, we are not looking for the "whole" that, through playing the right part, participants can simply become a part of. Rather, we need to examine how matters are being settled (or unsettled) by people as they go about their business. This applies to matters between different groups with different interests, but it also applies within groups and even to individuals themselves. The reason is that, for groups as well for individuals, there are competing possibilities for interpretation and conduct, competing narratives, and competing agendas.

Thus, in our approaches to researching nursing, at the same time that we need to explore what people as they work and interact make categories mean, we also need to be able to explore how people make meanings "stick" (Rabinow & Sullivan, 1979) and how they "dispose" (Latimer, 1997b; Munro, 1995; Strathern, 1999) of meanings. In these ways, the approach to studying nursing I have described stretches both the symbolic interactionist and ethnomethodological traditions to make explicit issues of power. The other researchers who I am suggesting can be thought of as in this same emergent tradition of critical constructionist nursing research have also stretched constructionist perspectives in different ways. But each of them has developed a methodology that, like the one I have featured here, allows the complexity of power relations in the world of health care to come into view and helps to make nurses' accomplishments in that world more visible.

• Notes

1. It should be noted that some of these researchers in this emergent tradition undertook doctoral studies at Edinburgh University School of Social Sciences and the Nursing Research Unit all at the same time, toward the end of the 1980s and the beginning of the 1990s.

2. By *knowing* here I do not mean something cognitive. Knowing can be tacit or embodied (Savage, 2003).

3. Elsewhere (Latimer, 1999, 2001, 2007; Latimer & Munro, 2006) I have, drawing on Strathern (1991) and Munro (1996b) suggested that a way to understand and explore the relation between materials, identity, and power effects is through the concept of extension.

4. Thanks to Marilyn Strathern for describing my way of working as *tracking* persons.

5. As Strathern argues (1991), in extension we are ourselves a kind of cultural material—extended through technology and other artifacts.

6. I have used Callon and Latour's (1981; Callon, 1986) ideas of enrollment and translation elsewhere (Latimer, 1995; Robinson et al., 1999) to help theorize how nurses, through drawing on particular kinds of technology and other cultural materials, align with, and thereby reproduce, managerial and other discursive effects.

• References

Abbott, P., & Wallace, C. (1990). The sociology of the caring professions: An introduction. In P. Abbott & C. Wallace (Eds.), *The sociology of the caring professions* (pp. 1–22). London: Falmer.

Allen, D. (2004a). Ethnomethodological insights into insider–outsider relationships in nursing ethnographies of healthcare settings. *Nursing Inquiry, 11,* 14–24.

Allen, D. (2004b). Re-reading nursing and re-writing practice: Towards an empirically-based reformulation of the nursing mandate. *Nursing Inquiry, 11,* 271–283.

Allen, D., & Cloyes, K. (2005). The language of "experience" in nursing research. *Nursing Inquiry, 12,* 98–105.

Allen, D. G. (1995). Hermeneutics: Philosophical traditions and nursing practice research. *Nursing Science Quarterly, 8,* 174–182.

Allen, D. G. (1996). Knowledge, politics, culture, and gender: A discourse perspective. *Canadian Journal of Nursing Research, 28,* 95–102.

Allen, D. G., & Hardin, P. (2001). Discourse analysis and the epidemiology of meaning. *Nursing Philosophy, 2,* 163–176.

Banonis, B. (1989). The lived experience of recovering from addiction: A phenomenological study. *Nursing Science Quarterly, 2*(1), 37–43.

Bauman, Z. (1997). *Life in fragments.* Oxford, UK: Blackwell.

Becker, H. S. (1993). How I learned what a crock was. *Journal of Contemporary Ethnography, 22*(1), 28–35.

Becker, H. S., Geer, B., Hughes, E. C., & Strauss, A. L. (1961). *The boys in white: Student culture in a medical school.* Chicago: University of Chicago Press.

Benner, P. (Ed.). (1994). *Interpretive phenomenology: Embodiment, caring and ethics in health and illness.* London: Sage.

Benner, P., & Wrubel, J. (1989). *The primacy of caring: Stress and coping in health and illness.* Menlo Park, CA: Addison-Wesley.

Berger, P., & Luckmann, T. (1991). *The social construction of reality: A treatise in the sociology of knowledge.* Harmondsworth, UK: Penguin Books. (Original work published 1966)

Bittner, E. (1965). The concept of organization. *Social Research, 32*(3), 239–255.

Bowers, L. (1992). Ethnomethodology: I. An approach to nursing research. *International Journal of Nursing Studies, 29*(1), 59–67.

Callon, M. (1986). Some elements of a sociology of translation: Domestication of the scallops and the fishermen of St Brieuc Bay. In J. Law J (Ed.), *Power, action and belief. A new sociology of knowledge?* (pp. 196–233). London: Routledge & Kegan Paul.

Callon, M., & Latour, B. (1981). Unscrewing the big Leviathan: How actors macro-structure reality and how sociologists help them do so. In K. D. Knorr-Cetain & A. Cicourel (Eds.), *Advances in social theory and methodology: Toward an integration of micro and macro-sociologies* (pp. 277–303). London: Routledge.

Cash, K. (1997). Social epistemology, gender and nursing theory. *International Journal of Nursing Studies, 34*(2), 137–143.

Coffey, A., & Atkinson, P. (1995). *Making sense of qualitative data: Complementary research strategies.* Thousand Oaks, CA: Sage.

Cohen, A. (1994). *Self-consciousness: An alternative anthropology of identity.* London: Routledge.

Crotty, M. (1996). *Phenomenology and nursing research.* Melbourne, Australia: Churchill Livingstone.

Darbyshire, P. (1994). Skilled expert practice: Is it "all in the mind"? A response to English's critique of Benner's novice to expert model. *Journal of Advanced Nursing, 19*(5), 755–761.

Darbyshire, P., Diekelmann, J., & Diekelmann, N. (1999). Reading Heidegger and interpretive phenomenology: A response to the work of Michael Crotty. *Nursing Inquiry, 6*(1), 17–25.

Davies, C. (1995). *Gender and the professional predicament of nursing.* Buckingham, UK: Open University Press.

Dingwall, R., & McIntosh, J. (Eds.). (1978). *Readings in the sociology of nursing.* Edinburgh, UK: Churchill Livingstone.

Douglas, M., & Isherwood, B. (1986). *The world of goods: Towards an anthropology of consumption.* Harmondsworth, UK: Penguin.

Foucault, M. (1976). *The birth of the clinic.* London: Tavistock.

Foucault, M. (1983). Afterword: The subject and power. In H. L. Dreyfus & P. Rabinow (Eds.), *Michel Foucault: Beyond structuralism and hermeneutics* (2nd ed., pp. 208–226). Chicago: University of Chicago Press.

Gamarnikow, E. (1978). Sexual division of labour: The case of nursing. In A. Kuhn & A. Wolpe (Eds.), *Feminism and materialism* (pp. 96–123). London: Routledge & Kegan Paul.

Garfinkel, H. (1967). *Studies in ethnomethodology.* Englewood Cliffs, NJ: Prentice Hall.

Garfinkel, H., & Sacks, H. (1986). On formal structures of practical actions. In H. Garfinkel (Ed.), *Ethnomethodological studies of work* (pp. 160–193). London: Routledge & Kegan Paul.

Geertz, C. (1983). *Local knowledge.* New York: Basic Books.

Geertz, C. (1993). *The interpretation of cultures: Selected essays.* London : Fontana Press.

Giddens A. (1989). *The constitution of society: Outline of structuration theory.* Cambridge, UK: Polity Press. (Original work published 1984)

Goffman, E. (1958). *The presentation of self in everyday life* (Monograph No. 2). Edinburgh, UK: University of Edinburgh, Social Sciences Research Centre.

Gullickson, C. (1993). My death nearing its future: A

Heideggerian hermeneutic analysis of the lived experience of persons with chronic illness. *Journal of Advanced Nursing, 18,* 1386–1392.

Haase, J. (1987). Components of courage in chronically ill adolescents: A phenomenological study. *Advances in Nursing Science, 9*(2), 62–80.

Hearn, J. (1982). Notes on patriarchy, professionalization and the semi-professions. *Sociology, 16,* 184–202.

Hughes, D. (1988). When nurse knows best: Some aspects of nurse/doctor interaction in a casualty department. *Sociology of Health and Illness, 10,* 1–22

Koch, T. (1995). Interpretive approaches in nursing research: The influence of Husserl and Heidegger. *Journal of Advanced Nursing, 21,* 827–836.

Koch, T. (1996). Implementation of a hermeneutic inquiry in nursing: Philosophy, rigour and representation. *Journal of Advanced Nursing, 24,* 174–184.

Latimer, (1994). *Writing patients, writing nursing: The social construction of nursing assessment of older people in an acute medical unit.* Unpublished doctoral thesis, University of Edinburgh, UK.

Latimer, J. (1995). The nursing process re-examined: Diffusion or translation? *Journal of Advanced Nursing, 22,* 213–220.

Latimer, J. (1997a). Figuring identities: Older people, medicine and time. In A. Jamieson, S. Harper, & C. Victor (Eds.), *Critical approaches to ageing and later life* (pp. 143–159). Milton Keynes, UK: Open University Press.

Latimer J. (1997b). Giving patients a future: The constituting of classes in an acute medical unit. *Sociology of Health and Illness, 19*(2), 160–185.

Latimer, J. (1999). The dark at the bottom of the stair: Participation and performance of older people in hospital. *Medical Anthropology Quarterly, 13*(2), 186–213.

Latimer, J. (2000a). *The conduct of care: Understanding nursing practice.* Oxford, UK: Blackwell Science.

Latimer, J. (2000b). Socialising disease: Medical categories and inclusion of the aged. *Sociological Review, 48*(3), 383–407.

Latimer, J. (2001). All-consuming passions: Materials and subjectivity in the age of enhancement. In N. Lee & R. Munro (Eds.), *The consumption of mass* (pp. 158–173). Oxford, UK: Blackwell.

Latimer, J. (2007). Diagnosis, dysmorphology and the family: Knowledge, motility, choice. *Medical Anthropology, 26,* 53–94.

Latimer, J., & Munro, R. (2006). Driving the social. In S. Bohm, C. Jones, & M. Pattison (Eds.), *Against automobility* (pp. 32–53). Oxford, UK: Blackwell.

Latour, B. (1986). The powers of association. In J. Law (Ed.), *Power, action and belief: A new sociology of knowledge?* (pp. 264–280). London: Routledge & Kegan Paul.

Lawler, J. (1991). *Behind the screens: Nursing somology and the problem of the body.* Melbourne, Australia: Churchill Livingstone.

Lawler, J. (1998). Phenomenologies as research methodologies for nursing: From philosophy to researching practice. *Nursing Inquiry, 5,* 104–111.

Lyotard, J. F. (1984). *The post-modern condition: A report on knowledge.* Manchester, UK: Manchester University Press.

May, C. (1991). *Individual care?: Power and subjectivity in therapeutic relationships.* Unpublished doctoral thesis, University of Edinburgh, UK.

May, C. (1992). Individual care?: Power and subjectivity in therapeutic relationships. *Sociology, 26,* 589–602.

May, C. (2003). Where do we stand in relation to the data? Being reflexive about reflexivity in health care evaluation. In J. Latimer (Ed.), *Advanced qualitative research for nursing* (pp. 17–31). Oxford, UK: Blackwell.

Melia, K. (1987). *Learning and working: The occupational socialisation of nurses.* London: Tavistock.

Mintzberg, H. (1983). *Power in and around organizations.* Englewood Cliffs, NJ: Prentice Hall.

Morse, J. M., Bottorff, J. L., & Hutchinson, S. (1994). The phenomenology of comfort. *Journal of Advanced Nursing, 20,* 189–195.

Munhall, P. (1994). *Revisioning phenomenology: Nursing and health science research.* New York: National League for Nursing Press.

Munro, R. (1995). Disposal of the meal. In D. Marshall (Ed.), *Food choice and the consumer* (pp. 313–325). London: Blackie.

Munro, R. (1996a). Alignment and identity-work: The study of accounts and accountability. In R. Munro & J. Mouritsen (Eds.), *Accountability: Power, ethos and the technologies of managing* (pp. 1–19). London: Thomson International Business Press.

Munro, R. (1996b). The consumption view of self: Extension, exchange and identity. In S. Edgell, K. Hetherington, & A. Warde (Eds.), *Consumption matters* (pp. 248–273). Oxford, UK: Blackwell.

Munro, R. (2005). Partial organization: Marilyn Strathern and the elicitation of relations. In C. Jones & R. Munro (Eds.), *Contemporary organization theory* (pp. 245–266). Oxford, UK: Blackwell.

Nelson, S. (1997). Reading nursing history. *Nursing Inquiry, 4,* 229–236.

Nelson, S. (2000). *A genealogy of care of the sick.* Southsea, Hants, UK: Nursing Praxis International.

Nelson, S (2001a). From salvation to civics: Care of the sick in nursing discourse. *Social Science and Medicine, 53*(9), 1217–1225.

Nelson, S. (2001b). *"Say little, do much": Nurses, nuns and hospitals in the nineteenth century.* Philadelphia: University of Pennsylvania Press.

Paley, J. (1998). Misinterpretive phenomenology: Heidegger, ontology and nursing research. *Journal of Advanced Nursing, 27*(4), 817–824.

Porter, S. (1992). Women in a women's job: The gendered experience of nurses. *Sociology of Health and Illness, 14*(4), 510–527.

Purkis, M. E. (1993). *Bringing practice to the clinic: An excavation of the effects of health promotion discourse on nursing practice in a community health clinic.* Unpublished doctoral thesis, University of Edinburgh, UK.

Purkis, M. E. (1999). Embracing technology: An exploration of the effects of writing nursing. *Nursing Inquiry, 6*(3), 147–156.

Rabinow, P., & Sullivan, W. M. (1979). The interpretive turn: Emergence of an approach. In P. Rabinow & W. M. Sullivan (Eds.), *Interpretive social science: A reader* (pp. 1–21). Berkeley: University of California Press.

Raffel, S. (1979). *Matters of fact.* London: Routledge and Kegan Paul.

Rafferty, A. M. (1996). *The politics of nursing knowledge.* London: Routledge.

Robinson, J., Avis, M., Latimer, J., & Traynor, M. (1999). *Interdisciplinary perspectives on health policy and practice: Competing interests or complementary interpretations?* Edinburgh, UK: Harcourt Brace/ Elsevier Science.

Rudge, T. (1997). *Nursing wounds: A discourse analysis of interactions between nurses and patients during wound care procedures in a burns unit.* Unpublished doctoral thesis, LaTrobe University, Melbourne, Australia.

Rudge, T. (1999). Situating wound management: Technoscience, dressings and "other" skins. *Nursing Inquiry, 6,* 167–177.

Salvage, J. (1985). *The politics of nursing.* London: Heinemann.

Sandelowski, M. (1999). Troubling distinctions: A semiotics of the nursing/technology relationship. *Nursing Inquiry, 6,* 198–207.

Sandelowski, M. (2000). *Devices and desires: Gender, technology, and American nursing.* Chapel Hill: University of North Carolina Press.

Sandelowski, M. (2003). Taking things seriously: Studying the material culture of nursing. In J. Latimer (Ed.), *Advanced qualitative research For nursing* (pp. 185–210). Oxford, UK: Blackwell.

Savage, J. (1995). *Nursing intimacy: An ethnographic approach to nurse–patient interaction.* London: Scutari Press.

Savage, J. (2000). Participative observation: Standing in the shoes of others? *Qualitative Health Research, 10,* 324–339.

Savage, J. (2003). Participative observation: Using the subject-body to understand nursing practice. In J. Latimer (Ed.), *Advanced qualitative research for nursing* (pp. 53–76). Oxford, UK: Blackwell.

Schutz, A. (1967). *The phenomenology of the social world.* Evanston, IL: Northwestern University Press.

Silverman, D. (1989). The impossible dreams of reformism and romanticism. In D. Silverman & J. Gubrium (Eds.), *The politics of field research: Sociology beyond enlightenment* (pp. 30–48). London: Sage.

Silverman, D., & Gubrium, J. (1989). Introduction. In D. Silverman & J. Gubrium (Eds.), *The politics of field research: Sociology beyond enlightenment* (pp. 1–12). London: Sage.

Simpson, I. H. (1979). *From student to nurse: A longitudinal Study of socialization.* Cambridge, UK: Cambridge University Press.

Stein, L. I. (1967). The doctor–nurse game. *Archives of General Psychiatry, 16,* 699–703.

Strathern, M. (1991). *Partial connections.* Savage, MD: Rowman & Littlefield.

Strathern, M. (1992). Writing societies, writing persons. *History of Human Sciences, 5*(1), 5–16.

Strathern, M. (1999). *Property, substance and effect: Anthropological essays on persons and things.* London: Athlone Press.

Tilley, S. (1990). *Negotiating realities: Making sense of interaction between patients diagnosed as neurotic and nurses in two psychiatric admission wards.* Unpublished doctoral thesis, University of Edinburgh, UK.

Traynor, M. (2006). Discourse analysis: Theoretical and historical overview and review of papers in the *Journal of Advanced Nursing,* 1996–2004. *Journal of Advanced Nursing, 54*(1), 62–72.

Turner, R. (1989). *Deconstructing the field.* In D. Silverman & J. Gubrium (Eds.), *The politics of field research: Sociology beyond enlightenment* (pp. 13–29). London: Sage.

Tyler, S. A. (1986). Post-modern ethnography: From document of the occult to occult document. In J. Clifford & G. Marcus (Eds.), *Writing culture: The poetics and politics of ethnography* (pp. 122–140). Berkeley and Los Angeles: University of California Press.

CHAPTER 9

Social Construction and Psychological Inquiry

● **Kenneth J. Gergen**
Mary M. Gergen

Not since the late 19th century and the emergence of psychology as a science have the dialogues on the nature of the discipline—its metatheory, methods, or subject matter—been livelier than they are today. In part, such dialogues are stimulated by what may be viewed as the threat of eradication through neurological reductionism. More profound, however, is a challenge to the very presumptions of psychology as a foundational science. Many would trace the origins of this turmoil to the critical ferment of the 1960s, but today such dialogues revolve centrally around issues in social construction. To be sure, critique and antagonism are pervasive; at the same time, current deliberations are suffused with enthusiasm and unparalleled creativity. As this *Handbook* also attests, what is taking place in psychology is also a reflection of a dynamic revolution occurring throughout the social sciences.

It is the purpose of this chapter to explore in greater detail the flowering of social constructionist inquiry in psychology. To this end we first touch on the emergence of constructionism in psychology and the major form that it takes today. We then take up the principle domains of constructionist inquiry, along with several movements currently gaining visibility. Although a detailed review of this substantial array of developments is beyond the scope of this chapter, we provide ample resources for more detailed exploration.

The Emergence of Social Construction in Psychology

There are many stories to be told about the development of social constructionism in psychology. We offer here but one, although one that is congenial with much common

171

understanding. To be sure, one may trace the intellectual roots of social constructionism to Vico, Nietzsche, Dewey, and Wittgenstein, among others. And, too, Peter Berger and Thomas Luckmann's *The Social Construction of Reality* (1966) was a landmark volume with strong reverberations in neighboring disciplines. However, the social movements and intellectual ferment that took shape in the late 1960s in the United States and Western Europe were perhaps more influential in paving the way for social constructionism in psychology. Resistance to the Vietnam War and to the country's political leadership was intense; profound skepticism of the established order was voiced. Much of the academic community was deeply engaged in political protest. The context was optimal for reassessing the established rationale and practices within the sciences and other scholarly traditions. In brief, one can locate at least three major forms of broadly shared critique that resulted from such reassessment. Each of them found expression in the psychological literature. Most important, the amalgamation of these forms of critique—often identified with postmodernism—largely serves as the basis for most social constructionist inquiry in psychology today.[1]

Perhaps the strongest and most impassioned form of critique of the dominant orders has been and continues to be *ideological*. In this case, critics challenge taken-for-granted realities and reveal the political ends that they achieve. In effect, such analysis discloses the constructed character of "the real" in the service of liberating the reader from its subtle grasp. Within the scholarly world more generally, such "unmasking" has played a major role, from Marxist and feminist contributions to the work of Michel Foucault (1979, 1980). In psychology, early representatives of the critical movement include Ronald Laing's (1965) work in antipsychiatry, Naomi Weisstein's (1971) critique of the sexism inherent in traditional psychology, Klaus Holzkamp's (1978) Marxist-based critique,

and Edward Sampson's (1985, 1993) critique of the ideology of self-contained individualism implicit in psychological research.

The second major form of critique may be viewed as *literary/rhetorical*. With developments in semiotic theory in general and literary deconstruction in particular (Derrida, 1976), attention was variously drawn to the ways in which linguistic convention serves as the forestructure for all claims to knowledge. Whatever reality may be, its representation is necessarily dominated by such conventions. Such ideas have been slower to manifest themselves in psychology, but the work of David Leary (1990) on metaphors of psychology and of Jan Smedslund (1978, 1988, 2004) on the linguistic circularity of knowledge claims in psychology are representative.

The third significant critique of foundational science was stimulated largely by the 1970 publication of Thomas Kuhn's *The Structure of Scientific Revolutions* (1962/ 1970). Kuhn portrayed normal science as guided by paradigms of theory and practice shared by particular communities. In effect, the outcomes of science are not demanded by the world as it is but are the result of communal negotiation. This social account of science was further buttressed by a welter of research in the sociology of knowledge and the history of science (see, e.g., Feyerabend, 1978; Latour & Woolgar, 1986). Within psychology, this view was reflected in Kenneth Gergen's (1973) article treating the interactive effects of cultural conceptions and empirical research in psychology. In his later work, *Toward Transformation in Social Knowledge* (1982/1994), Gergen specifically identified his orientation as social constructionist.

The convergence of scholarship in these three domains gave rise in the 1970s to intense debate on the nature of psychological inquiry (cf. Harré & Secord, 1972; Israel & Tajfel, 1972; Strickland, Aboud, & Gergen, 1977). Ultimately, however, one could begin to discern within this domain of debate the contours of a specifically "social constructionist movement" in psychology (K. Gergen, 1977, 1985; K. Gergen & Davis, 1985). Within this movement the phrase *social construction* typically refers to those social processes from which emerge commonly shared presumptions about the nature of the real, the rational, and the good. The social constructionist project does not exclude any category of existence, whether commonly viewed as physical, mental, or spiritual. Even death takes its meaning from a diversity of relational processes, whether in a hospital or a Hindu prayer circle (Edwards, Ashmore, & Potter, 1995).

The term *constructivism* is sometimes used interchangeably with *constructionism*. However, unlike social construction, early scholars tended to define constructivism in terms of cognitive processes within the individual mind. For these theorists, the focus was placed on the individual's perceptions and interpretative capacities as the originating source of their constructions of the world (see, e.g., Kelly, 1955). Drawing largely from the early work of Lev Vygotsky (1934/1962), and Mikhail Bakhtin (1981), recent scholarship has made it increasingly difficult to sustain the distinction between constructivism and constructionism. Constructivists increasingly find mental practices to be reflections or embodiments of social process (see, especially, Harré, 2003; Neimeyer, 2001; Shotter, 2007).

We are now positioned to consider significant developments in constructionist inquiry. However, before proceeding, an important caveat is required. In accounting for *research* in social construction, the central aim of this volume, there is a tendency to fall back on traditional empiricist conceptions. At the same time, the constructionist dialogues draw attention to major problems in this tradition, particularly in the separation of subject and object, claims to scientific neutrality, presumptions of cause and effect, and distinguishing representation from reality. In effect, social constructionist ideas provoke a revolution in conceptions of research. As a result, although there are some

who employ traditional empiricist methods and others who find qualitative methods more congenial, many constructionist scholars are at the cutting edge of redefining the very definition of research (see K. Gergen & M. Gergen, 2000; Marecek, 2003). In the present account, we thus employ the term *inquiry* as opposed to *research*.

Domains of Impact

The early ferment over social construction has given way to a new and significant range of initiatives in psychological inquiry. Such dialogues have played a particularly important role in the emergence of six major domains of exploration.

Critical Psychology

As outlined, ideological critique in the social sciences was a major stimulus to the development of social constructionist initiatives in psychology. Yet in psychology, the early critiques of the mental health professions, along with class- and gender-based criticism, have since expanded in both depth and breadth. Virtually all the emerging inquiry is based on demonstrating the constructed character of dominant discourses and practice, the otherwise hidden ideology thereby sustained, and the resulting impact on society. Such inquiry abandons the positivist attempt to "predict and control" human behavior (itself often characterized as sustaining an oppressive ideology) and replaces it with a goal of *liberation*. Once the ideological underpinnings of dominant reality claims are revealed, it is reasoned, one is liberated to pursue alternative activities of greater societal promise.

Such inquiry has moved in many directions. Particularly active have been participants in various politically sensitive wings of the discipline. Feminist psychologists have been among the vanguard of the critical movement, pointing to the gender biases pervading many of the concepts and research practices of the field at large (Crawford & Marecek, 1989; Hare-Mustin & Marecek, 1990; M. Gergen, 1988, 2001, in press; Sherif, 1987). Similarly active have been constituents of the gay and lesbian movement, much concerned with the constructed character of sexual categories, their implicit values, and their impact on cultural life (Bohan, 1996; Bohan & Russell, 1999; Kitzinger, 1987). Other researchers have studied gender formation, sexual identity, and sexual activity (Kessler & McKenna, 1978; Tiefer, 1995). At the same time, Marxist, social class, and societally relevant critique remains active (Burman et al., 1996; Fine et al., 2003a, 2003b; Henriques, Hollway, Urwin, Venn, & Walkerdine, 1984; Holzman & Morss, 2000; Parker & Shotter, 1990; Weis & Fine, 2005).

Yet critical work does not necessarily emanate from political subgroups alone. Within psychology, perhaps a major target of attack has been the assumptions and practices of the mental health professions. An extensive literature illuminates the constructed character of the psychiatric concepts of mental illness and points to the ideological and political interests served by diagnostic categorization. Thus an extensive literature has explored the historical, cultural, and political conditions giving rise to various illness classifications. These include, for example, the social construction of schizophrenia (Sarbin & Mancuso, 1980; Barrett, 1996), anorexia (Hepworth, 1999), depression (Blazer, 2005), attention-deficit disorder (Divorky & Schrag, 1975), and posttraumatic stress disorder (Quosh & Gergen, in press) (see also Dwight Fee, 2000, and Robert Neimeyer, 2000). These deconstructions of illness categories have been accompanied by critical assessments of the impact on both clients and the society more generally. For example, diagnostic categories are variously seen as devices used largely for purposes of social control (e.g., client management, insurance justification), that mystify the values agendas they express, and that sustain the myth of mental health practice as medical science in such a way that problems in living are increasingly treated with pharmaceutical suppressants (Kutchins & Kirk, 1997; Szasz, 1961). Furthermore, when "knowledge of mental illness" is disseminated to the culture, people cease to examine the societal conditions that may favor depression or hyperactivity, for example, and increasingly come to construct themselves in these terms (K. Gergen, 2006; Hare-Mustin, 1994). Furthermore, to be categorized as "mentally ill" frequently increases the anguish of those who bear the labels. To hear voices, to be hyperactive, or to be chronically sad, for example, is not inherently a diagnosis of an illness, and there are more beneficial constructions possible (Parker, Georgas, Harper, McLaughlin, & Stowall-Smith, 1995).

A large volume of work has also been devoted to pinpointing conceptual and ideological problems inherent in the cognitive movement (Coulter, 1979; Potter, 1996), evolutionary psychology (Oyama, 1991, 1993), positive psychology (Held, 1996), and experimental methods (K. Gergen, 1994; Weinstein, 2004), along with ways these professional investments are injurious to the culture.

Increasingly, psychologists have also turned their attention to the constructed worlds of the culture more generally and to some detrimental effects on human and environmental well-being. For example, Valerie Walkerdine's work has focused on how girls are evaluated in the math classroom (Walkerdine, 1988, 1990; Walkerdine & the Girls & Mathematics Unit, 1989); Michelle Fine, Lois Weis, and their colleagues' compilations (Fine, Freudenberg, et al., 2003; Weis & Fine, 2005) frame the lives of marginalized youths and women in prison; Paul Komesaroff, Philipa Rothfield, & Jeanne Daly's (1997) readings on cultural and philosophical issues resist the common interpretation of menopause; Michael Kimmel's work (1994) suggests that the social construction of masculinity is based on homophobia; and June Crawford, Sue Kippax, Jenny Onyx, Una Gault, and Pam

Benton (1992) detail the social production of emotional responses in girls, which train them in docility. Broad compilations and discussions of critical psychology may be found in Tomas Ibanez and Lupicinio Iniguez (1997), Ivan Prilletensky (1994), Dennis Fox and Isaac Prilletensky (1997), and Alexa Hepburn (2000). Although critical psychology has become increasingly robust, the movement also faces significant problems. As we have seen, critical inquiry is launched from many different value bases, with a resulting fragmentation of concerns. Internecine confrontations are pervasive. Furthermore, critical psychologists often disagree in their orientation toward social construction. Most critical work employs constructionist assumptions in its posture of attack, but many critical theorists do not wish to view their own positions as constructions. Many critics do not wish to see the identity category with which they are associated deconstructed; to do so, they reason, would be to abandon the very grounds of critique. Debates on these issues continue.

Discursive Psychology

As outlined earlier, the contributions of literary and rhetorical study were pivotal to the postmodern dialogues more generally and to social constructionist thought in particular. One outcome of these explorations was an acute consciousness of the significance of language in the construction of both the real and the rational. For most constructionist scholars, publicly shared discourse has served as the chief site of construction. As discourse has taken center stage in this way, so have research interests rapidly moved in this direction. To be sure, linguistic study in psychology already had a substantial tradition. The study of the relation of mind (or cognition) to language, along with research into grammar and syntax, for example, had generated a large corpus of literature. However, within a constructionist frame, such issues were no longer engaging. For one thing, the study of

the mind to language relation already presumed a dualism between mind and speech that many constructionists have found unacceptable. Furthermore, in its search for "the truth about language," traditional research is stripped of concern with political and ideological context and thus of little relevance for many constructionists.

Inquiries into discursive practices have not only been substantial but have also moved in myriad directions. To be sure, much constructionist inquiry in psychology has been devoted to deconstructing essentialist views of mental life. The targets in this case are the taken-for-granted assumptions about "what's in the mind," assumptions that are pivotal to psychological science and that play a central role in cultural life. Thus, for example, such inquiry illuminates the constructed character of the emotions (Averill, 1982; K. Gergen, 1995; K. Gergen & M. Gergen, 1995; Harré, 1986; Shields, 2002), memory (Shotter, 1990), the sense of smell (Corbin, 1986), erotic experience (Halperin, Winkler, & Zeitlin, 1990; Lockford, 2004), boredom (Spacks, 1995), intellectual disability (Rapley, 2004), and teenage desire (Jackson, 2005). Such research not only removes the foundations for an empirical science of psychology but also raises profound questions concerning the utility of empirical research on what amount to conversational objects. Such questions are actively explored in the theoretical circles.

Many scholars have employed discourse analysis to illuminate issues of broad cultural concern. For example, the early work of Margaret Wetherell and Jonathan Potter (1992) explored the subtle prejudices built into unremarkable utterances of daily life. More recent inquiry is illustrated in the work of Nicola Gavey (1989, 2005), concerned with the influence of discourse about sexual relationships on rape. Walkerdine and Helen Lucey (1989) have explored the ways that mothers and daughters are domesticated by the "kitchen" talk of everyday life; Rom Harré, Jens Brockmeier, and Peter Muhlhousler (1998) have formulated the discursive mechanisms underlying Green Party politics.

Perhaps the most active line of discursive inquiry has issued a major assault on the cognitive paradigm in psychology, proposing that an analysis of discursive processes is sufficient to account for most of what we take to be cognitive process. In one of the earliest provocations of this kind, Potter and Wetherell (1987) demonstrated the problems inhering in the supposition that attitudes in the head cause overt public actions. As they proposed, an attitude is more fruitfully understood as a public action in itself or, essentially, a position taken in a conversation. As Michael Billig (1987) went on to illuminate, most of what we take to be rational thought is more adequately viewed as a social process of argumentation. We do not argue because we have private thoughts, but, rather, private thinking comes into being through the social practice of argumentation. This line of reasoning has been a significant stimulus to one of the most significant lines of constructionist inquiry, namely, *communal memory*. With the volume by David Middleton and Derek Edwards (1990), the grounds were established for viewing memory not as a personal, mental process but as a social process (see Middleton & Brown, 2005, for a review of this work to date). As proposed by Edwards and Potter (2000), a fully discursive psychology should properly replace cognitive psychology.

To these discursive pursuits it is appropriate to add both narrative research and conversation analysis. The former constitutes a subdiscipline in its own right and is treated subsequently. The latter has concertedly shifted the focus from the content and form of particular discursive segments to relational interdependence as conversation unfolds over time (see, e.g., Antaki, 1981; Parker, 1998). Such inquiry has been useful, for example, in demonstrating the microprocesses of establishing power in relationships (see, e.g., Davies, 1982; Mishler, 1984). Although not restricted to conversation analysis, the concept of *positioning* (Davies & Harré,

1990; Van Langehove & Harré, 1998) has opened up a fruitful line of inquiry in its own right. The concern in this case is how individuals largely position or define each other through their discursive actions.

For more comprehensive accounts of discourse analysis in psychology, see Erica Burman and Ian Parker (1993), Carla Willig (1999), Wetherell, Taylor, and Yates (2001), Potter (1996), and Edwards (1997). Also see the journal *Discourse and Society*.

Narrative Psychology

As the literary and rhetorical movements within the intellectual world brought language into center stage, it carried with it a specific interest in narrative. Narrative is a pivotal form of construction used by people to intelligibly link events across time. Within the constructionist framework, early inquiry by James Mancuso and Theodore Sarbin (1983) and by Kenneth Gergen and Mary Gergen (1983, 1988) more fully linked narrative concerns with psychological inquiry. Later volumes by Sarbin (1986), Donald Polkinghorne (1988), and Jerome Bruner (1990) gave the study of narrative a prominent place in psychological study. Open for inquiry were such topics as the relationship of narrative to personal identity, moral behavior, social acceptability, personal memory, self-acceptance, social efficacy, intimacy, and even the intelligibility of psychological theorizing itself.

With a rich palette of possibilities open, narrative inquiry has become a fertile domain of study. In the field of personality, for example, the long-standing concern with life history has been highly congenial to narrative study (Rosenwald & Ochberg, 1990). The work of Dan McAdams (1985, 1993, 2006a) has been enormously important in its contributions to the understanding of narrative in personal life. His inquiry into resurrection narratives has also fired interest in the relationship of people's self-understanding to their spiritual traditions (McAdams, 2006b). James Holstein and Jay

Gubrium (2000a, 2000b) illuminate the continuous process of creating and performing the storied self in everyday life. The study of gender differences in psychology has also been illuminated through narrative study (M. Gergen, 2001). Mark Tappan and Martin Packer (1991) have explored the use of narrative in developing morality. The use of narrative in constructing intelligible history of both self and culture has been examined (K. Gergen, 2005; K. Gergen & M. Gergen, 2006). A series of 11 volumes edited by Ruthellen Josselson and Amie Lieblich, later joined by McAdams, has been critical in providing a venue for narrative researchers to present their work (i.e., Josselson & Lieblich, 1995; Josselson, Lieblich, & McAdams, 2003; Lieblich & Josselson, 1994). Among the vast array of topics covered have been the stories of Israeli Holocaust survivor families (Bar-on & Gilad, 1994); autobiographies and gendered bodies (M. Gergen & K. Gergen, 1993); the poetics of research (Rogers et al., 1999); professional practice within a mental hospital (Abma, 1999), and loneliness among older Southeast Asian refugee women (Bennett & Detzner, 1997). The rich productivity in narrative research has also stimulated critical reflection on narrative methods themselves (Duarte & Lightfoot, 2004; M. Gergen & Davis, 2003; Gubrium & Holstein, 2003).

For further coverage of narrative inquiry in psychology, the *Journal of Narrative and Life History* and *Narrative Inquiry* are useful resources. A comprehensive account of narrative inquiry can be found on Vincent Hevern's *Internet and Resource Guide* (*web.lemoyne.edu/~hevern/narpsych.html*).

Theoretical Psychology

In the constructionist view, the very conception of empirical research, along with "the phenomenon under study," is dependent on an a priori domain of shared understandings. Within scientific enclaves, this socially negotiated forestructure is more formally viewed as theory. Thus, as the theoretical

discourse of psychology is expanded or contracted, so are the possibilities for meaningful observation and acceptable methodology. In this sense, both the behaviorist and cognitive movements in psychology generated certain possibilities, but in both cases the range was narrow, and the door was closed on alternatives. As constructionist sensitivity in psychology has increased, interest has grown in discussions of the nature of psychological theory and its implications for the science and for practice and its place in culture. The interest is not so much in abandoning the empirical program altogether as it is in expanding exponentially the field of endeavor (K. Gergen, 2001b).

However, attempts to undermine the presumption of a universal and transhistorical account of mental life have also given rise to more positive developments in the theoretical construction of the person. In particular, theorists have opened a space for a major reconceptualizing of human action. Moving beyond the traditional image of biologically based, universal psychological processes, an image associated with Sampson's (1985) critique of self-contained individualism, there is active exploration of the potential of a relational ontology. In this account, relationships take prior place to individual functioning. Or, reflecting Vygotsky's early work (1978), the major ingredients of human functioning are given birth within social process. Those remaining closer to the Vygotskian tradition (e.g., Bruner, 1990; Wertsch, 1991) continue to speak of psychological process *sui generis*. Hubert Hermans and Harry Kempen's (1995) explorations into the discursive mind are illustrative; this work has also given birth to the online journal *The International Journal for Dialogical Science*. However, as one moves closer to constructionist premises, the focus on relationship becomes sharper, and the distinction between *inner* and *outer* begins to fade. Virtually all of the contributions to a discursive psychology, as discussed previously, lend themselves to this end. When attitudes and reason are viewed as discursive actions, psychology is removed from the head and placed within the relational sphere. It is this line of deliberation that is extended in Gergen's explorations of relational being (K. Gergen, in press).

Engaging inquiry has also extended the implications of social constructionist ideas to speak to spiritual and theological traditions (Hermans, Immink, de Jong, & van der Lans, 2002). As Buddhist practices have gained significant inroads into therapeutic community, so have its conceptual underpinnings become more open to deliberation. Such deliberation demonstrates a number of affinities, including between concepts of "no mind" in Buddhism and of "discursive deconstruction" in social construction (K. Gergen & Hosking, 2006; Kwee & Taams, 2006).

Methods of Inquiry

Although a constructionist view of knowledge does not eliminate any particular method of study, it has provided a vital stimulus for critical reflection on traditional empiricist methods and an invitation to consider alternative departures. For most constructionists, experimental research is avoided. The reasons are many, including a distaste for the trappings of truth that typically accompany such research, the reliance on human manipulation, the alienated relationship between the researcher and the "objects" of research, and the view that virtually all intelligible hypotheses about human behavior can be vindicated in at least some temporal and cultural location. If research is to carry with it an empirical base, constructionists tend to be far more comfortable, as we have seen, with more interpretive analysis of discourse or narrative (Gergen & Gergen, 2007).

Yet the invitation for inquiry into new ranges of representation is also compelling. Two significant directions are evident, the first concerned with the relationship of researcher to those represented by the research and the second with the relationship of the researcher to the profession and the culture. In the first case, many constructionists have experienced a certain discomfort in laying claims to fidelity in representation, which is to say, "making claims to knowledge about others." For many, psychology has long been at fault because its researchers dominate the process of description and explanation without offering their participants any right to voice. Certain of these sentiments pervade the narrative and life history areas mentioned earlier. Increasingly, researchers attempt to open spaces for various groups to represent themselves to the profession and public (Lather & Smithies, 1997). In her work with Guatemalan women, M. Brinton Lykes (1997) invited her "colleagues" from war-torn villages to express their perspectives with photographs made from cameras she provided. Others, who are most closely associated with action research methods, close the gap between researcher and researched by collaborating with communities working for social justice and economic security (Reason & Bradbury, 2000, 2007).

Other constructionist scholars have centered their concerns on the process of representation. From a constructionist viewpoint, there are no foundations of support for any particular form of representation. Thus a space is opened to consider the full range of representational devices available for communication. Furthermore, careful consideration is given to the forms of relationship fostered by one's means of representation. All writing invites a form of relationship with the reader (K. Gergen, in press). Thus, for example, much traditional writing in psychology both formalizes relationships in the discipline and is opaque to those outside. Such writing tends to be both divisive and elitist in form. With such concerns in mind, psychologists have begun to experiment with various forms of writing. For example, in her feminist work, M. Gergen (2001) has employed both dramatic monologue and fictitious dialogue. Other writing experiments include short stories (Diversi, 1998), dialogue (Tillmann-Healy, 1996), and dramatic scripts (Fox, 1996).

More radically, psychologists have begun to explore the potentials for performance to carry both theoretical and empirical content (M. Gergen, 2005; Gray & Sinding, 2002; Jones, 2006; Newman & Holzman, 1996). These psychologists have made significant theoretical contributions to the understanding of performance potentials, and they have written and staged a variety of psychologically important plays, vignettes, and Internet pieces. K. Gergen and M. Gergen (2001) have explored a variety of performance possibilities in their theoretical inquiries, including art, poetry, music, and drama. Of further significance, Glenda Russell (2000) has used interview data to create a musical piece, entitled "Fire," performed by choral groups. The work is based on research into reactions related to the elimination of certain civil rights provisions for gays and lesbians in Colorado.

For a more extended view of the range and innovation in qualitative inquiry in psychology and related disciplines, see the compendiums of Paul Camic, Jean Rhodes, and Lucy Yardley (2003) and Norman Denzin and Yvonne Lincoln (2005), along with the contents of the journals *Qualitative Inquiry*, *Narrative Inquiry*, and *Action Research* and the electronic journals *Forum Qualitative Sozialforschung/Forum: Qualitative Social Research* and *The Qualitative Report*.

Therapy as Social Construction

Finally, we wish to touch on contributions of social construction to therapeutic practice. It is in this domain that constructionist deliberations have played their most significant cultural role. With the splitting away of more research-oriented psychologists to form the American Psychological Society (now the Association for Psychological Science), the American Psychological Association was free to become the more practice-oriented professional group. Therapists were essentially liberated from the "super-ego" constraints of the positivist program. And, more attuned to the intellectual and cultural milieu, constructionist ideas soon became incorporated into much theory and practice. The first and most visible of these developments was narrative therapy (White & Epston, 1990). Committed to the view that people largely understand themselves in terms of storied constructions, the attempt in therapy is primarily to enable clients to develop new and more viable personal narratives (see also McLeod, 1997). Along similar lines, brief therapists focus on shifting from "problem talk" (which sustains the reality of the problem) to talking about solutions or new possibilities for action (de Shazer, 1994; O'Hanlon, 2003). In a related vein, Tom Andersen and his colleagues (Andersen, 1991; Friedman, 1993) have developed reflecting teams that open multiple spaces of meaning for clients. In postmodern therapy, Harlene Anderson (1997) emphasizes the importance of abandoning theoretical preconceptions and working as closely and sensitively as possible with clients' understandings of their lives. Closely tied to these developments in therapy are explorations into diagnostic practices that give voice to a wider circle of engaged parties (Seikulla, Arnkil, & Eriksson, 2003).

When considered as a whole, these therapeutic movements represent a fundamental transformation in the definition and practice of therapy. First, echoing the work of critical psychologists, they understand the illness categories so central to traditional psychiatry as constructed and thus of questionable value to the client. Along with this orientation comes a more judicious view of pharmacological "cures" and a search for more meaningful means to alleviate suffering. Furthermore, the traditional status of the therapist as the expert or "knowing one" is largely replaced by a view of therapist as an agent in the coconstruction of meaning. The emphasis on "deep psychological problems" is largely abandoned in the pursuit of more socially viable constructions of self and world. And for many, in abandoning the medical model of therapy, there is a more acute awareness of the social and political implications of therapeutic practice.

For more detailed accounts of these and related developments, see Angus (2004), Friedman (1993), Hoffman (2002), K. Gergen (2006), Hoyt (1998), McNamee and Gergen (1992), Rosen and Kuehlwein (1996), and G. Miller and Strong, Chapter 31, this volume.

The Expanding Dialogue

Within the six preceding domains one finds a substantial and continuing corpus of constructionist inquiry. At the same time, there are further sites of inquiry in psychology in which constructionist ideas have taken root, and with significant impact. Critical ferment, innovative ideas, and new frontiers of inquiry have appeared in each case. Several of these demand particular attention.

Health Psychology

Although health psychology is traditionally committed to empiricist research pursuits, constructionist ideas have made significant inroads. There is first the issue of defining health and illness. Empiricist researchers have traditionally presumed the reality of health and illness and then embarked on research to explore causal antecedents. In contrast, constructionists open inquiry into the categories of health and illness and, as we have seen previously, raise significant questions about the value of mental illness categories for clients, as well as for the culture more generally. David Karp's (1996) *Speaking of Sadness: Depression, Disconnection, and the Meanings of Illness* provides an example of such work. Such "deconstructive efforts" have allied constructionist psychologists with the efforts of ex-mental patients and other groups (e.g., people who hear voices or who are classified as autistic) in attempting to resist or subdue the effects of deficit discourse. However, efforts to demonstrate the constructed character of physical disease have now become prominent (Hurwitz & Greenhalgh, 1998; Lorber & Moore, 2002; Mattingly & Garro, 2000; Whitehouse, 2005). Kathy Charmaz's (1991) work on chronic illness is one such endeavor.

Such liberatory inquiry is also accompanied by numerous creative efforts to employ constructionism for healing purposes. Noteworthy is a substantial line of inquiry into the social construction of pain and its implications for pain management. As the groundbreaking work of Arthur Frank (1995, 2004) proposed, our experience of pain is lodged in narrative understanding. The same physical condition may be more or less burdensome depending on whether it is constructed in a narrative of helplessness or in one that places it in the service of a valued goal. Pain thus becomes a cultural phenomenon as opposed to merely a physical sensation (Morris, 1991). Also in terms of healing, Neimeyer (2001) has explored how irreconcilable grief can be treated through the renegotiation of meaning.

Developmental Psychology

Entering the developmental sphere at the dawn of the constructionist movement was Philippe Aries's 1962 volume, *Centuries of Childhood: A Social History of Family Life*. In this work Aries examined the ways in which the conception of the child was lodged in cultural history. In effect, a challenge was mounted (but largely ignored) to the universalizing impetus of research on child development. Aries's thesis was later amplified by the developmental psychologist William Kessen (1979). Further contributions by Erica Burman (1994), Ben Bradley (1989), and John Morss (1990) have enriched the dialogue by demonstrating ideological and political implications of widely accepted conceptions of child development.

With occasional exceptions (Bodor, 2003), resistance to constructionist ideas remains obdurate in research on child development. The field of lifespan development has been more receptive. Holstein and Gubrium (2000b) have brought attention to the ways construction of the person proceeds across the lifespan; Haim Hazan (1994) has furnished a detailed analysis of the construction of aging. In their work, Mary Gergen and Kenneth Gergen (2005) have brought critical attention to the negative constructions of aging broadly shared within the culture and initiated a move to reconstruct aging as a period of positive growth and enrichment. The results of this work are distributed in a bimonthly electronic newsletter, *Positive Aging* (*www. positiveaging.net*).

The History of Psychology

Traditional historical accounts in psychology have tended to be both realist and "presentist." That is, they have treated history as ideally an objective and value-neutral recounting of the past and have tended to view the present state of psychological knowledge (along with methods and research results) as superior to the past. However, scholars engaged in the constructionist dialogues have found this tradition vitally flawed. Historical accounts do not reflect the past so much as give it structure and shape. They create the intelligibility of the past. "Presentist" history is an endeavor that valorizes the present state of the field over the past. In doing so, such accounts presume the cumulative character of the positivist research and its self-serving conception of progress.

Constructionist scholars have mounted a significant challenge to this form of historical inquiry. In his work, Kurt Danziger (1990) has illuminated the way in which research practices shaped the very concept of the subject in psychological research. In his later work, Dangizer (1997) examined the cultural and professional origins of the discourse of mind shared within experimental psychology. Suzanne Kirschner (1996) has provided a sophisticated analysis of the

roots in religious history of developmental assumptions in psychoanalytic theory. In Jill Morawski's (1988) edited volume, contributors explored the ways in which research practices in psychology were shaped by cultural values. In Carl Graumann and Kenneth Gergen's (1996) work, contributors placed current conceptions of mental life in both historical and cultural perspective. Such historical analyses not only undermine the psychological essentialism inherent in traditional accounts but also open a space for self-reflexive dialogues on the future potential of theory and research (Rose, 1985).

Emergents in Practice

Social constructionist ideas have also entered into arenas of practice outside the therapeutic arena. Most closely related are developments in practices of counseling (Paré & Larner, 2004). In a similar vein, many psychologists are also realizing the limitations of the individualist view of knowledge (Steffe & Gale, 1995). In the educational sphere, for example, such limitations are realized particularly in traditional forms of pedagogy centered on the improvement of individual minds. Originating largely in Vygotskian orientations to education, interest has centered on the relationship of teacher to student (Holzman, 1997; Rogoff, Turkanis, & Bartlett, 2001). Constructionists have extended the reach of these concerns, with special emphasis placed on the potentials for collaborative pedagogies to replace hierarchical teaching (top down) with productive and more equalizing classroom dialogue (Bruffee, 1993; Wells, 1992). In the organizational sphere, we find again a strong movement concerned with the social construction of organizational realities (cf. Weick, 1995). Practitioners have developed a variety of new practices relying on narrative and metaphor for reducing conflict in organizations and inspiring positive change. Appreciative inquiry is among the leading new practices (see, e.g., Barrett & Fry, 2005; Cooperrider & Whitney, 2000). The Public

Conversation Project in the Boston area uses a dialogic approach to conflict resolution and the development of nonconfrontational techniques for generating intergroup tolerance (see *www.PublicConversationProject. net*). These various increments in practice have also stimulated a reconsideration of the relationship between theory and practice (see the special issue of *Theory and Psychology*, 2006, *16*(5)).

The Continuing Story

In the context of psychology, social constructionist ideas have been explosive in their consequence. In many quarters they have led to a full rethinking of the nature of knowledge, theory, research, and practice. The dialogues have opened multiple new lines of inquiry and heretofore undreamed possibilities for the profession and its relationship to the culture. A space has opened for much-needed critical reflection. Discourse study has become a full-fledged subdiscipline. Narrative study brings psychology closer than ever before to scholarship in the humanities. Grounds have emerged for a major reconceptualization of human action, and a new range of research methods and therapeutic practices have sprung to life. At the same time, constructionist ideas have made significant entry into arenas of health psychology, developmental psychology, and historical study in psychology.

Although these are significant accomplishments indeed, this is scarcely to say that constructionist ideas are in any way dominant. The vast majority of research in psychology remains hermetically committed to traditional (1930s) visions of science. In part because the current structure of power allows it to disregard the intellectual world outside itself, and in part because training in the empiricist paradigm ill equips its students for self-reflection, only occasionally have more traditional psychologists paused in their resistance to social construction

(e.g., Jost & Kruglanski, 2002). In fact, virtually all significant critique of social construction in psychology has originated among those outside the empiricist paradigm (see, e.g., Hibberd, 2005; Kvale, 1992; Nightingale & Cromby, 1999; Parker, 1998; and a special issue of *Theory and Psychology*, *11*, no. 3). Yet these latter critiques also play a productive role in the development of social construction. For the most part, they have stimulated the development of more highly nuanced accounts of social constructionist metatheory, along with its spaces of vulnerability. Such dialogue also brings with it new hybrids. Critique originating in humanistic and phenomenological quarters, for example, has given rise to new potentials for inquiry. For those participating in these various dialogues, the future is an exciting one.

• Note

1. For a more detailed account of these critiques within psychology, see K. Gergen (1982/ 1994, 1994). Additional accounts of social constructionist premises and potentials may be found in Burr (1995); K. Gergen (1999, 2001a); K. Gergen and M. Gergen (2004); and Potter (1996).

• References

Abma, T. A. (1999). Powerful studies: The role of stories in sustaining and transforming professional practice within a mental hospital. In R. Josselson & A. Lieblich (Eds.), *The narrative study of lives: Vol. 6. Making meaning of narratives* (pp. 77–106). Thousand Oaks, CA: Sage.

Andersen, T. (1991). *The reflecting team*. New York: Norton.

Anderson, H. (1997). *Conversation, language and possibilities: A postmodern approach to psychotherapy*. New York: Basic Books.

Angus, L. (2004). *The handbook of narrative and psychotherapy: Practice, theory and research*. Thousand Oaks, CA: Sage.

Antaki, C. (1981). *The psychology of ordinary explanations*. London: Academic Press.

Aries, P. (1962). *Centuries of childhood: A social history of family life*. New York: Vintage.

Averill, J. (1982). *Anger and aggression.* New York: Springer-Verlag.

Bakhtin, M. M. (1981). *The dialogic imagination: Four essays.* Austin: University of Texas Press.

Bar-on, D., & Gilad, N. (1994). To rebuild life: A narrative analysis of three generations of an Israeli Holocaust survivor's family. In A. Lieblich & R. Josselson (Eds.), *The narratives study of lives: Vol. 2. Exploring identity and gender* (pp. 83–112). Thousand Oaks, CA: Sage.

Barrett, F., & Fry, R. (2005). *Appreciative inquiry: A positive approach to building cooperative capacity.* Chagrin Falls, OH: Taos Institute.

Barrett, R. (1996) *The psychiatric team and the social definition of schizophrenia.* New York: Cambridge University Press.

Bennett, J. A., & Detzner, D. F. (1997). Loneliness in cultural context: A look at the life-history narratives of older Southeast Asian refugee women. In A. Lieblich & R. Josselson (Eds.), *The narrative study of lives, Vol. 5* (pp. 113–146). Thousand Oaks, CA: Sage.

Berger, P., & Luckmann, T. (1966). *The social construction of reality: A treatise in the sociology of knowledge.* New York: Doubleday/Anchor.

Billig, M. (1987). *Arguing and thinking.* London: Cambridge University Press.

Blazer, D.G. (2005). *The age of melancholy: Major depression: and its social origins.* New York: Routledge.

Bodor, P. (2003). *On emotions, A developmental social constructionist account.* Budapest, Hungary: Harmattan.

Bohan, J. S. (1996). *Psychology and sexual orientation: Coming to terms.* New York: Routledge.

Bohan, J. S., & Russell, G. M. (1999). *Conversations about psychology and sexual orientation.* New York: New York University Press.

Bradley, B. (1989). *Visions of infancy.* London: Polity Press.

Bruner, J. (1990). *Acts of meaning.* Cambridge, MA: Harvard University Press.

Bruffee, K. A. (1993). *Collaborative learning.* Baltimore: Johns Hopkins University Press.

Burman, E. (1994). *Deconstructing developmental psychology.* London: Routledge.

Burman, E., Aitken, G., Allred, P., Allwood, R., Billington, T., Goldberg, B., et al. (1996). *Psychological discourse practice: From regulation to resistance.* London: Taylor & Francis.

Burman, E., & Parker, I. (Eds.). (1993). *Discourse analytic research: Repertoires and readings of texts in action.* London: Routledge.

Burr, V. (1995). *An introduction to social constructionism.* London: Routledge.

Camic, P. M., Rhodes, J. E., & Yardley, L. (Eds.). (2003). *Qualitative research in psychology: Expanding perspectives in methodology and design.* Washington, DC: American Psychological Association.

Charmaz, K. (1991). *Good days, bad days: The self in chronic illness and time.* New Brunswick, NJ: Rutgers University Press.

Cooperrider, D., & Whitney, D. (2000). A positive revolution in change: Appreciative inquiry. In D. Cooperrider, P. Sorensen, D. Whitney, & T. Yaeger (Eds.), *Appreciative inquiry* (pp. 4–24). Champaign, IL: Stipes.

Corbin, A. (1986). *The foul and the fragrant: Odor and the French social imagination.* Cambridge, MA: Harvard University Press.

Coulter, J. (1979). *The social construction of the mind.* New York: Macmillan.

Crawford, J., Kippax, S., Onyx, J., Gault, U., & Benton, P. (1992). *Emotion and gender: Constructing meaning from memory.* London: Sage.

Crawford, M., & Marecek, J. (1989). Psychology reconstructs the female, 1968–1988. *Psychology of Women Quarterly, 13,* 147–165.

Danziger, K. (1990). *Constructing the subject: Historical origins of psychological research.* Cambridge, UK: Cambridge University Press.

Danziger, K. (1997). *Naming the mind: How psychology found its language.* London: Sage.

Davies, B. (1982). *Life in the classroom and playground: The accounts of primary school children.* London: Routledge.

Davies, B., & Harré, R. (1990). Positioning: The discursive production of selves. *Journal for the Theory of Social Behaviour, 20,* 43–63.

Denzin, N. K., & Lincoln, Y. S. (Eds.). (2005). *Handbook of qualitative research* (3rd ed.). Thousand Oaks, CA: Sage.

Derrida, J. (1976). *Of grammatology* (G. Spivak, Trans.). Baltimore: Johns Hopkins University Press.

de Shazer, S. (1994). *Words were originally magic.* New York: Norton.

Diversi, M. (1998). Glimpses of street life: Representing lived experience through short stories. *Qualitative Inquiry, 4,* 131–147.

Divorky, D., & Schrag, P. (1975). *The myth of the hyperactive child.* New York: Pantheon.

Duarte, C., & Lightfoot, C. G. (Eds.). (2004). *Narrative analysis: Studying the development of individuals in society.* Thousand Oaks, CA: Sage.

Edwards, D. (1997). *Discourse and cognition.* London: Sage.

Edwards, D., Ashmore, M., & Potter, J. (1995). Death and furniture: The rhetoric and politics and theology of bottom line arguments against relativism. *History of the Human Sciences, 8,* 25–49.

Edwards, D., & Potter, J. (2000). *Discursive psychology.* London: Sage.

Fee, D. (Ed.). (2000). *Pathology and the postmodern.* London: Sage.

Feyerabend, P. (1978). *Against method.* New York: Humanities Press.

Fine, M., Freudenberg, N., Payne, Y. A., Perkins, T., Smith, K., & Wanzer, K. (2003). Anything can happen with police around: Urban youth evaluate strategies of surveillance in public places. *Journal of Social Issues, 59,* 141–158.

Fine, M., Torre, M. E., Boudin, K., Bowen, I., Clarke, J., Hyulton, D., et al. (2003). Participatory action research: From within and beyond prison bars. In P. M. Camic, J. E. Rhodes, & L. Yardley (Eds.), *Qualitative research in psychology: Expanding perspectives in methodology and design* (pp. 173–198). Washington, DC: American Psychological Association.

Foucault, M. (1979). *Discipline and punish: The birth of the prison.* New York: Random House.

Foucault, M. (1980). *The history of sexuality* (Vol. 1). New York: Random House.

Fox, D. I., & Prilletensky, I. (Eds.). (1997). *Handbook of critical psychology.* Thousand Oaks, CA: Sage.

Fox, K. V. (1996). Silent voices: A subversive reading of child sexual abuse. In C. Ellis & A. Bochner (Eds.), *Composing ethnography: Alternative forms of qualitative writing* (pp. 330–356). Walnut Creek, CA: AltaMira Press.

Frank, A. W. (1995). *The wounded storyteller: Body, illness and ethics.* Chicago: University of Chicago Press.

Frank, A. W. (2004). *The renewal of generosity: Illness, medicine, and how to live.* Chicago: University of Chicago Press.

Friedman, S. (Ed.). (1993). *The new language of change: Constructive collaboration in psychotherapy.* New York: Guilford Press.

Gavey, N. (1989). Feminist poststructuralism and discourse analysis: Contributions to a feminist psychology. *Psychology of Women Quarterly, 14,* 459–476.

Gavey, N. (2005). *Just sex?: The cultural scaffolding of rape.* London: Routledge.

Gergen, K. J. (1973). Social psychology as history. *Journal of Personality and Social Psychology, 26,* 309–320.

Gergen, K. J. (1977). The social construction of self-knowledge. In T. Mischel (Ed.), *The self: Psychological and philosophical issues* (pp. 139–169). Oxford, UK: Blackwell.

Gergen, K. J. (1985). The social constructionist movement in psychology. *American Psychologist, 40,* 266–275.

Gergen, K. J. (1994). *Toward transformation in social knowledge* (2nd ed.). London: Sage. (Original work published 1982)

Gergen, K. J. (1994). *Realities and relationships.* Cambridge, MA: Harvard University Press.

Gergen, K. J. (1995). Metaphor and monophony in the twentieth century psychology of emotions. *History of the Human Sciences, 8,* 1–23.

Gergen, K. J. (1999). *An invitation to social construction.* London: Sage.

Gergen, K. J. (2001a). Psychology in a postmodern context. *American Psychologist, 56,* 803–813.

Gergen, K. J. (2001b). *Social construction in context.* London: Sage.

Gergen, K. J. (2005). Narrative, moral identity, and historical consciousness: A social constructionist account. In J. Straub (Ed.), *Narrative, identity and historical consciousness* (pp. 120–139). New York: Berghahn.

Gergen, K. J. (2006). *Therapeutic realities.* Chagrin Falls, OH: Taos Institute.

Gergen, K. J. (in press). *Relational being.* New York: Oxford University Press.

Gergen, K. J., & Davis, K.E. (1985). *The social construction of the person.* New York: Springer-Verlag.

Gergen, K. J., & Gergen, M. M. (1983). Narratives of the self. In T. R. Sarbin & K. E. Scheibe (Eds.), *Studies in social identity* (pp. 254–273). New York: Praeger.

Gergen, K. J., & Gergen, M. M. (1988). Narratives and the self as relationship. In L. Berkowitz (Ed.), *Advances in experimental social psychology* (Vol. 21, pp. 17–56). New York: Academic Press.

Gergen, K. J., & Gergen, M. M. (1995). What is this thing called love?: Emotional scenarios in historical perspective. *Journal of Narrative and Life History, 5,* 221–238.

Gergen, K. J., & Gergen, M. M. (2000). Qualitative inquiry: Tensions and transformations. In N. Denzin & Y. Lincoln (Eds.), *Handbook of qualitative research* (2nd ed., pp. 1025–1046). Thousand Oaks, CA: Sage.

Gergen, K. J., & Gergen, M. M. (2001). Ethnographic representations as relationship. In C. Ellis & A. Bochner (Eds.), *Ethnographically speaking* (pp. 11–33). Walnut Creek, CA: AltaMira Press.

Gergen, K. J., & Gergen, M. M. (2004). *Social construction: Entering the dialogue.* Chagrin Falls, OH: Taos Institute.

Gergen, K. J., & Gergen, M. M. (2006). Narratives in action. *Narrative Inquiry, 16,* 119–128.

Gergen, K. J., & Gergen, M. M. (2007). Social construction and research methods. Outhwaite & S. Turner (Eds.), *Sage handbook of social science methodology* (pp. 461–478). London, Thousand Oaks, CA: Sage.

Gergen, K. J., & Hosking, D. M. (2006). If you meet social construction along the road: A dialogue with Buddhism. In M. Kwee, K. J. Gergen, & F. Koshikawa (Eds.), *Horizons in Buddhist psychology: Practice, research, and theory* (pp. 299–314). Chagrin Falls, OH: Taos Institute.

Gergen, M. (1988). Toward a feminist metatheory and methodology in the social sciences. In M. Gergen (Ed.), *Feminist thought and the structure of knowledge* (pp. 87–104). New York: New York University Press.

Gergen, M. (2001). *Feminist reconstructions in psychology: Narrative, gender and performance.* Thousand Oaks, CA: Sage.

Gergen, M. (2005). Toward a performative psychology. In H. P. Mattes & Tamara Musfeld (Ed.), *Psychologische Konstruktionen: Der Diskurs des Performativen* (pp. 200–210). Gottingen, Germany: Vandenhoek & Ruprecht.

Gergen, M. (in press). Qualitative methods in feminist research. In W. Stainton-Rogers & C. Wittig (Eds.), *Handbook of qualitative research in psychology.* Thousand Oaks, CA: Sage.

Gergen, M., & Davis, S. (2003). Dialogic pedagogy: Developing narrative research perspectives through conversation. In R. Josselson, A. Lieblich, & D. McAdams (Eds.), *Up close and personal: The teaching and learning of narrative research* (pp. 239–258). Washington, DC: American Psychological Association.

Gergen, M., & Gergen, K. J. (1993). Narratives of the gendered body in popular autobiography. In R. Josselson & A. Lieblich (Eds.), *The narrative study of lives* (Vol. 1, pp. 191–218). Thousand Oaks, CA: Sage.

Gergen, M., & Gergen, K. J. (2005). Positive aging: Reconstructing the life course. In C. Goodheart & J. Worell (Eds.), *Handbook of women and girls* (pp. 416–426). London: Oxford University Press.

Graumann, C. F., & Gergen, K. J. (Eds.). (1996). *Historical dimensions of psychological discourse*. New York: Cambridge University Press.

Gray, R., & Sinding, C. (2002). *Standing ovation: Performing social science research about cancer*. Walnut Creek, CA: AltaMira Press.

Gubrium, J. F., & Holstein, J. A. (Eds.). (2003). *Postmodern interviewing*. Thousand Oaks, CA: Sage.

Halperin, D., Winkler, J., & Zeitlin, F. (Eds.). (1990). *Before sexuality: Erotic experience in the ancient Greek world*. Princeton, NJ: Princeton University Press.

Hare-Mustin, R. (1994). Discourse in a mirrored room: A postmodern analysis of therapy. *Family Process, 33*, 199–236.

Hare-Mustin, R., & Marecek, J. (Eds.). (1990). *Making a difference: Psychology and the construction of gender*. New Haven, CT: Yale University Press.

Harré, R. (Ed.). (1986). *The social construction of emotion*. Oxford, UK: Blackwell.

Harré, R. (2003). *The self and others: Positioning individuals and groups in personal, political and cultural contexts*. New York: Praeger.

Harré, R., Brockmeier, J., & Muhlhousler, P. (1998). *Greenspeak: Study of environmental discourse*. London: Sage.

Harré, R., & Secord, P. (1972). *The explanation of social behaviour*. London: Rowman & Littlefield.

Hazan, H. (1994). *Old age, constructions and deconstructions*. Cambridge, UK: Cambridge University Press.

Held, B. (1996). *Back to reality: A critique of postmodern psychotherapy*. New York: Norton.

Henriques, J., Hollway, W., Urwin, C., Venn, C., & Walkerdine, V. (1984). *Changing the subject: Psychology, social regulation and subjectivity*. London: Methuen.

Hepburn, A. (2000). On the alleged incompatibility between relativism and feminist psychology. *Feminism and Psychology, 10*, 94–103.

Hepworth, J. (1999). *The social construction of anorexia nervosa*. London: Sage.

Hermans, H. J. M., Immink, G. K., de Jong, A., & van der Lans, J. (Eds.). (2002). *Social construction and theology*. Leiden, The Netherlands: Brill.

Hermans, H. J. M., & Kempen, H. J. G. (1995). *The dialogical self: Meaning as movement*. San Diego, CA: Academic Press.

Hibberd, F. (2005). *Unfolding social constructionism*. New York: Springer.

Hoffman, L. (2002). *Family therapy: An intimate history*. New York: W. W. Norton.

Holstein, J. A., & Gubrium, J. F. (2000a). *Constructing the life course* (2nd ed.). Lanham, MD: AltaMira/ Rowman & Littlefield.

Holstein, J. A., & Gubrium, J. F. (2000b). *The self we live by: Narrative identity in a postmodern world*. New York: Oxford University Press.

Holzkamp, K. (1978). *Gesellschaftlichkeit des indivuums: Aufsatze 1974–1977*. Berlin: Atheneum-Verlag.

Holzman, L. (1997). *Schools for growth: A radical alternative to current educational models*. Mahwah, NJ: Erlbaum.

Holzman, L., & Morss, J. (Eds.). (2000). *Postmodern psychologies, societal practice and political life*. New York: Routledge.

Hoyt, M. (Ed.). (1998). *The handbook of constructive therapies: Innovative approaches from leading practitioners*. San Francisco: Jossey-Bass.

Hurwitz, B., & Greenhalgh, T. (1998). *Narrative based medicine: Dialogue and discourse in clinical practice*. London: BMJ.

Ibanez, T., & Iniguez, L. (Eds.). (1997). *Critical social psychology*. London: Sage.

Israel, J., & Tajfel, H. (1972). *Context of social psychology: A critical assessment*. New York: Academic Press.

Jackson, S. (2005). "I'm 15 and desperate for sex": "Doing" and "undoing" desire in letters to a teenage magazine. *Feminism and Psychology, 15*, 295–313.

Jones, K. (2006). A biographic researcher in pursuit of an aesthetic: The use of arts-based (re)presentations in "performative" dissemination of life stories. *Qualitative Sociological Review, 2*, 66–85.

Josselson, R., & Lieblich, A. (Eds.). (1995). *The narrative study of lives: Vol. 3. Interpreting experience*. Thousand Oaks, CA: Sage.

Josselson, R., Lieblich, A., & McAdams, D. (Eds.). (2003). *Up close and personal: The teaching and learning of narrative research*. Washington, DC: American Psychological Association.

Jost, J. T., & Kruglanski, A. W. (2002). The estrangement of social constructionism and experimental social psychology: History of the rift and prospects for reconciliation. *Personality and Social Psychology Review, 6*, 168–187.

Karp, D. A. (1996). *Speaking of sadness: Depression, disconnection, and the meanings of illness*. New York: Oxford University Press.

Kelly, G. A. (1955). *The psychology of personal constructs*. New York: Norton.

Kessen, W., (1979). The American child and other cultural inventions. *American Psychologist, 34*, 815–820.

Kessler, S., & McKenna, W. (1978). *Gender: An ethnomethodological approach.* New York: Wiley.

Kimmel, M. (1994). Masculinity as homophobia. In H. Brod & M. Kaufman (Eds.), *Theorizing masculinities* (pp. 119–141). Thousand Oaks, CA: Sage.

Kirschner, S. (1996). *The religious and romantic origins of psychoanalysis.* New York: Cambridge University Press.

Kitzinger, C. (1987). *The social construction of lesbianism.* Thousand Oaks, CA: Sage.

Komesaroff, P. A., Rothfield, P., & Daly, J. (Eds.). (1997). *Reinterpreting menopause: Cultural and philosophical issues.* New York: Routledge.

Kuhn, T. (1970). *The structure of scientific revolutions* (2nd ed.). Chicago: University of Chicago Press. (Original work published 1962)

Kutchins, H., & Kirk, S. A. (1997). *Making us crazy: DSM: The psychiatric bible and the creation of mental disorders.* New York: Free Press.

Kvale, S. (Ed.). (1992). *Psychology and postmodernism.* London: Sage.

Kwee, M. G. T., & Taams, M. (2006). A new Buddhist psychology: Moving beyond Theravada and Mahayana. In M. G. T. Kwee, K. J. Gergen, & F. Koshikawa (Eds.), *Horizons in Buddhist psychology: Practice, research, and theory* (pp. 299–314). Chagrin Falls, OH: Taos Institute.

Laing, R. D. (1965). *The divided self: An existential study in sanity and madness.* London: Penguin.

Lather, P., & Smithies, C. (1997). *Troubling with angels: Women living with HIV/AIDS.* Boulder, CO: Westview Press.

Latour, B., & Woolgar, S. (1986). *Laboratory life: The construction of scientific facts.* Princeton, NJ: Princeton University Press.

Leary, D. (1990). *Metaphors in the history of psychology.* Cambridge, UK: Cambridge University Press.

Lieblich, A., & Josselson, R. (Eds.). (1994). *The narrative study of lives: Vol. 2. Exploring identity and gender.* Thousand Oaks, CA: Sage.

Lockford, L. (2004). *Performing femininity: Rewriting gender identity.* Walnut Creek, CA: AltaMira Press.

Lorber, J., & Moore, L. J. (2002). *Gender and the social construction of illness.* Walnut Creek, CA: AltaMira Press.

Lykes, M. B. (1997). Activist participatory research among the Maya of Guatemala: Constructing meanings from situated knowledge. *Journal of Social Issues, 53,* 725–746.

Mancuso, J. X., & Sarbin, T. R. (1983). The self-narrative in the enactment of roles. In T. R. Sarbin (Ed.), *Studies in social identity* (pp. 233–253). New York: Praeger.

Marecek, J. (2003). Dancing through minefields: Toward a qualitative stance in psychology. In P. M. Camic, J. E. Rhodes, & L. Yardley (Eds.), *Qualitative research in psychology: Expanding perspectives in methodology and design* (pp. 49–69). Washington, DC: American Psychological Association.

Mattingly, C., & Garro, L. C. (Eds.). (2000). *Narrative and the cultural construction of illness and healing.* Berkeley: University of California Press.

McAdams, D. (1985). *Power, intimacy, and the life story: Personological inquiries into identity.* Homewood, IL: Dorsey Press.

McAdams, D. P. (1993). *The stories we live by: Personal myths and the making of the self.* New York: Morrow.

McAdams, D. P. (2006a). *Identity and story: Creating self in narrative.* Washington, DC: American Psychological Association.

McAdams, D. P. (2006b). *The redemptive self: Stories Americans live by.* New York: Oxford University Press.

McLeod, J. (1997). *Narrative and psychotherapy.* London: Sage.

McNamee, S., & Gergen, K. J. (Eds.). (1992). *Therapy as social construction.* Thousand Oaks, CA, London: Sage.

Middleton, D., & Brown, S. D. (2005). *The social psychology of experience: Studies in remembering and forgetting.* London: Sage.

Middleton, D., & Edwards, D. (Eds.). (1990). *Collective remembering.* London: Sage.

Mishler, E. G. (1984). *The discourse of medicine.* Norwood, NJ: Ablex.

Morawski, J. (Ed.). (1988). *The rise of experimentation in American psychology.* New Haven, CT: Yale University Press.

Morris, D. (1991). *The culture of pain.* Berkeley: University of California Press.

Morss, J. R. (1990). *The biologising of childhood: Developmental psychology and the Darwinian myth.* Hove, UK: Erlbaum.

Neimeyer, R. A. (Ed.). (2000). *Constructions of disorder: Meaning-making frameworks for psychotherapy.* Washington, DC: American Psychological Association.

Neimeyer, R. A. (2001). *Meaning reconstruction and the experience of loss.* Washington, DC: American Psychological Association.

Newman, F., & Holzman, L. (1996). *Unscientific psychology: A cultural–performatory approach to understanding human life.* Westport, CT: Praeger.

Nightingale, D., & Cromby, J. (1999). *Social constructionist psychology: A critical analysis of theory and practice.* Celtic Court, UK: Open University Press.

O'Hanlon, W. (2003). *In search of solutions: New directions for psychotherapy.* New York: Norton.

Oyama, S. (1991). Essentialism, women and war: Protesting too much, protesting too little. In A. E. Hunter (Ed.), *Genes and gender: Vol. 6. On peace, war, and gender: A challenge to genetic explanation* (pp. 64–76). New York: Feminist Press.

Oyama, S. (1993). How shall I name thee?: The construction of natural selves. *Theory and Psychology, 3,* 471–496.

Pare, D. A., & Larner, G. (Eds.). (2004). *Collaborative practice in psychology and therapy.* Binghamton, NY: Haworth Press.

Parker, I. (Ed.). (1998). *Social constructionism, discourse and realism*. London: Sage.

Parker, I., Georgas, E., Harper, D., McLaughlin, T., & Stowall-Smith, M. (1995). *Deconstructing psychopathology*. London: Sage.

Parker, I., & Shotter, J. (Eds.). (1990). *Deconstructing social psychology*. London: Routledge.

Polkinghorne, D. E. (1988). *Narrative knowing and the human sciences*. Albany: State University of New York Press.

Potter, J. (1996). *Representing reality*. London: Sage.

Potter, J., & Wetherell, M. (1987). *Discourse and social psychology: Beyond attitudes and behavior*. London: Sage.

Prilletensky, I. (1994). *The morals and politics of psychology*. Albany: State University of New York Press.

Quosh, C., & Gergen, K. J. (in press). Constructing trauma and treatment: Knowledge, power, and resistance. In T. Sugiman, K. J. Gergen, & W. Wagner (Eds.), *Meaning in action: Construction, narratives and representations*. New York: Springer.

Rapley, M. (2004). *The social construction of intellectual disability*. Cambridge, UK: Cambridge University Press.

Reason, P., & Bradbury, H. (Eds.). (2000). *Handbook of action research, participative inquiry and practice*. Sage: London.

Reason, P., & Bradbury, H. (Eds.). (2007). *Handbook of action research, participative inquiry and practice* (2nd ed.). Sage: London.

Rogers, A., Casey, M. E., Ekert, J., Holland, J., Nakkula, V., & Sheinberg, N. (1999). An interpretive poetics of languages of the unsayable. In R. Josselson & A. Lieblich (Eds.), *The narrative study of lives: Vol. 6. Making meaning of narratives* (pp. 77–106). Thousand Oaks, CA: Sage.

Rogoff, B., Turkanis, C. G., & Bartlett, L. (Eds.). (2001). *Learning together: Children and adults in a school community*. New York: Oxford University Press.

Rose, N. (1985). *The psychological complex*. London: Routledge & Kegan Paul.

Rosen, H., & Kuehlwein, K. T. (Eds.). (1996). *Reconstructing realities: Meaning-making perspectives for psychotherapists*. San Francisco: Jossey Bass.

Rosenwald, G., & Ochberg, R. (Eds.). (1990). *Storied lives*. New Haven, CT: Yale University Press.

Russell, G. M. (2000). *Voted out: The psychological consequences of anti-gay politics*. New York: New York University Press.

Sampson, E. E. (1985). The decentralization of identity: Toward a revised concept of personal and social order. *American Psychologist, 40*, 1203–1211.

Sampson, E. E. (1993). *Celebrating the other: A dialogic account of human nature*. Boulder, CO: Westview Press.

Sarbin, T. (Ed.). (1986). *Narrative psychology: The stories nature of human conduct*. New York: Praeger.

Sarbin, T., & Mancuso, J. (1980). *Schizophrenia: Medical diagnosis or verdict?* Elmsford, NY: Pergamon.

Seikulla, J., Arnkil, T., & Eriksson, E. (2003). Postmodern society and social networks: Open and anticipation dialogues in network meetings. *Family Process, 42*, 185–204.

Sherif, C. W. (1987). Bias in psychology. In S. Harding (Ed.), *Feminism and methodology* (pp. 37–56). Bloomington: Indiana University Press. (Original work published 1979)

Shields, S. A. (2002). *Speaking from the heart: Gender and the social meaning of emotion*. Cambridge, UK: Cambridge University Press.

Shotter, J. (1990). The social construction of remembering and forgetting. In D. Middleton & D. Edwards (Eds.), *Collective remembering* (pp. 120–138). London: Sage.

Shotter, J. (2007). *Conversational realities, reloaded*. Chagrin Falls, OH: Taos Institute.

Smedslund, J. (1978). Bandura's theory of self-efficacy: A set of common sense theorems. *Scandinavian Journal of Psychology, 19*, 1–14.

Smedslund, J. (1988). *Psycho-logic*. New York: Springer-Verlag.

Smedslund, J. (2004). *Dialogues about a new psychology*. Chagrin Falls, OH: Taos Institute.

Spacks, P. M. (1995). *Boredom: The literary history of a state of mind*. Chicago: University of Chicago Press.

Steffe, L. P., & Gale, J. (Eds.). (1995). *Constructivism in education*. Hillsdale, NJ: Erlbaum.

Strickland, L., Aboud, F., & Gergen, K. J. (Eds.). (1977). *Social psychology in transition*. New York: Plenum Press.

Szasz, T. (1961). *The myth of mental illness: Foundations of a theory of personal conduct*. New York: Hoeber-Harper.

Tappan, M. B., & Packer, M. J. (Eds.). (1991). *Narrative and storytelling: Implications for understanding moral development*. San Francisco: Jossey-Bass.

Tiefer, L. (1995). *Sex is not a natural act, and other essays*. Boulder, CO: Westview Press.

Tillmann-Healy, L. M. (1996). A secret life in a culture of thinness. In C. Ellis & A. Bochner (Eds.), *Composing ethnography* (pp. 76–105). Walnut Creek, CA: AltaMira Press.

Van Langehove, L., & Harré, R. (1998). *Positioning theory*. London: Blackwell.

Vygotsky, L. (1962). *Thought and language* (E. Hanfmann & G. Vakar, Eds. & Trans.). Boston: MIT Press. (Original work published 1934)

Vygotsky, L. S. (1978). *Mind in society: The development of higher psychological processes*. Cambridge, MA: Harvard University Press.

Walkerdine, V. (1988). *The mastery of reason*. London: Routledge.

Walkerdine, V. (1990). *Schoolgirl fictions*. London: Verso.

Walkerdine, V., & the Girls & Mathematics Unit. (1989). *Counting girls out*. London: Virago.

Walkerdine, V., & Lucey, H. (1989). *Democracy in the kitchen: Regulating mothers and socializing daughters*. London: Virago.

Weick, K. (1995). *Sensemaking in organizations.* Thousand Oaks, CA: Sage.

Weinstein, M. (2004). Randomized design and the myth of certain knowledge: Guinea pig narratives and cultural critique. *Qualitative Inquiry, 10,* 246–260.

Weis, L., & Fine, M. (2005). *Beyond silenced voices: Class, race, and gender in United States schools.* Albany: State University of New York Press.

Weisstein, N. (1971). Psychology constructs the female. In V. Gornick & B. K. Moran (Eds.), *Women in sexist society* (pp. 133–146). New York: Basic Books.

Wells, G. (1992). *Dialogic inquiry: Towards a sociocultural practice and theory of education.* Cambridge, UK: Cambridge University Press.

Wertsch, J. (1991). *Voices of the mind.* Cambridge, MA: Harvard University Press.

Wetherell, M., & Potter, J. (1992). *Mapping the language of racism: Discourse and the legitimation of exploitation.* New York: Columbia University Press.

Wetherell, M., Taylor, S., & Yates, S. J. (Eds.). (2001). *Discourse theory and practice: A reader.* London: Sage.

White, M., & Epston, D. (1990). *Narrative means to therapeutic ends.* New York: Norton.

Whitehouse, P. (2005). *Returning to normal: A cry for revival and reformation.* Chicago: Independent.

Willig, C. (Ed.). (1999). *Applied discourse analysis: Social and psychological interventions.* Buckingham, UK: Open University Press.

CHAPTER 10

Social Constructions in the Study of Public Policy

● **Anne L. Schneider**
Helen Ingram

S ocial construction theory has begun to play an important part in understanding how it is that public policy treats some people so much better (or worse) than others and what the implications are for citizenship and democracy (Ingram & Schneider, 1993, 2007; Schneider & Ingram, 1993, 1997, 2005). In a democracy, policymakers have to give reasons for their actions, and these reasons often involve the creation of positive and negative constructions that justify specific types of policy and policy impacts. Although public policy often reflects the prevailing social constructions of social groups, there are times when it acts as a powerful engine for change that mobilizes people for or against the policy and that alters prevailing constructions of events and people. Policy designs teach lessons to people affected by the policy and to the public at large about how one can expect to be treated by government, whether one is a "worthy" or "unworthy" person, and what kind of political participation is appropriate (Schneider & Ingram, 1997). The result is an unequal citizenship whereby those who are most vulnerable and receive the least from policy tend to have the lowest rates of political participation and sometimes are the least aware of their own interests.

Empirical research has confirmed the importance of social constructions of target populations and has shown how constructions are used, manipulated, reproduced, and changed in the policymaking process. Another important area of research emphasizes how policy designs carry messages that are interpreted by people in their daily experiences with public policy and that shape one's orientation toward government and subsequent political participation.

The constructionist perspective, with its focus on symbols, interpretation, and discourse, has had a profound impact on the study of public policy. This chapter reviews the theoretical work and the empirical research that has traced the role of social constructions across numerous policy fields and the implications for citizenship and democracy.

Background

The study of public policy generally is grounded in a very strong positivist tradition, and early studies of public policy examined whether and how policies achieved their stated goals. Politics was often treated as interference with rational management, and insofar as politics was afforded a role, the task assigned was simply to establish goals. Scientific analysis was considered the appropriate way to design policies that could achieve those goals. Political scientists who have traditionally studied public policy have been interested in policy processes and have treated public policy as merely a window through which to study process. Theodore Lowi's (1979) famous public policy typology saw public policy as both the cause and the result of different political processes. For instance, "iron triangles" of agencies, interest groups, and congressional committees were associated with distributive policies that rewarded narrow-gauged interests at the expense of long-term national welfare. Another prominent framework, advocacy coalitions, emphasizes the role of policy coalitions in policy formation and change (Sabatier, 1999). Path dependency/punctuated equilibrium theory focuses on empirical studies of how policies stay on the same course for long periods of time and then are suddenly changed (Baumgartner & Jones, 1993; Jones et al., 2003).

In the 1980s and 1990s, however, one strand of public policy analysis took a critical turn. Scholars such as Dryzek (1990), Stone (1997), Fischer (1980), deLeon (1997), Yanow (1996), and Bacchi (1999) went beyond the pluralist question of short-term winners and losers to consider the impact of public policy on democracy and citizenship. Public policies, it is argued, have impacts far beyond their putative goals and have profound effects on how the political system serves citizens (Ingram & Schneider, 1993; Landy, 1993; Schneider & Ingram, 1993; 1993; Stone, 1993). Researchers working in this critical vein examine the symbolic, interpretive, and multiple understandings found in political discourse and policy arguments (Edelman, 1964; Fischer, 1980; Rochefort & Cobb, 1994). Most of the work acknowledges an empirical, material, or "immediate" world but contends that the symbolic or interpretive aspects are crucial to understanding it. The path-breaking early work of Murray Edelman (1964, p. 5) put it this way:

> There is . . . the immediate world in which people make and do things that have directly observable consequences. In these activities men can check their acts and assumptions against the consequences and correct errors. There is feedback . . . relatively few are involved in politics in this direct way.
>
> Politics is for most of us a passing parade of abstract symbols, yet a parade which our experience teaches us to be a benevolent or malevolent force that can be close to omnipotent.

Empirical research has persistently documented very unequal access and resources in policymaking, thereby exposing the privileged positions held by politically powerful groups in actual contests over policy. Attention of scholars then turned to how issues come to public attention in the first place and how they make their way onto the formal policymaking agenda. Agenda-setting research embraced ideas from the social construction movement in sociology and other fields (Berger & Luckmann, 1967;

Best, 1989; Miller & Holstein, 1993; Specter & Kutsuse, 1977). Rochefort and Cobb (1994) contend that the social construction of issues is a critical factor in understanding how issues come to public attention and become part of the political agenda. Research also has documented the importance of issue framing and the role of social construction in which of several competing definitions of "the problem" will rise to the forefront and drive policy arguments (Majone, 1989). Yanow's interpretive methodologies, reflected in *How Does a Policy Mean?* (1996), and Fischer's (2003) explication of an interpretive policy analysis show how language underlies multiple meanings. Fischer has proposed multiple levels of evaluation research in an attempt to incorporate interpretive analysis and discourse into traditionally instrumental evaluation studies.

The Schneider–Ingram Framework

The original framework we developed moved the field forward in several ways: It brought the importance of social construction into the understanding of how power operates in policymaking; it brought the *design and content*, not just the process, of public policy into the discussion of symbols and values; and it connected policy design elements to messages that affect citizenship and participation. Building from our framework (Ingram & Schneider, 1993, 2005; Schneider & Ingram, 1993, 1997, 2005), many other scholars have conducted empirical research focused on the reciprocal relationships between social constructions and public policy.

Definitions

Social constructions refer to "world making," or the varying ways in which realities are shaped. Similar to the social construction tradition in sociology, we posited a societal context resembling a primeval soup, in which all the ingredients swirled about from which issues could be framed and public policies proposed. The process of socially constructing issues, people, and events, however, is viewed as one of competing perspectives in which extant public policy itself plays a prominent role. There is, in some respects, no easily demarcated "beginning" of a policy process, as policy and societal institutions at one point in time embed particular constructions that continue to exert influence for many years thereafter (Ingram & Schneider, 2005). At some point, a particular construction may become so entrenched that it is thought of as "real." "We live in a world of constructs that simply 'are' to most ways of thinking" (Schneider & Ingram, 1997, p. 73). Social constructions, however, are not always hegemonic, and countervailing points of view continue to be heard and to compete with the dominant construction.

Our framework goes on to contend that the policymaking process often involves the creation of "target populations" and then uses or creates images of the target groups that will justify the allocation of benefits or burdens to that group. Target populations are the groups actually identified in public policy as recipients of benefits or burdens or otherwise incorporated into the policy design. Policy may set the boundaries of targets so that they coincide with visible social groups, but policy often combines groups or subdivides them to create more specific target populations.

> The social construction of potential target populations refers to the images, stereotypes, and beliefs that confer identities on people and connect them with others as a social group who are possible candidates for receiving beneficial or burdensome policy. (Schneider & Ingram, 1997, p. 75)

We have proposed that in many policymaking institutions, all aspects of policy design—the way the issue is framed, the language used to justify the policy, the rules and tools actually employed within the design, the implementation and institutional structures, and the underlying assumptions—may be shaped differently, depending on the social construction of the target group.

The Typology

Our framework is centrally situated within the political science literature, as it recognizes the importance of political power resources such as the size of a group, intensity, wealth, organization, and access to decision making, as well as social constructions. These are combined into a two-dimensional typology (see Figure 10.1).

The horizontal axis in Figure 10.1 shows whether the social constructions of the group are positive or negative. Positive constructions include language such as *deserving, entitled, good, meritorious*. Negative constructions range from images such as *greedy, corrupt*, and *immoral* to *dangerous* or *inhuman*.

The vertical axis indicates whether the power resources are extensive or meager. Power resources refer to such things as the size of the group, their propensity to mobilize, access to decision points, wealth, and intensity of beliefs. Schneider and Ingram (2005) propose that the allocation of benefits and burdens falls heavily along the left–right diagonal, with benefits going primarily to groups that have significant political power, as well as constructions of "deservedness" or "entitlement." Burdens, in contrast,

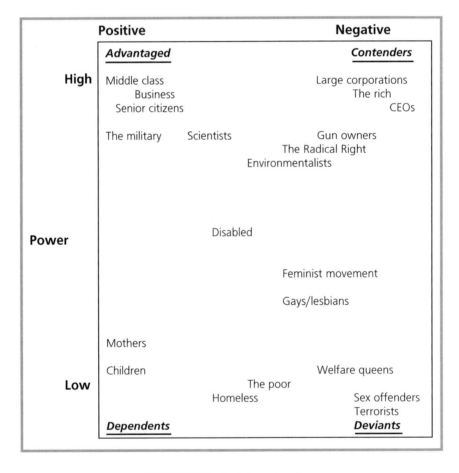

FIGURE 10.1. Social construction.

go mainly to those without power and who also are negatively constructed as undeserving and unworthy, if not downright dangerous. Schneider and Ingram extend the theory to explain how social constructions become embedded within the design itself, sending messages to the target group and the public at large about the worthiness (or lack of it) of the target group. These messages become internalized by the target populations themselves, with extensive implications for the identity, attitudes, and political participation patterns of the groups. Through these dynamic processes, public policy not only responds to social constructions but also helps create them and may either reproduce or modify them through policy design. A critical implication is that policy, through these processes, produces a distinctly unequal citizenship in which those who have the most to gain by increasing their participation are the least likely to do so. And those who receive the most remain disdainful of government but participate at very high levels to protect their privileges.

The policy space should be thought of as a two-dimensional continuum rather than as categories, but labels have been applied to the four corners. *Advantaged* groups have extensive resources for the influence of policy, such as size, wealth, mobilization potential, and positions of authority, but they also carry very positive social constructions as being deserving of the special benefits received from policy. These are widely assumed to be "worthy" people who have earned their position of respect in society and who contribute significantly to the public good. The specific groups shown in Figure 10.1 reflect the perspective of a hypothetical public official, as the actual placement of any group is an empirical issue. But many would agree that advantaged groups at this point in history include the middle class, business, senior citizens, the military, and scientists. The military are honored for their heroism and courage in protecting the homeland. Scientists are positively constructed as dedicated, intelligent people who seek new information

that will benefit society. The middle class has been extended to include just about everyone, as policy arguments today almost never acknowledge that the policy will actually benefit the rich or the working class.

Contenders also have considerable political power but generally carry negative constructions. Large corporations, for example, periodically carry a construction of being greedy and corrupt. The "rich" throughout history have been vilified as not deserving of all they receive. Gun owners are fearful of losing their once-positive image as "sportsmen" and "rugged individualists" to a more negative construction as irresponsible people who contribute to crime and schoolyard disasters such as Columbine. *Dependents* carry a positive construction as loving, sweet, blameless, helpless, "good" people such as mothers and children, but they exercise almost no political power. *Deviants* carry very heavy negative constructions, ranging from lazy and irresponsible ("welfare queens") to the dangerousness attributed to terrorists and "sex offenders."

Social Constructions, Policy Design, and Democratic Citizenship

The central set of propositions in our framework focus on explaining how social constructions are used by political leaders, how policies are designed in accordance with the social constructions of social groups, and how policies so designed affect subsequent political behavior.

Political leaders are strongly motivated, we argue, to pay attention both to the political power and to the social construction of social groups. Policymaking in a democracy is not simply a matter of raw political power, because leaders have to give reasons for their actions, and those reasons typically involve claims about the worthiness of various groups or claims about how providing benefits (or punishments) to some group will in fact benefit the entire nation. The most straightforward implication of the framework is that beneficial policy, which confers rights, subsidies, and regulations desired by the group, will go mainly to advantaged populations. Political leaders have much to gain from such policy, as support and loyalty from the groups themselves can be expected, and the larger public is not likely to object as they, too, believe that these policies are going to deserving people whose actions will serve the national interest. The rationales for such policies almost always stress the connection between the group and the putative national interest. The military and business sectors of society in the 1940s and 1950s were granted significant subsidies and positive regulations in order to combat Communism. Once the Communist threat was diminished through the collapse of the Soviet Union, these same groups continued to receive their bounty, but the rationale changed to become national economic competitiveness. Currently, the same groups are still benefited, but the rationale now is focused on combating the terrorist threats. Advantaged groups sometimes are recipients of burdensome policy, but this usually is rationalized on the grounds that the policy is needed to provide a level playing field among a number of equally advantaged groups.

Contenders also receive significant beneficial policy, but such policy tends to be *sub rosa* and deceptive. The efforts by Republicans in Congress, for example, to eliminate the inheritance tax and the claim that this benefits the middle class is an example. As of 2006, this "death tax" only applies to inheritances greater than $1 million—more accurately, a policy that would benefit the rich. Policymakers also may provide token burdens to contenders but leave avenues for avoiding these burdens during the implementation process. In the case of contenders, the strategy is to keep their issues off the public agenda and in the back rooms of politics, such that the groups themselves will know that they are getting advantages or avoiding burdens but the broader public will be unaware.

Policy designs for dependents tend to be heavy on rhetoric and light on actual funding. Congress tends to push such policies into the local arena, such as No Child Left Behind, by which the effort to strengthen schools was mandated at the federal level but with funding that most considered far less than what was needed. On the other hand, policymakers have to be careful not to appear to be mean-spirited when it comes to dependents, and regulations accompanied by positive rhetoric about the value of the group are common.

Policy for deviants is heavily punishment-oriented in the United States. These groups provide a scapegoating outlet by which policymakers can demonize the groups without fear of public retribution and mandate extensive punishment. Such policies are aided not only by the negative social construction and lack of political power of those who break the law but also by the very positively constructed notion of being "tough" rather than "soft." Policy designs that allocate funds even for punishment tend to have an intermediate target agency or population, such as private prisons or the contractors who help fight terrorists, that stands to benefit from expenditures. The political value of punishment policy to policymakers could not be more obvious, as the United States, over the past 30 years, has increased its penalties for crime to the point at which this country incarcerates a higher percentage of its population than any other nation in the world.

Social constructions become embedded in policy designs through the allocation of benefits and burdens, the rationales that accompany the policy, and also the actual tools and rules within the policy itself. Policy designs send messages to target populations and to the broader public that influence political orientations and participation. Advantaged groups get the message that they are good, intelligent people and that their problems are central to the national interest. They can expect to be treated with respect.

In turn, these groups are expected to be supportive of government even if disdainful that government can actually operate for the public good. They expect to participate in many ways, and they expect to "win" politically. Contenders, on the other hand, realize that they are controversial, that to "win" in politics they must work behind the scenes and engage in deceptive practices. Dependents recognize that they are helpless and needy, that their problems are mainly the responsibility of the civic society or faith-based institutions rather than government, and that other people's interests are more important than their own. Their level of participation in traditional activities such as voting, giving, campaigning, and so on is very low. Deviants get the message that they are "bad" and "dangerous" and will be treated with disrespect, hate, and disregard for their rights. Their participation is expected to be very low, and when they mobilize, if they do, it will be in the form of strikes, riots, or violent activities of some type. A key implication of the framework is that policy produces a distinctive unequal citizenship such that those who have the most to gain from being more active politically are the least likely to take such action. Thus negative and divisive social constructions manipulated by policymakers and embedded in policy designs have long-lasting consequences for future public policy, for citizenship, and for democracy.

This framework was designed for and has been useful in answering questions such as:

How is it that while every citizen is nominally equal before the law, policy design tends to distribute mainly benefits to some people, while almost always punishing others? Why is it that some policies are perpetuated and even enlarged despite their failure to achieve policy goals? How is it that some negatively constructed groups are able to gain a more positive social construction and better treatment by policy makers whereas others do not? And why and how does it happen that policy designs sometimes depart from the typical repro-duction of power and social constructions to introduce change in institutions, power relationships, and the social construction of target groups? (Ingramk, Schneider, & deLeon, 2007, p. 93)

The utility of this framework comes not so much from recognizing that social groups carry social constructions that sometimes are so entrenched as to be taken as God-given attributes—this has long been recognized by sociologists. Nor is its value confined to challenging the instrumental, positivist, pluralist traditions in political science, as others have also issued such challenges. Rather, its utility comes, first, in the integration of pluralist and symbolic traditions through its recognition of the *interaction* between political power and social constructions. It also integrates symbolic and interpretive traditions with behavioral studies—long a dominant force in political science—in its contention that public policymakers and the policy-making process itself *manipulate* constructions, bringing some to the forefront and pushing others into the background. Second, and equally important, this framework connects social constructions with *policy design*, proposing that the characteristics of public policies differ depending on whether the target groups are advantaged, contenders, dependents, or deviants. Perhaps even more significant is the idea that the social constructions of target populations become *embedded* in policy designs and in institutions that then send messages both to the target populations and to the society at large about the worth and value of social groups. This aspect of the theory again has an integrative role, as it connects the social construction and symbolic/interpretive movements in public policy scholarship with historical and institutional analysis, recognizing the influence that institutions have on people's lives. When policy and institutions embed certain constructions and assumptions about people, they send powerful messages that become internalized and have long-lasting impacts on the identity, political participation, and beliefs of target groups. In some cases, this has the unexpected effect of policy becoming the focal point for mobilization and creating a backlash that might not otherwise have occurred. The framework also complements theories of policy change—particularly path dependency and punctuated equilibrium—as it helps us understand why some policies are especially susceptible to long, uninterrupted periods on a particular trajectory and others to sudden punctuations (Schneider, 2006).

Finally, the framework lends itself to inquiry from a variety of social science traditions. Some scholars test propositions derived from the theory using traditional quantitative methods. Others conduct historical case studies of policy evolution and change. Some incorporate the ideas into institutional analysis or analysis of social movements. Still others use the framework to turn a critical eye on society and seek to improve the plight of disadvantaged populations by unmasking the role of social constructions and proposing alternative constructions that would justify vastly different types of policy.

This framework should not be treated in a rigid or slavish manner, as there are many nuances. Also, it is as important to find exceptions to the patterns as it is to document the general ideas (Schneider & Ingram 1997, 2005). For example, some people find themselves in more than one group—professional women, for example, are sometimes treated as advantaged people, sometimes as dependents, and sometimes as contenders, especially if they are feminists. The extremely well-off people, such as Bill Gates, are reviled as greedy on the one hand and lauded for their philanthropy on the other. Not all institutions and decision-making systems rely so heavily on social constructions as is implied by the framework. *Degenerative democracy* refers to policymaking systems or institutions in which social constructions and political power interact in the way specified here. Other institutions may rely almost exclusively on power, without the negative and

divisive social constructions; and still others may be grounded in the norms of scientific and professional analysis (Schneider & Ingram, 1997). Some institutions, such as the U.S. Congress, may use more than one decision-making style, focusing on social constructions in relation to some issues and paying far more attention to scientific analysis in other policy arenas.

What Has Been Learned from Empirical Research

As shown in Table 10.1, empirical research on social constructions and public policy stretches across many policy areas and involves a wide variety of methodological traditions. The table shows the studies arranged into four categories: social constructions and the policymaking process; social constructions and the allocation of benefits and burdens; social constructions and the choice of policy design elements (other than whether the recipients are slated for benefits or burdens), and social construction, identity, and political participation.

Social Constructions and the Policymaking Process

In the early days of the republic, as Jensen (2005) explains in her historical study of veterans' pensions, it was not the common practice to allocate subsidies to *groups* of people using general rules to set boundaries around a "target population." Instead, *individuals* who were in need could petition Congress for relief. Thus the emergence of a subsidy program for an entire group of people—veterans of the Continental Army in the Revolutionary War—was a marked departure from the past and was hotly debated. Jensen documents the arguments over who should be included (all veterans, or only those in the Continental Army and not those in the militia? Or only those who were poverty-stricken? Or perhaps only those who were wounded?) And if veterans,

TABLE 10.1. Summary of Empirical Studies

Author	Policy area	Comments
A. Social constructions and the policymaking process		
Anglund (1998)	Small-business procurement	Historical analysis (1953–1993) of small-business procurement policy finds that positive social constructions are central to understanding which of several competing problem definitions will be successful in policy change.
Anglund (1999)	Small-business procurement	Historical and comparative policy analysis of small-business procurement policies shows that social constructions of target groups are important in understanding when a "comparison effect" form of policy learning (i.e., target groups comparing themselves with others) is likely to lead to policy change.
Bensonsmith (2005)	Welfare	Author contends that the Moynihan report on the African American family and dependency on welfare provided negative construction of welfare mothers that set the stage for the negative constructions that still prevail.
Bundy (1994)	Health	The study finds that positive social constructions influence the ability of a group to mobilize in its own interests and that its participation in policy design influences the successful implementation of policy.
DiAlto (2005)	Minorities	Historical analysis shows how change in the social construction of Japanese Americans aided their struggle to become more positively viewed.
Ferrales (2004)	Health/AIDS	Qualitative analysis compares AIDS policy development in Mexico and in the United States, finding that the social constructions of target groups played a significant role in policy design in both countries.
Furlong (1993)	Health	Analysis of the agenda-setting process showed that policy was more likely to be initiated, to reach the formal agenda, and to be passed when target populations were positively viewed by Congress.
Harrison (2001)	Health/ environment	Study explains that the social construction of breastfeeding and contamination of breast milk by dioxin contribute to contamination of breast milk not being able to find a place on the policy agenda.
Hirshberg (2001)	Indigenous populations	Study shows how perceptions about race influence policy positions of Alaskan legislators in terms of health and social services for native Alaskans.
Ingram & Ingram (2006)	Organic agriculture	Analysis shows how the marginalized social movement supporting organic agriculture created for themselves a social construction of "expert" that led to policy change.
Itkonen (2004)	Education	Study of interest-group strategies shows that positive constructions of students with disabilities as contributing members of society are more effective in gaining positive legislation than constructions of disabled students as "different."

(continued)

TABLE 10.1. *(continued)*

Author	Policy area	Comments
A. Social constructions and the policymaking process *(cont.)*		
Jenness & Grattet (2001)	Crime (hate)	Study traces the development of the "hate crime" concept and how it made its way into public policy, as well as the diffusion of hate-crime policy across the United States.
Jensen (2003, 2005)	Veterans	Historical analysis of veterans' pensions shows how policymakers selected the initial target population (in the early 1800s), the rationales that were used, and how the positive construction of veterans became embedded in policy and society and how policy made in the 1800s has produced long-lasting effects on current policy, as well as on identity and participation of veterans.
Kelmes (2004)	Crime (drugs)	Qualitative study examines how change in the social construction of drug users led to passage of California's drug prevention act.
Kyle (2006)	Homelessness	Long historical analysis of the rhetoric of homelessness finds common themes across time and how these themes shape policy toward those without homes.
Lantz et al. (2003)	Health	Qualitative study of the Breast and Cervical Cancer Prevention and Treatment Act of 2000 shows that a "window of opportunity" is more apt to open up for a positively viewed target population.
Menahem (1998)	Water policy (Israel)	Finds that social constructions of target populations are important part of problem definitions and policy change in Israeli water policy.
Newton (2005)	Immigration	Narrative policy analysis of the 1986 immigration reform finds that rationales are central to policy design but that when benefits are provided the policy is less stable.
Nicholson-Crotty (2003)	Crime	Analysis finds that the negative social construction and meager power resources made punishment-oriented crime policy especially salient to federal officials, who relied on monetary and symbolic policy tools to bring about change at the state level.
Pride (1999)	Race/ minorities	Analysis shows that national and local factors converged to change the social construction of black Americans, which in turn changed the policy design.
Reeher (2003)	Health care	Study finds that those covered by means-tested insurance and publicly funded health care should not be in the "dependent" or "deviant" group and offers ideas on how they can break out of their position of relative powerlessness and negative constructions.
Reese (2006)	Welfare/ immigration	Analysis shows that broad-based policy threats of negative policy served as a point of mobilization for immigrant and welfare recipients, leading to success in overturning negative policy.

(continued)

TABLE 10.1. *(continued)*

Author	Policy area	Comments
A. Social constructions and the policymaking process *(cont.)*		
Schneider (1999)	Prisons/ privatization	Historical analysis of the emergence of private prisons shows that when policy overreaches in its conferral of punishment on those who break the law, opportunities for policy change occur.
Schneider (2006)	Incarceration	Time series (1890–2003) and comparative state study shows that punishment policy is especially susceptible to path dependency (failure to change even when needed) and that attempts to provide rehabilitation to offenders led to frequent policy change (punctuations).
Schriner (2005)	Voting	Historical analysis of how persons constructed as "idiots" and "insane" came to be excluded from voting in most states, even as the states opened up their voting rolls to almost everyone else.
Sidney (2003, 2005)	Housing	Studies examine the role of social constructions in the development of Congressional fair-housing policy.
Warner (1995)	Youth services	Analysis finds that when a coalition of youth advocates succeeded in combining target populations and creating positive social constructions of "youth," they were able to get Congress to pass PL 101-610, the National and Community Service Act of 1990.
Wisen (2000)	General	Contends that social constructions of target populations are one of the factors holding policies in place (path dependency) and that change in social constructions is one of the keys to policy change.
B. Social constructions and the allocation of benefits and burdens		
Birkland (2004)	National security	Using the September 11 attacks as a learning/focusing event, the study suggests that "deserving" victims will be the most popular recipients of federal largesse after a crisis or catastrophe.
Czech, Krausman, & Borkhataria (1998)	Endangered species	Study of endangered species shows that species with more positive social constructions were more apt to be better protected by policy than species with negative constructions.
Davies et al. (2002)	Health	Study of health care report cards finds that the most vulnerable groups suffered from systematic biases in health care report cards.
Donovan (1993)	Health/AIDS	Analysis of the Ryan White Act (HIV/AIDS) shows that research funds were disproportionately allocated to those suffering from AIDS who had more positive social constructions.
Hogan (1997)	Prison/AIDS	Analysis of prison policy regarding those with HIV/AIDS shows that the greatest protection went to the most advantaged groups (e.g., guards) and the least protected were those considered most deviant within a prison culture.

(continued)

TABLE 10.1. *(continued)*

Author	Policy area	Comments
B. Social constructions and the allocation of benefits and burdens *(cont.)*		
Houston & Richardson (2004)	Drunk driving	Survey research of automobile drivers' views of appropriate punishment for drunk driving finds that demand for more coercive policy is from those with most negative view of drunk drivers and that this policy is the least apt to have an impact on those who drink the most.
Hunter & Nixon (1999)	Housing	The discourse analysis of housing policy in the United Kingdom finds that social constructions of target populations influences the policy agenda, the rationales that legitimize policy choices, and the distribution of rewards and punishments to various target groups.
Maynard-Moody & Musheno (2003)	Police, teachers, child protective services	In-depth interviews with street-level bureaucrats (police, teachers, and child protective service workers) show that they "put the fix" on clients and adjust their service levels upward or downward based on the deservedness of the client.
Newton (2005)	Immigration	Comparative analysis of immigration policy shows that policymakers draw on positive constructions of Mexican Americans to justify generous/lenient policy and on negative constructions when justifying restrictions.
Nicholson-Crotty & Meier (2005)	Crime	Historical analysis of the 1909 ban on opium smoking and the 1984 crime control act show the importance of moral entrepreneurs and policy entrepreneurs in the translation of negative constructions and punishment-oriented policy.
C. Social constructions and choice of design elements (problem definition, tools, rules, rationales)		
Camou (2005)	Neighborhood-based organizations	Study finds that neighborhood-based organizations that had an institutional mission for "serving the poorest of the poor" were able to do so but that the techniques (policy tools) varied between voluntary groups, professionalized groups, and faith-based organizations.
Campbell (2003)	Social Security	Study concludes that the universalistic nature of Social Security, compared with means-tested eligibility rules for other kinds of welfare programs, was important in understanding participation patterns of seniors.
Chanley (2005)	Education	Study found that policy design elements (tools and rules) for dependent populations differed in expected ways from those of advantaged populations and that, over time, a policy originally designed to provide funding for environmental education actually provided funding for farmers, miners, and others opposed to strict environmental standards.
Chanley & Alozie (2001)	Battered women/ welfare	Study finds that benefits to battered women were largely rhetorical rather than substantive and that policy design elements included high levels of local discretion rather than mandates.
Crowley & Watson (in press)	Child support/ welfare	Study finds that policy rules systematically disadvantage fathers whose children are on welfare, compared with those whose children are not, and that orientations toward the state differ accordingly.

(continued)

TABLE 10.1. *(continued)*

Author	Policy area	Comments
C. Social constructions and choice of design elements *(cont.)*		
Jurik & Cowgil (2005)	Microenterprise loan programs	Case study and national survey find that microenterprise loan nonprofits "creamed" clients and changed rationales and other design elements in order to meet the definitions of a "successful" program, as defined by federal policy.
Nicholson-Crotty & Nicholson-Crotty (2004)	Prisons/health	Quantitative (comparative state) study finds that the extent of negative social constructions of criminals in a state is associated with choice of policy tools and with ineffective implementation.
Reichenbach (2002)	Health/cancer	Analysis shows that the social construction differential between breast cancer and cervical cancer affected the priority given to these in Ghana.
Schram (2005)	Welfare	Author contends that deceptive rationales, even if intended to empower negatively constructed groups (welfare recipients), are in the long run counterproductive.
Schroedel & Jordan (1998)	Health/AIDS	Analysis of Senate voting on multiple AIDS policies confirms linkage between social constructions of target groups and policy design elements, including distribution of benefits and burdens, *sub rosa* policy (to contenders), and rhetorical benefits (to dependents).
Sidney (2003, 2005)	Housing	Study shows that federal policy intended to assist low-income people and communities contained design elements that actually thwarted local mobilization and coalition-building. The negative social construction of targets was at least partly responsible for these design characteristics.
Silver & Miller (2002)	Mental health and crime	Study of mental health and crime shows that actuarial risk assessment tools are more apt to be used on marginal populations and exacerbate marginality.
Soss & Schram (2005)	Welfare/TANF	Survey study finds that Welfare Reform Act of 1996 has not led to a more positive construction of welfare recipients, at least partly because the policy design elements (especially rationales) did not challenge the negative social constructions.
D. Social construction, identity, and political participation		
Blumenthal (1994)	Juvenile justice	Qualitative study of male youths in juvenile prison finds that the negative messages in policy and institutions have turned a positive self-image into violent and angry behavior.
Campbell (2005)	Senior citizens	Historical analysis shows the importance of Social Security policy (and the elements of its design) on political participation and understanding of citizenship among seniors.
Frantz (2002)	Health/lepers	Study found that persons suffering from leprosy internalized the highly negative social construction imposed by a half century of public policy.
Ingram & Schneider (2006); Schneider & Ingram (2006)	General	Analysis makes the argument that when social constructions are heavily involved in policy design, it produces an unequal citizenship.

(continued)

TABLE 10.1. *(continued)*

Author	Policy area	Comments
D. Social construction, identity, and political participation *(cont.)*		
Kumlin (2004); Kumlin & Rothstein (2005)	Welfare	Survey research studies of how experiences with the design of welfare state institutions (universalism vs. needs testing) in Sweden affect political orientations of trust and social capital.
Link & Oldendick (1996)	Equal opportunity/ multiculturalism	Survey research study showing that the social construction of target groups is as important as (or more important than) social class as predictor of support for equal opportunity policy and multicultural policy.
Luna (2005)	Welfare	Qualitative analysis finds that some welfare mothers internalize the negative social constructions they experience in contact with welfare agencies but that others (especially black women familiar with discrimination) are more apt to resist the negative portrayals.
Mettler (2002); Mettler & Welch (2004)	Veterans	Historical analysis of the G.I. Bill and survey research study show how characteristics of the G.I. policy design affected attitudes and participation.
Mettler (2005)	Veterans	In-depth interviews with veterans show that some designs facilitate conventional participation, whereas others spark contentious participation.
Mettler & Soss (2004)	General	Synthesis of how characteristics of policy designs affect citizen attitudes and participation.
Schur, Shields, & Schriner (2003)	Disability	Survey research study finds that disabled populations show lower levels of external political efficacy, at least partly because of their negative social constructions.
Simon (2002)	Americorps	Survey research study finds that participation in Americorps had a positive impact on civic participation that equalized participation regardless of race or gender.
Soss (1999, 2000, 2005)	Welfare/Social Security Disability Income	Comparative analysis (survey research and in-depth interviewing) of AFDC and SSDI recipients shows differences in orientations, identity, and participation attributed to differences in the personal experiences people have with elements of the policy design.
Soss & Schram (2005)	Welfare	Study found that the Welfare Reform Act of 1996, which some expected to change the image of welfare recipients, did not have this effect, at least partly because the rhetoric and design elements did not embed a positive construction.
Stein (2001)	Title I Education	In-depth interview study finds that categories in policy design influence how teachers think about (and treat) students and how students think about themselves.
Williams (1996)	Citizen participation	Analysis of bureaucratic processes concludes that the institutional structure of the bureaucracy plus the characterizations of population groups held by administrators resulted in some groups being purposely excluded (the poor, minorities, those dependent on public services, and others negatively constructed by bureaucrats).

why not war widows and children? Jensen shows how the discourse supporting the initial entitlement was later used by those left out of the subsidy (those in the state militias, those who were not poverty-stricken) to make the case that the program should be expanded to include all veterans. This study illustrates how a policy, once put in place with its embedded constructions of the recipients, shapes the future discourse and future policy designs. Subsequent policy discourse focused not on whether it was an appropriate role for government in a democracy to provide subsidies to special groups of people but rather on the eligibility rules that would set the boundaries for the target population.

Jensen's (2005) study also shows the critical importance of the institutional context, as do many of the other studies of social constructions and policymaking. The new nation needed to bind the loyalty of the military and solidify the importance of a central government, the veterans' pensions and many other similar policies that followed were an essential part of nation building. Yet these policies almost always required the positive construction of recipients, whether these were railroad companies whose subsidies would benefit the nation's transportation system, farmers whose subsidies were need to ensure an adequate food supply, or the children of pioneers who needed access to free public education and higher education.

Kay Schriner's (2005) analysis shows how the right to vote was gradually expanded beyond white, male property owners, as additional groups were deemed worthy of this special privilege; yet negative constructions of women and those viewed as "idiots" or "insane" resulted in exclusionary rules that denied them the vote. As Schriner points out, "everyone knew" that the nation had to be protected from those who were not rational enough to help decide on political leadership. One of the most interesting aspects of her work is the evidence of how little attention was paid to definitions or mechanisms in deciding who was an "idiot" or was "insane" and why they should not be allowed to vote. Currently, only six states do not exclude such persons from the ballot box. The extremely long effects of policy on subsequent policy are clearly illustrated in this work.

Sandra Anglund's (1998, 1999) historical studies of small-business procurement policy also show how the rationales and discourse that justify a policy may later be used by others who view themselves as similarly situated to gain remediation—but that this dynamic process works only if the group has a positive social construction. Working from an institutional perspective, Anglund integrates institutional analysis with social construction but contends that institutional analysis alone is not sufficient. Social constructions drive problem definitions, she says, and problem definitions drive policy.

Some of the studies trace the efforts of negatively constructed groups to change their construction (DiAlto, 2005; Ingram & Ingram, 2006; Reese, 2006). Stephanie DiAlto's (2005) analysis of the strategies used by Japanese Americans to challenge and eventually overcome the construction that they were not worthy nor capable of American citizenship emphasizes the importance of institutions in this process. She finds that Japanese Americans turned to every type of institution available to them—media, courts, state legislatures, Congress—at one time or another, seeking to find a more favorable reception for their arguments. Their arguments were grounded in the notion that Japanese Americans were more truly American than most native-born Americans in their honesty, commitment to hard work, and dedication to family. A very important part of the change was the military service of Japanese Americans who served honorably in the military. This construction came to be spread over the entire group. Japanese Americans never accepted their negative image but challenged it at every turn. In contrast, Dionne Bensonsmith (2005) shows how a document, the

Moynihan report, containing negative images of African American women has dominated discourse to the present time, including the highly negative image of welfare "queens" who cheat the system. Welfare recipients could be constructed simply as mothers who are doing the best they can for their children, but that construction has not taken hold.

Other studies of the role of constructions in the policymaking process document that changes in construction may be a necessary but not sufficient factor in policy change. Glenda Kelmes (2004), for example, shows how a change in the social construction of drug users led to passage of California's drug prevention act of 2003. Lantz, Weisman, and Itani (2003), working from John Kingdon's framework that policy ideas need a "window of opportunity" if they are to become incorporated into statutes, found that such windows were more apt to open up for breast cancer prevention and treatment than for cervical cancer; apparently more "blameless" causes are attributed to breast cancer, whereas cervical cancer is constructed as being the product of promiscuity. Valerie Jenness and Ryken Grattet (2001) trace the emergence of hate-crime legislation, showing how social movements, institutions, and social constructions of hate converged to produce special sanctions for crimes reflecting hatred of certain groups.

Schneider's (2006) studies of incarceration versus rehabilitative policy for those who break the law shows that path dependency is more likely to occur when negatively constructed groups are being punished and far less likely when rehabilitative policies are directed toward offenders. She also contends that the insertion of a positively viewed target group (private prisons) to be the direct recipient of funding exacerbates the U.S. tendency to follow a path-dependent process in its incarceration policy that has resulted in the United States having the highest incarceration rate in the world.

Newton (2005) and Sidney (2005) explain how difficult it has been for Congress to provide beneficial policy to minorities and that success in doing so requires considerable manipulation of social constructions. Newton explains that Congress draws on laudatory constructions when they are attempting to benefit immigrants but resorts to negative portrayals of immigrants as illegal aliens and criminals when justifying "get tough" and "control the border" policies. Sidney's work documents how Congress created a new target population—the "black middle class"—and distinguished them from "urban rioters" in the development of housing policy that would benefit minority populations.

These studies all conclude that the social construction of target populations are centrally implicated in the historical policymaking processes. Policy creates the boundaries that identify target populations, uses existing constructions or creates new ones for these groups, embeds these images in the details of the policy design, and then reproduces these constructions within the society as a whole. Most of these studies take an implicit or explicit "new institutionalism" approach in which policy itself may be viewed as an institution or in which social constructions become embedded in the institutional fabric of the nation, making them exceptionally path dependent—especially positive constructions for the conferral of benefits and negative constructions for the conferral of punishment.

Social Constructions and the Allocation of Benefits and Burdens

The second category in Table 10.1 lists studies that address the relationship between social constructions of target populations and the allocation of benefits or burdens. Rather than make comparisons across widely divergent policy, these studies all are conducted within a single policy arena. Comparisons are made based on the *relative* extent of political power and positive or negative constructions of the various players in a particular policy arena. The expectations of the framework are that benefits will be disproportionately allocated to advantaged groups and punishments to deviants. Contenders are expected to receive benefits, though mostly delivered *sub rosa* and without discussion, and burdens that are highly publicized but with extensive loopholes that will enable the group to avoid them. Dependents are expected to be disproportionately the recipients of policy that sounds generous but lacks funding or that pushes the funding to a lower level or to the private sector.

One of the first studies of these patterns (Donovan, 1993) analyzes the target population and other relevant groups in the Ryan White Act. He finds that the rationales overwhelmingly claim that the act will take care of *innocent* victims of AIDS. Donovan contrasts children, hemophiliacs, and blood transfusion recipients with homosexuals and drug users and finds that the funding levels specified in the act are proportionate not to the number of people suffering from HIV/AIDS but to the social constructions. For example, the original act specified 15% to go to infants, children, women, and families with AIDS and 10% to hemophiliacs or American Indians. Thus 25% of the funds were mandated for "innocent" victims, who constituted an estimated 2% of the infected population. The act also prohibits states from using any of the funds for needle exchange programs.

Researchers have found that health care report cards are biased against dependent and deviant populations (Davies, Washington, & Bindman, 2002). AIDS policy in prisons granted the greatest protection to the most advantaged group (guards) within the prison culture (Hogan, 1997). Social constructions influenced housing policy in the United Kingdom such that the most favorable rules were granted for advantaged populations and the most restrictive for dependents and deviants (Hunter & Nixon, 1999). Street-level caseworkers (police, teachers,

and child protective service workers) were found to "size up" their clients and give more than required to those they consider deserving and less than required to others (Maynard-Moody & Musheno, 2003). Even after a disaster such as the September 11 attacks, victims constructed as more "deserving" will receive more than others (Birkland, 2004)

Social Constructions and the Choice of Policy Design Elements

Policy design refers to the substance and content of policy and to the specific elements or mechanisms that the policy contains. These typically include: (1) the *goals* or *problems* the policy is expected to address; (2) *rules*, such as eligibility rules; (3) *tools*, which are the mechanisms the policy uses to influence the behavior of lower level agents and target populations; (4) *rationales*, which are the justifications given for the policy; (5) the *implementation structure*, such as the number of intervening target populations and the amount of discretion available at various decision points; and (6) the underlying *assumptions*, especially the causal logic connecting policy elements or program activities to outcomes.

Several studies have examined whether the way clients are treated by policy differs depending on their political power and social construction. Advantaged targets—those both powerful and constructed as "deserving"—typically enjoy the professionalized and respectful treatment of federal career employees, whereas dependents are far more likely to be served by state or local administrators who have considerable discretion in whom they do or do not treat well (Campbell, 2003; Maynard-Moody & Musheno, 2003). As Joe Soss (2005) and Sanford Schram (1995) show, recipients of Social Security Disability Income (SSDI) have better access to decision makers and tend to be treated with respect—consistent with the rhetoric that they have earned their retirement—whereas welfare recipients have numerous rules and hurdles to overcome to prove that they are worthy. Sharon Chanley and Nick Alozie (2001) find that policy design for battered women—a dependent group—is mainly rhetorical and devoid of concrete assistance for the group. Policy rules, according to Crowley and Watson (in press), systematically disadvantage fathers who are attempting to collect child support if their children are on welfare compared with those whose children are not on welfare. Jean Schroedel and Daniel Jordan's (1998) study of Senate voting on AIDs policies confirms the linkage between social construction and policy design, not only in terms of benefits and burdens but also in the provision of *sub rosa* policy benefits to HIV sufferers who are constructed as contenders and mainly rhetorical benefits to dependents. Richardson and Houston (2003) find that the construction of drunk drivers ("killer drunks," "impaired drivers," "suffering from a disease of alcoholism," or "irresponsible but not criminal") is consistent with the kinds of policy recommendations that would follow. They went on to argue that the influence of social constructions on policy elements results in ineffective policy— a conclusion also reached by Nancy VanDeMark (2006) in her study of substance-abusing women.

Social Construction, Identity, and Political Participation

One of the most important areas of research pertains to how policy shapes the identity, orientation toward government, and political participation patterns of citizens. Policy, because it sends such powerful and persuasive messages about who is deserving, trustworthy, and important to the national interest and who is dangerous, greedy, dependent, or helpless is an important but typically overlooked factor (Mettler & Soss, 2004). Schriner's (2005) historical study of voting, for example, reveals that long-term disenfranchisement (of minorities, women,

the 18- to 21-year-old group) is associated with the lowest levels of voting turnout and other forms of participation for decades even after the restriction is lifted. Campbell (2003) finds that senior citizens participate at disproportionately high rates and that the characteristic income differential does not exist among senior citizens. Suzanne Mettler's (2002) study of the G.I. Bill finds extensive impacts on soldiers' orientations toward government and participation patterns. She attributes this not simply to the presence of a subsidy but to the actual design of the policy itself, such that the relationship between clients and government is a professionalized relationship in which recipients are made to feel empowered, deserving, and respected and that they have earned the benefit. Soss's (2005) comparison of SSDI recipients with Aid to Families with Dependent Children (AFDC) recipients also finds that the way welfare benefits are provided makes a difference in orientation toward government and participation. The message of SSDI, Soss says, is that these benefits are deserved. AFDC recipients, on the other hand, are not treated in the same way and are required to meet numerous regulations, prepare time-consuming documentation, and meet personally with their caseworkers. These constructions, again according to Soss, tend to be incorporated into the identity of welfare recipients, as most will agree that most welfare recipients are responsible for their own situation, although they exempt themselves from that category. Several studies compare the effects of universalistic welfare (in which everyone is eligible and one does not have to prove poverty) with particularistic, means-tested programs (Kumlin, 2004; Kumlin & Rothstein, 2005). All comment on the positive effects of the former on participation and the negative impact of the latter.

Democratic citizenship refers both to what government is expected to provide to citizens and to the obligations that citizens have to be informed and active in public life. Policy affects citizens in many ways, most strikingly through the messages it imparts, both instrumental and symbolic. Through instrumental effects it shapes the distribution of valued goods and services. Through rhetorical claims attached to material policy, as well as that which is purely symbolic, policy signals who is important. The result is unequal citizenship.Some scholars have sought to divide policy types into those with "instrumental" effects and those with "interpretive" effects, or those with "resource" effects and "symbolic" effects. Schneider and Ingram (1997, 2005) disagree, however, making a case that instrumental or material policy has substantial symbolic effects. We argue that even though it is true that some policy is mainly symbolic, rhetorical, or "hortatory," it is a mistake to think that material/instrumental policy is devoid of interpretive or symbolic value.

Conclusion

For many people drawn to the insights of social construction, the study of public policy would appear at best irrelevant. If policymaking is a "passing parade," as Murray Edelman (1964) termed it, then public policy would appear to be no more than costuming on transient political portrayals meant to hide what is really going on. If policy studies are the arid, empirical, means–ends, benefit–cost analyses pursued in many academic public policy programs, then policy is simply part of the rationality project blind to equity, democracy, and other value questions. The argument made here is that public policy is at the heart of social constructions of citizens in democracy and that understanding how policy works helps explain how people can have such different views about and experiences with politics.

The social construction of target group framework, first fully articulated in 1993, grew out of a strand of public policy study that had turned critical and reflective. We built upon the work of previous scholars who had begun to examine the adverse impacts of often well-meaning policies. Despite

millions in government money spent on social, educational, health, and poverty programs, economic and social differences among different segments of the population persist. Policies intended to help the disadvantaged often are not implemented or prove to be mainly symbolic. Moreover, many citizens continue to see government as an alien, negative force. Even more discouraging, those citizens with the largest stake in government programs are also least likely to participate in politics.

The social construction of target group framework and the large literature that has flourished from its insights has demonstrated that public policies carry messages to their intended targets and to the general public that some citizens are privileged and advantaged, whereas others are disadvantaged. Some people can expect only burdens and punishments from government. Still others can probably get what they want from politics, but they must wield their political power unobtrusively and secretly. Any attempt to redress the inequalities and lack of democracy in society must consider the powerful agency that public policy has to construct groups. Far greater attention needs to be directed at the implicit messages that policy sends about the nature of democracy.

The social constructions of target group framework was developed independently of the social construction movement in sociology. Indeed, we were initially unaware of that work, labeling our original concept as a "cultural construction." As we became aware of the social construction movement in sociology, the similarities were apparent, even though we did not want to become embroiled in the debate that seemed to drag down the sociological theory. This debate emphasized whether social problems were "real" or whether such problems actually did not exist, even for those who were suffering from them, until they had been socially constructed as a "problem." In the relationship between social constructions and public policy, the emphasis is on how social constructions are created and manipulated for political gain, how they change, and the role of policy in these dynamic processes. Perhaps it makes less difference in this kind of analysis whether there are "real" or "material" underlying conditions. Social constructions of groups, events, history, and target populations are "real" in the sense that they have consequences.

There is, however, a marked disconnection between those who study social constructions of social problems and those who study the relationships between social constructions and public policy, as it is rare for either to cite the other. Perhaps this is simply the outgrowth of disciplinary isolation, or it may be that neither wants to take on the disciplinary-specific controversies that each has generated. In any case, there is room for a very fruitful exchange of ideas between the social construction movement in sociology and in the study of politics and public policy.

• References

Anglund, S. M. (1998). How American core values influence public policy: Lessons from federal aid to small business, 1953–1993. *Governance: An International Journal of Policy and Administration, 11*(1), 23–50.

Anglund, S. M. (1999). Policy feedback: The comparison effect and small business procurement policy. *Policy Studies Journal, 27*(1), 11–27.

Bacchi, C. L. (1999). *Women, policy, and politics: The construction of politics.* London: Sage.

Baumgartner, F., & Jones, B. (1993). *Agendas and instability in American politics.* Chicago: University of Chicago Press.

Bensonsmith, D. (2005). Jezebels, matriarchs, and welfare queens: The Moynihan Report of 1964 and the social construction of African American women in welfare policy. In A. L. Schneider & H. Ingram (Ed.), *Deserving and entitled: Social construction and public policy* (pp. 243–260). Albany: State University of New York Press.

Berger, P. L., & Luckmann, T. (1966). *The social construction of reality: A treatise in the sociology of knowledge.* Garden City, NY: Doubleday.

Best, J. (1989). *Images of issues: Typifying contemporary social problems.* New York: Aldine de Gruyter.

Birkland, T. A. (2004). The world changed today: Agenda setting and policy change in the wake of the September 11 terrorist attacks. *Review of Policy Research, 21*(2), 179–200.

Blumenthal, J. M. (1994). *Do you hear me though?: Voices of young black males in Arizona's juvenile corrections system.* Unpublished DPA dissertation, Arizona State University.

Bundy, R. V. (1994). *Politics, health care policy and distributive justice: The Ryan White Comprehensive AIDS Resources Emergency (CARE) Act and the Breast and Cervical Cancer Mortality Act, 1990.* Unpublished doctoral dissertation, Claremont Graduate University.

Camou, M. (2005). Deservedness in poor neighborhoods: A morality struggle. In A. L. Schneider & H. Ingram (Ed.), *Deserving and entitled: Social construction and public policy* (pp. 197–222). Albany: State University of New York Press.

Campbell, A. (2003). *How policies make citizens: Senior citizen activism and the American welfare state.* Princeton, NJ: Princeton University Press.

Campbell, A. (2005, April). *Universalism, targeting, and participation.* Paper presented at the Conference on Making the Politics of Poverty and Inequality, Madison, WI.

Chanley, J. (2005). *An analysis of civic education policy making in Arizona using the advocacy coalition framework and policy design theory.* Unpublished PhD dissertation, Arizona State University, School of Public Affairs.

Chanley, S. A., & Alozie, N. O. (2001). Policy for the "deserving" but politically weak: The 1996 Welfare Reform Act and battered women. *Policy Studies Review, 18*(2), 1–25.

Crowley, J. E., & Watson, M. (in press). Understanding "power talk": Language, public policy, and democracy. *Perspectives on Politics.*

Czech, B., Krausman, P. R., & Borkhataria, R. (1998). Social construction, political power, and the allocation of benefits to endangered species. *Conservation Biology, 12,* 1103–1112.

Davies, H. T. L. A., Washington, E., & Bindman, A. B. (2002). Health care report cards: Implications for vulnerable patient groups and the organizations providing them care. *Journal of Health Politics, Policy and Law, 27*(3), 379–399.

DeLeon, P. (1997). *Democracy and the policy sciences.* Albany: State University of New York Press.

DiAlto, S. (2005). From "problem minority" to "model minority": The Changing Social Construction of Japanese Americans. In A. L. Schneider & H. M. Ingram (Eds.), *Deserving and entitled: Social construction of public policy* (pp. 81–110). Albany: State University of New York Press.

Donovan, M. C. (1993). Social constructions of people with AIDS: Target populations and United States policy, 1981–1990. *Policy Studies Review, 12*(3/4), 3–29.

Dryzek, J. S. (1990). *Discursive democracy.* Cambridge, UK: Cambridge University press.

Edelman, M. J. (1964). *The symbolic uses of politics.* Urbana: University of Illinois Press.

Ferrales, T. D. (2004). *Deconstructing AIDS policy: A comparative analysis between Mexico and the United States.*

Unpublished doctoral dissertation, University of Texas, Austin.

Fischer, F. (1980). *Politics, values, and public policy*. Boulder, CO: Westview Press.

Fischer, F. (2003). *Reframing policy analysis*. Oxford, UK: Oxford University Press.

Frantz, J. E. (2002). Political resources for policy terminators. *Policy Studies Journal, 30*(1), 11–28.

Furlong, E. A. (1993). *Agenda-setting and policy design of the National Center for Nursing Research legislative*. Unpublished doctoral dissertation, University of Nebraska, Lincoln.

Harrison, K. (2001). Too close to home: Dioxin contamination of breast milk and the political agenda. *Policy Sciences, 34*(1), 35–62.

Hirshberg, D. B. (2001). *Northern exploring: A case study of non-Native Alaskan education policymakers' social construction of Alaska Natives as target populations*. Unpublished doctoral dissertation, University of California, Los Angeles.

Hogan, N. (1997). The social construction of target populations and the transformation of prison-based AIDS policy: A descriptive case study. *Journal of Homosexuality, 32*(3/4), 77–114.

Houston, D. J., & Richardson, L. E., Jr. (2004). Drinking and driving in America: A test of behavioral assumptions underlying public policy. *Political Research Quarterly, 57*(1), 53–64.

Hunter, C., & Nixon, J. (1999). The discourse of housing debt: The social construction of landlords, lenders, borrowers, and tenants. *Housing, Theory, and Society, 16*, 165–178.

Ingram, H., & Schneider, A. (1993). Constructing citizenship. In H. Ingram & S. R. Smith (Eds.), *Public policy for democracy*. Washington, DC: The Brookings Institution.

Ingram, H., & Schneider, A. (2005). Introduction: Public policy and the social construction of deservedness. In A. Schneider & H. Ingram (Eds.), *Deserving and entitled: Social construction and the public policy* (pp. 1–32). Albany: State University of New York Press.

Ingram, H., Schneider, A. L., & deLeon, P. (2007). Social construction and policy design. In P. A. Sabatier (Ed.), *Theories of the policy process* (pp. 93–126). Boulder, CO: Westview Press.

Ingram, M., & Ingram, H. (2006). Creating credible edibles: The organic agriculture movement and the emergence of U.S. federal organic standards. In D. Meyer, V. Jenness, & H. Ingram (Eds.), *Routing the opposition: Social movements, public policy, and democracy* (pp. 121–148). Minneapolis: University of Minnesota Press.

Itkonen, T. (2004). *Stories of hope and decline: Interest groups and the making of national special education policy*. Unpublished doctoral dissertation, University of California, Santa Barbara.

Jenness, V., & Grattet, R. (2001). *Making hate a crime: From social movement to law enforcement*. New York: Russell Sage Foundation.

Jensen, L. (2003). *Patriots, Settlers, and the Origins of American Social Policy*. Cambridge, UK: Cambridge University Press.

Jensen, L. S. (2005). Constructing and entitling America's original veterans. In A. Schneider & H. Ingram (Eds.), *Deserving and entitled: Social construction and public policy* (pp. 35–62). Albany: State University of New York Press.

Jones, B. D., Sulkin, T., & Larsen, H. A. (2003). Policy punctuations in American political institutions. *American Political Science Review, 97*(1), 151–170.

Jurik, N., & Cowgill, J. (2005). The construction of client identities in a post welfare social service program: The double bind of microenterprise development. In A. Schneider & H. Ingram (Ed.), *Deserving and entitled: Social construction and public policy* (pp. 173–196). Albany: State University of New York Press.

Kelmes, G. (2004). *Taking the high road: A qualitative analysis of the passage and implementation of California's Substance Abuse and Crime Prevention Act of 2000*. Paper presented at the conference of the Society for the Study of Social Problems.

Kumlin, S. (2004). *The personal and the political: How personal welfare state experiences affect political trust and ideology*. New York: Palgrave Macmillan.

Kumlin, S., & Rothstein, B. (2005). Making and breaking social capital: The impact of welfare state institutions. *Comparative Political Studies, 38*, 339–365.

Kyle, K. (2006). *Contextualizing homelessness: Critical theory, homelessness, and federal policy addressing the homeless*. New York: Routledge.

Lantz, P. M., Weisman, C. S., & Itani, Z. (2003). A disease-specific Medicaid expansion for women: The Breast and Cervical Cancer Prevention and Treatment Act of 2000. *Women's Health Issues, 13*, 79–92.

Link, M., & Oldendick, R. W. (1996). Social construction and white attitudes toward equal opportunity and multiculturalism. *Journal of Politics, 58*(1), 149–168.

Lowi, T. (1979). *The end of liberalism*. New York: Norton.

Luna, Y. (2005). *Social constructions, social control, and resistance: An analysis of welfare reform as a hegemonic process*. Unpublished doctoral dissertation, Arizona State University.

Majone, G. (1989). *Evidence, argument, and persuasion in the policy process*. New Haven, CT: Yale University Press.

Maynard-Moody, S., & Musheno, M. (2003). *Cops, teachers, counselors: Stories from the front lines of public service*. Ann Arbor: University of Michigan Press.

Menahem, G. (1998). Policy paradigms, policy networks, and water policy in Israel. *Journal of Public Policy, 18*, 282–310.

Mettler, S. (2002). Bringing the state back in to civic engagement: Policy feedback effects of the G.I. Bill for World War II veterans. *American Political Science Review, 96*, 351–365.

Mettler, S. (2005). *Soldiers to citizens: The G.I Bill and the* making of the greatest generation. New York: Oxford University Press.

Mettler, S., & Soss, J. (2004). The consequences of public policy for democratic citizenship: Bridging policy studies and mass publics. *Perspectives on Politics, 2,* 55–73.

Mettler, S., & Welch, E. (2004). Civic generation: Policy feedback effects of the G. I. Bill on political involvement over the life course. *British Journal of Political Science, 34*(3), 497–518.

Miller, G., & Holstein, J. A. (1993). Constructing social problems: Context and legacy. In G. Miller & J. A. Holstein (Eds.), *Constructionist controversies: Issues in social problems theory.* New York: Aldine de Gruyter.

Newton, L. (2005). It is not a question of being anti-immigration: Categories of deservedness in immigration policy making. In A. Schneider & H. Ingram (Eds.), *Deserving and entitled: Social construction and public policy* (pp. 139–172). Albany: State University of New York Press.

Nicholson-Crotty, J., & Nicholson-Crotty, S. (2004). Social construction and policy implementation: Inmate health as a public health issue. *Social Science Quarterly, 85*(2), 240–255.

Nicholson-Crotty, S. (2003). *Punishment from the top down?: Federal influence on state-level criminal justice policy.* Unpublished doctoral dissertation, Texas A&M University.

Nicholson-Crotty, S., & Meier, K. J. (2005). From perception to public policy: Translating social constructions into policy design. In A. Schneider & H. Ingram (Eds.), *Deserving and entitled: Social construction and public policy* (pp. 223–242). Albany: State University of New York Press.

Pride, R. (1999). Redefining the problem of racial inequality. *Political Communication, 16,* 147–167.

Reeher, G. (2003). Reform and remembrance: The place of the private sector in the future of health care policy. *Journal of Health Politics, Policy and Law, 28*(2/3), 355–367.

Reese, E. (2006). Policy threats and social movement coalitions: California's campaign to restore legal immigrants' rights to welfare. In D. S. Meyer, V. Jenness, & H. Ingram (Eds.), *Routing the opposition: Social movements, public policy, and democracy* (pp. 259–287). Minneapolis: University of Minnesota Press.

Reichenbach, L. (2002). The politics of priority setting for reproductive health: Breast and cervical cancer in Ghana. *Reproductive Health Matters, 10*(20), 47–58.

Richardson, L. E., Jr., & Houston, D. H. (2003, April). *Attitudes and policy preferences of elites in the drinking-and-driving policy arena.* Paper presented at the meeting of the Midwest Political Science Association, Chicago.

Rochefort, D. A., & Cobb, R. W. (Eds.). (1994). *The politics of problem definition.* Lawrence: University of Kansas.

Schneider, A. L. (1999). Public–private partnerships in prison operation. *American Behavioral Scientist, 43*(1), 192–208.

Schneider, A. L. (2006). Patterns of change in the use of incarceration in the American states: A path dependency and punctuated equilibrium perspective. *Political Research Quarterly, 59*(3), 457–469.

Schneider, A., & Ingram, H. (1993). The social construction of target populations. *American Political Science Review, 87*(2), 334–346.

Schneider, A. L., & Ingram, H. M. (1997). *Policy design for democracy.* Lawrence: University Press of Kansas.

Schneider, A. L., & Ingram, H. M. (Eds.). (2005). *Deserving and entitled: Social construction and public policy.* Albany: State University of New York Press.

Schneider, A. L., & Ingram, H. M. (2006). Public policy and democratic citizenship: What kinds of citizenship does policy produce? In F. Fischer, G. J. Miller, & M. S. Sidney (Eds.), *Handbook of public policy analysis: Theory, politics, and methods* (pp. 329–346). Boca Raton, FL: CRC/Taylor & Francis.

Schram, S. F. (1995). *The words of welfare: The poverty of social science and the social science of poverty.* Minneapolis: University of Minnesota Press.

Schram, S. F. (2005). Putting a black face on welfare: The good and the bad. In A. Schneider & H. Ingram (Eds.), *Deserving and entitled: Social construction and public policy* (pp. 261–290). Albany: State University of New York Press.

Schriner, K. (2005). Constructing the democratic citizen: Idiocy and insanity in American suffrage law. In A. Schneider & H. Ingram (Eds.), *Deserving and entitled: Social construction and public policy* (pp. 63–80). Albany: State University of New York Press.

Schroedel, J. R., & Jordan, D. R. (1998). Senate voting and social construction of target populations: A study of AIDS policy making, 1987–1992. *Journal of Health Politics, Policy and Law, 23*(1), 107–131.

Schur, L., Shields, T., & Schriner, K. (2003). Can I make a difference? Efficacy, employment, and disability. *Political Psychology, 24*(2), 119–149.

Sidney, M. (2003). *Unfair housing: How national policy shapes community action.* Lawrence: University Press of Kansas.

Sidney, M. S. (2005). Contested images of race and place: The politics of housing discrimination. In A. Schneider & H. Ingram (Eds.), *Deserving and entitled: Social construction and public policy* (pp. 111–138). Albany: State University of New York Press.

Silver, E., & Miller, L. M. (2002). A cautionary note on the use of actuarial risk assessment tools for social control. *Crime and Delinquency, 48*(1), 138–161.

Simon, C. (2002). Testing for bias in the impact of Americorps service on volunteer participants: Evidence of success in achieving a neutrality program objective. *Public Administration Review, 62*(6), 670–678.

Soss, J. (1999). Lessons of welfare: Policy design, political learning, and political action. *American Political Science Review, 93*(2), 363–380.

Soss, J. (2000). *Unwanted claims: Politics, participation, and the U.S. welfare system.* Ann Arbor: University of Michigan Press.

Soss, J. (2005). Making clients and citizens: Welfare policy as a source of status, belief, and action. In A. Schneider & H. Ingram (Eds.), *Deserving and entitled: Social construction and public policy* (pp. 291–328). Albany: State University of New York Press.

Soss, J., & Schram, S. F. (2005, April). *A public transformed? Welfare reform as policy feedback.* Paper presented at the Conference on Making the Politics of Poverty and Inequality, Madison, WI.

Spector, M., & Kitsuse, J. (1977). *Constructing social problems.* Menlo Park, CA: Benjamin-Cummings.

Stein, S. (2001). These are your Title I students: Policy language in educational practice. *Policy Sciences, 34,* 135–156.

Stone, D. (1997). *Policy paradox.* New York: Norton.

Straus, R. M. (2005). Reconstructing magnet schools: Social construction and the demise of desegregation. Unpublished doctoral dissertation, University of California, Irvine.

VanDeMark, N. R. (2006). *Reintegration of women with histories of substance abuse into society.* Unpublished doctoral dissertation, University of Colorado, Graduate School of Public Affairs, Denver.

Warner, J. S. (1995). *A policy study of youth service: Synthesizing analysis of policy content and policy process over time.* Unpublished doctoral dissertation, University of Oklahoma.

Williams, E. H. (1996). *Citizen participation in administrative policy making: Bureaucratic impediments and social construction: Implications for democracy.* Unpublished doctoral dissertation, University of Nebraska, Lincoln.

Wisen, C. A. (2000). Policy regimes and policy change. *Journal of Public Policy, 20,* 247–274.

Yanow, D. (1996). *How does a policy mean?* Washington, DC: Georgetown University Press.

CHAPTER 11

Social Constructionism in Science and Technology Studies

● **Sal Restivo**
Jennifer Croissant

In this chapter, we use certain moments and tensions in science and technology studies to explore constructionism in this interdisciplinary field.[1] Our starting point is the publication of *Laboratory Life* (1979) by Bruno Latour and Steve Woolgar. They subtitled this seminal monograph in the ethnography of science *The Social Construction of Scientific Facts*. They removed the word *social* from the subtitle for the 1986 edition. We look at this decision in the light of certain developments sometimes referred to as "the death of the social" and of a historical Anglo–American resistance to a robust understanding and application of the concept *social*.

A second moment occurs with the 1999 debate between David Bloor and Latour about the strong program and its critics.[2] From a wider perspective, one of the most

significant moments in the discussions and debates over social constructionism is the emergence of the "science wars" in the mid-1990s.[3] There are other moments that ground this story, but we do not address them all to the same extent. These moments include Harry Collins's (2006) defense of a weak sociology of science, the Sokal affair, and the science wars (e.g., Segestråle, 2000a), Langdon Winner's (1996) views on social construction and the politics of technology, and debates over actor–network theory (e.g., Law & Hassard, 1999). Our objectives are (1) to demonstrate the centrality of social constructionism to any serious understanding of what is behind the classical slogans in science and technology studies (STS)—science is social relations, and artifacts have politics; (2) to underscore the fact that social constructionism is a key factor in

213

explanatory social theory; and (3) that social constructionism is not a philosophy or a philosophical idea but a core concept in sociological theory and reasoning.[4] Social constructionism is compatible with sociologically sophisticated notions of reality, objectivity, and truth. We endorse Dorothy Smith's (1999) notion that postmodernism has not undermined our capacities to tell the truth but rather enhanced them even while complicating them.

Social Construction as a Fundamental Theorem

Human beings socially construct their lives, their thoughts, their cultures. There is one and only one way that we can come to be, to know things, and to build cultures, and that is through our interactions with others. This is the great discovery of the 19th-century social theorists, iconographically represented by Durkheim and Marx above all, and including prominently Weber, Nietzsche, and Simmel, among others. Durkheim (1912/ 1995; see especially his remarks on logic, p. 440) already gives us a sociology (and therefore a social constructionism) of religion and logic. It is the realization of Durkheim's agenda in the application of sociological reasoning to scientific knowledge that we locate the origins of the contemporary sociology of science.

The key feature of the post-Mertonian sociology of science, associated with social studies of science and technology, or science and technology studies, is that scientific knowledge itself becomes an object of social analysis. The Mertonians[5] studied the social system of science but not the products of scientific practice. The products of science were considered to be outside of society, culture, and history. Mannheim (1936, p. 79) had asserted this in pioneering the sociology of knowledge; there cannot be, he wrote, a sociology of 2 + 2 = 4. Spengler (1926/1991, pp. 41–69), by contrast, was already making the case for a comprehensive culturological

analysis of mathematics in his *The Decline of the West*. The key moment for sociologists of science during this period was Fleck's (1935/1979) *Genesis and Development of a Scientific Fact*. Fleck's work fueled Kuhn's (1962) musings on "scientific revolutions," "paradigms," and "exemplars."

Kuhn and Merton aside, the early ethnographies of science helped give substance and visibility to the "social construction of science" and, in due course, the "social construction of technology." Along with increasing visibility came increasing confusion, criticism, and intellectual warfare. We consider social constructionism and the science wars in due course. For now, let us see what the post-Mertonian sociologists of science themselves had to say about the social construction of science.

Social Constructionism and the Ethnography of Science

Chapter 1 of Latour and Woolgar's *Laboratory Life* (1979) begins with an observer's notes on the comings and goings of people in a laboratory:

> Every ten minutes or so, there is a telephone call for one of the staff from a colleague, an editor, or some official. There are conversations, discussions, and arguments at the benches: "Why don't you try that?" Diagrams are scribbled on blackboards. Large numbers of computers spill out masses of print-out. Lengthy data sheets accumulate on desks next to copies of articles scribbled on by colleagues. (p. 16)

The authors begin straightaway to alert the reader that an anthropological excursion is under way—not in order to report on a primitive society but rather to study a tribe of scientists. They are at pains from the start to point out that their concern with the "social" is not confined to the sorts of variables traditional (read "Mertonian") sociologists of science paid attention to, such as norms and competition. Latour and Woolgar (1979,

p. 32) are concerned with the construction of "sense" in science, and this leads to the following working definition: "we are concerned with the *social* construction of scientific knowledge in so far as this draws attention to the *process* by which scientists make sense of their observations."

They illustrate this concern by concisely reviewing the process leading to the discovery of pulsars and, in particular, the observations made by research student Jocelyn Bell. Their aim is to demonstrate that technical events are not simple or mere psychological operations (Latour & Woolgar, 1979, p. 33):

> the very act of perception is constituted by prevalent social forces. Our interest, however, would be in the details of the observation process. . . . The processes which inform the initial perception can be dealt with psychologically. However, our interest would be with the use of socially available procedures for constructing an ordered account out of the apparent chaos of available perceptions.

Latour and Woolgar (1979, p. 40) thus focus their attention first on how facts are constructed in a laboratory and how sociologists can account for this construction. They are also interested in the differences, if any, between constructing facts and constructing accounts of what goes on in the laboratory. There is an important reflexive feature in their work. While the scientists are trying to construct order (an ordered account) out of the disorder in their observations, data, and interpretations, Latour and Woolgar are trying to construct an ordered account out of the chaos of everyday laboratory life.[6]

The details of this laboratory study need not concern us here. What is important sociologically (and for the "new" or post-Mertonian sociology of science) is the nature of this study as a paradigm or exemplar. In the end, we are given an "account of fact construction in a biology laboratory" that stands alongside the account produced by the scientists themselves. The two accounts are equal in their capacity to give us access to the realities of the laboratory. Already here we find the seeds of what will come to be known as the "science wars" (Latour & Woolgar, 1979, p. 257): "We do not claim to escape from our description of scientific activity: the construction of order out of disorder at a cost, and without recourse to any preexisting order. In a fundamental sense, our own account is no more than *fiction*."

In order to see to what extent Latour and Woolgar raise the dreaded specter of relativism here, it is worthwhile to follow the superscript that follows the word *fiction* to the footnote (Latour & Woolgar, 1979, p. 261):

> "Fiction" is to be taken as having a noncommittal or "agnostic" meaning that can be applied to the whole process of fact production but to none of its stages in particular. The production of reality is what concerns us here, rather than any one produced final stage. . . . Our main interest in using the word "fiction" is the connotation of literature and writing accounts.

They thus tie their approach to a tradition of linking science and literature that owes much to Michel de Certeau (1986) and Michel Serres (1997). Their use of the word *fiction*, however deliberately provocative, is nonetheless rather sophisticated and a far cry from the idea that science is not in some sense "true." If we tie this to their explicit disavowal of relativism (Latour & Woolgar, 1979, pp. 180, 238), it is difficult to see how a careful reading of their text could lead a reader to conclude that their work is a contribution to relativism in the sociology of science. They do not deny that facts exist; they do not deny reality. Their achievement is to contribute to our understanding of reality as an accomplishment, whatever its intuited quality of "out-there-ness." The "out-there-ness" of reality is a consequence of scientific work, both practical and rhetorical, not its cause. Here they are at one with other post-Mertonian science studies pioneers (see, e.g., Barnes & Bloor, 1982, pp. 44–45; Bloor, 1976, p. 141; Collins, 1985, pp. 165–167; Knorr-Cetina, 1979, p. 369; Restivo, 1988,

1994). The charge of relativism is in great part a reaction to the provocations of such words as *fiction, construction,* and *social* rather than to the content of the arguments and discussions. Indeed, the ethnographers of science could hardly be accused of relativism if they had undertaken to document ordering and orderly practices in the laboratory in relation to a material world. We say more about the distinction between relativism, realism, and absolutism further on.

The second edition of *Laboratory Life* appeared in 1986. The main body of the text was unchanged. Significantly, however, the subtitle was changed from *The Social Construction of Scientific Facts* to *The Construction of Scientific Facts*. This change is explained in the only major addition to the book, a postscript. By the time the second edition appeared, the term *social construction* had become notorious. It was about to become a contentious object in the "science wars" and to lead to such provocative works as Ian Hacking's *The Social Construction of What?* (1999). The problem was that the term had become associated with relativism. This was and continues to be a great curiosity, given the fact that the major advocates of the idea in science studies all explicitly associated themselves with the sciences and realism. As Bloor (see 1999 for a noteworthy example) has been wont to point out over and over, the issue has always been relativism versus absolutism, not relativism versus realism. None of the critics of the sociology of scientific knowledge as a relativistic or antiscience discipline (notably, e.g., Gross & Levitt, 1994; Nanda, 2003) deal with the scientific traditionalism at the core of the field. Not one of the critics, to our knowledge, has explicitly discussed Barnes and Bloor's (1982, p. 47, note) claim that relativism is nothing more than "disinterested inquiry," a classic definition of what we mean by science.[7] Many scientists and philosophers nonetheless argued (and continue to argue) that scientific facts were "real" and therefore could not be socially constructed because that would imply that they were arbitrary or fictions. Bloor (1999, p. 101), in his argument with Latour, writes:

> realists are said to believe that scientific controversies about how best to represent nature are settled by nature itself, while relativists are said to believe that "Nature will be the consequence of the settlement" (Latour, 1987, p. 99). Notice that Latour says "nature" not "beliefs about nature." Second, "relativism" is taken to be an evaluative position. Relativists are said to be committed to defending bodies of belief against various "charges," such as the charge of irrationality. Their aim, allegedly, will be to convince us that such a negative evaluation is unfounded or impossible to sustain, and that the body of belief in question can be defended on the grounds that it is really rational after all. Latour draws a legal parallel. Relativists, he says, are like defence lawyers, arguing for the innocence of their client. Whenever the scientific community rejects a theory, as they rejected phlogiston or caloric or Newtonian mechanics with its absolute space and time, the relativist must make the case for the defence— in the teeth of the scientific consensus.

What do Latour and Woolgar have to say, then, about deleting the word *social* from their subtitle? The reader of the 1986 postscript is reminded at the beginning of the section on "The Demise of the Social" that already in their first chapter (unchanged from the first edition) they disavow "social factors." They do this by arguing "that it is not necessary to attach particular significance to the achievement of a 'correct' balance between 'social' and 'intellectual' factors" (Latour & Woolgar, 1979, p. 27). Scientists themselves, they point out, routinely distinguish between "social" and "technical" factors. As anthropologists of science, Latour and Woolgar do not want to emphasize one set of factors over the other in order to understand science. Rather, they want to understand how this distinction works within science for the scientists. As anthropologists, they do not want to uncritically use concepts and terms used by the scientists to understand and explain the scientists' activities. In keeping with what was at this moment in science studies a commitment to focus on the "technical" and "intellectual" issues in science, Latour and Woolgar position themselves in a way that foreshadows the demise of the social in the 1986 edition. Let's see, then, how they explain the demise of the social.

The problem, Latour and Woolgar (1986, p. 281) argue, is that the term *social* no longer has any meaning. Their original intention was, in fact, to render the term *social* meaningless because of its "pervasive applicability." They claim that *social* had meaning when the Mertonians used it to define a sociology of science that excluded the study of the content of science. It also took on meaning in the context of the Edinburgh school's development of the sociology of scientific knowledge. Here the point was to offer a sociological alternative to internalist explanations of technical scientific knowledge.[8] We now know that everything is social, so we no longer need the term *social*.

This line of argument should appear strange indeed to sociologists. To claim that the term *social* can be dispensed with because "everything is social" compounds one misdirection with another. Or can we simply say the claim is specious? Supposing the phrase *everything is social* and the term *social* mean anything at all, they do not "mean" transparently. In both cases, we are obliged epistemologically and ontologically to unpack meaning. And so our first task must be to say what it is that *social* means. Rather than go straight on to a definition, let us stay the course within science studies and see what can be learned by following the term *social* and the phrase *social construction* beyond Latour and Woolgar (1979, 1986).

Perhaps the most important monograph in the ethnography of science appeared in 1981. Karin Knorr-Cetina's *The Manufacture of Knowledge* was subtitled *An Essay on the Constructivist and Contextual Nature of Science*. Her index includes the terms *social*, *con-struction*, and *constructive*, but not *social construction*. Several other less extensive ethnographies of science were in progress when Knorr-Cetina's book was published.[9] The preliminary results of the most important of these studies were presented at a conference on the social process of scientific investigation, organized by Roger Krohn at McGill University in 1979. Ideas about "practice," "contingencies," and "production" and "reproduction" figured more prominently than those about "social construction" and "construction" in the early ethnographies. This is the case, for example, in Zenzen and Restivo's (1982) study of a colloid chemistry laboratory. Only in their conclusion do they note that their results are consistent with the "constructivist interpretation" rapidly coalescing in science studies. The term *social construction* appears for the first time in their conclusion (Zenzen & Restivo, 1982, p. 470): "The social construction of scientific facts can be conceived, following Fleck (1979: 100), as events in the history of ideas, stylized by contemporary, local, social, cultural, and environmental factors."

What is striking about this conclusion is, first, that Zenzen and Restivo (1982) turn to Fleck, whose study on the "genesis and development of a scientific fact" was originally published in German in 1939, and not to Kuhn. Kuhn, of course, had already become the darling of the science studies movement in spite of his objections (which became stronger as the years went by) to being considered a contributor to the sociology of knowledge and science.[10] But second, and more important, they follow up the reference to Fleck with a realist manifesto. Already, the main science studies ethnographers were associating social construction or constructivism with a realist ontology. Latour and Woolgar, Knorr-Cetina, and Zenzen and Restivo argue for "construction" without denying that there is a recalcitrant reality and without *a fortiori* adopting relativism. In spite of these early commitments to a realist ontology (sustained to this day), science studies would provoke critics to label it antiscience and relativist in the decades to follow. The reasons for this are discussed further on in the chapter.

The key idea that came up in the various presentations at the McGill conference was not social construction or even construction but rather *contingency*. Scientific practice was beginning to come to anthropological light as a process of molding local contingencies into an orderly form that would eventually coalesce into a scientific fact. Knorr-Cetina (1979, p. 369) put it this way: "we see scientific products as selectively carved out, transformed and constructed from whatever is." Critics would mistake this claim, based on empirical observations, to imply an antiscientific, relativist attitude.

Knorr-Cetina (1981) approached her study of a plant protein research laboratory with a conception of facts as made, manufactured, fabricated. This is an etymologically correct understanding of the word *fact*, an understanding confirmed by observations of scientists at work. The seeds of the science wars are planted in this view of facts as made rather than given and in a conception of science as constructive rather than descriptive. What is sociologically at stake here is made clear early on in Knorr-Cetina's (1981, p. 5) study: "The thesis under consideration is that the products of science are contextually specific constructions which bear the mark of the situational contingency and interest structure of the process by which they are generated."

(Social) constructions in the laboratory are, to put it in the strongest terms, *constitutive* of truths, facts, and knowledge (Zenzen & Restivo, 1982, p. 470). Right at the beginning of the post-Mertonian sociology of science, the science studies movement, there is a move to eliminate the term *social* from the analysis and understanding of science as practice and discourse. Yet that very term is what has nourished our critics and even our colleagues in a struggle to uncover the meaning emerging from our studies of science as practice, process, and discourse.

Social Construction, Philosophy, and Sociology

It is more than a mere curiosity that in the one book that, more than any other of its time, signaled a sea change in the study of science—Bloor's *Knowledge and Social Imagery* (1976)—one does not find the words *social* or *construction*, or even *sociology*, in its index. With Emile Durkheim as his guide, one might imagine that Bloor would have heralded "social constructionism" more clearly. Bloor, however, was and is first and foremost a naturalistic investigator, a philosopher and scientist imbued with the sociological imagination. Interestingly, the index of the second edition, based on the original text, has many more *social* terms, but again the term *construction* does not appear. What was clear in the Durkheim-inspired first edition now makes a much stronger appearance in the new index as an explicit commitment to a sociology-of-knowledge approach.

It is hard to make the case that post-Mertonian sociologists of science went out of their way to sell "social construction" to a resistant community of scholars. Soon enough, however, social construction became the hallmark of science studies for critics inside and outside of the field. In particular, the term *social* became linked to *relativism* and the idea that scientific knowledge, objectivity, and truth were arbitrary, even whimsical, constructions in an "anything goes" world. To this day, nothing science studies researchers do or say seems capable of breaking this link. The social study of scientific knowledge entails, for some science studies observers—especially those in the physical and natural sciences—relativism. It seems clear to us that the objections to social construction, the indiscriminate use of the relativist label, and the general attack on science studies in the science wars have had more to do with defending jurisdictions and defending arenas of authority (see Gieryn's [1999] argument) than with grounded intellectual disagreements, disputes, and conflicts. We return to this issue later, but first we need to discuss the expansion of "social constructionism" into technology studies.

Social Constructionism and the SCOT Program

Known to a generation of graduate students as the "school bus book" for its vivid black-and-yellow dust jacket, Bijker, Hughes, and Pinch's 1987 edited volume stands as the consolidating moment for the social construction of technology (SCOT) framework. At that point in time, what would become actor–network theory (ANT) appears congenially as a variation on the theme, rather than as a separate school of thought. One might expect that ideas about the social construction of technology would have appeared prior to the social construction of knowledge; the stock language surrounding technology is one of invention and manufacture, not discovery. The fabrication of chairs and tables is superficially obvious. Resistance to the "social" in the construction of technology comes from several sources. The first is the continuing prevalence of an "internalist" history of technology, which focuses on technical details and generally presents a linear success story in which technological developments seem to be inevitable results of unilateral improvements rather than subtle trade-offs among constraints and competing definitions of problems. Second, economic ideologies also contribute to this progress-oriented narrative, as they mask the ways in which interests shape both problem formulation and technical negotiations around technologies. The academic origin of the history of technology as an offshoot of the history of science is a third factor, provoking disciplinary boundary work. Finally, the ideology of technological determin-

ism, the common belief that technological change is inevitable and unambiguously represents progress, distracts from understanding the multiple levels of sociality in technology.

Bijker (1995) has since elaborated the SCOT program from a general heuristic to an approach that, taking a cue from Bloor's (1976, p. 5) symmetry principle that the same social mechanisms that explain error are at work in the production of truth, argues that the "working" of a technology is entirely social. That is, despite bells ringing and gears turning (or enzymes reacting or atoms splitting), whether or not a technology moves beyond a superficial internal functionality and into society will depend on how the technology is both materially and rhetorically configured to meet perceived needs among the multiple users who must be enrolled to ensure the technology's survival.

ANT, however, resists further the technical–social distinction and argues that what is placed in each category, as technical or social, is the product of actors and their engagement in networks. Actors do not have distinct properties; properties are attributed—assigned—to them by other actors in the network. This complete rejection of essentializing attributes produces the same frustrations that ethnomethodological approaches to inquiry produce. In addition, ANT suffers from the same problems that network explanations generate in other social realms: Are networks explanatory? Or do networks need to be explained? If the structure of a network, and the flows of information and resources across it, can explain the end configuration of a new technology and its uses, what explains the structure of the network?

An additional resistance to SCOT emerges from historians and their professional ambivalence about theory. As the exchange between Scranton (1991) and Law (1991) suggests, this ambivalence rests on a false distinction between narrative and theory. As Hayden White (1987) reminds scholars, narratives, even the most simplistic chronological accounts, contain within them theories, because what is chronicled implies selection criteria and modes of causality (as well as enfolded worldviews). Thus the resistance to SCOT, based on the belief that it distorts historical descriptions when producing generalizing theories, rests on a false dichotomy.

SCOT has also been criticized and resisted on methodological and political grounds. SCOT organizes its explanations around "relevant social groups." This raises the question of whether or not those social groups would be recognized by participants or whether they need be adequate only for the analysts' generalizations. This concern is related to hesitations about theory-driven scholarship not capturing the lived experience of participants. There is also a question about the impact on social groups not directly involved in the construction but nonetheless engaged with the consequences. Groups apparently irrelevant to the immediate construction process often have to live with consequences, and, mimicking a weakness in political theories of pluralism, items that never make the agenda remain invisible to analysts. Furthermore, a latent positivist scientism inhibits normative analysis of the potential "shoulds" and "oughts" of technological change, depoliticizing the field (Winner, 1993, 1996).

We have reviewed the idea of social construction in the context of how the term has been used by sociologists of science and technology. What is it about the idea that science and technology (but especially science) are socially constructed that has led to controversies between sociologists of science on the one hand and philosophers of science and physical and natural scientists on the other? Why are science and technology studies researchers at war with each other on this issue? We devote the remainder of this chapter to exploring those questions and to further explicating our notion of social constructionism.

Whither Social Construction: I. The Variety of Constructionist Experience

There is an obvious place to root controversies about social construction, and that is in the mixed usage of the term. It is associated in sociology and especially in social problems research, with—and in some cases is synonymous with—labeling theory. In this sense, then, the social construction of knowledge implies that knowledge is literally created by social groups in the same way that deviance, for example, is created. Following Becker's (1963) classic formulation in *Outsiders: Studies in the Sociology of Deviance*, the labeling theory of deviance claims that deviance is created by groups and is not an inherent characteristic of a particular act or behavior.[11] Applied to knowledge, this would imply that anything a group labeled "knowledge" would be knowledge. By extension, any claim or fact labeled "true" or "objective" by a group would be true or objective. In a sense, this is something like what sociologists of scientific knowledge have claimed. But not even the anarchistically inclined philosopher of science Paul Feyerabend (1975) could sustain an "anything goes" epistemology.[12] Realism is a *sine qua non* of any science, including sociology and the social sciences in general. What is at issue in the sociology of knowledge and science is not whether there is a reality independent of human wishes, dreams, and whims but whether it is possible to know this reality in a way that is independent of who and what we are. And who and what we are is grounded in the fundamentally social nature of our selves and even of our individualities. The upshot of this is that we cannot know anything at all independently of our social and cultural heritages, contexts (or situatedness), and tools. There are things that are true and things that are false about the world, but things are not true and false in very simple noncontextual, unsituated ways. The truths of science are corrigible and tentative, but at some point their veracity becomes convincing enough through experience and communication so that we stop worrying very much about the possibility that we might be wrong. The earth is *not* flat, the moon is *not* made of green cheese. There does not seem to be much epistemological danger in adopting those positions. On the other hand, we could claim with equal conviction that the earth *is* an oblate spheroid wobbling in precession and still leave open the possibility that a novel conception of time, space, mass, and energy (let's say along the lines of the theories proposed by the late David Bohm [e.g., 1973]) might lead us to reconceptualizing the physical nature of the earth. It would be unreasonable to entertain the possibility, however, that we would return to a flat-earth view based on the continued unfolding of our sciences and our cultures.[13]

There is something else here, and that is that concepts, ideas, theories, and claims do not exist in vacuums. Every word is embedded in a network of all the words of its cultural contexts, and as the complexity of those contexts varies and changes, so do the meanings of terms. 1 + 1 = 2 looks harmless enough as an example of a statement of fact that can in principle claim universal assent across all human cultures (and even in settings without humans, according to Martin Gardner, 1981). And yet, if we look at what this term has meant to mathematicians and logicians across the ages, we discover that it meant different things in different times and places as we move from Plato to Russell and Whitehead by way of Leibniz and Peano. In the context of an everyday world of trees, cows, pigs, and lakes, the meaning of 1 + 1 = 2 is stable across time and place. So a Plato transported to early-20th-century Europe could readily trade two cows for two pigs with Russell or gather up one apple and one orange and agree with Russell that he now held two fruits. However, if Plato tried to step into the world of *Principia Mathematica*,

he would be lost and would not be able to grasp the notion of 1 + 1 = 2 in that logical world. Russell and Whitehead are heirs to a culture of mathematics grounded in more than 2,000 years of historical experience beyond what Plato experienced in his lifetime, plus about 200 years of specialized developments in the professional culture of mathematics. Cultural and professional developments take their toll on words, ideas, and concepts. All of our words, ideas, and concepts are mutable in the unfolding dramas of history. Logic and its relationship to mathematics had become a subject of complex debates by the early 1900s in a mathematical world that no longer mapped onto the world of mathematics Plato inhabited.

Some sociologists, let alone physical scientists and science studies critics, are convinced that the notion of "social construction" is controversial. The sociologists become confused by conflating social construction as a fundamental theorem with social construction as a synonym for labeling theory. This error is responsible, in part at least, for generating confusion among nonsociologists. Our claim is that it is nothing more or less than the fundamental theorem of sociology. We humans have no other way to become human, to be in the world, and to find our way through truths and falsities than as social beings and in social interactions. The "confusion" persists because certain philosophical biases persist.

Whither Social Construction: II. Reference

Philosopher and historian of science Ian Hacking (1999, p. 4–25) argued that there are few, if any, "universal constructionists." That is, few people would say, for example, that the sun or DNA are in and of themselves socially constructed and exist only by virtue of that social construction. Rather, our images and representations of objects in the physical world are socially constructed, and our social relationships to and interactions with those objects are socially constructed. The social sphere, however, is different, as important social realities (e.g., money) may exist by virtue of their social construction by people over time.

What, then, is the sun "in and of itself"? Sociologists do not—and certainly should not want to—claim that the sun is socially constructed in the same way that money is socially constructed. But the difference here is not the difference between institutional facts and brute facts. Critics of social construction in science must explain how "brute facts" make themselves known to us and how they become "brutes." Brute facts are the facts of naive realism, and once we dispense with naive realism (as we have done in every intellectual arena except for some radically resistant corners of philosophy in which metaphysics still rules), we dispense with brute facts. The "sun" does not come directly to individual humans, individual perceptual systems, or individual brains, which is the only way it could present itself to us as a brute fact (see Hanson, 1971, pp. 4–15, for an argument about sunrises). This is the move that philosophers in particular seem unable to make. If, like sociologists, they start from the fact that we are social beings, then every thing, event, and process is the result of our interaction rituals and interaction ritual chains (cf. Collins, 2004). Interaction rituals do not exist as independent social eddies of dancing individuals but rather as links in networked interaction ritual chains. This is the stumbling block for those philosophically inclined paradox mongers who demonstrated their cleverness by inventing the classical sociology-of-knowledge self-refutation claim (so elegantly refuted by Bloor, 1976, pp. 17–18). That is, if knowledge is social, then the sociology of knowledge itself is social, thus negating—what? If knowledge is social (socially constructed), then of course the sociology of knowledge is social (socially constructed), and if something is social, it must, in colloquial thinking, be wrong. There is no para-

dox here unless we want to claim that there is a pathway to knowledge that somehow bypasses interaction ritual chains. Hacking's argument that because everything is socially constructed, social construction itself thus cannot explain anything is spurious only because it collapses the different kinds of social analysis—important distinctions between levels of analysis and mechanisms appropriate to various scales of inquiry—into one term.

No one has been clearer, no one more consistent in defending social constructivism/ constructionism than Karin Knorr-Cetina. She recognizes that efforts to reconcile science studies with classical philosophy of science are biblical efforts to bring home "the sheep that has gone astray" (Knorr-Cetina, 1993, pp. 555, 557):

> science secretes an unending stream of entities and relations that make up "the world." Now whether this thesis is rejected . . . seems to me to hinge not on whether one grants the preexistence of an (unknown) material world, which to my knowledge every constructivist has granted, but on whether one assumes the pre-existence of specific objects before they have been delimited by science in precisely the way they are delimited by science.

Constructionism, as we are conceiving it here, rejects the latter view and seeks "a less transcendental view of ontology" (Knorr-Cetina, 1993, p. 557). Even when we grant the preexistence thesis, as Knorr-Cetina (1993, p. 558) shows, we have to confront the historicocultural contingency of pre-existence. Subatomic particles are granted preexistence status only after scientists make up their minds about entities brought forth through their laboratory interventions.

Who Is a Social Constructionist?

Is Latour a social constructionist? The answer is not quite. The word *social* was used in the first edition of *Laboratory Life* in 1979 and then dropped in the second edition. It seems as though everything has been demonstrated to be "socially constructed," but even then the meaning of *social* was more like that of *practice* and had nothing to do with an explanation of science in terms of interest, power, social structure, and so on. *The Practical Construction of Scientific Facts* might have solved the subtitle dilemma. Since then, Latour's method has always been to show how science is a better analyzer of society than society is an analyzer of science.

But if he is not a social constructionist, Latour is certainly a full-blooded constructionist (and even an unreconstructed constructionist at that!), meaning that things could have failed and that there is some risk entailed in making them what they are and in maintaining them in existence (cf. Whitehead, 1929/1969, pp. 269–270). A theory of how society constitutes itself is at the same time a theory of how human mentality constitutes itself. This means nothing more nor less than that society and mentality are products of interaction rituals and ritual chains. Knowledge about reality—the sun, DNA, money—is socially *accomplished.* Interaction ritual chains are collective representations in action. Consciousness, as Marx and Engels (1845/1947) argued in *The German Ideology*, is straightforwardly conscious existence, self-aware activity. Things do not exist in themselves but only actively in and through shared and shareable representations and interventions. Whether these representations, these social constructions, have some connection to the "thing in itself," "reality out there," is determined by how successful we are in using them to navigate the world and convincing each other of our success. The contexts and successes of these navigations can be local, regional, or global. Successes in one of these contexts may not necessarily translate into successes in one of the other contexts. And short-term successes may not lead to long-term successes. Local, culturally specific, short-term strategies for navigation and survival are not necessarily going to be compatible with long-term species survival, evolution, and quality of life.

Conclusion: Ways of Life and the Constructionist Debate

Our objective in this chapter has been to rehearse the emergence of social constructionism in science and technology studies and to describe its current theoretical and empirical viability. The history of this term is also a history of controversies, within STS and between STS and other fields of inquiry. These controversies are most virulent in the battles between sociologists of science and philosophers of science. We have every reason to expect that these controversies will not and cannot be resolved by way of standard methods of reasoned discourse. If we conceive of the claims and counterclaims by sociologists and philosophers as acts in defense of ways of life, then any sort of conventional resolution is not an option.[14] Barbara Herrnstein Smith (2006, pp. 166–167) reaches a comparable conclusion. Trying to make social constructionism "clearer" for our critics and opponents is not the answer. Because they are defending a way of life, as we are, "clarifications" will not put an end to their misreadings, misinterpretations, and mistranslations. We can legitimately ask whether all the fuss and furor means the end of sociology as we know it (as Latour, 2004, tends to argue) or the end of epistemology, metaphysics, and indeed of philosophy (as Restivo [1994, pp. 199–207]) tends to argue).

Social constructionism has had demonstrable success in ethnographically describing the social processes of the sciences and in revealing various kinds of interests at work in constituting knowledge. Nonetheless, the assessment of these successes by philosophers and physical and natural scientists has been that science and technology studies has given us at best a sociology of error and at worst relativism. This criticism has been repeatedly addressed by, for example,

Barry Barnes and David Bloor (1982; see, especially, Bloor, 1999), Knorr-Cetina (1993), and Restivo (1988; see also Restivo, 2005b, for an answer to social construction critics within science studies). The utility of social constructionism for articulating both pragmatic and normative analyses of knowledge production remains underdeveloped. Establishing traces of the construction process within texts and film is a hallmark of postmodern cinema and widely viewed as a legitimate theoretical and methodological strategy. Similarly, analysis of many consumer products (organic foods, fair trade goods, tourist and cultural wares) enhances the authenticity of the product, and certifications of various steps in the "construction" process are the hallmark of quality management for large-scale construction and infrastructure development. Culturally, and in various disciplines, the possibility that analyses of the constructedness of facts or worldviews might become a step in demonstrating veracity or otherwise add to their legitimacy remains only in the realm of imagination (Croissant, 2000, p. 233).

There are various ways in which social constructionism is undervalued and undermined from both within and outside of science and technology studies. Latour (2004) is the most extreme critic from within the field. But even among the most sociologically friendly science studies researchers, one finds views of sociology that are less than favorable to the discipline by comparison with the physical and natural sciences (e.g., Collins, 2006). One can contrast these positions with the strong versions of sociology defended by, for example, Randall Collins (e.g., 1975, 1998) and Restivo (1991).

Another way in which social constructionism is obscured and obstructed is by defining it as an extremist (e.g., Shakespeare & Erickson, 2000) or reductionist (e.g., van Kerkhove, 2004–2005) position. If, as we contend, social constructionism is neither more nor less than what humans do as social beings, then the extremism challenge is a category mistake. Putting social constructionism opposite biological determinism is thus putting sociology opposite biological determinism. Sociology is not characteristically a deterministic discipline, even among its most scientistic practitioners; and it is no more deterministic as a discipline than biology or, for that matter, physics and chemistry. The reductionism challenge is a function of not understanding "reductionism" and, indeed, not understanding science. When physicists study the physical world, they are not criticized for being reductionist. Yet when sociologists study the social world, they do hear such criticisms. This has to be a function of the apparent transparency of the physical world as a world of facts subject to scientific analysis versus the opaqueness (even invisibility) of the social world as a world of facts equally subject to (social) scientific analysis.[15] One final view of social constructionism is that it is opposed to "constructivism" by virtue of being more critically and politically engaged. As we note in endnote 1, this is the position Barbara Herrnstein Smith (2006) adopts. This position is not without merit, but it tends to obscure the term and the concept as a fundamental theorem of sociology as a discovery science.

Our conclusion is that sociology and social constructionism have been wildly successful in revolutionizing our understanding of science and technology. The very success of the sociology of science and technology in the post-Mertonian era has challenged traditional boundaries of metadiscourse on science and technology. The challenge has been most severely experienced by philosophers of science and physical and natural scientists. This challenge is grounded in a one-size-fits-all view of science. Historically, this view of science is expressed in what Restivo (Restivo & Loughlin, 2000, p. 139) has called "the grammar of the ever-present tense." Science, once it becomes established in the European "scientific revolution," becomes essentialized, and discussions about and references to science invariably take on the form "Science *is* this, science *is* that. . . ." Post-Mertonian science studies and postmodernist cultural studies of science have, as we have pointed out, given us a more critical and heterogeneous view of science as a pluralistic enterprise. Cultural theory (Thompson, Ellis, & Wildavsky, 1990; see also Douglas, 1973, pp. 77–92) provides a theoretical grounds for associating different forms of science with different ways of life. Social constructionism has contributed significantly to the final stages of the loss of our "unity of science" innocence. More positively, it has for many students of science and science watchers revolutionized their view of the sciences, scientific knowledge, and the world of our everyday experiences.

Social constructionism in science and technology studies is neither relativist, reductionist, nor naively deterministic. The focus on humans as quintessentially social does not eliminate the idea of humans as biological or thermodynamic systems. Stressing the social does not erase the various physical and natural substrata on which the social interactively nests. Genes and neurons are clearly part of the larger picture. It may be that the difficulties these ideas pose for us are rooted in a wrongheaded system of categories and classifications that separate mind, body, brain, and social order. Post-postmodern sociology may have to theorize genes and neurons, bodies, brains, and social orders at the general level of information systems.[16] We already see movements in the direction of conceiving new ways of categorizing and classifying these traditional units of our experiences and experiments in the writings of neuroscientists (e.g., Brothers, 1997; Rose, 2005), psychologists (e.g., Donald, 2001), biologists (Fausto-Sterling, 2005), and sociologists (e.g., Restivo, 2005a, p. 16). Social constructionism in science and technology studies is the social sciences' most promising route into this interdisciplinary convergence.

Notes

1. We are faced with the problem of choosing between two suffixes attached to the term *construct-*: *constructivism, constructionism; constructivist, constructionist.* The suffixes are used more or less interchangeably in some of the literature we are surveying, but some authors use one or the other suffix exclusively. One could perhaps argue that someone who advocates constructionism is a constructivist. Except where *-ist* is used by a quoted author, we use the terms *constructionism* and *constructionist* throughout. Our choice is in part arbitrary and in part principled, as we believe that our choice stresses the active, "making" aspect involved in social construction. We are of course encouraged in this choice by the title the editors chose for this volume. See Barbara Herrnstein Smith's (2006, pp. 4–5) explanation of the reason it is important to distinguish "constructivism" from "social constructionism." Smith views "social constructionism" as a critically and politically engaged set of views on knowledge and science. "Constructivism" is a broader set of views on the nature of knowledge and cognition. The position we adopt here is that social constructionism is a fundamental theorem of the sociological imagination.

2. The strong program (in the sociology of knowledge, introduced in Bloor, 1976, pp. 4–5) adopts the basic values of the scientific disciplines in the study of knowledge and science.

3. Philosophers of science and natural and physical scientists began to criticize and attack the ideas of sociologists of science, especially the idea that science is socially constructed. The science wars (Segestråle, 2000a) can be said to have emerged in the wake of the debate between sociologist of science Harry Collins and biologist Lewis Wolpert at the September 1994 meeting of the British Association for the Advancement of Science (Segestråle, 2000b, p. 7; Smith, 2006, p. 33). Segestråle (2000b, pp. 14–18) also describes and explains the Sokal hoax. Physicist Alan Sokal was able to publish a hoax paper on "transformative hermeneutics of quantum gravity" in the cultural studies journal *Social Text* in 1996. He claimed that this demonstrated that if you wrote in the right style and in the politically appropriate leftist jargon about science, cultural studies scholars would not be able to distinguish

between a hoax and a genuine paper. This hoax was, in fact, just another example of the absurdities that could follow from a failure to understand the nature and foundations of social and cultural studies of science.

4. Treating "social constructionism" philosophically robs it of its empirical grounding and significance. Philosophers transform it into just "another" idea subject to their rules of discourse. This reflects a widespread resistance to the idea of sociology as a discovery science. Latour's (2004) recent effort to systematically refute and reconceptualize sociology from the privileged positions of philosophy and metaphysics has been criticized by Restivo (2005a).

5. Merton (1973) collects Robert K. Merton's major contributions to the sociology of science; see also the work of his students and followers, including J. R. Cole and S. Cole (1973) and N. W. Storer (1966).

6. Sociologists may notice that this is a moment at which we might expect ethnomethodology to enter the sociology of science. And, indeed, Harold Garfinkel's ideas do have some influence on some of the new ethnographers of science. Ethnomethodologists produce some significant contributions to the new science studies (e.g., Livingston, 1986; Lynch, 1985; Lynch, Livingston, & Garfinkel, 1983). For a discussion of ethnomethodology and science studies, see Lynch, Chapter 37, this volume. It should be clear from Lynch's chapter that there is a significant tension between the view of social constructionism we espouse and trace within science and technology studies and ethnomethodology. Our approach is grounded in a Durkheimian-inspired science of social facts and a Marxian-inspired sociological materialism by contrast to phenomenological everyday-world assumptions that guide ethnomethodology.

7. This point is not always "buried" in a footnote. See Restivo's (1988, p. 207) examples from the field of sociology of scientific knowledge (SSK) and science studies generally demonstrating the explicit commitments of core researchers to the scientific worldview.

8. *Internalism* is sometimes taken to refer to the idea that we can know facts by reflection alone. More generally in the history, sociology, and philosophy of science, internalism is the idea that facts and artifacts have inherent, essential logics of unfolding in the world, that there is something inevitable about how they emerge and evolve independently of social, cultural, and historical contingencies.

9. For a list of the handful of ethnographies or anthropologies of science published or in progress at the time, see Knorr-Cetina (1981, p. 32, note 81). Almost all of the pioneers in this field were present at the social process of scientific investigation workshop organized by Roger Krohn at McGill University in Montreal in October 1979.

10. Mary Hesse (1980, p. 32), among the handful of critics who grasped Kuhn qua Kuhn, argued that he had, if anything, discouraged sociological studies of science. M. D. King (1971, p. 30) was one of the earliest critics to recognize the convergence between Kuhn and Merton. And see Bourdieu's (1975) critical remarks on Kuhn (Restivo, 1983). Kuhn himself made quite clear that *The Structure of Scientific Revolutions* (1962) was an homage to his teacher, Alexander Koyré, and from beginning to end was designed as an exercise in internalist history of science. This Kuhnian voice, instantiated in his post-*Structure* book on black-body theory (1978), could not penetrate the roar of his sociology-of-knowledge acolytes. Kuhn's public remarks upon receiving the Bernal Prize of the Society for Social Studies of Science in 1983 made his internalist nonsociological goals quite explicit but again fell on mostly deaf ears.

11. The editors of this volume remind us that Becker is not consistent in his commitment to labeling theory; realism leaks into his theory by way of his idea of "secret deviants" (see Pollner, 1987). The point here is that a strong version of social constructionism should be understood to support a sociological realism and not a labeling theory that supports "social realism" (or something like the [William I.] Thomas "definition of the situation" theorem). On the "anything goes" tone in labeling theory, see Gubrium (1993).

12. Paul Feyerabend, who began his book *Against Method* with a defense of an "anything goes" anarchist philosophy of science, quickly dropped anarchism in favor of Dadaism. By the end of his argument, he is siding with the more conservative agenda set out by Lakatos. The reason for this is that Feyerabend's radicalism might paralyze almost everyone's brains (Feyerabend, 1975, p. 214). One needed a less volatile approach to keep inquiry going.

13. We are currently addressing the complexities of classification and closure in the social con-

struction of facts in a study of the case of Pluto. We have (with the additional collaboration of Wenda K. Bauchspies of Pennsylvania State University) a book in progress titled *Pluto's Revenge: The Social Construction of the Solar System.*

14. See, for example, the approach to change and conflict outlined in *Cultural Theory*—neo-grid-group analysis—by Thompson, Ellis, and Wildavsky (1990); see also Hooker (1975). Hooker argued persuasively that philosophies of science (e.g., realism, empiricism, etc.) could not be compared "head to head" but had to be analyzed in terms of the various worldview categories latent in each philosophy. Restivo and Zenzen (1986) adapted Hooker's analysis for sociologies of science.

15. For a clarification of the meaning of *reductionism* and a discussion of the mistaken reasons given for identifying sociology as a reductionist discipline, see van den Berghe (1990, p. 180). On "society as mystery and illusion," see Collins and Makowsky (2005, pp. 1–14).

16. The implication here is that it is now time to integrate the sociology of mind, which has a long and distinguished history in the discipline from Durkheim, Marx, and Mead to C. Wright Mills, Randall Collins, and Sal Restivo, with a sociology of brain already emergent in Geertz (1973, pp. 74–75) and made more explicit in Geertz (2000, pp. 203–217); and see Crane (2001) for a model of how to move back and forth between sociocultural and biological frameworks to insightfully reveal how the brain works.

• References

Barnes, B., & Bloor, D. (1982). Relativism, rationalism, and the sociology of knowledge. In M. Hollis & S. Lukes (Eds.), *Rationality and Relativism: Studies in the Sociology of Deviance* (pp. 21–47). Cambridge MA: MIT Press.

Becker, H. (1963). *Outsiders.* New York: Free Press.

Bijker, W. E. (1995). *Of bicycles, Bakelites, and bulbs: Towards a theory of sociotechnical change.* Cambridge, MA: MIT Press.

Bijker, W. E., Hughes, T. P., & Pinch, T. (Eds.). (1987). *The social construction of technological systems: New directions in the sociology and history of technology.* Cambridge, MA: MIT Press.

Bloor, D. (1976). *Knowledge and social imagery.* London: Routledge & Kegan Paul.

Bloor, D. (1999). Anti-Latour. *Studies in the History and Philosophy of Science, 30*(1), 81–112.

Bohm, D. (1973). Quantum theory as an indication of a new order in physics: Part B. Implicate and explicate order in physical law. *Foundations of Physics, 3*, 139–68.

Bourdieu, P. (1975). The specificity of the scientific field and the social conditions of the progress of reason. *Social Science Information, 14*(6), 19–47.

Brothers, L. (1997). *Friday's footprints: How society shapes the human mind.* Oxford, UK: Oxford University Press.

Cole, J. R., & Cole, S. (1973). *Social stratification in Science.* Chicago: University of Chicago Press.

Collins, H. (1985). *Changing order.* Beverly Hills: Sage.

Collins, H. (2006). A personal introduction to sociology of science for nonsociologists. Retrieved September 19, 2006, from *www.cardiff.ac.uk/schoolsanddivisions/academicschools/socsi/staff/acad/collins/gravwave/personal.html*

Collins, R. (1975). *Conflict sociology.* New York: Academic Press.

Collins, R. (1998). *The sociology of philosophies.* Cambridge, MA: Harvard University Press.

Collins, R. (2004). *Interaction ritual chains.* Princeton, NJ: Princeton University Press.

Collins, R., & Makowsky, M. (2005). *The discovery of society* (7th ed.). Boston: McGraw-Hill.

Crane, M. T. (2001). *Shakespeare's brain.* Princeton, NJ: Princeton University Press.

Croissant, J. (2000). Critical legal theory and critical science studies: Engaging institutions. *Cultural Dynamics, 12*(2), 223–236.

de Certeau, M. (1986). *Heterologies: Discourse on the other.* Minneapolis: University of Minnesota Press.

Donald, M. (2001). *A mind so rare.* New York: Norton.

Douglas, M. (1973). *Natural symbols.* New York: Vintage Books.

Durkheim, E. (1995). *The elementary forms of religious life* (K. E. Fields, Trans.). New York: Free Press. (Original work published 1912)

Fausto-Sterling, A. (2005). The bare bones of sex. *Signs, 30*(2), 1491–1527.

Feyerabend, P. (1975). *Against method.* London: Verso.

Fleck, L. (1979). *Genesis and development of a scientific fact.* Chicago: University of Chicago Press. (Original work published 1935)

Gardner, M. (1981). Is mathematics for real? *New York Review of Books, 28*, 37–40.

Geertz, C. (1973). *The interpretation of cultures.* New York: Basic Books.

Geertz, C. (2000). *Available light: Anthropological reflections on philosophical topics.* Princeton, NJ: Princeton University Press.

Gieryn, T. (1999). *Cultural boundaries of science: Credibility on the line.* Chicago: University of Chicago Press.

Gross, P., & Levitt, N. (1994). *Higher superstition: The academic left and its quarrel with science.* Baltimore: Johns Hopkins University Press.

Gubrium, J. (1993). For a cautious naturalism. In G.

Miller & J. Holstein (Eds.), *Reconsidering social constructionism: Debates in social problems theory* (pp. 89–101). New York: Aldine de Gruyter.

Hacking, I. (1999). *The social construction of what?* Cambridge, MA: Harvard University Press.

Hanson, N. R. (1971). *Patterns of discovery*. Cambridge, UK: Cambridge University Press.

Hesse, M. (1980). *Revolutions and reconstructions in the philosophy of science*. Bloomington: Indiana University Press.

Hooker, C. A. (1975). Philosophy and meta-philosophy of science: Empiricism, Popperianism, and realism. *Syntheses, 32*, 177–231.

King, M. D. (1971). Reason, tradition, and the progressiveness of science. *History and Theory, 10*, 3–32.

Knorr-Cetina, K. (1979). Tinkering toward science: Prelude to a theory of scientific practice. *Theory and Society, 8*, 347–376.

Knorr-Cetina, K. (1981). *The manufacture of knowledge*. New York: Pergamon Press.

Knorr-Cetina, K. (1993). Strong constructivism—from a sociologist's point of view: A personal addendum to Sismondo's paper. *Social Studies of Science, 23*, 555–563.

Kuhn, T. (1962). *The structure of scientific revolutions*. Chicago: University of Chicago Press.

Kuhn, T. (1978). *Black-body theory and the quantum discontinuity, 1904–1912*. New York: Oxford University Press.

Latour, B. (2004). *Politics of nature: How to bring the sciences into democracy*. Cambridge, MA: Harvard University Press.

Latour, B., & Woolgar, S. (1979). *Laboratory life: The social construction of scientific facts*. Beverly Hills, CA: Sage.

Latour, B., & Woolgar, S. (1986). *Laboratory life: The construction of scientific facts* (2nd. ed.). Princeton, NJ: Princeton University Press.

Law, J. (1991). Theory and narrative in the history of technology: response. *Technology and Culture, 32*(2), 377–384.

Law, J., & Hassard, J. (1999). *Actor network theory and after*. Oxford, UK: Blackwell.

Livingston, E. (1986). *The ethnomethodological foundations of mathematics*. London: Routledge & Kegan Paul.

Lynch, M. (1985). *Art and artifact in laboratory science*. London: Routledge & Kegan Paul.

Lynch, M., Livingston, E., & Garfinkel, H. (1982). Temporal order in laboratory work. In K. D. Knorr-Cetina & M. Mulkay (Eds.), *Science observed: Perspectives on the social study of science* (pp. 205–238). London: Sage.

Mannheim, K. (1936). *Ideology and utopia*. London: Routledge & Kegan Paul.

Marx, K., & Engels, F. (1947). *The German Ideology*. New York: International. (Original work published 1845)

Merton, R. K. (1973). *The sociology of science*. Chicago: University of Chicago Press.

Nanda, M. (2003). *Prophets facing backward: Postmodern critiques of science and Hindu nationalism in India*. New Brunswick, NJ: Rutgers University Press.

Pollner, M. (1987). *Mundane reason: Reality in everyday and sociological discourse*. Cambridge, UK: Cambridge University Press.

Restivo, S. (1983). The myth of the Kuhnian revolution in the sociology of science. In R. Collins (Ed.), *Sociological theory* (pp. 293–305). New York: Jossey-Bass.

Restivo, S. (1988). Modern science as a social problem. *Social Problems, 35*(3), 206–225.

Restivo, S. (1991). *The sociological worldview*. Boston: Blackwell.

Restivo, S. (1994). *Science, society, and values: Toward a sociology of objectivity*. Bethlehem, PA: Lehigh University Press.

Restivo, S. (2005a). Politics of latour. *Organization and Environment, 18*(1), 111–115.

Restivo, S. (2005b, November). *Romancing the robots: Social robots and society, or: Can robots learn to dance (?), and why it matters*. Paper presented at the Eyebeam Open Lab Workshop, New York.

Restivo, S., & Loughlin, J. (2000). The invention of science. *Cultural Dynamics, 12*(2), 135–149.

Restivo, S., & Zenzen, M. (1986). A humanistic perspective on science and society. In W. K. Fishman & C. G. Benello (Eds.), *Readings in humanist sociology: Social, criticism, and social change* (82–116). New York: General Hall.

Rose, S. (2005). *The future of the brain*. Oxford, UK: Oxford University Press.

Scranton, P. (1991). Theory and narrative in the history of technology: Comment. *Technology and Culture, 32*(2), 385–393.

Segestråle, U. (Ed.). (2000a). *Beyond the science wars: The missing discourse about science and society*. Albany: State University of New York Press.

Segestråle, U. (2000b). Science and science studies: Enemies or allies. In U. Segestråle (Ed.), *Beyond the science wars: The missing discourse about science and society* (pp. 1–40). Albany: State University of New York Press.

Serres, M. (1997). *The troubadour of knowledge*. Ann Arbor: University of Michigan Press.

Shakespeare, T., & Erickson, M. (2000). Different strokes: Beyond biological determinism and social constructionism. In H. Rose & S. Rose (Eds.), *Alas, poor Darwin* (pp. 229–247). New York: Harmony Books.

Smith, B. H. (2006). *Scandalous knowledge*. Durham, NC: Duke University Press.

Smith, D. (1999). *Writing the social: Critique, theory, and investigations*. Toronto, Ontario, Canada: University of Toronto Press.

Spengler, O. (1991). *The decline of the West*. New York: Knopf. (Original work published 1926)

Storer, N. (1966). *The social system of science*. New York: Holt, Rinehart, & Winston.

Thompson, M., Ellis, R., & Wildavsky, A. (1990). *Cultural theory*. Oxford, UK: Westview Press.

van den Berghe, P. L. (1990). Why most sociologists don't (and won't) think evolutionarily. *Sociological Forum, 5*(2), 173–185.

Van Kerkhove, B. (2004–2005). *Naturalism and the foundations of mathematical practice: A metaphilosophical essay*. Unpublished doctoral dissertation, Vrije Universiteit Brussel, Brussel, Belgium

White, H. (1987). *The content of the form: Narrative discourse and historical representation*. Baltimore: Johns Hopkins University Press.

Whitehead, A. N. (1969). *Process and reality*. New York: Free Press. (Original work published 1929)

Winner, L. (1993). Upon opening the black box and finding it empty: Social constructivism and the philosophy of technology. *Science, Technology and Human Values, 18*(3), 363–378.

Winner, L. (1996). The gloves come off: Shattered alliances in science and technology studies. *Social Text, 14*(1/2), 81–91.

Zenzen, M., & Restivo, S. (1982). The mysterious morphology of immiscible liquids: A study of scientific practice. *Social Science Information, 21*(3), 447–473.

CHAPTER 12

Constructionism in Sociology

● **Scott R. Harris**

"**S**ocial constructionism" occupies a prominent place in sociology. Since the phrase was popularized by Berger and Luckmann's 1966 book *The Social Construction of Reality*, a substantively, methodologically, and theoretically diverse array of scholars have conducted research under the general rubric of constructionism. These constructionists have made significant contributions to the study of deviance, social problems, social movements, the self, gender, race, education, health, emotions, family, and other areas. As a simple library search indicates, there is a large and growing number of sociological books and articles titled *The Social Construction of X* or simply *Constructing X* (see Best, 2000; Hacking, 1999). The list grows exponentially when one considers constructionist works that are not explicitly titled as such or that

employ synonyms for *constructing*, such as *assembling, building, crafting, fabricating, fashioning, forming, making, manufacturing,* and *producing*. Terms that merely signal agency or creativity—*accomplishing, becoming, discovering, doing, inventing, managing*—are also popular concepts in constructionist titles and analyses. Constructionists enjoy gerunds. They use them to highlight the recurring processes (Prus, 1996), strategies (Lofland, 1976), and practices (Gubrium & Holstein, 1997) through which people actively generate, maintain, and transform reality.

Not all commentators consider the proliferation of constructionist analyses to be an entirely positive development, however. Philosopher and social theorist Ian Hacking (1999) has suggested that there is a great deal of vague thinking and superficial "bandwagon jumping" in these ostensibly constructionist analyses (see also Hollander & Gordon, 2006). Sociologist David Maines (2001, 2003) has argued that the adjective *constructionist* too often serves as an empty rhetorical device, as virtually all sociological analyses rest on the assumption that social life is somehow "constructed."

The concept of "constructing" is too entrenched and important to be dispensed with, however. What is needed is not the dismissal of that metaphor but more precise, careful, and self-conscious applications of it in authors' works. Constructionists need to specify their particular brands of constructionism. Readers, too, could bring more critical and discerning mindsets to constructionist research. This *Handbook* as a whole should make an important contribution to clarifying the many strains of constructionist thought, both across and within disciplines.

Whereas other chapters deal with the intellectual history and philosophical foundations of constructionism, this chapter focuses on two general forms of constructionism that are most frequently confused in the sociological literature: *objective constructionism* and *interpretive constructionism*. These are not currently accepted terms, but I believe they are helpful in distinguishing two dominant and competing (if only implicit) sociological uses of the constructionist perspective.[1]

This distinction between objective and interpretive constructionism is at first glance relatively simple to understand. Yet its implications are broad, and many complexities appear upon closer inspection. Interpretive and objective constructionists may use almost identical language to advance very different arguments. At the same time, there are overlapping concerns between the two approaches, and there can be intricate connections between the processes and outcomes of the interpretive and objective construction of social life (see Gubrium & Holstein, 1997; Hacking, 1999; Loseke, 1999).

Interpretive Social Constructionism

Interpretive social constructionism (ISC) is frankly what I would consider the more radical form of constructionism. It has roots in a number of diverse traditions, especially pragmatism, symbolic interactionism, phenomenology, and ethnomethodology.[2] Other orientations and developments, such as narrative analysis, cognitive sociology, semiotic sociology, and postmodernism also sometimes derive from and contribute to what might be called the interpretive constructionist movement.[3]

Although these approaches are sometimes difficult to define and compare and are by no means equivalent, it is possible to identify some fairly common themes. I begin by focusing on one in particular. For many scholars, the core principle of ISC is the idea that *the meaning of things is not inherent*. This assumption is reflected in Blumer's (1969, pp. 2–6) fundamental premises of symbolic interactionism, in which he argues that meanings are created, learned, used, and revised in social interaction. All objects—"objects" being cows, chairs, actions, selves, social problems, decades, or anything else that can be referred to—derive their meaning from the purposes and perspectives that people bring to them (Blumer, 1969; Mead, 1934). Schutz's (1964, p. 227) phenomenological sociology also presumes the "ambivalence of the meaning of all social phenomena," as does the ethnomethodological argument that descriptions "reflexively" constitute the situations they appear to report about—even as those descriptions "indexically" derive their sense from the circumstances surrounding their use (Coulon, 1995, p. 23; Heritage, 1984, p. 140).

Similarly, when Berger and Luckmann (1966) initially formulated the social constructionist project, the issue of meaning was central to it. Their goal was to expand the sociology of knowledge—previously preoccupied with abstract ideas, philosophies, and the like—to the realm of everyday life:

> The sociology of knowledge must first of all concern itself with what people "know" as "reality" in their everyday, non- or pre-theoretical lives. In other words, commonsense "knowledge" ... must be the central focus. ... It is precisely this "knowledge" that constitutes the fabric of meanings without which no society could exist. The sociology of knowledge, therefore, must concern itself with the social construction of reality. (Berger & Luckmann, 1966, p. 15)

Their frequent use (including scare quotes) of the terms "knowledge" and "reality" indicate that Berger and Luckmann were taking a highly relativistic stance toward issues of truth. What is "constructed," in their initial formulation of the constructionist perspective, was first and foremost the meaning of things.

For interpretive constructionists, the premise "meaning is not inherent" applies to everything. Although there may be some limits to what humans can get away with—for example, a chair usually cannot be eaten as food, and others may sanction an individual for trying—there are always many purposes and perspectives people can bring to things that interest them. What is taken to be a simple chair could be used as a strange weapon, as something to stand on, as something to burn or to sell, and so on (Blumer, 1969, p. 69). It might be viewed or described as beautiful or ugly or plain, as cheap or expensive or moderately priced, as an ordinary seat or a place of honor. A chair might be vaguely noticed but deemed irrelevant. And what holds for such a relatively simple and noncontroversial item of experience also holds for more complex and contentious examples. A war, a political leader, tattoos, animal cruelty, homelessness—the meaning of these and everything else is contingent on the actions of people, who must supply classifications, interpretations, and narratives to make sense of them.

Whole schools of interpretive constructionist thought have been founded on or at least inspired by the idea that meaning is not inherent: ISC studies of self-identity often hinge on the assumption that "who we are" is a socially created idea, negotiated in interaction (Gubrium & Holstein, 2001; Vryan, Adler, & Adler, 2003); ISC studies of deviance frequently assume that no behavior or personal attribute is inherently deviant, that people's actions and appearance must be defined as deviant to be seen that way (Becker, 1973, p. 9; Herman-Kinney, 2003; but see also Pollner's [1987] critique of Becker); ISC studies of family are sometimes premised on the idea that "family" can be defined in a number of different ways, that no set of social bonds is inherently familial or nonfamilial, and that there are no definitive versions of what is going on in any particular family relationship (Gubrium & Holstein, 1990; Knapp, 1999, 2002); ISC studies of social problems regularly assume that no social issue is troubling just as someone says it is, that interpretive claimsmaking gives order to indeterminate states of affairs (Blumer, 1971; Schneider, 1985; Spector & Kitsuse, 1977).

Thus ISC analyses tend to assume or argue that social phenomena are *interpreted* entities whose existence and qualities are dependent in large part on people's meaning-making practices. Human beings are construction workers in the sense that they create (or assemble, build, manufacture) meaning. Just as there is virtually always more than one way to build something, there is virtually always more than one way to define something. ISC scholars usually argue or assume that a particular understanding of "X" is not the only understanding possible, that what is taken as the "truth" of the matter depends on people's agendas and orientations. Everything can be seen or described or used in different ways. Interpretation is not a completely spontaneous or random process, however. It is guided by material and conceptual resources at individuals' disposal and conditioned by social and physical constraints (Gubrium & Holstein 1997, Chapter 8).

Again, this one simple yet profound theme—meaning is not inherent—is arguably the core principle of interpretive social constructionism. There are many other ideas associated with ISC, but all of them tend to cohere around the creation of meaning as the central guiding concern. Interpretive constructionists believe that researchers ought to study the meanings people live by and how those meanings are created. They are wary of methodologies and approaches that lead researchers to impose meanings onto those they study, rather than investigating meanings (Blumer, 1969). They are not principally concerned with discovering what things "really" mean in order to dispel myths or correct misunderstandings (Berger & Luckmann, 1966, p. 12). They try to suspend belief *and* disbelief in reality (Schutz, 1970) in order to examine how it is produced by and for members of various social settings (Garfinkel, 1967).

Objective Social Constructionism

Objective social constructionism (OSC) is different from what I have just described. Although important and useful, OSC[4] arguments do not focus on the creation of meaning, or at least not to the extent that ISC arguments do. For OSC analyses, what are made, built, or assembled are not interpretations but (for lack of a better phrase) real states of affairs. As a result, OSC arguments can be made without necessarily attending so much to what things mean to actors and the intricate processes through which those diverse meanings are created; OSC arguments can be made without suspending belief in the existence of the world as the analyst sees it.

OSC has roots in a broad range of sociological perspectives, too diverse and numerous to specify beyond the examples I provide later. Moreover, many scholars who

take an interpretive constructionist approach to some issues take an objective constructionist approach to other issues, even in the same report. ISC and OSC analyses are often interwoven in complex and even contradictory ways. But to put it simply: OSC deals with the creation of "real things" as opposed to "meanings." Consequently, OSC is reflected in any arguments that suggest that real social phenomena (e.g., actual family relationships vs. interpretations of putative relationships) are produced by the actions of individual actors and groups, by constraining social forces, by the operations of class, race, gender, politics, or religion, and so on. Culture and interpretation may play a role in an OSC analysis, but only insofar as these issues can be put to use in a more standard sociological account of what is really going on and why it is happening. For example, authors who identify "self-fulfilling prophecies" often incorporate an element of interpretation into their analyses, but they may do so within a framework that takes for granted the meaning of virtually everything in order to enter debates over the real causes of social behavior (e.g., Watzlawick, 2005). In the hands of somewhat more interpretive scholars, arguments about "self-fulfilling prophecies" may occupy an ambiguous middle ground between objective and interpretive constructionism (e.g., Loseke, 1999, pp. 167–168). But again, simply put, objective constructionists argue that something is "socially constructed" when a real phenomenon (as opposed to an interpretation or meaning) derives its existence or its dimensions from other social factors.

When Maines (2003) argues that all sociology is constructionist, it is largely OSC that he has in mind:

Sociology's fundamental domain proposition is that some combination of social things cause or are related to some other combination of social things. Insert whatever variables, factors, elements, or "constructed social realities" one wants, and the proposition holds. Parents influence their children through communication; inner-city schools disadvantage inner-city students; unemployment goes up when the economy shrinks; mobility opportunities are lower at the top and bottom of class systems; personal identities are expressed through narratives; divorce tends to have an array of negative effects on the children of divorced parents; and electronic and visual media technologies tend to give the capitalist class an advantage. We all know that [all of these factors] have been historically created and that they undergo change in different ways and at different rates, and that even some of them (e.g., television, cities, capitalism, schools) at one time did not exist at all. (p. 16)

This statement leans heavily toward the OSC side of the OSC–ISC continuum. The phrase "personal identities are expressed through narratives" seems potentially interpretive constructionist, as long as the verb *expressed* is read in the right (meaning-making) way. Most of the other examples in Maines's list refer to the objective construction of social life—that is, to the creation of real states of affairs through the operation of various social forces. If this is "social constructionism," then sociology truly is thoroughly constructionist and has been since its inception. Sociologists always have and probably always will try to explain *why things occur as they do*. However, this form of analysis overlaps with but is far from identical to the ISC focus on *how things are defined as they are*.

Take Maines's examples that "inner-city schools disadvantage inner-city students" and that "divorce tends to have an array of negative effects on the children of divorced parents." These kinds of arguments may employ verbs that imply a constructionist analysis—as in *manufacturing* students' careers, the social *creation* of children's experiences, or perhaps the *making* of delinquents. But this is fairly standard social-scientific thinking, and is certainly *not* what rigorously interpretive scholars would want to call "constructionist." An ISC scholar would more likely focus on how these issues are

interpretively constituted—that is, given meaning. For example, a social problems constructionist in the tradition of Spector and Kitsuse (1977) would study the different claims that are made about the issue of inner-city schools. The researcher would examine the diverse meanings that various claimsmakers create as they proffer competing interpretations of the putative problem at hand, the supposed causes and effects of the problem, the suggested solutions to the problem, and so on. An ISC scholar would study how narratives—those told by everyday folk as well as by OSC scholars—create meaning by making assertions about actors, motives, conditions, causes, effects, and remedies.

Certainly, an ISC scholar may be tempted to argue that meaning-making can lead to real, observable changes in a society. This type of argument has been a feature of ISC and OSC thought for decades. It takes us back to the middle ground I mentioned with respect to self-fulfilling prophecies. Blumer's (1969) first premise of interactionism ("People act based on what things mean to them") and the oft-cited Thomas theorem ("If people define things as real, they are real in their consequences") both imply a simultaneous concern with meaning and with objective reality. Berger and Luckmann (1966, p. 91) also encouraged analyses that considered the dialectical relationship between what people do and what they think. Controversies over constructionists' selective relativism (Best, 2003; Ibarra & Kitsuse, 2003; Woolgar & Pawluch, 1985) and solutions such as "analytical bracketing" (Holstein & Gubrium, 2003) in large part point as well to the ambiguous overlaps and "interactions" (Hacking, 1999, p. 31; see also Loseke, 1999, Chapters 6, 7) between what I am calling objective and interpretive constructionism.

My first priority in this chapter is not to clarify the ambiguous middle ground between ISC and OSC. Instead, my main goal is to describe these two forms of sociological constructionism in a somewhat stark but clear manner, so that the differences be-tween them can be appreciated. I want to reach a broad audience with a simple point: More sociologists need to recognize that the exact same constructionist language can be used in (at least) two very different kinds of analyses. Only then, once a clear image of each approach is apprehended, might read-ers better trace the complex moves that re-searchers sometimes make as they combine or alternate between one form of analysis and the other.

Objective and Interpretive Constructionism: Common Vocabularies, Different Arguments

In this section, I further explain the differ-ence between OSC and ISC by focusing on the vocabulary that analysts use in parallel but conflicting fashion. My discussion cen-ters on four key terms—*contingency*, *essen-tialism*, *reification*, and *work*—but will touch on other central constructionist concepts as well. Though OSC and ISC rely on the same terms and make similar-sounding argu-ments, there are often vast differences that go unrecognized. I wish to make these dif-ferences clearly apparent. Moreover, as an interpretive constructionist, I want to advo-cate for more consistent and self-conscious usage of the ISC perspective. In order to pursue these goals, I draw examples from widely read textbooks and anthologies, as well as journal articles and monographs. Given my own research interests, I pay most attention to constructionist writings on fam-ily, inequality, and social problems.

Contingency

Both ISC and OSC are in superficial agree-ment about the *contingent* nature of social life. The foil for constructionist analyses tends to be arguments, whether advanced by laypersons or scholars, that treat social phe-nomena as natural, inherent, or automatic. As Hacking (1999, p. 12) has noted, con-structionists of all sorts typically argue that what some people may take for granted and treat as inevitable actually should not be seen that way. But what is contingent? Inter-pretations or objective realities?

For an OSC analysis, what is contingent is some real trait, behavior, or state of affairs. Consider the following example, from a widely read text on sociological social psy-chology. The author/editor uses construc-tionist verbs but (in this passage) leans much more toward OSC than ISC:

> Social institutions are *created* and *maintained* through the active participation of individuals. To the extent that we are aware of our reasons for participating in various cultural produc-tions, we can be said to be mindfully engaged in the *construction* of reality. . . . Imagine [an at-torney] explaining to her spouse and children that she does not have time to celebrate birth-days and anniversaries because she is busy fighting for an important social cause. She is often absent from family meals and other ev-eryday rituals as well. One day she awakens to the discovery that she is no longer meaning-fully engaged with her family—they seem to be living their lives without her. This example il-lustrates the simple but profound point that if we do not actively participate in the *production* of those realities that we wish to maintain . . . they will be eroded by the forces of entropy. (O'Brien, 2005, p. 517; emphasis added)

This passage suggests that close relation-ships are "constructed"—created, main-tained, produced—by the careful effort peo-ple put into them. The argument is that even familial relationships are not automatic or inevitable and cannot be taken for granted. This is a useful way of thinking about things, but in my opinion it is not as *interpretive* as it could be. It lies closer to the other end of the OSC–ISC continuum.[5]

ISC analyses employ a different and (in my view) deeper sense of contingency.[6] In their book *What Is Family?* Gubrium and

Holstein (1990) adopt a more thoroughly and consistently interpretive form of constructionism. They are interested in how people *define* family affairs, an issue that arguably precedes discussions of whether a family exists, what qualities it may have, and what causal factors shape it. Here contingency centers on meaning: The meaning of any (putative) familial relationship is not inherent. According to Gubrium and Holstein's version of constructionism, people define the family into and out of being through their interpretive practices. People assign various qualities to families (e.g., closeness, distance, normality, deviance) as they think and talk about ambiguous states of affairs. It is in this different sense that the authors use the exact same verbs *construct* and *produce*: "We offer a view of family as a socially constructed object, a product of decidedly public actions and interactions" (Gubrium & Holstein, 1990, p. 12).

Consider an example derived from Gubrium and Holstein's (1990) observations of a family–patient support group. A father and his 22-year-old son with schizophrenia offer competing interpretations of the closeness of their relationship, as well as the behavior and motivations of the son. The father accuses the son of (among other things) not being around very often and then of being quiet and surly when he is present. The father assembles these three potential "facts"—absence, silence, surliness—into a narrative that his son was more a "stranger" than a loving family member. In response, the son recasts the same biographical elements into a different pattern. In the son's account, absence and silence and surliness are portrayed as signs of love, as well as struggles with mental illness, not as signs of alienation or disloyalty. The son says:

> Come on. You know I care. It's just hard for me. I come by, but I don't want to start you worrying, so I don't say too much. I don't want to complain because I don't want you to think that I'm not doing okay. I thought I was doing something good for you by trying to stay out of

> your hair. . . . I get pretty screwed up sometimes, so I try to stay away when I might have a bad day. (Gubrium & Holstein, 1990, p. 59)

Thus what Gubrium and Holstein are focusing on here is not the same kind of "contingency" as in the previous case. In O'Brien's example, what is contingent are real families, whose existence and qualities are not inevitable. This sort of objective contingency is common in the literature on families, whether the contingent factors are wide-scale cultural and economic conditions or the daily choices of spouses (e.g., Carrington, 2004; Hochschild, 1989). In Gubrium and Holstein's example, family again is contingent, but this time it is the meaning of family that is not inevitable and that must be constructed. This sort of interpretive contingency is somewhat less common in the literature, but it also has been pursued (e.g., Harris, 2006a; Knapp, 1999; Loseke, 1987; Miller, 1991).

Essentialism

All constructionists tend to emphasize contingency and argue against the foil of inevitability, but there are different degrees of inevitability. A potentially weak sense of inevitability may exist when someone takes a phenomenon for granted and does not question why something appears to be the way it is. A stronger form of inevitability is reflected in "essentialism," the belief that some phenomenon has an essence or inherent nature that makes it what it is. But this term too can be put to different uses depending on the version of constructionism at hand. An OSC definition of essentialism would be one that launches analysts into debates over the real causes of real behavior. In *The Social Construction of Difference and Inequality*, author/editor Ore (2003, p. 5) offers this explanation:

> [Essentialism is] the tenet that human behavior is "natural," predetermined by genetic, biologi-

cal, or physiological mechanisms and thus not subject to change. Human behaviors that show some similarity are assumed [by nonconstructionists] to be expressions of an underlying human drive or tendency. In the United States, gender and sexuality are among the last realms to have their natural or biological status called into question.

This version of essentialism can lead to OSC because it encourages scholars to enter debates over *why* mundane behavior occurs. The "nature versus nurture" debate is often treated as "essentialism versus constructionism," but in my view that contrast elides the OSC–ISC distinction. ISC is not preoccupied with nature versus nurture. Interpretive constructionists sidestep such debates in order to study more carefully what people *claim* to be the reasons for behavior, as well as how those claims are advanced, confirmed, and contested. In contrast, more objective constructionists try to separate myth from reality regarding human behavior, usually by arguing against innate tendencies.

For OSC, "essentialism" centers on the idea that people do what they do because it is in their nature: They are inherently nurturing, they possess natural genius or talent, or they are "born bad." The objective constructionist counterargument is that these real behaviors and traits are not simply inherent but are created by social factors: Women may be expected and pressured to act nurturing (Bellas, 2001; Crompton & Lyonette, 2005); genius and talent may be produced by access to high-quality instruction and other social factors quite apart from the inborn capacities a person may have (Chambliss, 1989; Scheff, 2005); deviance and conformity can be seen as socially elicited actions rather than innate propensities (Agnew, 2001; Becker, 1963/1973, pp. 26, 34). Although these sorts of OSC arguments are important, they are not the same as ISC arguments.

An interpretive constructionist take on essentialism focuses more squarely on the meaning of things—on how things are viewed or described—rather than on the causes of behavior. Representation, not causality, is the more central issue for ISC analyses.[7] Consequently, interpretive constructionism rebuts meaning-centered essentialism rather than causality-centered essentialism; its target are assertions that some actions (e.g., not wearing clothes, smoking pot, or even committing murder) are essentially or inherently wrong or that certain categories (e.g., the "alcoholic") simply reflect real features of the world. Consider Goode's (1994) definition of essentialism, from his text on deviance:

> Essentialism is the view that all phenomena in the world have an indwelling "essence" that automatically and unambiguously places them in specific, more or less unchanging categories. . . . Essentialists are comfortable with using the terms "true" and "real" when referring to categories or their representatives. Certain inherent, unchanging characteristics define, for example, "true" alcoholism or "true" homosexuality. . . . (Goode, 1994, p. 32)

I don't mean to imply that Goode's large book is uniformly interpretive. But in this passage, in this definition, essentialism is portrayed in ISC terms. Classifications, not causes of behavior, are what are at stake. The question is not What causes alcoholism? or What causes good parenting? but rather How do different people define what "alcoholism" or "homosexuality" mean and decide whether particular individuals should be described in those terms?

For a classic ISC treatment of essentialism, consider Howard Becker's (1963/1973) influential formulation of the labeling perspective on deviance. Although Becker wavers between a realist and a radically interpretive point of view (see Berard, 2003; Pollner, 1987), his famous dictum on deviance can be read as ISC. It is also interesting that he so long ago articulated in embryonic form the objective–interpretive distinction that is the subject of this chapter. Notice the dual meanings of the verb *create*, as well as his argument against essentialism:

> Deviance is *created* by society. I do not mean this in the way it is ordinarily understood, in which the causes of deviance are located in the social situation of the deviant or in "social factors" which prompt his action. I mean, rather, that social groups *create* deviance by making the rules whose infraction constitutes deviance, and by applying those rules to particular people and labeling them as outsiders. From this point of view, deviance is *not* a quality of the act the person commits, but rather a consequence of the application by others of rules and sanctions to an "offender." The deviant is one to whom that label has successfully been applied; deviant behavior is behavior that people so label. (Becker, 1973, p. 9; emphasis altered)

In this passage, the kind of essentialism that Becker is contrasting with constructionism is different than in Ore's (2003) case, mentioned earlier. Becker is arguing against absolutist notions of deviance and respectability, such as "Public nudity *is* immoral" or "Abortion *is* murder." An essentialist might consider public nudity or abortion to be morally wrong now and forever, irrespective of what human beings think about those actions. An interpretive constructionist would argue that meanings are never essential, because they are socially created. People define things as deviant, normal, and so on. The ISC agenda would then be to study in detail how those meanings are created (Holstein, 1993), rather than to move quickly back to examining the real causes of deviant actions, as Becker (1973, pp. 26, 34) does.

Reification

Along with essentialism, reification is a common antagonist for constructionist analyses. Berger and Luckmann (1966) provide a profound and oft-cited inspirational definition of reification, but one that can be read and used from either an OSC or an ISC perspective.

> Reification is the apprehension of human phenomena as if they were things, that is, in nonhuman or possibly super-human terms. Another way of saying this is that reification is the apprehension of the *products* of human activity as if they were something else than human *products*—such as facts of nature, results of cosmic laws, or manifestations of divine will. Reification implies that man is capable of forgetting his own authorship of the human world. (Berger & Luckmann, 1966, p. 89; emphasis altered)

Notice the ambiguity surrounding the constructionist idea of "production." What is being produced—actual social phenomena or interpretations of social phenomena?

For an objectivist, reification is treating an organization, a family, or an inequality as if they were "things"—as if they existed outside of the interactions through which people created, enacted, and transformed them. Consider Benson's (1977) programmatic article on organizations. He argues that many conventional scholars treat organizations as if they had an "autonomous, determinate structure" (p. 5). His constructionist approach, in contrast, treats organizations as always produced in an ongoing manner by human behavior: "Relationships are *formed*, roles are *constructed*, institutions are *built* from the encounters and confrontations of people in their daily round of life" (Benson, 1977, p. 3; emphases added). All of these italicized constructionist verbs seem to be used in a primarily objectivist manner as Benson argues against the reification of organizations (see also Hall, 1987, p. 16).

Similarly, Schwalbe and colleagues (2000, p. 420) critique sociologists who do not understand that "social entities"—and forms of inequality in particular—"must be understood as recurrent patterns of joint action." For example, they argue that "class" is too often treated as a thing—an explanatory variable. Instead, class should be studied as "a situated construction, accomplished through people's daily efforts to make a living; through struggles between workers and employers . . . ; and through cooperation among elites to control business, finance, and government" (Schwalbe et al., 2000, p. 441). Though they acknowledge the importance of meaning, Schwalbe and colleagues' argument against reification seems in many ways more objectivist than interpretive.[8]

Pollner (1987) provides, in my view, an ISC understanding of reification. He cites the same passage from Berger and Luckmann (1966) that I previously quoted but gives it a much different spin. For Pollner (1987, p. 100), reification occurs whenever people act or talk as if there are "determinate and objective or absolute entities"—that is, when someone posits an object whose meaning is independent of any human subject. As an example, Pollner describes how officers and judges act as if they are responding to an "independent field" of deviance, rather than (interpretively) creating the meaning of behavior through their responses to it. During the course of their everyday routines, these actors regularly reify deviance as a thing waiting to be found rather than an ongoing human product—"product" being an interpretation of indeterminate events. In contrast to Benson (1997) and to Schwalbe and colleagues (2000), Pollner is not interested in how social interaction creates the real properties of organizations or class inequality; he is interested in how people convince themselves that there are "organizations" and "inequalities" as real, independent entities in the world.

When I have cited Berger and Luckmann (1966) in my own work on equality in marriage, I have also given their work a decidedly interpretive spin (Harris, 2000, p. 131). Objectivist researchers, I have argued, are prone to reification when they assume that marital equality and inequality exist in the world and that

their job is to accurately define, measure, and explain those phenomena. Reification is evident whenever scholars specify the contingent factors, choices, and practices by which some couples succeed or fail at accomplishing marital equality (Blaisure & Allen, 1995; Schwartz, 1994). In contrast, a constructionist would dereify equality in order to focus on the contingent *definitional* processes that bring equality and inequality into being (Harris 2006a, p. 8).[9] Here marital equality and inequality are both *interpretive* accomplishments—that is, meanings. Although this approach strikes some as cynical and detached, it can more favorably be seen as a way to respect and study the truths people live by. What are the different ways that people define "marital equality"? How do they interpret ambiguous instances as examples of "power," "labor," "respect," or whatever else they regard important to equality? How does the issue of equality–inequality actually enter people's lived experiences? These are the questions I asked, which are more reflective of ISC than OSC.

Work

As constructionists highlight contingency and argue against essentialism and reification, they often do so by documenting the important kinds of "work" that human beings do. Reality is not automatic, natural, or self-generating; it is created by people's actions. This broad premise has led to the development of many interesting concepts that build directly on the metaphor of humans as construction workers. Here is an incomplete list:

- Authenticity work (Peterson, 2005)
- Biographical work (Holstein & Gubrium, 2000)
- Body work (Gimlin, 2002)
- Border work (Thorne, 1993) and boundary work (Lamont & Molnár, 2002)

- Care work (Herd & Meyer, 2002)
- Character work (Holyfield & Fine, 1997)
- Conversational work and interactional work (Fishman, 1978)
- Edgework (Lyng, 1990)
- Emotion work (Hochschild, 1979)
- Ethnicity work (Berbrier, 2000)
- Identity work (Snow & Anderson, 1987) and public identity work (Foley, 2005)
- Ideological work (Berger, 1981)
- Kin work (Stack & Burton, 1993)
- Money work (Schweingruber & Berns, 2003)
- Rape work (Martin, 2005)
- Reality work and time work (Flaherty, 1984, 2003)
- Risk work (Horlick-Jones, 2005)
- Self work (Spencer, 1992)
- Social problems work (Holstein & Miller, 2003)
- Surgical work (Pope, 2002)
- Symbolic work (Wanderer, 1987)
- Teamwork, face work, and remedial work (Goffman, 1959, 1967, 1971)
- Thought work, family work, food work, sociability work, and support work (Devault, 1991)
- Trajectory work, awareness context work, composure work, rectification work, sentimental work, and trust work (Strauss, Fagerhaugh, Suczek, & Wiener, 1982)

The kinds of "work" that these concepts imply are somewhat diverse, but they can be placed along the objective–interpretive continuum highlighted in this chapter. Consider the concepts of *conversational work* and *thought work*. Both emerged out of feminist analyses that sought to bring recognition to women's important contributions to social life. In Fishman's (1978) and Devault's (1991) analyses, the authors document the often invisible work (Daniels, 1987) that women perform in their close relationships.

Fishman carefully describes how women actively maintain conversations via subtle comments such as "Mmm," "Oh?," and "Yeah?" Women do more of this interactional work, Fishman argues, and it is largely unnoticed and taken for granted. Devault, in turn, highlights the planning and organizing that women (more than men) put into feeding their families. Such work goes well beyond selecting recipes and making shopping lists and includes frequently taken-for-granted actions such as attending to the contradictory food preferences of family members, maintaining variety, budgeting, fostering a desired mood at the table, and so on. The construction metaphor implicit in these two examples seems to be: just as it takes time, effort, and planning to build a real chair, it takes time, effort, and planning to feed one's family or to conduct an intimate conversation. Family meals and ordinary conversations, like chairs, do not exist automatically or inevitably. They are all dependent on the efforts of human beings.

Although useful and insightful, these conceptions of work seem potentially more objective than interpretive. Fishman's (1978) *interactional work* includes efforts that keep a real conversation going. Devault's (1991) *thought work* includes efforts that help put real food on the table. Much in these analyses does not entail a thoroughgoing bracketing of social reality and a consistent focus on the creation of meaning.[10] A more interpretive constructionist would probably not employ the concept of work in order to argue that our society should recognize as laborious some activities that have previously been classified as nonwork, such as volunteering, caring, and emoting (Daniels, 1987, p. 413). An interpretive constructionist would probably not, at least not under the guise of analysis, enter debates over what the public should count as important or real labor. Such debates about the objective status of work rely on various kinds of *interpretive* work that ISC is interested in (see also Besen, 2006; Gusfield, 1984; Spector & Kitsuse, 1977, pp. 70–71).

Whereas OSC analyses tend to focus on the work it takes to create reality, ISC analyses tend to focus on the work it takes to create a sense of reality. This latter version of "work" is reflected more prominently in some of the concepts I listed previously. Discursive constructionists, such as those associated with the concepts of *social problems work* (Holstein & Miller, 2003; Loseke, 1999, pp. 19, 198–199) and *biographical work* (Holstein & Gubrium, 2000), usually try to bracket as much of a social issue as possible—the actors, actions, conditions, causes, and so forth—in order to examine how they are categorized and given meaning. For example, analyses of social problems work might consider how types of people (e.g., the "inexpressive male" or the "battered woman") are invented and popularized, as well as how these categories are employed to make sense out of ambiguous situations in everyday life (e.g., Loseke, 1987, 2003). Analyses of biographical work might examine how past conversational actions (such as silence, interrupting, yelling, active listening) are given meaning by a spouse's, friend's, or therapist's narrative. An interpretive constructionist would emphasize the work it takes to link behavioral incidents into a meaningful pattern. Any social situation—a conversation, a family meal, or any other—contains "a number of evanescent, ambiguous difficulties" that may or may not be noticed and defined as some sort of "trouble" (Emerson & Messinger, 1977, p. 121). The process of selecting, classifying, and narrating elements of experience is the *interpretive* work that ISC analyses focus on (Gubrium & Holstein, 1997, p. 147; Riessman, 2002). OSC scholars tend to assume primary responsibility for this kind of work, rather than highlighting how members get the job done.

Conclusion

I close this chapter with three points about the OSC–ISC distinction I have drawn. First, the difference between objective and interpretive constructionism is a matter of degree. It is unlikely that any author or report could be placed utterly at one end or the other of this continuum. I have never met or read a truly "naive realist" who would deny that multiple interpretations are sometimes plausible or that some descriptors are merely arbitrary conventional symbols. Given the rise and influence of interpretive constructionism, it seems unlikely that even the most structural, quantitative, positivistic scholar would not express some recognition of the importance of meaning, culture, perspectives, and related constructionist notions. Indeed, Maines (2001) and Atkinson and Housley (2003) argue that many interactionist and constructionist ideas have pervasively infiltrated mainstream sociology, even if not all sociologists explicitly acknowledge the intellectual heritage of those ideas.

At the same time, an utterly interpretive constructionism also seems unlikely. As debates within the social problems literature have clarified, it is impossible for a scholar to bracket everything at once (Best, 2003; Woolgar & Pawluch, 1985). At least some assumptions about objective reality must enter even the most "strict" constructionist analyses.[11] Holstein and Gubrium's (2003) solution to this dilemma is for interpretive constructionists to be deliberate, minimalist, and explicit as they import realist assumptions into their analyses in order to highlight the local contextual factors that shape (and are shaped by) interpretations. Rather than attempting a wholesale bracketing of social reality, Holstein and Gubrium recommend a strategic "analytic bracketing" that alternates between the concrete "whats" and constitutive "hows" of social reality (see also Holstein & Gubrium, Chapter 19, this volume). Other interpretive constructionists recommend moving somewhat further toward objectivism. Best (2003) expresses confidence in analysts' abilities to focus on meaning making while simultaneously comparing lay interpretations with the "facts" of the matter and locating those interpretations within larger structural contexts.

My second point flows from the first: The fact that the difference between OSC and ISC is "only a matter of degree" does not mean that the distinction is eradicated. Degrees can be large and consequential. Degrees matter. For example, in my own work I have tried to argue that sociologists remain largely captivated with their own conceptions of inequality, despite the proliferation of qualitative and "constructionist" studies of this topic (Harris, 2001, 2003, 2004). Even scholars who acknowledge the idea that "meaning is not inherent" subsequently proceed to treat inequality as an objective fact whose features can be readily observed and explained by analysts (e.g., Collins, 2000; Heiner, 2002; Lamont & Molnár, 2002; Ore, 2003). The risk of this objectivism is that we may not fully understand the diverse meanings that "unequal situations" may have for people in everyday life, as well as how those meanings are created (Harris, 2006a, 2006b). In response to my critique, however, a more objectivist scholar might reasonably argue that a rigorously interpretive sociology entail risks of its own, such as missing the opportunity to correct the public's misunderstandings about the real extent and causes of inequality and other problems.

Adopting any orientation involves risks and benefits. All theoretical perspectives have strengths and weaknesses. So let many flowers bloom—but let's not treat them as if they were all the same plant. I suggest that the distinction between objective and interpretive constructionism provides one way to summarize and clarify the different kinds of constructionist work that have proliferated in sociology in the past few decades. Clearly, this distinction is only a starting point. OSC and ISC are themselves very broad labels, and I have not attempted to specify all of the subtypes of, as well as all the ambiguous overlaps between, these two approaches.

My third and final point is, thus, an endorsement of vigilance. Readers who arc interested in understanding and using constructionist ideas may benefit from increased alertness regarding the particular form of constructionism that is in play in any given publication or passage therein. Vigilance is required because even when two scholars invoke the same theoretical source, excerpt, and concept—such as Berger and Luckmann (1966, p. 89) on reification—there is still ample room for ambiguity and divergent agendas. These agendas shape what we know and what we try to learn.

Perhaps it is fitting that the basic premises of constructionism—that meaning is not inherent, that it depends on people's purposes and perspectives—apply reflexively to the concept of "social constructionism" itself. If you think about it, how could it be any other way?

• Acknowledgments

I thank Mitch Berbrier, Jay Gubrium, and Jim Holstein for commenting on earlier versions of this chapter. My work was supported by a Summer Research Award from Saint Louis University.

• Notes

1. This objective vs. interpretive distinction is similar to what Hacking (1999, p. 14) describes as the social construction of "objects" versus "ideas." It also at times parallels Gubrium and Holstein's (1997, pp. 215–216, note 3) discussion of performative versus constitutive "hows" and Edwards's (1997, pp. 47–48) contrast between ontological and epistemic constructionism. My goal is to elaborate on the differences implied by these authors' contrasts by showing how the exact same vocabulary is often put to two divergent uses in the sociological literature.

2. Among other sources, see Schutz (1970) and Berger and Luckmann (1966) on phenomenological sociology, Garfinkel (1967) and Heritage (1984) on ethnomethodology, and Blumer (1969) and Mead (1934) on symbolic interactionism and pragmatism. Textbooks and readers that discuss these perspectives include those by Cahill (2004), Coulon (1995), Hewitt (1997), Lindesmith, Strauss, and Denzin (1999), Musolf (2003), O'Brien (2005), Prus (1996), Reynolds (1993), Sandstrom, Martin, and Fine (2003), and others.

3. For examples, see Fontana (2002), Manning (2001), Riessman (2002), and Zerubavel (1997).

4. I use OSC and ISC as nouns (as in construction*ism*) and as adjectives (as in construction*ist*), depending on the context.

5. For other examples, see Ulmer and Spencer's (1999) review of interactionist research on *criminal career contingencies* and compare it with Holstein and Gubrium's (2000, pp. 162–163) discussion of *interpretive contingencies*. Whereas the research on *criminal career contingencies* involves carefully studying the various factors that shape real phases and stages of life, research on *interpretive contingencies* involves carefully studying the various factors that shape how the life course (including any putative phases, stages, or causes) is given meaning.

6. O'Brien herself alludes to this deeper form of contingency in other places in her book. For example, her own definition of constructionism (O'Brien, 2005, p. 55) is more interpretive than objective, despite her later uses of the perspective.

7. In ISC, causality or *why* questions enter in limited fashion and tend to revolve around the issue of *why interpretations happen the way they do*, with the goal of discerning the factors that shape the meaning-making process (see Gubrium & Holstein, 1997, Chapter 9).

8. Elsewhere (Harris, 2004) I explain this assertion in greater detail. Schwalbe and colleagues (2000) assume that inequality exists objectively and that it is the scholar's job to define inequality, decide what the most important kinds are, find examples, and explain the causal factors that "produce" it. A more rigorously interpretive approach would bracket the existence of inequality and study how people interpretively produce inequality meanings through their own definitions, examples, and explanations.

9. Similarly, Berard (2006, p. 12) treats reification as assuming that inequality (or any entity) exists "prior to and independent of social understandings and judgments."

10. Some of this analysis does move further down the continuum toward ISC, however. Fishman (1978) and Devault (1991), respectively, assert that "doing" conversations and "doing" family are ways of "doing gender." By coordinating an in-depth conversation or orchestrating a family meal, women can be seen as assembling signs of gender propriety and thereby performing what is taken to be "natural." Though this

analysis seems (to me) fairly inferential and overlaid onto the objective analysis, it does highlight the creation of meaning. It arguably occupies an ambiguous middle ground along the OSC–ISC continuum.

11. It is always possible to find realist assumptions in a constructionist's work—not the least of which is the assumption that it is possible to study and accurately describe the interpretive work that people do. Moreover, interpretive scholars are always finding something else in need of bracketing that has been overlooked by their fellow constructionists. For example, constructionist staples such as "mind" and "perspectives" have been examined as interpretive accomplishments (Edwards, 1997; Gubrium, 1986).

• References

Agnew, R. (2001). Building on the foundation of general strain theory: Specifying the types of strain most likely to lead to crime and delinquency. *Journal of Research in Crime and Delinquency, 38,* 319–361.

Atkinson, P., & Housley, W. (2003). *Interactionism: An essay in sociological amnesia.* London: Sage.

Becker, H. (1973). *Outsiders: Studies in the sociology of deviance.* New York: Free Press. (Original work published 1963)

Bellas, M. L. (2001). The gendered nature of emotional labor in the workplace. In D. Vannoy (Ed.), *Gender mosaics* (pp. 269–278). Los Angeles: Roxbury.

Benson, J. K. (1977). Organizations: A dialectical view. *Administrative Science Quarterly, 22,* 1–21.

Berard, T. J. (2003). Ethnomethodology as radical sociology: An expansive appreciation of Melvin Pollner's "Constitutive and mundane versions of labeling theory." *Human Studies, 26,* 431–448.

Berard, T. J. (2006). From concepts to methods: On the observability of inequality. *Journal of Contemporary Ethnography, 35,* 236–256.

Berbrier, M. (2000). Ethnicity in the making: Ethnicity work, the ethnicity industry, and a constructionist framework for research. In J. A. Holstein & G. Miller (Eds.), *Perspectives on social problems* (Vol. 12, pp. 69–88). Stamford, CT: JAI

Berger, B. (1981). *The survival of a counterculture: Ideological work and everyday life among rural communards.* Berkeley: University of California Press.

Berger, P. L., & Luckmann, T. (1966). *The social construction of reality: A treatise in the sociology of knowledge.* Garden City, NY: Doubleday.

Besen, Y. (2006). Exploitation or fun? The lived experience of teenage employment in suburban America. *Journal of Contemporary Ethnography, 35,* 319–340.

Best, J. (2000). The apparently innocuous "just," the law

of levity, and the social problems of social construction. In J. A. Holstein & G. Miller (Eds.), *Perspectives on social problems* (Vol. 12, pp. 3–14). Stamford, CT: JAI Press.

Best, J. (2003). But seriously folks: The limitations of the strict constructionist interpretation of social problems. In J. A. Holstein & G. Miller (Eds.), *Challenges and choices: Constructionist perspectives on social problems* (pp. 51–69). Hawthorne, NY: Aldine de Gruyter.

Blaisure, K. R., & Allen, K. R. (1995). Feminists and the ideology and practice of marital equality. *Journal of Marriage and the Family, 57*, 5–19.

Blumer, H. (1969). *Symbolic interactionism: Perspective and method.* Englewood Cliffs, NJ: Prentice Hall.

Blumer, H. (1971). Social problems as collective behavior. *Social Problems, 18*, 298–306.

Cahill, S. E. (2004). *Inside social life: Readings in sociological psychology and microsociology* (4th ed.). Los Angeles: Roxbury.

Carrington, C. (2004). The political economy of constructing family. In S. Coltrane (Ed.), *Families and society* (pp. 303–308). Belmont, CA: Wadsworth/Thompson.

Chambliss, D. F. (1989). The mundanity of excellence: An ethnographic report on stratification and Olympic swimmers. *Sociological Theory, 7*, 70–86.

Collins, R. (2000). Situational stratification: A micro–macro theory of inequality. *Sociological Theory, 18*, 17–43.

Coulon, A. (1995). *Ethnomethodology.* Thousand Oaks, CA: Sage.

Crompton, R., & Lyonette, C. (2005). The new gender essentialism: Domestic and family "choices" and their relation to attitudes. *British Journal of Sociology, 56*, 601–620.

Daniels, A. K. (1987). Invisible work. *Social Problems, 34*, 403–415.

Devault, M. (1991). *Feeding the family.* Chicago: University of Chicago Press.

Edwards, D. (1997). *Discourse and cognition.* Thousand Oaks, CA: Sage.

Emerson, R. M., & Messinger, S. L. (1977). The micropolitics of trouble. *Social Problems, 25*, 121–134.

Fishman, P. M. (1978). Interaction: The work women do. *Social Problems, 25*, 397–406.

Flaherty, M. G. (1984). A formal approach to the study of amusement in social interaction. *Studies in Symbolic Interaction, 5*, 71–82.

Flaherty, M. G. (2003). Time work: Customizing temporal experience. *Social Psychology Quarterly, 66*, 17–33.

Foley, L. (2005). Midwives, marginality, and public identity work. *Symbolic Interaction, 28*, 183–203.

Fontana, A. (2002). Postmodern trends in interviewing. In J. F. Gubrium & J. A. Holstein (Eds.), *Handbook of interview research: Context and method* (pp. 161–175). Thousand Oaks, CA: Sage.

Garfinkel, H. (1967). *Studies in ethnomethodology.* Englewood Cliffs, NJ: Prentice Hall.

Gimlin, D. L. (2002). *Body work: Beauty and self-image in American culture.* Berkeley: University of California Press.

Goffman, E. (1959). *The presentation of self in everyday life.* New York: Anchor Books.

Goffman, E. (1967). *Interaction ritual.* New York: Doubleday.

Goffman, E. (1971). *Relations in public.* New York: Basic Books.

Goode, E. (1994). *Deviant behavior* (4th ed.). Englewood Cliffs, NJ: Prentice Hall.

Gubrium, J. (1986). The social preservation of mind. *Symbolic Interaction, 9*, 37–51.

Gubrium, J. F., & Holstein, J. A. (1990). *What is family?* Mountain View, CA: Mayfield.

Gubrium, J. F., & Holstein, J. A. (1997). *The new language of qualitative method.* New York: Oxford University Press.

Gubrium, J. F., & Holstein, J. A. (Eds.). (2001). *Institutional selves: Troubled identities in a postmodern world.* New York: Oxford University Press.

Gusfield, J. R. (1984). On the side: Practical action and social constructivism in social problems theory. In J. W. Schneider & J. I. Kitsuse (Eds.), *Studies in the sociology of social problems* (pp. 31–51). Norwood, NJ: Ablex.

Hacking, I. (1999). *The social construction of what?* Cambridge, MA: Harvard University Press.

Hall, P. M. (1987). Interactionism and the study of social organization. *Sociological Quarterly, 28*, 1–22.

Harris, S. R. (2000). Meanings and measurements of equality in marriage: A study of the social construction of equality. In J. A. Holstein & G. Miller (Eds.), *Perspectives on social problems* (Vol. 12, pp. 111–145). Stamford, CT: JAI Press.

Harris, S. R. (2001). What can interactionism contribute to the study of inequality? The case of marriage and beyond. *Symbolic Interaction, 24*, 455–480.

Harris, S. R. (2003). Studying equality/inequality: Naturalist and constructionist approaches to equality in marriage. *Journal of Contemporary Ethnography, 32*, 200–232.

Harris, S. R. (2004). Challenging the conventional wisdom: Recent proposals for the interpretive study of inequality. *Human Studies, 27*, 113–136.

Harris, S. R. (2006a). *The meanings of marital equality.* Albany: State University of New York Press.

Harris, S. R. (2006b). Social constructionism and social inequality. *Journal of Contemporary Ethnography, 35*, 223–235.

Heiner, R. (2002). *Social problems: An introduction to critical constructionism.* New York: Oxford University Press.

Herd, P., & Meyer, M. H. (2002). Care work: Invisible civic engagement. *Gender and Society, 16*, 665–688.

Heritage, J. (1984). *Garfinkel and ethnomethodology.* Cambridge, UK: Polity.

Herman-Kinney, N. J. (2003). Deviance. In L. T. Reynolds & N. J. Herman-Kinney (Eds.), *Handbook of* symbolic interactionism (pp. 695–720). Walnut Creek, CA: AltaMira.

Hewitt, J. P. (1997). *Self and society: A symbolic interactionist social psychology.* Needham Heights, MA: Allyn & Bacon.

Hochschild, A. R. (1979). Emotion work, feeling rules, and social structure. *American Journal of Sociology, 85,* 551–575.

Hochschild, A. R. (with Machung, A.). (1989). *The second shift.* New York: Avon Books.

Hollander, J., & Gordon, H. R. (2006). The processes of social construction in talk. *Symbolic Interaction, 29,* 183–212.

Holstein, J. A. (1993). *Court-ordered insanity: Interpretive practice and involuntary commitment.* Hawthorne, NY: Aldine de Gruyter.

Holstein, J. A., & Gubrium, J. F. (2000). *Constructing the life course* (2nd ed.). Walnut Creek, CA: AltaMira Press.

Holstein, J. A., & Gubrium, J. F. (2003). A constructionist analytics for social problems. In J. A. Holstein & G. Miller (Eds.), *Challenges and choices: Constructionist perspectives on social problems* (pp. 187–208). Hawthorne, NY: Aldine de Gruyter.

Holstein, J. A., & Miller, G. (2003). Social constructionism and social problems work. In J. A. Holstein & G. Miller (Eds.), *Challenges and choices: Constructionist perspectives on social problems* (pp. 70–91). Hawthorne, NY: Aldine de Gruyter.

Holyfield, L., & Fine, G. A. (1997). Adventure as character work: The collective taming of fear. *Symbolic Interaction, 20,* 343–363.

Horlick-Jones, T. (2005). Risk-work: Professional discourse, accountability, and everyday action. *Health, Risk, and Society, 7,* 293–307.

Ibarra, P. R., & Kitsuse, J. I. (2003). Claims-making discourse and vernacular resources. In J. A. Holstein & G. Miller (Eds.), *Challenges and choices: Constructionist perspectives on social problems* (pp. 17–50). Hawthorne, NY: Aldine de Gruyter.

Knapp, S. J. (1999). Analyzing narratives of expertise: Toward the development of a Burkeian pentadic scheme. *Sociological Quarterly, 40,* 587–613.

Knapp, S. J. (2002). Authorizing family science: An analysis of the objectifying practices of family science discourse. *Journal of Marriage and Family, 64,* 1038–1048.

Lamont, M., & Molnár, V. (2002). The study of boundaries in the social sciences. *Annual Review of Sociology, 28,* 167–195.

Lindesmith, A. R., Strauss, A. L., & Denzin, N. K. (1999). *Social psychology* (8th ed.). Thousand Oaks, CA: Sage.

Lofland, J. (1976). *Doing social life: The qualitative study of human interaction in natural settings.* New York: Wiley.

Loseke, D. R. (1987). Lived realities and the construction of social problems: The case of wife abuse. *Symbolic Interaction, 10,* 229–243.

Loseke, D. R. (1999). *Thinking about social problems: An introduction to constructionist perspectives.* New York: Aldine de Gruyter.

Loseke, D. R. (2003). Conditions, people, morality, emotion: Expanding the agenda of constructionism. In J. A. Holstein & G. Miller (Eds.), *Challenges and choices: Constructionist perspectives on social problems* (pp. 120–129). Hawthorne, NY: Aldine de Gruyter.

Lyng, S. (1990). Edgework: A social psychological account of voluntary risk taking. *American Journal of Sociology, 95,* 851–886.

Maines, D. R. (2001). *The faultline of consciousness: A view of interactionism in sociology.* New York: Aldine de Gruyter.

Maines, D. R. (2003). Interactionism's place. *Symbolic Interaction, 26,* 5–18.

Manning, P. K. (2001). Semiotics, semantics and ethnography. In P. Atkinson, A. Coffey, S. Delamont, J. Lofland, & L. Lofland (Eds.), *Handbook of ethnography* (pp. 145–159). Thousand Oaks, CA: Sage.

Martin, P. Y. (2005). *Rape work: Victims, gender, and emotions in organization and community context.* New York: Routledge.

Mead, G. H. (1934). *Mind, self, and society.* Chicago: University of Chicago Press.

Miller, G. (1991). Family as excuse and extenuating circumstance: Social organization and use of family rhetoric in a work incentive program. *Journal of Marriage and the Family, 53,* 609–21.

Musolf, G. H. (2003). *Structure and agency in everyday life: An introduction to social psychology* (2nd ed.). Lanham, MD: Rowman & Littlefield.

O'Brien, J. (Ed.). (2005). *The production of reality* (4th ed.). Thousand Oaks, CA: Pine Forge.

Ore, T. E. (Ed.). (2003). *The social construction of difference and inequality* (2nd ed.). New York: McGraw-Hill.

Peterson, R. A. (2005). In search of authenticity. *Journal of Management Studies, 42,* 1083–1098.

Pollner, M. (1987). *Mundane reason: Reality in everyday and sociological discourse.* New York: Cambridge University Press.

Pope, C. (2002). Contingency in everyday surgical work. *Sociology of Health and Illness, 24,* 369–384.

Prus, R. (1996). *Symbolic interaction and ethnographic research.* Albany: State University of New York Press.

Reynolds, L. T. (1993) *Interactionism: Exposition and critique* (3rd ed.). Dix Hills, NY: General Hall.

Riessman, C. K. (2002). Analysis of personal narratives. In J. F. Gubrium & J. A. Holstein (Eds.), *Handbook of interview research: Context and method* (pp. 695–710). Thousand Oaks, CA: Sage.

Sandstrom, K. L., Martin, D. D., & Fine, G. A. (2003). *Symbols, selves, and social reality: A symbolic interactionist approach to social psychology and sociology.* Los Angeles: Roxbury.

Scheff, T. J. (2005). A theory of genius. In J. O'Brien

(Ed.), *The production of reality* (4th ed., pp. 296–308). Thousand Oaks, CA: Pine Forge.

Schneider, J. W. (1985). Social problems theory: The constructionist view. *Annual Review of Sociology, 11*, 209–229.

Schutz, A. (1964). *Collected papers* (Vol. 2). The Hague, Netherlands: Martinus Nijhoff.

Schutz, A. (1970). *On phenomenology and social relations.* Chicago: University of Chicago Press.

Schwalbe, M., Godwin, S., Holden, D., Schrock, D., Thompson, S., & Wolkomir, M. (2000). Generic processes in the reproduction of inequality: An interactionist analysis. *Social Forces, 79*, 419–452.

Schwartz, P. (1994). *Peer marriage: How love between equals really works.* New York: Free Press.

Schweingruber, D., & Berns, N. (2003). Doing money work in a door-to-door sales organization. *Symbolic Interaction, 26*, 447–471.

Snow, D., & Anderson, L. (1987). Identity work among the homeless: The verbal construction and avowal of personal identities. *American Journal of Sociology, 92*, 1336–1371.

Spector, M., & Kitsuse, J. I. (1977). *Constructing social problems.* Menlo Park, CA: Cummings.

Spencer, J. W. (1992). Negotiating role definitions and the working consensus in self-work. *Sociological Inquiry, 62*, 291–307.

Stack, C., & Burton, L. (1993). Kinscripts. *Journal of Comparative Family Studies, 24*, 157–170.

Strauss, A., Fagerhaugh, S., Suczek, B., & Wiener, C. (1982). Sentimental work in the technologized hospital. *Sociology of Health and Illness, 4*, 254–278.

Thorne, B. (1993). *Gender play: Girls and boys in school.* New Brunswick, NJ: Rutgers University Press.

Ulmer, J. T., & Spencer, J. W. (1999). The contribution of an interactionist approach to research and theory on criminal careers. *Theoretical Criminology, 3*, 95–124.

Vryan, K. D., Adler, P. A., & Adler, P. (2003). Identity. In L. T. Reynolds & N. J. Herman-Kinney (Eds.), *Handbook of symbolic interactionism* (pp. 367–390). Walnut Creek, CA: AltaMira Press.

Wanderer, J. J. (1987). Simmel's forms of experiencing: The adventure as symbolic work. *Symbolic Interaction, 10*, 21–28.

Watzlawick, P. (2005). Self-fulfilling prophecies. In J. O'Brien (Ed.), *The production of reality* (4th ed., pp. 382–394). Thousand Oaks, CA: Pine Forge.

Woolgar, S., & Pawluch, D. (1985). Ontological gerrymandering: The anatomy of social problems explanations. *Social Problems, 32*, 214–227.

Zerubavel, E. (1997). *Social mindscapes: An invitation to cognitive sociology.* Cambridge, MA: Harvard University Press.

PART III

THE SCOPE OF CONSTRUCTIONIST INQUIRY

CHAPTER 13

Foucauldian Constructionism

● **Leslie Miller**

Anyone who knows anything about Michel Foucault knows that he was a constructionist. In this chapter, we ask: what kind? To what extent do those many books and papers titled "The Social Construction of *X*," "The Making of *Y*," "Disciplining *Z*" draw on the insights of Foucault? Foucault was not a sociologist, but he had plenty to say about sociological matters, especially about language and power. In the ongoing conversation about his work, which continues more than two decades after his death, scholars debate his views on a set of distinctive questions that Foucault readers will immediately recognize: What does Foucault mean by power and why did he call it "productive"? Is all knowledge of another, or care for another, just an exercise in oppression? Did Foucault abandon his interest in power in his last books? Does his emphasis on discourse mean that there is nothing in the world but language?

In this chapter, I summarize some of Foucault's main ideas and concepts. But neither a summary nor an in-depth look at central concepts is my main goal; others have ably done both of these, at any rate.[1] My interest is much more specific: I propose to interrogate his work through the lens of our own concern—social constructionism. This will be the key to narrowing a vast literature. As it happens, I will be circling back to those familiar Foucauldian questions about subjectivity, power, resistance, and the rest, but in a focused way.

Beyond the question What is Foucauldian constructionism?, I want to raise two others. The first is: What makes his version of constructionism distinctive? The second: How have Foucault's insights—again, connected to constructionism—actually played out in empirical research, and have scholars extended his insights in important ways? As I show, Foucault's "offspring" are many and diverse. Whole fields of scholarship and practice have been challenged and reworked as a result of reading and assimilating Foucault: medicine, social work and various kinds of therapeutic practice, gender studies and the body, criminology and policing, policy studies, studies of large-scale people-processing institutions (the school, the hospital, the jail), and autobiographical narrative, to name just a few. In what follows I look at some of the ways researchers in these fields have taken up his constructionist agenda.

In this chapter, I adopt the practice of other scholars who divide Foucault's work into stages: an early period, up to the publication of *Discipline and Punish* in 1979 (in French in 1975) and *The History of Sexuality: Volume 1* in 1980 (in French in 1976)[2]; and a later period covering the remaining works, including his essay on "governmentality" (1991; French, 1978) and the last two volumes of *The History of Sexuality: The Use of Pleasure* (1990) and *The Care of the Self* (1988; both published in French in 1984). My purpose in adopting such a "stage" approach is not to suggest, as some others have, that Foucault abandoned his earlier concerns in his last period of work (e.g., McNay, 1992) but rather to highlight a shift in emphasis that we can see there, one that plays out in the different research directions I discuss over the course of the chapter. Specifically, I consider the bodies of research that take up, and take off from, Foucault's writings in stage 1 (on disciplinary power and the "panopticon") and in stage 2 (on "governmentality" and the "care of the self") in order to see how they put social constructionist tenets into play.

Stage 1: Disciplinary Power and the Construction of "Docile Bodies"

Constructing the Subject

I begin by asking a basic question: What is it that "gets constructed" in Foucault's work? Foucault has said that his goal "has been to create a history of the different modes by which, in our culture, human beings are made subjects" (as cited in Arney & Bergen, 1984, p. 4). What is constructed ("made"), then, are "subjects," and Foucault means here that when human beings are "made subjects," they are also *subjected*, that is, constructed as objects of power. William Arney and Bernard Bergen, whose early classic work I return to later, cite this well-known statement of Foucault's and mention the discourse of medicine as an example of such a mode. Arney and Bergen (1984) understand discourse, in Foucault's sense of the term, as a large-scale system of knowledge, a whole way of *constituting* the world through the ways we have to know and talk about it. It is important to note here that discourses do not describe or represent "the real"[3]; they bring realities (including who we are) into being. Religious discourses, for example, bring people into being as pious or sinful; the discourse of medicine brings people into being as doctors and as patients, ascribes to them certain interests (health matters), and positions them in specific relationships, including relationships of power, by virtue of that. A discourse thus asserts a preferred version of the world, one that disqualifies competing versions; in the hospital I am a patient (not a member of a church, let's say), and medical discourse stipulates *this* "me" as the real and true one. Discourses are thus forms of power, and Foucault underlines this dimension by calling them "regimes of truth" (1980b, p. 131).

Foucault argues that major discourses (e.g., medical discourse) emerge at identifiable points in history and that we can track their appearance, their effects in specific practical domains (such as the clinical setting), and their demise. His main interest is in the decades around 1800, when the new knowledges and discourses of the human sciences emerged in their modern forms. These discourses represented a distinctively modern form of power called *discipline* and gave us an answer to "who we are" as moderns, for they created us as "individuals." Foucault develops this argument in his best-known book, *Discipline and Punish: The Birth of the Prison* (1979). His analysis is well known, so I only summarize it here. In the *ancien régime*, says Foucault, power was "sovereign or juridical" and based on force; this was the power of kings over life and death. The power of kings was manifested in their might and in the awe they were able to inspire in their subjects, who were reminded of this power at public hangings and other occasions of public punishment (the "spectacle of the scaffold"; 1979, p. 32). The attention or "gaze" of the people, including writers, painters, and others who documented the lives of the powerful, was directed "up" to these figures; "the masses" remained in the shadows, so to speak, and only became of interest if they grew troublesome and rebellious—the historian Barbara Tuchman wrote that medieval peasants were sometimes called "the worms of the earth" (1978, p. 369).

In early modern Europe, says Foucault, the direction of the gaze reverses: Ordinary people become of interest to the new sciences, which bring them into existence in a new way and make their lives for the first time an object of observation, documentation—and control. Here, from *Discipline and Punish*, is Foucault's account of this reversal and the "construction of the individual":

> For a long time ordinary individuality—the everyday individuality of everybody—remained below the threshold of description. To be looked at, observed, described in detail, followed from day to day by uninterrupted writing was a privilege [e.g., of kings or popes] . . . part of the rituals of power. The disciplinary methods reversed this relation, lowered the threshold of describable individuality and made of this description a means of control and a method of domination. It is no longer a monument for memory, but a document for possible use. . . . [The new entity created by these knowledges] is the individual as he may be described, judged, measured, compared with others, in his very individuality; and [he] is also the individual who has to be trained or corrected, classified, normalized, excluded, etc. (1979, p. 191)

It is important to grasp what Foucault is saying in this passage. First, he makes it very clear that "how people are" *means* how they are made knowable or "describable." As a result, his approach can never offer answers to questions about the nature of anything (e.g., human nature, or femininity, or inequality, or history). Instead, he poses a different question: How, in different historical periods, have different modes of knowing (discourses) brought people—and other realities—into being in various ways, and what are the consequences of that? This will be his abiding concern.

In the early modern world, Foucault tells us in the preceding passage, the "individual" is brought into being by the very specific disciplinary methods of the new discourses of science. These methods are two, and as forms of control they would have a powerful impact on the research agenda that followed the assimilation of *Discipline and Punish*. The first technique was surveillance (*hierarchical observation*), the ever more detailed observation and documentation of ordinary people's lives (their conduct and their morals, their property, their births, deaths, and marriages). The second method was *normalizing judgment*, a technique that compared and judged each individual against a standard of normalcy (e.g., "normal" intelligence); those who fell short of the standard became targets of exclusion, improvement, or correction. The two techniques of disciplinary power came together in the examination, a concept that Foucault understood broadly to include any form of assessment, including medical and educational "tests" (1979, pp. 184–192).

Foucault called disciplinary power *panoptic*, or all-seeing, drawing here on Bentham's "panopticon," a model for an ideal prison in which prisoners would come to *monitor themselves* because they felt—but could never really know—that they were under scrutiny by the guards. Disciplinary power had other characteristics, too, which made it all the more insidious and effective: It spread beyond institutional settings into all crannies in the social landscape, especially into family life and the school; its source could never be pinpointed in a social class or group of people, because it circulated, capillary fashion, all through the social body; as a regime of truth, it was self-legitimating; it was control in the guise of care and reform; and, as in the panopticon, it enlisted subjects in their own policing. The new knowledge discourses thus cast a net of surveillance and control over the whole population in the name of science. What they produced was *docile bodies*—calculable, manageable, self-monitoring—the very sorts of people needed as a workforce for 19th-century capitalism's new industrial machine. In this sense, power is "productive." Foucault says:

> We must cease once and for all to describe the effects of power in negative terms: it "excludes," it "represses," it "censors," it "abstracts," it "masks," it "conceals." In fact, power produces; it produces reality; it produces domains of objects and rituals of truth. The individual and the knowledge that might be gained of him belong to this production. (1979, p. 194)

The Constructionist Research Agenda in the Aftermath of Discipline and Punish

I move now to a discussion of the research that emerged as a result of Foucault's critique of the role of the new human sciences in the construction of "docile bodies." Foucault's account of the subtleties of disciplinary power, especially his assertion that knowledge and control were inextricably tied, combined to effect a fundamental reshaping of many fields of scholarship—especially education, medicine, and social work, those fields (and there were more) whose practitioners saw themselves indicted as part of the apparatus of disciplinary power.

The result of *Discipline and Punish*, then, was a reworked research agenda that focused on the social construction of docile bodies in the disciplined society, or "policing." As a group, these studies asked: *What*

are the techniques of disciplinary power and how do they work to manage and control individuals? Researchers interrogated every site of social life for policing practices; titles such as "Disciplining the . . . ," "The Panopticon and . . . ," "Surveillance and . . . " flagged for the reader a research project that would show the social construction of docile bodies through the application of the techniques of power that Foucault had described in *Discipline and Punish* (1979). An early sign of the new sensitivity to this theme could be found in the renaming of courses and textbooks in the sociology of deviance: formerly called "Deviance," they were now called "Deviance and Social Control." In *Visions of Social Control* Stanley Cohen (1985) included a chapter called "Visions of Social Order," in which he described how city planners aimed to solve the "urban crisis" in post-1950s America by reconstructing city spaces to maximize order and the manageability of the citizenry; he notes especially the CPED movement (Crime Prevention Through Environmental Design), which combined elements of "territorial control, defensible space, close surveillance and, above all, the need to incorporate crime-control considerations into urban planning and design" (Cohen, 1985, p. 216; see also Richard Sennett, 1970, on the "purified city"). Other studies analyzed nursing homes, schools, and other "people-processing" institutions through the lens of the panopticon, their spatial and social organization interpreted as a technology for easy surveillance and control over the residents.[4] Students absorbed Foucault's critique eagerly and readily came up with examples of their own from the workplace and the street: surveillance cameras, time cards, electronically monitored exits, and so on. And they did not fail to grasp the university itself as a site of policing and discipline; the university, which of course featured as its hallmark the examination, a technique of power analyzed to devastating effect by Foucault and quickly understood by students not as a pedagogical tool designed to assist them but as a means of documenting, comparing, and correcting them—in short, as ways of constructing them as docile bodies (see Schmelzer, 1993).

Other early studies focused on the helping professions, notably social work and medicine, following Foucault's insight that here the intermeshing of care and control appeared in its most problematic and interesting form. Jacques Donzelot's study *The Policing of Families* (1979) traced the techniques of power that gradually brought the once-ignored life of French working-class and peasant families under the scrutiny and control of the church and the state, and implicated the strengthening alliance between medical experts and mothers as a crucial mechanism in the disciplining of the home (i.e., in its social construction as a respectable and orderly childrearing milieu; see also L. J. Miller, 1987). Arney and Bergen's study *Medicine and the Management of Living* (1984) took up Foucault's critique with a vengeance, and their analysis reconceptualized medicine not as a progressive force but as an ever-expanding "apparatus of power" that moved beyond its early interest in disease control to the managing of our whole lives (p. 105). To show how this apparatus disciplines us, the authors drew on several other classic Foucauldian insights, notably his emphasis on surveillance as a means of control the ("monitoring" of patients; p. 105). They added two further points: that the regulation of patients by medical expertise is seductive because it promises us rehabilitation and that this policing apparatus works far out in society beyond the halls of the hospital, notably in the "judgmentally benign" support group, which, they contended, in fact "synthesizes all aspects of the techniques of normalization" (Arney & Bergen, 1984, p. 107).

For scholars drawing on Foucault's concept of disciplinary power, the question of agency—the actor's autonomy or freedom to refuse or change the way he or she is constructed through dominant discourses—would prove to be a perennial concern. Arney and Bergen's (1984) early study supports the deterministic version of construc-

tionism attributed to Foucault at this period and analyzes medicine's efforts to empower patients (e.g., by listening more attentively to their experiences of illness) as ever more insidious expressions of the covert power of medical discourse to disarm potential challenges to its own interests or "gaze." They even frame this dispiriting rejection of the subject's agency as a new research agenda: How (they ask) can we see medicine's new openness to the patient's views of illness not as "a rebellion against immoral power [of medicine to alienate the patient] . . . [but rather] as a different form of the play of power"? (p. 6). In other words: How do the new "liberating" and progressive techniques of medicine function to construct patients as bodies complicit in their own policing? For Arney and Bergen, the power of medical discourse to translate all challenges to itself into its own language seemed endlessly inventive and succeeded in rendering them all "politically benign" (p. 168).[5]

It is clear from this early research on disciplinary power that scholars saw in *Discipline and Punish* and *The History of Sexuality* (1976/1980a) a top-down, totalizing, and deterministic model of the relationship between discourse and the actor. In social constructionist parlance, this interpretation meant that the actor or "subject" was entirely constructed—subject*ed*—by discourse, a stance that seemed to close off all possibility of agency. Thus Arney and Bergen's (1984) analysis produced a picture of the disciplinary power of medical discourse as all-pervasive and a picture of the patient's freedom or autonomy as an illusion. In short, one is an "actor" in only the most impoverished sense, as one is only *acted upon*. The "no way out" interpretation of Foucault that is so poignantly displayed in Arney and Bergen's work has a long reach and plays out in the continuing fear that all progressive developments in the human sciences, especially in the "caring professions," are nothing but covert forms of social control. A closer look at Foucault's concept of discursive power as a relationship and what he had to say about the matter of resistance to such dominant discourses would come later.

But in the early stage of Foucault's reception in the English-speaking world, the deterministic version of constructionism was undoubtedly the accepted one, and it could be seen in many other studies of disciplinary power besides Arney and Bergen's. Much of this work emphasized the resilience and power of dominant discourses to construct meaning for actors and to endow them with essentializing identities. A striking example is Bronwyn Davies' (1989) classic look at children in day care in New Zealand, which demonstrated how dominant discourses of masculinity and femininity had thoroughly shaped the self-identities of children as young as 5 and 6, how eager they were to take on these cultural constructions, and how enthusiastically they policed themselves and their buddies for signs of "error" (e.g., a boy who liked dancing) (Davies, 1989). The theme of disciplinary power as moral regulation was explored in a range of studies of mundane aspects of everyday life: in the production of girls' sexuality in routine family life in 1950s Germany (Haug et al., 1987); in the policing of immigrant families in late 19th- and early 20th-century Canada through the rhetoric of moral and physical hygiene (Valverde, 1991); and in the social construction of the "good mother" in the discourse of dentistry (Nettleton, 1991), to name just a few. Other research returned to the theme of the disciplinary power of science to classify and regulate "the elderly" (*Gerontology and the Construction of Old Age* [Green, 1993]; *The Disciplining of Old Age* [Katz, 1996]), their titles signaling their debt to Foucault. More recent research into disciplinary power, especially in institutional settings, has extended and complicated the early depiction of the docile body somewhat (e.g., Doran, 2002; Malacrida, 2005; Middleton, 1998). But disciplinary power remains a formidable conceptual tool for research, and studies drawing on it continue to flourish.

The early deterministic interpretation of Foucault's constructionism was provocative because the disciplinary gaze seemed to construct docile bodies everywhere. But it also drew attention because it stood in sharp contrast to the new interpretive sociology of the late 1960s and 1970s in the United States, which was gradually opening itself to the revolutionary concept of actors as reality constructors (i.e., producers of everyday realities) as it was being explored by Harold Garfinkel (1967) and by Peter Berger and Thomas Luckmann (1966), whose book title *The Social Construction of Reality* said it all. This work drew on a different European tradition, notably the social phenomenology of Alfred Schutz (1970; see Holstein & Gubrium, 1994, for a review of these developments). It would build into an influential strand of interpretive sociology whose centerpiece was the "artful" actor as meaning maker; this actor in turn would be at the center of a kind of constructionism that emphasized the importance of interaction in the construction of social realities—gender, for example (Holstein, 1987). This version of constructionism saw Foucault-style discourse as a resource on which actors could draw in their specific interactional projects. It was thus actors and their "interpretive work"—not discourses—that "brought things into being." *Discipline and Punish*—not to mention the first volume of *The History of Sexuality* (1976/1980a)—seemed to run entirely against this bottom-up narrative: Whatever power and agency Garfinkel's work (and that of other ethnomethodologists and interpretive sociologists) attributed to the actor was erased by Foucault's apparently top-down construction of actors as produced—scripted—by discourse.

Recent Research on Surveillance

Foucault's most memorable image—the panoptic society that produces us as docile bodies—continues to animate researchers who debate its relevance for our high-tech era (Lyon, 1993, 2003). Against arguments that the panopticon is obsolete (e.g., Mathiesen, 1997), other scholars reassert its viability, arguing that contemporary surveillance and screening activities still aim at the production of docile bodies despite shifts in their sites of application (Boyne, 2000; Norris, Moran, & Armstrong, 1998; Staples, 1997). Several studies explore the impact of new technologies on the policing of populations through the social construction of identity. In a timely book, John Torpey (2000) traces the invention and history of the passport as the state's effort to handle the threat to its power represented by the unregulated movement of people and, more recently, the possibility of "potentially unstable and counterfeit identities" (p. 166). Through the passport, says Torpey, we are constructed as "durable" and legitimate identities "for administrative and political purposes," just as a credit rating, one might argue, gives us a durable identity for economic purposes. In another article on surveillance, Kevin Haggerty and Richard Ericson (2000) argue that new technologies, notably the rise of computerized databases, no longer construct us as single entities but rather as a multitude of informational selves they call "data doubles," each one of these new "assemblages" created and utilized for specific and perhaps fleeting purposes of management, security, profit, and entertainment (2000, p. 619; see also Ericson & Haggerty, 2005).

These lines of analysis continue and extend Foucault's insight that "who we are" is not an unchanging essence but rather a shifting product of power, governed by an overall interest in administrative control and regulation. In this strain of research, at least, the question of agency and the freedom of the subject are equated with the possibility of invisibility and anonymity—a life lived under the radar of new technologies of surveillance. This analysis suggests that the chances of such a life—and with it "the possibilities of self-creation" (Haggerty & Ericson, 2000, p. 619)—are increasingly slim.

Resistance and the Return of Subjugated Knowledges

I commented earlier that the question of agency and the subject would be of continuing interest for Foucauldian scholars. We have already seen how some representatives of powerful disciplinary discourses (especially those in the helping professions) agonized over Foucault's argument that they were complicit in the subjection of their clientele (Cohen, 1985; L. J. Miller, 1984), a recognition that prompted, for some, a more careful look at Foucault's views on whether, and how, these discourses might be resisted.

It is no surprise, though, that the question of resistance was raised most urgently by scholars who themselves had felt the weight of "policing" most oppressively, especially over their bodies and sexualities—feminists and gay and lesbian scholars. Whereas some feminists scorned Foucault for asserting women's powerlessness (Moi, 1985), others recognized the resonances of his critique in their own silenced and disciplined lives (Haug et al., 1987; McWhorter, 1999; Middleton, 1998). Either way, the outcome was a second look at Foucault's discussion of power, and especially the top-down, deterministic social constructionism that had been the received interpretation of his work so far.

On such reexamination, another reading of power now came to light. First, it became clear that Foucault, as against the deterministic thesis, had always insisted that power was a relationship—and that whenever power was exercised, resistance was also always present (1991, p. 12). The oppressed, in short, were never entirely powerless. Second, Foucault had argued that dominant discourses and knowledges maintained their power by means of an ongoing struggle; in other words, by a process that actively pushed other "disqualified" knowledges to the margins—those ways of knowing and speaking belonging to society's subordinated groups (Foucault, 1980b, p. 83). And finally, as a consequence of this last point, he had recommended that we amplify these subjugated voices, for, he said, "it is through the reappearance of this knowledge, of these local, popular knowledges [of the psychiatric patient, the ill person, the delinquent,] that criticism performs its work" (1980b, p. 82).

This interpretation fragmented the earlier, totalizing sense of discourse attributed to Foucault and produced a picture of "truth" as the product of ongoing contestation between dominant discourses and marginalized ones. In all, it turned the earlier reading of Foucault on its head, and for some scholars amounted to a call to empower the silenced voice of the underdog. Feminists now began to debate Foucault's work in the context of resistance (Bordo, 1989; Diamond & Quinby, 1988[6]; Hartsock, 1990; Hekman, 1996). And it opened the way for new set of research questions, which would look at the process of marginalization and resistance. As Joan Scott (1990, p. 135) put it: (1) How have some ways of talking and knowing emerged as privileged or normative, while others have been eclipsed or silenced? And (2) What do these processes reveal about power and how it operates?[7]

This agenda developed in several directions. Social psychologists, for example, studied marginalized groups with an eye to the different "ways of knowing" that set them apart from the mainstream. Within first- and second-wave American feminism there already existed the idea that women spoke "in a different voice" (Addams, 1976; Belenky, Clinchy, Goldberger, & Tarule, 1986; Gilligan 1982)—in a language of sentiment, nurturance, or caring—one that posed an alternative to a masculinist language of reason and instrumentality. But these insights often carried with them essentialist assumptions about "women's nature," and Foucault's emphasis on power and contestation worked to politicize such theories of difference by implying that their distinctive features were the outcome of a marginalizing or discrediting process, rather than an essence.[8] Foucault's discussion of subjugated knowledges intersected with developments in other fields as well. In linguis-

tics appeared a new tradition exploring the display and reproduction of dominant and subordinate status in talk (e.g., Lakoff, 1990). Feminist historians and philosophers began to reformulate "women's ailments," such as anorexia and "hysteria," as "women's ways" of resisting their subordinate place in the social order through the distinctively feminine language of body (Bordo, 1989). And in the then-new field of cultural studies, the theme of "resistance from below" interpreted popular culture and subcultural styles as indications of how working-class youth and other disempowered groups reshape or resist mainstream "truths" about the way the social world works (Grossberg, Nelson, & Treicher, 1992). Finally, a number of "genealogies from below" have also documented how members of the working class resisted disciplinary power, and not just industrial capitalism, in the early 19th century (Doran, 1994, 1996).

These studies collectively resuscitated and described the kinds of subjugated knowledges that Foucault's discussion of power had pointed to and in so doing politicized previously passive and silenced subjects by reformulating them as actively—though indirectly and subtly—engaged in resisting their subjection to dominant discourses. This formulation had implications for the constructionist approach to social problems as well: It extended the definition of "claimsmakers" to all groups and sensitized social problems analysts to a larger range of styles that subordinated groups might employ to get their concerns on the agenda (L. J. Miller, 1993; and see Lowney, Chapter 17, this volume).

In the kinds of studies just described, the emphasis is on the form and style of subjugated knowledges and discourses—on the hidden languages of resistance. A second research direction shifted the focus to the actor more directly, to the ways actors take up dominant (but also marginalized) discourses and strategically rework them in specific social settings to pursue their own interests. These studies begin from the assumption that the actors are not passively constructed (or "positioned") by dominant discourses but can actively and strategically *position themselves* within them.

This, too, has proved a varied and fruitful body of work. Leslie Miller and Otto Penz (1991), for example, analyzed the ways women bodybuilders were able to use both dominant and subordinate discourses of femininity to move into a traditionally male sport; here, the actor is formulated as an active interpreter of the world who can maneuver within discourses previously assumed to be only confining. Gale Miller (1991) showed how clients in a work incentive program constructed strategic identities, problems, and solutions for themselves by drawing on local discursive formations in ways that were astutely crafted to the occasion. Other studies examined adolescent girls' efforts to explore their sexuality in nonstigmatizing ways (as in Amy Best's [2003] analysis of prom night beauty practices) or to resist dominant discourses of femininity through hairstyles (Weitz, 2003). Thomas J. Gershick and Adam S. Miller (1995) looked at men's struggles to negotiate alternative versions of masculinity for themselves away from the dominant discourse, especially when they were excluded from mainstream masculinity by serious physical disability. All of these studies take an approach that constitutes the subject as one who actively engages and negotiates with dominant discourses in strategic ways. Unlike earlier formulations of the subject who is disciplined and constrained, this is a subject who is can contest—resist—his or her subjection. And although these studies of the strategic actor go beyond Foucault's own concern with the actor, at least in his early work, they all owe a debt to his discussion of subjugated knowledges.

What Kind of Resistance? What Kind of Subjectivity?

Despite this new attention to the artfulness of the actor, we must not forget that Foucault's subject is always constituted ("subjected") in discourse and is never the autonomous maker of meaning that we encounter in some versions of symbolic interactionism, for example. So the question remains: What kind of resistance is this? Can subjects effect changes in discourses, or can they only reposition themselves within them? If actors are limited, as Foucault seemed to suggest, to maneuvering within the scripts that are "given" to them by the discourses in their historical and cultural environments, what kind of autonomy do they really have? Next we look at two directions that scholars have taken in response to what we can call "the problem of the subject." My goal in this discussion is not to survey the research but to indicate the outlines, with some illustrative examples, of different responses to this issue and what they imply for Foucauldian constructionism.

One approach to the problem of the subject starts from the assumption that such a "closed" relationship between discourse and the actor fatally limits the freedom of the subject. Scholars who take this view generally hold that "not everything is constructed" and invoke an extradiscursive realm, which, they argue, allows actors to escape the confining net of discourse. This argument typically suggests that our bodies make insistent and intrusive claims on our attention and thus that lived bodily experience (or "subjective experience") has a reality or authenticity that speaks to us prior to the meanings that culture assigns to it (Shilling, 1997; Wainwright & Turner, 2003). Thus it is claimed that we know our bodies directly and immediately, and it is this knowledge that is silenced or disciplined by the powerful discourses of the day, especially biomedicine. Accordingly, the source of the actor's agency or power to resist dominant discourses lies here, in the "reality" of lived experience, and the liberating project of research into subjective experience focuses on retrieving that reality from "behind" the discourses that are thought to obscure it. In this interpretation, then, research into "lived experience" (of disability, of aging, of bisexuality) privileges "experience" as authoritative and true knowledge; it is not just another story (but see Frank, 1998).

An early and influential version of this argument has been made by the Canadian feminist theorist Dorothy E. Smith (1987), who argues that women's subjective experience, especially of the family, has a truth value long marginalized by malestream knowledge. Because men's discourses of work, life, children, and women have dominated even the subjective knowledge of mothers themselves, women have developed a "bifurcated consciousness"—a split life that they require to survive in a patriarchal world, especially in the labor force. Smith's view owes something to Marx's concept of ideology: There are illusions that the powerful impose on us that serve their interests, and that smother our own consciousness of who we "really" are. Smith argues that we must treat women's subjective knowledge as true and real if we are to combat patriarchy; as she puts it, if we are to act politically, we have to know "who is right in arguments about what is" (1997, p. 177).

What would Foucault make of this critique? I suggest that these interpreters are correct in attributing to him the rejection of extradiscursive categories such as "the body" or "lived experience." Foucault is very clear that we cannot know the world directly, including those things that seem closest to us—our "lived experiences," our selves, our bodies, or our own histories (Foucault, 1991, pp. 2–3); the subject is "not accessible through the description of lived experience" (Gillan, 1991, p. 37). The reason is that he decisively rejects *all* foundational arguments (he would see them as "foundational discourses"); there are no natural categories or essences, no bedrock realities to be discovered in history or social life—only claims to have discovered them, such as have been made in the early modern era by the human (or natural) sciences. Any argument for such realities, he would contend, is a rhetorical move designed to establish a regime of truth, whose effect is to block resistance to itself. Moreover, the idea of the subject who

has a direct pipeline to the way the self or the world "really" is and thus to his or her own liberation from relations of power is an illusion, of a piece with other Enlightenment fantasies about progress and the advancement of knowledge toward truth.

Thus, whereas the scholars who take this view appreciate the value of Foucault's analysis of disciplinary power and the importance of the idea of discourse, they contend that his constructionist position leads to a conception of the subject as irretrievably limited. Other scholars take a more circumspect view of his scheme in this regard and note that his version of social constructionism, hampered by his lack of interest in the subject as other than an artifact of discourses, is poorly equipped to explore actors' strategies, performances, and creativity. In short, Foucault's is a constructionism that implies a weak concept of the actor.

A recent study by Julia Twigg (2003) lets us probe these very issues. Twigg explores the personal care of people in what is sometimes called "deep old age." Her article is especially useful because it is framed within the debates about Foucauldian discursive constructionism that we have just encountered; moreover, it takes up these questions—of discourses and meaning and the freedom of the subject—through an entirely accessible, everyday example. Twigg's article illustrates the second approach to the problem of the subject—that is, her perspective accepts Foucault's argument that the subject is constructed in discursive practices and explores the limits of agency *within* a discursive framework.

Twigg interviewed older men and women who need help with bathing, and her study shows how these people challenge the dominant discourse of nurses and other homecare service providers, an administrative language that constructs them as "clients" with "personal hygiene deficits" (2003, p. 148). Twigg begins by noting that "getting clean" hardly exhausts the meanings of the bath and reminds us of many senses of bathing that have accrued historically, including the bath as pleasurable and erotic, as an experience of well-being and luxury, and as a regimen of discipline and even punishment (pp. 149–150). Twigg's respondents drew on some of these other meanings as they talked with her about what a bath meant to them and the kind of help they liked, a homely discourse that drew on sociability and personal relations and likened "good help" to family and friendship rather than to nursing.

Twigg (2003) argues that the elders in her study wanted to be positioned (and to position themselves) within this discourse of body-in-social-care and rejected the biomedical–administrative version (in the person of nurses) as impersonal, hurried, and bossy. Her analysis displays the limits and possibilities of a Foucauldian social constructionism very well: Her respondents live in a rich world of meanings and are evidently able to draw on them in artful ways to assert their own preferences and feelings and especially to refuse the dominant discourse of the service provider. Thus they have considerable agency. But they are far from self-determining or autonomous meaning makers, for what they can say (including the ways they have to resist the administrative version of care) is clearly grounded in and circumscribed by the meanings available to them in their discursive environment. They cannot, within the Foucauldian problematic, reach beyond these other (discursively given) ways of making sense of the world. Nor does their account of the "subjective experience" of bathing draw, in Twigg's formulation, on some experiential reality of the body that lies outside language.[9] Thus Twigg does not frame her respondents as revealing to her the "real" bath experience that can be contrasted with the oppressive constructed reality of the nurses. Instead, they are conceptualized as considering their options (the meanings of bathing and care) from the limited hand that they are dealt.[10]

I have considered Twigg's article at some length because it seems to me to take up the version of Foucauldian constructionism that displays the strongest possible reading of agency within his paradigm. Chris Weedon's summary (as cited in Eckermann, 1997, p. 165) captures the crucial issues. She says:

> Although the subject [in Foucault's work] is socially constructed in discursive practices, she nonetheless exists as a thinking, feeling subject and social agent capable of resistance and innovations produced out of the clash between contradictory subject positions and practices. She is also a subject able to reflect upon the discursive relations which constitute her and the society in which she lives, and [is] able to choose from the options available.[11]

Stage 2: Governmentality, Risk, and the "Responsibilizing" Subject

To recap: It is above all Foucault's interest in the constitution of the subject—the self—that runs through his work. In his early writings, as we have seen, subjects are constructed in disciplinary practices as objects of knowledge to be observed, compared, and corrected. In later works (what we call here his *second stage*) Foucault's interest in power and the regulated subject remains constant, but his emphasis shifts to the ways in which subjects are able to regulate or govern ("subject") themselves. In his last books, published after his death (*The History of Sexuality*, 1984/1988, 1984/1990), he draws on insights from classical Greece to explore a specific form of self-governance—the ethical subject.

But Foucault's interest in governance began well before that. In 1979, shortly after the publication of *Discipline and Punish*, he began to explore forms of "governmental rationality" in the political domain—"ways of thinking about the nature and practice of government" (Gordon, 1991, p. 3). His short essay called "Governmentality" (Foucault, 1991) has given rise to a lively and productive body of research known as "governmentality studies."[12] In the following section

I outline major developments in this field, paying, as usual, special attention to the version of social constructionism that informs the research.

The "Governmentalized State" and the "Responsibilized" Subject

Foucault's discussion of governmentality begins at that point in European history at which the sovereign turned from an interest in protecting his own territory to the broader question, How shall the State govern so as to maximize the happiness of individuals and also the prosperity or welfare of the whole?[13] Foucault suggests that this new interest in "the arts of government" marked the emergence of the modern administrative state and was brought into being by a double-sided form of power he termed "biopower"—the control of both populations and individuals (the first through the gathering of information we would now call demographic, the second through efforts to regulate individual lives in minute detail) (Foucault, 1980b, p. 104). Biopower was a new mechanism of control, Foucault argued, because its reach encompassed all of life's processes (Gordon, 1991, p. 5; McHoul & Grace, 1997, pp. 62–63). In coining the term *governmentality*, Foucault extends and reworks the concept of biopower: He retains the latter's double-sided aspect but now connects the ways authorities govern populations with the "technologies" individuals employ to shape *themselves* (Garland, 1997).

Governmentality scholars, some sociologists, others with backgrounds in political science, criminology, and administrative studies, have focused on the programs that allow the modern state to manage the welfare of the population and also the individual, especially in the post–World War II era amid the rise of neoliberalism (or "advanced liberalism"). Taking their cue from Foucault's assertion that much writing on government overvalued the state (Foucault, 1991, p. 103), these scholars hold that "governmentalized" power (like disciplinary power) is enacted at many sites far out from the state—in schools, in health care settings, and especially in families—and often takes the form of moral regulation instead of direct coercion. The idea of governance "at a distance" is a hallmark of this work, and programs of governance have been explored in a host of empirical sites: in the regulation of pregnancy (Ruhl, 1999; Weir, 1996); in policies governing pub licensing (Valverde, 2003); in the regulation of workplaces and workplace safety (Duncan, 2003); in the governance of AIDS patients (Kinsmen, 1996; Mykhalovskiy, McCoy, & Bresalier, 2004); in the historical treatment of poverty (Dean, 1991); and especially, in the field of crime control and policing (Ericson & Haggerty, 1997; Garland, 1997).

Most important for our interest in social constructionism is the concept of the *responsibilized* actor (Garland, 1997), the subject that lies at the heart of this perspective.[14] The ideal actor in the governmentalized state, the responsibilized actor, actively participates in his or her own life management. No longer the docile subject of disciplinary power to be usefully integrated into the machinery of early capitalism, the responsibilized actor is endowed by governmentality discourse with an active desire to take responsibility for his or her own life. This version of the actor (as "enterprising" in his or her own governance) accords concretely with neoliberal programs that have, since the 1970s in Europe and North America, shifted responsibility for social welfare from the state to the individual citizen or to businesses in the private sector (e.g., the responsibility for child care and elder care, or for physical and financial security—401K and registered retirement savings plans being prime examples).

Throughout this discussion we need to bear in mind the distinctive Foucauldian aspects of this analysis: Neoliberal governmentality is not the disappearance of state power but rather its dispersion into new social sites, and the responsibilized actor, though cloaked in the "appearance of freedom," is nevertheless an effect—an artifact—of the larger apparatus of power that is the governmentalized state. Here again, Foucault is determined to overturn the Enlightenment version of history as progress toward individual freedom. This important aspect of Foucault's thought has been retained in varying degrees in governmentality research, as we shall see.

Governmentality and the Analysis of Risk

More recently, we have seen Foucault's insights on governmentality and the governmentalized subject extended to the analysis of risk (Lupton, 1999).[15] In this research, the responsibilized actor has evolved into the risk manager (or the "prudential" actor) who will actively manage all aspects of his or her life (health, finances, physical security) so as to minimize risk to him- or herself and subsequent cost to the state. Some scholars in this field speak of the "risk gaze," which maps the distribution of risk over the social terrain and produces a version of the state as the facilitator of risk management, rather than a provider of welfare (Rose, 2000). Nikolas Rose has suggested that risk discourse constructs a new version of the citizen, one who is not directly connected to the state (e.g., through voting) but rather through access to valued "circuits of consumption" (credit cards, passports, driver's licenses, mortgages, and the like) that are open only to those people who are able to take responsibility for managing risks to their own health and personal and financial safety (e.g., who don't smoke, who lock up their cars, who insure their mortgages, etc.). Those who will not or cannot responsibilize are denied access to valuable "spaces of consumption"—in effect, they are excluded from full citizenship. In such a society, says Rose, "citizenship becomes conditional on conduct and self-governance" (Rose, 2000, p. 33).

The discourse of risk also creates a new role for professional experts, notably medical doctors and the police, who now become information brokers and community advisers on risk and its management (Bunton, 1997; Ericson & Haggerty, 1997.) Robin Bunton's analysis of health-related articles in *Good Housekeeping* magazine since the late 1950s, for example, documents the gradual replacement of the doctor by a host of health interventions across a wide range of social sites, including self-help groups and help lines and popular forums such as the aforementioned magazine. Bunton (1997) also shows how subjects are differently positioned by such "magazine medicine" (and by cultural imperatives more generally): in the 1950s as obedient patient–recipients of the doctor's advice, later as active and watchful managers of their own health. Over the same period, he says, medical expertise has been subjected to a "marketization . . . focusing on risk analysis and population management" (1997, p. 241).

Ericson and Haggerty (1997) describe similar transformations in their provocative book *Policing the Risk Society*. They begin by noting the proliferation of knowledge that attributes ever new sources of risk to ever wider social terrain and the emergence, as a result, of a new group of "risk professionals" whose role is to "make risks visible and to advise and instruct on their management" (as cited in O'Malley, 1999, p. 139). Police are one such group, they argue (and doctors are another, Bunton would doubtless agree). Ericson and Haggerty assert that that risk discourse has transformed policing from crime control, maintenance of public order, and social service to the business of "risk-knowledge brokering" to a whole range of "customers," including schools, community organizations, and the retail and banking sectors.

Whereas some governmentality researchers explore variations on this trend (e.g., Valverde, 2003), most generally agree that the major strength of the approach lies in the attention it has drawn to the diverse and hybrid sites of governance away from the state, an insight directly attributed to Foucault. They have also begun a critical reappraisal of research in their own field. Here, they inevitably return to the perennial issues that run through any application of Foucauldian contructionism: the concern over possible top-down, totalizing theoretical frameworks, the question of the freedom and agency of the subject and the place of resistance and contestation, and the possibility of critique within this approach. Next I touch on some of these discussions, as they bear in interesting ways on matters related to social constructionism.

One important debate interrogates the issue of agency: Just how free is this free, "responsibilized" subject that is called into being by such a form of governance?

Some authors take a relatively benign view of power in the governmentalized state, emphasizing the subject's freedom to choose in a consumer society they describe as "advanced" (rather than "neo") liberal. Peter Miller and Nikolas Rose (1996), for example, who studied the then-novel collaboration between advertising agencies and psychology consultants after World War II in England, stress the "complexity" of the subject–consumer that was created in this collaboration (a personality "infused with psychological functions"; 1996, p. 31) and deemphasize the fact that such a subject is nonetheless an effect of the disciplinary power of expert knowledge. Others suggest that the fragmented concept of power at the heart of the governmentality model *builds in* a routinely questioning subject (e.g., think here of the medical "customers" who shop around in the cafeteria of "alternative" medical knowledges or who regularly challenge doctors' advice; Bunton, 1997, p. 234). At the other end of the spectrum are scholars who emphasize the limited agency possible within neoliberal programs of governance and point to the hidden constraints ("compulsions of choice"; Peterson, 2003, p. 196) on the responsibilized or prudential subject; they note, for example, the pressures exerted on "consumers" to become experts on their own medical problems in the guise of

autonomy or on women "not to say no" to fetal risk screening (Peterson, 2003, pp. 195–196) or on people with incurable illness to "do the responsible thing" and "choose" to die, just as the costs of prolonging life are escalating (Prado, 2003). These concerns echo Arney and Bergen's (1984) cynical view of the allegedly self-determining subject mentioned earlier and focus on the increasingly subtle ways actors are "encouraged" to actively enlist themselves in (cost-saving) state programs. In short, whereas governmentality scholars agree that the approach constructs a subject who has a limited form of autonomy, some stress the limits, and others the autonomy. Their different emphases play out the possibilities of agency in this version of constructionism.

Agency is also the issue in a second debate within the governmentality/risk literature. Here, critics complain that too much research takes a programmatic approach to governance (Hindess, 1997) and focuses on programs and policies instead of on the "messy realities of [their] application," thus closing off consideration of resistance to such programs (O'Malley, Weir, & Shearing, 1997, pp. 504–505; for a related critique of the risk research, see O'Malley, 1999, pp. 142, 144). As a corrective, they make the now familiar recommendation to examine the ways actors actually take up or challenge such programs—the bottom-up antidote to the top-down problem—a move that would open the governmentality agenda to the possibility of a stronger version of agency (Peterson, 2003).[16]

It is ironic to note that in making these recommendations, some of these critics call for governmentality scholarship to return to its origins in Foucault, who is here represented as the champion of bottom-up, detailed analyses of practice (O'Malley, 1999). Moreover, they take pains to distance the governmentality approach to risk from the "sociological" risk analysis of Ulrich Beck (1992), whose work is marred, they argue, by the totalizing concept of "risk society," which implies an "all-embracing grasp" and a "sweeping tide of risk" that allows the subject "no way out" (O'Malley, 1999, 2004). This tells us something important about the many Foucaults in Foucault scholarship: at one moment positioned as the theorist of "no agency" and totalizing frameworks, at another as the champion of resistance, subjugated knowledges, and contestation. Herein lies a cautionary tale for readers who are anxious to find the "right" Foucault.

The Construction of the Ethical Self

The picture of neoliberal society that governmentality scholars have drawn from Foucault's work seems realized all around us. As I have just noted, the "responsibilized" self that is constructed in this literature expresses its agency "in line with official goals," as Alan Peterson puts it (in particular, the goal of reducing the burden of individuals on the state; Peterson, 2003, p. 195; see also Garland, 1997, p. 176). Yet Foucault wanted to show that the version of the self we have inherited historically is not our only possibility, and in the final two volumes of *The History of Sexuality*, his main achievement is to open a space for a new concept of the self as the *ethical* subject who can maintain some critical distance from this and other regimes by reflecting on its own relationship to such forms of power.

Although the *responsibilized* self and the *ethical* self are thus importantly different concepts[17] and reflect Foucault's evolving thinking on regulation and the subject (McWhorter, 1999, p. 254), both have their origins in his early discussion of the "arts of governance" (How shall I best govern myself and others?). Yet the research agendas emerging from these two bodies of work (i.e., governmentality and the ethics of the self) have developed in very different directions—and, with some exceptions, have little connection with each other.[18]

I now turn to a brief account of Foucault's formulation of the ethical subject. Here

Foucault draws on insights from Greco-Roman culture, which, he argued, placed only very loose constraints on individual conduct (e.g., in law) and instead emphasized *self*-regulation—the self's governance (or "care") of itself. The goal of Greek education was the cultivation of the virtuous or moral citizen, a person who could participate thoughtfully in the public life of the city, or *polis*. This always implied a form of self-regulation, because morality could never be a natural state (and if it were, it would be of no interest to Foucault). Instead, morality is a way of governing ourselves and others according to certain principles of moderation: to be moral *means* to reflect on and to ask about the right relation to have with one's self and others. This is a version of self, then, that emphasizes self-reflection and self-regulation (which Foucault called *askesis*) as a basis for ethical relations with others (Foucault, 1988, pp. 39–68; 1990, pp. 25–32). We shall see how it is carried forward into research.

Foucault's exploration of Greek thought on self-formation has three important ramifications. First, he recognized that the freedom to choose that is implied in such a notion of the moral self set Greek culture on a crucially different path from that of early modern European thought, which sought an ever more detailed knowledge of—and control over—the individual's body, mind, and even soul (Rose, 1990) through the newly developing human sciences.[19] For Foucault, the Greek tradition provided the cultural grounds from which to challenge the essentialist "truths" about sex and the body that were stipulated by these sciences.

Second, it opened an expanded position of freedom for the subject of power: In terms of its relation to dominant discourses, the ethical subject has a certain freedom—a freedom within limits—to reflect on ways it is positioned by such discourses (e.g., the biomedical discourse of sex) and to consider other styles of self, together with the principles that inform them. This is Foucault's point about the moral self as a relation of power. I return shortly to a discussion of this self in Foucault's work and what it means for social constructionism, but it can be seen even here that this represents the most expansive version of agency to emerge from his work, one that goes well beyond the docile or self-policing body of *Discipline and Punish* and also beyond the "responsibilizing" actor who fits him- or herself to a program of neoliberal governance.

Third, Foucault's work on ethics has stimulated a new research agenda. Although his foray into Greek thought on right self-governance away from the paradigm of law was primarily intended to explore a new direction for philosophy (Bernauer, 1987/1991, p. 54; McWhorter, 1999[20]), it has also stimulated research that investigates "the care of the self," that is, practices in which subjects attempt to govern themselves and shape who they are. As many commentators on postmodern society have observed, the self has become an ongoing project, and practices of self-formation are all about us: in various kinds of body modification, notably cosmetic surgery and dieting; in self-help groups and therapies of various sorts; in "new social movements" of many kinds (Melucci, 1989)—veganism, for example—in which we see our participation as entwined with who we want to be; in efforts to tell a different story of our gendered selves; and in the new experts who set themselves up as "coaches" in this enterprise of self-formation. Insights from Foucault's ethics of the subject would suggest that all of these practices offer opportunities for analysis of the ways we choose to put ourselves together, so to speak, from the materials and meanings "on offer" in various popular and professional discourses and of the ways we reflect on our choices, as well as the principles that guide them.

Although this agenda circles back to an earlier research focus on the ways that subjects take up and sometimes contest dominant discourses, the analytic emphasis here

shifts away from the interest in resistance per se (and its associated version of the agent as the resister) to the struggles of the subject to form itself as ethical—as McHoul and Grace (1993, p. 124) put it, the struggles of the subject to make "a pleasurable and satisfying set of constructed experiences" for itself within relations of power. An example of such research is Catherine E. Foote and Arthur W. Frank's exploration of the ethical possibilities of narrative grief therapy. In their analysis, therapy is reformulated as a way of assisting bereaved clients to explore and expand their range of grieving selves and to help them establish some critical distance from the power of the dominant discourse of grieving—the expectation that "time heals," for example—to define them as normal or abnormal mourners. There is no "right" grief story on offer in this version of therapy, as the authors make clear; the goal instead is an intensified self-reflection on "who I am" and "who I can be," a process that holds at the forefront the question "To what stories do we want to subject ourselves?" (Foote & Frank, 1999).

Other studies of self-care look at practices of self-formation in autobiographical writing (Einat, 2003), in stories of illness (Frank, 1998), in erotic practices (Blasius, 1994), and in organizational initiatives that invite employees or clients to create themselves as professional (Kelly & Colquhoun, 2005) or empowered (McDonald, 2004) or healthy and fit (Markula, 2004). But although postmodern society would seem to offer many opportunities to apply Foucault's discussion of ethics to projects of self-formation, relatively few researchers explicitly draw on his "ethical period," and his insights here remain underexploited.[21] These insights would add value by moving beyond a discussion of agency framed by resistance to a fuller exploration of self-formation as an ethical project, the direction exemplified by Ladelle McWhorter (1999) and taken up in Catherine E. Foote and Arthur W. Frank's (1999) chapter on therapy and in the special issue of the *Journal of Medical Humanities* (2003), edited by Frank and Therese Jones, which specifically attempts to draw out the implications of Foucault's ethical writings for bioethics.

Care of the Self and Social Constructionism

I propose now to sift Foucault's ethical work for what it implies for the perspective of social constructionism. Perhaps most significant is that his insights offer us a new way of thinking about the sterile debates over social constructionism and "the real." Throughout his work, Foucault has maintained that "who we are" is inevitably a construction; it is never an entity, either within or outside us, "there" to be discovered. In his last work on the ethical self, he makes it clear that self-formation (and self-knowledge) requires reflection, taking a position with respect to our relations of power with self and others; therein is the struggle and possibility of the moral life. This possibility is closed off if we formulate who we are as natural or self-evidently revealed by "the voice of experience," by our bodies, or by scientific experts; all these voices *tell* us who we are "really" and thus deny us the opportunity to reflect on how we should relate to our self (and to others). If I, as one of the elderly people interviewed by Julia Twigg in her study of bathing, accept the dominant service provider's version of myself as a "hygiene problem," for example, then many spaces of reflection are closed off to me: the opportunity to think of myself as other than "difficult," should I resist; the chance to reencounter my body as pleasurable within a sociable relationship with another; the question of how to relate to myself and to others when I am in a position of vulnerability—of how to retrieve and sustain a strong story of "who I am" when privacy and independence are stripped away. These and other considerations that are important to me as an old person are silenced by the dominant discourse of hygiene.[22] How shall I govern my-

self and others? asks Foucault. The lesson he derives from the Greeks is that the opportunity to form an ethical self is not a lofty enterprise but a mundane, everyday one.[23]

Foucault's hostility to dominant discourses such as the aforementioned administrative one—those that stipulate the answer to the question of who I am and enforce it unequivocally as truth—is bound here to the way they close off the possibility of the ethical self by removing our opportunity to reflect and to choose. His work suggests that we need to be able to reflect on various stories of ourselves in order to form ethical relations with ourselves and others. The irrevocable fact that life can only ever be stories or "constructions"—a life within the limits of discourse—and the impossibility of escaping this limit through various foundational maneuvers is thus transformed from a constraint into the possibility of the moral life. Deprived of the security of foundational knowledge (of the "real me" or the "real world"), we are forced to struggle with the question Who/How should I be? and to call on our practical–moral principles, rather than falling back on the supposed "bedrock" authority of "reality" or the privileged discourses of the day.

The recognition that the self can *only* be a story is thus the ethical moment. Against this, critics of social constructionism have argued that in a world in which *everything* is a construction (a story) and nothing is real, we are led inevitably into relativism, according to which nothing counts—or everything counts equally—and nothing can be done. This critique thrives especially in the field of social problems analysis, in which it is argued that without the firm foundation provided by objective knowledge of the world, we are unable to tell real from spurious social problems. The constructionist position is thus claimed to disable critical inquiry and to make political action impossible.[24] (For a review of this debate, see G. Miller & Holstein, 1993, pp. 5–23.) But as we have seen, this same constructionism leads Foucault not to relativism and a retreat from political engagement but to the ethical life, in which, in fact, the most basic political issues–the "arts of government"–are put at the fore (see Seidman, 1991, 1994; Weeks, 2005). His ethical work therefore bears on arguments among social constructionists about how we change the world. For Foucault, how we act politically does not require knowing the real or true ("unconstructed") story; instead, it requires reflection on the right way to govern ourselves and others.

Although it has been underexploited as a research agenda–with significant exceptions, as I indicated earlier–Foucault's ethics of the self has important implications for debates in social constructionism. In the next section I move away from the ethical subject to a brief discussion of his broader contribution to the social constructionist agenda.

Some Final Reflections

In the opening paragraph of their introduction to this volume, Holstein and Gubrium describe the basic tenets of social constructionism. They say:

> [Social constructionism means] . . . that the world we live in and our place in it are not simply and evidently "there" for participants. Rather, participants actively construct the world of everyday life and its constituent elements. (Chapter 1, this volume, p. 3)

These sentences neatly frame what Foucault's work shares with this version of social constructionism and how it differs. Readers of this chapter will by now recognize Foucault's views echoed in the first part of this description. They should also see, however, that Foucault's interest in the interaction setting (in which actors "actively construct . . . the world") is secondary to his interest in larger discourses or bodies of knowledge and in the ways subjects are positioned–and position themselves–through these discourses. In this chapter I

have suggested that Foucault's work can be seen as an evolving account of the place of the subject within discursive limits, where this subject is always an effect of power. Subjects, as Foucault says, are always subjected, and this means that the actor's power to make and assign meaning in the world, although not determined, is strictly limited. More precisely, it is tied back to the range of meanings that specific discourses make available to them. Put crudely, if actors construct their worlds in interaction, it is because they are themselves discursively constructed.

But although Foucault's focus is not on the interaction order per se, his discursive constructionism certainly broadens our understanding of it. We see, for example, how discursive frameworks shape the interactional encounter by enabling and restricting the range of meaning actors deploy in specific settings, an insight captured in Jonathan Potter and Margaret Wetherell's (1987) discussion of the actor's "discursive repertoire" (see also Ibarra, Chapter 18, this volume). This insight has also influenced the constructionist approach to social problems analysis; Ibarra and Kitsuse (1993), for their part, have importantly extended our understanding of the claimsmaking process to include the kinds of moral discourses claimsmakers draw on to give their claims "the accent of truth" (e.g., the discourse of loss or the prestigious discourse of science). And despite frequent assertions that Foucault's "totalizing" version of discourse so enshrouds the subject as to make resistance to dominant discourses impossible, his discussion of subjugated knowledges has expanded the very idea of what counts as a claim, as indicated earlier. More generally, it has opened the door to a heightened awareness of the relationship between knowledge and power and to an ongoing discussion within feminist scholarship about alternative knowledges and realities, especially from the margins.

This in turn is reflected in new ways of thinking about the relationship between language and power. Foucault argues consistently that power struggles are struggles over interpretations of social reality, in which "we must hear the distant roar of battle" (Foucault, 1975/1979, p. 308): Whose version of the world will count as the true one? This means that the power that individuals wield (or not) in interactional encounters is crucially tied to their position in the discursive order and not to some "property" of actors themselves, such as social class or occupational status. The doctor's power over the patient, for example, is here conceptualized not as an effect of occupational status per se but instead as tied to the ways doctors can mobilize the privileged discourse of professional medicine in order to enforce their version of the patient's "problem" in the clinical setting. In an important sense, then, actors are empowered or not by discourse. This focus makes Foucault inattentive to the subtleties of interactional practice that are the concern of symbolic interactionists, for example, or conversation analysts. And in a way that these traditions of scholarship would very likely resist, his concept of power goes beyond the power of actors to the power of dominant discourses "themselves" as "truth games," self-legitimating systems of knowledge that are oriented to producing themselves as objective truths.

As for the more general social constructionist tenet—that "the world . . . is not simply and self-evidently 'there' . . . "—we suggest that Foucault adopted this stance as the touchstone for his scholarly work and also as a personal credo. His insistence on defamiliarizing our most cherished assumptions, "upsetting basic preconceptions" by "exposing seemingly natural categories as constructs, articulated by words and discourse" is widely recognized as his greatest overall contribution (Jones & Porter, 1994, p. 5; McWhorter, 1999, p. 36). As James Bernauer says, Foucault showed us "fresh ways to doubt the order of things" (1987/1991, p. 72). Intensely concerned with the power relations that have historically constituted us as knowable, he was especially hos-

tile to the "truths" of the emerging human sciences in early modern Europe, those discourses that sought to discover our essential selves and pin them to us as "identity." His refusal to offer up the real, the essential, Foucault to his followers and interpreters is thus entirely consistent with his constructionist view. Here is his response to their queries:

> Do not ask who I am and do not ask me to remain the same: leave it to our bureaucrats and our police to see that our papers are in order. (Foucault, as cited in Bernauer & Rasmussen, 1987, p. vii)

• Notes

1. For an excellent short introduction, see *A Foucault Primer*, by McHoul and Grace, 1993.

2. Many scholars who find the "stage" model useful as an organizing device see three stages, not two, in Foucault's work: for simplicity I have elided the first two stages into one.

3. And in *The Order of Things*, Foucault (1973) establishes the groundwork for this view by analyzing the history of the human sciences and their relations to language, asking how it came to be that language as the representation of something outside it became the accepted view of what language "really" is; see McHoul and Grace (1993, p. 14).

4. For early applications of the concept of the panopticon to policing, see Gordon (1986) and Marx (1988); to consumer surveillance, see Mosco (1989) and Poster (1990); to the workplace, see Zuboff (1988). For a slightly later collection that applies insights derived primarily from *Discipline and Punish* to the university and its disciplines, to the workplace, to law, and to healing institutions, see *Foucault and the Critique of Institutions* (Caputo & Yount, 1993). For essays especially focusing on disciplinary power, normalization, and the panopticon, see chapters by Dyke, Schmelzer, and Moore in Caputo and Yount (1993).

5. Thus mainstream biomedicine refers to other forms of healing, such as naturopathy, as "complementary" and to resistant patients as "noncompliant."

6. Even those feminists who recognize the

value for women of Foucault's insights on sub-ordination and resistance, however, note that Foucault himself largely ignores *women's* discourses of resistance (e.g., Diamond & Quinby, 1988, p. xvi).

7. This phrasing is slightly adapted from Scott's. Note also that the project of unearthing historically subjugated knowledges is described by Foucault as "genealogical research." See Foucault, 1980b, pp. 82–85.

8. See, in this connection, Hartsock's discussion of the characteristic features of fiction produced by writers who are members of marginal groups (Hartsock, 1990). For a discussion of the tendency to read the political out of the analysis by treating discursive styles as "different" rather than super- or subordinate, see Troemel-Ploetz's (1991) review of Deborah Tannen's *You Just Don't Understand: Men and Women in Conversation* (1991).

9. Moreover, Twigg is very critical of other (medical) versions of aging that treat "decline" as natural.

10. Foucault is quite clear here. Concerning "the way in which the subject constitutes himself, in an active fashion, by the practices of the self," he says:

> these practices are nevertheless not something that the individual invents by himself. They are patterns that he finds in his culture and which are proposed, suggested and imposed on him by his culture, his society and his social group. (1991, p. 11)

11. It is arguable, nevertheless, that some people may have no language available to "say" their problem; we are reminded here of the arguments that gays and lesbians sometimes make about their difficulties articulating their identities (saying "who I am") before they encountered discourses of (homo)sexuality that gave them a way of naming themselves. But Foucault would challenge this argument, as it claims a directly accessible knowledge of "who we are."

12. For a collection of this work, see Burchell, Gordon, and Miller (1991) and a special issue of the journal *Economy and Society*, 25(3). Governmentality work has emerged and flourished in the United Kingdom, Canada, and Australia/New Zealand, but has seen less interest or development in the United States. This is especially curious—or perhaps it is understandable—as the "responsibilized" actor is in the classic American

tradition of the independent, self-reliant individual.

13. Sociologists often encounter this idea first in the work of the Scottish Moralists, notably Adam Smith and Adam Ferguson, who theorized the relationship between the conduct or "propensities" of individuals and the welfare of the whole society; in the history of sociology, this is sometimes seen as an early attempt to consider the micro–macro link (see Schneider, 1967).

14. This very evocative phrase (the "responsibilized actor") is Garland's, not Foucault's.

15. Lupton's collection includes but is not confined to the governmentality approach to risk. In her introduction. she compares this and other perspectives.

16. These critics recommend, more generally, a closer examination of relevant insights from sociology and feminist thought—in particular, feminist work on subjugated knowledges, sociological work that explores the standpoint of the actor, and the strengthened version of agency that is implied in the concept of the strategic actor who is able to revise and contest programs.

Although some governmentality researchers are decidedly ambivalent about their relationship with sociology, others have productively appropriated and extended sociological insights. See, for example, Ewald (1991), and Lupton's discussion of constructionist approaches to risk (Lupton, 1999, pp. 5–6).

17. My own view is that they are importantly different, though they have a common source in Foucault's discussion of governmentality; see note 18 below. For discussions of the relationship between these two skeins in Foucault's work and of the different (or similar) versions of the subject constituted therein, see Hindess, 1997, and Peterson, 2003.

18. Thus, while the two bodies of research are usually called "governmentality studies" and "ethics," both are in fact about governance. But although some governmentality writers are clearly aware of Foucault's later work on ethics (e.g., Gordon, 1991, p. 1), there is little evidence that insights from this work have been integrated into governmentality research. Research emerging from Foucault's discussion of ethics, however, seems to have made better use of the discussion of neoliberalism and the responsibilized self; see, for example, Frank and Jones (2003).

19. Foucault called such power *pastoral* and identified its characteristic technique of power as

the "confessional," by which he meant not just what was spoken into the ear of the priest but also the "truths" elicited in secular, especially medical, settings all across the society—including therapies, examinations, treatments, and interviews. It was this outpouring of talk about sex in the 19th century, he contends, that undermined the stereotypic picture of the sexually repressive Victorian era (Foucault, 1976/1980a).

20. In her thoughtful and very readable book *Bodies and Pleasures*, McWhorter explicitly employs Foucault's notion of *askesis*—an "exercise of thinking that transforms its reader"—to describe her own personal and political transformation as a lesbian woman and feminist over 15 years.

21. For example, when we look at the evolution of feminist thinking on the matter of cosmetic surgery, we see that it has developed in a direction that parallels Foucault's thought neatly but fails (to my knowledge) to integrate his ethical work—from an early refusal of it as a disciplinary control strategy, to a (less pejorative) interest in how subjects take it up and use it strategically, to the beginnings of a discussion of its role in a postmodern aesthetics of the body that is undergirded by the questions: How shall I govern my body? Create my body? (see, e.g., Davis, 1997).

22. It is important to see that losses accrue also to the "service provider" if she enlists herself in the dominant administrative discourse of hygiene. She is also denied the opportunity of reflections on the nature of care (as other than providing a service, for example), especially for others who may be weak, unattractive, or unresponsive; she is denied, in short, the opportunity to form a professional self that is grounded in ethical principles rather than expediency.

23. Yet its mundane aspect has profound consequences. Volume 3 in *The History of Sexuality* (Foucault, 1984/1988) looks at the government or cultivation of the self in ancient Greek culture, as it is connected with bodily pleasure, conjugal relations, and homoerotic relations; as Foucault points out, the careful practice of personal virtues was thought to be the key to the good government of the ancient Greek city. In Greek culture, says Foucault, "The rationality of the government of others is the same as the rationality of the government of oneself" (1984/1988, p. 89).

24. On this dilemma and the resulting search for new foundational knowledges, see L. J. Miller (2000).

• References

Addams, J. (1976). *Jane Addams on peace, war and international understanding, 1899–1932*. New York: Garland.

Arney, W. R., & Bergen, B. B. (1984). *Medicine and the management of living: Taming the last great beast*. Chicago: University of Chicago Press.

Beck, U. (1992). *Risk society: Towards a new modernity*. London: Sage.

Belenky, M. F., Clinchy, B. M., Goldberger, N. R., & Tarule, J. M. (1986). *Women's ways of knowing: The development of self, voice and mind*. New York: Basic Books.

Berger, P. L., & Luckmann, T. (1966). *The social construction of reality*. Garden City, NY: Doubleday.

Bernauer, J. (1991). Foucault's ecstatic thinking. In J. Bernauer & D. Rasmussen (Eds.), *The final Foucault* (pp. 45–82). Cambridge, MA: MIT Press. (Original work published 1987)

Bernauer, J., & Rasmussen, D. (Eds.). (1991). *The final Foucault*. Cambridge, MA: MIT Press.

Best, A. L. (2003). Fashioning the feminine. In J. A. Holstein & J. F. Gubrium (Eds.), *Inner lives and social worlds* (pp. 405–418). Oxford, UK: Oxford University Press.

Blasius, M. (1994). *Gay and lesbian politics: Sexuality and the emergence of a new ethic*. Philadelphia: Temple University Press.

Bordo, S. (1989). The body and the reproduction of femininity: A feminist appropriation of Foucault. In A. M. Jaggar & S. R. Bordo (Ed.), *Gender/body/knowledge: Feminist reconstructions of being and knowing* (pp. 13–33). New Brunswick, NJ: Rutgers University Press.

Boyne, R. (2000). Post-panopticism. *Economy and Society, 29*, 285–307.

Bunton, R. (1997). Popular health, advanced liberalism and *Good Housekeeping* magazine. In A. Peterson & R. Bunton (Eds.), *Foucault, health and medicine* (pp. 223–248). London: Routledge.

Burchell, G., Gordon, C., & Miller, P. (1991). (Eds.). *The Foucault effect: Studies in governmentality*. London: Harvester.

Caputo, J., & Yount, M. (Eds.). (1993). *Foucault and the critique of institutions*. University Park: Pennsylvania State University Press.

Cohen, S. (1985). *Visions of social control*. London: Blackwell.

Davies, B. (1989). *Frogs and snails and feminist tales: Preschool children and gender*. Sydney, Australia: Allen & Unwin.

Davis, K. (1997). "My body is my art": Cosmetic surgery as feminist utopia? In K. Davis (Ed.), *Embodied practices: Feminist perspectives on the body* (pp. 168–181). London: Sage.

Dean, M. (1991). *The constitution of poverty: Toward a genealogy of liberal governance*. London: Routledge.

Diamond, I., & Quinby, L. (Eds.). (1988). *Feminism and*

Foucault: Reflections on resistance. Boston: Northeastern University Press.

Donzelot, J. (1979). *The policing of families*. New York: Pantheon Press.

Doran, N. (1994). Risky business: Codifying embodied experience in the Manchester Unity of Oddfellows. *Journal of Historical Sociology*, 7(2), 131–154.

Doran, N. (1996). From embodied "health" to official "accidents": Class, codification and British factory legislation, 1831–1844. *Social and Legal Studies*, 5, 523–546.

Doran, N. (2002). Medico-legal expertise and industrial disease compensation: Discipline, surveillance, and disqualification in the era of the "social." In G. M. MacDonald (Ed.), *Social context and social location in the sociology of law* (pp. 159–180). Peterborough, Ontario, Canada: Broadview Press.

Duncan, G. (2003). Workers' compensation and the governance of pain. *Economy and Society*, 32, 449–447.

Eckermann, L. (1997). Foucault, embodiment and gendered subjectivities: The case of voluntary starvation. In A. Peterson & R. Bunton (Eds.), *Foucault, health and medicine* (pp. 151–169). London: Routledge.

Einat, A. (2003). Impacts of truth(s): The confessional mode in Harold Brodkey's illness autobiography. *Literature and Medicine*, 22(2), 164–187.

Ericson, R. V., & Haggerty, K. D. (1997). *Policing the risk society*. Oxford, UK: Clarendon Press.

Ericson, R. V., & Haggerty, K. D. (Eds.). (2005). *The new politics of surveillance and visibility*. Toronto, Ontario, Canada: University of Toronto Press.

Ewald, F. (1991). Insurance and risk. In G. Burchell, C. Gordon, & P. Miller (Eds.), *The Foucault effect: Studies in governmentality* (pp. 197–211). London: Harvester.

Foote, C. E., & Frank, A. W. (1999). Foucault and therapy: The disciplining of grief. In A. S. Chambon, A. Irving, & L. Epstein (Eds.), *Reading Foucault for social work* (pp. 157–187). New York: Columbia University Press.

Foucault, M. (1973). *The order of things: An archaeology of the human sciences*. New York: Vintage Books. (Original work published 1966)

Foucault, M. (1979). *Discipline and punish: The birth of the prison*. New York: Vintage Books. (Original work published 1975)

Foucault, M. (1980a). *The history of sexuality: Vol. 1. An introduction* (R. Hurley, Trans.). New York: Vintage Books. (Original work published 1976)

Foucault, M. (1980b). *Power/knowledge: Selected interviews and other writings, 1972–1977*. New York: Pantheon Books.

Foucault, M. (1980c). Truth and power. In M. Foucault, *Power/knowledge: Selected interviews and other writings, 1972–1977* (pp. 109–133). New York: Pantheon Books.

Foucault, M. (1988). *The history of sexuality: Vol. 3. The care of the self* (R. Hurley, Trans.). New York: Vintage Books. (Original work published 1984)

Foucault, M. (1990). *The history of sexuality: Vol. 2. The use of pleasure* (R. Hurley, Trans.). New York: Vintage Books. (Original work published 1984)

Foucault, M. (1991). The ethic of care for the self as a practice of freedom: An interview. In J. Bernauer & D. Rasmussen (Eds.), *The final Foucault* (pp. 1–20). Cambridge, MA: MIT Press.

Foucault, M. (1991). Governmentality. In G. Burchell, C. Gordon, & P. Miller (Eds.), *The Foucault effect: Studies in governmentality* (pp. 87–104). Chicago: University of Chicago Press. (Original work published 1978)

Frank, A. W. (1998). Stories of illness as care of the self: A Foucauldian dialogue. *Health*, 2, 329–348.

Frank, A. W., & Jones, T. (Eds.). (2003). Bioethics and the later Foucault [Special issue]. *Journal of Medical Humanities, 24*.

Garfinkel, H. (1967). *Studies in ethnomethodology*. Englewood Cliffs, NJ: Prentice Hall.

Garland, D. (1997). "Governmentality" and the problem of crime: Foucault, criminology and sociology. *Theoretical Criminology, 1*, 173–214.

Gershick, T. J., & Miller, A. S. (1995). Coming to terms: Masculinity and physical disability. In M. Kimmel & M. Messner (Eds.), *Men's lives* (3rd ed., pp. 262–275). Boston: Allyn & Bacon.

Gillan, G. (1991). Foucault's philosophy. In J. Bernauer & D. Rasmussen (Eds.), *The final Foucault* (pp. 34–44). Cambridge, MA: MIT Press.

Gilligan, C. (1982). *In a different voice: Psychological theory and women's development*. Cambridge, MA: Harvard University Press.

Gordon, C. (1991). Governmentality: An introduction. In G. Burchell, C. Gordon, & P. Miller (Eds.), *The Foucault effect: Studies in governmentality* (pp. 1–51). Chicago: University of Chicago Press.

Gordon, D. (1986). The electronic panopticon: A case study of the development of the National Crime Records system. *Politics and Society, 15*, 483–511.

Green, B. (1993). *Gerontology and the construction of old age*. New York: Aldine de Gruyter.

Grossberg, L., Nelson, C., & Treicher, P. (Eds.). (1992). *Cultural studies*. New York: Routledge, Chapman and Hall.

Haggerty, K. D., & Ericson, R. V. (2000). The surveillant assemblage. *British Journal of Sociology, 51*, 605–622.

Hartsock, N. (1990). Foucault on power: A theory for women? In L. Nicholson (Ed.), *Feminism/postmodernism* (pp. 157–175). London: Routledge.

Haug, F., Andresen, S., Bünz-Elfferding, Hauser, K., Lang, U., Laudan, M., et al. (1987). *Female sexualization: A collective work of memory* (E. Carter, Trans.). London: Verso. (Original work published 1983)

Hekman, S. (Ed.). (1996). *Feminist readings of Foucault*. University Park: Pennsylvania State University Press.

Hindess, B. (1997). Politics and governmentality. *Economy and Society, 26*, 257–272.

Holstein, J. (1987). Producing gender effects in involuntary mental hospitalization. *Social Problems, 34*, 141–155.

Holstein, J. A., & Gubrium, J. F. (1994). Phenomenology, ethnomethodology and interpretive practice. In N. K. Denzin & Y. S. Lincoln (Eds.), *Handbook of qualitative research* (pp. 262–272). Thousand Oaks, CA: Sage.

Ibarra, P. B., & Kitsuse, J. I. (1993). Vernacular constituents of moral discourse: An interactionist proposal for the study of social problems. In J. A. Holstein & G. Miller (Eds.), *Reconsidering social constructionism: Debates in social problems theory* (pp. 25–58). New York: Aldine de Gruyter.

Jones, C., & Porter, R. (1994). *Reassessing Foucault: Power, medicine, and the body.* London: Routledge.

Katz, S. (1996). *Disciplining old age: the formation of gerontological knowledge.* Charlottesville: University of Virginia Press.

Kelly, P., & Colquhoun, D. (2005). The professionalization of stress management: Health and well-being as a professional duty of care? *Critical Public Health, 15*, 135–145.

Kinsman, G. (1996). "Responsibility" as a strategy of governance: Regulating people living with AIDS and lesbians and gay men in Ontario. *Economy and Society, 25*, 393–409.

Lakoff, R. T. (1990). *Talking power: The politics of language.* New York: Basic Books.

Lupton, D. (Ed.). (1999). *Risk and sociocultural theory: New directions and perspectives.* Cambridge, UK: Cambridge University Press.

Lyon, D. (1993). An electronic panopticon?: A sociological critique of surveillance theory. *Sociological Review*, pp. 653–678.

Lyon, D. (2003). *Surveillance after September 11.* Malden, MA: Polity Press.

Malacrida, C. (2005). Discipline and dehumanization in a total institution: Institutional survivors' descriptions of time-out rooms. *Disability and Society, 20*, 523–537.

Markula, P. (2004). "Tuning into one's self": Foucault's technologies of the self and mindful fitness. *Sociology of Sport Journal, 21*, 302–321.

Marx, G. T. (1988). *Undercover: Police surveillance in America.* Berkeley: University of California Press.

Mathiesen, T. (1997). The viewer society: Michel Foucault's "Panopticon" revisited. *Theoretical Criminology, 1*, 215–233.

McDonald, R. (2004). Individual identity and organizational control: Empowerment and modernization in a primary care trust. *Sociology of Health and Illness, 26*, 925–950.

McHoul, A., & Grace, W. (1993). *A Foucault primer: Discourse, power and the subject.* Washington Square, NY: New York University Press.

McNay, L. (1992). *Foucault and feminism: Power, gender and the self.* Cambridge, UK: Polity Press.

McWhorter, L. (1999). *Bodies and pleasures: Foucault and the politics of sexual normalization.* Bloomington: Indiana University Press.

Melucci, A. (1989). *Nomads of the present: Social movements and individual needs in contemporary society.* Philadelphia: Temple University Press.

Middleton, S. (1998). *Disciplining sexuality: Foucault, life histories, and education.* New York: Teachers College Press.

Miller, G. (1991). *Enforcing the work ethic.* Albany: State University of New York Press.

Miller, G., & Holstein, J. A. (1993). Reconsidering social constructionism. In J. A. Holstein & G. Miller (Eds.), *Reconsidering social constructionism: Debates in social problems theory* (pp. 5–23). New York: Aldine de Gruyter.

Miller, L. J. (1984). Intervention for what?: The question of paternalism. *Phenomenology and Pedagogy, 2*, 83–91.

Miller, L. J. (1987). Uneasy alliance: Women as agents of social control. *Canadian Journal of Sociology, 12*, 345–361.

Miller, L. J. (1993). Claims-making from the underside: Marginalization and social problems analysis. In J. A. Holstein & G. Miller (Eds.), *Reconsidering social constructionism: Debates in social problems theory* (pp. 349–376). New York: Aldine de Gruyter.

Miller, L. J. (2000). The poverty of truth-seeking: Postmodernism, discourse analysis and critical feminism. *Theory and Psychology, 10*, 313–352.

Miller, L. J., & Penz, O. (1991). Talking bodies: Female bodybuilders colonize a male preserve. *Quest, 43*, 148–163.

Miller, P., & Rose, N. (1996). Mobilizing the consumer: Assembling the subject of consumption. *Theory, Culture and Society, 14*, 1–36.

Moi, T. (1985). Power, sex and subjectivity: Feminist reflections on Foucault. *Paragraph: Journal of the Modern Theory Group, 5*, 95–102.

Mosco, V. (1989). *Pay-per society.* Toronto, Ontario, Canada: Garamond.

Mykhalovskiy, E., McCoy, L., & Bresalier, M. (2004). Compliance/adherence, HIV and the critique of medical power. *Social Theory and Health, 2*, 315–340.

Nettleton, S. (1991). Wisdom, diligence and the teeth: Discursive practices and the creation of mothers. *Sociology of Health and Illness, 13*, 98–111.

Norris, C., Moran, J., & Armstrong, G. (Eds.). (1998). *Surveillance, closed circuit television, and social control.* Aldershot, UK: Ashgate.

O'Malley, P. (1999). Governmentality and the risk society [Review of the book *Policing the risk society*]. *Economy and Society, 28*, 138–148.

O'Malley, P. (2004). *Risk, uncertainty and government.* London: Glasshouse Press.

O'Malley, P., Weir, L., & Shearing, C. (1997). Governmentality, criticism and politics. *Economy and Society*, *26*, 501–517.

Peterson, A. (2003). Governmentality, critical scholarship and the medical humanities. *Journal of Medical Humanities*, *24*, 187–201.

Poster, M. (1990). *The mode of information.* Oxford, UK: Polity Press.

Potter, J., & Wetherell, M. (1987). *Discourse and social psychology: Beyond attitudes and behavior.* London: Sage.

Prado, C. G. (2003). Foucaultian ethics and elective death. *Journal of Medical Humanities*, *24*, 203–211.

Rose, N. (1990). *Governing the soul: The shaping of the private self.* London: Routledge.

Rose, N. (2000). Government and control. *British Journal of Criminology*, *40*, 321–339.

Ruhl, L. (1999). Liberal governance and pre-natal care: Risk and regulation in pregnancy. *Economy and Society*, *28*, 95–117.

Schmelzer, M. (1993). Panopticism and postmodern pedagogy. In J. Caputo & M. Yount (Eds.), *Foucault and the critique of institutions* (pp. 127–136). University Park: Pennsylvania State University Press.

Schneider, L. (Ed.). (1967). *The Scottish moralists on human nature and society.* Chicago: University of Chicago Press.

Schutz, A. (1970). *On phenomenology and social relations.* Chicago: University of Chicago Press.

Scott, J. W. (1990). Deconstructing equality-versus-difference: Or, the uses of post-structuralist theory for feminism. In M. Hirsh & E. Fox Keller (Eds.), *Conflicts in feminism* (pp. 134–148). New York: Routledge.

Seidman, S. (1991). The end of sociological theory: The postmodern hope. *Sociological Theory*, *9*, 131–146.

Seidman, S. (1994). *Contested knowledge: Social theory in the postmodern era.* Cambridge, MA: Blackwell.

Sennett, R. (1970). *The uses of disorder: Personal identity and city life.* New York: Knopf.

Shilling, C. (1997). The body and difference. In K. Woodward (Ed.), *Identity and difference* (pp. 63–107). London: Sage.

Smith, D. E. (1987). *The everyday world as problematic: A feminist sociology.* Toronto, Ontario, Canada: University of Toronto Press.

Smith, D. E. (1997). Telling the truth after postmodernism. *Symbolic Interaction 19*, 171–202.

Staples, W. (1997). *The culture of surveillance: Discipline and social control in the United States.* New York: St. Martin's Press.

Tannen, D. (1991). *You just don't understand: Men and women in conversation.* New York: Ballantine Books.

Torpey, J. (2000). *The invention of the passport: Surveillance, citizenship and the state.* Cambridge, UK: Cambridge University Press.

Troemel-Ploetz, S. (1991). Selling the apolitical [Review of the book *You just don't understand*]. *Discourse and Society*, *2*, 489–502.

Tuchman, B. W. (1978). *A distant mirror: The calamitous 14th century.* New York: Ballantine.

Twigg, J. (2003). The body and bathing: Help with personal care at home. In C. A. Faircloth (Ed.), *Aging bodies: Images and everyday experience* (pp. 143–169). Walnut Creek, CA: AltaMira Press

Valverde, M. (1991). *The age of light, soap and water: Moral reform in English Canada 1885–1925.* Toronto, Ontario, Canada: McClelland & Stewart.

Valverde, M. (2003). Police science, British style: Pub licensing and knowledges of urban disorder. *Economy and Society*, *32*, 234–252.

Wainwright, S. P., & Turner, B. S. (2003). Aging and the dancing body. In C. A. Faircloth (Ed.), *Aging bodies: Images and everyday experience* (pp. 259–292). Walnut Creek, CA: AltaMira Press

Weeks, J. (2005). Remembering Foucault. *Journal of the History of Sexuality*, *14*, 186–201.

Weir, L. (1996). Recent developments in the governance of pregnancy. *Economy and Society*, *25*, 372–392.

Weitz, R. (2003). Women and their hair: Seeking power through resistance and accommodation. In R. Weitz (Ed.), *The politics of women's bodies: Sexuality, appearance and behavior* (pp. 135–151). New York: Oxford University Press.

Zuboff, S. (1988). *In the age of the smart machine.* New York: Basic Books.

CHAPTER 14

Discursive Constructionism

● **Jonathan Potter**
Alexa Hepburn

D iscursive constructionism (DC) is most distinctive in its foregrounding of the epistemic position of both the researcher and what is researched (texts or conversations). It studies a world of descriptions, claims, reports, allegations, and assertions as parts of human practices, and it works to keep these as the central topic of research rather than trying to move beyond them to the objects or events that seem to be the topic of such discourse. It is radically constructionist in that it is skeptical of any guarantee beyond local and contingent texts, claims, arguments, demonstrations, exercises of logic, procedures of empiricism, and so on. In this sense it can be described as antifoundationalist and poststructuralist. It takes seriously the work in rhetoric and the sociology of scientific knowledge that highlights the contingent, normative, and constructive work that goes into, say, logical demonstrations, mathematical proofs, or experimental replications. Like much work in the sociology of scientific knowledge, it is methodologically relativist in that it systematically avoids starting with one party's version of events, actions, or structures as true or given (Ashmore, 1989).

Although DC appears to have a narrow topic—discourse—its power comes from its central role in human affairs. Discourse is the fundamental medium for action. It is the medium through which versions of the world are constructed and made urgent or reworked as trivial and irrelevant. For social scientists working with DC, the study of discourse becomes the central way of studying mind, social processes, organizations, and events as they are continually made live in human affairs.

The first section of this chapter overviews the central elements of discursive constructionism and highlights what makes it distinctive from alternative constructionisms. The second section describes the operation of discursive constructionism as an analytic project that studies the procedures through which versions are built, established, and made independent of their authors. This is illustrated through an extended analysis of fact construction in a single account. The third section explores the power of a discursive constructionist approach by considering its operation in realms that on first sight appear to defy discourse constructionist analysis: death and furniture, social structure and context, embodiment, emotion, and experience. In each case discursive analyses are offered that illustrate the radical power and potential of this approach (also see Nikander, Chapter 21, this volume).

Elements of Discursive Constructionism

Discourse is most simply defined as texts and talk as parts of social practices (Potter, 1996). That is, it works with the sense of *discourse* as a verb rather than a noun. Thus discourse in DC can include conversations, arguments, talk in work settings, professional client interaction, the various situations in which interaction is mediated and supported by technology (phones, visual displays, instruments, etc.), and any occasion on which people are doing things involving some form of interaction. Occasionally, DC will work with open-ended interviews, but these will be treated as interactional events rather than as places in which participants' views can be excavated (Potter & Hepburn, 2005). This commitment to discourse involves considering the live delivery of talk with its stress and emphasis, silence and overlap. Although it does not have to be exclusively verbal and linguistic, there is a commitment to approaching nondiscursive material via the orientations of participants.

The focus on discourse rather than language signals an approach that is focused on action and practice rather than linguistic structure.

DC does not adopt the extended notion of discourse used in some of Foucault's work. For example, at points in *Discipline and Punish* (1979), Foucault treats discourse variously as including institutions, institutional practices (e.g., for dealing with abnormality), the archived set of "statements" that embody the founding of the institution, the rules of inclusion and exclusion, the physical architecture of prisons, decisions about sentencing, scientific criminology, moralizing, and philanthropy. DC has a more restricted notion of discourse; however, that does not mean that the sort of analytic work involved in DC might not address several of the phenomena that for Foucault constitute a discourse, nor that it might not draw on some of Foucault's insights about institutions, practice, and the nature of subjectivity. The virtue of the notion of discourse in DC is its precision and its fittedness to a particular analytic practice.

DC draws on conversation analytic (CA) methods and findings. It is distinctive from CA, however, precisely because of its foregrounding of construction as an issue. Nevertheless, in considering how versions are assembled in talk and texts, its practice parallels that of CA. There are differences in the approach taken to cognition, with some conversation analysts being willing to consider cognition as a realm to be connected to interaction rather than something that can be studied as an object in and for interaction in the manner of DC (Potter & te Molder, 2005). So the differences are subtle and, as Wooffitt (2005) shows, there are important areas of overlap. Indeed, in the past few years, CA work has started to bring to the fore the kinds of epistemic issues that have been at the center of DC (e.g., Clift, 2006).

One way of understanding DC is as a research tradition in which epistemics are perpetually live for both researchers and researched and in which any conclusions may apply just as much to the researcher's own discourse as to the discourse under study. In this sense, DC is a reflexively mature practice. Indeed, DC itself is an approach whose justification is not foundational. It is warranted by a weave of arguments and illustrations and stands insofar as it can counter or improve on or reinterpret analyses from alternative perspectives that work with assumptions that are realist, positivist, symbolic interactionist, social cognitionist, or other. Note that DC is not a program that suggests that social phenomena do not have objectivity reality (Hammersley, 2003); to deny such things would be as realist a move as endorsing them (Edwards, Ashmore, & Potter, 1995). Rather, DC considers the role of "phenomena" in terms of the different descriptions, glosses, categories, and orientations offered by social actors (Potter, 2003).

This approach to constructionism was developed by the discourse-analytic tradition within the sociology of scientific knowledge (e.g., Gilbert & Mulkay, 1984) and within the broader discourse-analytic tradition that developed within social psychology (e.g., Potter & Wetherell, 1987; see Hepburn, 2003, for an overview). This chapter will draw in particular on the systematic manifesto for a discursive constructionism by Jonathan Potter (1996). The chapter offers a constructionist and inevitably constructive account of a range of work in discourse analysis, discursive psychology, ethnomethodology, and conversation analysis. The latter approaches are not always identified as constructionist; however, this chapter is working with a specific sense of constructionism and a specific reading of parts of those literatures (see Wooffitt, 2005).

Senses of Construction

Discursive constructionism works with two senses of construction. On the one hand, discourse is construct*ed* in the sense that it is assembled from a range of different resources with different degrees of structural organization. Most fundamentally, these are words and grammatical structures, but also broader elements such as categories, metaphors, idioms, rhetorical commonplaces, and interpretative repertoires. For example, how is a description manufactured in a way that presents something that has been done as orderly and unproblematic? People are extremely skilled builders of descriptions; they have spent a lifetime learning how to do it. Part of the analytic art of DC is to reveal the complex and delicate work that goes into this seemingly effortless building.

On the other hand, discourse is construc*tive* in the sense that these assemblages of words, repertoires, and so on put together and stabilize versions of the world, of actions and events, of mental life and furniture. For example, how does one party in a relationship counseling session construct a version that presents the breakdown of a long-term relationship as primarily the responsibility of the other party, who might be the one most in need of counseling and under most pressure to change (Edwards, 1995)? Crucially, then, DC is dynamic; these assemblages of symbolic resources that construct versions are organized for action rather than by some abstract principle of accurate description.

In DC, discourse is understood as *situated*. First, it is situated in the sequential environment that is basic to interaction. It follows on, and orients to, the immediately prior talk and provides the environment for what immediately follows. In the case of texts, they may be invoked as a part of some practice. The screen prompts may be voiced by the dispatcher in an emergency 911 call; some elements of a medical record may be referenced in a multiprofessional team meeting to allocate elderly care; a newspaper report may be invoked or quoted in an argument about extremism and asylum. Second, discourse is situated institutionally. It is generated within, and gives sense and structure to, practices such as news interviews, air traffic instructions, and family meals. Third, discourse is situated rhetorically. That is, constructions in talk are often built in a way that counters relevant alternatives.

Linguistic and Discursive Constructionism

Let us try further to clarify this sense of construction by contrasting it to the influential linguistic constructionism of Benjamin Whorf (1956). Famously, linguistic constructionism, incorporating the work of the linguist Sapir in the Sapir–Whorf hypothesis, stimulated a large body of psychological research. The idea was that linguistic categories constructed the *perceptual* world for language users in a speech community. Thus Inuit tribes could "see" fine distinctions between different kinds of snow as a result of the elaborate snow vocabulary that they have available that allowed them to (mentally) categorize wet snow, snow that had just fallen, snow that had frozen hard, and so on. This kind of constructionism is linguistic (as it depends on the available linguistic categories) but is also cognitivist (as the construction processes are taken to operate at the levels of perception and cognition).

Whorf worked for a firm that assessed insurance risks, and he used this as an example to illustrate linguistic constructionism. Employees of a company had described a set of drums as "empty" and therefore safe; but the drums were actually "full" of inflammable gasoline vapor. The employees' use of linguistic categories such as "empty" structured their understanding in a misleading manner; if they had used a different category—"full"—they would have understood the drums as presenting much more of a risk. In Whorf's view, language constructs the *perception* of the world.

The DC outlined in this chapter takes a different approach to the operation of categories. Stimulated by work in ethnomethodology, and particularly the writings of Harvey Sacks (1992), it considers categories not as templates for perception and information processing but as resources for action. As Derek Edwards (1991) puts it, categories are for talking (not for seeing, thinking, or reasoning). DC is not treating language as a grid or system of classification lying between a static individual perceiver

and the world; rather, language operates in social practices. That is precisely why we are writing about *discursive* rather than *linguistic* constructionism.

Returning to Whorf's gasoline drums, Edwards (1994) wonders what the employees who talked to Whorf were *doing* with their descriptions. For example, in the context of an insurance claim, the categorization "the drums were empty" might be offered as an *account*. That is, not as a direct report of a way of seeing the world but as a practical move in a particular piece of institutional interaction in which blame (Whose fault was the fire?) and practical consequences (Who is going to pay for the damage?) are paramount. The point is not that Whorf's employee respondents are not describing the world and classifying it in a way that offers a particular construction. Rather, it is that we need to understand the way the construction is oriented to the particular actions. These actions are situated in what the employees said to Whorf and in the institutional practices of insurance assessment; the description "empty" rhetorically counters the relevant alternative that they are "full" of dangerous vapor.

Discourse, Construction, and Cognition

In Peter Berger and Thomas Luckmann's (1966) original manifesto for social constructionist sociology, they offer what in more recent sociology of scientific knowledge would be glossed as a "symmetrical" stance to knowledge (Collins, 1981). That is, they were concerned with what *passes as* knowledge, regardless of its validity, from the perspective of any social group. This symmetrical stance is a key element in the discursive constructionism described here.

For example, when approaching legal discourse from a DC perspective, we are not required to know the outcome of the trial, whether witnesses were lying, or whether an acquitted defendant was actually guilty. All these practical matters are for the various actors involved to argue over using the resources at their disposal (see, e.g., Drew, 1992). Just as sociologists of science need not know physics better than physicists do in order to study physics, so DC researchers do not need to know the law, say, better than lawyers do in order to study legal discourse. The domain of study is discourse practices and the constructive work embedded in those practices. None of this is to say that (1) work on legal discourse might not have broader implications, including implications for the verdicts of trials; (2) DC researchers might not develop a sophisticated understanding of legal practices; (3) that the researchers might personally have strong opinions about, say, the outcome of specific trials or issues such as politics or gender in sentencing, as these latter things come into the courtroom in terms of categories and orientations that are appropriate objects of study. The point of methodological relativism here is to avoid research being based on a particular version of the law or a particular side in court cases, which risks turning it into a social science restatement of any current legal status quo (see Potter, 1996, Chapter 1). Berger and Luckmann (1966) had an important early grasp of the general requirement for this kind of symmetry.

However, when Berger and Luckmann consider specific cases, they do so by starting with the phenomenology of individual experience:

> The reality of everyday life is organized around the "here" of my body and the "now" of my present. This "here and now" is the focus of my attention to the reality of everyday life. What is "here and now" presented to me in everyday life is the *realissimum* of my consciousness. (1966, p. 36)

That is, they offer a variety of cognitive constructionism. Instead of studying processes of constructing in texts and talk, the building of versions, and so forth, they are working with perception and understanding.

We outline three drawbacks of cognitive versions of constructionism. First, if construction is cognitive, what is the status of what is constructed? This is the question rightly highlighted by Ian Hacking (1999). Is it a representation? Is it therefore some mental image or picture? And if it is a mental picture, how can this be the topic of constructionist research? If it enters into research through a description (in an open-ended interview, say), this process will *itself* be using the *very category system* that is central to processes of construction. Should this further constructive process be ignored? For some critical linguists who take a broadly cognitive constructionist approach, these problems are not insurmountable (van Dijk, 1998; Wodak, 2006); however, DC avoids this set of problems by taking a practical and interactional approach rather than a cognitive one (for comments on broadly cognitive constructionist approaches in social psychology and sociolinguistics, see Potter & Edwards, 1999, 2001).

A second drawback of cognitive constructionism is that it separates representations from practices. The representations become things that are constructed within actors and that are carried around by actors in the form of cognitive representations. This separation makes it harder to focus on the way the representations (constructions, versions) are built within settings to perform particular actions. For example, we can consider, as Steven Clayman and John Heritage (2002) do, how news interview questions can include a preface that is specifically designed to raise issues (perhaps a topical agenda or an action agenda) that will challenge the interviewee and help generate a revealing answer that is "good television." To study this, Clayman and Heritage considered the different elements that can go into the building of such a preface and how it works as part of a broader news interview question. This analysis does not assume that the interviewer has a mental representation of the question preface, nor that it is something transported around with him or her. DC will start with the practical and analytically available version in the question and the rich interactional evidence that comes from studying the building of the question preface *in situ*.

The third drawback of cognitive constructionism is that cognition is pervasively both the topic of talk and a resource for constructing versions. DC is ontologically indifferent to whether the versions being studied are of some historical events or of some physical or geographical objects or whether they are part of the mental thesaurus of some culture, although of course distinctions between these realms may at times be highly consequential in all kinds of ways in the texts or interactions being studied. One of the features of talk highlighted by discursive psychology is that descriptions of "the world" and of "mind" are commonly mutually implicative (Edwards, 2005). People may bolster versions of events by using cognitive constructions (good memories, direct perception, and so on) and bolster versions of their cognition (their attitude toward something or their motive for acting) by developing specific versions of how the world is.

For example, when callers to a child protection help line develop their reasons for calling, they recurrently described themselves as "concerned" or "worried" about a child (Potter & Hepburn, 2003). Such "cognitive" constructions can be understood locally as building an appropriate psychological stance on the abuse for the help line (caring, concerned, not indifferent or enjoying it) and also building a finely tuned knowledgeability. The "concern" constructs the caller as not being in a state of certainty about the abuse (in which case they should already have contacted the police or social services); rather, they speak from a position of concern that can be collaboratively unpacked with the child protection officer. The psychological matters here are inseparable from the practical and institutional business of the help line. Attitude and knowledge are developed and attended to as matters of local relevance. In DC such things are studied in terms of their construction in discourse.

Accomplishing Constructions

The disciplines that study the operation of discourse—some varieties of discourse analysis, some styles of rhetorical analysis, discursive psychology, major parts of ethnomethodology, and conversation analysis—are constructionist insofar as they consider how talk and texts are assembled and how those assemblages work to accomplish actions. However, some of this work has focused in particular on the way descriptions are built *as* objective, *as* independent of the speaker and credible (Potter, 1996; Smith, 1978; Wooffitt, 1992). This work studied the practical task of accomplishing a construction that can shrug off its own constructed status. Potter (1996) distinguishes the *action orientation* of talk and texts from their *epistemological orientation*. The former body of work is focused on action orientation (how discourse accomplishes actions), whereas the latter work is focused on epistemological orientation (how discourse is built as factual). Of course, in practice, this distinction is heuristic rather than absolute. The construction of facts is itself done actively, and the accomplishment of actions continually implicates epistemic issues (cf. Heritage & Raymond, 2005).

Given the space limitations of a single chapter, we give a single illustrative example that brings together and introduces a range of the phenomena of fact construction in a compact way. This section focuses on the epistemological orientation of talk in a description of some strange events. In his path-breaking work on fact construction, Wooffitt (1992) focused on accounts of paranormal events. One of the features of accounts of ghosts, poltergeists, UFOs, and other extraordinary events is that when they are delivered to researchers or other "nonbelievers," they are built to resist skepticism. And precisely because they have so much work to do to build a convincing description of events, they provide an exquisite natural laboratory for the study of fact construction. We have chosen the following example from our own data, as it packs in a range of features of fact construction in a relatively short extract. The extract is transcribed using Gail Jefferson's (2004) now-standard system for representing the elements of speech (emphasis, overlap, etc.) that have been found to be interactionally live. This might seem unfamiliar or confusing at first but, as we show, these features of delivery are analytically consequential.

Carrie's Story

```
 1 Interviewer: Okay, so when you're ready can you tell
 2               me about your paranormal experience
 3               in your own words.
 4               (0.4)
 5 Carrie:      Oka:y, (.) UM (.) my house has got
 6               quite (.) a lot've (0.6) em stori:es,
 7               (0.2)
 8 Carrie:      Um main one was prob'lly whe:n (.) I
 9               woke up in the morning, (0.4) a:n:d um
10               I (0.2) >sorta< looked out in the garden.
11               ((tape disruption)) (and there was) a
12               figure, (.) standi:ng (0.5) quite far (up)
13               my garden (0.2) um: in a sor've night
14               dress, (0.2) .hh a:n my instant reaction
15               was: (.) it was: my mother:, (0.2) .hh
16               um an:d I sord've >I din't look< (0.3)
17               that lon:g, (.) but I went into: my parents'
18               bedroo:m, (.) and my mum was in bed?
19               (0.2)
20 Carrie:      .hh an >so I was like< (.) that's a bit
21               weir:d, (.) but (.) it was kind of (0.3)
22               (0.4) (the reason) why >it really freaked
23               me out a lot< was cos it was like a figure
24               in a night dress:, like looking
25               up at my bedroo:m?
26               (0.2)
27 Carrie:      .hh [an::d that's quite sc]ar:y I think.
28 Interviewer:     [ °o o h : : : : : °]
29 ((29 secs omitted; story about unexpected luck with dice))
30 Carrie:      .hh A:N:D: (0.2) U:H: once me and my
31               sister were- (.) u:m in the kitchen
32               cooking, (0.3) a::nd: (0.2) u:hh (0.4)
33               we both star'ed laugh:ing because there
34               was >sor've like< (.) a really: (0.9)
35               like <really deep growly> noise?
36               (0.2)
37 Carrie:      .Hh (.) an: we were both laughing
38               and going- I >said to her y'know<
39               why di'you make that noise.
40               (.)
41 Carrie:      and she got really freaked ou:t an
42               said that (0.2) I'd made it.
43               (0.2)
44 Carrie:      .h an it's because< it came from
45               right (.) (th'other) side of our
46               fa:ces,
47               (0.2)
48 Carrie:      .hh an it was like a properly (0.7)
49               scary kin've animal growling noise,
50               (0.4) .hh umm and we got quite
51               freaked out.
52               (0.3)
53 Carrie:      U::m (0.2)
54 Int:         Ur↑::uh:.
55               (0.2)
```

There are a large number of different discourse practices that are involved in the construction of versions that can be treated as solid or independent of the speaker. For simplicity, and somewhat arbitrarily, we have divided them into three classes: category entitlement and interest management, the discursive psychology of mind–world relationships, and practices of narration.

Category Entitlement and Interest Management

One of the things that Sacks emphasized in his early work on conversation was the relationship of categories to particular kinds of speaker entitlements (Sacks, 1992). For example, it is the *witness* to a horrific auto accident who has the right to the bad experience (to feel awful, have his or her day ruined). Categories can be normatively tied to a range of different psychological states and characteristics, including knowledge. In some cases this is explicit and institutionally warranted—doctors know about medicine through training, exams, and practice. Other categories are much more permeable and occasioned, with their memberships open to being rhetorically and interactionally built up, undermined, or discounted in a range of ways. For example, the categories "witness" and "ordinary person" do not require a uniform, a membership certificate, or other official and public category ratification. However, they are associated with particular kinds of knowledgeability.

On the one hand, categories can often entitle speakers to knowledge; on the other, interests can undermine or discount that entitlement. The notion of interests (and related notions such as stake) can be used to suggest that a speaker (in his or her individual or institutional capacity) has something to gain or lose; he or she has a *stake* in a course of action that the description relates to. Indeed, descriptions can be pervasively heard against a backdrop of potential competences, projects, motives, and allegiances. They can be understood as the product of prejudice or stupidity or a huge variety of other things that can undercut or reinterpret claims. Speakers pervasively attend to the potential for their talk being treated as interested, particularly (but not exclusively) in situations of conflict or dispute. At times interests that are counter to what might be expected in making a claim may be invoked ("stake inoculation"; see Potter, 1996).

We illustrate these features of the work of construction with examples from Carrie's account preceding. First, note how in line 6 Carrie does not restate (either in the same words or new but equivalent words) the interviewer's description "paranormal experience." The formulation Carrie uses is the much less epistemically committed "stories." Moreover, these stories are tied to the house rather than to the speaker. At the outset of the account, then, the speaker avoids explicit references that presuppose the reality of, or belief in, the paranormal event. Wooffitt (1992) found this kind of "oblique reference" to be a recurrent feature of the openings of paranormal accounts.

In a similar way, in line 14, Carrie describes her *first* reaction to the figure in the garden as that it was her mother. That is, she presents her first reaction as a mundane or ordinary one, the kind of reaction that *anyone* might have. Note also that it is presented as "instant"—something that came naturally rather something that is thought through. In terms of categories and interests, we can see

these kinds of descriptive practices as presenting the speaker as acting from a category of "mundane persons" and not from the sort of category (sci-fi nut? mystic?) that might have an interest in the reality of paranormal events (cf. Sacks, 1984). One of the features of these descriptive practices is that they are inexplicit; neither the categories nor the interests are spelled out in a way that might draw attention to them or open them to being easily countered.

Other details of the account work in the same way. Note how Carrie and her sister are described as cooking in the kitchen—the sort of mundane activity that ordinary people engage in. And, rhetorically and relevantly, they are *not* described as talking about ghosts and apparitions or their fascination with the occult. Then, when the noise happens, Carrie describes their first reaction as laughter. That is, their reaction is to something they immediately see as ordinary rather than strange or frightening. More generally, these descriptive practices illustrate the important and subtle attention that can be paid to category entitlement and interest management in factual accounts.

The Discursive Psychology of Mind–World Relationships

One of the features of the way talk and texts operate that has been highlighted in discursive psychology is that there are complex reflexive relationships between descriptions of the world and descriptions of mental states (Edwards, 2005). As speakers provide reports of events that attend to issues of causality, action, and accountability in those events, so, simultaneously, are they inevitably displaying or managing their own accountability in the provision of the report. This means that constructions of mind and constructions of reality operate together as parts of practices.

When we write about *constructions*, this term can suggest something simple, such as a picture or vignette of some kind. However, one of the features that CA work in particular has emphasized is the importance of considering not merely reports of mental states and furniture but *displays* of those things. Thus understanding, stance, and confusion become things that are displayed through talk in a variety of ways, and in doing so they make available inferences about actions, events, structures, and so on. The structuring here can be complex. For example, Edwards (2000) developed Anita Pomerantz's (1986) work on extreme case formulations (ECFs), which are constructions of events that use extreme expressions such as *always, brand new, as good as it gets, perfectly,* and so on. Edwards shows how such formulations can be ways of doing "nonliteral" (not accountably accurate) but also can be used to display some speaker investment in, or stance toward, what is described. For example, an ECF can be used to display a committed or caring stance toward what is described.

The materials in Carrie's story are a narrative account of events rather than elements in an action such as an invitation. Nevertheless, we can consider the role of the mutual implications of reality and psychology as developed in the account. Note, for example, the mental state construction "freaked out" in line 22. "Freaked out" is an idiomatic and somewhat extreme construction of the speaker's mental state; as such it implicates some feature of the world that is responsible for the "freaking out" and provides at least an outline construction of some of its features—it is capable of invoking a state of being freaked out. The point here is simple but fundamental: The psychological construction works to build the reality.

There are two more things to note about this that have broader relevance to studying construction in action. First, note that Carrie's (retrospective) construction of her mental state as "freaked out" does not just work to build the reality of the strange or paranormal object. It also simultaneously constructs her as someone who is freaked out by weird or strange events. That is, her response is a normal or mundane one; it simultaneously constructs the object as having that effect and her identity as someone who is a member of the appropriate category to give credible or perhaps disinterested accounts of paranormal events.

Second, note the interactional organization here. All of this work with categories, interest management, and displays of inferentially rich mental states unfolds interactionally. Although what Carrie produces is a story (or perhaps a series of stories) on a topic, it does not exist as an abstract text set against the interaction. It is elicited by a very specific question, and it is recipient designed throughout. Although a Bakhtinian perspective might tune us into the dialogic nature of even written texts such as novels, the CA understanding of recipient design combined with the attention it focuses on recipiency is particularly revealing.

Thus we can note that the first part of the story comes to a potential completion at the point at which Carrie describes finding her mother in bed (line 18). It is at this point that the instant, mundane explanation of the figure in the garden is revealed as wrong (to Carrie in the story narration and to the interviewer in "story time"). This completion is underscored by the questioning intonation on the term *bed* that indicates that some response is appropriate. However, what we see at this transition-relevant place is a brief but significant silence. The 0.2 seconds on line 19 is enough to cue Carrie that no response from the interviewer is forthcoming, and indeed she continues after a brief inbreath. What Carrie does is continue spelling out the upshot of the mother being in bed, which the interviewer failed to do (maybe because he or she has been inattentive or because he or she is following the interview guidelines to interact only minimally). It is "weird" (another psychologically inferential category), and then Carrie upgrades her reaction to "freaked out." However, even after this, the interviewer fails to come in at a new appropriate position for a response (line 26), and Carrie spells out the upshot one further time: "that's quite scary."

It is only at this point, and in overlap, that the interviewer produces an extended and expressive news receipt (cf. Heritage, 1984). The extreme extension of the news receipt may mark the lateness of the recognition of what is precisely newsworthy here, and the quietness is a way of providing emphasis that is perhaps appropriate for the ghost story genre. (Something similar happens in lines 52–54 when the interviewer responds late but again does an exaggerated and expressive news receipt.) As before, we see that the psychological display in the news receipt is a reflexive marker of the nature of the object of the story and shows the way it is here being jointly constituted. More generally, note the way DC analysis is here enriched by the extra interactional information provided by the Jeffersonian transcription.

Practices of Narration

When speakers assemble narrative descriptions of actions and events, they can draw on a wide range of resources to construct and manage the factuality of what is described. For example, the apparatus of footing that Goffman (1981) delineated is available for marking the positions and views of a set of narrative characters in consequentially different ways (e.g., as origin of a view or relayer of another's view). Wooffitt (1992) found in his study of paranormal accounts that "active voicing" of the words and even thoughts of the characters in the story was a common and important element in the construction of factuality. For example, corroboration can be produced by actively voicing different characters into agreement over some state of affairs, and using specific reported speech (often with vivid prosodic marking) to suggest that the speaker actually witnessed some event.

Edwards and Potter (1992) highlight the role of linguistic detail in the construction of narrative in both producing particular kinds of actions (such as criticisms or accounts) and providing a sense of being present as a witness. A description that is detailed and vivid, perhaps offering descriptions from a place or point of view (as might be seen by a single observer), can work through category entitlement. The category witness is one of the most powerful in factual accounting, and vivid detail is one way of showing membership in such a category.

In effect, narratives of this kind are protoforms of the novelist's art, in which plot, character, and motivation can be controlled. As with novels, the author is massively powerful, with control over the descriptive language used, where the narrative starts and finishes, and what is included and what is omitted (as understood from a competing narrative). In DC one of the features of narratives is that they are seen, as other discourse practices, as embedded in particular settings and having a particular interactional order. Conversation analysts have highlighted a range of structural properties of narrative (Schegloff, 1997a), whereas discursive psychologists have emphasized their rhetorical organization (Edwards, 1997).

Such an approach to narrative starts with stories or narratives told in settings, such as family telephone calls, relationship counseling sessions, or political controversies, rather than seeing narratives as something abstract that can be elicited as a complete and decontextualized entity such as a life story (e.g., Wortham, 2001). This approach contrasts with some other constructionist and postmodernist positions that tend to characterize narrative in terms of ideal templates that package descriptions of events (e.g., Gergen, 1999) and are even part of the "deep structure" of understanding (White, 1978). As Stokoe and Edwards (2006) show, DC resists these protocognitivist moves (important though the work is in other ways) in favor of considering narratives as situated practices and purveyors of action.

The stories offered by Carrie in the previous example can illustrate some of these issues. Note first the description in lines 11–14:

(and there was) a <u>figure</u>, (.) standi:ng (0.5) <u>quite</u> far (up) my garden (0.2) um: in a sor've <u>night</u> dress,

This is a description of a scene including vivid detail ("quite far up," "night dress"). It is a description offered from an observer's point of view (note that "quite far up" is a description given in relation to the observer). It is the kind of description, then, that works to entitle the speaker to the category of witness. The same is true of the description of the noise in the second story as a "really deep growly noise"—it is not a gloss or typification but offers a sense of the noise as it sounded.

A further element in Carrie's second story is the use of "active voicing." In lines 38 and 39 Carrie reports: "I >said to her y'know< <u>why</u> di'you make that <u>noise</u>." Here the actively voiced question neatly constructs Carrie's first mundane inference. Rather than being an inference about something paranormal, it is simply that her sister had made the noise. There is a lovely detail here. Carrie inserts "y'know" into this utterance just before the actively voiced question. It is easy to overlook such elements of talk or treat them as irrelevant clutter. However, as Edwards (1997) and others have shown, they can be a consequential part of the achievement and management of shared knowledge. In this case, the "y'know" constructs the question as just what anyone might understandably be expected to ask; Carrie would know what she was doing in asking such a question. Again, this works to establish her category membership as an ordinary person.

The final thing to note is the construction of the sister's response to the growly noise: "we <u>both</u> star'ed <u>laugh</u>:ing." This pulls together a number of features of fact construction. Laughing operates to provide a world–psychology inference—it presents a stance on the sound that has the first understanding as not a paranormal one. However, the description has this as a shared immediate response, and therefore has it as both consensual and corroborated. Then the reaction a few lines later is also presented as consensual—"we got quite freaked out" (note the "we")—and therefore the speaker uses her own construction of other's actions to corroborate her account. Again, this is the power of narrative of this kind—the author controls the content.

The general point of this discussion has been to show the way in which construction can be considered as an accomplishment of speakers and writers. Given that it has such a status, then one of the analytic tasks of DC is to document the procedures through which versions are solidified as factual, objective, and independent of the speaker or writer. We have illustrated some of the key procedures here, but this an area of research that needs much more development.

Mundane Epistemics

One area that is and should continue to be a major focus of work is what might be called *mundane epistemics*. This is the study of knowledge and understanding as things that are practical and interactional. Emanuel Schegloff (1991) picked up from Harold Garfinkel's (1967) observation that shared knowledge can be treated as something procedural. This transformed the traditional cognitive question of mental equivalence into a *practical* question of how particular members' methods might be used to confirm (or deny) that knowledge is "held in common." Drawing on CA findings, Schegloff notes that understanding is something that is socially organized and something that is consequentially different in different places in conversation.

Take invitations, for example. One crucial point at which understanding is socially live is in the turn that follows an invitation (in CA, the second turn). This is a place at which a range of confusions can be attended to if need be. The turn that follows is also crucial, because the second turn may reveal an understanding that the recipient finds problematic and that he or she can therefore fix in the third turn. In fact, Schegloff (1992) suggests that third turns are the last structurally provided-for place for sustaining shared understanding. He emphasizes the dangers (for relationships and individuals) that can arise from letting failures of understanding go by:

> When a source of misunderstanding escapes the multiple repair space, a whole institutional superstructure that is sustained through talk-in-interaction can be compromised. And since virtually anything in the talk can be such a source of misunderstanding, the potential for trouble for that institutional superstructure can be vast. It is against those systematic potentials for subversion of social order that repair after next turn is the last structurally provided defence. (1992, p. 1337)

In this world of mundane epistemics, common understanding is a procedural problem that is both an *analytic topic* for DC researchers and a *practical issue* for participants. Understanding is not something floating in a phenomenological space but something structurally located, with differential possibilities for checking and modifying. There is no independent check on understanding outside of such procedures.

Edwards (1999) further reworks the cognitivist notion of shared knowledge. He notes that the traditional idea of shared knowledge implies agreement in mental representations of some kind. However, if agreement is *procedural* rather than *abstract*, then it is something to be done, displayed, invoked, or denied. Instead of being achieved through a mental calculus, it is situated and defeasible; that is, it is open to reformulation and denial. This reworking of agreement supplements Schegloff's reworking of understanding. Edwards additionally notes that the knowledge that is considered to be shared is, in the practical situations of life, inseparable from descriptions. And as the central programmatic of discursive

psychology has shown (picking up from Wittgenstein, sociology of scientific knowledge, and poststructural philosophy), descriptions have their home as active elements of practices. The general point here is that when we consider carefully the idea of shared or agreed knowledge in practice (i.e., from the point of view of the participants in an actual situation), issues of structure, procedure, and description come to the fore. In contrast, the cognitivist notion of knowledge is sustained by the world of theory or in the procedures of cognitive science, in which its status is achieved definitionally (Edwards & Potter, 1992).

To take one final example of mundane epistemics, Heritage and Raymond (2005) studied the display of knowledge entitlement and authority. Heritage has shown over a series of studies the way the particle *oh* can suggest a "change of state." For example, in question–answer sequences, the questioner's "*oh*-receipt" can mark a change of state and ratify the answer as news; such receipts are absent in classroom or news interview contexts in which the questioner is not projecting him- or herself as uninformed on a topic (see Heritage, 2005). *Oh*-receipts are bound up with epistemic issues of who knows something and who does not, and they serve as an ongoing interactional marking of such matters. Note again that such analyses do not make the same assumptions as cognitive psychological work on knowledge, as the practices here are public, practical, and conversational and their sufficiency is for those things.

Heritage and Raymond (2005) build on this work and explore the relationship between *oh*-receipts and knowledge entitlement. They suggest that *oh*-receipts can be used to build epistemic authority with respect to another speaker. Take the following (p. 17):

```
Eve:  No I haven't seen it Jo saw it 'n she said
         she f- depressed her ter[ribly
Jon:                              [Oh it's [terribly depressing.
Lyn:                              [Oh it's depressing.
```

Heritage and Raymond (2005) note that Jon and Lyn, who have seen the film that is under discussion, do agree, but they *oh-*preface it. By doing this they suggest that they have independent access to the film and, therefore, that they have epistemic priority relative to Eve. Contrast the interviewer's news receipts in lines 28 and 54 in the paranormal account, which defer epistemic authority to Carrie. Heritage and Raymond suggest that conversation is suffused with indirect claims to authority of this kind, in which whose version is correct and who has the appropriate epistemic entitlement is acted out through different practices.

Constructionism without Limits

In this final main section we consider some of what have often been treated as the limits of CA. We press the case for DC as a thoroughgoing constructionism that does not exempt certain areas from study for one reason or another. This section thus lays out some of the arguments that DC has provoked, as well as indicating some of the areas of analytic development. We discuss the issue of limits in three parts. The first focuses on basic arguments against thoroughgoing constructionism and particularly what have been called "death and furniture" arguments. The second focuses on issues of social structure, history, and context. The third explores some of the analytic frontiers of DC in respect to embodiment, emotion, and perception.

Furniture and Death

There have been long-standing debates between the different varieties of constructionism and different forms of realism. These debates are occasioned and local, with different forms of constructionism (relativism, social constructivism, discourse analysis, and so on) pitted against different forms of realism (e.g., realism, critical realism, Marx-

ist materialism, experimental psychology). Such debates pick up from long-standing philosophical disputes. Although this is a picture with utility that has been much used, it is important to recognize the reflexive relationship between the picture and the argument(s) painted within it. From a DC perspective, the "constructionism–realism" debate is a literary construction. Indeed, the DC perspective *itself* is a literary creation, put together for this book, and inevitably (and usefully) systematizing and simplifying. This is consistent with its epistemic assumptions. And, for all that, DC is no *less* real, as sociology of scientific knowledge has shown us that such processes are generic, not just in the social and human "soft" sciences but across physics, astronomy, and even mathematics (see Ashmore, Myers, & Potter, 2002).

One of the moves in this debate between realism and constructionism (relativism, antifoundationalism) has been to offer "bottom line" arguments that propose some bedrock of reality that places limits on what is constructed:

> When relativists start talking about the social construction of reality, truth, cognition, scientific knowledge, technical capacity, social structure and so on their realist opponents sooner or later start hitting the furniture, invoking the Holocaust, talking about rocks, guns, killing, human misery, tables and chairs. (Edwards, Ashmore, & Potter, 1995, p. 26)

In their influential "Death and Furniture" article, Edwards, Ashmore, and Potter (1995) observe that there are two related argumentative tropes—the "furniture" trope (which makes reference to tables, rocks, etc., as the reality that *cannot* be denied) and the "death" trope (which invokes misery, genocide, poverty, etc., as the reality that *should* not be denied). The article approached these moves in a manner consistent with its constructionist, relativist perspective. That is, rather than attempt a direct rebuttal (that would risk getting caught up in the polarities and realist tropes of the moves), it focused on their rhetoric, exposing the way they were constructed to have their effect. Furthermore, the literary form of Edwards and colleague's article was designed to draw attention to its own rhetoric in the process of its explication, conveying its argument as much in its literary form as its propositional content (and, of course, making it resist the kind of summary that sits easily in a *Handbook* chapter).

Edwards and colleagues (1995) uncovered the reflexive nature of authoring in the "furniture and death" tropes that carried the arguments. That is, it showed the way these emblematic arguments were literary constructions assembled in a way that precisely obscures their literary basis. The article highlights the realist's dilemma. The very act of constructing a piece of the external world (a rock, a table) that is nonrepresented, external, "just there," is inevitably a construction, a representation in talk and text, or the semiotics of table thumping, and as such it threatens immediately to turn against the very position it is designed to support. The point to highlight here is how the discursive and epistemic basis of DC leads it to focus on the constructive work of the different arguments invoked.

Social Structure and Context

There are various approaches to issues traditionally glossed as social structure or history or context that formulate them as objects that transcend constructionist analysis. Indeed, some approaches formulate the key problem in social analysis as the joining of constructionist arenas to "the real" by way of a complex set of argumentative and epistemic bolts—compare, for example, Fairclough (1995) and Burr (1999). DC offers a number of ways of treating social structure and context as part of a coherent constructionist universe, rather than having them as separate realms with contrasting epistemologies. We briefly consider three

strands of argument: one that treats context as a member's concern, one that treats social structure as ongoing accomplishment, and one that explores the way social structure is formulated and constructed in accounts.

The issue of context has elicited wide-ranging debate. One traditional social science approach, sometimes glossed as positivist or realist, attempts to understand the context of discourse through historical, theoretical, statistical, or ethnographic means. These means are then used to provide supposedly "broader" or more "macro" analyses of the discourse. In contrast, Schegloff (1997b) presses the virtues of studying context through participants' own orientations. He notes that in any interaction there are a wide variety of possible relevant contextual particulars and that the crucial issue is which contextual particulars the participants *themselves* treat as relevant. It is not just that social scientists find people, according to Schegloff, "to be characterizable as 'president/assistant,' 'chicano/black,' as 'professor/student,' etc. But that for them, at that moment, those are terms relevant for producing and interpreting conduct in the interaction" (1992, p. 109). Furthermore, even when some contextual particular, structure, or description has been shown to be *relevant*, there is still an issue of how far it is *consequential* for the unfolding of the ongoing interaction. For example, if a particular style of questioning is found to be central to classroom teaching, there is still a further analytic challenge to show how this style of questioning is institutionally produced rather than being a style common elsewhere and simply drawn on in classroom practice.

These are challenging issues for researchers, and they have provoked considerable controversy (for responses, see Billig, 1999; Schegloff, 1998, 1999; Stokoe & Smithson, 2001; Wetherell, 1998). Schegloff has not presented these arguments as part of a constructionist problematic. Nevertheless, from DC they have a constructionist nucleus because they give primacy to the situated categorizations and displayed understandings of the participants and rigorously avoid the production of a privileged "offstage" story that situates and reframes the participants' discourse (see Stokoe, in press).

A second approach considers how social structure is an ongoing accomplishment of different parties. Rather than treating action in a setting as contextually determined by the institutional context—school, law court, therapeutic session—this approach considers the way different parties collaboratively and actively produce the relevant structures. These structures are normative and inferential; they do not determine what goes on in, say, a medical consultation, but they do provide the coherence of that interaction. There is a now a mature and large-scale research program of this kind, and many of the arguments and issues are familiar, so we do not spend a great deal of time discussing it. The classic treatments are available in Drew and Heritage (1992); methodological issues in studying institutional interaction are discussed in Heritage (2005); and, for an extended research illustration, see Clayman and Heritage (2002) on the news interview.

The third and final research approach here is rather different, although complementary. It considers the ways in which social structures of various kinds are constructed in and through talk and what those constructions are used to do. Studies of this kind have covered a range of topics that invoke constructions of social structure and organization, including racism (e.g., Hopkins & Kahani-Hopkins, 2006), nationalism (e.g., Condor, Figgou, Abell, Gibson, & Stevenson, 2006), and family (Gubrium & Holstein, 2005).

For example, Billig (1992) studied talk about the British royal family. He aimed to show how people drew on, reproduced, and reconstructed notions of privilege, equality, the nation state, and morality as they argued about the role of the royal family in the life of Great Britain. In particular, Billig high-

lighted a weave of contradictory and dilemmatic notions that were drawn on to obscure inequalities and legitimate current social arrangements. For Billig, the participants are engaged in conversational "acts of settlement": "common-sense talk about royalty settles ordinary people down into their place within the imagined national community" (1992, p. 23).

Billig (1992) suggests that common sense is fragmented in a way such that trouble and conflict are rhetorically settled and the political status quo is thereby perpetuated (see Billig et al., 1988). It provides one illustration of the way that social organization and structure can be studied as a flexible set of constructions that are drawn on as parts of broader practices of social legitimation (see also Wetherell & Potter, 1992). In terms of our interest in systematic discursive constructionism, we see in examples such as this a version of analysis that does not take a privileged analyst's version of social structure and use it to situate participants' accounts. Instead, the focus is on how participants themselves invoke, describe, and reconstruct social structure in the course of their practices.

Embodiment, Emotion, and Perception

Critics of constructionism from various perspectives have often picked up various "psychological" domains as limits or at least challenges to constructionist analysis (see, e.g., Burr, 1999). The body, perception, and emotion are three central examples. In this final section we indicate the sorts of ways in which these domains can be addressed in DC.

One DC way to address embodiment is deceptively simple, and that is to use video materials to analyze what is going on in a way that includes its "embodied" and "physically situated" nature. In itself, of course, this is not a distinctively DC approach to research. Indeed, the use of video might seem to suggest a vision of simple empiricism. However, video materials are analyzed in DC ways that keep the participants' own orientations to what is going on at the fore (Heath, 2005). Gaze and gesture, for example, are not studied for what the *analyst* can see going on but for how they are coordinated with and contribute to the ongoing interaction for the participants in that interaction. This approach contrasts with both traditional studies of nonverbal behavior that tend to see gesture in terms of information leakage that a skilled analyst can detect behind the backs of the participants and traditional sociological analyses of the visual that tend to interpret gesture and other visual elements according to theories from cultural studies and semiotics. With respect to DC, the visual (gesture, physical settings, etc.) are not the *limits* on what is constructed; instead, they are precisely and centrally part of the constructed world of ongoing interaction.

Another DC approach to embodiment is to consider bodily orientations in talk of a range of kinds. This could involve constructions of bodies and embodiment (accounts, descriptions, formulations) rather in the manner of DC studies of "social structure" and other objects of this kind. Or it could involve meaningful bodily displays of various kinds. For example, Wiggins (2002) studied expressions of "gustatory pleasure" and, in particular, the sorts of *mmm*s that people make when eating. She showed the way the *mmm*s are produced to deliver expressions of pleasure as spontaneous and immediate but are also socially organized and communicative (coordinated between speakers and helping to form actions such as compliments on food). They can be treated as "sensation receipts," presenting the body as itself seeming to inform the assessment. Again, instead of the body offering a solid boundary to constructionist analysis, it becomes something invoked, displayed, and enacted in a manner that is susceptible to DC analysis.

Emotion is similarly treated overwhelmingly in the social sciences as something emerging from the body, as something close to nature and rather distant from culture.

There is a relatively small literature on the social construction of emotion (see Harré, 1986, and Loseke & Kusenbach, Chapter 26, this volume). DC research has started to explore this area of work. For example, Buttny (1993) considers some of the ways that emotion categories can be part of the formation of actions such as blamings and apologies. Edwards (1997) considered the way in which emotion descriptions operate in relationship counseling talk. Through a detailed examination of the different moves of the parties to the counseling, Edwards shows that notions such as "anger" and "upset" can be used as parts of accounts that work to construct actions as reactions. This DC approach to emotion both brings it into analysis—rather than having emotion be a boundary or limit—and also highlights a realm of central human business virtually bypassed by traditional cognitive and cross-cultural models of emotion.

Edwards (1997) and Buttny (1993) concentrate in particular on the use of emotion descriptions and categories. Other work has considered emotion in terms of display. For example, Heath (2002) considered the use of gesture in medical consultation as patients displayed pain and suffering, and Hepburn (2004) focused on crying and the social, communicative, and interactional organization of upset.

A final domain that is sometimes seen as troubling for constructionist analysis is perception. Indeed, perception and its associated tropes are historically and tropically bound up with empiricism and other foundational epistemic systems (Rorty, 1980). Although perception has been undercut by a range of philosophical critiques, from Quine through Hanson, Popper, and Wittgenstein, that highlight its conventional or theory-laden nature (see Chalmers, 1992, for a useful review), the approach from DC has been to consider practices of seeing as topics for analysis.

Some of the most powerful research in this tradition was conducted by Goodwin and Goodwin (1996). They have conducted a rigorous series of studies of looking, seeing, and perception in the context of a range of professional settings. For example, they researched the way air traffic controllers "see" planes as part of getting their work done. This work shows that perception is neither simple nor a purely mental phenomenon sitting behind cognition and causing interaction. Perception is profoundly socially organized and can be an important and consequential area for constructionist study.

In this final section we have considered the way a range of conventional limits to constructionist analysis—furniture and objects, death, social structure, context, the body, emotion, and perception—can become major topics of DC study. Put another way, we have noted the way that these phenomena can come within the purview of constructionism rather than being rogue objects that require their own special analytic methods (phenomenology, Marxism, etc.).

DC has been a literary construction of this chapter, but it is reflexively and epistemically at peace with that status. As Davies (1998), Hepburn (2000), and Smith (1988), among others, have shown, this reflexive construction is not a requirement to accept that "anything goes" (that strange realist construction) nor that constructionists must work without any personal commitment to social critique, feminism, or visions of transformation. This is not to say that DC is a coherent and sealed system; there are a range of creative tensions between, for example, the more conversation analytic and more discourse analytic moments or between more epistemic focused and more ontologically focused versions of constructionism. Such tensions provide one of the motors for future development.

• Acknowledgments

We would like to thank Derek Edwards, Elizabeth Stokoe, and the editors of this volume for thoughtful comments on an earlier draft.

• References

Ashmore, M. (1989). *The reflexive thesis: Wrighting sociology of scientific knowledge*. Chicago: University of Chicago Press.

Ashmore, M., Myers, G., & Potter, J. (2002). Discourse, rhetoric and reflexivity: Seven days in the library. In S. Jasanoff, G. Markle, T. Pinch, & J. Petersen (Eds.), *Handbook of science, technology and society* (Rev. ed., pp. 321–342). London: Sage.

Berger, P. L., & Luckmann, T. (1966). *The social construction of reality*. Garden City, NY: Doubleday.

Billig, M. (1992). *Talking of the royal family*. London: Routledge.

Billig, M. (1999). Whose terms? Whose ordinariness?: Rhetoric and ideology in conversation analysis. *Discourse and Society, 10*, 543–558.

Billig, M., Condor, S., Edwards, D., Gane, M., Middleton, D., & Radley, A. R. (1988). *Ideological dilemmas*. London: Sage.

Burr, V. (1999). The extra-discursive in social constructionism. In D. Nightingale & J. Cromby (Eds.), *Social constructionist psychology: A critical analysis of theory and practice* (pp. 113–126). Buckingham, UK: Open University Press.

Buttny, R. (1993). *Social accountability in communication*. London: Sage.

Chalmers, A. (1992). *What is this thing called science?: An assessment of the nature and status of science and its methods* (2nd ed.). Milton Keynes, UK: Open University Press.

Clayman, S., & Heritage, J. C. (2002). *The news interview: Journalists and public figures on the air*. Cambridge, UK: Cambridge University Press.

Clift, R. (2006). Indexing stance: Reported speech as an interactional event. *Journal of Sociolinguistics, 10*, 569–595.

Collins, H. M. (1981). What is TRASP?: The radical programme as a methodological imperative. *Philosophy of the Social Sciences, 11*, 215–124.

Condor, S., Figgou, L., Abell, J., Gibson, S., & Stevenson, C. (2006). "They're not racist": Prejudice mitigation and suppression in dialogue. *British Journal of Social Psychology, 45*, 441–462.

Davies, B. (1998). Psychology's subject: A commentary on the relativism/realism debate. In I. Parker (Ed.), *Social constructionism, discourse and realism* (pp. 133–46). London: Sage.

Drew, P. (1992). Contested evidence in courtroom cross-examination: The case of a trial for rape. In P. Drew & J. Heritage (Eds.), *Talk at work: Interaction in institutional settings* (pp. 470–520). Cambridge, UK: Cambridge University Press.

Drew, P., & Heritage, J. C. (1992). Analyzing talk at work: An introduction. In P. Drew & J. Heritage (Eds.), *Talk at work: Interaction in institutional settings* (pp. 3–65). Cambridge, UK: Cambridge University Press.

Edwards, D. (1991). Categories are for talking: On the cognitive and discursive bases of categorization. *Theory and Psychology, 1*(4), 515–542.

Edwards, D. (1994). Whorf's empty gasoline drum and the Pope's missing wife. *Journal of Pragmatics, 22,* 215–218.

Edwards, D. (1995). Two to tango: Script formulations, dispositions, and rhetorical symmetry in relationship troubles talk. *Research on Language and Social Interaction, 28*(4), 319–350.

Edwards, D. (1997). *Discourse and cognition.* London: Sage.

Edwards, D. (1999). Shared knowledge as a performative and rhetorical category. In J. Verschueren (Ed.), *Pragmatics in 1998: Selected papers from the 6th International Pragmatics Conference* (Vol. 2, pp. 130–141). Antwerp, Belgium: International Pragmatics Association.

Edwards, D. (2000). Extreme case formulations: Softeners, investments and doing nonliteral. *Research on Language and Social Interaction, 33,* 347–373.

Edwards, D. (2005). Discursive psychology. In K. L. Fitch & R. E. Sanders (Eds.), *Handbook of language and social interaction* (pp. 257–273). Hillsdale, NJ: Erlbaum.

Edwards, D., Ashmore, M., & Potter, J. (1995). Death and furniture: The rhetoric, politics and theology of bottom-line arguments against relativism. *History of the Human Sciences, 8*(2), 25–49.

Edwards, D., & Potter, J. (1992). *Discursive psychology.* London: Sage.

Fairclough, N. (1995). *Critical discourse analysis.* London: Longman.

Foucault, M. (1979). *Discipline and punish.* Harmondsworth, UK: Penguin.

Garfinkel, H. (1967). *Studies in ethnomethodology.* Englewood Cliffs, NJ: Prentice Hall.

Gergen, K. J. (1999). *An invitation to social construction.* London: Sage.

Gilbert, G. N., & Mulkay, M. (1984). *Opening Pandora's box: A sociological analysis of scientists' discourse.* Cambridge, UK: Cambridge University Press.

Goffman, E. (1981). *Forms of talk.* Oxford, UK: Basil Blackwell.

Goodwin, C., & Goodwin, M. H. (1996). Seeing as situated activity: Formulating planes. In Y. Engeström & D. Middleton (Eds.), *Cognition and communication at work* (pp. 61–95). Cambridge, UK: Cambridge University Press.

Gubrium, J. F., & Holstein, J. A. (Eds.). (2005). *Couples, kids, and family life.* Oxford, UK: Oxford University Press.

Hacking, I. (1999). *The social construction of what?* Cambridge, UK: Harvard University Press.

Hammersley, M. (2003). Conversation analysis and discourse analysis: Methods or paradigms. *Discourse and Society, 14*(6), 751–781.

Harré, R. (Ed.). (1986). *The social construction of emotions.* Oxford, UK: Blackwell.

Heath, C. (2002). Demonstrative suffering: The gestural (re)embodiment of symptoms, *Journal of Communication, 52,* 597–617.

Heath, C. (2005). Analysing face-to-face interaction: Video, the visual and the material. In D. Silverman (Ed.), *Qualitative research: Theory, method and practice* (pp. 266–282). London: Sage.

Hepburn, A. (2000). On the alleged incompatibility between feminism and relativism, *Feminism and Psychology, 10*(1), 91–106.

Hepburn, A. (2003). *An introduction to critical social psychology.* London: Sage.

Hepburn, A. (2004). Crying: Notes on description, transcription and interaction. *Research on Language and Social Interaction, 37,* 251–290.

Heritage, J. (1984). A change-of-state token and aspects of its sequential placement. In J. M. Atkinson & J. Heritage (Ed.), *Structures of social action* (pp. 299–345). Cambridge, UK: Cambridge University Press.

Heritage, J. (2005). Conversation analysis and institutional talk. In K. Fitch & R. Sanders (Eds.), *Handbook of language and social interaction* (pp. 103–147). Mahwah, NJ: Erlbaum.

Heritage, J., & Raymond, G. (2005). The terms of agreement: Indexing epistemic authority and subordination in assessment sequences. *Social Psychology Quarterly, 68,* 15–38.

Hopkins, N., & Kahani-Hopkins, V. (2006). Minority group members' theories of intergroup contact: A case study of British Muslims' conceptualizations of "Islamophobia" and social change. *British Journal of Social Psychology, 45,* 245–264.

Jefferson, G. (2004). Glossary of transcript symbols with an introduction. In G. H. Lerner (Ed.), *Conversation analysis: Studies from the first generation* (pp. 13–31). Amsterdam: Benjamins.

Pomerantz, A. M. (1986). Extreme case formulations: A new way of legitimating claims. *Human Studies, 9,* 219–30.

Potter, J. (1996). *Representing reality: Discourse, rhetoric and social construction.* London: Sage.

Potter, J. (2003). Discursive psychology: Between method and paradigm. *Discourse and Society, 14,* 783–794.

Potter, J., & Edwards, D. (1999). Social representations and discursive psychology. *Culture and Psychology, 5,* 445–456.

Potter, J., & Edwards, D. (2001). Sociolinguistics, cognitivism and discursive psychology. In N. Coupland, S. Sarangi, & C. Candlin (Eds.), *Sociolinguistics and social theory* (pp. 88–103). London: Longman.

Potter, J., & Hepburn, A. (2003). I'm a bit concerned: Early actions and psychological constructions in a child protection helpline. *Research on Language and Social Interaction, 36,* 197–240.

Potter, J., & Hepburn, A. (2005). Qualitative interviews in psychology: Problems and possibilities. *Qualitative Research in Psychology, 2,* 281–307.

Potter, J., & te Molder, H. (2005). Talking cognition: Mapping and making the terrain. In H. te Molder & J. Potter (Eds.), *Conversation and cognition* (pp. 1–54). Cambridge, UK: Cambridge University Press.

Potter, J., & Wetherell, M. (1987). *Discourse and social psychology: Beyond attitudes and behaviour.* London: Sage.

Rorty, R. (1980). *Philosophy and the mirror of nature.* Princeton, NJ: Princeton University Press.

Sacks, H. (1984). On doing "being ordinary." In J. M. Atkinson & J. Heritage (Eds.), *Structures of social action: Studies in conversation analysis* (pp. 413–429). Cambridge, UK: Cambridge University Press.

Sacks, H. (1992). *Lectures on conversation* (Vols. I–II, G. Jefferson, Ed.). Oxford, UK: Blackwell.

Schegloff, E. A. (1991). Conversation analysis and socially shared cognition. In L. Resnick, J. Levine, & S. Teasley (Ed.), *Perspectives on socially shared cognition* (pp. 150–171). Washington, DC: American Psychological Association.

Schegloff, E. A. (1992). Repair after next turn: The last structurally provided defence of intersubjectivity in conversation. *American Journal of Sociology, 98,* 1295–1345.

Schegloff, E. A. (1997a). "Narrative analysis" thirty years later. *Journal of Narrative and Life History, 7,* 97–106.

Schegloff, E. A. (1997b). Whose text? Whose context? *Discourse and Society, 8,* 165–187.

Schegloff, E. A. (1998). Reply to Wetherell. *Discourse and Society, 9,* 413–416.

Schegloff, E. A. (1999). "Schegloff's texts" as "Billig's data": A critical reply. *Discourse and Society, 10,* 558–572.

Smith, B. H. (1988). *Contingencies of value: Alternative perspectives for critical theory.* Cambridge, MA: Harvard University Press.

Smith, D. (1978). K is mentally ill: The anatomy of a factual account. *Sociology, 12,* 23–53.

Stokoe, E. (in press). Categories, actions and sequences: Formulating gender in talk-in-interaction. In L. Litosseliti, H. Saunston, K. Segall, & J. Sunderland (Eds.), *Gender and language: Theoretical and methodological approaches.* London: Palgrave Macmillan.

Stokoe, E., & Edwards, D. (2006). Story formulations in talk-in-interaction, *Narrative Inquiry, 16,* 56–65.

Stokoe, E. H., & Smithson, J. (2001). Making gender relevant: Conversation analysis and gender categories in interaction. *Discourse and Society, 12,* 217–244.

van Dijk, T. A. (1998). *Ideology: A multidisciplinary approach.* London: Sage.

Wetherell, M. (1998). Positioning and interpretative repertoires: Conversation analysis and post-structuralism in dialogue. *Discourse and Society, 9,* 387–412.

Wetherell, M., & Potter, J. (1992). *Mapping the language of racism: Discourse and the legitimation of exploitation.* London/New York: Harvester and Columbia University Press.

White, H. (1978). *Tropics of discourse.* Baltimore: Johns Hopkins University Press.

Whorf, B. L. (1956). *Language, thought and reality: Selected writings of Benjamin Lee Whorf* (J. B. Carroll, Ed.). Cambridge, MA: MIT Press.

Wiggins, S. (2002). Talking with your mouth full: Gustatory *mmm*s and the embodiment of pleasure. *Research on Language and Social Interaction, 35,* 311–336.

Wodak, R. (2006). Dilemmas of discourse (analysis). *Language in Society, 35,* 595–611.

Wooffitt, R. (1992). *Telling tales of the unexpected: The organization of factual discourse.* London: Harvester/Wheatsheaf.

Wooffitt, R. (2005). *Conversation analysis and discourse analysis: A comparative and critical introduction.* London: Sage.

Wortham, S. (2001). *Narratives in action.* New York: Teachers College Press.

CHAPTER 15

Narrative Constructionist Inquiry

- Andrew C. Sparkes
  Brett Smith

Constructionist inquiry is a complex and varied field of scholarship. Various frameworks or dimensions are attached to it. One of these is narrative.[1] This dimension of constructionist inquiry has in part developed from and been grounded on various concerns and assumptions that have long historical roots. For example, according to Arthur Bochner (2002), the burst of enthusiasm for narrative—and a reason for turning to it—was partly inspired by the crises of representation and legitimization. For some people, it was also a consequence of a moral concern with imagining new, different, and better ways of living.

Intimately connected to these concerns, and fueling the development of narrative studies, has been the growing awareness that a person is essentially a storytelling animal (MacIntyre, 1981; Taylor, 1989) who natu-

rally constructs stories out of life (Freeman, 1999; McAdams, 2006). Narrative has also come to be understood in terms of, on the one hand, theories and, on the other hand, methods (Gubrium & Holstein, 1998; Lieblich, Tuval-Mashiach, & Zilber, 1998; McAdams, 1993; Riessman, 1993; Smith & Sparkes, 2005a, 2005b; Sparkes, 2005). Epistemologically, narratives have emerged as both a *way* of telling about our lives and a *method* or *means* of knowing (Bruner, 1990; Richardson, 2000). Furthermore, it has been postulated that human life is storied and that narrative is an ontological condition of social life (Sarbin, 1986; Somers, 1994). That is, we live in story-shaped worlds. Narratives, in significant measure, constitute human realities and our mode of being. They help guide action and are a socioculturally shared resource that gives substance, artfulness, and texture to people's lives. They form the warp and weft of who we are and what we might or might not do.

These concerns and assumptions on which narrative constructionist inquiry is partly based and justified in turn have led to an appreciation of people as active, socially constructed beings who live and lead storied lives. Indeed, a narratively oriented dimension of constructionist research has developed into a rich terrain with vistas of understanding and vocabularies for theorizing lives, doing empirical work, teaching, and shaping practical engagement with the world (Clandinin, 2007; Josselson, Lieblich, & McAdams, 2005; Smith & Sparkes, 2006). Here, for example, scholars have suggested that narrative is a form of social action (Atkinson & Delamont, 2006); that narratives *do* things (Frank, 2006); that storytelling is a meaning activity and important in making sense of our lives (Bruner, 1990; Freeman, 1999, 2001; Polkinghorne, 1988); that "experience" is constituted and made meaningful through narratives (Sarbin, 1986; Somers, 1994); that narration is a way of making people intelligible to each other (Gergen, 1999a); that narratives endow the human condition with plasticity and are vehicles for questioning all that is pregiven (Brockmeier & Harré, 1997); that narratives can be effective in social and individual transformation (Gergen, 1999a; McAdams & Janis, 2004); that memories and emotions are, at least in part, narratively created and often embedded within expressive bodily actions (Fivush & Haden, 2003; Neisser, 1994; Sarbin, 2001); and that stories are embodied (Frank, 1995; Peterson & Langellier, 2006; Smith, 2002).

Furthermore, scholars have suggested that narratives have moral force and provoke ethical reflection (Bochner, 2001; Frank, 2004); that narrative is a way of organizing our experience of time (Ezzy, 1998; Sparkes & Smith, 2003); that stories are subjectifiers of health (Frank, 2006); that storytelling has both health benefits and risks (Ramírez-Esparza & Pennebaker, 2006); that

selves and identities are constructed and performed in and through narratives (Ezzy, 1998; Nelson, 2001; Smith & Sparkes, in press); that narratives are performative, contextually framed, socially situated, emergent, and jointly constructed and take place within the flow of interaction (Bamberg, 2006; Chase, 2005); and that narratives, as resources, can be habitually used and cumulatively built across time, thereby being a source of self-continuity (Taylor, 2006). It has also been argued that researchers themselves are storytellers who may write in different ways (Ellis, 2004; Smith, 2002; Sparkes, 2002); that researchers cannot stand apart from the stories they generate (Atkinson & Delamont, 2006; Bochner, 2001; Coffey, 1999); that researchers call the stories they tell "theories" (Bochner, 2002); that researchers move back and forth between the *whats* and *hows* of narration (Gubrium & Holstein, 1998); that thinking both *about* stories and *with* them is important (Frank, 1995; Sparkes, 2003a, 2003b); that storytelling affirms the existence of the teller as human (Frank, 2004); and/or that people are shaped, enabled, and constrained not only by material conditions but also by a large yet ultimately limited repertoire of available social and cultural narrative resources (Somers, 1994; Sparkes, 1996; Taylor, 2006).

Thus framed by such assumptions and rationales, narrative has emerged as one important dimension of constructionist research. However, it is all too easy to celebrate the "narrative turn" and to neatly package a narratively framed line of inquiry in ways that deflect or gloss over its historical connections and debt to what has gone before it. Likewise, it is tempting to pass over the variety, tensions, diversification, and contestation currently within it. *Narrative constructionist inquiry* instead needs to be considered an umbrella term. It is a rubric for a mosaic of research efforts with diverse and shared theoretical musings, methods, and empirical groundings, all revolving around an interest in narrative (Atkinson &

Delamont, 2006; Chase, 2005; Clandinin, 2007; Josselson et al., 2005; Riessman, 1993; Smith & Sparkes, 2005a, 2006, in press; Sparkes, 2005). Given this situation, in this chapter our aspirations are modest. The main aim is to give a flavor of both the variation and common ground of constructionist inquir*ies* that have informed and been played out within narrative research. The first section highlights two strands of narrative constructionist thought via a focus on the concept of the self, or subjectivities, as it is known in some quarters. In the second section, we examine the ways in which the social construction of selves has been articulated within narrative research in relation to interrupted lives. Finally, a number of ideas regarding directions that future narrative constructionist inquiries may take are offered.

Narrative Constructivism and Narrative Constructionism

Narrative as a dimension of constructionist scholarship is a varied, ongoing, and contested enterprise rather than a singular, ossified, or monolithic one. In this context, therefore, it is useful to consider the *plurality* of social constructionist inquiry. Given the confines of space, we restrict ourselves to illuminating two strands of constructionist inquiry that have informed and been played out within narrative studies in recent years. The first is that of narrative constru*ctivism*. The second is that of narrative constru*ctionism*.

Narrative constructivism suggests that narratives and people's life stories are psychosocial or intersubjectively created (Smith & Sparkes, in press). This strand of constructionist inquiry recognizes the significance of sociocultural narratives in the construction of people's lives. That said, what goes on inside an individual's head when he or she is engaged in social interaction is the prime concern. Interest is in a person's experiences, psychological machinery, or inner

world. Indeed, the importance of narrative as a mode of thought is stressed (Bruner, 1990).[2] The relevance of imagination and the poetic construction of selfhood, experience, and cognition is emphasized (Freeman, 1999, 2001, 2006). Psychic realities are cherished (Day Sclater, 2003). Furthermore, the "real nature" of subjectivity, coherence, selves, and experience is prized (Crossley, 2003a; McAdams, 2001).

Such realms of interiority, however, do not remain locked away. Rather, for many constructivists, they can be "got at" and somehow known. They are accessible and knowable via the stories an individual tells. That is, a story reflects the inner workings of the person's mind: his or her identity, sense of meaning in life, moral commitments, emotions, and ways of understanding the past, present, and anticipated future. Consequently, instead of placing accent on narratives as social action, emphasis is often given to personal experience and the active engagement of the individual person in the process of self-construction. Furthermore, narrative is privileged as a means of accessing the person's interior realm. As Kenneth Gergen (1999a) points out, within constructivism it is argued that the mind is significantly informed by influences from social relationships. This inner, mental process, though, still "constructs reality in its relationship to the world" (Gergen, 1999a, p. 60).

In this sense, although constructivism does not deny the importance of the social in shaping lives, from a constructivist perspective narrative is woven into the fabric of life itself, is a cognitive structure that guides action, and/or is personally absorbed into one's own functioning. In other words, constructivism sees narratives as making explicit the meaning that is there in experience (Freeman, 1999). It views them as cognate schemas or scripts through which people understand the world (McAdams, 2006). Furthermore, although it locates narrative within social relationships, it considers narratives "as *incorporated into the personal functioning of the individual*" (Gergen &

Gergen, 2006, p. 119, original emphasis). In such ways, the individual holds or becomes a repository of narratives, meanings, and "inner" feelings and personal reflections. These, in turn, correspond to or are reflected in the stories he or she tells. All this is particularly evident, as a case in point, in the ways the process of narratively constructing the self and lived experience is discussed. For example, Ben Crewe and Shadd Maruna (2006, p. 112) state that "the storied identity can be seen as an active 'information-processing structure,' a 'cognitive schema' or a 'construct system' that is both shaped by and later mediates social interaction."[3]

Furthermore, Michele Crossley (2000, p. 40) suggests that narrative approaches to the self should recognize the need for a "realist epistemology which is able to accord sufficient respect to the experiences of specific individuals." Thus, with overtones of a correspondence theory of truth, she calls upon the (neo) " 'realist' assumption" that narratives "have the capacity to 'reflect' the realities of . . . personal experiences. In this sense . . . there is a congruent relationship between talking about life . . . and actually living that life" (p. 155). For Crossley, narratives provide an important means of access to the interiority of individuals' personal experiences, selves, and identities independent of our theories. They have a real nature, which can be found and known for what it actually is. Likewise, Crossley (2003a) proposes that narratives can tap into an individual's deep well of the self and identities and extract his or her innermost dimensions and that they are an important route to "the essentially personal, coherent and 'real' nature of individual subjectivity" (2003a, p. 289). Given this, the potential is opened to explore issues such as how a person feels "subjectively about a particular event, how it relates to their internal sense of themselves, their morality, and their sense of themselves as a person" (p. 289).

Narrative constructivism is also the pervasive—although not exclusive—theme in our reading, within the works of, for example, Jerome Bruner (1990, 2002), Shelley Day Sclater (2003), Corey Drake, James Spillane and Kimberly Hufferd-Ackles (2001), Giancarlo Dimaggio and Antonio Semerari (2004), Vilma Hänninen (2004), Nairán Ramírez-Esparza and James Pennebaker (2006), and Donald Polkinghorne (1988, 1996). Many other excellent examples might be added to this list. For instance, in his life-story model of identity, Dan McAdams (1993) argues that narrative identities are psychosocial constructions and that identity itself takes the form of an inner story. As he proposes, "the story is inside of us. It is made and remade in the secrecy of our own minds, both conscious and unconscious, and for our own psychological discovery" (p. 12). Yet this does not mean that life stories or narrative identities stay hidden inside of us. The story, for McAdams, "is there all along, inside the mind. It is a psychological structure that evolves slowly over time, infusing life with unity and purpose. An interview can elicit aspects of that [narrative], offering me hints concerning the truth already in place in the mind of the teller" (p. 20). Recently, McAdams (2005) reinforced these points when he commented that stories are "*in* people's heads" (p. 124) and "that the storied accounts we hear reflect an inner sense of narrative identity" (p. 129). Accordingly, like many of those within constructivism, he considers "the life story to be an internalized and evolving cognitive structure or script that provides an individual's life with some degree of meaning and purpose while often mirroring the dominant and/or the subversive cultural narratives within which the individual's life is completely situated" (McAdams, 2006, p. 11).

In contrast to constructivism, the primary emphasis of *narrative constructionism* is not on cognitive scripts or the inner realm of individuals but on narratives as a *vehicle* through which our world, lives, and selves are articulated and the way in which such narratives function within *social relationships* (Gergen, 1999a). Thus, in this strand of constructionist inquiry, there is a shift in emphasis from an individuated, psychologized image of the person to a perspective that stresses narrative as a form of social action and a relational, sociocultural phenomenon. As Mary Gergen and Kenneth Gergen (2006, p. 118, original emphasis) put it, "*narratives are discursive actions.* They derive their significance from the way in which they are employed within relationships." In addition, and without claiming that anything goes, constructionism does not make an appeal to (neo)realism but instead commits to relativism (see Smith & Hodkinson, 2005). Here, there is no such thing as theory-free observation, and all of our knowledge is socially and historically conditioned. Likewise, narratives never simply mirror some independent reality or tap into an inner world but help to construct, within relationships, the very reality itself.

Therefore, on the face of it, there would appear to be some contrasts and differences between narrative constructivism and narrative constructionism. Indeed, for scholars who favor constructionism, narratives are not viewed as embedded in the individual or their interiority, as constructivist accounts would suggest. Rather, they are lodged within relationships and appropriated by individuals for use in various contexts. They are ongoing social practices that people *perform* and *do* in relation to others as opposed to something they *have*. Furthermore, within constructionist inquiry, meaning is not considered a property within the interiority of individual actors that can simply be transmitted to others via narrative. Narratives instead generate meaning by virtue of their place within the realm of human interaction (Gergen, 1999a). Agency, too, is neither "in here" nor "out there" but is realized within the doing of storytelling relations (Gergen, 1999b). Furthermore, coherence is conceptualized as an achievement (Mishler, 1999). It is artfully created in storytelling and is consequently neither a natural impulse created inside us nor necessarily an indicator of well-being. Likewise, "experiences" such as

emotions or memories are not merely psychological states but also are narratively performed social enactments (Atkinson, Coffey, & Delamont, 2003).

Accordingly, when compared with narrative constructivism, narrative constructionism gives greater attention to *relatedness*. Instead of placing accent on the individual and his or her "inner self" or personal experience, it considers narratives more as forms of social action through which human life and our sense of self are constructed, performed, and enacted. This constructionism perspective is suggested in the work of Paul Atkinson and colleagues (2003). For them, narrative, rather than being considered a transparent window to an antecedent reality or merely an interior-based phenomena, is a form of social action, with its indigenous, socially shared forms of organization. As they suggest:

> People do things with words, and they do things with narratives. They use biographical accounts to perform social actions. Through them they construct their own lives and those of others. . . . Such accounts are certainly not private, and they do not yield accounts of unmediated personal experience. If we collect spoken (and indeed written) accounts of "events" or "experiences," then we need to analyze them in terms of the cultural resources people use to construct them, the kinds of interpersonal or organizational functions they fulfill, and the socially distributed forms that they take. (p. 117)

None of this, therefore, is to imply that phenomena such as "selves," "memories," or "emotions" remain locked away in an inaccessible and ineffable realm of interior personal experience. On the contrary, for Atkinson and colleagues (2003), it means that we ought to regard such things as constituted through storytelling and shared resources. They are rendered visible to ourselves and to others through joint actions and cultural-specific resources, such as narrative formats. In this regard, although narratives may be felt and expressed as if they were highly personal, they are culturally situated and rely for their success on culturally shared conventions about language, "tellability," and the hearing of stories. Thus, as Paul Atkinson and Sara Delamont (2006) point out, recognizing that narrative is a form of social action and inescapably a social phenomenon means more than acknowledging that narratives are produced and circulated in "social contexts." It also implies the recognition that they are based on and structured according to socially shared conventions of reportage (Plummer, 2001).

Narrative constructionism is also the pervasive—although, again, not exclusive—theme in our reading, within the works of, for example, Nigel Edley (2002), Kenneth Gergen (1994), Maria Medved and Jens Brockmeier (2004), Elliot Mishler (1999), Hilde Lindemann Nelson (2001), Cassandra Phoenix and Andrew Sparkes (2006), Catherine Riessman (2003), Brett Smith and Andrew Sparkes (2005b), and Margaret Somers (1994). This is particularly so when they discuss the concept of the self. Indeed, in contrast to social constructivist scholarship, which generally privileges the interiority and active engagement of the individual person in constructing self and identity, scholars placed under the umbrella of social constructionism give greater attention to relatedness and the social aspects of narrative in the self- and identity-construction process. For example, Somers (1994, p. 622, original emphasis) argues that "*all* identities . . . must be analyzed in the context of relational and cultural matrixes because they do not 'exist' outside of these complexities. Individualism, after all, is itself socially and relationally constructed."

Building on this argument, Somers offers a framework for conceptualizing narrative identities and narrativity along a number of dimensions. First, there are what she calls *ontological narratives*. These are "the stories that social actors use to make sense of—indeed, to act in—their lives. Ontological narratives are used to define who we *are*; this in turn is a precondition for knowing what to *do*. . . . Ontological narratives make identity and the self something that one becomes. Thus narrative embeds identities in time and spatial relationships" (Somers, 1994, p. 618, original emphasis).

Yet where do these narratives come from? How are people's stories constructed? For Somers (1994, p. 618), ontological narratives, although personalized over time, are drawn from a limited repertoire of available narrative resources that are "above all, social and interpersonal." That is, ontological narratives derive from and are intimately connected to and shaped by webs of relationality or interlocution that Somers calls *public narratives*. This second dimension refers to "those narratives attached to cultural and institutional formations larger than the single individual, to intersubjective networks of institutions, however local or grand" (1994, p. 619). These public narratives link to the third dimension of narrativity, which is *metanarrativity*. This refers to the "master narratives" in which, according to Somers, "we are embedded as contemporary actors in history and as social scientists. Our sociological theories and concepts are encoded within aspects of these master narratives—Progress, Decadence, Industrialisation, Enlightenment, etc." (Somers, 1994, p. 619). Such narratives, Somers notes, can be the epic dramas of our times—for example, individual versus society, capitalism versus communism, and barbarism/nature versus civility.

Also residing within narrative constructionism is the work of Gergen (1994). For him, self-narratives are not essentially private nor interior based, because they are linguistic products and language is a social act. As he argues, persons do not consult an internal script, cognitive structure, or apperceptive mass for guidance or information; they do not interpret the world through narrative lenses; they do not author their lives. Rather, "the self-narrative is a linguistic implement embedded within conventional sequences of action and employed in relationships in such a way as to sustain, enhance, or impede various forms of action" (1994, p. 188). As such, "relationship takes priority over the individual self" (p. 249). In a similar fashion, Theodore Sarbin (2005, p. 208) argues that one's identity is "formed and transformed by narrative-inspired social relationships. Whether engaged in formal conventional roles or in informal spontaneous encounters, the primary medium for the creation and development of relationships is dialogical."

Despite the rapid and partial tour we have offered through a complex terrain, there are clearly contrasts and tensions between narrative constructivism and narrative constructionism. These can be considered a sign of the vibrancy of the field of narrative inquiry. Indeed, as we have suggested, like Bochner (2002) and Richard Rorty (1982), it is preferable to treat differences not as issues to be ignored or resolved but as differences to be lived with (Smith & Sparkes, 2006, in press). That said, although there are contrasts and tensions that we might live and engage in dialogue with, differences are not absolute. Points of contact do exist, and co-existence is possible. This is particularly so when one considers the nonlinear *trajectories* on which researchers embark when they approach theorizing, empirical material, and practical engagement with the world.

For example, both constructivism and constructionism start off interested in the storied nature of human conduct (Sarbin, 1986). They share the conviction that—to a great or lesser extent—selves and identities are constituted via narrative. People understand themselves *as selves* through storytelling and the stories they feel part of. Furthermore, at the outset both strands recognize that stories are shaped by culture and that people may tell different ones in certain contexts over time. Moreover, there is a broad consensus that people have, in varying degrees, agency and freedom to construct the story they tell. They are not slaves to culture. Nor are stories determining. As Bochner (2002, p. 81) put it, "people are not condemned to live out the stories passed on

through cultural productions and institutional traditions. If our stories never thwarted or contested received and canonical ones, we would have no expectation of change, no account of conflict, no real demand to account for our actions, no sense of agency."

Yet, although people have agency, they are not free to thwart or fabricate narratives at will. For instance, people do not tell stories about themselves under conditions of their own choosing, nor can they always deploy them for purposes of their own choosing. Various institutional orders and their representatives (e.g., teachers and doctors) mandate narratives, each for different purposes and each in different forms. Likewise, when people tell a story about themselves, they draw upon a particular set of narrative resources that are at hand. These narrative resources, however, are not equally distributed. People are not free to take up or make up just any storyline they please; there are differential invitations and barriers involved—what Douglas Ezzy (1998, p. 249) refers to as the "politics of story telling." Therefore, people act on and are acted on by social and cultural contexts of a society and culture in which interaction occurs. They both actively position themselves in relation to and are positioned by narrating social beings (Davies & Harré, 1990; Harré & Moghaddam, 2003).

Many scholars influenced by constructivism and constructionism also share a commitment and have a point of contact when it comes to the body. That is, an *embodied* social science rather than a *disembodied* social science is often preferred (Ellis, 2004; Frank, 2006; Peterson & Langellier, 2006; Sarbin, 2001; Smith & Sparkes, 2002). This preference does not deny the living body or that the corporeality of bodies matters. Stories are felt in and through the body. They come out of the body, infusing our lives in and as social bodies, profoundly shaping our senses of self and identity. Yet bodies are also fleshy, physical biological entities. As Arthur Frank (1995) puts it, the corporeal character of bodies is an obdurate fact. That acknowledged, we not only tell stories *about* our bodies, but we also tell stories *out of* and *through* our bodies; the body is simultaneously cause, topic, and instrument of whatever story is told.

Last, but by no means least, both constructivist and constructionist research are united in their view that, quite simply, narratives matter. This does not mean that it is the royal road to understanding or that everything should be reduced to narrative. What it does imply is that narrative is of use and of value. For instance, stories potentially have practical benefit, such as being effective in social and personal change (Gergen & Gergen, 2006). Stories can also touch us where we live, in our bodies, allowing us to "step into the shoes of other human beings," to enter into relationships, and to make connections across differences in ways that do not finalize people (Frank, 2004, 2005). Moreover, as Riessman (1993, p. 5) notes, studying narratives is useful for what they reveal about social life, in that culture "speaks itself" through an individual's story: "It is possible to examine gender inequalities, racial oppression, and other practices of power that may be taken for granted by the individual speakers. Narrators speak in terms that seem natural, but we can analyze how culturally and historically contingent these terms are." Furthermore, for Mark Freeman (2003a), narrative inquiry bears within it the promise of fashioning a different kind of scholarship, one that is not only largely "qualitative" in its orientation but that seeks to practice a deep fidelity to lived experience in all of its variousness:

> [Narrative constructionist researchers] would argue vehemently against any and all renditions of human experience that were overly reductive or mechanical, disembodied or dis-languaged, substantialistic or animalistic. . . . They would reject simplistic forms of universalistic thinking and would, at the least, be suspicious about robust claims regarding human nature, set apart from the cultural world. Finally, and more positively, whether they are

avowed "humanists" or not, they would share an abiding respect for real human persons . . . and the real discourses, practices, and institutions within which they/we are enmeshed. (pp. 344–345)

Therefore, narrative is a dimension of constructionist inquiry that is valuable, has benefits, and is useful. It is one also characterized by tensions and connections, differences and similarities, and contrasts and disparity. This, though, is not a source of concern. Rather, for us, it is simply part and parcel of narrative constructionist inquiries that seek to understand and reveal—or indeed construct—the multilayered, unfinalized, and complex nature of human lives (see also Smith & Sparkes, 2006, in press).

Narrative Constructionist Inquiry in Action: Exemplars of Narrative Research

With all this *talk* about narrative constructionist inquiry in mind, let us now turn to examples of empirical work that we and other scholars have been *doing*. The four we present are all similar in that they focus on interrupted body-self projects, such as illness. That said, they are not offered as models. Neither is the point to synthesize them within some theoretical matrix over which narrative constructionist research presides. Instead, the complementary objectives are to illuminate the two different strands of narrative constructionist research in action, the various levels they operate on, and some possibilities they offer. For example, it is possible to hear the voices of constructivism in examples 1 and 4 and of constructionism in 2 and 3. The analytic focus of the researcher's empirical gaze in examples 2 and 4 is on the *whats* of storytelling. Example 1 is, in contrast, more concerned with the *hows*. Example 3, however, moves back and forth between *how* and *what* concerns. Furthermore, collectively they elucidate diverse techniques and sources for the collecting and generating of narratives, such as autobiographies, active interviews, and sociological introspection. They suggest that narratives might best be subjected to multiple forms of analysis. Together they also highlight the potential of using diverse writing strategies to represent one's findings.

Emplotting the Cancer Experience

Crossley (2003b) provides the first exemplar in her narrative study of what it is like to have to live as a cancer patient following diagnosis. This research has constructivist impulses running through it. It draws on the source of autobiography to bring into focus the *hows* of narration and to produce what Sparkes (2002) refers to as a *realist tale*. These are characterized by experiential authority, the participant's point of view, and interpretive omnipotence. Accordingly, Crossley focuses on an autobiographical account by John Diamond (2001) in his book *Snake Oil and Other Preoccupations*, which takes the form of diary extracts from the time of his suspected diagnosis of oral cancer in September 1996 until the week before his death in March 2001. Importantly, Diamond's diaries, she notes, "are unique in that they provide essential insight into what it is actually like to have to live as a cancer patient within the context of such 'therapeutic emplotment' " (Crossley, 2003b, p. 441).

According to Peter Brooks (1984), *emplotment* is an active process by which people creatively engage with and make sense of a story so as to determine what is really going on and what is likely to happen as the story progresses. This concept has been applied to making sense of illness by Mary-Jo Del Vecchio Good, Tseunetsugu Munakata, Yasuki Kobayashi, Cheryl Mattingly, and Byron Good (1994), who focused on people learning to live with a cancer diagnosis. They defined *therapeutic emplotment* as "the interpretive activity, present in clinical encounters, through which clinicians and patients create and negotiate a plot structure within clinical time, one which places therapeutic actions within a larger therapeutic story" (p. 855). They concluded that the emplotment of illness and the therapeutic course constitutes a major task in the treatment of cancer. They proceeded to illustrate how this operates from the perspective of oncologists and reveal how they attempt to formulate experiences for patients by structuring time and horizons in ways that instilled hope, encouraged investment in arduous and toxic treatments, and avoided a sense of despair.

Utilizing the concept of therapeutic emplotment and drawing on the diary extracts, Crossley (2003b) divides the time between suspected diagnosis and death into six main stages in order to depict the dominant themes and underlying temporal structure characterizing Diamond's attempts to adapt to the reality of oral cancer. These stages include (1) "Precancer: Touch wood"; (2) "Learning to live in 'therapeutic emplotment' "; (3) "In limbo: Holding one's breath"; (4) "Recurrence: 'Therapuetic emplotment' continued"; (5) "Through the mirror: The 'unspoken narrative'"; and (6) "Endings or the end?" Her analysis of each stage illustrates the ways in which Diamond's narrative very quickly appropriates the characteristic form of therapeutic emplotment used by oncologists. For example, DelVecchio Good and colleagues (1994) note one narrative strategy oncologists use that expresses time within specific or highly foreshortened horizons in order to create an experience of immediacy, of "living for the moment" rather than trivial chronology. Likewise, Crossley (2003b) notes how Diamond, from his early diagnosis to first recurrence, is largely focused on the "immediacy" of specific treatments, expressing (in retrospect) a naive faith in their efficacy. However, she goes on to show how, as time progressed, Diamond questioned the "surgical story," and a largely "unspoken narrative" of fear and uncertainty emerged that began to supersede the therapeutic plot. Thus Crossley's detailed case study of one individual via a realist tale illustrates how the process of therapeutic emplotment implicitly worked to structure the narrative produced by one man attempting to adjust to the reality of life with oral cancer.

Hope and Active Interviews

Our second example is Smith and Sparkes's (2005b) research on the meanings of hope in the lives of men who have suffered spinal cord injuries (SCI) and become disabled through playing sports. Like Crossley (2003b), they produce a realist tale. In contrast, however, narrative constructionism shapes their understanding of the men's stories, which they jointly create and coconstruct in dialogue via multiple active interviews. Rather than focus just on the *hows*, the authors turn their analytic attention to the *whats* of storytelling—that is, the content, plot, and structural features of narrative. Accordingly, drawing on transcribed data and building on previous work (e.g., Smith & Sparkes, 2002, 2004; Sparkes & Smith, 2002, 2003, 2005), they illuminate the most common kind of hope used by the men in telling their stories post-SCI. In their analyses, important differences were identified in the kinds of hope used and the influences of these in reconstructing body-self relationships. They suggested that the differences were due, in part, to the power of three narrative types that circulate in Western cultures to shape their lives in general and the kinds of hope used in their stories in particular.

For the majority of the men in Smith and Sparkes's (2005b) study, their ontological narratives were shaped by the metanarrative of *restitution*, as defined by Frank (1995). The plot of the restitution narrative has the basic storyline: "Yesterday I was healthy, today I'm sick, but tomorrow I'll be healthy again" (Frank, 1995, p. 77). For the men in Smith and Sparkes's research, this translates to "Yesterday I was able-bodied, today I'm disabled, but tomorrow or at some point in the future I'll be able-bodied again." For the participants who told restitution narratives, *concrete hope* was prominent in their stories.

This kind of hope is oriented to specific or material results and is linked to the positive expectation of realizing desirable outcomes.

According to Smith and Sparkes (2005b), hope in restitution narratives is linked to concrete outcomes that revolve primarily around the discovery of a "cure" via medical and technological advancements in the future. They also suggest that the metanarrative of restitution and the public narrative (Somers, 1994) of concrete hope operate in combination to help create and sustain a *restored* self and an *entrenched* self, as described by Kathy Charmaz (1987). These kinds of self are linked to notions of a "comeback" that returns the individual to a former, more desirable state of being that he or she had in the past. As such, the individual becomes locked into his or her past body–self relationships and ways of being in the world, with the belief that he or she will return to this state. To be ready for this return, the body itself must remain disciplined and adhere to various therapeutic regimens so that its former predictability can be embraced when the opportunity arises. This process does not, though, occur in a social vacuum. As Smith and Sparkes argue, stories of restitution and hope might be thought of as extremely personal and private, because, in one sense, people often depend on and act to defend what they experience as their personal, authentic stories. Yet their narratives are couched in terms of shared cultural forms or plots. They also reverberate, shaping others' stories. They are social actions. As Smith and Sparkes (p. 178) state, "concrete hope and the restitution narrative that helps enact entrenched selves need to be considered in relational terms and as culturally and historically contingent. This is because narratives do not spring from the minds of individuals but are social creations."

Whereas the majority of the men in Smith and Sparkes's (2005b) research drew on the restitution narrative, two of the men in their study understood themselves as selves through a different type of story they told and felt part of—that is, a *quest* narrative.

This metanarrative meets suffering head on. It accepts impairment and disability and seeks to *use* it. As Frank (1995) points out, just what is quested for may never be wholly clear, but the quest is defined by the person's belief that something is to be gained from the experience. Furthermore, in contrast to the restitution narrative, which incorporates concrete hope, quest stories foster and embrace *transcendent hope*. This kind of hope is not oriented to achieving a fixed and specific outcome but instead embraces uncertainly and finitude, celebrating surprise, play, novelty, mystery, and openness to change. In this sense, the hopeful person, rather than being defined (or enslaved) by certain wishes, is continually open to the possibility that reality will disclose as yet unknown sources of value and meaning.

According to Smith and Sparkes (2005b), for these two men in their study, becoming disabled through sport was reframed, with the aid of a quest narrative and transcendent hope, as a challenge and an opening to other ways of being. As such, the past is placed securely behind them, life is lived in the present, and the future is a vista of possibilities. Furthermore, in these circumstances, a *developing* self, as described by Charmaz (1987), emerges. Rather than simply committing to an outcome tied to a cure and being locked into specific prior activities and former identities, the two men are concerned about the directions of their lives, as well as the characters of the selves they shape along the way. Indeed, they commit themselves to growing and developing in the future. By opting for a developing self, these men emphasize their ability to reconstruct their sense of self over time; they display an openness to change; and they show a willingness to explore new identities as possibilities emerge. This is enabled further, Smith and Sparkes argue, by the *counternarratives* of the *social model* and *affirmative model* of disability. These may help in the process of reconstructing identities by providing a sense of communal consciousness and by expanding the cultural repertoire of stories on which to draw when replotting a life. In so doing, they con-

test and displace the tragedy storyline that restricts opportunities to engage with a range of future possible identities that are a necessary part of becoming a developing self.

In contrast to the restitution narrative that attempts to outdistance mortality by rendering disability transitory and to the quest narrative that meets disability head on is the *chaos* narrative. According to Frank (1995), this narrative imagines life never getting better. These stories are chaotic in their absence of narrative order. They are told by a storyteller who inhabits a chaotic body about how life is experienced; that is, without sequence or discernable causality. Not surprisingly, within chaos, despair is foregrounded and hope vanishes. Furthermore, the self in this narrative is fragmented.

According to Smith and Sparkes (2005b), it might be suggested, but not finalized (Frank, 2005), that a person in chaos feels swept along, without control, by life's fundamental contingency. He or she may be an alienated storyteller, wounded in the lack of narrative resources he or she can access, connect with, and take on board. According to Freeman (2003b), in situations in which certain outcomes are anticipated as inevitable, in which things cannot be otherwise, individuals may experience what he calls *narrative identity foreclosure*. This involves the premature conviction that one's life story is effectively over. In such instances, Freeman suggests, if one already knows or *believes* that one knows what lies ahead, then one may become convinced that there is little value in lasting to the very end. Consequently, one's life may seem a foregone conclusion. The individual in this circumstance might feel that he or she can no longer move creatively into the future.

The Artfully Persuasive Storyteller

The third example related to interrupted lives is Sparkes's (2003a) work on illness, identities, and body-self relationships. Like Smith and Sparkes's (2005b) study, it can be considered as oriented toward narrative constructionism. However, it takes very different positionings on a number of levels. For example, rather than write a realist tale, for various purposes Sparkes chooses the creative analytic practice (Richardson, 2000) of *autoethnography*[4] to show and tell the consequences of an interrupted body project and what this means for who he thought he was, who he thinks he is, and who he thinks he might be in the future. In this kind of representation, the analytic gaze also shifts between the *hows* and *whats* of storytelling as opposed to privileging either what was said or how it was told. Furthermore, although it is neither easy nor without risks, Sparkes does not act as a story analyst who conducts an analysis of narrative and thinks *about* stories but instead operates as a storyteller who performs a narrative analysis and calls for thinking *with* stories (Frank, 2000; Smith & Sparkes, 2006). As part of this process, he relinquishes the role of declarative author/persuader and writes as an artfully persuasive storyteller (Barone, 1995, 2000; Sparkes, 2002).

With these issues in mind and drawing strength from the narrative turn in the social sciences that helped him realize that writing is a method of inquiry, a way of knowing, and a method of discovery and analysis (Richardson, 2000), Sparkes (2003a) constructed a text that draws on his body's memory via sociological introspection (Ellis, 2004). As part of an autoethnographic trilogy (Sparkes, 1996, 2003a, 2003b), his narrative focuses on the interplay of his feelings about inhabiting a (then) 45-year-old, anxious, clinically depressed, white, heterosexual, "middle-class" male, "failed" and problematic body and his early memories of an elite, performing, working-class body that housed a *fatal flaw* in the form of a lower back problem.

Accordingly, Sparkes's (2003a) autoethnography offers a series of stories related to sports, identity, masculinities, bodies, selves, and, for example, social class. However, despite some readers who might have liked an "ending" to the stories, he resists an authori-

tative final interpretation. In the end, no answers are given, but many questions are asked of the reader. Similarly, he raises a range of methodological issues and invites the reader to feel and engage with various theories and concepts that frame his story, rather than simply to know them. For example, in considering the relationship between narrative and reality, the work of Ulric Neisser (1994) could be used to draw conclusions from Sparkes's story. Neisser (1994, p. 2) provides four controversial categories, not accepted by everyone, with regard to memory: "(1) actual past events and the *historical self* who participated in them; (2) those events as they were experienced, including the individual's own *perceived self* at the time; (3) the *remembering self*, that is, the individual in the act of recalling those events on some later occasion; and (4) the *remembered self* constructed on that occasion."

Neisser (1994, p. 8) later speaks of the *oblivious self* and notes how "autobiographical memory is best taken with a grain of salt. The self that is remembered today is not the historical self of yesterday, but only a reconstructed version. A different version—a new remembered self—may be reconstructed tomorrow." With these points in mind, Sparkes (2003a) could have included this as a direct quotation, adopted a more distanced writing stance, and *told* the reader about how these different selves operate in relation to identity construction and reconstruction within parts of his story. However, in his stories, he chooses to *show* the reader these selves in action.

For example, in the story "Jars" (Sparkes, 2003a, p. 51), the remembering self is signaled when, having picked up the three jars, "I suddenly get the urge to smell these remains. The lids come off, I inhale, I inhale memories" (p. 51). The remembered selves are there in jars that contain the corporeal debris of surgical operations in 1988, 1994, and 2000 and that are preserved "long after they would have rotted outside of my body" (p. 51). These remembered selves are connected to the historical selves created in the stories he tells when "I'm 17," "I'm 39," "I'm 45," and "Still 45" years of age. These, in turn, are informed by the perceived selves who experienced the events at the time.

Thus a number of stark contrasts are offered to the reader. For instance, there is the nonproblematic, performing, 17-year-old, sinewy, sporting body-self that cuts air and feels speed oozing though it. This body moves so fast "the world turns molten, melting in wavy space around me" (Sparkes, 2003a, p. 52). In contrast, the 39-year-old body-self is problematic. It hobbles and limps. It feels useless, anxious, fearful, embarrassed, and guilty: "My uselessness makes me angry with my body. At that moment I hate it intensely" (p. 52). Accordingly, the various selves that Neisser (1994) talks of are actually woven into and played out within the story of "Jars" and his other stories. As a consequence, Sparkes (2003a) invites the reader to feel his interruptions and various bodies and selves in action and to engage with them in relation to their own historical, perceived, remembering, remembered, and oblivious selves as they read the text.

The Psychotherapeutic Impulse

A focus on narrative and interrupted lives is also evident in the work of Dimaggio and Semerari (2004). Like the work of Crossley (2003b), this fourth and final example in our reading has *constructivist* impulses running through it (see also McAdams & Janis, 2004, and various contributors to the issue of *Journal of Constructivist Psychology*, 2006, 19(2)). It is also a *realist* tale, thus having a commonality with Crossley, as well as with Smith and Sparkes (2005b). That said, Dimaggio and Semerari's work adds a different layer to the variety of narrative constructionist inquiry we have presented thus far in terms of its focus and explicit possibilities. That is, they explicitly attend to the ways in which narrative research can function within the practical and professional setting of psychotherapy.

Of course, the link between psychotherapy and narrative is not new. Indeed, most if not all forms of therapy are lodged within some form of narrative. As Gergen and Gergen (2006) remind us, psychoanalysis, for instance, is based on a story of emerging repression, with cure depending on the lifting of such repression via psychoanalytic treatment. That said, in recent years the increasing consciousness of narrative has culminated in an explicitly narrative-informed therapeutic movement (see Angus & McLeod, 2004; White & Epston, 1990). There are various ways in which narratives are employed in such work, including those driven by constructionism (see, e.g., McLeod, 2004).

The narrative constructivist work of Dimaggio and Semerari (2004), in contrast, places emphasis on how therapy can be used for rewriting patients' stories through the construction of more adaptive narratives, assisting patients in overcoming their conflicts and tackling the world's complexities. For them, storytelling is one of the psyche's basic functions. Furthermore, Dimaggio and Semerari argue, the stories that one's mind constructs, incorporates, and portrays to itself are tied to one's bodily state. Thus an interruption to this condition, such as an illness, can create a sense of inner turmoil and disorganization. Indeed, what is specifically narrative about their approach is that they pay particular attention to structural alterations in patients' narratives, noting that they can suffer not only through the subject matter of their story but also by the way in which it is organized and put together. That is, some peoples' narratives are poor in content, whereas those of others are littered with interruptions and are disorganized.

According to Dimaggio and Semerari (2004), with patients who have disorganized narratives, therapists find themselves faced with a difficult task, that is, entering a chaotic scenario in which numerous voices are all crowding together and a vast number of fragments of different stories are intertwined. The emotions in these cases are almost always intense and difficult to modulate. Therapists get easily caught up in a relationship that is intense, occasionally irritating, sometimes threatening, and constantly confusing. Given this situation, Dimaggio and Semerari (2004) propose a therapeutic strategy that involves certain actions aimed at treating the structural narrative dysfunction in a way the enhances the context for working, "observing, and modifying the life themes, the quality of relationships, and the dialogue between the characters inhabiting a patient's mental world" (p. 278).

The first type of action suggested by Dimaggio and Semerari (2004, p. 278) is aimed at acquiring a higher degree of "metacognitive skills and at encouraging an Observing-I position that can endow patients' inner chaos with meaning and acknowledge the breathless multiplicity of their narrative." With this action, they argue, patients are able to experience their internal chaos in a less threatening way and to communicate in a more comprehensible fashion with their therapists. By starting with a sharing of the problems caused by the chaos in the narrative within the individual, patients and therapists are facilitated in identifying the dominant life themes, the characters that represent these themes, and the way to build more adaptive life narratives.

The second type of action proposed by Dimaggio and Semerari (2004) is aimed at recovering the ability to distinguish between fantasy and reality where this has been lost. The goal is not to immediately change the contents of the narratives but to allow the patient to acknowledge that an imaginary narrative is taking the place of the world, with pernicious consequences. For them, self-disclosure by therapists can be a valuable tool in this context. The effect of these actions is a change in the quality of the therapeutic relationship. When patients "acquire a better level of metarepresentative skills, their position vis-à-vis the therapist changes. Emotions shift flexibility in the context of new narrative scenarios" (2004, p. 279). Dimaggio and Semerari go on to add that a patient and a therapist, working together

collaboratively to implement treatment, see the individual patient as the object of threats, seductions, and abuses by others. Distinguishing between imagined and actual narrative scenarios makes it possible later to modify the ones in which problematical contents and interpersonal relationships appear. Thus this vision of narrative constructivism in action opens up a range of possibilities for personal change following an interruption to one's body-self project.

Future Directions

In this chapter, we have attempted to make sense of and give some shape to what can broadly be called narrative constructionist inquiry. We now reflect on some future directions that narrative constructionist inquiry might take. Of the many future directions that may be taken, we briefly consider seven.

First is the relationship between narrative constructionist inquiry and methods.

The primary technique for inviting and generating stories is a certain kind of interview, such as life story or interactive interviews (Chase, 2005). These are very useful and important sources of narrative. However, we need to expand the ways in which we critically think about interviews and analyze the stories jointly created in them. For example, deeper awareness of the *contextual* dimensions of face-to-face interviewing, including the implications of *where* (e.g., the place or space) and *when* (the time) storytelling occurs, is needed (Holstein & Gubrium, 2004). Likewise, the *performative* aspects of interviewing require further attention (Riessman, 2003). More work is desired on what is *done* in interaction and how people *do* things in dialogue *with* others (Bamberg, 2006). The complexities related to *being* and *having* a body and the effects of entering or not entering into relationships with other living, feeling, talking bodies during interviews needs to be explored. Equally, we need more stories concerning the embodied impact and aftermath of both being interviewed and being an interviewer.

Not only is it vital that we expand our understandings of interview narratives, but our techniques for inviting and generating stories also need expanding. Put more strongly, relying on and privileging interviews would not serve the narrative study of lives well. Interviews can be useful, but they are only one among a number of viable techniques, rather than the one and only source of inviting and gathering stories. Accordingly, without advocating discarding interviews or the elevation of one kind of source over another, other techniques for the collection and analysis of data might be more critically and responsibly explored in the future. These techniques may include e-mail, blogs, online support groups, instant messaging, autobiographies, letters, ethnographic field notes, diaries, obituaries, photographs, newspapers, magazines, television, music, and "naturally occurring" conversation. All of this, moreover, needs to be done in relation to both *how* and *what* questions, as well as to the *whens* and *wheres* of storytelling (Holstein & Gubrium, 2004). It also might consider taking into account, we feel, not only big stories but also small ones (Bamberg, 2006; Freeman, 2006; Georgakopoulou, 2006); that is, stories that are short, spontaneously told in everyday settings, and perhaps not traditionally seen as particularly interesting.

The second possible direction involves the relationship between narratives and representation. Creative analytic practices (CAPs; Richardson, 2000), such as poetry, ethnodrama, autoethnography, visual presentations, music, layered accounts, and fiction (see Ellis, 2004; Smith, 1999; Sparkes, 2002; and contributors to the special issue of *Journal of Contemporary Ethnography*, 2006, *35*(4)), have been advocated by various narrative constructionists as useful and vital ways to transform their "data" and represent them. There is, however, still much to be considered and discussed (Bochner, 2001). For example, in our opinion, with the in-

crease in CAPs, there has simultaneously been a decline in the way they are creatively written. That is, the actual writing of CAPs often now seemingly follows a formula or template set by previous ones. They are becoming a formulistic, uniform, and ossified textual product. As a result, some CAPs—but certainly not all—are clichéd, boring, apolitical, theoretically vacuous, and/or lacking in such characteristics as verisimilitude, evocation, embodied life, fidelity, relevance, impact, and a connection with society and culture. Equally, the critics of CAPs are provided with fuel to inflame their arguments, and the spaces to publish potentially different and important ways of writing could shrink.

Given such points, and as promoters of "good quality" CAPs, we hope that in the future analytic practices seek to disturb such a trend and strive to regain their creativity while not imposing themselves as the best or only viable form of research. As part of this, researchers might consider showing the complexities of human life in ways that seek to affect, inspire, and change people's lives and the world they live in. One way to do this is by writing from the heart, well, and in an informed manner (Pelias, 2004). In doing so, although it is certainly not easy, CAPs may in the future, as good ones have done in the past, inspire people to want to reach out and take action. They do not simply *state* that they evocatively connect the personal to the sociocultural, that they show rather than tell, that they turn the personal into the political and the political into the personal, that they use stories to perform the work of analysis and theory, and/or that they open a door, both conceptually and emotionally, into a world of relational, embodied lives. They actually *do* such things.

Third, we consider the relationship between narrative inquiry and the people it focuses on. For example, the narrative study of lives has emerged in recent years as an interdisciplinary effort to write, interpret, and disseminate people's life stories to different audiences, with special attention paid to the groups and people whose lives and whose stories have historically been ignored or marginalized. This should continue. But, given that our lives are relationally constructed, it is important, too, to expand the types of people we talk with. For instance, stories from people who are in privileged positions, who are considered healthy rather than ill, who are non-Western, who govern institutions and society, and who lead what may be viewed on the surface as unremarkable lives also need to be explored. Moreover, they need to be audiences to our research. This, in turn, raises various questions.

Who receives the stories we create? How are they received? What are the effects on certain people and groups, such as health care professionals or disabled persons, who listen to certain kinds of tales? What types of stories incite and/or hinder individual and collective action? And to what effect? When and where is storytelling most effective for creating change, empathy, and dialogue in various audiences? How can indigenous, queer, ethnic, postcolonial, and feminist standpoints infuse narrative constructionist inquiry more directly?

The fourth direction involves the relationship between narrative inquiry and theory. As we have pointed out here and elsewhere (Smith & Sparkes, 2006, in press), there are various theoretical tensions within this dimension of constructionist inquiry. More needs to be said about not just these but also others. For example, how might we navigate between contrasting perspectives that suggest that narrative is woven into the fabric of life and makes explicit meaning that is there in the experience (Freeman, 2001), draws out the meaning that inheres in the events (Nelson, 1998), or imposes the meaning that we imagine we see in mere happenings (White, 1978)? What is the theoretical adequacy of constructivist and constructionist inquiry in terms of research and practice (Gergen & Gergen, 2006)? We also need to discuss the possible tensions and similarities between other dimensions of construction-

ist inquiry, such as discursive research. This is especially important given the notion of *sociological* or *psychological amnesia*. That is, in the search for novel ideas and to help create and sustain a career in academia, researchers sometimes ignore the past, as well as the present, and periodically reinvent the wheel (Atkinson, 2006; Atkinson et al., 2003; Maines, 2001). Is narrative constructionist inquiry really the same as discursive constructionism (see Potter & Hepburn, Chapter 14, this volume)? Are both essentially forms of interactionism?

Fifth, researchers interested in the relationship between narratives and the body might consider more explicitly addressing, debating, incorporating, and theorizing bodies as lived—social, storied, practical, and biological (Williams, 2006). As part of this inquiry, one might explore what Oscar Gonçalves, Margarida Henriques, and Paulo Machado (2004) call the *narrative brain*. For them, at the biological level, narrative seems to be an essential process that facilitates the integration of our experiences "by means of coordinated action from a diverse array of brain structures and process. Almost every brain structure is involved in the process of narrative construction, and thus, we may say that human mind is, indeed, a *narrative brain*" (p. 103). Given such issues and the availability of techniques such as magnetic resonance imagining scanners, exploring the narrative brain could be an interesting future line of inquiry.

The sixth possible direction involves the relationship between narrative constructionist inquiry and the conception of dialogue. According to Frank (2005), little attempt has been made to apply Mikhail Bakhtin's (1981) conception of dialogue to the conduct of research and the production of research reports. Yet it offers great promise. This is especially so in relation to ethics. For example, as Frank argues, the research report ought to understand itself not as a final statement of who the research participants are but as one move in a continuing dialogue through which those participants will continue to form themselves as they continue to become who they may yet be. As such, researchers in the future need to consider ways in which they do not *finalize* the people they generate stories with. Likewise, they might reflect on how *monological* narratives that claim to utter the last word are to be avoided. For Frank (2005), what is required is a *dialogical* research report that leaves the person unfinalized.

The seventh and final issue revolves around the relationship between narrative and judgment criteria. John Smith and Phil Hodkinson (2005) and Sparkes (2002) remind us that discussions about criteria are unequivocally important and demand ongoing attention. For example, some scholars argue for foundational criteria, whereas others would call for nonfoundational criteria. It is unlikely that such tensions will disappear imminently. However, it is important that in the future *both* positions get together and start to talk with and respond to each other—that is, engage in dialogue. Indeed, it is no good if only one position responds to the other and does not hear anything back in return. We need responses to critiques if constructionist inquiry and qualitative research in general are to continue developing and avoid being ghettoized. This is particularly vital for the future development of narrative constructionist inquiry, because as Smith and Hodkinson point out, there are governmental attempts to mandate research criteria in the United States and the United Kingdom that may limit and restrict the potential of qualitative-based narrative research. Social scientists who collaborate in this process, the Research Assessment Exercise (an exercise conducted nationally to assess the quality of research and to inform the selective distribution of public funds for research by higher education funding bodies) in the United Kingdom, and the obsession with journal impact factors make this all the more disconcerting and the need for future discussion on criteria even more urgent.

Narrative constructionist inquiry, therefore, presents both challenges and promises for the future. Constructivism and constructionism each have important parts to play in this process. Certainly, theorizing and having dialogues about them, as well as doing and producing constructionist research of either strand that is useful and effective and that works, is no easy task. However, it is not impossible. For us, the effort and risks involved are worth taking, because when narrative constructionist inquiry, of either strand or variety, is done well and does work, it provides a powerful means of understanding human beings in new, different, and exciting ways. As such, we feel not only that narrative is a worthy dimension of constructionist inquiry but also that there are exciting and interesting times ahead.

• Notes

1. Acutely aware that it is difficult to give a clear-cut definition of story or narrative, here we try to use *story* when referring to actual tales people tell. A story is a verbal or nonverbal telling. In contrast, narrative is delineated as a dynamic structure embedded in society. It is, unlike a chronicle, a report, or a question-and-answer exchange, a cultural frame, frequently taken for granted, that comprises various particular stories and that has, for example, a plot—a sequence of events that is temporally ordered—characters, a consequence, a point, intentionality, and a teleological quality or a valued ending (Gergen, 1999a; Maines, 2001; Riessman & Quinney, 2005). But, as Frank (1995) reminds us, because narratives exist only in particular stories and all stories are narratives, the distinction is hard to sustain.

2. Bruner (1990) proposed that there are two different but complementary ways of knowing and cognitive functioning. One is narrative. The other he calls the *logicoscientific* or *paradigmatic* mode. Many scholars have taken up and relied on this distinction to formulate their arguments related to narrative research. Interestingly, though, Bruner (2002) has recently left this idea behind. He now says he was profoundly mistaken in suggesting that there are two mutually translatable worlds of mind—the narrative and the logical–paradigmatic.

3. Some of the people we have placed under the label *constructivism*, and later *constructionism*, will no doubt not see themselves as being signed-up members of the constructionist club. For heuristic purposes, what matters is not direct influence or whether they see themselves as constructionists but rather that it is possible to hear a constructionist voice in their work.

4. *Autoethnography* is defined by Carolyn Ellis and Arthur Bochner (2000) as an "autobiographical genre of writing and research that displays multiple layers of consciousness, connecting the personal to the cultural. Back and forth autoethnographers gaze, first through an ethnographic wide-angle lens, focusing outward on social and cultural aspects of their personal experience; then, they look inward, exposing a vulnerable self that is moved by and may move through, refract, and resist cultural interpretations. . . . Autoethnographers vary in their emphasis on the research process (*graphy*), on culture (*ethnos*), and on self (*auto*)" (pp. 739–740).

• References

Angus, L. E., & McLeod, J. (Eds.). (2004). *The handbook of narrative and psychotherapy*. London: Sage.

Atkinson, P., Coffey, A., & Delamont, S. (2003). *Key themes in qualitative research*. Oxford, UK: AltaMira Press.

Atkinson, P., & Delamont, S. (2006). Rescuing narrative from qualitative research. *Narrative Inquiry, 16*, 164–172.

Bakhtin, M. (1981). *The dialogic imagination: Four essays* (C. Emerson & M. Holquist, Eds. & Trans.). Austin: University of Texas Press.

Bamberg, M. (2006). Stories: Big or small—Why do we care? *Narrative Inquiry, 16*, 139–147.

Barone, T. (1995). Persuasive writings, vigilant readings, and reconstructed characters: The paradox of trust in educational storysharing. *Qualitative Studies in Education, 8*, 63–74.

Barone, T. (2000). *Aesthetics, politics, and educational inquiry*. New York: Lang.

Bochner, A. (2001). Narrative's virtues. *Qualitative Inquiry, 7*, 131–157.

Bochner, A. (2002). Perspectives on inquiry: III. The moral of stories. In M. Knapp & J. Daley (Eds.), *The handbook of interpersonal communication* (3rd ed., pp. 73–101). London: Sage.

Brockmeier, J., & Harré, R. (1997). Narrative: Problems and promises of an alternative paradigm. *Research on Language and Social Interaction, 30*(4), 263–283.

Brooks, P. (1984). *Reading for the plot: Design and intention in narrative*. New York: Knopf.

Bruner, J. (1990). *Acts of meaning*. Cambridge, MA: Harvard University Press.

Bruner, J. (2002). *Making stories*. Cambridge, MA: Harvard University Press.

Charmaz, K. (1987). Struggling for a self: Identity levels of the chronically ill. In J. Roth & P. Conrad (Eds.), *Research in the sociology of health care: A research manual* (Vol. 6, pp. 283–321). Greenwich, CT: JAI Press.

Chase, S. (2005). Narrative inquiry: Multiple lenses, approaches, voices. In N. Denzin & Y. Lincoln (Eds.), *Handbook of qualitative research* (3rd ed., pp. 651–679). London: Sage.

Clandinin, D. J. (Ed.). (2007). *Handbook of narrative inquiry*. London: Sage.

Coffey, A. (1999). *The ethnographic self*. London: Sage.

Crewe, B., & Maruna, S. (2006). Self-narratives and ethnographic fieldwork. In D. Hobbs & R. Wright (Eds.), *The Sage handbook of fieldwork* (pp. 109–123). London: Sage.

Crossley, M. (2000). *Introducing narrative psychology*. Buckingham, UK: Open University Press.

Crossley, M. (2003a). Formulating narrative psychology: The limitations of contemporary social constructionism. *Narrative Inquiry, 13*(2), 287–300.

Crossley, M. (2003b). "Let me explain": Narrative emplotment and one patient's experience of oral cancer. *Social Science and Medicine, 56*, 439–448.

Davies, B., & Harré, R. (1990). Positioning: The discursive production of selves. *Journal for the Theory of Social Behaviour, 20*, 43–63.

Day Sclater, S. (2003). What is the subject? *Narrative Inquiry, 13*(2), 317–330.

DelVecchio Good, M. J., Munakata, T., Kobayashi, Y., Mattingly, C., & Good, B. (1994). Oncology and narrative time. *Social Science and Medicine, 38*(6), 855–862.

Diamond, J. (2001). *Snake oil and other preoccupations*. London: Vintage.

Dimaggio, G., & Semerari, A. (2004). Disorganized narratives: The psychological condition and its treatment. In L. E. Angus & J. McLeod (Eds.), *The handbook of narrative and psychotherapy: Practice, theory, and research* (pp. 263–282). London: Sage.

Drake, C., Spillane, J., & Hufferd-Ackles, K. (2001). Storied identities: Teacher learning and subject-matter context. *Journal of Curriculum Studies, 33*(1), 1–23.

Edley, N. (2002). The loner, the walk and the beast within: Narrative fragments in the construction of masculinity. In W. Patterson (Eds.), *Strategic narrative* (pp. 127–145). Oxford, UK: Lexington Books.

Ellis, C. (2004). *The ethnographic I*. Oxford, UK: AltaMira Press.

Ellis, C., & Bochner, A. (2000). Autoethnography, personal narrative, reflexivity: Researcher as subject. In N. Denzin & Y. Lincoln (Eds.), *Handbook of qualitative research* (3rd ed., pp. 733–768). London: Sage.

Ezzy, D. (1998). Theorising narrative identity: Symbolic interactionism and hermeneutics. *Sociological Quarterly, 39*(2), 239–252.

Fivush, R., & Haden, C. A. (Eds.). (2003). *Autobiographical memory and the construction of a narrative self.* Mahwah, NJ: Erlbaum.

Frank, A. (1995). *The wounded storyteller.* Chicago: University of Chicago Press.

Frank, A. (2000). The standpoint of storyteller. *Qualitative Health Research, 10*(3), 354–365.

Frank, A. W. (2004). *The renewal of generosity.* Chicago: University of Chicago Press.

Frank, A. (2005). What is dialogical research, and why should we do it? *Qualitative Health Research, 15,* 964–974.

Frank, A. (2006). Health stories as connectors and subjectifiers. *Health, 10*(1), 421–440.

Freeman, M. (1999). Culture, narrative, and the poetic construction of selfhood. *Journal of Constructivist Psychology, 12,* 99–116.

Freeman, M. (2001). From substance to story: Narrative, identity, and the reconstruction of the self. In J. Brockmeier & D. Carbaugh (Eds.), *Narrative and identity: Studies in autobiography, self and culture* (pp. 283–293). Amsterdam: Benjamins.

Freeman, M. (2003a). Identity and difference in narrative inquiry: A commentary. *Narrative Inquiry, 13*(2), 331–346.

Freeman, M. (2003b). When the story's over: Narrative foreclosure and the possibility of self-renewal. In M. Andrews, S. Day Sclater, C. Squire, & A. Treader (Eds.), *Lines of narrative* (pp. 81–91). London: Routledge.

Freeman, M. (2006). Life "on holiday"? In defense of big stories. *Narrative Inquiry, 16*(1), 131–138.

Georgakopoulou, A. (2006). Thinking big with small stories in narrative and identity analysis. *Narrative Inquiry, 16*(1), 122–130.

Gergen, K. (1994). *Realities and relationships.* Cambridge, MA: Harvard University Press.

Gergen, K. (1999a). *An invitation to social construction.* London: Sage.

Gergen, K. (1999b). Social construction and relational action. *Theory and Psychology, 9,* 113–115.

Gergen, M., & Gergen, K. (2006). Narratives in action. *Narrative Inquiry, 16,* 112–121.

Gonçalves, Ó., Henriques, M., & Machado, P. (2004). Nurturing narrative: Cognitive narrative strategies. In L. Angus & J. McLeod (Eds.), *The handbook of narrative and psychotherapy* (pp. 103–117). London: Sage.

Gubrium, J., & Holstein, J. (1998). Narrative practice and the coherence of personal stories. *Sociological Quarterly, 39*(1), 163–187.

Hänninen, V. (2004). A model of narrative circulation. *Narrative Inquiry, 14*(1), 69–85.

Harré, R., & Moghaddam, F. (Eds.). (2003). *Positioning individuals and groups in personal, political and cultural contexts.* Westport, CT: Praeger.

Holstein, J., & Gubrium, J. (2004). Context: Working it up, down and across. In C. Seale, G. Gobo, J. Gubrium, & D. Silverman (Eds.), *Qualitative research in practice* (pp. 297–311). London: Sage.

Josselson, R., Lieblich, A., & McAdams, D. (Eds.). (2005). *Up close and personal.* Washington, DC: American Psychological Association.

Lieblich, A., Tuval-Mashiach, R., & Zilber, T. (1998). *Narrative research: Reading, analysis and interpretation.* Thousand Oaks, CA: Sage.

MacIntyre, A. (1981). *After virtue.* Notre Dame, IN: Notre Dame University Press.

Maines, D. (2001). *The faultline of consciousness.* New York: Aldine de Gruyter.

McAdams, D. (1993). *The stories we live by.* New York: Morrow.

McAdams, D. (2001). The psychology of life stories. *Review of General Psychology, 5,* 100–122.

McAdams, D. (2005). A psychologist without a country, or living two lives in the same story. In G. Yancy & S. Hadley (Eds.), *Narrative identities* (pp. 114–130). London: Kingsley.

McAdams, D. (2006). The role of narrative in personality psychology today. *Narrative Inquiry, 16*(1), 11–18.

McAdams, D., & Janis, L. (2004). Narrative identity and narrative therapy. In L. Angus & J. McLeod (Eds.), *The handbook of narrative and psychotherapy: Practice, theory, and research* (pp. 159–173). Thousand Oaks, CA: Sage.

McLeod, J. (2004). Social construction, narrative, and psychotherapy. In L. Angus & J. McLeod (Eds.), *The handbook of narrative and psychotherapy: Practice, theory, and research* (pp. 351–365). Thousand Oaks, CA: Sage.

Medved, M., & Brockmeier, J. (2004). Making sense of traumatic experiences: Telling a life with fragile X syndrome. *Qualitative Health Research, 14*(6), 741–759.

Mishler, E. (1999). *Storylines: Craft artists' narratives of identity.* Cambridge, MA: Harvard University Press.

Neisser, U. (1994). Self-narratives: True and false. In U. Neisser & R. Fivush (Eds.), *The remembering self* (pp. 1–18). Cambridge, UK: Cambridge University Press.

Nelson, H. (2001). *Damaged identities, narrative repair.* Ithaca, NY: Cornell University Press.

Nelson, K. (1998). Meaning in memory. *Narrative Inquiry, 8*(2), 409–418.

Pelias, R. (2004). *A methodology of the heart.* Walnut Creek, CA: AltaMira Press.

Peterson, E., & Langellier, K. (2006). The performance turn in narrative studies. *Narrative Inquiry, 16*(1), 173–180.

Phoenix, C., & Sparkes, A. C. (2006). Young athletic bodies and narrative maps of aging. *Journal of Aging Studies, 20,* 107–121.

Plummer, K. (2001). *Documents of life: 2. An invitation to a critical humanism.* London: Sage.

Polkinghorne, D. (1988). *Narrative knowing and the human sciences.* Albany: State University of New York Press.

Polkinghorne, D. (1996). Explorations of narrative identity. *Psychological Inquiry, 7,* 363–367.

Ramírez-Esparza, N., & Pennebaker, J. (2006). Do good stories produce good health? Exploring words, language, and culture. *Narrative Inquiry, 16*(1), 211–219.

Richardson, L. (2000). Writing: A method of inquiry. In N. Denzin & Y. Lincoln (Eds.), *Handbook of qualitative research* (2nd ed., pp. 923–948). London: Sage.

Riessman, C. K. (1993). *Narrative analysis.* London: Sage.

Riessman, C. K. (2003). Performing identities in illness narrative: Masculinity and multiple sclerosis. *Qualitative Research, 3*(1), 5–33.

Riessman, C. K., & Quinney, L. (2005). Narrative in social work. *Qualitative Social Work, 4*(4), 391–412.

Rorty, R. (1982). *Consequences of pragmatism: Essays, 1972–1980.* Minneapolis: University of Minnesota Press.

Sarbin, T. (Ed.). (1986). *Narrative psychology: The storied nature of human conduct.* New York: Praeger.

Sarbin, T. (2001). Embodiment and the narrative structure of emotional life. *Narrative Inquiry, 11*(1), 217–225.

Sarbin, T. (2005). If these walls could talk: Places as stages for human drama. *Journal of Constructivist Psychology, 18,* 203–214.

Smith, B. (1999). The abyss: Exploring depression through a narrative of the self. *Qualitative Inquiry, 5*(2), 264–279.

Smith, B. (2002). The (in)visible wound: Body stories and concentric circles of witness. *Auto/Biography, 10*(1&2), 113–121.

Smith, B., & Sparkes, A. C. (2002). Men, sport, spinal cord injury, and the construction of coherence: Narrative practice in action. *Qualitative Research, 2*(2), 143–171.

Smith, B., & Sparkes, A. C. (2004). Men, sport, and spinal cord injury: An analysis of metaphors and narrative types. *Disability and Society, 19*(6), 509–612.

Smith, B., & Sparkes, A. C. (2005a). Analyzing talk in qualitative inquiry: Exploring possibilities, problems, and tensions. *Quest, 57*(2), 213–242.

Smith, B., & Sparkes, A. C. (2005b). Men, sport, spinal cord injury, and narratives of hope. *Social Science and Medicine, 61*(5), 1095–1105.

Smith, B., & Sparkes, A. C. (2006). Narrative inquiry in psychology: Exploring the tensions within. *Qualitative Research in Psychology, 3,* 169–192.

Smith, B., & Sparkes, A. C. (in press). Contrasting perspectives on narrating selves and identities: An invitation to dialogue. *Qualitative Research.*

Smith, J. K., & Hodkinson, P. (2005). Relativism, criteria, and politics. In N. Denzin & Y. Lincoln (Eds.), *Handbook of qualitative research* (2nd ed., pp. 915–932). London: Sage.

Somers, M. R. (1994). The narrative constitution of identity: A relational and network approach. *Theory and Society, 23,* 605–649.

Sparkes, A. C. (1996). The fatal flaw: A narrative of the fragile body–self. *Qualitative Inquiry, 2*(4), 463–494.

Sparkes, A. C. (2002). *Telling tales in sport and physical activity: A qualitative journey.* Champaign, IL: Human Kinetics Press.

Sparkes, A. C. (2003a). Fragmentary reflections of the narrated body-self. In J. Denison & P. Markula (Eds.), *"Moving writing": Crafting movement and sport research* (pp. 51–76). New York: Lang.

Sparkes, A. C. (2003b). From performance to impairment: a patchwork of embodied memories. In J. Evans, B. Davies, & J. Wright (Eds.), *Body knowledge and control* (pp. 157–172). London: Routledge.

Sparkes, A. C. (2005). Narrative analysis: Exploring the whats and the hows of personal stories. In M. Holloway (Ed.), *Qualitative research in health care* (pp. 191–209). Milton Keynes, UK: Open University Press.

Sparkes, A. C., & Smith, B. (2002). Sport, spinal cord injury, embodied masculinities and the dilemmas of narrative identity. *Men and Masculinities, 4*(3), 258–285.

Sparkes, A. C., & Smith, B. (2003). Men, sport, spinal cord injury and narrative time. *Qualitative Research, 3*(3), 295–320.

Sparkes, A. C., & Smith, B. (2005). When narratives matter. *Medical Humanities, 31,* 81–88.

Taylor, C. (1989). *Sources of the self.* Cambridge, MA: Harvard University Press.

Taylor, S. (2006). Narrative as construction and discursive resource. *Narrative Inquiry, 16*(1), 94–102.

White, H. (1978). *Tropics of discourse.* Baltimore: Johns Hopkins University Press.

White, M., & Epston, D. (1990). *Narrative means to therapeutic ends.* New York: Norton.

Williams, S. J. (2006). Medical sociology and the biological body: Where are we now and where do we go from here? *Health, 10*(1), 5–30.

CHAPTER 16

Interactional Constructionism

● **Amir Marvasti**

nteractional constructionism (IC) is a useful way of referring to a body of research that is explicitly concerned with everyday practices and contingencies that mediate social life. Like other constructionists, IC researchers believe that reality is inseparably linked with interpretive actions. They view society as a collection of actors whose interpretations construct reality in relation to the variable "demands" of everyday settings. Following George Herbert Mead (1934) and Herbert Blumer (1969), IC takes for granted that (1) social objects are not inherently meaningful and (2) social reality is made meaningful and is changed through human interaction. Interactional constructionists aim to empirically investigate *situated practices* that create reality. The key feature of IC's approach to understanding social life is an uncompromising attention to the construction process as it is enacted in concrete settings. Although texts, rhetoric, or discourse can be considered manifestations of reality (Best, 1993; Goode & Ben-Yehuda, 1994; Gusfield, 1963; see also Gubrium, 1993a), for IC analysts social objects and their texts ultimately are realized in everyday practice.

Key Questions and Concerns of Interactional Constructionism

IC's analytic project can be broadly depicted through three of its central topics of concern: self, conditions of reality, and practice. These concerns, along with related theoretical and empirical questions, are listed in Table 16.1.

The IC approach varies from another predominant approach in sociology: the rhetorical claimsmaking approach. A construction-

TABLE 16.1. Key Questions and Topics of Interactional Constructionist Research

Broad analytic questions	Specific empirical questions	Topics of concern
How can human agency be conceptualized and studied?	Who and where is the empirical subject in the research?	Agency, subject, self, or identity
What social contingencies are at play when people use particular rhetorical claims?	What are the historical, institutional, and discursive environments of the empirical?	Conditions of reality or institutional or social structures
What is social action and how is it presented in everyday life?	What are the sites and sources of empirical realities that represent social interaction?	Social action or practice

ist research agenda focused on rhetorical claims, such as Peter Ibarra and John Kitsuse's (1993) "vernacular constituents" model, considers features of widespread public claims through which social phenomena are constructed but tends to gloss over the interactional *work* that underlies the making of social objects. As the Table 16.1 suggests, in contrast, IC emphasizes the real-time interactional contingencies of the social construction process. The questions listed point to the ongoing and nuanced dimensions of human interaction. As David Snow (2001) notes under the rubric of symbolic interaction, and similarly under IC, every dimension of human existence is constantly in the making or "emergent." First, the self, the building block or agent of interaction, is made and remade repeatedly within the boundaries of, and through, cultural resources. Second, social conditions are perpetually in the making, as they are interpreted and employed in practice. And, finally, practice itself is variable and contingent on the demands of the setting.

Some of these questions and related analytic issues are discussed in detail in James Holstein and Gale Miller's (1993) edited volume *Reconsidering Social Constructionism*. Borrowing from this book and other sources, in what follows I explain how questions related to self, to social conditions, and to practice form the basis of a distinctive constructionist research program. Follow-

ing that, I exemplify this from my own empirical work on the everyday construction of clients and clienthood in a homeless shelter.

Self and Identity in Everyday Life

IC's conceptualization of identity draws heavily from Mead's (1934) notion of the interactional self. This view begins with the premise that meaningful communication and human conduct (unlike reflexes and instinctual responses) are possible because we assume that others will respond to our actions based on a set of shared expectations. In this context, "expectations" are not fixed norms of conduct, but they are drawn through socially significant interpretive activity in relation to the contingencies of everyday life. In other words, expectations both define and are defined by the situation. As English speakers, for example, we could expect to invoke an argument when we utter the phrase "That's nonsense!" Or, depending on the context, we could solicit agreement and consensus. The point is that expectation (i.e., the structure of the interaction) is always and continually subject to how what is expected is construed in the context of unfolding social situations (i.e., interactive practice). The Meadian actor is both the subject and the object of social reality and can shape what is expected to fit developing circumstances. On the one hand, he or she is an agent who interpretively intervenes in the social world (this is what Mead refers to as the "I"). At the same time, to the extent that he or she takes the role of others (i.e., anticipates and perceives his or her own and others' actions), the individual him- or herself is a shared object of the social world, created and treated by its rules and expectations (this is what Mead refers to as the "Me").

This interactionist view of agency envisions a fluid and ongoing subject. Jay Gubrium (1993a) refers to this kind of Meadian subject as an "artful practitioner," or a self who is eternally and creatively embedded in his or her social surrounding. In Meadian terms, this "self is social in its origins." For interactional constructionists, participants in social interaction are not static, fixed in time and place. Therefore, they cannot be located solely in documents and their analyses or in fully structured and predetermined frameworks of social action. These active selves are mediated by concrete conditions and interpretive actions. Indeed, the conditions become part of the actor's identity. As I discuss next, IC's view of social contingencies is far more flexible than the traditional model of social structures.

The selves in IC studies are always in the making. Such research has focused on a wide range of identities in process. These include: the homeless self (Snow & Anderson, 1987), the artistic self (Stalp, 2006), the bankrupt self (Thorne & Anderson, 2006), the moral self (Green, South, & Smith, 2006; Presser, 2004), the abused self (Loseke, 1992), the nondepressed self (LaFrance & Stoppard, 2006), the nonimmigrant self (Killian & Johnson, 2006), and the alcoholic self (Denzin, 1987). In many cases, these studies are especially concerned with "stigmatized" selves (Goffman, 1970) and their management in everyday life and in social institutions (Gubrium & Holstein, 2001). Feminist studies of marginalization of women in everyday life (see, e.g., Dorothy Smith's seminal book *The Everyday World as Problematic*, 1987) have also contributed to

this body of work on identities in the making.

Conditions of Everyday Life

For IC, social conditions are not mere structures that dictate human conduct. IC rejects a deterministic view of social conditions in favor of a more malleable model in which social structures are interpreted, invoked, and/or enacted in everyday practice. Instead of broad conceptualizations (i.e., "culture," "poverty," "race"), interactional constructionists employ a more limited and locally circumscribed definition of social contingencies. For example, in *Out of Control* (1992), Gubrium compares "the local cultures" of two family therapy centers to show how each constitutes a different sense of "troubled families." Rather than treating "troubled families" and their purported "troubled selves" as universal and invariable social categories, Gubrium's research shows how these social objects are achieved locally and interactionally.

In addition to variations in local cultures, IC analysts are also concerned with how actors might interpret the same setting differently. For example, Gubrium's *Speaking of Life* (1993b) shows how the institutional circumstances of the same nursing home are seen from different perspectives, or different "horizons of meaning," by its residents. Thus the same nursing home can be described as either hospitable or harsh, depending on the particular actor's narrative standpoint.

According to IC, discourses can also be viewed as social conditions in the sense that they constitute languages of possibility. Following Foucault (1975), interactional constructionists approach discourse as a set of descriptive resources with practical implications. However, whereas Foucault studied the genealogical origins of discourses as conditions of possibility, interactional constructionists are more interested in "discourse in practice" (Gubrium & Holstein, 2000), the use of discursive resources to inform and guide everyday practices. For example, in their study of arthritis patients, Dana Rosenfeld and Christopher Faircloth (2004) examine how the patients' narratives of their illness and their practices are informed and bounded by the discourse of "functional mobility" and its mandate for patients to remain physically active even at the risk of causing themselves additional pain.

The attention to the convergence of language and social conditions in practice is also evident in the field of "discursive psychology" (Edwards & Potter, 1992), particularly as represented by the "discourse and rhetoric group" at Loughborough University in the United Kingdom. Like IC analysts, discursive psychologists are interested in how social reality is produced through site-specific uses of language. For example, discursive psychology offers "interpretive repertories" as analytic devices for connecting "the details of participants' descriptive practices to the broader ideological and historical formations in which those practices are situated" (Edwards, 2004, p. 506). In their groundbreaking book *Mapping the Language of Racism* the discursive psychologists Margaret Wetherell and Jonathan Potter (1992) employ interpretive repertoire to illustrate how "racism" operates as a set of discursive categories in use. The analytic project informing this work is described by the researchers thus: "We want to develop a discourse analysis which might utilize a double movement between styles of reading that emphasize the constitution of subject and objects and those that emphasize the ideological work of discourse" (1992, p. 93).

As is evident throughout this chapter, the analysis of discourse in use or in practice is similarly the hallmark of IC. It is also worth noting that as an analytic framework, IC, whether it goes by this title or not, is employed across social science disciplines. The common element across its various applications is IC's emphasis on the fluid and practical nature of all things social.

The Practice of Everyday Life

IC's take on practice is complicated. Let me begin to explain by noting that IC rejects individualistic and acontextual interpretations of practice. Similarly, IC does not reduce practice to behavior or verbal utterances that presumably manifest an actor's motive or intentions. Instead, practice is viewed as ongoing and purposeful action directed at others and mediated by the social context. This view of practice is, of course, at odds with positivistic readings of human conduct as universal cause-and-effect relationships, sociohistorical movements, or rhetorical strategies. As Gubrium (2005, p. 527) notes, "Practice is anything but neatly and empirically compartmentalized into institutional and social movement concerns."

How do we then grasp this admittedly messy view of practice? Here I try to answer this question by listing four ways in which IC researchers conceptualize social objects as ongoing concerns (Gubrium, 2005). The first conceptualization is denoted by inserting the word *practice* after the research topic. An example of this is Gubrium and Holstein's (2000) use of the term *interpretive practice* to refer to the everyday work of giving meaning to objects and events in particular social settings. Another example is the same authors' concept of *narrative practice* (1998), which refers to the convergence of discourse, rhetoric, and practice to construct site-specific, usable stories. Narratively based concepts have been important to my own constructionist work, and I take these up later in discussing empirical examples of interactional constructionist research.

A second way in which IC analysts emphasize the constructed quality of social action is to describe ongoing concerns as "work." Arlie Hochschild's *The Managed Heart* (2003) is a marvelous example of research focused on situated practice. In this work, Hochschild informs us that so-called pure emotions could in fact be deliberately performed for job-related tasks. For

Hochschild, *emotion work* refers to the activities and circumstances that help produce the "right" emotion for the "right" occasion. In a related study, Simon Gottschalk (2003) uses *emotion work* to explain the self-presentation styles of the children of Nazi Holocaust survivors. Similarly, Jack Spencer (1994) develops the term *client work* to describe constructive practices surrounding client processing in human service organizations. Specifically, he shows how clients use various themes to craft locally sensible identities that support their "service worthiness," or, as Spencer puts it: "clients constructed their narratives as rhetorical devices which could accountably cast themselves in ways which would guarantee their reception of services" (1994, p. 39).

A third way to key the construction process is to use the active word *doing* before a concept. For example, Trautner's (2005) "Doing Gender, Doing Class: The Performance of Sexuality in Exotic Dance Clubs" considers how gender, social class, and sexuality intersect in practice and are enacted in different locations in accordance with the customers' and club owners' expectations. As Trautner puts it, "expressions and performances of sexuality . . . are not homogeneous. Clubs construct distinctive working-class and middle-class performances and performers of sexuality that are consistent with popular ideas of how class and sexuality intersect" (2005, p. 785). Similarly, in "Doing Money Work in a Door-to-Door Sales Organization," David Schweingruber and Nancy Berns (2003) show how the meaning of money is interactionally achieved and put into practice by college students who are recruited to sell books door to door.

Finally, practice in IC research can be indicated with the *-ing* suffix. For example, in my own research on Middle Eastern American ethnic identity, I use *accounting* (Marvasti, 2005) to refer to the interactional dynamics of self-presentation in situations in which ethnic others are treated with suspicion and are asked to show themselves to be docile

and conventional. Using participant observation and in-depth interview data, I in a sense study the "interpretive repertoire" of Middle Eastern Americans who encounter public mistreatment. Essentially, this study amounts to an empirical analysis of how minority members "de-other" themselves using certain descriptive resources and self-presentation strategies.

In writing about "narrative practice," "client work," "doing gender," or "accounting," for IC, practice and its conditions are never far from analytic view. As Gubrium (2005, p. 527) states regarding the analysis of narratives, even the most artful and nuanced descriptions are embedded in tangible environments that "reflexively shape the realization of the problems in question, and mediate their sustenance or transformation." My own ethnography of a homeless shelter (Marvasti, 2003) showed how the client work was informed by the organizational mission of helping only those who were "responsive" to treatment and declining services to those who were deemed "treatment resistant." This contextual mandate thus provided an institutional gaze, or an "interpretive repertoire," for perceiving, classifying, and responding to "needy" clients.

Similarly, Kathleen Lowney and James Holstein's "Victims, Villains, and Talk Show Selves" alerts us that the troubles and characters presented in talk shows are formulaically manufactured "to arouse the viewer's passions" (2001, p. 24) or to generate higher ratings for the show. In the same vein, Gale Miller's "Changing the Subject: Self-Construction in Brief Therapy" (2001) illustrates how discursive environments provide different opportunities for defining clients and their problems. Susan Chase's "Universities as Discursive Environments for Sexual Identity Construction" (2001) is another example of how discursive resources (p. 155) the construction of identities.

Collectively, this body of research demonstrates IC's relentless attention to the contexts in which the work of constructing social objects is done. However, IC's commitment to conditioned practice is tempered with an analytic requirement to avoid reifying discursive or narrative environments. Accordingly, discursive environments are to be treated as simply conditions of possibilities, to borrow a phrase from Foucault, that mediate artful practices. As the excerpts from my own research detail in the next section, although the conditions provide a framework for what is possible, the outcomes of interaction are never predictable from the start.

Exemplifying the Key Concerns

In the remainder of this chapter, I use two examples from my own research on homelessness to underline IC's appreciation of how selves and conditions coalesce in practice. In these studies I focus on the work of constructing site-specific selves or clients. My goal is to understand how homelessness is interactionally achieved given the contingencies of the setting. I am especially interested in the dynamic relationship between the telling of experiential accounts and their narrative environments. These examples are from two locations in which homelessness was showcased in practice. The first study is from a public presentation in which people with a "homeless" past told their stories to student activists. The second is from an emergency shelter where homeless clients were required to tell their stories to a social worker as part of the screening process that determined their eligibility for services.

The empirical data for these studies come from ethnographic observations, interviews, and analysis of public documents. Note that in these examples, as is often the case with IC, the research methods are themselves interactional (see Holstein & Gubrium's *The Active Interview*, 1995). The data collection procedures and analyses reflect IC's underlying assumptions about the fluidity of social objects and conditions. Ethnographic methods are favored over the more statistically based procedures by IC researchers not be-

cause of a deep-seated ideological divide but for a more practical reason—namely, qualitative data, particularly from multiple perspectives, allow us to better understand the interactional *use* of discourse in *practice* (Gubrium & Holstein, 2000). Whereas the science of statistics by definition is aimed at capturing the *status* of things (from the word's Latin roots), IC researchers rely on qualitative techniques to describe the interactional "flow" of social objects in time and place.

Homelessness as Narrative Redemption (Marvasti, 1998)

Research Question and Background

How are accounts of homelessness *used* in everyday life to construct a situated identity? Social science literature often portrays homelessness as a "stigma," a concrete social condition or quality of certain individuals, fixed in time and place with little or no variation. Instead, I show how "homelessness" is contextually and interactionally bound. The policy implication of the study is that the so-called "one-size-fits-all" approach oversimplifies the experience and reduces social service recipients to victimized caricatures.

Setting and Analysis

There were, in fact, several settings for this ethnographic study. The research began at an emergency shelter when I met a homeless client, Shorty (all names have been fictionalized), who subsequently accompanied me on a trip to a nearby university to give an invited talk about being homeless. When we arrived there, we were greeted by a conference organizer, Todd, who coached Shorty and several other speakers on what the audience expected from them:

Todd: What I'd like everybody to talk about is to talk about what your life is like, if you have a son or daughter [for example]. Give a little bit about your background and whatever kind of information you feel comfortable sharing. (*Puts his hands on his heart.*) I want you to go into the *pain* from when you were homeless on the streets. . . . And guys, this is a student audience. They've had a lot of interaction with homeless people but they never had a chance to listen to homeless people tell their stories. . . . I will be the time keeper. . . . If I sense that you're really connecting with the audience, I'll give you the chance to wrap it up.

Todd's instructions for the speakers provides a context and clues about what descriptive resources or discourses are best suited for this particular audience and setting. This suggests that narratives of homelessness do not materialize in experiential vacuums but, as this case shows, are grounded in purposeful, setting-bound interaction.

Todd's interaction with the speakers went on in what Goffman (1959) calls "backstage." What comes next is the "frontstage" narrative performance. In a sense, the backstage provides the conditions and boundaries for the identities that are to be performed on the frontstage. The following presents two examples of the interactional construction of homelessness through redemptive or salvation narratives, which were deemed particularly suited for this event. The first is Dean's story of economic crisis and the second is Jim's account of emotional collapse.

Dean: I am Dean Lewis. I'm a formerly homeless person. . . . [The foregrounding of the downfall to homelessness] I kept getting laid off in the '90s and could not stay employed. My expenses exceeded my income and I tend to want to look at things from that point of view. . . . After not being able to pay my rent . . . I lived in a shelter for a while. Didn't want to do that. I hated it. I tried to hide my homelessness as much as possible. I was ashamed of it. So I went to the greatest efforts not to appear homeless. . . . [The

narrative turns to recovery and redemption] I started working for longer periods of time. . . . I am now working in my field. I am a children's mental health counselor. I have a place to live and enjoy being around my girlfriend and experiencing all the things that reinforce that I am a warm, loving, creative, zestful, human being who deserves a place on this planet. I am no longer angry as I had been toward service providers. And I ask people I may have offended to please forgive me. And I thank God for every day I am not homeless. And I thank you for letting me be a part of my recovery.

Jim: My name is Jim . . . I am very glad to be here today. . . . [The foregrounding of the downfall to homelessness] At the time I became homeless I had a good job, I had an apartment. I had plenty of possessions. I had plenty of money in the bank. Then after a death in the family in 1991, I felt like an emotional collapse, mental illness, ended up in a state hospital. . . . I also had a drinking problem which was related to my mental illness. I know that now, but at the time I didn't. . . . I found myself on the streets of North Carolina with nowhere to go. . . . At that point I didn't trust people too much. I mean I didn't realize I had problems. . . . I tried for the next couple of years to get a job, tried to find a place to stay, but I kept ending up in the same site, I'd be on the street. . . . I didn't have too much hope for a couple of years. I was alone with my problem. [The narrative turn to recovery and redemption] Today, I know I'm not alone. There are a lot of people who care. And by caring I care. . . . I would not wish this on anyone but I'm glad it happened to me, a lesson about life and a lesson about myself.

These stories unfolded literally on the stage in front of tens of students. The identities were unique and artful, in that they reflected the narrators' particular experiential standpoints. These individual variations constituted the speakers' "narrative horizons" (Gubrium & Holstein, 1997). At the same time, there were two sources of commonalities or two conditions of possibility for these stories. First, the stories were anchored discourses of insurmountable life disruptions. Whether homelessness was attributed to putative external causes (e.g., economic crisis or abusive spouses) or internal ones (e.g., mental illness or drug abuse), the precursor condition to becoming homeless was cast as an unendurable aberration in one's life course. After this was foregrounded for the audience, narrative redemption, the preferred style of telling, followed.

IC's concerns with self, conditions, and practice converge in this analysis. The actors construct useful biographies using salvation narratives that seem to suit the purpose at hand (i.e., to inform student activists about the plight of the homeless with an emphasis on hope for change, the potential for redemption). The interactional context (the public address, the coaching from a veteran activist, the well-publicized "down-and-out" discourse of homelessness) is used in the particular autobiographical performances here. Although there is variation in the experiences (e.g., emotional collapse, economic crisis, alcoholism), there is also a unifying discursive environment. Let us now consider the second study in which IC thematic concerns are manifest.

Constructing "Service-Worthy" Clients through Narrative Editing (Marvasti, 2002)

Research Question and Background

Given their limited resources, how do human service organizations decide which clients are worthy of services and which ones are turned away? This study exemplifies how we can get a nuanced appreciation of the social construction of service-worthy clients by simultaneously attending to identities and discursive environment as they become apparent in "narrative editing," or a type of interpretive practice that "constantly monitors, manages, modifies, and revises the

emergent story" (Gubrium & Holstein, 1998, p. 164). I specifically focus on how a social worker and her clients jointly work on stories of homelessness to achieve an client profile that fits the mission of this emergency shelter and facilitates the administration of its limited resources. Like the previous study, the research is aimed at understanding how useful, practical selves are achieved given the discursive conditions in place.

Setting and Analysis

The data for this study were collected at an emergency shelter for the homeless. As a charity organization, the main mission of the shelter was to provide free services and goods to people without housing. To determine which clients were deemed "truly" in need of help, a full-time social worker, Ann, was charged with conducting intake interviews to assess clients' needs. Through these interviews the staff established whether a particular client was a feasible investment for the shelter's limited resources.

Overall, the intake interviews with the social worker were occasions for constructing service-worthy narratives (Spencer, 1994). Consequently, accounts of medical disability, sudden and unexpected financial misfortune, and family crises were common institutionally *usable* stories that constituted the boundaries of this narrative environment. Still, the particulars of the clients' narratives were altered, shaped, or in some cases ignored by the social worker as these descriptive resources were put into practice during the intake interview. The conditions did not dictate the substance of the stories. In the course of narrative practice, client narratives sometimes produced differing or competing realities of service worthiness.

Following are two examples of client processing with different results. In the first instance (collaborative editing), a couple's story about homelessness is significantly helped by the social worker to establish their service worthiness. In the second (dismissive editing), a female client's story is dismissed as incredible. I recorded both interviews, along with more than 20 others, in the social workers' office with the clients' permission.

Collaborative Editing

Connie and Ray were admitted to the shelter as an "unmarried couple." In addition to having to convince the social worker of their neediness, this couple had to establish that their relationship was intimate and serious enough to meet the shelter's informal definition of "family." This in turn would allow Connie and Ray to share a room and to receive priority with rent assistance and other services. After the usual waiting and the introductions, the intake interview began. Note how in this interview the narrative environment of an emergency shelter mediates the story of a "homeless couple."

Social Worker: Well, let's see, Ray and Connie.

Ray: Yes.

Social Worker: My name is Ann, if you hadn't already figured that out. Sorry you had to wait a little bit. (Looks through her papers for a few seconds.) That signature doesn't look like it says Ray Williams. Is that your signature?

Ray: I was writing in Korean in the army. I picked up the signature then.

Connie: He used to write like that all the time. Every time he signed something, he'd write like that.

Ray: It used to be a lot worse.

Social Worker: So when were you in the service?

Ray: '87 to '92.

Social Worker: And you served in Korea at one point?

Ray: Yeah, for about six weeks until I caught something called Chinese food poisoning sickness, or some word like that. So they sent me home. So I was very sick, that's how they shipped me. I've been here [back in the United States] since then and it's never bothered me. So I don't know what they were talking about. Maybe they just wanted to get rid of me. I don't know.

Social Worker: Well, it is a very real syndrome.

Ray: Oh, okay. They called it Chinese something something.

Social Worker: Yeah, Chinese restaurant syndrome or something like that. I don't know if they do so much anymore, but they used to use a lot of MSG [monosodium glutamate] in their cooking. My mother used to use a lot of it years ago and as the truth came out about it, she realized it was the source of some of her depression and headaches and she stopped using it. That made a difference.

Connie: He had a lot of headaches.

Social Worker: (*Goes back to writing notes.*)

As we examine the interactional dynamics of this exchange, we see that the social worker does not challenge the reasonability of Ray's insistence on signing his name in Korean; instead, she just uses it as a narrative link (Gubrium & Holstein, 1998) to probe the client's background in the military, which may point to Ray's special needs as a veteran. As Ray explains how he was sent back home because of "Chinese food poisoning," Ann collaborates with him in creating his account by saying: "Well, it is a very real syndrome," and she goes on to provide the client with the appropriate medical jargon: "the Chinese restaurant syndrome," a label that is in fact used in medical literature as a synonym for "MSG symptom complex."

Ann makes the applicants' joint narrative relevant by comparing it to her own mother's problems with "depression and headaches," at which point Connie also validates the account by saying: "He had a lot of headaches." Through this act of collaborative editing, Ray's story smoothly moves from his Korean signature to the validation of his medical status, a matter that is of immediate organizational relevance.

Connie's story of illness is similarly shaped.

Social Worker: They wrote down, Connie, under medical problems that your heart races when you get hot. What is that all about?

Connie: When out in the sun too much, it's like someone is sticking a knife in my back.

Social Worker: Have you got medical treatment for that?

Ray: She's applied for SSI [Supplemental Security Income]. They're going to give her something tomorrow. The lawyer said her appeal is going to go in in February. They're going to give her something to fix it. They told her pretty much, "When it happens again, then you come in and give your paper work and then you go to HRS [Florida Department of Health and Rehabilitative Services] with the paper work."

Social Worker: What's the diagnosis? Do you know? Have they given it a name?

Connie: I have no idea what caused it. When I'm out in the sun for a period of time riding my bike or something, then it hits me.

Ray: Or when she's trying to go up a hill on her bike.

Social Worker: Your SSI claim is based solely on that, or are there other issues?

Connie: Oh, it's just based on—I have a little bit of asthma every now and then, but I'm getting that taken care of. So there's no problem with that. It's going be based on me having a situation where I can't go out and get a job. Like most other people, they can just go out and wham! They get a job. When I go out to get a job that gets in my way. I mean I tried, tried, and tried to get a job.

Ray: She never graduated from high school.

Social Worker: So you have a learning disability, is that part of it?

Ray: She was born 2 months early—7 months.

Connie: I was born premature.

Ray: She lived in an incubator. I'm not trying to sound like a doctor but it sounds like that attention-deficit disorder. She can read a book and 10 minutes later she won't remember having put it down.

Social Worker: I don't know if attention-deficit disorder will cause you to not recall something, but it may be a related condition.

Connie: I think my family has something similar to that and that's the reason why.

Ray: Her mom did about every kind of drug there was when she was pregnant with her. She shot up, she smoked this and that, and probably a few things we've never even heard of.

Connie: My mom did this and that when she was pregnant with me. She didn't want to feed me, she didn't change my diaper—

Ray: Okay, we're talking about your *mental health*.

Social Worker: Well, what a mother does when she's pregnant can certainly affect the mental functioning of her child. Though it sounds like the attorney is basing the claim on a combination of all those issues. Although February is long way off to wait for that funding.

Connie: I hope something comes through. (*Pause*)

Exposure to the sun, learning disability, asthma, premature birth, and parental negligence are all marshaled as discursive resources to establish Connie as a "needy" client. At one point in the story, sensing that Connie's litany is losing coherence as she recounts how infrequently her diaper was changed, Ray monitors the narrative by reminding her, "Okay, we're talking about your *mental health*." His professed knowledge of the details of his companion's condition and the entitlement to intervene in her story also help to establish that Ray and Connie are indeed an intimate couple.

Again, we can see here how discursive conditions and resources are artfully put into practice to construct a useful identity for this site. This example demonstrates how through narrative practice inconsistencies and irrelevancies are transformed into locally relevant information. However, client work is not always geared toward consensus and serving needs. In some cases, client work is geared toward ridding the shelter of unusable selves.

Dismissive Editing

Sometimes the failure of the parties to preserve the narrative enterprise results in the patent rejection of the client's claims regarding service worthiness. This is illustrated in the following intake with Paula, a black woman in her late 20s, who came to the shelter several times during my volunteer shift to make an appointment with the social worker. Though not a shelter resident, she insisted on seeing Ann about "getting help," refusing to disclose the specifics of her request.

She was eventually given an interview, which began with her explanation of how a criminal record made her ineligible for government-subsidized housing. In response, the social worker probed:

Social Worker: How old are the charges?

Paula: About maybe a year or two.

Social Worker: What's the nature of them?

Paula: They said I was trying to obtain they didn't even have, what you call it, they couldn't even define what the charge was. I was trying to get my son some medicine

for his tooth and they were saying I was trying to obtain a prescription for drugs. And I'm not a drug addict, never have been.

Social Worker: But I mean were you convicted of something?

Paula: That's what they say.

Social Worker: How come *they* say that and *you* seem a little puzzled?

Paula: Yeah, because they're saying I was trying to "obtain" a prescription for drugs. I did it for his toothache, and they said it was, what you call it, a drug.

Social Worker: But you were unable to fight that through the public defender or somebody?

Paula: I wasn't able to do it. Sure wasn't.

Social Worker: And what type of sentence did you receive?

Paula: It was probation.

Social Worker: Uh-huh. (*Waits for the client to go on.*)

Social Worker: Well, that probably is going to be somewhat of an obstacle. I can't make that go away.

Paula: I can't either, you know. I just deal with it.

At first, the social worker attempts to transform the client's narrative into a usable client story by focusing on specific dates and objective facts (Emerson, 1994). However, because the client's story contradicts "official" accounts of her story, Ann tries to resolve the matter by asking, "How come *they* say that and *you* seem a little puzzled?" The client's criminal background, coupled with her vague explanation of the criminal charges, makes the work of constructing a service-worthy client particularly difficult in this case. Therefore, Ann's narrative editing becomes dismissive, as signaled by the statement: "I can't make that go away."

Nonetheless, the service applicant is not ready to accept the rejection and uses a moral appeal (Spencer, 2001) to persuade the caseworker. Paula states, "I can't either, you know. I just deal with it," and goes on to expand on her narrative, explaining how she and her two children were forced to leave her husband because of "domestic problems" caused by a "divorce situation." Paula adds that she is currently living with "a friend" under a temporary arrangement and that she is looking for public housing. As seen in the following excerpt, Ann dismisses Paula's moral claims with an impromptu interpretation of the shelter policies, or what Spencer and McKinney (1997) call a "policy rap."

Social Worker: I'm not sure what you're asking. Be more specific.

Paula: Like maybe rental assistance or something like that.

Social Worker: Oh, okay. The only rent money we have available is for people living in the shelters. It is not available to someone who's not living in a shelter.

Ostensibly, the client's request is dismissed solely on the grounds that it does not fit the procedural parameters of the organization, but in reality, based on my previous observations, as in most organizational matters, the caseworker had a good deal of discretion in granting requests of this kind. Nevertheless, Ann's somewhat extemporaneous application of the shelter policies makes it possible to forgo the expenditure of valued and limited resources on a difficult case. Listing other agencies that might be of use to Paula, the caseworker reminds her that she is not qualified for emergency services because she is not literally without a place to stay. Yet, Paula makes a final moral plea:

Paula: Ms. Allen (*referring to the social worker by her last name*)? You know, no one knows what it's like to be in a place where they're not family. And those people are just

reaching out, because—I'm pretty sure God has a lot to do with it, you understand?

Social Worker: Uh-huh.

Paula: Sometimes people look at you and they think you aren't in need, but if they only knew, you understand me? Because a lot of times you keep the best for the outside, you know? And you go on, you know, and you try to make it like that. But if people only knew what you feel and what your situation really is. You know, it's like you cry for help and you wonder: Do God hear you? Do other people? You reach out and reach out, and reach out.

Social Worker: Well, unfortunately, a lot of times agencies' hands are tied because of limited funding or the rules that they have.

Paula: Yeah.

Social Worker: I mean the rules on our rent program are prescribed by the federal government. If I don't follow the rules, they may decide next year they're not gonna give us the money. So, there are consequences if I don't follow the rules.

Paula: Right, right.

Social Worker: So we don't always have the freedom to help out of compassion because we have guidelines that we have to follow.

Paula: Right. I'm just speaking up about, you understand, in general, about society.

Social Worker: Oh, sure. (*Short pause*) Well, these are the places with food pantries (*pointing to a map that shows the location of other charity organizations*).

The client's use of the discourse of morality (Spencer, 2001), as indicated by the explicit plea for sympathy and the expression of dire needs, is dismissed and rebutted by the policy rap (Spencer & McKinney, 1997), or the organization's need to "follow the rules." The social worker's statement, "So we don't always have the freedom to help out of compassion because we have guidelines that we have to follow," is very telling in this regard because it shows how the staff uses the discourse of rationality (Spencer, 2001) to resolve the recurring tension between the professed desire to help the needy and the organizational necessity of managing limited resources.

As seen in this example, IC does not assume that conditions determine outcomes. Ann's interpretation of shelter policies is artful and variable. It is through the study of practice that we can fully appreciate the variations and complexities of how "claims," "rhetoric," or "conditions" are used. The narrative practice styles discussed here show that the construction of homeless clients and their service worthiness, although grounded in a specific discursive environment, are nonetheless variable and artful in practice. The social worker and her clients have at their disposal a repertoire of discourses and editing styles to artfully guide the telling of homeless narratives. Staff–client interactions are fluid and reflexive. Clients do not passively follow editing cues from their service workers. On the contrary, they often pursue, at least initially, what they believe is a relevant story. On the other hand, the staff and the institutional mission of the shelter constantly mediate how homelessness is articulated. As Gubrium and Holstein's (2000) analytic reflexivity would suggest, the social construction of service-worthy clients involves a dialectical relationship between the organizational conditions of possibility and "how members artfully put discourses to work as they constitute their subjectivities and related social worlds" (p. 497).

The narrative editing styles explicated in this analysis illustrate variations in how discourses are put into practice to achieve or disregard accounts of service worthiness. Given that institutional conditions of possibility allow for a range of interpretations, staff members have several interpretive op-

tions for how they respond to client narratives. The variability in these responses does not necessarily represent capricious or arbitrary interpretive work on the part of staff members. To the contrary, the narrative editing styles may be seen as a fairly stable institutional repertoire of possible responses from which staff members draw to respond to clients. They form an "institutional menu of possible ways of dealing with clients' stories, and like any menu, they limit possibilities without dictating choices" (J. Holstein, personal communication, October 1, 2001).

Conclusion

In these examples from my research, identities were interactionally achieved for locally relevant purposes. In the first example, we see that the "homeless" self and its presumed stigma are not universal realities that transcend time and place; rather, they are social categories artfully crafted for the task at hand, in this case for inspiring college students "to get involved." In the second example, the analysis shows that the work of constructing "service-worthy" homeless clients is not accomplished in a unified and consistent manner. Rather, the social worker and her clients have at their disposal a repertoire of discourses and editing styles to artfully guide the telling of homeless narratives.

Both studies are conceptually grounded in the understanding that the social construction of reality is embedded in the reflexive give-and-take between the substance of everyday life (i.e., *whats*) and its practitioners' constructive practices (i.e., *hows*; Gubrium & Holstein, 1997). According to Gubrium and Holstein (1997, p. 119), a complete analysis of social life requires "alternately bracketing the *whats*, then the *hows*, in order to assemble a more complete picture of practice." This approach, loosely named "analytic bracketing," simultaneously attends to the artful qualities of everyday practice and its substantive conditions and thus embodies the core elements of IC (self, conditions, and practice). As Gubrium and Holstein (1997, p. 12, original emphasis) explain:

> analytic bracketing *does not privilege conditions or artfulness*. Being the two sides of interpretive practice, conditions and artfulness are reflexively intertwined so that the reification of one in service to the analysis of the other is virtually impossible. While a simultaneous focus on the artful *and* the substantial is a practical impossibility, analytic bracketing allows us to appreciate their respective contributions to interpretation while respecting their reflexive relationship.

Similar to Wetherell and Potter's (1992) dual focus, discussed earlier in this chapter, research informed by this reflexive approach treats social objects simultaneously as conditions of possibility and artful practices. For example, in their edited book, *Institutional Selves: Troubled Identities in a Postmodern World*, Gubrium and Holstein (2001) present a number of studies that look at how institutional settings and their policies provide contingencies without necessarily determining outcomes of everyday practices.

These studies and the related IC literature cited in this chapter suggest that reality cannot be fully comprehended through textual representations, isolated and stripped from discursive environments and practice, as Ibarra and Kitsuse (1993) contend. A textually driven analysis of claimsmaking takes for granted the topic of the analysis by ignoring the interpretive context that provides its meaning and coherence. Ironically, this violates the very ethnomethodological mandate about bracketing that Ibarra and Kitsuse claim to follow. To borrow from Mead's (1934) classic baseball metaphor, it is absurd to suggest that the totality of the game of baseball can be understood by studying instructional manuals about the sport. The game is not just a set of rules, textually represented, modified, and updated. Rather, the game ultimately involves practice, players, and settings that collectively define how it is played and what it means to the actors. Likewise, the game of social life is far too complex to be reduced to a mechanical analysis of rhetorical claims as found in public texts. People do things under certain conditions and for certain purposes.

It is important to note that IC's point of departure from Ibarra and Kitsuse (1993) does not center on rejecting rhetoric as a constituent element of social reality. On the contrary, to the extent that rhetoric is understood as the artful *use* of language in everyday *practice*, IC analysts are very much interested in its analysis. However, if rhetoric is stripped of its contextualized use, then IC would contend that its analysis is at best incomplete and at worst simply wrong. (See Dorothy Smith's, 1990, similar interactional and institutionally based approach to texts.)

A few words of caution are in order here. IC is so comprehensive in its scope that it is reasonable to expect novice readers to find the approach evasive or pretentiously out of reach. IC researchers are at once interested in everything and nothing in particular. Although their research agenda encompasses many perennial topics of social science (e.g., identity, power, social order), they take none of these topics for granted. In this chapter, to convey the ambitious project of IC, I began by artificially separating its constituent elements to explain the interactionist conceptualization of self, social conditions, and practice. I then reassembled these parts using Gubrium and Holstein's analytic reflexivity and narrative practice models. My intention was to present a glimpse of the elemental "trees" before plunging into the whole "forest" of IC. Some of the researchers cited in this chapter may be unpleasantly surprised that their work has been labeled *interactional constructionist*. If that is the case, I apologize and hope that the instructive purpose of this chapter justifies my unintentional error.

In his famous essay "Science without Concepts," Blumer (1969, p. 169) admonished us against "manufacturing [concepts] with reckless abandon, with no concern as to whether there is need for them." He suspected we do so to satisfy a "pretension to be scientific" (p. 169). Ultimately, we will do well to remember Blumer's quintessentially pragmatic advice that conceptual frameworks, such as IC, are meant to be used as "synthesizing" tools for the practice of research.

• References

Best, J. (1993). *Threatened children: Rhetoric and concerns about child-victims.* Chicago: University of Chicago Press.

Blumer, H. (1969). *Symbolic interaction: Perspective and method.* Los Angeles: University of California Press.

Chase, S. E. (2001). Universities as discursive environments for sexual identity construction. In J. F. Gubrium & J. A. Holstein (Eds.), *Institutional selves: Troubled identities in a postmodern world* (pp. 142–157). New York: Oxford University Press.

Denzin, N. (1987). *The alcoholic self.* Newbury Park, CA: Sage.

Edwards, D. (2004). Interpretative repertoire. In M. Lewis-Beck, A. Bryman, & T. F. Liao (Eds.), *Encyclopedia of social science research methods* (pp. 506–507). Thousand Oaks, CA: Sage.

Edwards, D., & Potter, J. (1992). *Discursive psychology.* London: Sage.

Emerson, R. M. (1994). Constructing serious violence and its victims: Processing a domestic violence restraining order. In J. A. Holstein & G. Miller (Eds.), *Perspectives on social problems* (Vol. 6, pp. 3–28). Greenwich, CT: JAI Press.

Foucault, M. (1975). *Discipline and punish: The birth of the prison.* New York: Random House.

Goffman, E. (1959). *The presentation of self in everyday life.* Harmondsworth, UK: Penguin.

Goffman, E. (1970). *Stigma: Notes on the management of spoiled identity.* New York: Penguin.

Goode, E., & Ben-Yehuda, N. (1994). *Moral panics: The social construction of deviance.* Oxford, UK: Blackwell.

Gottschalk, S. (2003). Reli(e)ving the past: Emotion work in the Holocaust's second generation. *Symbolic Interaction, 2*(3), 355–380.

Green, G., South, N., & Smith, R. (2006). "They say that you are a danger but you are not": Representations and construction of the moral self in narratives of "dangerous individuals." *Deviant Behavior, 27,* 299–328.

Gubrium, J. F. (1992). *Out of control: Family therapy and domestic disorder.* Thousand Oaks, CA: Sage.

Gubrium, J. F. (1993a). For a cautious naturalism. In J. A. Holstein & G. Miller (Eds.), *Reconsidering constructionism: Debates in social problems theory* (pp. 89–101). New York: Aldine de Gruyter.

Gubrium, J. F. (1993b). *Speaking of life: Horizons of mean-ing for nursing home residents.* New York: Aldine de Gruyter.

Gubrium, J. F. (2005). Narrative environments. *Social Problems, 52*(4), 525–528.

Gubrium, J. F., & Holstein, J. A. (1997). *The new language of qualitative method.* Thousand Oaks, CA: Sage.

Gubrium, J. F., & Holstein, J. A. (1998). Narrative practice and the coherence of personal stories. *Sociological Quarterly, 39,* 163–187.

Gubrium, J. F., & Holstein, J. A. (2000). Analyzing interpretive practice. In N. Denzin & Y. S. Lincoln (Eds.), *Handbook of qualitative research* (2nd ed., pp. 487–508). Thousand Oaks, CA: Sage.

Gubrium, J. F., & Holstein, J. A. (2001). *Institutional selves: Troubled identities in a postmodern world.* Thousand Oaks, CA: Sage.

Gusfield, J. (1963). *Symbolic crusades: Status politics and the American temperance movement.* Champaign: University of Illinois Press.

Hochschild, A. (2003). *The managed heart: Commercialization of human feeling* (2nd ed.). Berkeley: University of California Press.

Holstein, J. A., & Gubrium, J. (1995). *The active interview.* Thousand Oaks, CA: Sage.

Holstein, J. A., & Miller, G. (Eds.). (1993). *Reconsidering social constructionism: Debates in social problems theory.* New York: Aldine de Gruyter.

Ibarra, P., & Kitsuse, J. (1993). Vernacular constituents of moral discourse: An interactionist proposal for the study of social problems. In J. A. Holstein & G. Miller (Eds.), *Reconsidering social constructionism: Debates in social problems theory* (pp. 25–58). New York: Aldine de Gruyter.

Killian, C., & Johnson, C. (2006). "I'm not an immigrant!": Resistance, redefinition, and the role of resources in identity work. *Social Psychology Quarterly, 69*(1), 60–80.

LaFrance, M., & Stoppard, J. (2006). Constructing a non-depressed self: Women's accounts of recovery from depression. *Feminism and Psychology, 16*(3), 307–325.

Loseke, D. (1992). *The battered woman and shelters: The social construction of wife abuse.* New York: State University of New York Press.

Lowney, K., & Holstein, J. A. (2001). Victims, villains and talk show selves. In J. F. Gubrium & J. A. Holstein (Eds.), *Institutional selves: Troubled identities in a postmodern world* (pp. 23–45). New York: Oxford University Press.

Marvasti, A. (1998). Homelessness as narrative redemption. In J. A. Holstein & G. Miller (Eds.), *Perspectives on social problems* (Vol. 10, pp. 167–182). Greenwich, CT: JAI Press.

Marvasti, A. (2002). Constructing the service-worthy client through narrative editing. *Journal of Contemporary Ethnography, 10,* 220–221.

Marvasti, A. (2003). *Being homeless: Textual and narrative constructions.* Lanham, MD: Lexington Books.

Marvasti, A. (2005). Being Middle Eastern American: Identity negotiation in the context of the war on terror. *Symbolic Interaction, 28*(4), 525–547.

Mead, G. H. (1934). *Mind, self, and society.* Chicago: University of Chicago Press.

Miller, G. (2001). Changing the subject: Self-construction in brief therapy. In J. F. Gubrium & J. A. Holstein (Eds.), *Institutional selves: Troubled identities in a postmodern world* (pp. 64–83). New York: Oxford University Press.

Presser, L. (2004). Violent offenders, moral selves: Constructing identities and accounts in the research interview. *Social Problems, 51*(1), 82–101.

Rosenfeld, D., & Faircloth, C. (2004). Embodied fluidity and the commitment to movement: Constructing the moral self through arthritis narratives. *Symbolic Interaction, 27*(4), 507–529.

Schweingruber, D., & Berns, N. (2003). Doing money work in a door-to-door sales organization. *Symbolic Interaction, 26*(3), 447–471.

Smith, D. (1987). *The everyday world as problematic: A feminist sociology.* Boston: Northeastern University Press.

Smith, D. (1990). *The conceptual practices of power.* Boston: Northeastern University Press.

Snow, D. (2001). Extending and broadening Blumer's conceptualization of symbolic interactionism. *Symbolic Interactionism, 24,* 367–377.

Snow, D., & Anderson, L. (1987). Identity work among the homeless: The verbal construction and avowal of personal identities. *American Journal of Sociology, 92*(6), 1336–1371.

Spencer, J. W. (1994). Homeless in River City: Client work in human service encounters. In J. A. Holstein & G. Miller (Eds.), *Perspectives on social problems* (Vol. 6, pp. 29–46). Greenwich, CT: JAI Press.

Spencer, J. W. (2001). Self-presentation and organizational processing in a human service agency. In J. F. Gubrium & J. A. Holstein (Eds.), *Institutional selves: Troubled identities in a postmodern world* (pp. 158–169). New York: Oxford University Press.

Spencer, J. W., & McKinney, J. L. (1997). "We don't pay for bus tickets, but we can help you find work": The micropolitics of trouble in human service encounters. *Sociological Quarterly, 38*(1), 185–203.

Stalp, M. (2006). Creating an artistic self: Amateur quilters and subjective careers. *Sociological Focus, 39*(3), 193–216.

Thorne, D., & Anderson, L. (2006). Managing the stigma of personal bankruptcy. *Sociological Focus, 39*(2), 77–97.

Trautner, M. N. (2005). Doing gender, doing class: The performance of sexuality in exotic dance clubs. *Gender & Society, 19*(6), 771–788.

Wetherell, M., & Potter, J. (1992). *Mapping the language of racism: Discourse and the legitimation of exploitation.* New York: Columbia University Press.

CHAPTER 17

Claimsmaking, Culture, and the Media in the Social Construction Process

● **Kathleen S. Lowney**

Be it pain, anger, grief, fear, despair, or even the hope for a better future, emotions push individuals out of their private lives and into the public arena, ready to perform claimsmaking (Jasper, 1998; Loseke, 1993). Whether it is the solitary individual whose voice is the quiet whisper drowned out by all the hustle and bustle of our lives or thousands of individuals acting in concert, claimsmaking, first and foremost, begins by harnessing passions. It was, for example, just one person's earnest plea that moved so many citizens of the state of Washington to form the social movement known as the Tennis Shoe Brigade. Ryan Hade, Helen Harlow's son, was in middle school when he was savagely attacked—beaten, sexually assaulted and mutilated, and left for dead—by a just-released sex offender. The heinousness of the act, the young age of the victim, and his mother's dignified but quiet fury ensured media coverage. Harlow appealed to those who were appalled by what had happened to her son and to so many other children who were similarly attacked by sexual predators to send a child's tennis shoe to the governor to force him to call a special session to discuss how to protect children from violent predators. She thus became the leader of a movement that changed American jurisprudence. Although sexual-predator laws are still debated (Corrigan, 2006; Janus, 2000), no one could argue that the Tennis Shoe Brigade nearly single-handedly forced the Washington State governor and legislature to act. Of course, these actions were embedded within the state's cultural context of heightened worries about sexual predators and concerns about numerous escapes from the state's mental health hospital, as well as criticisms of its staff, both in terms of the level of security they provided the community and in the care they gave, and the more widespread cultural context of a moral panic about crimes against children that has been present in the United States since the 1980s (Best, 1990; Shaw, 1990; Turner, 2004).

Individuals such as Helen Harlow or social movements such as the Tennis Shoe Brigade, agitating for social change in order to fix what they perceive to be a moral injustice, are called *moral entrepreneurs*. Becker (1963) described a moral entrepreneur in this manner:

> The existing rules do not satisfy him because there is some evil which profoundly disturbs him [*sic*]. He feels that nothing can be right in the world until rules are made to correct it. He operates with an absolute ethic; what he sees is truly and totally evil with no qualifications. Any means is justified to do away with it. The crusader is fervent and righteous, often self-righteous. . . . The crusader is not only interested in seeing to it that other people do what he thinks right. He believes that if they do what is right it will be good for them. Or he may feel that his reform will prevent certain kinds of exploitation of one person by another. (pp. 147–148)

Emotions, then are one of the primary motivations that drive moral entrepreneurs to do something—anything—in order to make the world right. "Since feeling is a form of pre-action, a script or a moral stance toward it is one of the culture's most powerful tools for directing action" (Hochschild, 1983, p. 56). By persuading others to feel empathy and sympathy for the victims being harmed and to direct their anger and even hatred toward the villains who inflict the damage, they often are able to attract others to their cause, creating a social movement. Their claims-making activities, if done well, situate themselves, those who respond to them, and the victims and villains they identify within a shared moral universe. That shared moral universe is itself embedded within a larger

cultural milieu that shapes the rhetoric, imagery, and emotions that are available for claimsmakers to use.

In this chapter we examine the complex interplay between culture and claimsmaking practices, with a special focus on how these come together in media stories about distressing social conditions. Of course, sociological discourse about social problems is not the only location for constructionism within academe. Many disciplines now utilize constructionist discourse. Some of these include: anthropology (e.g., Casper & Koenig, 1996), the counseling disciplines (e.g., Asen, 2004; Friedlander, Heatherington, & Marrs, 2000; Holstein & Gubrium, 1995; Lyon, 1995; Mancuso, 1996; Wong, 2006), criminology and criminal justice (e.g., Armour, 2002; Burns, 2001; Chermak, 2003; Chiricos & Eschholz, 2002; Chiricos, Padgett, & Gertz, 2000; Dunn, 2002; Mertz, 1994; Muehlenhard & Kimes, 1999), housing (Jacobs, Kemeny, & Manzi, 2004), science and medicine (e.g., Berg, 1992; Courtenay, 2000; Nicolson & McLaughlin, 1988), environmental studies (Ali, 2002; Burningham, 1998; Burningham & Cooper, 1999; Clarke & Short, 1993; Cunter & Harris, 1998; Greider & Garkovich, 1994; Hannigan, 2006; Murphy, 2004; Tierney, 1999; Woodward, 2000), even marketing (Hackley, 1998). As each discipline utilizes constructionism to elucidate its central questions, each adheres to the proposition that reality, however it might be experienced by human actors in any particular social setting, is actively created and sustained through human interaction.

We begin this chapter by tracing how troublesome conditions become constructed as social problems, what Best (2008) has called the *social problems process*. Who are the social actors involved in this process and what is the nature of their interactions? What role does culture play in this process? What cultural messages do claimsmakers need to absorb in order to become successful? The chapter then analyzes one kind of claimsmaker—the mass media—in particular and discusses the key status the media hold in the social problems process. We will end with a more speculative discussion of issues that constructionists—both those writing now and the next generation to come—will likely face.

The Social Problems Process

The process begins with moral entrepreneurs who are roused by a troubling condition in the social or physical world—a potential social problem. Their often visceral concern necessitates that they call attention to the condition in the hope that it can be changed, for they believe it must be addressed. Moral entrepreneurs—also referred to in constructionism as *primary claimsmakers* or *activists*—need to fashion their concerns into successful packages of claims (sets of words, behaviors, and symbols/images) if they wish to persuade others. That is to say, they need to create claims that are convincing, holistic, and seem to have a reasonable chance of success, as judged not only by themselves but also by their audience(s), those whom they are attempting to win over. The most successful claimsmakers recognize that the audience needs to be provided with a certain amount of information in order to even consider supporting the claim. Individuals need to know about the troubling condition in order to be persuaded that it is important enough to be concerned about, and thus individual claimsmakers construct a diagnostic frame that discusses, among other things, how many people the troubling condition supposedly affects, how seriously they are harmed, the best orientation to the troubling condition (i.e., is it a medical condition, a legal issue, etc.?), and so on. Diagnostic frames are used to provide "facts and figures" that are persuasively argued, but claimsmakers need to realize that support can be best generated if they make people feel as well as think (Loseke, 1993). Providing one or two typifying examples—real-life examples of those who have been se-

verely harmed by the troublesome condition that shape the audience's perceptions of it—to illustrate the problem often rounds out the diagnostic frame. Emotional work is critical to building a consensus that the condition must be changed; claimsmakers, therefore, need to carefully choose the typifying examples they will use and select those that evoke emotions that will, they hope, lead to their desired actions.

But successful claims need to give their audiences more than a diagnostic frame; they should also provide a prognostic frame, which outlines their means of solving, or at least ameliorating, the troubling condition. Prognostic frames can be challenging to construct; activists need to provide enough detail to make people feel confident that the solutions proffered could work yet not too much detail, for that might lead to premature disputes about implementation, which could decrease support. Solutions proffered should offer a sense of hope to audience members, a vision of a time not far away when the suffering of the victims could be ameliorated, and the promise that they can help to make that better time a reality. To support that vision, claimsmakers also construct a motivational frame for their audiences. These frames explain why people should care about the troubling condition, its victims, and even its villains. Although motivational frames are often less visible to audience members than the diagnostic and prognostic frames, they are in large measure crucial to the success of the claimsmaking campaign. Activists must find ways to tap into the reserve of cultural images, values, and themes and use them to create feelings that can draw together various constituencies into a social movement focused on achieving change. A variety of framing strategies can be used to increase the likelihood that any one audience member will be persuaded.

This process can be fraught with the possibilities for claimsmakers to make, if not mistakes, at least poor decisions that might put off potential members instead of bringing them into the cause. So activists, who are initially often unsophisticated in claimsmaking, may have to try numerous approaches in order to gain the attention they feel they need to right the troubling condition. For every unsuccessful attempt, they may feel frustrated by their lack of success, but they are also determined to try again, for they feel they *must* fix the troubling condition; it is their mission in life to make the world a better place.

Activists often need others to help "sell" their claims, and so they seek out expert claimsmakers, so labeled because they bring to the claimsmaking process a specialized body of knowledge about the troubling condition or similar ones. Experts legitimize claims (or are supposed to) by grounding them in professional discourse, including theories, statistics, and the dramaturgical trappings of credibility (i.e., professional titles, symbols, etc.). That is not to say that expert claimsmaking never utilizes emotional techniques, for obviously it does. But experts frequently background emotions, highlighting the seemingly objective nature of their claimsmaking contributions. They stress "facts and figures," leaving activists to personify them with typifying stories that will pull at our heartstrings (Best, 1987, 1990; Loseke, 1992; Lowney & Best, 1995).

Activists, the social movements they begin, and experts rarely are able to propagate their claims strongly enough to create the social change they desire. They need another social actor in the social problems process to help spread the word about the troublesome condition; thus, in the second step, the media are involved in the claimsmaking process. Most often the claimsmakers seek out the media to disseminate their views more broadly, but there are times when the media find the claimsmakers first—sometimes in a cooperative spirit, though at other times, the media can be downright hostile. Media coverage therefore can be a mixed blessing for claimsmakers (Kruse, 2001). Their claims may reach a larger number of potential supporters and bring additional resources to

the cause, but their claimsmaking is especially vulnerable because they no longer have complete control over how their message is communicated (Gamson, Croteau, Hoynes, & Sasson, 1992; Kensicki, 2001). Despite the risk, in nearly every claimsmaking campaign, even a small, localized one, media coverage will be necessary in order to reach the numbers of people needed to create social change.

Although we may naively believe that the media are there to inform us about important information, that is, "news," constructionist scholars have long pointed out how reporters use specific techniques to tell a good story. Often this means that complex events are translated into visually wrenching images of sympathetic victims and despicable villains in order to elicit emotions (Best, 1987, 1990; Best & Horiuchi, 1985; Gitlin, 1983; Loseke, 1993; Lowney & Best, 1995). Such melodramatic presentation of stories increases viewership and thus the advertising revenue and profit margin, as well.

The media may have the power to alter, edit, amplify, or modify activists' and experts' claimsmaking in significant ways, but what counts is how the various intended audiences respond to the claims. Fishman's (1978) research on how the media constructed a crime wave against senior citizens showed that the general public can be highly influenced by claimsmaking done by the media. And so the third step in the social problems process (Best, 2008) focuses on public reaction to the claimsmaking campaign. Have the claimsmakers been able to package their claims in a way that arouses the hoped-for emotions in the general public or in their more narrow, targeted audiences who have the power to make policy? If they succeed, then they increase the likelihood that these individuals will institute change. If they do not succeed, savvy claimsmakers will tweak their campaign in ways that—they hope—will improve their subsequent chances of success.

The concept of "public reaction" needs to be interpreted broadly; certainly opinion polls, the outcomes of elections, and the like are ways to measure claimsmakers' success, but audiences can respond in a variety of ways to claims. Constructionists—for obvious reasons centered around the ease of measurement—often turn to examining how individuals or groups react to media stories as the primary means of assessment, but other ways of assessing what audiences are thinking and feeling should not be overlooked. For instance, folklore that individuals spread, whether it be via e-mail, word of mouth, or through emerging technologies such as viral video websites (e.g., *YouTube.com*), allows individuals to register their responses to claimsmaking (Lowney & Best, 1996). Of course, like all audience responses, interpreting folklore is difficult. Could it be that people passed on a rumor about a troubling condition because they agreed with it, because they were angry about it, or because they were amused by it (Turner, 1991)? Even if analysts can discern these answers, they often cannot provide nuanced interpretations. Consider the situation whereby an audience member shared a claim with another over e-mail, only to critique it. What part of the claim was upsetting? Did she or he agree that the condition is troublesome but disagree with the prognostic frame or solution? Was there basic agreement on the "facts," the diagnostic frame, but a difference of opinion over why action was necessary (the motivational frame)? Rarely can scholars evaluate all of the nuances of folklore transmission in order to assess transmitters' and receivers' motivations.

One possible audience reaction is to become a counterclaimsmaker, beginning a rival social movement that stands in opposition to the initial activism. To take such action requires that the audience member feels negatively toward the original claim intensely enough to compel her or him to enter the public sphere and engage in a morality contest. Constructionists have devoted a good deal of attention to the interactional dance that claimsmakers and their op-

position perform (see, e.g., Einwohner & Spencer, 2005; Esacove, 2004; Kruse, 2001; Leahy & Mazur, 1980; Lowney, 1994, 2003; McCright & Dunlap, 2000; Rohlinger, 2002). In part the reason is that the interplay between different social actors makes the social problems process more visible to the analyst.

The fourth step in the social problems process is policymaking (Best, 2008). In this step there is a shift away from the activists and experts who were so intimately involved in the identification of the troubling condition to those who have the power to create and institute social change. Activists must watch, often from the sidelines, as policymakers (e.g., politicians, their staffs, boards of directors of nonprofits, organizations, lobbyists, etc.) take up their cause. These new players in the process often have less emotional commitment to solving the troubling condition; it might be, for example, one of hundreds that they must confront during a legislative session. The minutia of policymaking often requires different types of claimsmaking skills, and insider claimsmakers (Best, 2008), those whose full-time jobs are steeped in policy and often government rhetoric and diplomacy, are often needed to guide a prognostic frame to fruition. They know how to construct a good causal story (Stone, 2002), involving victims, villains, proposed solutions, and such, that will motivate individuals to push the proposed policy forward through the maze of the policymaking process.

Many different social scientists have analyzed the policy process, but one model that many constructionists (see, e.g., Best, 2008; Stone, 2002) have used is Kingdon's (1984) model of policy streams. He argued that policy is more likely to be created when there is confluence between the problem recognition (in effect, the social problems process), the policy proposal stream, and the political stream. Put differently, when claimsmaking activities correspond with prevailing ideological arguments available in the culture that are shared by most audience members and fit with the political realities of the time, then there is a greater likelihood that prognostic frames will become actual policy.

Here, too, understanding the role of emotions is crucial for analysts. At least some politicians become active policymakers because they are responding to constituents' fears, worries, and concerns rather than because they "believe" in the activists' mission to make the world a better place. Other politicians care about their own reelection and so will more join claimsmaking campaigns that they believe will help this endeavor. Still other policymakers succumb to the bureaucratization of policymaking and specialize in one or more areas that they may care passionately about and more or less "go through the motions" with policies in other arenas, trusting in others, often in their own party, to guide their choices. Of course, external events, such as those of September 11, 2001, in New York, Washington, DC, and Shanksville, Pennsylvania, can intervene, and even the most self-absorbed policymaker becomes caught up in the national moment of grief, anger, and vengeance, participating in the rush to create new policy so that "it can never happen again."

The fifth step in the social problems process is to take the newly created policy and decide how to implement it (Best, 2008). Policy implementation shifts the analyst's observational gaze from the "big picture" to the micropolitics of people working in, coping with, and being processed by institutions and bureaucracies. How, then, do staff members of social agencies go about this social problems work (Holstein & Miller, 1993a, 1993b)? How are workers socialized to perform the way their bosses want them to? What kind of feeling management (Hochschild, 1983) must they learn in order to do their jobs well? How are they to feel about, let alone interact with, their clients—whether they be, for example, battered women (Loseke, 1992), rape victims (Frohmann, 1998), or individuals fighting possible institutionalization (Holstein, 1993)? An agency needs its staff members to handle clients in the most efficient manner possible, given its mission. So staff members must develop processes to manage both the people and the paperwork their jobs require, often while suppressing or denying their emotions on the altar of "efficiency." People become transformed into cases to be managed, paperwork to be finished, and so on. These processes depersonalize the interactions between staff members and clients as they are more efficiently routinized (Chambliss, 1996). Of course, clients (or whatever term the institution or bureaucracy favors) have feelings about staff members and the ways they are treated and often make them known, in formal and informal ways (Loseke, 1992).

The policy implementation stage of the social problems process centers around the interactional negotiation of power. Funding agencies, boards of directors, accrediting agencies, primary claimsmakers, and so on feel the need to check up on the agency to see whether the mission they set is being fulfilled. They often demand significant paperwork as "proof" of that. That requirement forces supervisors to compel their staff members to create a paper trail to explain their case management processes and use of resources in order to show the data to the outsiders. Supervisors and staff members jointly create routines to process clients efficiently, thus normalizing their interactions. And clients, those with the least amount of power, often demand a more humane interactional process. Staff members often feel squeezed both by supervisors and outsiders, as well as by clients below them on the status hierarchy in the agency. They may try to cut corners, breaking the norms if it means they can help clients get what they need or if it means they can speed up their work processes. With little outlet for their feelings of frustration, anger, and empathy, they often become burnt out, victims of what is called secondary trauma (see, e.g., Adams, Boscarino, & Figley, 2006; Geller, Madsen, & Ohrenstein, 2004).

The last step in the social problems process refers to policy outcomes (Best, 2008), the "what next" stage in the claimsmaking process. Once a policy is created and has been "lived with" for a while in the implementation stage, there will be a variety of reactions to it. Some individuals—often those who did not support the policy in the first place—will be hostile, making claims that it should be abolished or at least reduced in significant ways so as to minimize its damage. These counterclaimsmakers, who might have lost in a claimsmaking contest, may see the implementation stage as a good time to launch a barrage of criticism. Because no policy ever completely lives up to its vision, they can seize on these contradictions to use in their diagnostic frame. Other people may have the opposite reaction and will see the policy as a success; indeed, they often want to expand it to encompass new victims and villains, encouraging either domain or range expansion or both. More nuanced reactions will also arise; some will agree that the policy has merit but question its effectiveness as currently implemented. These people will often want studies done to assess how successful the policy *truly* is and will raise questions of measurement. Some of these claimsmakers truly are supportive of the policy and want to make it even more effective, but others may use the language of assessment as a means to undercut a policy they never truly supported.

If a policy is perceived as successful by other claimsmakers, it might become piggybacked (Loseke, 1999; Lowney & Best, 1995) by a similar movement trying to attain audience attention. Piggybacking—"when a new problem is constructed as a different instance of an already existing problem" (Loseke, 2003a, p. 61)—allows persuasive claimsmaking campaigns to become role models for others wanting to copy their success. Or its leaders might be sought out by other social movement organizations in an effort to create a broad coalition. Often such coalitions involve the use of a master frame (Benford, 1993; Snow & Benford, 1992) that encompasses all the distinct movements.

The last step in the social problems process, then, brings us full circle; one cycle of claimsmaking may come to an end with a policy being created and implemented, but the accomplishment often sparks renewed interest among many more claimsmakers, who have a variety of claimsmaking positions. Such a natural history model of social problems claimsmaking has been extensively debated in sociology (Leahy & Mazur, 1980; McCright & Dunlap, 2000). Some theorists have worried that such a model portrays a facticity that may not be historically accurate. Critics allege that seeing each step as necessarily following another in time might be too simplistic a model of what happens during a complex claimsmaking. Constructionist arguments, however, rarely have argued that proposition. These scholars hold that, although the steps might be discussed as analytically discrete, they often operate in claimsmakers' lives simultaneously (Best, 2008; Loseke, 2003a). Claimsmakers are bombarded with countless decisions to make—decisions about how to manage feelings (their own and others'), how to control and respond to individuals and groups, how to construct, edit, and analyze rhetoric—nearly every moment in which they seek to create a better world.

The Cultural Context of Claimsmaking

All social actors involved in the social problems process are situated within particular cultural contexts; these need to be analyzed carefully if any one social movement's claimsmaking is to succeed. Therefore, one of the most important decisions that claimsmakers face is how to utilize cultural resources in their claims. Successful claimsmakers, it is clear, need to develop an openness to cultural processes in order to learn how to advance their claims, create shared meanings, and build legitimacy with their audiences and allies, all while being engaged in interaction with other players in the "social problems game" (Loseke, 2003b), including those who might be hostile to them:

> Whatever else social movement actors do, they seek to affect interpretation of reality among various audiences. . . . Meanings are derived (and transformed) via social interaction and are subject to differential interpretations. Hence meaning is problematic; it does not spring from the object of attention into the actor's head, because objects have no intrinsic meaning. Rather meaning is negotiated, contested, modified, articulated, and rearticulated. In short, meaning is socially constructed, deconstructed, and reconstructed. (Benford, 1997, p. 410)

The social problems process, constructionism argues, is an ongoing act of meaning making. At any one historical moment hundreds of claimsmakers may be clamoring for policymakers' and the general public's attention, and those who are able to frame their concerns in ways that tap into larger cultural patterns may be better equipped for success. But how are activists to use culture in their claimsmaking campaigns? Answering that question takes us to some of the most important decisions claimsmakers must make.

Culture is ubiquitous; we know it is there and that it affects us, but we rarely spend time considering precisely how it shapes our lives. Claimsmakers, though, have to respect cultural messages and, especially, popular wisdom, as audiences—especially the general public but even targeted audiences—will often weigh social problems claims through its filter. Popular wisdom, those "taken-for-granted ideas about how the world works" (Loseke, 2003a, p. 30), shape audiences' receptivity; audience members will pay closer attention to those that "make sense" based on what they know from culture, and they will likely find it easier to dismiss claims that do not fit with cultural content. Audiences have grown up surrounded by a cultural repertoire of aphorisms about social problems and deviance (i.e., in the United States, some

of these are that "one bad apple spoils the barrel," and that "too many cooks spoil the soup") that, although often contradictory, can linger in the background as they assess claims.

Because activists are trying to construct a system of shared meanings between themselves, movement members, audience members, and policymakers, rhetorical strategies that marshal popular culture resources can benefit these claimsmakers in the social problems process. But how do they go about shaping their claims in ways that mesh with elements of the cultural milieu? Social-movement scholars answer this question by discussing the framing process. Framing is:

> used to explain the contingent interpretive processes involved in building understandings about the world. It highlights the interactive *process* by which definitions are constructed that specify the nature of problems and ways to confront them (Blumer, 1969). In short, framing raises the problem of understanding the cognitive orientations shaping protest and movement formation within a social context. (Futrell, 2003, p. 361)

Frames by necessity involve the use of symbols, be they linguistic or visual, that unify while simultaneously collapsing meaning for those who agree with them. Few Americans who were alive on September 11, 2001, will be able to forget the images of the twin towers, first one and then the other, falling down in a rush of noise, debris, and death. Those images seemed almost sacred, so revered that even newscasts did not repeat the images too often for fear of deepening the psychic wounding (Goldberg, 2002). More than 5 years later, the iconic images of the towers—known before that day as a feat of engineering—have come to represent fear and helplessness. The choice of symbols to represent one's campaign, therefore, necessitates claimsmakers' careful consideration. What elements of culture can be condensed into their symbol? Will people be able to "read" it correctly, decoding it in only the ways the claimsmakers wish? Will the symbol tap into the depth of emotion they need in order to spur people to join the crusade, to donate time and money to help make the world a better place? There are practical decisions, of course, involved here, but even they spring from and are rooted in the cultural context. Color, we know, is often symbolic, and claimsmakers often portray colors as emblematic of their cause; we understand that red ribbons stand for AIDS prevention, purple ribbons represent domestic violence prevention, pink ribbons symbolize the campaign against breast cancer, and so on (Heilbronn, 1994; Tuleja, 1994).

Rhetoric is used to condense frames into a few words capable of being reproduced on bumper stickers, on yard signs, in advertising, and the like. So the creation of slogans is another framing decision that claimsmakers must carefully consider. Slogans not only create an identity for one's side but also simultaneously help to construct the opposition negatively, as well. This dualistic nature of framing is captured especially cogently in Esacove's work (2004) on "partial-birth" abortion frames. She described how the anti-abortion claimsmakers went through several designations until they hit on the "right" one, which provoked the right mix of emotion in their intended audiences and described their opponents in ways that undercut any claims they might make:

> Early in the framing/counterframing process AR [abortion rights] opponents struggled with terminology. The ad to defeat the Freedom of Choice Act called the procedure a dilation and extraction. "Partial-birth" was not introduced until 1994. In the months surrounding the introduction of the first federal bill, AR opponents often included a list of terms in their materials, "the 'D&X,' or dilation and extraction abortion—also known as 'brain-suction abortions' or 'partial-birth abortions' " (National Right to Life Committee, 1995e, p. 4). The ultimate choice of terminology had a large impact on the meanings that could be employed through the frame/counterframe. Dilation and extraction was not only too sterile and scientific to produce an emotional response, it

was also the term used by AR supporters. Unless opponents of AR were able to change the social meaning associated with this term, its use evoked the discourse of AR supporters. "Brain-suction" abortion, on the other hand, was too extreme, provoking a nervous, almost comical, response and was dropped after the first bill was introduced. (p. 75)

These claimsmakers had to find the proper mix of words and images that would create in audiences the emotions that they believed would motivate recruitment to the cause. Thus their pamphlets, full of text that used terms emblematic of their claimsmaking campaign, also contained powerful visuals; " 'the drawings illustrate a gruesome new abortion technique being used in the second and third trimester of pregnancy' " (Esacove, 2004, p. 75, citing a National Right to Life Committee brochure).

> Meaning was ascribed to the frame/counterframe by the strategic employment of components of the larger abortion narrative and related narratives. One can think of these components as strands of the overall [partial-birth abortion] frame/counterframe. The visual images in the five drawings and the accompanying description were initially the most powerful component of the meaning-construction effort. (Esacove, 2004, p. 75)

Frames are constructed through a dialogic process (Esacove, 2004; Nichols, 2003) involving interaction by various types of claimsmakers; oppositional social movements construct their proposed policies in a complex interactive dance, in which each side must listen intently in order to counter the other. Esacove argued that what appeared to be two constructed processes, one made by the social movement and the other by the countermovement, are really just one intricate interactive process:

> A frame/counterframe is never purely the creation of one side of the framing/counterframing process. It is always constructed in response to something else, whether the efforts of a countermovement or the conditions that

motivated action in the first place. Social movement actors are further constrained and supported by the larger cultural, social, and historical context. (p. 95)

Claimsmakers, then, need to be cognizant of the sociopolitical situation in which they are making claims. It is often easier to get claims heard when they reflect, in whole or in part, the particular political ideology that dominates at the moment. Of course, it helps even more if that shared ideology is supported by a significant portion of their intended audience for claimsmaking. This is more complicated than it might at first seem. If the political culture—especially government—espouses a particular ideology, then any actions it might accomplish that reflect that ideology will likely garner media attention; so if a social movement can use such a moment for its own purpose, to advance its own claim, then it has seized what scholars have called a "critical discourse moment" (Gamson & Modigliani, 1989).

On the other hand, seizing such a critical discourse moment would be much more difficult if one's claims were considered contrary to the operative cultural context. While facing such an external ideological obstacle, activism is still possible, but it will demand a certain amount of claimsmaking sophistication in order to (re)package a claim in a way that will attract audience and media attention without simply offering up one's social movement as "cannon fodder" for one's opponents and, possibly, the media. In Rohlinger's (2002) analysis of the National Organization for Women (NOW) and the Concerned Women of America's (CWA) morality contest over abortion, she showed how one side was less willing to adjust its message than the other:

> Unlike NOW, CWA did not tailor its message to the political environment. One CWA representative explained that the sanctity of human life is the foundation of every CWA issue. Abortion, then, is a moral absolute that does not change over time. . . . [The] CWA's packages remained constant even as the po-

litical environment and oppositional tactics changed. (p. 492)

Of course, the CWA's moral steadfastness could be analyzed as both a claimsmaking success and a tactical failure. The choice to remain morally consistent aroused feelings of unity and solidarity among members in a way similar to the way ACT UP (a radical AIDS activist group) was "also involved in activities . . . whose primary principle [was] expressive" (Gamson, 1989, p. 354) and built internal unity. But by being unwilling or unable to adjust its claimsmaking activities to alternations in political realities, counterclaimsmaker's tactics, and media coverage, the CWA increasingly talked only to its members and the like-minded. Opportunities for outreach to new constituencies were lost by the inability to adjust to changing cultural contexts. Movements must decide whether feelings of moral resoluteness and heightened internal bonding are worth the possible costs of persuading others who might disagree on some issues but with whom useful claimsmaking bridges might be able to be built. Clearly, during the same relative time period, movements similar to the CWA have been able to reach out to feminist activists on other topics, such as the fight against pornography (Cottle, Searles, Berger, & Pierce, 1989; Downs, 1989; West, 1987). Movements, therefore, have to choose where—no matter the claimsmaking ramifications—they will draw the line and remain unwavering in their beliefs. It is likely that there will be criticism from both within and without of the movement, no matter where the movement chooses to draw such a moral boundary, so leaders need to be prepared for it and to craft a response that stays true to the movement's political goals and beliefs so as to maintain as many members as possible and to keep spirits high.

Framing provides claimsmakers the means by which they can organize their thoughts, evidence, resources, and emotions in ways that they hope will be persuasive to others. Rooted in the cultural milieu, the processes of creating and using frames are central to the social problems process. When they are done well, others will join the crusade, eager to work for change; policymakers will stand ready to do their part to create and implement new policies; and opponents' claims will be marginalized. But although the centrality of framing is acknowledged in the literature, it is also much debated.

Part of the debate has focused on the different ways that constructionists and social movement analysts examine framing. Constructionists have tended to use the language of grounds ("the facts" used to explain the troubling condition—statistics, typifying examples, etc.), warrants (why individuals ought to care about the troubling condition), and conclusions (the proposed solution), whereas social movement thinkers have used the terminology of diagnostic frame (for "grounds"), motivational frame (for "warrants"), and prognostic frame (for "conclusions") to discuss these tasks that social movements must accomplish. Recently, some leading constructionists have begun to use framing language (Best, 2008; Loseke, 1999, 2003b) in place of grounds, warrants, and conclusions, while maintaining their constructionist meanings. Social movement analysts have often generated a long list of frames that movements have used to make claims (see Benford, 1997, for a partial list, as well as a criticism of this trend in the social movement literature). In keeping with this chapter's analytic focus on examining claimsmaking, in particular how it is rooted in emotion management, I now analyze some of the claimsmaking decisions about framing that activists and social movements must make if audiences are to share the emotions needed to create change.

Diagnostic Framing: Using Cultural Feeling Rules

At first glance, it might seem difficult to construct a diagnostic frame that is built on arousing emotions in the audience, because a good deal of the frame is concerned with "facts and figures" related to the troubling condition; but this is indeed essential for activists to accomplish. There are claimsmaking decisions that can, if decided well, build commitment among those already in the social movement, increase membership, and attract policymakers' attention. One of the most important is how to "people" the claims with those afflicted by the troubling condition and those who caused it.

Constructing Victims

Claimsmakers must select typifying examples to act as representational symbols of their campaign. Such typifying stories—also called atrocity stories or horror stories (Johnson, 1989)—are narratives that narrowly focus on how one or a few individuals have been victimized by the social problem. But these should not be just any run-of-the-mill victim; typifying examples should be chosen because they have been horrifically harmed, often scarred physically or emotionally for life (i.e., such as the way Ryan Hade's penis was cut off by his molester) due to no fault of their own. These narratives of devastation provide ways for the audience to apprehend the activists' urgency about making things better, for other victims might be enduring the same horrible harm right now if no action is taken.

Successful activists, therefore, need to understand how their society's cultural feeling rules operate (Clark, 1997; Hochschild, 1983), in order to more effectively employ them in the construction of emotions that can motivate action. Loseke (2003a, p. 79, original emphasis), writing about how these feeling rules are constructed in the United States, noted that "we tend to reserve the status of victim for people we feel sympathy toward and we feel sympathy when our evaluations lead us to conclude that *morally good people are greatly harmed through no fault of their own.*" Activists, therefore, need to find victims to put before their audiences who fit as many of these requirements as possible.

Then they need to construct their stories in such a way as to make listeners respond in particular ways. First, they want to create two kinds of emotions in listeners; sympathy for the horrendously harmed victim and, second, righteous anger toward whomever or whatever caused the harm (Holstein & Miller, 1990; Loseke, 2003a). Second, activists hope that hearing these painful typifying stories will mobilize people into action, in particular to join their cause.

Claimsmakers, then, must search for victims whose stories will likely evoke such feelings and behaviors. They are not likely to find such typifying stories by looking at cases that reflect statistical measures of central tendency (i.e., the mean, the median, or the mode) of the social problem about which they are concerned. Instead, they look at statistical outliers, in particular those extreme cases that show the social problem at its worst, damaging those most innocent. These are more likely to be effective typifying stories, for the victims have endured extreme suffering, which is likely to garner sympathy. Regardless of the constructionist terminology used, these narratives are not about showcasing "typical" victims but rather about manufacturing audience concern, and the way to do that is to highlight those narrative details that will build sympathy and garner action.

Constructing Enemies

The social problems process requires claimsmakers to spend time developing a picture of those individuals who have been harmed by the problem for the audience. But the process is even more elaborate, requiring claimsmakers to make more complex constructionist decisions: Are their claims about the social problem and its victims likely to be persuasive enough that there is less of a need to construct a tangible villain to hate? Are their constructions under attack by a counterclaimsmaker, and do they therefore need to offer ongoing constructions in response to counterattacks? Or have

they, in fact, established social problems ownership—"when one particular social problem diagnostic frame becomes the taken-for-granted frame for that problem" (Loseke, 2003a, p. 69; see also Gusfield, 1981)—allowing claimsmakers to relax just a bit, knowing that their perceptions of the social problems are accepted by most of the public, at least for now? The answers to these questions determine whether claimsmakers feel compelled to construct villains.

In one sense, the moment that activists construct typifying examples of victims who have been incredibly hurt by the social problem, they are also constructing a villain (Holstein & Miller, 1990). The two statuses are interactionally intertwined. Claimsmakers need to construct a strong narrative of victimization in order to garner audience sympathy, and how they construct the villain can assist this goal. Again, cultural feeling rules can help clarify the process:

> First, we tend to assign blame only when we believe things or people who do harm *intended* to do harm.... Yet assigning blame does not necessarily mean we will feel the emotion of hatred. We continue by asking another evaluation: Was there a *good reason* for creating harm?... The cultural feeling rule encourages feeling hatred only when the harm is done for "no good reason." (Loseke, 2003a, pp. 83–84; original emphasis)

Intriguingly, though, in some ways it is more difficult to assign a villain to blame than to construct a victim. More individuals in the audience might disagree about whether the harm was done for a "good reason" or about whether the villain perchance was also a victim and therefore should receive less blame (e.g., an abused child, now adult, who attacks his or her abuser; or a violently abused domestic partner who finally reaches a mental breaking point and kills the abusive other), and so constructing villains can be even more contentious than constructing victims. Frequently, then, claimsmakers may choose to let the villain remain under- or unconstructed (Best, 1999; Conrad & Schneider, 1980; Loseke, 1987; Lowney, 1999) in hopes of not diminishing audience support. This can be a viable strategy so long as the victim narrative is more fully developed and achieves its goal of channeling emotions into action.

Social problem ownership (Gusfield, 1981) is a desired state for claimsmakers, but it does not often occur. Instead, claimsmaking is usually contested activity; there are activists and experts on many sides, endorsing their own opinions while opposing others' views. Thus activists must not only construct victims and sometimes villains but also must do so in relation to other activists, who stand in opposition to what they believe, as they participate in the "dialectical dance of meaning-making" (Sewell, 1999, p. 57).

Esacove (2004, p. 71) noted that "[m]eaning-making is a contested process and frames continuously evolve as movement and countermovement actors interact with each other and the social environment." Recently, constructionists have displayed a growing interest in the interactional dynamics between claimsmakers and counterclaimsmakers, recognizing the importance of morality contests between competing claimsmakers in shaping claims (see, e.g., Einwohner, 2002; Esacove, 2004; Fetner, 2001; Kruse, 2001; Levin, 2005; Lowney, 2003; McCright & Dunlap, 2000; Rohlinger, 2002; Stein, 1998; Tamura, 2004; Youngman, 2003). This dialectical dance is not easy for claimsmakers to negotiate; for example, counterclaimsmakers, especially powerful and vocal ones, might attract more media attention. Claimsmaking disputes can provide ready-made stories for reporters, but they might be counterproductive to what the original claimsmaker desired. Movement–countermovement interaction requires ongoing maintenance, so that any changes in framing, symbology, or rhetoric can be quickly observed and a response created. Because social movements can have different amounts of power and resources at any particular moment, these disparities often affect the response to the other organization.

How should a social movement respond to counterclaimsmakers? There is no easy answer to such a question. In part it depends on what the nature of the counterclaim is, how available it is to the intended audience of the first movement, and how different responses might be interpreted. On the one hand, the creation of countermovements could be a sign that the activists are succeeding, for "a countermovement is likely to emerge if the [original] movement appears to be accomplishing its goals" (Zald & Useem, 1987, p. 254, as cited in McCright & Dunlap, 2000, p. 505). In that case, spending too much time and energy on the countermovement could send the confusing message to audience members that its oppositional claims have merit, or else why would they be worried about them? Ignoring them unless they rise to a certain level of audience and media attention might be an effective strategy. But the existence of countermovements could also illustrate that the original social movement's claimsmaking has not been effective; in that case, ignoring or ridiculing counterclaimsmakers might backfire and lose audience members' support. Social movements need to assess what critiques their countermovements are proffering; are they offering new grounds but sharing the same desired conclusions? In that case, it might behoove the original activists to consider adding these additional grounds into their claims, if they feel they can. That would perhaps allow for movements to work together. More likely, however, a countermovement may not be so easily managed, and the "dance" between them will continue, with each social movement adjusting its framing process in light of the other's claims. Sometimes one cause will be more advanced, but then the other might surge ahead (Benford & Hunt, 2003). They must circle around each other but stay cognizant of the larger cultural context in which their claimsmaking occurs; they cannot, however, become so immersed in each other that they forget their audiences, nor their mission to combat the social problem:

> The collective action of a counter movement is a purposeful attempt to affect the social and political world (see Lo, 1982; Meyer & Staggenborg, 1996; Mottl, 1980) regarding a particular set of grievances. . . . The actions, statements, and political presence of a counter movement can alter the political terrain in which social movement actors are accustomed to working. Social movement organizations choose strategies, frame political claims, and develop protest tactics which they believe will be appropriate to the political context, effective for accomplishing their goals, and consistent with their organizational values (Meyer & Staggenborg, 1996). Counter movements, by shifting political venues, disputing social movement claims, lobbying politicians, and introducing new frames, alter the political context and create new problems for opposing SMOs [social movement organizations]. (Fetner, 2001, p. 413)

Claimsmaking in general, but particularly social movement–countermovement interaction, often involves another critical social actor, the media. Media workers can have significant impact on claimsmaking success, in both subtle and overt ways.

The Media and Claimsmaking

Most members of the general public learn about claims secondhand, transmitted from activists and experts to media workers to them. But this process is even more complicated. Media workers do not just passively transmit claims; they have the power to frame them, modify them, or edit them in a variety of ways and for a variety of reasons (Best, 1991; Fishman, 1978; Gamson & Modigliani, 1989). Media workers, then, are critical in the claimsmaking process, for they can have significant power to shape what the public perceives about claimsmakers and their motivations for claimsmaking.

Media workers—especially those involved in the production of news—have professional standards (norms) that they strive to follow (Croteau & Hoynes, 2003; Gitlin, 1983; Schudson, 2003), but exactly how these are operationalized while covering any one story is less clear (see, e.g., Chiricos & Eschholz, 2002; Fishman, 1978). One norm is that media workers strive for "balance" in their reporting and so seek out spokespersons for both social movements and countermovements. This search for balance, however, can give to audience members the impression that each side is relatively equal in the social problems process, accurate or not. Such "balanced" attention can significantly improve lesser known counterclaimsmakers' opportunities to promulgate their beliefs, for otherwise they might have struggled to reach a larger audience. There are times, however, when media workers feel less need to balance their stories; this is especially true when activists' claims are felt to be so outlandish, so outside the cultural norm, that media workers want to highlight this for the audience (e.g., in claims of large-scale UFO abductions, experts are rarely recruited to discount the stories). Providing balance in these kinds of stories might seem to lend too much credibility to claimsmakers perceived as "too far out," and so their claims are allowed to stand alone, as a way to highlight how far removed from reality they truly are.

A second standard that media workers observe is that of novelty. This is especially true for those who work in the news industry; the very nature of what they do requires that stories be fresh and "new." This means that claimsmakers whose passion is a long-standing social problem need to work harder to attract media attention by finding novel twists to their claims so that reporters do not feel the issue is "tired" and not worth covering. If claimsmakers can keep providing new twists to their stories (i.e., new kinds of victims, new kinds of solutions, etc.), then they are more likely to be successful at keeping the issue in front of media workers, and thus it is more likely that media workers will allow the story to reach the audience.

Closely related to novelty is a third media standard—that stories be interesting. This is important to media workers for a number of reasons. First, they are people, too, and would prefer to work, day in and day out, on stories that are exciting and not monotonous and repetitive. Second, the media industry is a capitalist enterprise, which means that profit making is the bottom line. Coverage that is boring and feels repetitious is not likely to maintain audience levels, let alone bring in new viewers. When that happens, advertisers are more likely to become unhappy, which can affect profit margins. So media workers feel pressured to look for interesting stories or at least stories that can be told in interesting ways. One way to build interest in audience members, especially for television reporters, is to be sure to tell a good story. Melodramatic narratives that portray innocent victims so damaged, so traumatized, so in need of assistance due to the actions of dastardly villains make good media stories (Berns, 2004; Best, 1990, 1999; Loseke, 1993, 2001, 2003b; Loseke & Fawcett, 1995; Lowney, 1999; Lowney & Holstein, 2001; Prasad, 1994). Careful selection by activists of their typifying stories, then, can heighten the chance that media workers will cover a claim. Another way for television media workers to tell a good story is to use arresting visual images, because they make for more interesting stories than mere "talking heads" giving a verbal account of the news. Claimsmakers need to consider carefully their symbology to ascertain whether it is helping them to obtain media coverage.

But which images will be used in a story are not necessarily in the control of the claimsmaker. I found that out the hard way in 1988. NBC had been running ads for a 2-hour primetime special by Geraldo Rivera on Satanism to be aired the following week. The local NBC station contacted me, as an "expert" on adolescent Satanism, and asked to conduct an interview with me to be aired on the 6:00 P.M. local news the night the special would air. It was my first televised interview, and I made several errors in judgment. I agreed to take the camera crew to one of the sites where local teens practiced Satanism—that was my first mistake. (I now conduct interviews in my campus office, surrounded by the "appropriate" faculty accoutrements.) Then, we got out of the car and walked around while the interview was conducted. Somewhat nervous, I did not really examine the locale that thoroughly, for I had been there just a few days before conducting research and felt comfortable—my second mistake. When I watched the interview later that night, I was appalled. The reporter had not edited my words, thank goodness, but instead had paired my words with visual pictures that seemed to directly contradict them. So while I was saying off camera, "there has been no animal sacrifice," the decaying, partially skeletonized carcass of a dead dog was on screen for nearly 30 seconds, in a quite dramatic closeup shot. I vaguely recalled seeing the dog lying in a ditch quite far away from where the reporter and I conducted most of the interview and that the cameraperson wandered around taking pictures for about 20 minutes after the end of the interview, but I never put all those things together until I watched the piece on the air.

Which message would claimsmakers be more likely to remember, my voice-over words or that quite dramatic carcass? I was, unfortunately, confident that it would be the visual one. My educated guess was confirmed by the number of friends and colleagues who started calling my house or stopping by my office the next day talking about the animal sacrifice that I had said teens were doing! The site was known as a place where families often dumped dead family pets—I had told the reporter that fact during the interview, but those words were never put on the air—but the image of the rotting carcass was all that most people re-called from the interview. I called the station immediately after the piece aired in order to voice my concerns. The reporter listened courteously to me but said that she had done nothing wrong—"after all, the dog's body was there; it wasn't like that was a lie, was it?" Still unhappy, I immediately spoke with my university's public relations staff, who managed to get the story pulled from the 11:00 P.M. show, where it was supposed to air again. However unwittingly, I had probably contributed to boosting the ratings for the Geraldo Rivera special locally. It was a lesson that I have never forgotten; claimsmakers lose control when their claims are covered by media workers, who might choose interesting visual images that could mitigate their claims.

Claimsmakers, therefore, are likely to be more successful in attracting media coverage if they can construct claims in ways that fit with media standards and media conventions (Fiske, 1987). Conventions are

the structural elements of genre that are shared between producers and audiences. They embody the crucial ideological concerns of the time in which they are popular and are central to the pleasures a genre offers its audience. Conventions are social and ideological. . . . Genres are popular when their conventions bear a close relationship to the dominant ideology of the time. (Fiske, 1987, pp. 110, 112)

Although each medium has its own conventions—social constructions that allow the audience to rapidly ascertain the kind of media product they are consuming—an analysis of one medium can be illustrative. Daytime talk shows have three primary conventions (Lowney, 1999)—patterns of show construction to which the host, production staff, and audience can easily relate and that shape the show's narrative. First, there is the entertainment convention, in which celebrities sit down with the host, often to talk about their latest movie, television show, or CD. These shows are hour-long teases for the other media product, mixed in with some personal stories told by the celebrities. *The Oprah Winfrey Show* does a fair number of these shows; perhaps the most well-known recent episode was Tom Cruise's "couch jumping" declaration of love for actress Katie Holmes. A second convention is the informational convention, wherein expert guests share their expertise with the in-studio and at-home audience. Medical experts, usually physicians, discuss a specific illness and its treatment. Given the predominantly female audience for daytime talk shows, the medical problems selected are often those that afflict women. Usually, in these informational convention shows, additional guests appear who are afflicted by the disease, so that the audience is not overloaded with only highly technical information but also learns about the day-to-day existence of those who suffer with the illness. However, informational shows do not have to be about medical problems. They can, for instance, revolve around social policy or politics. Again, *The Oprah Winfrey Show* can illustrate this convention. During the 2000 U.S. presidential campaign, both then–Vice President Al Gore and Governor George W. Bush appeared (separately) as guests. Both men did one-on-one interviews with Winfrey. Some in the press credit her interview with Governor Bush for raising his poll numbers with women and perhaps giving him the election. Intriguingly, Winfrey did not extend a similar offer to the 2004 presidential candidates.

But the most common media convention on talk shows—and the one for which the production staff needs an endless supply of claimsmakers—is the salvational show (Lowney, 1999). Here the show's emphasis is on rescuing a person from the clutches of a destructive, if not outright evil, lifestyle choice, relationship, group, and so forth. These shows play with and utilize both the religious revival roots of television talk shows and also to a lesser extent the freak show–carnival root of the genre. The salvational show requires the construction of *dramatis personae* (Benford & Hunt, 1992) who fit the convention and "sell it" to the audience. The first guests are those who have been victimized in some way by a lifestyle choice, relationship, or group. Victims are treated tenderly by the hosts, for they are fragile and spent from the damage that has been inflicted on them. They are allowed to tell their highly emotional stories relatively uninterrupted save for commercial breaks. If need be, victims are protected using disguises, wigs, heavy makeup, voice distortion, or even screens behind which they sit; everything possible is done to allow them to narrate their pain for the audience. Usually a few victims will grace the small screen, weaving a complex though often incomplete portrait of the hurt that had been done to them. Claimsmakers need to consider which victims can best articulate the movement's story, fit with the visual nature of the medium, and generate the most sympathy. Then they need to manage the interactions with the production staff in order to get their victims on the air. Sometimes this might mean calling the show's 800 hotline number and suggesting a topic or names of possible guests; at other times it might involve trying to get the production staff not to air countermovement's typifying examples; and so on.

Victims' narratives of pain usually take nearly half the show; only then is the next type of guest introduced: the villain. They come out and receive an entirely different reception from the host and the in-studio audience; they are harshly treated. Their narratives are frequently interrupted by the host, and any attempt by them to minimize their culpability is repudiated. They get few opportunities to present a positive presentation of themselves, as that would invalidate their status in the convention. Once the villains have been thoroughly discredited in the eyes of the audience, experts are brought out in the closing minutes who rubber-stamp the views of the host, diagnose the problem with therapeutic labels, and offer some sort of counseling or 12-step program as a way to "fix" the victim and villain. For daytime talk shows, the salvational convention is even more specific; talk shows are considered to be a female medium, with a largely female audience. Typifying stories by claimsmakers that showcase innocent women and children victims who have been harmed by bad men best mirror the pop psychology and brand of cultural feminism promulgated on these shows (Abt & Mustazza, 1997; Gamson, 1998; Rapping, 1996).

When claimsmakers want to persuasively influence their intended audience, most of the time they must utilize the media to accomplish that task. Media workers then make decisions that shape how audiences hear and see claims. They decide not only which claimsmakers to showcase but also in what order they appear. Editors must decide which stories are important enough to be on the front page of the newspaper and, of these, which are so significant as to merit being above the fold. Television news editors decide not only what stories will be covered (Fishman, 1978) but also what the length of the story will be, whether and what visuals will be added to the story or whether it will simply be a "talking head" story, where the story will appear in the broadcast, and so on. Time and space (i.e., what those in the media often call the "news hole," the space available in a particular kind of media product; for instance, the total column inches in a newspaper or the number of minutes of on-air content minus the commercials) in media products, therefore, are scarce resources that must be carefully managed by media workers (Croteau & Hoynes, 2003; Hallin, 1986). The more that claimsmakers can learn about media production rhythms, norms, and conventions and can situate that information in the broader cultural context, the more influence they will have in the social problems process.

Claimsmaking and the Media: The Tasks Ahead for Constructionists

Perhaps one of the most studied aspects of the social problems process has been the nature of the relationship between claimsmakers and the media (see, e.g., Baylor, 1996; Gamson et al., 1992; Gamson & Modigliani, 1989; Johnson, 1989; Kensicki, 2001; Kruse, 2001; Loseke & Fawcett, 1995; Lowney, 1994, 1999, 2003; Lowney & Best, 1995, 1996; Lynxwiler & Gay, 2000; Meyers, 1997; O'Neal, 1997; Prasad, 1994; Rohlinger, 2002; Rosenberg, 2005; Ryan, Carragee, & Meinhofer, 2001; Schudson, 2003; Smith, McCarthy, McPhail, & Boguslaw, 2001; Tuchman, 1978). But there are long-standing issues that have not been analyzed thoroughly, as well as emerging issues that will need constructionists' attention. Certainly this list is speculative and reflects my own concerns about where constructionism needs to go as a discipline, but I offer them in the spirit of dialogue.

First, I think we need to pay more attention to the media as claimsmakers. Is coverage different when the media report on other claimsmakers than when they *are* the primary claimsmakers? If so, in what ways? This possible variation in coverage illustrates the complex ways the media function in the social problems process, I believe. When acting to lift a social problem onto the public's list of important social problems—in other words, when they are acting as agenda setters (Kingdon, 1984; Stone, 2002)—media often are primary claimsmakers, creating claims that garner attention and move a new topic into the policymaking process. More often, however, media workers are secondary players, simply broadcasting claims already formulated by others. Are there systematic differences in the ways the two kinds of stories get constructed? If so, in what ways?

Second, I think that constructionism needs to consider its methods and how they have shaped the body of knowledge thus produced. Most constructionist work thus far—and I include my own here—has usually analyzed one single incidence of claimsmaking, be it an individual claimsmaker or a social movement. Although the work is interesting to read, I wonder how much new analysis can be obtained using only this method. We need more comparative studies across social movements in order to deepen our analysis. Others have already suggested this (see Benford, 1997) and scholars are responding (e.g., Carroll & Ratner, 1999; Chesters & Welsh, 2004; DeLuca, 1999; Fine & Christoforides, 1991; Kolker, 2004; McVeigh, Myers, & Sikkink, 2004; Stein, 1998; Walton & Bailey, 2005). Ideally, such comparative studies will examine movements that are contemporaneous in time, as well as those are not, in order to assess how claimsmaking practices have evolved. So, too, much of the constructionist literature is about U.S. or other industrialized nations' claimsmaking activities. We need to begin to examine the social problems process in other nations, especially those in which media resources are quite different. How might that shape claimsmaking practices? How do claimsmakers go about promulgating their claims in a society with different kinds of media resources? With different kinds of national political structures?

Along with these methodological issues, there are still other issues to consider. How do we find representative samples of claimsmaking activities to study? What does that mean sociologically when studying a localized social movement? An international movement? An ongoing media product whose content changes from day to day, such as a newspaper or a television talk show? Two movements across time and space? Do we talk enough about sampling in our published research? Can we better address this scientific question in our work? Should we?

And what about the changing nature of the media industry? How will this social fact shape our constructionist research agenda?

One line of potential research would be to study how the fragmentation of media audiences (what is sometimes called *audience segmentation*) affects claimsmakers and the overall social problems process. Although it might be easier to target claims to those audience members most likely to become involved in one's cause now (what might be called *narrowcasting*), will this necessarily be a good thing? What are the ramifications—both positive and negative—for claimsmakers? For the media? For policymakers trying to gauge public opinion? Another line of research focuses on claimsmaking on the Internet. How does a media resource that is, for all intents and purposes, limitless bear on claimsmaking? Today, any person with access to a computer and some knowledge of computer software can prepare a website chock full of social problems claims. But the quandary is how to attract like-minded others to the website, let alone get them to participate in collective action. How will claimsmakers approach this resource mobilization issue? Will search engines such as Google and Yahoo! become major social problems players, with their ability to channel viewers to certain sites? Should constructionists think of search engines the same way we do, for example, a television channel? Or will the magnitude of the service these engines provide—sifting vast amounts of information into a measured list—require us to revise our theories of the role of the media? The social problems process? How can we assess claims on the Internet when they change so rapidly? Just log onto a viral video site such as *YouTube.com* for an hour, or watch the "most popular" ranking on *Amazon.com* change when Oprah Winfrey announces her next book club selection, to see how rapidly public opinion can shift. What will this fast-paced rate of audiences' interpretation of claims mean for claimsmakers? For policymakers? Although in one sense any measure of public opinion, such as the results of a poll, is a snapshot of attitudes at one particular time and in one particular cultural context, now such measurement can be even more fleeting than ever before if we use such websites as data.

The last issue that constructionism needs to address is that of failed claims. Admittedly, this is a difficult topic to research; claimsmaking campaigns that are not successful rarely come to the public's, let alone the analyst's, attention. But such claims can give us insight—perhaps even more insight than successful claims can—into the claimsmaking process. Probably claims that fail utterly will be difficult to investigate if their advocates then refrain from further claimsmaking, but many activists will take failure as a challenge. They will come back with a revised campaign, modifying frames and the like in order to try again, because their passion tells them they need to do this (Lowney & Best, 1995). What changes will they make? How successful are these revised claims? If they are, what could account for this second-time-around success? Was it what they did or a shift in the cultural context or a change in countermovements or something else? These are the kinds of questions that could lead to an elaboration of constructionist theory.

• References

Abt, V., & Mustazza, L. (1997). *Coming after Oprah: Cultural fallout in the age of the TV talk show.* Bowling Green, OH: Bowling Green State University.

Adams, R. E., Boscarino, J. A., & Figley, C. R. (2006). Compassion fatigue and psychological distress among social workers: A validation study. *American Journal of Orthopsychiatry, 76*(1), 103.

Ali, S. H. (2002). Dealing with toxicity in the risk society: The case of the Hamilton, Ontario plastics recycling fire. *Canadian Review of Sociology and Anthropology, 39*(1), 29–48.

Armour, M. P. (2002). Journey of family members of homicide victims: A qualitative study of their post-homicide experience. *American Journal of Orthopsychiatry, 72*(3), 372–382.

Asen, E. (2004). Collaborating in promiscuous swamps: The systematic practitioner as context chameleon? *Journal of Family Therapy, 26*(3), 280–285.

Baylor, T. (1996). Media framing of movement protest: The case of American Indian protest. *Social Science Journal, 33*(3), 241–256.

Becker, H. (1963). *Outsiders: Studies in the sociology of deviance.* New York: Free Press.

Benford, R. D. (1993). "You could be the hundredth monkey": Collective action frames and vocabularies of motive within the nuclear disarmament movement. *Sociological Quarterly, 34*(2), 195–216.

Benford, R. D. (1997). An insider's critique of the social movement framing perspective. *Sociological Inquiry, 67*(4), 409–430.

Benford, R. D., & Hunt, S. A. (1992). Dramaturgy and social movements: The social construction and communication of power. *Sociological Inquiry, 62,* 36–55.

Benford, R. D., & Hunt, S. A. (2003). Interactional dynamics in public problems marketplaces: Movements and the counterframing and reframing of public problems. In J. A. Holstein & G. Miller (Eds.), *Challenges and choices: Constructionist perspectives on social problems* (pp. 153–186). Hawthorne, NY: Aldine de Gruyter.

Berg, M. (1992). The construction of medical disposals: Medical sociology and medical problem solving in clinical practice. *Sociology of Health and Illness, 14*(2), 151–180.

Berns, N. (2004). *Framing the victim: Domestic violence, media, and social problems.* Hawthorne, NY: Aldine de Gruyter.

Best, J. (1987). Rhetoric in claims-making: Constructing the missing children problem. *Social Problems, 34*(2), 101–121.

Best, J. (1990). *Threatened children: Rhetoric and concern about child-victims.* Chicago: University of Chicago Press.

Best, J. (1991). "Road warriors" on "hair-trigger highways": Cultural resources and the media's construction of the 1987 freeway shootings problem. *Sociological Inquiry, 61,* 327–345.

Best, J. (1999). *Random violence: How we talk about new crimes and new victims.* Berkeley: University of California Press.

Best, J. (2008). *Social problems.* New York: Norton.

Best, J., & Horiuchi, G. T. (1985). The razor blade in the apple: The social construction of urban legends. *Social Problems, 32,* 488–499.

Burningham, K. (1998). A noisy road or noisy resident? A demonstration of the utility of social constructionism for analysing environmental problems. *Sociological Review, 46*(3), 536–563.

Burningham, K., & Cooper, G. (1999). Being constructive: Social constructionism and the environment. *Sociology, 33*(2), 296–316.

Burns, R. (2001). Constructing images of workplace homicide. *Western Criminology Review, 3*(1). Retrieved from *wcr.sonoma.edu/v3n1/burns.html*

Carroll, W. K., & Ratner, R. (1999). Media strategies and political projects: A comparative study of social movements. *Canadian Journal of Sociology, 24*(1), 1–34.

Casper, M. J., & Koenig, B. A. (1996). Reconfiguring nature and culture: Intersections of medical anthropology and technoscience studies. *Medical Anthropology Quarterly, 10*(4), 523–536.

Chambliss, D. F. (1996). *Beyond caring: Hospitals, nurses, and the social organization of ethics.* Chicago: University of Chicago Press.

Chermak, S. (2003). Marketing fear: Representing terrorism after September 11. *Journal for Crime, Conflict, and Media, 1*(1), 5–22.

Chesters, G., & Welsh, I. (2004). Rebel colours: "Framing" in global social movements. *Sociological Review, 52*(3), 314–335.

Chiricos, T., & Eschholz, S. (2002). The racial and ethnic typification of crime and the criminal typification of race and ethnicity in local television news. *Journal of Research in Crime and Delinquency, 39*(4), 400–420.

Chiricos, T., Padgett, K., & Gertz, M. (2000). Fear, TV news, and the reality of crime. *Criminology, 38*(3), 755–786.

Clark, C. (1997). *Misery and company: Sympathy in everyday life.* Chicago: University of Chicago Press.

Clarke, L., & Short, J. F., Jr. (1993). Social organization and risk: Some current controversies. *Annual Review of Sociology, 19*(1), 375–399.

Conrad, P., & Schneider, J. (1980). *Deviance and medicalization: From badness to sickness.* St. Louis, MO: Mosby.

Corrigan, R. (2006). Making meaning of Megan's Law. *Law and Social Inquiry, 31,* 267–312.

Cottle, C. E., Searles, P., Berger, R. J., & Pierce, B. A. (1989). Conflicting ideologies and the politics of pornography. *Gender and Society, 3,* 303–333.

Courtenay, W. H. (2000). Engendering health: A social constructionist examination of men's health beliefs and behaviors. *Psychology of Men and Masculinity, 1*(1), 4–15.

Croteau, D. R., & Hoynes, W. (2003). *Media/society: Industries, images, and audiences.* Thousand Oaks, CA: Sage.

Cunter, V. J., & Harris, C. K. (1998). Noisy winter: The DDT controversy in the years before *Silent Spring. Rural Sociology, 63*(2), 179–198.

DeLuca, K. M. (1999, Summer). Unruly arguments: The body rhetoric of Earth First! ACT UP, and Queer Nation. *Argumentation and Advocacy, 36,* 9–21.

Downs, D. A. (1989). *The new politics of pornography.* Chicago: University of Chicago Press.

Dunn, J. (2002). *Intimate stalking, culture, and criminal justice.* Hawthorne, NY: Aldine de Gruyter.

Einwohner, R. E. (2002). Motivational framing and efficacy maintenance: Animal rights activists' use of four fortifying strategies. *Sociological Quarterly, 43*(4), 509–526.

Einwohner, R. E., & Spencer, J. W. (2005). That's how we do things here: Local culture and the construction of sweatshops and anti-sweatshop activism in two campus communities. *Sociological Inquiry, 75,* 249–272.

Esacove, A. W. (2004). Dialogic framing: The framing/counterframing of "partial-birth" abortion. *Sociological Inquiry, 74*(1), 70–101.

Fetner, T. (2001). Working Anita Bryant: The impact of Christian anti-gay activism on lesbian and gay movement claims. *Social Problems, 48*(3), 411–428.

Fine, G. A., & Christoforides, L. (1991). Dirty birds, filthy immigrants, and the English Sparrow War: Metaphorical linkage in constructing social problems. *Symbolic Interaction, 14*, 375–393.

Fiske, J. (1987). *Television culture.* London: Methuen.

Fishman, M. (1978). Crime waves as ideology. *Social Problems, 25*, 531–543.

Friedlander, M., Heatherington, L., & Marrs, A. L. (2000). Responding to blame in family therapy: A constructionist/narrative perspective. *American Journal of Family Therapy, 28*(2), 133–146.

Frohmann, L. (1998). Constituting power in sexual assault cases: Prosecutorial strategies for victim management. *Social Problems, 52*, 79–101.

Futrell, R. (2003). Framing processes, cognitive liberation, and NIMBY protest in the U.S. chemical-weapons disposal conflict. *Sociological Inquiry, 73*(3), 359–386.

Gamson, J. (1989). Silence, death, and the invisible enemy: AIDS activism and social movement "newness." *Social Problems, 36*, 351–367.

Gamson, J. (1998). *Freaks talk back: Tabloid talk shows and sexual nonconformity.* Chicago: University of Chicago Press.

Gamson, W. A., Croteau, D., Hoynes, W., & Sasson, T. (1992). Media images and the social construction of reality. *Annual Review of Sociology, 18*, 373–393.

Gamson, W. A., & Modigliani, A. (1989). Media discourse and public opinion on nuclear power: A constructionist approach. *American Journal of Sociology, 95*, 1–37.

Geller, J. A., Madsen, L. H., & Ohrenstein, L. (2004). Secondary trauma: A team approach. *Clinical Social Work Journal, 32*(4), 415–430.

Gitlin, T. (1983). *Inside prime time.* New York: Pantheon.

Goldberg, J. (2002, March 20). Bring back the horror: I want to be disturbed. *National Review.* Retrieved June 6, 2006, from *www.nationalreview.com/goldberg/goldberg032002.asp*

Greider, T., & Garkovich, L. (1994). Landscapes: The social construction of nature and the environment. *Rural Sociology, 59*(1), 1–24.

Gusfield, J. R. (1981). *The culture of public problems: Drinking-driving and the symbolic order.* Chicago: University of Chicago Press.

Hackley, C. E. (1998). Social constructionism and research in marketing and advertising. *Qualitative Market Research: An International Journal, 1*(3), 125–131.

Hallin, D. C. (1986). Network news: We keep America on top of the world. In T. Gitlin (Ed.), *Watching television* (pp. 9–41). New York: Random House.

Hannigan, J. A. (2006). *Environmental sociology: A social constructionist perspective.* New York: Routledge.

Heilbronn, L. M. (1994). Yellow ribbons and remembrance: Mythic symbols of the Gulf War. *Sociological Inquiry, 64*, 151–178.

Hochschild, A. R. (1983). *The managed heart: Commercialization of human feeling.* Berkeley: University of California Press.

Holstein, J. A. (1993). *Court-ordered insanity: Interpretive practice and involuntary commitment.* New York: Aldine de Gruyter.

Holstein, J. A., & Gubrium, J. F. (1995). Deprivatization and the construction of domestic life. *Journal of Marriage and the Family, 57*(4), 894–908.

Holstein, J. A., & Miller, G. (1990). Rethinking victimization: An interactional approach to victimology. *Symbolic Interaction, 13*, 103–122.

Holstein, J. A., & Miller, G. (1993a). *Reconsidering social constructionism: Debates in social problems theory.* New York: Aldine de Gruyter.

Holstein, J. A., & Miller, G. (1993b). Social constructionism and social problems work. In J. A. Holstein & G. Miller (Eds.), *Reconsidering social constructionism: Debates in social problems theory* (pp. 151–172). New York: Aldine de Gruyter.

Jacobs, K., Kemeny, J., & Manzi, T. (Eds.). (2004). *Social constructionism in housing research.* Burlington, VT: Ashgate.

Janus, E. S. (2000). Sexual predator commitment laws: Lessons for law and the behavioral sciences. *Behavioral Sciences and the Law, 18*, 5–21.

Jasper, J. M. (1998). The emotions of protest: Affective and reactive emotions in and around social movements. *Sociological Forum, 13*(3), 397–424.

Johnson, J. (1989). Horror stories and the construction of child abuse. In J. Best (Ed.), *Images of issues: Typifying contemporary social problems* (2nd ed., pp. 5–17). New York: Aldine de Gruyter.

Kensicki, L. J. (2001). Deaf president now! Positive media framing of a social movement within a hegemonic political environment. *Journal of Communication Inquiry, 25*(2), 147–166.

Kingdon, J. W. (1984). *Agendas, alternatives, and public policies.* New York: HarperCollins.

Kolker, E. S. (2004). Framing as a cultural resource in health social movements: Funding activism and the breast cancer movement in the US, 1990–1993. *Sociology of Health and Illness, 26*(6), 820–844.

Kruse, C. R. (2001). The movement and the media: Framing the debate over animal experimentation. *Political Communication, 18*, 67–87.

Leahy, P. J., & Mazur, A. (1980). The rise and fall of public opposition in specific social movements. *Social Studies of Science, 10*(3), 259–284.

Levin, D. (2005). Framing peace policies: The competition for resonant themes. *Political Communication, 22*, 83–108.

Loseke, D. (1987). Lived realities and the construction

of social problems: The case of wife abuse. *Symbolic Interaction, 10*(2), 229–243.

Loseke, D. (1992). *The battered woman and shelters: The social construction of wife abuse.* Albany: State University of New York Press.

Loseke, D. (1993). Constructing conditions, people, morality, and emotion: Expanding the agenda of constructionism. In G. Miller & J. A. Holstein (Eds.), *Constructionist controversies: Issues in social problems theory* (pp. 207–216). New York: Aldine de Gruyter.

Loseke, D. R. (1999). *Thinking about social problems: An introduction to constructionist perspectives.* New York: Aldine de Gruyter.

Loseke, D. R. (2001). Lived realities and formula stories of "battered women." In J. F. Gubrium & J. A. Holstein (Eds.), *Institutional selves: Troubled identities in a postmodern world* (pp. 107–126). New York: Oxford University Press.

Loseke, D. R. (2003a). *Thinking about social problems: An introduction to constructionist perspectives* (2nd ed.). New York: Aldine de Gruyter.

Loseke, D. R. (2003b). "We hold these truths to be self-evident": Problems in pondering the pedophile priest problem. *Sexualities, 6*(1), 6–14.

Loseke, D. R., & Fawcett, K. (1995). Appealing appeals: Constructing moral worthiness, 1912–1917. *Sociological Quarterly, 36*(1), 61–77.

Lowney, K. S. (1994). Speak of the devil: Talk shows and the social construction of Satanism. In J. A. Holstein & G. Miller (Eds.), *Perspectives on social problems* (Vol. 6, pp. 99–128). Greenwich, CT: JAI Press.

Lowney, K. S. (1999). *Baring our souls: TV talk shows and the religion of recovery.* New York: Aldine de Gruyter.

Lowney, K. S. (2003). Wrestling with criticism: The World Wrestling Federation's ironic campaign against the Parents Television Council. *Symbolic Interaction, 26,* 427–446.

Lowney, K. S., & Best, J. (1995). Stalking strangers and lovers: Changing media typifications of a new crime problem. In J. Best (Ed.), *Images of issues: Typifying contemporary social problems* (2nd ed., pp. 33–57). New York: Aldine de Gruyter.

Lowney, K. S., & Best, J. (1996). What Waco stood for: Jokes as popular constructions of social problems. In J. A. Holstein & G. Miller (Eds.), *Perspectives on social problems* (Vol. 8, pp. 77–97). Greenwich, CT: JAI Press.

Lowney, K. S., & Holstein, J. A. (2001). Victims, villains, and talk show selves. In J. F. Gubrium & J. A. Holstein (Eds.), *Institutional selves: Troubled identities in a postmodern world* (pp. 23–45). New York: Oxford University Press.

Lynxwiler, J., & Gay, D. (2000). Moral boundaries and deviant music: Public attitudes toward heavy metal and rap. *Deviant Behavior: An Interdisciplinary Journal, 21,* 63–85.

Lyon, M. L. (1995). Missing emotion: The limitations of cultural constructionism in the study of emotion. *Cultural Anthropology, 10*(2), 244–263.

Mancuso, J. C. (1996). Constructionism, personal construct psychology and narrative psychology. *Theory and Psychology, 6*(1), 47–70.

McCright, A. M., & Dunlap, R. E. (2000). Challenging global warming as a social problem: An analysis of the conservative movement's counter-claims. *Social Problems, 47*(4), 499–522.

McVeigh, R., Myers, D. J., & Sikkink, D. (2004). Corn, Klansmen, and Coolidge: Structure and framing in social movements. *Social Forces, 83*(2), 653–690.

Mertz, E. (1994). A new social constructionism for sociolegal studies. *Law and Society Review, 28*(5), 1243–1266.

Meyers, M. (1997). *News coverage of violence against women.* Thousand Oaks, CA: Sage.

Muehlenhard, C. L., & Kimes, L. A. (1999). The social construction of violence: The case of sexual and domestic violence. *Personality and Social Psychology Review, 3*(3), 234–245.

Murphy, R. (2004). Disaster or sustainability: The dance of human agents with nature's actants. *Canadian Review of Sociology and Anthropology, 41*(3), 249–266.

Nichols, L. T. (2003). Voices of social problems: A dialogical constructionist model. *Studies in Symbolic Interaction, 26,* 93–123.

Nicolson, M., & McLaughlin, C. (1988). Social constructionism and medical sociology: A study of the vascular theory of multiple sclerosis. *Sociology of Health and Illness, 10*(3), 234–261.

O'Neal, G. S. (1997). Clothes to kill for: An analysis of primary and secondary claims-making in print media. *Sociological Inquiry, 67*(3), 336–349.

Prasad, B. D. (1994). Dowry-related violence: A content analysis of news in selected newspapers. *Journal of Comparative Family Studies, 25*(1), 71–90.

Rapping, E. (1996). *The culture of recovery: Making sense of the self-help movement in women's lives.* New Brunswick, NJ: Transaction Books.

Rohlinger, D. A. (2002). Framing the abortion debate: Organizational resources, media strategies, and movement–countermovement dynamics. *Sociological Quarterly, 43*(4), 479–507.

Rosenberg, J. (2005). Newspaper deconstruction. *Editor and Publisher, 138*(2), 38–44.

Ryan, C., Carragee, K. M., & Meinhofer, W. (2001). Framing the news media, and collective action. *Journal of Broadcasting and Electronic Media, 45*(1), 175–182.

Schudson, M. (2003). *The sociology of news.* New York: Norton.

Sewell, W. H. J. (1999). The concept(s) of culture. In V. Bonnell & L. Hunt (Eds.), *Beyond the cultural turn* (pp. 35–61). Berkeley: University of California Press.

Shaw, L. (1990, November 19). Campaign paying off for victims of crime. *The Seattle Times,* p. A1.

Smith, J., McCarthy, J. D., McPhail, C., & Boguslaw, A. (2001). From protest to agenda building: Description bias in media coverage of protest events in Washington, D.C. *Social Forces, 79*(4), 1397–1423.

Snow, D., & Benford, R. (1992). Master frames and cycles of protest. In A. D. Morris & C. M. Mueller (Eds.), *Frontiers in social movement theory* (pp. 133–155). New Haven, CT: Yale University Press.

Stein, A. (1998). Whose memories? Whose victimhood?: Contests for the Holocaust frame in recent social movement discourse. *Sociological Perspectives, 41*(3), 519–540.

Stone, D. (2002). *Policy paradox: The art of political decision making* (rev. ed.). New York: Norton.

Tamura, Y. (2004). Illusion of homogeneity in claims: Discourse on school rules in Japan. *High School Journal, 88*(1), 52–63.

Tierney, K. J. (1999). Toward a critical sociology of risk. *Sociological Forum, 14*(2), 215–242.

Tuchman, G. (1978). *Making news: A study in the construction of reality.* New York: Free Press.

Tuleja, T. (1994). Closing the circle: Yellow ribbons and the redemption of the past. *Journal of American Culture, 17*, 23–30.

Turner, J. (2004, February 21). Tennis Show Brigade marches for predator law. *The News Tribune* (Tacoma, WA), p. B01.

Turner, P. (1991). The Atlanta child murders: A case study of folklore in the black community. In S. Stem & J. A. Cicalia (Eds.), *Creative ethnicity: Symbols and strategies of contemporary ethnic life* (pp. 75–86). Logan: Utah State University Press.

Walton, B. K., & Bailey, C. (2005). Framing wilderness: Popularism and cultural heritage as organizing principles. *Society and Natural Resources, 18*, 119–134.

West, R. (1987). The feminist–conservative antipornography alliance and the 1986 Attorney General's Commission on Pornography Report. *American Bar Foundation Research Journal, 12*(4), 681–711.

Wong, Y. J. (2006). Strength-centered therapy: A social constructionist, virtues-based psychotherapy. *Psychotherapy: Theory, Research, Practice, Training, 43*(2), 133–146.

Woodward, R. (2000). Warrior heroes and little green men: Soldiers, military training, and the construction of rural masculinities. *Rural Sociology, 65*(4), 640–657.

Youngman, N. (2003). When frame extension fails: Operation Rescue and the "triple gates of hell" in Orlando. *Journal of Contemporary Ethnography, 32*(5), 521–554.

CHAPTER 18

Strict and Contextual Constructionism in the Sociology of Deviance and Social Problems

● Peter R. Ibarra

The idea that reality is socially constructed has proven both fertile and contentious. The contention is nowhere more notable than among scholars who use constructionist insights to generate investigable topics and problems. Although such scholars may be viewed from the outside as constituting a "school of thought" with unique and identifiable contributions to specific bodies of literature, fissures and divisions among these practitioners are recognized from within, coalescing around preferred methods of analytic practice. Of chief importance to the emergence of these divisions is the question of whether (and how) a relationship between so-called objective and subjective realms of reality ought to be taken into account when analyzing and depicting how reality is socially constructed. The theoretical significance of and epistemological grounds for making these analytic "moves" are subject to contention as well.

The idea of viewing the so-called objective–subjective split as a problem that must be addressed or resolved via constructionist analytic practice stems from a disagreement among social constructionists over whether and how the seeming radicality of social constructionism can or should be contained, limited, or compromised. This point is evident in the very terms that are used to identify the varying analytic approaches to the problem, most recently expressed in the distinction between those who adopt a "contextual" as opposed to a "strict" interpretation of the perspective's prescriptions, and which has elsewhere been delineated in terms of parallel distinctions between "weak" and "strong" readings of constructionism and between "balanced" and "constitutive" orientations (see, e.g., Best, 1989, 1995; Holstein & Gubrium, 2003; Ibarra & Kitsuse, 1993; Kitsuse & Spector, 1975; Pollner, 1978; Rains, 1975). These distinctions encapsulate distinctive analytic stances on the extent to which constructive processes (such as by way of interpretive or definitional practice) can be viewed in and of themselves as productive of social realities in either a proximate or taken-for-granted sense, as opposed to being best approached in connection with stable, fixed, and/or unchanging "properties" or "aspects," construed as constraining (and remaining impervious to) the world-making potential of social construction.

There are broadly shared notions and sensibilities among social constructionists, regardless of substantive field, including such specializations as deviance, social problems, and science studies, and these bear mention. Chief among them is that social constructionism aims to document and trace the emergence, distillation, diffusion, institutionalization, and social implications of "understandings," whether their study entails examining, for example, the categories through which someone is classified as "deviant"; the routine methods through which scientists working in a laboratory arrive at, or confirm, a "scientific discovery"; or the rhetorical resources that enter into the development of a "public awareness" campaign targeting a particular "social problem."

Social constructionists ground the study of shared and conflicted understandings within the context of social milieus, which may be conceived as work groups, laboratories, families, hospitals, communities, political organizations, mass media venues, and so forth. These milieus can manifest themselves "in action" or "in text." In a certain sense it doesn't matter, because whether the "data" are utterances (e.g., communicated in social interaction) or inscriptions (e.g., communicated through some kind of written or textual device), such expressions can be examined for patterns of inference, association, definition, and contrast that, taken together, function as "claims" about realities that exist independent of the *in situ* means that were used to uncover or posit them, which is to say they can be treated as natives' reports or insiders' accounts. Familiarity with both the content produced and the forms taken by reality-constituting practices, as well as the local standards employed in those settings in which such devices are deployed, is essential to the doing of constructionist work, again irrespective of the substantive field in which such scholarship is being carried out. On these points, there appears to be unanimity among social constructionists; the question remains as to the origins and ramifications of divergences in constructionist thought that are manifested around notions of "contextual" and "strict," or "compromise" and "constitutive" readings of social construction.

This chapter discusses the origins and development of social constructionism in the areas of deviance and social problems, tracing the roots and evolution of the distinction between what came to be called "strict" and "contextual" constructionism. The intellectual links between these two fields are strong, especially with respect to processes of social construction (e.g., the importance of definition, labeling, and interpretation) and the involvement of particular theorists (John I. Kitsuse especially); hence they are well suited for a discussion of conceptual continuities. Although the distinction between strict and contextual constructionism emerged within discussions in the sociology of social problems, it was foreshadowed in deviance studies, in which the analytic importance that ought to be accorded to the objectivity of deviance (and the normative structures by which it could presumably be identified) was in dispute and handled differently by various theorists. A parallel discussion might be undertaken regarding developments in social studies of science (e.g., Bloor, 1991; Latour & Woolgar, 1979); see Restivo and Croissant (Chapter 11, this volume) for an extended discussion of constructionism in studies of science and technology.

The Objective–Subjective Problem in Early Constructionism: Sociology of Deviance

The sociology of deviance was the first of the two fields addressed in this chapter to develop an approach that can be considered "constructionist," and the manner in which debate unfolded there informed how social constructionists later formulated an orientation toward the sociology of social problems. The objective–subjective problem reemerged in the latter as a topic of in-school divergence, so to speak, in spite of efforts to apply lessons learned in the former. The terms in which these concerns were addressed were remarkably similar, testimony to the multiple agendas that are encapsulated by the distinction, in spite of the best intentions to render it theoretically irrelevant or theoretically uncontroversial within a generally constructionist framework.

The sociology of deviance was one of the most important areas within the discipline in the 1960s, inspiring much fieldwork-based research, as well as lively theoretical and political discussion. At the forefront of this dialogue were the writings of such authors as Howard Becker (1963), Aaron Cicourel (1968), Erving Goffman (1961), John Kitsuse (1962), and Edwin Lemert (1951, 1967), who made social interaction central to the sociological examination of deviance. The roots of the emergent conception are traceable to Lemert's (1967) distinction between primary and secondary deviation, which directs attention away from the deviant or his or her deviance per se (primary deviation) and toward the consequences of being perceived and reacted to as deviant:

> Primary deviation, as contrasted with secondary, is polygenetic, arising out of a variety of so-

cial, cultural, psychological, and physiological factors, either in adventitious or recurring combinations. While it may be socially recognized and even defined as undesirable, primary deviation has only marginal implications for the status and psychic structure of the persons concerned. . . . Secondary deviation refers to a special class of socially defined responses which people make to problems created by the societal reaction to their deviance. These problems are essentially moral problems which revolve around stigmatization, punishments, segregation, and social control. Their general effect is to differentiate the symbolic and interactional environment to which the person responds, so that early or adult socialization is categorically affected. They become central facts of existence for those experiencing them, altering psychic structure, producing specialized organization of social roles and self-regarding attitudes. Actions which have these roles and self attitudes as their referents make up secondary deviance. The secondary deviant . . . is a person whose life and identity are organized around the facts of deviance. (pp. 40–41)

Secondary deviance was the central focus of the new conception in Lemert's (1967) formulation. Through this idea, Lemert developed an alternative to the traditional view of deviance. Conventionally, deviance was viewed as giving rise to social control–the deviant brought upon himself the terms of his own ostracism. Lemert inverted this notion, suggesting that social control could prove fateful in unanticipated and powerful ways, generating or amplifying the social meanings and forms of deviant behavior. Societal reaction selected from among naturally occurring human variations those statistically "outlying" forms of behavior that ought to be negatively sanctioned, leading to the "differentiated" (e.g., deteriorated or marginalized) social situations in which deviants often found themselves. By contrast, in the absence of a societal reaction, there really was nothing for a sociologist of deviance to consider: where primary deviance per se did not occasion a reorganization of the deviant's identity, fate, perspective, and so forth, there was no sociologically based deviantization. A negative societal reaction, then, was essential to identifying a phenomenon of interest, as well as suggesting a uniquely powerful sociological dynamic, one productive of the social reality of deviance.

The logic of Lemert's innovation did not hinge on a distinction between deviance as objective or subjective so much as it relied on a distinction between deviance that was socially marked (secondary) and that was unmarked (primary). It was an emphasis on the former that constituted the innovative thrust of his conception. Primary deviation was without sociological significance unless the unmarked status was attributable to secretive behavior (discussed later) on the part of the deviant to avoid detection, behavior that was effectively incorporated into manifestations of secondary deviation. Lemert's formulation essentially rested on a theoretically indifferent view toward primary deviance. It is not that primary deviance did not exist; rather, it was that primary deviance was socially unprocessed, as it were, hence without interest to the sociologist. Lemert's innovation, then, was one that sidestepped the question of "objective" (socially unmediated) deviance on theoretical grounds. It is not that we are precluded from knowing the "objective" (i.e., socially unmediated) reality so much as there is no theoretical rationale for its study in his social-interaction-based conception of deviance.

Lemert's student, John Kitsuse, along with Aaron Cicourel, jointly and singly published influential work that advanced the study of societal reaction in the construction of deviance and hence was indebted to Lemert's work (although their formulation was also influenced by ethnomethodology, as then being developed by Harold Garfinkel; see Rains, 1975). However, Kitsuse and Cicourel's work was developed without the encumbrance of the etiological agenda that was central to Lemert's work (even if Lemert's focus on the origins of secondary deviance was of a strictly sociological

sort), and it did not rely on a notion of fundamentally observable departures from central tendencies in a statistical-normative sense. Their modestly titled joint paper, "A Note on the Uses of Official Statistics" (Kitsuse & Cicourel, 1963), featured an inversion that paralleled Lemert's own, while at the same time turning the study of societal reaction away from secondary deviance. The subject of the paper concerns the underlying conception of deviance that ought to accompany the use of crime statistics and other sorts of administrative data produced by social control–welfare agencies. Historically, such statistics have been criticized for their unreliability: categories weren't applied uniformly (because of discretionary decisions, errors, or poor training), and the categories themselves were not created with the sociologist's purposes and concepts in mind, making the use of the resulting data problematic in testing hypotheses about the social and cultural determinants of (primary) deviance.

Addressing this traditional critique, Kitsuse and Cicourel (1963) make a distinction between a behavior-producing process and a rate-producing process. The former refers to the "social and cultural" conditions that sociologists theorize about and investigate as productive of units or rates of deviant behavior (e.g., poverty, anomie, a culture of violence, or socially disorganized environments); the latter refers to *the actions taken by persons in the social system* which define, classify and record certain behaviors as deviant" (Kitsuse & Cicourel, 1963, p. 135, original emphasis). By way of the alternative conception, such statistics bear the indicia of societal reaction:

> If a given form of behavior is not interpreted as deviant by such person it would not appear as a unit in whatever set of rates we might attempt to explain. . . . The persons who define and activate the rate-producing processes may range from the neighborhood "busybody" to officials of law enforcement agencies. From this point of view, *deviant behavior* is behavior which is organizationally defined, processed, and treated as "strange," "abnormal," "theft," "delin-

quent," etc., by the personnel in the social system which has produced the rate. (Kitsuse & Cicourel, 1963, p. 135)

Kitsuse and Cicourel's (1963) notion of a "rate construction process" provides an early version of what would come to be characteristic of social construction, namely, a focus on the definitional practices and organizational considerations that are embedded in the moral differentiation of populations, a kind of sorting out process that collectively comes to yield an official reality: a crime rate, a marked group of persons. Crime rates, rather than being used as evidence in support of one or another criminological theory of predisposing social conditions, can be "accounted for" by close consideration of the practical situations in which, and systems of classification through which, actors make sense of "putatively" deviant acts and persons.

Cicourel and Kitsuse (1963, 1968) applied this conception to the processing of deviance in two high schools, focusing on the "social typing" through which students with "adolescent problems" are made sense of by school personnel, interpretations that serve to ground referrals and nonreferrals to other school officials, as well as to various agencies beyond the school. "The social processes by which the members of the social organization impute motives and perceive regularities in their construction of the deviant, the grounds for such decisions, and the subsequent treatment of persons so defined" (Cicourel & Kitsuse, 1968, p. 126) are thereby made the phenomena that are described and analyzed. Adolescent problems may be "found" to originate in academic issues, in emotional issues, or in delinquency issues. Depending on the social-typing framework that is invoked and applied, different responses will be warranted in terms of the disciplinary ideologies and resources within the organization. Perhaps the "problem" can be "solved" by putting the student in a more or less academically challenging track; perhaps psychiatric counseling is

called for; or perhaps it is time to invoke the juvenile justice system. The sense that is made of the "problem" shapes the "adolescent career," including whether it is organizationally processed as deviant.

The societal reaction theorists outlined a framework for the study of deviance that did not make or rest on substantive assumptions about the "underlying nature" of the phenomenon; it could be examined strictly from the perspective of those parties constructing the phenomenon in everyday circumstances, by way of their ordinary language and routine practices. Because there were no assumptions made about an underlying deviant nature—such as what was "true" or "untrue" about the deviant, notwithstanding how he or she was reacted to or defined—the imputers of deviancies could, from the sociologist's observational standpoint, do no wrong. To the extent that there was error, poor training, or discretionary decision making to be found, it was from a practitioner's perspective, as documented in and expressed through the ordinary language and routine practices of those making determinations of deviance. These represented "technical" problems among more or less expert users of those languages and routines, rather than a failing that the academic sociologist was obligated to "correct" (Matza, 1969). Thus, in his writings, when discussing "what is being reacted to," Kitsuse (1962) wrote about "putative deviance," an especially interesting term because it sidesteps questions about "actual" deviance. For Kitsuse, deviance could be understood sociologically as constructed through imputation, "without regard for warrant" (Rains, 1975, p. 10). Questions about the underlying reality of deviance or the accuracy of deviance designations could be bracketed or momentarily set aside, with attention instead focused on the talk and action that communicated understandings about, as well as providing mechanisms for the social differentiation of, deviant populations.

To be sure, Kitsuse and Cicourel (1963) acknowledged that any full-scale theory of deviance should be able to account for both the constructions, as per societal reaction, and what "produced" those populations in a prereaction state. Societal reaction theorists did not assert that there are no social or cultural conditions that might produce deviant behavior; nor did they assert that there are no "actual" behaviors that are being reacted to as deviant. However, these latter matters were not accorded conceptual weight in the formulation, and there was no effort to integrate them into the research directives stemming from the framework. Thus societal reaction theorists produced a conceptual framework for research that would be considered (vis-à-vis contemporary theoretical language) an approximation of strict constructionism (Best, 1989). If they did not engage the "objectivity" of deviance, it was because their "sensitizing concept" (Blumer, 1969) that deviance is constructed through definitions did not logically mandate it.

Howard S. Becker's *Outsiders* (1963), a text that offered the most celebrated exposition of "labeling theory," took a somewhat different tack in formulating a constructionist orientation to deviance studies. He begins with premises closely aligned with societal reaction as formulated by Kitsuse and Cicourel, arguing that "the deviant is one to whom that label has successfully been applied; deviant behavior is behavior that people so label" (Becker, 1963, p. 9). On its face this maxim is clearly reminiscent of the position taken by Kitsuse and Cicourel regarding the "official" differentiation of deviant populations, but Becker departs from them in ways that foreshadow difficulties that would bedevil later social constructionists who attempted to reconcile "objective" and "subjective" realities. According to Becker:

> deviance is not a simple quality, present in some kinds of behavior and absent in others. Rather it is the product of a process which involves responses of other people to the behavior. The same behavior may be an infraction of the rules at one time and not at another; may be an infraction of the rules at one time and

not at another; may be an infraction when committed by one person, but not when committed by another; some rules are broken with impunity, others are not. In short, whether a given act is deviant or not depends in part on the nature of the act (that is, whether or not it violates some rule) and in part on what other people do about it. . . . Deviance is not a quality that lies in behavior itself, but in the interaction between the person who commits and act and those who respond to it. (p. 14)

Becker's placement of deviance within a rule-breaking model undermines the explicit relativism in this statement, namely, that its sense, meaning, and reality changes with the perspective of the labeling party. Constructionism adopts a relativist stance, as does Becker when he asserts that "outsiders" (deviants) may view the standards by which they are found to be lacking unacceptable to them, just as they may condemn those who condemn them. However, the normative model of social process that underlies the conception of deviance results in inconsistencies, because transformative, reality-constituting capacities of labeling are hamstrung by the constant, fixed nature of deviance. The inconsistencies are condensed in Becker's famous fourfold typology of the labeling process, which generated the anomalous categories "falsely accused deviant" and "secret deviant." This model presumed and incorporated into its structure the idea that there was objectivity to deviance that transcended the deviant label, namely, conformity with or departure from normative standards (Becker, 1963, p. 20). The label was not as essential to deviance as was rule-breaking behavior; on the contrary, the label was a kind of ornamentation that might be aptly or inaptly applied. In that sense the radical implication that deviance could be studied as strictly constructed through ordinary people's everyday language and practices was reined in and subverted.

Thomas Scheff (1984) offered an extension of Becker's model in his book, *Being Mentally Ill*. In this text, Scheff attempted to further intertwine the conception of labeling within a rule-breaking model in his theory of the genesis of mental illness through his concept of "residual deviance" (p. 37), which is defined as rule-breaking "for which our society provides no explicit label and which, therefore, sometimes leads to the labeling of the violator as mentally ill" (p. 38). The violator, in turn, adopts a "patient role" that "confirms" the diagnosis. Scheff's elaboration of Becker's labeling theory attempts to offer an analysis of how someone becomes "mentally ill" that can stand as an alternative to nonconstructionist perspectives, but what results is a dialogue that turns on the extent to which labeling explains what Lemert (1967) referred to as *primary deviation*. For societal reaction becomes construed as a variable, thus stating as a proposition the question of how much labeling versus something else might account for mental illness. Returning to the terms of our earlier discussion, societal reaction is put to the service of explaining the behavior-producing process, a debate that the perspective never really sought to join. Framing the discussion this way only succeeds in emboldening positivists, who are now invited to think of labeling as a variable with greater or lesser "effects" or impact compared with other such "inputs" (see Holstein, 1993, pp. 7–13, for a parallel discussion of Scheff's version of labeling theory).

The societal reaction perspective need not be utilized in this way if one wishes to study mental illness, of course. One can look to such exemplars of analysis as Dorothy Smith's "K is Mentally Ill: The Anatomy of a Factual Account" (1978), which is concerned with explicating how an account of someone's "becoming mentally ill" is intricately structured through the use of various communicative devices that encourage auditors to "hear" no other reasonable conclusion but that such a development in fact has occurred. Smith's analysis makes no assumptions about K's actual condition: Her alleged mental illness is constructed by way of another per-

son's accounting practices. Therefore, the focus of explication falls on the methods through which the reality of someone's becoming mentally ill is discursively organized as a commonsense, accountable conclusion.

Melvin Pollner (1978) provided a valuable summation of the analytic currents and countercurrents to be found within the emerging conception of deviance. Referring to "mundane" and "constitutive" versions of labeling theory, Pollner argued that influential formulations of the labeling perspective enacted a "fusion of lay and analytic perspectives" that resulted in "conceptual knots" that undermined the promise of the new conception of deviance. The power of labeling theory was that it had the potential to display how " 'deviance' was not a given property of acts but rather the name of the process through which such designations were received" (Pollner, 1978, p. 269), generating an examination of deviance as a concerted accomplishment expressed through that corpus of reasoning practices that classified, sorted, and theorized about deviant behavior while simultaneously masking the very interpretive work that constituted deviant acts as known-in-common entities. According to Pollner (1987), however, Becker's (1963) model of the labeling process did not identify a distinctively sociological conception but rather offered a formalization of commonsense notions about deviance rooted in a mundane ontology, including the idea that deviance is constituted through something other than a community reaction, hence undermining the very innovation that labeling theory advanced in the first place:

In the mundane version, the features of an act that require one or another kind of response from a community are treated as nonproblematic givens and even, occasionally, as objective, inherent properties. The deviant or nondeviant, the rule-violating or conforming character of an act are regarded, in one fashion or another, as defined by some criterion other than the reaction of the community. In the mundane version, a community's "reaction," "response," or "labeling" activities consist essentially of its judgments about the deviant or nondeviant character of acts and persons. The community is conceived as an umpire whose task is to call balls and strikes. The relevant questions about the community's judgments focus on the extent to which they correspond to the act's "real" properties and the conditions affecting the degree of correspondence. (p. 270)

In essence, the conception of the "deviant-making enterprise" that is promoted in Becker's (1963) text rests on the idea of contingent errors, which presumes that an analyst can compare the presence or absence of community reaction with what the analyst "knows" to be the "real" status of the deviance to be found or not found in actuality. The constructive process is thereby understood to logically presume an intervention on the part of an analyst in possession of inside knowledge regarding the ontological status of the putative deviance. It is not evident from what perch a constructionist analyst can make such determinations without conceding the limits of construction itself.

The conceptual intermingling of constructive processes and objective "properties" that was embedded in Becker's typology is bypassed in the "constitutive" version of labeling theory, which asserts that

from the sociological point of view, there is absolutely nothing else to consider other than the praxis through which persons orient to, display, detect, make observable, and thereby accomplish an act's status as deviant. As a sociological entity, the deviant act exists only in and through the praxis through which it is responded to as such, and the procedures that members have establishing and sustaining the response as warrantable. (Pollner, 1978, p. 280)

In this statement, the focus is clearly fixed on societal reaction, now seen from a more explicitly ethnomethodological perch. The constitutive version of labeling theory pro-

posed to forgo all concerns with deviant acts either as objective (having fixed, determinate attributes), or as subjective (that is, viewed from the perspective of the alleged deviant actor). Instead, emphasis was returned to those parties who in effect produced deviance in the very act of identifying, discovering, or otherwise "responding" to it, without regard for whether such deviance-making was produced in ways consistent or at variance with what the sociologist considers norms, rules, values, common sense, and so forth. Such a conception rested on a bet: that deviance could be sociologically addressed without concern for anything other than the perspective and practice that implicitly or explicitly constituted it as such. The problem with such a bet is that the sociologist appears to give up the expertise that he or she is often called on to employ, including "objective" knowledge of deviance itself, irrespective of the "definitions" of ordinary members of society. This "giveaway" was both in principle and in practice difficult—a point that would be underscored when social constructionism came to focus on what for many is the bread and butter of sociology: the study of "social problems."

The Social Construction of Social Problems: Lessons Learned or Forgotten?

Regardless of the area of social life they may examine, social constructionists are typically studying phenomena that are studied by nonconstructionists as well, and this means that they have to, in some way, address whether and how their conception does or does not build on the terms through which nonconstructionists conceive of the nature and investigability of the same topic. Although this principle of "ground clarification" applies to any area in which different theoretical premises inform approaches to social inquiry, it is an especially important matter when attempting to fashion a mode of scholarship that is dedicated to understanding the very senses in which something can be taken as a meaningful reality in the first place. Proceeding with inquiry by assuming that a nonconstructionist understands a phenomenon identically to a constructionist is likely to result in incoherencies downstream. In the postlabeling and societal reaction period, with the appreciation for paradigms in sociology (Wilson, 1970) and paradigm shifts in science (Kuhn, 1970) more generally that emerged from the intractable debates over the value of the "new conception" of deviance (e.g., Gove, 1980), this was a crucially important insight, and it was incorporated into the formulation of "social problems as social construction" that was developed by John Kitsuse and his younger colleague, Malcolm Spector, in a series of articles published in the 1970s in the journal *Social Problems* (subsequently revised for the 1977 book *Constructing Social Problems*). Spector and Kitsuse (1977/1987) here developed a research program that attempted to extend the logic of societal reaction to the sociology of social problems, now in a more self-consciously social constructionist and reflexive direction (although whether it was reflexive enough would eventually emerge as an issue in subsequent decades).

Although Spector and Kitsuse were basically inexplicit about the philosophical foundations of their approach, their approach is one whose roots lie in the phenomenology of Alfred Schutz (1962) and the ethnomethodology of Harold Garfinkel (1967), as well as in the definitional sensibility promoted by symbolic interactionism (Loseke, 1999, p. 197). Notwithstanding the presuppositional understatement, theirs was a conception that stood at some remove from conventional sociology's orientation to social problems. As they put it, their formulation "will not offer a rival explanation for a commonly defined subject matter. We argue for a different subject matter for the sociology of social problems" (Spector & Kitsuse, 1977/1987, p. 39). Spector and Kitsuse's approach located social problems not in "so-

cial conditions" but in "claims-making activities" about "putative conditions." In so redefining the phenomenon, they wished to make the process of definition central and the "underlying reality" of the condition theoretically irrelevant, in a manner reminiscent of Kitsuse's earlier writings on the sociology of deviance (e.g., Kitsuse, 1962). Spector and Kitsuse's call to sociologists to focus on definitions when studying social problems was in that sense not new—even positivists (nonconstructionists) had occasion to examine subjective perspectives via public opinion on those social problems they studied. The novelty of Spector and Kitsuse's formulation came less from their call for social constructionists to rigorously examine "claimsmakers" definitional activities in order to reveal the "institutional careers" of definitions and more from their recommendation that the analyst be conscious of the role of the sociologist in the very construction of those social problems under investigation.

The pivotal article, vis-à-vis the present discussion, is Kitsuse and Spector's 1975 article, "Social Problems and Deviance: Some Parallel Issues." The authors are concerned with preventing the derailment of their fledging conception into the analytically compromised terrain previously visited by definitional approaches to deviance, as well as by earlier protoconstructionist perspectives on social problems. Their review of previous efforts by like-minded scholars such as Willard Waller, Richard Fuller, and Richard Myers (on the social problems side), as well as Becker and Lemert (on the deviance side), emphasizes the failure to remain mindful of "the symbolic processes through which the meanings of [deviant] behaviors and [social problem] conditions are generated and institutionalized" (Kitsuse & Spector, 1975, p. 585). According to Kitsuse and Spector, these earlier authors were "sensitive" to being accused of "subjectivism" and so developed "balanced approach[es] that acknowledged the importance of objective, as well as subjective aspects of deviance and social problems" (p. 585). The problem with the "balanced approach," however, is that it implies that

> definitions of social problems may be understood as reactions to conditions. "Competent" socialized members of society do not see and complain about conditions that do not exist. Therefore the existence of the objective condition itself helps explain the societal reaction to it. This reduces the definition from a social construction of reality, an accomplishment of members of the society, to a mere mechanical reaction to exterior forces. The integrity of the definitional process is sacrificed for the balanced view. (p. 589)

In Kitsuse and Spector's reading, previous sociologists' difficulties in remaining trained on the constructive processes stemmed from "three kinds of memberships"—as "members of society," as "members of a profession," and as "experts" who are accorded the authority to speak to questions about public policy:

> As members of society they fail to examine their own interpretive activities. As members of an aspiring profession in a competitive organizational environment, vested interests make them compete in traditionally defined areas. Finally, as individual experts they are expected to address the practical policy questions and thus accept their underlying positivistic assumptions. (1975, p. 593)

Each kind of membership exerts a kind of gravitational pull on interpretive sociologists, leading them to turn away from addressing the sociological intricacies and implications of the definitional process in favor of more traditional (e.g., etiological, diagnostic, or remedial) concerns. Thus Kitsuse and Spector's research program presumes that analysts will be prepared to ask themselves at each point in the examination of the definitional process: Who is speaking here? Who is identifying condition X as the problem? Who is according person Y the status of "claimant" in this definitional process? At times, these questions may reveal that the

analyst has moved away from the periphery and toward the center, such as in those scenes depicted in field notes in which the researcher is doing participant observation, or when an analyst participates as a policymaker or activist, or later, away from the field, in the creation of an analytic narrative that uses interpretive relevancies that belong more to the analyst than to the participants involved in the definitional process.

Kitsuse and Spector clearly prefer that the analyst remain detached, "on the side," because such a stance presumably keeps the analyst from blurring the distinction between the process of analyzing a social problem's construction and the process of constructing a social problem: The point of the former is to understand the latter. However, should the analyst take a more participatory role in the process, he or she should be prepared to examine how and whether his or her participation shaped the ultimate construction of the social problem. Needless to say, the sociologist cannot presume that he or she will be accorded weight or authority by others involved in the construction of the social problem; this is a contingent issue, amenable to empirical documentation, and itself testimony to the sociology of social problems processes. Note, too, that such expert enrollment would be unlikely to result from the analyst's work on the social problems process, because the knowledge furnished by such research is less about the "facts" of the social problem than about the institutional career of the definitions, which presumably holds less interest to claimants and policymakers.

In spite of their concern with urging on constructionists a sensitivity to the distinction between an analytic stance and a participants' stance (or members' stance) and their suggestion that sociologists be prepared to monitor and document their own role in the construction of the social problems under study, research inspired by Spector and Kitsuse's framework came under critical scrutiny that found it to be lacking in reflexivity. The 1985 publication of Steve Woolgar and Dorothy Pawluch's "Ontological Gerry-mandering" was a signal event for the field, appearing in the same year as Joseph Schneider's review essay on work done by social constructionists (Schneider, 1985). The latter, appearing in the *Annual Review of Sociology*, furnished proof that the approach had in a sense arrived, citing a plethora of published studies that documented the versatility of the framework for analyzing a wide range of substantive controversies. The former honed in on patterns of analytic practice embedded within those same studies. Woolgar and Pawluch's analysis centered on two points. First, they argued that social constructionists lapsed into a tacit objectivism in that their analysis of social problems centered on "the variability of the definitions vis-à-vis the constancy of the conditions to which they relate" (p. 215). In other words, the social construction amounted to a kind of wrapping or packaging of an otherwise unchanging object. What the object is called, how it is reacted to, and who is entrusted with managing it may change, but the thing itself does not. Woolgar and Pawluch noted that even Spector and Kitsuse, in *Constructing Social Problems* (1977/1987), had made this kind of theoretically compromised error, in their discussion of marijuana, when they stated in passing that the chemical composition of marijuana had not changed, unlike the responses it elicited. Such a statement implies that the analyst knows something that social problems participants do not, even though what participants "know and use" (Sacks, quoted in Heritage, 1984, p. 233) is supposed to form the basis for the analyst's depiction of the constructive process.

Presumably, the authors note, such lapses into "selective relativism" conceivably are avoidable, through what Prudence Rains (1975, p. 3) referred to as "ostentatiously careful talk," for example. However, Woolgar and Pawluch's (1985) second point was a thornier matter altogether, for the second sense in which social constructionists practiced selective relativism had to do with

their handling of their own analytic tools; constructionists failed to turn their tools back on themselves. Going beyond Spector and Kitsuse's call for sociologists to take note of their involvement in the process of constructing problems, the issue is that there is no call to examine how the tools of constructionist analysis themselves are contingent and constructive. It is as if everything else is up for grabs *except* constructionist precepts and practices: The definitional practices under study are viewed as contingent and constructive, but the tools of analysis are treated as unproblematic, hence acquiring a kind of omniscience that is elsewhere (in the critique of objectivism) implicitly considered impossible to attain. Selective relativism in the first sense is more straightforwardly dealt with than in the second sense, and to date there has been no convincing response demonstrating how constructionism may be reconciled with it.

Woolgar and Pawluch (1985) offered a trenchant reading of the "anatomy" of constructionist practice as applied to the study of social problems, one that galvanized discussion and resulted in a variety of responses, with some constructionists taking their statement to heart and attempting a kind of reformulation of their approach (e.g., Schneider, 1991, 1993) and others viewing the critique as so much metatheory that held little significance for the goals and practices associated with the perspective (e.g., Gusfield, 1985). Woolgar and Pawluch did not offer a new definition of social problems, for example; nor did they propose to reorient empirical or theoretical investigations of social problems. In that sense, the critique struck many as an interesting comment on the limits of constructionism but not a real challenge to the study of social problems through such a perspective, since as Woolgar and Pawluch point out, the problem they noted was likely to be endemic in *any* mode of analysis that takes as its goal the explication of constructive processes. Indeed, Woolgar (1983) was raising the issue of selective relativism in constructionist science studies contemporaneously with the ontological gerrymandering critique of social problems studies.

Peter Ibarra and John Kitsuse's 1993 chapter, "Vernacular Constituents of Moral Discourse: An Interactionist Proposal for the Study of Social Problems," offered a recasting of *Constructing Social Problems* (Spector & Kitsuse, 1977/1987) in light of the problem of selective relativism in the first sense but neglected to address the problem of selective relativism in the second sense (Pollner, 1993). The authors suggested retracting the concept "putative condition" from the constructionist formulation because it logically implied the possibility of an object constancy to the conditions that presumably organized claimsmaking activities; instead of putative conditions, they suggested the term "condition category," more closely positioning the object of claimsmaking within the domain of members' talk and symbolization, enabling an analytic focus on process-based disjunctures and pivots that might be precluded in a condition-centered analysis. Alongside this alteration, they proposed reconceiving of social problems processes as akin to language games, replete with rhetorical figures, stylizations, and common motifs, taken together amounting to a kind of moral discourse enacted in constructions of social problems.

Ibarra and Kitsuse (1993) proposed these alterations to draw social constructionists away from unproductive debates with objectivist sociologists (who after all were studying social problems in a different sense) and to suggest how the intermingling of objectivism and subjectivism might be avoided. This proposal engendered a substantial set of responses that appeared in two volumes (Holstein & Miller, 1993; Miller & Holstein, 1993), throughout many of which the problem of subjectivism–objectivism ran as an underlying theme. Ibarra and Kitsuse's chapter was subse-

quently taken to exemplify the "strict constructionist" view, a term proposed by Joel Best (1989) to refer to constructionist approaches that "avoid making assumptions about objective reality" (pp. 245–246). According to Best, strict constructionism entails sacrifice of much that is conceivably of interest to constructionists and their readers. These self-imposed limits constrain constructionism from making statements or pursuing investigations that might yield insight into the *whys* of social construction (Bogard, 2003). Furthermore, Best is dubious that strict constructionism is even possible, claiming that "it may be possible to avoid overt 'lapses'—outright declarations about objective reality—but implicit assumptions about objective conditions will almost inevitably guide researchers" (Best, 2003, p. 59).

Instead, Best favors a "contextual constructionist" approach to social problems analysis, which effectively makes a virtue out of the analyst's ability to move between objective and subjective dimensions of social problems, that is, ontological gerrymandering. So long as the analyst does not succumb to a "vulgar" mixture of such intermingling (Best, 1995), and so long as the analyst stays focused on constructionist processes, there should be no unsurpassable problem. Best, in other words, recommends a return to the very approach that concerned Spector and Kitsuse in the first place, namely a "balanced view" of constructionism, in which the procedures for intermingling were ad hoc, arbitrary, and apt to be responsive to the social situation of the analyst more than the social situation of the claimants. Presumably, sometimes the analyst would be satisfied that in *this* circumstance further problematizing of claimants' beliefs is necessary, and in *that* circumstance not so much, but who is to say when and why? As Donileen Loseke puts it:

> once we argue it's acceptable for analysts to bring statements about objective conditions

into their examinations, where do we draw the line? How many assumptions or statements about the existence of conditions do we allow before it's no longer an example of social constructionism? Also, and critically, if we allow analysts to compare claims and assess their truth, what guidelines do we use to judge truthfulness? Will we simply accept government statistics as the truth and not examine their socially constructed nature? Or, conversely, will we simply accept claims made by powerless people as the truth? (1999, p. 207)

Such contextual approaches generate direct parallels to Becker's category of secret deviance. Richard Ball and J. Robert Lilly's (1984) notion of "potential social problems," defined as "activities which might reasonably be expected to provoke claims-making responses" (p. 114) were they not hidden from view, and Joel Best and Gerald Horiuchi's (1985) notion of "unconstructed social problems," defined as conditions that have the "potential to be defined as social problems, [but which] never reach this status" (p. 495), suggest that the problematic nature of social problems inheres in conditions rather than in the perspective and definitional praxis that would construct them as morally objectionable phenomena of collective concern. Obstructions in the proper exercise of ordinary members' perceptual acuities, whether because of material interests, ideology, "sociocultural strain," or deflection practices, prevent glimpses of that which is otherwise readily available for apprehension: a genuine social problem. Such a view stands in stark contrast to the idea that the definitional practices and collective actions of ordinary members/participants, rather than the sociologist's interpretive relevancies, constitute social problems—unless, of course, the sociologist's own definitional practices form part of the process under documentation. If the latter is the case, however, we are likely to be left once again to puzzle over whether the analyst's fundamental task is to construct social problems or to reconstruct constructions of social problems.

Conclusion

The problem of how or whether to reconcile objective and subjective dimensions of social problems and deviance within a constructionist formulation is a long-standing one, and it is unlikely that there will be a resolution to the problem that would be satisfactory to all. Having said that, however, the analytic divide to be found among scholars working within these fields has not exactly resulted in paralysis, either. To the contrary, constructionist scholarship flourished (and continues to flourish, in the social problems area, in particular) irrespective of these disputes. In the meantime, constructionist sensibilities have been dispersed throughout substantive areas of sociology, as well as beyond sociology, to which the present volume attests, often with lesser degrees of interest in the problem.

Although it is possible to do work that is more akin to *strict* constructionism than *contextual* constructionism (e.g., Jaworski, 1994; Lynxwiler & DeCrote, 1996), it is apparent that most contemporary scholars employing the perspective have taken to a so-called contextual approach (Holstein & Gubrium, 2003)—"so called" because even "strict" approaches are ever mindful of context. It has always been so, however. As noted earlier, in Kitsuse and Spector's reading, the position of the sociologist, as a member of society, of a profession, and of an expert class, seems to cultivate a "balanced" or compromised constructionism. Perhaps there is a lesson in this, but it would not appear that the analytic power of what phenomenologists call "bracketing" has been allowed to develop to full advantage in these cases. For bracketing is pursued to understand precisely the experientially obdurate, objective nature of things, as well as that which is on its surface subjective. Bracketing is an interpretive orientation demanded by rigorous constructionism. It is likely to counteract the influence of "memberships" that can become unwittingly embedded within our work—

however real the worlds we study may seem—permitting analytic leverage useful for discerning the constituents of reified phenomena, which is to say, that which would otherwise be taken for granted as the proximate foundations for sensible and accountable inference.

An intriguing effort at developing the analytic value of bracketing in service of "constructionist analytics" has been offered by James Holstein and Jaber Gubrium (2003, p. 194) that "stands somewhere between, or apart from, the 'strict' and 'contextual' designations that have come to define the constructionist landscape." These authors remind us that "context" is itself always already constructed and that bracketing is a useful way of capturing the contours—here apparently fixed, there apparently breachable—that govern and animate discursive and interpretive practice in everyday life, inclusive of such phenomena as social problems and deviance. As they put it:

> Analytic bracketing provides us with an orienting procedure—a method for flexibly attending to the *hows*, *whats*, and related *whens*, and *wheres* of social life in order to assemble both a contextually scenic and contextually constructive picture. Either constitutive interactional sequential environments or available discursive resources become the provisional phenomenon of interest, while the other is temporarily consigned to the analytic periphery. In a sense, the constant interplay in the analysis mirrors the lived interplay between social interaction, its immediate interactional environment, and its more distal interpretive resources and going concerns (Hughes, 1984). By conceiving of context in terms of this reflexive interplay, constructionist researchers can escape the endless philosophical debate that results from invidious comparisons between "strict" and "contextual" frameworks. (p. 203)

Holstein and Gubrium note that there is no inconsistency between an insistence that context must be constantly attended to, both in the sense of something that is emergent and something that is taken for granted, and

a demand that we not succumb to the substantive reification that inevitably undermines the promise of constructionism—namely, that active, everyday praxis can be examined for its role in generating the social reality of social problems and deviance that we seek to document in our research.

The history of how the object–subject split has been addressed in the sociologies of deviance and social problems suggests that constructionists need not make an ontological choice. There is no need to definitively declare that social problems are only or merely constructed or that deviance is only or merely that which exists in spite of labels. However, this same history does suggest that constructionists always must make methodological choices, including whether to remain committed to the rigorous documentation of the process of reification that can result in known-in-common phenomena such as "deviance" and "social problems."

• References

Ball, R., & Lilly, J. R. (1984). When is a "problem" not a problem?: Deflection activities in a clandestine motel. In J. Schneider & J. Kitsuse (Eds.), *Studies in the sociology of social problems* (pp. 114–139). Norwood, NJ: Ablex.

Becker, H. S. (1963). *Outsiders: Studies in the Sociology of Deviance.* New York: Free Press.

Best, J. (1989). Afterword. In J. Best (Ed.), *Images of issues* (pp. 243–253). Hawthorne, NY: Aldine.

Best, J. (1995). Constructionism in context. In J. Best (Ed.), *Images of issues* (2nd ed., pp. 337–354). Hawthorne, NY: Aldine de Gruyter.

Best, J. (2003). But seriously folks: The limitations of the strict constructionist interpretation of social problems. In J. A. Holstein & G. Miller (Eds.), *Challenges and choices: Constructionist perspectives on social problems* (pp. 51–69). Hawthorne, NY: Aldine de Gruyter.

Best, J., & Horiuchi, G. T. (1985). The razor blade in the apple. *Social Problems, 32,* 488–499.

Bloor, D. (1991). *Knowledge and social imagery* (2nd ed.). Chicago: University of Chicago Press.

Blumer, H. (1969). *Symbolic interactionism.* Englewood Cliffs, NJ: Prentice Hall.

Bogard, C. (2003). Explaining social problems: Addressing the *whys* of social constructionism. In J. A.

Holstein & G. Miller (Eds.), *Challenges and choices: Constructionist perspectives on social problems* (pp. 187–208). Hawthorne, NY: Aldine de Gruyter.

Cicourel, A. V. (1968). *The social organization of juvenile justice*. New York: Wiley.

Cicourel, A. V., & Kitsuse, J. I. (1963). *The educational decision-makers*. Indianapolis, IN: Bobbs-Merrill.

Cicourel, A. V., & Kitsuse, J. I. (1968). The social organization of the high school and deviant adolescent careers. In E. Rubington & M. S. Weinberg (Eds.), *Deviance: The interactionist perspective* (2nd ed., pp. 124–135). New York: Macmillan.

Garfinkel, H. (1967). *Studies in ethnomethodology*. Englewood Cliffs, NJ: Prentice Hall.

Goffman, E. (1961). *Asylums*. New York: Doubleday.

Gove, W. (1980). *The labeling of deviance: Evaluating a perspective*. Beverly Hills, CA: Sage.

Gusfield, J. (1985). Theories and hobgoblins. *SSSP Newsletter, 17,* 16–18.

Heritage, J. (1984). *Garfinkel and ethnomethodology*. Cambridge, UK: Polity Press.

Holstein, J. (1993). *Court-ordered insanity*. Hawthorne, NY: Aldine de Gruyter.

Holstein, J., & Gubrium, J. (2003). A constructionist analytics for social problems. In J. A. Holstein & G. Miller (Eds.), *Challenges and choices: Constructivist perspectives on social problems* (pp. 187–208). Hawthorne, NY: Aldine de Gruyter.

Holstein, J., & Miller, G. (1993). *Reconsidering social constructionism*. Hawthorne, NY: Aldine de Gruyter.

Ibarra, P. R., & Kitsuse, J. I. (1993). Vernacular constituents of moral discourse: An interactionist proposal for the study of social problems. In J. A. Holstein & G. Miller (Eds.), *Reconsidering social constructionism* (pp. 25–58). New York: Aldine de Gruyter.

Jaworski, G. D. (1994). Debunking the drug scare: A rhetorical analysis. *Perspectives on Social Problems, 5,* 55–73.

Kitsuse, J. I. (1962). Societal reaction to deviant behavior: Problems of theory and method. *Social Problems, 9,* 247–256.

Kitsuse, J. I., & Cicourel, A. V. (1963). A note on the uses of official statistics. *Social Problems, 11,* 131–139.

Kitsuse, J. I., & Spector, M. (1975). Social problems and deviance: Some parallel issues. *Social Problems, 22,* 584–594.

Kuhn, T. S. (1970). *The structure of scientific revolutions* (2nd ed.). Chicago: University of Chicago Press.

Latour, B., & Woolgar, S. (1979). *Laboratory life: The construction of scientific facts*. Beverly Hills, CA: Sage.

Lemert, E. (1951). *Social pathology: A systematic approach to the theory of sociopathic behavior*. New York: McGraw-Hill.

Lemert, E. (1967). The concept of secondary deviation. In E. Lemert (Ed.), *Human deviance, social problems, and social control* (pp. 40–64). Englewood Cliffs, NJ: Prentice Hall.

Loseke, D. R. (1999). *Thinking about social problems: An introduction to constructionist perspectives*. Hawthorne, NY: Aldine de Gruyter.

Lynxwiler, J., & DeCrote, C. (1996). Claims-making and the moral discourse of hard core rap music. *Perspectives on Social Problems, 7,* 3–28.

Matza, D. (1969). *Becoming deviant*. Englewood Cliffs, NJ: Prentice Hall.

Miller, G., & Holstein, J. (1993). *Constructionist controversies*. New York: Aldine de Gruyter.

Pollner, M. (1978). Constitutive and mundane versions of labeling theory. *Human Studies, 1,* 269–288.

Pollner, M. (1987). *Mundane reason*. New York: Cambridge University Press.

Pollner, M. (1993). The reflexivity of constructionism and the construction of reflexivity. In J. A. Holstein & G. Miller (Eds.), *Reconsidering social constructionism* (pp. 199–212). New York: Aldine de Gruyter.

Rains, P. (1975). Imputations of deviance: A retrospective essay on the labeling perspective. *Social Problems, 23,* 1–11.

Scheff, T. J. (1984). *Being mentally ill: A sociological theory* (2nd ed.). New York: Aldine.

Schneider, J. (1985). Social problems theory: The constructionist view. In R. Turner (Ed.), *Annual review of sociology* (pp. 209–229). Palo Alto, CA: Annual Reviews.

Schneider, J. (1991). Troubles with textual authority in sociology. *Symbolic Interaction, 14,* 295–319.

Schneider, J. (1993). "Members only": Reading the constructionist text. In J. A. Holstein & G. Miller (Eds.), *Reconsidering social constructionism* (pp. 103–116). New York: Aldine de Gruyter.

Schutz, A. (1962). *Collected papers: The problem of social reality*. The Hague, Netherlands: Martinus Nijhoff.

Smith, D. (1978). "K is mentally ill": The anatomy of a factual account. *Sociology, 12,* 23–53.

Spector, M., & Kitsuse, J. I. (1987). *Constructing social problems*. New York: Aldine de Gruyter. (Original work published 1977)

Wilson, T. P. (1970). Normative and interpretive paradigms in sociology. In J. Douglas (Ed.), *Understanding everyday life* (pp. 57–79). Chicago: Aldine de Gruyter.

Woolgar, S. (1983). Irony in the social study of science. In K. Knorr-Cetina & M. Mulkay (Eds.), *Science observed* (pp. 239–266). London: Sage.

Woolgar, S., & Pawluch, D. (1985). Ontological gerrymandering: The anatomy of social problems explanations. *Social Problems, 32,* 214–227.

PART IV

STRATEGIES AND TECHNIQUES

CHAPTER 19

Constructionist Impulses in Ethnographic Fieldwork

● **James A. Holstein**
Jaber F. Gubrium

Across sociology, anthropology, and other disciplines with observational traditions, the common thread running through ethnographic fieldwork is the empirical scrutiny of social situations *in vivo*. Whether sited in households, in small groups, on street corners, in villages, or distributed within organizations and societies, the fieldworker capitalizes on being immersed in a social situation to study its social practices (Bernard, 1998). If, for some, ethnography has become synonymous with qualitative methods (Atkinson & Hammersley, 1994), its traditional method of *in situ* participant observation remains a distinguishing and accepted source of empirical material and analytic inspiration throughout the social sciences.

A long-standing interest in the realistic representation of lives and experience has shaped ethnographic fieldwork into a predominantly naturalistic endeavor, aimed at documenting social worlds and their subjective meanings. Recently, constructionist impulses have captivated the enterprise, altering the goal from naturalistic representation to understanding the indigenous organization of representational practices. Questions arise regarding the sited "thereness" of naturalistic inquiry, prompting epistemological concerns associated with the "being there" assumption of traditional ethnographic fieldwork (Geertz, 1988). How is "there" constructed as a field of inquiry? From what does the field's organization derive? What are the practices and conditions that shape the construction process?

The aim of this chapter is to highlight the ways in which ethnographic fieldwork can be transformed by constructionist sensibilities, focusing mainly on modes of conceptualizing the field, collecting empirical material, and analyzing data. The chapter is less concerned with the writing of ethnography or ethnographic representation; that issue, by now, has had a vibrant history of debate across the social sciences, especially in anthropology and sociology (see, e.g., Behar, 1996; Clifford & Marcus, 1986; Clough, 1992; Ellis & Bochner, 1996; Fox, 1991; Geertz, 1988; Goodall, 2000; Rosaldo, 1993; Tedlock, 2000, 2004; Van Maanen, 1988, 1995; see also Amit, Chapter 39; Ellingson & Ellis, Chapter 23; Faubion & Marcus, Chapter 4; and J. Schneider, Chapter 38, all in this volume). We are well aware that procedural, analytic, and representational practices are interwoven throughout qualitative inquiry, and researchers do well to keep this mind in formulating and assessing ethnography. At the same time, it is useful to consider fieldwork in its own rights in order to sort out the particulars of the research process.

Of course, constructionist impulses play out differently in fieldwork dealing with distinct settings, bound to specific disciplines, and located within particular national traditions (see, e.g., Barth, Gingrich, Parkin, & Silverman, 2005). But constructionist sensibilities, in our view, harbor impulses that transcend disciplinary boundaries. This chapter draws from an ongoing program of research on the social organization of everyday life to provide an orientation to the infusion of constructionist perspectives into fieldwork (Gubrium & Holstein, 1997). The chapter is not a cross-disciplinary survey so much as a presentation of a framework of understanding or "analytics" for conducting fieldwork from a constructionist point of view.

Naturalistic and Constructionist Agendas

Naturalism is arguably the predominant orientation to ethnographic fieldwork (Gubrium & Holstein, 1997). As John and Lyn Lofland (1995) put it, naturalistic studies of social settings minimize presumptions about the empirical world while striving for close, searching descriptions of everyday life. The naturalistic goal in ethnography is to understand social reality on its own terms, "as it really is," to describe what comes naturally, so to speak. It seeks rich descriptions of people and interaction as these exist and unfold in their native habitats. Eschewing representational concerns beyond matters of veridical accuracy, this approach to ethnographic description becomes a matter of documenting and communicating true-to-life depictions of social worlds—the more thickly described the better (Geertz, 1973).

Naturalistic ethnography is replete with prescriptions and injunctions for capturing social reality on its home turf and in its own terms. One of the earliest and most impassioned pleas came from Robert Park, a founder of the "Chicago School" of field research. Reacting to what he called "armchair sociology," Park insisted that social researchers immerse themselves in the "real world" (Bulmer, 1984). Park encouraged researchers to get close to the sources of their data. Insisting that his students get "their hands dirty in real research," Park steered them toward firsthand observation of city streets, dance halls, hotels, and other natural areas of the city rather than the library or official statistics. He implored his students to find data in the real-life settings that captured their interest: "Go get the seat of your pants dirty in real research" (McKinney, 1966, p. 71). This admonition to get involved with the people and communities under study permeates the ethnographic perspective to this day (see Bulmer, 1984; Emerson, Fretz, & Shaw, 1995; Gubrium & Holstein, 1997).

Whereas naturalistic ethnography aims to delve deeply into social worlds, constructionist impulses promote a different perspective. One way of describing the difference is in terms of what we call *what* and *how* questions. Whereas the naturalistic impulse in fieldwork is typically to ask "*What* is going on?" with and within social reality, constructionist sensibilities provoke questions about *how* social realities are produced, assembled, and maintained. Rather than trying to get inside social reality, the constructionist impulse is to step back from that reality and describe *how* it is socially brought into being. Although still deeply interested in *what* is going on, constructionist sensibilities also raise questions about the processes through which social realities are constructed and sustained. The analytic focus is not so much on the dynamics within social realities as it is on the construction of social realities in the first place.

A constructionist agenda spurs ethnographers to look at and listen to the activities through which everyday actors produce the orderly, recognizable, meaningful features of their social worlds. This is an explicitly *action* orientation, focusing intently on interaction and discourse as productive of social reality (see, e.g., Edwards & Potter, 1992). Whereas the naturalistic fieldworker attends to what his or her informants say about their lives and worlds in order to understand what things mean to them (the informants), constructionist sensibilities focus the researcher on aspects of social life that reveal how social reality and an attendant social order are formulated and organized through talk and interaction. At the heart of constructionist inquiry is an abiding concern for the ordinary, everyday procedures that society's members use to make their experiences sensible, understandable, accountable, and orderly.

If many constructionists retain an appreciation of naturalists' desire to describe "what's going on," they combine such interest with decided emphasis on how these *whats* are sustained as realities of everyday life. Instead of treating social facts or social worlds either as objective parameters or as subjective perceptions, constructionist ethnographers approach them as achievements in their own right. Both inner lives and social worlds are epiphenomenal to the constructive practices of everyday life (Holstein & Gubrium, 2003b). Constructionist researchers are interested in the practical activities in which persons are continually engaged, moment by moment, to construct,

manage, and sustain the sense that their social worlds exist as factual and objectively "out there," apart from their own actions.

Given their concern with reality-constituting practices, constructionists tend to focus on the communicative processes of everyday life. Moving beyond naturalistic description of the more or less stable experiential contours of everyday life, constructionist ethnographers examine how these contours are assembled through everyday talk and interaction (Heritage, 1984). The commonplace phenomena that interest the traditional ethnographer remain important—indeed, vital—but take a temporary back seat to the interactional processes through which those phenomena are assembled and sustained. This requires ethnographic field methods and an analytic orientation that center on constructive actions more than on objects, on reality-constituting practices more than on the realities themselves.

Talk and interaction are the everyday engines driving reality construction. All forms of discourse fuel the process, including discourses that coalesce into regimes and regimens of knowledge and understanding (see L. Miller, Chapter 13, this volume). Because constructionists are deeply concerned with what is done with language to construct field realities, they not only watch but also especially *listen* in order to discern how the realities are produced and sustained. Taking reality as an interactional project (Mehan & Wood, 1975), constructionist ethnography becomes the study of what people "do with words." This requires interactionally and communicatively reflexive fieldwork (see Gubrium, 1988; Mehan, 1979; Miller, 1994, 1997b; Spencer, 1994b).

A Constructionist Analytics for Ethnography

The leading question of a constructionist analytics is, How are the realities of everyday life and their related social worlds constructed and sustained? Closely related are the questions, Constructed from what? and

Constructed under what circumstances? Clearly, answers to these questions implicate naturalistic concerns. In formulating a constructionist analytics, we have come to refer to the inclusive bailiwick of the *whats* and *hows* of social reality as *interpretive practice* (Gubrium & Holstein, 1997, 2000; Holstein, 1993; Holstein & Gubrium, 1994, 2000b). Both *what* and *how* concerns may be accommodated by formulating constructionist ethnography's empirical research horizons in terms of the procedures, resources, and conditions through which reality is apprehended, understood, organized, and conveyed. If a focus on interpretive practice is constructionist in its empirical bearings, the grounds for this focus are empirically substantive. It is our view that the constructive *hows* of communicative practice must take account of experientially real social objects lest the social conditions that bear on constructive activity be shortchanged in our understanding of the organization of everyday life.

A constructionist analytics of interpretive practice provides a way of addressing reality-constituting processes without blindly reifying, nor needlessly ignoring, the contexts, conditions, and resources of the construction process. Centered on communicative action *in context*, it is an analytic framework eminently suited to understanding the practice of everyday life. If the social construction process is artful, as Harold Garfinkel (1967) put it, the analytics also hearkens back to Karl Marx's (1956) view that participants actively construct their worlds but that they do not do so completely on their own terms. Put differently, a constructionist analytics recognizes that reality-constituting "language games" (Wittgenstein, 1958) are frequently institutionalized, which sets the practical conditions for talk and interaction. The experientially real is simultaneously and reflexively constitutive of, and constituted through, ongoing social relations. Constructionist ethnographers gaze both at and beyond immediate discursive activity to examine the ways in which broader—if still socially

constructed—circumstances, conditions, and interpretive resources mediate the reality-construction process.

In this regard, a constructionist analytics incorporates three enduring sociological preoccupations. One is interactional and concrete: an abiding interest in everyday *discursive practice*. A second is more experientially distant or transcendent: *discourse-in-practice*. The third concern is for the conditions and circumstances of interpretation that both reflexively shape and are shaped by discursive practice and discourse-in-practice. The following sections discuss how the three concerns bear on key objects of constructionist inquiry in the context of ethnographic fieldwork.

Discursive Practice

Although Peter Berger and Thomas Luckmann's *The Social Construction of Reality* (1966) is often cited as the foundational inspiration for constructionist inquiry, Alfred Schutz not only provided the impetus for Berger and Luckmann's contribution but also set methodological benchmarks for constructionist fieldwork. Schutz (1962, 1964, 1967, 1970) drew on Edmund Husserl's (1928/1970) phenomenological philosophy to develop an approach to empirical inquiry that centers on the ways that members of society orient to and relate to each other in their social worlds. Stressing the constitutive or reflexively constructive nature of consciousness and social interaction, Schutz (1964) argues that the social sciences should focus on the ways that the lifeworld—that is, the lived world that every person takes for granted—is produced and experienced. To view this world as under construction requires that we temporarily set aside the experiential assumptions of the "natural attitude" (Schutz, 1970), that is, the everyday cognitive stance that views the world and its objects as principally "out there" or "in here," separate and distinct from acts of perception or interpretation. In the natural attitude, the constitutive role of language is overlooked as we assume that the life world exists independent of members' presence and activity.

Schutz argues that we need to escape the natural attitude in order to effectively view and describe empirical reality. To do so, we need to "bracket" the life world. By this, he means that the researcher temporarily sets aside a taken-for-granted orientation to the objective world. The goal is to become "agnostic" regarding the reality of the social world in order to focus on how that world is constituted as real. Bracketing allows constructionist researchers to see, hear, and analyze the processes by which social reality becomes real for its participants. This is a methodological move. The question of the ultimate reality of social forms, which is ontological, is not at issue. The constructionist researcher thus temporarily suspends judgment about the nature and essence of things being studied and focuses instead on the ways in which members of the life world constitute recognizable social structures. This opens to view the commonsense knowledge, everyday reasoning, and discursive practices that members use to construct and objectify social reality. Similarly, bracketing provides the first step for constructionist ethnographers in orienting to the lifeworld and its social forms.

Ethnomethodology shares Schutz's orientation to the lifeworld but is exclusively concerned with the everyday *hows* of real-time talk and social interaction. As Douglas Maynard and Steven Clayman (1991) explain, ethnomethodology addresses the problem of order in everyday life by combining a "phenomenological sensibility" with a paramount concern for constitutive social practice. Garfinkel's (1967) pioneering ethnomethodological studies posited a model of social order built on the contingent, embodied, ongoing interpretive work of ordinary members of society. Society's members, he argued, possessed the practical linguistic and interactional skills through which the observable, accountable, and orderly features of everyday reality were meaningfully produced. As John Heritage (1984) puts it, social order from an ethnomethodological point of view is virtually "talked into being." Many constructionist ethnographers borrow from this, explicitly or implicitly bringing ethnomethodological sensibilities to bear on constructionist projects (see Gubrium, 1988; Gubrium & Holstein, 2000; Holstein & Gubrium, 2005; McHugh, 1968; Mehan, 1979; Miller, 1994, 1997b; Moerman, 1974, 1988; Pollner, 1987; Spencer, 1994b; Sudnow, 1972; Turner, 1974).

More than other constructionist approaches, ethnomethodologically informed studies have paid close attention to the fine details of talk and interaction (see, e.g., Drew, Raymond, & Weinberg, 2006). How this attention is focused, however, varies across different ethnomethodological modalities. Ethnographically oriented studies emphasize the situated content of talk as constitutive of local meaning (e.g., Wieder, 1988). Other ethnomethodologically oriented studies emphasize the conversational machinery of everyday interaction (see Heritage, 1984; Sacks, Schegloff, & Jefferson, 1974). Conversation analysis (CA)—which is arguably a close relative, if not an essential component, of ethnomethodology (see Atkinson, 1988; Lynch & Bogen, 1994)—attempts to describe and explicate the socially constructive and collaborative practices within sequences of talk that speakers use and rely upon when they engage in social interaction. Both the production of conduct and its interpretation are viewed as accountable products of conversation's turn-taking apparatus. Through this machinery, members accomplish the intelligibility of their social worlds.

Regardless of emphasis or specific method, these perspectives place discursive practice at the forefront of empirical inquiry. The constructionist ethnographer thus finds him- or herself squarely within the domain of everyday interaction, dealing with the discursive procedures of reality construction. Communication *in situ* is scrutinized for the ways it works to produce, manage, and secure locally recognizable social structures. Rather than concentrating on everyday conduct *in* the world, this ethnographer examines the practices of what Melvin Pollner (1987) calls "worlding," the linguistic actions that constitute the social world and its forms.

This is a theoretically minimalist approach in that, as a consequence of bracketing, there is no a priori social order available to theorize. There are no preexisting social forms in view to link analytically or to correlate. Propositions and hypotheses concerning the relationship between social structures, specified as variables, cannot be formulated because they have been set aside in order to make their discursive practices visible. Indeed, such propositions and hypotheses *must not* be formulated because they would compromise bracketing and analytic indifference. On this front, the constructionist ethnographer's theoretical concerns are typically limited to members' own indigenous theorizing and the ways in which they apply their theoretical skills to the business of making sense of everyday life. The ethnographer's aim is to document how members themselves *use* theory in everyday talk and interaction to construct their everyday realities.

Discourse-in-Practice

Studying *how* reality is constructed inevitably leads us to questions regarding the discursive resources, or the *whats*, from which social realities are produced. Michel Foucault's historical studies of systems of discourse suggest one method for discerning the interpretive options that are available for reality construction at any particular time or place. Broad configurations of meaningful action—which Foucault called *discourses*—set the conditions of possibility for usage and supply ways of considering questions relating to the discursive resources with which reality is constructed. The available discourses at any particular

time and/or place set the *conditions of possibility* (Foucault, 1977) for how lives and worlds are constructed. The constructionist impulse to examine the discursive possibilities of everyday life thus prevents an exclusive accent on discursive practice that might overemphasize social mechanisms and fail to distinguish distinctive social realms and their forms.

Foucault's constructionism was assiduously attuned to distinct regimes of reality. In *Discipline and Punish* (1977), for example, he informs us that the construct of the "self" as we know it was not in common usage before the rise of panopticism. The social structure we now call the individualized self would have been literally "incredible" at a time before a discourse of individualized subjectivity had widespread currency. But today, at a time when virtually hundreds of social organizations and institutions promote discussion of the personal self, the discursive options for recognizably constructing who we are are nearly endless (Gubrium & Holstein, 2001; Holstein & Gubrium, 2000b). Constructionist sensibilities direct the ethnographer to explore the available discursive possibilities for reality construction, not just the interactional processes of construction.

Another way of viewing constructionist impulses is in terms of what Ludwig Wittgenstein (1958) calls socially situated *language games*. Occupying an analytic space distant from Foucault's, Wittgenstein offers an interactional way to think about the discursive resources that advance the constructionist interest in discursive possibilities. His primary concern is how to understand the meaning of words. Arguing against a correspondence theory of meaning, Wittgenstein contends that meaning is always derived from the context of a word's use—from the practical way a word is deployed. Wittgenstein refers to different contextual configurations of usage as *language games*. These are ways of communicating that have working (if unspoken) "rules" that provide a practical sense for "what goes with what," so to speak. Language games are systems of usage or "forms of life" in which speakers and other participants articulate more or less recognizable linkages between words and things, drawing from well-established connections. Put differently, language games virtually constitute their own everyday realities (Holstein & Gubrium, 2000b).

Existing in a different empirical register from Foucault's "discourses," language games provide the basis for the interactional construction of local realities. Although Wittgenstein appears at first glance to be more in tune with ethnomethodological concerns regarding discursive practice, his notion of socially situated language games also provides analytic tools for understanding the sources and resources of discursive constructions. The argument that meaningful realities are built up within particular language games clearly resonates with Foucauldian arguments about the constructive role of discourses and discursive structures. Both perspectives suggest that discursive resources reflexively constitute the realities that words are commonsensically thought to merely describe. To engage a discourse or language game is not simply a matter of representing reality; it simultaneously constitutes that reality as it is meaningfully embedded in the discourse itself.

The procedural point that constructionists can glean from Foucault and Wittgenstein is that ethnographic attention should attend to the discursive *environments* (Gubrium & Holstein, 2001) of talk and interaction. The objective would be to describe the communicative resources (e.g., discourses, language games) available at any particular time and place. The constructionist ethnographer would therefore place discourse-in-practice squarely within the field of inquiry.

A concern for discourse-in-practice clearly complements the study of discursive practice, but it focuses more on historical, institutional, or cultural resources than on the present-time actions of social construction. At times, this focus may be somewhat distant from face-to-face interaction. Still, if the aim is more abstract, it remains theoretically minimalist. An analytics of discourse-in-practice does not—indeed, should not—seek to formulate causal or determinate relations between discourses and/or language games and local processes of reality construction. It does not strive for a priori definitions of social structure, nor to theorize social structure's associations or effects. Instead, the goal is to describe how systems of discourse mediate the social construction process, providing the practical, substantive groundings of everyday life.

Conditions of Construction

A focus on discourse-in-practice draws the conditions of social construction explicitly into ethnographic purview. It raises questions about the material, social, and cultural limits of discursive practice. The conditions of interpretation—some clearly visible and others somewhat nebulous in practice—are already "there" in the sense that people take them more or less for granted. These conditions and circumstances provide working groundings, borders, themes, and materials for constructing realities. Reality construction always takes place somewhere, under some conditions. Their discernible presence prompts questions such as why discursive practice moves in particular directions and what the consequences might be for the lives of those under consideration.

This impulse turns us to the varied working "contexts" that shape reality construction. Although the social construction process may be discursively artful and agentic, it is also subject to both local and more distal influences. It is always substantively mediated by the interpretive resources and circumstances at hand. As Emile Durkheim (1961) might have put it, everyday interpretation is inevitably conditioned by practical exigencies, relying on existing cultural categories or "collective representations" that are diversely articulated with the particulars of social construction.

Local culture, organizational settings, and institutional structures all mediate talk and interaction. They shape the ways individuals understand and represent local realities. They should not be viewed as prescriptions, rules, or norms for the social construction processes but rather seen as offering more or less regularized, localized ways of assigning meaning and responding to things. They provide discernible frames of interpretation and standards of accountability to which members orient as they engage in constructive activities. The ordinary, situated particulars of everyday interaction—local aspects of discursive environments—are constantly taken into account and used to construct meaningful objects of experience (see Gubrium & Holstein, 1997, 2000, 2001; Holstein & Gubrium, 2000b).

This is a constructionist's way of orienting to discursive process as more or less institutionalized, a process that is shaped by its location in relation to shared concerns (see Berger & Luckmann, 1966). Social life is replete with what Everett Hughes (1942/1984) referred to as "going concerns." For him, going concerns could be as expansive as bureaucracies or as limited as families, as insular and insidious as terrorist cells or as loosely organized and innocuous as toddlers' play groups. Hughes was always careful not to reify the patterns of interaction that constitute institutions. Such patterns were established through concerted activity and were subject to variable contingencies. For Hughes, going concerns were always emergent, continually in process.

On this front, constructionist sensibilities situate the social construction process within the context of local culture, organizational structure, going concerns, and any number of other socially organized circumstances. Accordingly, the constructionist ethnographer balances interactional with institutional or contextual analysis. Critical questions emerge: What are the cultural codes and resources available for constituting local realities? How are they locally applied? What regulates the use of particular accounts and vocabularies of motive? These and similar questions direct ethnographic inquiry to the meaningful conditions of everyday life, conditions that influence reality construction. They direct attention to ongoing talk and interaction as it unfolds in distinct circumstances, giving as much attention to circumstances as it does to discursive practice in its own right.

An orientation to socially *situated* reality construction takes us into complex territory. As Foucault notes, discourse is not owned by anyone in particular, nor is it centered in formal authority. The same might be said of language games. Rather, power/knowledge and influence are brought to bear through socially conditioned discursive practice. Discourse works locally and contingently. Discourses are not fixed templates to be automatically employed. The categories of available discourses are articulated in practice, using available interpretive resources, fueling the work of reality construction.

Reorienting to the Field

Ethnography's naturalistic data-gathering practices and analytic conventions require retooling to accommodate constructionist impulses. Naturalistic ethnography typically draws on indigenous materials collected through observation and interviewing. Its aim, most generally, is to collect data that aid in the description, reconstruction, and/or explanation of subjects' social worlds or worldviews from the subjects' perspectives. In this approach, indigenous talk and other forms of discourse—language use in general—are viewed as *resources* that researchers themselves draw on, a means through which indigenous actors convey information that researchers seek to summarize, systematize, and generalize. Bringing constructionist sensibilities to bear on ethnography transforms the appreciation of language use. It is reconceptualized as a form of social action through which social worlds and regularities are constructed. As such, it becomes the research *topic* in its own right, not merely a means for formulating information *about* a topic. Although this topic–resource distinction has been central to ethnomethodological inquiry from the beginning (see Cicourel, 1964; Garfinkel, 1967; Zimmerman & Pollner, 1970), it is equally pertinent to the constructionist project as well.

Following from the analytics previously presented, constructionist ethnography takes situated language use as its field of inquiry, paying close, detailed attention to linguistic activity *in situ*. Whereas naturalistic ethnography moves relatively quickly from the words of research subjects to researchers' formulations and summaries, constructionist impulses lead the ethnographer to examine practices, structures, and circumstances of language use, asking, most generally, what people are doing with their talk or discourse. The aim is to describe and analyze talk and discourse in terms of their constructive contributions instead of treating them as mere conveyances of what is going on.

Orienting to Discursive Practice

The constructionist impulse directs ethnographic interest toward the *production* of social forms and structure. For example, a naturalistic ethnographer might approach a social setting and begin to consider the various ways that standard analytic constructs or variables might relate to one another within the setting. The researcher might scrutinize a setting for ways in which members' gender relates to differential outcomes in (or beyond) that setting. Such was the case in a series of studies of the effects of candidate patients' gender on involuntary commitment decisions (see Holstein, 1987). These research reports produced equivocal results, and even Carol Warren's (1982) richly descriptive naturalistic ethnography of a mental health court was inconclusive about the relationship between candidate patients' gender and the likelihood of their commitment. Although they vary in their approach

and focus, these studies held in common the naturalistic assumption that gender was a fixed characteristic (variable) of candidate patients, one that might influence courtroom outcomes.

Bringing constructionist sensibilities to this line of inquiry, however, orients us to a different field of action. Instead of asking, How does gender affect commitment hearing outcomes? a constructionist impulse raises this question: How is gender (talk) *used* to affect hearing outcomes? This question leads us directly to discursive practice and the reality-structuring work accomplished by courtroom talk. Rather than treating gender as a fixed element of the scene, a constructionist project would attend to the situated construction of gender and its effects.

This was the orientation to talk and interaction of James Holstein's (1987, 1993) ethnography of involuntary commitment proceedings. The study showed that courtroom participants typically argued cases in terms of the "tenability" of the proposed fit between mentally ill candidate patients and community living situations putatively available to them (Holstein, 1984, 1987, 1993). Candidate patients' vulnerability and manageability were key dimensions of these arguments. A mentally ill person viewed as especially vulnerable to life's unpredictable exigencies would be a poor candidate for community release and thus would likely be committed. Conversely, a candidate patient who was viewed as easily manageable in a community setting was more likely to be released. In the course of such commitment arguments, gender was frequently—but variably—brought to the discursive forefront.

For example, Kathleen Wells, a 32-year-old white female, became a candidate for commitment when she was found living in a large cardboard box beneath a railroad overpass. At her hearing, the viability of this shelter was the focus of concern. In presenting arguments for commitment, the district attorney referred to the deficiencies of this dwelling and then used the candidate patient's gender as a lens for viewing this arrangement as especially untenable:

> Now I know Miss Wells claims that this [the cardboard box] is as good as the subsidized public housing programs the DSS [Department of Social Services] has suggested she look into, but we have to consider more than its construction aspects. . . . You can't allow a woman to be exposed to all the other things that go on out there under the [railroad] tracks. Many of those men have lived like that for years, but we're talking about a woman here. A sick and confused woman who doesn't realize the trouble she's asking for. She simply cannot live like that. That's no place for a woman, especially after dark. . . . She's not taking it [being a woman in the midst of men] into account. She doesn't realize how dangerous it is for her. It's up to the court to protect her. (Holstein, 1987, pp. 146–147)

In analyzing this case, Holstein (1987, p. 147) noted that the district attorney implied that the proposed living arrangement might have been tolerable, if not entirely acceptable, for men, but it was unequivocally unacceptable *for a woman*. The tenability of the living circumstance depended on the version of the candidate patient's gender that was rhetorically summoned on this occasion. Not only was gender situationally invoked as an important concern, but its meaning was also circumstantially crafted as an interpretive framework for understanding the situation at hand. Gender and its meaning were *made* relevant as they were locally constructed. The use of "gender talk" was thus a key rhetorical action leading to a decision to commit.

To illustrate that gender talk is highly circumstantial and artful, Holstein juxtaposed a similar commitment hearing. In the second instance, Sharlene Fox, a 27-year-old African American female, was released into the care of her mother and aunt instead of being involuntarily committed. The judge in the case offered the following explanation:

> I'm releasing this woman if she'll go and stay with her family, her mother and her aunt. They'll take her in . . . and give her a good place to stay. [*To Ms. Fox*: But you gotta do what they say or you'll be right back in here.] Her mother should be able to deal with her this time. Her [Sharlene's] husband's not around [he had been portrayed as an irresponsible troublemaker] and she should be able to take care of her daughter all right Her symptoms seem to be under control and I think that between the two of them they can manage her. It's not like she's some 200 pound guy who they'd have to put in a straight jacket if he got off his medication. . . . We're talking about a woman here who isn't going to be able to cause much trouble. (Holstein, 1987, p. 147)

In this case, the analysis (p. 147) focused on how gender was invoked as a component of Ms. Fox's manageability. The judge explicitly contrasted how a woman, as opposed to a man, could be appropriately housed in the available circumstances. Gender was used to portray the candidate patient as easily managed and her living arrangements as tenable, under the circumstances. The larger point to be gleaned is that it was discursive *work* that produced a "gender effect," and this effect is visible only by paying close attention to reality-constituting practices.

A wide variety of ethnographic studies evince this constructionist appreciation for discursive practice. Hugh Mehan's (1979) "constitutive ethnography" of schools and classrooms examines the social structuring activities that assembled everyday realities in educational settings. Grounded in ethnomethodological and CA traditions, *Learning Lessons* (Mehan, 1979) pays extremely close attention to the details of talk-in-school-interactions. Also displaying ethnomethodological sensibilities, David Buckholdt and Jaber Gubrium's (1979) *Caretakers* ethnographically examined the discursive construction of emotional disturbance and its treatment. Paralleling Mehan in their orientation to discursive practice, Buckholdt and Gubrium, however, are less concerned with the sequential conversational construction of local realities as they are with narrative accounting practices. Holstein's ethnography of involuntary commitment proceedings (1993) falls somewhere in the middle, looking at both sequential and narrative production. Nonetheless, all of these ethnographies share an explicit focus on how talk is used to produce the local realities of concern. They represent only the tip of the iceberg of constructionist ethnographies. Studies of "client work" (Spencer, 1994a) and "person production" (Holstein, 1992) illustrate how individuals are differentially constructed as social objects, either institutionally or otherwise. Constructionist ethnography also has examined the discursive practices through which a wide variety of social forms are constructed, including family (Gubrium, 1992; Gubrium & Holstein, 1990), the life course (Holstein & Gubrium, 2000a), homelessness (Marvasti, 2003), and insanity and addiction (Weinberg, 2005).

Orienting to Discourse-in-Practice

If studies of discursive practice tend to emphasize talk and interaction or other forms of discursive exchange, ethnographies of discourse-in-practice use historical, cultural, or textual material and field observations to document the production of systems of discourse. Foucault's groundbreaking work is illustrative. Foucault provides compelling historical examinations of the emergence of regimes of power/knowledge through which reality is produced and apprehended. He describes discourses that constitute social forms as widely varied as the self (1977, 1988), medicine and the clinic (1975), sexuality (1978), and madness, insanity, and psychiatry (1965). Traces of Foucault's approach and procedures can be found in more contemporary ethnographic applications (see Kendall & Wickham, 1999)

If not expressly Foucauldian, other contemporary examinations of discourse-in-practice have ethnographic components that focus on social problems. These include

studies of the emergence of discourses of social problems (Holstein & Miller, 1993, 2003a; Spector & Kitsuse, 1977), homelessness (Spencer, 1996), hate crime (Jenness & Broad, 1997; Jenness & Grattet, 2004), rape (Martin, 2005), fatness and thinness (Sobal & Maurer, 1999), domestic violence (Berns, 2004), and marital equality and inequality (Harris, 2006), among many others. Many of these and similar studies are descriptions of social movements, involving significant ethnographic examinations of the dynamics of organizational action, as well as resource and media mobilization, and inter- and intragroup contentiousness (see Benford & Hunt, 2003), all of which deal with discourses of various kinds.

Working in a related vein, Gale Miller (1997a) has conducted an exemplary "ethnography of institutional discourse" (1994, p. 280) that documents the emergence and use of discursive resources in organizing the therapeutic work of a therapy agency. Miller's study is especially instructive because it is an ethnography of the discourse structures and discursive resources that characterized the same agency in two different historical periods. This 12-year study of Northland Clinic, an internationally prominent center of brief therapy, describes a marked shift in the discourse of client subjectivity that accompanied a conscious alteration of treatment philosophy. When Miller began his fieldwork, Northland employed ecosystemic brief therapy, which emphasized the social contexts of clients' lives and problems. In this therapeutic environment, clients' subjectivity was linked with the systems of social relationships that were taken to form and fuel their problems. The approach required the staff to discern and discuss the state of these systems and to intervene so as to alter their dynamics and thereby effect change. Miller notes that this approach was informed by the modern discourse of real psychological and relational problems.

Several years after Miller's fieldwork began, Northland shifted to a more postmodern discourse, which articulated intervention in a solution- (as opposed to problem-) oriented, constructivist discourse. Therapists began to practice solution-focused brief therapy, which meant viewing troubles as distinctive ways of talking about everyday life. This prompted the staff to orient to the therapy process as a set of language games, consciously appropriating Wittgenstein's sense of the term. The idea was that troubles were as much constructions—ways of talking or forms of life—as they were real difficulties for the clients in question. This conception transformed clients' institutional subjectivity from that of being relatively passive agents of systems of personal troubles and negative stories to a conception of them as active problem constructors and solvers with the potential to formulate positive stories about themselves and design helpful solutions. An everyday language of solutions, not a discourse of problems, became the basis of intervention. Changes in the therapy agency clearly displayed the alternate discourses-in-practice, which, in turn, were mobilized in talk and interaction. This resulted in the construction of distinctly different "clients" and "problems" (subsequently "solutions"). Miller's (1997a) study vividly highlights the emergence and use of contrasting discursive resources, as well as the constraints that the discourses entail.

Attending to Discursive Conditions

The work of Erving Goffman provides a point of departure for attending to the circumstances that shape the construction process. In *The Presentation of Self in Everyday Life* (1959), for example, he portrays interaction in highly active, creative, agentic terms. But he also attends to the conditions of interaction, most importantly those that bear on the construction of moral order. According to Randal Collins (1980, p. 200), Goffman stresses the "hard external constraints of society upon what individuals can afford to do and believe," but he also allows

for considerable flexibility. For Goffman, ever-changing situational demands produce interpretive variability.

Goffman's concern for the production and management of the moral order leads to his interest in the situational contours of social life: "My perspective is situational, meaning here a concern for what one individual can be alive to at a particular moment, this often involving a few other particular individuals and not necessarily restricted to the mutually monitored arena of face-to-face gatherings" (Goffman, 1974, p. 8). For Goffman (1964, p. 134), "Social situations at least in our society constitute a reality *sui generis* as he [Durkheim] used to say, and therefore need and warrant analysis in their own right, much like that accorded other basic forms of social organization." "Social situatedness" thus assumes a commanding role in Goffman's ethnography. His analytic vocabulary of situated action directs empirical attention to the contours of the "interaction order" (1983) within which people conduct their everyday lives, conveying the artfulness of reality-defining action.

Studies of the circumstances of social construction may take into consideration the working objectives motivating reality construction, the audiences who are involved with these realities, the accountability structures that operate in particular circumstances, and the interpretive resources that are locally available (Gubrium & Holstein, 1997). In addition, Goffman would not let the constructionist ethnographer forget the physical features of a setting as they relate to talk and interaction. Some of the most important contingencies of reality construction are such material features of a social setting as bodies, rooms and doors, furniture arrangements, and lighting. Consider, for example, how Gubrium attended to the role of an ordinary physical object—a ticking clock—as it was used to represent the self in the midst of an Alzheimer's disease support group meeting (Gubrium & Holstein, 1995, pp. 709–710). During a discussion of the burdens of home care, the wife of a dementia sufferer described the challenge of deciding whether or not to place her husband in a nursing home. Pointing to a ticking clock on a nearby shelf, she remarked, "That there clock's me. It'll keep ticking away until it's time [to decide] and won't stop for a minute, until it winds down, I guess." Focusing on the discursive use of the clock, Gubrium shows the reader how, for the wife and others, "winding down" signifies the gradual decline of the caregiving wife. She needlessly wastes away, martyring herself for someone who has become the "mere shell" of a former self.

In the preceding analysis, the clock is a culturally recognizable symbol conscripted for self-construction. Its familiar characteristics are used metaphorically, but its concrete, physical presence is also crucial in communicating the dilemma at hand. Concrete references to the clock visibly represent a self whose incessant temporal progression into ill health might not be readily communicated on its own. The clock, according to Gubrium, is taken on board rhetorically to concretize the experience in question. A virtual cultural cliché, presumably recognizable to other competent members of society and certainly familiar to those who have participated in the Alzheimer's disease movement (Gubrium, 1986), it becomes a device for shared understanding. It is crucial to this setting and the social construction process because it serves to *materially* mediate the transmission of cultural meaning. The material setting—the concrete physical circumstances of interaction—thus become important parameters of the ethnographic field. We see this even more prominently in Gubrium's comparative ethnography of family therapy agencies (1992), which underscores the importance of engaging the sheer scenic presence of reality-constructing material. This study shows vividly how tissue boxes, teddy bears, waiting rooms, and clients' chairs, among many other physical objects, are used to mediate and convey personal meaning in the therapy environment.

Procedural Adaptations

Bringing constructionist sensibilities to ethnographic fieldwork also involves procedural adaptations to traditional field methods and analytic strategies. It does not require reinventing the wheel, but it does demand that research techniques explicitly attend to the social construction process. Naturalistic ethnography, of course, deals explicitly with interaction. In their superbly detailed guide to *Writing Ethnographic Fieldnotes*, Robert Emerson, Rachel Fretz, and Linda Shaw (1995, p. 14) urge researchers to "value close, detailed reports of interaction." Although this suggestion is aimed primarily at a naturalistic audience, it is true even more so for the constructionist ethnographer. For the constructionist ethnographer, however, the focus is as much on the *hows* as the *whats* of everyday life.

Fieldnotes, Recordings, and Transcripts

In light of their deep concern for socially situated discourse, constructionist ethnographers collect documents of discourse and discursive environments. Data collection focuses on capturing the communicative, as well as the interactive, details of settings of interest. The constructionist ethnographer is drawn to settings as scenes in which reality-construction *work* is taking place. There has long been debate concerning the relative advantages and disadvantages of "natural" versus "contrived" or "provoked" data (e.g., observation vs. interviewing and intentionally elicited or experimentally induced conversation and actions—see Atkinson & Coffey, 2002; Becker & Geer, 1957; Lynch, 2002; Potter, 2002; Speer, 2002). Although naturally occurring talk and interaction may be widely preferred, in principle there is no reason to exclude "provoked" communication—as long as analysis focuses on the discursive work being done in the talk that has been elicited in one way or another.

Beyond capturing the details of settings and their events, the constructionist ethnographer is especially concerned with recording discursive data. Most standard ethnographic data collection techniques remain useful but require modification (see Emerson et al., 1995; Jackson, 1995; Sanjek, 1990). Fieldnotes, for example, include as much indigenous discursive detail as possible. A higher degree of attention to the actual talk in interaction generally characterizes constructionist ethnography.

All fieldnotes are *inscriptions*—not literal reproductions—of field realities (Emerson et al., 1995; Geertz, 1973). They unavoidably transform witnessed events and scenes according to preconceptions, conventions, framing, and other forms of selectivity. Whereas naturalistic fieldnotes strive for rich snapshots of the field, which can be used to describe and summarize those scenes, constructionist ethnography is more concerned with what members do with words. Although selectivity is imposed in choosing what to record or inscribe, the constructionist fieldworker typically strives to capture as much *in situ* verbatim detail as possible, preserving the opportunity to later "unpack" talk-in-interaction for the constructive work entailed. Sometimes this amounts to close-to-verbatim records of key spates of talk, noted as much as possible in speakers' own words. Sometimes constructionist projects require greater detail in terms of conversational sequencing and structure.

Audio- (or video-) tape recordings of interactions can be advantageous, as they allow for a more detailed reconstruction of what has discursively transpired. Of course, a transcribed tape recording cannot fully substitute for an actually observed interaction, especially in terms of context and scenic presence, but it does provide the opportunity to repeatedly consult the data to uncover patterns that might not have been initially apparent. Candace West (1996) has argued persuasively that if ethnographers' analyses focus on talk, there is much to be gained from the use of detailed transcriptions and/or the detailed preparation of fieldnotes that approximate verbatim records (so-called do-it-yourself transcripts; Atkinson & Drew, 1979).

Of course tape recording is often impossible in field settings, and do-it-yourself transcripts are possible only under special conditions—often highly regimented institutional circumstances such as court hearings in which turns at talk are preallocated (see Holstein, 1993, Appendix; West, 1996). Nevertheless, if one's aim is to show precisely, in talk-in-interaction, how social order and meaning are talked into being, then less than perfect, do-it-yourself transcripts can be valuable despite their imperfections.

Consider another example from Holstein's (1993) involuntary commitment study. One analytic point of his research report related to the collaborative production of "crazy talk" during the hearings. Holstein argued that talk that was ostensibly and commonsensically considered evidence of mental illness and interactional incompetence in the hearings was empirically the result of competent collaboration in conversational practice.

The following extract is a segment of the district attorney's cross-examination of Henry Johnson that a judge cited in his account for hospitalizing Mr. Johnson. Among other things, the judge noted that Johnson's testimony was "confused and jumbled." As he put it, "He [Johnson] didn't know what to say. He was stopping and starting, jumping from one thing to another. You can see that he can't focus on one thing at a time" (Holstein, 1993, p. 108).

1. DA:	How you been feeling lately?
2. HJ:	OK
3.	((Silence))

4. HJ:	I been feeling pretty good.
5.	((Silence))
6. DA:	Uh huh
7.	((Silence))
8. HJ:	Pretty good, ummm all right
9.	((Silence))
10. HJ:	Got a job with (several words inaudible)
11.	((Silence))
12. HJ:	Pays OK, not bad.
13.	((Silence 4 seconds))
14. HJ:	My car got hit, an accident, really messed it up
15.	((Silence))
16. HJ:	Got to get it on the street
17.	((Silence 5 seconds))
18. HJ:	They gonna let us go to the truck out front?
19. DA:	When you're all done here they might.

In his analysis, Holstein (1993, pp. 108–110) notes that this stretch of talk is discontinuous and multifocused. It is a speech environment characterized by failed speaker transition and recurrent silence. In court, the talk was heard as Mr. Johnson's own doing, interpreted as symptomatic or probative of Johnson's interactional incompetence. But, Holstein argued, it is possible to consider this halting, disjointed movement from one line of talk to another as a *collaborative* phenomenon. If one frames discontinuous utterances as proffered solutions to the problems that witnesses confront as they attempt to produce responsive testimony in a nonresponsive environment, one can interpret Mr. Johnson's testimony in an entirely different light. The detailed transcription of the talk, including the notation and placement of silences, provides the basis for claiming that silences and topic shifts resulted from the DA's refusal to assume a turn at talk at appropriate or expected junctures or to minimally acknowledge that Mr. Johnson had satisfactorily completed an utterance in his turn at talk. Arguing that silences and topic changes often result from failures at speakership transition, Holstein was able to demonstrate empirically that the disjointed talk was explainable in CA terms,

suggesting that Mr. Johnson's "jumbled" speech resulted from his competent attempt to sustain conversation in a speech environment in which his conversational partner (the DA) was not fulfilling his turn-taking responsibilities. Such an analysis would not be possible without transcriptions written with the requisite level of detail.

West (1996) enumerates several ways in which recording and transcription of talk in field settings benefits the ethnographic enterprise. But she also notes both practical and analytic limitations. There are two crucial points that constructionists should take from West's thoughtful assessment of the utility of transcription in field research. First, it is imperative to collect data at the level of detail necessary and appropriate to the goals of analysis. Second, the researcher should be careful not to make analytic claims that cannot be supported by the level of detail available in the recorded data.

Maynard (2003) also considers the relationship between ethnography and the fine-grained, sequential analysis of talk-in-interaction that characterizes CA. He draws an important distinction between collecting data to analyze an activity (which is the aim of CA) and collecting data to describe a setting (which is major goal of naturalistic ethnography). Calling for mutual appreciation between CA and ethnography, Maynard (2003) specifies two approaches to their joint use in research projects: "mutual affinity" and "limited affinity." At the risk of oversimplifying, the former approach is likely to begin from a more naturalistic, ethnographic standpoint. The focus would be on what might be transpiring in a setting, and analysis would work toward explication of how local realities might come about, perhaps using discourse and CA techniques in the process. Working from a standpoint of limited affinity, however, the researcher would be more cautious about the unexplicated use of contextual material at the expense of shortchanging the sequentially emergent context of interaction within which all speech acts are embedded. The tendency would be to work more closely with carefully recorded and transcribed spates of talk, mining them for the properties of social organization displayed within.

Anthropologists Michel Moerman (1988) also has proposed a more symbiotic relationship between ethnographic fieldwork and CA. In *Talking Culture*, he suggests that ethnographic studies of how people make sense of their lives should try to find out how the organization of talk influences the sensemaking process. This call has been echoed in several other proposals for more conversationally sensitive ethnographic approaches (e.g., Gubrium & Holstein, 1997; Miller, 1994, 1997b; Spencer, 1994b). Although Moerman's companion suggestion that CA be more sensitive to surrounding context has not been warmly embraced across the CA community, West (1996) argues that a number of fruitful developments in CA have stemmed from debates over Moerman's proposal.

Interviews

Interviews are a staple of ethnographic fieldwork. There are, however, important differences in how they are used and analyzed as part of a constructionist project. Harboring both *what* and *how* concerns, constructionist ethnographers engaged in interviewing need to keep in mind the distinction between collecting data in order to analyze discursive activity and collecting data to describe a setting.

Traditional approaches to interviewing tend to see the interview as a medium for the transmission of information (Holstein & Gubrium, 1995; Kvale, 1996; Wooffitt & Widdicombe, 2006). The informant or respondent is treated as a vessel of answers about his or her social world, and the interview is viewed as a means of extracting, in an uncontaminated fashion, that information that naturally lies within (Holstein & Gubrium, 1995). From a constructionist perspective, however, the interview should be conceived as more active. It is the site of social interaction from which meaningful accounts of social life are assembled and conveyed. The knowledge or information produced is therefore both collaboratively produced and continually under construction (Holstein & Gubrium, 1995).

Following this perspective, ethnographic interviewing guided by constructionist impulses proceeds much like the many variants of traditional naturalistic interviewing (see Gubrium & Holstein, 2002). Although the constructionist would be more aware of the unavoidably collaborative nature of interviewing, he or she would nevertheless observe many of the conventional guidelines and strictures governing the interview process. Although the interview process itself might be indistinguishable from conventional, informal interviewing, there would be analytic justification for more active exchanges between all participants, if desired. Constructionist impulses, however, would be clearly evident in the analysis of interview data, which, as the following section shows, orients to interview data more as social action than as retrieved information.

Data Analysis

Ethnographic data analysis guided by constructionist concerns orients to the constitutive work done by interaction, discourses-in-practice, and their mediating circumstances. Several descriptions of constructionist discourse analyses are included in this *Handbook* (see L. Miller, Chapter 13; Potter & Hepburn, Chapter 14; and Nikander, Chapter 21, this volume). Other forms of analysis are more narratively oriented and more or less ethnographic (e.g., Chase, 2005; Gubrium & Holstein, in press; Riessman, 1993). CA and ethnomethodological approaches and techniques may also be informative (see Drew et al., 2006; Garfinkel, 1967; Heritage, 1984; Holstein, 1993; Maynard, 2003; Mehan, 1979; Mehan & Wood, 1975; Silverman, 2004, 2006; ten Have, 1999; West, 1996; Wieder, 1988).

Long-standing guides to data analysis have been adapted to the constructionist enterprise, including the grounded theory approach (Glaser & Strauss, 1967). In Chapter 20 of this volume, Kathy Charmaz suggests that grounded theory strategies can fruitfully be used to create and interrogate constructionist data. The familiar procedures of coding, categorization, and comparison can be applied to constructionist data when proper attention is paid to the work of constructing social forms. The distinguishing feature of a constructionist application would be the emphasis on describing reality-constructing social processes in the data.

Another feature distinguishing constructionist studies is their analytic vocabulary. Constructionist vocabulary is replete with categories of action; its terminology and idioms virtually constitute empirical horizons of discursive activity. At the risk of oversimplifying, constructionist ethnography is characterized by key analytic terms that refer to members' reality work. These terms typically take the form of gerunds—wording derived from verbs but functioning as nouns, as in "*producing* reality" or "*accomplishing* social order." These verbs are given the form of nouns in order to name types of constructive activity. Other common features of the vocabulary include expressions of "practices," such as in descriptive practice and narrative practice, or types of "work," such as biographical work (Holstein & Gubrium, 2000a), identity work (Gubrium & Holstein, 2001), and social problems work (Holstein & Miller, 2003b). The unifying thread of this vocabulary is its utility in highlighting reality-constituting activity.

The analysis of ethnographic interview data nicely illustrates other differences between constructionist and naturalistic analysis. In naturalistic analyses, interview data are copiously presented as evidence of informants' experience and point of view. Their descriptions, accounts, and narratives are taken as representative of the key variables, themes, and frameworks of meaning that members of settings recognize and appreci-

ate. The analyst scours the corpus of interview data to extract generalizable observations and analyses from what informants have said, then offers exemplary interview extracts to corroborate or illustrate orienting hypotheses, themes emerging from the analysis, and generalizations about the field in question (Mehan, 1979; Zimmerman & Pollner, 1970). Data extracts tend to be used illustratively but are not *analyzed* per se.

Consider, for example, the naturalistic use of interview data in Robert Prus's and Styllianoss Irini's (1980) study of a hotel community, *Hookers, Rounders, and Desk Clerks.* One would be hard pressed to find an ethnography that contained more excerpts of informants' interview talk; a conservative estimate suggests that well over 50% of the 266 pages of core text are devoted to informants' talk. Typically, the authors describe a feature of community life, offer an extrapolated generalization, then proffer extended interview extracts in illustration, often prefaced with the following sort of explication: "The following extracts indicate both the sorts of concerns the girls have and the sorts of approaches they encounter" (p. 12). Following the extracts, the text typically moves to a new topic, with further illustration of the new topic. Interview data used in this fashion offer insights—in the "authentic" voices of the informants themselves—into what informants think is going on. There is, however, little analysis on the part of the researcher. Instead, the interview talk is left to "speak for itself." As descriptively interesting as such a report might be in terms of what is going on from the informant's point of view, the researchers say little about *how* social worlds and meanings are created and sustained.

In contrast, constructionist sensibilities lead the analyst to look for what informants are "doing with words" in the interview. The analyst would typically present a data extract, then analyze, in considerable detail, what is going on in the extract—that is, what discursive work is being done by the spate of talk. The analysis might proceed in terms of narrative analysis (see, e.g., Chase, 1995; Holstein & Gubrium, 1995; Marvasti, 2003), discourse analysis (e.g., Wooffitt & Widdicombe, 2006), ethnomethodology (e.g., Baker, 2002), or CA (e.g., Maynard, Houtkoop-Steenstra, Schaeffer, & van der Zouwen, 2002), just to name a few possibilities. All these approaches would attempt to unpack the constitutive practices imbedded in the talk. The interview data would *not* be left to speak for themselves.

For example, in his interview study of nursing home narratives, *Speaking of Life* (1993), Gubrium uses nursing home residents' own words and voices to convey aspects of life in the nursing home. But the study's constructionist impulses yield an analytic vocabulary of "biographical work," "horizons of meaning," and "narrative linkage" that help the analyst (and reader) understand *how* residents produce and structure the meaning of life and death, aging, health, illness, family, God, and the past, present, and future. The study focuses on how, in "speaking of life," nursing home residents construct the lives in question. The study is as much about *how* life is spoken as it is about what is said. We find similar analytic developments in many other constructionist interview studies. For example, we can see the social construction of various social forms in studies of the production of homelessness (Marvasti, 2003), equality and inequality (Harris, 2006), sexual identity (Chase, 2001), and divorce (Hopper, 2001), just to mention a very few constructionist interview studies.

Analytic Bracketing

As is evident in the preceding sections, discursive practice, discourse-in-practice, and discursive conditions are intimately intertwined and mutually constitutive. Dealing with the interplay poses procedural challenges. Constructionists need a way to consider discursive practice without depicting it as unconditionally artful and unconstrained by resources and circumstances, but without, in turn, letting practice be overwhelmed by the resources and circumstances in which it is embedded. At the same time, they need to highlight the resources available to discursive practice without simply casting discourses as mere artifacts of situated interaction. And there is the need to consider conditions of interpretation without reifying discursive context in order to document the constructed grounds of everyday life.

Phenomenological bracketing can open the construction process to view, but it does little to help us take account of the prevailing discourses and conditions of social life. As a stride in this direction, we suggest an analytic practice located at the crossroads of social interaction, discursive environments, local culture, and material circumstance. This practice might purposefully "misread" strictures from naturalistic, Foucauldian, and ethnomethodological traditions, coopting useful insights in order to appreciate the possible complementarity of different analytic idioms. It centers on the interplay, not the synthesis, of situated discursive practice, discourse-in-practice, and discursive conditions.

To achieve analytic footing for viewing both the *hows* and *whats* of interpretive practice, we refer to a procedural imperative we have called *analytic bracketing* (Gubrium & Holstein, 1997, 2000; Holstein & Gubrium, 2000b, 2003a, 2005). Analytic bracketing is similar in some respects to the a priori bracketing employed in phenomenology and ethnomethodology. It differs in that it employs an alternating or oscillating indifference to the realities of everyday life, allowing the analyst to momentarily focus on the *hows* and *whats* of the construction process.

This is a methodological move, not an ontological one. The more phenomenological or ethnomethodological versions of bracketing begin analysis by setting aside all assumptions about forms of social organization and structure in order to view the everyday practices by which subjects, objects, and events come to have an accountable sense of being observable, rational, and orderly. The analytic project advances from there, documenting how discursive practices constitute the realities in question. The aim is to make visible how language is used to construct the objects it is otherwise viewed as principally describing.

Analytic bracketing operates somewhat differently. It is applied throughout analysis, not just at the start. As analysis proceeds, the investigator intermittently orients to everyday realities as both the *products* of members' reality-constructing procedures and as *resources* from which realities are constituted. At one stage, the research may be indifferent to the structures, conditions, and available discourses of everyday life in order to document their production through discursive practice. In the next analytic move, the analyst brackets discursive practice in order to assess the local availability, distribution, and/or regulation of resources and conditions of reality construction. This leads to alternating considerations of locally fine-grained discursive practices at one juncture, of discourse-in-practice at another, and of the conditions of construction at still other points in the analysis. The objective is to move back and forth between discursive practice, discourse-in-practice, and discursive conditions, documenting each in turn and making informative references to the others in the process.

The emphasis on the interplay between the *hows* and *whats* of the construction process is paramount in analytic bracketing. The technique carefully avoids analytically emphasizing discursive practice, discourse-in-practice, or discursive conditions at the expense of the others. The aim is to document the interchange between the interactional, discursive artfulness entailed in assembling everyday reality, on one hand, and the cultural, institutional, and contextual circumstances, resources, and discourses that mediate discursive practice on the other. Because these are viewed as mutually constitutive, one cannot argue that analysis should necessarily begin or end with any particular aspect. Wherever one chooses to focus, nei-

ther the cultural, institutional, or material foundations of discourse nor the constructive dynamics of interaction predetermines the other. If we set aside the need to formally resolve the question of which comes first or last or has priority, we can designate a reasonable starting point from which to begin and proceed from there, so long as we keep firmly in mind that the interplay requires that we move back and forth analytically. Of course, researchers of different stripe may be inclined to start at different places and that, no doubt, will shape how analysis proceeds.

The back-and-forth movement of analytic bracketing is far from arbitrary; it is keyed to emergent analytic needs. As the researcher documents constructive activities, questions regarding what is being constructed, what resources are used, and what conditions shape the process provoke a shift in analytic stance—a change in analytic brackets that is necessary to address such questions. Subsequently, the analyst's attention to the *whats* under consideration will, in turn, prompt the researcher to ask *how* these features of lived experience came to be regarded as real, inducing yet another shift in brackets.

It is unlikely, if not improbable, that any single study will become a full-scale exercise in analytic bracketing. Social scientists tend to work in units corresponding to book chapters or journal articles. As a practical matter, most constructionist ethnographies will be presented incrementally, focusing on one component of the social construction process, then taking up another aspect at a later time. There are occasions, however, on which the various aspects of the construction process may be alternatively bracketed and described within the same report. This was the case when Gubrium undertook an ethnographic study of the Alzheimer's disease experience in the 1980s (Gubrium, 1986). In this study, Gubrium alternately focused on *what* people knew Alzheimer's disease to be and *how* it was descriptively constituted. The study maintained several analytic focal points. One part of the study bracketed the organic components of the condition in order to look at how the discourse of "the disease" was publicly formulated and took currency. This part of the analysis drew mostly on documents and public statements—publicity directed at constituting Alzheimer's disease as a new sort of disease entity.

A second aspect of the study focused on the "public culture" of Alzheimer's disease. This involved a series of bracketing moves that allowed the analyst to describe discourses-in-practice as resources for interpreting a newly emergent "disease." Then, the focus would shift again as analysis turned to the ways in which the public culture was expressed and communicated through mass media and other forms of publicity.

Once again shifting brackets, the study then turned to the discursive practices by which the new experience of Alzheimer's disease was articulated in the daily lives of persons serving as caregivers to Alzheimer's sufferers. The focus here was on discursive practice, highlighting the ways in which participants in the growing public culture of the disease interactionally constituted it and its ill effects as a practical feature of their everyday lives. This portion of the study examined the way a new discourse literally was put into experiential practice in face-to-face interaction. Of course, the description of interactional practice also led, in turn, to discussions of how local circumstances conditioned the new discourse in place.

Over the course of this study, the analytic focus shifts repeatedly from the *whats* to the *hows* of interpretive practice, from discourse-in-practice to discursive practice, to conditions of interpretation, and back again. In doing so, it becomes evident that continual analytic bracketing is required in order to gain access to—if not fully capture—the reflexive and emergent relation between social action and its varied contexts and resources.

Conclusion

Bringing constructionist impulses to ethnographic fieldwork invites assumptions, an analytic vocabulary, and procedural guidelines that differ from those of naturalistic inquiry. At the same time, it is our view, as constructionist ethnographers, that naturalistic inquiry draws attention to "realities" of the social world that must be taken into account lest social reality be conveyed as a mere swirl of communicative moves. Thus we have offered a view of constructionist impulses infused with considerable naturalistic sentiments. This demands an appreciation for the continually emergent contexts that bear on the construction of social realities. The constructionist ethnographer portrayed here is not likely to be satisfied with descriptions of local constitutive practices but also must describe how resources from beyond the interaction at hand mediate these practices.

It bears repeating that the constructionist impulse in ethnographic fieldwork does not evoke a theory of social life. Rather, it calls forth a minimalist analytics to sensitize researchers to the myriad elements of reality construction. Although this may not appeal to researchers seeking definitive descriptions of social settings or causal explanations, it does provide the basis for documenting and understanding social worlds and structures that operate in circumstances continually under construction.

• References

Atkinson, J. M., & Drew, P. (1979). *Order in court*. Atlantic Highlands, NJ: Humanities Press.

Atkinson, P. (1988). Ethnomethodology: A critical review. *Annual Review of Sociology, 14,* 441–465.

Atkinson, P., & Coffey, A. (2002). Revisiting the relationship between participant observation and interviewing. In J. F. Gubrium & J. A. Holstein (Eds.), *Handbook of interview research* (pp. 801–814). Thousand Oaks, CA: Sage.

Atkinson, P., & Hammersley, M. (1994). Ethnography and participant observation. In N. Denzin & Y. Lincoln (Eds.), *Handbook of qualitative research* (pp. 248–261). Thousand Oaks, CA: Sage.

Baker, C. (2002). Ethnomethodological analyses of interviews. In J. F. Gubrium & J. A. Holstein (Eds.), *Handbook of interview research* (pp. 777–796). Thousand Oaks, CA: Sage.

Barth, F., Gingrich, A., Parkin, R., & Silverman, S. (2005). *One discipline, four ways: British, German, French, and American anthropology.* Chicago: University of Chicago Press.

Becker, H. S., & Geer, B. (1957). Participant observation and interviewing: A comparison. *Human Organization, 16,* 28–32.

Behar, R. (1996). *The vulnerable observer: Anthropology that breaks your heart.* Boston: Beacon.

Benford, R., & Hunt, S. (2003). Interactional dynamics in public problems marketplaces: Movements and the counterframing and reframing of public problems. In J. A. Holstein & G. Miller (Eds.), *Challenges and choices: Constructionist perspectives on social problems* (pp. 153–186). Hawthorne, NY: Aldine de Gruyter.

Berger, P. L., & Luckmann, T. (1966). *The social construction of reality: A treatise in the sociology of knowledge.* New York: Doubleday.

Bernard, H. R. (Ed.). (1998). *Handbook of methods in cultural anthropology.* Walnut Creek, CA: AltaMira.

Berns, N. (2004). *Framing the victim.* Hawthorne, NY: Aldine de Gruyter.

Buckholdt, D. R., & Gubrium, J. F. (1979). *Caretakers.* Newbury Park, CA: Sage.

Bulmer, M. (1984). *The Chicago school.* Chicago: University of Chicago Press.

Chase, S. E. (1995). *Ambiguous empowerment: The work narratives of women school superintendents.* Amherst: University of Massachusetts Press.

Chase, S. E. (2001). Universities as discursive environments for sexual identity construction. In J. F. Gubrium & J. A. Holstein (Eds.), *Institutional selves* (pp. 142–157). New York: Oxford University Press.

Chase, S. E. (2005). Narrative inquiry: Multiple lenses, approaches, voices. In N. Denzin & Y. Lincoln (Eds.), *Handbook of qualitative research* (3rd ed., pp. 651–680). Thousand Oaks, CA: Sage.

Cicourel, A. V. (1964). *Method and measurement in sociology.* New York: Free Press.

Clifford, J., & Marcus, G. (Eds.). (1986). *Writing culture.* Berkeley: University of California Press.

Clough, P. T. (1992). *The end(s) of ethnography: From realism to social criticism.* Newbury Park, CA: Sage.

Collins, R. (1980). Erving Goffman and the development of modern social theory. In J. Ditton (Ed.), *The view from Goffman* (pp. 170–209). London: Macmillan.

Drew, P., Raymond, G., & Weinberg, D. (2006). *Talk and interaction in social research methods.* London: Sage.

Durkheim, E. (1961). *The elementary forms of the religious life.* New York: Collier Books.

Edwards, D., & Potter, J. (1992). *Discursive psychology.* London: Sage.

Ellis, C., & Bochner, A. P. (1996). *Composing ethnography: Alternative forms of qualitative writing.* Walnut Creek, CA: AltaMira.

Emerson, R. M., Fretz, R. I., & Shaw, L. L. (1995). *Writing ethnographic fieldnotes.* Chicago: University of Chicago Press.

Foucault, M. (1965). *Madness and civilization: A history of insanity in the age of reason.* New York: Random House.

Foucault, M. (1975). *The birth of the clinic.* New York: Vintage.

Foucault, M. (1977). *Discipline and punish: The birth of the prison.* New York: Vintage.

Foucault, M. (1978). *The history of sexuality* (Vol. 1). New York: Vintage.

Foucault, M. (1988). *Technologies of the self.* Amherst: University of Massachusetts Press.

Fox, R. G. (Ed.). (1991). *Recapturing anthropology: Working in the present.* Santa Fe, NM: School of American Research Press.

Garfinkel, H. (1967). *Studies in ethnomethodology.* Englewood Cliffs, NJ: Prentice Hall.

Geertz, C. (1973). *The interpretation of cultures.* New York: Harper.

Geertz, C. (1988). *Works and lives: The anthropologist as author.* Stanford, CA: Stanford University Press.

Glaser, B. G., & Strauss, A. L. (1967). *The discovery of grounded theory.* Chicago: Aldine.

Goffman, E. (1959). *The presentation of self in everyday life.* New York: Doubleday.

Goffman, E. (1964). The neglected situation. *American Anthropologist, 66*(1), 133–136.

Goffman, E. (1974). *Frame analysis.* New York: Harper & Row.

Goffman, E. (1983). The interaction order. *American Sociological Review, 48*(1), 1–17.

Goodall, H. L. (2000). *Writing the new ethnography.* Lanham, MD: AltaMira Press.

Gubrium, J. F. (1986). *Oldtimers and Alzheimer's.* Greenwich, CT: JAI Press.

Gubrium, J. F. (1988). *Analyzing field reality.* Newbury Park, CA: Sage.

Gubrium, J. F. (1992). *Out of control: Family therapy and domestic order.* Newbury Park, CA: Sage.

Gubrium, J. F. (1993). *Speaking of life.* Hawthorne, NY: Aldine de Gruyter.

Gubrium, J. F., & Holstein, J. A. (1990). *What is family?* Mountain View, CA: Mayfield.

Gubrium, J. F., & Holstein, J. A. (1995). Individual agency, the ordinary, and postmodern life. *Sociological Quarterly, 36*(3), 555–570.

Gubrium, J. F., & Holstein, J. A. (1997). *The new*

language of qualitative method. New York: Oxford University Press.

Gubrium, J. F., & Holstein, J. A. (2000). Analyzing interpretive practice. In N. Denzin & Y. Lincoln (Eds.), *Handbook of qualitative research* (2nd ed., pp. 487–508). Thousand Oaks, CA: Sage.

Gubrium, J. F., & Holstein, J. A. (Eds.). (2001). *Institutional selves.* New York: Oxford University Press.

Gubrium, J. F., & Holstein, J. A. (Eds.). (2002). *Handbook of interview research.* Thousand Oaks, CA: Sage.

Gubrium, J. F., & Holstein, J. A. (in press). Narrative ethnography. In S. Hesse-Biber & P. Leavy (Eds.), *Handbook of emergent methods.* New York: Guilford Press.

Harris, S. (2006). *The meanings of marital equality.* Albany: State University of New York Press.

Heritage, J. (1984). *Garfinkel and ethnomethodology.* Cambridge, UK: Polity.

Holstein, J. A. (1984). The placement of insanity: Assessments of grave disability and involuntary commitment decisions. *Urban Life, 13*(1), 35–62.

Holstein, J. A. (1987). Producing gender effects on involuntary mental hospitalization. *Social Problems, 34*(2), 141–155.

Holstein, J. A. (1992). Producing people: Descriptive practice in human service work. *Current Research on Occupations and Professions, 6,* 23–39.

Holstein, J. A. (1993). *Court-ordered insanity: Interpretive practice and involuntary commitment.* Hawthorne, NY: Aldine de Gruyter.

Holstein, J. A., & Gubrium, J. F. (1994). Phenomenology, ethnomethodology, and interpretive practice. In N. Denzin & Y. Lincoln (Eds.), *Handbook of qualitative research* (pp. 262–271). Thousand Oaks, CA: Sage.

Holstein, J. A., & Gubrium, J. F. (1995). *The active interview.* Thousand Oaks, CA: Sage.

Holstein, J. A., & Gubrium, J. F. (2000a). *Constructing the life course.* Dix Hills, NY: General Hall.

Holstein, J. A., & Gubrium, J. F. (2000b). *The self we live by.* New York: Oxford University Press.

Holstein, J. A., & Gubrium, J. F. (2003a). A constructionist analytics for social problems. In J. A. Holstein & G. Miller (Eds.), *Challenges and choices: Constructionist perspectives on social problems* (pp. 187–208). Hawthorne, NY: Aldine de Gruyter.

Holstein, J. A., & Gubrium, J. F. (Eds.). (2003b). *Inner lives and social worlds.* New York: Oxford University Press.

Holstein, J. A., & Gubrium, J. F. (2005). Interpretive practice and social action. In N. Denzin & Y. Lincoln (Eds.), *Handbook of qualitative research* (3rd ed., pp. 483–506). Thousand Oaks, CA: Sage.

Holstein, J. A., & Miller, G. (Eds.). (1993). *Reconsidering social constructionism: Debates in social problems theory.* New York: Aldine de Gruyter.

Holstein, J. A., & Miller, G. (2003a). *Challenges and choices: Constructionist perspectives on social problems.* Hawthorne, NY: Aldine de Gruyter.

Holstein, J. A., & Miller, G. (2003b). Social constructionism and social problems work. In J. A. Holstein & G. Miller (Eds.), *Challenges and choices: Constructionist perspectives on social problems* (pp. 70–91). Hawthorne, NY: Aldine de Gruyter.

Hopper, J. (2001). Contested selves in divorce proceedings. In J. F. Gubrium & J. A. Holstein (Eds.), *Institutional selves* (pp. 127–141). New York: Oxford University Press.

Hughes, E. C. (1984). *The sociological eye.* New Brunswick, NJ: Transaction Books. (Original work published 1942)

Husserl, H. (1970). *Logical investigation.* New York: Humanities Press.

Jackson, J. E. (1995). "Déjà entendu": The liminal qualities of anthropological fieldnotes. In J. Van Maanen (Ed.), *Representation in ethnography* (pp. 37–78). Thousand Oaks, CA: Sage.

Jenness, V., & Broad, K. (1997). *Hate crimes: New social movements and the politics of violence.* Hawthorne, NY: Aldine de Gruyter.

Jenness, V., & Grattet, R. (2004). *Making hate a crime.* New York: Russell Sage.

Kendall, G., & Wickham, G. (1999). *Using Foucault's method.* London: Sage.

Kvale, S. (1996). *InterViews.* Thousand Oaks, CA: Sage.

Lofland, J., & Lofland, L. H. (1995). *Analyzing social settings* (3rd ed.). Belmont, CA: Wadsworth.

Lynch, M. (2002). From naturally occurring data to naturally organized ordinary activities: Comment on Speer. *Discourse Studies, 4*(4), 531–537.

Lynch, M., & Bogen, D. (1994). Harvey Sacks's primitive natural science. *Theory, Culture, and Society, 11*(1), 65–104.

Martin, P. Y. (2005). *Rape work.* New York: Routledge.

Marvasti, A. (2003). *Being homeless.* Lanham, MD: Lexington Books.

Marx, K. (1956). *Selected writings in sociology and social philosophy* (T. B. Bottomore, Ed.). New York: McGraw-Hill.

Maynard, D. W. (2003). *Bad news, good news: Conversational order in everyday and clinical settings.* Chicago: University of Chicago Press.

Maynard, D. W., & Clayman, S. E. (1991). The diversity of ethnomethodology. *Annual Review of Sociology, 17,* 385–418.

Maynard, D. W., Houtkoop-Steenstra, H., Schaeffer, N. C., & van der Zouwen, J. (Eds.). (2002). *Standardization and tacit knowledge: Interaction and practice in the survey interview.* New York: Wiley Interscience.

McHugh, P. (1968). *Defining the situation.* Indianapolis, IN: Bobbs-Merrill.

McKinney, J. C. (1966). *Constructive typology and social theory.* New York: Appleton-Century-Crofts.

Mehan, H. (1979). *Learning lessons: Social organization in the classroom.* Cambridge, MA: Harvard University Press.

Mehan, H., & Wood, H. (1975). *The reality of ethnomethodology.* New York: Wiley.

Miller, G. (1994). Toward ethnographies of institutional discourse. *Journal of Contemporary Ethnography*, *23*(3), 280–306.

Miller, G. (1997a). *Becoming miracle workers: Language and meaning in brief therapy*. New York: Aldine de Gruyter.

Miller, G. (1997b). Building bridges: The possibility of analytic dialogue between ethnography, conversation analysis and Foucault. In D. Silverman (Ed.), *Qualitative research: Theory, method and practice* (pp. 24–44). London: Sage.

Moerman, M. (1974). Accomplishing ethnicity. In R. Turner (Ed.), *Ethnomethodology* (pp. 54–68). Harmondsworth, UK: Penguin.

Moerman, M. (1988). *Talking culture*. Philadelphia: University of Pennsylvania Press.

Pollner, M. (1987). *Mundane reason*. New York: Cambridge University Press.

Potter, J. (2002). Two kinds of natural. *Discourse Studies*, *4*(4), 539–542.

Prus, R., & Irini, S. (1980). *Hookers, rounders, and desk clerks*. Salem, WI: Sheffield.

Riessman, C. K. (1993). *Narrative analysis*. Thousand Oaks, CA: Sage.

Rosaldo, R. (1993). *Culture and truth*. Boston: Beacon.

Sacks, H., Schegloff, A., & Jefferson, G. (1974). A simplest systematics for the organization of turn-taking in conversation. *Language*, *50*(4), 696–735.

Sanjek, R. (Ed.). (1990). *Fieldnotes: The makings of anthropology*. Ithaca, NY: Cornell University Press.

Schutz, A. (1962). *The problem of social reality*. The Hague, Netherlands: Martinus Nijhoff.

Schutz, A. (1964). *Studies in social theory*. The Hague, Netherlands: Martinus Nijhoff.

Schutz, A. (1967). *The phenomenology of the social world*. Evanston, IL: Northwestern University Press.

Schutz, A. (1970). *On phenomenology and social relations*. Chicago: University of Chicago Press.

Silverman, D. (Ed.). (2004). *Qualitative research: Theory, method and practice* (2nd ed.). London: Sage.

Silverman, D. (2006). *Interpreting qualitative data: Methods for analyzing talk, text and interaction* (3rd ed.). London: Sage.

Sobal, J., & Maurer, D. (Eds.). (1999). *Weighty issues: Fatness and thinness as social problems*. Hawthorne, NY: Aldine de Gruyter.

Spector, M., & Kitsuse, J. I. (1977). *Constructing social problems*. Menlo Park, CA: Cummings.

Speer, S. A. (2002). Natural and contrived data: A sustainable distinction? *Discourse Studies*, *4*(4), 511–525.

Spencer, J. W. (1994a). Homeless in River City: Client work in human service encounters. In J. A. Holstein & G. Miller (Eds.), *Perspectives on social problems* (Vol. 6, pp. 29–46). Greenwich, CT: JAI Press.

Spencer, J. W. (1994b). Mutual relevance of ethnography and discourse. *Journal of Contemporary Ethnography*, *23*(3), 267–279.

Spencer, J. W. (1996). From bums to the homeless: Media constructions of persons without homes from 1980–1984. In J. A. Holstein & G. Miller (Eds.), *Perspectives on social problems* (Vol. 8, pp. 39–58). Greenwich, CT: JAI Press.

Sudnow, D. (Ed.). (1972). *Studies in social interaction*. Middlesex, UK: Penguin.

Tedlock, B. (2000). Ethnography and ethnographic representations. In N. Denzin & Y. Lincoln (Eds.), *Handbook of qualitative research* (2nd ed., pp. 455–486). Thousand Oaks, CA: Sage.

Tedlock, B. (2004). Narrative ethnography as social science discourse. *Studies in Symbolic Interaction*, *27*(1), 23–31.

ten Have, P. (1999). *Doing conversation analysis*. London: Sage.

Turner, R. (Ed.). (1974). *Ethnomethodology*. New York: Penguin.

Van Maanen, J. (1988). *Tales of the field: On writing ethnography*. Chicago: University of Chicago Press.

Van Maanen, J. (1995). *Representation in ethnography*. Thousand Oaks, CA: Sage.

Warren, C. A. B. (1982). *The court of last resort*. Chicago: University of Chicago Press.

Weinberg, D. (2005). *Of others inside: Insanity, addiction, and belonging in America*. Philadelphia: Temple University Press.

West, C. (1996). Ethnography and orthography: A (modest) methodological proposal. *Journal of Contemporary Ethnography*, *25*(3), 327–352.

Wieder, D. L. (1988). *Language and social reality*. Landham, MD: University Press of America.

Wittgenstein, L. (1958). *Philosophical investigations*. New York: Macmillan.

Wooffitt, R., & Widdicombe, S. (2006). Interaction in interviews. In P. Drew, G. Raymond, & D. Weinberg (Eds.), *Talk and interaction in social research methods* (pp. 28–49). London: Sage.

Zimmerman, D. H., & Pollner, M. (1970). The everyday world as a phenomenon. In J. Douglas (Ed.), *Understanding everyday life* (pp. 80–104). Chicago: Aldine.

CHAPTER 20

Constructionism and the Grounded Theory Method

● **Kathy Charmaz**

In the introduction to this *Handbook*, James A. Holstein and Jaber F. Gubrium suggest that a social constructionist approach deals best with *what* people construct and *how* this social construction process unfolds. They argue that the constructionist vocabulary does not as readily address the *why* questions that characterize more positivistic inquiry.[1] In their earlier methodological treatise, *The New Language of Qualitative Method* (Gubrium & Holstein, 1997), they proposed that naturalistic qualitative researchers could address *why* questions "by considering the contingent relations between the *whats and hows* of social life" (p. 200). To date, however, most qualitative research has not addressed *why* questions.

In contrast, the grounded theory method has had a long history of engaging both *why* questions and *what* and *how* questions. What is grounded theory? The term refers to both the research product and the analytic method of producing it, which I emphasize here. The grounded theory method begins with inductive strategies for collecting and analyzing qualitative data for the purpose of developing middle-range theories. Examining this method allows us to rethink ways of bringing *why* questions into qualitative research.

A social constructionist approach to grounded theory allows us to address *why* questions while preserving the complexity of social life. Grounded theory not only is a method for understanding research participants' social constructions but also is a method that researchers construct throughout inquiry. Grounded theorists adopt a few strategies to focus their data gathering and analyzing, but what they do, how they do it, and why they do it emerge through interacting in the research setting, with their data, colleagues, and themselves.

How, when, and to what extent grounded theorists invoke social constructionist premises depends on their epistemological stance and approach to research practice. From its beginnings, grounded theory has offered explicit guidelines that promise flexibility and encourage innovation. Paradoxically, these guidelines also provided sufficient direction such that some researchers have treated the method as a recipe for stamping out qualitative studies. These researchers emphasize *application* of the method—often a narrow and rigid application at that. Such application limits the potential of grounded theory and fosters the production of superficial studies. In contrast, a social constructionist approach encourages *innovation*; researchers can develop new understandings and novel theoretical interpretations of studied life. The value of social constructionism for grounded theory studies has only begun to be mined.

Distinguishing between a social constructionist and an objectivist grounded theory (Charmaz, 2000, 2002, 2006) provides a heuristic device for understanding divisions and debates in grounded theory and indicates ways to move the method further into social constructionism. The form of constructionism I advocate includes examining (1) the relativity of the researcher's perspectives, positions, practices, and research situation, (2) the researcher's reflexivity; and (3) depictions of social constructions in the studied world.[2] Consistent with the larger social constructionist literature, I view action as a central focus and see it as arising within socially created situations and social structures. Constructionist grounded theorists attend to *what* and *how* questions. They emphasize abstract understanding of empirical phenomena and contend that this understanding must be located in the studied specific circumstances of the research process.

Objectivist grounded theory (Glaser, 1978, 1992, 1998) has roots in mid-20th-century positivism. It explicitly aims to answer *why* questions. Objectivist grounded theorists seek explanation and prediction at a general level, separated and abstracted from the specific research site and process. Unlike my version of grounded theory, which I have previously called constructivist grounded theory (Charmaz, 2000, 2006), 20th-century constructionism treated research worlds as social constructions, but not research practices.

The two respective emphases on understanding and explanation are not entirely mutually exclusive. An abstract understanding of particular sites and situations can allow social constructionists to move from local worlds to a more general conceptual level. The close attention that social constructionist grounded theorists give their research problems builds the foundations for generic statements that they qualify according to particular temporal, social, and situational conditions.

In this chapter, I show how a grounded theory informed by social constructionism can lead to vibrant studies with theoretical implications that address *why* questions. To provide a backdrop for the discussion, I outline the development of grounded theory and delineate distinctions among proponents. By distinguishing between objectivism and constructionism in grounded theory, I explicate their underlying assumptions and point out the tensions between explanation and understanding. How might grounded theorists resolve these tensions? How might the ways in which they construct their studies foster developing explanations *and* understandings and thus attend to both the particular and the general? What principles might researchers adopt? To address these questions, I offer several guidelines and look at how two grounded theorists, Susan Leigh Star (1989) and Monica Casper (1998), constructed their respective analyses.

Reconstructing Contested Logics of Grounded Theory

Barney G. Glaser and Anselm L. Strauss's (1967) original conception of grounded theory assumed a social constructionist approach to the empirical world. Like other social scientists of the time, they adopted a more limited form of social constructionism than what I advocate here. Glaser and Strauss did not attend to how they affected the research process, produced the data, represented research participants, and positioned their analyses.[3] Their research reports emphasized generality, not relativity, and objectivity, not reflexivity.

Nonetheless, Glaser and Strauss laid the foundation for constructing sound methods, as well as analyses. By adopting a few flexible guidelines, grounded theorists could construct their specific methodological strategies, as well as the content of their research.[4] Both method and content then emerge during the research process rather than being preconceived before empirical inquiry begins.

Until 1990, most scholars saw grounded theory as a single method based on a shared logic. As both the originators and their students worked with the method, changes emerged and debates ensued about what grounded theory entails, whose version is "correct," and which direction the method should take. How did these discussions unfold? What are their implications for a grounded theory founded in social constructionism? To understand these issues, I take a brief look back at the emergence of contested logics of the method(s).

Glaser had supplied much of the original logic and form of grounded theory. *Theoretical Sensitivity* (1978) depicted his concept-indicator logic and focus on core variables. Beyond Glaser and Strauss's (1967) original statement, however, Strauss's *Qualitative Analysis for Social Scientists* (1987) and Strauss and Corbin's *Basics of Qualitative Research* (1990, 1998) brought grounded the-

ory tools to researchers who had not studied with either Glaser or Strauss or their students.[5] Many qualitative researchers relied solely on the justificatory ammunition that Glaser and Strauss (1967) had fired in defense of qualitative research; however, other researchers sought specific analytic guidelines. Strauss and Corbin (1990, 1998) did not simply offer guidelines; they prescribed procedures as a path to qualitative success. *Basics of Qualitative Research* became something of a bible for novices, who often interpreted the method in concrete ways that muted the social constructionist elements in the method.[6]

Meanwhile, the "qualitative revolution" that Denzin and Lincoln (1994, p. ix) proclaimed had grown exponentially in and across fields. As I (Charmaz, 2000, 2006) have argued previously, the entire qualitative revolution owed much to Glaser and Strauss's (1967) initial statement. Glaser and Strauss made qualitative research defensible—even respectable—at a time when quantitative researchers had controlled the framing definitions of what counted as research: that is, only what these methodologists could count. Glaser and Strauss provided a strong justification for inductive qualitative inquiry that many researchers seized to legitimize their own work; but these researchers only loosely adopted the strategies, if at all.

Still, Glaser and Strauss (1967) inspired the democratization of qualitative research—and of theorizing itself. No longer must a qualitative researcher have the analytic acumen of an Erving Goffman or Anselm Strauss. No longer must qualitative research be a mysterious endeavor conducted by anointed elites. Qualitative research could spread beyond the confines of Chicago and its reach. Moreover, all qualitative researchers could aspire to theorizing and achieve their goals by following a handful of flexible guidelines.

Because grounded theory was decidedly inductive, scholars commonly viewed it as a social constructionist method. Yet was it? Certainly its emphasis on building an analysis, studying processes, and attending to how people create and view their worlds had strong social constructionist leanings. Strauss's Chicago roots made the method compatible with symbolic interactionist, social constructionist currents in the discipline. Both Glaser and Strauss emphasized emergence, but subtle differences between them may be discerned. Glaser emphasized the emergence of the grounded theorist's ideas through studying the data. Strauss's use of the term also suggests the influence of George Herbert Mead's (1932) analysis of time. Fundamentally social and temporal processes result in the present emerging as new and different from the past.

By 1990, grounded theory had become something of an orthodoxy (see Bryant & Charmaz, 2007). Strauss and Corbin's (1990, 1998) book fostered an orthodox view—but it differed from Glaser and Strauss's original statement and undermined Glaser's emphasis on emergent codes and categories and, in his view, diminished his considerable contribution to the classic statement of grounded theory. Glaser (1992) objected and asked for retraction of the book. Other scholars framed the differences between Glaser and Strauss and Corbin as a debate, although the latter two did not respond publicly to Glaser's charges. No debate followed from Strauss and Corbin. To date, perhaps the closest statement to a response came from Corbin (1998) after Strauss's death. Other scholars (Atkinson, Coffey, & Delamont, 2003; Charmaz, 2000; La Rossa, 2005; Locke, 1997; Kelle, 2005), however, gave the differences between the two versions substantial discussion and debate from the 1990s to the present, particularly in nursing (see, e.g., Boychuk Duchscher & Morgan, 2004; May, 1996; Melia, 1996; Stern, 1994; Wilson & Hutchinson, 1996).

Although Glaser's version of grounded theory differed from that of Strauss and Corbin in conception and concrete strategies, they shared basic premises about an ex-

ternal reality, the discovery of provisional truths in this reality, the role of the observer, and an unproblematic representation of research participants. Neither belabored accuracy, but Strauss's empirical studies with Corbin (Corbin & Strauss, 1984, 1988) demonstrate thorough description and data collection in the social constructionist tradition.

By the early 1990s, qualitative inquiry in general and grounded theory in particular had gained credibility in numerous disciplines. It was a short-lived victory. Contested views continued to develop as postmodernists challenged assumptions in social theory and qualitative research (see, e.g., Clough, 1992; Daly, 1997; Denzin, 1992). Grounded theory came to exemplify the criticisms these scholars leveled at ethnography and qualitative research more generally. Traditional qualitative research had roots in Enlightenment values, including beliefs in reason, objectivity, scientific authority, and notions of progress through science. Grounded theory became known as the most realist and positivist of the modernist qualitative methods (Van Maanen, 1988). For postmodernists, grounded theory epitomized distanced inquiry by objective experts who assumed their training licensed them to define and represent research participants. Glaser (1992) reappeared in methodological discussions and reaffirmed his objectivist stance; however, his views have exerted more influence in professional disciplines such as nursing and management than in the social sciences.

The postmodernist turn renewed—and intensified and generalized—epistemological critiques that theorists and several qualitative sociologists had made in the 1960s (Berger & Luckmann, 1966; Bruyn, 1966; Cicourel, 1964).[7] Postmodernist critiques challenged positivist assumptions in classic grounded theory statements and questioned its continued relevance. As a form of "naturalist inquiry" (Gubrium & Holstein, 1997; Lincoln & Guba, 1985; Lofland & Lofland, 1995), critics included grounded theory among those approaches castigated as epistemologically naive, voyeuristic, and intrusive in the lives of the research participants (see, e.g., Clough, 1992). From postmodernist perspectives, the underlying assumptions in earlier grounded theory statements mirrored a modernist epistemology. Simultaneously, the narrative turn theorized and valorized respondents' full stories, unlike the grounded theory strategy of using excerpts of their stories to build theoretical statements. Not surprisingly, some sociologists who had previously adopted grounded theory methods (Ellis, 1995; Richardson, 1993; Riessman, 1990) sought new approaches.

Other critics either misunderstood or rejected grounded theory emphases on theory building rather than storytelling and on a particular process or problem rather than on the whole of research participants' lives. In actuality, few grounded theory studies build theory, but many provide an analytic handle on a specific experience. Still, the growing emphasis on storytelling caused some critics to question grounded theorists' use of data and their representation of research participants, and other critics disdained grounded theory analytic practices and claims to scientific authority.

Most critics could not see beyond Glaser and Strauss's (1967) early statements of the grounded theory method—and other critics still cannot (Dey, 1999, 2004; Layder, 1998). As a result, until recently (Bryant, 2002; Charmaz, 2000, 2002, 2005, 2006; Clarke, 2003, 2005, 2006; Henwood & Pidgeon, 2003; Willig, 2001) the flexibility and potential versatility of the method remained hidden—and its promise for innovative social constructionist study remained unfulfilled. By fusing grounded theory strategies with the way Glaser and Strauss had used the method, critics had relegated grounded theory to being an outdated modernist method. Discarding grounded theory guidelines, along with Glaser and Strauss's objectivist assumptions, precluded revitalizing the method through social constructionism.

The Constructionist Renewal of Grounded Theory

Postmodern challenges from without combined with positivistic inclinations from within grounded theory spurred efforts to reclaim its strategies for social constructionist inquiry. Those of us who adhered to a relativist epistemology never concurred with grounding grounded theory in Glaser's mid-20th-century positivism. Strauss's students and colleagues (see, e.g., Charmaz, 1991, 2000; Clarke, 1998, 2005; Lempert, 1997; Maines, 1984; Reif, 1975) particularly imbued grounded theory with social constructionism, whether or not they articulated epistemological reasons for their actions. No doubt, for some, grounded theory was inherently social constructionist; yet, paradoxically, Strauss and Corbin's methodological procedures gave grounded theory an objectivist cast.

The Objectivist–Constructionist Dichotomy

Those grounded theorists who endorse a social constructionism informed by recent epistemological critiques have made explicit efforts to distinguish between key grounded theory strategies and their positivist antecedents (see, e.g., Bryant, 2002, 2003; Castallani, Castallani, & Spray, 2003; Charmaz, 2000, 2002, 2005, 2006; Clarke, 2003, 2005; Henwood & Pidgeon, 2003; Mills, Bonner, & Francis, 2006; Seale, 1999). Numerous scholars have merged grounded theory strategies with the positivism inherent in Glaser's (1978, 1992, 1998) and Strauss and Corbin's (1990, 1998) versions of the method.

Grounded theory strategies are just that—strategies for creating and interrogating our data, not routes to knowing an objective external reality. Objectivist versions of grounded theory assume a single reality that a passive, neutral observer discovers through value-free inquiry. Assumptions of objectivity and neutrality make data selection, collection, and representation unproblematic; they become givens, rather than constructions that occur during the research process, and they shape its outcome. A naive empiricism results. Objectivists assume that data are self-evident and speak for themselves. Possibilities of partial, limited, or missing data and multiple readings of them remain unseen (see also Clarke, 2005, 2006). Objectivists aim to generalize through abstractions that separate the completed grounded theory from the conditions and contingencies of its data collection and analysis (see Glaser, 1998, 2001). As abstraction increases, so does decontextualization of the research that gave rise to this abstraction. Objectivists seek generalizations that provide explanations and predictions. The completed grounded theory aims for fit, work, relevance, and modifiability (Glaser, 1978).

My constructionist approach makes the following assumptions: (1) Reality is multiple, processual, and constructed—but constructed under particular conditions[8]; (2) the research process emerges from interaction; (3) it takes into account the researcher's positionality, as well as that of the research participants; (4) the researcher and researched coconstruct the data—data are a *product* of the research process, not simply observed objects of it. Researchers are part of the research situation, and their positions, privileges, perspectives, and interactions affect it (Charmaz, 2000, 2006; Clarke, 2005, 2006). In this approach, research always reflects value positions. Thus the problem becomes identifying these positions and weighing their effect on research practice, not denying their existence. Similarly, social constructionists disavow the idea that researchers can or will begin their studies without prior knowledge and theories about their topics. Rather than being a *tabula rasa*, constructionists advocate recognizing prior knowledge and theoretical preconceptions and subjecting them to rigorous scrutiny.

The comparative method inherent in grounded theory helps researchers to scruti-nize and conceptualize data but does not render the data objective, as Glaser (2003) asserts. From my constructionist view, objectivity is a questionable goal, and what researchers define as objective still reflects partial knowledge and particular perspectives, priorities, and positions. Subjectivities are embedded in data analysis, as well as in data collection. Methodological procedures neither make research objective nor preclude responsibility to locate research relative to time, place, and situation. Grounded theorists' awareness of the relativism in research practice fosters their reflexivity about how they construct their actions. Both constructionist and objectivist versions of grounded theory adopt a realist position, but constructionists view learning about and portraying the studied world as problematic.

This constructionist version of grounded theory redirects the method from its objectivist, mid-20th-century past and aligns it with 21st-century epistemologies (Charmaz, 2000, 2006).[9] Rather than assuming that theory emerges from data, constructionists assume that researchers construct categories of the data. Instead of aiming to achieve parsimonious explanations and generalizations devoid of context, constructionists aim for an interpretive understanding of the studied phenomenon that accounts for context. As opposed to giving priority to the researcher's views, constructionists see participants' views and voices as integral to the analysis—and its presentation.

These differences between objectivist and constructionist grounded theory offer researchers a frame to clarify their starting assumptions and research actions. In practice, however, grounded theory inquiry ranges between objectivist and constructionist approaches and has elements of both. Objectivist grounded theory strategies encourage researchers to be active analysts of their data. The reflexivity and relativity in this constructionist approach fosters taking researchers several steps further through critically examining their construction of the research process as they seek to analyze how their research participants construct their lives (Charmaz, 2006).

Enacting 21st-Century Constructionist Principles

Reconstructing grounded theory with 21st-century methodological sensibilities can preserve a grounded theory while simultaneously answering varied criticisms of the method. When stripped of their epistemological clothing, Glaser and Strauss's (1967) original flexible strategies still make for sound research practice that researchers can invoke to produce useful—and innovative—social constructionist analyses.

A 21st-century social constructionist grounded theory rests on certain principles, as I have implied earlier. Thus grounded theorists who adhere to this position:

* Treat the research process *itself* as a social construction

* Scrutinize research decisions and directions

* Improvise methodological and analytic strategies throughout the research process

* Collect sufficient data to discern and document how research participants construct their lives and worlds.

In brief, the first principle means that using grounded theory involves more than applying a recipe for qualitative research. This principle belies the current notion of treating the grounded theory method as something to apply and then treating the analysis as something a computer program compiles. Using grounded theory strategies means responding to emergent questions, new insights, and further information and simultaneously constructing the *method of analysis*, as well as the analysis. No set of rules can dictate what a researcher needs to do and when he or she needs to do it (see Sanders, 1995).

The second principle follows. To make these kinds of decisions, researchers must think through what they are doing and how and why they are doing it. Such thinking implicates the researcher, who does not stand outside the studied process but is a part of it, as I detail subsequently. Reflexivity is central to this constructionist revision and renewal of grounded theory. The scrutiny that grounded theorists give their method and—by extension—themselves leads to the third principle: improvising their methods and analytic strategies.

The fourth principle assumes that in order to understand how research participants construct their world, researchers need to know that world from their participants' standpoints (Blumer, 1969; Goffman, 1989). Invoking grounded theory as a "quick and dirty" method impedes gaining this understanding because achieving it includes defining tacit meanings and implicit actions, as well as what is directly observable and explicitly stated. Obtaining thorough, rich data, in contrast, facilitates seeking and seeing tacit meanings and actions and constructing useful grounded theories, as the subsequent research accounts attest.

Social Constructionism in Grounded Theory

Explicating a Basic Social Process

Studying a basic social process is—or was—a fundamental objective of classic grounded theory method.[10] How do grounded theorists go about it? How might a social constructionist approach inform their research? Several studies in the sociology of science exemplify adopting a social constructionist approach in grounded theory (see, e.g., Baszanger, 1998; Bowker & Star, 1999; Clarke, 1998). As a case in point, I analyze Susan Leigh Star's (1989) grounded theory in *Regions of the Mind: Brain Research and the Quest for Scientific Certainty*. In this book, she adopts social constructionist logic in her argument about how scientific theories become entrenched.

By looking at scientific work in a specific area and era, Star (1989) reconstructs what happened and how it occurred and simultaneously constructs a theoretical argument about scientific theorizing. She pieces together how 19th-century brain researchers, the localizationists, constructed certainty about their theory. These early brain researchers earned the name *localizationists* because they contended that local areas of the brain controlled specific neurological functions. Consistent with classical grounded theory (Glaser, 1978; Glaser & Strauss, 1967), Star defines a process, "creating and maintaining certainty" (1989, p. 87), and identifies subprocesses constructed through individual and collective actions that constitute the major process. Localizationists transformed the uncertainty that they witnessed in their laboratories and clinics into what Star calls "global certainty at the institutional level" (p. 87). She addresses *what* and *how* questions here. In examining the mechanisms of transformation, Star scrutinizes what localizationists did—a process—and how they did it—actions. Thus, she analyzes how localizationists' ordinary actions accomplished this institutional transformation and, simultaneously, rendered local contradictions invisible.

Through studying her data, Star (1989) defines a set of actions that, taken together, accomplished the hegemony of localization theory of the brain. To create and maintain certainty, localizationists engaged in the following actions: borrowing evidence from other fields, evaluating their operational procedures rather than actual technical failures, substituting ideal clinical pictures for anomalous findings, generalizing from case results, and reducing epistemological questions to debates about technique (Star, 1989, pp. 87–93). Star's depiction of how localizationists substituted ideal types for irregular cases exemplifies key dimensions of her reconstruction of their emergent constructions of views and actions. She points out

that medical researchers and clinicians demanded accurate textbooks and atlases of typical neurological conditions. Star (pp. 89–90) writes:

> In the process of resolving taxonomic uncertainty, researchers thus created *typical* pictures of diseases that were eagerly adopted by the medical community. These representations include functional anatomical maps—such as maps that could indicate the anatomical point in the brain that was the source of loss of speech. These maps became substitutes, in the building of localization theory, for case data that contained irregular or anomalous findings. The demand for functional anatomical representations in medical education, diagnosis, and texts represented a market intolerant of ambiguity and of individual differences. The theory became unambiguously packaged into the atlas. The ideal types represented in such maps were presented as context-independent (that is, as *the* brain, not *a* brain).

In the preceding excerpt, the relationship between interaction and action with the subsequent result is clear. The demand came first; a neurology textbook followed that contained functional atlases, which erased anomalies and ambiguities. The subsequent widespread adoption of the textbook made the localizationists' views the standard in the field. The ideal type had become more than a source of comparison; it became the only serious measure. Thus Star (1989) implies that these early neurologists had accomplished significant boundary work that prevented other theories of brain function to be entertained.

Star's attention to the sequencing of action reveals the interconnections between knotty work problems and localizationists' attempts to resolve them. Establishing an ideal typical clinical picture through the textbook atlas is just one kind of action the localizationists undertook. Star similarly traces how localizationists routinely constructed each kind of the aforementioned actions in which they engaged. These actions arose in the exigencies of problem solving at work. Localizationists' other actions reflected how they acted on their professional ideologies by explicitly constructing strategies to defeat brain diffusionists' opposing theory of brain function.

Note how Star (1989) moves from action to outcome in the excerpt. Earlier in the book, she provides the historical, professional, and work contexts in which the reader can situate the actions she describes in this section. Hence she can move directly to delineating the conditions under which actions arose. Clinicians urgently needed to make definitive diagnoses. Brain researchers needed to categorize diseases accurately. They both sought certainty. The lack of tolerance for ambiguity made localization theory appealing. Later, Star tells us that localizationists' financial sponsors also pressed for generality and standardization. When the sponsors' referees found irregular findings in localizationists' experimental reports, they requested that the localizationists standardize their existing results rather than redo the experiments. Here, significant external bodies buttress the construction of "facts," and subsequently having their imprimatur on the written reports serves to reify this construction.

Star (1989) makes a strong case for accepting her interpretation of what localizationists did and how they did it. She weaves specific evidence and telling incidents through her narrative that support her assertions. The range and thoroughness of her evidence make her argument compelling. She specifies how actions construct processes and answers *what* and *how* questions. Star's use of grounded theory logic and construction of categories is transparent at this level. However, Star does not stop with *what* and *how* questions. As she merges processes into major categories and chapter titles, she brings the reader back to her major topics and places them on center stage. Subsequently, the grounded theory style and logic recede to the backstage. Rather than provide a parsimonious statement of relationships between abstracted categories, Star

synthesizes what localizationists did and how they did it in one clear, direct statement: "Localizationists eventually intertwined questions about the nature of phenomena, the strategies for organizing information and resources, and political commitments" (p. 196). Then, to end her book, she raises *why* questions and answers them in the following discussion of the implications of analyzing scientific work:

> *The Implications of Analyzing Science as Work*
>
> Research on scientific theories has rarely taken into account the processes in dimensions described above, especially the degree with which these complex multiple dimensions are interactive and developmental. What are the implications of looking at theories in this way? A conversation with Anselm Strauss provided a partial answer to this question. As I was describing to him the many participants in the debate about localization, and the various kinds of work and uncertainties faced by participants, I began to frame the concept, "inertia." I saw the questions becoming extraordinarily complex and, at the same time, taken for granted by participants. In the middle of explaining this, and when I was feeling overwhelmed with the complexity and interdependence of all the issues, Strauss asked me: what would it have taken to overthrow the theory? (p. 196)

By addressing what overthrowing the theory would have taken and when it could have occurred, Star answers why it did not. Moreover, by showing how localization became and remained entrenched, she offers a new explanation of change and stability in scientific theorizing. Star's strong answers to *how* questions provide the foundation for advancing *why* questions. Throughout the book, she pieces together diverse sources of evidence that permit her to trace chronology and to make connections between actions, incidents, and outcomes.

Star (1989) presents an analysis thoroughly grounded in data. Her sorting and categorizing of data make sense. She takes simple, direct, but intermediate categories as her headings and subheadings such as "Diplomacy" (p. 134), "Compiling Credibility" (p. 138), "Manipulating Hierarchies of Credibility" (p. 140), "Organizational Tactics" (p. 144), "Controlling the Focus of the Debate" (p. 145), and "Modes of Debate and Tacit Debates" (p. 152) to build an abstract analysis. Star describes and explains each category and often details a series of actions that constitutes the category, as she did with "Creating and Maintaining Certainty," discussed earlier. Most of these intermediate categories are gerunds; they depict actions. As such, the categories not only give the reader a sense of people's intentions and concerns, but they also specify and anchor the analysis. When Star uses gerunds, her categories provide more information and a clearer point of view than her other categories. They enliven her narrative and inform the reader of its direction. Taken together, Star's intermediate categories outline her chapters and organize her argument.

Like other qualitative researchers, grounded theorists are often deservedly criticized for moving too quickly from the specific study to a general level.[11] The strength of Star's analysis permits her to move from the particular case of localization theory to considering why scientific theories do or do not change. Star challenges Thomas S. Kuhn's (1970) explanation that a critical mass of anomalous findings forces a paradigm change. In contrast, she shows that "practical negotiations with and about anomalous events are constitutive of science at every level of organization" (Star, 1989, p. 64). Star closes her book with the following explanation of the significance of her study:

> The study of how theories take hold and become seen as "natural" is important in answering some basic questions in the sociology of knowledge and epistemology. This book argues that problems/theories/facts/perspectives are a form of collective behavior, and I have provided some data about the processes and conditions of that behavior. Implicit in this

approach is an equation between knowing and working. These two kinds of events do not proceed in parallel: they are the same activity, but differently reported. (1989, p. 197)

Adapting Constructionist Grounded Theory for General Audiences

Grounded theory, particularly in its constructionist versions, can serve audiences in multiple disciplines and beyond the academy. As many critics have observed, authors often claim that grounded theory guided their inquiry, but their work bears no resemblance to it. Other authors use the method but do not claim it.[12] And numerous others adopt a couple of strategies, such as coding and some kind of memo writing, but do not engage in theoretical sampling or explication of a major category.

Monica J. Casper's (1998) book on fetal surgery, *The Making of the Unborn Patient: A Social Anatomy of Fetal Surgery*, acknowledges the influence of grounded theorists Clarke and Strauss, but its grounded theory origins are less clear than Star's. Nonetheless, Casper based her book on her dissertation, which used grounded theory. Like many authors, Casper outlines her diverse sources of data for her multisite ethnography, but she does not claim grounded theory analytic strategies.

The social constructionism stands out in Casper's book, from the title through the analysis. Proponents have created fetal surgery and, with surgical techniques, have created the unborn patient. Making the unborn into viable patients deserving of surgical interventions took sustained effort, which continues to be subject to disagreement and debate. Fetal surgery is not simply a natural sequel of medical progress; rather, it emerges from political advocacy, collective support, creation of a market, and cultural values. The notion of the unborn patient and the legitimacy of fetal surgery are both crafted social constructions that occurred within a particular historical moment and entered into larger public debates about reproductive politics. Informed consent is not simply signed and documented. The consent form itself is manufactured after many discussions and iterations, but it often implies that the procedure represents the last hope and understates its risks and consequences.

Casper (1998) builds a detailed constructionist story and places herself and her multiple positions and situations in it. She acknowledges multiple actors and contested realities, her struggles with rendering them, and the relativity of her analysis.[13] She began her study as an engaged feminist and argues that no work—whether of fetal surgeons or of sociologists—stands outside of its contexts (p. 20). She states:

> I care too much about the issues raised by fetal surgery and the unborn patient to assume a polite, reasonable distance, and instead embrace a politics of engagement that recognizes my own immersions in the worlds I study. I have been moved and transformed by this research in multiple ways, and fetal surgery is something I shall continue to think and talk about long after this book is published. My politics and intellectual assumptions have been shaken time and again, precisely because fetal surgery evokes persistent debates about fetuses, abortion, women's roles, the health-care system, and rescued technologies. (p. 25)

Note how Casper's statement corresponds with constructivist assumptions. She acknowledges her starting points and continued immersion in this world as a social actor. Yet Casper also became immersed as a researcher and subsequently found her views challenged and changed. Like the studied phenomenon, the research process itself is never neutral or without context. It, too, is an emergent social construction. The political weight of Casper's topic magnified this social construction of the research process. Respondents and gatekeepers alike quizzed her about her views and commitments. Some gatekeepers stalled, limited, or refused access to data. Others welcomed Casper into their worlds knowing that she took a critical stance toward their work. Contested positions surrounding a topic such as fetal surgery, however, can force the researcher to maintain a problematic view of the data and not uncritically accept one or another position, including one's own.

Several commitments shaped Casper's work. She locates her work as contributing to the dialogue of feminist scholars who had begun to theorize the fetus and to keep women in their theories. Thus this perspective leads her to keep women at the center of attention. As a result she takes into account how fetal surgery affected their lives; she does not reduce women to passive objects who were acted upon. Casper acknowledges that some critics might see her stance as biased. True, but her work implicitly conveys an alternative interpretation of the consequences of her perspective. She did not limit her study to the boundaries of inquiry set by fetal surgeons because theirs erased women as central participants and, by extension, erased questions of the effects of fetal surgery on their health.

Feminist theory and practice gave Casper a series of sensitizing concepts from which to develop. Starting points frame but do not determine the content of constructionist grounded theory. Thus Casper remains attuned to cultural practices, conceptions of personhood, and the place of women's bodies and health in the unfolding scenarios that she witnessed. Casper's feminist perspective no doubt informed her of earlier lengthy debates between prochoice and antiabortion activists about establishing if or when a fetus had human qualities and whose rights—the mother's or the unborn's—took precedence. She detects meanings attached to representations of the fetus as a free agent with its own needs and interests, a unique, autonomous individual, a visible presence, a separate being from the mother, and worthy of protection (Casper, 1998, p. 16). In keeping with sociological treatment of work, Casper aims to show how fetal surgery is a particular type of work that occurred in special work sites.

Casper's book tells a complex tale and involves multiple types of data, ranging from documents to oral histories to firsthand observations. How might its grounded theory underpinnings be discerned? First, Casper sees the history of fetal surgery as a socially constructed process and titles a chapter "Breaching the Womb." Second, she inserts telling *in vivo* codes into the headings and subheadings of her chapters. Among them are: "A Bona Fide Patient" (p. 51), "Not God's Will" (p. 67), "A Spirit of Cooperation" (p. 110), "Folks Are Always Rubbing Shoulders" (p.115), and "It's a Reality Dump" (p.151). Third, Casper shows how actions, conditions, and contingencies contribute to the larger processes of conducting and legitimizing fetal surgery.

Does Casper develop complex grounded theory categories? Does she explain one core variable? Does she offer precise generalizations abstracted from their sources? No. Casper skillfully constructs the social construction of the unborn patient; her theorizing remains embedded in the narrative. She presents a complex analysis of complicated worlds, and does so in accessible terms. Although Casper's use of grounded theory bears little resemblance to objectivist grounded theory, it contains crucial elements of social constructionism consistent with my approach. These elements include (1) the attention to context; (2) the locating of actors, situations, and actions; (3) the assumption of multiple realities; and (4) the subjectivity of the researcher, noted previously. Casper produces an interpretive understanding of the arenas she entered and points out that both her interpretations and the studied scenes could change as emergent contingencies unfold.

We must look at Casper's purposes to understand her strategies. From the start, she aimed to write a book free from the esoteric obscurity of academic discourse. Thus she intended to make her book a vibrant specific sociological story anchored to a larger story of contemporary politics and culture, and she fulfilled her goal.

Summary and Conclusion

Throughout this chapter, I have built an argument explaining how and why social constructionists can adopt grounded theory guidelines to deepen and broaden their analyses and thus address *why* questions. A social constructionist approach to grounded theory encourages researchers to make measured assessments of their methods and of themselves as researchers. A close attention to *what* and *how* questions builds the foundation for moving to *why* questions, as Star's (1989) analysis demonstrates. Thus social constructionists can invoke the generalizing logic of objectivist grounded theory but do so in full view of their measured assessments, not in absence of them. The result promises to be a nuanced analysis that acknowledges and analyzes positionality and partiality, as Casper's (1998) analysis testifies. The subsequent social constructionist analysis resists the tendency in objectivist grounded theory to oversimplify, erase differences, overlook variation, and assume neutrality throughout inquiry. Simultaneously, this analysis grapples with *why* questions and offers qualified explanations.

Grounded theory is a method of explication and emergence. The method itself explicates the kinds of analytic guidelines that many qualitative researchers implicitly adopt. It also fosters explicating analytic and methodological decisions—each step along the way. By explicating their decisions, grounded theorists gain control over their subject matter and their next analytic or methodological move. The construction of the process, as well as the analytic product, is emergent. As I stated earlier, immediate exigencies in the field and concerns of gatekeepers and participants affect this construction, and the contextual positioning of the research frames it. All become grist for analysis. In short, when social constructionists combine their attention to context, action, and interpretation with grounded theory analytic strategies, they can produce dense analyses with explanatory power, as well as conceptual understanding. Simultaneously, their analyses attest to how furthering the social constructionist elements in grounded theory strengthen the method.

• Acknowledgments

I thank Jay Gubrium and Jim Holstein for their careful reviews of an earlier draft and Tina Balderrama for helping with the references.

• Notes

1. David Silverman (2005) has made a similar argument about qualitative research. He contends that by studying phenomena that occur naturally, qualitative researchers can define how interaction ensues and what meanings it holds. For Silverman, answering the "how" and "what" questions must precede the "why" questions.

2. In earlier works, I have referred to my approach as *constructivist grounded theory* to distinguish it from objectivist iterations. The present chapter continues my earlier approach but frames the discussion under the more general rubric of social constructionism to be consistent with the purpose of this volume. Constructivist grounded theory assumes relativity, acknowledges standpoints, and advocates reflexivity. My use of constructivism assumes the existence of an obdurate, real world that may be interpreted in multiple ways. I do not subscribe to the radical subjectivism assumed by some advocates of constructivism. Consistent with Marx, I assume that people make their worlds but do not make them as they please. Rather, worlds are constructed under particular historical and social conditions that shape our views, actions, and collective practices. Constructivist grounded theory (Bryant, 2002; Charmaz, 2000, 2002, 2005, 2006; Clarke, 2003, 2005, 2006) has fundamental epistemological roots in sociological social constructionism. My position on social constructionist grounded theory in this chapter relies on the preceding definition and its premises.

3. They did claim that their method was phenomenological (Glaser & Strauss, 1967). Social constructionist approaches had a long and varied history but moved to the forefront of qualitative sociology in the late 1960s. Harold Garfinkel pub-

lished *Studies in Ethnomethodology* in 1967. Peter Berger and Thomas Luckmann's *The Social Construction of Reality* (1966) came out almost simultaneously with *The Discovery of Grounded Theory* (Glaser & Strauss, 1967) and built on the phenomenological tradition of Alfred Schutz (1967). In contrast, Strauss's social constructionism drew on the pragmatist and symbolic interactionist traditions of Blumer (1969), Dewey (1958), Mead (1932, 1934), and Peirce (1958). These three developments remained relatively independent of each other. Neither Strauss nor Glaser was influenced by the other developments, but Strauss remained in frequent contact with his Chicago school colleagues. Much of Strauss's (1993) and Corbin and Strauss's (1984, 1988) subsequent research and writing contained strong constructionist elements; Glaser's much less so.

4. A number of works describe the method and its variations, so I do not detail them here. See Charmaz (2000, 2003, 2006); Clarke (2005, 2006); Glaser (1978, 1998, 2003); Glaser and Strauss (1967); Strauss (1987); Strauss and Corbin (1990, 1998).

5. Their students' locations also influenced the dissemination of grounded theory. Many more of the University of California, San Francisco, nursing doctoral students of the early years later took positions in doctoral training programs in their profession than did the sociology students of the same era. Graduate programs in nursing emerged and expanded from the mid-1970s through the 1980s, whereas positions in graduate sociology programs shrunk.

6. Paradoxically, the social constructionist logic of Corbin and Strauss's (1988) empirical work often is apparent.

7. See Bryant and Charmaz (2007) for a discussion of the epistemological climate of the mid-1960s.

8. I come close to the Marxist view of history here because I acknowledge human agency but assert that it always occurs within a preexisting social frame with its constraints—of which we may be unaware and which may not be of our choosing (see also Charmaz, in press).

9. My subsequent comparisons draw on Charmaz (in press).

10. Now Glaser (2003) disavows his earlier insistence on finding and studying a basic social process. I have long argued that the quest for a basic social process can mislead the researcher or

mask many processes, and therefore I agree with his recent view (see also Clarke, 2005).

11. Any qualitative study without extensive data can make only limited claims; small interview studies that make general claims stand on shaky ground. The generality of the claims needs to be proportionate to the thoroughness of the data collection.

12. The genre matters here. Academic disciplines and journals vary in their prescriptions for methodological detail. Many require authors to specify their logic of sampling and data collection, but not their analytic strategies. Books differ markedly in the amount and complexity of methodological explanation, depending on the publisher and projected audience. Trade and crossover books (those published as scholarly works that will reach general educated audiences) seldom provide more than minimal information and may not include a methodological section or appendix.

13. These dimensions of Casper's work align her with the constructivist grounded theory that I have previously delineated.

• References

Atkinson, P., Coffey, A., & Delamont, S. (2003). *Key themes in qualitative research: Continuities and changes.* New York: Rowman & Littlefield.

Baszanger, I. (1998). *Inventing pain medicine: From the laboratory to the clinic.* New Brunswick, NJ: Rutgers University Press.

Berger, P. L., & Luckmann, T. (1966). *The social construction of reality.* Garden City, NY: Doubleday.

Blumer, H. (1969). *Symbolic interactionism.* Englewood Cliffs, NJ: Prentice Hall.

Bowker, G. C., & Star, S. L. (1999). *Sorting things out: Classification and its consequences.* Cambridge, MA: MIT Press.

Boychuk Duchscher, J. E., & Morgan, D. (2004). Grounded theory: Reflections on the emerging vs. forcing debate. *Journal of Advanced Nursing, 48*(6), 605–612.

Bruyn, S. T. (1966). *The human perspective in sociology. The methodology of participant observation.* Englewood Cliffs, NJ: Prentice Hall.

Bryant, A. (2002). Re-grounding grounded theory. *Journal of Information Technology Theory and Application, 4*(1), 25–42.

Bryant, A. (2003, January). A constructive/ist response to Glaser. *FQS: Forum for Qualitative Social Research, 4*(1). Retrieved March 14, 2003, from *www.qualitative-research.net/fqs/-texte/1-03/1-03bryant-e.htm*

Bryant, A., & Charmaz, K. (2007). Grounded theory in historical perspective: An epistemological account. In A. Bryant & K. Charmaz (Eds.), *The Sage handbook of grounded theory.* London: Sage.

Casper, M. (1998). *The making of the unborn patient: A social anatomy of fetal surgery.* New Brunswick, NJ: Rutgers University Press.

Castallani, B., Castallani, J., & Spray, L. (2003). Grounded neural networking: Modeling complex quantitative data. *Symbolic Interaction, 23,* 577–589.

Charmaz, K. (1991). *Good days, bad days: The self in chronic illness and time.* New Brunswick, NJ: Rutgers University Press.

Charmaz, K. (2000). Constructivist and objectivist grounded theory. In N. K. Denzin & Y. Lincoln (Eds.), *Handbook of qualitative research* (2nd ed., pp. 509–535). Thousand Oaks, CA: Sage.

Charmaz, K. (2002). Grounded theory analysis. In J. F. Gubrium & J. A. Holstein (Eds.), *Handbook of interview research* (pp. 675–694). Thousand Oaks, CA: Sage.

Charmaz, K. (2003). Grounded theory. In J. A. Smith (Ed.), *Qualitative psychology: A practical guide to research methods* (pp. 81–110). London: Sage.

Charmaz, K. (2005). Grounded theory in the 21st century: A qualitative method for advancing social justice research. In N. K. Denzin & Y. E. Lincoln (Eds.) *Handbook of qualitative research* (3rd ed., pp. 507–535). Thousand Oaks, CA: Sage.

Charmaz, K. (2006). *Constructing grounded theory: A practical guide through qualitative analysis.* London: Sage.

Charmaz, K. (in press). Reconstructing grounded theory. In L. Bickman, P. Alasuutari, & J. Brannen (Eds.), *Handbook of social research.* London: Sage.

Cicourel, A. V. (1964). *Method and measurement in sociology.* Glencoe, IL: Free Press.

Clarke, A. E. (1998). *Disciplining reproduction: Modernity, American life sciences, and the problems of sex.* Berkeley: University of California Press.

Clarke, A. E. (2003). Situational analyses: Grounded theory mapping after the postmodern turn. *Symbolic Interaction, 26,* 553–576.

Clarke, A. E. (2005). *Situational analysis: Grounded theory after the postmodern turn.* Thousand Oaks, CA: Sage.

Clarke, A. E. (2006). Feminisms, grounded theory, and situational analysis. In S. Hess-Biber & D. Leckenby (Eds.), *Handbook of feminist research methods* (pp. 345–370). Thousand Oaks, CA: Sage.

Clough, P. T. (1992). *The end(s) of ethnography: From realism to social criticism.* Newbury Park: Sage.

Corbin, J. (1998). Comment: Alternative interpretations—valid or not? *Theory and Psychology, 8*(1), 121–128.

Corbin, J., & Strauss, A. L. (1984). Collaboration: Couples working together to manage chronic illness. *Image, 4,* 109–115.

Corbin, J., & Strauss, A. L. (1988). *Unending work and care: Managing chronic illness at home.* San Francisco: Jossey-Bass.

Daly, K. (1997). Replacing theory in ethnography: A postmodern view. *Qualitative Inquiry, 3*(3), 343–365.

Denzin, N. K. (1992). *Symbolic interactionism and cultural studies: The politics of interpretation.* Oxford, UK: Basil Blackwell.

Denzin, N. K., & Lincoln, Y. S. (1994). Preface. In N. K. Denzin & Y. S. Lincoln (Eds.), *Handbook of qualitative research* (pp. ix–xii). Thousand Oaks, CA: Sage.

Dewey, J. (1958). *Experience and nature.* New York: Dover.

Dey, I. (1999). *Grounding grounded theory.* San Diego, CA: Academic Press.

Dey, I. (2004). Grounded theory. In C. Seale, G. Gobo, J. F. Gubrium, & D. Silverman (Eds.), *Qualitative research practice* (pp. 80–93). London: Sage.

Ellis, C. (1995). Emotional and ethical quagmires of returning to the field. *Journal of Contemporary Ethnography, 24*(1), 68–98.

Garfinkel, H. (1967). *Studies in ethnomethodology.* Englewood Cliffs, NJ: Prentice Hall.

Glaser, B. G. (1978). *Theoretical sensitivity.* Mill Valley, CA: Sociology Press.

Glaser, B. G. (1992). *Basics of grounded theory analysis.* Mill Valley, CA: Sociology Press.

Glaser, B. G. (1998). *Doing grounded theory: Issues and discussions.* Mill Valley, CA: Sociology Press.

Glaser, B. G. (2001). *The grounded theory perspective: Conceptualization contrasted with description.* Mill Valley, CA: Sociology Press.

Glaser, B. G. (2002). Constructivist grounded theory? *Forum: Qualitative Social Research, 3*(3). Retrieved March 15, 2007, from *http://www.qualitative-research. net/fqs-texte/3-02/3-02glaser-e-htm*

Glaser, B. G. (2003). *Conceptualization contrasted with description.* Mill Valley, CA: Sociology Press.

Glaser, B. G., & Strauss, A. L. (1967). *The discovery of grounded theory.* Chicago: Aldine.

Goffman, E. (1989). On fieldwork. *Journal of Contemporary Ethnography, 18,* 123–132.

Gubrium, J. F., & Holstein, J. A. (1997). *The new language of qualitative method.* New York: Oxford University Press.

Henwood, K., & Pidgeon, N. (2003). Grounded theory in psychological research. In P. M. Camic, J. E. Rhodes, & L. Yardley (Eds.), *Qualitative research in psychology: Expanding perspectives in methodology and design* (pp. 131–155). Washington, DC: American Psychological Association.

Kelle, U. (2005, May). "Emergence" vs. "forcing" of empirical data?: A crucial problem of "grounded theory" reconsidered. *Forum: Qualitative Social Research, 6*(2), Art. 27. Retrieved May 30, 2005, from *http/www.qualitative-research.net/fqs.texte-2-05/05-2-27-e. htm*

Kuhn, T. S. (1970). *The structure of scientific revolutions* (2nd ed.). Chicago: University of Chicago Press.

LaRossa, R. (2005, November). Grounded theory methods and qualitative family research. *Journal of Marriage and Family, 67,* 837–857.

Layder, D. (1998). *Sociological practice: Linking theory and social research.* London: Sage

Lempert, L. (1997). The other side of help: The negative effects of help seeking processes of abused women. *Qualitative Research, 20,* 289–309.

Lincoln, Y. S., & Guba, E. G. (1985). *Naturalistic inquiry.* Newbury Park, CA: Sage.

Locke, K. (1997). Rewriting the discovery of grounded theory after 25 years? *Journal of Management Inquiry, 5*(1), 239–245.

Lofland, J., & Lofland, L. (1995). *Analyzing social settings: A guide to qualitative observation and analysis.* Belmont, CA: Wadsworth.

Maines, D. (1984). The social arrangements of diabetic self-help groups. In A. L. Strauss, J. Corbin, S. Fagerhaugh, B. G. Glaser, D. Maines, B. Suczek, et al. (Eds.), *Chronic illness and the quality of life* (2nd ed., pp. 111–126). St. Louis, MO: Mosby.

May, K. (1996). Diffusion, dilution or distillation? The case of grounded theory method. *Qualitative Health Research, 6*(3), 309–311.

Mead, G. H. (1932). *The philosophy of the present.* La Salle, IL: Open Court.

Mead, G. H. (1934). *Mind, self and society.* Chicago: University of Chicago Press.

Melia, K. M. (1996). Rediscovering Glaser. *Qualitative Health Research, 6*(3), 368–378.

Mills, J., Bonner, A., & Francis, K. (2006). The development of constructivist grounded theory. *International Journal of Qualitative Methods, 5*(1), 1–10.

Peirce, C. S. (1958). *Collected papers.* Cambridge, MA: Harvard University Press.

Reif, L. (1975). Ulcerative colitis: Strategies for managing life. In A. L. Strauss & B. G. Glaser (Eds.), *Chronic illness and the quality of life* (pp. 81–88). St. Louis, MO: Mosby.

Richardson, L. (1993). Interrupting discursive spaces: Consequences for the sociological self. In N. K. Denzin (Ed.), *Studies in symbolic interaction* (Vol. 13, pp. 77–84). Greenwich, CT: JAI Press.

Riessman, C. K. (1990). *Divorce talk.* New Brunswick, NJ: Rutgers University Press.

Sanders, C. R. (1995). Stranger than fiction: Insights and pitfalls in post-modern ethnography. In N. K. Denzin (Ed.), *Studies in symbolic interaction* (Vol. 17, pp. 89–104). Greenwich, CT: JAI Press.

Schutz, A. (1967). *The phenomenology of the social world.* Evanston, IL: Northwestern University Press.

Seale, C. (1999). *The quality of qualitative research.* London: Sage.

Silverman, D. (2005, August). Instances or sequences?: Improving the state of the art of qualitative research. *Forum: Qualitative Social Research, 6*(3), Art. 30. Retrieved October 15, 2006, from *http://www. qualitative research.net/fqs-texte/3-05/05-3-30-e.htm*

Star, S. L. (1989). *Regions of the mind: Brain research and the quest for scientific certainty.* Stanford, CA: Stanford University Press.

Stern, P. N. (1994). Eroding grounded theory. In J.

Morse (Ed.), *Critical issues in qualitative research methods* (pp. 212–223). Thousand Oaks, CA: Sage.

Strauss, A., & Corbin, J. (1990). *Basics of qualitative research: Grounded theory procedures and techniques.* Newbury Park, CA: Sage.

Strauss, A., & Corbin, J. (1998). *Basics of qualitative research: Grounded theory procedures and techniques* (2nd ed.). Thousand Oaks, CA: Sage.

Strauss, A. L. (1987). *Qualitative analysis for social scientists.* Cambridge, UK: Cambridge University Press.

Strauss, A. L. (1993). *Continual permutations of action.* New York: Aldine de Gruyter.

Van Maanen, J. (1988). *Tales of the field: On writing ethnography.* Chicago: University of Chicago Press.

Willig, C. (2001). *Introducing qualitative research in psychology: Adventures in theory and method.* Buckingham, UK: Open University Press.

Wilson, H. S., & Hutchinson, S. A. (1996). Methodologic mistakes in grounded theory. *Nursing Research, 45*(2), 122–124.

CHAPTER 21

Constructionism and Discourse Analysis

● Pirjo Nikander

The term *discourse analysis* (DA) is best understood as an umbrella designation for a rapidly growing field of research covering a wide range of different theoretical approaches and analytic emphases (see Potter & Hepburn, Chapter 14, this volume). What discursive approaches in different disciplinary locations share, however, is a strong social constructionist epistemology—the idea of language as much more than a mere mirror of the world and phenomena "out there" and the conviction that discourse is of central importance in constructing the ideas, social processes, and phenomena that make up our social world. The discourse analysis described in this chapter is particularly influenced by discussions and developments within discursive psychology (e.g., Edwards, 1997; Potter, 1996; Potter & Wetherell, 1987). Key theoretical underpinnings, starting points, and traditions of discursive constructionism are discussed in detail elsewhere in this volume (see, e.g., L. Miller, Chapter 13, and Potter & Hepburn, Chapter 14). The scope and topic of the current chapter is therefore also more notably aimed at practical implementation and based on numerous empirical examples of "doing discourse analysis."

The chapter is divided into three sections. In the first, I briefly discuss some underlying commonalities, analytic themes, and guiding principles of DA. In the process, I provide a thumbnail sketch of the scope of different analytic emphases and of the data sets available to a discourse researcher. Second, I discuss two empirical examples: one from a research project focusing on constructions of age and aging in interview data, the second an example of the analysis of naturally occurring videotaped materials on institutional decision making in meeting settings. I hope that these examples from my own work will clarify some of the key questions about conducting discursive research on different types of materials. They also show how constructionist epistemology guides the formulation of research questions and explicate the various decisions and considerations that go into the process of analysis and writing. The final section of the chapter takes stock of the practical and evaluative side of analysis: transcription, reliability, and validity.

The Field of DA

Specifying DA as a method in any traditional way is difficult, if not impossible. Instead, DA is often described as a methodology or as a theoretical perspective rather than a method (e.g., Phillips & Hardy, 2002, p. 3), as a general epistemological perspective on social life containing both methodological and conceptual elements (Wood & Kroger, 2000, p. 3), as an analytic mentality (Gill, 1996, p. 144; Schenkein, 1978), or as craft skill or form of scholarship (Billig, 1988; Potter, 1997). DA cuts across academic and disciplinary boundaries and neighboring methodological traditions in the fields of rhetoric (e.g., Billig, 1996), membership categorization analysis, and conversation analysis (Silverman, 1998). To add to the variety, DA as an academic enterprise and construction is itself emerging. Researchers' philosophies, research interests, and assumptions as to how DA should be defined also vary, and different analytic interests, schools of thought, and understandings of "discourse" can easily be identified, both within and across disciplines (e.g., Burr, 1995; Nikander, 1995; Parker, 1998; Wetherell 2001a; Wodak, 2006).

The range also bridges critical perspectives. For example, critical discourse analysts adopt an explicitly sociopolitical or ideological stance toward data and analysis (e.g., Burman & Parker, 1993; Fairclough, 1995; Fairclough & Wodak, 1997). Some emphasize the applied and transformative nature of analysis (e.g., Willig, 1999), whereas others, particularly those closer to the conversation analytic tradition, focus more explicitly on the fine-grained microdynamics of interaction and on speakers' orientations instead of analyst's concerns.

The different styles and analytic dimensions in discursive research are conveyed by Figure 21.1. Any particular discourse analytic study can be located within this field, which represents different analytic emphases. Critical DA, for instance, aims at explaining the processes of power from the outset—how power is legitimated, reproduced, and enacted in the talk and texts of dominant groups or institutions—whereas more pronounced data-driven bottom-up approaches to discourse only attend to features that participants *themselves* clearly orient to. Power, in the latter case, is limited to *in vivo* references to notions of oppression and power in ways that make them analyzable and hearable in interaction.

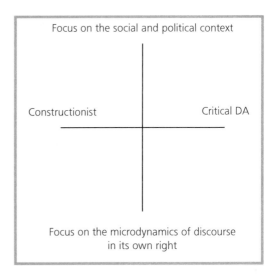

FIGURE 21.1. The field of discourse analysis (DA). Based on Phillips and Hardy (2002, p. 62).

Common Themes

Given the heterogeneity of the field of discursive research, we need to ask what is common within it. What themes, in other words, hold the enterprise together? The foremost theme is the habit of attending to discourse and talk in a multitude of interactional contexts and texts and focusing on the close study of language use. Regardless of the particular form it takes, DA interrogates the nature of social action by dealing with how actions and/or meanings are constructed in and through text and talk. In practice, a discourse researcher looks for pattern and order in how text and talk are organized and for how intersubjective understanding, social life, and a variety of institutional practices are accomplished, constructed, and reproduced in the process. How do people, for instance, make sense of their own identities, and how are collectives and groups—various types of "us" and "them"—discursively formed and maintained through text and talk? Another potential layer for analysis focuses on the construction of psychological categories in interaction. How do we make sense of and use (references to) emotions or memories in interaction, and what are the social functions of psychological categories in interaction (Harré, 1986)? A discourse researcher may also focus on historical and longer term features of discursive formation, for instance, on how meaning making concerning a particular institution, such as the university or the European Union, have developed over time. In general, topics such as hospital culture, attitudes, everyday descriptions and opinions, institutional practices, emotions, and identity are not approached as abstract structures or as being separate from the interactions, conversations, and textually mediated practices that are an intrinsic part of their makeup. Instead, discursive researchers prefer to approach these phenomena in terms of how they are talked into being, and in relation to their social and interactional functions.

Potential data sets in DA include all forms of talk transcribed into written format from audio or video recordings and a wide variety of written documents. Data in DA range, then, from naturally occurring dyadic or multiparty conversations in everyday and institutional settings to interviews and focus groups and the analysis of documents, records, diaries, and newspaper items; media products such as political gatherings, speeches, or interviews; and, increasingly, visual materials and semiotic structures of place (Scollon & Scollon, 2004).

A second common theme is the consideration of everyday language for its occasioned and situated functions. The *action orientation* of discourse refers to the notion that people *do things with words* (Austin, 1962); they account for, explain, blame, make excuses, construct facts, use cultural categories, and present themselves to others in specific ways, taking the interpretive context into account. The discourse researcher is interested in identifying recurrent patterns in language use, not some internal psychological or in-the-world entity that lies "behind" and explains it. Explicating the dynamics and dilemmas of people's active sense-making, the details of people's practices of categorization, accounting, and explaining all lie at the heart of this analytic task. Consequently, the focus is on how versions of our social realities are achieved in and through texts and talk.

Consider, for instance, the following exchange (from Drew, 1992, p. 489) between an attorney (A) and a witness (W) in a rape trial cross-examination.[1]

A: It's where uh (.) gi:rls and fella:s
    meet isn't it?
W: People go there

The business at hand in this courtroom is to establish—on the basis of evidence given—whether characteristics of rape apply to the case at hand. In the preceding extract, the attorney and the witness produce alternative descriptions of the location where the victim and the defendant met. Their mutually competing versions clearly project different motives, scenarios, and interpretations of the actions on the night in question, and the witness's choice of words works to dispute those of the attorney. Formal institutional contexts such as courtrooms or meetings are typical sites at which people clearly do things and establish facts with words. In such contexts, talk is often rife with discourse that is carefully crafted to fit the context. The same holds true—perhaps less dramatically and obviously—for our everyday discourse, in which, on the surface, neutral descriptions, accounts, and categorizations are, in similar ways, about the "facts of the matter," possibly about our moral character or trustworthiness, and about orienting to the particular interpretive context and recipient. The process of becoming a skilled discourse analyst thus includes making the familiar strange (Gill, 1996, p. 144) and taking a step back from the taken-for-granted nature of language. This requires developing a constructionist analytic eye and ear—an appreciation of the detailed artfulness of text, talk, and interaction. In other words, the task of the discourse analyst is to study "how people do the transparently obvious" (Sacks, 1974).

The third common theme in DA, which takes a special emphasis in discursive psychology, is a focus on *rhetorical* organization, on the persuasive and morally consequential aspects of language use. DA is sensitive to the notion that discourse is guided toward persuasion and that this typically results in the argumentative organization of talk and texts (see Billig, 1996). In practical terms this means that talk and texts can be analyzed in terms of how they orient to or take into account culturally available opposing argumentative positions. Such mutually contrasting argumentative positions were evident in our earlier data extract from the rape trial, but similar rhetorical structures—particularization and categorization (Billig, 1985)—also form the basis of our everyday argumentation and discourse. In addition,

newspaper reports, parliamentary discussions, election campaigns, and debates, which are materials that discourse researchers commonly work with, all represent further potential data sets in which the analysis clearly stands to gain from rhetorical analysis. The construction of facts in the news coverage on the September 11, 2001, attacks and their aftermath, the political discourse of New Labour, and the political argumentation concerning European Union expansion are thus all examples of potential data for a discourse analyst.

Doing DA

A constructionist epistemology leads the discourse analyst toward a specific kind of analytic orientation and interpretative take on data. Discourse and interaction are topics in their own right, and language use is constructive action with specific rhetorical characteristics. At the same time, however, there is no one method in the sense of some formally specified set of procedures or calculations, and constructionist theory does not directly guide DA in particular ways. Instead, discourse researchers often argue that the best way to learn the analytic craft skills is through practice and example (e.g., Potter & Wetherell, 1994; Widdicombe, 1993, p. 97).

Analysis of Age in Interaction

Consider first a study of the construction of age identities in interaction. In this project, I wanted to look at how people talk about, make sense of, and manage their membership in a particular age category (Nikander, 2000, 2002). To do this, I analyzed interview accounts: the answers, anecdotes, and stories by men and women who by their chronological age had turned, or were about to turn, 50. My motivation for investigating this topic was the fact that social scientific studies still largely seemed to treat age as an unproblematic, independent, and uninteresting background variable, as a simple quantifiable individual denominator. Unlike discursive research on other social categories, such as gender (e.g., Stokoe, 1998; Wetherall, 2002; Wilkinson & Kitzinger, 1995), race, and national background, for example (Rapley, 1998; Wetherell & Potter, 1992), research on age and aging seemed relatively slow to adopt language-centered, discursive, or interactional approaches. The study was thus geared to elucidate the advantages and analytic mileage resulting from more systematic cross-fertilization of discursive analysis and life course research.

Formulating Explicit Research Questions

Formulating clear-cut, creative, and precise research questions provides a basic frame for any successful research project (Phillips & Hardy, 2002, p. 60). Setting out to look at how baby boomers "do age" in interaction, my research questions were first formulated broadly and clumsily, as: How do people position themselves and others in lifetime terms? How are age identities ascribed and rejected, displayed and refused in interaction? These questions already convey the basic constructionist starting point that categories of age, like any cultural categories by which we understand and organize the world around us, are "for talking" and sensemaking (Edwards, 1991, 1998). After going through literature from the identities-in-interaction tradition (e.g., Antaki & Widdicombe, 1998; Shotter & Gergen, 1989; Widdicombe & Wooffitt, 1995) and empirical and theoretical work on age in interaction (e.g., Coupland & Nussbaum, 1993; Holstein & Gubrium, 2000), I formulated more explicit questions that also defined and guided the analytic take and the theoretical and methodological contributions I wished to make to the existing literature. Important revelations as to the nature of the object of my study and the analytic niche available came from various sources. Consider the following example on age in interaction.

A: How old are you Mr. Bergstein?
B: I'm 48, I look much younger. I look about 35, and I'm quite ambitious and quite idealistic and very inventive and conscientious and responsible.
(Sacks, 1992, Vol. 1, p. 44)

In this example from his lectures, Harvey Sacks points out how the speaker's list of added modifiers to the disclosure of his chronological age—"I'm 48"—does discursive work to preempt possible negative attributes applied to someone in that age category (that someone who is 48 is past their prime, "over the hill," etc.). With the help of empirical research literature and examples such as the preceding, I started to acknowledge and incorporate the positioned and factual characteristics of stage-of-life categories into my research questions. Reading my data, I also began to understand that they could be approached as a showcase of moral and factual discourse in interaction (see Bergmann, 1998; Jayyusi, 1984; Nikander, 2000). In the end, the study was framed as one making empirically grounded observations (Nikander, 2002, p. 15):

1. On how people orient to and display the factual nature of the human life course as a progression, and how overlap between age categories is managed.
2. On the discursive practices through which membership in an age category is either warranted or resisted.
3. On the discursive formulations of personal change and continuity.
4. On the patterns of moral discourse in age in interaction.

Working with Interviews in DA

The data in the baby-boom study consisted of interviews. The field of discourse research is, however, of two minds when it comes to using such materials as data. In the *natural versus contrived debate* the relative advantages of using "naturally occurring" or "naturalistic" data as opposed to "researcher-provoked" or "artificial" data have been explicitly contrasted. In a recent thorough overview of the debate, Speer (in press) recommends caution in applying the natural–contrived distinction too rigidly and suggests that strict and hard lines not be drawn in haste. Justification for this line of argument can, in fact, be found in the appreciation that much of the influential work in DA originates from studies using interviews. Dorothy Smith's (1978) and later Wooffitt's (1992) groundbreaking work on fact construction and factual discourse, analysis of construction of authenticity (Widdicombe & Wooffitt, 1995), work on the construction of professional and gender identity (Marshall & Wetherell, 1989), and on gender discrimination (Gill, 1993), as well as analysis of interpretative repertoires in talk about race (e.g., Wetherell & Potter, 1992), are all ample examples of the analytic force and richness of findings that originate from interview data.

The discursive field is unanimous, however, on the point that, in contrast to realist or factist social science perspectives (ten Have, 2004, p. 73), interview data within discourse analysis are viewed "as interaction in their own right" (e.g., Potter & Wetherell, 1987; Wetherell & Potter, 1992). This entails understanding questions not as a medium into the inner world or opinions of respondents, but, rather, as a central part of the data. DA also addresses and analyzes participants' orientations to the relevance of their talk as interview talk (e.g., Baker, 1997). In recent texts the constructed nature of interviews as interaction is also embraced as a specific social context, as constituting a specific category of institutional talk that can be studied in itself. As a result, the research interview as a discursive act opens up to a rich variety of analytic and theoretical perspectives (e.g., van den Berg, Wetherell, & Houtkoop-Steenstra, 2003). It seems, then, that interview data continue to yield analyses that, along with work on other types of similarly important data, enrich the DA tradition.

Creating Data Collections from Materials

Data collection in discursive research is always followed by a time-consuming period during which the researcher immerses himor herself in the materials by thorough reading and rereading. When audiotaped or videotaped interaction is in question, it is recommended that this process be done side by side with the original recorded material. Next, the body of texts or the transcribed talk is coded according to the researcher's interests, and initial analytic questions are often further specified and refined at this stage. Developing and finessing a coding system and coming up with suitable organizing principles for the material is where DA practice turns into a craft skill. Precise procedural guidelines are impossible to come by in any conventional sense, and the sorting of materials is always more or less specific to the data and research questions. Familiarity with choices made in earlier empirical research, method textbooks, and software packages can be of assistance at this stage (see, e.g., Phillips & Hardy, 2002; Taylor, 2001; Wood & Kroger, 2000).

Coding in DA is more than simply a mechanical procedure that precedes analysis proper. It is guided by constructionist sensitivities and assumptions about language, interaction, and society and by theoretical underpinnings and research questions. Reading of the data may in part also take place in joint data sessions with colleagues. This allows multiple opinions and observations to emerge and functions as a sounding board for preliminary coding, analysis, and interpretations. Reading the data may include asking specific questions such as the following: What do speakers produce as relevant in this account? How do participants interpret what is being said? What is their uptake? Why this particular category/detail/silence here? Is the speaker doing some extra discursive work or accounting? Why do I feel that some topic is avoided or only alluded to? What are participants orienting to in their talk? Posing such questions to the material, as well as reading for variation, detail and pattern, all work as gateways into analysis and the actual writing up (see also Potter & Wetherell, 1994; Wood & Kroger, 2000).

The reading of materials often takes place in phases. The researcher first reads or observes variation in the text or notices particularly striking moments in the interaction. Very soon one might start reading and searching for recurrent patterns and gathering these into collections that then become a corpus of data. Collections are pieces of text and talk that have several discrete components in common that warrant their examination together. According to Wood and Kroger (2000, p. 117), discourse patterns may be synchronic (e.g., used by a particular participant) or diachronic (recurrent in the turn taking of participants). They may be found across participants, within or across sections and occasions, and so on. In the

case of the 50-something interviews, this work stage involved, first, reading the 800 pages of transcribed interview talk in detail and identifying and developing a coding system for the variety of points at which age, in various ways, became topical in the interaction. Further immersion yielded several recurrent discursive patterns on which the analysis subsequently focuses. For instance, I identified one particular recurrent discursive structure by which speakers seemed to acknowledge physical, psychological, and other change as a common norm and fact of life and aging while at the same time placing themselves, at least temporarily, outside such change. Extracts 1 through 3, transcribed in both English and Finnish, provide examples from this collection. What struck me in these extracts and others like them was how notions of continuity (in the present day) and impending change and decrement (possibly in the future) are constructed using a three-component structure (marked

---

Extract 1. **PN: M4: Mikael (Cas 1, A: 3.2–3.9)**
Speakers: M, Mikael; A, Anna; L, Laura; PN, Interviewer.

1.	M:	Well I'd (.) this is still <u>quite</u>	No mää (.) täähän on vielä <u>ihan</u>
2.		a good age when you're <u>healthy</u>	hyvä ikä kun on <u>terve</u>
3.	PN:	mm	mm
4. →	M:	There's like nothing <u>yet</u>	Eihän tässä <u>vielä</u> mitään oo
5.		(.) <u>otherwise</u> to worry about	(.) <u>muute</u> hätää oo
6.	PN:	ye-es	joo-o
7. →	M:	mm (0.2) you of course (.) little	mm (0.2) sitä tietysti (.) pikkuhiljaahan sitä
8.		by little start to <u>calm</u> down and	rupee ihminen vähän <u>rauhottumaan</u> ja
9.		(0.4) with the <u>years</u>	(0.4) ku ikää <u>tulee</u>
10. →		but like I wouldn't <u>otherwise</u> see	mutta tuota en mä <u>muuten</u> näkis tässä
11.		it as any sort of a problem	minkäänlaisena probleemana
12.		this <u>age</u> of mine yet=	tätä <u>ikääni</u> vielä=
13.	PN:	°yes?°	°joo°
14	M:	as long as you have your <u>health</u>	=niin kauan kuin että <u>terveyttä</u> on

---

Extract 2. **PN: W12: Anna (Cas 1, A: 3.6–4.6)**

1. →		>it hasn't been a< reason	>se ei oo myöskään ollu
2.		for <u>crisis</u> for me personally (.)	mikään< <u>kriisin</u> aihe mulle itselle (.)
3. →		for the <u>time-being</u> don't know if it	<u>toistaseks</u> vielä en tiedä
4.		turns into one some day but like	vaikka tulee sit joskus mut että
5.	PN:	mm	mm
6.	A:	growing old and age	vanheneminen ja ikä
7. →		so like (0.2) at least at this	et tota (0.2) ainakaan tällä
8.		moment (.) I don't feel that way	hetkellä (.) en koe sitä

Extract 3.   **PN: W1: Laura 1 (Cas 1, A: 10.3–10.4)**

1. →	L:	So there's like <u>nothing</u> yet (.)	Ettei oo niinkun <u>mitään</u> (.)
2.		that would've <u>clearly</u> marked	tämmöistä jossa ois <u>selkeesti</u>
3.		(.) that now your age comes in	tullu vielä että (.) et nyt se ikä
4.		the way	haittais
5.	PN:	yeah	joo
6. →	L:	I mean it will surely sta(h)rt	Et kyllä niitä varmaan sit
7.		<u>litt</u>le by little when you start to	<u>pikk</u>uhiljaa rupeen tulema(h)an
8.		ache here and there	kun rupee kolottaan sieltä ja täältä
9. →		But not like (2.0) I can't	Mut ei niinkun (2.0) en ainakaan
10.		say that <u>yet</u> at least	<u>vielä</u> osaa sanoa

by arrows). Note how in the first part of this format, personal change with age is denied, often by using an extreme case formulation (Pomerantz, 1986) of the type: "nothing has changed yet." This statement is followed by an account that works to soften the extremity of the previous claim by acknowledging the impending possibility of change or by acknowledging that some change may have happened. The second part also typically includes reference to common sense with acknowledgement tokens such as "of course" or "surely." The third part is then produced contrastively, with a *but* and a temporal marker (*yet, at least at this moment*). This reestablishes the speaker's no-change status in the present. This recurrent pattern in my data seemed, in other words, to function as an excellent practical tool for the discursive management of the factual commonsense existence of change in the life course.

Making Cross-Reference to Other Studies and Findings

One additional subject that I wish to address in relation to this research is the use of existing discourse studies as a comparison point for one's own material and analysis. This is where reading and being familiar with the literature and other pieces of analysis helps not only to build the analytic acuity needed but also to make relevant and sustainable interpretations in ways that add to the existing body of analyses. Returning to the baby-boom interview material, this meant that the identification of specific patterns such as the one just described led me to look for in-

stances as to how it might apply across different contexts. What I found was that the discursive pattern identified carried considerable family resemblance to what Charles Antaki and Margaret Wetherell (1999) call "show concessions," as well as to other data, in which speakers are talking about change. The following extract comes from Sue Widdicombe and Robin Wooffitt's (1995, p. 168) study on youth subcultures. Here is an exchange between the interviewer (I) and a participant who identifies himself as a punk rocker (R):

1.	I:	is being a punk very ((smiley voice))
2.		important for you?
3.	R:	yeah very indeed
4. →		I couldn't imagine myself being
5.		straight at all
6.		(.) like dressing neatly in tidy
7.		nice clothes an' having my hair
8.		down and all that .hh
9. →		na I can't imagine=probably
10.		in a couple of years times
11. →		I'll be like that but I-I-
12.		at the moment I can't imagine it at all

Note how a discursive formulation somewhat similar to those found in my data functions here. This time the linguistic pattern is used to describe one's personal style of dressing as open to possible change in the future but also as something that nonetheless remains continuous and unchanged in the present day. The point I wish to make here is that using earlier research and analytic observations as a reference and comparison point can render research more generalizable. More important, it gives credit to earlier findings, supports the analytic choices made, and helps form new, more solid bases on which future empirical observations can be built.

Perspectives on Institutional Decision Making

Resonating with concerns for the institutional contexts of interaction, the same data set often affords multiple analytic angles and points of interrogation. I use an empirical study of institutional decision making as a case in point. The data derive from a project in which extensive naturally occurring video data were collected in the same institution during a period of 1 year (see Nikander, 2003, 2005). The data consist of 42 hours of team meetings between professionals within the social service and heath sector, including doctors, nurses, home-help personnel, social workers, and a secretary. The practical task for the team meetings is to make concrete decisions either about financial support to elderly clients still living at home or about long-term nursing home placements. The data thus represent one focal interactional site at which the practical work of people processing in human service organizations is done, largely through talk. The study can also be located within the construction of social problems tradition (e.g., Holstein & Miller, 1993) in that the data concern the so-cial processes of situational definition and claimsmaking by institutional actors in interaction.

The normal flow of interaction in the team meetings consists of a chain of client case descriptions. Case presentations that are normally produced in monologue are followed by collegial discussion that varies in length and usually by a turn that marks that a decision about a client case has been reached. After this, the next client case is introduced. The aim is to go through a number of client cases and to provide criteria and arguments either for or against placing a particular client into a category of care receipt.

Extract 4 is an example in both English and Finnish of a case description that is presented in a comparatively short, consensual, and uncomplicated fashion.

As pointed out already, any DA audio or video data set affords multiple analytic angles. One obvious choice for a unit of analysis here was the detail in which case descriptions were constructed. Analysis of the discursive detail through which individual clients are talked into being in case talk includes analysis of what gets produced as relevant for decision making (Edwards, 1998) and how specific categorizations in themselves already project and index specific out-

---

Extract 4: M10: C12 21:21
Speakers: HHH, head of home help; HN, head nurse (district); S, secretary. Pseudonyms: Sunnybrook (Mikonmaa), hospital; Greyfield (Harmaaharju), nursing home

1.	HHH: yes .hhh ↑well then there's	joo .hhh ↑no sitten on
2.	((last name + first name)) (0.8)	((sukunimi + etunimi)) (0.8).
3.	and she's er (1.2) now, (0.5)	ja hän on tuota (1.2) nytten (0.5)
4.	in Sunnybrook hospital and	Mikonmaan sairaalassa ja
5.	has: ↑gone there on the fifteenth of	on: sinne viidestoista
6.	Mayhh (0.8) ↑<u>due</u> to decline in	viidettähhh (0.8) ↑mennyt
7.	general con<u>di</u>tion (0.5)	<u>y</u>leiskunnon <u>l</u>askun (0.5)
8.	for<u>get</u>fulness and disorientation	<u>m</u>uistamattomuuden ja sekavuuden <u>vuoksi</u>
9.	(0.6) after falling at home	(0.6) kaaduttuaan kotona
10.	up till now she's been living	hän on tähän asti asunut
11.	al<u>o</u>ne secured by relatives	<u>y</u>ksin siellä omaistenhhh ja
12.	and three daily visits from	kolme kertaa päivässä käyvän
13.	home help (0.5) there's a	kotiavun turvin (0.6) tänne on
14.	(2.8) assistant senior doctor N	(2.8) apulaisylilääkäri N
15.	has been con<u>s</u>ulted	tehny <u>k</u>onsultaation
16.	on the twelfth of June and (.)	kahdestoista kuudetta ja (.)

17.		hhh noted that ((the patient))	hhh todennut ettei ((potilas))
18.		doesn't need <u>hospital</u> care	tarvitse <u>sairaalahoitoa</u>
19.		but that all means of non-	mutta (.) avohuollon mahdollisuudet
20.		institutional care have run up and	on käytetty loppuun ja\
21.		given this (0.5) he suggests this	näin ollen (0.5) ehdottaa tätä
22.		placement (.) in Greyfield (.)	Harmaaharjun (.) paikkaa (.)
23.		and home help? (.) °agrees?	ja kotihoito? on (.) °samaa? mieltä
24.		(1.2) so I guess we'll accept°	mieltä (1.2) että hyväksyttäneen°
25.	HN:	[accepted	[hyväksytty
26.	S:	[mm	[mm
27.	HHH:	°good? ° (4.0) <then> next we have	°hyvä?° (4.0) <sitte> meillä on seuraavana

comes and decisions. In Extract 4, the routine mention of the absent client's name is this time followed by mention of her current whereabouts, medical condition, and network of care.

In some cases, however, specific categories may be produced early on. Consider the material in Extract 5 for a contrasting case: This is a compact example of how specific detail, the marital status and the gender of the client, in an economical way already indicate that this woman does not have a spouse or children to fall back on. Despite its demographic, "checking-a-box" character, the categorization therefore already moves the client into a specific cluster of action-worthy cases and indicates that an institutional intervention may be needed.

Looking at how client cases are discursively constructed is thus one crucial analytic angle to these as well as to other data and studies consisting of professional–client encounters. Other possibilities include reading the data in terms of the social functions of psychological or emotion discourse in decision making (Nikander, 2007); mapping the practices whereby professionals move between written documents or computer files

and their own firsthand eyewitness knowledge of the clients; and identifying how professional boundaries and power structures are alluded to, constructed, and demarcated through discourse or how moral responsibilities of the community, the professionals, and the families of the elderly clients are negotiated (Nikander, 2005). The data may also yield methodological points of view, such as analyzing the data in terms of participants' orientations to the camera. In DA studies, common claims about data contamination can easily be turned around into an analyzable topic.

The richness of data and the potential for multiple analytic viewpoints is a further benefit of working with audio and video. Faced with such ample range of choice, the researcher zooms in on particular interactional phenomena with a specific analytic and theoretical contribution to the wider field of DA studies in mind. The richness of data is also a practical issue that concerns writing up results in separate articles or chapters or in more practice-oriented pieces that help take the analytic observations of a discourse analyst back to the institutional field from which they originated.

Extract 5. M4. Nursing home placements (12.32-)
Speaker: HSW, Hospital social worker; Fairfield (Teukka), a hospital

1.	HSW:	Okay the first one is	Okei ensimmäisenä
2.		((last name + first name))	((sukunimi + etunimi))
3.		(0.8) on page what <u>three</u>	(0.8) sivulla mikä <u>kolme</u>
4.		(3.8) ((page leafing))	(3.8) ((monisteiden selailua))
5.	HSW:	A: (0.8) er never married female	Tämmöne:n (0.8) eh neiti-ihminen
6.		who has come to us in	joka on meille tullu
7.		Fairfield (1.2) in Ju<u>l</u>y a:nd	Teukkaan (1.2) h<u>ei</u>näkuussa ja:

Transcripts, Validity, and Reliability

Finally, let me address some key points of producing good-quality DA. Good quality in all social scientific work builds on generally agreed-upon norms such as ethically sound starting points and principles (e.g., Taylor, 2001). Here, however, the focus is more specifically on the validity and reliability in research when working with texts and on good practice in our analysis. We can start with a list of questions that is by no means exhaustive:

- What are the specific strengths of working with transcripts?
- Does translating transcripts affect validity?
- What are the special characteristics of the data that are collected through audio- or videotaping?
- What kinds of social and interactional processes are missed?
- Are transcripts enough, or should data also be gathered by other means?

Specific Strengths in Working with Transcripts

The most common rationale for working with transcripts is that recordings and the transcripts based on them provide a highly detailed and accessible representation of social action (Peräkylä, 1997, p. 203). In DA, the detail of empirical material is presented in a form that allows readers and researchers "to make their own checks and judgements" (Potter & Edwards, 2001, p. 108). Transcripts bring immediacy and transparency to the phenomenon under study, and the audience is given access to inspect the data on which the analysis is based, along with the researcher. In addition to immediacy, the analysis of transcripts, particularly conversation analysis, is "rigorous in its requirement of an empirical grounding for any description to be accepted as valid" (Peräkylä, 1997,

p. 202). In DA, the requirement to anchor analytic observations firmly in the data is also imperative. Compared with conversation analysis, more latitude is sometimes allowed, however, and the final evaluation of the persuasiveness of an analytic claim is left to the reader (see Seale, 1999). So, in addition to analytic grounding, DA has emphasized the rhetorical persuasiveness, or the convincing qualities of the research report, as well as the reader's active judgment on its validity.

The reasons and justifications for working with transcripts are typically presented in contrast to and comparison with ethnography, particularly in contrast to the use of field notes. According to Anssi Peräkylä (1997, p. 203), working with transcripts "eliminates at one stroke many of the problems that ethnographers have with unspecified accuracy of field notes and with the limited public access to them" (see also discussions in Maynard, 1989, 2003; West, 1996). He is not alone in saying this. The problem with the reliability of field notes is that they are observations turned into texts; they are reconstructions from an observer's notes and, as such, based on the memory of their writer. The reader has no direct access to the actual goings-on but must take on trust that the descriptions and observations do justice to the "reality" and to the initial interactions that the descriptions present. One can therefore suspect, as Paul Atkinson (1992) does, that field notes are based on rhetorical construction and active selection by the author. Working with transcripts efficiently solves such problems and builds a solid ground for analysis.

Peräkylä (1997, p. 203) also points to Jerome Kirk and Marc Miller's (1986) definition of reliability "as the degree to which the finding is independent of accidental circumstances of the research" (p. 20). Securing superior reliability and transparency when working with transcripts, according to Peräkylä (pp. 205–207) requires adequate and high technical quality of the recordings they are based on and that proper attention be paid to data selection. A further source of quality in DA research results from collective analysis in data session. These can be taken as an exercise in interrater reliability. That is, results are rarely based on an individual researcher's reading but, rather, collectively produced interpretative testing feeds into and informs the analyses prior to publication.

Translated Transcripts

The discourse methods literature has produced several excellent overviews on the best practices in producing transcripts and discussions of the rationale of not producing tidied-up versions of them and of using specific transcription notations (e.g., Silverman, 1993; Taylor, 2001; West, 1996). One largely overlooked question in the literature concerns the fact that a large proportion of DA work is done in languages other than English. Discussion about the additional complications that follow from having to produce and translate transcripts of data originally in another language for an English-speaking and reading audience remains a rarity in the DA literature (e.g., Nikander, 2002, in press; ten Have, 1999). A few points deserve mention here. First, it seems that presenting the original data alongside the translation into the language of the publication (often English) is a norm that fits the principle of validity and reliability through transparency, outlined earlier. Second, translating data extracts is not merely a question of "adopting" a "transcription technique" but, rather, includes a range of practical and ideological questions as to the level of *detail* in the transcription and of the way in which the translations are *physically* presented in print. Third, if we understand transcripts as central to guaranteeing the publicly verifiable nature of DA research, generally agreed-upon rules concerning the layout and publication practices of these data should be in place. One example of a possible layout has been used in this chapter.

Special Characteristics of Data Collected through Audio- or Videotaping: Is Something Missed?

All types of research methods inevitably include delimiting the data in some ways. All data are produced. They are limited presentations of the social world and, in themselves, already a product of specific choices made by the researcher (e.g., Hester & Francis, 1994). Despite the acclaimed accuracy and public accessibility of audio and video materials, some critics argue that the use of such technologies, particularly when studying various work or institutional settings, is in danger of shaping our research questions and the occupations studied and, therefore, potentially also in danger of producing distorted representations of work practices (Hak, 1999). Tony Hak's (1999) criticism is directed specifically against conversation analysis in institutional settings, but it can, in part, be extended to discursive research, as well.

According to Hak, the use of audio or video recordings sets certain limits to what can be studied and what kinds of questions are asked. For instance, a considerable amount of research has been done on relatively stationary situations such as consultations, meetings, or ward rounds, whereas the multitude of goings-on in corridors, by the bedside, and in ad hoc informal discussions between the staff members and between the staff and clients are lost to what Hak calls the "discursive gaze." Another limitation in working with recordings is that the discursive gaze means that only work situations that are done through a lot of talk are focused on. Hak claims that this also means that research easily concentrates on data recorded among professions with a higher status, whereas menial work, unremarkable aspects of work practices, and certain tasks such as bathing, cleaning, and cooking meals are overlooked (1999, p. 440). This situation has some political implications: Being a focus of research often brings positive effects to the category of workers studied.

According to Hak, it is therefore regrettable that studies of discourse in work settings often focus on professions with higher status.

These are only a few important points made by Hak (1999), but they raise serious concerns worth considering. Simultaneously, however, Hak's criticism clearly misrepresents and does injustice to discursive (and conversation analytic) research and fails to appreciate the rapidly broadening range of empirical analyses. The collection of video-recorded material in institutions inevitably includes fieldwork in some form, the nonverbal side of interaction is often an integral part of DA, and related technological developments already enable a variety of mobile data collection in different interactional settings. Hak's criticism is also built on simple juxtaposition between research based on the use of recordings and transcripts and the ethnographic tradition, which in itself is a rather arbitrary distinction.

Other Forms of Data

Still, the question remains, are transcripts enough, or should data also be gathered by other means? In practice, discourse analytic research rarely limits itself purely to video- or audiotaped data. In fact, the research literature offers a number of helpful suggestions for combining ethnography and interviews with discursive analysis, for using textual materials, and for following longer term interactional processes. According to Douglas Maynard, for instance (1989; 2003, pp. 64–87), analysis of discourse episodes may deemphasize the institutional context wherein those episodes occur. Similarly, however, granting uncontrolled primacy to ad hoc ethnographic knowledge in the wider social environment and the setting surrounding the interaction may result in data loss (Maynard, 2003, p. 71). According to Maynard (2003, p. 72): "ethnographic insistence on the relevance of larger and wider institutional structures can mean a loss of data in and as the interaction, for attention shifts from actual utterances in the fullness of their detail and as embedded within a local interactional context to embrace narrative or other general accounts concerning social surrounding." He proposes limited affinity between ethnography and discourse and conversation analytic research and points to three precise ways in which ethnography can complement close analysis of video and audio data: in descriptions of settings and identities of parties; in explications of key terms, phrases, and course of action that the researcher is unfamiliar with; and in explaining "curious" patterns that prior analysis may reveal (2003, p. 73).

In the end, imposing strict restrictions as to what types of data DA research should be restricted to is futile, and discourse researchers continue to vary in the degree and style in which social structure is incorporated and what is granted primacy, set at the foreground or background in their analyses. David Silverman (1999) has argued for collaboration between different traditions and against establishing sectarian armed camps based on animosity. It is through surprising and ongoing exchange and dialogue between research traditions that new outlooks emerge. Using transcripts, collecting observational data, using documents, and conducting interviews do not rule one another out, and in practice DA researchers are encouraged to combine a wide range of different materials.

Conclusion

Translating a skill into a technique (Hepburn, 1997, p. 33) is always a difficult task. Simple linear "cookbook" models of DA can never do justice to the complexity and its different versions, traditions, and debates. Instead of attempting to pin down discourse analysis as a "constructionist method," the goal in this chapter has been to give a taste of the rationale for doing discursive research and to provide general guidelines and empirical examples of what the analyses in this tradition have to offer. Critical voices, tensions, and ongoing debates are always a sign of lively and fruitful academic enterprise. Therefore, such voices were also included, not silenced.

The future development of the field of DA depends, however, on how members new to the field adopt existing versions and traditions, how they add to, transform, and further extend the body of analytic findings and agendas, and how they find new, insightful means of analyzing empirical material. The construction of new forms of DA will continue as theoretical boundaries shift and new and exciting approaches emerge.

• Note

1. All data extracts in the chapter follow the transcription conventions originally developed by Gail Jefferson (see, e.g., Atkinson & Heritage, 1984, for details).

• References

Antaki, C., & Wetherell, M. (1999). Show concessions. *Discourse Studies*, *1*(1), 7–27.

Antaki, C., & Widdicombe, S. (Eds.). (1998). *Identities in talk*. London: Sage.

Atkinson, J. M., & Heritage, J. (Eds.). (1984). *Structures of social action: Studies in conversation analysis*. Cambridge, UK: Cambridge University Press.

Atkinson, P. (1992). *Understanding ethnographic texts*. Newbury Park, CA: Sage.

Austin, J. L. (1962). *How to do things with words*. Oxford, UK: Clarendon Press.

Baker, C. D. (1997). Membership categorization and interview accounts. In D. Silverman (Ed.), *Qualitative research: Theory, method and practice* (pp. 130–143). London: Sage.

Bergmann, J. R. (1998). Introduction: Morality in discourse. *Research on Language and Social Interaction*, *31*(3–4), 279–294.

Billig, M. (1985). Prejudice, categorization and particularization: From a perceptual to a rhetorical approach. *European Journal of Social Psychology*, *15*, 79–103.

Billig, M. (1988). Methodology and scholarship in understanding ideological explanation. In C. Antaki (Ed.), *Analyzing everyday explanation: A case book of methods* (pp. 199–215). London: Sage.

Billig, M. (1996). *Arguing and thinking: A rhetorical approach to social psychology* (2nd ed.). Cambridge, UK: Cambridge University Press.

Burman E., & Parker, I. (Eds.). (1993). *Discourse analytic research: Repertoires and readings in action*. London: Routledge.

Burr, V. (1995). *An introduction to social constructionism*. London: Routledge.

Coupland, N., & Nussbaum, J. F. (Eds.). (1993). *Discourse and lifespan identity*. Newbury Park, CA: Sage.

Drew, P. (1992). Contested evidence in courtroom cross-examination: The case of a trial for rape. In P. Drew & J. Heritage (Eds.), *Talk at work: Interaction in institutional settings* (pp. 470–520). Cambridge, UK: Cambridge University Press.

Edwards, D. (1991). Categories are for talking: On the cognitive and discursive bases of categorization. *Theory and Psychology*, *1*(4), 515–542.

Edwards, D. (1997). *Discourse and cognition*. London: Sage.

Edwards, D. (1998). The relevant thing about her: Social identity categories in use. In C. Antaki & S. Widdicombe (Eds.), *Identities in talk* (pp. 15–33). London: Sage.

Fairclough, N. (1995). *Critical discourse analysis: The critical study of language*. London: Longman.

Fairclough, N., & Wodak, R. (1997). Critical discourse analysis. In T. A. van Dijk (Ed.), *Discourse as social interaction* (Vol. 1, pp. 258–284). London: Sage.

Gill, R. (1996). Discourse analysis: Practical implementation. In J. T. E. Richardson (Ed.), *Handbook of qualitative research methods* (pp. 141–156). Leicester, UK: British Psychological Society.

Hak, T. (1999). "Text" and "con-text": Talk bias in studies of health care work. In S. Sarangi & C. Roberts (Eds.), *Talk, work and institutional order: Discourse in medical, mediation and management settings* (pp. 427–451). Berlin: Mouton de Gruyter.

Harré, R. (Ed.). (1986). *The social construction of emotions*. Oxford, UK: Blackwell.

Hepburn, A. (1997). Teachers and secondary school bullying: A postmodern discourse analysis. *Discourse and Society*, *8*, 27–48.

Hester, S., & Francis, D. (1994). Doing data: The local organization of a sociological interview. *British Journal of Sociology*, *45*(4), 675–695.

Holstein, J. A., & Gubrium, J. F. (2000). *Constructing the life course* (2nd ed.). Dix Hills, NY: General Hall.

Holstein, J. A., & Miller, G. (Eds.). (1993). *Reconsidering social constructionism: Debates in social problems theory*. New York: Aldine de Gruyter.

Jayyusi, L. (1984). *Categorisation and the moral order*. London: Routledge & Kegan Paul.

Kirk, J., & Miller, M. L. (1986). *Reliability and validity in qualitative research*. London: Sage.

Marshall, H., & Wetherell, M. (1989). Talking about career and gender identities: A discourse analysis perspective. In S. Skevington & D. Baker (Eds.), *The social identity of women* (pp. 106–129). Sage: London.

Maynard, D. W. (1989). On the ethnography and analysis of discourse in institutional settings. In J. A. Holstein & G. Miller (Eds.), *Perspectives on social problems: A research annual* (pp. 127–146). Greenwich, CT: JAI Press.

Maynard, D. W. (2003). *Bad news, good news: Conversational order in everyday talk and clinical settings.* Chicago: University of Chicago Press.

Nikander, P. (1995). The turn to the text: The critical potential of discursive social psychology. *Nordiske Udkast: Journal for Critical Social Science, 2,* 3–15.

Nikander, P. (2000). "Old" vs. "little girl": A discursive approach to age categorisation and morality. *Journal of Aging Studies, 14*(4), 335–358.

Nikander, P. (2002). *Age in action: Membership work and stage of life categories in talk.* Helsinki: Finnish Academy of Science and Letters.

Nikander, P. (2003). The absent client: Case description and decision-making in interprofessional meetings. In C. Hall, K. Juhila, N. Parton, & T. Pösö (Eds.), *Constructing clienthood in social work and human services: Identities, interactions and practices* (pp. 112–128). London: Kingsley.

Nikander, P. (2005). Managing scarcity: Joint decision making in interprofessional meetings. In T. Heinonen & A. Metteri (Eds.), *Social work in health and mental health: Issues, developments and actions* (pp. 260–279). Toronto, Ontario: Canadian Scholar's Press.

Nikander, P. (2007). Emotions in meeting talk. In A. Hepburn & S. Wiggins (Eds.), *Discursive research in practice: New approaches to psychology and interaction* (pp. 50–69). Cambridge, UK: Cambridge University Press.

Nikander, P. (in press). Working with transcriptions and translated data. *Qualitative Research in Psychology.*

Parker, I. (Ed.). (1998). *Social constructionism, discourse and realism.* Thousand Oaks, CA: Sage.

Peräkylä, A. (1997). Reliability and validity in research based on tapes and transcripts. In D. Silverman (Ed.), *Qualitative research: Theory, method and practice* (pp. 201–220). London: Sage.

Phillips, N., & Hardy, C. (2002). *Discourse analysis: Investigating processes of social construction.* Thousand Oaks, CA: Sage.

Pomerantz, A. (1986). Extreme case formulations: A way of legitimizing claims. *Human Studies, 9,* 219–229.

Potter, J. (1996). Discourse analysis and constructionist approaches: Theoretical background. In J. T. E. Richardson (Ed.), *Handbook of qualitative research methods* (pp. 125–140). Leicester, UK: British Psychological Society.

Potter, J. (1997). Discourse analysis as a way of analysing naturally occurring talk. In D. Silverman (Ed.), *Qualitative research: Theory, method and practice* (pp. 144–160). London: Sage.

Potter, J., & Edwards, D. (2001). Discursive social psychology. In W. P. Robinson & H. Giles (Eds.), *The new handbook of language and social psychology* (pp. 103–118). Chichester, UK: Wiley.

Potter, J., & Wetherell, M. (1987). *Discourse and social psychology: Beyond attitudes and behaviour.* London: Sage.

Potter, J., & Wetherell, M. (1994). Analyzing discourse. In A. Bryman & R. G. Burgess (Eds.), *Analysing qualitative data* (pp. 41–66). London: Routledge.

Rapley, M. (1998). "Just an ordinary Australian": Self-categorisation and the discursive construction of facticity in "new racist" political rhetoric. *British Journal of Social Psychology, 37,* 325–344.

Sacks, H. (1974). On the analyzability of stories by children. In R. Turner (Ed.), *Ethnomethodology: Selected readings* (pp. 216–232). Harmondsworth, UK: Penguin.

Sacks, H. (1992). *Lectures on conversation* (Vols. 1 & 2). Oxford, UK: Blackwell.

Schenkein, J. (1978). Sketch of the analytic mentality for the study of conversational interaction. In J. Schenkein (Ed.), *Studies in the organization of conversational interaction* (pp. 1–6). New York: Academic Press.

Scollon, R., & Scollon, S. W. (2004). *Discourses in place: Language in the material world.* London: Routledge.

Seale, C. (1999). *The quality of qualitative research.* London: Sage.

Shotter, J., & Gergen, K. J. (Eds.). (1989). *Texts of identity.* London: Sage.

Silverman, D. (1993). *Interpreting qualitative data: Methods for analysing talk, text and interaction.* London: Sage.

Silverman, D. (1998). *Harvey Sacks: Social science and conversation analysis.* Cambridge, UK: Polity Press.

Silverman, D. (1999). Warriors or collaborators: Reworking methodological controversies in the study of institutional interaction. In S. Sarangi & C. Roberts (Eds.), *Talk, work and institutional order: Discourse in medical, mediation and management settings* (pp. 401–425). Berlin: Mouton de Gruyter.

Smith, D. (1978). K is mentally ill: The anatomy of a factual account. *Sociology, 12,* 23–53.

Speer, S. (in press). Natural and contrived data. In L. Bickman, J. Brannen, & P. Alasuutari (Eds.), *Handbook of social research.* London: Sage.

Stokoe, E. H. (1998). Talking about gender: The conversational construction of gender categories in academic discourse. *Discourse and Society, 9*(2), 217–240.

Taylor, S. (2001). Locating and conducting discourse analytic research. In M. Wetherell, S. Taylor, & S. J. Yates (Eds.), *Discourse as data: A guide for analysis* (pp. 5–48). London: Sage.

ten Have, P. (1999). *Doing conversation analysis: A practical guide.* London: Sage.

ten Have, P. (2004). *Understanding qualitative research and ethnomethodology.* London: Sage.

van den Berg, H., Wetherell, M., & Houtkoop-Steenstra, H. (Eds.). (2003). *Analyzing race talk: Multidisciplinary approaches to the interview.* Cambridge, UK: Cambridge University Press.

West, C. (1996). Ethnography and ortography: A (modest) methodological proposal. *Journal of Contemporary Ethnography, 25*(3), 327–352.

Wetherall, A. (2002). *Gender, language and discourse.* New York: Routledge.

Wetherell, M. (2001). Debates in discourse research. In M. Wetherell, S. Taylor, & S. J. Yates (Eds.), *Discourse theory and practice: A reader* (pp. 380–399). London: Sage.

Wetherell, M., & Potter, J. (1992). *Mapping the language of racism: Discourse and the legitimation of exploitation.* London: Sage.

Widdicombe, S. (1993). Autobiography and change: Rhetoric and authenticity of "Gothic" style. In E. Burman & I. Parker (Eds.), *Discourse analytic research:* *Repertoires and readings in action* (pp. 94–113). Routledge: London.

Widdicombe, S., & Wooffitt, R. (1995). *The language of youth subcultures: Social identity in action.* Hemel Hempstead, UK: Harvester Wheatsheaf.

Willig, C. (Ed.). (1999). *Applied discourse analysis: Social and psychological interventions.* Buckingham, UK: Open University Press.

Wilkinson, S., & Kitzinger, C. (1995). *Feminism and discourse: Psychological perspectives.* London: Sage.

Wodak, R. (2006). Dilemmas of (discourse) analysis. *Language in Society, 35,* 595–611.

Wood, L. A., & Kroger, R. O. (2000). *Doing discourse analysis: Methods for studying action in talk and text.* Thousand Oaks, CA: Sage.

Wooffitt, R. (1992). *Telling tales of the unexpected: The organization of factual discourse.* London: Harvester Wheatsheaf.

CHAPTER 22

A Social Constructionist Framing of the Research Interview

● **Mirka Koro-Ljungberg**

Scholars use, read, and interpret theories differently, but they cannot conduct research without drawing on theory, if only implicitly (see Hatch, 2002; LeCompte & Preissle, 1993; St. Pierre, 2004). Theoretical awareness shapes scholars' use of research methods (see Coe, 2001), and theory locates researchers within discourses that use specific language and argumentation systems. Furthermore, theoretical perspectives influence the research process by setting a particular epistemological frame around various stages of the research process. Questions such as, What do we believe about the nature of reality? What is worth knowing (ontology)? How do we know what we know (epistemology)? and How should we study the world (methodology)? guide research designs and interpretation processes.

Epistemology and theoretical perspective influence how researchers utilize and implement interviews in research projects. Epistemological orientation and theoretical perspectives assist researchers in organizing their research and making sense of interview data (see LeCompte & Preissle, 1993; Plummer, 1983). Theories not only provide methods of arranging, prioritizing, and legitimizing what researchers see and do during the interviews but also offer scholars the space in which to construct identity and plan research (see Tuhiwai Smith, 2001).

Social Constructionist Perspective

Social constructionism brings a variety of distinctive sensibilities to research methodology. Vivien Burr (1995), for example, highlights how constructionist ways of knowing relate to taken-for-granted knowledge. From a social constructionist perspective (see Crotty, 1988, for more about theoretical perspectives), knowing occurs during socially negotiated processes that are historically and culturally relevant and that ultimately lead to social action. Mary Gergen and Kenneth Gergen (2003) argue that "constructionist ideas place an emphasis on the power of relationships over individual minds, multiple worlds over singular realities, collaborative interdependence over individual heroism, and dialogue over monologue" (p. 158). Peter Berger and Thomas Luckmann (1967) also propose that knowing and the reality of everyday life are founded in an intersubjective world in which individuals cannot exist without interacting and communicating with others. Furthermore, there is a connection between individuals' meanings and the meanings of others. Barnett Pearce (2002) contends that the social world is based on conversations that include "game-like patterns of conjoint activities" (p. 202). These "conjoint activities" shape the meaning-making processes and are controlled by social rules and obligations.

Taken together, these constructionist perspectives on knowledge cast the research interview as more than a set of predetermined research techniques or well-structured methods that can be mastered through research training: Constructionist interviews are dialogical performances, social meaning-making acts, and cofacilitated knowledge exchanges. In order for researchers to understand the meaning-making activities that take place during an interview, they must focus on the actions of individuals that influence the immediate social process and context of the interview, as well as those actions that have been influenced by other sociopolitical contexts or discourses.

In the following sections, I briefly outline some constructionist approaches to interview research and share one possibility for social constructionist researchers to conceptualize and formulate the interview process.

The subsequent illustration considers all individuals engaged in the interview process and event as "knowing subjects." This approach to socially constructed interviews has several important implications. First, the concept of knowing subjects implies shared epistemological authority and ownership. *All* interview participants create knowledge and thus carry responsibility for the created knowledge. Second, *all* knowing subjects are actively and intentionally engaged in knowledge production during the interview. As a result, one's subjective knowing and epistemological agency are in constant flux and are continuously shaped by other knowing subjects and interactions (see Holstein & Gubrium, 2003). This particular version of the socially constructed interview project is illustrated with data from my own research involving teacher focus-group interviews. The chapter concludes with suggestions as to how a social constructionist framing of the research interview can alter conventional notions of the interview process and product.

Constructionist Knowing, Sensibilities, and Interview Data

The social ways of knowing and socially constructed character of interviews have been acknowledged by a wide range of qualitative researchers. For example, James Holstein and Jaber Gubrium (1995, 2003) refer to interviews as reality-constructing and interactional events during which the interviewer and interviewee construct knowledge together. Holstein and Gubrium (2003) add that an interview is "a site of, and occasion for, producing knowledge itself" (p. 4). Andrea Fontana and James Frey (2005) similarly propose that an interview can be defined as a collaborative, contextual, and active process that involves two or more people. William Miller and Benjamin Crabtree (2004), in turn, view interviewing as a "partnership on a conversational research journey" (p. 185).

Constructionist perspectives also tend to focus on the emergent, socially constructed character of the "data" that are produced through the interview. Furthermore, the constructionist perspective highlights the role of the interview process itself and the continuous and dynamic unfolding of participants' perspectives within it (Anderson & Jack, 1998). Charles Briggs (1986), for example, argues that the social circumstances of interviews fundamentally, not incidentally, affect the form and content of what is said. Similarly, Fontana and Frey (2005) emphasize the importance of shared meaning that is based on the contextualized understandings of experiences. They propose that due to these shared contextualized understandings, interviews can be viewed as negotiated texts. Katherine Borland (1998) also discusses how the interpretive space created during the interviews promotes an understanding of other perspectives. Aaron Cicourel (1974) likewise maintains that interviews impose particular ways of understanding reality. In essence, interviewers are deeply and unavoidably implicated in creating meanings that are typically treated as residing within respondents. In addition, it is clear that constructionist approaches to interviewing legitimate both interviewer and interviewee as active knowers.

These realizations lead constructionists to reconsider the ways in which interview data should be analyzed. Cicourel (1964, 1974), for example, offers insightful suggestions as to how to make sense of typical interview interactions. Elliot Mishler (1986) points out the contextual and narrative complexities of the research interview, suggesting that interview narratives must be analyzed in a cultural context. Brad Olsen (2006), in his analysis of interviews, focuses on the various dimensions of the interviewer–interviewee relationship, including how the participants interact with each other, talk about their practices, and enact practices in particular contexts. These authors all express the need to develop a better understanding of the meanings conveyed by both interviewer and respondent.

A conception of the interview as collaborative suggests that the interview process yields actively produced narratives (Holstein & Gubrium, 1995). Holstein and Gubrium (1995) argue that this conception prompts researchers to examine the dynamic and unfolding narrative processes that are revealed in interview data. As a constructionist project, analyzing interview data involves looking at both the *whats* of the content and the *hows* of the production. A wide variety of approaches to linguistic methods, particularly narrative analysis, have been developed in conjunction with the constructionist analysis of interview data (e.g., Harris, 2006; Riessman, 1993). The major implication of a constructionist approach to interview data has been to treat interview narratives as situated, constructed reports, not actual representations of facts or "true" experiences.

Conceptualizing the Socially Constructed Interview

I argue in this chapter that constructionist perspectives of interviewing should shift the focus from mining individual minds to the coconstruction of (temporarily) shared discourses. Jennifer Greenwood (1994) makes a case that social reality is "a function of shared meanings, it is constructed, sustained and reproduced through social life" (p. 85). Rather than the researcher studying what participants know about a particular topic or what kind of experiences they have had, they instead engage in dialogue with participants and thus actively contribute to the knowledge production. The goal of the interview is to examine how knowing subjects (researchers and study participants) experience or have experienced particular aspects of life as they are coconstructed through dialogue. No meaning or shared experience can be isolated from the socially constructed knowledge-production event, and no meaning can be examined outside the performance itself. In other words, the analytic and interpretive focus of the interview shifts from individual responses to shared knowledge and meaning making that occurs during the interaction. Consequently, constructionist sensibilities lead researchers to consider the *polyvocality* of knowing and thus of interviews.

Before I introduce some commonly referenced concepts related to socially constructed knowledge, as exemplified in Figure 22.1, it is important to mention that similar to Gayatri Spivak (1997), who explains that many labels are inaccurate, I acknowledge that the label of *interview* might not be the most appropriate to describe the social exchange and interaction that takes place when knowing subjects engage in a dialogue with each other about a particular topic. But at the same time, I am bound by my disciplinary knowledge and the discourse of research methodology. As such, I use the term *interview* throughout this chapter, but I expand the meaning associated with the label by interpreting how interviews can be conceptualized from the social constructionist perspective and how this conceptualization might change conventional meanings.

The bidirectional arrows in Figure 22.1 illustrate the interchange and social interaction that takes place between subjects. Knowing subjects are interlinked with other subjects, an interchange that influences the responses produced during the interview. For example, when a subject assumes the role of the student, the role and how it is performed during the interview is influenced by the discourse of being a student. This discourse includes the relationship with teachers and peers outside the immediate context of the interview.

Additionally, knowing subjects are not only discursive and psychological social beings who construct their sense of selves in relation to discourses and other individuals, but they are also embodied subjects who have a sense of physical body, emotional self, and biological functions. Thus it is important to highlight that all knowing subjects are constituted by the historical and cultural context of the interview and the other subjects involved. As a result, power and materiality are ever-present conditions that shape the interview and the relational selves of knowing subjects.

Social Interaction: Space for Knowledge Construction

How can one characterize various forms of socially constructed knowledge that are applicable to interview studies? Knowledge is interactive, coconstructed, and negotiated, as well as historical, situational, and changing, and thus difficult to duplicate. In addition, knowledge is plural and fallible, and conversations and social interactions are the ultimate contexts in which knowledge is produced and understood (see Kvale, 2002; Rorty, 1979). According to Thomas Schwandt (1998), "knowledge is one of the many coordinated activities of individuals and as such is subject to the same processes that characterize any human interaction (e.g., communication, negotiation, conflict, rhetoric)" (p. 240).

In this chapter, I use the label *social interaction* to describe a space in which knowing subjects engage in social activities and socially constructed knowledge production. However, my interpretation and the use of the term *interaction* is not a Cartesian dualistic connotation that separates the knower from the known or the subject from the object. Instead, when I think about interaction from a social constructionist perspective, I assume that knower and known are inseparable and conditioned by each other. The idea that an observer becomes a part of the observation is at the very heart of social construction.

Barbara Thayer-Bacon (2003) proposes that from a relational *(e)pistemological*[1] perspective, knowing is a process, reality cannot be separated from the subject, and fallibility must be compensated for through plurality. Thus data produced during the interviews

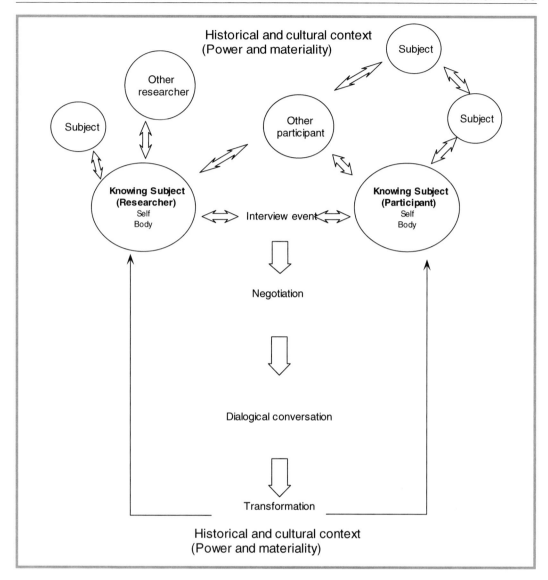

FIGURE 22.1. Socially constructed interview.

or research findings cannot be distinct from the subjects of knowledge production or knowers involved in the interaction (e.g., researcher, participant, community, and readers). Furthermore, any knowing subjects, including the interviewer, cannot act as neutral and external spectators in knowledge construction, and knowing subjects cannot claim privilege of knowledge or interpretation—instead, all representations are partial perceptions of realities. Researchers do not have access to privileged information; rather, they must enter into the state of learning with other knowing subjects, in which all subjects learn from one another by acknowledging their state of not-knowing and vulnerability. In this form of interviewing, Carolyn Ellis and Leigh Berger (2003) consider all participants both researchers and research participants.

Furthermore, transformative collaboration and connectedness between various knowers requires an epistemological movement away from foundationalism to ontological flexibility and epistemological plurality. This movement can be characterized by a dismissal of rationality and cultural modernism. All claims to knowledge are founded in communities of meaning making (Gergen, 2001), and each meaning construction is situated and contextualized; any meanings are open to resignification and are constantly remade. In other words, truth is situational, and contextual and knowledge construction is a circular process (see Pearce, 2002). The ways in which knowing subjects describe truth in their lives and create particular narratives based on their lived experiences are valid and noteworthy.

Epistemological Agency within Relationships

Many social constructionists propose that individuals are relational beings and that there are no independent selves without the social context (Gergen, 1999, 2001; McNamee & Gergen, 1999). Kenneth Gergen (1999) calls the self formed within relationships the *relational self*. Relational selves are subject to change according to the differing social structures that simultaneously limit and maintain cultures and discourses. Thus individuals' cultural milieu and group affiliations provide them with lenses through which they view relationships, themselves, and others and endow them with meaning (Crotty, 1998). However, social construction of the self does not oppose agency; rather, the construction is "the necessary scene of agency, the very terms in which agency is articulated and becomes culturally intelligible" (Butler, 2003, p. 130). Once the constructionist view proposes that identity is constructed, the constructed nature of identity opens up possibilities for agency, in comparison with the view of identity categories as foundational and fixed (Butler, 2003).

Socially constructed identities cannot be viewed only as a psychological phenomenon, and knowing subjects do not exist in a sociophysiological vacuum. John Cromby and David Nightingale (1999) argue that subjects and bodies encountered in social interactions need to be viewed as biological, physiological, emotional, hormonal, and phenomenological rather than solely mental or neutral constructions. Furthermore, knowing subjects are influenced not only by their perceptions of themselves in relation to others but also by their embodiment and physical bodies. Anne Cranny-Francis (1995) refers to the societal function of embodied subjects as important because embodied subjects intentionally operate between various social positions, which enable them to transform traditional practices. Additionally, individuals feel and sense their bodies as a result of social interactions, social expectations, and current societal norms, values, and beliefs.

Cartesian separation of mind and body becomes problematic from some social constructionist perspectives because the separation promotes narrow understandings of knowing subjects, limits the types of dialogue and transformation that can occur, and devalues the embodied engagement with other knowing subjects. Also, when viewed from the transactional perspective, cognitive and affective sides of the individual are not separate. "Instead, both aspects of meaning—which might be termed the public and the private—are always present in our transactions with the world" (Rosenblatt, 1993, p. 383). As a result, knowing subjects engage in interactions and transactions with their environments on the self–body continuum.

Human bodies are subjects of desire, despair, tragedy, and joy, which can all be socially constructed and certainly influence social interactions during interviews (see also Cromby & Nightingale, 1999, p. 10). Margaret Hagood (2005) wrote that "the body is a cultural interweaving and production of nature as influenced by factors such as people, culture, and experiences" (p. 22). Furthermore, according to Hagood, the body is socially (re)produced by the practices it has been exposed to. For example, interview practices limit and enable different types of bodily functions. Additionally, knowing subjects expose their thoughts and emotions through various verbal, nonverbal, visual, and emotional messages (see Mishler, 1986). In other words, bodies as physiological, emotional, or phenomenological entities read each other during interactions and interview events.

The knowing subjects in a research project are not predefined, predetermined, or completely known ahead of time. Rather, the subjects are emerging and actively made during the interview process: "Although the imagined subject behind the respondent is eventually conceptualized, perhaps as a rational or an emotional agent, the image emerges as part of the project, not beforehand" (Holstein & Gubrium, 1995, p. 14). Additionally, knowing subjects continuously reflect upon themselves and "monitor who they are in relation to the person questioning them" (Holstein & Gubrium, 1995, p. 15). In other words, the knowing subject is contextualized and actively produced.

Exemplifying the Socially Constructed Interview

In order to both illustrate how knowing subjects operate and exemplify my arguments regarding socially constructed interviews, I present data examples from teacher focus groups within a qualitative core of a longitudinal mixed-method study designed to describe experiences that have helped or hindered help-seeking for attention-deficit/hyperactivity disorder (ADHD). The exemplary 1-hour focus group included seven white middle and high school teachers, both men and women, and three facilitators. It is also important to note that even though the empirical examples have been drawn from the particular focus-group interactions, it does not mean that one-to-one interviews cannot support similar arguments or illus-

trate my conceptualization of socially constructed knowledge in practice.

The first data example (Table 22.1) illustrates the beginning of the focus-group interview during which I, the researcher, construct myself as a group member, establish rapport with the participants, and set up the operational rules for group interaction. Furthermore, the excerpt demonstrates my negotiation of the rules of engagement that shape the progress of the interview. In addition, at the beginning, I attempt to read the nonverbal clues of the participants to find out who is willing to answer the question first. However, my conclusion about the possible candidate to begin the conversation is incorrect. Susan (pseudonym) resists beginning the conversation both verbally and physically (e.g., shifting her position on the seat and having a worried look on her face). Additionally, I react to my misinterpretation of Susan's willingness to begin the conversation by laughing. As a result of Susan's resistance, a change in the operational rules of the interview takes place. Instead of going around the table, subjects take turns in random order. Not only are the construction of rules of engagement exemplified in this example, but also the ways in which I respond to the participants' resistance indicate the continuous creation process of relational selves and my uncertain power position.

Table 22.2 demonstrates how different knowing subjects build their relational selves during the interview. Participating teachers compare their own experiences with those of others. For example, Paul reflects on his classroom experiences and concludes by constructing a self of a teacher whose students do not have serious behavioral problems. Paul's construction of self is influenced by the fact that he works in the general education classroom in a high-performing school. As a response to Paul's construction of self as a general education teacher, Mike and Ella establish themselves as special education teachers who experience serious student behavioral problems in their classrooms.

TABLE 22.1. Interview Excerpt

Interview text	Author's commentary
Lisa: Do we go around the room on this one?	Lisa is not certain how the group will function.
Mirka (researcher): Yes, we can. We can start with Susan.	Mirka considers what should be done and who should begin. She looks around the table to find the clues indicating who would be ready to begin the talk.
Susan: Oh, um, wow. I kind of think I need a minute to think about that.	Susan is not ready to start. She feels secure enough to resist the facilitator's suggestion. She takes her time.
Mirka: Okay. You can have a minute.	Mirka realizes her misjudgment regarding Susan's willingness to begin the conversation based on Susan's nonverbal communication. As a result, Mirka confirms that it is okay for Susan to take time to formulate her answer.
Susan: Okay.	Susan responds and passes her turn.
Mirka: Do we all need a minute, or are we ready?	Mirka reacts to Susan's suggestion more generally, wondering if all participants need more time with the first question.
Mike: I don't need a minute.	Mike indicates that he is ready to answer. By volunteering, Mike also allows other participants to have more time to respond.
Mirka: Okay. Go ahead! (*Laughs*.)	Mirka is relieved and indicates her gratitude to Mike for beginning the conversation.

TABLE 22.2. Interview Excerpt

Interview text	Author's commentary
[Teachers have previously discussed serious problems that they have encountered in their classrooms.]	
Paul: Sounds like I might have the most main-stream classroom out of the bunch. . . . The things that I have to react to the most are like kids sitting sideways in their seat, or kids, um, maybe looking at each other, and I have to say, you know, "So and so, have your eyes forward, please."	Paul reflects on his own classroom situation and notes that he has the most mainstream class compared with other focus-group members. He illustrates his argument by sharing examples that other teachers recognize as "easy" compared with more serious detention or juvenile justice problems that were discussed earlier in the group.
Mike: [I am jealous.] **Ella:** [Yes.] (*Laughs*.)	Mike and Ella respond simultaneously to Paul's comment, indicating that Paul is right—he has the easiest classroom situation. Mike and Ella construct themselves as "teachers with serious classroom situations."

Even though dialogical exchange often occurs between two knowing subjects during the interview (e.g., if overlapping talk is discouraged for transcription reasons), the resultant interaction is always shaped by previous discussions and responses. From the social constructionist perspective, interviewers or knowing subjects are no longer seen as sympathetic listeners but rather as comrades in world construction. Table 22.3 illustrates the complexities of social knowledge construction by examining the notions of individual knowledge and subjects as passive listeners, but it is not clear whose knowledge, content, or selection of terminology characterizes the exchange. For example, Debra introduces the idea of work-related interests of teenagers. Susan and Diane redefine Debra's content by specifying the focus and using the word *vocational*. Debra maintains her position and continues with her original construction but is also de-

lighted that Susan and Diane can connect with her ideas and experiences. Paul concludes the discussion by affirming that the term *vocational* sounds great and introduces his experiences to expand the content of the discussion even further.

Transformation: A Goal for Social Constructionist Dialogue

As illustrated previously, the dialectics and dialogical exchanges during interviews transform individuals (see Berger & Luckmann, 1967). During the transformation, individual and collective subjectivities, social roles, dialogue, and constructed talk are turned into something new. New discourses then mediate conditions of life and subjective experiences of knowing subjects related to these conditions. Furthermore, individuals do not act on their fixed roles, but each dialogue is a new creation. Existing dis-

TABLE 22.3. Interview Excerpt

Interview text	Author's commentary
Debra: They are not going to go to college. Many of these children I have seen, maybe that will change next year, but I would like to see. I cannot think of the word now. I am sorry. It has been a long day. (*Laughs.*) Um, work-related, you know, something that might . . .	Debra draws examples from her student population but cannot find the words to describe the appropriate training or type of education that meet the interests of her students.
Susan: Vocational.	Susan interrupts Debra by suggesting a term for her to use.
Diane: Vocational.	Diane finds Susan's proposed term appropriate and agrees.
Debra: Yes, yes, yes. (*Laughs.*) Work-related. That's all I could do. Um, a little more of even that in, in, uh, middle school where these kids just, they don't need to, go to, you know, college.	Debra approves the suggested word and demonstrates her approval with laughter. Nevertheless, Debra returns to her previous word choice "work-related" instead of applying Susan and Diane's suggestion.
Susan: Uh-huh.	Susan acknowledges Debra's point of view.
Paul: "Vocational" sounds great. Um, I would only add that, that the more I can individualize them, the better.	Paul confirms the content of Debra's talk ("work-related"), but he prefers the term "vocational" and he wants to emphasize the individualization of curriculum and instruction.

courses are used to define, situate, and realize current interests, positions, and newly created meanings. Furthermore, "premises for action are problematized and the tensions between the individual's short- and long-term interests [are] identified" (Willig, 1999, p. 43).

Moreover, from the social constructionist perspective I exemplify here, discourses and language are not reflections of the world or simply conversations; rather, they are transformative sociopolitical mediums, constituting the world and forming individuals' actions in the world (see Gergen, 2001). Transformation through dialogue aims to move beyond "an alienated existence to a more promising way of going on together" (Gergen, 1999, p. 148). Dialogue also enables a relationship in which the relational selves of participating individuals change and grow, fostering new understandings and thereby encouraging the dialogue to move toward relational responsibility and negotiation.

Additionally, it is important to emphasize that transformation and dialogue from social constructionist perspectives do not include the romantic notions of care and empathy. Instead, dialogue that is transformative in nature is often painful, revealing, and impolite. According to Steinar Kvale (2006), the conceptualizations of interviews as dialogues are misleading but common; he further explains that "domination and inequality can be masked through authentic and egalitarian dialogical conceptions of hierarchical and commercial social relationships" (p. 489). Kvale continues that interview dialogue "gives an illusion of mutual interests in conversation, which in actuality takes place for the purpose of just the one part—the interviewer" (p. 483). I agree with Kvale in that a dialogue can provide an illusion of mutual interest. Nonetheless, I believe that everything we create during the interviews can be labeled as illusions or as limited and particular perceptions of reality. In fact, any subjective and constructed perception of reality can carry elements of illusion and deception when viewed from other perspectives or contexts.

Despite the fact that in-depth and active interviews might create an illusion of mutual interest, which I argue does not necessarily need to be avoided but rather acknowledged, open communication, negotiation, and respect for other points of view facilitate fruitful dialogue and change. Transformation is further accelerated by self-reflexivity, a critical questioning of one's own beliefs and positions, and the coconstruction of a new reality that supports contributions from all knowing subjects. Moreover, the achieved polyvocality and mutual constructions of reality can broaden perspectives and shape the relational selves of all individuals involved in the relationship (see Gergen, 1999).

Table 22.4 illustrates how knowing subjects engage in dialogue that transforms not only the individuals but also the content of the conversation. Susan and Paul build on each other's sentences, asking questions that continuously foster the content of their talk. In this way, both participants contribute to the constructed knowledge. Additionally, this example complicates the ownership of the data—both Susan and Paul collaboratively argue for seating charts and their usefulness in creating structure in the classroom. Even though Susan originally introduces the concept of separating boys and girls in the classroom, Paul mentions his practical application of separation: the seating chart.

Similar to the previous example, Table 22.5 represents one transformative aspect of a dialogue. However, in Table 22.4, both knowing subjects contribute rather equally to the knowledge construction, whereas here one subject has knowledge and experiences that the other subject desires to learn from. The following example shows how Rose (one of the researchers) learns from other knowing subjects and thus expands her understandings of successful intervention strategies from the teacher's perspective. This example also demonstrates that Di-

TABLE 22.4. Interview Excerpt

Interview text	Author's commentary
Susan: I don't know that's it's an ADHD thing. I know it's a teenage thing, but, um, it's helped actually, a little bit, to [separate boys and girls in the classroom].	Susan introduces the concept of separating boys and girls, but she does not refer to the practical details of how to do it.
Paul: I, uh, could not agree more.	Paul identifies with Susan's idea and indicates that he has similar practices.
Susan: So you do too?	Susan gets excited about Paul's response, but she is not sure exactly what Paul is referring to. As a response to this uncertainty, Susan proposes a rhetorical question to Paul.
Paul: Seating charts.	Paul answers with specifics of how he separates boys and girls in his classroom.
Susan: Yes, oh, yes!	Susan connects with Paul's idea with enthusiasm.
Paul: . . . are *the* biggest, you know, uh . . .	Paul emphasizes the importance of seating charts and thus highlights the significance of Susan's idea even more.
Susan: for structure.	Susan completes Paul's sentence to illustrate agreement.

TABLE 22.5. Interview Excerpt

Interview text	Author's commentary
Rose (researcher): So, did, is that a strategy that works then?	Rose is not certain if she understood Diane's idea correctly.
Diane: Yes.	Diane confirms the usefulness of her strategy.
Rose: That is where you literally . . .	Rose is still uncertain whether she understands what Diane means and asks for clarification.
Diane: Yes, but, yes, yes.	Diane confirms and provides clues that indicate that Rose understood what Diane meant with that particular strategy.
Rose: Literally send them on a . . .	Rose still illustrates her uncertainty by trying to reframe what Diane said but at the same time not finishing her sentence.
Diane: Yes, the bouncing.	Diane provides a concrete example in order to assist Rose in conceptualizing the proposed idea.
Rose: Like a scavenger hunt.	Rose provides another example and thus demonstrates that she understands what Diane proposed.
Diane: The bouncing around works, but not suspending them, and timing out does not really work.	After Rose's accurate alternative example, Diane is ready to continue her line of reasoning and finish describing her original idea.
Rose: Okay, do we have that on our list? Sending them out to errands? I am interested.	Rose is aware of her learning and notes the importance of new insight. She also makes sure that the new insight is recorded on the board among other important ideas coming from the group. Finally, Rose demonstrates that it was a significant insight and that she is interested in learning more about it.

ane is responsive to Rose's questioning and will not finish or expand on her original idea until Rose is ready to follow Diane's line of reasoning.

Negotiation: A Tool to Confront Conflicts

Gergen (1999) argues that transformative dialogue is based on reflexivity, equal opportunities for communication, and negotiation. In order to enable transformation, it is important to negotiate and discuss how all knowing subjects can ask questions during the interview event, how decisions are made about the acceptable topics, when it is time to end the dialogue, how data can be shared, and what will happen to the recorded data. Furthermore, contextual and emotional shifts that occur during the interviews not only require continuous reflexivity and self-disclosure but also openness and a willingness to negotiate. It is in negotiating the conflicts that arise, within ourselves as well as between oneself and the other, that we are able to cocreate a new world in which "the conversation about 'who is wrong' is replaced by joint deliberation on what kind of *relationship* we might build together" (Gergen, 1999, p. 164).

Moreover, each socially created meaning can be "vulnerable to reconstitution as a failed project" (Gergen, 2003, p. 154), and in order to avoid socially constructed meaning to become a failed project, negotiation is required. Negotiation enables knowing subjects to continue their interaction beyond differing assumptions, worldviews, discourses, and unequal social structures. Thus "the production of interaction as meaningful entails active and continual 'negotiation' of differences of meaning; the 'norms' of interaction as a moral order are oriented to and interpreted differently by different social actors, and these differences are negotiated" (Fairclough, 2003, p. 41). Ideally, the negotiations of possible differences and differing expectations lead to increased rapport, a strengthened relationship, and richer communication between subjects that can assist transformation and decrease resistance to change.

From the social constructionist perspective I apply, interviews provide an analytically fruitful social context in which to observe and investigate the production and negotiation of ideas, normative influences, commonalities, and differences (see Finch & Lewis, 2003). Because the social interaction between knowing subjects most often involves normative differences and an unequal balance of power, interpersonal dimensions (such as gender, race, and age) might either enable or hinder and prohibit successful negotiation. Negotiation can also be complicated by differing values, preestablished understandings, and role expectations of the interviewer and interviewee. For example, research training and experience and prior knowledge about the topic influence the perceptions, understandings, and resources that knowing subjects create and utilize during the negotiation.

Table 22.6 displays the complexity of negotiation and Diane's uncertainty and resistance in accepting other possible explanations or perspectives. At the beginning, Diane discusses how little her students care. As an indicator for possible disagreement, Mike poses a rhetorical question that introduces one socioeconomical justification for the lack of care. However, Diane is not willing to completely support Mike's proposition or invitation to explore other explanations. Nevertheless, she admits that she cognitively knows how socioeconomical influences shape children's lack of care but she does not find these explanations sufficient in explaining the mothers' lack of care. Mirka, in turn, invites Diane to elaborate on her response. At the same time, Mirka encourages other participants to join the conversation and put forward their perspectives. Mirka attempts to facilitate transformative dialogue and consensus building. However, despite Mirka's intentions, Diane restates her position by rephrasing how none of her 12 kids care but at the same time she expresses uncertainty about her argu-

---

TABLE 22.6. Interview Excerpt

Interview text	Author's commentary
Diane: They don't care about any of that. None, none of that.	Diane proposes that children in her class don't care about learning or homework.
Mike: Have you visited some of their houses?	Mike asks Diane to consider children's home situations as one possible explanation for the lack of caring. He is not ready to accept Diane's position without raising concerns about children's socioeconomical context.
Diane: Well, I know that's why, but, you know, then why don't their mothers care? But they have to care because their parents care.	Diane is cognitively aware that socioeconomical context plays a role, but she further challenges Mike's response by asking why parents don't care. She is not willing to accept socioeconomical context as a justification for mothers' lack of care.
Mirka: So, do you think that it is related to motivation or is the care a different issue?	Mirka clarifies whether Diane is referring to the fact that children don't care because they lack motivation or that they don't care for other reasons. In this way, Mirka encourages more conversation about this topic and she invites other participants to express their opinions and share their experiences. Mirka hopes that further conversation will promote meaning negotiation and deepen knowers' understandings.
Diane: Well, I don't know because, none, out of my twelve kids, none of them care. Zero of the twelve care, and some have good parents and some don't. So, I don't if it is the parents or them, their motivation.	[*Diane shows hesitation*] Diane reemphasizes the fact that none of her students care. She is still not quite ready to accept Mike's explanation. Diane also rules out parental influence by stating that some kids have good parents and some don't. Consequently, she illustrates her uncertainty about the topic and she opens the conversation for other possible explanations.
Susan: I think the part of, one of the things that troubles me the most this year is the fact that the children are so, seems like they are coming in really beaten down, and that's part of the reason why they are not caring.	Susan responds to Diane and Mike by introducing yet another explanation that addresses the lack of caring: physical and mental conditions of children.

---

ment and concludes her turn by not knowing how the lack of care originates and what causes it. Additionally, Diane's self-questioning prompts Susan to speak. Susan's comment puts forward another explanation that addresses the lack of care. It could be argued that this example illustrates how transformation can be partial, limited, and difficult to achieve at the level of each knower but socially constructed dialogue can still promote sensitization to alternative interpretations and explanations. Additionally, this data excerpt exemplifies how socially constructed interviewing cannot dis-

solve all conflicts between different interpretations or overcome all power differentials, but socially constructed frame to research interviews support scholars' investigations of the ways in which collaborators and knowers relate to each other dialogically, may be less research-controlled and more reflective in ways.

Conclusion

Gergen (2001) proposes that interviews can be viewed as "methodologies of sensitization" (p. 160) during which collaborators are sensitized to the alternative interpretations of individuals' experiences in the world. Socially constructed interviewing cannot dissolve conflicts between different interpretations or overcome all power differentials, but they allow collaborators to relate to each other in dialogical, maybe less researcher-controlled and more reflective and sensitizing ways. Additionally, Holstein and Gubrium (2004) describe the usefulness of active and sensitizing interviews: "It would seem far more productive to devote our attention to finding rigorous ways of examining social context and the ways that the *hows* and the *whats* (as well as the *whens* and *wheres*) of interaction reflexively constitute that which can be situationally construed as consequential social context" (p. 309).

Situationality of socially constructed knowledge also implies that particular discourses are available, as well as unavailable, to groups and individuals. In addition, these discourses are deployed in various ways due to the historical and material conditions (see Willig, 1999). For example, some of the focus group teachers had special education training or had worked in special education classrooms, whereas others had been exposed to general education settings. Additionally, some teachers had teaching experience in socioeconomically disadvantaged communities, and others had taught children mainly in middle-class neighborhoods. Consequently, the differences in discourses that were available for teachers affected the socially constructed dialogue and relational selves of the participants.

In other words, based on these examples, "discourses cannot be independent from material structures; rather, they are historically and culturally variable ways of making different kind of sense of the phenomena and events generated by intransitive structures" (Willig, 1999, p. 45). Furthermore, materiality embedded in discourses "embraces the distribution of resources, the location of bodies, the organization of space and the irreversible fact of time" (Cromby &

Nightingale, 1999, p. 11). This more critical approach to social constructionism brings about the methodological and interpretative move from description to sociopolitical and material considerations and toward collaborative activism. Thus it becomes important to further investigate how materiality and oppressive historicity create visible and invisible borders for socially constructed interviews and, as a result, prohibit cultural and sociopolitical change. Additionally, it would be interesting to study how these borders can be identified, interpreted, and transformed into productive exchanges among knowing subjects. Moreover, it could be meaningful to consider how the borders might separate objects and subjects of knowledge by questioning whether stories and knowledge constructed during the interview belong to the knowing subjects or to the organizational structures that shape occurring discourses (see Holstein & Gubrium, 2003). Last, it would be important to further investigate the differences between conventional and socially constructed interview data and to consider how to analyze the latter and what kind of conclusion can be drawn from it.

To conclude, what does the social constructionist framing of interviews require from the researchers, and how does it change conventional notions of interviews? First, the interaction, and consequently the research process itself, is a sociocultural and sociopolitical phenomenon rather than an individual- or researcher-driven independent project. From this perspective, the facilitation of transformative, interactive, and dialogical practices is essential. Kvale (2006) expresses concern that interviewers not only dominate the dialogue and interaction but also control the data and consequential interpretations. Ideally, from the social constructionist perspective, the role of knowing subjects does not end when the interview is over. Instead, as a part of interactive and dialogical practices, decision making during the entire research process is shared. The knowing subjects negotiate the research design, interview agenda and topics, data analysis methods, analytic insights, and preferred representation of the data. Ongoing negotiations also imply that no knowledge is privileged and that knowing subjects cannot predetermine what they desire to know. Rather, knowledge construction is evolving, constantly moving toward transformation. However, knowers' agency and individual commitment change the degree of involvement in the research process. For example, some of the subjects might become more involved in coanalyzing and cowriting the data stories and reports, whereas others might want only to check the accuracy of constructed data or data representations.

In addition, during the socially constructed interviews that I advocate, all knowing subjects are exposed to their emotions and desires. Subjects, including the researcher, are asked to express themselves, negotiate, and ultimately transform. This transformation requires openness and acceptance of diverse opinions, experiences, and worldviews. All interview questions posed by knowing subjects are asked from a position of curiosity (Gergen & Gergen, 2003).

The researcher must also be able to collaborate and negotiate with other knowers who may or may not agree with him or her. Coconstructed data might take knowing subjects to unanticipated areas of inquiry, scholarship, or action. Gergen (2001) asks, "What forms of [interviewing] practice may be generated that move away from isolation and insulation and towards the cross-fertilization of identities, the intermingling of practices, the interweaving of selves and ever-broadening forms of coordinated action?" (p. 180)

Finally, it should be clearly communicated that every knowing subject carries social and political consequences of coconstructed knowledge. Knowing subjects speak as individuals located in a socially constructed setting from situated perspectives. In these ways, the coconstructed data become unpredictable, uncertain, and fallible. If knowing subjects are willing to take risks, open their minds to new ways of knowing, and move away from predetermined ideas and hypothesis-driven research models, a social constructionist frame of interviewing provides a fruitful place for growth, transformation, and sociopolitical change.

• Note

1. The expression *(e)pistemological* is used to separate Thayer-Bacon's (2003) use of the term *epistemology* from the transcendental uses of the term.

• References

Anderson, K., & Jack, D. (1998). Learning to listen: Interview techniques and analyses. In R. Perks & A. Thomson (Eds.), *The oral history reader* (pp. 157–171). London: Routledge.

Berger, P., & Luckmann, T. (1967). *The social construction of reality: A treatise in the sociology of knowledge.* New York: Anchor Books.

Borland, K. (1998). "That's not what I said": Interpretive conflict in oral narrative research. In R. Perks & A. Thomson (Eds.), *The oral history reader* (pp. 320–332). London: Routledge.

Briggs, C. (1986). *Learning how to ask.* Cambridge, UK: Cambridge University Press.

Burr, V. (1995). *An introduction to social constructivism.* London: Routledge.

Butler, J. (2003). Identity, deconstruction, and politics. In M. Gergen & K. Gergen (Eds.), *Social construction: A reader* (pp. 129–131). London: Sage.

Cicourel, A. V. (1964). *Method and measurement in sociology.* New York: Free Press.

Cicourel, A. V. (1974). *Theory and method in a study of Argentine fertility.* New York: Wiley.

Coe, C. (2001). Learning how to find out: Theories of knowledge and learning in field research. *Field Methods, 13*(4), 392–411.

Cranny-Francis, A. (1995). *The body in the text.* Melbourne, Australia: Melbourne University Press.

Cromby, J., & Nightingale, D. (1999). What's wrong with social constructionism? In D. Nightingale & J. Cromby (Eds.), *Social constructionist psychology: A critical analysis of theory and practice* (pp. 1–19). Buckingham, UK: Open University Press.

Crotty, M. (1998). *The foundations of social research.* London: Sage.

Ellis, C., & Berger, L. (2003). Their story/my story/our story: Including the researcher's experience in interview research. In J. A. Holstein & J. F. Gubrium

(Eds.), *Inside interviewing: New lenses, new concerns* (pp. 467–493). Thousand Oaks, CA: Sage.

Fairclough, N. (2003). *Analysing discourse: Textual analysis for social research.* London: Routledge.

Finch, H., & Lewis, J. (2003). Focus groups. In J. Ritchie & J. Lewis (Eds.), *Qualitative research practice: A guide for social science students and researchers* (pp. 170–198). London: Sage.

Fontana, A., & Frey, J. (2005). The interview: From neutral stance to political involvement. In N. Denzin & Y. Lincoln (Eds.), *The Sage handbook of qualitative research* (3rd ed., pp. 695–727). Thousand Oaks, CA: Sage.

Gergen, K. (1999). *An invitation to social construction.* London: Sage.

Gergen, K. (2001). *Social construction in context.* London: Sage.

Gergen, K. (2003). Meaning in relationship. In M. Gergen & K. Gergen (Eds.), *Social construction: A reader* (pp. 148–155). London: Sage.

Gergen, M., & Gergen, K. (Eds.). (2003). *Social construction: A reader.* London: Sage.

Greenwood, J. (1994). Action research and action researchers: Some introductory considerations. *Contemporary Nurse, 3*(2), 84–92.

Hagood, M. (2005). Bodily pleasures and/as the text. *English Teaching: Practice and Critique, 4*(1), 20–39.

Harris, S. R. (2006). *The meanings of marital equality.* Albany: State University of New York Press.

Hatch, A. (2002). *Doing qualitative research in education settings.* Albany: State University of New York Press.

Holstein, J. A., & Gubrium, J. F. (1995). *The active interview.* Thousand Oaks, CA: Sage.

Holstein, J. A., & Gubrium, J. F. (2003). Inside interviewing: New lenses, new concerns. In J. A. Holstein & J. F. Gubrium (Eds.), *Inside interviewing: New lenses, new concerns* (pp. 3–30). Thousand Oaks, CA: Sage.

Holstein, J. A., & Gubrium, J. F. (2004). Context: Working it up, down, and across. In C. Seale, G. Gobo, J. F. Gubrium, & D. Silverman (Eds.), *Qualitative research practice* (pp. 297–311). London: Sage.

Kvale, S. (2002). The social construction of validity. In N. Denzin & Y. Lincoln (Eds.), *The qualitative inquiry reader* (pp. 299–325). Thousand Oaks, CA: Sage.

Kvale, S. (2006). Dominance through interviews and dialogues. *Qualitative Inquiry, 12*(3), 480–500.

LeCompte, M., & Preissle, J. (1993). *Ethnography and qualitative design in educational research* (2nd ed.). San Diego, CA: Academic Press.

McNamee, S., & Gergen, K. (1999). *Relational responsibility: Resources for sustainable dialogue.* Thousand Oaks, CA: Sage.

Miller, W., & Crabtree, B. (2004). Depth interviewing. In S. Hesse-Biber & P. Leavy (Eds.), *Approaches to qualitative research* (pp. 185–202). New York: Oxford University Press.

Mishler, E. G. (1986). *Research interviewing.* Cambridge, MA: Harvard University Press.

Olsen, B. (2006). Using sociolinguistic methods to uncover speaker meaning in teacher interview transcripts. *International Journal of Qualitative Studies in Education, 19*(2), 147–161.

Pearce, B. (2002). New models for communication: Shifts from theory to praxis, from objectivism to social constructionism, and from representation to reflexivity. In D. Schnitman & J. Schnitman (Eds.), *New paradigms, culture and subjectivity* (pp. 197–208). Cresskill, NJ: Hampton Press.

Plummer, K. (1983). *Documents of life.* London: Allen & Unwin.

Riessman, C. K. (1993). *Narrative analysis.* Newbury Park, CA: Sage.

Rorty, R. (1979). *Philosophy and the mirror of nature.* Princeton, NJ: Princeton University Press.

Rosenblatt, L. (1993). The transactional theory: Against dualism. *College English, 55*(4), 377–386.

Schwandt, T. (1998). Constructivist, interpretivist approaches to human inquiry. In N. Denzin & Y. Lincoln (Eds.), *The landscape of qualitative research: Theories and issues* (pp. 221–259). Thousand Oaks, CA: Sage.

Spivak, G. (1997). Translator's preface. In J. Derrida (Ed.), *Of grammatology* (Corrected ed., pp. ix–lxxxvii). Baltimore: John Hopkins University Press.

St. Pierre, E. (2004). Refusing alternatives: A science of contestation. *Qualitative Inquiry, 10*(1), 130–139.

Thayer-Bacon, B. (2003). *Relational "(e)pistemologies."* New York: Lang.

Tuhiwai Smith, L. (2001). *Decolonizing methodologies: Research and indigenous peoples* (4th ed.). London: Zed Books.

Willig, C. (1999). Beyond appearances: A critical realist approach to social constructionist work. In D. Nightingale & J. Cromby (Eds.), *Social constructionist psychology* (pp. 37–51). Buckingham, UK: Open University Press.

CHAPTER 23

Autoethnography as Constructionist Project

- **Laura L. Ellingson**
  Carolyn Ellis

everal years ago, we published an essay in which we claimed that qualitative research can be productively thought of as existing along a continuum. Artistic interpretivists anchor one end, whereas scientific positivists hold down the other. In between is a vast and varied middle ground wherein most qualitative researchers locate themselves (Ellis & Ellingson, 2000). We constructed a nuanced range of possibilities to describe what many others have socially constructed as dichotomies (mutually exclusive, paired opposites), such as art–science, hard–soft, and qualitative–quantitative (see Potter, 1995). Dichotomous thinking remains the default mode of the academy. "Language, and thus meaning, depends on a system of differences," explains Gergen (1994, p. 9). "These differences have been cast in terms of binaries. . . . All are distin-

guished by virtue of what they are not." Nowhere is this evidenced more strongly than in the quantitative–qualitative divide. Even in qualitative work itself polarities mark the differences between interpretivists and realists (Atkinson, Coffey, Delamont, Lofland, & Lofland, 2001; Bochner & Ellis, 1999). Recently autoethnographers have begun to distinguish themselves from one another by separating evocative from analytic autoethnography. Analytic autoethnographers focus on developing theoretical explanations of broader social phenomena, whereas evocative autoethnographers focus on narrative presentations that open up conversations and evoke emotional responses (Hunt & Junco, 2006).

When Carolyn invited me (Laura) to coauthor this chapter, I accepted with enthusiasm, excited to be working with her again.

Perusing the *Handbook* prospectus, I chuckled at the irony of the two of us jointly constructing a story about the intersections between autoethnography and social constructionism once again. Those familiar with Carolyn's methodological novel on autoethnography (Ellis, 2004) might recognize me as the witty, weak-bladdered woman in Carolyn's qualitative methods seminar. Whereas Carolyn cheerfully explores my bodily weakness to add levity to her story, her discussion of my dissertation only hints at the lengthy, intense saga of my negotiation with her and my committee over the role autoethnography would play in my ethnographic construction of an interdisciplinary geriatric oncology team. Thankfully, the story had a happy ending; together we resisted the art–science dichotomy and embraced crystallization, a postmodern form of methodological triangulation that utilizes multiple methods of analysis and multiple genres of representation (Richardson, 2000). I combined narrative ethnography, grounded theory analysis, autoethnography, and feminist analyses into a single dissertation project, now revised into a book (Ellingson, 2005a). In this chapter, Carolyn and I continue that conversation, developing our conception of autoethnography as a constructionist project.

When I (Carolyn) asked Laura to coauthor this chapter with me, I hesitated at first as I thought about how insistent she had been in her dissertation on including everything but "the kitchen sink." She wanted to engage in crystallization and approach the oncology team she studied from a variety of perspectives. Her goal was to illuminate the socially constructed world of the team while simultaneously revealing the constructed nature of her multiple accounts of the team. Yes, perhaps I would have preferred at the time that Laura do it "my" way. Don't we all want to reproduce ourselves? But I also pride myself on helping students to find their particular and unique voices, especially if they are different from mine. I was leery of Laura's proposed project because I've discovered in my many years of directing dissertations that the main roadblock for students is that they try to do too much. Then they encounter difficulty doing any one thing deeply or thoroughly enough. Laura was among the very best students I had ever mentored, and I wanted her to succeed. Laura persevered, and I guess I shouldn't have been surprised, given that she was as astute at traditional analysis as she was talented as a narrative writer, that she pulled off an excellent dissertation that incorporated multiple perspectives and methods. In light of our experience, I thought she would be the perfect coauthor for this chapter.

In this chapter, we explore autoethnography as a social constructionist project. We want to resist the tendency to dichotomize and instead explore how autoethnography makes connections between seemingly polar opposites. Though we see it as a sign of progress that authors desire to tease out differences in autoethnographic projects, we argue that concentrating on dichotomies is counterproductive, given that autoethnography by definition operates as a bridge, connecting autobiography and ethnography in order to study the intersection of self and others, self and culture.

After further detailing in this chapter the limits of dichotomous thinking, we sketch the meanings and goals of autoethnography. We then discuss social constructionist concepts pertinent to autoethnography by deconstructing various methodological dichotomies.

The Limits of Dichotomous Thinking

I (Laura) often feel I am channeling Carolyn when I introduce the continuum of qualitative methods to my undergraduate qualitative students, so tied to our personal relationship is my knowledge of and passion for qualitative methods. I recall with fondness Carolyn's chart of qualitative research with the squiggly, broken line down the middle between the art and science sides. "Qualitative as art and qualitative as science," she says adamantly, "are endpoints of a continuum. You have to decide where you want to locate yourselves in terms of your identity and in every research project you do. That location will determine your goals, the procedures you use, and the claims you make" (Ellis, 2004, pp. 25–31, 359–363).

I address the limits of dichotomous thinking early in my qualitative methods course, right after introducing social constructionism as the epistemology that underlies the methodological continuum. "The central premise of social constructionism," I tell students, "is that meaning is not inherent. The central concerns of constructionist inquiry are to study what people 'know' and how they create, apply, contest, and act upon these ideas" (Harris, 2006, p. 225).

My undergraduate students sit with their desks arranged in a circle, faces not yet drooping with late-term fatigue but more than a few evidencing the mild resentment born of taking required courses. I discuss the politics of the field of qualitative research and how hotly contested many issues are within the field, referencing their reading of James Potter (1995). My students look at me with naked disbelief when I add with a smile, "And some of us actually care so deeply and passionately about this stuff that we have ongoing debates and dialogues and even get *mad* at each other sometimes!" The students shake their heads, mystified as to how anyone could care so much about such a topic.

Then I tell them that making sense of the world through dichotomous thinking is unproductive. "Dichotomies are pervasive in Western thinking," I add, warming to my topic, my excitement growing. The circle of students remains quite unexcited, but I continue.

"Knowledge is not 'out there' waiting to be found. Instead, we socially construct knowledge in relationships, through for-

mal channels, such as academic journals, and through informal, interpersonal interaction with others [Gergen, 1994]. Unfortunately, we are so schooled in some ways of thinking that we no longer notice how limiting those mental patterns can be. There are three ways in which dichotomies limit our thinking. You'll want to take notes on this and ask me questions if you don't understand, since this isn't in the reading, and it will be on the exam."

This last comment brings them to rapt attention, and they poise their pens above their notebooks as I explain.

"First, dichotomies present as opposites what are actually interdependent. Socially constructed opposites actually *depend* upon each other for existence; without women there would be no men, only people; without hard, there would be no soft, only a single texture.

"Second, dichotomies limit the possibilities to two and only two, negating the near-infinite possibilities present between any two poles. Thus we can resist the limitations of femininity and masculinity as mutually exclusive opposites and imagine them instead as poles between which there are many degrees of androgyny, blended identities, and possible performances of sex, gender, and sexuality.

"Finally, when we limit possibilities to only two, one will inevitably be valued over the other. It is not possible to view the world in terms of equal opposites; one side is *always already* privileged."

As I finish the statement I notice I am leaning forward, gesturing enthusiastically, my voice effortlessly projecting throughout the room. One of my students, a lovely young woman who works in my department office, looks up at my impassioned soliloquy and gives me an amused smile.

As my students dutifully scribble away, I think back to my own courses in qualitative methods with Carolyn, narrative inquiry and social constructionism courses with Art Bochner, and feminist theory and methods courses in women's studies, all of which challenged me to think beyond, through, and around accepted (dichotomous) norms for research and knowledge construction in academe. The fundamental axiom that culture and meaning are socially constructed undergirded my graduate coursework, opening up for me bountiful possibilities for challenging the taken-for-grantedness of everyday life. I try to offer my students the same.

I recall that Carolyn constructed qualitative methods not only as a continuum but as a passionate pursuit. "I love method, as you know," she reaffirmed in a recent e-mail. "I like to figure out the process of *how* to know. I am passionate about making methods dovetail with life as lived, rather than with rigid procedures." I couldn't have agreed more, and her enthusiasm reinfected me immediately. Though I don't have as much success teaching undergraduates to love qualitative methods in a 10-week quarter as Carolyn does teaching committed graduate students in her interpretive studies program, many of my students report that they find it at least palatable. I try to be content with that.

Both of us teach the entire continuum but locate ourselves between the middle and artistic ends. Carolyn more comfortably inhabits the near regions of the artistic pole than Laura does, and Laura indulges more often in systematic, middle-ground analyses than Carolyn does (e.g., Ellingson, 2002, in press-b; Ellis, 1995, 2002c). But Carolyn has done grounded analysis in the past (Ellis, 1986) and sometimes now grounds her narratives in theory and other voices (Ellis, 1998, 2000, 2002b), and Laura writes artistic narratives and often includes long portions of narrative in her grounded analysis pieces (Ellingson, 2003, 2005a).

Both of us write from a social constructionist perspective, which provides the epistemological underpinnings for autoethnography and other boundary-spanning qualitative methods we embrace (Gubrium & Holstein, 1997). Social constructionism,

we believe, is an approach particularly adept at challenging fundamental dichotomies, not only those in society in general but also those that structure traditional approaches to research, such as:

- Self–other
- Subject–object
- Humanities–social science
- Process–product
- Personal–political
- Emotional–rational
- Passionately involved–neutral
- Evocative–analytic

We view autoethnography as a social constructionist approach that enables critical reflection on taken-for-granted aspects of society, groups, relationships, and the self. Autoethnography becomes a space in which an individual's passion can bridge individual and collective experience to enable richness of representation, complexity of understanding, and inspiration for activism.

Defining Autoethnography

Autoethnography is research, writing, story, and method that connect the autobiographical and personal to the cultural, social, and political (Ellis, 2004, p. xix). It is the study of a culture of which one is a part, integrated with one's relational and inward experiences. The author incorporates the "I" into research and writing, yet analyzes self as if studying an "other" (Ellis, 2004; Goodall, 2000). Autoethnography displays multiple layers of consciousness, connecting the personal to the cultural. Autoethnographic texts appear in a variety of forms—short stories, poetry, fiction, novels, photographic essays, personal essays, journals, fragmented and layered writing, and social science prose. In these texts, the workings of the self are expressed emotionally, physically, and cognitively. These texts feature concrete action, emotion, embodiment, spirituality, and introspection, which appear as relational and institutional stories influenced by history, social structure, and culture, which themselves are revealed dialectically through action, feeling, thought, and language. Autoethnography portrays meaning through dialogue, scenes, characterization, and plot, claiming the conventions of literary writing (Ellis, 2004, p. xix; Ellis & Bochner, 2000).

Similar to many terms used by social scientists, the meanings and applications of *autoethnography* have evolved in a manner that makes precise definition difficult. We include under the broad rubric of autoethnography those studies that have been referred to by other similarly situated terms, such as: *personal narratives* (Personal Narratives Group, 1989), *narratives of the self* (Richardson, 1994), *personal experience narratives* (Denzin, 1989), *personal essays* (Krieger, 1991), *ethnographic short stories* (Ellis, 1995), *writing stories* (Richardson, 1997), *self-ethnography* (Van Maanen, 1995), *emotionalism* (Gubrium & Holstein, 1997), *radical empiricism* (Jackson, 1989), and many others (see Ellis & Bochner, 2000, pp. 739–740). Autoethnography is a blurred genre. Whether we call a work an *autoethnography* or an *ethnography* depends as much on the claims made by authors as anything else (Ellis & Bochner, 2000). We desire to be inclusive rather than exclusive, to focus on commonalities among terms and projects rather than differences. Autoethnography as a genre frees us to move beyond traditional methods of writing (Gergen & Gergen, 2002), promoting narrative and poetic forms, displays of artifacts, photographs, drawings, and live performances (Ellis, 2004). The predominant form consists of short stories written by researchers who systematically introspect and record their experience with the intent of evoking emotional response from readers. Thus autoethnographers connect the imaginative style of literature with the rigor of social science ethnography.

Autoethnographers vary in their emphasis on the writing and research process

(*graphy*), culture (*ethnos*), and self (*auto*) (Reed-Danahay, 1997, p. 2). Different exemplars of autoethnography fall at different places along the continuum of each of these three axes. For example, Laurel Richardson sees herself as a writer and focuses on *graphy*, often writing about writing (Richardson, 2000; Richardson & Lockridge, 2004). Carolyn often focuses on the self, and Laura often focuses on culture. In all these cases, however, the authors include all three dimensions in their works, and how much of each is included differs in the various projects they do.

Although some types of autoethnographic writing focus on the voice and point of view of the primary author (Jago, 2006; Kiesinger, 2002; Secklin, 2001; Spry, 1997), the genre also includes multivoiced narratives in which authors weave their stories with those of other participants (Boylorn, 2006; Drew, 2001; Ellingson, 2005a; Holman Jones, 1998) and coauthors (Ellis, Kiesinger, & Tillmann-Healy, 1997). Coconstructed narratives, interactive interviews, and interactive focus groups are variations of this interactive approach (Davis & Ellis, in press; Ellis & Bochner, 2000; Ellis et al., 1997). These techniques allow autoethnographers to more fully understand the lived experiences and relationship practices that occur in interaction with others and in groups and systems, as well as the multiple interpretations, experiences, and voices that emerge in lives and stories.

Autoethnography as a Social Constructionist Project

The practice of autoethnography presumes that reality is socially constructed and that meaning is constructed through symbolic (language) interaction (Berger & Luckmann, 1966). Presuming that reality is socially constructed enables autoethnographers to counter accepted claims about "the way things are" or "the way things always have been." As described earlier, autoethnography is a broad and wonderfully ambiguous category that encompasses a wide array of practices. As authors, we remain ever cognizant of how we participate in the social construction of the field of autoethnography by participating in this discourse that is both autoethnographic and about autoethnography.

On the one hand, we have much in common: Laura seeks multigenre crystallization in her work (Ellingson, 2005a), and Carolyn advocates that "analysis and story also can work together" (Ellis, 1993; Ellis & Bochner, 2006, p. 444). Laura learned about autoethnography from Carolyn, who mentored her throughout her PhD program and beyond, thus significantly influencing Laura's understanding of herself as an ethnographer and autoethnographer. On the other hand, our goals as researchers and authors often diverge. Carolyn publishes primarily personal autoethnographic narratives (e.g., Ellis, 1995), coconstructed narratives (e.g., Ellis & Bochner, 1992), and methodological commentaries for those who appreciate and work at the intersection of social sciences and humanities (e.g., Ellis et al., 1997), thus troubling the distinction between humanities and social sciences. Laura offers systematic qualitative analyses to more conventional social science audiences in health communication and family communication (Ellingson, 2002, 2003, in press-a; Ellingson & Sotirin, 2006), alongside her narrative and autoethnographic writing (Ellingson, 1998; 2005b), gleefully troubling the distinctions within genres of social science (Ellingson, 2005a).

Socially constructed categories such as autoethnography do not exist in a vacuum. Social institutions, laws and regulations, media, advocates representing various positions, and more make up the matrix in which ideas are created, maintained, and changed over time (Hacking, 1999). In no context is this more apparent than in universities and research institutions. Social constructionists posit that the conventional standards of scientific inquiry developed during the Enlightenment—to remain dis-

passionate, control the conditions, convert observations to numerals, search for *the* answer, and separate truth from practice—are rhetorically constructed to privilege the powerful elite and marginalize other voices (Gergen, 1999, pp. 91–93). Although not suggesting that such research is without value, Gergen counters its claims to a privileged status in the process of knowledge production.

Autoethnography developed in large part as a response to the alienating effects on both researchers and audiences of impersonal, passionless, abstract claims of truth generated by such research practices and clothed in exclusionary scientific discourse (Ellis, 2004). It attempts to disrupt and breach taken-for-granted norms of scientific discourse by emphasizing lived experience, intimate details, subjectivity, and personal perspectives. Thus autoethnography as a method participates in the ongoing social construction of research norms and practices at the same time that it seeks to influence the social construction of specific phenomena (e.g., child abuse; Hacking, 1999).

Troubling Dichotomies and Socially Constructing Alternative Research Modes

We now turn to a discussion of dichotomies that pervade research and explore how autoethnography troubles these divisions, often providing alternative modes of experiencing the process of research. We invite readers to think through and beyond polarities such as researcher–researched, objectivity–subjectivity, process–product, self–others, art–science, and personal–political.

Researcher–Researched

The researcher–researched dichotomy is undone, or at least unraveled, by autoethnographies in which the author becomes a participant and the author's experiences, emotions, and meanings become data for exploration. To a greater or lesser extent, researchers incorporate their personal experiences and standpoints in their research by starting with a story about themselves, explaining their personal connection to the project, or by using personal knowledge to help them in the research process (e.g., Holman Jones, 1998; Linden, 1992). Feminism contributed significantly to legitimizing the autobiographical voice associated with reflexive ethnography (e.g., Behar, 1996; Personal Narratives Group, 1989; Richardson, 1997).

Qualitative methodologists refer to the process of researching the self as introspection (Ellis, 1991b). Introspection involves the researcher in generating diaries, journals, freewriting, field notes, and narratives of his or her lived experiences, thoughts, and feelings, and then using these as data. "Resurrecting introspection (conscious awareness of awareness or self-examination) as a systematical sociological technique will allow social constructionists to examine emotion as a product of the individual processing of meaning as well as socially shared cognitions" (Ellis, 1991b, p. 23). I (Carolyn) used this technique to construct the experience of grief for my family, my neighbors, and myself in my story of my brother's sudden death:

> Even with the planning, we did not anticipate the effect seeing the flag-draped casket would have on my mother on Sunday night when our family went to the funeral home to receive friends. Silently, we walk through the bitter cold weather and into the funeral home. When my mother sees the casket, she screams, "My baby. Oh my baby is dead." She collapses to the floor, while the rest of us stand rooted to our spots. It is like a play rehearsal, and my mother has messed up her lines. In slow motion, we finally help her up and support her still sobbing to a chair. My once-powerful and imposing father looks helplessly on, confused, as someone approaches to remove his coat.
>
> Several hundred people have come to pay respects. [My brother] Art and I shake hands or hug each one, thank them for their expressions of sorrow, exchange light talk, smile, sometimes even laugh. "It is God's will." "God will look after him," they say to make us and themselves feel better. I nod. The same sentences are uttered over and over. It doesn't matter. There are no points for originality. (Ellis, 1993, pp. 720–721)

Using my own experiences, reflections and memories, I reconstructed myself and people emotionally close to me and to the tragic event I describe as a story told within the context of my ongoing relationships with family and friends. By looking inward for data, I, the researcher, became both the subject and object of research.

I (Laura) also turned an analytic lens on myself, but as part of a larger ethnographic project. I engaged in sensemaking about myself and my participants in my fieldwork in an interdisciplinary geriatric oncology program at a regional cancer center (Ellingson, 1998). I wrote a layered piece that was essentially an account of how I constructed an understanding of my relationship to the patients, their loved ones, and the staff, to whom I was a researcher and cancer survivor. Unlike Carolyn, I constructed accounts of patients I met only briefly and staff I knew but who were not part of my intimate circle. In order to explore connections among my own previous experiences as a cancer patient and my understanding of the people in the clinic in which I was conducting an ethnography, I both wrote narratives based on memories and reconstructed events based on accounts in my personal journals written at the time of my diagnosis and treatment for bone cancer: that is, "the process of opening inward [allowed] me to reach outward toward understanding" others (Berger, 2001, p. 515).

The following excerpt tells of spending Christmas in the hospital in Vermont while suffering from septicemia, a serious illness brought on by infection and the compromising of my immune system due to chemotherapy. After going out for lunch with my brother and father, I cry in my hospital bed:

Dad and Mark leave early to beat the storm home, and, with a lump in my throat, I watch them go. They take my presents with them, since I have no use for them in the hospital. *How can they leave? Why didn't Mom come? When will this end?* I think bitterly to myself that they all care, but then they get to go home. It is not their bodies pierced with needles. Too weak to make it to the toilet on crutches, having to use a bedpan. Schedule determined by blood counts and temperature. Leg aching, stomach queasy, buttocks numb from sitting in the bed day after day. Alone I lay flat on my back and stare at the ceiling all evening. My constant, silent tears creep slowly from the outer corners of my eyes and drip into my ears. (Ellingson, 1998, p. 506)

The inspiration for this story was a line in my journal, written at the lowest point of my spirits during treatment, in which I had written, "I discovered that when I cry while laying flat on my back, my tears drip into my ears." I analyzed my own experiences and joined them with my analysis of field notes of my participants. Through autoethnography, I demonstrated that the taken-for-granted demarcation between staff and patient is slippery, for all bodies bespeak vulnerability.

Objectivity–Subjectivity

Being labeled *subjective* or *biased*, as it is often called, commits the worst of the deadly sins within the positivists' worldview. Scientists socially constructed the rules of science centuries ago, and these rules remain entrenched in academic discourse and in Western societies in general. Supporters construct and present objectivity and subjectivity as a dichotomy with clear points of demarcation, and they prize objectivity and dismiss or even ridicule subjectivity. From a social constructionist perspective, objectivity is not fundamental or inherent in science but "is primarily a linguistic achievement that draws on the machine metaphor of human functioning" (Gergen, 1994, p. 165). Claiming objectivity does not make it so but rather signifies the power and authority of a

person or group to assert their particular perspective over that of other persons or groups. Because power and knowledge intricately intertwine, the authority to judge and label some knowledge as objective—and thus valuable—ensures that the powerful remain so, as knowledge disputing the status quo power relations is always already delegitimated (see Foucault, 1975).

Autoethnography interferes with this dichotomy by drawing blurry lines between detached, external knowledge and personal, internal knowledge. Much of the rhetorical force of this dichotomy lies in the invocation of objective accounts as rational and of subjective ones as emotional. In actual practice, however, reading emotions of self and other often forms a necessary precursor for rational action (Ellis, 1991a). Autoethnographers weave their own emotions into their research accounts and "plunge directly into the subjective fray, at times becoming passionately engrossed" (Gubrium & Holstein, 1997, p. 59).

For example, I (Laura) not only admit but celebrate my subjectivity. I wrote in an account of the geriatric oncology clinic:

While many confessional tales have as their goal the reassurance of the reader that their findings are "uncontaminated" and hence "scientific" and "valid" (Van Maanen, 1988), I have as my goal the opposite: to reassure the reader that my findings are *thoroughly* contaminated. This contamination with my own lived experience results in a rich, complex understanding of the staff and patients of the clinic in which I am observing (and of my own cancer experience). . . . For the first time, I now enter the oncology context with no immediate implications for my own health or that of a loved one. Yet, I do not study the patients and staff of the clinic with detachment; my own experiences as a patient filter what I see, hear, and feel. (Ellingson, 1998, p. 494)

In reclaiming contamination, I move beyond confessing my subjectivity to reveling in the possibilities of subjectivity for understanding a complex topic.

I (Carolyn) also eschew the objectivity–subjectivity dichotomy. In addition to advocating for the impossibility of detachment in research (Ellis, 2004), I demonstrate the importance of subjective understanding by allowing some narratives to stand on their own without any analysis, explanation, or contextualization within a field of research. For example, in a narrative about my mother's hospitalization, I tell of lovingly caring for her:

> Taking care of her feels natural, as though she is my child. The love and concern flowing between us feels like my mom and I are falling in love. The emotionality continues during the four days and nights I stay with her in the hospital. My life is devoted temporarily to her well-being. She knows it and is grateful. I am grateful for the experience. I do not mind that she is dependent on me. I am engrossed by our feeling, by the seemingly mundane but, for the moment, only questions that matter. Are you dizzy? In pain? Comfortable? Do you want to be pulled up in bed? (Ellis, 1996, p. 242)

This embodied tale provides concrete details of caring for an elderly parent. I do not attempt to establish distance from the experience. My sensemaking is visceral and in the moment. I tell the tale as I understand it so that others can experience the particularity of my experience through my story. My choice to publish an openly personal (read: subjective) story without the scaffolding of detachment that frames most qualitative work, including much autoethnography—theories, reviews of literature, methodological details—radically refuses to reify the opposition of objectivity and subjectivity. In so doing, I celebrate the individual's view as sufficient for making meaning, and I participate in troubling the taken-for-grantedness of the objectivity–subjectivity dichotomy in research.

Process–Product

Autoethnography encompasses both process—what one does—and product—what one gets after it is done. Autoethnography reflexively celebrates and often explicitly integrates processes into the product (Ellis,

2004). Revealing and interrogating the processes of research is critical to autoethnography and counters the historical imperative to obscure the details of the construction of research findings using sanitizing strategies such as passive voice (e.g., *the data were collected; it was found that*) (Gergen, 1994; Richardson, 2000). In the field, during solitary introspection, and/or while participating in interactive reflection with others, autoethnographers engage in embodied action, not just report on distant processes (Ellingson, 2006). Often this takes the form of revealing the researcher's complex role in a study of a specific context and of acknowledging the messiness and mistakes that inevitably imbue the process of conducting such research.

Ethnographers—Laura included—tend to want to publish the most credible and persuasive version of our stories when we seek to influence policy, practice, and/or theory (Ellingson, in press-a). Hence we often sanitize our accounts, omitting missteps as irrelevant, tangential, or overly personal; historically, such confessional tales were kept separate from authoritative accounts of research (Tedlock, 1991; Van Maanen, 1988). Granted, we take a risk when we combine confessions of embarrassing moments with passionate calls for social, political, and professional change based on our findings; many will dismiss out of hand work that admits to a messy process (see Ellingson, 2005a, in press-a). However, when we pretend that research progresses smoothly, we provide inaccurate and deceptively simplistic maps for those who read our work. In addition to field work, the writing of accounts of our work also reflects an embodied, messy process that is inextricably bound to the final products of our research.

For example, here I (Laura) give a glimpse of the story of writing my ethnography of the geriatric oncology clinic:

> I have *had* it with my body. I am sick to *death* of laying around my little house recovering from my knee replacement surgery and trying to write with my laptop balanced precariously on

my uneven lap . . . to write so personally about my understanding of the clinic seems impossible from the primarily prone, pain-filled position I grudgingly inhabit these days. Somehow, I can engage in systematic and detached writing, but the combination of my physical pain and the psychic wounds that accompany it are so fresh, so immediate, that attempting to dig into my body memories for insights is like rubbing salt into open wounds. Unwelcome memories of the repeated violations of my body . . . surface every time a wave of nausea hits or the pain spikes. I have no energy for embodiment right now. (Ellingson, 2005a, pp. 77–78)

Of course, my example also illustrates a profound resistance to the socially constructed mind–body dichotomy that deeply influences Western cultures. Social constructionists do not deny that material bodies exist apart from discourse but argue that their meanings are inseparable: "bodies are not only constrained or damaged but also constituted by discursive relations, social practices, and historical processes" (Ziarek, 2005, p. 88). My body always forms part of the process of research, and openly discussing how that happens troubles the process–product divide.

In more personal-focused autoethnography, the process of constructing the tale may be alluded to or included explicitly. I (Carolyn) tell the story of sharing with my mother a narrative I had written about our relationship (Ellis, 2001). The story chronicles my mother's verbal and nonverbal reactions to hearing the former story I had written about taking care of her. Then, in an italicized parallel narrative interwoven into the story, I reflect upon my own reactions to sharing the story with my mother:

As I read this to her, I notice tears in her eyes. I think again of how difficult it is to know what to say in these situations. I also think that bluntly acknowledging that she may never get better might be difficult for both of us. Our relationship, to some extent, is based on joy. I come home to make her feel better, and it usually works. Yes, perhaps feeling better might mean accepting the pain and living the best life

she can in spite of it. Certainly, I don't want her to feel like she has to play down the pain or pretend to think she will get better just to make me feel good. Or do I? Do I want a relationship based upon reality and truth? Could I stand it? . . . I know there will come a time when she and I will have this conversation. But not yet. (Ellis, 2001, p. 604)

The account of modifying my story as I read it to my mother displays the usually hidden processes of adapting to one's audience and considering the effects of one's words upon those who are characters in my stories. Moving beyond merely using active voice and owning one's own involvement in research processes, I resist the process–product dichotomy by highlighting the processes that led to the product, thus destabilizing the product as a fixed interpretation of an event and opening up possibilities for multiple understandings. I try to show how research findings, as well as hope and truth, are socially constructed in relationships, and how negotiation might change as the research and illness progress. I also show what I learned about the product from focusing on the process of research.

Self–Others

In social constructionist theory, the self exists only in relation to others. The self is not a discrete, individual, fixed entity as promoted in Enlightenment philosophy but connected to others for understanding. We understand the self "not as an individual's personal and private cognitive structure but as *discourse* about the self—the performance of languages available in the public sphere . . . the self as narrative rendered intelligible within ongoing relationships" (Gergen, 1994, p. 185; see also Holstein & Gubrium, 2000). Autoethnography points to the self as embedded in cultural meanings. Doing autoethnography affects the social construction of the author's self. People make sense of their experiences through the stories they develop about them (Bruner, 1990). These stories are continually altered, never static; we can retell them in ways that make them fit better the "I" who tells them (see Jago, 2006). Doing autoethnography affects individuals who do the work of "re-storying" their lives; the autoethnographic story becomes part of the life, an element of the ongoing construction of self. At times the story stands in for the experience itself and becomes what one remembers as the experience (Ellis, 2004).

Often autoethnographies feature stories of resistance to stigmatizing labels. As Kenneth Gergen (2006) suggests, "When one commits to the dominant logics, values, and sanctioned patterns of action within a group, it is often at the expense of hushed but valued impulses to the contrary" (p. 122). Giving voice to those hushed impulses becomes a political act because language is indeterminate and imbued with power relations. Autoethnography troubles the socially constructed categories by showing how they play out in the world and how we incorporate them into our identities—or do not. "Ways of classifying human beings interact with the human beings who are classified" (Hacking, 1999, p. 31). Hacking calls this an "interactive" kind of classification, as those who are classified modify their behaviors and beliefs because they are affected by the classification label (as opposed to labeling an element as iron, which causes no change in the element's particles).

The process can work both ways, as Carolyn demonstrates in her story about the role of personal details and analysis in her study of minor bodily stigma:

> I doubt that I would have been able to move outside the category of minor bodily stigmas without first immersing myself in it. Categories too often limit us without our being aware of their influence; once we are aware, too often we assume there is no use in trying to break through them. Telling and analyzing my personal story not only helped generate and make visible the category of minor bodily stigma, it also provided a way through. The categorical story offered a name to my experiences where

before there was only dread; the personal story connected real people with feelings to the labels, where before there were only tactics of concealment and denial. This research helped me understand the inextricable connections between categorical and personal knowledge. (Ellis, 1998, p. 535)

Often labels become essentialized, taken as inherent to a group instead of recognized as socially constructed (Ziarek, 2005). Focusing on individual narratives of self-categorization troubles the naturalness of such categories.

Collaborative self-making, such as that which occurs in interactive interviews and focus groups, provides another opportunity in autoethnography to produce meaning that is "neither subjective nor objective but *intersubjective*" (Onyx & Small, 2001, p. 775, original emphasis). In interactive research, participants act in an equal relationship as coresearchers with other authors/researchers, share authority, and author their own lives in their own voices. The group helps each member to construct the self. These approaches give us a way to include the voice and feedback of all participants (Hawes, 1994; Reed-Danahay, 2001) and to understand how participants "assign meaning to their realities," rather than how we as researchers evaluate their realities (Daly, 1992, p. 8; see also Davis & Ellis, in press).

Bringing the idea of interactive interviews to traditional focus groups, Carolyn, Cris Davis, and associates (Davis, Ellis, Myerson, Poole, & Smith-Sullivan, 2006) have developed a methodological approach called *interactive focus groups*. More than simply a large interactive interview, this method borrows characteristics from traditional focus groups and other methods, such as interactive interviewing (Ellis et al., 1997; Holstein & Gubrium, 1995), interactive group interviews (Patton, 2002), leaderless discussion groups (Stewart & Shamdasani, 1990), and the therapy practice of reflecting teams (e.g., Andersen, 1987, 1995). In an ongoing project on re/claiming middle age, Carolyn and four other women—all middle-aged (45–60 years old) white professionals—discuss aging for women in 2006. These conversations take place in interactive focus groups.

> "I think that women like us are socially constructing a different story [from our mothers]," Mary says. "We're not buying the canonical story about what it's like to be an older woman."
>
> Carolyn interjects, "What was one of the first conversations everyone had when we first walked in the door?"
>
> Kendall laughs. "Oh my age, oh my this, oh my allergies. My innards are so, blah, blah blah."
>
> "Right," Carolyn says. She turns to Marilyn. "Look what we talk about when we go walking every week."
>
> Marilyn and Carolyn respond together. "How are your aches and pains today?"
>
> "Yeah," Carolyn says, "and it feels a lot like the conversations I used to hear my mother have." (Davis et al., 2006, p. 10)

As researchers and participants, we probe the prevailing social constructions of middle-aged women and debate how such constructions reflect and do not reflect our lived realities as women.

The highlighting of process in autoethnography complements the work that the product, or representation, does in the world—in academia and beyond. "Human science inquiry is itself a form of social action. Knowledge and application are not fundamentally separable" (Gergen, 1994, p. 140). Readers take a more active role as they are invited into the author's world, as feelings are evoked about the events being described, and as they are stimulated to use what they learn there to reflect on, understand, and cope with their own lives. Autoethnographers write meaningfully and evocatively about topics that matter and that may make a difference, include sensory and emotional experience (Shelton, 1995), and write from an ethic of care and concern (Denzin, 1997; Richardson, 1997). Carolyn invites readers to connect and identify with

her and even to be inspired by her to write their own stories:

> I provide my story as an incentive for you to put your own into words, compare your experience to mine, and find companionship in your sorrow (Mairs, 1993). I speak my story so that you feel liberated to speak yours without feeling guilty that others suffered more and therefore your story is not worth telling, your feelings unjustified. I believe we each need to find personal and collective meaning in the events that have transpired and in the disrupted and chaotic lives left behind. (Ellis, 2002b, p. 378)

Autoethnography intentionally blurs the lines between self and others, between the author's particular experiences and the universality of those same experiences. Whereas autoethnographies of tragic and painful or at least difficult circumstances, such as most of Carolyn's and Laura's work, emphasize making meaning and forging connections, others call to joy and playfulness, to making connections with autoethnographers who want to share positive experiences as opportunities for others to celebrate their own strengths, successes, and pleasures (e.g., Drew, 2001; Ellis, 2006; Lockford, 2004; Tillmann-Healy, 2001). It may be that we feel the connection between ourselves and others most readily in the wake of pain, fear, and loss, but we also construct our positive meanings in relationship to others.

Art–Science

In the writing of evocative accounts, autoethnographers blend analysis and narrative, troubling the socially constructed chasm between science and the arts (Ellis, 2004). The choice of a genre influences perception of the audience regardless of the intended meaning of the piece:

> for the constructionist, there is good reason to be concerned with the form of writing . . . our accounts of the world are not maps of the

world, but operate performatively, to do things with others. [We ask] what kind of world do we build together through our forms of inscription? (Gergen, 1999, p. 185)

Autoethnographers seek to build a world, largely within the academy but also beyond, in which art and science do not exist as a rigid and fixed dichotomy but instead form a continuum of practices. Rather than opposing traditional social science, most autoethnographers (Carolyn and Laura among them) instead choose to engage in productive play with social science writing and research conventions, shedding light on the constructed nature of the art–science dichotomy and casting doubt on its inevitability or exclusive claims to truth.

One way to accomplish that goal involves framing a narrative in a discussion of research and theory before and/or after the narrative as I (Carolyn) did in writing about my brother's death. I followed the story with an analysis of surviving the accidental death of a loved one and a discussion of my desire to reposition social scientists and their readers closer to literature. I wrote:

> This article brings ["after death"] into the open, allowing us to converse about and try to understand it. As such it accomplishes what Rorty (1982) says we should expect from social scientists—"to act as interpreters for those with whom we are not sure how to talk." . . . This is, after all, what we "hope for from our poets and dramatists and novelists" (Rorty, 1982, p. 202). . . . I seek to reposition readers vis á vis the authors of texts of social science research, evoking feeling and identification as well as cognitive processing. As you read this story, some of you may have felt empathy with me, as you would in watching a "true-to-life" movie; some of you may have been reminded of parallels in your own lives, as in reading a good novel. Perhaps reading my work evoked in you emotional experience that you could then examine, or led to recall of other emotional situations in which you have participated. Acknowledging a potential for optional readings gives readers license to take part in an experience that can reveal to them not only how it was for me (the au-

thor), but how it could be or once was for them. (Ellis, 1993, pp. 725–726)

Laura's social science autoethnographies usually contain citations to other academics and use an academic, disciplinary vocabulary. Layered accounts (Ronai, 1995) move back and forth between academic prose and narrative, revealing their constructed nature through the juxtaposition of social science and narrative ways of knowing. In her ongoing ethnography of an outpatient dialysis unit, Laura experiments with layering poetic representation of interview transcript excerpts with academic discussion of the social construction of professionalism in health care to explore the knowledge construction of the dialysis technicians. Medical professionals whose formal education far exceeds that of the technicians largely ignore or even scorn these paraprofessionals' expertise. Technicians resemble artisans, with a great deal of hands-on, tactile knowledge that is vital to caregiving but difficult to transmit.

One poem, entitled "Joking Around," describes how the technicians adapt to the preferences of the patients they work with over long periods of time:

> Yeah, you joke around with him, 'cause I
>   remember when he first came
> to this clinic, he was
> well to me he still is,
> a grumpy old man
> . . .
> It took me a week or so until I figured
> him out.
> Give him a bad time.
> Argue with him
> and it makes him happy. That's him.
> You've got to be   I hate to say it
> To him it's not disrespectful, but
> you got to be
> kind of like disrespectful towards him
> and speak to him   basically in his own
>   language
> in order for him to be happy.
> And he has to complain
> to be happy   ha ha
> Oh I love that old man.

He's one of those patients that when it's
    time
for him to go   it's gonna hurt.
And other patients it's "Yes ma'am, No
    ma'am"
'cause that's the way they want it and
with no joking around. (Ellingson, 2007)

These excerpts from the poem reflect my editing of the technician's words and, as such, reveal my views of his role in the dialysis unit. I constructed the poem to show what I appreciated about this man—his earthy charm, innate kindness and gentleness, what I perceived to be his sincere attempts to serve his patients "as a professional." This blurring of the boundaries of art and science in my writing enriches readers' understanding of the culture of this dialysis unit.

Personal–Political

The impetus for arguing that something is socially constructed generally arises when a phenomenon appears to be natural and inevitable (Hacking, 1999). Feminists have long argued that the personal is political. Resisting the dichotomy of what should be private and what should be public, what is an individual issue and what is a matter for the collective to address, often figures prominently in autoethnography. Autoethnographers address issues such as child sexual abuse (Ronai, 1995), bulimia (Tillman-Healy, 1996), the ravages of irritable bowel syndrome (Defenbaugh, in press), and the death of a parent (Berger, 1997), bringing painful, intimate topics to share with others. Many times autoethnography sheds light on uncomfortable issues that others wish would remain hidden.

The article I (Carolyn) coauthored with my partner Art on our abortion experience exemplifies the politics of a personal choice and the personal implications of a hotly contested political issue. We wrote:

No doubt, other persons who have faced abortion have felt the sense of not knowing how to feel about or interpret what was happening to them. Others surely have been as bruised as we were by the contradictions and ambivalence associated with the constraints of choice. The absence of personal narratives to detail the emotional complexities and ambivalence often attributed generally to abortion . . . may be only the result of people feeling forced to accept these blows of fate passively or being subjected to taboos against expressing these disturbing feelings openly. Because abortion may still be deemed immoral . . . it can become nearly impossible to find the words to talk about what happened. Making public and vivid some of the intricate details of abortion may break the barriers that shield public awareness and prevent marginalized voices of both women and men from being heard. (Ellis & Bochner, 1992, p. 99)

As narrators and performers of this story, we gained a perspective on our experience and a sense of what it meant that we did not have before. The responses of others to our performance and text strongly suggest that they have been moved to feel and think about themselves and others in new and important ways and to grasp and feel the ambivalence, confusion, and pain associated with experiences of abortion such as ours. The response to the content of this story has been both positive and negative, which of course met our intent of opening up conversations, though it remains difficult to hear some of the condemning remarks.

Bodily details are certainly another one of those personal details that many people would rather not know. I (Laura) include many of those in my book on an interdisciplinary team, showing my experiences as a cancer patient receiving chemotherapy, using my own suffering to connect me to the patients and hospital where I did my research. For example:

A sharp pain in my lower abdomen startled me into wakefulness and I groaned in recognition. I searched the bed for my nurse-call button and pushed it. Glancing over at the rapidly dripping IV line, I cursed the need for continuous hydration to save my kidneys from the onslaught of toxic chemicals that was injected in that morning. The bone cancer had left my right leg a mess of grafts, stitches, and staples; there was no way I could get out of the bed, find my crutches, and hobble to the bathroom without losing control of my bladder. I was beyond exhaustion, and by the time I woke up, my bladder was so full it hurt. I'd have to wait for my nurse, Chris, to bring a bed pan. . . . The hot yellow liquid streamed from my urethra without my consent and the searing flames of shame swept over my face. Defeated, I let the tears flow with the urine. My pelvic muscles relaxed gratefully even as my buttocks cringed in retreat from the growing wetness that surrounded them. (Ellingson, 2005a, p. 87)

We engage in political work when we openly discuss bodily details that society tells us are shameful, for we resist the social imperative to remain ashamed and hence complicit in our powerlessness (Mairs, 1997).

We embrace troubling the taken-for-grantedness of the world in order to give voice to oppression and move people to action or new beliefs and understandings. Yet social constructionist projects such as autoethnography are not inherently liberating; material realities do not change simply because we reveal their origins and sociopolitical complexities; poverty, for example, may be shown to be socially constructed as being the fault of the poor, but noting unjust portrayals does nothing to alleviate the crushing oppression of poverty. People must be in a position to benefit from the critical analysis offered by autoethnography and other critical methods: "Social construction theses are liberating chiefly for those who are on the way to being liberated . . . [those] whose consciousness has already been raised" (Hacking, 1999, p. 2). Some methods claim liberation as an explicit intent of their project: Practitioners of the memory-work method suggest it "is thus explicitly liberationist in its intent" (Onyx & Small, 2001, p. 774). The connection between intention and action may blur, however.

Ian Hacking (1999) describes six "grades" of commitment invoked by different constructionist projects. His continuum spans from *historical* constructionism, which analyzes a phenomenon and posits that it is the result of historical events and social processes and hence not inevitable, through *revolutionary* constructionism that overtly moves beyond writing and "the world of ideas" (1999, p. 20) to strive to bring about concrete change in the world. Autoethnography may reflect any grade of commitment to change. Many people's lives have been transformed through the process of composing their own stories and of hearing those of others; others have been moved to action through telling and reading personal narratives (Ellis, 2002a). Thus autoethnography certainly can be one tool in the social change tool box, particularly in its potential to spark creative and productive discourse. Dialogue moves us toward constructing a better world (Gergen, 2006). Many, if not most, researchers publish autoethnography in academic outlets. Those who seek broader audiences and revolutionary social change may need to move beyond traditional academic outlets, such as journals, handbooks, and edited collections, to mainstream outlets, such as trade and popular books.

Could Dichotomies Be Useful?: A Concluding Dialogue

Carolyn: Laura, after cowriting this chapter with you, I was thinking about how dichotomies come to seem so natural and inevitable; "the reality of everyday life is taken for granted *as* reality" (Berger & Luckmann, 1966, p. 23). We seldom notice how often we invoke these socially constructed norms within social science simply because they are so foundational to our sense of methodological reality. While autoethnography troubles taken-for-granted dichotomies, this method can also reinscribe them.

You operate primarily in the large middle ground of the methodological continuum, so nondichotomous thinking may be to your advantage. For me, working on the humanities end, which traditional ethnographers view as more marginal, that might be less true. Politically, it might be smart for me to encourage people to think in terms of dichotomies, at least for a while, because it brings focus to what I do. For example, Leon Anderson's (2006) article, which views analytic and evocative autoethnographies as dichotomous, actually had the unintended consequence of calling the attention of an audience of realist ethnographers to the kind of autoethnography I do. It provided a venue for autoethnographers to speak back and "claim" territory, which is important in this phase of the interpretive "social movement" going on in ethnographic circles. The resistance of Art [Bochner] and me to the realists' attempt to claim and rename autoethnography put us in the center of the debate. We have something other, more mainstream ethnographers want. I recognize this as dichotomous thinking, but I still think it can be useful as long as we see it for what it is—a political strategy rather than necessarily useful for knowledge production.

Laura: You're arguing for strategic essentialism a la Gayatri Spivak (1988), who suggests that we can't fight for women's (or other groups') rights if we unrelentingly deconstruct the category of women. Thus you can't uphold the value of what you do as an autoethnographer if you can't define it and stake some territory.

Carolyn: I believe that. But we need not have a rigid definition of autoethnography, in terms of what's included and what's excluded from the category (Ellis, 2004). Autoethnography is an evolving and fluid approach. But to call a work autoethnography means it should share at least some, if not all, of the most important elements of the category—a focus on personal story, evocation, and narrative writing. Anderson's conception of autoethnography didn't em-

phasize any of these. I am concerned that those in power positions or who fear losing relative power may try to appropriate autoethnography primarily by watering it down so much that it is unrecognizable and thus no longer potentially challenging to their definitions of what is included in ethnography and what is not.

Laura: I recognize the political necessity of challenging existing power structures and their policing of disciplinary and methodological boundaries (Blair, Brown, & Baxter, 1994). But relying on existing dichotomies to take our stand concedes most of the ground to those in power before we even begin. As Audre Lorde (1984) explained, "The master's tools will never dismantle the master's house" (p. 110). Reifying positivist dichotomies in order to challenge the socially constructed boundaries of methodological legitimacy seems no more effective as a dismantling strategy. The question for me becomes, then, how do we help everyone to stake their ground—including my boundary spanning, crystallizing ground—in ways that go beyond defining our stories dichotomously—as *not* analysis, our analysis as *not* loose or weak, our personal details as *not* distant, our grounded theory as *not* merely one case?

This recalls Gergen's ideas about how we define things in opposition. Scholars understand the positivist rules of social science primarily through what they exclude—subjectivity, intimacy, stories, and so on—and autoethnographers have challenged these socially constructed standards by flagrantly violating them (Gergen, 1999). I can see why that is helpful. When Leon uses the analytic versus evocative dichotomy, he enables you to speak up for your position. However, this also recollects what I said about how dichotomies present as opposites what are actually interdependent for meaning. Thus we cannot have autoethnography if there isn't realist ethnography for contrast.

Carolyn: Though the realists would like to think they can have realist ethnography without autoethnography because they think realist ethnography *is* ethnography and autoethnography, if it should exist at all, would be subsumed under their label. That's what can happen if we don't honor dichotomies, I'm afraid. We all become one category, like women all used to be lumped under *mankind*, and masculine pronouns stood for all of us.

I think nuanced disagreement is important. Don't new ways of thinking come out of this kind of dialogue? And aren't things sometimes improved with new paradigms that address gaps and holes that older paradigms ignore or miss? Conflict can be useful; it can point the way for change. Sometimes it's productive to get our dander up, feel a little angry, and be determined to show the value of our position. You might argue that adrenaline could limit our perspective, but I also think feeling revved up about something can help us do deeper work. I feel that's been the case for me.

Besides, too much lukewarm agreement, which I predict would happen if we gave up entirely on dichotomies, would interfere with the word games that academics like to play. Sometimes when I argue with realists over meanings, I wonder if that's all we're doing—acting as wordsmiths. I don't know how important these games are in the whole scheme of things. Sometimes I think this kind of debate isn't really important at all, except to protect the few measly resources represented in the struggle. I doubt word mining and position defending contribute to making the world a better place. Maybe these disagreements simply entertain us until rigor mortis sets in.

Laura: I'm not sure how entertaining they are. In the beginning of autoethnography, it made sense to harness that adrenaline to reinforce the differences—and hence value—inherent in our position. Someone else had all the methodological power, and so we began by getting angry and critiquing them to stake our ground. Feminists started with similar opposition—race scholars, queer theorists, and now autoethnographers have,

too. But haven't we already made the case that autoethnography is useful, meaningful, and legitimate? What comes after anger and defensiveness? Shouldn't we explore interdependency instead of opposition?

Carolyn: That sounds good in theory, but in practice it's difficult because the goals of autoethnographers and realists are different. To be interdependent we have to agree on goals for our research, or at least agree that it is legitimate and worthwhile to have different goals. Autoethnographers honor meaning, intelligibility, and interpretation as their goals, whereas the realists look more to facts and representation. Given these differences, it's hard to agree on how to go about achieving our purposes (Bochner, 1985). Then there's also power politics.

This conversation makes me laugh, because I'm usually the "let's get along" and "here are the ways in which we overlap rather than divide" person, and you're more into power politics. Now we've switched sides. I've become more watchful. I don't want to give in to people who then, instead of meeting me halfway, view my giving in as a weakness and an opportunity to control my voice with theirs.

I try not to think in terms of power politics, but I also know that if I ignore that reality, I stand to lose a lot of ground. Granted, my work has flourished from my concentrating on what I do well, rather than defending it and debating with people who criticize what I do. But sometimes that debate becomes important, because many graduate students and young professors need senior scholars to take a position and speak back, to help them in their quest for their autoethnographic projects to be taken seriously. So sometimes I think we need to come on strong and show that we're not going to roll over and play dead. We're resisting encroachment and defending what we care about. But I'm aware that this position is inconsistent with what I've argued in the past and has its consequences, such as conflict with people who have more similarities with me than differences.

Laura: Exactly. Perhaps the first step toward mutual accommodation with productive, collaborative debate is to find a language of interdependency to replace or at least augment the language of war and opposition. You present something along this line in your response to Bill Tierney, who critiqued autoethnography (Ellis, 2002a).

Carolyn: Yes—I suggested that we respond to critique with "yes, and . . . " rather than "yes, but. . . ."

Laura: Yes, and a language of interdependency would explain how autoethnography *needs* realist ethnography, how stories *call out* for theory, how theories *require* specific cases. We need to surrender the battle metaphors about "laying claim," "seizing ground," "defending our turf," and "giving power" to the other side and imagine new ways of relating—sharing the loaf, swimming alongside each other, planting a bountiful garden with many varieties of fruits, vegetables, and flowers, and so on. The use of warlike metaphors fosters an equation of argument with violence (Lakoff & Johnson, 1980). Because "through language an entire world can be actualized" (Berger & Luckmann, 1966, p. 39), we should consider carefully the implications of our choice to actualize a pervasively violent world. I don't want to suggest that we pretend there is no conflict but that we introduce language into our debates that offers some hope of accommodation rather than merely reinvoking the same old power struggle over who's right and who's wrong.

Carolyn: Part of a solution is to see oneself as interdependent with members of a relevant community, such as the community of ethnographers. For example, in the response to Anderson (Ellis & Bochner, 2006), I pointed out commonalities among all of us who do ethnography, no matter how we label ourselves. I worry sometimes that we aren't accomplishing as much as we could if all ethnographers joined together and thought of themselves as a community with multiple shared goals and mutual standards.

That would make us a stronger coalition against the positivists, with whom we have more differences than we do with each other. Of course, that just changes the oppositional group.

Laura: I'd like to know if it is possible to stand *next to* the positivists rather than *against* them.

Carolyn: I'm not sure we have enough in common with them, or they with us, to make standing next to each other a worthwhile goal.

Laura: Aren't you and I the perfect example? Within the context of our relationship, we care deeply about each other. We stand together. Yet we do different work, and we disagree, if not on what is legitimate, then on priorities, on what is most valuable and worthy of spending our time on. This realization pained me at first, because I not only cared about you but also wanted you to be proud of me. Perhaps it disappointed you as well. But we moved past that and constructed a way of relating that celebrates our commonalities and respects our differences. As in our relationship, methodologists could address differences of opinion by making room for commonalities *and* differences (oh no—is that dichotomy!?). I don't want to sound hopelessly optimistic, and I know material outcomes are at stake (like tenure).

Carolyn: You and I get along because we love and respect each other but also because we see ourselves as having more commonalities than differences in the areas that matter. We are both academics, ethnographers, social scientists, communication scholars, women, responsible people, and so on. Besides, you're not a positivist! Just kidding. Our differences really don't amount to much. What's more interesting to me is when the differences *do* matter. If you wrote a piece that attacked autoethnography, then our differences would be more salient. The same might be true if I attacked the work you do, which is some of what you felt in the initial stages of your dissertation. It's not as though our work and relationships can't survive some criticism and disagreement; they can. And sometimes they're enhanced as a result, as I said before. But if all we hear is critique, especially disrespectful critique . . . well, it has an effect. At some point, it would be nice to show some appreciation for the work of others. Maybe academics just don't show enough respect for what those doing different work are achieving. We're schooled in the "shootout at the OK Corral" mode. That's hard to get rid of—try as we might—for us as well as "them."

Laura: I agree that more traditional researchers seldom express respect for autoethnographers, at least not overtly, and many offer criticism. And I am continually amazed by how much casual bashing of others' work I hear in the hallways at conferences (let alone in sessions), by people ranging all across the methodological continuum. Perhaps I find this particularly painful because my work spans a larger than average chunk of the continuum, leaving me vulnerable to critique from a great number of positions. I am left to ponder, could we move past tolerance to appreciation of differences? And can we do that without reinforcing dichotomies? Maybe not. Maybe I'm too idealistic, and dichotomies really are needed for clarification and debate.

Carolyn: No, don't give up that easily. We need the large, messy middle ground to hold us all together, and right now I feel pretty messy. This conversation makes me aware that I can and often do construct my position about dichotomies from both sides . . . I mean, at numerous points along the continuum. While I see this kind of questioning and messiness as functional for helping me think through what's going on, it's not a strength that is appreciated often in the academy. The academy rewards us for "taking and defending a position." Maybe that's what leads to dichotomies—the push to take a position, make a case, defend our work.

Laura: As you know, I'm happiest in the messy middle ground. Do you think we can ever find a peaceful academic corral to replace the oppositional "shootout" one?

Carolyn: I surely hope so. But wait a second. . . .

Laura and Carolyn (Together): Oh, no, isn't that another dichotomy?

• References

Andersen, T. (1987). The reflecting team: Dialogue and metadialogue in clinical work. *Family Process, 26,* 415–428.

Andersen, T. (1995). Reflecting processes: Acts of informing and forming. In S. Friedman (Ed.), *The reflecting team in action: Collaborative practice in family therapy* (pp. 11–37). New York: Guilford Press.

Anderson, L. (2006). Analytic autoethnography. *Journal of Contemporary Ethnography, 35*(4), 373–395.

Atkinson, P., Coffey, A., Delamont, S., Lofland, J., & Lofland, L. (Eds.). (2001). *Handbook of ethnography.* Thousand Oaks, CA: Sage.

Behar, R. (1996). *The vulnerable observer: Anthropology that breaks your heart.* Boston: Beacon Press.

Berger, L. (1997). Between the candy store and the mall: The spiritual loss of a father. *Journal of Personal and Interpersonal Loss, 2,* 397–409.

Berger, L. (2001). Inside out: Narrative autoethnography as a path toward rapport. *Qualitative Inquiry, 7,* 504–518.

Berger, P., & Luckmann, T. (1966). *The social construction of reality.* Garden City, NY: Doubleday.

Blair, C., Brown, J. R., & Baxter, L. A. (1994). Disciplining the feminine. *Quarterly Journal of Speech, 80,* 383–409.

Bochner, A. (1985). Perspectives on inquiry: Representation, conversation, and reflection. In M. Knapp & G. Miller (Eds.), *Handbook of personal communication* (pp. 27–58). Beverly Hills, CA: Sage.

Bochner, A., & Ellis, C. (1999). Which way to turn? *Journal of Contemporary Ethnography, 28,* 485–499.

Boylorn, R. (2006). E pluribus unum (Out of many, one). *Qualitative Inquiry, 12,* 651–680.

Bruner, J. (1990). *Acts of meaning.* Cambridge, MA: Harvard University Press.

Daly, K. (1992). The fit between qualitative research and characteristics of families. In J. Gilgun, K. Daly, & G. Handel (Eds.), *Qualitative methods in family research* (pp. 3–11). Newbury Park, CA: Sage.

Davis, C., & Ellis, C. (in press). Emergent methods in autoethnographic research. In S. Nagy Hesse-Biber & P. Leavy (Eds.), *The handbook of emergent methods.* New York: Guilford Press.

Davis, C., Ellis, C., Myerson, M., Poole, M., & Smith-Sullivan, K. (2006, November). *The menopause club: Five hot middle-aged women sitting around talking about their bodies.* Paper presented at the conference of the National Communication Association, San Antonio, TX.

Defenbaugh, N. (in press). "Under erasure": The absent "ill" body in doctor–patient dialogue. *Qualitative Inquiry.*

Denzin, N. (1989). *Interpretive biography.* Newbury Park, CA: Sage.

Denzin, N. (1997). *Interpretive ethnography: Ethnographic practices for the 21st century.* Thousand Oaks, CA: Sage.

Drew, R. (2001). *Karaoke nights: An ethnographic rhapsody.* Walnut Creek, CA: AltaMira Press.

Ellingson, L. L. (1998). "Then you know how I feel": Empathy, identification, and reflexivity in fieldwork. *Qualitative Inquiry, 4,* 492–514.

Ellingson, L. L. (2002). The roles of companions in the geriatric oncology patient–interdisciplinary health care provider interaction. *Journal of Aging Studies, 16,* 361–382.

Ellingson, L. L. (2003). Interdisciplinary health care teamwork in the clinic backstage. *Journal of Applied Communication Research, 31,* 93–117.

Ellingson, L. L. (2005a). *Communicating in the clinic: Negotiating frontstage and backstage teamwork.* Cresskill, NJ: Hampton Press.

Ellingson, L. L. (2005b, November). *Ritual, repetition, and difference: Perceptions of time in a dialysis unit.* Paper presented at the conference of the National Communication Association, Boston.

Ellingson, L. L. (2006). Embodied knowledge: Writing researchers' bodies into qualitative health research. *Qualitative Health Research, 16,* 298–310.

Ellingson, L. L. (2007). *The poetics of professionalism among dialysis technicians.* Unpublished manuscript.

Ellingson, L. L. (in press-a). Ethnography in applied communication research. In L. R. Frey & K. Cissna (Eds.), *The handbook of applied communication research.* Mahwah, NJ: Erlbaum.

Ellingson, L. L. (in press-b). The performance of dialysis care: Routinization and adaptation on the floor. *Health Communication, 22*(2).

Ellingson, L. L., & Sotirin, P. (2006). Exploring young adults' perspectives on communication with aunts. *Journal of Social and Personal Relationships, 23,* 499–517.

Ellis, C. (1986). *Fisher folk: Two communities on Chesapeake Bay.* Lexington: University Press of Kentucky.

Ellis, C. (1991a). Emotional sociology. In N. Denzin (Ed.), *Studies in symbolic interaction* (Vol. 12, pp. 123–145). Greenwich, CT: JAI Press.

Ellis, C. (1991b). Sociological introspection and emotional experience. *Symbolic Interaction, 14,* 23–50.

Ellis, C. (1993). "There are survivors": Telling a story of sudden death. *Sociological Quarterly, 34,* 711–730.

Ellis, C. (1995). Speaking of dying: An ethnographic short story. *Symbolic Interaction, 18,* 73–81.

Ellis, C. (1996). Maternal connections. In C. Ellis & A. Bochner (Eds.), *Composing ethnography* (pp. 240–243). Walnut Creek, CA: AltaMira Press.

Ellis, C. (1998). "I hate my voice": Coming to terms with minor bodily stigma. *Sociological Quarterly, 39,* 517–537.

Ellis, C. (2000). Negotiating terminal illness: Communication, collusion, and coalition in caregiving. In J. Harvey & E. D. Miller (Eds.), *Loss and trauma: General and close relationship perspectives* (pp. 284–304). London: Brunner-Routledge.

Ellis, C. (2001). With mother/with child: A true story. *Qualitative Inquiry, 7,* 598–616.

Ellis, C. (2002a). Being real: Moving inward toward social change. *International Journal of Qualitative Studies in Education, 15*(4), 399–406.

Ellis, C. (2002b). Shattered lives: Making sense of September 11th and its aftermath. *Journal of Contemporary Ethnography, 31,* 375–410.

Ellis, C. (2002c). Take no chances. *Qualitative Inquiry, 8,* 170–175.

Ellis, C. (2004). *The ethnographic I: A methodological novel about autoethnography.* Walnut Creek, CA: AltaMira Press.

Ellis, C. (2006). The emotional life: A tribute to Ron Pelias. In N. Denzin (Ed.), *Studies in symbolic interaction* (Vol. 29, pp. 9–16). Amsterdam: Elsevier.

Ellis, C., & Bochner, A. P. (1992). Telling and performing personal stories: The constraints of choice in abortion. In C. Ellis & M. Flaherty (Eds.), *Investigating subjectivity: Research on lived experience* (pp. 79–101). Newbury Park, CA: Sage.

Ellis, C., & Bochner, A. P. (2000). Autoethnography, personal narrative, reflexivity: Researcher as subject. In N. K. Denzin & Y. S. Lincoln (Eds.), *Handbook of qualitative research* (2nd ed., pp. 733–768). Thousand Oaks, CA: Sage.

Ellis, C., & Bochner, A. P. (2006). Analyzing analytic autoethnography: An autopsy. *Journal of Contemporary Ethnography, 35,* 429–449.

Ellis, C., & Ellingson, L. L. (2000). Qualitative methods. In E. F. Borgatta & R. J. V. Montgomery (Eds.), *Encyclopedia of sociology* (2nd ed., Vol. 4, pp. 2287–2296). New York: Macmillan.

Ellis, C., Kiesinger, C., & Tillmann-Healy, L. (1997). Interactive interviewing: Talking about emotional experience. In R. Hertz (Ed.), *Reflexivity and voice* (pp. 119–149). Thousand Oaks, CA: Sage.

Foucault, M. (1975). *Discipline and punish: The birth of the prison* (A. Sheridan, Trans.). New York: Vintage Books.

Gergen, K. J. (1994). *Realities and relationships: Soundings in social construction.* Cambridge, MA: Harvard University Press.

Gergen, K. J. (1999). *An invitation to social construction.* Thousand Oaks, CA: Sage.

Gergen, K. J. (2006). Social construction as an ethics of infinitude: Reply to Brinkmann. *Journal of Humanistic Psychology, 46,* 119–125.

Gergen, M. M., & Gergen, K. J. (2002). Ethnographic representation as relationship. In A. P. Bochner & C. Ellis (Eds.), *Ethnographically speaking: Autoethnography, literature, and aesthetics* (pp. 11–33). Walnut Creek, CA: AltaMira Press.

Goodall, H. L. (2000). *Writing the new ethnography.* Walnut Creek, CA: AltaMira Press.

Gubrium, J., & Holstein, J. (1997). *The new language of qualitative method.* New York: Oxford University Press.

Hacking, I. (1999). *The social construction of what?* Cambridge, MA: Harvard University Press.

Harris, S. R. (2006). Social construction and social inequality: An introduction to a special issue of *JCE. Journal of Contemporary Ethnography, 35,* 223–235.

Hawes, L. C. (1994). Revisiting reflexivity. *Western Journal of Communication, 58,* 5–10.

Holman Jones, S. (1998). *Kaleidoscope notes: Writing women's music and organizational culture.* Walnut Creek, CA: AltaMira Press.

Holstein, J. A., & Gubrium, J. F. (1995). *The active interview.* Thousand Oaks, CA: Sage.

Holstein, J. A., & Gubrium, J. F. (2000). *The self we live by: Narrative identity in a postmodern world.* New York: Oxford University Press.

Hunt, S. A., & Junco, N. R. (2006). Analytic autoethnography [Special issue]. *Journal of Contemporary Ethnography, 35*(4).

Jackson, M. (1989). *Paths toward a clearing: Radical empiricism and ethnographic inquiry.* Bloomington: Indiana University Press.

Jago, B. (2006). A primary act of imagination: An autoethnography of father-absence. *Qualitative Inquiry, 12,* 398–426.

Kiesinger, C. (2002). My father's shoes: The therapeutic value of narrative reframing. In A. P. Bochner & C. Ellis (Eds.), *Ethnographically speaking: Autoethnography, literature, and aesthetics* (pp. 95–114). Walnut Creek, CA: AltaMira Press.

Krieger, S. (1991). *Social science and the self: Personal essays on an art form.* New Brunswick, NJ: Rutgers University Press.

Lakoff, G., & Johnson, M. (1980). *Metaphors we live by.* Chicago: University of Chicago Press.

Linden, R. R. (1992). *Making stories, making selves: Feminist reflections on the Holocaust.* Columbus: Ohio State University.

Lockford, L. (2004). *Performing femininity: Rewriting gender identity.* Walnut Creek, CA: AltaMira Press.

Lorde, A. (1984). *Sister outsider: Essays and speeches.* Freedom, CA: The Crossing Press.

Mairs, N. (1997). Carnal acts. In K. Conboy, N. Medina, & S. Stanbury (Eds.), *Writing on the body: Female embodiment and feminist theory* (pp. 296–305). New York: Columbia University Press.

Onyx, J., & Small, J. (2001). Memory-work: The method. *Qualitative Inquiry, 7,* 773–786.

Patton, M. Q. (2002). *Qualitative research and evaluation methods.* Thousand Oaks, CA: Sage.

Personal Narratives Group. (Eds.). (1989). *Interpreting women's lives: Feminist theory and personal narratives.* Bloomington: Indiana University Press.

Potter, W. J. (1995). *An analysis of thinking and research about qualitative methods.* Mahwah, NJ: Erlbaum.

Reed-Danahay, D. (1997). *Auto/Ethnography: Rewriting the self and the social.* Oxford, UK: Berg.

Reed-Danahay, D. (2001). Autobiography, intimacy, and ethnography. In P. Atkinson, A. Coffey, S. Delamont, J. Lofland, & L. Lofland (Eds.), *Handbook of ethnography* (pp. 407–425). London: Sage.

Richardson, L. (1994). Nine poems: Marriage and the family. *Journal of Contemporary Ethnography, 23,* 3–14.

Richardson, L. (1997). *Fields of play: Constructing an academic life.* New Brunswick, NJ: Rutgers University Press.

Richardson, L. (2000). Writing: A method of inquiry. In N. K. Denzin & Y. S. Lincoln (Eds.), *Handbook of qualitative research* (2nd ed., pp. 923–949). Thousand Oaks, CA: Sage.

Richardson, L., & Lockridge, E. (2004). *Travels with Ernest.* Walnut Creek, CA: AltaMira Press.

Ronai, C. (1995). Multiple reflections on childhood sex abuse: An argument for a layered account. *Journal of Contemporary Ethnography, 23,* 395–426.

Rorty, R. (1982). *Consequences of pragmatism.* Minneapolis: University of Minnesota Press.

Secklin, P. (2001). Multiple fractures in time: Reflections on a car crash. *Journal of Loss and Trauma, 6,* 323–334.

Shelton, A. (1995). Foucault's madonna: The secret life of Carolyn Ellis. *Symbolic Interaction, 18,* 83–87.

Spivak, G. C. (1988). Subaltern studies: Deconstructing historiography. In R. Guha & G. C. Spivak (Eds.), *Selected subaltern studies* (pp. 3–34). New York: Oxford University Press.

Spry, T. (1997). Skins: A daughter's reconstruction of cancer: A performative autobiography. *Text and Performance Quarterly, 17,* 361–365.

Stewart, D. W., & Shamdasani, P. N. (1990). *Focus groups: Theory and practice.* Newbury Park, CA: Sage.

Tedlock, B. (1991). From participant observation to the observation of participation: The emergence of narrative ethnography. *Journal of Anthropological Research, 41,* 69–94.

Tillmann-Healy, L. (1996). A secret life in a culture of thinness: Reflections on body, food, and bulimia. In C. Ellis & A. P. Bochner (Eds.), *Composing ethnography: Alternative forms of qualitative writing* (pp. 77–109). Walnut Creek, CA: AltaMira Press.

Tillmann-Healy, L. (2001). *Between gay and straight: Understanding friendship across sexual orientation.* Walnut Creek, CA: AltaMira Press.

Van Maanen, J. (1988). *Tales of the field: On writing ethnography.* Chicago: University of Chicago Press.

Van Maanen, J. (1995). An end to innocence: The ethnography of ethnography. In J. Van Maanen (Ed.), *Representation in ethnography* (pp. 1–35). Thousand Oaks, CA: Sage.

Ziarek, E. P. (2005). The abstract soul of the commodity and the monstrous body of the sphinx: Commodification, aesthetics, and the impasses of social construction. *Differences: A Journal of Feminist Cultural Studies, 16,* 88–115.

CHAPTER 24

Documents, Texts, and Archives in Constructionist Research

● **Annulla Linders**

There are still too many points at which, when faced with alternatives, the only available advice seems to amount to "use your judgment," or "use common-sense." Judgment and commonsense are fine things, but notoriously differ from one person to another. . . . If anything, documentary research needs to employ more, not less, systematic and explicit procedures than other types of research, since the possibility of replication is reduced by the shortage of data. . . .
—PLATT (1981, p. 64)

Numerous qualitatively oriented researchers rely on documents to make their case, but the literature on how to find, select, and draw conclusions on the basis of documents is notably sparse. This situation is particularly unfortunate because the analytic demands of different traditions push the methodological concerns associated with documents in somewhat different directions. This chapter provides an overview of some of the general issues that all scholars who use documents have to confront, but it focuses especially on the more particular concerns associated with the use of documents in constructionist research.

Research conducted in the constructionist tradition spans a wide range of disciplines, covers an expansive substantive territory, and is used to satisfy a number of analytic goals. Some scholars use constructionism primarily as a theoretical orientation, others as a methodological tool, and yet others as part of a hybrid research approach. Such analytic diversity inevitably invites debate about the nature, purpose, viability, and future of constructionism as a scholarly enterprise (e.g., Best, 1993; Hacking, 1999; Sterne & Leach, 2005; Woolgar & Pawluch, 1985). The aim of this chapter is not to engage the particulars of these debates but instead to hone in on that which brings constructionist projects together, whether they are conducted by scholars who are deeply committed to some principle of constructionism or by scholars who use the tools provided by constructionism for purposes that otherwise may violate some of those principles.

What all constructionist projects share is a commitment to documenting how some aspect of reality is constructed through the efforts of social actors; that is, to trace the process whereby some element of social life—meanings, institutions, identities, norms, problems, routines, and all other conceivable aspects of social reality—comes into being, emerges, takes shape, becomes understandable, acquires visible and meaningful boundaries, and takes on constraining and/or facilitating characteristics. Thus, although those of us who engage in projects loosely defined as constructionist may disagree on the *extent* to which reality is socially constructed, as well as on the implications of a constructionist orientation for our ability to formulate and answer questions about the constructions of reality that concern us (Can we ask *why* questions? Can we evaluate the truth of constructions? Can we place our constructions in a larger sociohistorical context?), we must all contend with similar issues regarding the methodological approach we use to demonstrate that something is socially constructed. Those issues, more specifically, refer to our ability to conclude with confidence that we have accurately—*accurately* here refers to the relationship between our stated research goals, our data, and our conclusions—documented the process whereby something became constructed; that is, that we have detailed the *hows* and/or *whats* of the social constructions we have identified in such a way that our findings can be replicated (Gubrium & Holstein, 2003).

The emphasis throughout the chapter is on the methodological decision-making process that precedes issues related to the actual analysis of documents via coding schemes, categorization, the development of new concepts, and various content analysis tools. Although most of the discussion here is focused on textual documents, it is important to keep in mind that the documentary universe is more expansive than that and includes a variety of other material products as well, including photographs, films, music, images, and various other traces of human activity (e.g., Bauer, 2000; Harper, 2000; Hodder, 2000; Loizos, 2000; Penn, 2000; Pole, 2004; Rose, 2000; Webb, Campbell, Schwartz, Sechrest, & Belew Grove, 1981). This decision-making process involves a number of issues that, in various ways, affect our ability both to draw conclusions and to persuade our readers that the conclusions we have drawn are the right ones.

First, the most fundamental problem that all scholars who engage in empirical research must deal with—how to ensure that the data we use can answer the questions we raise—poses particular challenges for documentary researchers who, with few exceptions (e.g., Bell, 1999; Bornat, 2004; Harper, 2000), have no control over the production of the data they rely on. Simply put, we must contend with what is available. Second, and related, not all data sources are equal. The kinds of information that can be extracted from documents such as newspapers, legislative records, organizational literature, personnel records, official statistics, research reports, and personal correspondence differ quite a bit. In other words, documents are produced for different purposes, with different audiences in mind, and under different conditions, and therefore come with different methodological constraints.

For constructionists the challenges associated with the nature and availability of documents are somewhat different from those facing scholars who use documents primarily to resurrect some true state of the social world (and hence must evaluate documents in terms of their truth value), but the general principle that the kinds of documents we choose or have to contend with affect our ability to draw conclusions applies to all scholars who rely on documents. Generally speaking, the concerns for constructionists relate to the appropriateness and utility of particular sets of documents for the purpose of revealing or identifying a process of social construction. This means, with some variation for different research goals, that we must determine *who* the participating actors are, *how* they go about constructing or contesting the aspect of reality we are interested in, what the interpretive *content* of their activities and claims are, and what documentary *venues* for identifying these processes we might consult. In other words, our ability to trace and document a process of social construction is intricately tied up with the quality and appropriateness of the documents that we choose.

Third, the "truth" of documents and texts matters for all documentary researchers, albeit in somewhat different ways for constructionists. Although constructionists do not ultimately evaluate texts in terms of their truth value (i.e., the correspondence between textual accounts of reality and that reality itself), we must nevertheless confront and address truth-related issues such as biases inherent in data sources (e.g., newspapers tied to political parties) and the general accuracy of the data and/or documents themselves (e.g., typographical and unintended factual errors, incompleteness of data). The problems associated with the errors that sprinkle many documents are typically less pressing analytically (keep in mind, though, that the extent to which documents are error prone is not entirely coincidental insofar as it takes time, resources, and determination to check for errors) but, if left unaddressed, can affect the persuasiveness of our accounts. The challenges linked to systematic biases are analytically more significant but, for constructionists, less tied up with the biases themselves—we expect different collective actors to present different pictures of the world—than with the determination of (1) how particular biases push reality constructions in distinct directions, (2) which particular aspects of reality, if any, are subject to conflicting interpretations (or, in

the absence of conflict, which are generally agreed upon), and (3) where the sources of interpretive divergence are located (e.g., in collective interests, in documentary conventions, or in the setting in which documents are produced).

Finally, documents, like other forms of data, do not speak for themselves but must be made to speak by the analyst (Tierny, 1997). Given the suspicion with which constructionists approach the detached but all-knowing analyst, the issues involved in making sense of our data are particularly important and have already generated a lively debate among constructionists. For the purposes of this chapter, however, I will not directly engage the extensive debates about how to deal analytically with the widely divergent claims about reality that might show up in our documents (Best, 1993; Ibarra & Kitsuse, 1993; Sarbin & Kitsuse, 1994) or what analytic considerations should guide the treatment of context in reality constructions (Best, 1989; Bogard, 2003a; Cicourel, 1987; Holstein & Gubrium, 2003; Miller & Holstein, 1993; Rafter, 1992). Rather, I address a few of the issues that, methodologically speaking, come before these thorny analytic questions; namely, the issues involved in drawing conclusions on the basis of, or about, the document itself, its author, and the events described in the document.

In what follows I first elaborate on these problems in a discussion that draws on the insights and contributions that documentary scholars from a range of substantive areas have already generated and then illustrate several of the issues raised in a more comprehensive exemplar from my own research on capital punishment.

The Problem of Availability

Generally speaking, this problem relates to the ability of researchers to identify and locate documents that pertain to the questions they pose. Although the problem of document availability is particularly acute for historically oriented researchers, whether constructionists or not (Abrams, 1982; Ben-Yehuda, 1995; Gardner, 1994; Laslett, 2005; Skocpol, 1984), the issues involved apply to all documentary scholars, even those who might worry more about data abundance than scarcity; that is, both scarce and abundant data sources are more or less available, more or less complete, and more or less accessible. This is so for a number of different reasons, some associated with the very production of documents, others with the preservation and organization of documents, and yet others with the authority and control over documents.

For nonconstructionists, the problem associated with document availability directly affects their ability to describe reality accurately on the basis of spotty records pertaining to that reality. This is a challenge akin to repainting a long-forgotten picture of a puzzle with the help of only a limited number of pieces, some of which are faded or otherwise damaged beyond recognition, and none of which holds the key to the puzzle's solution. That is, although extracted from the traces left by various social actors, the reality sought by nonconstructionists is located not in the traces themselves, which are always incomplete, but instead in the analyst's assembly of those traces into a coherent whole. For constructionists, in contrast, the analytic focus is precisely on the pieces of the (putative) puzzle that, we assume, give rise to different versions of reality, none of which is truer in an absolute sense than any of the others. From this perspective reality is not to be found somewhere beyond the different accounts of it that social actors generate but, instead, within those accounts. This means that the challenges associated with document availability for constructionists are much more closely linked to the pieces themselves than with the presumed distance between the pieces and the reality they describe.

Much constructionist research focuses on contemporary issues that are surrounded by an abundance of documentary materials that are relatively easy to access, including media items, political records, legal opinions, reports produced by various professional groups, statistical sources, organizational records, and, increasingly, Internet activity. It is perhaps for this reason that constructionists, generally speaking, are less likely to address how, if at all, the availability of documents might enter into our findings and/or conclusions than we are to address the appropriateness of different document types. However, there are numerous issues to consider, both in terms of the potential data gaps themselves (incomplete data) and the reasons for these gaps (the historical deterioration of documents does not affect all documents equally; not all social activities leave documentary traces). Some of these issues are discussed in the next section in terms of missing documents, never-produced documents, and inaccessible documents.

Missing Documents

To address the problem of missing documents, we must first try to get a handle on what it is that is missing. This involves a determination not only of how many data are missing of what kind (articles from a medical journal, arrest records from certain periods, a few volumes of official documents, meeting minutes from select years, spotty records of tabloid newspapers) but also of the reasons why they are missing (e.g., court records consumed in a fire; incomplete library holdings; lost in the dustbin of history). Once these determinations are made, we must tackle the question of how the data gaps might affect the conclusions that can be drawn on the basis of remaining data. Apart from the general observation that the fewer and less systematic the data gaps the better, it is not always the case that more voluminous data sources yield better answers than sparse ones. Although the challenges associated with scarce data are somewhat different from those associated with abundant data, it would obviously be a mistake to conclude that abundance in itself constitutes a protection against the problems associated with data gaps due to missing documents (e.g., lots of data from one source, e.g., *The New York Times*, does not always compensate for data that might be missing from another source, e.g., the *National Police Gazette*).

In practice, the determination of how missing data might affect a constructionist analysis can be made only on a case-by-case basis; but, generally speaking, it must take into account which contributions to a process of reality construction are insufficiently documented. The problems here are especially urgent, perhaps, in scholarship directed at the activities of those at the social margins. This is so for the simple reason that not all social groups leave documents behind (Gubrium, 1993; Prior, 2004) and those that do leave documents of varying depth and quality. Generally speaking, the production and preservation of documents are linked to the distribution of power and resources in any given social setting; governments, for example, produce much more comprehensive documentary records about their activities than do radical protest groups. There are exceptions to this rule, of course, and in some cases power and resources are associated with the absence of records (e.g., time cards are produced by hourly employees, not salaried executives), but, in general, those with more power in a relationship (e.g., police vs. criminals or government vs. citizens) are also in a better position to define—to make an audience see the relationship through their eyes—the confines of that relationship through the documents they produce. For instance, if we are interested in the competing interpretations of 18th-century infanticide pursued by priests and women who have killed their infants, we would be hampered in our investigation if had access to an abundance of sermons by parish priests but only one or two diaries by women addressing the practice.

Never-Produced Documents

For constructionists who are interested in how documents themselves, including how and by whom they are produced, are impli-cated in the construction of reality (e.g., the construction of infanticide by church and state), the problem with never-produced documents can be less urgent than for those concerned with discovering some truth lying beyond the documents that were not produced. There are at least two other ways, however, that the close relationship between the construction of some portion of reality and the documentary evidence thereof can become problematic for constructionists. First, the widespread reliance on documents circulated in the public sphere—newspapers, for example—might lead constructionists to conclude that groups marginalized in public sources play no active role in the construction of the issue at hand (Gubrium, 1993). Second, because the construction of various social conditions is often accompanied by a plethora of new documentary evidence—official statistics, for example—the constructionist who is interested in tracing a construction historically sometimes has difficulties locating the underlying (putative) condition in a different interpretive constellation (Best, 1990; Pfohl, 1977).

But there are numerous other ways in which never-produced documents can cause methodological problems for constructionists. The design of comparative constructionist projects, for example, relies on the availability of comparable (if not identical) data across nations or other collectivities (Abu-Laban & Garber, 2005; Kuipers, 2006; Linders, 1998), but given that nations generate different kinds of documents and that the generation of documents varies across time, researchers often have to compensate for never-produced documents in creative ways. Take 19th-century state legislative records in the United States, for example; some states provide transcripts (or edited summaries) of actual debates, and other states simply record that an issue was discussed and what action was taken. In such a scenario, a researcher might be able to use newspaper accounts of such debates as an alternate data source but must then consider the ways in which this particular document form differs from legislative records.

A somewhat different aspect of the problem of never-produced documents, and a more difficult one to resolve, refers to contents that were never produced (this problem is further addressed later, in discussing what documents say and what inferences can be made). That is, it is not only what is actually in a document that might be relevant or of interest to a researcher trying to document a process of social construction but also what is not in the document (Silverman, 1993). In cases in which the researcher has reason to suspect that the omission of content is intentional, the methodological problem becomes one of bias, which is somewhat different from the kinds of omissions generated by the sociohistorical context in which the text was originally produced. In practice, these two sources of omissions are often blurred. In my own research on the construction of womanhood in 19th-century execution accounts, for example, I can easily find evidence of the interpretive work that accompanies the execution of white, married, middle-class women who kill their husbands but have much more trouble locating such interpretive work in the context of poor, black women, including slave women, who kill someone in the course of a robbery.

Liz Stanley's (1995) study of a set of diaries produced by men and women in Britain in the 1930s and 1940s at the behest of a team of researchers (the so-called Mass-Observation Diaries), provides another good example of the problem of omissions that are neither intentional nor accidental; men and women observe and/or record somewhat different things about their daily lives, leading to the ironic conclusion that "women have servants and men never eat." In other words, both the production and consumption of texts are dependent on and affected by a backdrop of taken-for-granted experiences, bodies of knowledge, assumptions, and various other cultural competencies. If in the preceding example it might strike us as too self-evident to warrant further comment to conclude that men, just like women, eat and have servants, from a methodological perspective the analytic leap is no different from that required when the missing content is more ambiguous or about an issue we are less familiar with. Imagine, for example, that the preceding conclusion was "men drink and women never fight" and consider whether it would be appropriate to "correct" the accounts in the same way as we might in the case of food and servants.

Inaccessible Documents

A final dilemma relating to missing documents refers to inaccessible documents; that is, documents that exist but for various reasons are inaccessible to the researcher. This problem involves both researcher limitation (e.g., language barriers, resource constraints) and restricted access (e.g., documents involving national security). At first glance, missing data due to the limitations of researchers may not look like a particularly urgent methodological problem, but if we consider this issue in conjunction with the problems associated with doing research on marginalized groups more generally (Collins, 1989; Miller, 1993), the limitations that we as researchers bring to documents do have consequences for our ability to describe and understand the social world from the perspective of those who live in worlds we ourselves have difficulties making sense of or who speak languages we cannot decipher. The constraints imposed by limited resources, similarly, are in part practical in nature (how many archives can I afford to visit? How many months can I spend on this?), albeit with methodological consequences, but because the costs associated with accessing data are not evenly distributed across all data sources, they are also in part direct methodological problems (e.g., the accessibility of historical *New York Times* issues—first through the index, now through electronic access—makes it a vastly more affordable and accessible data source than other newspapers; hence, the *New York Times* is more often used as an indicator of public discourse than other newspapers).

Access to existing documents can be restricted in a number of other ways, some of which are the result of deliberate efforts to restrict access and others of which are basically incidental, for example, through archaic recordkeeping of documents or any number of other factors associated with the preservation, storage, and organization of materials (e.g., Featherstone, 2006; Landes & Tilly, 1971; Stoler, 2005; Wheeler, 1969).[1] In this sense, we might think of the institutions that store documents as "mediating" institutions; that is, they mediate in various ways the "material and symbolic practices that constitute collective understandings of culture" (Marontate, 2005, p. 286). How to deal with deliberately restricted documents (e.g., by finding alternate data sources or by trying to get limited access for specific research purposes) depends in part on why the documents are restricted in the first place (e.g., to protect governments or individual privacy) and in part on who has the power to place restrictions and/or release access to the documents.

The problem of incidental restrictions has no one solution, of course, and sometimes—especially in cases in which researchers are unaware of the existence of a document—becomes resolved only over time as a result of a slowly accumulated body of knowledge by a community of scholars (new documents, as well as contents within documents, are discovered all the time). However, documentary access provided by the labors of others and made available through a secondary literature is not without pitfalls (Altheide, 1999). This is so both because documents are rarely reproduced in their entirety and because the content selected for presentation is always colored by the specific argument or thesis they are meant to support or the social processes they are meant to illustrate. Nevertheless, information pertaining to the existence of a document, as well as to its precise location, enables subsequent scholars to access it for

their particular purposes (hence, researchers should always provide detailed information about sources). In cases in which researchers have good reason to think that the documents (or specific contents within documents) they need exist but are difficult to access, either as a result of document storage practices (e.g., insufficient detail in the records of archival holdings) or as a result of the form of the document itself (e.g., no index to legislative debates or newspaper contents), they must weigh the anticipated benefits of accessing the document, which can be as tedious and time-consuming as finding the proverbial needle in the haystack, against the resources it would take to secure such access.

How to Choose (the Right) Documents

The determination of which kinds of documents to choose as data sources is first and foremost linked to the research questions asked (Phillips & Hardy, 2002). The selection and sampling of document types, as well as the selection of subsets or subsegments of those documents, go hand in hand with the evaluation of how, by whom, for what purpose, and with what audience in mind particular documents are produced, all of which affect the content and structure of documents in various ways (Fleury, Sullivan, Bybee, & Davidson, 1998; Hallgrimsdottir & Benoit, 2006; Holbrook, 1996). If the topic is the construction of abortion by major political actors, for example, then newspapers are much more appropriate data sources than private diaries, but if the issue is how individual women make sense of abortion, then private diaries are more appropriate than newspapers.

For constructionists, one of the most prominent challenges is to ensure that our findings are not artifacts of the particular documents we have chosen to interrogate (unless that is a purpose of the study). The concerns here have less to do with the accuracy of the information provided in different documents, although some do center their research questions precisely on the divergence across different document sources (Ben-Yehuda, 1995; Best, 2001; Burgess, 2004; Orcutt & Turner, 1993), than with the particular aspects of a process of social construction that a document reveals or participates in. The literature on the construction of social problems, for example, provides numerous examples of studies that document how a particular condition or issue became understood in a particular way by a particular group of social actors (e.g., Gusfield, 1981; Johnson, 1995; Orcutt & Turner, 1993; Rafter, 1992). It probably strikes most of us as self-evident that a Canadian newspaper, for example, would not be a particularly good source from which extract the construction of problems in the United States or that the sole reliance on prochoice literature would not be sufficient to grasp the contours of the abortion issue in the United States; but such commonsense solutions to the problem of how to select sources are often used in lieu of a more detailed discussion of how the particular sources we do end up with might influence our findings. The challenge here, in other words, is to understand how different document sources yield different kinds of information of relevance to the construction process.

How to Select Document Types

Given that different document types constrain the information contained in them in more or less distinct ways, it is important to consider the ramifications of such variations for our ability to reconstruct a process of social construction. Media scholars, for example, have demonstrated how the organization and financing of newspapers and other news organizations influence the substance and ordering of news in systematic ways (Gans, 1980; Schudson, 1978; Tuchman, 1978). Hence, and as a general recommendation, analyses of the news (or other documents) should ideally be based in

an understanding of how the news (or other documents) are produced (Ahlkvist & Faulkner, 2002; Altheide, 1999). This is an easier task for some documents than for others, however; first, some document-producing settings are less transparent than others (e.g., deliberations by Supreme Court justices); second, the production and organization of documents change over time (e.g., the universe of newspapers available via LexisNexis is not the same for all time periods; *The New York Times* only recently started to publish marriage announcements submitted by gay and lesbian couples); and third, historical distance sometimes makes it difficult to reassemble a long-forgotten production context (e.g., the structure of 18th-century execution sermons).

As a distinct document type, institutionally generated data, especially in the form of statistics, warrant special consideration (Prior, 2003; Silverman, 1993). It is not uncommon for constructionists to use official and expert data as a backdrop against which to compare other types of claims (e.g., Duwe, 2005; Reinarman & Levine, 1995; Ruddell & Decker, 2005; Yanich, 2004), but it is important to keep in mind that the tendency to treat official data as information (neutral, in no need of explanation) and activist data as misinformation (biased, in need of explanation) constitutes a methodological quagmire for constructionists and one that should give us pause (Yar, 2005). First, the link between social conditions and their representation in facts, including statistics, is always ambiguous (Best, 2001; Kitsuse & Cicourel, 1963; Zuberi, 2003); that is, the very process whereby a messy social world is translated into orderly categories of people and activities inevitably reduces that world to the categories devised to describe it. Second, and more directly linked to the problems discussed in this section, official data do not emerge by themselves but instead are contingent on decisions to fund, gather, and select particular kinds of information for public distribution and storage (Delaney, 1994; Foucault, 1990; Gusfield, 1981). The

problem here is not only that official statistics are distinctly political in nature (e.g.,
think about the current debate over whether
data should be collected on racial categories,
and if so, which categories) and not simply
that the generation of official data is implicated in many construction processes, but
also that the very presence and categorization of certain kinds of information influence how we as researchers see and represent the world we write about.

How to Select Documents within a Type

The problems associated with choosing
which documents to analyze do not end with
document types, of course, but also involve
selecting documents within types (Bauer &
Aarts, 2000). This aspect of the data selection process, however, has received much
less attention from constructionists thus far,
even though the implications of the methods we use for selecting documents within a
type can be far reaching (e.g., which issues of
a newspaper, which articles in medical journals, which television ads?). Generally speaking, there are three distinct strategies for selecting documents, and constructionists use
them all (albeit to varying degrees and in different combinations): proportionate selection, targeted selection, and "anything you
can lay your hands on." Although all three
methods are used to generate a manageable
and meaningful sample of documents to
work with, the differences among them are
not simply technical in nature but also have
consequences for the types of questions that
can be posed and the kinds of answers that
can be generated.

Although *proportionate selection* in the
form of random or weighted samples is
more commonly associated with nonconstructionist projects (Gobo, 2004), it can
serve limited constructionist ends as well, especially when used in combination with
other methods. As a preliminary step to an
analysis of the transformation of meanings
over time, it can be useful to draw a series of
proportionate samples at strategic moments

in time to trace changes regarding such
things as the frequency and structuring of information within particular document types;
this is what Sarah Byrne did, for example, in
her analysis of the construction of racialized
identities in personal ads over time (Byrne,
2003). It is important to keep in mind, however, that a proportionate selection of documents requires that the pool from which the
documents are selected is clearly and meaningfully defined. To draw a random selection of newspaper articles from an online archive such as LexisNexis, for instance, is not
particularly useful, methodologically speaking, because the newspapers included in the
archive do not constitute a meaningful unit
for most research purposes. (This is not to
suggest that such easy access to a range of
newspapers is not helpful; it is, and tremen-
dously so for the purpose of gaining a quick
picture of the spread of a particular news
item.)

The strategy most commonly used among
constructionists is *targeted sampling* of documents pertaining to the emergence, persis-
tence, and/or evolution of a particular social construction. Although the utility and
appropriateness of targeted samples, in contrast to proportionate samples, do not ultimately rely on the extent to which they are
representative of some imaginable population of documents and/or document producers, the selection of a targeted sample
nevertheless requires researchers to draw
clearly defined and conceptually meaningful
boundaries around the particular documents to be included. More specifically, the
challenges involved in drawing a good targeted sample are linked to the constructionist aim of placing the analytic spotlight on a
particular process of social construction in
conjunction with the requirement that the
findings are not predetermined by the particular selection of documents and the conclusions not foregone in the sense that we
pick only documents that fit. In this sense,
the generation of a targeted sample is analytically more demanding than that of a proportionate sample and rests on the analyst's

ability to identify documents in which the features and/or elements that capture a process of social construction come into clear relief. Technically, this can be accomplished in several different ways, including via huge, comprehensive samples (Duwe, 2005), with comparisons of analytically defined and contained samples (Bogard, 2003b), or through a single carefully selected case (Fine, 1997).

The third strategy for selecting documents, *anything you can lay your hands on*, if used appropriately, is neither a poor relative of the two sampling methods just discussed nor a license to cut the strings of methodological rigor. Instead, it is sometimes the only possible strategy for locating enough information pertaining to research involving marginal, obscure, delicate, or clandestine topics, either because the pool of data itself is so scarce as to make any example an important find (e.g., authentic slave narratives) or because a particular content is only rarely addressed directly in the documents we are searching (e.g., interviews with clients in news reports about prostitution).

A final issue concerning the selection of documents refers to the problem of knowing when we have enough data. Here the concerns are somewhat different, depending on the aims of the researcher. As a general methodological rule of thumb for projects that do not rely on a predetermined sample size, which few constructionist projects do, we have enough data when we learn nothing new by adding additional items (Bauer & Aarts, 2000).

Are the Documents Telling the Truth?

For constructionists, the problems associated with the truth value and credibility of documents are not primarily about the extent to which documents conceal or skew an otherwise unbiased reality, which is the dominant worry among nonconstructionists. In fact, as constructionists we assume that documents are skewed in certain ways,

we take for granted that there is no such thing as a true and unbiased picture of anything, and we rarely begin our research projects with the intent of providing a distilled and supposedly objective description of the world. But this general orientation does not absolve us from dealing methodologically with the potential problems associated with issues of document credibility. More specifically, the challenge for constructionists is how to identify and incorporate the various untruths, half-truths, biases, omissions, inclusions, and mistakes that characterize, and sometimes constitute, the documents we work with into our own accounts in ways that are methodologically sound and make sense analytically (Silverman, 1993).[2] In other words, bias for constructionists is less about trying to distill an unbiased truth from biased accounts than it is about securing against data collection procedures that might yield a biased selection of accounts (e.g., favoring official over marginal sources); that is, a selection of accounts that is inappropriate and/or insufficient for the purpose of describing a process of social construction.

Leaving aside for the moment the issues of credibility that are implicated in the constructionist project itself, there are numerous ways, for a variety of reasons, that documents give a skewed, limited, or sometimes faulty picture of that which they are meant to represent or describe. What I have in mind here are the less systematic and seldom intended errors and inaccuracies that creep into most documents (a glance at the "corrections" published by daily newspapers provides a good entry point into the many ways that documents can be inaccurate), such as typos, wrong or mixed-up names of people and places, mistaken gender attribution, inaccurate information about laws and regulations, people and events placed in the wrong time period, messed-up quotations, and numerous other such errors. The best strategy for catching such inaccuracies, apart from the general advice of gaining as much familiarity as possible with our topic and the documents implicated in it, is to seek a wide enough range of documents pertaining to the particular process of social construction we are examining in order to get facts of this nature as straight as possible. Although inaccuracies along these lines may not directly implicate the particular process of reality construction we are documenting, the credibility of our research efforts may nevertheless be questioned if we reproduce such errors in our own accounts without acknowledging them (e.g., placing a significant congressional vote in the wrong presidential term, misattributing achievements, getting names and dates mixed up).

More significant for the constructionist analysis are the untruths, half-truths, biases, omissions, and inclusions that we have good reason to suspect are more systematically linked to either the documents themselves or to the producers of those documents. Two general strategies are available to constructionists for dealing with these kinds of problems; first, to gather data from multiple sources (both within and across document types) in order to ease the interpretive burden on particular documents; second, to try to get a handle on the credibility issue through an examination of who produced the documents for what purposes under what conditions and constraints (e.g., a report by a politically motivated think tank is likely to be different from one by a professionally motivated scientist). Both of these strategies come with methodological challenges that push in somewhat different directions depending on the kinds of untruths, half-truths, biases, omissions, inclusions, and mistakes that characterize the documents in question. Some of these issues I have already touched on in the preceding sections, so the discussion here is relatively brief.

Biases Associated with Documents

The kinds of credibility issues that are tied up with the structure and organization of distinct document types can be particularly insidious in that they typically do not simply refer to a biased content, although that obviously is an issue, too (see later in the section), but also to the production of the very categories and identities we use to organize and understand the world (Prior, 2003). Think about the ways in which police records (Komter, 2006) and patient records (Berg, 1996), for example, not only describe an aspect of reality but also in various ways define and bring order to that reality through patterns of inclusion, exclusion, and ordering of materials. For constructionists whose primary research goal is the uncovering of the ways in which documents are constitutive of the aspects of reality they purportedly describe, the methodological challenge is precisely how to ensure that the documents at hand, given the variations, exceptions, and idiosyncrasies that characterize most document types, however regulated and formulaic they are, are appropriate for demonstrating such constitutive processes.

Constructionist researchers who are intent on revealing how particular processes of documentation work in tandem with particular configurations of power and domination in such a way that some interpretations, experiences, and social groups are favored and others marginalized face the additional challenge of making visible the marginal voices that are concealed in various ways in the product(ion)s of power (Butler, 1999; Foucault, 1990; Szasz, 1970). How exactly to accomplish this is not altogether self-evident, however, considering that documents are more often produced by the powerful than the powerless and therefore do not typically reveal that which they are organized to conceal. For such research purposes, it can be methodologically justifiable "to make a mountain out of a molehill" should we find traces of alternate interpretations, accounts, experiences, or descriptions in our documents.

A final credibility issue linked to the structure and organization of documents refers to the meaning content of documents. Constructionist studies designed to reconstruct the clusters of meaning that define issues, social problems, events, and/or various categories of people typically extract those meaning clusters from a range of documents, including especially newspapers and other media, but also expert reports, political documents, judicial opinions, and various other documents that serve as repositories of meaning. The methodological challenge here is not primarily the identification of the many ways in which the meanings embedded in documents can and do depart from some benchmark measure—although many researchers using constructionist tools attempt such comparisons as well—but instead the determination of the extent to which, if at all, the meaning clusters we identify are artifacts of the particular document types we are relying on as opposed to penetrating the documents from without. To take an example from my own research on the social construction of executions (to be further discussed later in the chapter), I am frequently faced with significantly different descriptions of the same execution in different documentary outlets (e.g., different newspapers, legislative debates, legal documents). Some of these differences are factual (e.g., blood or no blood) and others more about impression (the audience was *aghast*). In order to make sense of such differences, and to make decisions about how to use them, a necessary first step is to consider the constraints under which the various document types are produced.

Biases Associated with Document Producers

When it comes to truth issues associated with the producers or authors of documents, constructionists are on firm conceptual ground in that one of our most enduring contributions to the larger research community is precisely the identification of the many ways that truths, facts, meanings, and all other aspects of social life are caught up with the activities of distinct social actors. By now, a large body of constructionist research has demonstrated how seemingly objective social conditions and categories are better viewed as accomplishments of the social groups that in various ways have participated in the process of constructing those conditions and categories (Reinarman, 2005; Sarbin & Kitsuse, 1994; Spector & Kitsuse, 1977). Methodologically speaking, however, constructionists could do better when it comes to detailing the particular decisions we make about the selection of documents and contents pertaining to the activities of different social actors.

The challenges facing constructionists who focus on the more or less intentional efforts by particular social actors to name and define some aspect of reality (e.g., a new social problem, a new psychiatric condition, a new form of deviance) are somewhat different from those associated with constructionist projects aimed at uncovering the kinds of taken-for-granted interpretive categories that characterize a distinct historical period and somehow penetrate the activities and accounts of social actors from the outside (e.g., 19th-century ideas about women), but both types of projects require a methodology that clearly explicates how our conclusions are warranted by the data as opposed to being superimposed on the data. That is, one of the greatest difficulties for analysts tracing meaning constructions via actors' words and deeds is to let the documents do the speaking—that is, to reign in and highlight the particular meaning clusters that our documents reveal—instead of treating documentary evidence as a see-through grab bag that lets us take only that which we are looking for and ignore the rest.

Some of the most recurrent sources of systematic document untruths, half-truths, and biases that constructionists have identified are those linked to the sociopolitical interests and intentions of the document producers, including those derived from political affiliations, professional interests, and membership in various other more or less distinct collectivities (e.g., social movements, religious groups). Thus one of the first steps of any constructionist analysis must be to subject the producers (and/or authors, should they be different) of documents to an examination: who are they, with what purposes in mind do they produce the documents they do, what are the conditions or constraints under which they produce their documents, and what, if any, are the areas of disagreement (Prior, 2003)? This strategy is especially important for research that for various reasons must rely on documents that are disproportionately produced by only a limited range of social actors (Yar, 2005). As a general rule, the closer the document author is in terms of interests to the content of a document, the greater the likelihood that the content is deliberately filtered through those interests and, hence, the greater the likelihood that the document provides a distinct and identifiable view of a particular issue. For example, a report by a prolife organization about the consequences of abortion for women is likely to look very different from a report on the same issue by a prochoice organization.

More difficult to deal with are the more or less pervasive taken-for-granted assumptions or meaning clusters that, without being clearly linked to the interests and intentions of particular document producers, permeate documents in various ways. The constructionist literature is filled with studies aimed at uncovering such meaning clusters and provides numerous examples of how documentary sources can be used to arrive at persuasive conclusions regarding their emergence and transformation (e.g., Ariès, 1962; Gusfield, 1981; Lesko, 2001; Rafter, 1992). And yet analysts dealing with meaning constructions that are somehow lodged at the larger cultural level must be particularly careful not only to describe and document the process whereby particular sources were selected but also to explicate the decision-making rules involved in identifying the presence or absence of particular contents. The challenge here is particularly acute when we ourselves view the world through the same lens as the document producers and hence might be less inclined to interrogate the process whereby what strikes us as a sensible as opposed to a less sensible construction of meaning was accomplished. Nevertheless, biases of this type are problematic only insofar as we take such partial or skewed document contents to be representative of much larger social constellations.

Documents Do Not Speak for Themselves

Documents, like other forms of data, do not speak for themselves but must be made to speak by the analyst. The process whereby documents are made to speak involves the linking together of three separate activities (Stanley, 1995): *writing* (or otherwise producing) the document in the first place, *reading* the document (understanding and making sense of what was written), and *(re-)writing* a new document (placing the document and our reading of it in a larger interpretive context). If the preceding discussion has been primarily focused on the methodological challenges involving the first two of these activities, this section confronts more directly the third activity: What inferences can we make on the basis of our documents and how do we use the documentary data to support our conclusions? Here I do not directly engage the thorny theoretical and analytic issues involved in making sense of the data (e.g., Denzin, 2000; Gubrium & Holstein, 1997; Lee, 2000) but rather focus on three different types of inferences or conclusions that are direct outgrows of the methodological issues raised earlier: (1) about the documents themselves, (2) about the author(s) of documents, and (3) about the social material (e.g., events, meanings) that constitutes the contents of documents.

For some constructionist research purposes, conclusions about the document itself constitute an important research contribution. For projects aimed at establishing authenticity (whether this document is what it purports to be), this is obviously a primary task. The discussion by Henry Louis Gates (2002) in the introduction to *The Bondwoman's Narrative* is a good illustration of both what this process might look like and the pitfalls of drawing conclusions about how people view the world on the basis of inauthentic documents. In other cases, it is precisely the conventions guiding a particular document type that are subject to analysis. The identification of the conventions, or distinguishing forms, that characterize various documents, such as newspapers (Schudson, 1978), mediation hearings (Garcia, 1991), personal correspondence (Chartier, Boureau, & Dauphin, 1997), death certificates (Bloor, 1991), and criminal biographies (Printz, 2003), are not only important contributions in themselves but also inform subsequent scholars in their efforts to make sense of such documents and to determine how documentary conventions are implicated in or inform the construction of particular aspects of reality. In fact, and generally speaking, what a document tells us cannot be completely grasped unless we know what kinds of conventions guide its structure and contents.

Inferences about the authors of documents are so commonplace in constructionist projects, and the assumption that such inferences not only can but must be made is so pervasive, that it is not altogether surprising that the question of just how to make such inferences is often left unaddressed. The danger here is not only that we draw faulty (or insufficiently supported) conclusions about the connection between various individual author attributes (motivations, values, interests, actions) and the documents they produce but also that we make questionable inferences about the extent to which, and, if so, how, authors are constrained and influenced by the social locations they occupy and often are made to represent in our studies (e.g., gender, race, class, professional, historical, geographical). The procedural safeguards that qualitative researchers who do ethnographic work have adopted to make sure they do not misrepre-

sent their subjects—by letting the subjects read and comment on the researcher's text prior to publication, for example (e.g., Stacey, 1990)—are not typically available to documentary researchers (Hodder, 2000). Moreover, although the ambition to accurately represent peoples' lives is pervasive in much qualitative research, it can be difficult to meet when our subjects' desire to present themselves in a favorable light comes up against the demands of the larger interpretive context into which those subjects' lives are placed. This is a particularly thorny issue when dealing with people and lives that we ourselves find offensive and repulsive, as Kathleen Blee so cogently has described in her study of women in racist organizations (2002).

For documentary researchers who do not have direct contact with the subjects who people our documents—often just names on a page—the most urgent problem may not be how to ensure that we do not misrepresent those subjects in the sense of not offending them (although the issue of what, if any, our responsibility toward such distant subjects might be does warrant further consideration; see Fine, Weis, Weseen, & Wong, 2003) but instead how to reconstruct their participation in a process of social construction from the glimpses that documents provide. That is, insofar as we attribute their actions to motives we cannot see or their motives to actions we cannot see, then we must devise explicit methods for stepping outside of the data to make such connections (Boyce, 2000; Prior, 2003). The burden on theory is heavy here, of course, but that burden gets lighter the better our methodological decisions are in terms of data collection and the better our strategies are for selecting, extracting and comparing document contents.

The problem of how to draw inferences about the contents of documents has already been partially addressed in the earlier discussion about the truth of documents. Here I focus more directly on some of the links between documents and the social elements they describe or constitute parts of that affect our ability to make inferences about those elements (Ekecrantz, 1997). Those who provide records of social life do so from different vantage points—some are directly implicated in the aspects of social life that are described, some are more distant observers, and yet others rely on secondhand information—and these different vantage points obviously influence what the document producer "sees" (Wagner-Pacifici, 2005). It is not always the case, however, that the "best" (however defined) descriptions come from those who are the closest (whether conceived in temporal, geographical, or experiential terms) to an event. Rather, different vantage points affect the production and organization of contents in different ways.

Finally, and more tentatively for the purposes of this chapter (this is otherwise a huge issue), there is the problem of how to draw inferences about the larger social and cultural forces that may not be directly addressed or visible in our documents but that nevertheless can be assumed to penetrate those documents in various ways (Hall, 2003; Spencer, 2000). The issue itself has been discussed extensively, especially by historically oriented scholars (Abrams, 1982; Laslett, 2005; Skocpol, 1984) but also by constructionists who consider how, if at all, the context of reality constructions should be dealt with analytically (Best, 1989; Bogard, 2003a; Cicourel, 1987; Holstein & Gubrium, 2003; Miller & Holstein, 1993; Nichols, 1995; Rafter, 1992). However, these debates are more often situated in the intersection of theory and methods than in that of methods and documents. That is, we know more about the problems involved in identifying social and cultural forces from whatever documents we have at hand than we do about how the selection of those documents in the first place might affect our ability to identify such forces.

For analysts who use constructionist tools to extract evidence of such larger forces from various documents (e.g., newspapers,

advertisements, scientific reports), the methodological challenge becomes not only how to identify features that indicate the presence and influence of such forces and to distinguish them from features that do not but also how to ensure that our expectations of what to find do not blind us to contrary evidence. For example, if we are interested in documenting how white femininity was constructed in the 19th century or black masculinity in the 20th century, and if our basic intellectual orientation points us in the direction of inequality, we would find a wealth of data from any number of documentary sources to support a conclusion that such constructions are distinct, pervasive, and derogatory (e.g., Jackson, 2006; Russett, 1989). But the question we must (always) ask ourselves is: Could we have found something different, and, if so, what would it look like? The danger, then, is not only that we miss, or dismiss as insignificant, evidence that might point in a different direction but also that we close off analytic access to potentially very significant constructionist processes that hover at the edges of that which is readily visible (Thorne, 1993).

The Construction of Meanings about Capital Punishment

With this brief exemplar, I want to illustrate a series of methodological problems that I have been faced with in my own research on capital punishment. Some of these problems are particularly relevant to the construction of meanings, whereas others are more about my ability to accurately locate the events (e.g., particular executions) and mileposts (e.g., legislative activity) that in various ways are implicated in different construction processes.

My interest in capital punishment originates in my dissertation research, a comparative-historical analysis of moral politics, specifically about abortion and capital punishment, in Sweden and the United States. Considering that I was dealing with two issues, two nations, and some 200 years, the methodological challenges were not insignificant. Theoretically, I assumed that the formation and distribution of political meanings (including moral meanings) are at all times tentative and open-ended outcomes of an ongoing sociohistoric process of meaning construction but also that the construction of political meanings does not take place in a vacuum; actual historical locations are filled with memories, procedures, ideas and understandings, social and political cleavages, institutions, organizations, technologies, and so forth, that constitute a baggage that efforts to construct meaning must and do contend with in various ways. This baggage is both constraining and enabling, and its impact is as great on conventional political procedures and decisions as it is on the so-called moral issues.

Given these overarching concerns, I needed a methodological approach that would allow me to both illustrate the evolving process through which moral meanings get constructed—via a historical–interpretive perspective—and explore what factors might influence the extent to which, and to what ends, political actors engage in moral politics—via a cross-national comparison. In subsequent studies I have pursued more specific (and somewhat more manageable) questions arising out of this larger project pertaining to both abortion and capital punishment. For the purpose of this discussion, I focus on some of the issues I have encountered in my research on capital punishment in the 19th and early 20th centuries, especially those associated with finding, selecting, evaluating, and drawing inferences from appropriate documents.

How to find and select data? First, because political decisions are almost always accompanied by interpretive negotiations, political records from the legislature, courts, and other governmental institutions were necessary. In Sweden, where complete transcripts of parliamentary sessions were available for the entire period, and where bills, propositions, hearings and reports are generally preserved and accessible (e.g., at the Parliament Library), this was a relatively easy task. These types of records were more problematic to collect for the United States, however, especially because capital punishment has been handled legislatively primarily at the state level, rapidly turning 1 case into 50. Moreover, as I found out when I started this phase of the data collection effort (at the Library of Congress, which has the most comprehensive holding of state legislative records outside the individual states), records at the state level are much less complete than at the federal level and vary extensively in terms of content and organization across states (e.g., only occasional transcripts of debates; sometimes no index to bills or issues; missing volumes). So how did I deal with the United States? First, I pulled as much information as I could out of the secondary literature, including dissertations and theses, on conflict and policy regarding capital punishment in the various states. Second, I searched *The New York Times* index (which is relatively comprehensive from about the 1870s) for any entry dealing with capital punishment, executions, the death penalty, and, in some cases, murder. Although this search produced significantly more information about New York than other states, it nevertheless yielded lots of useful, if somewhat arbitrary, information on developments in other states. Here it helps that capital punishment has been a contentious and highly symbolic issue for a very long time. Finally, once I had a better sense of when and where things happened, I turned to state-level newspapers, none of which have indexes, for more comprehensive and detailed information about state-level happenings at the political level (I again relied on the holdings of the Library of Congress, which are impressive but incomplete). The result of these various strategies is a relatively complete, if bare in many cases, picture of when and where capital punishment was subject to political debate and what the outcomes of those debates were in terms of policy.

In order to gain a deeper understanding of the meanings attached to political decisions, however, I deemed it necessary to go back one step and examine the major collective sources of political positions, such as political parties and various interest groups and organizations (e.g., medical, religious, legal, and social movements). Here both my efforts and the results of those efforts were more scattered, in part because these types of materials can be more difficult to locate and access (except for medical journals, which are well preserved and, toward the end of the 19th century, sufficiently indexed across different journals to access relatively easily) and in part because I feared "drowning" in primary documents that were only potentially relevant. Nevertheless, I made a serious but, in the end, futile effort to retrieve primary materials from the major political parties in Sweden, where the parties were somewhat more likely to develop a party position on capital punishment than they were in the United States. I was somewhat more successful regarding the activities of the Social Democratic party, which has been the dominant party in Sweden since the 1930s and which maintains its own archive. Some historical records for the other parties are maintained by the National Archive, but the material is incomplete and not organized in a way that gives ready access to particular substantive issues. Moreover, I was not convinced, given what I had learned from the legislative records, that there would be a significant payoff from spending too much effort searching for party records.

Regarding the records of other types of interest groups, I relied in part on a scattered but sometimes very useful secondary literature (for both nations) and in part, especially for the United States, on a wide array of magazines (some of which were tied to particular interests) that by the end of the 19th century attracted commentaries on a wide range of subjects from a wide range of interest groups. Here I relied heavily on the extensive holdings of my home institution, the State University of New York at Stony Brook, and the invaluable services of interlibrary loan. Not only are many of the 19th-century magazines available and indexed (again, it helps to work with a subject that is well defined and recurrent enough to have warranted an index entry), but also a unified index (the *Readers' Guide to Periodical Literature*) that covers a range of magazines is available from the beginning of the 20th century. In addition, legislative records sometimes contain reports and petitions submitted by various interest groups that have taken an interest in the issue of capital punishment, including professional groups, social movement organizations, and religious organizations. I also searched for and located several 19th-century books and pamphlets (many self-published) addressing the issue of capital punishment from a number of vantage points. From these varied data sources I gained a fairly comprehensive picture of the positions and roles of various interest groups in the debate and policy-making surrounding capital punishment in both nations.

Regarding newspapers, I first used them primarily as complementary sources of information (e.g., places, dates, and legislative and interest group activities), but as I was browsing the coverage of capital punishment, it became increasingly clear to me that newspapers constituted a major force of their own in channeling, even shaping, the debate over capital punishment. As intermediaries between the public and various political actors, in other words, newspapers are prime locations for identifying images of dominant and competing meanings. Newspapers aimed at a mass public mushroomed in the United States during the latter half of the 19th century, and by the end of the century several daily papers had reached a circulation of more than a million copies. Widespread circulation, commercialism and competition, and the emergence of journalism as a new profession all combine to make newspapers an excellent source of information about public controversies and, occasionally, to make newspapers themselves the originators of, or at least contributors to, political controversy. More specifically, it became evident to me that newspaper stories about murder and executions revealed much more about the symbolic and rapidly shifting tensions permeating capital punishment than the more "reasoned" and principled arguments delivered by legislators and professionals on either side of the debate. Hence, I began to view newspapers as a much more central data source than I had originally anticipated, which, in turn, led me to pose research questions that more directly pertained to the role of newspapers in constructing meanings about capital punishment. But this shift also raised new methodological issues concerning how exactly to treat newspapers as a data source.

Here I discuss in more detail a few of the challenges I have faced, and continue to face, in two different research endeavors that involve newspapers: (1) the transformation of the American execution audience, which raises issues about data selection, and (2) the role of women in 19th-century conflicts surrounding capital punishment, with a particular focus on the execution of women, which, in addition to selection issues, also raises issues of inference. My interest in the execution audience emerged slowly as I began reading stories about executions and eventually resulted in a file folder entitled "the audience" in which I stuck notes and references pointing to the audience; but it was not until I read a conference call for papers dealing with various aspects of "the audience" that I realized I could probably do something sociological with my disparate notes. What I set out to do was to trace the process whereby the audience was transformed from a rowdy crowd to a few select witnesses and to place that transformation in the context of both the interpretive conflicts over capital punishment and 19th-century cultural change more generally. And I had plenty of data, I thought, once I reviewed all the execution stories I had collected for other purposes. With some embarrassment I confess that it was not until I got the first round of reviews back (once

the paper was submitted to a journal) that I was forced to confront the data issue more directly: "A bit more detail about the data—what it consists of, how it was analyzed—would be helpful. This latter question is particularly important: was there any attempt made to ensure that the data were analyzed systematically?" This small and polite comment by one of the reviewers set in motion a process that resulted in more data and a much greater awareness on my part about the particular methodological issues I was faced with. On the editor's urging, the article ended with an appendix in the published version describing some of the problems and how I solved them (Linders, 2002). What follows is an elaboration of some of the issues addressed in that appendix.

Had I analyzed the data "systematically"? Definitely not, if by this we mean that the execution stories I analyzed were randomly selected, either from the total pool of executions (such a sample would actually have been possible to draw from an extraordinary data file of American executions assembled by Watt Espy and Ortiz Smykla [1994]) or from the total pool of execution stories published in 19th-century newspapers (this sample would not have been possible to draw given the gaps in the collections of historical newspapers). More important, I concluded that neither a random sample of executions nor a random-like sample of execution accounts would have served the ends of this article very well. Rather, I made an attempt to target execution depictions from different geographical regions (to ensure that I did not rely too heavily on the urban papers in the Northeast), different types of newspapers (both tabloids and so-called respectable papers), and different kinds of controversies (e.g., over execution methods, women as convicts, mishaps). These efforts produced a pool of execution accounts that, I concluded, were relatively typical in their variety of the range of stories that newspapers printed.

Moreover, given the links I had already uncovered between execution controversies and the politics of capital punishment, I made an effort to select stories about executions that for various reasons came to represent critical events in the history of capital punishment, either locally or nationally—for example, the first execution in a county, the first execution of a woman, the first electrocution, the first so-called private execution, the first state-centralized execution, and various other newsworthy aspects involving convicts and/or their crimes. The result of this selection process was a data set deliberately skewed in the direction of controversy and sensationalism. As descriptions of controversial executions, however, the range of accounts are fairly typical in the sense that any one account of a controversial execution generally could have been substituted for another in a similar outlet, and, in fact, many accounts were replicated in more than one newspaper, a practice facilitated by the emergence of central news organizations such as the Associated Press but begun much earlier. The total pool of execution stories I ended up working with for that particular article involved some 200 executions drawn from about 140 different newspapers.

Although they shared a general approach to reporting executions, newspapers nevertheless produced accounts that for each individual execution could differ markedly in ways that involved not only details (e.g., dress, appetite, general demeanor of the convict) but also for my purposes potentially more significant aspects of the execution (e.g., mishaps, blood, visible expressions of pain, disturbances, audience depictions). Thus different newspapers not infrequently gave different accounts of the same execution, some claiming a flawless and orderly arrangement, whereas others emphasized mishaps, drama, and confusion. The discrepancies in such cases have multiple origins, I determined, including different journalistic practices, different editorial stances regarding capital punishment, and, occasionally, different responses to official gag orders (several states tried to suppress sensationalistic newspaper accounts of executions). Had my ambition been to evaluate

these different accounts in terms of how accurately they described the execution and its audience, I would evidently have faced some real difficulties, not only because of the differences in newspaper coverage but also because much of the secondary literature about 19th-century crowds generally, and execution crowds in particular, is filtered through various interpretive lenses that directly affect depictions of the audience. However, given that my argument was built on claims, not objective features, both the discrepancies themselves and the subsequent debates about how newspapers should report on executions ended up strengthening rather than weakening the conclusions drawn.

The second project, involving capital punishment and gender, also emerged slowly as I read more and more stories of and about executions, but it became more focused as a result of the project on the execution audience, which clearly revealed a significant gender dimension (women disappeared as audience members once executions became private). Some of the selection problems discussed previously have carried over into this project, but with a few new twists. One of my research goals is to use capital punishment generally, and the execution of women particularly, as an especially vibrant site for exploring the constructions and contradictions of womanhood in the 19th century. Specifically, I want to document the process whereby meanings surrounding both capital punishment and gender produced a state of affairs in which the execution of women produced major public controversies that split open the fragile foundation upon which the bourgeois notion of womanhood rested. Here I address only the first step toward this goal, which involves the vanishing female audience members.

My contention in the audience article that women audience members brought trouble to the legitimacy of public executions was accepted by the reviewers of that paper but challenged on evidentiary grounds by a subsequent reviewer of a paper that focused more directly on this issue, thus forcing me to review the link I thought I had established between the data and the conclusion. This process is not concluded at the time of writing this chapter, so what I am describing here is an as yet unresolved methodological problem. Could my inference be wrong? If not, how will I be able to convince the reviewer that the inference is appropriate and justified by the data? The evidence I used to make the inference was primarily a series of quotes from accounts of public executions that singled out, and sometimes overtly criticized, women audience members, but I also included a sketch of an execution (drawings were part of the 19th century newspaper landscape, especially in the tabloids) with a prominently displayed group of women and children among the audience. This drawing, I asserted, supported my contention that such representations added tension and drama to the story *because* they involved women and children. Problem number one: I have a few other such drawings involving different executions, with a near replica of the group of women and children, which add credence to my claim. However, in one case, the information about which paper the drawing comes from has somehow gotten lost (if I ever had it), which means I cannot use it; and in another case, the quality of the copy, printed from a grainy microfilm, is so poor as to make reproduction almost impossible. But knowing that that these other examples exist increases my confidence that I am right about the first drawing, which gives me two options. I can either try to retrieve the missing citation and/or try to get a better copy, or I can turn to the secondary literature for more information on the representation of women in 19th-century drawings (e.g., the showing of feet signals questionable respectability).

About the textual evidence I used, the reviewer similarly was unconvinced that the sheer mentioning of women as audience members added tension to the stories and indicated something significant about gender. Problem number two: Although it is true that a number of execution stories comment on women audience members, numerous other stories say nothing about the gender composition of the audience, or simply state without further comment that the audience was composed of women as well as men, thus weakening my claims. But given that mentions of women, but never of men, often were accentuated, by italics or exclamation marks, for example, I remain convinced that my inference is basically right. That does not solve the problem of how to persuade an unconvinced reader, however. So, what to do? One option is to find additional evidence, both by locating more execution stories from the critical time period I am interested in that comment on women audience members and by locating more stories from an earlier period that do not contain such comments. I am in the process of doing these things, even though the second of these strategies is made more difficult by the availability of fewer newspapers with much more limited circulation, by a greater time lag between events and stories, and by a much less pronounced news emphasis on crime and punishment). Another option, again, is to dig deeper into the secondary literature, which has already provided me with useful additional evidence about how gender entered into the realm of capital punishment in the 19th century that dovetails with my own evidence.

Conclusion: Documents Matter

The most basic conclusion of this chapter is precisely that documents matter. And they matter in particular ways for those engaging in constructionist research. And yet the constructionist literature is filled with studies that gloss over the process whereby the documentary sources used to draw conclusions from were located and selected (though this is not to suggest that constructionist literature as a whole is methodologically worse off than other literatures). This glossing over does not necessarily mean that the methodology guiding the selection of documents is wanting in any way, but it does indicate that the disciplinary tradition among historians, for example, to provide detailed accounts about sources and decision-making rules has no established constructionist counterpart. Given both the potentially far-reaching consequences of different documentary sources for our ability to draw persuasive conclusions and the limited (but certainly not non-existent) utility of the methodological rules developed by practitioners in other research traditions for constructionist analysts, this is unfortunate.

This chapter, therefore, should be read not only as prescription of sorts for solving particular methodological problems associated with the use of documents in constructionist research but also as a more general attempt to instill a greater awareness among constructionists about the importance of clear, and clearly explicated, strategies for dealing with documents. Those strategies, as I have tried to show, ultimately are not about using our common sense but instead involve a series of more systematic considerations including (1) the availability of documents, (2) the methods we use for locating particular documents to analyze, both across and within document types, (3) the extent to which various documentary biases and inaccuracies might influence our analysis, and (4) the inferences that can be drawn from the particular documents we use. Taken together, these considerations point to the critical importance of a solid documentary foundation on which to build our analyses of reality construction.

• Notes

1. The *Journal of Documentation* is an excellent starting point for anyone interested in the range of issues involved in storing, organizing, and accessing documentary information regarding, for example, cataloging library holdings (Šauperi, 2005), the process of indexing novels (Saarti, 2002) and holdings at a film archive (Hertzum, 2003), and the standardization of digital information resources (Chaudhry & Jium, 2005).

2. For the purposes of this discussion, I am not dealing with questions related to the authenticity of documents—that is, whether a document is in fact what it purports to be (e.g., a real as opposed to fake Picasso painting)—but instead focus on truth issues of otherwise authentic documents. However, it is important to keep in mind that questions of authenticity are paramount to some research purposes, for example, the analysis of slave narratives (Gates, 2002).

• References

Abrams, P. (1982). *Historical sociology*. Ithaca, NY: Cornell University Press.

Abu-Laban, Y., & Garber, J. A. (2005). The construction of the geography of immigration as a policy problem: The United States and Canada compared. *Urban Affairs Review, 40*(4), 520–561.

Ahlkvist, J. A., & Faulkner, R. (2002). "Will this record work for US?": Managing music formats in commercial radio. *Qualitative Sociology, 25*(2), 189–215.

Altheide, D. L. (1999). Qualitative media analysis. In A. Bryman & R. G. Burgess (Eds.), *Qualitative research* (Vol. II, pp. 235–255). London: Sage.

Ariès, P. (1962). *Centuries of childhood: A social history of family life*. New York: Vintage Books.

Bauer, M. W. (2000). Analysing noise and music as social data. In M. W. Bauer & G. Gaskell (Eds.), *Qualitative researching with text, image and sound: A practical handbook* (pp. 263–281). London: Sage.

Bauer, M. W., & Aarts, B. (2000). Corpus construction: A principle for qualitative data collection. In M. W. Bauer & G. Gaskell (Eds.), *Qualitative researching with text, image and sound: A practical handbook* (pp. 19–37). London: Sage.

Bell, L. (1999). Public and private meanings in diaries: Researching family and childcare. In A. Bryman & R. G. Burgess (Eds.), *Qualitative research* (Vol. II, pp. 263–278). London: Sage.

Ben-Yehuda, N. (1995). *The Masada myth: Collective memory and mythmaking in Israel*. Madison: University of Wisconsin Press.

Berg, M. (1996). Practices of reading and writing: The constitutive role of the patient record in medical work. *Sociology of Health and Illness, 18*(4), 499–524.

Best, J. (Ed.). (1989). *Images of issues: Typifying contemporary social problems*. New York: Aldine de Gruyter.

Best, J. (1990). *Threatened children: Rhetoric and concern about child-victims*. Chicago: University of Chicago Press.

Best, J. (1993). But seriously, folks: The limitations of the strict constructionist interpretation. In G. Miller & J. A. Holstein (Eds.), *Constructionist controversies: Issues in social problems theory* (pp. 109–127). New York: Aldine de Gruyter.

Best, J. (2001). *Damned lies and statistics: Untangling numbers from the media, politicians, and activists.* Berkeley: University of California Press.

Blee, K. (2002). *Inside organized racism: Women in the hate movement.* Berkeley: University of California Press.

Bloor, M. (1991). A minor office: The variable and socially constructed character of death certification in a Scottish city. *Journal of Health and Social Behavior, 32*(3), 273–287.

Bogard, C. J. (2003a). Explaining social problems: Addressing the whys of social constructionism. In J. A. Holstein & G. Miller (Eds.), *Challenges and choices: Constructionist perspectives on social problems* (pp. 209–235). Hawthorne, NY: Aldine de Gruyter.

Bogard, C. J. (2003b). *Seasons such as these: How homelessness took shape in America.* New York: Aldine de Gruyter.

Bornat, J. (2004). Oral history. In C. Seale, G. Gobo, J. F. Gubrium, & D. Silverman (Eds.), *Qualitative research practice* (pp. 34–47). London: Sage.

Boyce, R. W. D. (2000). Fallacies in interpreting historical and social data. In M. W. Bauer & G. Gaskell (Eds.), *Qualitative researching with text, image and sound: A practical handbook* (pp. 318–335). London: Sage.

Burgess, A. (2004). *Cellular phones, public fears, and a culture of precaution.* Cambridge, UK: Cambridge University Press.

Butler, J. (1999). *Gender trouble: Feminism and the subversion of identity.* New York: Routledge.

Byrne, S. (2003). *Constructing racialized identities in the search for intimate relationships: An analysis of personal advertisements, 1974–2002.* Unpublished doctoral dissertation, University of Cincinnati.

Chartier, R., Boureau, A., & Dauphin, C. (1997). *Correspondence: Models of letter-writing from the Middle Ages to the nineteenth century.* Princeton, NJ: Princeton University Press.

Chaudhry, A. S., & Jium, T. P. (2005). Enhancing access to digital information resources on heritage: A case of development of a taxonomy of the integrated museum and archives system in Singapore. *Journal of Documentation, 61*(6), 751–776.

Cicourel, A. V. (1987). The interpenetration of communicative contexts: Examples from medical encounters. *Social Psychology Quarterly, 50*(2), 217–226.

Collins, P. Hill. (1989). The social construction of invisibility: Black women's poverty in social problems discourse. *Perspectives on Social Problems, 1,* 77–93.

Delaney, K. (1994). The organizational construction of the "bottom line." *Social Problems, 41*(4), 497–518.

Denzin, N. K. (2000). The Practices and Politics of Interpretation. In N. K. Denzin & Y. S. Lincoln (Eds.), *Handbook of qualitative research* (2nd ed., pp. 897–922). Thousand Oaks, CA: Sage.

Duwe, G. (2005). A circle of distortion: The social construction of mass murder in the United States. *Western Criminology Review, 6*(1), 59–78.

Ekecrantz, J. (1997). Journalism's "discursive events" and sociopolitical change in Sweden 1925–87. *Media, Culture and Society, 19,* 393–412.

Espy, M. W., & Smykla, J. O. (1994). *Executions in the United States, 1608–1991: The Espy file* [Computer file] (3rd ICPSR ed.). Ann Arbor, MI: Inter-university Consortium for Political and Social Research.

Featherstone, M. (2006). Archive. *Media, Culture and Society, 23*(2/3), 591–596.

Fine, G. A. (1997). Scandal, social conditions, and the creation of public attention: Fatty Arbuckle and the "problem of Hollywood." *Social Problems, 44*(3), 297–323.

Fine, M., Weis, L., Weseen, S., & Wong, L. (2003). For whom? Qualitative research, representations, and social responsibilities. In N. K. Denzin & Y. S. Lincoln (Eds.), *The landscape of qualitative research: Theories and issues* (2nd ed., pp. 167–207). Thousand Oaks, CA: Sage.

Fleury, R. E., Sullivan, C. M., Bybee, D. J., & Davidson, W. S., II. (1998). What happened depends on whom you ask: A comparison of police records and victim reports regarding arrests for woman battering. *Journal of Criminal Justice, 26*(1), 53–59.

Foucault, M. (1990). *The history of sexuality: Vol. I. An introduction.* New York: Vintage Books.

Gans, H. J. (1980). *Deciding what's news: A study of* CBS Evening News, NBC Nightly News, Newsweek *and* Time. New York: Vintage Books.

Garcia, A. (1991). Dispute resolution without disputing: How the interactional organization of mediation hearings minimizes argument. *American Sociological Review, 56*(6), 818–835.

Gardner, C. B. (1994). The social construction of pregnancy and fetal development: Notes on a nineteenth-century rhetoric of endangerment. In T. R. Sarbin & J. I. Kitsuse (Eds.), *Constructing the social* (pp. 45–64). London: Sage.

Gates, H. L., Jr. (Ed.). (2002). *The bondwoman's narrative: Hannah Crafts.* New York: Warner Books.

Gobo, G. (2004). Sampling, representativeness and generalizability. In C. Seale, G. Gobo, J. F. Gubrium, & D. Silverman (Eds.), *Qualitative research practice* (pp. 435–456). London: Sage.

Gubrium, J. F. (1993). For a cautious naturalism. In J. A. Holstein & G. Miller (Eds.), *Reconsidering social constructionism: Debates in social problems theory* (pp. 89–101). New York: Aldine de Gruyter.

Gubrium, J. F., & Holstein, J. A. (1997). *The new language of qualitative method.* New York: Oxford University Press.

Gubrium, J. F., & Holstein, J. A. (2003). Analyzing interpretive practice. In N. K. Denzin & Y. S. Lincoln (Eds.), *Strategies of qualitative inquiry* (pp. 214–248). Thousand Oaks, CA: Sage.

Gusfield, J. R. (1981). *The culture of public problems: Drinking–driving and the symbolic order.* Chicago: University of Chicago Press.

Hacking, I. (1999). *The social construction of what?* Cambridge, MA: Harvard University Press.

Hall, J. R. (2003). Cultural history is dead (long live the Hydra). In G. Delanty & E. F. Isin (Eds.), *Handbook of historical sociology* (pp. 151–167). London: Sage.

Hallgrimsdottir, H. K., & Benoit, C. (2006). Fallen women and rescued girls: Social stigma and media narratives of the sex industry in Victoria, B.C., from 1980 to 2005. *Canadian Review of Sociology and Anthropology, 43*(3), 265–280.

Harper, D. (2000). Reimagining visual methods: Galileo to neuromancer. In N. K. Denzin & Y. S. Lincoln (Eds.), *Handbook of qualitative research* (2nd ed., pp. 717–732). Thousand Oaks, CA: Sage.

Hertzum, M. (2003). Requests for information from a film archive: A case study of multimedia retrieval. *Journal of Documentation, 59*(2), 168–186.

Hodder, I. (2000). The interpretation of documents and material culture. In N. K. Denzin & Y. S. Lincoln (Eds.), *Handbook of qualitative research* (2nd ed., pp. 703–715). Thousand Oaks, CA: Sage.

Holbrook, T. L. (1996). Document analysis: The contrast between official case records and the journal of a woman on welfare. *Marriage and Family Review, 24*(1/2), 41–56.

Holstein, J. A., & Gubrium, J. F. (2003). A constructionist analytics for social problems. In J. A. Holstein & G. Miller (Eds.), *Challenges and choices: Constructionist perspectives on social problems* (pp. 187–208). Hawthorne, NY: Aldine de Gruyter.

Ibarra, P. R. & Kitsuse, J. I. (1993). Vernacular constituents of moral discourse: An interactionist proposal for the study of social problems. In G. Miller & J. A. Holstein (Eds.), *Constructionist controversies: Issues in social problems theory* (pp. 21–54). New York: Aldine de Gruyter.

Jackson, R. L. (2006). *Scripting the black masculine body: Identity, discourse, and racial politics in popular media.* Albany: State University of New York Press.

Johnson, J. M. (1995). Horror stories and the construction of child abuse. In J. Best (Ed.), *Images of issues: Typifying contemporary social problems* (pp. 17–31). New York: Aldine de Gruyter.

Kitsuse, J. I., & Cicourel, A. V. (1963). A note on the use of official statistics. *Social Problems, 11*(2), 131–139.

Komter, M. L. (2006). From talk to text: The interactional construction of a police record. *Research on Language and Social Interaction, 39*(3), 201–228.

Kuipers, G. (2006). The social construction of digital danger: Debating, defusing and inflating the moral dangers of online humor and pornography in the Netherlands and the United States. *New Media and Society, 8*(3), 379–400.

Landes, D. S., & Tilly, C. (Eds.). (1971). *History as social science.* Englewood Cliffs, NJ: Prentice Hall.

Laslett, P. (2005). The wrong way through the telescope: A note on literary evidence in sociology and in historical sociology. In J. A. Hall & J. M. Bryant (Eds.), *Historical methods in the social sciences* (Vol. III, pp. 199–226). London: Sage.

Lee, A. (2000). Discourse analysis and cultural (re)writing. In A. Lee & C. Poynton (Eds.), *Culture and text: Discourse and methodology in social research and cultural studies* (pp. 188–202). Lanham, MD: Rowman & Littlefield.

Lesko, N. (2001). *Act your age! A cultural construction of adolescence.* New York: Routledge Falmer.

Linders, A. (1998). Abortion as a social problem: The construction of "opposite" solutions in Sweden and the United States. *Social Problems, 45*(4), 488–509.

Linders, A. (2002). The execution spectacle and state legitimacy: The changing nature of the American execution audience, 1833–1937. *Law and Society Review, 36*(3), 607–656.

Loizos, P. (2000). Video, film and photographs as research documents. In M. W. Bauer & G. Gaskell (Eds.), *Qualitative researching with text, image and sound: A practical handbook* (pp. 93–107). London: Sage.

Marontate, J. (2005). Museums and the constitution of culture. In M. D. Jacobs & N. Weiss Hanrahan (Eds.), *The Blackwell companion to the sociology of culture* (pp. 286–301). Malden, MA: Blackwell.

Miller, G., & Holstein, J. A. (1993). Constructing social problems: context and legacy. In G. Miller & J. A. Holstein (Eds.), *Constructionist controversies: Issues in social problems theory* (pp. 3–18). New York: Aldine de Gruyter.

Miller, L. J. (1993). Claims-making from the underside: Marginalization and social problems analysis. In J. A. Holstein & G. Miller (Eds.), *Reconsidering social constructionism: Debates in social problems theory* (pp. 349–376). New York: Aldine de Gruyter.

Nichols, L. T. (1995). Cold wars, evil empires, treacherous Japanese: Effects of international context on problem construction. In J. Best (Ed.), *Images of issues: Typifying contemporary social problems* (2nd ed., pp. 313–334). New York: Aldine de Gruyter.

Orcutt, J. D., & Turner, J. B. (1993). Shocking numbers and graphic accounts: Quantified images of drug problems in the print media. *Social Problems, 40*(2), 190–206.

Penn, G. (2000). Semitic analysis of still images. In M. W. Bauer & G. Gaskell (Eds.), *Qualitative researching with text, image and sound: A practical handbook* (pp. 310–323). London: Sage.

Pfohl, S. (1977). The "discovery" of child abuse. *Social Problems, 24,* 31–24.

Phillips, N., & Hardy, C. (2002). *Discourse analysis: Investigating processes of social construction.* Thousand Oaks, CA: Sage.

Platt, J. (1981). Evidence and proof in documentary research: 1. Some specific problems of documentary research. 2. Some shared problems of documentary research. *Sociological Review, 29*(1), 31–66.

Pole, C. J. (Ed.). (2004). *Seeing is believing? Approaches to visual research.* Amsterdam: Elsevier.

Printz, J. K. (2003). "Every like is not the same," or is it?: Gender, criminal biographies, and the politics of indifference. In K. Kittredge (Ed.), *Lewd and no-*

torious: Female transgression in the eighteenth century (pp. 165–196). Ann Arbor: Michigan University Press.

Prior, L. (2003). *Using documents in social research.* London: Sage.

Prior, L. (2004). Documents. In C. Seale, G. Gobo, J. F. Gubrium, & D. Silverman (Eds.), *Qualitative research practice* (pp. 375–390). London: Sage.

Rafter, N. (1992). Claims-making and socio-cultural context in the first U.S. eugenics campaign. *Social Problems, 39*, 17–34.

Reinarman, C. (2005). Addiction as an accomplishment: The discursive construction of disease. *Addiction Research and Theory, 13*(4), 307–320.

Reinarman, C., & Levine, H. G. (1995). The crack attack: America's latest drug scare, 1986–1992. In J. Best (Ed.), *Images of issues: Typifying contemporary social problems* (2nd ed., pp. 147–186). New York: Aldine de Gruyter.

Rose, D. (2000). Analysis of moving images. In M. W. Bauer & G. Gaskell (Eds.), *Qualitative researching with text, image and sound: A practical handbook* (pp. 246–262). London: Sage.

Ruddell, R., & Decker, S. H. (2005). Kids and assault weapons: Social problem or social construction? *Criminal Justice Review, 30*(1), 45–63.

Russett, C. E. (1989). *Sexual science: The Victorian construction of womanhood.* Cambridge, MA: Harvard University Press.

Saarti, J. (2002). Consistency of subject indexing of novels by public library professionals and patrons. *Journal of Documentation, 58*(1), 49–65.

Sarbin, T. R., & Kitsuse, J. I. (1994). A prologue to constructing the social. In T. R. Sarbin & J. I. Kitsuse (Eds.), *Constructing the social* (pp. 1–18). London: Sage.

Šauperi, A. (2005). Subject cataloging process of Slovenian and American catalogers. *Journal of Documentation, 61*(6), 713–734.

Schudson, M. (1978). *Discovering the news: A social history of American newspapers.* New York: Basic Books.

Silverman, D. (1993). *Interpreting qualitative data: Methods for analysing talk, text and interaction.* London: Sage.

Skocpol, T. (Ed.). (1984). *Vision and method in historical sociology.* Cambridge, UK: Cambridge University Press.

Spector, M., & Kitsuse, J. I. (1977). *Constructing social problems.* Menlo Park, CA: Cummings.

Spencer, J. W. (2000). Appropriating cultural discourses: Notes on a framework for constructionist analyses of the language of claims-making. *Perspectives on Social Problems, 12*, 25–40.

Stacey, J. (1990). *Brave new families: Stories of domestic upheaval in late twentieth century America.* New York: Basic Books.

Stanley, L. (1995). Women have servants and men never eat: Issues in reading gender, using the Mass-Observation's 1937 day-diaries. *Women's History Review, 4*(1), 85–102.

Sterne, J., & Leach, J. (2005). The point of social construction and the purpose of social critique. *Social Epistemology, 19*(2–3), 189–198.

Stoler, A. L. (2005). Colonial archives and the art of governance. In J. A. Hall & J. M. Bryant (Eds.), *Historical methods in the social sciences* (Vol. III, pp. 247–271). London: Sage.

Szasz, T. S. (1970). *The manufacture of madness: A comparative study of the inquisition and the mental health movement.* New York: Harper Colophon Books.

Thorne, B. (1993). *Gender play: Girls and boys in school.* New Brunswick, NJ: Rutgers University Press.

Tierny, W. G. (1997). Lost in translation: Time and voice in qualitative research. In W. G. Tierny & Y. S. Lincoln (Eds.), *Representation and the text: Re-framing the narrative voice.* Albany: State University of New York Press.

Tuchman, G. (1978). *Making news: A study in the construction of reality.* New York: Free Press.

Wagner-Pacifici, R. (2005). Dilemmas of the witness. In M. D. Jacobs & N. Weiss Hanrahan (Eds.), *The Blackwell companion to the sociology of culture* (pp. 302–313). Malden, MA: Blackwell.

Webb, E. T., Campbell, D. T., Schwartz, R. D., Sechrest, L., & Belew Grove, J. (1981). *Nonreactive measures in the social sciences* (2nd ed.). Boston: Houghton Mifflin.

Wheeler, S. (Ed.). (1969). *On record: Files and dossiers in American life.* New York: Russell Sage Foundation.

Woolgar, S., & Pawluch, D. (1985). Ontological gerrymandering: The anatomy of social problems explanations. *Social Problems, 32*, 214–27.

Yanich, D. (2004). Crime creep: Urban and suburban crime on local TV news. *Journal of Urban Affairs, 26*(5), 535–563.

Yar, M. (2005). The global "epidemic" of movie "piracy": Crime wave or social construction? *Media, Culture and Society, 27*(5), 677–696.

Zuberi, T. (2003). *Thicker than blood: How racial statistics lie.* Minneapolis: University of Minnesota Press.

PART V

THE SOCIAL CONSTRUCTION OF WHAT?

CHAPTER 25

The Constructed Body

● Bryan S. Turner

Social constructionism in general is a critical theory that shows how social structures are merely "man-made" rather than immutable conditions, but, paradoxically, various forms of constructionism are deterministic and preclude human agency. In this analysis, a traditional theoretical distinction between agency and structure is employed in order to identify six types of constructionist theory. In broad terms, constructionism can produce deterministic (antihumanist) accounts of the processes by which social reality is constructed without significant reference to human agency; or it can emphasize social agency, by which social reality is constructed without significant reference to the constraints of social structure. This typology of six forms of constructionism identifies two versions of determinism, two forms of nondeterminism, and two schemes that combine agency and structure. For example, philosophical anthropology and various forms of structuralism that have been influenced by the legacy of Martin Heidegger tend to preclude human agency and to see the constructed nature of reality as socially determined. By contrast, "political constructionism" and "technological utopianism" both emphasize the role of agency in transforming the political context of official discourses. Finally, there are two versions of social constructionism, namely, symbolic interactionism and pragmatism, that implicitly embrace the notion of "structuration," (Giddens, 1984) in which agency produces structure and structure produces agency. To paraphrase Karl Marx, this final epistemological position argues that people construct their own classificatory schemes, but not under conditions of their own choosing.

This typology is intended to fulfill a heuristic role, and it is not offered as definitive or conclusive. There may be other cases, and different typologies are possible. For example, although feminist arguments tend to occur across all six theoretical positions, feminist epistemology has been influential particularly in antihumanist, technological, and political versions of constructionism. In addition, each type has a strong and a weak version. However, there is no need to complicate the typology further; the basic typology of six possible positions is sufficiently flexible to present an effective account of constructionism.

This typology is employed in considering the various ways in which sociologists have understood the human body as socially constructed (Turner, 1984, 1992). Taking the human body as a point of departure, my aim is to work toward a more general position that integrates the construction of the body as a cultural object with the embodiment of the agent in the everyday world. This integration is theoretically important for the somewhat conventional argument that sociology (like economics and politics) requires a theory of action, and because action requires agency and an actor, the human agents of social action and interaction are embodied. Such an interpretation of sociology does not involve methodological individualism, because sociology also presupposes the institutionalization of action. Actions are never wholly random or individual; they are produced by and shaped through institutionalization. In order to develop this sociology of actions and institutions, we need a conception of practical embodiment rather than simply a theory of classification. In particular, we should seek to develop a sophisticated understanding of embodiment in order to develop a richer view of the everyday world. Finally, the debate about social constructionism raises important issues about human agency, the no-

tion of social rights, and the assumption that human agents, unlike nonhuman agents, can be held responsible for their actions.

Social and Anthropological Structuralism

The body has been conceptualized by social anthropologists as a system of signs; that is, as a conduit of meaning and symbolism. Ritual preparation, scarification, and cultural transformations of the body in rites of passage have been central topics of cultural and social anthropology (Blacking, 1977). In 20th-century anthropology, this theoretical tradition was developed in the work of Mary Douglas (1966), for whom the body is an important source of metaphor about the organization of society. Disorganized bodies express social disorganization, as illustrated by magical attacks upon the body. Douglas captured the idea that the body is a metaphor of social equilibrium in her analysis of pollution and taboo. As a consequence, the input and output of the human body as a system has been used as a method of expressing social transformations and exchanges. Through this understanding of the symbolic richness of the body, Douglas sought to avoid a naturalistic conception of the body. Pollution is not a problem of hygiene, but a problem of classification.

For social anthropology, the body is a means of thinking about metaphorical relations. Thus the dietary rules of Judaism, as they are expressed in Leviticus, are in fact a means of thinking about social relationships and a means of expressing social harmony. The prohibition on pork was not a hygienic measure based on scientific knowledge; rather, it expressed an anxiety about category confusions, in that pigs have cloven feet but do not ruminate.

Two aspects of this tradition of social anthropology can be noted. First, the focus of the theory is on "the body" as a classificatory scheme, and second, the theory is a form of structuralism, because the agents exercise little active control over the contradictory nature of classification. It might be said that human agents do not decide, for example, whether the basic laws of Frege's system of logic are true, because the truth of these propositions is a function of the system as a whole. In a similar fashion, the structure of a classificatory scheme in religious culture is, as it were, given to the agent. In the terms of Émile Durkheim's sociology of religion, the dichotomy of the sacred and the profane is a "social fact" (Durkheim, 2001). There is little evidence in this tradition of anthropology and sociology of classificatory systems that agents have much scope to contest or to re-negotiate the structure of the classificatory scheme. The classificatory scheme is a cultural construct, but it is also a social fact.

There is another tradition of philosophical anthropology that has been influential in the development of social constructionism. In its modern form, this tradition has been articulated in Peter L. Berger and Thomas Luckmann's sociology of knowledge, which is overtly and self-consciously based on the traditions of classical sociology. *The Social Construction of Reality* (Berger & Luckmann, 1966) can be regarded as the classical text of social constructionism within sociology. Whereas their constructionism was generated by debates in sociology over the legacy of Marx, Durkheim, and Mead, Berger's general sociology has been dominated by the philosophical anthropology of Arnold Gehlen (Turner, 2001). In his foreword to *Man in the Age of Technology* (Gehlen, 1980), Berger (1980) was explicit about the importance of Gehlen's philosophical anthropology in the development of his own work (Berger & Kellner, 1965). The tension between the conservative impulse of Gehlen's theory of institutions and the radical agenda of the sociology of knowledge makes Berger's sociology interesting but also ambiguous. In *Invitation to Sociology*, Berger (1963) developed a critical perspective that deconstructed everyday reality by uncovering its taken-for-granted assumptions. This humanistic sociology promised to expose the disguises and masks that cloak our social worlds, but, paradoxically, he also demonstrated that we need these disguises—these sociological conceits—to make our world orderly. We need a "sacred canopy" (Berger, 1967).

Following Nietzsche, Gehlen (1988) had argued in the 1950s that human beings are not yet finished animals. Human beings are poorly equipped biologically to deal with the world into which they are involuntarily thrown; they have no finite instinctual basis that is specific to a given environment and depend on a long period of socialization in order to adapt themselves to their world. In order to cope with this world openness, human beings are compelled to construct a cultural world to supplement their underdeveloped instinctual world. Berger and Luckmann (1966) went on to argue that, because human beings are biologically impoverished, they have to construct a social canopy around themselves. Social institutions are the cultural bridges between human groups and their natural environment, and it is through these institutions that human life becomes meaningful. In filling the gap created by instinctual deprivation and the world, institutions provide humans with psychological relief from the tensions generated by their undirected instinctual drives. Over time, these institutions are taken for granted and become part of the background assumptions of social action. By contrast, the social foreground is taken over by more reflexive, conscious practices. With modernization, however, deinstitutionalization occurs, and the social background becomes less reliable and more negotiable and, increasingly, an object of reflection. As the foreground expands, social life becomes more uncertain, risky, and reflexive.

It is interesting, therefore, that Berger and Luckmann's contribution to the debate about social constructionism was in fact based on a foundationalist ontology. We need to construct a social canopy because we are underequipped to inhabit our natural world. Berger and Luckmann have had relatively little to say about the body as such, and their main preoccupation has been with human biology, which they have interpreted through Gehlen's theory of instincts. In speaking about the body, they note that humans are bodies, in the same way that other mammals are bodies. But they also assert that "man *is* a body" and he has "that body at his disposal" (Berger & Luckmann, 1966, p. 68). This observation did not lead them, however, to develop the idea that humans have to be trained to use those bodies at their disposal. The peculiar character of human embodiment means that social order has to be constructed, but equally humans have to "forget" that social construction if their plausibility structures are to remain in place.

Berger's version of social constructionism has become unfashionable, because it is not easily reconciled with postmodern relativism, with the radical deconstruction of sexual categories by feminist theory, with the attack on racialized identities by subaltern studies, or with the rejection of determined and fixed homosexual identities by queer theory. In short, popular forms of social constructionism are basically antiessentialist, whereas Berger's sociology is rooted in a foundationalist ontology that recognizes the biological need for social order. Berger and Luckmann came to accept the argument of Helmut Schelsky (1969) that it is practically impossible to institutionalize a continuously critical questioning of social reality without undermining its credibility, thereby making the everyday world an insecure haven for humans.

This foundationalist ontology in the sociology of Berger and Luckmann helps to expose the underlying political nature of constructionist theories. As I discuss in the case of political constructionism, one could argue historically that radical social constructionism has emerged for the very reasons outlined by Gehlen, namely, that our background assumptions can no longer be taken for granted and that as a result they are foregrounded. Hence their legitimacy is constantly, if only implicitly, challenged. Insofar as the social world has become postmodern, there is skepticism about the legitimacy of grand narratives. For example, the notions that sexual identity is socially constructed and that gender is social rather than biological represent a challenge to many conventional, specifically Christian evangelical assumptions. It is because we cannot rely on our background institutions and characters that sexual identity is seen to be increasingly historically and socially contingent. Sexuality is no longer a taken-for-granted aspect of character; it is a negotiated feature of personality.

Despite the ironic nature of Berger and Luckmann's sociology, their position is deterministic in the sense that society cannot exist without adequate plausibility structures, and the sacred canopy, in order to be sacred, must exist in society as an incontrovertible social fact. Berger's ironic constructionism ultimately retreats from political radicalism in the interests of social cohesion (Berger, 1998), and, in his recent retrospective reflections on his study of religion, he has argued that we are witnessing a process of desecularization—a position that is ideologically and theoretically somewhat remote from radical constructionism (Berger, 1999).

Antihumanist Structuralism

Various forms of structuralism and poststructuralism have influenced the ways in which sociologists have approached the constructed nature of the social world. I refer here in a generic fashion to "antihumanism" to signify a range of modern philosophical traditions that, starting with Martin Heidegger's critique of humanism, reject the human subject as the source of rational knowledge and action. Heidegger's concept of Being (*Dasein*) involved a decisive attempt to separate himself from both existentialism and humanism. In his "letter on humanism" in 1946, Heidegger rejected any notion of the importance of intersubjective meaning and interaction and separated any notion of human subjectivity from the idea of Being (Heidegger, 1962). Critics of Heidegger have argued that this antihumanism in his later work is an implicit indication of his sympathy for national socialism as an ideology, in which the will of the folk is overwhelmingly more important than interpersonal subjectivity and individual will (Wolin, 1990). There are many contemporary manifestations of this legacy, but generally any philosophical system that gives language a central place in the determination of what can be known tends toward structuralism. Both the linguistic and cultural turns are formulations of this theoretical strategy. To argue that the body is a text is to embrace what we might call "language determinism." It is also clear that, in his desire to reject the existentialism of Jean-Paul Sartre, Michel Foucault (1970) took over Heidegger's position by claiming that the human is only ever the product of an "order of things."

In the social sciences, the legacy of Louis Althusser and structural Marxism has also been influential. For example, the work of Judith Butler provides a valuable illustration of feminist theories of the body, which seek to deconstruct our conventional notions of materiality. Following her earlier study of *Gender Trouble* (1990), Butler (1993) elaborates a theory of gender by considering the effects of power on the material dimensions of sex and sexuality. In developing a philosophical critique of the regime of heterosexuality, which she perceives to be hegemonic in modern societies, she generates a distinctive approach to the materiality of the body through a consideration of how sex is produced and constrained by a heterosexual hegemony of power. The focus of this theoretical position is on the contributions of discourse analysis to our understanding of sexuality. She seeks to recast the matter of bodies as the consequence of a dynamic of power in which the materiality of bodies cannot be disassociated from the regulatory norms that produce their materialization

and signification. "The body" emerges through social iteration of "sex" within a hierarchy of power relations. It is this "performativity" of the reiterative power of discourse that produces the bodily phenomena that it constrains and regulates. Within this theoretical framework, "sex" can no longer be understood as simply a given fact of biology on which culture constructs various norms. There is no prediscursive reality of nature before language constitutes the self or the body. In approaching this materiality of the sexed body, she also wants to understand the subject as that which is produced through the very process of assuming a sex. This identification of the subject by the allocation of sex is connected with the discursive means through which the heterosexual power imperative generates certain social foreclosures on other forms of identity (Butler, 1993).

It is useful to approach this theory of performativity in terms of reiteration and citation via Althusser's notion of ideological interpellation (Althusser, 1971), in which the subject is hailed by ideology in terms of being called a name. Sexual identity involves the interpellation of gendered subjects by heterosexual regimes in which identification is citation. This approach becomes clear in her view of sexual difference and differentiation. Following the work of Luce Irigaray, Butler notes that "psychoanalysis has been used by feminist theorists to theorise sexual difference as a distinct and fundamental set of linguistic and culture relations" (Butler, 1993, p. 167). Sexual hierarchies interpolate individuals into a subjected status as a sexed subject; in this sense, the heterosexual call is an iterative performative sequence. When we give a child a personal name such as *Mary* we also put into place a process of social location, or "girling."

Butler's (1993) main focus is "sex" as a position within a space determined by the hegemonic discourse of heterosexuality, but it is not a contribution to the analysis of the materiality of the body in the sense that it might have for the anthropology of Marcel

Mauss (1979), in which material embodiment requires "body techniques." By this phrase, Mauss identified the different ways by which people learn how to use their bodies. He observed, for example, that British and French soldiers during World War I had entirely different techniques for digging. He also argued that children had to be taught to keep their eyes open under water, contrary to their instinctive ocular reflexes. In short, we need to be trained how to use our bodies. By contrast, Butler's approach indicates both the strength and weakness of textual and rhetorical studies. Sexuality is more than a position in a social space; it is a potentiality organized by disciplinary practices. Sex is a body technique, like digging and swimming under water, for which we need magazines on sexual positions. Furthermore, there is, in fact, little interest here in the materiality of the phenomenal body in the sense that sociologists might be concerned with understanding the effects of odor, secretions, and bodily decay on social interactions.

The issue of the aging body is always a useful test of the nature of any theoretical attempt to come to terms with human embodiment (Turner, 1995, 2004). Age, like sex, can be regarded as a position that is interpolated within a social hierarchy, but aging also involves a largely ineluctable transformation of the body and the body image via physical decline and decay. It is the discrepancy between the aging of the body in natural reality and the aging of the body in social reality that constitutes the existential problem of age for an individual. Social constructionists collapse the phenomenology of physical aging into an account of the discourses of social positions that aging people might occupy. The sociological study of elderly people leads us to the view that aging is a continuous process of disruptions through the life course, but age as a status is a classificatory system of exclusion, and gerontology is a discipline that contributes to the social construction of age and aging as social phenomena.

Foucault was also influenced by anti-humanist structuralism. He was both a student and friend of Althusser, and Althusserian methods of reading a text were important in his approach to both theory and methods. In retrospect, it is now clear that Foucault made two specific contributions to contemporary social science, namely, an analysis of power and the emergence of the modern self through technologies. His analysis of power has proved particularly useful in understanding the functions of the medical profession, particularly the functioning of the clinic (Foucault, 1973). Foucault's theory of power was a critical reaction against both French Marxism and the existentialism of Sartre. He attempted to challenge the Marxist conceptualization of power as a macrostructure, such as the state, which functioned to support capitalism and which was displayed through major public institutions such as the police, the law, and state agencies. Foucault saw power as a relationship that was localized, dispersed, and diffused through the social system, operating at a micro, or covert, level through sets of specific practices. Power is embodied in the day-to-day practices of the medical profession within the clinic, through the activities of social workers, through the day-to-day decision making of legal officers, and through the religious practices of the church as they operate through everyday life in the confessional. This view of power is very closely associated with Foucault's fascination with discipline, namely, that power exists through the disciplinary practices that produce particular individuals, institutions, and cultural arrangements. The disciplinary management of society results in a carceral that is a form of society in which the principles of Bentham's panopticon are institutionalized in society through everyday arrangements. These ideas about power were further elaborated through Foucault's interest in "governmentality," a system of power that articulated the triangular relationship between sovereignty, discipline, and government. Governmentality (Foucault, 1991), which emerged in the 18th century, is a mechanism for regulating and controlling populations through an apparatus of security. This governmental apparatus required a whole series of specific *savoirs* and was the foundation for the rise of the administrative state.

With the translation of his work into English, it became clear that for Foucault the study of medicine was part of a larger intellectual program that examined the evolution of sexuality in European societies from classical Greece and how that evolution was intimately bound up with the transformation of medicine. In his final publications, Foucault appeared to turn more and more to an analysis of the self in the context of medical history and the development of sexuality (Foucault, 1987, 1990). His interest in how the self in Western societies was an effect of discourse and disciplines of the self became increasing obvious in his studies of "technologies of the self" (Foucault, 1988).

For Foucault, the body was the crucial target in the evolution of these regulative practices. The normalization of the body was the outcome of new forms of knowledge and surveillance associated with the control of captive populations, such as armies, prisoners, and the mentally ill. The Foucauldian critique of modern medicine was that it represented a form of government that controlled individual transgression through a network of local normative constraints. It was an effective, localized institution of normative coercion to produce compliant patients. Although there was significant evolution and change in Foucault's social philosophy, it is clear that the body and populations played a major role in the analytic structure of his work. The body was the focus of military disciplinary practices, but it was also subject to the monastic regulation of medieval Catholicism. In these inquiries into the historical construction of the self through the truth of the body, there was no space for agency, because the power relations endlessly reproduced a regime of knowledge in which human subjectivity and agency have played no part.

Political Constructionism

Social constructionism has been important in a variety of social movements and political conflicts as a basis for advocacy. Political deployments of constructionist theories arise in contexts within which traditional categories of behavior have been challenged and contested. Political confrontation means that conventional patterns of behavior are no longer taken for granted, and hence their "plausibility structures" are shattered. For example, the idea that anorexia is socially constructed typically arises in a situation in which feminists want to deny the importance of physiology in social behavior and in which commercial norms of feminine beauty are regarded as problematic for both health and politics. By contrast, when categories of behavior or disease are not politicized, the question of their social construction tends not to occur. For example, gout does not appear to be a politically sensitive category, and thus there is little evidence of any desire on the part of medical sociologists to deconstruct or criticize this medical term. Social constructionism is therefore probably best regarded as a historical account of how certain diseases or sickness categories become accepted over time by the medical profession or by society and how that historical process is shaped by political struggles and economic interests. The historical reception of repetitive strain injury (RSI) is a particularly good illustration of this idea. RSI as a nonspecific discomfort or condition was constructed over time as a distinctive disease entity as a consequence of the lobbying of the victims of the condition (Turner, 1987).

The sociology of the body has also been developed around the questions of patriarchy, gender, sex, and sexuality. The question of the gendered nature of power has been facilitated by feminist and gay writing on the body. Much of the development of feminist theory about the body has been developed through French social theory, especially by Julia Kristeva, Hélène Cixous, and Luce Irigaray (Pateman & Gross, 1986), and then further elaborated by feminists such as Juliet Mitchell through a return to psychoanalytic theory, especially that of Jacques Lacan (Elliott, 1999). The specific application of this theoretical tradition to the body has been undertaken by a variety of feminist writers for very different purposes, but there are common aspects to the logic of the underlying argument. Both Cixous and Irigaray challenged the view of feminine sexuality in Freud and Lacan and turned to the body to valorize female difference. They defined female sexuality as open, dispersed, and multiple and developed a vision of female otherness as a challenge to male power. The notion of female specificity brought a criticism of essentialism against this tradition, and, as a counterweight to the prevailing ideological assumptions of biological determinism, feminist theory following Kristeva has emphasized the importance of symbolic power in the creation of the male–female dichotomy. The politics of sexual difference has thus established the centrality of the socially constructed body; it also requires the view that alleged emotional and moral differences between men and women are also social products and therefore can be changed and transformed.

One objection to this form of social constructionism might be to argue that, although social roles are constructed, anatomy is not. Whatever the role of culture in shaping personality, men and women just have different bodies, and these bodies are real (Evans & Lee, 2002). Recent historical writing on the history of anatomy is instructive in this context. For example, in his *Making Sex*, Thomas Lacqueur (1990) has shown how medieval theories of sexuality held to the doctrine of a single sex with dichotomous genders. The female body was simply a weakened, deformed, or inverted form of the male body. Anatomical investi-

gation was unable to transform this rigid ideological notion into an alternative discourse until the emergence of Freudian psychoanalysis. A considerable amount of contemporary scholarship, therefore, has gone into the historical analysis of the impact of Christian ideology on the presentation of gender differences as differences of a moral order (Ariès & Béjin, 1985; Bynum, 1991; Delany, 1998). Although much of this analysis is concerned with the historical shaping of the difference between men and women, gender differences continue to play a major role in the representation of power and authority in contemporary industrial societies. For example, Martin (1992) in *The Woman in the Body* has presented a fascinating analysis of the relationship between industrial production and reproduction, in which, for example, the reproduction of children is still referred to as "labor."

Political constructionism, unlike antihumanist structuralism, must retain a strong sense of human agency, because it is closely associated with political and social movements that seek to criticize taken-for-granted notions of an objective social order and that want to change the world through political action.

Technological Utopianism

A further field of sociological research involving constructionism is the relation between the body and technology. This form of constructionism is based on the literal notion that the human body could be rebuilt or reconstituted by the interventions of modern technology. I refer critically to this position as utopian, because it often approximates a science-fiction view of reality in which anything, in principle, is (technologically) possible. It is the utopian side of the normally dystopian, or Frankenstein, view of gender, science, and the human body. Technological utopianism celebrates or promotes a "mirage of health" (Dubois, 1960), in which the traditional afflictions of humanity could be removed by science, the earth could be made more abundant, and the modern killers (heart condition, strokes, and cancer) could be eliminated. Genetic counseling, artificial reproduction, genetic engineering, and cloning are in many senses spectacular illustrations of the possibilities opened up by the new genetics. These changes are forging a new imagination in constructing genetic maps of human life (Rothman, 1998). These scientific developments thus suggest a very special meaning for social constructionism that is close to social engineering but through the application of genetic science. These scientific changes present society—or, more specifically, governments—with an opportunity for political and social control through eugenics.

For example, the development of modern technology provides the potential to replace bodily functions and organs and to repair and upgrade the performance of the human body (Turner, 2004). It can do this in two ways. First, by directly altering the infrastructure of the body, genetic engineering is a further step in a series of increasingly radical techniques that will literally produce posthumans. Second, by constructing artificial devices and altering the immediate near-to-body environment, technology can augment and replace human capacities through systems designed to increase empowerment. In the former case, the inner structure of the body is changed or redesigned with technological replacement parts or devices, and in the latter case the body is fitted into a new "outer skin" of specially designed devices, machines, and technological environments. There has been considerable interest in the social implications of machine–body fusions, or cyborgs. There has long been a strong association between technology and masculinity. In popular culture, the film *Robocop* portrays the ultimate cyborg, the merging of machine and organism, but also incorporates very traditional gender themes about power and sexuality. The *homo faber* perspective of man as the maker and builder, in which hands are potent tools, is a pervasive modern myth that elevates a particular form of masculinity and denies the potential of alternative relations between the body and technology. In recent years, however, feminists have begun to confront the relationship between women and technology and to explore the potential benefits for women not only of reproductive technologies but also of the reproductive and emancipatory implications of new forms of technology (Haraway, 1991). Important here has been the interest in the new information technology and the potential of virtual reality and cyberspace. Computer simulations and networks create the possibilities of new experiences of disembodiment, reembodiment, and emotional attachment that threaten to transform many of the conventional assumptions about the nature of social relationships. The use of "e-mail sex" would be simply one illustration.

Technological constructionism, as an implicit framework, can also be said to include the political statements of performance artists such as Stelarc and Orlan. In the case of Orlan, the surgical reconstructions of her face are intended to be performances in which she ironically calls into question the transformation of women's bodies by cosmetics and cosmetic surgery. She is literally showing that medical technology can socially reconstruct her body. Here we see the body being used as a site upon which a performance occurs that delivers a powerful political statement (Featherstone, 2000). Although this type is an underdeveloped aspect of social constructionism, I include it here as a contrast to more deterministic models of the cultural production of the body. Orlan's surgery ironically displays the power of medical technology while also calling it into question as part of the apparatus of a consumer society.

Cosmetic surgery involves, therefore, the actual reconstruction of the "natural" body in order to produce social—that is, aesthetic—effects. The most common procedures for women are breast and facial surgery. In the United States, the cosmetic industry is clearly much larger and more acceptable. Whereas aesthetic surgery is becoming routine, the negative effects of cosmetic surgery have come to public attention through sensational cases such as the death of Lolo Ferrari, whose 18 operations created what were reputed to be the largest breasts in the world, with a 54G cup. There are other celebrity cases, such as Jocelyne Wildenstein, who has shaped her face around the image of a leopard. Orlan's surgical performances are thus designed to bring into question the alliance between medicine, market, and aesthetics in a consumer society in which the human (typically female) body is being simultaneously physically and socially reconstructed.

If the body is socially constructed, then some theorists of postmodern cyborgs suggest that the body—with its narratives or inscriptions of sex and gender—is disappearing with the rise of the "techno-body." For postmodern theories of hypermodernity (Kroker & Kroker, 1987), the natural body has no ontological status and has been deconstructed by a series of invasions to produce the "panic body." These are merely "inscribed surfaces" that function as the conduits for the debris of technological civilization. This postmodern analysis of the impact of hypermodernity on the body is rhetorically provocative (Balsam, 1995), but it is a remarkably limited view of the body in society. It does not touch on another aspect of how bodies in modern medicine might be reconstructed, namely through the exchange of organs. The global market in body "spare parts" should alert us to profound differences in the place of "the body" in rich and poor societies. The sale of organs and the gross inequalities in the organ marketplace conjure up a radically different picture of the "disappearance of the body." This postmodern body belongs to the utopian vision of the disappearing body, because it has little conceptual space not only for death and violence in the third world (Scheper-Hughes, 1992) but also for the routine problems of aging and decay in the everyday

world of rich societies. This image of the disappearing "pure body" of a cybernetic society has obviously no connection with ordinary people and their embodiment in mundane social relations (Riggs & Turner, 1999).

This techno-perspective on the body is utopian in one additional sense: It pays little attention to the alienation and exploitation of the body by a consumer-driven technological society. Far from disappearing, the body becomes increasingly obtrusive in a smooth technological society because its structures and rhythms do not always or easily fit into the demands of a machine age. It appears likely that the emergence of RSI among office workers in the 1980s was a consequence of the rapid introduction of computers into white-collar and professional occupations. In recent years, with the development of global call centers, telephone operators have complained of a new illness called "acoustic shock." New technologies have radical implications for the body, but we have yet to fully understand the long-term impact on health of computerization, mobile phones, or microwaves. For each new technology there is a corresponding disaster—airplanes are necessary in order to have plane crashes, the nuclear bomb is necessary to Hiroshima (Virilio, 2000). What disaster awaits the technologically enhanced body? However, technological determinism can also take a utopian direction in arguing, for example, that medical technologies could transform the human condition and, through stem cell research, could reverse the aging of the human body, permitting us literally to live forever. The body would no longer be a constraint on human agency, and biological determinism would be a thing of the past.

Symbolic Interactionism

Symbolic interactionism involves three principal claims (Blumer, 1969). First, the meanings of social reality are not fixed or intrinsic but the product of human interaction. The meanings of social reality emerge out of the constant flux of social exchange and are thus embedded in their local cultural context. Meaning and significance have no general or transsocial relevance. Second, when social actors from different settings or cultures interact, the meaning and importance of basic concepts are not necessarily shared and thus have to be negotiated. Unless common norms emerge from these negotiations, interaction will be confused and involve conflict. Third, agreement in interaction is achieved by negotiation between individuals or parties with different resources in terms of power and skill. Because misunderstanding and disagreement constantly threaten the micro-order of social action, social interaction involves teamwork. Thus social meanings can never be taken for granted, because they are constantly contested in everyday interactions, and human beings are self-reflexive about these meanings and constantly intervene to discuss and to change them. Such a perspective has been useful in studying the processes by and through which patients and doctors negotiate the meaning or significance of illness. This perspective also goes on to argue that these meanings of illness at the microsocial level are also conditioned by and have an impact on the more general macro-belief systems that surround health and illness concepts. At this general level, concepts of health and well-being become inextricably connected to fundamental notions of self-identity.

In a recent review of the history of symbolic interactionism, Ken Plummer (2000, p. 205) laments the fact that sociology has neglected the contributions of symbolic interactionism to the study of identity, the body, and habitus in recent writing about intimacies, structuration, and embodiment. In more specific terms, it is clear that, whereas medical sociology was dominated in the 1960s and early 1970s by symbolic interactionism, more recent approaches have been influenced by the poststructuralism of Foucault and by postmodernism. The irony is that, as Plummer points out, many of these approaches, especially with respect to the notion that the social world is socially constructed, are either compatible with or were produced by symbolic interactionism. The idea that the social world is continuously negotiated by social actors and that the everyday world is consequently produced by collective strategies was a core assumption of interactionism. We need to understand time as a dimension of this negotiated order. More important for medical sociology, we need to conceptualize time from the point of view of embodied social actors who are both individually and collectively passing through a life cycle.

In order to focus this discussion, I consider the contributions of Anselm L. Strauss. The principal component of symbolic interactionism is the notion of the social world as a negotiated order. This idea characterized the whole of Strauss's approach, from his early essays on "The Hospital and Its Negotiated Order" (Strauss, 1963) and "Mirrors and Masks" (Strauss, 1959) to his later work in *Negotiations* (Strauss, 1978). Society is something that is continuously produced by endless micro-negotiations about resources, identities, and meanings. Strauss's work has been specifically concerned with the negotiation of workplace settings such as hospitals and, specifically, how the social interface between technology, work organization, and occupational clusters is resolved or managed. The notion that settings are negotiated was not, of course, unique to Strauss. Much of the impetus for such a view of social reality came from Erving Goffman, especially in *Asylums* (1961), in which the organizational structure of social interactions involves, for example, constant negotiations between front and back stage.

In his final work, Strauss (1993) argued that these settings of action should be thought of as "continual permutations of action." Within this framework, he spoke of "the conditional matrix" and the conditional paths of action through it. The social was conceptualized as a series of circles from the global to the setting of action itself. The task of sociology is to chart the pathways of action through such conditional matrices. The paths through such social circles can be "short, long, thick, thin, loose, tight, startling, commonplace, visible, invisible" (Strauss, 1993, p. 60). The point of this analysis of action is to demonstrate that the micro–macro distinction is untenable.

Symbolic interaction, as its name indicates, gives a central place to action in sociological theory within the constraints of situational conditions and necessities. When symbolic interactionists paid special attention to the ceremonial order of interaction, then their theoretical position was close to that of Durkheim and hence to a deterministic vision of culture. Within this account of order, the body played a central role, especially in the work of Goffman. Following Durkheim, Goffman was concerned with understanding how a symbolic order was sustained through a myriad of actions that are the continual mutations of action. In this theory, the body became an important medium of order in terms of face work and embarrassment in interaction. Rather like social anthropological accounts, Goffman (1959) showed how disruptions to action are manifest in uncontrolled face work and gestures. Insofar as this symbolic order was a product of dramatic engagements, the dramaturgical approach suggested that agents could play strategic games within the broad context of fixed roles, stages, and actors. The body became important because many of its gestures—the flushing face of the deeply embarrassed person—were not easily controlled, and hence actors would need to undertake remedial work to restore a symbolic order. In the case of stigma, however, the body typically gave off signs that were beyond the active control of the agent, and hence there was once more a significant loss of face (Goffman, 1964). The social order is, from this perspective, constantly constructed through negotiations that typically involve interpretations of the signs given off by the body.

Symbolic interactionism can therefore be seen theoretically as a form of structuration in which social actions produce situational circumstances that in turn determine actions. In this account, the body is an indispensable component of action, but it also functions as an aspect of the context of actions.

Pragmatism

In the American sociological tradition, symbolic interactionism is normally interpreted as the product of American philosophical pragmatism. For example, the social philosophy of G. H. Mead provided one account of the relationship between the body, the self, and society, and his work was particularly important in the development of symbolic interactionism. Meadian social psychology has provided inspiration for sociologists for decades (Diggins, 1994; Joas, 1996). In this discussion of constructionism, it is useful to treat pragmatism somewhat separately from symbolic interactionism in order to draw out more specifically the rich and complex philosophical legacy of pragmatism. For example, the philosophical legacy of Mead raises the complex issue of whether a pragmatist can also be a realist (Dickstein, 1998). Although we can show that, for example, the work of Pierre Bourdieu is related to the pragmatist tradition, we cannot meaningfully argue that Bourdieu was a symbolic interactionist (Aboulafia, 1999). Therefore, there is some merit in treating symbolic interactionism and pragmatism separately.

Pragmatism suggests that philosophical problems in the everyday world are solved by routine practices. The answer to the question "Is this an apple?" is essentially practical—"Eat it!" So-called natural realism accepts that there is a real world that can be known through such empirical practices as looking, touching, and eating. At the same time, Mead argued that we live in a world that is symbolic and that these symbols define our social reality. This apparent tension in Meadian pragmatism between realism and antirealism has received no convincing solution in contemporary theory. In contemporary social theory, Richard Rorty's radical version of pragmatism has been influential as a criticism of empirical naturalism.

Rorty's reputation in modern philosophy was originally built on the foundations of his philosophy of science, namely, *Philosophy and the Mirror of Nature* (1979). One aspect of his argument is to claim that philosophers should give up the fantasy that philosophical truths could be a mirror of (or to) nature. If there are any philosophical truths, they are not representations (mirrors) of an objective reality. Because Rorty holds that all observations of nature are theory-dependent and that a correspondence theory of truth is untenable, he rejects realism as a plausible position. In many respects, his criticisms of representational theories of truth remain his principal contribution to what we might regard as mainstream or professional philosophy. His philosophy of science has been widely debated and reviewed (Malachowski, 1990; Margolis, 1986).The pragmatism that drives his view of the limited nature of philosophy is the same pragmatism that drives his view of political theory and politics. Thus his criticisms of representational theories of truth in *Philosophy and the Mirror of Nature* form the basis of his social philosophy, in which the attack on representational or correspondence theory is necessarily combined with his (somewhat idiosyncratic) version of liberalism.

Rorty's approach to science and truth claims owes a great deal to both John Dewey and Ludwig Wittgenstein, for whom the validity and authority of truth claims is a function of language and language is a set of social practices. The result of Dewey's pragmatism, for Rorty, was to demolish the Cartesian tradition that Truth can be grasped by a Mind Apart, and it introduces the social into the heart of any debate about truth and reality. In fact, it brings Rorty very close to ethnomethodology, because the social practices that interest Rorty are not the practices

of Humanity but what you and I do when we try to make sense of our everyday world. What you and I do with our bodies in the everyday world should therefore be of interest to pragmatist philosophers.

In his recent work, Rorty identified himself with the commonsense tradition of Hume against the rationalist and universalistic tradition of Kant and Hegel. The down-to-earth commonsense tradition of Scottish philosophy appears to have some similarity with Rorty's often rather homespun approach to philosophizing. Certainly in his treatment of Hume Rorty has been influenced by feminist theories, particularly in the analysis of Hume's moral philosophy—for example, in *A Progress of Sentiments: Reflections on Hume's Treatise* (Baier, 1991). Whereas Kant attempted to regard moral judgments as a branch of rational inquiry and treated aesthetic appreciation of beauty as a disinterested neutral judgment, Hume gave a central place to sentiment and affect in moral debate and aesthetic inquiry. Critical social thought, following Nietzsche's rejection of the Kantian approach to aesthetics, has argued that aesthetic judgment is essentially bound up with an emotional orientation to reality and cannot be divorced from sentiment. In my view, aesthetic judgments cannot be separated from the embodiment of the social beings who are doing the judging.

This implication of the body in practical reasoning about the everyday world from within a pragmatist set of assumptions has been developed by Richard Shusterman (1992, 2000, 2002) in a number of publications in which he has developed an approach to aesthetics to show how embodiment is central to aesthetic appreciation, such as rap musical performance. Shusterman (1992, 2000), drawing on the work of Bourdieu (1977, 2000) has argued that an aesthetic understanding of performance such as hip-hop cannot neglect the embodied features of artistic activity. The need for an understanding of embodiment and the lived experience of the body is crucial in understanding performing arts and also in the study of the dancing body (Turner, 2005). Although choreography is in one sense the text of the dance, performance takes place outside or beyond the strict directions of the choreographic work. Dance has an immediacy, which cannot be fully captured by discourse analysis or by representational study. It is important to recapture the intellectual contribution of the phenomenology of human embodiment in order to avoid this reduction of bodies to cultural texts.

Bourdieu's concepts of habitus, field, and capital are relevant, therefore, to the sociology of the performing body (Turner & Wainright, 2003). Although Bourdieu has clearly been the target of much critical assessment in recent years (Shusterman, 1999), the most interesting critical response has come from Shusterman in *Pragmatist Aesthetics* (1992) and *Surface and Depth* (2002). Shusterman makes an important contribution to aesthetic theory by examining the relationship between the pragmatist legacy of Dewey and Bourdieu's cultural sociology. In his emphasis on the body in relation to aesthetics, Shusterman (1992, 2000) makes the interesting point that Bourdieu's analysis of the cultural field is exclusively concerned with the audible (musical taste) and the visual (conventional works of art). Performance is not addressed by Bourdieu, despite the centrality of the concept of practice to his sociology as a whole. Shusterman argues that Bourdieu's sociology of the aesthetic is implicitly parallel to Adorno's critique of popular culture. Visual culture, such as a Baroque painting, or literary culture, such as a Shakespearean sonnet, have more cultural capital than a performance such as a dance routine. For example, Shusterman has been interested in rap music as a critique of society, but he does not regard rap as merely an expression of inauthentic popular culture. Claiming that Bourdieu's treatment of the everyday habitus as compatible with but superior to the social philosophy of language and rule following in Austin and Wittgenstein,

Shusterman (2002) argues that Bourdieu failed to provide an adequate sociology of experience, particularly aesthetic experience. He claims that Bourdieu's reluctance to treat experience (of movement) seriously is associated with the fact that appreciation of rap or tango falls outside the cultural privilege accorded to intellectual self-consciousness and reflection. Reliance on such intellectual introspection will not help us penetrate to "the deeper, unconscious, socially structured strata of the self that help shape individual consciousness" (Shusterman, 2002, p. 224). Despite Bourdieu's own protests to the contrary, Shusterman (2002, p. 221) claims that Bourdieu failed to deal with lived experience, especially an ephemeral experience of a dance gesture: "No sympathetic attention is given to the phenomenological dimension of lived experience, its power of meaningful, qualitative immediacy, and its potential for the transformation of attitudes and habits." Shusterman takes rap as a powerful instance of these problems, but dance in general provides as it were a litmus test of the scope of traditional aesthetic theory in which the Kantian legacy of disinterested, rational judgment is still omnipresent.

Conclusion: The Stuffness of Life and Social Action

By way of conclusion, I want to argue that our consideration of the constructed body has produced two general criticisms of social constructionism. The first is that most constructionist accounts of the body neglect or deny our experiences of embodiment (Seymour, 1998). This absence becomes especially important when we want to engage as sociologists in the analysis of pain, suffering, and impairment. It has the consequence of denying the very humanity of the agent. As the human body disappears behind the social and cultural constructions that produce it, the vulnerability of the human agent is obscured. What we share in common is our human vulnerability, which exposes us to pain and indignity, and for which we need the protection of human rights (Turner, 2006). In order to understand this vulnerability, we must not allow social construction wholly to obscure the phenomenological body. This argument entails our recognition of the "stuffness" of life. However, to recognize the importance of social rights in protecting us vulnerable beings—that is, beings who are not entirely at home in the world—we also have to engage in arguments about whether as rights-bearing agents we can be held responsible for our actions. If we recognize agency, then we must also recognize responsibility. Structuralist and deterministic perspectives on social construction tend to deny agency and hence must accept that people cannot be held responsible for the social structures that determine their lives. By contrast, if social actors produce the social structures that come to determine their social world, they can be held to account for the social world they have produced. In this discussion of constructionist views of the body, I have tried to show that a sociology of the body does not have to be deterministic, especially when it pays attention to the idea of practice. The position one takes on these issues—the embodied experiences of the everyday world and the agency behind social action—is ultimately a question of epistemology.

Social science, and specifically sociological, approaches to health and illness have been typically bifurcated around a dichotomy between what, for convenience, we might call "naturalism" and "social constructionism." Naturalistic explanations seek physical causes of health and illness on the assumption that disease can be effectively controlled or eliminated by targeted medical intervention. This approach historically involved treating the human body as a machine that could be manipulated by medical science without the distractions of such dubious entities as "mind" or "subjectivity." The spectacular treatment of the infectious diseases of childhood in the late 19th and early 20th centuries provides the ideal model of medical science and its therapeutic potency. Of course, critics of this vision of medical history argue that these treatments were successful only after the social and physical environment had been improved by the introduction of sewerage, clean water, and an adequate food supply. Perhaps more important in the present context, although the physical etiology, for example, of measles has been successfully identified, there is far less scientific consensus as to the physical "substance" that produces alcohol addiction or mental illness. Similarly, the quest to discover genes that explain specific forms of social deviance is like a fable from *Don Quixote* in the sense that deviancy, because it is paradoxically a product of law or moral convention, does not lend itself to such explanations. The classic sociological argument is that the search for a genetic explanation of deviancy involves a category mistake. As Durkheim argued, social facts can be explained only by social facts. Is homosexuality a genetic disorder, a socially constructed category, or a lifestyle choice? Is there a gene to explain the prevalence of divorce in modern society? Perhaps, but first we need to find the gene that will explain the prevalence of matrimony. We tend to assume that matrimony does not need a causal explanation at all, simply because it is a "normal" relationship between men and women that has the blessing of the law. Because we take heterosexuality for granted as a natural state of affairs, we tend to look for causal explanations of homosexuality, which is in commonsense terms a deviation from the normal. We tend to look for naturalistic explanations in the social sciences only when phenomena appear to be untoward.

The naturalistic research strategy looks particularly unpromising if our effort is, for example, to explain the link between mental disability and patterns of social exclusion, such as homelessness. At least some aspects of homelessness will be a function of macro-social and economic changes, such as interest rates, property prices, the rental market, the supply of affordable housing, local governmental policies, and so forth. The complex causal processes behind the housing market do not allow for simple biological explanations of homelessness as a social condition. Moreover, at the individual level, the social reality of alcoholism is profoundly shaped by local circumstances. Homeless men consuming alcohol in public spaces in Britain or America are very likely to come to the attention of the police, whereas businessmen having a "liquid lunch" are not. In the everyday world, my consumption preferences may very well constitute someone else's stigmatizing addiction. These arguments are well known. In order to avoid these pitfalls of naive naturalism, sociologists have contested clinical labels, arguing, for example, from the standpoint of social constructionism that pathology is in the eye of the beholder. Addiction exists if a professional person can deploy expert knowledge to secure the social acceptance of the label.

Although the Foucauldian perspective has been productive in research terms, the approach has difficulty in accounting for the growth of social rights. In particular, the Foucauldian perspective on knowledge and power has problems accounting for the fact that new rights (or claims on the state) are often predicated on findings or proof of disability. Disability as a condition is plainly not just a matter of social rights denial, because being successfully defined as disabled can be necessary in order to acquire rights to some forms of welfare entitlement. The analytic limit of social constructionist in its Foucauldian or antihumanist perspective is further illustrated when we consider the phenomenology of physical disability. Social constructionism has not fully succeeded in explaining the real performative impediments associated with disability status. We might contrast the Foucault-inspired sociology of mental illness as a system of governmentality with rich ethnographical accounts of the performative peculiarities of Tourette syndrome (Sacks, 1995). Neither

Althusser's notion of interpellation nor Foucault's concept of governmentality can tell us anything about the everyday world of mental illness, such as the involuntary swearing, twitching, and grimacing of the victim of Tourette syndrome. We must as sociologists attend to quiddity, or the "stuffness" of life. Now quiddity has interesting properties for the sociological imagination. It can refer to philosophers engaging in (largely useless) debates about whether things exist or, alternatively, refers to the nature or essence of a thing. A *quid* is that which a thing is. Social construction appears to involve an approach that misses the obvious "thing-ness" (quid) of a condition, or what we might call the "throwness" of social phenomena.

Sociology is at its best a critical discipline that produces its own type of discomfort, inviting us to see the world as an alien place by breaking down taken-for-granted assumptions. The social constructionist argument, which is clearly a powerful vision of the world, is also discomforting; it helps us to question what Bourdieu has called the "doxic," or unquestioned, qualities of our objective realities. But it also has some unfortunate shortcomings (Hacking, 1999). In recognizing the ways in which social circumstances are socially caused, we must not lose sight of the agency in social action, and hence sociological explanations should not rule out human agency by regarding all social phenomena as determined by the unalterable social constructions that produce it. The very idea of action as opposed to behavior in sociological accounts of social reality must presuppose the possibility of human responsibility or accountability. If this argument cannot be sustained, then political advocacy (which we have detected in political constructionism) would be a largely pointless strategy. At its best, social constructionism should critically expose those circumstances that obscure human understanding in order to make human agency more, rather than less, efficacious and palpable.

• References

Aboulafia, M. (1999). A (neo) American in Paris: Bourdieu, Mead and pragmatism. In R. Shusterman (Ed.), *Bourdieu: A critical reader* (pp. 153–174). Oxford, UK: Blackwell.

Althusser, L. (1971). *Lenin and philosophy and other essays.*, London: New Left Books.

Ariès, P., & Bejin, A. (1985). *Western sexuality: Practice and precept in past and present times.* Oxford, UK: Blackwell.

Baier, A. (1991). *A progress of sentiment: Reflections on Hume's treatise.* Cambridge, MA: Harvard University Press.

Balsam, A. (1995). Forms of technological embodiment: Reading the body in contemporary culture. In M. Featherstone & R. Burrows (Eds.), *Cyberspace, cyberbodies, cyberpunk: Cultures of technological embodiment* (pp. 215–237). London: Sage.

Berger, P. L. (1963). *Invitation to sociology.* Garden City, NY: Doubleday.

Berger, P. L. (1967). *The sacred canopy.* Garden City, NY: Doubleday.

Berger, P. L. (1980). Foreword. In A. Gehlen, *Man in the age of technology* (pp. vii–xvi). New York: Columbia University Press.

Berger, P. L. (1998). *The limits of social cohesion: Conflict and mediation in pluralist societies.* Boulder, CO: Westview Press.

Berger, P. L. (1999). The desecularization of the world: A global overview. In P. L. Berger (Ed.), *The desecularization of the world* (pp. 1–18). Grand Rapids, MI: Eerdmans.

Berger, P. L., & Kellner, H. (1965). Arnold Gehlen and the theory of institutions. *Social Research, 32*(1), 110–113.

Berger, P. L., & Luckmann, T. (1966). *The social construction of reality: A treatise in the sociology of knowledge.* New York: Doubleday.

Blacking, J. (Ed.). (1977). *The anthropology of the body,* London: Academic Press.

Blumer, H. (1969). *Symbolic interactionism.* Englewood Cliffs, NJ: Prentice Hall.

Bourdieu, P. (1977). *Outline of a theory of practice.* Cambridge, UK: Cambridge University Press.

Bourdieu, P. (2000). *Pascalian meditations.* Cambridge, UK: Polity Press.

Butler, J. (1990). *Gender trouble: Feminism and the subversion of identity.* New York: Routledge.

Butler, J. (1993). *Bodies that matter: On the discursive limits of "Sex."* New York: Routledge.

Bynum, C. W. (1991). *Fragmentation and redemption: Essays on gender and the human body in medieval religion.* New York: Zone Books.

Delany, S. (1998). *Impolitic bodies: Poetry, saints and society in fifteenth–century England.* Oxford, UK: Oxford University Press.

Dickstein, M. (Ed.). (1998). *The revival of pragmatism: New essays on social thought, law and culture.* Durham, NC: Duke University.

Diggins, J. P. (1994). *The promise of pragmatism: Modernism and the crisis of knowledge and authority.* Chicago: University of Chicago Press.

Douglas, M. (1966). *Purity and danger: An analysis of the concepts of pollution and taboo.* London: Routledge & Kegan Paul.

Dubois, R. (1960). *Mirage of health: Utopias, progress and biological change.* London: Allen & Unwin.

Durkheim, E. (2001). *The elementary forms of religious life.*, Oxford, UK: Oxford University Press.

Elliott, A. (1999). *Social theory and psychoanalysis in transition: Self and society from Freud to Kristeva.* London: Free Association Books.

Evans, M., & Lee, E. (Eds.). (2002). *Real bodies: A sociological introduction.* Basingstoke, UK: Palgrave.

Featherstone, M. (Ed.). (2000). *Body modification.* London: Sage.

Foucault, M. (1970). *The order of things: An archaeology of the human sciences.* London: Tavistock.

Foucault, M. (1973). *The birth of the clinic.* London: Tavistock.

Foucault, M. (1987). *The use of pleasure: The history of sexuality* (Vol. 2). Harmondsworth, UK: Penguin Books.

Foucault, M. (1988). Technologies of the self. In L. H. Martin, H. Gutman, & P. H. Hutton (Eds.), *Technologies of the self* (pp. 16–49). London: Tavistock.

Foucault, M. (1990). *The care of the self: The history of sexuality* (Vol. 3). Harmondsworth, UK: Penguin Books.

Foucault, M. (1991). Governmentality. In G. Burchell, C. Gordon, & P. Miller (Eds.), *The Foucault effect: Studies in governmentality* (pp. 87–104). London: Harvester Wheatsheaf.

Gehlen, A. (1980). *Man in the age of technology.* New York: Columbia University Press.

Gehlen, A. (1988). *Man: His nature and place in the world.* New York: Columbia University Press.

Giddens, A. (1984). *The constitution of society: Outline of the theory of structuration.* Cambridge, UK: Polity Press.

Goffman, E. (1959). *The presentation of self in everyday life.* Garden City, NY: Doubleday Anchor.

Goffman E. (1961). *Asylums: Essays on the situation of mental patients and other inmates.* Harmondsworth, UK: Penguin Books.

Goffman, E. (1964). *Stigm: Notes on the management of a spoiled identity.* Englewood Cliffs, NJ: Prentice Hall.

Hacking, I. (1999). *The social construction of what?* Cambridge, MA: Harvard University Press.

Haraway, D. (1991). *Symians, cyborgs and women: The reinvention of nature.* London: Free Association Books.

Heidegger, M. (1962). *Being and time.* Oxford, UK: Blackwell.

Joas, H. (1996). *The creativity of action.* Chicago: University of Chicago Press.

Kroker, A., & Kroker, M. (Eds.). (1987). *Body invaders: Panic sex in America.* New York: St. Martins Press.

Laqueuer, T. (1990). *Making sex: Body and gender from the Greeks to Freud.* Cambridge, MA: Harvard University Press.

Malachowski, A. R. (Ed.). (1990). *Reading Rorty: Critical responses to philosophy and the mirror of nature (and beyond).* Oxford, UK: Blackwell.

Margolis, J. (1986). *Pragmatism without foundations: Reconciling realism and relativism.* Oxford, UK: Blackwell.

Martin, E. (1992). *The woman in the body.* Boston: Beacon Press.

Mauss, M. (1979). Body techniques. In *Sociology and psychology: Essays by Marcel Mauss* (pp. 97–123). London: Routledge & Kegan Paul.

Pateman, C., & Gross, E. (Eds.). (1986). *Feminist challenges: Social and political theory.* Sydney, Australia: Allen & Unwin.

Plummer, K. (2000). Symbolic interactionism in the twentieth century. In B. S. Turner (Ed.), *The Blackwell companion to social theory* (pp. 193–222). Oxford, UK: Blackwell.

Riggs, A., & Turner, B. S. (1999). The expectation of love in older age: Towards a sociology of intimacy. In M. Poole & S. Feldman (Eds.), *A certain age: Women growing older* (pp. 193–208). St. Leonards, UK: Allen & Unwin.

Rorty, R. (1979). *Philosophy and the mirror of nature.* Princeton: Princeton University Press.

Rothman, B. K. (1998). *Genetic maps and human imaginations: The limits of science in understanding who we are.* New York: Norton.

Sacks, O. (1995). *An anthropologist on Mars.* New York: Knopf.

Schelsky, H. (1969). Can continual questioning be institutionalized? In N. Birnbaum & G. Lenzer (Eds.), *Sociology of religion: A book of readings* (pp. 418–422). Englewood Cliffs, NJ: Prentice Hall.

Scheper-Hughes, N. (1992). *Death without weeping: The violence of everyday life in Brazil.* Berkeley: University of California Press.

Seymour, W. (1998). *Remaking the body: Rehabilitation and change.* St. Leonards, UK: Allen & Unwin.

Shusterman, R. (1992). *Pragmatist aesthetics: Living beauty, rethinking art.* Oxford, UK: Blackwell.

Shusterman, R. (Ed.). (1999). *Bourdieu: A critical reader.* Oxford, UK: Blackwell.

Shusterman, R. (2000). *Performing live: Aesthetic alternatives for the ends of art.* Ithaca, NY: Cornell University Press.

Shusterman, R. (2002). *Surface and depth: Dialectics of criticism and culture.* Ithaca, NY: Cornell University Press.

Strauss, A. (1959). *Mirrors and masks: The search for identity.* Glencoe, IL: Free Press.

Strauss, A. (1963). The hospital and its negotiated order. In E. Freidson (Ed.), *The hospital in modern society* (pp. 147–169). New York: Free Press.

Strauss, A. (1978). *Negotiations: Varieties, processes, contexts, and social order.* San Francisco: Jossey-Bass.

Strauss, A. (1993). *Continual permutations of action.* New York: Aldine de Gruyter.

Turner, B. S. (1984). *The body and society.* Oxford, UK: Blackwell.

Turner, B. S. (1987). *Medical power and social knowledge.* London: Sage.

Turner, B. S. (1992). *Regulating bodies: Essays in medical sociology.* London: Routledge.

Turner, B. S. (1995). Ageing and identity: Some reflections on the somatization of the self. In M. Featherstone & A. Wernick (Eds.), *Images of aging: Cultural representations of later life* (pp. 245–260). London: Routledge.

Turner, B. S. (2001). Peter Berger. In A. Elliott & B. S. Turner (Eds.), *Profiles in contemporary social theory* (pp. 107–116). London: Sage.

Turner, B. S. (2004). *The new medical sociology: Social forms of health and illness.* New York: Norton.

Turner, B. S. (2005). Bodily performance: On aura and reproducibility. *Body and Society, 11*(4), 1–18.

Turner, B. S. (2006). *Vulnerability and human rights.* University Park: Penn State University Press.

Turner, B. S., & Wainwright, S. (2003). Corps de ballet: The case of the injured ballet dancer. *Sociology of Health and Illness, 25*(3), 269–288.

Virioli, P. (2000). *Polar inertia.* London: Sage.

Wolin, R. (1990). *The politics of being: The political thought of Martin Heidegger.* New York: Columbia University Press.

CHAPTER 26

The Social Construction of Emotion

- Donileen R. Loseke
  Margarethe Kusenbach

Theoretical attention to the importance of emotion in social life has a long history beginning with Aristotle, who argued that effective rhetoric involves a mix of appeals to logic and to emotion (Waddell, 1990). Modern leading social theorists such as Marx, Comte, Durkheim, Weber, Simmel, Freud, and the members of the Frankfurt school likewise argued that emotion was critical to social life (Beatty, 2005; Shilling, 2002). Regardless of this long history of theoretical interest, empirical attention to emotion in the United States was limited to psychologists until the 1930s, when anthropologists began cross-culture research on this topic (Beatty, 2005). Until the late 1970s, sociologists were not interested in emotion because it was conceptualized as a private, biological, or psychological phenomenon not governed by social rules (Hochschild, 1979). Likewise, because social historians prior to the 1980s tended to assume that people's feelings in the past did not differ from those in current eras, emotion was of no historical interest (Stearns & Stearns, 1985).

The reasons for such empirical neglect of emotion are located deep in Western body–mind dualisms that became embedded in the social sciences during the late 19th and early 20th centuries (Lyon, 1995). Modernist frameworks dichotomized cognitive and affective phenomena into separate realms (White, 2000), science was about objective phenomena and privileged the value and examination of cognition (Waddell, 1990). Within this framework, emotion was not of interest because it was disparaged as noncognitive, irrational, and subjective (Harré, 1986; Lutz, 1986).

In stark comparison to earlier eras, the "scientific literature on emotions has reached enormous proportions" in recent years (Gergen, 1994, p. 219). Observers note its ascendancy in sociology (Thoits, 1989), anthropology (Leavitt, 1996), and social history (Stearns & Stearns, 1985). The genesis of this new interest had its sources both inside and outside academia. Within academia, many scholars in the late 1970s were becoming dissatisfied with the then-dominant view of humans as mechanical "information processors." This dissatisfaction led to an increasing popularity of interpretive approaches to social life. Because questions from this perspective focus on how humans create and understand meaning, emotion became of center-stage interest (Lutz & White, 1986). Increased academic interest in emotion also reflects general changes in the social world. By the 1980s, observers were arguing that truth and logic were becoming relativized, making what we feel more important than what we think (McCarthy, 1989; Turner, 1976). Americans in particular were becoming increasingly conscious of their feelings and prone to "daily emotional temperature-taking" (Stearns & Stearns, 1985, p. 815).

Emotion now has become an important topic of social scientific study, and research findings have challenged previous assumptions. There is considerable evidence that Western binary conceptions that pit emotion against reason, feeling against thinking, subjectivity against objectivity, and body against mind are reflections of our "folk model of the person" (White, 1990, p. 46), or what some scholars call Western ethnopsychologies (see Lutz, 1986, for a review of the assumptions about emotion in Western ethnopsychologies). Scholars today generally agree that emotion decidedly affects cognition (see Schwarz, 2000, for a review) and that emotion is critical to moral judgments (Solomon, 1995).

But what is "emotion"? The literature is characterized by considerable conceptual untidiness, which is understandable given that interest in the topic is quite new and that examinations of emotion now occur in several academic disciplines that use quite different theoretical and methodological frameworks. Researchers ask very different kinds of questions about emotion, such as which situations typically provoke particular physiological feelings; how these internal feelings are subjectively experienced, socially shaped, and publicly expressed; which particular emotions are associated with which particular behaviors; how feelings are—and are not—talked about; and how emotion expectations and expressions change depending on cultural and historical contexts (Beatty, 2005; Mesquita & Frijda, 1992; Russell, 1991). Underlying such diverse interests are various theoretical frameworks that lead to different types of questions, as well as to different interpretations of the meaning of research findings. Our purpose in this chapter is to describe the social constructionist perspective on emotion.

The Social Constructionist Perspective on Emotion

The social constructionist perspective has been called the "great new theoretical paradigm of the late twentieth century in emotions research" (Stearns, 1995, p. 39). Historically, constructionist views were developed as an alternative to traditional conceptualizations of emotion commonly identified as naturalist, universalist, evolutionist, or positivist. There are multiple versions of these traditional theories, and we cannot do them justice here. What is important is that they all conceptualize emotion as first and foremost a natural and innate physiological phenomenon. Such traditional views of emotion in philosophy, psychology, and anthropology often reference the work of Charles Darwin, who claimed that emotion is a species adaptation (see Leavitt, 1996; Solomon, 1995, for reviews). Basic emotions, such as fear, anger, and surprise, are conceptualized within such a framework as "evolutionally important" and "cross-culturally universal" (Kemper, 1987, p. 263), whereas social influences on emotions are considered merely epiphenomenal, "pointing to the mere surface of the phenomenon, rather than to its explanatory core" (Kemper, 1981, p. 345).

Constructionist perspectives were developed in opposition to these traditional views, and they pose deep challenges to both naturalist frameworks and Western ethnopsychologies. In stark contrast to naturalist views of emotion as biological phenomena rooted in physiology, social constructionists understand emotion as *social* phenomena rooted in culture. Feelings are like other experiences in that they are social products based on beliefs, shaped by language, and therefore derived from culture (Armon-Jones, 1988). Simply put, "not only ideas, but emotions, too, are cultural artifacts" (Geertz, 1973, p. 81). Within constructionism, feelings are not "natural." It is culture, not biology, that "shapes the occasion, meaning, and expression of affective experience" (Gordon, 1981, p. 562).

Although the constructionist privileging of the social over the biological defies Western understandings that emotion is embodied, there is scientific support for this assertion that culture, not biology, shapes emotion. The most widely known study is a controlled laboratory experiment done by Stanley Schachter and Jerome Singer (1962) that demonstrated how commonly accepted physiological indicators of emotion require cognitive interpretation in order to be experienced as bodily signs of emotion. Schachter and Singer told study participants that they were to be in an experiment about the effects of a "vitamin supplement" on their vision. In actuality, study participants were given shots of epinephrine. Although epinephrine leads to typical physiological effects (trembling hands, rapid heartbeat, flushed and warm face), only some study participants were told this (the epinephrine-informed group). Others were told that their feet would feel numb and that they

might get a headache and experience an itching sensation over their bodies (the epinephrine-misinformed group), and a third group of research participants were told nothing about anticipated physiological effects (the epinephrine-ignorant group). Study participants then were told they needed to wait 15 minutes before the vision tests could be done and that they would be spending this "waiting" time with another study participant. In actuality, they were placed in a room with a research confederate who followed a predetermined script encouraging either "happiness" or "anger." Dependent measures included observations through a one-way mirror of the research participants during this 15 minutes, as well as subjects' self-reports of their moods. The findings of this study indicated that research participants who received a shot of epinephrine *did* have higher pulse rates than those who received a placebo; this is the physiological arousal effect of epinephrine. But physiological indicators of arousal did *not* explain either respondents' self-reports of mood or observers' tallies of behaviors during the 15 minutes. Although statistical analysis of these data yielded many intriguing findings, the most important support for the constructionist framework came from the fact that respondents who did *not* have ready explanations for their bodily states (those who were misinformed and those who were not informed about the physiological effects of epinephrine) were statistically more likely to mimic the mood (both in behavior and in self-report) of the confederate than were those whose expectations matched their bodily feelings (the epinephrine-informed group). As summarized by Schachter and Singer (1962, p. 396): "Given a state of sympathetic activation, for which no immediately appropriate explanation is available, human subjects can be readily manipulated into states of euphoria, anger, and amusement."

The Schachter and Singer (1962) study was merely the beginning of what now is a long line of research demonstrating a distinct lack of association between bodily sensations and emotion. Measures of physiology associated with emotion (such as facial expressions and peripheral nervous system functioning) "do not reliably differentiate emotion categories" (Lindquist, Barrett, Bliss-Moreau, & Russell, 2006, p. 135) and "physiological, behavioral and experiential components of each emotion category are only weakly interrelated" (Barrett, 2006, p. 23). Hence, while naturalists argue that emotion is a natural, physiological phenomenon, a "century of research has not produced a strong evidentiary basis for this belief" (Barrett, 2006, p. 27). Scientific research therefore supports the constructionist argument that experiencing emotion requires complex understandings of what sorts of events evoke what sorts of emotions and how those emotions can be suitably expressed (White, 1990). The experience of emotion depends on evaluations of events and situations, and the expression of emotion depends on evaluations of the imagined social implications of those expressions (Evers, Fischer, Mosquera, & Manstead, 2005). Hence emotion is a "cultural phenomena, embedded in beliefs, symbols, and language, inextricably linked to social and cultural processes" (McCarthy, 1989, p. 51).

Prioritizing the social and cultural over the personal and biological is a defining characteristic of a social constructionist perspective that explores meaning. This leads to two broad areas of interest: *what* types of emotional meaning are constructed and *how* this meaning is experienced, understood, and used by social actors (see Gubrium & Holstein, 1997, for elaboration of this distinction, as well as research methods following such agendas). In addition, scholars of social theory often distinguish between "strong" (or "strict") and "weak" (or "contextual") versions of constructionism. Within a traditional constructionist analytic vocabulary, strong versions are those that focus entirely on the cultural level of meaning creation and do not ask questions about the experiences or understandings of social

actors. In comparison, weak versions of constructionism examine relationships between socially constructed meaning and how social actors experience, understand, and use this meaning. Although there is ongoing dialogue about strong and weak versions of constructionism (see, e.g., Best, 1993), these primarily are theoretical discussions that are not an important aspect of empirical research on emotion. It is, however, important for us to note that, although the label of "strong" implies that such an orientation is better than the "weak," in practice there are theoretical, analytic, and practical costs *and* benefits of both strong and weak versions of constructionism.

We turn now to examining the varieties of research associated with social constructionist questions about emotion. This fills in our skeleton description of this framework, offers empirical support for constructionist arguments, and illustrates what types of knowledge about social life can be gained by examining emotion within this perspective. In the final section, we consider what types of questions about emotion are *not* addressed within a social constructionist framework.

Empirical Research

Constructionist perspectives on emotion lead to myriad questions about relationships between emotion and culture. Within this larger theme, important issues regarding emotion and power, status, and authority come into focus. We begin with the construction of emotion in and through language.

Emotion as Language

Constructionist perspectives conceptualize emotion as a matter of social meaning, which raises questions about how meaning is communicated. Although human emotion can be communicated through gestures (many modern-day Westerners recognize a clenched fist as indicating anger and crying as indicating sadness), constructionists are interested in the larger cultural systems of meaning and hence have focused on exploring the formation of emotion in language. Emotion language is critical because it furnishes the cognitive structures or schemata (Lutz & White, 1986) that can be used to make sense of internal states and to communicate perceived internal states to others. Because early discussions of constructionist perspectives on emotion declared that linguistic examinations should be a priority (Harré, 1986), considerable research has examined the significance of specific emotion words (White, 2000, p. 33), and a major focus in discursive psychology is on the rhetorical design and use of emotion categories (Edwards, 1999; Harré & Stearns, 1995).

A wealth of cross-cultural research demonstrates the variability in emotion vocabularies. There are emotion words in some languages for which no words exist in English; there are emotion words in English not found in other languages. Languages also "sort" emotions differently: The English-language distinction between "shame" and "fear," for example, is not universal; nor do all languages allow differentiating among annoyance, fury, rage, and irritation, which are familiar categories to Western English speakers (see Russell, 1991, for a review of these studies). There also can be marked differences over time within specific languages. For example, Westerners no longer speak of feeling melancholy or accidie, which were important emotions in past eras. Westerners now rather talk about feeling depressed, anxious, or stressed, feelings that would have made little sense even a century ago (Gergen, 1994).

Despite myriad methodological problems in cross-cultural and historical comparisons (Beatty, 2005; Mesquita & Frijda, 1992; Russell, 1991), such research is important to constructionists in their ongoing debate with naturalists. Just as Schachter and Singer's (1962) research demonstrated how bodily sensations require interpretation before they are perceived as emotion, cross-cultural and historical studies on emotion vocabularies demonstrate that emotions are not an innate aspect of human physiology. How could they be when some languages have no words to label or communicate specific feelings, when terms to label specific emotions are historically situated? Yet, critically, evidence of variability in emotion vocabularies is of far greater importance than simply as support for constructionist arguments with naturalists: This research demonstrates the symbolic and constructed aspects of the English language (White, 2000). In so doing, these empirical findings can be used to deconstruct Western beliefs about emotion, a particularly important project given that the taken-for-granted goodness of the English-speaking world is the justification for creating the rest of the world in its image (Gergen, 1994, p. 137).

Studies of language also attend to emotion in interactive discourse (Lutz & White, 1986). These studies show how emotion is *talk* that performs social actions (Edwards, 1999), talk that is a "tool for shaping the social construction of reality" (White, 2000, p. 39). Such studies sometimes focus on discourse about emotions—how emotion is talked about by both scientists and practical actors (Abu-Lughod & Lutz, 1990). Findings from these studies illustrate that talk about emotions is intimately bound with power. Power relations determine what can—and what cannot—be said about the self and emotion, and hence talk about emotion works to establish, assert, challenge, or reinforce power and status differences (Abu-Lughod & Lutz, 1990, p. 14). The most obvious Western example of relationships between emotion discourse and power is that of the correspondence between discourses about emotion and about gender. Emotion is a binary discourse in the Western world. It associates emotion with irrationality, subjectivity, the chaotic, and other characteristics *not* associated with social power, while identifying cognition with rationality, objectivity, and other characteristics that *are* associated with social power. This emotion discourse is mapped onto a binary gender discourse, identifying women with emotion and men with cognition. Within a world in which objectivity and rationality are identified with power, this emotion–gender discourse is a critical, yet often unnoticed, reinforcement of the ideological subordination of women, who are identified with the subjective and irrational (Cancian, 1987; Lutz, 1986).

Studies of emotion discourse also include examinations of talk that seems to have "some affective content or effect" (Abu-Lughod & Lutz, 1990, p. 10). Researchers explore how written or oral talk is constructed in ways that encourage emotional responses in audiences. Appeals to emotion are a common feature of mass media presentations (Richards, 2004), talk surrounding social activism (Goodwin, Jasper, & Polletta, 2000), social problems (Loseke, 2003), science policy (Waddell, 1990), political advertisements (Brader, 2005), and presidential speeches (White, 2004).

The study of emotion vocabularies and emotion discourse is a path to examining the social construction of meaning and relationships between power and the discourses of emotion. Constructionists can examine what emotion discourse is, what it does, and how it reflects, perpetuates, or challenges systems of power and social hierarchy (Abu-Lughod, 1990). This is a complicated project because language and meaning *always* are contextualized. It is not possible to argue that talk "appeals to emotion" without unraveling the content of emotion cultures surrounding that talk (Solomon, 1995).

Emotion Cultures

Emotion discourse is one aspect of a larger concept that we call *emotion cultures* but that goes by other names, such as *emotional culture* (Gordon, 1990), *feeling rules, framing rules,* and *expression rules* (Hochschild, 1990), and *emotionologies* (Stearns & Stearns, 1985). Emotion cultures include emotion vocabularies (words) and emotion discourse (the structure of talk), as well as complexes of expectations, standards, and ideals surrounding emotion.

Modern-day Western emotion cultures include widely held notions of which feelings are expected for which social actors in given situations: Westerners typically expect that wives will grieve when their husbands die and that parents will be happy when a daughter or son wins a university scholarship. Emotion cultures also include expectations about the intensity and duration of emotions: Westerners expect that parental emotions surrounding the birth of a baby will be more intense and longer lasting than will pet owners' emotions surrounding the birth of a litter of kittens. Emotion cultures additionally include expectations about whether or not emotions should be displayed: Employees are expected not to openly show anger toward their supervisors and to show gratitude when their supervisors show them kindness. Emotion cultures also include expectations about how emotions will be outwardly displayed: Westerners expect that sadness, and perhaps extreme happiness, will be expressed through tears and that anger can be communicated by shouting. Still further, emotion cultures include expectations about the objects of emotions: Westerners expect that husbands and wives should love one another and that fathers should not feel lust toward their daughters. Finally, emotion cultures include moral evaluations: Westerners tend to believe that anxiety is bad and should be avoided and that personal pride is good and should be pursued. In brief, emotion cultures are complex *cognitive* models (Russell, 1991). As socially circulating constellations of ideas, the elements of emotion cultures are resources that "allow members of a society to identify and discuss emotions, evaluate them as desirable or undesirable, and regulate them in line with values and norms" (Gordon, 1990, p. 29).

Empirical examinations of emotion cultures are of several types. Because the complexes of ideas surrounding emotion are socially constructed, research examines how social actors *create* emotion cultures. Historical studies show how the most important creators of emotion cultures in the Victorian era in the United States were clergymen and the wives and daughters of clergymen. In that era, novels and children's schoolbooks were critical in promoting such cultures (Stearns, 1993). Our modern era, in contrast, is characterized by incredible diversity among the originators and promoters of emotion cultures and in the methods of dissemination of ideas. Creators of emotion cultures now include psychiatrists, counselors, advice book writers, and clergy; they include social movement activists who construct victims as the types of people deserving of sympathy and victimizers as the types of people deserving of condemnation (Loseke, 2003). Emotion cultures are created and popularized by the countless "relationship experts" who appear on television talk shows and write newspaper advice columns, by films and novels, and by product advertisements that instruct consumers as much about how to feel as about how to think about products. Creating and modifying elements of emotion cultures are pervasive activities in the modern Western world.

There also is much cross-cultural research that demonstrates *variability* in what particular types of situations call for what particular emotions, in how emotions should be expressed, and in how particular emotions are morally evaluated (see Mesquita & Frijda, 1992, for a review). There are multiple examples of how a particular emotion that is common and encouraged in one culture might be absent or discouraged in another (see Harré, 1986), as well as of historical changes within cultures concerning what events are taken to be emotionally significant and how emotion should be expressed (Harré & Finlay-Jones, 1988). There also are explorations of elements of emotion cultures in the United States. These include studies of the emotion cultures of anger (Lambek & Solway, 2001; Stearns, 1987; Tavris, 1982; White, 1990), jealousy

(Stearns, 1989, 1990); sympathy (Clark, 1997), love (Cancian, 1987; Swidler, 2001), and fear (Altheide, 2002; Furedi, 1997; Glassner, 1999).

Studies of emotion cultures also examine how the *moral* evaluations of particular emotions change over time. Considerable attention has been paid to changes in evaluations of anger. Once prized for his spirit, the "angry boy" now is evaluated as a menace whose anger must be controlled (Stearns, 1993). "Job-based" anger also once was assumed to be a positive force but now is condemned (Stearns & Stearns, 1985). Additionally, there have been changes in the evaluations of emotions associated with family life. Prior to the 1970s, jealousy within adult relationships was evaluated as a positive emotion, a proof of love, but jealousy now is evaluated as a personal weakness, an emotion to overcome (Clanton, 1989). So, too, evaluations of love have changed. "Mother love" in the 1800s was evaluated as a positive force in child rearing, yet by the mid-1900s, it was evaluated as potentially dangerous (Stearns, 1993), a passion that continually threatens to grow out of control (Shields & Koster, 1989). Finally, and increasingly, relationship manuals targeted to audiences of adult women evaluate "too much" love as a dangerous emotion that should be avoided (Hazleden, 2004).

Many studies therefore explore how elements of emotion cultures change over time. Critically, what all such research demonstrates is that the elements of emotion cultures reflect characteristics of the surrounding social orders. "Job anger," for example, was transformed from a positive to a negative emotion as more women entered the workforce and experts urged men to curb their anger because of its perceived negative effect on women workers (Stearns, 1993). The increasing prevalence of consumer culture with its reverence for consumer goods can be understood as transforming "envy" in children from a near sin in the late 1800s to a neutral or even positive emotion by the mid-1930s (Matt, 2002). Mounting criticisms

518 • THE SOCIAL CONSTRUCTION OF WHAT?

of adult jealousy and "too much" love reflect and perpetuate a culture increasingly prizing self-development (Cancian & Gordon, 1988; Hazleden, 2004). Efforts to explore the meanings and contents of emotion cultures therefore must place emotions within cultural and social structural contexts, and these studies are important in examining more general questions about sociohistorical change (Stearns & Stearns, 1985).

Whether called *emotion cultures* or *emotional culture* (Gordon, 1990), *feeling rules, framing rules, and expression rules* (Hochschild, 1990), or *emotionologies* (Stearns & Stearns, 1985), the concept has yielded remarkable insights about how understandings of emotion are socially constructed. At the same time, this concept is prone to three types of misunderstandings that reduce its usefulness and distort its findings. First, we have used the plural, *emotion cultures*, in order to avoid the implication of cultural coherence. Although it is obvious and expectable that emotion cultures vary historically and cross-culturally, these cultures also reflect "local moral orders" (Harré, 1986), which are "local cultures" (Holstein & Gubrium, 2000). So, for example, the local culture in one "family therapy" social service agency might be very different from that of another such agency in the same town (Gubrium, 1992), and the local cultures of two different "soup kitchens" for the poor can be vastly dissimilar (Allahyari, 2000; see the collection of studies edited by Holstein & Gubrium, 2000, for further empirical examples). Conceptualizing culture in a plural sense is extremely important in advanced industrialized societies characterized by social, economic, and political differentiation that leads to heterogeneity among social members in experiences, understandings, and moral evaluations. Typical emotion cultures of middle-class Anglos are not necessarily those of poor people of color; new immigrants might have emotion cultures that differ from those who are native born; and so on. Furthermore, and also critically, social actors in such complex societies typically en-

counter multiple, and sometimes conflicting, emotion cultures over periods of time or even over the course of a single day: A woman might work in the emotion culture of a particular attorney's office, and this might vary dramatically from the emotion culture of her family. The emotion culture of any given attorney's office or any particular family also might change remarkably over time. In brief, although anthropologists and historians have produced considerable empirical evidence that the elements of emotion cultures are historically and culturally situated, it also is critical to conceptualize these cultures as locally situated. We return to this important point in the conclusion.

Second, and related, although constructionists sometimes talk about emotion cultures using terms such as *rules*, or *norms*, cultural guidelines of any sort *always* are situated. So, although Western emotion cultures typically associate the emotion known as grief with the death of a spouse, it might be quite understandable if a battered wife reacts with glee when her abusive partner dies. Likewise, it might make sense that a parent feels anger, not happiness, when a son or daughter accepts a university scholarship rather than continues a family business, as expected. Any rules, norms, expectations, and so on associated with emotion cultures apply to particular people and must be investigated within the contexts of particular situations, particular locations, and particular times.

Third, *emotion cultures* is a macrolevel concept. As such, it does not explain or predict individual subjectivity. Unfortunately, erroneously predicting individual subjectivity from cultural characteristics can be encouraged by research within a strong constructionist tradition. Because such research does not empirically examine aspects of individual subjectivity, it can invite the assumption that emotion as subjectively experienced by individual social actors will more or less reflect the relevant emotion cultures pertaining to that person, event, place, and time.

For such an assumption to be true, however, social actors would need to be conceptualized as "cultural dopes" who are without agency. This assumption merely replaces the biological determinism of naturalists with a cultural determinism of constructionists. Critically, this does not need to be the case. Cultural determinism is theoretically and empirically rejected by many constructionists influenced by ethnomethodology, who argue that elements of culture must be understood as resources that can be used by social actors to make sense of their own experiences and the experiences of others (see Gubrium & Holstein, 1997; especially Chapter 3). Social actors have agency: On a case-by-case basis they can decide to use, ignore, or creatively transform elements of an emotion culture.

Despite these warnings and disclaimers, there is more than enough evidence to support the constructionist claim that specific emotions are surrounded by cultures of social expectations about when and where and toward whom or what emotions should be experienced, how they should be displayed, and how they should be morally evaluated.

Socialization into Emotion Cultures

As the research by Schachter and Singer (1962) and others has demonstrated, emotion cannot be explained via human physiology, and it should be obvious that humans are not born understanding the complex, situated, and variable characteristics of whatever emotion cultures dominate in their particular times and places. It therefore follows that bodies as well as minds are socialized (Burkitt, 1997; Leavitt, 1996). Another type of research flowing from a constructionist framework examines the "socialization and acquisition of emotional competence" (Lutz & White, 1986, p. 424). Attaining emotional competence requires social actors to learn the countless and situated elements of emotion cultures, including how to name, categorize, subjectively experience, regulate, evaluate, elicit, suppress, change, and

display various emotions. People have "emotional competence" when they have been adequately socialized in the emotional ways of whatever emotion cultures pertain in their particular times and places.

The most general socialization for emotional competence is part and parcel of primary socialization, accomplished early in life by others in the infant's and young child's environment. The research on this is clear and unequivocal: On a situation-by-situation basis, parents, siblings, other family members, and caregivers explicitly teach children how to *feel*, as well as how to think. Children's peers become further teachers of emotion cultures that also are transmitted in children's books and movies (for references to these studies, see Cervantes, 2002; Leavitt & Power, 1989; Pollak & Thoits, 1989; see also journals such as *Early Education and Development*, *Child Development*, and *Early Childhood Education* for such studies).

Building from primary socialization that teaches general, transsituational emotional competence, secondary socialization teaches elements of emotion cultures associated with particular settings or groups. American sociologists have paid considerable attention to the processes of this secondary socialization in the area of employment. For example, although emotion cultures in the Western world generally associate feelings such as grief and sadness with illness or death, a variety of professionals, such as physicians, nurses, psychiatrists, psychologists, and social workers, routinely deal with such troubles in the course of their work. Because it would not be possible for them to do their jobs if they regularly were overcome with sadness or grief, it is not surprising that professional training includes learning new ways of feeling (Loseke & Cahill, 1986; Smith & Kleinman, 1989; Yanay & Sharah, 1998). The case of funeral directors offers an interesting example of relationships between primary and secondary socialization: People who select this profession typically come from families of funeral directors, meaning that from their earliest days they have been socialized into how to feel about death and deceased people. Secondary emotional socialization for professional funeral directing builds on this basic socialization (Cahill, 1999).

Researchers have argued that workers of many types are explicitly trained in how to feel about their work and how to properly express their feelings while at work. Corporations train their professional employees in how to feel loyalty toward the company (Kunda & Van Maanen, 1999), and airlines train flight staff in how to calm anxious or angry passengers (Hochschild, 1983). Service workers are trained in how to smile, and insurance sales agents are given detailed scripts for responding to various emotional reactions in their clients (see Leidner, 1993; Schweingruber & Berns, 2005; Steinberg & Figart, 1999, for references to many studies of such occupational socialization).

Teaching the elements of emotion cultures also is done in countless organizations and groups for people who define themselves as "troubled" or who are so defined by others. Studies demonstrate how these organizations and groups first and foremost are concerned with what might be called emotional resocialization: changing clients' understandings of emotion cultures. For example, gay and ex-gay Christian support groups work to transform what their members experience as the emotion of shame into the emotion of pride (Wolkomir, 2001), whereas court-mandated counseling for men accused of wife abuse encourages group members to experience shame, rather than pride, about their abusive behavior (McKendy, 1992). Weight Watchers seeks to give members techniques for *managing* the feeling of shame associated with weight, Overeaters Anonymous works to *increase* the feeling of shame associated with weight, and groups sponsored by the National Association to Advance Fat Acceptance (NAAFA) seek to *eliminate* the association between shame and weight (Martin, 2000).

So far, we have focused primarily on questions about emotions associated with the strong constructionist perspective that brackets questions about how individuals understand and experience emotion. For two reasons, the topic of emotional socialization in general and the case of programs for troubled people in particular lead us to move to a weaker version of constructionism in order to examine questions about how individual social actors understand and experience emotion. First, parents, teachers, employers, and social service providers might indeed attempt to "teach" their versions of emotional competence, but that does not necessarily mean these lessons are "learned." Whereas that assumption requires conceptualizing humans as passive information receivers, a wealth of research on the social processes in organizations and groups for emotionally troubled people demonstrates that service providers and clients alike actively collaborate to make sense of emotional trouble. There are agreements and disagreements, and providers and clients sometimes use, sometimes modify, and sometimes simply discard elements of particular emotion cultures (see Gubrium, 1992; Holstein & Gubrium, 2001; McKendy, 1992).

Second, the case of support groups for people with troubled emotional lives makes visible a pervasive feature of modern social life: Social actors can evaluate their own or others' subjective feelings or displays as different in kind or degree from what they believe *should* be experienced and displayed in given situations (Thoits, 1990). Such routine disparities between subjective experience and socially circulating understandings should be expected: People in complex and mass-mediated societies are bombarded with often conflicting messages regarding what should be felt about the self and others; lives are lived in a variety of constantly changing, and sometimes conflicting, emotion cultures, and the heterogeneity of experience leads to multiple understandings of, and reactions to, these emotion cultures.

Although a strong version of social constructionism offers a theoretical scaffolding on which to explore the social sources and social shaping of emotions, it does not empirically address questions of relationships between the social and the personal. We thus turn to a weaker version of constructionism in order to examine relationships between the social aspects of emotion and the lived emotional experience of social actors. In so doing, we retain a key constructionist assertion: what social actors subjectively feel, as well as how social actors evaluate and express these feelings, is social in origin.

Emotion Work in Daily Life

At times, differences between subjective feeling and understandings of social expectations can be so great that modern actors become immobilized. We defer those cases to psychologists and continue our exploration of the social construction of emotion by examining the *emotion work* surrounding the routine conflicts between subjective feelings and perceived social expectations. There are two interrelated types of emotion work: what social actors do to align their *own* subjectively experienced feelings and their emotion displays with their understandings of what they should feel and display and what social actors do to encourage particular emotional reactions and displays in *others*.

The most influential framework for examining emotion work was proposed by Arlie Hochschild (1979, 1983). Her interest was in examining the characteristics of "emotional labor," which she defined as emotion work that is a *job requirement* in paid employment. According to Hochschild, workers in jobs that demand emotional labor are required to produce desired emotions in their customers, and this requires workers to manage their own emotions and expressions. One of Hochschild's major examples was that of flight attendants, who, for instance, are expected to calm anxious passengers. This might be accomplished by managing emotion display: An attendant can express the emotion of sympathy by offering an anxious passenger a soothing smile. In such "surface acting," the attendant does not subjectively feel sympathy; the emotion work lies in eliciting the bodily expression of sympathy—in this case, a soothing smile. Hochschild, however, argued that flight attendants' employers want them to display "authentic" emotions, meaning they want attendants to subjectively feel the emotion they are displaying. Flight attendants, therefore, are explicitly taught how to do the emotion work of "deep acting," such as conjuring an image of a passenger, such as "a poor guy, he must be having a difficult time at home." When deep acting is successful, the soothing smile *is* authentic because it reflects the sympathy the attendant subjectively feels (Hochschild, 1983).

Following Hochschild's lead, researchers have compiled considerable evidence that a variety of jobs demand workers to manage the emotions of customers, clients, and patients and that this routinely requires workers to manage their own emotions. Much research in this tradition examines emotional labor in interactive service occupations, such as the work of waitresses (Erickson, 2004), fast food workers (Leidner, 1993), supermarket cashiers (Rafaeli & Sutton, 1987; Tolich, 1993), domestic workers (Hochschild & Ehrenreich, 2003), insurance salesmen (Leidner, 1993), personal trainers (Maguire, 2001), and adventure guides (Holyfield, 1995). Emotion work also is a requirement in a variety of other jobs, such as those of paralegals (Pierce, 1995), models (Mears & Finlay, 2005), criminal interrogators and bill collectors (Rafaeli & Sutton, 1991), doctors, nurses, social workers, psychiatrists, psychologists, and others in the helping professions (see Yanay & Shahar, 1998, for an overview), and those working in high-tech corporations (Kunda & Van Maanen, 1999).

Hochschild's (1979, 1983) framework has been immensely influential on researchers examining employment in a postindustrial society in which "our feelings and those of others have become paramount features of our encounters with the world, a world of personalities at work on one another" (McCarthy, 1989, p. 65). Although influential, this framework nonetheless can be criticized. First, observers who follow Hochschild's lead typically emphasize the negative consequences of emotional labor, said to lead workers to experience "burnout, fatigue, and emotional inauthenticity" (Steinberg & Figart, 1999, p. 12). Others, however, have argued that the image of employer control over employees' emotions is overstated and that both surface acting and deep acting that produce "happy customers" can be positive experiences, leading workers to feel great pride in and control over their work (see Abiala, 1999; Tolich, 1993). Second, and related, Hochschild's framework conceptualizes emotional labor as an *employer* demand, which logically leads to criticisms that emotions have been commodified. Although sensible, stopping the analysis after placing blame on employers misses a larger point: Employers' demands for such labor—as well as workers' subjectively felt need to do emotion work—can be understood as reflecting characteristics of Western beliefs that emotion arises from the inside and that displays of emotion *should* match what one "really" feels. Within modern Western emotion cultures, people judge themselves and are judged by others "on the sincerity . . . of their performances" (Clark, 1997, p. 58). Although social actors routinely and without discomfort perform surface acting in daily life, the most highly prized expressions in both the self and others are those evaluated as "authentic." For that reason, employers' demands for deep acting make sense: Customers, clients, and patients typically are emotionally competent social actors, so they will judge the apparent sincerity of emotional expression being offered. As evaluated through Western beliefs, an emotional performance judged as insincere is worse than no performance of emotion at all. Furthermore, and critically, because Westerners experience greater satisfaction when

emotional expression matches inner feeling, social actors typically feel more satisfied when they offer what they believe is an authentic emotional expression. In brief, employer demands, as well as worker preferences, for "authentic" emotional displays can be understood as reflecting socially dominant ideas about emotion.

The concept of emotion work has relevance far beyond examining the emotional labor associated with employment. We already discussed how workers and clients in services for people with troubled identities do the emotion work to make sense of these troubles, and there are many other indications of the pervasiveness of emotion work in daily life. For example, researchers have demonstrated how animal-loving employees and volunteers in pet shelters do considerable emotion work when they must euthanize unwanted dogs and cats (Arluke, 1994), how people who lost family members in the Holocaust work to suppress negative emotions and elevate positive emotions toward these lost family members (Gottschalk, 2003), how women in prison manage their emotional lives while incarcerated (Greer, 2002), and how emotion work on the self is necessary to cope with dehumanizing factory jobs (Thompson, 1983). The emotion work concept has been used to describe all caregiving and interpersonal support in families (DeVault, 1999), the work close relational partners do to normalize problematic emotions in conversations (Staske, 1998), and the interactional work parents do to maintain their "good parent" identities despite their teens' rebellion (Godwin, 2004) and to get their children admitted to elite private high schools (Chin, 2000). The emotion work concept also has been used to describe what wheelchair users do to manage the emotions of others who seem uncomfortable around them (Cahill & Eggleston, 1994). Furthermore, researchers have found that women victims of rape (Konradi, 1999) and stalking (Dunn, 2002) very deliberately manage their emotional expressions, and sometimes engage in deep acting, in order to appear as "expectable victims," which they believe is necessary for their offenders to be found guilty in court. Finally, politicians do emotion work in order to present themselves as "authentic" individuals with the particular emotional makeup they believe voters find compelling (Richards, 2004).

What these and many other studies indicate is that, regardless of the multiplicity, contradictions, indeterminacy, and situated nature of emotion cultures, social actors understand and manage their basic contours. Social actors expect themselves, and are expected by others, to feel and act in ways defined as "emotionally competent." They can use their skills to reconcile perceived discrepancies between subjectivity and social expectations, and they can use their skills to manage the emotions of others. Critically, emotion work in daily life can have political consequences. For instance, much of the burden of emotional labor in the workforce and emotion work in families falls on women, and observers argue that this reinforces gender inequality (DeVault, 1999; Hochschild, 1983). Displays of anger by bosses (Rafaeli & Sutton, 1991) and others in high-status positions (Clark, 1997) can serve to intimidate and control subordinates, and expectations for "appropriate" emotion displays can be conceptualized as the politics of emotion in everyday life (Shields, 2005). In brief, emotion work is part and parcel of daily life, and this work can have important political consequences.

Evaluating and Expanding Constructionist Perspectives on Emotion

In this chapter, we have attempted to show how constructionist perspectives are valuable in examining relationships between emotion, history, culture, politics, and individual experience. We focus our final comments on questions that can and should be asked about *any* theoretical perspective: What are its limits? What are its uses?

The primary criticism of the constructionist perspective on emotion is that it ignores the "guts" of emotion (Lyon, 1995). This criticism is well placed: As subjectively experienced by Westerners, the "guts" of emotion is a bodily experience, yet constructionists often ignore this. Obviously, because a foundational claim of constructionism is the primacy of the social, it is not possible to integrate into constructionist theory ideas from evolutionary biology, with its proclamation of species-wide physiology. At the same time, a constructionist analysis does not require denying the subjective bodily experience of emotion. Indeed, some supporters of constructionism argue that more attention should be given to bodily dimensions of emotion (Burkitt, 1997; Leavitt, 1996; Stearns, 1995), which is possible because, within constructionism, bodies are socialized (Leavitt, 1996).

When observers complain that constructionists ignore the "guts" of emotional experience, they also note that this framework pays too little attention to how emotion is experienced as deeply personal. Indeed, in strong versions of constructionism, emotion is about language and discourse; it examines the world of ideas entirely disconnected from subjective feelings (Craib, 1995). Weaker versions of constructionism do ask questions about how individuals subjectively experience emotion, but interest is limited to examining the effects of the social on the individual and to how individuals use their understandings of emotion to make sense of their individual feelings. There is truth, therefore, in Norman Denzin's (1992, p. 20) complaint that constructionist views on emotion are not really that much different from those of the naturalists in that both seek an "objective, scientific account . . . of this phenomenon called 'emotionality.'"

These, then, are the limits of the social constructionist perspective on emotion. Although it is possible for constructionist examinations to bring the body into sharper focus, it must be a socialized body (Boellstorff & Lindquist, 2004) rather than a "natural" body that is deemed to be the source of emotion. In the same way, although it is possible within constructionism to explore questions about the individual subjective experience of emotion, it is *not* possible to examine subjectivity "on its own terms, and not merely as epiphenomenal to other levels of analysis" (Ellis & Flaherty, 1992, p. 6) because that would privilege the individual over the social.

Privileging the cognitive, social aspects of emotion over its subjective, embodied qualities makes the social constructionist framework unattractive to those who believe that emotion is primarily about human physiology or that individuals can have distinctly unique feelings. That said, our review of the existing literature demonstrated the important insights on human social life that are gained by using constructionism as a theoretical guide. We conclude by describing three specific areas of research in which examining emotion through a social construction lens could prove particularly beneficial.

First, we need more examinations of the production of *emotional meaning*, especially as it enters political discourse (White, 2004). Emotion cultures are implicated in how people construct symbolic boundaries, which are the "conceptual distinctions made by social actors to categorize objects, people, practices, and even time and place" (Lamont & Molnár, 2002, p. 168; Zerubavel, 1996). Typically, attention is on how such distinctions reflect deeply held *symbolic codes* (Alexander, 1992), a term for complex systems of ideas about how the world works, how the world should work, and the rights, responsibilities, and relationships among people in the world. Our observation is that, although analysts focus on symbolic codes as ways of *thinking*, these codes include moral judgments, which are inextricably related to ways

of *feeling* (Solomon, 1995). Consider political discourse in the United States surrounding war (Coles, 2002; Moerk & Pincus, 2000). This discourse invariably includes elements of the classical "citizen–enemy" symbolic code (Alexander, 1992, p. 293) in that it constructs Americans as citizens who are rational, realistic, and sane, whereas enemies are constructed as irrational, unrealistic, and mad. Our point is that these cognitive constructions of "citizens" and "enemies" are supported by underlying emotion cultures: Typical discourse justifying war constructs Americans as virtuous victims who can become heroes by vanquishing evil. Such a discourse encourages the emotion of "pride," and pride invites citizens into a "collaboration of virtue" (Coles, 2002, p. 599). Conversely, dramatizing enemies as "evil, bloodthirsty, and animalistic" (Merskin, 2004, p. 157) encourages the emotion of hatred, and this supports waging war. In brief, scholars argue that "the internal structure of the civil code must become an object of study" (Alexander, 1992, p. 291). We agree and add that it is not possible to understand cultural ways of *thinking* without understanding cultural ways of *feeling* (Loseke, 2000).

Second, and related, emotion cultures are implicated in the social inequality reflected in, and perpetuated by, *social policy*. Observers argue that social policy is responsive to public images of the *types* of people who will be affected by policy (Asen, 2002; Schneider & Ingram, 1993), so policy decisions cannot be understood without examining the influence of ideas circulating in the surrounding culture (Mazzeo, Rab, & Eachus, 2003). This argument again implicates emotion cultures: As judged within the emotion cultures of sympathy and hatred, some types of people are evaluated as worthy of the emotion of sympathy, resulting in its behavioral expression of help (Clark, 1997); other types of people are evaluated as worthy of the emotion of hatred, resulting in its behavioral expression of punishment (Loseke, 2003). This statement is confirmed by empirical findings that sympathy leads to support for policies that will help, whereas hatred leads to support for policies that will punish (Schwarz, 2000). Consider, for example, the "get tough on welfare" policy transformations in the United States in the mid-1990s. Policy hearings constructed a story of the "welfare queen" as an African American woman who was lazy and promiscuous. When read through the symbolic codes of racism and individualism, such a woman logically "needs" to become responsible, and a new welfare policy encouraging work and setting limits on welfare eligibility did just that. Yet underlying this logic were emotions associated with the "welfare queen" that aptly can be characterized as the "politics of disgust" (Hancock, 2004). Again, it is not enough to know what citizens and legislators think; attention must be focused on what they feel, and this means examining the characteristics of emotion cultures that influence social policy.

Our third and final example in which constructionist examinations of emotion are needed is the most basic: Far too little attention is devoted to examining the *variability* of emotion cultures in political, academic, and social life. Policymakers, for example, most often assume that the emotion cultures of the dominant classes are, or at least should be, shared by the targets of social policy. This results in flawed social policy, because the emotion cultures of the dominant classes are not typically shared by all and, indeed, cannot be. Different structural positions necessarily lead to different values and views of the world (Hancock, 2004). Ignorance of variability in emotion cultures also results in flawed academic theory that is unwittingly biased in terms of class and race. Historians, for example, all too often study—and then morally judge—working-class and poor people of the past through the prism of their own modern-day, middle-class emo-

tion cultures (Stearns & Stearns, 1985). Likewise, studies of emotional labor in employment tend to assume that all workers and clients share Anglo middle-class emotion cultures, although different racial and class locations produce very different sets of expectations (Kang, 2003).

Finally, ignorance of the variability of emotion cultures across time, place, and status leads to very practical misunderstandings. Members of ethnic minority groups in the United States, for example, are less likely than Anglos to seek professional treatment for the emotion that dominant class members call *depression*. Expensive education campaigns to encourage members of minority groups to seek professional help often are unsuccessful because they do not recognize that different emotion cultures include different ideas about the cause of, and therefore the solution to, emotional distress (Karasz, 2005). In brief, and as we mentioned earlier, although historians and anthropologists have done considerable work examining the cross-cultural and historical variability of emotion cultures, far too little attention has been given to examining how such cultures are "local cultures" (Holstein & Gubrium, 2000). Given the current struggles of opinion concerning immigration both in the United States and around the world, exploring the diversity of emotion cultures is a particularly important political project.

When emotion is conceptualized as socially constructed meaning, questions about natural bodies and unique individual subjectivities drift into the background. What is left is distinctly social. The constructionist focus on the creation and use of social meaning shows how emotion is socially shaped in ways that reflect and either reproduce or challenge social hierarchy and how the meanings of emotion are learned and creatively used by social actors to make sense of themselves and their lives. Emotion conceptualized in this way is about daily life, and it is about power and politics.

• References

Abiala, K. (1999). Customer orientation and sales situations: Variations in interactive service work. *Acta Sociologica, 42,* 207–222.

Abu-Lughod, L. (1990). Shifting politics in Bedouin love poetry. In C. A. Lutz & L. Abu-Lughod (Eds.), *Language and the politics of emotion* (pp. 24–45). New York: Cambridge University Press.

Abu-Lughod, L., & Lutz, C. A. (1990). Introduction: Emotion, discourse, and the politics of everyday life. In C. A. Lutz & L. Abu-Lughod (Eds.), *Language and the politics of emotion* (pp. 1–23). New York: Cambridge University Press.

Alexander, J. C. (1992). Citizen and enemy as symbolic classification: On the polarizing discourse of civil society. In M. Lamont & M. Fournier (Eds.), *Cultivating differences: Symbolic boundaries and the making of inequality* (pp. 289–308). Chicago: University of Chicago Press.

Allahyari, R. A. (2000). *Visions of charity: Volunteer workers and moral community.* Berkeley: University of California Press.

Altheide, D. L. (2002). *Creating fear.* New York: Aldine de Gruyter.

Arluke, A. (1994). Managing emotions in an animal shelter. In A. Manning & J. Serpell (Eds.), *Animals and human society: Changing perspectives* (pp. 145–165). New York: Routledge.

Armon-Jones, C. (1988). The thesis of constructionism. In R. Harré (Ed.), *The social construction of emotions* (pp. 32–56). New York: Blackwell.

Asen, R. (2002). Imagining in the public sphere. *Philosophy and Rhetoric, 35,* 345–367.

Barrett, L. F. (2006). Solving the emotion paradox: Categorization and the experience of emotion. *Personality and Social Psychology Review, 10,* 20–46.

Beatty, A. (2005). Feeling your way in Java: An essay on society and emotion. *Ethnos, 70,* 53–78.

Best, J. (1993). But seriously folks: The limitations of the strict constructionist interpretation of social problems. In J. A. Holstein & G. Miller (Eds.), *Reconsidering social constructionism: Debates in social problems theory* (pp. 129–150). New York: Aldine de Gruyter.

Boellstorff, T., & Lindquist, J. (2004). Bodies of emotion: Rethinking culture and emotion through Southeast Asia. *Ethnos, 69,* 437–444.

Brader, T. (2005). Striking a responsive chord: How political ads motivate and persuade voters by appealing to emotions. *American Journal of Political Science, 49,* 388–405.

Burkitt, I. (1997). Social relationships and emotions. *Sociology, 31,* 37–55.

Cahill, S. E. (1999). The boundaries of professionalization: The case of North American funeral direction. *Symbolic Interaction, 22,* 105–119.

Cahill, S. E., & Eggleston, R. (1994). Managing emotions in public: The case of wheelchair users. *Social Psychology Quarterly, 57,* 300–312.

Cancian, F. M. (1987). *Love in America: Gender and self-development.* Cambridge, UK: Cambridge University Press.

Cancian, F. M., & Gordon, S. (1988). Changing emotion norms in marriage: Love and anger in U.S. women's magazines since 1900. *Gender and Society, 2,* 308–342.

Cervantes, C. A. (2002). Explanatory emotion talk in Mexican immigrant and Mexican American families. *Hispanic Journal of Behavioral Sciences, 24,* 138–163.

Chin, T. (2000). Sixth grade madness: Parental work in the private high school application process. *Journal of Contemporary Ethnography, 29,* 124–163.

Clanton, G. (1989). Jealousy in American culture, 1945–1985: Reflections from popular literature. In D. Franks & E. D. McCarthy (Eds.), *The sociology of emotions* (pp. 179–196). Greenwich, CT: JAI Press.

Clark, C. (1997). *Misery and company: Sympathy in everyday life.* Chicago: University of Chicago Press.

Coles, R. L. (2002). War and the contest over national identity. *Sociological Review, 28,* 586–609.

Craib, I. (1995). Some comments on the sociology of emotions. *Sociology, 29,* 151–158.

Denzin, N. K. (1992). The many faces of emotionality: Reading *Persona.* In C. Ellis & M. G. Flaherty (Eds.), *Investigating subjectivity: Research on lived experience* (pp. 17–30). Newbury Park, CA: Sage.

DeVault, M. L. (1999). Comfort and struggle: Emotion work in family life. *Annals of the American Academy of Political and Social Science, 561,* 52–63.

Dunn, J. L. (2002). *Courting disaster: Intimate stalking, culture, and criminal justice.* New York: Aldine de Gruyter.

Edwards, D. (1999). Emotion discourse. *Culture and Psychology, 5,* 271–291.

Ellis, C., & Flaherty, M. C. (1992). An agenda for the interpretation of lived experience. In C. Ellis & M. C. Flaherty (Eds.), *Investigating subjectivity: Research on lived experience* (pp. 1–13). Newbury Park, CA: Sage.

Erickson, K. (2004). To invest or detach?: Coping strategies and workplace culture in service work. *Symbolic Interaction, 27,* 549–572.

Evers, C., Fischer, A. H., Mosquera, P. M. R., & Manstead, A. S. R. (2005). Anger and social appraisal: A "spicy" sex difference? *Emotion, 5,* 258–266.

Furedi, F. (1997). *Culture of fear: Risk-taking and the morality of low expectation.* London: Cassell.

Geertz, C. (1973). *The interpretation of cultures.* New York: Basic Books.

Gergen, K. J. (1994). *Realities and relationships: Soundings in social construction.* Boston: Harvard University Press.

Glassner, B. (1999). *The culture of fear: Why Americans are afraid of the wrong things.* New York: Basic Books.

Godwin, S. E. (2004). Managing guilt: Personal responsibility rhetoric among parents of "troubled" teens. *Sociological Quarterly, 45,* 575–596.

Goodwin, J., Jasper, J. M., & Polletta, F. (2000). The return of the repressed: The fall and rise of emotions in social movement theory. *Mobilization: An International Journal, 5,* 65–84.

Gordon, S. L. (1981). The sociology of sentiments and emotion. In M. Rosenberg & R. H. Turner (Eds.), *Social psychology: Sociological perspectives* (pp. 562–592). New York: Basic Books.

Gordon, S. L. (1990). Social structural effects on emotions. In T.D. Kemper (Ed.), *Research agendas in the sociology of emotions* (pp. 134–179). Albany: State University of New York Press.

Gottschalk, S. (2003). Reli(e)ving the past: Emotion work in the Holocaust's second generation. *Symbolic Interaction, 26,* 355–380.

Greer, K. (2002). Walking an emotional tightrope: Managing emotions in a women's prison. *Symbolic Interaction, 25,* 117–139.

Gubrium, J. F. (1992). *Out of control: Family therapy and domestic disorder.* Thousand Oaks, CA: Sage.

Gubrium, J. F., & Holstein, J. A. (Eds.). (1997). *The new language of qualitative method.* New York: Oxford University Press.

Hancock, A. (2004). *The politics of disgust: The public identity of the welfare queen.* New York: New York University Press.

Harré, R. (1986). An outline of the social constructionist viewpoint. In R. Harré (Ed.), *The social construction of emotions* (pp. 2–13). New York: Blackwell.

Harré, R., & Finlay-Jones, R. (1988). Emotion talk across times. In R. Harré (Ed.), *The social construction of emotions* (pp. 220–233). New York: Blackwell.

Harré, R., & Stearns, P. (1995). Introduction: Psychology as discourse analysis. In R. Harré & P. Stearns (Eds.), *Discursive psychology in practice* (pp. 1–8).Thousand Oaks, CA: Sage.

Hazleden, R. (2004). The pathology of love in contemporary relationship manuals. *Sociological Review, 52,* 201–216.

Hochschild, A. R. (1979). Emotion work, feeling rules, and social structure. *American Journal of Sociology, 85,* 551–575.

Hochschild, A. R. (1983). *The managed heart: Commercialization of human feeling.* Berkeley: University of California Press.

Hochschild, A. R. (1990). Ideology and emotion management: A perspective and path for future research. In T. D. Kemper (Ed.), *Research agendas in the sociology of emotions* (pp. 117–142). Albany: State University of New York Press.

Hochschild, A. R., & Ehrenreich, B. (2003). *Global women: Nannies, maids and sex workers in the new economy.* New York: Metropolitan Books.

Holstein, J. A., & Gubrium, J. F. (Eds.). (2000). *The self we live by: Narrative identity in a postmodern world.* New York: Oxford University Press.

Holstein, J. A., & Gubrium, J. F. (2001). *Institutional selves: Troubled identities in a postmodern world.* New York: Oxford University Press.

Holyfield, L. (1995). Manufacturing adventure: The buying and selling of emotions. *Journal of Contemporary Ethnography, 28,* 1–23.

Kang, M. (2003). The managed hand: The commercialization of bodies and emotions in Korean immigrant-owned nail salons. *Gender and Society, 17,* 820–839.

Karasz, A. (2005). Cultural differences in conceptual models of depression. *Social Science and Medicine, 60,* 1625–1635.

Kemper, T. D. (1981). Social constructionist and positivist approaches to the sociology of emotions. *American Journal of Sociology, 87,* 336–362.

Kemper, T. D. (1987). How many emotions are there? Wedding the social and autonomic components. *American Journal of Sociology, 93,* 263–289.

Konradi, A. (1999). "I don't have to be afraid of you": Rape survivor's emotion management in court. *Symbolic Interaction, 22,* 45–77.

Kunda, G., & Van Maanen, J. (1999). Changing scripts at work: Managers and professionals. *Annals of the American Academic of Political and Social Science, 561,* 64–80.

Lambek, M., & Solway, J. S. (2001). Just anger: Scenarios of indignation in Botswana and Madagascar. *Ethnos, 66,* 49–72.

Lamont, M., & Molnár, V. (2002). The study of boundaries in the social sciences. *Annual Review of Sociology, 28,* 167–195.

Leavitt, J. (1996). Meaning and feeling in the anthropology of emotions. *American Ethnologist, 23,* 514–539.

Leavitt, R. L., & Power, M. B. (1989). Emotional socialization in the postmodern era: Children in day care. *Social Psychology Quarterly, 5,* 35–43.

Leidner, R. (1993). *Fast food, fast talk: Service work and the routinization of everyday life.* Berkeley: University of California Press.

Lindquist, K. A., Barrett, L. F., Bliss-Moreau, E., & Russell, J. A. (2006). Language and the perception of emotion. *Emotion, 6,* 125–138.

Loseke, D. R. (2000). Ethos, pathos, and social problems: Reflections on formula narratives. In J. A. Holstein & G. Miller (Eds.), *Perspectives on social problems* (Vol. 12, pp. 41–54). Stamford, CT: JAI Press.

Loseke, D. R. (2003). *Thinking about social problems: An introduction to constructionist perspectives* (2nd ed.). New York: Transaction.

Loseke, D. R., & Cahill, S. E. (1986). Actors in search of a character. *Symbolic Interaction, 9,* 245–258.

Lutz, C. (1986). Emotion, thought, and estrangement: Emotion as a cultural category. *Cultural Anthropology, 1,* 287–309.

Lutz, C., & White, G. M. (1986). The anthropology of emotions. *Annual Review of Anthropology, 15,* 405–436.

Lyon, M. (1995). Missing emotion: The limitations of cultural constructionism in the study of emotion. *Cultural Anthropology, 10,* 244–263.

Maguire, J. S. (2001). Fit and flexible: The fitness industry, personal trainers and emotional service labor. *Sociology of Sports Journal, 18,* 379–402.

Martin, D. D. (2000). Organizational approaches to shame: Avowal, management, and contestation. *Sociological Quarterly, 41,* 125–150.

Matt, S. J. (2002). Children's envy and the emergence of the modern consumer ethic, 1890–1930. *Journal of Social History, 36,* 283–302.

Mazzeo, C., Rab, S., & Eachus, S. (2003). Work-first or work-only: Welfare reform, state policy, and access to postsecondary education. *Annals of the American Academy of Political and Social Science, 586,* 144–171.

McCarthy, E. D. (1989). Emotions are social things: An essay in the sociology of emotions. In D. D. Franks & E. D. McCarthy (Eds.), *The sociology of emotions: Original essays and research reports* (Vol. 9, pp. 51–72). Greenwich, CT: JAI Press.

McKendy, J. P. (1992). Ideological practices and the management of emotions: The case of "wife abusers." *Critical Sociology, 19,* 61–80.

Mears, A., & Finlay, W. (2005). Not just a paper doll: How models manage bodily capital and why they perform emotional labor. *Journal of Contemporary Ethnography, 34,* 317–343.

Menskin, D. (2004). The construction of Arabs as enemies: Post–September 11 discourse of George W. Bush. *Mass Communication and Society, 7,* 157–175.

Mesquita, B., & Frijda, N. H. (1992). Cultural variations in emotions: A review. *Psychological Bulletin, 112,* 179–204.

Moerk, E. L., & Pincus, F. (2000). How to make wars acceptable. *Peace and Change, 25,* 1–22.

Pierce, J. L. (1995). *Gender trials: Emotional lives in contemporary law firms.* Berkeley: University of California Press.

Pollak, L. H., & Thoits, P. A. (1989). Processes in emotional socialization. *Social Psychology Quarterly, 52,* 22–34.

Rafaeli, A., & Sutton, R. I. (1987). Expression of emotion as part of the work role. *Academy of Management Review, 12,* 23–37.

Rafaeli, A., & Sutton, R. I. (1991). Emotional contrast strategies as means of social influence: Lessons from criminal interrogators and bill collectors. *Academy of Management Journal, 34,* 749–775.

Richards, B. (2004). The emotional deficit in political communication. *Political Communication, 21,* 339–352.

Russell, J. A. (1991). Culture and the categorization of emotions. *Psychological Bulletin, 110,* 426–450.

Schachter, S., & Singer, J. E. (1962). Cognitive, social, and physiological determinants of emotional state. *Psychological Review, 69,* 379–399.

Schneider, A., & Ingram, H. (1993). Social construction of target populations: Implications for politics and policy. *American Political Science Review, 87,* 153–180.

Schwarz, N. (2000). Emotion, cognition, and decision making. *Cognition and Emotion, 14,* 433–440.

Schweingruber, D., & Berns, N. (2005). Shaping the selves of young salespeople through emotion management. *Journal of Contemporary Ethnography, 34,* 679–706.

Shields, S. A. (2005). The politics of emotion in everyday life: "Appropriate" emotion and claims on identity. *Review of General Psychology, 9,* 3–15.

Shields, S. A., & Koster, B. A. (1989). Emotional stereotyping of parents in child rearing manuals, 1915–1980. *Social Psychology Quarterly, 52,* 44–55.

Shilling, C. (2002). The two traditions in the sociology of emotions. In J. Barbalet (Ed.), *Emotions and sociology* (pp. 10–32). Oxford, UK: Blackwell.

Smith, A. C., III, & Kleinman, S. (1989). Managing emotions in medical school: Students' contacts with the living and the dead. *Social Psychology Quarterly, 52,* 56–69.

Solomon, R. C. (1995). Some notes on emotion: East and West. *Philosophy East and West, 45,* 171–202.

Staske, S. A. (1998). The normalization of problematic emotion in conversations between close relational partners: Interpersonal emotion work. *Symbolic Interaction, 21,* 59–86.

Stearns, P. N. (1987). The problem of change in emotions research: New standards for anger in twentieth-century childrearing. *Symbolic Interaction, 10,* 85–99.

Stearns, P. N. (1989). *Jealousy: The evolution of an emotion in American history.* New York: New York University Press.

Stearns, P. N. (1990). The rise of sibling jealousy in the twentieth century. *Symbolic Interaction, 13,* 83–101.

Stearns, P. N. (1993). Girls, boys, and emotions: Redefinitions and historical change. *Journal of American History, 80,* 36–74.

Stearns, P. N. (1995). Emotion. In R. Harré & P. Stearns (Eds.), *Discursive psychology in practice* (pp. 37–54). Thousand Oaks, CA: Sage.

Stearns, P. N., & Stearns, C. Z. (1985). Emotionology: Clarifying the history of emotions and emotional standards. *American Historical Review, 90,* 813–836.

Steinberg, R. J., & Figart, D. M. (1999). Emotional labor since *The managed heart. Annals of the American Academy of Political and Social Science, 561,* 8–26.

Swidler, A. (2001). *Talk of love: How culture matters.* Chicago: University of Chicago Press.

Tavris, C. (1982). *Anger: The misunderstood emotion.* New York: Touchstone.

Thoits, P. A. (1989). The sociology of emotions. *Annual Review of Sociology, 15,* 317–342.

Thoits, P. A. (1990). Emotional deviance: Research agendas. In T. D. Kemper (Ed.), *Research agendas in the sociology of emotions* (pp. 180–203). Albany: State University of New York Press.

Thompson, W. E. (1983). Hanging tongues: A sociological encounter with the assembly line. *Qualitative Sociology, 6*, 215–237.

Tolich, M. B. (1993). Alienating and liberating emotions at work: Supermarket clerks' performance of customer service. *Journal of Contemporary Ethnography, 22*, 361–381.

Turner, R. H. (1976). The real self: From institution to impulse. *American Journal of Sociology, 81*, 989–1016.

Waddell, C. (1990). The role of *pathos* in the decision-making process: A study in the rhetoric of science policy. *Quarterly Journal of Speech, 76*, 381–400.

White, G. M. (1990). Moral discourse and the rhetoric of emotions. In C. A. Lutz & L. Abu-Lughod (Eds.), *Language and the politics of emotion* (pp. 46–68). New York: Cambridge University Press.

White, G. M. (2000). Representing emotional meaning: Category, metaphor, schema, discourse. In M. Lewis & J. M. Haviland-Jones (Eds.), *Handbook of emotions* (2nd ed., pp. 30–44). New York: Guilford Press.

White, G. M. (2004). National subjects: September 11 and Pearl Harbor. *American Ethnologist, 31*, 293–310.

Wolkomir, M. (2001). Emotion work, commitment, and the authentication of the self: The case of gay and ex-gay Christian support groups. *Journal of Contemporary Ethnography, 30*, 305–334.

Yanay, N., & Sharar, G. (1998). Professional feelings as emotional labor. *Journal of Contemporary Ethnography, 27*, 346–373.

Zerubavel, E. (1996). Lumping and splitting: Notes on social classification. *Sociological Forum, 1*, 421–433.

CHAPTER 27

Constructing Gender
THE DANCER AND THE DANCE

- Judith Lorber

How can we know the dancer from the dance?
—W. B. YEATS

In the course of everyday life, gender is a constant part of who and what we are, how others treat us, and our general standing in society. Our bodies, personalities, and ways of thinking, acting, and feeling are gendered. Because we are gendered from birth by naming, clothing, and interaction with family, teachers, and peers, our identities as boys or girls, and then as men or women, are felt as, and usually explained as, a natural outcome of the appearance of our genitalia, the signs of our biological sex. Just as our anatomy was determined by XX or XY chromosomes and grew in utero in response to fetal hormones, we believe that

our brains and therefore our subsequent behavior also have to be determined by physiology. Then how can women and men be so different over time and space? Sex-differences proponents attribute variation to cultural overlays and social environments that do not affect an immutable baseline of sex differences.

Social constructionists argue that gender is not sex. Rather, gender is an organizing principle of social orders that divides people into two major categories: "men" and "women." They are expected to be different, are treated differently, and so become different. Social constructionists explain the historical and cross-cultural variability of gender differences by social processes and by hierarchical power differences between women and men. These social processes are carried out without thinking: Because we are gendered, we "do gender," and doing gender constructs our behavior, identities, and work and family lives (West & Zimmerman, 1987). Throughout our lives, we dance a gendered dance, and through the dance we are gendered.

These social processes reflect and sustain the gendering of all the institutions of society. The invidious effect of gender divisions is the disadvantageous status of women in most societies. Although societies can ensure that differences are not used to legitimate unequal legal rights or discriminatory practices, there is always debate over how equal women and men can be, given what seems to be a substantially wide and unbridgeable gap between female and male "natures." If, as social constructionists argue, the gendered social order and its constant reproduction and maintenance are the source of the differences between women and men, then the gendering processes can be altered, reversed, diminished, or erased altogether.

Change does not come easily, however, because many of the foundational assumptions of the gendered social order and its ubiquitous processes are legitimated by religion, taught by education, upheld by the mass media, and enforced by systems of social control. But the strongest element in the continued conventional construction of gender is its invisibility. Put simply, we are gendered because we do gender, and we do gender because we are constantly subject to gendered social processes and structures—yet we rarely notice the gendered dance we are dancing.

As a feminist, I believe that as pervasive as gender is, it can be resisted and reshaped through making the gender processes that produce inequality visible and altering or eliminating them. The social construction perspective argues that people create their social realities and identities, including their genders, through their actions with others—their families, friends, and colleagues. Gendering may be an individual dance, but the choreography is shaped by cultural expectations, workplace norms, and state laws. Both the dancer and the choreography have to change for gender to change. And that takes individual agency, group pressure, and social movements.[1]

Themes in the Constructionist Concept of Gender

The concept of gender as socially constructed has two main themes. One is gender as process: People construct gender for themselves and those they interact with by doing or performing gender. The other is gender as structure, regime, or institution: Gender divisions and the gendered organization of social worlds are iron cages that allow for little resistance or rebellion. The two themes are both complementary and in conflict. Process and structure are complementary in that processes create and maintain structures. They are in conflict because structuration delimits process.

Initially, the constructionist perspective focused on processes of gendering. Making them visible seemed to be liberating, allowing individual agents to bring about change (Bem, 1983). More recently, constructionists have focused on gendered structures that prescribe practices and thwart individual and group attempts to change them (Connell, 1987; Lorber, 1994). Empirical work in gender studies on small-group interaction (Webster & Foschi, 1988) and family dynamics (Potuchek, 1997) certainly continue, but the theoretical focus has shifted to structural issues in the organization of work (Acker, 1990; Britton, 2000); systems of social control, such as law (Bartlett & Kennedy, 1991) and medicine (Lorber & Moore, 2002); and knowledge production, especially in science (Harding, 1991; Keller, 1985). The structural focus tends to be critical of social constraints and pessimistic about the possibilities of change.

Theoretically and empirically, one cannot neglect process in analyzing structure nor forget the power of structure when describing process. Gender is a building block of the social order, with gender divisions and roles built into all major social institutions of society, such as the economy, the family, politics, culture, religion, and the law. Its production and maintenance are dependent on the interactive gendered behavior of people that reflects their position within the gender structure. Whether they are privileged or oppressed, people do gender because not to do so is to be shamed as unmanly or unwomanly. In this dual sense of doing and being done to lies the power of gender as a socially constructed system of inequality. This power is enormously strengthened by the invisibility of gender processes, the lack of reflection in doing gender, and the belief that the gender order is based on natural and immutable sex differences.

In the following sections, I discuss key theorists and researchers who developed the ideas of gendering as process and gender as structure. Using a feminist social construction perspective, I then discuss ways of *not* constructing gender.

Gendering as Process

Ethnomethodological Insights into Gender Construction

Gender as a construct first appeared in Harold Garfinkel's *Studies in Ethnomethodology* (1967) in the story of Agnes. Agnes was a 19-year-old with fully developed breasts, penis, and testicles who came to a University of California center for the study of people with "severe anatomical irregularities." Agnes presented as an "intersexual" but in actuality was a transsexual who had been taking female hormone pills stolen from her mother since the age of 12. What was important to Garfinkel was the way that Agnes achieved the gender display of a "natural, normal female" through voice pitch, gestures, dress, and other mannerisms that today we would call "emphasized femininity." The construction of gender identity by transgenders has subsequently been described in many accounts and is now a staple of the constructionist literature.[2] Another stream in the deliberate construction of cross-gender display is the literature on drag queens and drag kings.[3]

Buried in Garfinkel's chapter on Agnes but spotlighted by gender studies analysts is the idea that it is not only transgenders or drag performers who create a gender identity; everyone produces a version of masculinity or femininity socially and culturally acceptable enough to meet the expectations of normality in the eyes of others in their social groups.[4] Building on Garfinkel's work, Suzanne Kessler and Wendy McKenna, in *Gender: An Ethnomethodological Approach* (1978/1985), showed how gender is produced as a social fact: "The gender attribution process is the method by which we construct our world of two genders" (p. 18).

According to Garfinkel, the "natural attitude" is that there are two and only two genders, that everyone has to be one or the other, and that biology is the source of gender distinctions. As Kessler and McKenna (1978/1985) show, gender attribution reproduces the dichotomous reality of gender by ignoring anomalies and assuming anatomical congruence with outer appearance. Genitalia may be the signs used in the initial assignment of an infant to a sex category, but in gender attribution, the genitalia under clothing are assumed; Kessler and McKenna call them "cultural." In their ethnomethodological account of gender construction, Kessler and McKenna focus on the role of the "other" in the validation of gender, but they end their book by coming back to the doer: "All persons create both the reality of their specific gender and a sense of its history, thus at the same time creating the reality of two, and only two, natural genders" (p. 139).

Garfinkel (1967) did not address the question of the extent of consciousness and complicity in the construction of gender because he did not know until years after that Agnes had been lying about the source of her bodily anomalies (breasts and a penis). In a feminist reanalysis of the story of Agnes, Mary Rogers (1992) argued that Garfinkel was an unwitting "gender collaborator" who displayed the masculinity Agnes needed as a contrast. Although most "normals" present themselves as women or men without the deliberate impression management of transgenders, there were times when Garfinkel was well aware that he played up to Agnes's emphasized femininity by a complementarily emphasized masculinity—holding doors open, seating her in a car, and so on. What was below the surface of his awareness, according to Rogers, were the power differentials in his relationship with Agnes. He was older, a professional, in control of the interview sessions, and, with the other men in the research–clinic situation, the ultimate decider of whether or not Agnes would get the desired sex-change surgery. And so, like other Western women in the 1950s, Agnes had to be manipulative and secretive to get what she wanted from men who had power over her.

Constructionist feminist theory and research subsequently focused on how girls and women consciously learn heterosexual gender displays and subservient behavior as strategies to attract a husband but seemed to assume that boys and men absorbed the attitudes of patriarchal privilege much less consciously. Because consciousness-raising was at one time a radical feminist political strategy, it would seem that without the "click" of self-awareness, women are no more conscious of the gender construction of their lives than men are.

The use of Agnes in the feminist literature as a model of the production of femininity by "normal, natural females" greatly expanded the concept of gender construction. A huge body of empirical research shows how girls and women in Western societies are made docile, submissive, emotional, and nurturant through socialization by parents, teachers, and peers and through imitation of constantly presented media depictions of heterosexual attractiveness. Later work on masculinity shows that the same process takes place in the making of assertive, emotionally repressed, sexually aggressive boys and men, with the addition of sports as an arena for reward and emulation of violent behavior.[5]

An early and ongoing thread in gender construction homed in on sexist language that demeaned women and rendered them invisible through the generic *he*. Excellent research on cross-gendered conversations shows how men ignore and contradict women (Tannen, 1993; Thorne & Henley, 1975). Another continuing thread is the gendered body. In a change from the earlier bracketing of the body to concentrate on social processes of gendering, recent empirical studies do not see female and male bodies as separate from gender construction but show them to be shaped by and integrated into gender displays and identities (Lorber & Moore, 2007).

Doing Gender

The signature term in constructionist gender studies is *doing gender*, the title of an article published in *Gender & Society* in 1987 by Candace West and Don Zimmerman.[6] Building on the work of Garfinkel, Kessler and McKenna, and Erving Goffman (1967, 1977), West and Zimmerman argued that

> gender is not a set of traits, not a variable, nor a role, but the product of social doings of some sort. . . . Doing gender means creating differences between girls and boys and women and men, differences that are not natural, essential, or biological. Once the differences have been constructed, they are used to reinforce the "essentialness" of gender. (pp. 129, 137)

Given membership in a sex category, doing gender is inevitable and unavoidable. What is more, one's gender performance is evaluated by others, and one is accountable for its appropriateness. The end result is not only personal and interpersonal gendering but gendered workplaces, politics, medical and legal systems, religions, and cultural productions: "Doing gender furnishes the interactional scaffolding of social structure, along with built-in mechanisms of social control" (West & Zimmerman, 1987, p. 147).

These statements, widely accepted now but path-breaking at the time, provided a new paradigm for gender studies in the social sciences and generated reams of research that built on earlier work now seen to be empirical evidence for "doing gender." Areas that have been particularly fruitful have been studies of the family, the workplace, and the professions as sites of gender doings.[7] These studies show how the differentially gendered behavior of women and men is induced and sustained. For example, tacitly or openly, the underlying assumptions of family responsibilities influence the recruitment, retention, and advancement policies of workplace managers:

> For men, real, imagined or potential domestic responsibilities were usually evaluated as a positive indication of stability, flexibility, compatibility and motivation, while for women, they were often viewed negatively as confirmation of unreliability and a short-term investment in work. However, these selector assumptions could be reversed, where the jobs on offer were low paying, low status, and mundane with little career potential. For such jobs, it was often decided, on the basis of the stereotype of the dependent female homemaker, that women would be more stable, flexible and able to "fit in." (Collinson, Knights, & Collinson 1990, pp. 193–194)

The consequences are the now-familiar phenomena of tokenism, the glass ceiling, and the wage penalty for motherhood.

To the extent that women conform to norms of femininity, they could be said to be complicit in their own oppression, just as men who benefit from the privileges of mas-culinity are complicit in reproducing that oppression (Martin, 2001, 2003). However, even in our supposedly enlightened times, the pressures of accountability for doing gender properly still create family–work conflicts among successful women (Blair-Loy, 2003; Hochschild, 1997). These pressures constrain their career and family choices in ways that are often not of their own choosing.

Just as sexist language produced the ubiquitous devaluation of women until feminists made it visible in the 1970s, the discourse that shapes the norms of work and family reflects invidious gendered assumptions and values. Julia Nentwich (2004), a Swiss psychologist, suggests alternative language to construct different realities. Within a work organization, she says, women can be different—exotic, not the norm, a problem to integrate. Or they can be similar, so that treating them differently is discrimination. In the family, the language of the traditional division of labor puts children and job in conflict and makes a paid job a privilege for mothers and spending time with the family a privilege for fathers. In contrast, the language of equal partnership assumes that her paid work is important to the woman, that fathers take care of their children, and that both participate in work and family. Concerning full-time versus part-time work, in the dominant language framework, full time has to be the norm because the demands of the job come first; performance is measured by time spent at the job; and work and private life are two separate spheres. In an alternative language framework, performance is measured by fulfilling objectives, jobs can be partitioned, and work, family, and other life concerns are overlapping spheres (also see Epstein, Seron, Oglensky, & Sauté, 1999).

Gender as Performativity

If "doing gender" has been the touchstone of gender construction in the social sciences, Judith Butler's concept of *performativity*, from *Gender Trouble* (1990/1999), has been the prevailing concept in the humanities. Based in philosophy and psychoanalytic theory, Butler's concept of performativity encompasses the unconscious process of making gendered selves that reiterate social norms of femininity and masculinity and inscribe femaleness and maleness on the body and heterosexuality on the psyche. Performance and identity are one and the same; one does not precede or exist without the other.[8] And in that lies the possibility for "gender trouble." Gendering has to be done over and over, almost ritualistically, to reproduce the social norms. But different ways of gendering produce differently gendered people. So, with conscious deliberation, one might create oneself differently gendered, and, indeed, transgenders do just that. By 1993, Butler was rethinking aspects of gender performativity. In *Bodies That Matter* (1993), she took up the materiality or "bodiedness" of gender performativity and analyzed the ways that it encompassed sex and sexuality as well.

Butler ended *Gender Trouble* by arguing for the subversive political possibilities inherent in gender performativity. She said,

The loss of gender norms would have the effect of proliferating gender configurations, destabilizing substantive identity, and depriving the naturalizing narratives of compulsory heterosexuality of their central protagonists: "man" and "woman." (1990, p. 146)

Since 1990, postmodernists and queer theorists, following Butler's lead, have questioned the twofold divisions of gender, sexuality, and even sex, undermining the solidity of a world built on men–women, heterosexuals–homosexuals, and male–female (Beemyn & Eliason, 1996; Herdt, 1994; Warner, 1993). However, in the preface to the 10th anniversary edition of *Gender Trouble* in 1999, Butler says that she was somewhat too elated about these possibilities, forgetting normative gender's deep tentacles into our psyches and bodies. In *Undoing Gender* (2004), a collection of essays,

Butler mourns the destructiveness of imposed gendering, especially on those who are differently gendered. It is not the supposed active agent who undoes gender, she says, but rather gender that undoes the gender doer:

Does it turn out that the "I" who ought to be bearing its gender is undone by being a gender, that gender is always coming from a source that is elsewhere and directed toward something that is beyond me, constituted in a sociality that I do not fully author? If that is so, then gender undoes the "I" who is supposed to be or bear its gender and undoing is part of the very meaning and comprehensibility of that "I." (2004, p. 16)

Constructing Gendered Structures

In the late 1980s, especially in social science gender studies, the focus turned from process to structure. Structuration is the congealing of the situationally based rules of interactive processes and practices and their enforced application across time and space (Giddens, 1984, Chap. 1). Concepts of gendered organizations, gender regimes, and gender as an institution convey stability and solidity, in contrast to the fluidity and mutability of gendered processes. Gendered structures are not just the accumulation of gender doings; they constitute and organize a major part of the social order. With structuring, gendered practices (process) are imposed by institutionalized patterns of social interaction embedded in legal and bureaucratic rules and regulations. Most significantly, these institutionalized patterns are imbued with domination and power.[9]

Gendered Workplaces

A prime arena for research on gender structuration is the organization of workplaces (Acker, 1990; Britton, 2000; Ferguson, 1984). A workplace is more or less structurally gendered on several levels. One is the extent of the division into women's and men's jobs; another is the steepness or flatness of the hierarchy of authority and prestige and the gender clustering at each level; still another is the range of the wage and benefits scale and where women and men workers fall on it. The extent of gendering depends on the decisions, policies, and history of the particular workplace, which reflect and reproduce its structure through the interactions of workers as colleagues, bosses, and subordinates.

Work structures are legitimated by cultural rationales for the selection and placement of new workers and the advancement of some and not others (Gherardi, 1995; Hearn & Parkin, 2002; Ridgeway & Correll, 2004). When workers are recruited to a heavily gendered workplace, a belief in the importance of gendered characteristics influences the search for candidates who are "masculine" or "feminine." In Westernized cultures, "masculine" traits would be physical strength, rationality, objectivity, aggressiveness; "feminine" traits would be dexterity, emotional sensitivity, psychological perceptivity, ability to mediate and compromise. In a nongendered workplace, the search would be for workers who exhibited "neutral" characteristics, such as intelligence, honesty, experience, and mental agility. The gender designations of attributes as masculine, feminine, or neutral are culturally contingent, and the skills needed for a job are frequently regendered as the gender composition of the workforce changes (Jacobs, 1989; Reskin & Roos, 1990). The same jobs can be stereotyped as masculine "dangerous work" in one country and feminine work needing "nimble fingers" in another (Poster, 2001).

The end result of the attribution of desired characteristics is the valuation of men workers over women workers, men's jobs over women's jobs, and "masculine" over "feminine" work capabilities. However the workplace is gendered, the economic outcome seems to be stubbornly uniform in advantaging men. Salaries are highest in occupations in which men are the predominant

workers, whether the worker is a woman or a man, and lowest in occupations in which women are the predominant workers, again whether the worker is a man or a woman. Looked at from the perspective of the worker, men have the advantage no matter what the gender composition of the occupation or workplace, because they earn more than women in occupations in which men are the majority or women are the majority, and in those that are gender-balanced.

The pervasive cultural beliefs about women and men workers that perpetuate gender inequality support the devaluation of women's competence by men. Women themselves help to sustain the devaluation because they frequently compare themselves with other women, not men, at the same level. The unequal salary scales and opportunities for career advancement thus seem fair because there are no challenges to the beliefs that sustain them. In sum, the processes that produce gender inequality in the workplace are both interactive and structural. As Cecilia Ridgeway says,

> The result is a system of interdependent effects that are everywhere and nowhere because they develop through multiple workplace interactions, often in taken-for-granted ways. Their aggregate result is structural: the preservation of wage inequality and the sex segregation of jobs. (1997, p. 230)

Gender Regimes

Gender regimes are the ways that gender structures nation-states. Just as organizations are not aggregates of gendered practices but have a logic of their own, gender regimes are not aggregations of gendered organizations. Gender regimes stratify women and men across organizations, so that they are valued more or less over a matrix of statuses that determine their access to power, prestige, and economic resources (Collins, 1990; Yuval-Davis, 1997). Commonly, gender intertwines with racial, ethnic, and class stratification, so that gender is only one aspect of a complex of inequality (Acker, 2006; Collins, 1998, 2004; McCall, 2001).

Many gender regimes privilege one group of men. In *Masculinities*, Raewyn Connell (1995) contrasted hegemonic men and subordinated men.[10] Hegemonic men have economic and educational advantages and institutionalized patriarchal privileges, and their characteristics are the most valued attributes of masculinity. Subordinated men are not necessarily devalued, but they have fewer opportunities for advancement and little of the power, prestige, and wealth of hegemonic men. Connell describes how Western hegemonic masculinity is produced through college education, in which young men are trained to be rational and technically expert, and reproduced in professional and managerial careers in hierarchically organized workplaces, in which hegemonic men expect eventually to have positions of authority over other men. Hegemonic and subordinated groups of men shift with changing historical conditions, but according to Connell (1993, 1998, 2005), the hegemony of white European men over the past 500 years has spread globally through colonization, economic control, and state violence.

The gender regimes of Middle Eastern Islamic theocracies that were established after successful religious revolutions have not privileged college-educated men. In Iran after the overthrow of the shah, as Shahin Gerami (2003) notes, new masculine prototypes were in favor—mullahs as the leaders of revolution; martyrs as its soul; and working-class men as its beneficiaries. With a high birthrate and low levels of economic development, college-educated men find that urban jobs are hard to come by or pay too little to sustain a middle-class life style. An alternative route to hegemonic masculine status has been to become heroic soldiers and martyrs, protectors of women and their country's honor (Kimmel, 2003). When martyrs die heroically, their families reap the economic and prestige benefits of their new hegemonic status.

Islamic women live in the same gender regimes as Islamic men, but the economic, educational, and status opportunities for women are different from those of men in the same societies. The political shifts that reversed men's gender hierarchies, bringing hegemonic status to formerly subordinated men, made college-educated and professional women, who were dominant over some men, subordinate to all men. Formerly subordinated, poor religious women could attain positions of dominance over other women as enforcers of purity codes of dress and behavior (Gerami & Lehnerer, 2001). The nationalistic and revolutionary movements in Muslim countries have produced pendulum swings of Westernized, secular regimes and the counterestablishment of tradition-based theocracies. Women have had a more equal status with men under secular regimes and have lost many rights with theocratic revolutions, but there is considerable cross-national variation (Moghadam, 1999).

Gender as a Social Institution

According to Giddens, society-wide structural principles that extend over time and space can be considered *institutions* (1984, p. 17). In *Paradoxes of Gender* (Lorber, 1994), I claimed that gender was a social institution based on three structural principles: the division of people into two social groups, "men" and "women"; the social construction of perceptible differences between them; and their differential treatment, legitimated by the socially produced differences.[11] In complex societies, the binary division by gender overrides individual differences and intertwines with other major social statuses—racial categorization, ethnic grouping, economic class, age, religion, and sexual orientation—to create a hierarchical system of dominance and subordination, oppression, and exploitation. The members of the dominant gender status, usually hegemonic men, legitimate and rationalize the gender order through politics, the media, the education system, religion, and the production of knowledge and culture. Gendered kinship statuses reflect and reinforce the prestige and power differences of the different genders and institutionalize heterosexuality as an intrinsic part of gender (Butler, 2002; Ingraham, 2006).

The concept of gender as a social institution makes change seem impossible, but institutions do evolve or are drastically altered through political movements. Through feminist political activism and other political and social forces, the institution of gender has certainly evolved in Western societies: Women and men now have formal equality in all the major social spheres (Jackson, 1998). No laws prevent women from achieving what they can, and many laws help them do it by preventing discrimination and sexual harassment. More and more countries are ratifying laws to protect women's procreative and sexual rights and to designate rape, battering, and genital mutilation as human rights crimes. However, despite formal and legal equality, discriminatory treatment of women still regularly occurs in the economy and in politics. Gender equality has not significantly penetrated the family division of labor, and conflicts over who takes care of the children spill over and are exacerbated by gender inequities in the paid job market. Women have not gained the power or economic resources in most Western societies to ensure the structural bases of gender equality, and so their successes are constantly being undermined by the vicissitudes of the economy, a war, or the resurgence of religious fundamentalism.

Deconstructing Gender

The obverse of the construction of gender is its deconstruction, a term that has a double meaning. In queer theory and postmodern feminism, gender is deconstructed to describe the myriad processes of construction, emphasizing their fluidity, situational contingency, and malleability. Gender rebel-

lions by transgenders (cross-dressers, sex changers, intersexual and bisexual people) who do not want to pass as members of the other gender but rather refuse to abide by gender norms and expectations in performance, display, and identity have deconstructed gender by undermining its binary basis. The insistence on third terms—*intersex*, *bisexuality*, and *transgender*—call into question the opposition of one to the other that the binaries imply. Indeed, in queer theory, three is hardly the limit to sex, sexuality, and gender categories (Beemyn & Eliason, 1996; Garber, 1995; Warner, 1993).

If the concepts of gender structures, regimes, and institutions neglect individual actions or agency, postmodernism and queer theory have the opposite problem. Their emphasis on agency, impression management, and presentation of the self in the guise and costume most likely to produce, parody, or confront conformity implies that people are free to consciously and deliberately construct the gender they want. Neglected are the controlling discourses embedded in organizational, legal, religious, and political texts that inhibit free agency and bury creative, conscious impulses with the weight of tradition and "naturalness." Gender resisters and rebels do, of course, challenge gender construction, but they need to form their own communities to avoid ostracism. Someone whose presentation of self is unconventionally gendered, whose body has ambiguous sex markers, and whose sexuality is fluid has no place in a binarily gendered social world. We do not even know how to refer to gender refusers.

Doing Degendering

Feminists argue that the whole point of making gendering visible is to show the ways it produces inequalities in power, resources, and opportunities. Once that is done, ways can be devised to counteract the invidious effects by not constructing gender differences and to compensate for inequality by affirmative action or gender mainstreaming.

In *Breaking the Bowls: Degendering and Feminist Change* (Lorber, 2005), I suggest strategies of not constructing gender—*degendering*.

Degendering goes back to the processes of constructing gender divisions and differences, makes them visible and conscious, and then proceeds to *not do* them. If gender is constructed in unthinking complicity, degendering is constructed in conscious refusal. The areas that need degendering are the everyday ways that gender sorts people and allocates tasks in work organizations, schools, small groups, families, and other familiar social groupings. Degendering would entail not assigning tasks in the home and workplace by gender and not grouping children by gender in schools. Doing degendering would challenge gender expectations in face-to-face interaction and underplay gender categories in language (not saying "ladies and gentlemen" but "colleagues and friends"). Many people already use the degendered terms *partner, constant companion, significant other*, or *beloved* for the other person in a long-term emotional relationship, rather than *boyfriend, girlfriend, husband, wife*. Degendered kinship designations, such as *child, parent*, and *sibling*, could liberate us further from stereotypical gendered expectations. Where language itself is built on gender categories, developing gender-neutral ways of addressing and referring to people would be a major enterprise, but its accomplishment would go a long way toward degendering. Similarly, in theocracies in which the dominant state religion separates women and men and treats them markedly unequally through religious law, degendering cannot take place unless personal status laws are secularized and made gender-neutral.

As degendering agents in our everyday lives, we can confront the ubiquitous bureaucratic and public gender binaries just as transgendered people do—by thinking about whether we want to conform or challenge. We could stop ticking off the "M/F" boxes at the top of every form we fill out or question the need for them. Shannon Faulkner, a girl, got into the Citadel, an all-boys' military school, because the admission form did not have an M/F check-off box; it was assumed that only boys would apply. All her credentials and biographical information qualified her for admission, but when the Citadel administration found out she was a girl, she was immediately disqualified. The person did not change; her qualifications remained the same. It was on that basis that she successfully claimed gender discrimination and challenged the all-male status of the Citadel (Kimmel, 2000).

Making gender statuses irrelevant is precisely what degendering would do. The goal is to undercut the conventional assumptions and valuation built on gender comparisons ("boys will be boys," "just like a woman"). Diminishing the constant invocation of gender differences would also undermine the practices based on those assumed differences. Degendering, in short, is constantly questioning the ordinarily unquestioned construction of gendered behavior.

In place of an ideology that roots gender in sex differences and imposes heterosexuality on gendered sexual scripts, an ideology of degendering assumes that sex is biological, physiological, and procreative, not a basis for social categorization; that sexual desire is fluid, not bound by gendered opposites; and that gender is not a valid basis for organizing societies. Degendering would eliminate binary gender statuses—and the norms and expectations for behavior, bodies, gestures, speech, attitudes, and emotions that are built into them.

Because degendering would eliminate allocation by gender, barring the intervention of other statuses, allocation of jobs, tasks, and occupations and professions would be done on the basis of credentials, experience, and abilities. Rewards—economic and prestigious—would accrue to the type of work, as they do today; but the distribution of people to work of different sorts would vary by capabilities. Superiors and subordinates in workplaces would relate to each other the way people of the same gender do today.

Degendering kinship would necessitate some way in which to regularize responsibility for dependents through legalized civil unions or household contracts with built-in structures of equality for the adults involved and shared legal responsibility for dependents. Personality development would reflect family dynamics that are not structured by gender. With degendering, sexual scripts could be fluid and open. Degendered marriage contracts or legal partnerships could help protect the rights of the economically less advantaged partner in long-term relationships.

Degendering would mean no stratification or control by gender, but it would not eliminate other forms of valuation and resource allocation. Dominance and exploitation would not be eliminated if social class, racial ethnic, or other stratified statuses permeated the structure of a degendered society. It is unlikely that gender will stop being constructed, but it is mind-opening to imagine a world that does not constantly construct gender and that does not insist that everyone dances a gendered dance.

• Acknowledgment

Parts of this chapter have been adapted from Lorber (2005). Copyright 2005 by W.W. Norton & Company, Inc. Adapted by permission. Permission of the author is needed to reproduce all or parts of this chapter.

• Notes

1. For recent research on feminist social movements, see Taylor and Whittier (1998, 1999).

2. See, for example, Bolin (1988), Devor (1997), and Ekins (1997).

3. See, among others, Rupp and Taylor (2003), Troka, Lebesco, and Noble (2002), Schacht (2004).

4. Garfinkel's statement that "Agnes was self-consciously equipped to teach normals how normals make sexuality happen in commonplace settings as an obvious, familiar, recognizable, natural, and serious matter of fact" does not appear until almost the end of a very long account (1967, p. 180).

5. For some work on women and girls, see Berk (1985), Bordo (1993/2005), Brumberg (1997), Davis (1995), DeVault (1991), Gimlin (2002), Hobson (2005), Hochschild (1983), Lamb and Brown (2006). For some of the literature on men and boys, see Connell (1995, 2000), Gilmore (1990), Kimmel & Messner (2007), Messner (1992), Wacquant (2004). Messner (2002) deals with sports' usage and effects in constructing masculinity and femininity in girls, boys, women, and men. Thorne (1993) shows how schools construct gender for boys and girls.

6. "Doing Gender" was originally given as a paper at the annual meeting of the American Sociological Association in 1977. It was rejected for publication for 10 years, until the creation of *Gender & Society* by Sociologists for Women in Society. This history validated the need for a publication with a constructionist perspective (personal communication between Judith Lorber, the founding editor, and Candace West).

7. Important studies in gender construction are Berk (1985), Chodorow (1978), Epstein (1971, 1988), Hochschild (1989), Kanter (1977), and Lorber (1984).

8. The "dancer and the dance" metaphor is most applicable to Butler's concept of performativity.

9. Foundational books are Connell (1987), Lorber (1994), MacKinnon (1989), Smith 1990a, 1990b).

10. For a rethinking of the concept of masculine hegemony, see Connell & Messerschmidt (2005).

11. For a discussion of the concept of gender as a social institution, see Martin (2004).

• References

Acker, J. (1990). Hierarchies, jobs, and bodies: A theory of gendered organizations. *Gender & Society, 4*, 139–158.

Acker, J. (2006). *Class questions: Feminist answers.* Latham, MD: Rowman & Littlefield.

Bartlett, K. T., & Kennedy, R. (Eds.). (1991). *Feminist legal theory: Readings in law and gender.* Boulder, CO: Westview Press.

Beemyn, B., & Eliason, M. (Eds.). (1996). *Queer studies: A lesbian, gay, bisexual, and transgender anthology.* New York: New York University Press.

Bem, S. L. (1983). Gender schema theory and its implications for child development: Raising gender-aschematic children in a gender-schematic society. *Signs: Journal of Women in Culture and Society, 8,* 598–616.

Berk, S. F. (1985). *The gender factory: The apportionment of work in American households.* New York: Plenum Press.

Blair-Loy, M. (2003). *Competing devotions: Career and family among women executives.* Cambridge, MA: Harvard University Press.

Bolin, A. (1988). *In search of Eve: Transsexual rites of passage.* South Hadley, MA: Bergin & Garvey.

Bordo, S. R. (2005). *Unbearable weight: Feminism, Western culture, and the body.* Berkeley: University of California Press. (Original work published 1993)

Britton, D. M. (2000). The epistemology of the gendered organization. *Gender & Society, 14,* 418–434.

Brumberg, J. J. (1997). *The body project: An intimate history of American girls.* New York: Vintage.

Butler, J. (1999). *Gender trouble: Feminism and the subversion of identity.* New York: Routledge. (Original work published 1990)

Butler, J. (1993). *Bodies that matter: On the discursive limits of "sex."* New York: Routledge.

Butler, J. (2002). Is kinship always already heterosexual? *Differences: A Journal of Feminist Cultural Studies, 13,* 14–44.

Butler, J. (2004). *Undoing gender.* New York: Routledge.

Chodorow, N. (1978). *The reproduction of mothering.* Berkeley: University of California Press.

Collins, P. H. (1990). *Black feminist thought: Knowledge, consciousness, and the politics of empowerment.* Boston: Unwin Hyman.

Collins, P. H. (1998). *Fighting words: Black women and the search for justice.* Minneapolis: University of Minnesota Press.

Collins, P. H. (2004). *Black sexual politics: African Americans, gender, and the new racism.* New York: Routledge.

Collinson, D. L., Knights, D., & Collinson, M. (1990). *Managing to discriminate.* New York: Routledge.

Connell, R. (1987). *Gender and power.* Stanford, CA: Stanford University Press.

Connell, R. (1993). The big picture: Masculinities in recent world history. *Theory and Society, 22,* 597–623.

Connell, R. (1995). *Masculinities.* Berkeley: University of California Press.

Connell, R. (1998). Masculinities and globalization. *Men and Masculinities, 1,* 3–23.

Connell, R. (2000). *The men and the boys.* Berkeley: University of California Press.

Connell, R. (2005). Change among the gatekeepers: Men, masculinities, and gender equality in the global arena. *Signs: Journal of Women in Culture and Society, 30,* 1801–25.

Connell, R., & Messerschmidt, J. W. (2005). Hegemonic masculinity: Rethinking the concept. *Gender & Society, 19,* 829–859.

Davis, K. (1995). *Reshaping the female body: The dilemma of cosmetic surgery.* New York: Routledge.

DeVault, M. L. (1991). *Feeding the family: The social organization of caring as gendered work.* Chicago: University of Chicago Press.

Devor, H. (1997). *FTM: Female-to-male transsexuals in society.* Bloomington: Indiana University Press.

Ekins, R. (1997). *Male femaling: A grounded theory approach to cross-dressing and sex-changing.* New York: Routledge.

Epstein, C. F. (1971). *Women's place: Options and limits in professional careers.* Berkeley: University of California Press.

Epstein, C. F. (1988). *Deceptive distinctions: Sex, gender and the social order.* New Haven, CT: Yale University Press.

Epstein, C. F., Seron, C., Oglensky, B., & Sauté, R. (1999). *The part-time paradox: Time norms, professional lives, family, and gender.* New York: Routledge.

Ferguson, K. E. (1984). *The feminist case against bureaucracy.* Philadelphia: Temple University Press.

Garber, M. (1995). *Vice versa: Bisexuality and the eroticism of everyday life.* New York: Simon & Schuster.

Garfinkel, H. (1967). *Studies in ethnomethodology.* Englewood Cliffs, NJ: Prentice Hall.

Gerami, S. (2003). Mullahs, martyrs, and men: Conceptualizing masculinity in the Islamic Republic of Iran. *Men and Masculinities, 5,* 257–274.

Gerami, S., & Lehnerer, M. (2001). Women's agency and household diplomacy: Negotiating fundamentalism. *Gender & Society, 15,* 556–573.

Gherardi, S. (1995). *Gender, symbolism and organizational cultures.* Thousand Oaks, CA: Sage.

Giddens, A. (1984). *The constitution of society.* Berkeley: University of California Press.

Gilmore, D. D. (1990). *Manhood in the making: Cultural concepts of masculinity.* New Haven, CT: Yale University Press.

Gimlin, D. L. (2002). *Body work: Beauty and self-image in American culture.* Berkeley: University of California Press.

Goffman, E. (1967). *Interaction ritual: Essays in face-to-face behavior.* Chicago: Aldine de Gruyter.

Goffman, E. (1977). The arrangement between the sexes. *Theory and Society, 4,* 301–333.

Harding, S. (1991). *Whose science? Whose knowledge? Thinking from women's lives.* Ithaca, NY: Cornell University Press.

Hearn, J. R., & Parkin, W. (2002). *Gender, sexuality and violence in organizations: The unspoken forces of organization violations.* Thousand Oaks, CA: Sage.

Herdt, G. (Ed.). (1994). *Third sex third gender: Beyond sexual dimorphism in culture and history*. New York: Zone Books.

Hobson, J. (2005). *Venus in the dark: Blackness and beauty in popular culture*. New York: Routledge.

Hochschild, A. R. (1983). *The managed heart: Commercialization of human feeling*. Berkeley: University of California Press.

Hochschild, A. R. (with Machung, A.) (1989). *The second shift*. New York: Viking.

Hochschild, A. R. (1997). *The time bind: When work becomes home and home becomes work*. New York: Metropolitan Books.

Ingraham, C. (2006). Thinking straight, acting bent: Heteronormativity and homosexuality. In K. Davis, M. Evans, & J. Lorber (Eds.), *Handbook of gender and women's studies* (pp. 307–321). London: Sage.

Jackson, R. M. (1998). *Destined for equality: The inevitable rise of women's status*. Cambridge, MA: Harvard University Press.

Jacobs, J. A. (1989). *Revolving doors: Sex segregation and women's careers*. Stanford, CA: Stanford University Press.

Kanter, R. M. (1977). *Men and women of the corporation*. New York: Basic Books.

Keller, E. F. (1985). *Reflections on gender and science*. New Haven, CT: Yale University Press.

Kessler, S. J., & McKenna, W. (1985). *Gender: An ethnomethodological approach*. Chicago: University of Chicago Press. (Original work published 1978)

Kimmel, M. S. (2000). Saving the males: The sociological implications of the Virginia Military Institute and the Citadel. *Gender & Society, 14*, 494–516.

Kimmel, M. S. (2003). Globalization and its mal(e)contents: The gendered moral and political economy of terrorism. *International Sociology, 18*, 603–620.

Kimmel, M. S., & Messner, M. A. (Eds.). (2007). *Men's lives* (7th ed.). Boston: Allyn & Bacon.

Lamb, S., & Brown, L. M. (2006). *Packaging girlhood: Rescuing our daughters from marketers' schemes*. New York: St. Martin's Press.

Lorber, J. (1984). *Women physicians: Careers, status, and power*. London: Tavistock.

Lorber, J. (1994). *Paradoxes of gender*. New Haven, CT: Yale University Press.

Lorber, J. (2005). *Breaking the bowls: Degendering and feminist change*. New York: Norton.

Lorber, J., & Moore, L. J. (2002). *Gender and the social construction of illness* (2nd ed.). Lanham, MD: Rowman & Littlefield.

Lorber, J. & Moore, L. J. (2007). *Gendered bodies: Feminist perspectives*. New York: Oxford University Press.

MacKinnon, C. A. (1989). *Toward a feminist theory of the state*. Cambridge, MA: Harvard University Press.

Martin, P. Y. (2001), "Mobilizing masculinities": Women's experiences of men at work. *Organization, 8*, 587–618.

Martin, P. Y. (2003). "Said and done" versus "saying and doing": Gendering practices, practicing gender at work. *Gender & Society, 17*, 342–366.

Martin, P. Y. (2004). Gender as social institution. *Social Forces, 82*, 1249–1275.

McCall, L. (2001). *Complex inequality: Gender, class, and race in the new economy*. New York: Routledge.

Messner, M. A. (1992). *Power at play: Sports and the problem of masculinity*. Boston: Beacon Press.

Messner, M. A. (2002). *Taking the field: Women, men and sports*. Minneapolis: University of Minnesota Press.

Moghadam, V. M. (1999). Revolution, religion, and gender politics: Iran and Afghanistan compared. *Journal of Women's History, 10*, 172–195.

Nentwich, J. (2004). *Die Gleichzeitigkeit von Differenz und Gleichheit: Neue Wege für die Gleichstellungsarbeit* [The simultaneousness of difference and sameness: New ways for equal opportunities]. Königstein/Taunus, Germany: Ulrike Helmer Verlag.

Poster, W. R. (2001). Dangerous places and nimble fingers: Discourses of gender discrimination and rights in global corporations. *International Journal of Politics, Culture and Society, 15*, 77–105.

Potuchek, J. L. (1997). *Who supports the family?: Gender and breadwinning in dual-earner marriages*. Stanford, CA: Stanford University Press.

Reskin, B. F., & Roos, P. A. (1990). *Job queues, gender queues: Explaining women's inroads into male occupations*. Philadelphia: Temple University Press.

Ridgeway, C. (1997). Interaction and the conservation of gender inequality: Considering employment. *American Sociological Review, 62*, 218–235.

Ridgeway, C. L., & Correll, S. J. (2004). Unpacking the gender system: A theoretical perspective on gender beliefs and social relations. *Gender and Society, 18*, 510–531.

Rogers, M. F. (1992). They were all passing: Agnes, Garfinkel, and company. *Gender and Society, 6*, 169–191.

Rupp, L. J., & Taylor, V. (2003). *Drag queens at the 801 Cabaret*. Chicago: University of Chicago Press.

Schacht, S. (with Underwood, L.). (Eds.). (2004). *The drag queen anthology*. New York: Harrington Park Press.

Smith, D. (1990a). *The conceptual practices of power: A feminist sociology of knowledge*. Toronto, Ontario, Canada: University of Toronto Press.

Smith, D. (1990b). *Texts, facts, and femininity: Exploring the relations of ruling*. New York: Routledge.

Tannen, D. (Ed.). (1993). *Gender and conversational interaction*. New York: Oxford University Press.

Taylor, V., & Whittier, N. (Eds.). (1998). Gender and social movements: Part 1. *Gender & Society, 12*, 621–769.

Taylor, V., & Whittier, N. (Eds.). (1999). Gender and social movements: Part 2. *Gender & Society, 13*, 5–151.

Thorne, B. (1993). *Gender play: Girls and boys at school*. New Brunswick, NJ: Rutgers University Press.

Thorne, B., & Henley, N. (Eds.). (1975). *Language and sex: Difference and dominance.* Rowley, MA: Newbury.

Troka, D., Lebesco, K., & Noble, J. (Eds.). (2002). *The drag king anthology.* New York: Harrington Park Press.

Wacquant, L. (2004). *Body and soul: Notebooks of an apprentice boxer.* New York: Oxford University Press.

Warner, M. (Ed.). (1993). *Fear of a queer planet: Queer politics and social theory.* Minneapolis: University of Minnesota Press.

Webster, M., Jr., & Foschi, M. (Eds.). (1988). *Status generalization: New theory and research.* Stanford, CA: Stanford University Press.

West, C., & Zimmerman, D. (1987). Doing gender. *Gender & Society, 1,* 125–151.

Yeats, W. B. (1951). Among school children. In *The collected poems of W. B. Yeats* (p. 214). New York: Macmillan.

Yuval-Davis, N. (1997). *Gender and nation.* London: Sage.

CHAPTER 28

The Construction of Sex and Sexualities

Sara L. Crawley
K. L. Broad

The physical sexual activity of two men when one of them is defined as berdache among the Western Plains Indians is identical with the sexual activity of two men in ancient Greece or in a modern Western society; but the meanings attached to the behavior and its functions for the society are so disparate in these cases that seeing them as aspects of the same phenomena except in the most superficial way is to vitiate all we know about social analysis.

—GAGNON AND SIMON (1973/2005, pp. 4–5)

Sexuality is not a somatic fact; it is a cultural effect. Sexuality, then, does have a history—though not a very long one.

—HALPERIN (1993, p. 416)

Thinking of sex as social pushes us to consider what sorts of rules should organize sexuality; it compels us to furnish arguments defending these rules instead of simply invoking nature or religion.

—SEIDMAN (2003, pp. 137–138)

Every study of a "deviant" group is by corollary a study of the dominant group. Such is the case with the development of the study of lesbian/gay/bisexual/transgendered (LGBT) ontologies, people, communities, and social and political movements. As with many studies of "the other," research that began presumably to study causes of lesbian and gay people as "deviants" has shifted to the broader theorization of the concept "deviance" (Irvine, 2003), which asks a much more sociological question: How does heteronormativity happen? Social constructionism, in its many forms—symbolic interactionism, feminist theory, and queer theory—and across many disciplines has made this critique of the notion of sexual ontologies and practices possible.

This chapter tracks many of the inputs into the literature on the social construction of LGBT sexualities[1] over the past four decades, attempting to connect some previously disconnected literatures and to propose future directions for interdisciplinary study.

One goal in this chapter is to connect area studies that are often discussed and debated academically as separate worlds. Whereas sociology is written as social science and women's studies and queer studies often favor the humanities, this false dualism in the academy has impeded students in finding and reading works that might inform each other (Plummer, 2003, 2005a). Both of us have been trained as sociologists and women's studies scholars and have felt this divide. As we see it, symbolic interactionism lends attention to the local and particular (Gubrium & Holstein, 1997; Plummer, 2003); many forms of feminist thought (including at a minimum black feminist thought, Chicana feminism, feminist standpoint theory, and postcolonial feminist theories) call for articulating the variety and diversity of women's (and men's) lives; and (poststructuralist) queer theorists abhor grand theory and the normalization that comes from institutional categories. Hence there are many commonalities to these approaches (Plummer, 2005a). We hope to trace the connection between early constructionist sociological sexuality studies, second-wave feminist arguments, and later queer theory, recognizing the place of all three traditions and the potential of each to inform the others.

Like many other area studies, sexualities studies have branched out into a rich literature that works to document the varieties of sites or areas in which sexualities, identities, practices, politics, relationships, and communities play out. Thus a second goal of this chapter is to map the areas of analysis in which sexualities have been studied by constructionists—in particular, we discuss self, subjectivity and identity; community studies; and the development and politics of

social movements. In this section of the chapter, we hope to encourage students to think about sexualities in the particular, not in some grand scheme. "Sexualities" is a general subject matter rather than a specific study, and even sexualities theorists vary in their approaches and theoretical questions. Here we show some of the diversity of theoretical questions pursued by sexualities theorists and demonstrate the various levels of their focus.

A final goal is to consider future directions in theorizing sexualities. With the broad impact of queer theory and strong reception of constructionist approaches to sexualities in the past 30 years, where do we go from here? Students often feel as though all the good theory has already been written. We assume this feeling has been common in every academic era, and the goal is to look toward what has as yet received insufficient attention. To conclude this chapter, we attempt to map out some such directions, reminding readers of what others have suggested and offering, we hope, a few new ideas.

The Development of Constructionist Sexualities Studies

According to the current canon in the humanities, it would seem that all poststructuralist sexualities studies began with Michel Foucault and that no one wrote about the performative aspects of gender (for which students of sexualities find much overlap in theories and issues) before Judith Butler. Both these assumptions are wrong (Epstein, 1996; Rubin & Butler, 1994; Simon & Gagnon, 2003; Weeks, 1998). A full decade before Foucault's *History of Sexuality, Part I* (1978) came to the United States in English translation, several constructionist scholars (Gagnon & Simon, 1973/2005; Humphreys, 1970; Katz, 1976; McIntosh, 1968; Newton, 1972; Weeks, 1977, 2003) in sociology, anthropology, and history were offering theories on the impact of meaning systems in our sexual worlds and documenting the lives of LGBT people (Seidman, 2003). Likewise with gender studies, Harold Garfinkel (1967), Erving Goffman (1976, 1977), Suzanne J. Kessler and Wendy McKenna (1978), Spencer E. Cahill (1986, 1989), and Candace West and Don H. Zimmerman (1987) were all offering performative approaches to gendered bodies before Butler's canonized *Gender Trouble* (1990). Offering just this critique, Jeffrey Weeks (1998) writes:

> It is frustrating for those of us who have been toiling in this particular vineyard since the turn of the 1960s and 1970s to have our early efforts in understanding sexuality in general, and homosexuality in particular, refracted back to us through post-Foucauldian abstractions (and I say that as someone who has been deeply influenced by Foucault's work), and then taken up as if the ideas are freshly minted. (p. 132)

Our goal here is not to detract from Foucault's or Butler's important works. Clearly each has had profound impacts on their fields. In the most practical sense, our approach is to recover a longer history of sexualities studies for our students. We begin by outlining the basics of what might be called the queer theory canon and then detail some earlier movements that we believe contributed to this academic movement, perhaps with less recognition than is deserved.

A Queer Canon

The queer canon has tended to be attributed to a relatively small group of authors who became popularized around the early 1990s,[2] in particular Michel Foucault, Judith Butler, Eve Kosofsky Sedgwick, and perhaps David Halperin. Oddly, none of these authors articulates a specific definition or concept of queer theory (although given the aversion to fixity and boundaries espoused by queer theorists, perhaps this is not surprising), and each of these authors takes up distinct argu-

ments that are not clearly related. Here we want to describe four general characteristics of what often is called queer theory and offer contributions from a few more authors than often receive attribution for the genesis of this theory. First, power is not physical power over another by which to exert one's will (as in armies that repress an underclass) but rather *power is the deployment of discourse* (ideas), which creates the possibility of *subjectivities*. Power to control populations lies in ruling ideologies (discourses) that create the notion of real social positions (subjectivities—i.e., man, women, lesbian, mother), which each of us takes up by virtue of succumbing to the ruling ideology of any historical period (Foucault, 1978, 1980). In *History of Sexuality, Part I* (1978) and *Power/ Knowledge* (1980), Foucault outlines his notion that power is not deployed as simply repressive *power over* another (as in the Marxist, up–down, hierarchical model) but is a swirling hurricane of discourses that are powerfully persuasive in populations. Hence, rulers do not rule by threat of physical violence but by deployment of convincing ideas that sway the popular masses.[3] (Hetero)sexuality is simply one of those ruling discourses (Foucault, 1978). In *History of Sexuality, Part I*, Foucault argues against both Freudian ideas of repressed natural urges and Marxist notions of a ruling class. By asserting that sexuality is not repressed but productive of many, many new identities, including "gay" and "lesbian," Foucault disconnects the previously determinist tradition of the neo-Freudians and asserts a distinctly historically constructionist model. In *Discipline and Punish* (1977), Foucault outlines that this deployment of discourse is exacted through social surveillance. It is not some police force that compels us each to act in certain ways but actually the surveillance of each other in everyday life that encourages each of us to behave according to the ruling discourses. Importantly, after we have been exposed to such constant and ever-present surveillance, each of us begins to impose normative surveillance on ourselves. We become our own jailers, in the sense that we begin to simply "feel funny" if we know we are breaking a social edict (such as the taboo against erotically kissing a member of the same sex).[4]

Second and related to the first issue we introduced above, is that *sexuality is always practiced in a specific cultural context* (i.e., it is not innate) *and should be interpreted through historical and cultural context* (Foucault, 1978; Halperin, 1993; Laqueur, 1990; Monro & Warren, 2004; Patton, 1993; Rubin, 1993; Rust, 1995; Schwartz & Rutter, 1998; Scott, 1993; Stone, 1991; Weeks, 1977). This leads to the anthropological-style argument (similar to arguments made by Black feminist thought and postcolonial feminisms) that all sexual societies should be studied in their own context, not through the lens of recent Western heteronormative ideals. David Halperin's (1993) article, "Is There a History of Sexuality?" persuasively argues that in classical Athens there was no notion of sexual orientation; rather, sexuality was organized around citizenship (which was only available to adult, male land owners) and the power to exert one's will sexually on noncitizens (male or female). Citizenship, not "natural" urges or biological sex, defined who might have sex with whom and how. Furthermore, Joan Scott (1993) calls for all experience to be historicized in the sense that it cannot simply be experienced outside of longer historical analysis of ruling discourses. As such, common sense or personal experience cannot be understood, transhistorically, as evidence of some truth.

Third, in our historical moment, *sexuality and all of current social life is defined by the heterosexual/homosexual binary*, which is a control mechanism enacted on all people to encourage participation in the heteronormative power structure (Best, 2000; Ingraham, 1999; Sedgwick, 1990). Sedgwick (1990) argues that, since at least the late 1800s, it is the threat of a spoiled homosexual identity (the so-called "closet") that keeps most heterosexual-identified people overtly rejecting even the most minor hint of affilia-

tion for the same sex. Hence, she sees the hetero/homo binary as a ruling force in the lives of everyone in Western culture. Much of queer theory calls for questioning binary ontological categories common to Western ways of thinking and for understanding the world—nature, social categories, meaning systems—as composed of falsely bounded categories that give the impression of fixity and permanence where none "naturally" exists.

Fourth, the consistency of *gender performativity causes the belief in discrete biological sex categories*, not vice versa (Butler, 1990, 1993, 1996; West & Zimmerman, 1987). That is, the traditional idea that biological sex causes gendered behavior is backward. Rather, consistent dualistic gendered performances of the body give the illusion that masculinity and femininity and discrete categories of biological sex are real. Importantly, according to Butler, gender feels "natural" because it is well practiced via performativity. As such, the belief in a binary biological sex is the *effect* of performativity, not its precursor.[5] Thomas Laqueur (1990) shores up this argument by suggesting that at various points in history bodies have been understood variously—in some eras as the same but inverted; in others, as two different creatures. Indeed, he writes, "Sometime in the eighteenth century, sex as we know it was invented" (p. 149).

Following Foucault's notion of power, Butler (1993, 1996) goes on to note that gender performance can also be a source of powerful resistance if deployed in unconventional ways. To resist the confines of heteronormativity, one "does" gender in recognizable ways that are simply outside the binary prescriptions of male = masculinity/female = femininity. Hence, butch lesbians doing masculinity (Crawley, 2002c; Halberstam, 1998) and butch/femme couples holding hands in public (Case, 1989) are examples of subverting heteronormativity.

The popularity of Butler's work emphasizes a significant overlap of queer theory and sexualities theories with feminist gender theories. So for the sake of completeness, we briefly discuss them here, although these theories receive a more thorough treatment in Lorber, Chapter 27, this volume. We want to outline at least two major trends in gender theory that overlap with sexualities literatures—feminist critiques of the gendered body in medical literatures and a longer tradition of feminist gender theories preceding Butler but with similar impacts for sexualities theories.

Trained as a biologist, Anne Fausto-Sterling (1986, 1995, 2000) questions biologists' common causal assumption that biology precedes social impacts on bodies in every instance. Drawing on the example of Chinese foot binding, Fausto-Sterling notes that physiological difference can be trained into the organic body. In "Sexing the Body" (2000), she offers theories that recognize an interplay of nature and the social in a much more thoroughgoing manner than we have found elsewhere. Other authors have offered content analyses of historical and current biology texts, critiquing them on sexist and racist constructions of the body (Myerson et al., 2007; Schiebinger, 1993), and content analyses of medical texts, critiquing how the medical establishment describes intersexed infants as needing to be surgically altered to fit normative genital appearances (Kessler, 1998).

Although feminist gender theorists have tended to take up Butler as their hero *de rigueur*, a similar sociological tradition began to theorize the production of gender prior to Butler primarily via ethnomethodology. In 1978, Suzanne J. Kessler and Wendy McKenna published *Gender: An Ethnomethodological Approach*, which argues that gender is a social accomplishment that is both produced by the individual and agreed on by the participation of others in social interaction. They followed the lead of Garfinkel's 1967 study of Agnes, a male-to-female transsexual whose accomplishment of femininity obviously did not originate from some innate place in her male body. In the late 1980s

several authors were working on performance theories of gender (Cahill, 1986, 1989; West & Zimmerman, 1987). Spencer E. Cahill published a pair of articles outlining gender acquisition through appearance management, socialization recruitment processes, and language practices. In 1987, Candace West and Don H. Zimmerman published " 'Doing' Gender," which not only reiterates the ethnomethodological challenge to the "natural attitude" of gender as biological but also beats Butler to the punchline by arguing the falsity of fixed biological sex with their concept of "sex category," the social accomplishment of a belief in and performance of finite dualistic body types.

We offer these citations by way of pointing out that queer theory, sexualities theories, and gender theory have a long and broad tradition that often suffers from politics between disciplines. Like "queer theory," a tradition for which the name would suggest a unitary and succinct group of ideas, feminist gender and sexualities theories are more accurately described as long and complex theoretical traditions.

The Story of Sexualities Studies: Early Constructionist Works

Long before Foucault's work emerged in English translation in the 1980s and before Butler's work was widely read in the 1990s, similar ideas resonated in early studies of sexualities. Gayle Rubin (2002) documents the impact of the so-called Chicago School of sociologists, with their urban ethnographic focus, as a precursor to the current social science of sexualities. During the first half of the 20th century, Rubin argues, the flourishing of pragmatist and symbolic interactionist approaches at the University of Chicago laid the groundwork for considering sexual communities as worthy of ethnographic study. Indeed, Rubin recognizes Thomas's 1907 publication of *Sex and Society: Studies in the Social Psychology of Sex* as the beginning of conceptualizations of sex as a potential field of social study. Hence the ideas emanating from the Chicago School, unlike the reigning essentialist ideas of psychologists (Sigmund Freud) and sexologists (Havelock Ellis, Richard Von Krafft-Ebbing) of the time, provided a path for the original era of constructionist theorists.

The constructionist scholars of mid-century laid the direct groundwork for the first recognized constructionist sexualities studies. Garfinkel's (1967) famed ethnomethodological study of Agnes, a male-to-female transsexual, and Goffman's (1959, 1963a, 1963b) attentiveness to the performance and negotiation of self in everyday interaction are important precursors to the study of sexual identity. Additionally, the advent of the sociological study of deviance and ensuing constructionist study of social problems, influenced greatly by students of Howard Becker (1963), opened the door to studying sex and sexuality as a construction.

Today we often explain the emergence of constructionist understandings of sex and sexuality as an origin story of sexualities studies, and that story is often told by pointing to foundational works (Kitzinger, 1995; Nardi & Schneider, 1998; Plummer, 2003; Seidman, 2003). According to these accounts, the defining original works of constructionist social theory of sexualities emerged in the late 1960s and 1970s and included: Mary McIntosh's (1968) short but powerfully innovative article, "The Homosexual Role," John H. Gagnon and William Simon's (1973/2005) broad constructionist approach to sexual interaction in *Sexual Conduct*, and Kenneth Plummer's (1975) study of homosexuality, *Sexual Stigma*.[6]

Almost forgotten in most arenas of social theory, McIntosh's (1968) article should be understood as a turning point in the conceptualization of sexuality (Weeks, 1998). Although others have marked McIntosh's work as important (Greenberg, 1988; Nardi & Schneider, 1998), Weeks (1998) argues most forcefully that McIntosh, not Foucault, should be recognized as the "locus classicus of approaches that attribute the emergence of the homosexual category in the 19th cen-

tury to medicalization" (p. 139). Weeks argues that McIntosh's primary goal was to argue against sexologists, psychologists, and even prevailing political thought of the gay assimilationist "homophile" political movements of that time that took as a basic assumption the notion that homosexuality was a fixed and inflexible set of characteristics of the mind or body. As such, McIntosh's work, very much like Foucault's and yet preceding his, interprets sexuality as historical, sociological, and, importantly, political.

Gagnon and Simon's (1973/2005) work on sexual scripts is also often today understood as foundational to constructionist theories of sexualities (Plummer, 2005b; Seidman, 2003). Overtly responding to the likes of Alfred C. Kinsey and coauthors (Kinsey, Pomeroy, & Martin, 1948; Kinsey, Pomeroy, Martin, & Gebhard, 1953), Freud, and William H. Masters and Virginia E. Johnson (1966), which lend themselves to biological determinist approaches, Gagnon and Simon's (1973) *Sexual Conduct* offered the important argument that sex is scripted. As Steven Seidman (2003, p. 26) explains, by applying the idea of a social script to sexuality, Gagnon and Simon presented an understanding of sexuality not as body mechanics but as socially learned behaviors, complete with social meanings—notions of appropriateness and taboo.

Around the same time, Ken Plummer (1975) was working on similar ideas, albeit with an emphasis on case studies of homosexuality. Like Gagnon and Simon, Plummer advanced a distinctly social perspective of sexuality that challenged biological and pathological psychological explanations of homosexuality (Plummer, 2003; Seidman, 2003). By combining his symbolic interactionist perspective, interpretations of early constructionist works, and case studies of gay life, Plummer produced what we can now understand as an early constructionist statement on homosexuality. By his own account, Plummer (2003, p. 518), in *Sexual Stigma*, outlined some central constructionist ideas:

There was a critique of essentialism and the language of perversion; the importance of emergent and contested sexual meanings; a sense of the "constructed" nature of human sexualities; an awareness of the significance of variation and diversity in sexual life; and a growing sensitivity to the role of metaphor in thinking about the erotic.

Because all these works challenged prevailing biological and pathological psychological views of heteronormativity as natural and same-sex desire as unnatural, the debate between essentialism and constructionism came to define the field of sexualities studies, especially in the 1980s and 1990s (Nardi & Schneider, 1998, p. 4). Arguing for some inherent, human component to sexuality (which commonly assumed a heteronormative link to reproduction), essentialists relied on a sense of sex and sexuality as natural. Social constructionists, such as McIntosh, Gagnon and Simon, and Plummer, offered a strong and diametric opposition in which sexuality is inherent not in the body but in the social rules of the culture or structure of a society. Peter M. Nardi and Beth E. Schneider (1998) portray the constructionism versus essentialism debate by featuring McIntosh's (1968) piece as a classic constructionist statement and Frederick Whitam's (1998) response in essentialist terms. Whitam's response argues against conceiving of homosexuality as a "role," suggesting instead that it is an "orientation," a perspective he supports with examples of young men who participate in homosexual behaviors with little or no exposure to a gay subculture. The crux of Whitam's argument against McIntosh is the notion that a core orientation leads to behavior before any subculture or role is established. These two works illustrate the way in which sexualities scholars (even within sociology) initially constructed polar understandings of sexualities.

Later, the works of Stephen Epstein and Carol Vance detail how the essentialism-versus-constructionism debate continued in more nuanced ways (Nardi & Schneider,

1998). Epstein (1987/1998) illustrates how academic circles tend to favor constructionist perspectives while the gay movement in the United States has simultaneously been portraying itself in more essentialist terms (p. 135). Ultimately, he proposes a way to approach an understanding of ethnic identity from a modified constructionist position because, as he argues, "Neither strict constructionism nor strict essentialism are capable of explaining what it means to be gay" (1987/1998, p. 151). Vance (1998) points to many misunderstandings of constructionist perspectives by discussing how some assume that if an assertion is made that sexualities are constructed, this implies that gay and/or lesbian identities are not real or significant. She clarifies that sexual identity is quite real for those living through it. Rather than becoming burdened by misreads of constructionism, Vance advocates better understanding of the differences between and among constructionists, in terms of discipline (e.g., sociology vs. anthropology) and more complex arguments about what might be constructed (sexual acts, sexual desires, or sexual identities).

At heart, both Epstein (1987/1998) and Vance (1998) challenge readers to think beyond a simplified binary of essentialism versus constructionism, and their work forecasts the ways constructionist sexualities studies have developed in the past decade. Celia Kitzinger (1995, p. 136) suggests that the debate continued into the 1990s without fully resolving. She writes:

> It is a debate which no longer attracts the same passion it did then—not because one theory has gained precedence, but rather because the adversaries apparently became weary of the argument, and the debate itself came to be seen as impeding developments within each paradigm.

Finally, one last body of work important to the story of the emergence of constructionist sexualities studies is lesbian, gay, bisexual, and/or transgender ethnography and history. Using empirical studies of existing communities to subvert essentialist arguments, certain ethnographies significantly foreshadowed the coming of queer theory (Green, 2002). Two of these ethnographies are repeatedly mentioned by those telling the story of sexualities studies: Laud Humphrey's (1970) *Tearoom Trade* and Esther Newton's (1972) *MotherCamp: Female Impersonators in America*. Humphreys's (1970) research observed (often heterosexually identified and married) men who sought and had impersonal sex with other men in public restrooms. Although his work is often critiqued in mainstream sociology for the ethical boundaries it may have crossed, its constructionist contributions tend to be glossed over (Irvine, 2003b; Nardi, 1995). Humphreys's study emerged from a growing tradition of interpretivist work that complicated a simple definition of homosexual orientation and highlighted how categories of sexuality and stigma are socially maintained and defined, including how context or "geography" (urban or suburban settings) have an impact on social practices. Similarly, Newton's ethnography of gay men and drag demonstrated how sexual and gender identities are constructed and maintained. Notably, Newton's work detailed the stages a gay man goes through to become a female impersonator, offering new understandings of gender in the gay world and helping to denaturalize gender, as well as sex (Irvine, 2003b, p. 448).

Similarly, historical research is also often featured as illustrating the potential of constructionist sexualities theories (Seidman, 2003), including the following key pieces: Weeks (1977), Jonathan Ned Katz (1976), Carroll Smith-Rosenberg (1975), and Lillian Faderman (1981). As Seidman (2003) explains, Weeks and Katz both demonstrate the multiple and changing meanings attached to male homosexuality in England and the United States, respectively, over approximately 200 years. Smith-Rosenberg and Faderman both demonstrate similar understandings about how sexuality is historically situated, albeit with a focus on the experience of women, by documenting the existence of romantic friendships (intimate public relationships regarded as marriage-like) between women in 19th-century America.

Here we have provided but a brief portrait of how the story of the development of sexualities studies is often told. Certainly this is not a comprehensive portrait. By foregrounding key foundational works, the significance of the essentialism-versus-constructionism debate, and exemplary ethnographies and histories, these stories highlight how constructionist ideas, within the auspices of sexualities studies, emerge from interdisciplinarity, qualitative research and revolve around symbolic interactionist understandings of constructionism (Irvine, 2003b; Kitzinger, 1995; Nardi & Schneider, 1998; Plummer, 2003; Seidman, 2003).

Radical Feminist Constructions of Sexualities

Developing over a similar historical period as the sociological constructionist sexualities literature, radical, or sometimes called separatist, feminism originated from many disciplines and foreshadowed the coming of queer theory by questioning the naturalness of heterosexual relationship roles and their implicit division of labor and sexual power imbalances. Although the queer theory works of Eve Kosofsky Sedgwick (a scholar of English) and Judith Butler (a scholar of rhetoric and comparative literature) are commonly used by feminists today, we feel certain traditions within feminism, especially radical or separatist feminism, contributed to the advent of these important works, and we wish to reclaim that relationship here.

Often called *lesbian feminism*, even by its proponents, we prefer the term *radical* or *separatist feminism* because these terms recognize the staunchly constructionist notion of "lesbianism" that the theory intended. For radical feminism, lesbianism was less a sexual identity than a political position that refused to engage with patriarchy and, in particular, patriarchal men (Kitzinger, 1987). Developing from the second-wave feminist slogan, "the personal is political," radical feminism focused on critiquing the inequality of heteronormative power differences constructed into intimate relationships between women and men. Critiquing the notion that women and men had "natural" roles in the world based on an expectation of sexual difference, radical feminism focused primarily on power relations resulting from the organization of sexuality whereby, for each couple, the man is intended to be at least 2 inches taller, 2 years older, stronger (in particular, able to lift her, as in carrying a bride over the threshold), and richer than the woman. Radical feminists see this design as a signifier of the patriarchy in which men are intended to dominate women, sexually, financially, physically, and emotionally, first in intimate relationships and ultimately in all parts of social life. Perhaps foreshadowing queer theory, radical feminists recognize the arrangement as social, not natural, and fully able to change with a shift in consciousness.

The most radical extreme of radical feminist paradigms calls for the separatist or "lesbian" feminist to *separate* from men—emotionally, financially, and sexually (Frye, 1983; Jeffreys, 1996; Radicalesbians, 1970/2005). Disconnected from any sense of "natural" physical urge, "lesbian" feminism especially called for women to cease "sleeping with the enemy" and encouraged women to find intimacy and sexual fulfillment with women, as well as establishing households and raising children outside the influence of dominance that men expected in heteronormative relationships.

Now part of the canon of feminist theory, poet Adrienne Rich's (1986) "Compulsory Heterosexuality and the Lesbian Existence" redefines *lesbian* as a woman who foregrounds the role of women in her life. Interestingly, Rich's famous article is often used

as a means to suggest that women can identify with other women and foreground relationships with women in their lives without implying a need to have sex with women. Perhaps this move foreshadows queer theory's next step—to declare the falsity of all identities and the historical construction of all sexualities.

Having contributed at least three oft-cited articles, philosopher Marilyn Frye is also a major figure regularly included in the canon of feminist theory. Her piece, "On Separatism and Power" (1983), is often cited as an original call for separatism from patriarchy. Additionally, two further articles by Frye, "Sexuality" (1983) and "Lesbian 'Sex'" (1992) continue to be relevant not just historically but also in our current era, in our opinion. In "Sexuality," Frye foreshadows the work of queer theory's gender performativity authors such as Butler (1990, 1993) and West and Zimmerman (1987) by pointing out the use of clothing styles and bodily actions to emphasize the notion of biological sex as dualistic.[7] Critiquing all "natural" categories of gender and ultimately biological sex, Frye calls all gender "drag," especially the gender performances of heteronormative people. Indeed, she is clear to point out that at least drag queens doing drag are aware of their performance, unlike heteronormative people in everyday life who seem to be fooled by the notion that gender is real.

Even more innovative (and queer?), in our opinion, is Frye's article "Lesbian 'Sex'" (1992) in which Frye asserts that lesbians do not have sex because the word *sex* is so thoroughly infused with the connotation of male orgasms that it cannot apply to what two women do with each other sexually. Her point is that the notion of what two women do when having "sex" simply is not comparable to what is heteronormatively defined as sex in dominant culture (i.e., man-on-top, male-active–female-recipient, missionary style sex in which one "act" can be counted by his orgasm). Importantly, her point illustrates that asking the question, "what do two women do when they have sex?" demonstrates that, as a culture, we do not know what one woman does when she has sex. That is, the definition of sex is so thoroughly androcentric that there is no strongly developed cultural understanding of how any woman experiences sexuality except through men, an argument we believe continues to be relevant to constructionist sexualities theorists and queer theorists.

Still other feminists of the so-called second-wave era use constructionist notions of sexuality to call for social activism. In "Uses of the Erotic," poet Audre Lorde (1984) calls on women to reclaim erotic enjoyment in their lives. Her intent is to broaden the concept of the erotic to include all forms of expressions of humanity and the spirit to enjoy passionately all parts of life, even those unrelated to the sexual. Activist and essayist Barbara Smith (1990/1993) comments on how sexual orientation is still a socially acceptable target for discrimination and calls for feminists to recognize sexual orientation as an important form of inequality that should be of concern for feminists. In perhaps one of the most radical stances taken by a radical feminist, activist Shulamith Firestone (1970) argues that gender inequality cannot end until reproductive differences are made unnecessary by technology with which women's bodies will be no longer needed to gestate babies.[8]

Importantly, feminists of that era tended to theorize inequality on the basis of sexuality (i.e., discrimination against lesbians) but did not theorize sexuality itself (i.e., How does sexual orientation happen?). In "Thinking Sex," anthropologist Gayle Rubin (1984) recognizes that feminism has not questioned sexual hierarchies beyond those driven by gender inequality. Feminists at that point had yet to critique heteronormative rules of morality or pathologized sexual identities. As such, this article by Rubin stands at the historical intersection between radical feminist critiques of androcentric sexualities and the coming of queer theory.

Areas of Sexualities Studies

The second goal of this chapter relates to mapping the areas of study of sexualities. Apart from historical development, sexualities studies can be divided by the focus of the scholar, for scholars are often focused on the construction of sexualities in various areas of social life. We outline three common areas of analysis: self and identity, community ethnographies, and social movements.

Self, Subjectivity, and Identity

A popular and highly contested area of study among sexualities scholars includes theories of the self or identity. Many works orient around postmodern questions of the origin or authenticity of identity—that is, does the individual determine their identity, or is it given to the individual by the discourses available in a historical period? Queer postmodern notions of subjectivity originated as critiques of the modern self (Plummer, 2005a). The modern self is envisioned as the independent, free-thinking actor that Enlightenment philosophies ordained as part of the Enlightenment era that spawned such notions as inalienable civil rights and that encouraged the French and American revolutionary wars. Postmodernists such as Foucault, Jean Baudrillard, and Jacques Derrida wrote against the individual authenticity of each individual's personhood, arguing that the ruling discourses of each historical era created subjectivities rather than authentic selves. Subjectivities are basically simulated and repetitive social positions that individuals fill by conforming to the institutional contexts of their cultures and lives. As such, the actor is not an authentic individual agent, as modernists argue; rather, individuals simply fill the identities compelled by the social discourses. As such, postmodernists tend to argue for subjectivites, whereas modernists tend to refer to the development of selves.

As a result, identity is a contested notion, sometimes argued as the property of individuals, other times argued as the property of institutions and coercive social groups.

A related issue is the degree to which an individual has agency—the ability to change or amend the person they choose to be. If individuals do not author their own identities, can any individual make decisions on their own behalf—that is, have agency? If the identity of a person—for example, gay man—is a product of the institutional context that needs gay men to demonstrate stigmatized subjectivities, can any "gay man" speak or behave in ways that are authentic and exert his will on his own behalf?

In terms of sexualities, this debate is closely tied to the debate over identity politics versus queer politics. Supporters of identity politics tend to argue that sexual orientation is real and to be determined by the individual. For example, a lesbian is a person who says she is one because only she can interpret her urges. Supporters of queer politics argue that there are no "real" identities because the notion of "real" sexual orientations is purported to be constructed within powerful institutions that support the dominant heteronormative discourse and discourage all other forms of sexual expression (Foucault, 1978; Katz, 1995; Messner, 2000; Sedgwick, 1990; Tiefer, 2004). Those in favor of identity politics will argue that coming-out narratives are powerful stories asserting the will of the individual to subvert oppression, whereas queer theorists will argue there is no need to "come out" because doing so only supports the notion that identities are in some way fixed and authentic (Seidman, 2001).

Several authors have engaged the debate about the origin and authenticity of the subjectivities or selves (Almaguer, 1993; Brown, 1997; Chase, 2001; Trumbach, 1994). Indeed, the transgender and intersexed movements have in a sense renewed the age-old debate between essentialism and constructionism in which many authors have engaged discussions of the origin of the

individual (Bornstein, 1994; Dozier, 2005; Feinberg, 1996; Green, 2004; Nestle, Howell, & Wilchins, 2002; Prosser, 1995; Rubin, 2003; Schleifer, 2006; Schrock, Reid, & Boyd, 2005; Valerio, 2006). Many authors have debated the meanings and significations of subjectivities (Case, 1989; De Lauretis, 1989; Faderman, 1992; Halberstam, 1994). Still other authors have studied the self stories and self performances of LGBT people and their families, including stories of "coming out" (Broad, 2002b; Crawley & Broad, 2004; Plummer, 1995; Weston, 1991, 1993; Whisman, 1996), stories of gendered sexual identity (Crawley, 2002a; Halberstam, 1998), and changing identities related to age and aging (Crawley, 2002a; Rosenfeld, 2003).

Some newer approaches to self, subjectivity, and identity attempt to merge the possibilities of agentic selves with institutionalized subjectivities (Cahill, 1998; Holstein & Gubrium, 2000). In a direction that we find fruitful, these authors avoid the dualistic debate of either–or approaches and attempt to tease out how identities can be both deeply entrenched in institutional discourses and practices while still allowing for some individual decision making.

Community Ethnographies

The most common and perhaps theoretically uncontroversial form of LGBT research comes in the form of community ethnographies. Following the paradigmatic anthropological style, most ethnographies do not purport to be generalizable to other times or places but only record the existence of geographic communities at a particular point in time. Often these are ethnographies of historical communities. Commonly, the standard anthropological ethnography would offer a window into the world that most people from the dominant culture do not access. That is, ethnographies have tended to be studies of deviance communities. Ethnographies of LGBT communities have changed that paradigm somewhat, because they tend to be written by gay- and lesbian-identified scholars whose political interests are less in documenting the deviants than in demonstrating in full, vivid color the humanity of groups that had previously been taken to be outcast. As a result, these ethnographies tend to describe the workings of communities, the negotiation of safety and community by people with stigmatized identities. Some key examples of this type of work include studies of drag performance in the late 1960s (Newton, 1972), lesbian feminist community dynamics (Krieger, 1983), the gay men's community in early-20th-century New York City (Chauncey, 1994), butch and femme in mid-century Albany, New York (Lapovsky Kennedy & Davis, 1993), the growth of New York's Fire Island as a gay summer mecca (Newton, 1993), queer San Francisco (Boyd, 2003), lesbian feminist communities (Stein, 1992/1998), conservatism and gay and lesbian identity in Washington state (Linneman, 2003), and drag queen communities in Key West (Rupp & Taylor, 2003).

Sexualities in Social Movements

Sexualities keep marching out of the Diagnostic and Statistical Manual and on to the pages of social history. At present, several other groups are trying to emulate the successes of homosexuals. Bisexuals, sadomasochists, individuals who prefer cross-generational encounters, transsexuals, and transvestites are all in various states of community formation and identity acquisition. (Rubin, 1993, p. 18)

Rubin's observation is often noted, not only because it seems to forecast the emergence of certain forms of group formation (e.g., transgender) but also because she names a central concern that is highlighted when sexualities are understood as social—activism, politics, and social movements. Seidman (2003, p. 53) succinctly explains, "Every society has a system of sexual stratification. Sexual politics is about the making and contesting of these sexual hierarchies."

Importantly, the field of sexualities studies and constructionist research on sexualities has always been centrally concerned with sexual politics. In this section we highlight some of that more recent social movement work on sexual politics. In general, constructionist understandings of social movements stress two aspects of social movement processes of social construction—identity work and framing.

Paralleling the work on self and identity in sexualities studies, a great deal of research on social movements and sexualities has focused on identity work (so for the purposes of this chapter we focus on identity work, not framing).[9] Verta Taylor and Nancy Whittier's (1998) study, today, might be understood as foundational to that work. Taylor and Whittier examine the emergence of a lesbian-feminist identity in the United States and detail processes of forming a lesbian feminist consciousness, the construction of boundaries as far as who was a lesbian feminist and who was not, and the negotiation of being a lesbian feminist in everyday life. They contribute to constructionist understandings of identity-building strategies in social movements by identifying processes for constructing a collective identity that include the creation of a shared consciousness, the establishment of ingroup/out-group boundaries, and the negotiation of this identity in everyday life. But they also contribute to a constructionist understanding of sexualities by detailing how new categories of sexuality (and gender) are created via group work and interaction.

Yet, as many who are even slightly familiar with trends in lesbian, gay, bisexual, transgender, or queer politics over the past two decades are aware, the construction of a cohesive collective identity is not the only way in which identity work is engaged in social movements about sexualities. Indeed, even as Taylor and Whittier (1998) articulated the processes of constructing lesbian-feminist identity, Arlene Stein (1992/1998) was detailing how a cohesive lesbian identity was increasingly fragmented. Stein's work details a lesbian movement that "consists of a series of projects, often wildly disparate in approach, many of which incorporate radical and progressive elements" (p. 553). Similarly, Joshua Gamson's (1995) analysis of 75 letters from a San Francisco newspaper about "queer" challenges to a cohesive sense of "gay and lesbian" identity similarly details new forms of "queer" identity work. Gamson terms these processes *identity-blurring* processes of deconstruction, in contrast to the *identity-building* strategies of constructing collective identity identified by Taylor and Whittier. Deconstructive processes, according to Gamson (p. 390), both "disrupt categories" of identity and refuse (rather than embrace) ethnic minority status. To do so, activists assert an "in-your-face difference" by reveling in outsider status and engaging in border skirmishes over membership conditions and group boundaries (Gamson, 1995). These two examples of constructionist-oriented research explain identity work typical of the queer turn in sexual politics.

Since these works, our constructionist understandings of identity work in social movements related to sexualities and gender have continued to develop (see, e.g., Armstrong, 2002; Broad, 2002a, 2002b, 2004; Broad, Crawley, & Foley, 2004; Crawley & Broad, 2004; Gamson, 1996, 1997; Rupp & Taylor, 2003; Seidman, 2001). Here we highlight two examples. First, Mary Bernstein's (1997) work on strategic use of identities by different lesbian and gay rights campaigns offers important understandings of identity construction in a political context. She suggests that sexualities activists often engage in "identity deployment," a form of collective action whereby activists assess political conditions and strategically decide whether to celebrate or suppress differences in sexual categories. Importantly, assessment of those political conditions arises from interactions between social movement organizations, state actors, and the opposition. Bernstein's work nicely complements and explains the different ways that Taylor and Whittier

(1992), Stein (1992/1998), and Gamson (1995) observed identity work that contains or emphasizes differences in sexual categories. Another example is Crawley and Broad's (2004) "Be Your [Real Lesbian] Self." Grounded in participant observation in LGBTQ educational panels, the authors detail a tension in personal-storytelling-as-activism—the way in which individual sexualities and genders are constructed through personal narrative in tension with an audience expectation of typifying LGBT experience. Like Bernstein's work, this research relies on earlier work about identity construction but complicates it by emphasizing audience response and individual identity work.

New Directions

As a third goal of this chapter, here we relate new directions for the field of sexualities studies. Having outlined much of the history and some of the major debates of sexualities studies, we wish to offer some brief ideas for future work, as well as cite suggestions published elsewhere that we find particularly cogent.

Bodies and Sex Acts

One arena of research that is oddly missing from constructionist work on sexualities is explicit research on the sexual, in a bodily, lustful sense (not, e.g., in terms of identity, community, and politics). As Plummer (2003, p. 522) explains, "There are odd flashes of innovation, but in the main we could speak of a 'vanishing sexuality'—a certain absence of the sexual in much contemporary constructionist/interactionist research on the sexual." Indeed, he even suggests that the solution is autoethnographic research about the sexual researcher as a sexual self (although he modestly notes that he is not brave enough or interesting enough to do so himself).

The absence of constructionist work on bodies and sex acts is probably most notable in HIV/AIDS research, much of which has not been constructionist. It seems that constructionist questions of sexuality revolve around things we can imagine as social but not the actual practices of bodies. Plummer (2003) writes this critique most succinctly:

> There is little humping and bumping, sweatiness or sexiness in much sociological work. Instead we have discourses, identities, cultures, patriarchies, queer theories, transgender politics . . . you name it. Anything but the lustily erotic. (pp. 525–526)

Given that much of queer culture—newspaper, magazines, film—is oriented toward the erotic, it seems a significant absence that scholars have not addressed this component of sexual life. If we are to take embodiment seriously, we are going to have to address the body in all its messy practices.

Intersections of Race Categorization and Sexualities

Another arena that sexualities studies are only just beginning to understand is that of sexuality at the intersections of racial categories and ethnic cultures and practices. Queer theorists and scholars of black feminist thought should push themselves to focus on more than one or two intersections simultaneously. In the tradition of bell hooks, we must push ourselves to truly pursue the promise of understanding how gender, sexual orientation, race, and social class intersect simultaneously. As a result, queer theorists need to focus more on how racial categorization (whiteness and nonwhite status) play into sexuality formation (Valocchi, 2005). Similarly, scholars working with critical race perspectives, especially those concerned with the intersections of race, class, gender, sexuality, and nation, need to bring more theoretical focus on heteronormativity.[10] Some queer scholars have begun these critiques (Almaguer, 1993; Alonso,

1993; Mercer, 1993; Nagel, 2003; Sommerville, 2000), but in the interest of studying the particularities of sexual communities, we must push toward always recognizing the impact of racial category, including dominant whiteness, as a component of sexual identities and communities.

Methodological Currents and a Call for the Renewing of the Empirical

Given the argument introduced by queer theorists that categories are falsely constructed, sociologists of sexualities are left with an important methodological debate: Can there be a sociology without sex or sexual orientation (Seidman, 1996)? The tradition of sociology involves analysis of trends and social phenomena of people interacting in groups. Can this study legitimately continue if the categories on which social analysis traditionally has been based—sexual orientation, race, and indeed even biological sex—are shown to be themselves socially produced?[11]

The solution is not to negate the possibility of study but rather to undertake greater care with the particularity of the people and phenomena to be described. Ingraham (1996) provides a striking example of this in critiquing the common usage of the term *gender*. Emphasizing the importance of heteronormativity implicit in gender systems, Ingraham argues that scholars' common use of the term *gender* masks their own heteronormative expectations. A more accurate term, according to Ingraham, is *heterogender*. She argues that the term *heterogender* makes clear the heteronormative sexuality implicit in gender analyses and marks the possibility of styles of gender that do not implicitly include heterosexuality.

In response to the queer turn in sexualities studies, one major aspect for sociologists has been a reassertion of the empirical as an important arena of scholarship. In particular, sociologically minded sexualities scholars increasingly call for the relevance of social constructionist empirical studies and methodological developments. Although the sentiment has been articulated by many, we discuss two authors who have written recently about it, Adam Isaiah Green (2002) and Ken Plummer (1995, 1998, 2003).

Green (2002) asserts the centrality of an empirical sociology in his consideration of the next step for sexualities studies. While appreciating the complexity that queer theory has offered our understandings of sexualities, he warns that it has also resulted in the creation of a "theoretical cataract that permits only a dim view of the contribution of the 'social' to the sexual" (Green, 2002, p. 522). In essence, he reminds scholars of sexualities that empirical research is necessary to address what has become a construction of queer theory: "the undersocialized 'queer' subject with little connection to the empirical world and the sociohistorical forces that shape sexual practice and identity" (Green, 2002, p. 522). Although he does not explicitly outline the best methodological avenues by which to reinsert empirical sociology, he features Connell's (1992) life history study of masculinity among Australian men as a key example of postqueer empirical work because it combines attention to queer concerns (sexological categories and understandings of gay identity as potentially subversive) with social constructionist analyses and observations (the relevance of sexual categories to how gay men construct and form attachments to community institutions and these men's apolitical construction of identities).

Similarly, Plummer (1995, 1998, 2003) speaks staunchly as a sociologist and social constructionist, reminding us of the importance of empirical study and symbolic interactionism in the development of sexualities studies to date. Specifically, Plummer (1998) explicitly calls for "rediscovering ethnography," especially because of the reflexive turn in ethnographic methodologies, and "transcending discourse" to return to an understanding of the complex, concrete living social worlds of lesbians and gay men. Also, Plummer (2003) suggests that although symbolic interactionism has been a minority position in constructionist sexualities work, it need not be, primarily because of interactionism's "grip" on the reality of everyday life (in contrast to queer theory). Not only is interactionist dedication to the empirical important, but recent interactionist contributions to methodology also offer important ways for sexualities scholarship to advance, according to Plummer (2003, p. 521). In Kong, Mahoney, and Plummer (2002), the authors observe how the rise in queer approaches (to sexuality and methodology) make some methodological concerns resonate: issues of representation, challenges of legitimation (validity), reflexivity, and ethical concerns. In essence, this work concretely suggests how we might bring together concerns of queer theory with pragmatic methodological challenges of interviewing in order to better produce constructionist understandings of sexualities.

Both Green (2002) and Plummer (1995, 1998, 2003) provide us a forecast of the way constructionist work in sexualities may be headed, toward methodologically queered but still sociologically grounded empirical studies that capture the social in the sexual and the sexual in the social (research). In keeping with our previous argument about the need to engage racial and ethnic social locations in sexualities studies, we also suggest that empirical work with people of various identities is a logical next step to connecting the abstraction of queer theories with the lived context of power and identity construction in the lives of everyday people engaging in all sorts of sexualities.

Pragmatism and Performance Beyond Psychoanalytic Theories

Related to these critiques for methodological grounding, our students often offer the concern that queer theory may not have meaningful explanatory power for LGBT people in their everyday lives. Negotiating between the "linguistic turn" of queer theory and the material body, scholars would find it quite beneficial to study everyday life as interpreted by social actors (Plummer, 2003, 2005b). Although identity categories and the meanings they imply are a social construction, the practices they compel and social structures about which they are constructed create a sense of concrete lived "reality" for people in their everyday lives. Although identities may be constructed, they certainly feel real for the people who inhabit them. In defense of constructionist approaches and shoring up the importance of this work in bridging the humanities–natural science divide, Weeks (1998) writes:

> David Halperin, for example, though lauded or execrated, depending on your taste, as a high priest of social constructionism, and a devotee of Foucault, once admitted that if he were shown conclusive proof of the genetically determined nature of homosexuality, he would have to revise all his historical theories. But this is nonsense. Halperin's interpretation of the sexuality of the classical world may or may not be historically accurate; but it does not depend one iota on whether homosexuality is inherent or acquired. It is a fairly banal point to make, but it still seems important to make it: social categorizations have effects in the real world, whether or not they are direct reflections of inherent qualities and drives, whether or not their genealogies can be traced in a murky history of power and resistance. (p. 137)

As such, the so-called nature–nurture argument is entirely moot, or, conversely, any data from the natural sciences that shore up some link to sexuality should not be seen as a threat to linguistic or social theories of sexuality, because regardless of such linkages, what matters for most of us throughout most of our lives is how we interpret urges or social interaction. What is "real" for us is the social realm of interpretation through which we come to understand our lives, regardless of the origins of these instructions. Symbolic interactionist approaches, then, bridge the false dualisms of language or biology, learned or innate sexualities in favor of describing what Blumer (1969) referred to

as the "obdurate character" of social life (p. 22). Identities do not have to originate in the body to have a long-term effect in the social world. And so we suggest that pragmatist approaches—phenomenology, ethnomethodology, symbolic interactionism, among others—allow us to meet people where they live in their social worlds and describe the realities people understand in practice and which, for all practical purposes, organize their lives.

In addition to taking care with particularity of various lived experiences, the impact of queer theory argues for further investigation of the impact of ruling discourses in our lives. Queer theorists' arguments for deconstruction of categories call for scholars to focus on recognizing ways that dominant discourses and practices place subjectivities onto people, prescribing social categories and proscribing difference. This is the very work of constructionist sociologists—to study the effects of dominant discourses and social structures on people's lives. In our own work (Crawley & Broad, 2004), we demonstrate how social movement identity work compels each of us to claim an identity category, even when we purport to be speaking as individuals and feel uncomfortable claiming category membership in other settings. Hence, regardless of the "realness" or origins of social categories, their existence *in practice* is itself valuable to study.

For example, we would argue that gender and sexuality are often force-placed on social actors by others by being held accountable to particular visible characteristics, especially biological sex (Crawley, 2002a, 2002c; Crawley, Foley, & Shehan, in press). For example, in everyday interaction, female-bodied (and sometimes male-bodied) people are held accountable by others in interaction to being "women" and receive differential treatment on that basis. Hence, there is some recognizable basis for an analysis of a unitary experience of what it means to be "women" if in social interaction others enforce that sex category on people who might otherwise have very diverse interests and self-definitions. In other words, sex category is inescapable in interaction if others recognize and apply the interactional gender rules.[12] Although the particularities of their experiences cannot be ignored or glossed over, scholars can study what it means to be held accountable to "woman" in our culture. In particular, we agree with various critiques of Butlerian performance theories that continue to foreground psychoanalytic approaches unnecessarily (Dunn, 1997; Emery, 2002; Jackson & Scott, 2001). We argue that a more pragmatist approach avoids the tendancy toward a Freudian, heteronormative grand narrative of socialization. There is no need to assume a heteronormative psyche or its opposite, the queer psyche. Instead we find pragmatist approaches, based on the work of G. H. Mead (1964), to provide a broader set of human possibilities that are not restricted to heteronormative grand narrative (Crawley et al., in press). In our estimation, Meadian approaches to identity are more explanatory than neo-Freudian ones and provide far more flexibility of human interpretation, making the possibility of equality much more hopeful.

• Notes

1. Throughout this chapter we refer to sexualities in the plural to recognize the vast array of sexualities practiced, interpreted, and taken on as identities in the everyday world and over the course of history. By referring to *sexualities*, we hope the reader will begin to understand the insight that we should never assume that practices of sexuality are static, nor are meanings about them consistent across cultures or time. Additionally, this chapter is not intended as an exhaustive review of the literature on sexualities. Like other area studies, the literature on sexualities has grown into several subfields, many of which overlap with other subfields; for example, the sociology of gender. Certainly a sexualities scholar might review many of these important subfields such as women's sexuality (Brumberg, 1993; Holland, Ramazanoglu, & Thomson,

1996/2002), masculinity and sexuality (Bordo, 1998; Connell, 1987, 2005), sexuality and reproduction (Loe, 2004; Tiefer, 2004), motherhood and fatherhood, and so forth. Although these are significant studies of sexualities, they are beyond the scope of this chapter. Last, we want to acknowledge that much of the work that we discuss, as Green (2002) articulates, "might fall under the rubric of 'lesbian and gay studies'" but, like Green (2002, p. 542), we do not engage this term because it "excludes important recent efforts to problematize heterosexuality."

2. In concert with the development of constructionist sociological sexualities theories and radical feminist theories, historical events of the 1980s, especially the advent of HIV/AIDS, also became an important political and practical precursor to queer theory and the so-called linguistic turn. Initially labeled a "gay disease" because many gay men were mysteriously dying, scholars and public health officials early on recognized the need to change public consciousness about the disease by changing the discourse around it. (This is an example of the first characteristic of queer theory that we outline below—the deployment of discourse as power; see, e.g., Crimp, 1993.) The lethal context of AIDS/HIV increased the priority of sex research and encouraged scholars to critique positivistic methods and fixed sexual ontologies, which perhaps in part led to the so-called linguistic turn.

3. Dorothy Smith (1987) offers a similar notion with her concept of "relations of ruling" and "bifurcated consciousness," although Smith relies more on a Marxist structural analysis. Interestingly, her work has not made significant inroads outside sociology, perhaps because it was not related to the substantive study of sexualities, as is Foucault's.

4. All taboos, of course, are established within specific cultural, historical contexts, so they will differ across societies and over time.

5. Notice that, consistent with Sedgwick's ideas, Butler recognizes how social performances create the illusion of binaries.

6. Political events of a historical era likely also have a large impact on the potential for academic exploration. Similar to our previous argument about the impact of the emergence of AIDS on the development of queer theory (see note 2), the politics of the civil rights era, especially the emergence of the gay liberation movement, likely had an impact on or developed in concert with con-

structionist sexualities theories. It is not coincidental that these theories were emerging in the late 1960s and 1970s.

7. The authors would like to thank Kim Emery of the University of Florida for this insight.

8. Considered a bit of a fringe idea at the time (recall it was written almost 10 years before the first so-called "test tube baby"), the technological possibility of her call to action seems less and less impossible in the 21st century.

9. Although we have briefly outlined one branch of that here, constructionist social movement scholarship on sexualities also details and complicates processes of framing, constructing the issues of a movement (see, e.g., Broad, Crawley, & Foley, 2004; Jenness, 1995; Jenness & Broad, 1994).

10. Of course this is the central contribution of black feminist thought—the critique that we cannot talk about "women" as a unitary group without erasing racial and ethnic differences, as well as class- and sexuality-based differences (Combahee River Collective, 1981/2005; Hill Collins, 1991; Moraga & Anzaldúa, 1981). Our critique here is to truly support "intersectional" perspectives by asking how we can better talk about identity in a way that is more inclusive, particular, and specific.

11. Not coincidentally, symbolic interactionism and ethnomethodology allow us to consider these very particulars of intersecting experiences without essentializing any of these experiences (Valocchi, 2005).

12. In the most extreme case, such as that of Michael Kantaras, a female-to-male transsexual may not be seen as a "real man" if his birth sex is known. In Mr. Kantaras's case, a Florida court ruled that he could not have custody of his previously adopted child, not on the basis of his parenting skills but because he is not a male person and therefore should never been allowed to adopt the child in the first place. (Under Florida law, same-sex parents cannot adopt children.) So, for all practical purposes, Florida law treats Mr. Kantaras as a woman (*www.nclrights.org/cases/kantaraskantaras.htm*). Although his experience as a white, female-to-male man is clearly different from that of, for example, a Cuban heterosexual grandmother, both are still held accountable to what it means to be a woman in current-day, U.S. social context.

• References

Almaguer, T. (1993). Chicano men: A cartography of homosexual identity and behavior. In H. Abelove, M. A. Barale, & D. M. Halperin (Eds.), *The lesbian and gay studies reader* (pp. 255–273). New York: Routledge.

Alonso, A. M., & Koreck, M. T. (1993). Silences: "Hispanics," AIDS, and sexual practices. In H. Abelove, M. A. Barale, & D. M. Halperin (Eds.), *The lesbian and gay studies reader* (pp. 110–126). New York: Routledge.

Armstrong, E. A. (2002). *Forging gay identities: Organizing sexualities in San Francisco, 1950–1999*. Chicago: University of Chicago Press.

Becker, H. (1963). *Outsiders: Studies in the sociology of deviance*. Glencoe, IL: Free Press.

Bernstein, M. (1997). Celebration and suppression: The strategic uses of identity by the lesbian and gay movement. *American Journal of Sociology, 103*(3), 531–565.

Best, A. L. (2000). *Prom night: Youth, schools, and popular culture*. New York: Routledge.

Blumer, H. (1969). *Symbolic interactionism: Perspective and method*. Berkeley: University of California Press.

Bordo, S. (1998). Pills and power tools. *Men and Masculinities, 1*(1), 87–90.

Bornstein, K. (1994). *Gender outlaw: On men, women, and the rest of us*. New York: Routledge.

Boyd, N. A. (2003). *Wide-open town: A history of queer San Francisco to 1965*. Berkeley: University of California Press.

Broad, K. L. (2002a). Is it G, L, B *and* T?: Gender/sexuality movements and transgender collective identity (de)constructions. *International Journal of Sexuality and Gender Studies, 7*(4), 241–264.

Broad, K. L. (2002b) Social movement selves. *Sociological Perspectives, 45*(3), 317–336.

Broad, K. L. (2004). Institutional selves in social movements: The interpretive production of ftm/transmen. *Research in Political Sociology, 13*, 1.

Broad, K. L., Crawley, S. L., & Foley, L. (2004). Doing "real" family values: The interpretive practice of "families" in the glbt movement. *Sociological Quarterly, 45*(3), 509–527.

Brown, L. (1997). *Two spirit people: American Indian lesbian women and gay men*. New York: Haworth Press.

Brumberg, J. J. (1993). "Something happens to girls:" Menarche and the emergence of the modern American hygienic imperative. *Journal of the History of Sexuality, 4*, 99–127.

Butler, J. (1990). *Gender trouble: Feminism and the subversion of identity*. New York: Routledge.

Butler, J. (1993). *Bodies that matter: On the discursive limits of "sex."* New York: Routledge.

Butler, J. (1996). Imitation and gender insubordination. In D. Morton (Ed.), *The material queer* (pp. 180–192). Boulder, CO: Westview Press.

Cahill, S. E. (1986). Language practices and self-definition: The case of gender identity acquisition. *Sociological quarterly*, 27(3), 295–311.

Cahill, S. E. (1989). Fashioning males and females: Appearance management and the social reproduction of gender. *Symbolic Interaction*, 12(2), 281–298.

Cahill, S. E. (1998). Towards a sociology of the person. *Sociological Theory*, 16, 131–148.

Case, S. (1989). Toward a butch–femme aesthetic. In L. Hart (Ed.), *Making a spectacle* (pp. 282–298). Ann Arbor: University of Michigan Press.

Chase, S. E. (2001). Universities as discursive environments for sexual identity construction. In J. F. Gubrium & J. A. Holstein (Eds.), *Institutional selves: Troubled identities in a postmodern world* (pp. 142–157). New York: Oxford University Press.

Chauncey, G. (1994). *Gay New York: Gender, urban culture, and the makings of the gay male world, 1890–1940*. New York: Basic Books.

Combahee River Collective. (2005). A black feminist statement. In W. K. Kolmar & F. Bartkowski (Eds.), *Feminist theory: A reader* (2nd ed., pp. 311-317). Boston: McGraw-Hill. (Original work published 1981)

Connell, R. (1987). *Gender and power*. Stanford, CA: Stanford University Press.

Connell, R. (1992). A very straight gay: Masculinity, homosexual experiences, and the dynamics of gender. *American Sociological Review*, 57, 735–751.

Crawley, S. L. (2001). Are butch and fem working class and anti-feminist? *Gender & Society*, 15, 175–196.

Crawley, S. L. (2002a). *Narrating and negotiating butch and femme: Storying lesbian selves in a heteronormative world*. Unpublished doctoral disssertation, University of Florida.

Crawley, S. L. (2002b). Prioritizing audiences: Exploring the differences between stone butch and transgender identifications. *Journal of Lesbian Studies*, 6, 11–24.

Crawley, S. L. (2002c). "They *still* don't understand why I hate wearing dresses": An autoethnographic rant on dresses, boats and butchness. *Cultural Studies-Critical Methodologies*, 2, 69–92.

Crawley, S. L., & Broad, K. L. (2004). "Be your [real lesbian] self": Mobilizing sexual formula stories through personal (and political) storytelling. *Journal of Contemporary Ethnography*, 33, 39–71.

Crawley, S. L., Foley, L. J., & Shehan, C. L. (in press). *Gendering bodies*. New York: Rowman & Littlefield.

Crimp, D. (1993). The boys in my bedroom. In H. Abelove, M. A. Barale, & D. M. Halperin (Eds.), *The lesbian and gay studies reader* (pp. 344–349). New York: Routledge.

De Lauretis, T (1989). *Technologies of gender: Essays on theory, film, and fiction*. Bloomington: Indiana University Press.

Dozier, R. (2005). Beards, breasts, and bodies: Doing sex in a gendered world. *Gender & Society*, 19, 297–316.

Dunn, R. G. (1997). Self, identity, and difference: Mead and the poststructuralists. *Sociological Quarterly*, 38, 687–705.

Emery, K. (2007). *The lesbian index: Pragmatism and lesbian subjectivity in the twentieth-century United States*. Albany: State University of New York Press.

Epstein, S. (1998). Gay politics, ethnic identity: The limits of social constructionism. In P. N. Nardi & B. E. Schneider (Eds.), *Social perspectives in lesbian and gay studies: A reader* (pp. 134–159). New York: Routledge. (Original work published 1987)

Epstein, S. (1996). A queer encounter: Sociology and the study of sexuality. In S. Seidman (Ed.), *Queer theory/sociology* (pp. 145–167). Cambridge, MA: Blackwell.

Faderman, L. (1981). *Surpassing the love of men: Romantic friendship and love between women from the Renaissance to the present*. New York: Morrow.

Faderman, L. (1992). The return of butch and femme: A phenomenon in lesbian sexuality of the 1980s and 1990s. In J. Fout & M. Tantillo (Eds.), *American sexual politics: Sex, gender and race since the Civil War* (pp. 333–351). Chicago: University of Chicago Press.

Fausto-Sterling, A. (1986). *Myths of gender: Biological theories about women and men*. New York: Basic Books.

Fausto-Sterling, A. (1995). How to build a man. In M. Berger, B. Wallace, & S. Watson (Eds.), *Constructing masculinity* (pp. 127–135). New York: Routledge.

Fausto-Sterling, A. (2000). *Sexing the body: Gender politics and the construction of sexuality*. New York: Basic Books.

Feinberg, L. (1996). *Transgender warriors: Making history from Joan of Arc to Dennis Rodman*. Boston: Beacon Press.

Firestone, S. (1970). *The dialectic of sex: The case for feminist revolution*. New York: Morrow.

Foucault, M. (1977). *Discipline and punish: The birth of a prison*. New York: Random House.

Foucault, M. (1978). *The history of sexuality: An introduction* (Vol. 1). New York: Vintage Books.

Foucault, M. (1980). *Power/knowledge: Selected interviews and other writings, 1972-1977* (C. Gordon, Ed.). New York: Pantheon.

Frye, M. (1983). *The politics of reality: Essays in feminist theory*. Freedom, CA: Crossing Press.

Frye, M. (1992). Lesbian "sex." In M. Frye, *Willful virgin: Essays in feminism* (pp. 109–119). Freedom, CA: Crossing Press.

Gagnon, J. H., & Simon, W. (2005). *Sexual conduct: The social sources of human sexuality*. New Burnswick, NJ: AldineTransaction. (Original work published 1973)

Gamson, J. (1995). Must identity movements self-destruct?: A queer dilemma. *Social Problems*, 42(3), 390–407.

Gamson, J. (1996). The organizational shaping of collective identity: The case of lesbian and gay film festivals in New York . *Sociological Forum, 11*(2), 231–261.

Gamson, J. (1997). Messages of exclusion: Gender, movements, and symbolic boundaries. *Gender and Society, 11*(2), 178–199.

Garfinkel, H. (1967). *Studies in ethnomethodology.* Englewood Cliffs, NJ: Prentice Hall.

Goffman, E. (1959). *The presentation of self in everyday life.* New York: Anchor Books.

Goffman, E. (1963a). *Interaction ritual.* New York: Anchor Books.

Goffman, E. (1963b). *Stigma: Notes on the management of spoiled identity.* New York: Simon & Schuster.

Goffman, E. (1976). *Gender advertisements.* New York: HarperCollins.

Goffman, E. (1997). The arrangement between the sexes. *Theory and Society, 4*, 301–331.

Green, A. I. (2002). Gay but not queer: Toward a post-queer study of sexuality. *Theory and Society, 31*, 521–545.

Green, J. (2004). *Becoming a visible man.* Nashville, TN: Vanderbilt University Press.

Greenberg, D. E. (1988). *The construction of homosexuality.* Chicago: University of Chicago Press.

Gubrium, J. F., & Holstein, J. A. (1997). *The new language of qualitative method.* New York: Oxford University Press.

Halberstam, J. (1994). F2M: The making of female masculinity. In L. Doan (Ed.), *The lesbian postmodern* (pp. 210–228). New York: Columbia University Press.

Halberstam, J. (1998). *Female masculinity.* Durham, NC: Duke University Press.

Halperin, D. M. (1993). Is there a history of sexuality? In H. Abelove, M. A. Barale, & D. M. Halperin (Eds.), *The lesbian and gay studies reader* (pp. 416–431). New York: Routledge.

Hill Collins, P. (1991). *Black feminist thought.* Boston: Unwin Hyman.

Holland, J., Ramazanoglu, C., & Thomson, R. (2002). In the same boat? In S. Jackson & S. Scott (Eds.), *Gender: A sociological reader* (pp. 326–337). London: Routledge. (Original work published 1996)

Holstein, J. A., & Gubrium, J. F. (2000). *The self we live by: Narrative identity in a postmodern world.* New York: Oxford University Press.

Humphreys, L. (1970). *Tearoom trade: Impersonal sex in public places.* Chicago: Aldine de Gruyter.

Ingraham, C. (1996). The heterosexual imaginary: Feminist sociology and theories of gender. In S. Seidman (Ed.), *Queer theory/sociology* (pp. 168–193). Malden, MA: Blackwell.

Ingraham, C. (1999). *White weddings: Romancing heterosexuality in popular culture.* New York: Routledge.

Ingraham, C. (2003). The sociologist as voyeur: Social theory and sexuality research, 1910–1978. *Qualitative Sociology, 26*(4), 429–456.

Jackson, S., & Scott, S. (2001). Putting the body's feet on the ground: Towards a sociological reconceptualization of gendered and sexual embodiment. In K.

Backett-Milburn & L. McKie (Eds.), *Constructing gendered bodies* (pp. 9–24). New York: Palgrave.

Jeffreys, S. (1996). Heterosexuality and the desire for gender. In D. Richardson (Ed.), *Theorising heterosexuality: Telling it straight* (pp. 75–90). Buckingham, UK: Open University Press.

Jenness, V. (1995). Social movement growth, domain expansion, and framing processes: The gay/lesbian movement and violence against gays and lesbians as a social problem. *Social Problems, 42*(1), 145–170

Jenness, V., & Broad, K. L. (1994). Antiviolence activism and the (in)visibility of gender in the gay/lesbian and women's movements. *Gender & Society, 8*(3), 402–423.

Katz, J. N. (1976). *Gay American history.* New York: Crowell.

Katz, J. N. (1995). *The invention of heterosexuality.* New York: Dutton.

Kessler, S. J. (1998). *Lessons from the intersexed.* New Brunswick, NJ: Rutgers University Press.

Kessler, S. J., & McKenna, W. (1978). *Gender: An ethnomethodological approach.* Chicago: University of Chicago Press.

Kinsey, A. C., Pomeroy, W. B., & Martin, C. E. (1948). *Sexual behavior in the human male.* Philadelphia: Saunders.

Kinsey, A. C., Pomeroy, W. B., Martin, C. E., & Gebhard, P. (1953). *Sexual behavior in the human female.* Philadelphia: Saunders.

Kitzinger, C. (1987). *The social construction of lesbianism.* London: Sage.

Kitzinger, C. (1995). Social constructionism: Implications for lesbian and gay psychology. In A. R. D'Augelli & C. J. Patterson (Eds.), *Lesbian, gay and bisexual identities over the lifespan: Psychological perspectives* (pp. 136–165). New York: Oxford University Press.

Kong, T. S. K., Mahoney, D., & Plummer, K. (2002). Queering the interview. In J. F. Gubrium & J. A. Holstein (Eds.), *Handbook of interview research: Context and method* (pp. 239–258). Thousand Oaks, CA: Sage University Press.

Krieger, S. (1983). *The mirror dance: Identity in a women's community.* Philadelphia: Temple University Press.

Lapovsky Kennedy, E., & Davis, M. D. (1993). *Boots of leather, slippers of gold: The history of a lesbian community.* New York: Routledge.

Laqueur, T. (1990). *Making sex: Body and gender from the Greeks to Freud.* Cambridge, MA: Harvard University Press.

Linneman, T. (2003). *Weathering change: Gays and lesbians, Christian conservatives and everyday hostilities.* New York: New York University Press.

Loe, M. (2004). *The rise of Viagra: How the little blue pill changed sex in America.* New York: New York University Press.

Lorde, A. (1984). The uses of the erotic: The erotic as

power. In A. Lorde, *Sister/outsider: Essays and speeches* (pp. 53–59). Freedom, CA: Crossing Press.

Masters, W. H., & Johnson, V. E. (1966). *Human sexual response*. Boston: Little, Brown.

McIntosh, M. (1968). The homosexual role. *Social Problems, 16*, 182–192.

Mead, G. H. (1964). *Mind, self, and society* (C. W. Morris, Ed.). Chicago: University of Chicago Press. (Original work published 1934)

Mercer, K. (1993). Looking for trouble. In H. Abelove, M. A. Barale, & D. M. Halperin (Eds.), *The lesbian and gay studies reader* (pp. 350–359). New York: Routledge.

Messner, M. (2000). Becoming 100% straight. In M. Baca-Zinn, P. Hondagneu-Sotelo, & M. A. Messner (Ed.), *Gender through the prism of difference* (pp. 205–210). Boston: Allyn & Bacon.

Monro, S., & Warren, L. (2004). Transgender citizenship. *Sexualities, 7*, 345–362.

Moraga, C., & Anzaldúa, G. (Eds.) (1981). *This bridge called my back: Writings by radical women of color*. Watertown, MA: Persephone Press.

Myerson, M., Crawley, S. L., Anstey, E., Kessler, J., & Okopny, C. (2007). Who's zoomin' who?: A feminist queer content analysis of "interdisciplinary" human sexuality textbooks. *Hypatia, 22*, 92–113.

Nagel, J. (2003). *Race, ethnicity, and sexuality: Intimate intersections, forbidden frontiers*. New York: Oxford University Press.

Nardi, P. M. (1995). The breastplate of righteousness. Twenty-five years after Laud Humphrey's tearoom trade: Impersonal sex in public places. *Journal of Homosexuality, 30*(2), 1–10.

Nardi, P. M., & Schneider, B. E. (Eds.). (1998). *Social perspectives in lesbian and gay studies: A reader*. London: Routledge.

Nestle, J., Howell, C., & Wilchins, R. (2002). *Genderqueer: Voices from beyond the sexual binary*. Los Angeles: Alyson Books.

Newton, E. (1972). *MotherCamp: Female impersonators in America*. Englewood Cliffs, NJ: Prentice Hall.

Newton, E. (1993). *Cherry Grove, Fire Island: Sixty years in America's first gay and lesbian town*. Boston: Beacon Press.

Patton, C. (1993). From nation to family. In H. Abelove, M. A. Barale, & D. M. Halperin (Eds.), *The lesbian and gay studies reader* (pp. 127–138). New York: Routledge.

Plummer, K. (1975). *Sexual stigma: An interactionist account*. Boston: Routledge & Kegan Paul.

Plummer, K. (1995). *Telling sexual stories: Power, change and social worlds*. London: Routledge.

Plummer, K. (1998). The past, present and futures of the sociology of same-sex relations. In P. N. Nardi & B. E. Schneider (Eds.), *Social perspective in lesbian and gay studies: A reader* (pp. 605–614). New York: Routledge.

Plummer, K. (2003). Queers, bodies and postmodern sexualities: A note on revisiting the "sexual" in symbolic interactionism. *Qualitative Sociology, 26*(4), 515–530.

Plummer, K. (2005a). Critical humanism and queer theory. In N. K. Denzin & Y. S. Lincoln (Eds.), *The Sage handbook of qualitative research* (3rd ed., pp. 357–373). Thousand Oaks, CA: Sage.

Plummer, K. (2005b). Permanence and change: Sexual conduct—thirty years on. In J. H. Gagnon & W. Simon (Eds.), *Sexual conduct: The social sources of human sexuality* (2nd ed.). New Brunswick, NJ: AldineTransaction.

Prosser, J. (1995). No place like home: The transgendered narrative of Leslie Feinberg's *Stone Butch Blues. Modern Fiction Studies, 41*, 483–514.

Radicalesbians. (2005). The woman-identified woman. In W. K. Kolmar & F. Bartkowski (Eds.), *Feminist theory: A reader* (2nd ed., pp. 239–242). Boston: McGraw-Hill. (Original work published 1970)

Rich, A. (1986). *Blood, bread and poetry: Selected prose, 1979–1986*. New York: Norton.

Rosenfeld, D. (2003). *The changing of the guard: Lesbian and gay elders, identity, and social change*. Philadelphia: Temple University Press.

Rubin, G. (1993). Thinking sex: Notes for a radical theory of the politics of sexuality. In H. Abelove, M. A. Barale, & D. M. Halperin (Eds.), *The lesbian and gay studies reader* (pp. 3–44). New York: Routledge.

Rubin, G. (2002). Studying sexual subcultures: Excavating the Ethnography of gay communities in urban North America. In E. Lewin & W. L. Leap (Eds.), *Out in theory: The emergence of lesbian and gay anthropology* (pp. 17–68), Urbana: University of Illinois Press.

Rubin, G., & Butler, J. (1994). Sexual traffic. *Differences, 6*(2–3), 62–99.

Rubin, H. (2003). *Self-made men: Identity and embodiment among transsexual men*. Nashville, TN: Vanderbilt University Press.

Rupp, L. J., & Taylor, V. (2003). *Drag queens at the 801 Cabaret*. Chicago: University of Chicago Press.

Rust, P. C. (1995). *Bisexuality and the challenge to lesbian politics: Sex, loyalty, and revolution*. New York: New York University Press.

Schiebinger, L. (1993). *Nature's body*. Boston: Beacon.

Schleifer, D. (2006). Make me feel mighty real: Gay female-to-male transgenderists negotiating sex, gender, and sexuality. *Sexualities, 9*, 57–75.

Schrock, D., Reid, L., & Boyd, E. M. (2005). Transsexuals' embodiment of womanhood. *Gender & Society, 19*, 317–335.

Schwartz, P., & Rutter, V. (1998). *The gender of sexuality*. Thousand Oaks, CA: Pine Forge Press.

Scott, J. (1993). The evidence of experience. In H. Abelove, M. A. Barale, & D. M. Halperin (Eds.), *The lesbian and gay studies reader* (pp. 397–415). New York: Routledge.

Sedgwick, E. K. (1990). *Epistemology of the closet*. Berkeley: University of California Press.

Seidman, S. (Ed.). (1996). *Queer theory/sociology*. Malden, MA: Blackwell.

Seidman, S. (2001). From identity to queer politics: Shifts in normative heterosexuality. In S. Seidman & J. C. Alexander (Eds.), *The new social theory reader* (pp. 353–361). London: Routledge.

Seidman, S. (2003). *The social construction of sexuality*. New York: Norton.

Simon, W., & Gagnon, J. H. (2003). Sexual scripts: Influences and changes. *Qualitative Sociology, 26*(4), 491–497.

Smith, B. (1993). Homophobia: Why bring it up? In H. Abelove, M. A. Barale, & D. M. Halperin (Eds.), *The lesbian and gay studies reader* (pp. 99–102). New York: Routledge. (Original work published 1990)

Smith, D. E. (1987). *The everyday world as problematic*. Boston: Northeastern University Press.

Smith-Rosenberg, C. (1975). The female world of love and ritual. *Signs, 1*.

Somerville, S. B. (2000). *Queering the color line*. Durham, NC: Duke University Press.

Stein, A. (1998). Sisters and queers: The decentering of lesbian feminism. In P. Nardi & B. Schneider (Eds.), *Social perspectives in lesbian and gay studies*. New York: Routledge. (Original work published 1992)

Stone, S. (1991). The empire strikes back: A posttranssexual manifesto. In J. Epstein & K. Straub (Eds.), *Body guards*. New York: Routledge.

Taylor, V., & Whittier, N. (1998). Collective identity in social movement communities: Lesbian feminist mobilization. In P. Nardi & B. E. Schneider (Eds.), *Social perspectives in lesbian and gay studies* (pp. 349–365). New York: Routledge.

Thomas, W. I. (1907). *Sex and society: Studies in the social psychology of sex*. Chicago: University of Chicago Press.

Tiefer, L. (2004). *Sex is not a natural act and other essays*. Boulder, CO: Westview Press.

Trumbach, R. (1994). The origins and development of modern lesbian role in the Western gender system: Northwestern Europe and the United States, 1750–1990. *Historical Reflections, 20*, 287–320.

Valerio, M. W. (2006). *The testosterone files*. Emeryville, CA: Seal Press.

Valocchi, S. (2005). Not yet queer enough: The lessons of queer theory for the sociology of gender and sexuality. *Gender & Society, 19*(6), 750–770.

Vance, C. S. (1998). Social construction theory: Problems in the history of sexuality. In P. N. Nardi & B. E. Schneider (Eds.), *Social perspectives in lesbian and gay studies: A reader* (pp. 160–170). New York: Routledge.

Weeks, J. (1977). *Coming out: Homosexual politics in Britain from the 19th century to the present*. London: Quartet.

Weeks, J. (1998). The "homosexual role" after 30 years: An appreciation of the work of Mary McIntosh. *Sexualities 1*(2), 131–152.

Weeks, J. (2003). *Sexuality* (2nd ed.). London: Routledge. (Original work published 1986)

West, C., & Zimmerman, D. H. (1987). Doing gender. *Gender and Society, 1*, 125–151.

Weston, K. (1991). *Families we choose: Lesbians, gays, kinship*. New York: Columbia University Press.

Weston, K. (1993). Do clothes make the woman?: Gender, performance theory, and lesbian eroticism. *Genders, 17*, 1–21.

Whisman, V. (1996). *Queer by choice*. New York: Routledge.

Whitam, F. L. (1998). The homosexual role: A reconsideration. In P. M. Nardi & B. E. Schneider (Eds.), *Social perspectives in lesbian and gay studies: A reader* (pp. 77–83). London: Routledge.

CHAPTER 29

The Diverse Construction of Race and Ethnicity

● **Mitch Berbrier**

In *Black Skin, White Masks*, Frantz Fanon (1967) described a series of appalling interactions with others that influenced his identification as a Negro in mid-20th-century North Africa. Years later, David Theo Goldberg (1990) cited Fanon's work as seminal to our understanding of *"blackness* not as a natural fact but as socially and historically constructed" (p. xvii). But frankly, Frantz Fanon does not spring to my mind when considering seminal works on constructionism from the 1960s. On the other hand, and consistent with the editors' introduction to this *Handbook*, most of us who identify as constructionists would usually include Peter Berger and Thomas Luckmann (1966) among our major influences. But I reckon that Goldberg would not. Indeed, young scholars would get a much better sense of what to expect from

Goldberg's work if I labeled him a critical race theorist, a postmodernist, or both, rather than a constructionist.

Generally, when scholars address race or ethnicity as social constructs, the most common reference is not Fanon. Rather, that designation might just go to *Who Is Black?*, F. James Davis's (1991) highly readable account of the one-drop rule in the United States. Still, like Goldberg, Davis also makes no mention of Berger and Luckmann. In fact, he does not discuss "constructionism" at all. *Indeed, from my review of the literature, I find that when scholars in the social sciences and the humanities address race or ethnicity as constructs, they only rarely address the literature on constructionism.* So although there is unmistakably a trend in race and ethnic studies to recognize that race and ethnicity are socially constructed, to call this trend "constructionist" might suggest far too much affinity with a coherent constructionist epistemology and theory. These days, scholars and researchers who argue that race and ethnicity are social constructs occupy extremely diverse positions—from rather neo-essentialist to more radically constitutive constructions. In particular, dramatic variation exists among scholars in terms of their indebtedness and commitment to the well-articulated constructionist tradition that has infused social science, as well as this *Handbook*.

This chapter considers the wide range of scholarship that deals with the social construction of race and ethnicity—the multiple constructionisms that are brought to bear on the study of race and ethnicity. In this overview, I discuss the extent to which various approaches engage and highlight constructionist epistemology, tradition, and methodology. I begin by distinguishing between race and ethnicity—or, rather, tracing efforts to do so that, although ultimately futile, have effects on the way the literature is divided up. Then I follow the literature along a continuum that begins with those who take a liberal approach to reifying (or even essentializing) race and ethnicity and ends with more conservative approaches.

This spectrum corresponds well with Scott Harris's distinction between "objective" constructionists, who are interested largely in *why real things* are constructed, versus "interpretive" constructionists, who are focused on *how meanings* are constructed (Harris, Chapter 12, this volume). And it turns out that this also moves us from approaches that are primarily macrosociological in their analytic and evidentiary preferences to those that are more focused on individuals. Specifically, I first discuss the critical race theorists, then the political constructionists of ethnicity, followed by those who emphasize culture and identity, and ending with those who study ethnicity as a linguistic accomplishment. I conclude by analyzing the half-hearted commitment to constructionist principles in so many of the studies, suggesting that fruitful construc-

tionist research into the formation of race and ethnicity would focus on them less as topics of study and more as practical categories and distinctions that have major consequences for contemporary social life.[1]

Is It "Race" or "Ethnicity" or Both?

The practice of defining what one is examining in advance of studying it—either implicitly or explicitly—has long been a difficult and contentious issue in constructionist circles (Gubrium & Holstein, 1997; Woolgar, 1988). It often seems to constructionists that those engaged in defining are really fitting what they think they know about one or more groups or types (e.g., "Negroes" or "ethnicity") into an abstraction *so that they fit* it. As Virginia Domìnguez (1986) put it, "those who formulate and advocate particular definitions of identity seek, often unconsciously, to collapse description with prescription" (p. 11).

However, of the scholars who indicate that they are examining race and ethnicity as social constructs, only a few take this approach. Indeed, perhaps because of my own constructionist leanings, one thing that struck me repeatedly in reviewing their studies was the time and energy many scholars put into establishing a priori definitions that distinguished race from ethnicity and the virtual lack of consensus that emerged. In this regard Fenton and May (2002) describe "a tendency either to struggle unsuccessfully to make sustainable distinctions, or to admit that frequently the distinctions cannot be sustained" (p. 10). More incisively, Rogers Brubaker (2004) characterized this "intricate and ever-recommending definitional casuistry" as having "done little to advance the discussion" (p. 11).

An approach that might resonate more with the constructionist tradition would be to proceed more empirically and inductively, looking at how these terms are used in practice. This yields both less certitude and less dissension: Unanimously, it seems, scholars recognize that in both scholarly and nonscholarly discourse, *race* and *ethnicity* are routinely conflated, and not only with each other but also with several other contentious categories, such as *tribe, nation,* and *minority group.* There is consensus that all of those terms have a history and a historiography and that we can empirically document changes in their common application (if not always explain how or why things change).[2] Moreover, there is agreement that all of these labels are used to typify human groups and are both externally imposed and assertively claimed. The characteristics imposed or asserted frequently overlap, generally being used to connote shared experiences, culture, history, or heritage—each adjoined to place and/or ancestry.

The terminological choices of both analysts and actors seem to be highly correlated with—and constrained by—the contexts to which they are applied. We can note some general patterns there as well: *Tribes* are regularly associated with indigenous communities in former European colonies; *nations* come to be associated with increasingly politicized groups, as with the *nation-state* (see Stråth, Chapter 32, this volume); and *minorities* seem to become subordinated and victimized groups (Berbrier, 2002b; Fenton & May, 2002). Meanwhile, *ethnicities* are fairly consistently construed either as voluntary migrants to today's culturally plural nation-states *and/or* as indigenous cultural groups who do not seek statehood, whereas *ethnonationalist* is often used to characterize those among the latter who do seek statehood (e.g., via secession, such as in the cases of the Basques in Spain or Quebeçois in Canada).[3]

But, as is well known, there is much more discord regarding the term *race*—perhaps especially among scholars. As I discuss further later, races are constructed either as ethnic groups that happen to also be identifiable by physical appearance or descent, *or* as different kinds of groups that, although also identified by physical appearance or descent, are assigned racial status with the clear purpose

of creating or maintaining hierarchies of power and wealth (e.g., Bonilla-Silva, 1999; Eipper, 1983; Jenkins, 1996; Loveman, 1999a). Rather presciently, L. Singer (1962) seems to have anticipated this cleavage in his article in *Social Research* titled "Ethnogenesis and Negro Americans Today." Rather than a simple a matter of definition, Singer held that the issue was whether we are dealing with phenomena distinguished by "where" groups of people are hierarchically positioned or by "what they are," that is, by "groupness" itself:

> I had asked the question: In sociological terms, *what* are the Negroes in American society? And, at first, the answer appeared to be: They are a caste, or a race—and the whites must be one or the other also. Upon further consideration, however, it became clear that caste—as defined by . . . [Gunnar] Myrdal—and race—as defined by [Oliver] Cox—are not answers to the substantive question. The writers answer the question: *Where?* That is to say, they tell us the position of the Negroes in the structure of Negro–white relations. They do not indicate *what* the Negroes are, *what* they constitute as a social entity. (p. 419)

Singer's point corresponds to the two distinct streams that I see bifurcating the more macrosociological approaches in these areas, to which I turn next. The first stream derives from what its proponents call "critical race theory." This stream focuses on *race* and its relation to hierarchy, inequality, and injustice. In this literature, *ethnicity* is often explicitly disdained as a distraction: At best it masks stratification; at worst, it is used to deny it altogether. It is a secondary subdivision of races—a finer distinction, if you will—within a racially stratified system.

In the second stream—scholarship on "the social construction of ethnicity"—it is race that is secondary. That is, *ethnicity* is the broader category, differentiating peoples primarily along cultural lines, and race is but one form of ethnic distinction, the one that emphasizes both physical *and* cultural characteristics even though it is often recognized as the form most strongly correlated with hierarchy. With that in mind, I turn to a closer look at the critical race theorists' approach to constructionism.

The Critical Race Scholars and Their Whiteness Studies

One highly influential treatise in this area has been Ruth Frankenberg's *White Women, Race Matters: The Social Construction of Whiteness* (1993). Frankenberg's work is also interesting here in that she clearly employs a naturalistic approach, quoting extensively from interview data in order to interpret meaning from her informants' points of view. Hence her book has the trappings of a more "interpretive" constructionist account (Harris, Chapter 12, this volume). Moreover, Frankenberg holds that it is "most useful [to] view race as a socially constructed rather than inherently meaningful category" (p. 11). But she does not stop there. This sentence, and the definitional work it evinces, then indicates that race is a category that is both "linked to relations of power and processes of struggle, *and* [italics added] one whose meaning changes over time" (Frankenberg, 1993, p. 11).

In this variant of constructionism, although the meaning of *race* changes over time, there is an emphatic (and not very constructionist) exception to the change: its essence. Race, we are told, is really about power and advantage. Hence, Eduardo Bonilla-Silva (1999) writes that "race is *intrinsically* [italics added] connected to power relations and hierarchy; ethnicity is not" (p. 903), and Frankenberg elsewhere holds that whiteness in particular "refers to a set of locations that are historically, socially, politically, and culturally produced and, moreover, are *intrinsically* [italics added] linked to unfolding relations of domination" (1993, p. 6).

Moreover, when Frankenberg (1993) makes a point of citing studies that empha-size "race as a socially constructed rather than inherently meaningful category" (p. 11), she—like Goldberg—does not associate this with constructionism as it has been derived from Berger and Luckmann. Rather, she lists prominent scholars associated primarily with cultural studies—Stuart Hall, Cornel West, Paul Gilroy, and Goldberg himself. More notably for our purposes, she draws most directly from sociologists Michael Omi and Howard Winant's (1994) *Racial Formation in the United States*, which became, along with Frankenberg's own book and several works by historian David Roediger (e.g., 2005), standards in critical whiteness studies—the "must-cite" pieces.

Omi and Winant begin *Racial Formation* by deconstructing "ethnicity"—critiquing the "ethnicity paradigm" in social science that had erroneously reduced racial minorities to ethnic minorities. They indicate that for most of the 20th century biological claims about "race" were *de*constructed by social scientists, especially by anthropologists, who had hitherto been largely responsible for its scientific cachet. Meanwhile, social scientists became enamored of a newer concept and, for some, an entirely new term, *ethnicity*. Culture—the putative essence of ethnicity—was seen as real and was already the focus of much study, especially (again) among anthropologists. The study of race thereby came to be subsumed under the paradigm of ethnicity, and "racial groups" increasingly were seen by academics in the same way as those ethnic groups that are distinguished on the basis of their appearance. Their cultural distinctiveness just happened to correlate perfectly with a visible one.

Omi and Winant (1994) held that turning racial groups into ethnic groups by definitional fiat, and thereby equating processes of ethnicization and racialization, engendered invidious distinctions. Thus critical theorists argue time and again that equating race with ethnicity in the United States results in applying a success myth to white immigrants (i.e., ethnics) versus racial others—particularly blacks, Latinos, and Native

Americans. That is, when racial difference is reduced to ethnic difference, economic inequalities and power conflicts become matters of culture. The racial character of stratification is thereby denied (as is the stratified character of racial systems), bolstering political views that racial minorities demand too much from society or government and that "racialized communities had to shape up in terms of habits and values, not that an oppressive system had to change" (Roediger, 2005, p. 30).

In whiteness studies, such things as race, racialization, and racial formation are never at root boundary markers, categories, or identities, but rather really about conflict, power, and inequality.[4] Whiteness, they argue, is socially constructed and sustained in order to enhance domination, and the success of its realization can be explained by the advantages it has conferred on whites. Other peoples are socially constructed as races primarily in order to maintain or extend those advantages. The existence of race thereby implies the existence of racism, just as whiteness implies "white privilege."

Anti-Racism as a Constructionist Project

Yet whites—these days, anyhow—are empirically found to be in denial about this privileged status. This "unconsciousness" (Leistyna, 1998) is reproduced each generation, and that is the reason that whites so strongly resist the idea that the so-called mainstream values are in actuality "white mainstream values." Meanwhile, nonwhites who adhere to and/or advocate for such norms (e.g., by supporting assimilation to the dominant culture) must be falsely conscious, having accepted their groups' inferior status assignment and capitulated to it. Furthermore, when whites—or, for some scholars, any people—emphasize their "ethnic" heritage, critical race theorists often see "color-blind racism" operating in the form of cultural deficiency explanations of subordinate status that, in the final analysis, perform the same function as biologically ratio-

nalized forms of racism—separating people in order to perpetuate a system of racialized stratification.

Moreover, because race is understood as a structural principle of social organization, it is therefore akin (but not reducible) to class and gender and *entirely unlike ethnicity.* So when those operating within the ethnicity paradigm conflate, equate, or subsume race under the study of ethnicity, they obscure this objective structural role and thereby advance the interests of the ruling classes (e.g., Eipper, 1983). For the United States in particular, the racialization of blacks was not created and is not sustained because of prior cultural difference but because of dependence on cheap manual labor; thus if race is to be conflated with anything, it ought to be conflated with racism and not ethnicity. Because subordination on the basis of phenotype is part and parcel of colonialism, race and racism come into being together as coequal elements in the racialization process. The social reality of almost all race and ethnicity is interpreted through a lens that is primarily focused on the domination by whites and subordination of Africans (Winant, 2001).[5]

Some critical theorists hold that it was early scholarly activist rejection of racialism that laid the groundwork for the intellectual deconstruction of race that would follow. In this vein, Faye Harrison (1995) associates Franz Boas's (e.g., 1912) famous deconstruction of racist essentialism with W. E. B. DuBois's classic studies (e.g., 1899), which attributed the inferior health status of black Americans to their social conditions and not "racial" characteristics (see also Gates, 1990; Mullings, 1994). Although DuBois was using "normal" social science—in the sense of identifying and measuring social causes of things—he was simultaneously engaged in a pointed and iconoclastic refutation of scientific racism, which some critical race theorists see as a crucial precursor to all of today's social constructionist scholarship on race.[6]

In this spirit, Janet Shim's (2000) look at the racial gap in rates of heart disease provides an interesting update of DuBois, using the more current conceptual apparatus of Omi and Winant (1994). Shim compared epidemiologists' constructions of race with those of a group of patients. She found that the black patients tended to explain correlations of their health with their race in social terms—describing the cumulative consequences, over a lifetime, of confronting discrimination and segregation. On the other hand, the epidemiologists who uncovered this "social fact" explain the racial differences in health outcomes in apolitical and cultural terms, describing them as basically "cultural or ethnic" in nature, rooted in "differential behaviors and beliefs" (p. 414). The implication, consistent with critical theory, was that the individuals had to be changed, not society. "The routine attributions of racial difference to cultural difference," Shim writes, entails both "the pathologization of such behaviors, and the lack of attention given to the social structures and forces that give rise to and sustain them" (p. 419). Whereas Shim here uses racial construction as an independent variable, Omi and Winant's model has also been used to look at race as an *outcome*—for example, in Jorge Duany's (1998) comparative study of race among Puerto Ricans and Dominicans—and also as part of the *process*—for example, in Annegret Staiger's (2004) study on "whiteness as giftedness," which builds on Omi and Winant's concept of the "racial project."

The Macrosocial Approach to the Construction of Ethnicity

Although they are less integrated as a group than the critical race theorists, other scholars counter, in equally unequivocal terms, that by drawing such stark a priori distinctions between race and ethnicity or by ignoring the latter altogether, inquiry into social processes is stifled. For example, Randall

Collins (2001, p. 18) argued that because "there is no deep and analytically important distinction" between ethnicity and race, imposing such a distinction is "pernicious, because it obscures the social processes" that we are supposedly investigating—namely, "what elevates particular kinds of ethnic distinctions into an absolute break" that is often called "race." Thus race is seen as a form of ethnic distinction, but not as distinct from ethnicity itself. Mara Loveman (1999a) adds that the criticalist distinction between ethnicity and race is based on a narrow preoccupation with United States history, reflects a North American bias, and thereby (again) precludes inquiry into social processes:

> The arbitrary theoretical isolation of "race" from "ethnicity" discourages the comparative research needed to discover what, if anything, is unique about the operation or consequences of "race" as an essentializing practical category, as opposed to other categorization schemes that naturalize social differences between human beings. (p. 895)

Similar understandings of the race–ethnic distinction have long played a part in the empirical literature on "the social construction of ethnicity," under which banner the study of "race" has been both presumed and subsumed. In an influential review and reformulation of this body of work, Joane Nagel (1994) wrote that ethnicity was "constructed out of the material of language, religion, culture, appearance, ancestry, or regionality. The location and meaning of particular ethnic boundaries are continuously negotiated, revised and revitalized, both by ethnic group members themselves as well as by outside observers" (pp. 152–153). By emphasizing terms such as *continuously negotiated* and the agency of ethnic group members, Nagel moves us in a direction that is rhetorically open to a more inductive and process-oriented interpretive constructionism. And by including appearance and ancestry in her definition of ethnicity, Nagel also precludes a clear distinction of it from race. Moreover, one of the two examples that she directly discusses is "the black–white ethnic boundary" in the United States. Distinctly racial to critical race theorists, it was clearly subsumed under ethnicity by Nagel.

It is also the case that that 1994 article in *Social Problems*, together with Nagel's close subsequent publications (1995, 1996), were possibly the capstones of the first 15 years of concentrated sociological investigation into the social construction of ethnicity. In the 1980s Nagel and several others, particularly Susan Olzak and Cynthia Enloe, began publishing work in a tradition that I came to know as the *political construction of ethnicity* (Enloe, 1981; Olzak & Nagel, 1986). It was a largely instrumentalist body of work that was influenced by three fairly independent streams of scholarship in sociology and anthropology—but not by Berger and Luckmann (1966).

First of all, for sociologists it was through the American urban sociology of the mid-20th century that "ethnicity" became established as a commonplace dependent variable, something that might or might not emerge out of activities, specifically those of second-wave European immigrants and their progeny. One work cited with particular frequency was a 1976 article in the *American Sociological Review* titled "Emergent Ethnicity" (Yancey, Eriksen, & Juliani, 1976). In the article, the authors defined ethnicity as an interactive phenomenon, referring to "frequent patterns of association and identification with common origins . . . [catalyzed] by structural conditions" (p. 392) that produce concentrations of certain people in jobs, neighborhoods, and organizations. These network ties can promote what anthropologists call *sodality*—an extended social network (both nonkin and kin) distinguished by a satisfying sense of fellowship and intimacy (Hughey & Vidich, 1998), akin to Tönnies's (1957) better-known concept of *Gemeinschaft*. Moreover, under ideal conditions, neighborhoods may approach what Raymond Breton (1964) had called "institutional completeness"—a situation in which

ethnically associated employment, goods, services, and recreation are all available within a single territorial community. Thus, if a critical mass could live almost entirely within a neighborhood, minimally dependent on the rest of society, it was held that vibrant ethnic sodalities could then emerge.[7]

During the same era, notable scholars such as Abner Cohen (1974) in anthropology, as well as Nathan Glazer and Daniel Patrick Moynihan (1975) in sociology, were developing instrumentalist and functionalist interpretations of ethnic groups as political interest groups. They held that because people come together to pursue like interests, then, when interests correspond to ethnicity, people will mobilize and identify along ethnic group lines. One implication of that was that, as culture alone, ethnicity could not survive—that without practical material functions it becomes "merely" symbolic and voluntary (Gans, 1979; Waters, 1990) or "thin" (Cornell & Hartmann, 2007)—that is, decreasingly relevant—resulting in a moribund "atrophy" (Steinberg, 1981, p. 58).

The third stream derives from the highly influential anthropologist Fredrik Barth, who claimed in 1969 that his fellow anthropologists had for too long been excessively concerned with (their own interpretations of) the "cultural content" of ethnic groups. Instead (as in Weber's concept of "social closure") he held that the aspects of culture that are ultimately relevant are those that are made relevant by people when differentiating their group from others:

> The features that are taken into account are not the sum of objective differences, but only those which the actors themselves regard as significant. . . . One cannot predict from first principles which features will be emphasized and made organizationally relevant by the actors. In other words, ethnic categories provide an organizational vessel that may be given varying amounts and forms of content in different socio-cultural systems. (Barth, 1969b, p. 14)

Thus, although a group may survive indefinitely as a recognizable entity (vessel), the characteristics that are accepted as criteria for group membership or for a group's essential "groupness" will vary over time and under different conditions. In addition, in this formulation, ethnicity is systemic—that is, ethnicization is dependent on people recognizing and interacting with members of other putatively ethnic groups within a social setting.

In one of his empirical accounts, Barth (1969a) had investigated the Pathan—a group known to most Westerners these days as the Pashtuns, who live in the mountainous areas of eastern Afghanistan and western Pakistan.[8] Forty years ago Barth described them as a "highly self-aware ethnic group . . . widely extended over an ecologically diverse area and . . . in contact with other populations of diverse cultures" (Barth, 1969a, p. 117), actively maintaining ethnic boundaries between themselves and several other geographically dispersed groups (such as Baluchs, Indus, and Hazaras). Although the "native model" of what demarcates the Pathan includes such things as patrilineal descent, Islam, and Pathan custom (including language), Barth argues that these criteria do not often actually distinguish Pathans:

> The cultural diversity which we observe between different Pathan communities, and which objectively seems to be of an order of magnitude comparable to that between any such community and neighboring non-Pathan groups, does not provide criteria for differentiating persons in terms of ethnic identity. On the contrary, members of this society select only certain cultural traits, and make these the unambiguous criteria for ascription to the ethnic group. (p. 119)

Rather, Barth went on to argue, elements of political autonomy and structural organization were more relevant in the boundary work among people in those interactive settings.

Because of his emphases on agency and systemicity, Barth's approach is *prima facie* closer to the core constructionist tradition of this *Handbook*; I am referring specifically here to the importance of investigating how actors in diverse contexts actually do the work of maintaining group boundaries, which are necessarily constructed by reference to proximate others (cf. Berbrier, 2002b). His formulation explicitly discourages scholars from presuming in advance or from afar which features will be emphasized and made relevant by the actors. Rather, just as Bruno Latour (1987) would later suggest that we study scientific fact *making*, we are enjoined to follow those involved in the construction and to induce from those observations whether there exist patterned characteristics or processes (cf. Berbrier, 2000)—a theme to which I later return.

However, back in the 1980s, most sociologists working in this area took Barth's work in a different sort of constructionist direction, interpreting his disregard for cultural content as a call to explain ethnicity via social structure. It was argued that major structural change (e.g., industrialization, modernization) affects ethnicity and its social systems just as it affects other social institutions. "The formation of an ethnic group is a specific response of a collective to particular historical and structural conditions" wrote Judith Herbstein (1983, p. 31); the main difference between a mere ethnic population (people in the same category) and an ethnic *group* (with a consciousness) is manifest in collective action. Sociologists thus began looking at ethnicity less as emerging from organization and more as emerging from "ethnic mobilization" said to be driven by economic and political competition along group lines. Drawing on the work of organizational sociologist Michael Hannan (1979), Nagel wrote that "political and economic modernization should increase the likelihood that successful ethnic mobilization will occur along broader rather than narrower . . . identities" (Nagel, 1986, p. 95). That is, political and economic modernization was seen to increase the scale of all institutional interaction; for ethnicity, this meant that mobilization around larger scale identities was more likely to be successful in influencing other large-scale entities (e.g., the state, large corporations).

As indicated earlier, all of these strands were drawn on in the development of a "political constructionism" emphasizing the effect of the state (as opposed to economic or other structures) on ethnic mobilization and organization (Nagel, 1986). The idea is that the politicization of ethnicity both increases the level of ethnic mobilization and also constrains that mobilization within officially recognized categories. Sometimes this occurs through policy rules that stipulate membership in one or another group as a criterion for state-sanctioned entitlement, as in some forms of affirmative action. In other cases some states structure political access along ethnic lines, basing political representation on ethnic group affiliation and numbers.

In this vein, political scientist Paul Brass (1991) wrote about "consociation"—a form of political organization whereby representation in a parliament or congress is officially apportioned along ethnic lines. Brass explored this in a case study of India, and a much more current example may be the fragile new system of apportioning of power among Shi'a, Sunni, and Kurdish Iraqis. In such situations, the state has hypostatized ethnicity and affirmed its legitimacy as a political (and presumably social and cultural) device. It has also likely affected the boundaries of specific ethnicities. That is, by empowering some and weakening other group categories, an incentive is created to be recognized as among the empowered and not the weakened, thereby possibly expanding the boundaries of the former and contracting the boundaries of the latter.

The political constructionists were only slightly more tied into the "constructionist" project than are today's critical race activists. But, as I indicated earlier, the sense left from these studies of "ethnicity" has been one that fairly explicitly encourages more inductive and constitutive studies of ethnicity and race. Indeed, an active program of constructionist studies develops out of Barth's work

in anthropology, as well as sociology (including the political construction studies). Increasingly, the focus in these fields is on the meanings and uses of ethnicity to and by people being studied and on their construction of ethnic identity, as well. Indeed, in explicitly constructionist terms, Nagel (1994) anointed "identity and culture" as the basic "building blocks" of ethnicity. So I move on now to discuss those two building blocks.

Constructing Authentic Cultures

Ordinarily, scholars and social actors understand ethnicity as some kind of collection of cultural things. That is, almost every definition or explanation of ethnicity includes culture as a component, and sometimes the singularly necessary component. If that is the case—or, more precisely, if that is believed to be the case in a given setting—"cultural" can become the key interactive signifier for a designation as "ethnic" versus other categorical statuses. Put another way, in order to be recognized and treated as genuinely ethnic by others in social interaction, a group may first have to be recognized as "cultural" (Berbrier, 2004).

In the context of political construction, then, when ratifying one or another group as officially ethnic, a government might have to confront, or claim, that group's legitimacy as a cultural group. Laurie Kroshus Medina (1997), for example, illustrated how postcolonial governments that wished to define the Belizean nation as "multiethnic" thereby became involved in officially asserting and defining a national cultural sameness and subnational ethnic cultural differences, such that throughout this process "the idea of culture took centre stage" (p. 766). However, the state recognized the mutability of culture only in the abstract and imposed an ethnic classification system that conveyed images of immutable ethnicities rooted in long-standing customs and traditions. Each of the official groups—Creole, Mestizo, Garifuna, Yucatec, Mopan, and

Kekchi Maya—came to be associated with a distinct ancestry, language, and culture. Yet Medina cited data indicating that many Belizians have difficulty identifying with any single category, and that the two largest categories—Mestizo and Creole (respectively 44% and 30% of the population)—nominally reflect their own historical novelty and constructedness.

In another vein, Nagel (1994) presciently invoked the then-recent turn to cultural analysis in the social movements literature (e.g., Benford & Snow, 2000; Williams, 2003) and its potential for exploring how ethnic activists might engage available (and, by implication, broad and general) cultural themes and symbols to achieve their goals: "Ethnic movements often challenge negative hegemonic ethnic images and institutions by redefining the meaning of ethnicity in appealing ways or by using cultural symbols to effectively dramatize grievances and demands" (Nagel, 1994, p. 166). In my research on gay, Deaf,[9] and white racial activists I looked at a very similar phenomenon—how activists challenged negative images by claiming that, because of culture, their groups were akin to groups that were more generally recognized as ethnic or racial minorities and hence were equally legitimate (or "normal"). The "cultural symbols" they used were very often associated with other groups, particularly black Americans and civil rights movement icons (Berbrier, 2002b). One example would be claiming that discriminatory treatment is akin to being sent "to the back of the bus"—a powerful cultural symbol of unfair discrimination in the wake of the legal and cultural successes of the civil rights movement (see, e.g., Berbrier, 2002a, p. 3; Berbrier & Pruett, 2006, pp. 271, 274).

More often, culture is presented as constructed from the bottom up. The putative culture of a putative racial or ethnic group is never "simply an historical legacy . . . a shopping cart that comes to us already loaded with a set of historical cultural goods. Rather we construct culture by picking and choos-

ing items from the shelves of the past and the present" (Nagel, 1994, p. 162). For example, Zuleyka Zevallos (2003) described how the Australian "Latin" ethnicity of South and Central Americans is assembled by invoking food, language, music and dancing, and festivity. For Yolanda Flores Niemann and her colleagues (Niemann, Romero, Arredondo, & Rodriguez, 1999), Mexican ethnicity in the United States is a combination of three characteristics: (1) cultural uniqueness (family values, work ethic, and food and festivity), (2) identity (restricted to "heritage/roots" here), and (3) "minority status" (discrimination, low status, and collective struggle for justice). Festivity was also at the heart of Kathleen Conzen's (1989) interpretation of 19th-century German ethnicity in the United States. In all of these cases, constructing "culture" was central to ethnicity construction. It effectively represented the ends to which actors were striving, and the interpretations were that in expressing and highlighting those chosen cultural markers the actors were engaging in ethnic boundary work.

A closely related approach is to look at how groups become involved in "the reconstruction of historical culture, and the construction of new culture" (Nagel, 1994, p. 162). Thus, in the introduction to their edited volume on ethnic folklore, Stephen Stern and John Cicala (1991) indicate that "it is as common for traditional ethnic sentiments to be modified, to take on new meanings, to be communicated through newly created folklore, as it is for recently introduced practices to be labeled as traditional" (p. xii). Similarly, historians Eric Hobsbawm and Terence Ranger's influential book on "invented traditions" described how " 'traditions' which appear or claim to be old are often quite recent in origin and sometimes invented" (Hobsbawm, 1983, p. 1).

An important example, because it also became a cautionary tale for researchers, is anthropologist Allan Hanson's 1989 article "The Making of the Maori: Culture Invention and its Logic" in *American Anthropolo-*

gist. Hanson traced the origins of a putatively ancient oral tradition among the Maori in New Zealand to the 20th century. Although part of what Hanson was doing was adding to the long-standing reflexive turn in his discipline, wherein anthropologists became increasingly concerned about their role in "inventing" rather than just describing "culture" and "cultures" (Barth, 1969a; Clifford & Marcus, 1986; Wagner, 1981), he also made a broader claim, saying that "anthropological interpretations and misinterpretations have joined the contributions of other scholars, government officials, and Maoris themselves (including some Maori anthropologists) in the inventive process" (Hanson, 1989, p. 890). The resulting uproar, especially among Maori activists, laid bare what may be an inherent conflict of interest between constructionist scholarship and some kinds of racial or ethnic activism. Immanuel Wallerstein (1987) pithily put it this way:

> Maybe a people is something that is supposed to be inconstant in form. But if so, why the passion? Maybe because no one is supposed to observe upon the inconstancy. If I am right, then we have a very curious phenomenon indeed— one whose central features are the reality of inconstancy and the denial of this reality. (pp. 379–380)

In many ways this "reality of inconstancy"— the mutability of cultures, the shifting boundaries of a racial group, and so forth—is the theoretical soul of constructionist inquiry (whereas empirical accounts of such inconstancy are its heart). But "the denial of this reality" is implicit in many activist claims of authenticity. Thus, for activists, part of constructing their race or ethnicity often involves skillfully managing the impression that it is *not* constructed—that is, rather, essential, primordial, or even just ancient— because it is from this primordial essence that it draws its unique meaning and potential for powerful forms of collective action. People who strongly feel the reality of their race or ethnicity *as primordial* (typically people with a strong ethnic or racial "identity") will logically encounter some dissonance when trying to reconcile that with constructionist accounts of their "groupness." So this premise can run up against some real-world resistance. Wallerstein's explanation of the "passion" seems accurate: You just cannot have everyone running around reflexively remarking on the inconstancy.

The constructionist response to such potential resistance is twofold. One is to point out the potency inherent in constructionism's skepticism of received wisdom, as when Nagel noted the many instances in which ethnic activists can benefit from constructionist work and use it as a "counter-hegemonic" weapon for the weak to undermine essentialist and inferiorizing ideologies of dominant groups (Nagel, 1996, Chap. 3). The other is a more constitutive response that turns authenticity into the topic of examination. In this regard, Cornell and Hartmann (2007) argue that the constructionist stance is one of "constructed primordiality." Analysts can (and should) simultaneously recognize that although the peoplehood is constructed, the most successful peoples are constructed precisely so that the people will *feel* as if they were primordial: "The best-constructed identities show the least evidence of their construction. Assumed and sometimes even celebrated by those who carry them and by the society at large, they come to seem natural. Those who doubt constructionism verify its success" (Cornell & Hartmann, 1998, pp. 93–94). So, many constructionists argue that authenticity itself can, and should, become a theme in constructionist studies. As Brubaker (2004) wrote: "Reification is precisely what ethno-political entrepreneurs are in the business of doing. . . . As analysts we should certainly try to *account* [italics in original] for the ways in which—and conditions under which . . . this powerful crystallization of group feeling, can work" (p. 10).

Historian Karl Hagstrom Miller's (2001) analysis of the construction of Mexican ethnicity in San Antonio's Market Square incorporates both of the preceding responses and offers an interesting twist on the notion of authenticity as a tool of subordinate groups. Miller describes Market Square as a place that in the early 20th century was transformed from a cosmopolitan and multicultural economic center into a tourist destination—a "site of invented Mexican traditionalism . . . ethnic homogeneity and cultural authenticity" (p. 209). As the neighborhood in which the market is situated became increasingly segregated, efforts were made to attract white tourists to the market by selling it as a site of authentic Mexican culture. This resulted in a very consciously "performed ethnic essentialism," the style and content of which ratified stereotypes of Mexican culture in order to satisfy tourist expectations and pay the bills. As Miller interprets it, the locals (i.e., the ethnic performers) had only rational economic interest in this version of their ethnicity, a version to which they claimed no primordial attachment. In this case, it was not the insider activists who were most concerned with authenticity, but the outsider tourists who were sightseeing and paying to see authentic places. Miller's delightful article also points us toward thinking of constructions as emplaced phenomena (cf. Gieryn, 2000): It is not that these people do not feel their Mexican identity; it is that the ethnicity being constructed is particular to the material site at which it is performed.

It is also important to note that within putative ethnic and racial communities there is usually some debate about "authenticity." Indeed, the most active claimsmakers become strongly vested in legitimating (or maintaining the legitimacy of) some version of authenticity and spend a lot of time and energy patrolling the group boundaries, as they see them marked. One example was my examination of discursive claims for an essential Deaf culture. Among some people, being unable to hear would make people "small-d deaf," but significantly more was expected in order to be an authentic member

of the (large-D) Deaf culture—especially a native fluency in American Sign Language (Berbrier, 2000).

Another take on this issue regards the controversial question of whether poor black American schoolchildren patrol racial boundaries by accusing their scholarly cohorts of "acting white" (Fordham & Ogbu, 1986). In an interesting and critical engagement with this view, Prudence Carter (2003) provides several examples of in-group boundary work, describing such episodes in terms of "nondominant" cultural capital. Meanwhile, in *Real Black: Adventures in Racial Sincerity*, John Jackson (2005) queries authenticity itself, arguing that it is too often used to impose clarity and fixity on what is inherently ambiguous and protean.

A Note on Studying Race and/or Ethnicity as Identities

Before moving on to discuss identity studies directly, I first caution the reader that the study of "ethnicity and race" construction has often been conflated with the study of "identity" construction. Such was the case with several chapters in Werner Sollors's (1989) edited volume *The Invention of Ethnicity* that were limited to autobiographical accounts or literary analyses of individual experiences and "identities." More generally, in the racial and ethnic arena of cultural studies, "identity" is routinely indicated as the topic, but frequently in an idiographic style (see note 2 at the end of the chapter and the subsection "Problem Area 3" later). More rigorous accounts—in which the main aim is to contribute insights about social identity processes—are offered by social psychologists, some of whom explicitly reduce race and ethnicity to social identities (Howard, 2000). In the symbolic interactionist tradition, this means that the research is about "the self" rather than "race" or "ethnicity" per se.

On the other hand, sometimes scholars who say they are talking about racial or ethnic "identity" and who even limit their discussion to such terminology seem to be getting at much more than that. Cornell and Hartmann's (2007) signal text *Ethnicity and Race*, for example, was subtitled *Making Identities in a Changing World*. The title seems to reduce ethnicity and race to "making identities," but the text itself clearly addresses far more than that. Moreover, scholarship that is characterized as examining "racial or ethnic identity" has also tended to be more agent-centered in focus and more likely to address the means and manners by which people adopt these socially constructed categories as meaningful or affect that meaning itself. Scholars likely to identify themselves as "constructionists" tend to see these "how" questions about messy and seemingly indeterminate processes from category to meaning and back as central to their enterprise. So I restrict the following discussion to the sort of "identity" studies that leverage actors' identity orientations in order to elucidate ethnic and/or racial processes (rather than the inverse: using ethnicity to study identity).

Race and Ethnicity as Fluid Sets of Claims

In a series of articles and a textbook, Stephen Cornell laid out an orientation to the construction of race and ethnicity that focuses on process, meaning, interaction, and identity (e.g., 1988, 1996; Cornell & Hartmann, 2007). The creation of ethnic or racial (or other) groups, he wrote,

> is a complex process that takes place through extended interactions between particular populations and their social environments. People claim certain identities, reflecting their own notions of who they are and of the relevant bases of action. These identities are variously embedded in organization, producing group boundaries which may be variable or fixed, highly organized or not, permeable or impermeable, and so forth. (1988, p. 27)

At root, then, ethnicity and race are recognized here as a series of interactive processes involving sets of claims that go in many directions (cf. Loseke, 1999):

> People's notions of who they are, and their ability to organize and act accordingly, are shaped by the ideas, interests, and actions of others, and not least by the conceptions other populations may have of the group. Self-concept and organization, in other words, are to some extent asserted and to some extent imposed or assigned. Group formation–the emergence of a self-conscious, more or less solidary population–is a product of the complex interplay between these processes of assertion and assignment. (Cornell, 1988, p. 27)

Although some might find such a paragraph rather dissembling ("to some extent," "more or less"), the analytic language of assignment and assertion–the idea that the process involves a dialectic between "what you think your ethnicity is, versus what they think your ethnicity is" (Nagel, 1994, p. 154)–and the image of extended interplay among populations and in contexts accords well with myriad studies across the range of disciplines. That is, diverse literatures evince strikingly similar notions of such complex interplay among categories and group identities (e.g., Roosens, 1989; Whisnant, 1983).

Perhaps the most enduring approach to this identity dialectic is found in research on "panethnicity." Initially developing out of the political constructionist school reviewed earlier, *panethnicity* refers to agglomerations of different ethnic groups into a larger category based on some putative cultural or linguistic similarity. The theme in these studies is that some people are effectively targeted by more established and influential people who make certain that official and/or dominant categorical schemes stick, at least to some degree (assignment). However, in the wake of this, the newly constituted panethnic or racial category develops a collective consciousness, and people become actively involved in characterizing their own identities (assertion). Common examples include the five major "racial" categories in the United States: black, white, Indian, Latino/Latina, and Asian American.[10]

The most influential text has been Yen Le Espiritu's (1992) study, *Asian American Panethnicity*. Espiritu described how the weakening of economic, residential, and linguistic barriers among second- and third-generation descendants of Asian immigrants yielded increased interaction and familiarity, particularly on college campuses, beginning in the 1960s. Inspired by the civil rights activism of black Americans during that decade, many of these young activists presented themselves as uniting to confront distinctly "Asian" experiences of oppression. Associations and organizations were formed that increasingly reflected and used the name *Asian American*. In doing all of these things, they became "cultural entrepreneurs creating a community of culture out of diverse Asian peoples" (Espiritu, 1992, p. 52).

Espiritu's detailed listing and description of the activists, community organizers, and their formal associations fits well with what I have described programmatically as *ethnicity work* in an *ethnicity industry* (Berbrier, 2000; see also Harris, Chapter 12, this volume). Specifically, I defined ethnicity work as "making claims on behalf of a putative ethnic community, or the collective representation of ETHNICITY" (p. 79). *Ethnicity workers* include the organization leaders, teachers, professional or lay heritage preservers, pluralism advocates, and so on who constitute the webbed networks of people and institutions at the heart of any ethnicity industry. Building on actor-network theory (Latour, 1987), I suggested moreover that when associations of any ethnic kind (e.g., social, cognitive, associational, etc.) are bound to ETHNICITY, they make the concept more stable and obdurate. Similarly, when such associations are bound to a particular group, they make it more likely that claims made on behalf of the concept or group will be recognized as ethnic claims.

An example of this web of associations and an ethnicity industry can be inferred from Espiritu's (1992) account of how discrimination and prejudice fostered "reactive solidarity" along panethnic lines. She reported on the horrific case of Vincent Chin, who was murdered by a disgruntled autoworker during the height of the anti-Japanese fear mongering of the 1970s. The assailant either mistook Chin for Japanese or did not care to distinguish among East Asians. The incident galvanized pan-Asian organizing in Detroit, and the ethnicity industry networks were crucial to that development: Espiritu reports that the Japanese, Korean, and Filipino community leaders who came together already knew each other because, prior to that time, many had worked together on the city's ethnic festivals. These urban multicultural festivals, which are found in most large cities, create and reflect local ethnicity industries. In this case the network of heterogeneous associations brought together "experienced hands from the NAACP, the Anti-Defamation League of the B'nai Brith, and the Detroit Association of Black Organizations [who] provided invaluable contacts and information" (Espiritu, 1992, p. 150). Elsewhere, Espiritu describes the institutions that are built (be they Asian American studies programs or ethnic studies programs) and how they, too, legitimate and buttress historically new claims of common bond and experience across groups.

This and other empirical work dovetails well with Cornell's point about "extended interactions," but only if it is amended to note that these interactions occur not only between groups and their environments, as Cornell had them, but also within putative groups. Thus, in Espiritu's study, Asian American identity and culture were insignificant prior to activism, and it was only "by participating in these pan-Asian institutions [that] Asian Americans [began] to develop common views of themselves and of one another, and similar interpretations of their experiences and of the larger society" (1992, p. 165). Similarly, Nazli Kibria's (1997) interviews with Chinese and Korean Americans who were neither ethnic nor panethnic activists revealed a consonant pattern: "Asian American" identification seemed to be a function of interactively sharing similar experiences—discrimination, slurs, stereotypes, immigrant narratives, and childhood experiences. Of course, much of this interactive "sharing" is messy—laden with conflict and disagreement—and Espiritu documented multiple debates among activists about the "Asian" label, its relevance, and its reality.

Moreover, just as macrolevel historical and cultural research indicates the fluidity of categories, identities can also change with changes in contexts of social interaction. As Nagel put it, "a Native American is a Pine Ridge Sioux in Wounded Knee, South Dakota, but an Indian in Rapid City" (1986, p. 96). She calls this the "layering" of ethnic identities. Similarly, in Kibria's (1997) study, one Chinese American discussed her upbringing in this manner:

> Chinese parents are stricter than American parents. Study hard, no dating till you're in college, that kind of thing. It was different for my [white] friends. . . . I do know that a lot of other Asian kids go through the same thing, having strict parents and rules. It's an Asian thing. (p. 537)

Thus, for Kibria's respondents, some things were interpreted as immigrant experiences, others as Asian, and still others as Korean or Chinese. She argues that this is not a zero-sum identity game—that is, the strengthening of a panethnic identity does not necessarily entail a weaker "ethnic" identity (Chinese, Korean, etc.).[11]

In general, these kinds of studies, in which I would generally include my own work, move us still further away from objective and toward interpretive constructionism but retain a highly naturalistic approach to reality (of ethnicity as well as culture) by focusing on how its substance is constructed rather than the more ethnomethodological and interpretive focus on practices of con-

struction (cf. Gubrium & Holstein, 1997; Harris, Chapter 12, this volume). Thus, on the one hand, much of this work is animated by symbolic interactionist concerns—that is, the research asks how social actors manage and strategically present meanings of and for particular groups (see Gubrium & Holstein, 1997, on the "performative"). Yet, on the other hand, the work retains a focus on the reality of representations (e.g., as "claims" and "frames") and thereby on the role of representations as both enabling and constraining devices (Williams, 2003). This is rather different from those studies of race and ethnicity—as either identity or culture—that take us decidedly into ethnomethodological territory (at least in theoretical terms), wherein race and ethnicity are accomplished only in and by social interactions, such that the interpretive processes involved in calling things "racial" and/or "ethnic" entirely constitute the phenomena (cf. Gubrium & Holstein, 1997; Holstein & Miller, 2003; Pollner, 1974).[12] It is to these that we now turn.

Ethnicity as Linguistic Accomplishment

The findings that I elaborate in this section generally accord well with ethnomethodologist Michael Moerman's (1993) refusal to define ethnicity completely:

> What ethnographers have found out during the last 30 years requires [that any list of characteristics defining ethnicity] be unordered and incomplete. Each of the factors of ethnicity is itself a social accomplishment. What counts as a language among languages, like Hindi and Urdu, and what as a mere dialect, like *langue d'Oc*, is produced and contested no less than the histories that transform chaotic events into a story about "a people." . . . No factor is always the one critical to ethnicity. (p. 88)

It is in this tradition that Alan Hansen (2005) analyzed a school board meeting, called to discuss the pros and cons of a proposed charter school. Hansen combined "membership categorization analysis" and conversation analysis[13] in order to investigate "how ethnicity is locally organized"—that is, how it "is assembled as an issue of particular importance and is utilized as a resource" (p. 68) in meeting participants' discourse. As a resource, ethnicity is used to accomplish mundane goals of interaction. It is "a situated practical accomplishment" (p. 63) that emerges as the "participants attend to moment-to-moment exigencies" (p. 69) of their conversation. Hansen notes that because of its sensitive nature (at least in this conversation) the participants often talk around ethnicity rather than addressing it directly, characterizing the discourse of one participant in terms of " 'off record,' ambiguous, and sporadic *hearable*" [original emphasis] references to and about ethnicity in talk (Hansen, 2005, p. 85).

Strictly speaking, the techniques of conversation analysis are designed to elucidate the "conversational machinery of interaction" (Gubrium & Holstein, 1997, p. 55)—how talk is structured and how social order is thereby accomplished. But because of their affiliation with ethnomethodology, many conversation analysts veer into more substantive concerns about the accomplishment of particular social realities—in Hansen's case, "ethnicity." Similarly, in an article titled "Language and Negotiation of Ethnic/Racial Identity among Dominican Americans," Benjamin Bailey (2000) described how phenotypically black Dominican youths may resist being labeled as black in favor of a Hispanic identity. "In using language to resist such hegemonic social categorization," Bailey wrote, "the Dominican second generation is contributing to the transformation of existing social categories and the constitution of new ones in the US" (p. 555; see also Waters, 1994).

Other approaches also focus on ethnicity at the level of talk and draw similar conclusions using different methods. Some approaches to social identity theory have moved in a decidedly constructionist direction, with an empirical predilection for analyzing talk (Billig, 1985; Potter & Wetherell, 1987).[14] In this vein, Verkuyten, De Jong, and Masson (1995) emphasized fluidity in how native Dutch people in inner-city Rotterdam characterize themselves (the "Dutch") and various others when asked to engage in focus group discussions about "social renewal" (or "urban renewal," in U.S. parlance) in an ethnically diverse inner-city neighborhood. Although underlying all the discourse was the basic "us versus them" divide that is central to this scholarly perspective, in the discourse "the others" were placed into a highly variable list of broad categories, including "foreigners," "migrants," "Turks," "Surinamese," and still more subcategories. Moreover, in terms of the content or characterization of these groups, the researchers held that the construction of ethnic categories in talk was so variable that "it makes it difficult to define ethnic categories as fixed sets of attributes" (Verkuyten et al., 1995, p. 263).

Finally, and somewhat in contrast, ethnolinguists focusing on the social construction of ethnicity have noted that the *stability* of ethnic identity is, as Natalie Schilling-Estes (2004) put it, "reflected in, and partially created by, each interlocutor's overall alignment with the ethnolinguistic patterns associated with his own ethnic group" (p. 190)—patterns that have been quantitatively evidenced in sociolinguistic analyses. But that overall stability and alignment will still, of course, vary by context. This was Schilling-Estes's message in "Constructing Ethnicity in Interaction," which focused on such patterns in Robeson County, North Carolina—an area with a long history of recognized divisions among Lumbee Indians, blacks, and whites. These divisions are manifested in many ways (church membership, residential patterns), among which are divergent English dialects. The article focuses its empirical eye on a conversation between two residents and friends, one who self-identifies as African American (Alex), the other as Lumbee (Lou). It measures the ethnic components of their discussion as it moved across a variety of topics. Focusing on Alex's use of Robeson County African American Vernacular English and Lou's Robeson County Lumbee English, Schilling-Estes found more "ethnic distance" when the topic was local race relations and less when the topic was "family and friends" or even global race relations. In other words, when talking about the local blacks, Lumbee, and whites of Robeson County, the participants' linguistic performances were more distinctly "ethnic."

Conclusion: Race, Ethnicity, and the Constructionist Project

Over the past several decades scholars in the humanities and the social sciences have been proclaiming, in increasingly certain terms, that race and ethnicity are socially constructed. Many now believe that this constructedness is common knowledge (but see Morning, 2004).[15] At the very least, this does seem to be a basic premise of almost all social science scholarship on race and ethnicity. In this field constructionism is problematic not because it is resisted but because everyone wants a piece of it. Constructionism is hot in racial and ethnic studies. (Hence, I have only scratched the surface in this review). Yet although this may reflect a triumph of sorts, it may also indicate that constructionism is being spread too thinly, as others in this volume have noted (see, e.g., Best, Chapter 3, and Harris, Chapter 12, this volume).

Indeed, many published works that invoke the term *constructionism* have little to do with constructionism as it is articulated in this *Handbook* and they seem to operate with only a very general sense of the theoretical work, evincing very little commitment to constructionism as an approach to scholarship. Many of them were so far afield that I did not discuss them here, and they therefore escape direct critique. On the other hand, those that are a bit more in tune with

the constructionist project are both included earlier and critiqued in this section. So, I conclude here by discussing three things that I find somewhat disconcerting about the scholarship herein reviewed and suggest an orientation to overcome these. Specifically, my concerns include (1) the neo-essentialism expressed by critical race theorists, (2) the general focus (e.g., among scholars in the "construction of ethnicity" school) on single cases of putatively bounded groups, and (3) the conflation of race and/or ethnicity with identity. Before addressing these directly, however, I will discuss what I see as the root of these problems, and hence what must be acknowledged to overcome them: insufficient attention to the basic constructionist idea that scholars ought to presume as little as possible about what is being constructed and analytically enter construction processes while they are "in the making" (Latour, 1987). Although this is an argument I have been advancing throughout my career (Berbrier, 1996), here I draw more directly from the works of Rogers Brubaker and Mara Loveman, whose recent prescriptions regarding the social construction of "race" are almost interchangeable with suggestions that I have made about both "ethnicity" and "minority" status.[16]

Taking Constructing Seriously

Let us be clear: From a constructionist perspective, ethnicity and race are neither culture, nor skin color, nor power, nor intellectual capacity, nor some set of such characteristics. Rather, and emphatically, they are claims about these and innumerable other possible things. Races and ethnicities are constituted when people (often via institutions such as states) divide themselves along what they perceive to be racial or ethnic lines. Culture, language, or appearance are devices commonly used by people to delineate, categorize, contrast, and identify. It is in this regard that I explored "Ethnicity in the Making" (Berbrier, 1996, 2000) and

"Making Minorities" (Berbrier, 2002b), and Mara Loveman (1999b) urged "Taking Making Seriously." Loveman (1999a) wrote:

> The assumption that "races" exist as collective actors cannot be the starting point if the goal is to understand what "race" means, and how, and with what consequences, it operates as a principle of vision and division of the social world across time and place. The analyst should focus on the groupness itself, and hence on the processes of boundary making and unmaking in relation to systems of categorization and processes of social inclusion and closure. This requires an analytical framework that is not built on a reified conceptualization of "race." (p. 894)

Both Loveman and Brubaker (e.g., 2004) have put this in terms of that constructionist methodological principle that is regularly misunderstood and rather difficult to implement—that our analytic vocabulary must distinguish between their "categories of practice" and our "categories of analysis." In other words, we must be careful not to conflate social actors' meaningful uses of race, ethnicity, minority, nation, state, and so forth with those meaningful uses of analysts. This is the same distinction that is at the heart of the claimsmaking approach that I have outlined (Berbrier, 2000). Whereas Loveman and Brubaker draw from Pierre Bourdieu (e.g., 1991) and use his terminology, I derive the point largely from Malcolm Spector and John Kitsuse's (1977) *Constructing Social Problems* and Bruno Latour's (1987) *Science in Action*. It is also practically identical to Pollner's (1987) entreaty that ethnomethodologists not confuse our "topics" with their "resources."[17] Although there are myriad difficulties in consistently accomplishing this distinction (the "methodological horrors," as Woolgar, 1988, depicted them), we—at least those of us who are "contextual constructionists"—feel that these can be worked through or at least are preferable to the alternatives (see Best, Chapter 3, this volume).[18]

Problem Area 1: The Neo-Essentialism of Scholarly Activism

For the critical theorists, the distinction between categories of analysis and practice is rarely engaged. Doing so, I believe, would denude them of their *raison d'être*, which is to advance not the constructionist project but a particular political program for social justice. That is, in reading this material one gets a very clear sense—usually rather quickly—that it is not about construction processes but about racial stratification and, moreover, that constructionism is important only if and to the extent that it can move us in the direction of "racial justice." In this manner, it becomes a curious form of constructionism in that, while it trumpets the "social construction" of race, it simultaneously deploys a highly selective essentialism.

Identity-based activist scholars, in particular, confront a practical contradiction between their officially antiessentialist scholarly standpoint and a form of activism that often urges people to rally around a given racial or ethnic label. As discussed earlier in the section on authenticity, it is difficult to ask people to care profoundly about status in a category if you are saying (to other people) that it is a fiction of sorts, because something akin to a primordialist meaningfulness seems necessary in order to rally masses to make personal sacrifices for change, even for just cause.

The putative resolution to this conflict is to emphasize the structured, hard reality of race—or at least racial things. Critical race theorists hold that we all know what race is and that we must deal with it as a hard social fact. Race thereby is reified behind empirical observations of power relationships and becomes a contingent construction, but, as we saw above, one with "intrinsic" properties. Moreover, if "race" is otherwise deployed in practice either by scholars or people in society, then they are just wrong—perhaps falsely conscious. In this approach there is no use in distinguishing between our categories of analysis and their categories of practice, because we are not interested in reality construction processes but in truth and justice (as we know them to be).

Do not get me wrong here: Critical race theorists have produced an incredible body of fascinating and important scholarship in a short time, particularly vis-à-vis whiteness. Overall, they constitute a very prolific, engaged, committed, and well-networked community of researchers. I find much of this material immensely useful for my own work.[19] But as I see it, because their primary interests and reasons for being "critical" sociologists are rooted in activism and/or ideology, these scholars become captive to certainties that will help them pursue those interests and are hostile—in the political sense—to alternative formulations that might not help the activist project. At the very least, they are not deriving much at all from Berger and Luckmann and their intellectual progeny (or cousins) and are unconcerned about meaning construction processes in general. More substantively, for many constructionists there are limitations when the a priori motivation is uncovering how racial constructs serve the dominant group or its ideology, rather than uncovering social processes more broadly involved in reality construction. Although there is much to be gained by focusing on the construction activities of governments and/or the economically powerful and/or the whites, reducing our constructionist outlook to these leaves readers without an appreciation of the diversity, complexity, contingency, and nuance of construction processes.

Problem Area 2: Single-Group Focus and Inattention to the Very Idea of Race or Ethnicity

In order for constructionism to develop, we need more openness to cross-case comparative study—the kind of detail-oriented inquiry that connects cases not only with each other but also with the "very ideas" of ethnic-

ity and race (Berbrier, 2000). There remains insufficient attention to comparison across places, times, and groups and especially to cross-continental work. This may be difficult to overcome because of two prevailing zeitgeists—a methodological taste for the depth of case studies and an empirical penchant for reducing either race or ethnicity to identity.

Moreover, there is a postmodernist sensibility among many scholars attracted to "construction" that, because of its localizing implications, seems to have become associated with a dogmatic resistance to tracing connections among people or groups. For some, this is a straightforward humanistic faith that each individual or group is unique and special and that we ought to respect that. Others see such connections in more political terms—that efforts to accumulate a more general knowledge will inevitably become imperialistic impositions of one sort or another. Either might result in statements such as this one: "There is no guarantee that the knowledge [of racial and ethnic studies] will be cumulative or even that the background training will offer any insight into ethnic division in a new location. The diligent student can only use his/her familiarity with other examples to guess the significant aspects of ethnic division for a new set of people" (Bhattacharyya, 2003, p. 525).[20] I emphatically disagree and do not see how such a planned incommensurability advances the constructionist project. My own comparative work on frame diffusion (Berbrier, 2002b, 2004) empirically shows this happening, as do other comparative studies in this and other areas.

This problem is not merely a philosophical one but a methodological issue of unit of analysis. Even in the literature that is "most constructionist," the putative racial and ethnic groups "seem to be always already in existence" (Sollors, 1989). Although the best studies look nicely at how groups are constructed, performed, strengthened, and legitimated, the great majority of those presume "ethnicity-ness" or "race-ness" in advance. And this lends itself well to ideological posturing about cultural uniqueness and against comparative analysis. That is, because scholars ordinarily "know" (presume in advance) *who the ethnic groups are*, this means that they see the categorization process as rather settled and unproblematic. In this sense, although they fervently eschew crass primordialism (the idea that ethnicity is rooted in kinship or genetics), they seem oblivious to their own essentialism (the idea that there *is* something fundamental and even immutable about certain groups that makes *them* ethnic or racial or neither). This very problem is also inherent in the metaphor of ethnicity as either vessel (Barth, 1969b) or shopping cart (Nagel, 1994), mentioned earlier (the idea that a label such as *Pathan* or *Cree* are things into which varying characteristics may be deposited or removed over time). Although this directs us to explore evolutionary changes in the meaning of a group, it also indicates that no matter what changes are made, the group will nonetheless always remain an "ethnic" or "racial"one.

My point is that beyond all the careful defining and distinguishing analytically between ethnicity and race, insufficient attention is given to the "very idea" of race (vs. a racial group) and especially to the "very idea" of ethnicity (vs. an ethnic group; cf. Berbrier, 2000). In this way much of the literature is simultaneously antiprimordialist—in that the meaning and makeup of the group varies—and yet, once again, essentialist—in that there is such a thing as ethnicity and race and that this "vessel" is always an example of it.

Problem Area 3: Conflating Race and Ethnicity with Racial and Ethnic Identity

The constant and confusing interchangeability of "race and ethnicity" with "racial and ethnic identity" in many studies derives in part, I believe, from both of the problems addressed here. As with the problems of critical theory, we have here "identity" researchers whose primary interest is not race and ethnicity construction processes. But in this case, the problem is not the lack of interest in the construction process (as with the critical theorists); it is rather a lack of interest in "race" and/or "ethnicity." And whereas critical race theorists know very well what their primary concerns are, many of the identity researchers seem to genuinely think that they are studying ethnicity and race rather than identity (as it is manifested in ethnic and racial terms). Hence the ambiguous terminology.

Although there is, of course, nothing wrong with studying identity processes, it is misleading to think that we are thereby studying ethnicity and race. We must, therefore, get far "beyond identity" (Brubaker & Cooper, 2000). We need to attend to ethnic and racial meanings not only as identification for individuals but also as collective representations, as symbols (Berbrier, 2002b). Ethnicity and race are cultural tools—things used as resources in social action. In Brubaker's (2004) cognitive formulation, race and ethnicity are "perspectives on the world." Methodologically, there are a variety of approaches to accomplishing this, mostly focusing on discourse and action (e.g., Benford & Snow, 2003; Loseke, 1999), which are compatible both with more objectivist constructionism (which might offer historical and sociological accounts of culture) and with more ethnomethodologically inspired interpretive constructionism.

In summary, paying closer attention to the distinction between race and ethnicity as categories of practice provides a number of advantages. Focusing on the actors' practices directs us away from the essentialist traps we get into in our analytic work. Focusing on the action directs us away from reducing race and ethnicity to mere identity. Focusing on process entails neither defining these as stable things nor defining them in advance, thereby avoiding that tortuous "casuistry." And focusing on processes also brings us to a level of abstraction that facilitates cross-case comparison, thereby promoting an accumulation of scientific knowledge about the social construction of race and ethnicity.

Acknowledgments

I would like to thank Jim Holstein and Jay Gubrium for their guidance and sage comments on an earlier draft of this chapter. This chapter would also not have been possible were it not for Elaine Pruett's hard work of tracking down and organizing volumes of material. I would also like to thank Linda Vaughan and the Interlibrary Loan staff at the University of Alabama in Huntsville for being so patient and diligent with our avalanche of requests, and our student assistants Sara Neale and Alisha Sullivan for their invaluable help in proofreading the document and developing the References section.

Notes

1. In setting about to write this chapter I undertook the impossible task of collecting and cataloguing everything; in practice, to procure as many relevant articles and books as resources allowed. Frankly, most of this hard work was ably done by my research assistant, Elaine Pruett, with my guidance. We relied most heavily on *Sociological Abstracts*, which focuses on sociology, and the sociological approach dominates here. But the database includes sources from all social sciences and humanities. We also searched via public Internet search engines, generally looking for published material that appeared to have *some* connection to and *some* interest in discussing race and/or ethnicity as constructs.

No doubt the choices I made excluded some approaches. In particular, I discuss less material from the literary criticism side of cultural studies scholarship than was uncovered in our search; this choice reflects either on my own inadequacies or on the limitations of that approach.

2. For example, in the late 19th- and early 20th-century United States, the terms *race* and *nationality group* were regularly invoked to refer to groups of immigrants from Europe who would become "the ethnics" a few decades later, whereas blacks would continue to be seen (by whites) as *the* "racial" group. Meanwhile, "nationality" is still the preferred term in parts of Europe (Brubaker, 2004). Yet "nation" is also sometimes

applied these days to some groups heretofore labeled "tribal" (as in the First Nations of Canada). And so on.

3. There is a large literature connecting ethnicity and race to "nation," and I use some of that here, but I do not delve deeply as "nationality" is addressed in Stråth, Chapter 32, in this *Handbook*.

4. In a thoughtful discussion, Omi and Winant (1994) avoid the essentializing terminology of intrinsic properties and define race as a signifier of conflict. Specifically, "race is a concept which signifies and symbolizes social conflicts and interests by referring to different types of human bodies" (p. 55).

5. Of course, some disagree with this characterization, or at least its emphasis. Christopher Taylor (2004), for example, argues that divisions in Rwanda among Tutsi, Hutu, and Twa predated European colonization.

6. But see Goldberg (1990), who traces the intellectual deconstruction of race to the Enlightenment, and Stuart Hall (1989), who traces the crisis of collective identity to a decentering arising from countercurrents within Western thought to rationalism—in the writings of Marx, Freud, de Saussure, Nietzsche, and Foucault. In these crowds, of course, Berger and Luckmann are not found.

7. Contemporary versions of this approach are echoed in studies of immigrant enclaves (e.g., Portes & Jensen, 1989).

8. This is the group that spawned most of the Taliban, as well as their current nemesis, Afghan President Hamid Karzai, and that has been rumored to be harboring Osama bin Laden.

9. Deaf with a capital *D* is explicitly opposed to deaf with a small *d* in the boundary work of these activists (Berbrier, 1998).

10. The term *panethnicity* has been very stimulating for research but seems misleading. In some way almost everything that people call ethnicity or race is *pan*—that is, a mixing or combining of what is or was otherwise seen as several distinct groups. In another vein, Howard Winant (1994) holds that panethnicity is really a racialization process.

11. For a take on the methodological side of this issue, see De Andrade (2000). She explores the researcher's role in her participants' construction of a "Cape Verdean" identity.

12. This is not to say that the scholarship heretofore cited painted a structurally reductionistic

picture, nor that it was dismissive of agency, nor ignorant of the underlying theoretical issues (e.g., Nagel, 1996, chapters 1, 2, or 3).

13. These two represent somewhat divergent approaches of ethnomethodologists to conversation analysis (CA) as elaborated by and often attributed to Harvey Sacks (1992). Traditional CA focuses heavily on the structure and sequence of talk, whereas membership categorization analysis focuses more specifically and substantively on the situated and emergent uses of categories (in this case, ethnic categories). Hansen (2005) implies that these approaches are ordinarily seen as incommensurable but argues that "the sequential and membership categorization aspects of talk are mutually constitutive" (p. 67).

14. Social identity theory comprises a school of British social psychology that focuses, in part, on the contrasts effected by social categorization that create both in-group cohesion and inter-group prejudices (Tajfel, 1982).

15. Ann Morning's recent dissertation (2004) exploring the transmission of constructionist ideas on race within the college setting—among faculty and between faculty and students—provides reason to be skeptical. She found that the idea that race is a social construct is not shared throughout the social sciences and is strongly resisted and questioned among biologists. In terms of teaching, it seemed that only students of anthropology were reliably constructionist and that in the teaching of constructionism what students often get is a lot of rhetoric and little evidence. The dissertation is packed with such nuggets. In a nutshell, it makes the case that we need to transmit constructionist ideas better and *with evidence.*

16. This is not to say that I was the first to see it this way.

17. I am indebted to the editors for reminding me of this. For further insight, see their discussion of such issues in Gubrium and Holstein (1997, pp. 34–44).

18. That is, focusing on categories of practice does not (necessarily) mean strict, context-free analysis of talk (cf. Best, 1993). We need to be much more careful about not presuming in advance that which is to be explained as the outcome of our analysis; we analytically bracket out other things. To do this (and this is the trick, I believe) we need to develop and adhere to an analytic vocabulary that aids us in this pursuit. This is made even more horrifically difficult by the fact

that sometimes our analytic categories can *become* their practical ones and that sometimes we have been both the social actors (e.g., claiming ethnic status) and the putative analysts. Although that is precisely the situation that Loveman and I both urge researchers to avoid, it is already frequently a *fait accompli* (Berbrier, 2004), and we need to be aware of the recursive complexities of that as well.

19. In fact, one might argue that the critical approach has some "intrinsically" constructionist elements, particularly its emphasis on the relational characteristic of race—that races, or racial meanings, are dependent on other meanings, and particularly other racial meanings in a context. Whites and whiteness derive their very conceptual existence from contrast.

20. Bhattacharyya does make one delightful point (even though he evaluates it differently than I do): "Cultural studies has . . . fulfilled the important institutional role of making Sociology look like a 'real' discipline" (2003, p. 524).

• References

Bailey, B. (2000). Language and negotiation of ethnic/racial identity among Dominican Americans. *Language in Society, 29,* 555–582.

Barth, F. (1969a). *Ethnic groups and boundaries: The social organization of culture difference.* Boston: Little, Brown.

Barth, F. (1969b). Introduction. *Ethnic groups and boundaries: The social organization of culture difference* (pp. 9–38). Boston: Little, Brown.

Benford, R., & Snow, D. (2000). Framing process and social movements: An overview and assessment. *Annual Review of Sociology, 26,* 611–39.

Berbrier, M. (1996). *Ethnicity in the making: Cultural space and the ethnic/minority claims of the deaf, gays, and white supremacists.* Unpublished doctoral dissertation, Indiana University.

Berbrier, M. (1998). "Being Deaf has very little to do with one's ears": Boundary work in the Deaf culture movement. *Perspectives on Social Problems, 10,* 79–100.

Berbrier, M. (2000). Ethnicity in the making: Ethnicity work, the ethnicity industry, and a constructionist framework for research. *Perspectives on Social Problems, 12,* 69–88.

Berbrier, M. (2002a). Disempowering minorities: A critique of Wilkinson's "Task for social scientists and practitioners." *Journal of Sociology and Social Welfare, 29*(2), 3–19.

Berbrier, M. (2002b). Making minorities: Cultural space and the categorical status claims of gay, Deaf, and white supremacist activists in late 20th century America. *Sociological Forum, 17,* 553–591.

Berbrier, M. (2004). Assimilationism and pluralism as cultural tools. *Sociological Forum, 19,* 29–62.

Berbrier, M., & Pruett, E. (2006). When is inequality a problem? *Journal of Contemporary Ethnography, 35*(3), 257–284.

Berger, P. L., & Luckmann, T. (1966). *The social construction of reality.* Garden City, NY: Anchor Books.

Best, J. (1993). But seriously, folks: The limitations of the strict constructionist interpretation of social problems. In J. A. Holstein & G. Miller (Eds.), *Reconsidering social constructionism: Debates in social problems theory* (pp. 109–127). New York: Aldine de Gruyter.

Bhattacharyya, G. (2003). In defense of amateurism: On not professionalizing ethnic and racial studies. *Ethnic and Racial Studies, 26*(3), 523–527.

Billig, M. (1985). Prejudice, categorization, and particularization: From a perceptual to a rhetorical approach. *European Journal of Social Psychology, 15,* 79–103.

Boas, F. (1912). Changes in the bodily form of descendants of immigrants. *American Anthropologist, 14,* 530–562.

Bonilla-Silva, E. (1999). Reply: The essential social fact of race. *American Sociological Review, 64*(6), 899–906.

Bourdieu, P. (1991). *Language and symbolic power.* Cambridge, MA: Harvard University Press.

Brass, P. R. (1991). *Ethnicity and nationalism: Theory and comparison.* Newbury Park, CA: Sage.

Breton, R. (1964). Institutional completeness of ethnic communities and the personal relations of immigrants. *American Journal of Sociology, 70,* 193–205.

Brubaker, R. (2004). *Ethnicity without groups.* Cambridge, MA: Harvard University Press.

Brubaker, R., & Cooper, F. (2000). Beyond "identity." *Theory and Society, 29*(1), 1–47.

Carter, P. L. (2003). "Black" cultural capital, status positioning, and schooling conflicts for low-income African American youth. *Social Problems, 50,* 136–155.

Clifford, J., & Marcus, G. (Eds.). (1986). *Writing culture: The poetics and politics of ethnography.* Berkeley: University of California Press.

Cohen, A. (1974). Introduction: The lessons of ethnicity. In A. Cohen (Ed.), *Urban ethnicity* (pp. ix–xxiv). London: Tavistock.

Collins, R. (2001). Ethnic change in macro-historical perspective. In E. Anderson & D. S. Massey (Eds.), *Problem of the century* (pp. 13–46). New York: Russell Sage.

Conzen, K. N. (1989). Ethnicity as festive culture. In W. Sollors (Ed.), *The invention of ethnicity* (pp. 44–76). New York: Oxford University Press.

Cornell, S. (1988). The transformations of tribe: Organization and self-concept in native American ethnicities. *Ethnic and Racial Studies, 11*(1), 27–47.

Cornell, S. (1996). The variable ties that bind: Content and circumstance in ethnic processes. *Ethnic and Racial Studies, 13,* 368–388.

Cornell, S., & Hartmann, D. (2007). *Ethnicity and race: Making identities in a changing world* (2nd ed.). Thousand Oaks, CA: Pine Forge Press.

Davis, F. J. (1991). *Who is black?* University Park: Pennsylvania State University Press.

De Andrade, L. L. (2000). Negotiating from the inside: Constructing racial and ethnic identity in qualitative research. *Journal of Contemporary Ethnography, 29*(3), 268–290.

Dominguez, V. (1986). *White by definition.* New Brunswick, NJ: Rutgers University Press.

Duany, J. (1998). Reconstructing racial identity: Ethnicity, color, and class among Dominicans in the United States and Puerto Rico. *Latin American Perspectives, 25*(3), 147–172.

DuBois, W. (1899). *The Philadelphia Negro.* Philadelphia: University of Pennsylvania Press.

Eipper, C. (1983). The magician's hat: A critique of the concept of ethnicity. *Australia and New Zealand Journal of Sociology, 19*(3), 427–446.

Enloe, C. (1981). The growth of the state and ethnic mobilization: The American experience. *Ethnic and Racial Boundaries, 4*(2), 123–136.

Espiritu, Y. L. (1992). *Asian American panethnicity: Bridging institutions and identities.* Philadelphia: Temple University Press.

Fanon, F. (1967). *Black skin, white masks.* New York: Grove Press.

Fenton, S., & May, S. (2002). Ethnicity, nation, and 'race': Connections and disjunctures. In S. Fenton & S. May (Eds.), *Ethnonational identities* (pp. 1–20). New York: Palgrave.

Fordham, S., & Ogbu, J. U. (1986). Black students' school success: Coping with the burden of "acting white." *Urban Review, 18*(3), 176–206.

Frankenberg, R. (1993). *The social construction of whiteness: White women, race matters.* Minneapolis: University of Minnesota Press.

Gans, H. J. (1979). Symbolic ethnicity: The future of ethnic groups and cultures in America. *Ethnic and Racial Studies, 2*(1), 1–19.

Gates, H. L., Jr. (1990). Critical remarks. In D. T. Goldberg (Ed.), *Anatomy of racism* (pp. 319–329). Minneapolis: University of Minnesota Press.

Gieryn, T. F. (2000). A space for place in sociology. *Annual Review of Sociology, 26,* 463–496.

Glazer, N., & Moynihan, D. P. (Eds.). (1975). *Ethnicity: Theory and experience.* Cambridge, UK: Cambridge University Press.

Goldberg, D. T. (1990). Introduction. In D. T. Goldberg (Ed.), *Anatomy of racism* (pp. xi–xxiii). Minneapolis: University of Minnesota Press.

Gubrium, J. F., & Holstein, J. A. (1997). *The new language of qualitative method.* New York: Oxford University Press.

Hall, S. (1989). Ethnicity: Identity and difference. *Radical America, 23,* 9–13.

Hannan, M. T. (1979). The dynamics of ethnic boundaries in modern states. In J. Meyer & M. T. Hannan

(Eds.), *National development and the world system* (pp. 253–275). Chicago: University of Chicago Press.

Hansen, A. D. (2005). A practical task: Ethnicity as a resource in social interaction. *Research on Language and Social Interaction, 38*(1), 63–104.

Hanson, A. (1989). The making of the Maori: Culture invention and its logic. *American Anthropologist, 91*(4), 890–902.

Harrison, F. (1995). The persistent power of "race" in the cultural and political economy of racism. *Annual Review of Anthropology, 24,* 47–74.

Herbstein, J. (1983). The politicization of Puerto Rican ethnicity in New York: 1955–1975. *Ethnic Groups, 5,* 31–54.

Hobsbawm, E. (1983). Introduction: Inventing traditions. In E. Hobsbawm & T. Ranger (Eds.), *The invention of tradition* (pp. 1–14). Cambridge, UK: Cambridge University Press.

Holstein, J. A., & Miller, G. (2003). A fork in the road. In J. A. Holstein & G. Miller (Eds.), *Challenges and choices* (pp. 1–11). Hawthorne, NY: Aldine de Gruyter.

Howard, J. (2000). Social psychology of identities. *Annual Review of Sociology, 26,* 367–393.

Hughey, M. W., & Vidich, A. J. (1998). The new American pluralism: Racial and ethnic sodalities and their sociological implications. In M. W. Hughey (Ed.), *New tribalisms: The resurgence of race and ethnicity* (pp. 173–196). New York: New York University Press.

Jackson, J. L., Jr. (2005). *Real black: Adventures in racial sincerity.* Chicago: University of Chicago Press.

Jenkins, R. (1996). Ethnicity et cetera: Social anthropological points of view. *Ethnic and Racial Studies, 19*(4), 807–822.

Kibria, N. (1997). The construction of "Asian America": Reflections on intermarriage and ethnic identity among the second-generation Chinese and Korean Americans. *Ethnic and Racial Studies, 20*(3), 523–544.

Latour, B. (1987). *Science in action: How to follow scientists and engineers through society.* Cambridge, MA: Harvard University Press.

Leistyna, P. (1998, Spring). White ethnic unconsciousness. *Cultural Circles, 2,* 33–51.

Loseke, D. (1999). *Thinking about social problems.* New York: Aldine de Gruyter.

Loveman, M. (1999a). Comment: Is "race" essential? *American Sociological Review, 64*(6), 891–899.

Loveman, M. (1999b). Making "race" and nation in the United States, South Africa, and Brazil: Taking making seriously. *Theory and Society, 28*(6), 903–927.

Medina, L. K. (1997). Defining difference, forging unity: The co-construction of race, ethnicity, and nation in Belize. *Ethnic and Racial Studies, 20*(4), 757–780.

Miller, K. H. (2001). Mexican past and Mexican presence in San Antonio's Market Square: Capital, tourism, and the creation of the local. In M. P. Smith & T. Bender (Eds.), *City and nation: Rethinking place and*

identity (pp. 206–239). New Brunswick, NJ: Transaction.

Moerman, M. (1993). Ariadne's thread and Indra's net: Reflections on ethnography, ethnicity, identity, culture, and interaction. *Research on Language and Social Interaction, 26*(1), 85–98.

Morning, A. (2004). *The nature of race: Teaching and learning about human difference.* Unpublished doctoral dissertation, Princeton University.

Mullings, L. P. (1994). Race, inequality and transformation. *Identities, 1*(1), 123–129.

Nagel, J. (1986). The political construction of ethnicity. In S. Olzak & J. Nagel (Eds.), *Competitive ethnic relations* (pp. 93–112). Orlando, FL: Academic Press.

Nagel, J. (1994). Constructing ethnicity: Creating and recreating ethnic identity and culture. *Social Problems, 41,* 152–176.

Nagel, J. (1995). American Indian ethnic renewal: Politics and the resurgence of identity. *American Sociological Review, 60,* 947–965.

Nagel, J. (1996). *American Indian ethnic renewal: Red power and the transformation of identity and culture.* New York: Oxford University Press.

Niemann, Y. F., Romero, A. J., Arredondo, J., & Rodriguez, V. (1999). What does it mean to be "Mexican"?: Social construction of an ethnic identity. *Hispanic Journal of Behavioral Sciences, 21*(1), 47–60.

Olzak, S., & Nagel, J. (1986). *Competitive ethnic relations.* Orlando, FL: Academic Press.

Omi, M., & Winant, H. (1994). *Racial formation in the United States.* New York: Routledge.

Pollner, M. (1974). Sociological and common sense models of the labeling process. In R. Turner (Ed.), *Ethnomethodology* (pp. 27–40). Middlesex, UK: Penguin.

Pollner, M. (1987). *Mundane reason.* Cambridge, UK: Cambridge University Press.

Portes, A., & Jensen, L. (1989). The enclave and the entrants: Patterns of ethnic enterprise in Miami before and after Mariel. *American Sociological Review, 54,* 929–949.

Potter, J., & Wetherell, M. (1987). *Discourse and social psychology.* London: Sage.

Roediger, D. (2005). *Working toward whiteness.* New York: Basic Books.

Roosens, E. E. (1989). *Creating ethnicity: The process of ethnogenesis.* Newbury Park, CA: Sage.

Sacks, H. (1992). *Lectures on conversation.* Cambridge, MA: Blackwell.

Schilling-Estes, N. (2004). Constructing ethnicity in interaction. *Journal of Sociolinguistics, 8,* 163–195.

Shim, J. K. (2000). Constructing "race" across the science–lay divide: Racial formation in the epidemiology and experience of cardiovascular disease. *Social Studies of Science, 35*(3), 405–436.

Singer, L. (1962). Ethnogenesis and Negro-Americans today. *Social Research, 29,* 419–432.

Sollors, W. (Ed.). (1989). *The invention of ethnicity.* New York: Oxford University Press.

Spector, M., & Kitsuse, J. I. (1977). *Constructing social problems*. Menlo Park, CA: Cummings.

Staiger, A. (2004). Whiteness as giftedness: Racial formation at an urban high school. *Social Problems, 51,* 161–181.

Steinberg, S. (1981). *The ethnic myth*. Boston: Beacon Press.

Stern, S., & Cicala, J. A. (Eds.). (1991). *Creative ethnicity: Symbols and strategies of contemporary ethnic life*. Logan: Utah State University Press.

Tajfel, H. (1982). *Social identity and intergroup relations*. Cambridge, UK: Cambridge University Press.

Taylor, C. (2004). Dual systems in Rwanda: Have they ever really existed? *Anthropological Theory, 4,* 353–371.

Tönnies, F. (1957). *Community and society*. Lansing: Michigan State University Press.

Verkuyten, M., De Jong, W., & Masson, C. (1995). The construction of ethnic categories: Discourses of ethnicity in the Netherlands. *Ethnic and Racial Studies, 18,* 251–276.

Wagner, R. (1981). *The invention of culture*. Chicago: University of Chicago Press.

Wallerstein, I. (1987). The construction of peoplehood: Racism, nationalism, ethnicity. *Sociological Forum, 2*(2), 373–388.

Waters, M. C. (1990). *Ethnic options: Choosing identities in America*. Berkeley: University of California Press.

Waters, M. C. (1994). Ethnic and racial identities of second-generation black immigrants in New York City. *International Migration Review, 28*(4), 795–820.

Whisnant, D. (1983). *All that is native and fine: The politics of culture in an American region*. Chapel Hill: University of North Carolina Press.

Williams, R. H. (2003). The cultural contexts of collective action. In D. A. Snow, S. A. Soule, & H. Kriesi (Eds.), *The Blackwell companion to social movements* (pp. 91–115). Malden, MA: Blackwell.

Winant, H. (1994) *Racial conditions*. Minneapolis: University of Minnesota Press.

Winant, H. (2001). *The world is a ghetto*. New York: Basic Books.

Woolgar, S. (1988). *Science: The very idea*. London: Tavistock.

Yancey, W. L., Ericksen, E. P., & Juliani, R. N. (1976). Emergent ethnicity: A review and reformation. *American Sociological Review, 41,* 391–403.

Zevallos, Z. (2003). "That's my Australian side": The ethnicity, gender, and sexuality of young women of south and central American origin. *Journal of Sociology, 39*(1), 81–98.

CHAPTER 30

Constructions of
Medical Knowledge

- **Paul Atkinson**
  Maggie Gregory

The constructionist analysis of biomedical phenomena is a key aspect of sociological, anthropological, historical, and cultural research (e.g., Jordanova, 1995; Lachmund & Stollberg, 1982; Lupton, 1994, 2000; Wright & Treacher, 1982). It has a long history: One of the earliest of all constructionist texts is Ludwik Fleck's (1935/ 1979) *Genesis and Development of a Scientific Fact*, first published in 1935 and in many ways anticipating Thomas Kuhn's (1970) *Structure of Scientific Revolutions* (Löwy, 1988). Virtually all of the relevant disciplines and analytic strategies have been used to examine medical and biomedical phenomena. There has also been a noteworthy convergence of analytic perspectives between the sociology of medical knowledge and the sociology of scientific knowledge. At one time those academic subdisciplines operated with

a high degree of mutual isolation and ignorance. The increasing prominence of biomedical issues in contemporary science (including genomic and postgenomic life sciences) has meant that distinctions between natural science and medicine are becoming increasingly blurred. In the same way, sociological and anthropological research on medical knowledge and practice have become increasingly convergent. Moreover, a number of theoretical perspectives in the social sciences, including interpretative, feminist, poststructuralist, and postmodernist, all imply a broadly constructionist analytic strategy, notwithstanding that there are important differences between them. One of the advantages residing in a review of medical topics is the extent to which it reveals the diversity of social science approaches that can be defined, broadly, as constructionist. We do not suggest that there is a single, but inconsistent or incoherent, strategy of "constructionism," and we do not wish away such differences in order to impose a spurious unity on the diverse research traditions.

The various perspectives provide a powerful set of conceptual tools and case studies that reveal the mechanisms of stability and change in medical thought, the conventional nature of medical practice, the plasticity of medical categories, and the cultural variability of medical classifications. Such analyses are not inherently antagonistic to the knowledge claims of any particular medical system, nor does their value reside in "debunking" medicine. Some constructionist analyses may have that function, and some constructionist perspectives derive from critical engagements with medical orthodoxy. Constructionist analysis does not, however, necessarily entail an oppositional stance toward medicine and its practitioners. Nevertheless, a constructionist approach—however defined—and a culturally relativist standpoint are inescapable elements in any serious sociological or anthropological treatment of medicine as a cultural system or as a site of everyday social action (Collins & Pinch, 2006).

A constructionist account does not depend on a denial of or blindness to the material circumstances of disease, injury, or death. A constructionist perspective certainly should not be a disembodied view of medicine. On the contrary, the management of the body and the interpretation of its appearances are vital to the production of medical understanding (Mol, 2005). Although constructionist accounts of the body are beyond the scope of this chapter, that body of scholarship should be understood as a backdrop to our discussion. The same is true for the growing body of research in science and technology studies that documents the organizational and cultural settings in which biomedical phenomena are produced and reproduced through the collective practices of scientists, technicians, clinical spe-

cialists, and others (e.g., Keating & Cambrosio, 2003). We return to these issues briefly at the end of this chapter.

Historical and Cultural Diversity

The clearest evidence for the fundamental variability of medical phenomena is provided by historical and cross-cultural studies. These studies also introduce some of the most significant analytic perspectives in this field. The historical and anthropological imagination documents not merely variation or change but also radical differences and disjunctures. Above all, therefore, these studies show that we are not dealing merely with different interpretations of "the same" natural phenomena but with differently constituted phenomena. The physical, corporeal bases of the body and of disease are by no means irrelevant to such definitions or constructions, but they underdetermine them. We do not suggest, therefore, that the biological is to be rendered immaterial; rather, the categories of medical thought and practice are emergent phenomena, arising out of the intersection of the material and the cultural.

The categories of medical perception and thought have changed radically over time, and they continue to change. There are, for instance, relatively "modern" medical conditions that are now barely visible within the pantheon of diagnostic categories and illness experiences. For instance, the late 19th and early 20th centuries witnessed several conditions that are no longer current. The condition of *chlorosis* ("green sickness") was widely diagnosed and managed. It was a condition of adolescent females and young adult women. It would not now be recognized by most practitioners as a clinical entity. The same can be said of *neurasthenia*, a condition of the nervous system that was widely identified as a characteristic syndrome of the *fin de siècle*. It was part of a more general "nervous" discourse of late Victorian and Edwardian medical thought.

Although neurasthenia may still appear in medical textbooks and diagnostic handbooks, it is not part of the regular diagnostic discourse of medicine a century and more later. (It is, however, intriguing to note that many contemporary accounts of the postmodern condition have very similar things to say about culture and identity as did commentators on metropolitan life in America and Europe in the late 19th and early 20th centuries.) These are but among the many medical disorders that were regularly diagnosed but that do not now form any part of regular medical discourse. Ian Hacking (1999) has used the medical category of "fugue" (pathological, unconscious wandering) to illustrate some of the features of construction.

If one can point to a huge variety of conditions that are no longer current, then there are also more fundamental epistemological differences revealed in historical perspectives. The work of Michel Foucault has provided one major reference point. Viewed from a characteristically Parisian standpoint, Foucault (1973) identifies a significant epistemological fault line and the emergence of a distinctively modern form of knowledge in the first decades of postrevolutionary medicine in France (Petersen & Bunton, 1997). He suggests that the distinction between 18th-century and 19th-century medicine is far from being a story of gradual change and incremental progress. Rather, there is a radical break. The earlier premodern period is marked by a natural history of illness. It is a medicine of symptoms. Diseases inhabit the body and can migrate around it, but they are not necessarily anchored in specific pathologies or specific organs. Distinctively modern medicine is transformed into a medicine of signs. The body—including its interior—is open to direct inspection (the stethoscope, the thermometer), and the rise of clinical pathology means that hospital doctors can marry observed clinical signs with pathology in particular organs by means of the postmortem examination. Foucault overstates these dif-ferences in order to deploy his distinctive argument concerning discontinuous transformations in forms of knowledge, and his Parisian analysis would not necessarily hold for other centers of medical innovation (such as Leyden in Holland or Edinburgh in Scotland). Nevertheless, his overall approach is at least suggestive, and his work has been productive of a good deal of empirical research on medical knowledge, practice, and power. It is important to point out that Foucault's work is not in itself the origin of this strand of Parisian analysis. Foucault's work was inspired by the earlier work of Georges Canguilhem (1989) on the category of "pathology" in 19th-century biomedical thought. Canguilhem claims that the discourse of clinical knowledge rendered pathology a different domain of knowledge from that of normal biology. Pathology—and hence the clinic—consequently was asserted to be a domain *sui generis*, independent from the sciences of the "normal."

David Armstrong's (1983, 2002a, 2002b) analysis of the changing forms of medical knowledge is one of the most sustained applications of Foucault's analytic strategies to the genealogies of medical knowledge. He traces how normality and pathology are identified in different regimes of knowledge—in the clinic, in the dispensary, in the populations defined by public health, in the distribution of values in the survey, and in the stages of normal child development. These are not phases in a single trajectory of scientific and medical progress but a palimpsest of practices, social relations, and modes of medical knowledge production. Nettleton's (1992) analysis of dentistry deploys a similar analytic perspective, stressing the relations of knowledge and power, as does William Arney's (1983) account of power and expertise in obstetrics.

This perspective is dealt with in a more sociological and historically better informed way by Lester King (1982), whose work has been less fashionable than that of the French school but deserves to be more central to contemporary analyses. King, in a way that parallels the reflections of Canguilhem, stresses the distinctive character of clinical thought. King and Foucault, each from a different perspective, describe the cultural system that ascribes a particular privilege and status to clinical knowledge. Clinical knowledge, experience, and judgment are frequently portrayed as especially privileged, exceptional forms of knowledge production and reproduction (Atkinson, 1995; Freidson, 1970).

If the historical sociology of knowledge emphasizes some of the temporal specificities of medical knowledge, then the anthropology of medicine is replete with examples of its cultural specificity. The entire field is far too broad to summarize in one section of this chapter. The overall thrust of medical anthropology is, however, clear: Ideas about health and disease, systems and practices of healing, and the esoteric knowledge of healers are culturally variable. Here we note that the categories of clinical medicine are constantly developing and changing. New clinical entities are regularly created. The construction of a named clinical entity implies more than just the recognition of a novel constellation of signs or symptoms. The production of a named "disease" or "syndrome" involves a series of judgments and decisions. A clinical entity is an ideal type (Aronowitz, 1998, 2001). Its identification involves extrapolation beyond the variations and differences between and within cases to create a relatively stable object of description that can be enshrined in textbooks and can also be the object of management regimes (Brown, 1995). The identification of a named condition can trigger health care services, health insurance entitlement, and intervention from social services that might be absent or much harder to mobilize in the absence of such an identifiable entity. Recently identified and constructed entities include Lyme disease (Aronowitz, 1991) and multiple chemical sensitivities (Lax, 1998). Indeed, it is important to emphasize that constructions do not encompass only "obsolete" or "discredited" medical categories. Histori-

cal examples serve merely to throw into relief the more general issue of cultural and historical specificity.

Recurrent changes in medical technology repeatedly shift the boundaries and categories of orthodox nosography. In recent years, the emergence of the "new genetics" has inspired a considerable research literature, not least a body of work focused on the classification and reclassification of medical categories on the basis of genetic technologies (see, e.g., Hedgecoe, 2002, 2003; Kerr, 2000, 2005). It is not just the disease categories that are subject to such processes of definition and redefinition. So, too, are reported *rates* of incidence (see, e.g., Lantz & Booth, 1998).

Culture-Bound Syndromes

The discipline of medical anthropology has repeatedly documented cultural variations in knowledge systems and therapeutic practices. Indeed, the entire subdiscipline is predicated on the demonstration of such systems of cultural difference. Cultural systems display characteristic nosographies—descriptions of symptoms and diseases—and nosologies—classifications of diseases. These are highly variable and cannot be assumed to map onto the categories of conventional Western biomedical knowledge. The *emic* categories of local cultures cannot necessarily be translated into universalistic *etic* categories. We are not able to review all of the extensive literature of medical anthropology in order to substantiate the issues. General overviews and exemplary studies may be found elsewhere (e.g., Good, 1994; Green, 1999; Helman, 1985; Kleinman, 1980).

One strand of medical anthropology illustrates this line of analysis quite clearly; that is the description of *culture-bound syndromes* (Karp, 1985). This is associated with the more specialized field of ethnopsychiatry, the literature being grounded in anthropological accounts of culture-specific psychological conditions. Cultures furnish idioms of suffering through which personal troubles and disturbances are classified and given a culture-specific etiology (Guarnaccia & Rogler, 1999; Jilek & Jilek-Aall, 1985). There has, for instance, been a wide range of conditions that can be glossed as having connotations of "nerves," "fright," and similar kinds of unease (Low, 1985). Well-documented syndromes include *ataques de nervios* (Guarnaccia, Rubio-Stipec, & Canino, 1989; Jenkins, 1988; Oquendo, Horwath, & Martinez, 1992), *susto* (Mysyk, 1998; Rubel & Moore, 2001); *empacho* (Weller, Pachter, Trotter, & Baer, 1993), and *mal de ojo* (Baer & Bustillo, 1993). Various other anxiety-related states include the Japanese *shinkeishitsu* and *taijinkōfushī* (Russell, 1989), Punjabi *sinking heart* (Kraue, 1989), Chinese *shenjing shuairuo* (Lee & Wong, 1995), *old hag* in Newfoundland (Ness, 1978), Malay *amok* (Carr, 1978), Indian *dhat* syndrome (Malhotra & Wig, 1975; Sumathipala & Bhugra, 2004), Korean *hwabyung* (Pang, 1990), *koro* (Edwards, 1984) and Mongolian *yadargaa* (Kohrt, Hruschka, Kohrt, Panebianco, & Tsagaankjuu, 2004), or Yemeni *fijaʿ* (Swagman, 1989).

It would, however, be quite wrong to assume that "culture-bound syndromes" are the preserve of non-Western "others." We have already referred to the historical category of "neurasthenia," which was a culture-bound syndrome of a particular period of American and European modernity. There is a florid cultural history of "shattered nerves" and "shock" that encompasses many such syndromes (Oppenheim, 1991). Panic disorder is a contemporary version that has its own genealogy (Orr, 2005), as is posttraumatic stress disorder (Das-Munshi, 2005; Farrell, 1998; Jones et al., 2003; Summerfield, 2001). There are arguments to suggest that one can possibly regard conditions such as anorexia as culture-bound syndromes (Banks, 1992; Katzman & Lee, 1998; Keel, 2003; Lee, 1996; Prince, 1985; Swartz, 1985). Equally, some literature suggests that menopausal syndrome can be regarded as culture specific (Townsend & Carbone, 1980), and

Margaret Lock's monograph on menopause in Japan suggests a very different constellation of physical and personal responses from those described in Europe or North America (Lock, 1995). Likewise, Mari Rodin (1992) and Thomas Johnson (1987) explore the social construction of premenstrual syndrome. There is no need to consult only the exotic non-Western manifestations of ill health or distress in order to identify "culture bound" conditions.

From a strictly constructionist perspective, however, there is no such thing as a culture-bound syndrome. Or, rather, there is no separate category. All diagnostic entities are culture bound to the extent that there are culture-specific interpretations of any and all medical phenomena. Medical knowledge, whether lay or professional, is therefore culture bound. Western cosmopolitan concepts are culture bound. Orthodox biomedicine is culture bound. The cultural milieus are broader than the culture-specific concepts referred to previously, perhaps, but they are no less culturally produced and constrained than are the more "exotic" expressions of suffering we have just referred to.

Indeed, in recent decades a growing body of work has examined the production of biomedical knowledge and its categories from a number of perspectives, combining perspectives from the sociology and anthropology of medicine and from science and technology studies. These studies all extend the scope of the social sciences to include the cultural shaping of the very categories of life itself: the boundaries between the natural and the cultural; the categories and boundaries of the body in sickness and in health; the transformation of the body through prosthetic extensions and new biomedical technologies. Key texts in this genre include those by Franklin and Lock (2003), Clarke (1998), Franklin (1997), Stacey (1997), Martin (1987, 1994), and Smith and Moore (2006). The professional and cultural understanding of pain likewise forms a topic of inquiry for sociologists and anthropologists alike (Baszanger, 1998; DelVecchio Good, Brown, Good, & Kleinman, 1992).

Medical Work and Clinical Categories

Sociologists of medical knowledge have been located particularly within a tradition of interactionist and interpretative research (cf. Atkinson & Heath, 1981; Atkinson & Housley, 2003). This tradition has established a number of key themes in the performance of medical work and medical encounters, within which medical definitions and realities are defined and managed. These themes include the interactional management of the medical encounter, the narrative construction of illness, the discursive creation of cases, the textual enactment of medical phenomena, and techniques of biomedical representation. Clearly, these do not exist in mutual isolation in the everyday contexts of knowledge production and routine practice. We discriminate between them for analytic purposes. They all exemplify the same general phenomenon—that medical categories are produced and reproduced through socially shared, conventional means. There is no realm of medicine that is not mediated by the practices of spoken language, written language, or equally conventional means of representation.

We take here just a few examples from the vast research literature that help to establish some of these parameters. Sociologists and anthropologists have thoroughly documented the construction of medical diagnoses and disposals (Berg, 1992). As with all systems of science and practical knowledge, medical diagnosis is underdetermined by the observable and measurable phenomena. The processes of diagnosis and decision making depend on a series of judgments and are the outcomes of practical reasoning. They are susceptible to personal differences between practitioners and to more systematic organizational and cultural framing. Local preferences and the nuances of different

medical specialties are transmitted through the oral cultures of medical education (Atkinson, 1997). Michael Bloor's classic study of adenotonsillectomies demonstrates precisely how institutional routines and individual preferences lead to differential decision making and rates of surgical intervention (Bloor, 1976).

Elliot Mishler's work (1984) has informed a major series of publications on the discursive organization of the clinical encounter. These publications illustrate how the domain of orthodox biomedicine is asserted by medical practitioners in contrast to the world of everyday experience, as expressed by the patient. Paul Atkinson (1995) and Mary Hunter (1991) demonstrate how clinical cases and the "facts" of the case are constructed through the narrative performances that doctors create. Renee Anspach (1988) shows how recurrent discursive devices are used to frame physicians' descriptions—and hence their constructions—of medical cases and opinions. Paul Atkinson (2004) and Pamela Hobbs (2003), among others, have also documented how the formats of physicians' talk frame the credibility of medical evidence and professional opinion.

As Geoffrey Bowker and Susan Leigh Star (2000) have documented, medical constructions are enshrined in classificatory schemes. Such documentary sources do not merely describe conditions: They create and confirm them. Practices of inscription, such as the certification of causes of death, also contribute to the creation of medical categories and their distribution (Bloor, 1991). Within the organizational culture of clinics and hospitals, the medical record also constructs cases in accordance with socially shared conventions of writing, reading, and description (Barrett, 1988; Berg, 1996; Macintyre, 1978; Pettinari, 1988; Raffel, 1979; Rees, 1981). The written record provides the textual counterpoint to the narrated case (Will, 2005).

Likewise, the technologies of representation and imaging are not neutral methods of inspecting the structures, processes, and pathologies of the body but also of constructing its very nature through conventions of representation and reading. For instance, medical imaging provides a genealogy of moments of medical and anatomical reconstruction (see Heath, 1998; Holtzmann Kevles, 1997; Pasveer, 1989; van Dijck, 2005). Health technologies more generally provide modalities of biomedical construction (Brown & Webster, 2004; Cambrosio, Guttman, & Keating, 1994; Heath, Luff, & Svensson, 2003), from the simple technologies of staining cells (Atkinson, 1995) to the high-technology techniques of brain imaging (Dumit, 2004). The classifications of medical knowledge area, therefore, inscribed in material tools and representations. They are also reflected in the institutional ecology of medical institutions, including the architecture of hospitals and clinics, and their internal design (e.g., Prior, 1988; Stevenson, 2000). These various *forms* of representation and classification reflexively shape the forms of medical knowledge.

Contested Categories

Although a strong program of constructionist analysis would insist that all categories of medical thought are equally subject to social construction, it is easier to grasp some of the specificities of medical knowledge through a consideration of contested categories and entities. There are many clinical entities that are controversial and that are subject to dispute. Medical controversies, like controversial knowledge in the natural sciences, are perfectly normal features of the intellectual fields in which they take place. Also, like controversies in natural science, they are rarely susceptible to resolution simply by appeals to the evidence. Evidence itself is interpreted; the authority attributed to experts and interested parties is contested; the ownership of knowledge is rarely disinterested (Dumit, 2006).

Recent years have seen a good number of contested medical entities. They include hypoglycemia (Singer, Fitzgerald, & Von, 1984), myalgic encephalomyelitis (ME; Cooper, 1997; Moss & Dyck, 1999), chronic fatigue syndrome (CFS; Abbey & Garfinkel, 1991; Åsbring & Närvänen, 2003; Clarke & James, 2003; Richman, Jason, Taylor, & Jahn, 2000; Ware, 1992; Wesseley, Hotopf, & Sharpe, 1998), repetition/repetitive strain injury (Arksey, 1994, 1998; Arksey & Sloper, 1999; Hall & Morrow, 1988; Lucire, 2003; MacEachen, 2005; Reid, Ewan, & Lowy, 1991; Reid & Reynolds, 1990), and Gulf War syndrome (Brown et al., 2000; Sartin, 2000). They are contested in the sense that sufferers have identified their own health problems with a specific clinical entity, whereas the very existence of that entity has been disputed by medical scientists and practitioners themselves.

In a similar vein are conditions that have become medicalized. The medicalization of personal troubles is itself a terrain of considerable debate and political contest. A full review of medicalization is beyond the scope of this chapter, and Peter Conrad, among others, has undertaken the task already (Conrad, 1992; see also Bartholemew, 2000). Here we point out that medicalization implies the translation of everyday issues and troubles into medical categories. The medicalization of deviant identities and actions is a major class of such categories. Medicalized conditions range from shyness to attention deficit to alcoholism. What they have in common is that behaviors and dispositions that might in previous generations, or under different circumstances, or in other cultural settings, be regarded as failings of character are translated into medical, diagnostic categories (Molloy & Vasil, 2002). For example, Susie Scott (2006, 2007) documents the process whereby shyness has—at least in some contexts—been translated into a medical condition. It can even be graced with a medical label; *social phobia, social anxiety disorder*, and *avoidant personality disorder* have all been applied in recent years. The medicalization of obesity is yet another currently fashionable preoccupation among some professional and popular commentators alike (Ritenbaugh, 1982). The clinical entity of *autism* provides a site of contested etiologies and of contested rates of incidence (Nadesan, 2005).

Contested versions of medicalization are relatively frequent. Recent high-profile cases include the identification of Munchausen syndrome by proxy, claimed to be a medical condition in which parents (usually mothers) intentionally harm their children (Fish, Bromfield, & Higgins, 2005). The use of pediatricians as expert witnesses in the trials of parents suspected of killing their children has rendered this an especially visible site of contestation, not least because that expert testimony has been largely discredited and set aside in a series of successful appeals. The career of this particular "medical" condition and its identification highlights some of the processes whereby limited evidence can be transformed into medical facts when mediated by the authority of a senior medical practitioner. The self-referential nature of this aspect of knowledge production is underscored by the fact that the experts in question gained their reputations by creating the syndrome in the first place. In a similar way, the contested legitimacy of shaken-baby syndrome is performed in medicolegal contexts (Timmermans, 2006).

It is not necessary to restrict constructionist analysis to categories and classifications that are self-evidently controversial. Karin Garrety (1997), for instance, demonstrates the very complex and contingent nature of orthodox medical understandings of cholesterol levels and heart disease. The very "facts" on which well-established health policies are based are themselves contested. Indeed, the very status of knowledge and practice as "orthodox" is itself the outcome of processes of negotiation between different sets and networks of social actors, different professional segments, and different interest groups.

Medical Knowledge and Interests

A constructionist view of medical knowledge does not have to remain blind to the role of interests in the production of medical entities or to the promotion of particular versions of medical knowledge. On the contrary, a claim that medical knowledge is socially constructed does not imply that it is whimsically conjured out of thin air or that it bears no particular relation to material circumstances. Medical knowledge reflects socially distributed interests, including the interests of employers and insurers and the interests of medical practitioners themselves. Medical knowledge and its categories are embedded in cultural systems of differences, distinction, and discrimination; gender and race pervade medical knowledge.

The organized practices of medical specialists themselves are a key source in framing knowledge and reflecting sectional interests. Historically, for instance, many authors have identified the recurrent tensions between scientific researchers and clinical practitioners in the development of modern European medicine. The repeated affirmation of the privileged character of clinical knowledge and experience is one of the symbolic means whereby the elites of teaching-hospital consultants maintain a hierarchy of status and prestige that is naturalized in terms of distinctive forms of knowledge. Equally, repeated redefinitions of medical systems in terms of reductionist explanations (such as autoimmune conditions, viral infections, or genetic susceptibilities) can reflect the sectional interests of particular medical specialisms.

Wider sources of interest and ideology are discernible, however. There are, for instance, multiple instances suggesting that gender and race are implicated in the kinds of diagnostic, medical categories that are invoked. Feminist scholarship has treated medicine, both historically and from a contemporary perspective, as a major site in which the multiple meanings of sex and gender have been enacted. Historical examples include a series of female conditions. Hysteria is one of the most significant of these (Veith, 1965). Primarily a malaise of women, and originally associated with the displaced, wandering womb, hysteria became a type case of female susceptibility. Its history was linked intimately to yet broader assumptions and imagery concerning female psychopathology (Showalter, 1997). Recent anthropologies and sociologies of biomedical knowledge have highlighted the significance of gender in its production and circulation—especially the cultural marking of women's bodies as naturally problematic (e.g., Haraway, 1991; Martin, 1987). Likewise, Liz Lockyer and Michael Bury (2002) have demonstrated the gendered nature of nursing, medical, and social science constructions of the epidemiology of coronary heart disease.

Interest groups are directly implicated in the institutions and processes whereby medical conditions are contested and legitimated (Shriver, White, & Kebede, 1998). Activists were prominent actors in the disputes surrounding repetition/repetitive strain injury and its potential recognition as a problem of occupational health. The actions of veterans and their families have been instrumental in the legal processes surrounding posttraumatic stress disorder (Young, 1996) and Gulf War syndrome (Kilshaw, 2004; Zavetoski et al., 2004). Interests have been represented through court actions. They have real consequences in terms of compensation claims and insurance liabilities. The legal challenges to diagnoses of Munchausen syndrome by proxy in the United Kingdom have highlighted the extent to which legal proceedings have, first, legitimated the condition through high-profile expert testimony and second, placed in question that legitimacy by repudiating the expert opinion. As Stefan Timmermans (2006) shows, "shaken-baby syndrome" is also, in part, a product of forensic construction. Medical constructions are not the sole

preserve of medical practitioners, nor even of medical institutions. Indeed, there are multiple sites in which the contested realities of medical conditions are debated and made culturally visible. The mass media have significant roles to play in agenda setting and publicizing campaigns for and against the recognition of clinical conditions. Sometimes they may take the form of something like moral panics. Press campaigns can endorse the attempts of campaigners to seek recognition and redress. The popular press may also engage in sustained derision against activists' claims; ME or CFS may be labeled "Yuppie flu," for instance. In themselves the media do not provide the arena for the adjudication of contested entities, but they can help to create a cultural context and to frame the debates through which medical, legal, and lay interests are negotiated and contested.

In the case of Gulf War syndrome, of course, it is transparently clear that the interests of the military and of the State are involved, as are those of the veterans and their families. Likewise, repetitive strain injury (RSI) is embedded in industrial relations and health and safety regulations. Both conditions are implicated in the legal frameworks of compensation claims. Bloor's (2000, 2002) analysis of Welsh miners' claims for compensation for lung disease also reveals the interests of employers and their own medical experts in constructing diagnoses in one way while the miners and their representatives constructed it in another (see also Smith, 1987).

Constructionism Revisited

There have been and continue to be misconceptions as to the general implications of constructionist analyses of biomedical knowledge. We conclude our discussion, therefore, by reviewing the limits of constructionism. In the organization of this chapter, we have tried to reflect the range of connotations of "construction" in this field. It should be apparent by now that there are a variety of different analyses of biomedical knowledge and its social shaping. We continue by reviewing those different usages.

As we have already discussed, we confront the variability of biomedical systems—between cultures, between professional and layperson, and between historical periods. Even if we ascribe the broad features of those different configurations to differences in the sophistication of medical understanding and to progress in scientific and medical understanding, it is clear that we cannot attribute everything to science and enhanced knowledge. "Science" itself is socially accomplished, in any case, and cannot be invoked as if it provided a bedrock of knowledge that resisted social production. There are many discontinuities in medical knowledge; we are not confronted by smooth transitions from misunderstanding and ignorance to scientific and medical enlightenment.

Medical knowledge is also marked by high levels of controversy and contestation. Although some sociologists and anthropologists identify a hegemonic system of "biomedicine," close inspection always reveals cleavages and challenges. In contemporary Western societies, for instance, the apparent increase in reliance on alternative or complementary systems of therapy suggests that conventional biomedical knowledge does not hold sway to the exclusion of all else. Major systems of medical practice that run counter to professional orthodoxy, such as homeopathy, osteopathy, acupuncture, and chiropractic, are often incorporated selectively into "orthodox" practice. Alongside them, however, are systems of iridology, reflexology, aromatherapy, and the like that have little or no claim to biomedical legitimacy. Orthodox medicine has opposed such systems on an organized basis ever since an organized "profession" of medicine has existed. As Toby Murcott (2005) has pointed out in his discussion of complementary medicine and the gold standard of clinical trials, it is especially difficult to incorporate such practices within the scope of established biomedical tests of efficacy (cf. Cant & Sharma, 2000).

Lines of tension and cleavage are not confined to the boundaries between the orthodox and the unorthodox. What passes for orthodoxy is also subject to differentiation. There can be quite sharp differences between medical specialties. The professional perspective of the general surgeon can be quite different from that of the hematologist, for instance, and that difference is a source of professional identity for each type of practitioner. Psychiatry is not only sharply differentiated from other medical specialties but also internally differentiated by quite dramatically differing versions of medical orthodoxy, ranging from "talking cures" such as psychoanalysis and therapeutic communities to pharmaceutical interventions.

It is sometimes assumed, however, that the idea of "social constuction" implies something more radical, as if it sought to deny the material basis of disease or trauma. One occasionally encounters the "commonsense" retort: "You can't socially construct a broken leg," as if that provided a knockdown (fall down?) argument. Of course, nobody claims that an event such as a broken leg or any similar trauma can be conjured up out of nothingness by a process of social construction. Equally, nobody would seriously entertain the notion that the effect of a broken bone could be wished away. On the other hand, even the brute "fact" of a broken bone must be brought into the domain of cultural categories and social practices before the counterexample takes on any effect. There is, for example, a well-documented type of folk practitioner known as a bonesetter. It is a specialty often associated with particular families, who are credited with having especially well-developed skills. We can, therefore, begin by asking ourselves whether a broken bone is "the same" phenomenon to a traditional bonesetter and to a contemporary orthopedic surgeon. Clearly not: For each specialist the broken bone is culturally embedded in a specific set of diagnostic, classificatory systems. Each brings a different mode of perception to the limb. The modern surgeon, of course, also has recourse to a number of perceptual aids. We should not overlook the significance of the X-ray or the magnetic resonance imaging (MRI) scan. They are not merely passive tools. The opportunity to image the interior of the body transforms the way in which injuries and diseases are conceptualized. Furthermore, as we have seen, images, like other forms of biomedical evidence, have to be read and interpreted. This depends on socialized competence and rests on a set of conventions. If we add to the surgeon and the bonesetter the cultural possibility of faith in miracle-based healing, that adds to the possible interpretations of our broken bone and its consequences. These are not based on a simple, linear scale of greater medical sophistication and scientific progress; they reflect different *systems* of perception and action.

Furthermore, there need be no crude contrast between "reality" and "construction." Everything that we have been discussing is "real," in the sense that it is grounded in practical actions by embodied actors. Medical scientists and practitioners are engaged in material practices. They work with bodies and their physical traces. They use physical, material methods to investigate, manipulate, and treat those bodies. Their sensual readings of the body—based on sight, touch, or smell—are the products of embodied work. The traces that they inspect and interpret, such as tissue samples or images, are derived from material practices and are inscribed in material forms. Even the so-called virtual bodies derived from contemporary digital practices such as telemedicine are generated through technologies and representations that are material, Likewise, the practices that are used to legitimate or contest medical categories are undoubtedly real, whether they be the legal processes through which activists seek to establish the validity of their claims, the development of new diagnostic criteria, the professional confirmation of new diagnostic classifications, or the practices of record keeping. These are all real practices that are observable and susceptible to analysis by social scientists.

There is, therefore, no substance to a distinction between realism and constructionism when both are interpreted in adequately sociological terms. The practices—including the linguistic practices of describing and classifying medical phenomena—are real in themselves. The use of language is as much a material, physical activity as any other that we are discussing. Equally, physical objects and observable phenomena are open to interpretation. These are, we repeat, modes of social construction to the extent that they are dependent on socially organized actions and conventions. None of these phenomena is conjured up out of thin air by whimsical acts of imagination and will; their consequences are equally real. We repeat, therefore, that a thoroughgoing sociological or anthropological analysis of medicine and biomedical knowledge is inescapably constructionist. Like any system of knowledge and belief, it is *produced* through a diverse array of materials, techniques, interpretative frames, and discursive practices. We adopt such a stance in order to study precisely *how* such productions are accomplished. This is a methodological stance that allows us to study the complex of practical actions that go into those productions.

It is, therefore, vital to recognize that any *relativism* implied in constructionist analyses is an *analytic* stance. It reflects the sort of methodological commitment implied by the "strong program" in the sociology of scientific knowledge. In both fields we suspend assumptions concerning the relative value of forms of knowledge, such as between the categories of orthodox biomedicine and the categories of local belief systems. But this need not represent a general relativism whereby the sociologist or anthropologist endorses the (patently absurd) claim that all forms of knowledge are equally valid, well founded, or efficacious. The point is that we shall not understand, say, alchemy or phrenology simply by dismissing them as the outcomes of error. Equally, we shall not understand the practices of contemporary, conventional medicine simply by privileging its knowledge and practice. The relativist, constructionist step is an analytic necessity but not an ontological or epistemological judgment, nor yet a moral commitment. But as Stefan Timmermans and Marc Berg (2003) have so ably demonstrated, there is no absolute standard of medical evidence that can exist independently of the judgments and constructions that go into its creation. Even the "gold standard" of contemporary, evidence-based medical science is itself a series of constructions.

• References

Abbey, S. E., & Garfinkel, P. E. (1991). Neurasthenia and chronic fatigue syndrome: The role of culture in the making of a diagnosis. *American Journal of Psychiatry, 148*(12), 1638-1646.

Anspach, R. (1988). Notes on the sociology of medical discourse: The language of case presentation. *Journal of Health and Social Behavior, 29*, 357-375.

Arksey, H. (1994). Expert and lay participation in the construction of medical knowledge. *Sociology of Health and Illness, 16*, 448-468.

Arksey, H. (1998). *RSI and the experts: The construction of medical knowledge*. London: UCL Press.

Arksey, H., & Sloper, P. (1999). Disputed diagnoses: The cases of RSI and childhood cancer. *Social Science and Medicine, 49*(4), 483-497.

Armstrong, D. (1983). *Political anatomy of the body: Medical knowledge in Britain in the twentieth century*. Cambridge, UK: Cambridge University Press.

Armstrong, D. (2002a). *A new history of identity: A sociology of medical knowledge*. Cambridge, UK: Polity Press.

Armstrong, D. (2002b). Social theorizing about health and illness. In G. Albrecht, R. Fitzpatrick, & S. C. Scrimshaw (Eds.), *The handbook of social studies in health and medicine* (pp. 24–35). London: Sage.

Arney, W. R. (1983). *Power and the profession of obstetrics*. Chicago: University of Chicago Press.

Aronowitz, R. A. (1991). Lyme disease: The social construction of a new disease and its social consequences. *Milbank Quarterly, 69*(1), 79–112.

Aronowitz, R. A. (1998). *Making sense of illness: Science, society and disease*. Cambridge, UK: Cambridge University Press.

Aronowitz, R. A. (2001). When do symptoms become a disease? *Annals of Internal Medicine, 134*(9, Pt. 2), 803–808.

Åsbring, P., & Närvänen, A.-L. (2003). Ideal versus reality: Physicians' perspectives on patients with chronic fatigue syndrome (CFS) and fibromyalgia. *Social Science and Medicine, 57*(4), 711–720.

Atkinson, P. (1995). *Medical talk and medical work*. London: Sage.

Atkinson, P. (1997). *The clinical experience: The construction and reconstruction of medical reality* (2nd ed.). Aldershot, UK: Ashgate.

Atkinson, P. (2004). The discursive construction of competence and responsibility in medical collegial talk. *Communication and Medicine, 1*(1), 13–24.

Atkinson, P., & Heath, C. (Eds.). (1981). *Medical work: Realities and routines*. Farnborough, UK: Gower.

Atkinson, P., & Housley, W. (2003). *Interactionism*. London: Sage.

Baer, R. D., & Bustillo, M. (1993). *Susto* and *mal de ojo* among Florida farmworkers: Emic and etic perspectives. *Medical Anthropology Quarterly, 7*(1), 90–100.

Banks, C. G. (1992). "Culture" in culture-bound syndromes: The case of anorexia nervosa. *Social Science and Medicine, 34*(8), 867–884.

Barrett, R. J. (1988). Clinical writing and the documentary construction of schizophrenia. *Culture, Medicine and Psychiatry, 12*(3), 265–299.

Bartholomew, R. E. (2000). *Exotic deviance: Medicalizing cultural idioms from strangeness to illness*. Boulder: University Press of Colorado.

Baszanger, I. (1998). *Inventing pain medicine: From the laboratory to the clinic*. New Brunswick, NJ: Rutgers University Press.

Berg, M. (1992). The construction of medical disposals: Medical sociology and medical problem solving in clinical practice. *Sociology of Health and Illness, 14*, 151–180.

Berg, M. (1996). Practices of reading and writing: The constitutive role of the patient record in medical work. *Sociology of Health and Illness, 18*(4), 499–524.

Bloor, M. (1976). Bishop Berkely and the adenotonsillectomy enigma: An exploration of variation in the social construction of medical disposals. *Sociology, 10*(1), 43–61.

Bloor, M. (1991). A minor office: The variable and socially constructed character of death certification in a Scottish city. *Journal of Health and Social Behavior, 32*, 273–287.

Bloor, M. (2000). The South Wales Miners Federation, Miners' lung and the instrumental use of expertise, 1900–1950. *Social Studies of Science, 30*(1), 125–140.

Bloor, M. (2002). No longer dying for a living: Collective responses to injury risks in South Wales mining communities. *Sociology, 36*(1), 89–105.

Bowker, G., & Star, S. L. (2000). *Sorting things out: Classification and its consequences*. Cambridge, MA: MIT Press.

Brown, N., & Webster, A. (2004). *New medical technologies and society: Reordering life*. Cambridge, UK: Polity Press.

Brown, P. (1995). Naming and framing: The social construction of diagnosis and illness. *Journal of Health and Social Behavior*, pp. 34–52.

Brown, P., Zavestoski, S., McCormick, S., Linder, M., Mandelbaum, J., & Luebke, T. (2000). A gulf of difference: Disputes over Gulf War–related illnesses. *Journal of Health and Social Behavior*, *42*, 235–257.

Cambrosio, A., Guttman, R. D., & Keating, P. (1994). New medical technologies and clinical practice: A survey of lymphocyte subset monitoring. *Clinical Transplantation*, *8*, 532–540.

Canguilhem, G. (1989). *The normal and the pathological*. New York: Zone Books.

Cant, S., & Sharma, U. (2000). Alternative health practices and systems. In G. Albrecht, R. Fitzpatrick, & S. C. Scrimshaw (Eds.), *The handbook of social studies in health and medicine* (pp. 426–439). London: Sage.

Carr, J. E. (1978). Ethno-behaviorism and the culture-bound syndromes: The case of *amok*. *Culture, Medicine and Psychiatry*, *2*(3), 269–293.

Clarke, A. (1998). *Disciplining reproduction: Modernity, American life sciences, and the problems of sex*. Berkeley: University of California Press.

Clarke, J. N., & James, S. (2003). The radicalized self: The impact on the self of the contested nature of the diagnosis of chronic fatigue syndrome. *Social Science and Medicine*, *57*(8), 1387–1395.

Collins, H., & Pinch, T. (2006). *Dr. Golem: How to think about medicine*. Chicago: University of Chicago Press.

Conrad, P. (1992). Medicalization and social control. *Annual Review of Sociology*, *18*, 209–232.

Cooper, L. (1997). Myalgic encephalomyelitis and the medical encounter. *Sociology of Health and Illness*, *19*(2), 186–206.

Das-Munshi, J. (2005). Post-traumatic stress disorder: Or how to make yourself a traumatized body without organs. *Social Theory and Health*, *3*(1), 16–38.

DelVecchio Good, M.-J., Brown, P. E., Good, B. J., & Kleinman, A. (Eds.). (1992). *Pain as human experience: An anthropological perspective*. Berkeley: University of California Press.

Dumit, J. (2004). *Picturing personhood: Brain scans and biomedical identity*. Princeton, NJ: Princeton University Press.

Dumit, J. (2006). Illnesses you have to fight to get: Facts as forces in uncertain, emergent illnesses. *Social Science and Medicine*, *62*, 577–590.

Edwards, J. W. (1984). Indigenous *Koro*, a genital retraction syndrome of insular Southeast Asia: A critical review. *Culture, Medicine and Psychiatry*, *8*(1), 1–24.

Farrell, K. (1998). *Post-traumatic culture: Inquiry and interpretation in the nineties*. Baltimore: Johns Hopkins University Press.

Fish, E., Bromfield, L., & Higgins, D. (2005, Spring). A new name for Munchausen syndrome by proxy: Defining fabricated or induced illness by carers. *Issues*, *23*, 1–11.

Fleck, L. (1979). *Genesis and development of a scientific fact* (T. J. Trenn & R. K. Merton, Eds.). Chicago: University of Chicago Press. (Original work published 1935)

Foucault, M. (1973). *Birth of the clinic*. London: Tavistock.

Franklin, S. (1997). *Embodied progress: A cultural account of assisted conception*. London: Routledge.

Franklin, S., & Lock, M. (Eds.). (2003). *Remaking life and death: Toward an anthropology of the biosciences*. Santa Fe, NM: School of American Research Press.

Freidson, E. (1970). *Profession of medicine*. New York: Dodd Mead.

Garrety, K. (1997). Social worlds, actor-networks and controversy: The case of cholesterol, dietary fat and heart disease. *Social Studies of Science*, *27*(5), 727–773.

Good, B. J. (1994). *Medicine, rationality and experience: An anthropological perspective*. Cambridge, UK: Cambridge University Press.

Green, E. C. (1999). *Indigenous theories of contagious disease*. Walnut Creek, CA: AltaMira Press.

Guarnaccia, P. J., & Rogler, L. H. (1999). Research on culture-bound syndromes: New directions. *American Journal of Psychiatry*, *156*, 1322–1327.

Guarnaccia, P. J., Rubio-Stipec, M., & Canino, G. (1989). *Ataques de nervios* in the Puerto Rican diagnostic interview schedule: The impact of cultural categories on psychiatric epidemiology. *Culture, Medicine and Psychiatry*, *13*(3), 275–295.

Hacking, I. (1999). *Mad travellers: Reflections on the reality of transient mental illness*. London: Free Association Books.

Hall, W., & Morrow, L. (1988). "Repetition strain injury": An Australian epidemic of upper limb pain. *Social Science and Medicine*, *27*(6), 645–649.

Haraway, D. (1991). *Simians, cyborgs, women: The reinvention of nature*. New York: Free Press.

Heath, C., Luff, P., & Svensson, M. S. (2003). Technology and medical practice. *Sociology of Health and Illness*, *25*, 75–96.

Heath, D. (1998). Locating genetic knowledge: Picturing Marfan syndrome and its traveling constituencies. *Science, Technology and Human Values*, *23*(1), 71–97.

Hedgecoe, A. (2002). Reinventing diabetes: Classification, division and the geneticization of disease. *New Genetics and Society*, *21*(1), 7–27.

Hedgecoe, A. (2003). Expansion and uncertainty: Cystic fibrosis, classification and genetics. *Sociology of Health and Illness*, *25*, 50–70.

Helman, C. (1985). Psyche, soma, and society: The social construction of psychosomatic disorders. *Culture, Medicine and Psychiatry*, *9*(1), 1–26.

Hobbs, P. (2003). The use of evidentiality in physicians' progress notes. *Discourse Studies*, *5*(4), 451–478.

Holtzmann-Kevles, B. (1997). *Naked to the bone: Medical imaging in the twentieth century*. New Brunswick, NJ: Rutgers University Press.

Hunter, K. M. (1991). *Doctors' stories: The narrative struc-

ture of medical knowledge. Princeton, NJ: Princeton University Press.

Jenkins, J. H. (1988). Ethnopsychiatric interpretations of schizophrenic illness: The problem of *nervios* within Mexican-American families. *Culture, Medicine and Psychiatry, 12*(3), 301–329.

Jilek, W. G., & Jilek-Aall, L. (1985). The metamorphosis of "culture-bound" syndromes. *Social Science and Medicine, 21*(2), 205–210.

Johnson, T. M. (1987). Premenstrual syndrome as a Western culture-specific disorder. *Culture, Medicine and Psychiatry, 11*(3), 337–356.

Jones, E., Vermaas, R. H., McCartney, H., Beech, C., Palmer, I., Hyams, K., et al. (2003). Flashbacks and post-traumatic stress disorder: The genesis of a 20th-century diagnosis. *British Journal of Psychiatry, 182*, 158–163.

Jordanova, L. (1995). The social construction of medical knowledge. *Social History of Medicine, 8*(3), 361–381.

Karp, I. (1985). Deconstructing culture-bound syndromes. *Social Science and Medicine, 21*(2), 221–228.

Katzman, M. A., & Lee, S. (1998). Beyond body image: The integration of feminist and transcultural theories in the understanding of self-starvation. *International Journal of Eating Disorders, 22*(4), 385–394.

Keating, P., & Cambrosio, A. (2003). *Biomedical platforms: Realigning the normal and the pathological in late-twentieth-century medicine*. Cambridge, MA: MIT Press.

Keel, P. K. (2003). Are eating disorders culture-bound syndromes?: Implications for conceptualizing their etiology. *Psychological Bulletin, 129*(5), 747–769.

Kerr, A. (2000). (Re)constructing genetic disease: The clinical continuum between cystic fibrosis and male infertility. *Social Studies of Science, 30*, 847–894.

Kerr, A. (2005). Understanding genetic disease in a socio-historic context: A case study of cystic fibrosis. *Sociology of Health and Illness, 27*(7), 873–896.

Kilshaw, S. M. (2004). Friendly fire. *Anthropology and Medicine, 11*(2), 149–160.

King, L. S. (1982). *Medical thinking: A historical preface*. Princeton, NJ: Princeton University Press.

Kleinman, A. (1980). *Patients and healers in the context of culture*. Berkeley: University of California Press.

Kohrt, B. A., Hruschka, D. J., Kohrt, H. E., Panebianco, N. L., & Tsagaankjuu, G. (2004). Distribution of distress in post-socialist Mongolia: A cultural epidemiology of *yadargaa*. *Social Science and Medicine, 58*(3), 471–485.

Kraue, I.-B. (1989). Sinking heart: A Punjabi communication of distress. *Social Science and Medicine, 29*(4), 563–575.

Kuhn, T. (1970). *The structure of scientific revolutions*. Chicago: University of Chicago Press.

Lachmund, J., & Stollberg, G. (Eds.). (1982). *The social construction of illness: Illness and medical knowledge in*

past and present. Stuttgart, Germany: Franz Steiner Verlag.

Lantz, P. M., & Booth, K. M. (1998). The social construction of the breast cancer epidemic. *Social Science and Medicine, 46*(7), 907–918.

Lax, M. B. (1998). Multiple chemical sensitivities: The social construction of an illness. *International Journal of Health Services, 28*(4), 725–745.

Lee, S. (1996). Reconsidering the status of anorexia nervosa as a Western culture-bound syndrome. *Social Science and Medicine, 42*(1), 21–34.

Lee, S., & Wong, K. C. (1995). Rethinking neurasthenia: The illness concepts of Shenjing Shuairuo among Chinese undergraduates in Hong Kong. *Culture, Medicine and Psychiatry, 19*(1), 91–111.

Lock, M. (1995). *Encounters with aging*. Berkeley: University of California Press.

Lockyer, L., & Bury, M. (2002). The construction of a modern epidemic: The implications for women of the gendering of coronary heart disease. *Journal of Advanced Nursing, 39*(5), 432–440.

Low, S. M. (1985). Culturally interpreted symptoms or culture-bound syndromes: A cross-cultural review of nerves. *Social Science and Medicine, 21*(2), 187–196.

Löwy, I. (1988). Ludwik Fleck on the social construction of medical knowledge. *Sociology of Health and Illness, 10*(1), 133–155.

Lucire, Y. (2003). *Constructing RSI: Belief and desire*. Sydney, Australia: University of New South Wales Press.

Lupton, D. (1994). *Medicine as culture: Illness, disease and the body in Western societies*. London: Sage.

Lupton, D. (2000). The social construction of medicine and the body. In G. Albrecht, R. Fitzpatrick, & S. C. Scrimshaw (Eds.), *The handbook of social studies in health and medicine* (pp. 50–63). London: Sage.

MacEachen, E. (2005). The demise of repetitive strain injury in sceptical governing rationalities of workplace managers. *Sociology of Health and Illness, 27*(4), 490–514.

Macintyre, S. (1978). Some notes on record taking and making in an antenatal clinic. *Sociological Review, 26*, 595–611.

Malhotra, H. K., & Wig, N. N. (1975). *Dhat* syndrome: A culture-bound sex neurosis of the Orient. *Archives of Sexual Behavior, 4*(5), 519–528.

Martin, E. (1987). *The woman in the body*. Milton Keyes, UK: Open University Press.

Martin, E. (1994). *Flexible bodies: Tracking immunity in American culture from the days of polio to the age of AIDS*. Boston: Beacon Press.

Mishler, E. (1984). *The discourse of medicine: Dialectics of medical interviews*. Norwood, NJ: Ablex.

Mol, A. (2005). *The body multiple: Ontology in medical practice*. Durham, NC: Duke University Press.

Molloy, H., & Vasil, L. (2002). The social construction of Asperger syndrome: The pathologising of difference? *Disability and Society, 17*(6), 659–669.

Moss, P., & Dyck, I. (1999). Body, corporeal space, and

legitimating chronic illness: Women diagnosed with M.E. *Antipode, 31*(4), 372–397.

Murcott, T. (2005). *The whole story: Alternative medicine on trial?* London: Macmillan.

Mysyk, A. (1998). *Susto*: An illness of the poor. *Dialectical Anthropology, 23,* 187–202.

Nadesan, M. H. (2005). *Constructing autism: Unravelling the "truth" and understanding the social.* London: Routledge.

Ness, R. C. (1978). The old hag phenomenon as sleep paralysis: A biocultural interpretation. *Culture, Medicine and Psychiatry, 2*(1), 15–39.

Nettleton, S. (1992). *Power, pain and dentistry.* Buckingham, UK: Open University Press.

Oppenheim, J. (1991). *"Shattered serves": Doctors, patients, and depression in Victorian England.* Oxford, UK: Oxford University Press.

Oquendo, M., Horwath, E., & Martinez, A. (1992). *Ataques de nervios*: Proposed diagnostic criteria for a culture specific syndrome. *Culture, Medicine and Psychiatry, 16*(3), 367–376.

Orr, J. (2005). *Panic diaries: A genealogy of panic disorder.* Durham, NC: Duke University Press.

Pang, K. Y. C. (1990). *Hwabyung*: The construction of a Korean popular illness among Korean elderly immigrant women in the United States. *Culture, Medicine and Psychiatry, 14*(4), 495–512.

Pasveer, B. (1989). Knowledge of shadows: The introduction of X-ray images in medicine. *Sociology of Health and Illness, 11,* 360–381.

Petersen, A., & Bunton, R. (Eds.). (1997). *Foucault, health and medicine.* London: Routledge.

Pettinari, C. (1988). *Task, talk and text in the operating room: A study in medical discourse.* Norwood, NJ: Ablex.

Prince, R. (1985). The concept of culture-bound syndromes: Anorexia nervosa and brain-fag. *Social Science and Medicine, 21*(2), 197–203.

Prior, L. (1988). The architecture of the hospital: A study of spatial organization and medical knowledge. *British Journal of Sociology, 39*(1), 86–113.

Raffel, S. (1979). *Matters of fact.* London: Routledge & Kegan Paul.

Rees, C. (1981). Records and hospital routine. In P. Atkinson & C. Heath (Eds.), *Medical work: Realities and routines* (pp. 55–70). Farnborough, UK: Gower.

Reid, J., Ewan, C., & Lowy, E. (1991). Pilgrimage of pain: The illness experiences of women with repetition strain injury and the search for credibility. *Social Science and Medicine, 32*(5), 601–612.

Reid, J., & Reynolds, L. (1990). Requiem for RSI: The explanation and control of an occupational epidemic. *Medical Anthropology Quarterly, 4*(2), 162–190.

Richman, J. A., Jason, L. A., Taylor, R. R., & Jahn, S. C. (2000). Feminist perspectives on the social construction of chronic fatigue syndrome. *Health Care for Women International, 21*(3), 173–185.

Ritenbaugh, C. (1982). Obesity as a culture-bound syndrome. *Culture, Medicine and Psychiatry, 6*(4), 347–361.

Rodin, M. (1992). The social construction of premenstrual syndrome. *Social Science and Medicine, 35*(1), 49–56.

Rubel, A. J., & Moore, C. C. (2001). The contribution of medical anthropology to a comparative study of culture: *Susto* and tuberculosis. *Medical Anthropology Quarterly, 15*(4), 440–454.

Russell, J. G. (1989). Anxiety disorders in Japan: A review of the Japanese literature on *shinkeishitsu* and *taijinkofushi*. *Culture, Medicine and Psychiatry, 13*(4), 391–403.

Sartin, J. S. (2000). Gulf War illnesses: Causes and controversies. *Mayo Clinic Proceedings, 75,* 811–819.

Scott, S. (2006). The medicalisation of shyness: From social misfits to social fitness. *Sociology of Health and Illness, 28*(2), 133–153.

Scott, S. (2007). *Shyness and society: The illusion of competence.* London: Palgrave.

Shorter, E. (1992). *From paralysis to fatigue: A history of psychosomatic illness in the modern era.* New York: Free Press.

Showalter, E. (1997). *Hystories: Hysterical epidemics and modern media.* New York: Columbia University Press.

Shriver, T. E., White, D. A., & Kebede, A. (1998). Power, politics, and the framing of environmental illness. *Sociological Inquiry, 68,* 458–475.

Singer, A., Fitzgerald, M., & Von, L. (1984). Hypoglycemia: A controversial illness in US society. *Medical Anthropology, 8*(1), 1–35.

Smith, B. E. (1987). *Digging our own graves: Coal miners and the struggle over black lung disease.* Philadelphia: Temple University Press.

Smith, M., & Moore, J. (Eds.). (2006). *The prosthetic impulse: From a posthuman present to a biocultural future.* Cambridge, MA: MIT Press.

Stacey, J. (1997). *Teratologies: A cultural study of cancer.* London: Routledge.

Stevenson, C. (2000). *Medicine and magnificence: British hospital and asylum architecture, 1660–1815.* New Haven, CT: Yale University Press.

Sumathipala, S. H., & Bhugra, D. (2004). Culture-bound syndromes: The story of *dhat* syndrome. *British Journal of Psychiatry, 184,* 200–209.

Summerfield, D. (2001). The invention of post-traumatic stress disorder and the social usefulness of a psychiatric category. *British Medical Journal, 322,* 95–98.

Swagman, C. F. (1989). Fijaʿ: Fright and illness in highland Yemen. *Social Science and Medicine, 28*(4), 381–388.

Swartz, L. (1985). Anorexia nervosa as a culture-bound syndrome. *Social Science and Medicine, 20*(7), 725–730.

Timmermans, S. (2006). *Postmortem: How medical exam-

iners explain suspicious deaths. Chicago: University of Chicago Press.

Timmerman, S., & Berg, M. (2003). *The gold standard: The challenge of evidence-based medicine and standardization in health care.* Philadelphia: Temple University Press.

Townsend, J. M., & Carbone, C. L. (1980). Menopausal syndrome: Illness or social role—A transcultural analysis. *Culture, Medicine and Psychiatry, 4*(3), 229–248.

van Dijck, J. (2005). *The transparent body: A cultural analysis of medical imaging.* Seattle: University of Washington Press.

Veith, I. (1965). *Hysteria: A history of a disease.* Chicago: University of Chicago Press.

Ware, N. C. (1992). Suffering and the social construction of illness: The delegitimation of illness experience in chronic fatigue syndrome. *Medical Anthropology Quarterly, 6*(4), 347–361.

Weller, S. C., Pachter, L. M., Trotter, R. T., II, & Baer, R. D. (1993). *Empacho* in four Latino groups: A study of intra- and intercultural variation in beliefs. *Medical Anthropology, 15,* 109–136.

Wesseley, S., Hotopf, M., & Sharpe, M. (1998). *Chronic fatigue and its syndromes.* Oxford, UK: Oxford University Press.

Will, C. M. (2005). Arguing about the evidence: Readers, writers and inscription devices in coronary heart disease risk management. *Sociology of Health and Illness, 27*(6), 780–801.

Wright, P., & Treacher, A. (Eds.). (1982). *The problem of medical knowledge: Examining the social construction of medicine.* Edinburgh, UK: Edinburgh University Press.

Young, A. (1996). *The harmony of illusions: Inventing posttraumatic stress disorder.* Princeton, NJ: Princeton University Press.

Zavestoski, S., Brown, P., McCormick, S., Mayer, B., D'Ottavi, M., & Lucove, J. C. (2004). Patient activism and the struggle for diagnosis: Gulf War illness and other medically unexplained physical symptoms in the US. *Social Science and Medicine, 58*(1), 161–175.

CHAPTER 31

Constructing Therapy and Its Outcomes

- **Gale Miller**
  Tom Strong

his chapter examines the promise of social constructionist perspectives and research methods for analyzing therapy and counseling practices. We treat *therapy* and *counseling* as interchangeable terms. In most cases, we use the term *therapy* to refer to both. Our decision reflects typical usage in society and the widespread sharing of assumptions, practices, and concerns among professionals who call themselves therapists and counselors. The term *clients* is used to refer to the persons served by therapists, although some therapists prefer other terms, such as patients. We define therapy as the activities that therapists do. Therapists consult with clients about problems in clients' lives and how they might be managed. Therapists may also consult with representatives of nontherapy institutions, mediate conflicts,

administer and evaluate the results of psychological tests, and serve as gatekeepers, such as when court-ordered therapy is a condition for parents regaining custody of their children. They also sometimes act as imputational specialists, that is, as experts at discovering and classifying deviance (Pfohl, 1978).

The chapter is not a comprehensive review of constructionist research on therapy. Rather, we draw from aspects of this literature in discussing empirical and analytic strategies for furthering social constructionists' interest in studying reality construction, maintenance, and change in therapy sites. Our approach represents a *social constructionism of therapy*. We treat therapy philosophies, practices, and relationships as objects for study and analysis. Our orientation to therapy and social constructionism, although not inherently opposed, differs from that of therapists and social scientists who use social constructionist perspectives to advance particular therapy approaches and philosophies (Franklin & Nurius, 1998; Hall, 1997; McNamee & Gergen, 1992; Parton & O'Byrne, 2000; see also Gergen & Gergen, Chapter 9, this volume). The latter use of social constructionist perspectives might be called social constructionism in therapy (Franklin, 1995; Franklin & Jordan, 1996).

We emphasize the close relationship between the qualitative research methods typically employed by social constructionist researchers and the perspectives that they use in analyzing data. These methods and perspectives form a basis for analyzing diverse therapies as institutional discourses (Miller, 1994; Miller & Fox, 2004). This perspective calls attention to the way therapy realities are shaped by persons' talk in social interaction, by the local contexts within which the interactions occur, and by broad-based historical formations within which diverse therapies have evolved. The perspective takes account of how socially constructed therapy realities are shaped by the contingencies of concrete therapy interactions and by wider sociohistorical factors. The latter factors have implications for the way the purposes and goals of therapy interactions are defined. On the other hand, it is within concrete therapy interactions that these purposes and goals are given practical form and are applied to the practical circumstances at hand.

The methods and perspectives emphasized by the institutional discourse perspective contribute to a social constructionism of therapy that recognizes the relativity of social realities while also being empirically and analytically rigorous. We discuss these methods and perspectives in later sections, but first we consider how therapy is nested within an institutional environment that both supports and constrains the actions of therapists and clients.

Therapy Environment

Therapy occupies a distinctive niche within human service institutions. Therapists are trained in several different academic disciplines, notably in medicine, education, psychology, social work, psychiatric nursing, and the ministry. They work in a variety of institutional settings (including clinics, hospitals, schools, the military, residential treatment centers, correctional facilities, and the mass media), deal with many different kinds of problems (such as chronic health issues, interpersonal and intergroup conflicts, crime and delinquency, chemical addictions, depression, academic and career problems, and grief) and serve diverse clients (including individuals, families and other small groups, and communities). Many therapists are also accountable to organizations that refer clients to therapy, pay therapists, establish and enforce standards of professional conduct, and assess the effectiveness of therapists' interventions. The rise of managed care programs over the past 30 years is particularly significant (Hoyt, 2000). The programs are regulatory arrangements within which third parties (insurers and reviewers) influence the nature and length of therapy (Hoyt, 1995)

These aspects of the therapy environment point to the ways diverse therapies emphasize different social concerns, interests, and formulations of social reality. The differences have implications for therapists' orientations to their clients' problems, to how change is most effectively achieved through therapy, to what indicators should be used in evaluating therapy interventions, and to what constitutes appropriate therapist–client relationships.

Consider, for example, the differing social realities associated with therapies based on the medical model and those influenced by social constructionist perspectives. Medically oriented therapists treat clients' problems as disease-like and caused by underlying biomedical and psychic conditions that are often undetectable to the untrained observer (Herson & Turner, 1994; Perry, Frances, & Clarkin, 1990; Polatin, 1966). Medically oriented therapists address these conditions by diagnosing their clients' problems and prescribing treatments (often including, but not limited to, medications) that are designed to ameliorate, if not cure, the problems (Forman, Jones, & Francis, 1995; Oakley & Potter, 1997; Reid, 1989). Many of the categories used by medically oriented therapists and clients are codified in the *Diagnostic and Statistical Manual of Mental Disorders* (DSM-IV-TR; American Psychiatric Association, 2000), which also describes the typical or expected course of development for each disease category if it is left untreated.

Constructionist-oriented therapists, on the other hand, stress that clients' problems are socially constructed realities and that solving the problems involves developing alternative orientations to clients' lives (Dean, 1993; Efran, Lukens, & Lukens, 1988; Laird, 1993). Although they do not deny the reality of the pain felt by clients, constructionist-oriented therapists emphasize the ways clients' senses of their lives as troubled are sustained in their use of language (Anderson, 1997; de Shazer, 1994; White & Epston, 1990). They do not diagnose or look for the underlying causes of clients' problems, although these therapists sometimes ask clients to consider how their problems might be related to inequalities in society. Constructionist-oriented therapists emphasize that change in therapy involves helping clients to use available resources to assert greater control over their lives.

The differences between medically and constructionist-oriented therapies suggest the range of philosophical and practical orientations practiced by therapists. The differing social concerns and interests that shape medically oriented, constructionist-oriented, and other therapies are conditions of possibility that influence the range and types of social realities constructed in concrete therapy relationships and settings. The conditions include the ideological emphases (such as the medical and constructionist orientations) in different therapies, the typical patterns of interaction associated with them, and the institutional contexts in which the therapies are practiced. Next, we consider the research methods and analytic perspectives that constructionist researchers use in studying how social realities are constructed in differing institutional discourses.

Observing Therapy Realities

The qualitative research methods used by constructionist researchers are standpoints for observing therapy. They also shape researchers' relationships with participants in therapy settings. The relationships range from face-to-face encounters (including various degrees of participation by researchers in therapy settings) to more distanced relationships, such as the analysis of video recordings of therapy sessions and of texts written by and about therapy. Thus the methods used by constructionist researchers are more than simple or neutral means of collecting data about therapy settings; they are empirical and interpretive frameworks for knowing therapy. We discuss three such frameworks in this section.

Microinteractional Approaches

The first framework consists of microinteractional research methods and perspectives focused on the intricacies of talk and social interaction (Arminen, 1998; Bavelas, McGee, Phillips, & Routledge, 2000; Czyewski, 1995; Edwards, 1995; Gale, 1991). This research focus casts therapy as a series of interactional encounters that researchers often audio- and video-record. Analysts subscribing to different theoretical orientations attend to different aspects and implications of the interactions that they observe. For example, Alfred Scheflin (1973) concentrates on the social organization and meaning of bodily movements (gestures, posture, bodily shifts, etc.) in analyzing therapy interactions. William Labov and David Fanshel (1977), on the other hand, stress spoken language in their study, which focuses on the social frames or definitions of the situation within which therapy interactions occur. Labov and Fanshel explain that the significance of interactional details "can be defined only when the situation in which they are used is well known" (p. 27). Irit Kupferberg and David Green's (2005) study of metaphorical negotiation in therapy interactions occurring in the mass media and cyberspace represents yet another empirical and theoretical orientation to therapy talk and interaction.

An especially promising microinteractional approach is conversation analysis (Atkinson & Heritage, 1984; Boden & Zimmerman, 1991; Sacks, Schegloff, & Jefferson, 1974). Conversation analysts examine how social interaction is organized as turns at talk—that is, how speakers make and take speaking turns in pursuing their social purposes in interaction. As with its methodological cousin, ethnomethodology (Garfinkel, 1967), conversation analysis focuses on the mundane and taken-for-granted aspects of social interaction. Conversation analysts observe how therapists, clients, and others *show* how they make sense of each others' actions through their words and actions. No attempt is made to get "inside of" people's heads; instead the focus is on what interactants observably do with their own and others' talk.

Conversation analysts ask, for example, How does a short pause of only three-tenths of a second matter to talk between speakers? How might a momentarily averted gaze be related to a speaker's decision to change what she is saying in the middle of a speaking turn? These questions point out that therapy interactions are reflexively dialogic. A therapist's raised eyebrow or noted uninterest, as a client says something important, can cue the client to modify what is

said, which, in turn, would elicit new responses from the therapist. In this way, microinteractional developments become consequential for the ways interactants make sense of and respond to each other.

We see these aspects of conversation analysis in Anssi Peräkylä's (1995) and David Silverman's (1997) studies of systemic AIDS counseling, which defines clients' problems as recurring patterns of action within social relationships. Systemic therapists treat the problematic patterns as products of clients' social relationships and as sources for sustaining the relationships. A major purpose of systemic therapy is to "interrupt" the problematic patterns in order to change clients' social relationships. Peräkylä's and Silverman's studies explore how systemic therapists and their clients interactionally construct problems, social systems, and interventions designed to change clients' social systems. They also analyze how therapy participants use their interactional turns to show concern for others' emotions.

Ethnographic Approaches

The second methodological standpoint for knowing therapy consists of ethnographic studies. These studies involve observing therapy settings and interviewing the participants. Ethnographic researchers differ from conversation analysts, however, in their greater interest in how therapy interactions are influenced by the institutional contexts within which they take place (Bosk, 1992; Miller, 1986, 1987; Vandewater, 1983). For example, Kathleen Lowney (1999) analyzes how therapy becomes entertainment when it is incorporated into the moral dramas of television talk shows. She discusses how therapists appearing on the shows advance the individualistic discourse of the recovery movement, which is perhaps most clearly represented by Alcoholics Anonymous. Within this movement, personal and interpersonal problems are defined as addictions stemming from persons' dysfunctional relationships.

As with microinteractional researchers, ethnographers vary in their theoretical orientations. For example, Cheryl Mattingly (1998) uses a phenomenological perspective to analyze how therapists and clients in occupational therapy settings construct new life stories for clients. The narratives address the biomedical goals of occupational therapy, but they also speak to clients' changed social and emotional circumstances. Ethnomethodological ethnography focuses on the interpretive methods that people use in making sense of their experiences (Garfinkel, 1967; Pollner, 1987). Ethnomethodologists treat the social construction of reality as practical activity, that is, as reality work. These ethnographers describe the reality work done by therapy participants and highlight its social implications. For example, Stephen Pfohl (1978) and James Holstein (1993) analyze the reality work done by therapists in assessing the levels of dangerousness posed by patients in a maximum-security prison and by persons recommended for involuntary hospitalization.

The question of how therapy realities are constructed to fit with their institutional contexts is central to several recent comparative studies of therapy. For example, Gale Miller and David Silverman (1995) comparatively analyze how the discourse of enablement is implemented in an HIV counseling center in England and a family therapy agency in the United States. They define the discourse of enablement as "a professional strategy for inciting preferred forms of troubles talk and encouraging preferred forms of change in clients' lives" (p. 732). Other comparative ethnographies focus on the social construction of family, emotion, intrapsychic forces, and moral community. For example, Jaber Gubrium (1992) analyzes how orientations to the social reality of family order and disorder are embedded in the assumptions, interests, and practices of two therapy settings. Also, Darin Weinberg (2005) examines the practical conditions that shape therapy realities that are constructed in two treatment centers serving persons diagnosed as addicted and mentally ill.

Philosophical–Historical Approaches

The third framework for knowing therapy is philosophical and historical research (Edelman, 1977; Foucault, 1977; Sass, 1992). These constructionist researchers use methods and perspectives associated with the humanities in analyzing texts of various sorts. The researchers use the word *text* to refer to both the objects of their analysis (e.g., books, pictures, and social interactions) and to their "attitudes" toward the objects. They assume that texts' significance is not predetermined but emerges as "readers" interpret them. For example, Sander Gilman (1988) analyzes images of madness, the asylum, and the therapist role in the writings and art of Charles Dickens, Vincent van Gogh, and Sigmund Freud. Gilman (1988, p. 2) explains that his study shows how therapy realities are "constructed on the basis of specific ideological needs and structured along the categories of representation accepted within that ideology."

Gilman's study highlights the critical constructionist impulse in many philosophical and historical studies of therapy. Critical constructionists draw on several theoretical perspectives in critiquing the assumptions and implications of diverse therapies. For example, Louis Sass (1994) uses aspects of Foucauldian, Wittgensteinian, and phenomenological theory to critique 20th-century therapists' formulation of schizophrenic delusion as the absence of human reason. He also uses autobiographical texts to reframe schizophrenia as an alternative—solipsistic—reality that emerges from within human reason. Philip Cushman (1995) applies a hermeneutic perspective in discussing how ideologies of self and of therapy are intertwined in history and culture. He examines how therapy ideologies are embedded in the cultural practices and understandings of particular eras. Trends in therapy (e.g., 1950s lab-coat behaviorism and the tie-dyed human-potential movement of the 1970s) illustrate this point. He also emphasizes how psychological theories shape their historical eras, such as how post–World War II therapy theories construct an "empty self" that needs to be filled through consumerism.

The critical impulse of philosophical and historical studies is perhaps most sharply developed in critical discourse studies. These studies analyze how the use of language comes freighted with the values, understandings, and rhetorical practices associated with particular cultural formations (Fairclough, 1992; Foucault, 1972; Voloshinov, 2006). When clients and therapists talk, their dialogue refracts the discourses from which each draws specific languages, interpretations, and actions. To illustrate, a client may present concerns in a relational discourse (heartbreak, bereavement, interpersonal conflict), whereas a therapist might hear these concerns in the discourse of a diagnostic system. Each language maps problems and solutions differently. For a critical discourse analyst, any choice of discourse means that other discourses go unused. No discourse can totally represent the experiences or values of speakers, because language is always partial and allied to particular values. A major aim of critical discourse analysts is to make evident the ways in which dominant therapy discourses exclude alternative possibilities for thought and action (Wainwright & Calnan, 2002).

We have treated microinteractional, ethnographic, and philosophical–historical approaches as distinct in this section. This treatment reflects the fact that each approach brings distinctive concerns and strengths to the study of therapy. But they also overlap and complement each other. The areas of complementarity are central to the institutional discourse perspective and related approaches to constructionist research, such as discursive constructionism (Buttny, 2004) and discursive psychology (Edwards, 1992). We develop this emphasis in the institutional discourse perspective in the next section by discussing how it might

stimulate a constructionist imagination about therapy. Researchers express a constructionist imagination in considering the ways in which therapy realities are interactional, contextual, and historical–cultural constructions.

Toward a Constructionist Imagination

It is important to begin by pointing out that the institutional discourse perspective is itself an empirical and interactional framework for knowing therapy. Like the other frameworks discussed here, it allows researchers to readily see and understand therapy in particular ways, while offering limited opportunities for other "seeings" and understandings. This point is important because the institutional discourse perspective might appear to be a triangulating strategy that offers researchers comprehensive, objective, or privileged access to empirical reality (Denzin, 1978). This is not the case. For us, the value of the perspective rests on its usefulness to constructionist researchers of therapy in pursuing their research goals and interests. One such interest involves developing a constructionist imagination about the interconnections among therapy philosophies, practices, relationships, and contexts.

We see a constructionist imagination in Michael Billig's (1999) critical constructionist critique of Sigmund Freud's concept of repression (Brill, 1938). For Freud, repression is an internal—biological—process through which individuals monitor and control their thoughts and desires. It occurs within the unconscious and operates to keep troublesome impulses secret from both other people and from ourselves. This approach to repression also justifies a depth psychology designed to get beyond appearances and to the underlying reality of repression. Billig accepts the existence of repression as a form of avoidance, but he disagrees with Freud's claim that it is a hidden or biological process. Repression, for Billig, is an observable aspect of social interaction and occurs when people in interaction close off or avoid potential topics of discussion. Indeed, there is a commonplace word for such practices. It is *politeness*, an activity that may involve self-censorship or conversational collaboration with others.

Billig (1999, p. 52) highlights how "we are able to change the subject, pushing conversations away from embarrassing or troubling topics." He further notes that the topics (particularly sexual issues) that were repressed in Freud's conversations with his patients were also topics to be avoided in public conversations in Freud's Vienna. They were historically and culturally grounded taboos. Within Billig's constructionist imagination, then, repression is a socially organized activity. He also notes that repression may become institutionalized as unnoticed habits within the conventions of polite conversation in social groups.

Billig's (1999) reformulation of repression suggests that conversation analytic, ethnomethodological, and historical perspectives are useful in examining therapy realities. His analysis is further developed by considering conversation analysts' studies of affiliation in social interaction (Heritage, 1984). These studies detail the noticed and unnoticed "habits" used by interactants in managing conversational topics and relationships. They also show that polite avoidance is only one way of dealing with potentially troublesome issues. We have already noted, for example, Peräkylä's (1995) and Silverman's (1997) analyses of the ways HIV therapists delicately encourage clients to talk about delicate topics.

Ethnographic studies of therapy realities extend Billig's analysis by analyzing conversational repression across therapy settings. Whereas these studies might consider how clients avoid troublesome topics, a potentially more promising research focus is studying how therapists avoid and divert undesired topics raised by clients and other therapy participants. For example,

Gubrium's (1992) comparative ethnography points out how therapists' theories about family systems and troubles are related to the ways they attend and disattend to aspects of clients' talk Comparative ethnographies extend ethnographic research on the discourse of enablement (Miller & Silverman, 1995) by exploring the ways that therapists signal their lack of interest in particular conversational topics. Constructionist researchers also examine how clients acquiesce or resist such therapist moves and the consequences of clients' responses for therapy. The studies would link ethnographers and microinteractional analysts to critical constructionists' interest in attending to what is excluded from therapy. The studies would show that repression in therapy is not predetermined but is an accomplishment of participants in therapy settings.

Constructing Inner Realities

Few ideas are more associated with therapy than the assumption that human behavior is driven by inner forces that are—to varying degrees—beyond the control of the individual. This idea is central to Freud's highly influential ideas, but it is not limited to him or even to the world of therapy. It is a broad-based cultural theme that may be observed in the everyday conversations of nontherapists, in art and literature, and in popular culture. Social critics emphasize two implications of this cultural practice. First, it individualizes human behavior by removing it from its social contexts. In this way, attention is directed toward individual characteristics (including inner mental and emotional states) as most salient in making sense of people's behavior. The second implication is that it positions some people as authorities on what should count as normal and abnormal behavior.

Nikolas Rose (1990, 1998) uses the term *psy complex* in analyzing the fact that psychologists are often defined as experts on normal or appropriate personhood, development, and interpersonal conduct and, by implication, what is not normal or appropriate. Rose adds that psychology's discursive mapping of "individualization" constructs a base of normative understandings and techniques, as well as justifications, for "disciplining difference" (see also Burman, 1994; Hoshamand, 2001; Parker, 1999; Parker & Shotter, 1990; Shweder, 1991). When linked to governmental policies, these psychological understandings and techniques can be used to homogenize educational curricula, mental health treatment, or correctional services. Human differences become the focus of therapies designed to "help" people become "normal" by accepting and complying with dominant cultural realities. Accordingly, the justness of cultural practices is treated as given and bypasses critical scrutiny.

The critical constructionist methods and perspectives discussed here are beginning points for addressing these issues as research topics. For example, Cushman's (1995) analysis of the relationship between cultural orientations to self and the knowledges and practices of therapy points to the historical relativity of the psy complex. His study challenges claims to value-free and universally applicable scientific knowledge by therapists. It is also a standpoint from which to question therapists' qualifications to define what should count as acceptable and unacceptable behavior. Jeff Coulter's (1979), George Herbert Mead's (1934) and L. S. Vygotsky's (1978) approaches to mind and discursive psychologists' analyses of psychological constructs as interactional phenomena are also useful starting points (Edwards, 1997).

Another important research strategy is offered in Dorothy Smith's (1978) analysis of a text describing an interview about a respondent's belief that a friend ("K") is mentally ill. Smith stresses that the respondent's attribution of mental illness to K turns on the use of contrast structures. The structures include one part that might be heard as an instruction for interpreting the situation at hand and a second part that reports on the friend's behavior within the situation. Mental illness may be seen in the contrast between the instruction (which defines appropriate or normal behavior) and the person's reported behavior. Consider, for example, the following excerpt from the text. Please notice how this statement points to a troubled inner reality that is made observable in K's "inappropriate" behavior:

> K is so intense about everything at times, she tries too hard. Her sense of proportion is out of kilter. When asked casually to help in a friend's garden, she went at it for hours, never stopping, barely looking up. (Smith, 1978, p. 29)

Kathryn Fox's (1999a, 1999b, 2001) ethnography of a cognitive self-change program in several correctional faculties further illustrates how a constructionist imagination is useful in addressing aspects of the psy complex. This therapy approach treats criminal behavior as rooted in the cognitive distortions of the criminal personality. Much of the treatment program involves instructing inmates on how to interpret and describe their feelings and behavior as expressions of their criminal personalities. Fox details the rhetorical and interpretive methods used by the staff to correct the inmates' distorted cognitions and instruct them on how to properly think, feel, and talk about their past, present, and future lives. The instructions also justify staff members' claims to privileged knowledge about inmates' inner mental states and about what is appropriate behavior.

Smith's and Fox's studies call attention to the ongoing reality work that organizes and sustains the psy complex. People do reality work by assigning meanings to events and behavior, thus transforming them into instances of culturally shared realities. In this way, culturally honored orientations to mind and difference are affirmed, and interpreters' preferred definitions of appropriate and inappropriate behavior are justified.

Weinberg's (2005) comparative ethnography of two treatment programs extends this approach to the psy complex by showing how it is shaped by practical organizational contingencies. This study reminds us to notice how therapy settings are organized to produce different kinds of troubled minds and troubled behaviors.

These studies also speak to issues raised by Ian Hacking (1986) in analyzing how people are constructed as instances of troubled-person categories in institutional interactions (see also Hall, Juhila, Parton, & Pösö, 2003). The studies reveal the interpretive practices used by reality constructors to define troubled minds, which are then assumed to be the essential core of troubled persons' selves. Microinteractional studies are useful in showing how therapists elicit client accounts of experience that they later reformulate as proof of psychopathology, such as delusions (Georgaca, 2000), disability (Antaki, 2001), or addictions (Halonen, 2006). Conversely, therapists can be shown inviting clients to contest and negotiate pathologizing cultural and professional discourses (e.g., Avdi, 2005), or trying on more preferred discourses to construct clients' predicaments and aspirations (Strong, Zeman, & Foskett, 2006). Steven Kogan (1998) sees such "politics" as an inescapable aspect of constructing therapy realities.

Social Construction of Evidence

The evidence-based movement in medicine took off in the 1990s and not long thereafter in therapy. The purpose of the movement is to standardize the knowledge and practices of therapy into a common diagnostic language (that of the DSM-IV-TR) and to emphasize therapy interventions shown to be empirically supported by research. For example, the clinical division of the American Psychological Association has formed a task force to examine empirically validated treatments. Many therapists welcome this development, as do many persons who administer therapy programs (including managed care programs), who enforce ethical rules and standards, and who train graduate students in therapy. The movement promises to bring together the disparate approaches and interests of the therapy world through the adoption of a common vocabulary and scientifically tested practices.

But critics of the movement see it as an attempt to legislate therapy practice to conform to a flawed scientific perspective and to serve the interests of some therapy communities over others, especially the interests of the psy complex. Critics also stress that the evidence-based movement privileges medically oriented therapies by treating therapy interventions as similar to doses of medication (Stiles & Shapiro, 1989). For example, a cognitive therapy intervention (such as stopping criminal thinking) is "administered" to clients. Psychological tests are then used in ways that are analogous to blood samples to measure outcomes purportedly resulting from the therapy intervention. Critics of such studies note that several assumptions are at work in such studies, including the assumptions that psychological tests are a good measure of outcome and that it is the intervention (not other factors in the therapy setting and in clients' lives) that "causes" change.

It is not surprising that one group of critics of evidence-based practice consists of advocates for interactional, constructionist, and humanist therapies (Bohart, 2005; Larner, 2004; Strong, Busch, & Couture, in press; White & Stancombe, 2003). These critics point out that many of the problems reported by therapy clients are unrelated to the dysfunctions stressed by medically oriented researchers (e.g., Dumont & Fitzpatrick, 2005; Wampold, Ahn, & Coleman, 2001). They also stress that the emotions, memories, thoughts, and attitudes expressed by clients are interactional creations. Therapists' actions are implicated in clients' expressed mental and emotional states, because the expressions are responsive to what others are saying and doing.

Viewed this way, therapy is not about using interventions designed to treat clients' diagnosed disorders. It is, instead, an interactional process of "working up" definitions of social reality that make sense to clients and therapists and that point to practical actions clients might take in changing their lives.

The assumptions and claims of these critics clearly resonate with important themes in constructionist research. Thus it would be reasonable for constructionist researchers to want to enter into this debate to support the interests of interactional, constructionist, and humanist therapists. For example, critical constructionists might examine how the evidence-based movement has emerged to advance some ideological, economic, and political interests within therapy and its environment. The researchers might also analyze the ways in which scientific evidence is a socially constructed reality (Knorr-Cetina & Mulkay, 1983). Such studies are useful in relativizing claims that scientific research reveals universally applicable practices for addressing client problems that fit into particular diagnostic categories. A related line of critical constructionist inquiry is found in the ethnographic literature on rate-producing behavior (Bogdan & Ksander, 1980). This literature challenges the evidence-based research assumption that quantitative measures are objective, value-neutral depictions of social reality by analyzing the ways in which categorization and counting are reality work.

Another promising use of the constructionist imagination involves expanding discussions about evidence among therapists. Such constructionist studies might begin with Donald Schön's (1983) research on professional practice as reflection-in-action. Schön examines the ordinary, unacknowledged, and artful ways that psychotherapists (but also architects, scientists, and city planners) reflexively participate in problem-solving situations. Reflection-in-action is an ongoing process of making sense of problematic situations as practitioners seek to change them. Meaning and action are linked in this process, with each working together as foreground and background in socially constructing evidence for understanding and solving practical problems. Mattingly (1998) further develops this perspective in her phenomenological analysis of reality construction in occupational therapy.

Susan White and John Stancombe (2003) go further in discussing how social constructionist methods and perspectives are useful in identifying and analyzing tacit aspects of clinical judgment and practices that usually go unnoticed by therapists and evaluation researchers. They explain that constructionist studies of clinical practices do not strive so much for scientific objectivity as for ethnomethodological indifference (Garfinkel & Sacks, 1970), that is, "suspending any presuppositions on what constitutes 'good' and 'bad' clinical judgment" and focusing on what participants in therapy settings actually do in addressing clients' problems (White & Stancombe, 2003, p. 145). Constructionist researchers are positioned to develop this focus through microanalytic, ethnographic, and critical discourse studies of therapy settings, practices, and interactions. Each of these research strategies expands the evidence base that therapists, administrators, and teachers use in assessing effective therapy practices, seeking not to eliminate existing evidence-based research but to expand its scope and make it more realistic.

Applying Constructionist Research

Any discussion of applying social constructionist research must address questions about the epistemological status of constructionists' knowledge. For example, should we regard constructionists' research findings as facts, as impressions, or as something else? Treated as facts, constructionists' findings represent objectively real structures and processes that therapy participants cannot wish away. Such "facts" might be used to legislate therapist practices, much as evidence-based research is used. Defined as impressions, constructionists' findings are expressions of researchers' perceptions, biases, and opinions. Although therapy participants might consider these findings interesting, they face no practical imperative to try to apply the findings. Given the assumptions of social constructionist perspectives, it is difficult to argue for the "constructionist findings as facts" position, although this does not mean that social constructionist research is devoid of facts or concern for objective realities (Edwards, Ashmore, & Potter, 1995; Weinberg, 2005). But constructionist research findings are also more than impressions; they speak to practical and moral issues associated with observable patterns of activity and relationship in therapy settings.

Several of the studies discussed earlier suggest other ways of using constructionist research in therapy settings. For example, Janet Bavelas and colleagues (2000) used microinteractional methods to examine how therapists guide and shape therapy interviews by using particular words, paraphrasing clients' answers, and asking questions. These therapist actions create conditions of possibility for the co-construction (by clients and therapists) of therapy realities. Such studies illustrate that microinteractional research is a valuable resource for sensitizing therapists to the ways their talk influences what is likely to be said in therapy (Gale & Lawless, 2003).

Schön's (1983), Mattingly's (1998), and White and Stancombe's (2003) analyses of therapists' tacit knowledge illustrate how constructionist research calls attention to otherwise unnoticed aspects of therapy settings. Such research is not designed to produce facts that others must accept and live with but that can serve as sources for discussions among therapy participants and researchers. This use of the sociological imagination treats constructionist research as part of ongoing processes of social construction.

For example, Cheryl Mattingly and Maureen Fleming (1994) discuss how constructionist research can give language to practice. New languages emerge collaboratively as researchers suggest new framings of therapy and as therapy participants develop new vocabularies for describing and explaining what they do. Researchers and therapy participants also build distinctive—local—contexts for engaging questions about the evidence base of therapy by continuously exploring and describing what goes on in particular therapy settings.

This orientation treats constructionist research as a resource for therapy participants. Particularly noteworthy are its potential uses in constructionist-oriented therapies. These uses involve the overlapping assumptions and concerns of constructionist researchers and constructionist-oriented therapists. Arguably, therapeutic practice that is informed by constructionist understanding involves different kinds of expertise about the ways in which therapists orient to and contextually use language in therapy (Strong, 2002). For example, once one acknowledges the constructive or strategic potentials in articulating and answering questions (Tomm, 1988), research and therapy become more than benign exercises in gathering information. This is where the line between therapy and research can blur. Curiosity and collaboration have become central features of the constructionist therapies (e.g., Anderson & Goolishian, 1992). Unlike therapists who answer clients' questions with clinical wisdom, constructionist-oriented practitioners treat them as invitations to shared inquiry (Heron, 1996). This practice parallels the recent hybridization of constructionist research methods (Denzin & Lincoln, 2006; McLeod, 2001).

Much constructionist research focuses on contesting dominant understandings of therapy, identifying generative discursive practices, and contributing to participant-preferred outcomes (Guilfoyle, 2003; House, 2003; Wade, 1997). Sometimes these aims meet in studies that engage participants in deconstructing taken-for-granted understandings while inviting the construction of more useful understandings (e.g., Avdi, 2005; Morgan & O'Neill, 2001). An interesting spin-off of constructionist research involves therapists' adoption of qualitative research methods as therapeutic methods. Critical discourse analysis has furnished questions for narrative therapists, action research (a community empowerment tool), and heuristic inquiry (a powerful means by which resources and preferred experiences can be built upon). Recent efforts to coconstruct locally developed therapeutic methods for personal and community transformation are also consistent with the hybridization of methods (e.g., Heron, 1996; Newman & Holzman, 1997). Other therapists see the therapeutic interview as an opportunity to elicit, then innovatively join, clients' constructions of what change should entail (Duncan, Miller, & Sparks, 2000).

Micro- and macrointeractional research on how forms of knowledge, actions, and relationships are constructed or sustained has promoted a "discursive wisdom" (Paré, 2002) to be added to Schön's (1983) notion of reflective practice. New ethical domains of practice open up when therapists recognize their rhetorical capacity to supplant, hijack, or thwart clients' and others' efforts to articulate experience in constructs and idioms different from their own (Strong, 2004). Some use this knowledge to assist in clients' emancipatory efforts (e.g., Waldegrave, Tamasese, Tuhaka, & Campbell, 2003), whereas others turn to the imaginative and motivating potentials of questions and action-engendering answers they can promote (Cooperrider, Whitney, & Stavros, 2003). Recognizing that some questions and responses can "help" others sustain particular constructions and discourses whereas other responses and questions can disrupt them carries a kind of discursive burden usually unconsidered by nonconstructionist therapists.

Studying Constructionist-Oriented Therapies

The constructionist research agenda discussed in this chapter focuses on the interactional processes within which therapy realities are constructed, the various contextual factors that influence therapy practices and relationships, and the cultural assumptions and commitments embedded in therapy approaches. These aspects of our constructionist research agenda have equal relevance for studies of both constructionist-oriented therapies and realist-oriented therapies. Carolyn Taylor and Susan White (2000) state that constructionist studies are sources for developing reflexive consciousness and practices that help therapists to critically examine their routine reality-creating practices. Constructionist-oriented therapists are no less susceptible to unreflexive routinizing influences in therapy settings than are realist-oriented therapists. Nor are they immune from the human tendency to construct realities that express and serve their self-interests.

We have noted, for example, how the concept of collaboration has emerged as a central defining aspect of many constructionist-oriented therapies (Duncan & Miller, 2000; Madsen, 1999; Paré & Larner, 2003). Constructionist-oriented therapists define collaboration as a distinctive therapist–client relationship in which the expertise and desires of clients and therapists are treated as equal. They also contrast this approach to therapy relationships with the "noncollaborative" approach of other (especially medically oriented) therapies. Constructionist studies of therapy offer a reflexive standpoint from which to empirically examine these claims. Microinteractional studies of therapy interactions focus on the details of therapist–client interactions that therapists call equal and collaborative. The studies would not treat collaboration as an inherent feature of some therapy approaches and not others but as a practical accomplishment in therapy interactions.

Constructionist researchers ask how a sense of equality is constructed in social interactions that are often organized as a division of interactional labor—for example, clients have problems in need of remedy, therapists do not; therapists ask questions, clients answer them; therapists give advice, clients receive it. A critical perspective is introduced by also asking what is repressed in the collaborative interactions of constructionist-oriented therapy. And, finally, ethnographic research is useful in considering how the practical meaning of collaboration and equality in therapy is influenced by contextual and ideological factors. Weinberg's (2005) research suggests that the practical meaning of collaboration differs in therapy settings situated in different institutional environments, even if the therapists in the settings subscribe to the same therapy approaches. It is also clear from the literature on contemporary constructionist-oriented therapies that proponents of these therapies differ in how they define collaboration and equality.

Constructionist studies of the concept of collaboration in constructionist-oriented therapies call attention to these approaches to therapy as also being social theories. For example, solution-focused brief therapies borrow from Wittgensteinian philosophy in describing problems and solutions as different language games (Miller, 1997). The studies further develop this theory of language, problems, solutions, and therapeutic change by explaining how particular solution-focused brief therapy practices form a solutions-language game. Constructionist researchers might also examine the ways in which narrative therapy is a social theory of language, problems, solutions, and therapeutic change. These therapist–theorists apply Foucauldian philosophy in arguing that clients' problems are often related to clients' internalization of dominant cultural narratives (Freedman & Combs, 1996). Thus an important emphasis in narrative therapy involves exposing and externalizing problem narratives in order to create new ones.

Thus another way in which the constructionist imagination might be used by researchers is by studying the relationship between constructionist-oriented therapists' social theories and their practices. These studies might look at the interactional and interpretive methods that organize reality work in these therapies. They might also explore how constructionist-oriented therapies operate to elicit some and discourage other forms of talk. A critical view is introduced by considering whether and how constructionist-oriented therapies are organized to construct power relations (Foucault, 1978). Microinteractional and ethnographic methods might also be used to examine the concrete ways in which therapists and clients construct relations of power in their talk and interactions. Critical constructionist perspectives might be used to analyze the assumptions and interests at stake in constructionist-oriented therapists' social theories, including how they might draw on and affirm aspects of dominant cultural discourses and narratives.

Finally, it is important to remember that constructionist-oriented therapists often practice in environments that are oriented to realist assumptions and concerns. We have pointed out how these concerns are associated with institutional pressures to diagnose clients' problems, follow evidence-based practices, and differentiate between appropriate and inappropriate behavior. We should also mention clients' realist assumptions and concerns about addressing their "real" problems. Thus constructionist researchers might also study the ways in which constructionist-oriented therapists interpret and respond to these environmental pressures, including how they acquiesce to and resist them. We conclude by suggesting some ways that constructionist studies might be further developed.

Conclusion

We have discussed the ways in which therapy is a site for microinteractional, ethnographic, and critical constructionist research. Therapy is a rich and diverse context for observing how social realities are proposed, assessed, negotiated, chosen, and acted on by therapy participants. Constructionist studies of therapy might be developed to address issues in a variety of substantive specialties in the social and behavioral sciences. These include studies of interpersonal relations, human development, the life course, mind, emotions, health, and illness. Constructionists specializing in the study of social institutions (such as family, law, religion, education, and medicine) might also find therapy a promising research site. The chapter also points to some of the ways that therapy might be of interest to applied social and behavioral scientists. Each of these research strategies involves treating therapy as the object of constructionist researchers' observations and analysis.

There is, however, another way in which constructionist researchers might orient to therapy. This approach treats therapy as a site for reflecting on constructionist researchers' assumptions and practices and as a source of ideas about how constructionist research might be done differently. The researchers might ask, for example, how their observations and analyses are influenced by the institutional environments (particularly academic environments) of their research. Constructionist researchers might also consider the language games that organize constructionist research and, more generally, the ways in which their research methods and analytic perspectives are reality-creating resources. Applied constructionist researchers might critically examine how their suggestions are adapted to fit with the social contexts and interests of therapy.

Alternatively, constructionist researchers might examine therapy sites for ideas about how they might better achieve their research goals. Our emphasis on therapy as a discourse of enablement (Miller & Silverman, 1995) points out that both realist- and constructionist-oriented therapists are experts at asking questions designed to invite conversations about preferred topics. Constructionist researchers might borrow from and adapt therapy strategies and techniques in their research. Therapy interviews are especially promising sites of learning for active interviewers (Holstein & Gubrium, 1995) who ask questions intended to reveal the diverse interpretive methods used by respondents in socially constructing realities.

• References

American Psychiatric Association. (2000). *Diagnostic and statistical manual of mental disorders* (4th ed., text rev.). Washington, DC: Author.

Anderson, H. (1997). *Conversation, language, and possibilities: A postmodern approach to therapy.* New York: Basic Books.

Anderson, H., & Goolishian, H. (1992). The client as the expert: A not-knowing approach to counseling. In S. McNamee & K. Gergin (Eds.), *Therapy as social construction* (pp. 23–39). Newbury Park, CA: Sage.

Antaki, C. (2001). "D'you like a drink then do you?": Dissembling language and the construction of an impoverished life. *Journal of Language and Social Psychology, 20,* 196–213.

Arminen, I. (1998). *Therapeutic interaction: A study of mutual help in the meetings of Alcoholics Anonymous.* Helsinki: Finnish Foundation for Alcohol Studies.

Atkinson, J. M., & Heritage, J. (Eds.). (1984). *Structures of social action.* Cambridge, UK: Cambridge University Press.

Avdi, E. (2005). Negotiating a pathological identity in the clinical dialogue: Discourse analysis of a family therapy. *Psychology and Psychotherapy: Theory, Research and Practice, 78,* 493–511.

Bavelas, J. B., McGee, D., Phillips, B., & Routledge, R. (2000). Microanalysis of communication in psychotherapy. *Human Systems, 11*(1), 47–66.

Billig, M. (1999). *Freudian repression: Conversation creating the unconscious.* Cambridge, UK: Cambridge University Press.

Boden, D., & Zimmerman, D. H. (Eds.). (1991). *Talk and social structure: Studies in ethnomethodology and conversation analysis.* Berkeley: University of California Press.

Bogdan, R., & Ksander, M. (1980). Policy data as a social process: A qualitative approach to quantitative data. *Human Organization, 39*(4), 302–309.

Bohart, A. C. (2005). Evidence-based psychotherapy means evidence-informed, not evidence driven. *Journal of Contemporary Psychotherapy, 35,* 39–53.

Bosk, C. L. (1992). *All God's mistakes: Genetic counseling in a pediatric hospital.* Chicago: University of Chicago Press.

Brill, A. A. (Ed.). (1938). *The basic writings of Sigmund Freud.* New York: Modern Library.

Burman, E. (1994). *Deconstructing developmental psychology.* New York: Routledge.

Buttny, R. (2004). *Talking problems: Studies of discursive construction.* Albany: State University of New York Press.

Cooperrider, D., Whitney, D., & Stavros, J. (2003). *The appreciative inquiry handbook.* San Francisco: Berrett-Koehler.

Coulter, J. (1979). *The social construction of mind: Studies in ethnomethdology and linguistic philosophy.* Totowa, NJ: Rowman & Littlefield.

Cushman, P. (1995). *Constructing the self, constructing America: A cultural history of psychotherapy.* Cambridge, MA: Perseus.

Czyzewski, M. (Ed.). (1995). *Mm hm tokens as interactional devices in the psychotherapeutic intake interview.* Washington, DC: University Press of America.

de Shazer, S. (1994). *Words were originally magic.* New York: Norton.

Dean, R. (1993). Constructivism: An approach to clinical practice. *Smith College Studies in Social Work, 63,* 127–146.

Denzin, N. K. (1978). *Sociological methods: A sourcebook.* New York: McGraw-Hill.

Denzin, N. K., & Lincoln, Y. S. (Eds.). (2006). *Handbook of qualitative research* (3rd ed.). Thousand Oaks, CA: Sage.

Dumont, F., & Fitzpatrick, M. (2005). Faultlines in the great EST debate. *Journal of Contemporary Psychotherapy, 35*(1), 67–81.

Duncan, B. L., Miller, S., & Sparks, J. (2000). Mental health mythology. In B. L. Duncan & S. Miller (Eds.), *The heroic client: Doing client-directed, outcome-informed therapy* (pp. 18–63). San Francisco: Jossey-Bass.

Duncan, B. L., & Miller, S. D. (Eds.). (2000). *The heroic client: Doing client-directed, outcome-informed therapy.* San Francisco: Jossey-Bass.

Edelman, M. (1977). *Political language: Words that succeed and policies that fail.* New York: Academic Press.

Edwards, D. (1992). *Discursive psychology.* London: Sage.

Edwards, D. (1995). Two to tango: Script formulations, dispositions, and rhetorical symmetry in relationship troubles talk. *Research on Language and Social Interaction, 28*(4), 319–350.

Edwards, D. (1997). *Discourse and cognition.* London: Sage.

Edwards, D., Ashmore, M., & Potter, J. (1995). Death and furniture: The rhetoric, politics and theology of bottom line arguments against relativism. *History of the Human Sciences, 8*(2), 25–49.

Efran, J. S., Lukens, R. J., & Lukens, M. D. (1988). Constructivism: What's in it for you? *Family Therapy Networker, 12*(5), 27–35.

Fairclough, N. (1992). *Discourse and social change.* Cambridge, UK: Polity Press.

Forman, I. M., Jones, C., & Francis, A. (1995). The multiaxal system in psychiatric treatment. In G. O. Gabbard (Ed.), *Treatment of psychiatric disorders* (2nd ed., pp. 3–21). Washington, DC: American Psychiatric Press.

Foucault, M. (1972). *The archaeology of knowledge* (A. M. S. Smith, Trans.). New York: Harper & Row.

Foucault, M. (1977). *Madness and civilization: A history of insanity in the age of reason.* London: Tavistock.

Foucault, M. (1978). *The history of sexuality* (Vol. 1, R. Hurley, Trans.). New York: Random House.

Fox, K. J. (1999a). Changing violent minds: Discursive correction and resistance in the cognitive treatment of violent offenders in prison. *Social Problems, 46*(1), 88–103.

Fox, K. J. (1999b). Reproducing criminal types: Cognitive treatment for violent offenders in prison. *Sociological Quarterly, 40*(3), 435–453.

Fox, K. J. (2001). Self-change and resistance in prison. In J. F. Gubrium & J. A. Holstein (Eds.), *Institutional selves: Troubled identities in a postmodern world* (pp. 176–192). New York: Oxford University Press.

Franklin, C. (1995). Expanding the vision of the social constructionist debates: Creating relevance for practitioners. *Families in Society: The Journal of Contemporary Human Services, 76,* 395–406.

Franklin, C., & Jordan, C. (1996). Does constructivist therapy offer anything new to social work practice? In B. A. Thayer (Ed.), *Controversial issues in social work practice* (pp. 16–28). Boston: Allyn & Bacon.

Franklin, C., & Nurius, P. S. (Eds.). (1998). *Constructivism in practice: Methods and challenges.* Milwaukee, WI: Families International.

Freedman, J., & Combs, G. (1996). *Narrative therapy: The social construction of preferred realities.* New York: Norton.

Gale, J. E. (1991). *Conversation analysis of therapeutic discourse.* Norwood, NJ: Ablex.

Gale, J. E., & Lawless, J. (2003). Discursive approaches to clinical research. In T. Strong & D. Paré (Eds.), *Furthering talk: Advances in the discursive therapies* (pp. 125–144). New York: Kluwer Academic/Plenum.

Garfinkel, H. (1967). *Studies in ethnomethodology.* Englewood Cliffs, NJ: Prentice Hall.

Garfinkel, H., & Sacks, H. (1970). On formal structures of practical actions. In J. C. McKinney & E. A. Tiryakian (Eds.), *Theoretical sociology: Perspectives and developments* (pp. 337–366). New York: Appleton-Century-Crofts.

Georgaca, E. (2000). Reality and discourse: A critical

analysis of the category of "delusions." *British Journal of Medical Psychology, 73*, 227–242.

Gilman, S. L. (1988). *Disease and representation: Images of illness from madness to AIDS*. Ithaca, NY: Cornell University Press.

Gubrium, J. F. (1992). *Out of control: Family therapy and domestic abuse*. Newbury Park, CA: Sage.

Guilfoyle, M. (2003). Dialogue and power: A critical analysis of power in dialogical therapy. *Family Process, 42*, 331–343.

Hacking, I. (1986). Making up people. In T. C. Heller, M. Sosna, & D. E. Wellbery (Eds.), *Reconstructing individualism: Autonomy, individuality, and the self in Western thought* (pp. 222–236). Stanford, CA: Stanford University Press.

Hall, C. (1997). *Social work as narrative: Storytelling and persuasion in professional texts*. Adlershot, UK: Ashgate.

Hall, C., Juhila, K., Parton, N., & Pösö, T. (Eds.). (2003). *Constructing clienthood in social work and human services: Interaction, identities and practices*. London: Kingsley.

Halonen, M. (2006). Life stories used as evidence of addiction in group therapy. *Discourse and Society, 17*, 283–298.

Heritage, J. (1984). *Garfinkel and ethnomethodology*. Cambridge, UK: Polity Press.

Heron, J. (1996). *Cooperative inquiry*. London: Sage.

Herson, M., & Turner, S. M. (Eds.). (1994). *Diagnostic interviewing* (2nd ed.). New York: Plenum Press.

Holstein, J. A. (1993). *Court-ordered insanity: Interpretive practice and involuntary commitment*. New York: Aldine de Gruyter.

Holstein, J. A., & Gubrium, J. F. (1995). *The active interview*. Thousand Oaks, CA: Sage.

Hoshamand, L. (2001). Psychotherapy as an instrument of culture. In B. D. Slife, R. N. Williams, & S. H. Barlow (Eds.), *Critical issues in psychotherapy: Translating new ideas into practice* (pp. 99–118). Thousand Oaks, CA: Sage.

House, R. (2003). *Therapy beyond modernity: Deconstructing and transcending profession-centred therapy*. London: Karnac.

Hoyt, M. F. (Ed.). (1995). *Brief therapy and managed care: Readings for contemporary practice*. San Francisco: Jossey-Bass.

Hoyt, M. F. (2000). Likely future trends and attendant ethical concerns regarding managed mental health care. In M. F. Hoyt (Ed.), *Some stories are better than others: Doing what works in brief therapy and managed care* (pp. 77–98). Philadelphia: Brunner/Mazel.

Knorr-Cetina, K. D., & Mulkay, M. (1983). *Science observed: Perspectives on the social study of science*. London: Sage.

Kogan, S. (1998). The politics of making meaning: Discourse analysis of a "postmodern" interview. *Journal of Family Therapy, 20*, 229–251.

Kupferberg, I., & Green, D. (2005). *Troubled talk: Metaphorical negotiation in problem discourse*. Berlin: Mouton de Gruyter.

Labov, W., & Fanshel, D. (1977). *Therapeutic discourse: Psychotherapy as conversation*. New York: Academic Press.

Laird, J. (1993). Family-centered practice: Cultural and constructionist reflections. *Journal of Teaching in Social Work, 8*, 77–110.

Larner, G. (2004). Family therapy and the politics of evidence. *Journal of Family Therapy, 26*, 17–39.

Lowney, K. S. (1999). *Baring our souls: TV talk shows and the religion of recovery*. New York: Aldine de Gruyter.

Madsen, W. C. (1999). *Collaborative therapy with multistressed families: From old problems to new futures*. New York: Guilford Press.

Mattingly, C. (1998). *Healing dramas and clinical plots: The narrative structure of experience*. Cambridge, UK: Cambridge University Press.

Mattingly, C., & Fleming, M. H. (1994). *Clinical reasoning: Forms of inquiry in a therapeutic practice*. Philadelphia: Davis.

McLeod, J. (2001). *Qualitative research in counseling and psychotherapy*. Thousand Oaks, CA: Sage.

McNamee, S., & Gergen, K. J. (Eds.). (1992). *Therapy as social construction*. London: Sage.

Mead, G. H. (1934). *Mind, self and society: From the standpoint of a social behaviorist*. Chicago: University of Chicago Press.

Miller, G. (1986, Spring/Summer). Depicting family troubles: A micro-political analysis of the therapeutic interview. *Journal of Strategic and Systemic Therapies, 5*, 1–13.

Miller, G. (1987, Fall). Producing family problems: Organization and uses of the family perspective and rhetoric in family therapy. *Symbolic Interaction, 10*, 245–265.

Miller, G. (1994). Toward ethnographies of institutional discourse: Proposal and suggestions. *Journal of Contemporary Ethnography, 23*(3), 280–306.

Miller, G. (1997). *Becoming miracle workers: Language and meaning in brief therapy*. New Brunswick, NJ: Transaction.

Miller, G., & Fox, K. J. (2004). Building bridges: The possibility of analytic dialogue between ethnography, conversation analysis, and Foucault. In D. Silverman (Ed.), *Qualitative analysis: Issues of theory and method* (2nd ed., pp. 35–55). London: Sage.

Miller, G., & Silverman, D. (1995). Troubles talk and counseling discourse: A comparative study. *Sociological Quarterly, 36*(4), 725–747.

Morgan, A., & O'Neill, D. (2001). Pragmatic poststructuralism: II. An outcomes evaluation of a stopping violence programme. *Journal of Community and Applied Social Psychology, 11*, 277–289.

Newman, F., & Holzman, L. (1997). *The end of knowing*. New York: Routledge.

Oakley, L. D., & Potter, C. (1997). *Psychiatric primary care*. St. Louis, MO: Mosby.

Paré, D. A. (2002). Discursive wisdom: Reflections on

ethics and therapeutic knowledge. *International Journal of Critical Psychology, 7*, 30–52.

Paré, D. A., & Larner, G. (Eds.). (2003). *Collaborative practice in psychology and therapy*. New York: Haworth Press.

Parker, I. (Ed.). (1999). *Deconstructing psychotherapy*. New York: Routledge.

Parker, I., & Shotter, J. (Eds.). (1990). *Deconstructing social psychology*. London: Routledge.

Parton, N., & O'Byrne, P. (2000). *Constructive social work: Towards a new practice*. New York: St. Martin's Press.

Peräkylä, A. (1995). *AIDS counselling: Institutional interaction and clinical practice*. Cambridge, UK: Cambridge University Press.

Perry, S., Frances, A., & Clarkin, J. (1990). *A DSM-III-R casebook of treatment selection*. New York: Brunner/Mazel.

Pfohl, S. J. (1978). *Predicting dangerousness: The social construction of psychiatric reality*. Lexington, MA: Lexington Books.

Polatin, P. (1966). *A guide to treatment in psychiatry*. Philadelphia: Lippincott.

Pollner, M. (1987). *Mundane reason: Reality in everyday life and sociological discourse*. Cambridge, UK: Cambridge University Press.

Reid, W. H. (1989). *The treatment of psychiatric disorders*. New York: Brunner/Mazel.

Rose, N. (1990). *Governing the soul: The shaping of the private self*. London: Routledge.

Rose, N. (1998). *Inventing our selves: Psychology, power and personhood*. New York: Cambridge University Press.

Sacks, H., Schegloff, E. A., & Jefferson, G. (1974). A simplest systematics for the organization of turn-taking in conversation. *Language, 50*(4), 696–735.

Sass, L. A. (1992). *Madness and modernism: Insanity in the light of modern art, literature, and thought*. Cambridge, MA: Harvard University Press.

Sass, L. A. (1994). *The paradoxes of delusion: Wittgenstein, Schreber, and the schizophrenic mind*. Ithaca, NY: Cornell University Press.

Scheflin, A. E. (1973). *Communicational structure: Analysis of a psychotherapy transaction*. Bloomington: Indiana University Press.

Schön, D. A. (1983). *The reflexive practitioner: How professionals think in action*. New York: Basic Books.

Shweder, R. A. (1991). *Thinking through cultures: Expeditions in cultural psychology*. Cambridge, MA: Harvard University Press.

Silverman, D. (1997). *Discourses of counselling: HIV counselling as social interaction*. London: Sage.

Smith, D. E. (1978). "K is mentally ill": The anatomy of a factual account. *Sociology, 12*, 23–53.

Stiles, W., & Shapiro, D. (1989). Abuse of the drug metaphor in psychotherapy process-outcome-research. *Clinical Psychology Research, 9*, 521–543.

Strong, T. (2002). Collaborative "expertise" after the discursive turn. *Journal of Psychotherapy Integration, 12*, 218–232.

Strong, T. (2004). Ethical "construction zones" in psychology's big tent. *International Journal Critical Psychology, 11*, 131–152.

Strong, T., Busch, R., & Couture, S. (in press). Conversational evidence in therapeutic dialogue. *Journal of Marital and Family Therapy*.

Strong, T., Zeman, D., & Foskett, A. (2006). Introducing new topics and discourses into counselling interactions: A micro-analytic examination. *Journal of Constructivist Psychology, 19*(1), 67–89.

Taylor, C. E., & White, S. (2000). *Practising reflexivity in health and welfare: Making knowledge*. Buckingham, UK: Open University Press.

Tomm, K. (1988). Interventive interviewing: Part III. Intending to ask lineal, circular, strategic or reflexive questions. *Family Process, 27*(1), 1–15.

Vandewater, S. R. (1983). Discourse processes and the social organization of group therapy sessions. *Sociology of Health and Illness, 5*(3), 275–296.

Voloshinov, V. N. (2006). *Marxism and the philosophy of language*. Cambridge, MA: Harvard University Press.

Vygotsky, L. S. (1978). *Mind in society: The development of higher psychological processes*. Cambridge, MA: Harvard University Press.

Wade, A. (1997). Small acts of living: Everyday resistance to violence and other forms of oppression. *Contemporary Family Therapy, 19*(1), 23–39.

Wainwright, D., & Calnan, M. (2002). *Work stress: The making of a modern epidemic*. Buckingham, UK: Open University Press.

Waldegrave, C., Tamasese, T., Tuhaka, F., & Campbell, W. (2003). *Just Therapy: A journey: A collection of papers from the Just Therapy Team*. Adelaide, Australia: Dulwich Centre.

Wampold, B. E., Ahn, H., & Coleman, H. L. K. (2001). Medical model as metaphor: Old habits die hard. *Journal of Counseling Psychology, 48*, 268–273.

Weinberg, D. W. (2005). *Of others inside: Insanity, addiction and belonging in America*. Philadelphia: Temple University Press.

White, M., & Epston, D. (1990). *Narrative means to therapeutic ends*. New York: Norton.

White, S., & Stancombe, J. (2003). *Clinical judgement in the health and welfare professions: Extending the evidence base*. Buckingham, UK: Open University Press.

CHAPTER 32

Constructionist Themes in the Historiography of the Nation

● Bo Stråth

Constructionist themes in contemporary historiography often draw on the concepts of culture, public remembrance, commemoration, collective memory, and myth. This chapter compares constructionist and nonconstructionist approaches to the concepts as they play out in contemporary understandings of "nation" and "community." I take "community" to be the central problematic, asking how a collection of people and/or inhabitants of a particular geographical space come to have enough in common so that a sense of national identity emerges. Of course, the problematic itself has historical contours, and the chapter will also address those. Of particular concern is the way in which the myth of the nation has been constructed in the European context.

I begin by considering some conceptual tools used in the construction of nation and community: culture, collective memory, and myth. I then move to a discussion of the more general issue of the concept of "construction" in the context of history. The chapter then takes up the construction of the "myth of the nation" in relation to recent German history. Finally, I conclude with a discussion of challenges and problems that confront constructionist historiography.

Culture and History

The concepts of culture, collective memory, and myth are central to historical constructionist approaches. Culture is the overarching concept, operating like a software program that shapes the construction process. In describing community, culture often has been used to explain cohesion and homogeneity, which typically establish sharp boundaries between insiders and outsiders and tend to essentialize differences (Persson & Stråth, 2007, p. 14). In recent years, the approach has been designated "essentialist." The contrast with the nonessentialist themes of constructionism has historical resonances and is hardly limited to contemporary differences.

In the constructionist nonessentialist view, culture stands for openness and permanent interaction between settings and invites the transgression of borders. The demarcation between outsiders and insiders is fluid and contextual. The relationships of cultures to one another are performative and may be described in terms of entanglement as much as demarcation. Culture is thus a process of symbolic work that frames interpretation and community; it is emergent and not pregiven in its expressions. Culture is a matter of communication and negotiation; it is a discourse without essence, although culture is, or was, more often than not presented as the most essential entity.

For example, when culture has been used as a homogenizing term, such as *Kultur* and *Kulturkampf* in the German unification process, the French term *civilisation* was a kind of counterconcept radiating Enlightenment values of tolerance toward diversity and openness rather than closure. The latter signaled flexibility rather than rigid adherence to a symbolic space.

Today, the relationships between the two concepts are rather the opposite when culture stands for openness and civilization represents homogenization and closure ("clash of civilization").

Culture as an arena of symbolic work uses concepts, myths, and public remembrance as tools for understanding community and the nation state. The politics and practices of remembrance deal with the translation of experiences into future action orientations and horizons of expectation, with unfolding community in time and space. The image of the past is continuously reconsidered in the light of an ever-changing present. History is an *image* of the past, rather than *the* past *wie es eigentlich gewesen*, as it really was. In this context, the traditional opposition of history and remembrance can no longer be maintained. Rather, history and commemoration are mutually constitutive. From this perspective, history is both remembrance *and* oblivion; it is a *translation* or *representation* of the past done in the present (Ankersmit, 1998). Moreover, the distinction between history and myth is blurred. History as science, in a more conventional understanding of the term, signals an opposition between history and myth. Myths can be the object of objective historical science only in a critical and destructive way; they must be revealed and unmasked. Scientific historiography and myth are, in this positivistic or objectivist view, insurmountable, antagonistic entities. In a constructionist approach, viewing history as an ongoing process of reconsidering the past means that demystification is remystification.

Public Remembrance and History

Collective memory is a frequently used concept in constructionist analyses of community, with many references harkening back to Maurice Halbwachs's (1925/1994) usage. Although Halbwachs himself used the concept with clear ideological dimensions, its application during the recent decades has instead led to an essentialization of memories. In this application, collective memory becomes a more or less intrinsic property of a population. Therefore, I prefer an alternative conceptualization to that of "collective memory," which, moreover, connotes the image of *one* generally shared memory, whereas, as a matter of fact, cultural processes of remembering are contested issues and outcomes of contentious social work on coming to terms with the past. On this point, one should note Reinhart Koselleck's (1979/2004) argument that individuals have memories, collectives do not. Collective social forms such as nations, local communities, or an aggregation of nations such as Europe are unified not least through shared experiences, which they communicate and accommodate through attempts to come to terms with the past. In the process, individual experiences become shared experiences; they are not epiphenomena of collective memory writ large. Experiences are translated into public remembrance, which connotes much less cohesion than does a concept such as "collective memory." Public remembrance is a discourse not a property.

The symbolic work that constructs a shared, collective experience is a process of *Vergangenheitsbewältigung*, a coming to terms with the past from the perspective of the present. Coming to terms with the past through symbolic work of collective experience is a process of public remembrance. This is not pregiven but emerges through the symbolic construction of a memory by those concerned under social contention. In nonconstructionist formulation, the concept of collective memory is used the other way around, as something that determines social forms through its preexistence. The interpretation of the experiences and their translation into public remembrance is in the constructionist approach always made from a changing present, constantly provoking new views on the past and new outlines of future horizons. Remembrance emerges at the crossroads of experience and expectation. In this view, the connection between past, present, and future history is preliminary and permanently under revision from new points of departure. New experiences require new interpretation of the past (Koselleck, 1979/2004). Accordingly, as the construction of public remembrance goes, so does the history of a nation.

Public remembrance is both a matter of practice and a matter of politics and substance. Practices of remembrance manifest themselves in public acts such as commemorations, publications, exhibitions, speeches, and legal processes, in which group-specific experiences, interpretations, and expectations are negotiated. Commemoration is concrete and clear ritual and is action-oriented, whereas remembrance is a "softer" concept of something being remembered "out there" but less thematized than commemoration. Thus commemoration is the manifest political and ritual dimension of public remembrance. This requires the problematization of the principles of inclusion and exclusion, of what is remembered and what is not, and of the existence of different communities of remembrance in a society (Assmann, 1999; Eschebach, 2005, p. 39; Winter & Sivan, 1999, p. 9). Of particular interest in this context is the tension between various remembrance communities and the inclusion and exclusion strategies by which the substance of public remembrance is negotiated.

The key question here is what role myth (which I shortly consider in its own right) and public remembrance and/or commemoration play in the cultural construction of communities. Myth and remembrance unify a community and shape its identity in a way that *gives* it essential proportions. What is essential, in other words, is a matter of essentializing *practices*. According to Pierre Nora (1996, p. xi), the act of remembering is always related to "the repository of images and ideals that constitute the social relations of which we partake." Public remembrance and commemoration occur within the matrix or the plot that a myth provides. Such a matrix or plot constitutes tropes in which legitimacy and historical meaning are sought and confirmed by emphasizing certain values, such as French glory, British imperial rule, German social organization, American technological superiority, Danish smallness, Swedish welfare and neutrality, and Irish poverty. If, as a result, history takes on primordial proportions, in a constructionist perspective myth does not evolve from the "nature" of things. History is never eternal but, rather, has specific historical foundations that reflexively assemble it (see Barthes, 1972, pp. 109–110).

Johann Gottfried von Herder (Heinz, 1994), the Grimm brothers Jakob and Wilhelm (1854/1960), and other interpreters of the world among their contemporaries did not make a distinction between *Mythos* and *Märchen*, myth and fairy tale. However, with the Enlightenment discourse, a separation gradually emerged between myth and science, a development that was also visible in theology and biblical exegesis, for example. As this division widened, so there developed the positivistic program based on essentialism. This separation is now questioned by concepts such as postmodernity, in which historical signs are not as tied to concrete events as they are constructively linked to events through related narrative practices.

Historians do not stand above or beyond the processes they are analyzing but are part of them through the language that, by means of the act of translation or representation, connects the present with the past. In the wake of Michel Foucault's contributions, it is not only history but also epistemological schemes in general that are ideological and political. This perspective has become particularly clear with the emergence of radical constructionism. The first generation of constructionist perspectives—Benedict Anderson (1990) with "imagined nations," Eric Hobsbawm and Terence Ranger (1983) with "invented traditions," and Gareth Stedman Jones (1983)—certainly observed the constructions made by the past actors and societies they analyzed, but they hardly questioned their own role, which they saw as outsider observers of the processes they studied. In contrast, Hayden White (1974) argued for a more radical approach 10 years earlier in his groundbreaking book *Metahistory*. He emphasized not only the role of narrative structures in historiography but also the roles, including his own, of those who wrote the narratives. They were viewed as part of the narrative rather than outside of it, thus opening historiographic practice to consideration.

In emphasizing that social cohesion and community are constructed or invented rather than discovered, constructionist historians refuse to treat public remembrance ("collective memory") as straightforwardly "out there" or derivable, for example, from real economic structures. This does not mean, of course, that events as such are *merely* invented. Rather, the impulse is to orient to facts as constructed through reflection on the documents that attest to the occurrence of the events. This distinction between fact and event is important (White, 2000), as it forms a point of departure for the consideration of public remembrance that recognizes its concrete bearings in the world of history and its communication in the world of historical interpretation.

To say that community is constructed means that images and myths emerge from the transformation of existing inventories of historical heritage and culture. Successful construction appeals to certain cultural chords and conceptual tropes, to narrative plots or discursive frames. Such tropes and plots are, of course, not primordial; they, too, are the products of human imagination. In these processes of community construction, the *idea* of a "collective memory" and a specific history is a tool that bridges the gap between high political and intellectual levels and the levels of everyday life. What constitutes public remembrance and what is consigned to collective oblivion (i.e., taboos and what we do not talk about) is a highly disputed question, reflecting power relations in the definition of social problems. Nora (1996, pp. xv–xxiv) holds that each nation has its canonical memories and myths that bind the community together and create social identities. Myth and memory give the community a narrative through which it can continue to forge its identity. The act of remembering is related to the repository of images and ideals that constitute the social ties of a community. In this formulation, Nora comes close to an essentialization of the nation. A more constructionist formulation would be that nations do not have memories in the sense of a pregiven property or characteristic but that they develop public remembrance and acts of commemoration through debate and contention. Public remembrance and commemoration might draw on, as well as develop, national stereotypes.

The new symbolic topography around concepts such as identity and memory should be understood in light of experiences of intellectual disorientation and the erosion of earlier established frameworks of interpretation since the 1970s. These experiences have been the result of fundamental changes in epistemology, technology, and the organization of economies, international relations, work, and labor markets. These shifts have produced new views, both of the past and of the preconditions for history. History as "science" is a translation from the German *Wissenschaft*. Since the 19th century, the writing of the past in Germany has been seen as analogous to the description of nature, the *Naturwissenschaften*. The term in German is a derivation from *schaffen*, "to make" or "to create knowledge." In English-speaking cultures, history was never a science but belonged to the liberal arts. This distinction between the two linguistic cultures was long ignored, but it has recently been seen as more consequential. The view that the writing of history is a matter of the unproblematic discovery of a past "out there" has faded. It is now widely accepted that history is dependent on the context of the present in which questions about the past arise. The recognition of the role of narration poses further problems along the science–art axis, in which the symbolic practices of art are viewed as parallel to the symbolic practices of historiography.

The so-called linguistic or rhetoric turn, which argues that language sets the limits of reality construction, brought with it the insight that there is a connection between myth and historiography through the form of narration, through the very way in which the story is told. Historiography is much more dependent on its literary–textual organization than has been recognized in more conventional views. Historiography cannot, as a matter of fact, be easily separated from myths and myth building. In the most radical versions of the linguistic/rhetoric methodological approach, historiography and mythography become more or less identical. Such views, however, are much older than the rhetorical turn. The idea that truth is contextual, rather than immutable and absolute, and that founding myths are expressions of power was clearly present in the works of Baruch Spinoza, Giovanni Battista Vico (1725/1977), Friedrich Nietzsche (1852–1889/1980), Max Weber and Benedetto Croce (1941/1963) long before White and Foucault (Foucault, 1969; Hippler, 2000; Peukert, 1989; Szakolszai, 1998).

Myth and History

Myths assume the dimensions of reality to the extent to which people believe in them. From this perspective, they cannot be separated or distinguished from reality and truth; rather, they constitute this reality and truth through language. This means that reality and truth are contested and contextual entities. Foundational myths—the historical beliefs about the origins from which societies and nations ultimately emerge—often draw their legitimizing power from some specific connection to God, say, or to fantasy, or to the truths of the social and economic sciences. It is within this context of legitimation, or the *doxa* of everyday life, that right and wrong are defined and laws are promulgated that separate the proclaimed communities of destiny from the arbitrary and capricious.

Myth is not only the *object* of historiography; it is also its *product* in the form of constructed remembrance—which, at the same time, also means constructed oblivion. Processes of meaning production are processes of selection. The Holocaust and its preliminary stages took place before and during World War II, but it became a theme only in the 1960s, raising the question of why these events were more or less ignored in the late 1940s and throughout the 1950s. When, in the name of science, figures such as John F. Kennedy and Bill Clinton, Adolf Hitler and Winston Churchill, Catherine II and Voltaire, Kemal Atatürk and Attila, or abstractions such as Europe, the nation, democracy, and dictatorship, are described and discussed, the point of departure is the myths created by history. This does not mean that these are lies but, rather, that the truths they convey are truths constructed from an *ex post facto* position.

Myth, in this sense of constructed memory and oblivion, is emancipated from its pejorative connotation and assumes the role of an originary provider of meaning, becoming a constituent element of politics and social cohesion. In this context, emancipation takes on a meaning different from that in positivist historiography, in which activity in the name of science and source criticism are viewed as an emancipation or liberation of sources from the myths that enshroud them. This positivist approach was developed with references to Leopold von Ranke and his followers in 19th-century German historiography, who were argued to believe that they stood outside and above the processes they studied, although as a matter of fact they were more sophisticated than to do so. They were argued to believe that they were the judges or referees who were capable of disclosing the truth, *wie es eigentlich gewesen*, and who failed to realize that this very myth hid their role in the production of the past. As a matter of fact, Ranke, when he wrote his well-known phrase about *wie es eigentlich gewesen,* demonstrated that he was well aware that the past was more complex than just being a matter of reproduction in the scale 1:1.

In the European *Mythosforschung* of the 19th and 20th centuries, myth implied irrationality and was thus separated from rationality in the form of *logos* and reason. The key theoretical question that this dichotomy produced was whether mythical thought was prior to or parallel to scientific thought. It was through this debate that the myth of rational science emerged. From a construc-

tionist perspective, we can never recreate the past as it really was. We can only try to translate the past to produce meaning for ourselves, in our present. In this context, translation thus becomes a key methodological concept. This translation can be made only from our point of view today, and never from the point of view of that past's present. In this sense, concepts such as objectivity and Ranke's *wie es eigentlich gewesen* become ideology (Iggers, 1999, pp. 281–301). Both *wie es eigentlich gewesen* and the cumulative view of history as an inexorable process of mapping reality in a total and definitive sense through the addition of more and better data become vain undertakings. The truths about the past are conditional and dependent upon the present in which they are formulated.

This was the point of view promoted by Claude Lévi-Strauss (1978) when he described myth as something that orders and gives meaning to the universe. It provides us with a sense that we understand the universe. Roland Barthes (1972, pp. 124–125) defines myth as both a semiological system (form) and an ideology (content) consisting of three elements—form (signifier), concept (signified), and signification (sign). A myth hides nothing, but it does assemble understanding, that is, it functions in such a way as to give historical intention a natural justification.

Myths help build community and collective identities, and in these meaning-creating processes there are connections between remembrance, myth, and nationhood. What means are then available to enable us to study such connections? Nora (1996) studies the metamorphoses of "collective memory" by investigating the history of the *lieux de mémoire*, by which he means any significant entity—a monument, for instance—which, by dint of human will or the work of time, has become a symbolic element in the memorial heritage of a community. Jacques Le Goff (1985) suggests focusing on the connection between collective memory and power, because power lies with those who control memory. Lévi-Strauss (1978) holds that when studying a myth, one should not ask whether it is true but, rather, why people do or did believe in it. According to Barthes, myths can be studied either diachronically or synchronically, in time or in relation to each other. It is through the deconstruction of the myth that its "distortion" is revealed. This is a somewhat different view from that of Jacques Derrida (1972, 1979), who considers the meaning of deconstruction to be the disconnection of truth from reason in order to discern the fundamental divide between the two. The combination of the sacred and the good with the rational and the reasonable is nothing other than Plato's project of logocentrism, which should be seen as yet one more cultural construction among others that therefore must also be deconstructed.

The ouevre of Derrida provides a language for theorizing *difference*. His point of departure is that Western systems of knowledge depend on some original moment of truth or immanence from which our whole hierarchy of meaning springs. It is this guarantee of meaning transcending signification that is termed *logocentrism*. By invoking a claim to universal truth, a system of knowledge belies cultural diversity and conceals the power structures that preserve the hierarchical relations of difference. Binary oppositions and distinctions are central to this logocentric form of thinking. The binary juxtaposition of "Europe" and the "Other" is one case in point. Another example is the construction of sexual difference through dichotomies such as masculine–feminine, active–passive, rational–emotional, hard–soft, and so on (see Rutherford, 1990). François Lyotard (1979) expresses a similar view when he argues that master formulations of myth shatter under postmodern conditions, in which no metanarrative is possible. In particular, he considers that postmodern conditions are distinguished by their reliance on mass media for information and communication. In the absence of alleged master narratives, discourses in

these media are legitimized by micronarratives that shape the message transmitted and give meaning to the flow of information (Combs & Nimmo, 1990). (For an illustration of how such media micronarratives operate within the larger structure of a plot, see White, 2000.)

Approaching the Concept of Construction

Although a constructionist perspective frees us from the quest for absolute truth, we should not accept the concept uncritically. In the framework outlined in this chapter, the concept of construction, which has become so central in the linguistic or cultural approach during the past decades, *is* problematic in its own right. Its great merit is that it has mediated a view in which history is no longer seen as an object lying out there waiting to be discovered. But what do we then mean when we say that nations and their histories are constructed?

There are many different ways to consider the connections between culture, remembrance, myth, and history and many different ways to approach the problems associated with construction. At first these perspectives might appear mutually exclusive, but, on closer inspection, it becomes apparent that they are not necessarily incompatible. Much of the tension between the various views derives from the concepts of construction and invention. What do these concepts mean with reference to myth, memory, and history? At one extreme, the connection to some kind of elite activity, manipulation or otherwise, is emphasized. At the other extreme, weight is given to the structural preconditions of this activity. These structural preconditions might be something similar to the prevailing epistemes in Foucault's sense or like popular everyday practices and sentiments of a more anthropological kind. *Con*struction presupposes a *de*struction of something else, a fragmentation of a structure. The fragments can then be used to construct another one. In a verbatim sense, *con*struction is *re*construction by combining materials already at hand; constructing a society implies remaking it out of elements already present. However, this image of remaking is incompatible with the idea of modernity, which presumes a qualitative difference between present and past. When the fragments are recomposed, it is not the old building that emerges but images of something new. A case in point is the best known reconstruction of all, that which ostensibly took place after World War II.

Is it, then, the aim to combine the two extremes, action and structure, into one conceptual framework, one cohesive *Denkfigur*? Would it not be a vain undertaking to try to dissolve and merge dichotomies and contradictions such as action–structure, discontinuity–continuity, and elite–everyday life? Would not a more complex understanding of the past mean that the past can be understood in various ways dependent on the points of departure and viewpoints rather than looking for *the* past? Consider, in this connection, the distinction between *disaster*—in the literal sense of "bad star," that is, a society's exposure to ill fate—and *catastrophe*—a term from Greek drama that indicates a turn for the worse that will eventually result in the revelation of meaning in the final scene. Whereas *disaster* suggests misfortune, *catastrophe* is consciously staged; it is constructed (White, 2000).

The issue of action versus structure has an analogy in Freudian theory. From one perspective, myth and remembrance, like Freud's dreams, simply surface as expressions of the mental state of society. They are not governed or controlled. They provide a kind of cultural depository or heritage, and this depository is activated through specific codes. From another perspective, this depository is used in discursive struggles over political, economic, and social power. Myths and remembrances are interpreted and given form for political purposes. From this point of view, there is a clear element of con-

struction or invention in the process, at least within certain limits. In this sense, remembrance and myth should be seen as multiple and subject to continuous contestation, even if, at certain historical moments, one view enjoys almost complete domination.

There are connections from such a perspective to Cambridge speech act theory, founded in the language philosophy of Ludwig Wittgenstein (1989) and first developed by John Austin (1975), with Quentin Skinner (2002) and John Pocock (Pocock & Skinner, 2004). Instead of studying intellectual thoughts and political ideologies as long chains of ideas through history, as used to be the case in the conventional study of the history of ideas, speech act theory emphasizes the context in which arguments from a broad depository of intellectual thought are selected and used for specific purposes. In this strategy, arguments with very different origins can be combined. The connection between speech and action is emphasized. Michael Freeden (1996) has drawn attention to the tendency of the speech act approach to assume a somewhat too-intentional view of the connection between speech and act—first comes the thought and then the action—ignoring situations in which the action comes first and then the thought as an *ex post* legitimization of the action. One should here also refer to the German conceptual history school developed by Reinhart Koselleck (Brunner, Conze, & Koselleck, 1979–1992; see Palonen, 2004, for a comparison of the Cambridge school methodology and Koselleck's conceptual history approach). Politics is based on conceptual struggle over key concepts with a mobilizing capacity and therefore with a high attraction. Politics deals with the competitive attempts to define and shape such concepts and thereby appropriate positions of interpretive priority.

Koselleck (1959/1989) is especially relevant to constructionism for his philosophy of time. He views modernity as a movement from critique to crisis, in which *critique* means translation of experiences into horizons of expectation, which, in turn, provoke situations of crisis, claims for action, and developments in new directions. As the organizing basis for action in the present, the "space of experiences" has been replaced by "horizons of expectation." In an age of accelerating time, characterized by an unceasing accumulation of new problems, experience becomes a category of limited capacity, in Koselleck's view. The acceleration of time means that the space of experience shrinks, failing to make "modernity" comprehensible. Instead, the horizons of expectation became the guide for those trying to cope with modernity. Because this horizon itself is constructed out of politically pregnant concepts, the study of how these concepts are constructed becomes central (Koselleck, 1979/2004).

Adopting constructionist impulses, Koselleck has studied historical transition in Prussia in the wake of the French Revolution and of Napoleon, especially the historical connotation of change. Before *the* Revolution, *revolution* had a connotation of repetition and return. One impact of the Revolution was that the future, in contrast, became open and constructible, *machbar*. This provided a space for the transformation of policy and economy and a space for the development of social movements that sought to design and implement their visions of the future world. Within such a framework, there is great scope for the consideration of how the conceptual structure of the social world could be reconsidered as "modernity."

In many respects, Lynn Hunt's (1983) approach resembles Koselleck's. In her perspective, words in the French Revolution came "in torrents." Words have a unique, magical quality in her view. Revolutionary language during the French Revolution was charismatic. Wherever names were identified with Old Regime values, they were supplanted by new revolutionary appellations. Language did not simply reflect the reality of revolutionary changes "but rather was itself transformed in the process of making a revolution"(Hunt, 1983, p. 79). Language

participated in the very transition, so to speak. Revolutionary rhetoric opened the field of politics to its broadest possible limits. One of the initial accomplishments of the new revolutionary rhetoric was its invention of the Old Regime. Once French society was rhetorically divided into a new nation and an old, or former, regime, the revolution had been put into motion. The revolutionary discourse was not fashioned by a class in the Marxist sense, but the "language of class struggle" emerged nevertheless. In the American Revolution, the reactionary/conservative (British) forces were experienced as much more distant and less palpable. Therefore, American revolutionary rhetoric did not foster the development of a revolutionary tradition; instead, it fed into constitutionalism and liberal politics. The difference in France was an emphasis on rejecting all models from the national past. The specific French rhetoric of revolution made the revolution revolutionary. "Without the conviction and ability to act on their will to be new, the revolutionaries would not have been able to found modern politics," Hunt (1983, p. xx) explains. The revolutionary rhetoric broke through the confines of past politics by positing the existence of a new community rather than the revival of a purer, former one, as in the traditional meaning of the term *revolution*: *revolvere*, rolling back to an idealistic ancient past and starting again from scratch (Hunt, 1983, pp. 79, 89–91).

Concepts are developed by social actors to establish interpretive frameworks and to identify important problems and propose resolutions to these problems in order to come to terms with the present and the future. The outcome of these processes is always an open issue that never can be determined beforehand. It is emergent, not causal. The concepts that emerge in such processes produce interests and meaning. Meaning is multidimensional and relationally formed in an existing discursive field at the same time as new fields are created. In this sense, meaning is reflexive. Positive defi-

636 • THE SOCIAL CONSTRUCTION OF WHAT?

nitions are dependent on negative ones, and vice versa. One important conclusion of a related debate between Joan Scott (1988) and Gareth Stedman Jones (1983) is that a concept such as "class" is established through distinction and exclusion as much as by inclusion. "Class" and other similar identification categories are politically constructed. Therefore, they must be relativized and historicized instead of being reified. Instead of being seen as objective structures *an sich*, they must be seen as potential social forms that can be mobilized through language. Only in this way does class become a useful tool for constructionist analysis. Class should not be looked for in "objective" material structures but in the language of the political struggle. Language mediates the conditions for political coalitions and produces comparability between social groups. Language in this sense is not the enumeration of words but the production of meaning through distinction and separation. In this regard, political movements develop tactically, not logically, through improvisation in the search for support and through the incorporation and adjustment of different ideas to specific goals. They are a mixture of interpretations and programs, rather than being uniform social forms free from contradiction.

What Scott (1988) and Stedman Jones (1983) say about the construction of social classes is applicable to the construction of nations. If concepts such as class and nation are treated as discursive rather than ontological realities, the implication is that languages of class and nation are related to their usage. Stedman Jones argues that concepts such as experience and consciousness conceal the problematical nature of language itself. Language seems to have been transparent in the typical usage of historians, accepted as a simple medium through which "experience"—and, cumulatively derived from "experience," "class consciousness"—found expressions, being referred back to some primary anterior reality. The starting point of the analysis, as a rule, was a

class concept, in which different expressions of class were measured against socioeconomically derived conceptions of class position. The implicit assumption was that opposing and preexisting interests found their rational expression in the political arena. Nations were similarly analyzed before the cultural or linguistic turn in the 1980s, a turn within which Koselleck, Hunt, Scott, and Stedman Jones were prominent figures. They no doubt had a point when they argued that historians should look at changes in the political discursive struggle itself to explain changes in political practice.

A focus on political discursive struggle leads to a view of interests that are constructed and established in a linguistic field. This plays out in the political struggle over concepts such as class and nation and through the introduction of new concepts and metaphors. Thus interests themselves are linguistically constructed. Nations do not have interests prior to their formulation. The convincing and mobilizing capacity of concepts mediate how and what interests are expressed and how they are dealt with.

These perspectives on the concept of construction between (elite) action–reflection–construction and (everyday) structure–practice and on the role of language when narratives are constructed are not mutually exclusive. They are presented here simply as points of orientation toward a more inclusive constructionist view. The intention is not to set up a dichotomy but to draw together a range of approaches to myth and remembrance and place them in a context in which they can be constructively confronted and compared.

Public remembrance and the contention between various commemorative narratives as a key dimension of the construction of community supports or even creates the assumption of stability that demarcates identity distinct from the incessant change of the phenomenal world. Remembrance recalls lost paradises and promised lands, founding heroes, and the traumas of defeat. The stability established through memory provides the bridge to outlines of the horizons of the future and of expectations. Past and future are not exclusive categories but represent a continuum. From this point of view, it is clear that myth and remembrance cannot be clearly demarcated and that there is a link between the construction of the past and the construction of the future. In this context, in Germany, the year 1945 becomes a zero hour of remembrance and, at the same time, a pact of silence. The image of the 1930s as the last time that the plague of unemployment occurred is a further example of the construction of temporal divides, which in this case was constructed during the bonanza years of the 1960s. The generational confrontation of the zero-hour myth in Germany of the 1960s is a third example in which the goal was to see a new world emerge in the 1960s instead of 1945.

The Myth of the Nation

One of the most frequent points of departure for myth construction has been the nation. Why have questions about memory and the nation become so topical? How should the national identity boom be understood? A few decades ago, there was no discourse on either national memory or national identity. This section illustrates the methodological and theoretical considerations of constructionism in relation to recent German history.

In the case of Germany, one answer to these questions can be found in the end of the Cold War and in the social and cultural fragmentation that ensued in East and West alike. World War II had produced cohesion through the resistance to Nazism, and many foundation myths that contributed to the construction of national identity were built on this idea. (For a general discussion of historians, foundation myths, and World War II, see Bosworth, 1993.) These myths continued to give meaning and cohesion during the Cold War. The issue of resistance and collaboration during World War II has come

under increasing scrutiny since the end of the Cold War, and many established truths have been questioned and challenged. The consequence has been an erosion of interpretative frameworks, which, in turn, has brought the issue of collective memory and identity to the forefront. Questions about, for example, German national identity—about who Germans are and where they come from—are raised in situations in which the answers are not known. When we feel confident about who we are, we do not talk about it, and it is generally only in periods of identity crisis that we look for new identity and social community. Simply put, and perhaps counterintuitively, more national identity discourse occurs at the precise time at which national identity is on the wane.

A second reason that identity, memory, and nation came to the forefront of academic preoccupations against the backdrop of the end of the Cold War is the emergence of a new epistemology, indicated by concepts such as "construction" and "postmodernity." The developments in 1989 made the future much more open. The fall of the Berlin Wall in that year marked the end of the Cold War, which had produced stability through the clear distinction between "Good" and "Evil." This new openness provoked an increasing interest in rethinking the past in search of new points of national reference. The established truths and images of good and evil lost their convincing power. The German national foundation myths based on 1945 as the zero hour, developed to fit within the Cold War, were no longer credible. This new rethinking of the past fit well into the new epistemology implied in the constructionist approach. The epistemic opportunity to rethink the past offered a virtual testing ground for the constructionist impulse.

History and the construction of periods, phases, and temporal divides are the modeling clay of foundation myths. History structures numerous configurations of public remembrance and commemoration. The resonance of myths derives from their claim to universality, which, in turn, provides legitimacy. Myths are tightly woven fabrics of data and ideologies, of semantics and aesthetics, of values and practices. They represent extremely highly condensed cultural codifications that tell us "quote me, use me, believe me, but don't ask me." A case in point is the myth of the Baltic as the "Sea of Peace." At the end of the Cold War, a history of the Baltic Sea region was constructed, drawing on the myth of peace that recalled the Hanseatic web of cooperative trade relations. This myth was a counternarrative that connected to and tamed the Soviet Union's narrative about the Baltic as the "Sea of Peace" that referenced threats and empire. The Hanseatic myth served to circumvent one of the sharpest circum-Baltic divides in the nuclear terror balance. If these myths, in their Cold War and post-Cold War versions, are interrogated critically, with a point of departure in insights of how myth functions in society, a bellicose past emerges, one that is not characterized by peace but by division and war, hot and cold.

The construction of community is not only a matter of temporal divides but also of spatial separation. The construction of borders, for example, is a contested issue. The Baltic as division and unification is a case in point. One issue of spatial division deals with who is in and who is out. The answer varies from nation to nation, of course, and relates to language, religion, ethnicity, and particular forms of social organization ("social" or "welfare" vs. "capitalism"), among other bearings of national identity. Borders in time and space are not essential, but they offer important resources for the construction of national and, in the Baltic case, regional identity (Persson & Stråth, 2007).

The construction of community through myth and remembrance is not a test of historiographic truth. Rather, the question is, how do myths emerge and what is the role of historians and other social scientists in their production? More specifically, how do different views of history emerge when community is constructed through the process of demarcation between, say, *us* and *them*, *now* and *then*? How are these views, these foundation myths, transformed, and what is the role of media, politicians, artists, architects, writers, film producers, and so on? Such are the leading concerns of the constructionist impulse. Like all players in the national identity game, professional historians and social scientists also have a role to play, and they do it in their own particular way, through theoretical inclinations and methodological preferences. At the same time, we cannot expect academics to have a privileged position in this process, whereby others develop myths and the critical academics reveal these myths and tell the truth. These questions are linked to the general issue of how community is constructed in the *Spannungsfeld* between images of the past and visions of the future and how history has been interpreted and mediated in various settings, implicating everyone who addresses historiographic issues.

This raises the question of why symbols and myths so often emerge in the framework of the nation and become *Geschichtsmässig* (of historical value) (Schmale, 1997). Antifascism can be seen as an example, albeit an extreme one, of how myths become *Geschichtsmässig*. As a matter of fact, antifascism in the German Democratic Republic (GDR) represented the failure to purge the state and the SED (*Sozialistische Einheitspartei Deutschlands*, i.e., the Communist party) adequately of Nazi adherents. West German authors, as well as Simon Wiesenthal, have observed that some former Nazis were allowed to find their way back into political life in the GDR. At the same time, the Federal Republic of Germany (FRG) was accorded fascist heritage in the East German history construction. Fascism was argued to continue in West German capitalism, which also had given birth to it. Historian Ernst Engelberg would later write his great biography of Bismarck (Brinks, 1992, 2000; Engelberg, 1985), which relates to this point. In the 1980s, Luther, Friedrich the Great, and Bismarck were all taken on board as a legitimizing historical heritage by the regime and merged with antifascism as elements in the historical justification of the GDR.

An opposite history, in which the Western *Bundesrepublik* comes out looking like a hero whereas the GDR is nothing more than a propaganda construction, would be too simple. In the West, as Bernhard Giesen (1998, 2000) has shown, the combination of memory and oblivion after the war played down the Nazi past. This was a remembrance strategy that was not only supported by the Allied powers after the war but also actually initiated by them in order to prevent a repetition of the feelings of revenge provoked by the Treaty of Versailles. This strategy formed an important part of the framework of mental mobilization during the Cold War that assigned guilt to the Nazi leaders for having seduced the German people, who, in turn, were seen as being separate from the regime. Only with the Eichmann trial and the youth revolt in the 1960s did ideas of collective guilt emerge, in which Nazi terror was not confined to a ruling core but interpreted in the framework of a broader and, at the same time, more specific German history—the *Sonderweg*, or German exceptionalism.

The process of *Vergangenheitsbewältigung* (coming to terms with the past) that followed the changing view of the war experience in the 1960s shifted again in the 1990s, when the Holocaust was seen in less absolute terms and was related to the gulag system of repression and Stalinism in the Soviet Union. The *Historikerstreit* (dispute among historians about how World War II and the Holocaust should be understood and contextualized, pitting left- and right-wing historians against each other) in the late 1980s was the pivot of this shifting view (see Habermas, 1989; Nolte, 1987; Wehler, 1988). Germany was seen less as the *Sonderweg* in opposition to an imagined Western standard development—in which Germany was thought of as a deviating case—and more in terms of one *Sonderweg* among others. The role of the Germans as victimizers was later

relativized in relation to the theme that many Germans also were victims of the war.

That today the salute "Sieg Heil" can once more be heard in the former GDR cannot be attributed to a single cause but must be seen in the framework of a complex mythology (Brinks, 2000). One element of this framework was the antagonistic and permanent dichotomy that emerged between Communism and Nazism. When Communism collapsed, radical adversaries of the state could tap into the process of interaction between remembrance and oblivion and turn it in new directions with existing symbols. This example shows that myths and collective identities, although they may appear to offer a clear demarcation between *us* and *them*, *now* and *then*, contain within them contradictions and overlaps. Victor Klemperer, whose diaries span the decades of the 1940s and the 1950s in the GDR, was a contemporary who emphasized the continuity in language between Nazism and Communism (1999). Already at the beginning of the Cold War, or even before it had become a concept, he observed contradictions and such overlaps. In July 1945, we find him asking whether there is any difference between Hitler's creation of language and truth and that of Stalin: "Every day I observe the continuity from the Third Reich's *lingua Tertii Imperii* to the *Lingua Quarti Imperii* in the Soviet sphere," he added in October of that year (Klemperer, 1999). When the Communist regime collapsed almost half a century after Klemperer made his observations, the connection to the Nazi language was reactivated in an East German historical framework, which had had a form of liberal democratic experience for less than 14 years (the Weimar Republic, 1919–1933) and decades of authoritarian abuse and manipulation of the *Volk* concept.

The general pattern that emerges from this and other examples seems to indicate that foundation myths often emerge in times of crisis, and particularly in response to a collective yearning to come to terms with these situations. They provide a framework for interpretation and understanding and seem to offer consolation, if not compensation, for present and past suffering and injury. Public remembrance makes it possible to forget in the same sense in which Reinhart Koselleck (2004) has argued that, for public monuments, to reveal is to conceal: *zeigen ist verschweigen*. But perhaps, rather than forgetting, it is a matter of not being reminded, and uncontested monuments signify a kind of agreement on the meaning of history, as well as on the values of the present. We do not notice what we see around us every day, and it is in this context that myths take on the dimensions of common sense and truth that are never questioned. However, in new situations of crisis and loss of meaning, such as during and after World War II and in the 1990s, when the Cold War no longer provided meaning through the clear demarcation of *us* and *them*, myths become problematic and subject to renegotiation and revision (for France, for instance, see Rousso, 1987, 2000; Rousso & Conan, 1994).

Explanatory Challenges and Problems of Constructionist Historiography

There are three explanatory challenges or problems with the concept of historical construction in social science methodology. First, *construction* can connote a building industry or social engineering and, indeed, may even connote manipulation. Given this, it is not unreasonable to argue that the production of symbols, images, and myths is an elite undertaking, that the construction/invention processes discussed here are simply the elite's manipulation of the masses. But cohesion and community may also be constructed from the grassroots level and may challenge the meaning assigned to events and situations by elite groups. Indeed, social protest and social integration have been key dimensions of the construction of the nation.

A second and related explanatory problem with the concept of historical construction is that, in modern Western-style societies at least, this process of production is something that occurs in a conflicting and oppositional context marked by social bargaining and negotiation, with the aim of finding compromises. The ideas on the agenda are continuously transformed, so much so that it is often difficult to identify their origin. Symbols and myths, like other politically fertile concepts, can be seen in many different ways and are therefore open to contestation. They do not mediate one indivisible view emanating from an originating elite. Their production is marked by conflict and compromise, as is their mass reception. Unfortunately, the terms *construction* and *invention* may not readily convey the idea that the processes under consideration are not one-sided but emerge out of the interaction of many actors and stakeholders in national identity. This is how it must be studied if we are to understand the full implications of myth, commemoration, and community construction (Gerber, 2000; Stråth, 2000).

A third explanatory problem with constructionism stems not so much from the concept itself but from how it has been applied. It has been used to portray actors in the society under scrutiny but has been much less applied to those who perform the analyses. This fails to attend to the place of historical interpretation itself as part of the construction process. In other words, there is a problem of double construction. In their efforts to have history recognized as a science, professional historians have failed to recognize an important dimension of their discipline—namely, that history as a discipline is, like philosophy, a branch of ethics. The resulting double or radical constructionism highlights the role historians themselves play in the construction of nations, the fact that the historians are not outside the ideologies and language games they analyze but part of them, a fact that has created the now well-known methodological problems of postmodern history.

Constructionism leads to relativization of concepts such as truth and reality, which previously had been understood in absolute terms. The end of the Cold War and new epistemological views have meant new challenges for professional historiography, even giving a concept such as history new perspectives, not the least of which is the insight that there is no reality that can be conceptualized and analyzed beyond the limits that language sets on meaning. One might choose to see this as a burden, but it also justifies a certain optimism as a result of the interpretative freedom that the new view provides. In this context, it is well worth emphasizing the trade-off that, in being multivocal, language constitutes a huge semantic field with vast ranges; and, for this reason, it offers a space for national identity construction to be filled in broader terms than ever before.

• References

Anderson, B. (1990). *Imagined communities: Reflections on the origin and spread of nationalism.* London: Verso.

Ankersmit, F. R (1998). Danto on representation, identity and indiscernibles. *History and Theory, 37*(4), 44–70.

Assmann, J. (1999). *Das Kulturelle Gedächtnis: Schrift, Erinnerung und Politische Identität in Frühen Hochkulturen.* Munich, Germany: Beck.

Austin, J. L. (1975). *How to do things with words* (J. O. Urmson & M. Sbisà, Eds.). Oxford, UK: Clarendon Press.

Barthes, R. (1972). *Mythologies.* London: Cape.

Bosworth, R. J. B. (1993). *Explaining Auschwitz and Hiroshima: Historians and the Second World War, 1945–1990.* London: Routledge.

Brinks, J. H. (1992). *Die DDR-Geschichtswissenschaft auf dem Weg zur deutschen Einheit: Luther, Friedrich II und Bismarck als Paradigmen politischen Wandels.* Frankfurt, Germany: Campus.

Brinks, J. H. (2000). *Fatherland: Germany's Post-war right-wing politics.* London: Tauris.

Brunner, O., Conze, W., & Koselleck, R. (1979–1992). *Geschichtliche Grundbegriffe: Historisches Lexikon zur politisch-sozialen Sprache in Deutschlen* (Vols. 1–7). Stuttgart, Germany: Klett-Cotta.

Combs, J. E., & Nimmo, D. (1990). *Mediated political realities.* London: Longman.

Croce, B. (1963). *Il carattere della filosophia moderna.* Bari, Italy: Laterza. (Original work published 1941)

Derrida, J. (1972). *La dissémination.* Paris: Seuil.

Derrida, J. (1979). *Lécriture et la différence.* Paris: Seuil.

Engelberg, E. (1985). *Bismarck: Urpreusse und Reichsgründer.* Berlin, Germany: Siedler.

Eschebach, I. (2005). *Öffentliches Gedenken. Deutsche Erinnerungskulturen seit der Weimarer Republik.* Frankfurt, Germany: Campus.

Foucault, M. (1969). *L'archéologie du savoir.* Paris: Gallimard.

Freeden, M. (1996). *Ideologies and political theory: A conceptual approach.* Oxford, UK: Oxford University Press.

Gerber, G. (2000). Doing Christianity and Europe: An inquiry into memory, boundary and truth practices. In B. Stråth (Ed.), *Europe and the other and Europe as the other.* Brussels, Belgium: P I E-Peter Lang.

Giesen, B. (1998). *Intellectuals and the German nation: Collective memory in an axial age.* Cambridge, UK: Cambridge University Press.

Giesen, B. (2000). National identity as trauma: The German case. In B. Stråth (Ed.), *Myth and memory in the construction of community: Historical patterns in Europe and beyond.* Brussels, Belgium: P I E-Peter Lang.

Grimm, J., & Grimm, W. (1960). *Deutsches Wörterbuch.* Leipzig, Germany: S. Hirzel. (Original work published 1854)

Habermas, J. (1989). *The new conservatism: Cultural criticism and the historians' debate.* Cambridge, UK: Polity Press.

Halbwachs, M. (1994). *Les cadres sociaux de la mémoire.* Paris: Albin Michel. (Original work published 1925)

Heinz, M. (1994). *Sensualistischer Idealismus: Untersuchungen zur Erkenntnistheorie des jungen Herder (1763–1778).* Hamburg, Germany: Meiner.

Hippler, T. (2000). Spinoza on historical myths. In B. Stråth (Ed.), *Myth and memory in the construction of community: Historical patterns in Europe and beyond.* Brussels, Belgium: P I E-Peter Lang.

Hobsbawm, E., & Ranger, T. (Eds.). (1983). *The invention of tradition.* Cambridge, UK: Cambridge University Press.

Hunt, L. (1983). The rhetoric of revolution in France. *History Workshop Journal, 15,* 78–94.

Iggers, G. (1999). Historiography and the challenge of postmodernism. In B. Stråth & N. Witoszek (Eds.), *The postmodern challenge: Perspectives East and West.* Amsterdam: Rodopi.

Klemperer, V. (1999). *So sitze ich denn zwischen allen Stühlen: Tagebücher 1945–1959* (Vols. 1 & 2, W. Nowojski & C. Löser, Eds.). Berlin, Germany: Aufbau-Verlag.

Koselleck, R. (1989). *Critique and crisis.* Cambridge, UK: Cambridge University Press. (Original work published 1959)

Koselleck, R. (2004). *Futures past: On the semantics of historical time.* New York: Columbia University Press. (Original work published 1979)

Le Goff, J. (1985). *Histoire et mémoire.* Paris: Gallimard.

Lévi-Strauss, C. (1978). *Myth and meaning.* London: Routledge & Kegan Paul.

Lyotard, F. (1979). *La condition postmoderne: Rapport sur le savoir.* Paris: Minuit.

Nietzsche, F. (1980). *Werke in sechs Bänder.* Berlin, Germany: Hanser. (Original work published 1852–1889)

Nolte, E. (1987). *Der Europäische Bürgerkrieg 1917–1945: Nationalsozialismus und Bolschewismus.* Berlin, Germany: Propyläen.

Nora, P. (1996). *Realms of memory: Rethinking the French past.* New York: Columbia University Press.

Palonen, K. (2004). *Die Entzauberung der Begriffe: Das Umschreiben der politischen Begriffe bei Quentin Skinner und Reinhart Koselleck.* Münster, Germany: LIT Verlag.

Persson, H.-Å., & Stråth, B. (2007). *Reflections on Europe: Defining a political order in time and space.* Brussels, Belgium: P I E-Peter Lang.

Peukert, D. (1989). *Max Weber's Diagnose der Moderne.* Göttingen, Germany: V&R.

Pocock, J. G. A., & Skinner, Q. (2004). The history of politics and the politics of history. *Common Knowledge, 10*(3), 532–550.

Rousso, H. (1987). *Le syndrome de Vichy de 1944 à nos jours.* Paris: Seuil.

Rousso, H. (2001). *Vichy: l'événement, la mémoire.* Paris: Gallimard.

Rousso, H., & Conan, E. (1994). *Vichy: Un passé qui ne passé pas.* Paris: Fayard.

Rutherford, J. (1990). Identity: A place called home. In J. Rutherford (Ed.), *Identity: Community, culture, difference.* London: Lawrence & Wishart.

Schmale, W. (1997). *Scheitert Europa an seinem Mythendefizit?* Bochum, Germany: Winkler.

Scott, J. (1988). *Gender and the politics of history.* New York: Columbia University Press.

Skinner, Q. (2002). *Visions of politics: Vol. I. Regarding method.* Cambridge, UK: Cambridge University Press.

Stedman Jones, G. (1983). *Languages of class: Studies in English working class history, 1832–1982.* Cambridge, UK: Cambridge University Press.

Stråth, B. (2000). Introduction: Myth, memory and history in the construction of community. In B. Stråth (Ed.), *Myth and memory in the construction of community: Historical patterns in Europe and beyond.* Brussels, Belgium: P I E-Peter Lang.

Szakolszai, A. (1998). *Max Weber and Michel Foucault: Parallel life-works.* London: Routledge.

Vico, G. (1977). *La scienza nuova.* Milan, Italy: Rizzoli. (Original work published 1725)

Wehler, H.-U. (1988). *Entsorgung der deutschen Vergangenheit? Ein polemischer Essay zum "Histrikerstreit."* Munich, Germany: Beck.

White, H. (1974). *Metahistory: The historical imagination in nineteenth-century Europe.* Baltimore: John Hopkins University Press.

White, H. (2000). Catastrophe, communal memory and mythic discourse: The uses of myth in the reconstruction of society. In B. Stråth (Ed.), *Myth and memory in the construction of community: Historical patterns in Europe and beyond.* Brussels, Belgium: P I E-Peter Lang.

Winter, J., & Sivan, E. (1999). *Setting the framework.* In J. Winter & E. Sivan (Eds.), *War and remembrance in the twentieth century.* Cambridge, UK: Cambridge University Press.

Wittgenstein, L. (1989). *Tractatus logico-philosophicus.* Frankfurt, Germany: Suhrkamp.

PART VI

CONTINUING CHALLENGES

CHAPTER 33

The Reality of Social Constructions

● **Stephen Pfohl**

> How to have simultaneously an account of radical historical contingency for all knowledge claims and knowing subjects, a critical practice for recognizing our own "semiotic technologies" for making meanings, and a no-nonsense commitment to faithful accounts of a "real" world, one that can be partially shared and friendly to earth-wide projects of finite freedom, adequate material abundance, modest meaning in suffering, and limited happiness.
>
> —HARAWAY (1991, p. 187)

> Its not that nothing is real; rather everything is real.
>
> —K. ACKER (cited in Pfohl, 1992, back cover)

All meaningful accounts of the real world are mediated by the social contexts in which such accounts are constructed. Effective social constructions bestow a "taken-for-granted" sense of "naturalness" to some things but not others. Under the spell of dominant (or hegemonic) social constructions, artificial things become "second nature" to those they most captivate, blessing a particular order of things while cursing others. This is a core tenet of social constructionist theory and methods—

that, for language-dependent humans, things are never simply present in a direct and unadorned fashion. Things are, instead, partially shaped and provisionally organized by the complex ways in which we are ritually positioned in relation to each other and to the objects we behold materially, symbolically, and in the imaginary realm.

The ritual historical positioning of humans in relation to cultural objects and stories that we both make and are made over by—this, perhaps, is the elementary form of an effective social construction. This elementary form casts a social circle of believability around artificially constructed accounts of the world. At the same time, the believability of the social constructions that lie inside this circle depends on what the circle expels to the outside. In this sense, social constructions are, at once, constituted and haunted by what they exclude. This is true regardless of the content of specific social constructions. Constructions of gender and sexuality, war and peace, science and religion, race and coloniality, deviance and social control, economy and value, normal climate change and catastrophic global warming—each is mediated by the social force fields of power and knowledge in which they are produced, reproduced, or challenged.

To suggest that all meaningful accounts of reality are socially constructed does not imply that things are simply relative. Nothing is simply relative. "Relativism is a way of being nowhere while claiming to be everywhere equally, . . . a denial of responsibility and critical inquiry" (Haraway, 1991, p. 191). Instead of being simply relative, social constructions are relational and complexly systemic. Social constructions may be relative, but only to things that are natural and historical at the same time. Social constructions are relative to complex dynamics of power in the here and now and to ritual filters that shape human perceptions and stories about things in some ways to the exclusion of others.

Just as it is incorrect to state that social constructions are simply relative, it is wrong to argue that, because social understandings of reality are constructed, reality as such does not exist. The social construction of reality is never equivalent to the complexities of the real world of which it is but a part. But neither is the creative artifice of construction ever entirely separate from what is real. To suggest that social reality is constructed means only that, from a human point of view, reality is forever dependent on the natural–historical and psychic–social con-

texts in which selective knowledge of the real world is assembled. This is not to dismiss the role of biochemical processes, global economic circumstance, or brute physical forces in also influencing the character of human perceptions and knowledge. It is, however, to insist that such factors never operate independently of the ways in which our notions about the world are mediated by powerful cultural and historical constructions. This morning in Iraq, three U.S. soldiers were killed by IRDs (improvised roadside devices). This is reality. But the meaning and ethical–political implications of this reality vary with the constructs used and the stories told to make sense of this event. Did the soldiers die at the hands of freedom-hating terrorists? Or were they killed by insurgents fighting an army of unlawful foreign invaders? The answer depends on how this tragic loss of human life is framed and filtered, transformed by powerful interpretive screens, mediated by social constructions.

The Social Construction of Sociological Reality

Like many other sociologists, my initial engagement with social constructionist thought was sparked by both empirical and theoretical concerns. As a university student in the late 1960s and early 1970s, I was troubled by fierce disputes over what to do about the contested realities of white supremacy, gendered hierarchy, structured economic differences between entire classes of people, and the geopolitical meaning of the Vietnam War. Theoretically, constructionism helped me to glimpse how seemingly well-meaning people could arrive at decidedly different viewpoints on such matters. Peter Berger and Thomas Luckmann's book *The Social Construction of Reality* (1966) was particularly important. Influenced by the social phenomenology of Alfred Schutz, Berger and Luckmann urged sociologists to suspend judgment about the objective reality of social life in order to describe reality as it is constructed in the minds of everyday people.

Schutz (1970) viewed the experience of everyday life as filtered through a set of categorical definitions, or "typifications," about what the world is and how people should act within it. Typified stocks of meaning and recipes for action were said to provide people with a common sense about the nature of reality. For Schutz, common sense is graced by the *natural attitude*—a sense of the everyday world as taken-for-granted and structured independently of one's immediate experience. Commonsensical reality is also organized in accordance with the belief that—for all practical purposes—other "normal" people experience the world in more or less the same way as oneself. Combining Schutz's theories with ideas drawn from philosophical anthropology and the sociologies of Max Weber, Emile Durkheim, Karl Marx, and George Herbert Mead, Berger and Luckmann (1966) arrive at a dialectical approach to the construction of social reality. Their treatise begins with the suggestion that—unlike other species of animals—humans lack built-in or imprinted biological instincts capable of providing a stable sense of social order. To compensate for this lack, we rely on an evolved central nervous system that enables us to use symbols and language to construct an artificial world order.

The first step in this process is *externalization*—reaching out with words and images to classify the world around us. But soon the names we affix to things take on a life of their own, and we become prisoners of the artificial worlds we create. In this, we are positioned, not unlike Victor Frankenstein in Mary Shelley's terrifying novel, as creators whose lives come to be ruled by creatures we ourselves construct. Berger and Luckmann (1966) use the term *objectification* to denote the process whereby humanly created symbols are transformed into constraining social realities. Forgotten, or pushed outside common sense, is the fact that taken-

for-granted symbols are, in actuality, nothing but arbitrary and conventional ways of naming the ebb and flow of things in time.

Congealed into forceful social institutions by habit-forming "reciprocal typifications," the perceptual constraints of social constructions are taken inside the self through the rituals of socialization. When socialization is effective, artificial symbolic constructs are experienced as if they were natural realities. Objectification is extended by *legitimation*, an envelopment of typified constructs by a higher or more encompassing level of symbols. Legitimations are, in turn, backed up by social control mechanisms of various sorts. Although artificial, institutionalized social constructions come to selectively frame what counts as reality, shaping human perception, judgment, and habitual courses of action in the world.

Berger and Luckmann's (1966) treatise in the sociology of knowledge did much to expand the nature and scope of this subfield of sociological inquiry. It also helped "move the sociology of knowledge from the periphery to the very center of sociological theory" (Berger & Luckmann, 1966, p. 18). The notion of socially constructed reality appealed widely to sociologists concerned with the effects of symbolic interaction and with the historical shaping of cultural meanings and action. Moreover, in addition to its relevance to an empirical sociology of ideas and science, constructionism aligned with critical questions about how some actions, but not others, came to be labeled as deviant or viewed as social problems. Radical and constructivist criminologists asked why certain forms of harm were criminalized and other harms ignored. Questions pertaining to the power of interest groups and dominant social classes in shaping commonsensical worldviews and ideological ways of seeing also became associated with the constructionist perspective.

One area of inquiry, however, was explicitly excluded from Berger and Luckmann's (1966) early formulation of constructionist thought. This concerned epistemological and methodological questions pertaining to the reality of social science constructions. It is not that Berger and Luckmann saw no problems in this realm. Indeed, they remark that "the sociology of knowledge, like all empirical disciplines that accumulate evidence concerning the relativity and determination of human thought, leads toward epistemological questions concerning sociology itself as well as any other scientific body of knowledge" (p. 13). Likening problems posed by the sociology of knowledge to related "trouble for epistemology" generated by history, psychology, and biology, Berger and Luckmann contend that the

> logical structure of this trouble is basically the same in all cases: How can I be sure, say, of my sociological analysis of American middle-class mores in view of the fact that categories I use for this analysis are conditioned by historically relative forms of thought, that I myself and everything I think is determined by my genes and by ingrown hostility to my fellowmen, and that, to cap it all, I am myself a member of the American middle class? (p. 13)

While recognizing the importance of such problems, Berger and Luckmann contend "that these questions are not themselves part of the empirical discipline of sociology. They properly belong to the methodology of the social sciences, an enterprise that belongs to philosophy and is by definition other than sociology" (1966, p. 13). As such, efforts to develop a reflexive sociology of sociology are deliberated excluded by Berger and Luckmann. In their discussion of the social construction of reality, they "firmly bracket . . . any epistemological or methodological questions about the validity of sociological analysis" (1966, p. 14). Despite the generative character of Berger and Luckmann's work, this strikes me as a problematic exclusion, and one that unwarrantedly transfers to another discipline (philosophy) crucial questions about the reality and scope of sociological analyses of the social constructions of others.

In what ways are sociological constructions of reality also social constructions? In what ways are sociological constructs conditioned by the power-charged and historically specific social contexts in which they are produced? What, in other words, is the nature and scope of the reality produced by sociologists and other social scientists who deploy a constructionist perspective? What, moreover, distinguishes the constructions of sociologists from those of other social actors in history and everyday life? To address these questions is to take up the challenge of issues deliberately excluded by Peter Berger and Thomas Luckmann in their influential formulation of a constructionist framework 40 years ago. This chapter takes up this challenge.

In exploring the reality of social constructions, and specifically those produced by social analysts, I ask you to imagine the *ritual labor of social construction* as situated at the crossroads of four interdependent vectors of influence—*natural historical materiality*, *psychic social subjectivity*, *power*, and *knowledge*. These vectors both shape and are energetically shaped by the social constructions they together beget. Each vector is real, yet restricted in scope by the way that it contributes selectively to the social construction of what is taken for granted by specific cultures in history. By examining each vector in turn I hope to demonstrate sociological complexities that bear on the character of reality implicated in the work of social construction. Together, these vectors partially shape the ritual labor involved in producing hegemonic social constructions and what these constructions sacrifice. This raises questions about similarities and differences between hegemonic social constructions and reflexive sociological accounts. Is it possible for social constructionists to attend to the ways in which their own categories, frames, and stories are partially shaped by the complex systems of reality to which they belong? The chapter concludes with a discussion of *power-reflexive approaches* to constructionist theory and methods.

The Natural Historical Materiality of Social Construction

This first vector of influence pictures the reality of social construction as a constitutive material feature of human animal nature itself. Three considerations are of particular importance: (1) assumptions pertaining to species survival, (2) the restrictive economic character of a given society's dominant mode of production, and (3) the general economy of living energetic matter. Each plays a part in any natural history of social construction.

With regard to species survival, it is vital to recognize that, like all other living species, we human animals need relative stability in relation to our environments in order to maintain ourselves and reproduce. Without some modicum of stability we would be swept up in chaos, unable to effectively secure food, nurturance, shelter, and ordered approaches to governance, social exchange, and sexual procreation. In other words, we would not know how to interact with our environments in ways that enable species continuity across time and the spaces we cohabit with other species and our fellow humans. Nevertheless, as Berger and Luckmann (1966) suggest, when it comes to survival, unlike virtually all other species of animals, humans enter the world with a deficit. Despite the complexities of our genetic inheritance, we are not born with built-in or instinctual technologies that enable us to secure the rudimentary conditions of species survival. Nor are we biologically imprinted at an early age in ways that guarantee a repetition of stable action patterns over the course of our lives. In this sense, our bodies are not structured for the purposes of survival by biology alone.

Despite our precarious human condition, our lack of instinctual technologies for survival is compensated for in another bodily realm. Over the course of evolution, we have acquired a highly developed central nervous system. This is a material basis for the world-constructing artifice of human language. It enables us to engage productively with the world around us through signs, symbols, images, and gestures. Rooted in our bodily capabilities, language is also historically situated. Its constructs, classifications, and narrative possibilities are rooted in specific interactions between people who learn to exchange words for things and make meanings. In this sense, language is a constitutive feature of human nature, a material technology that enables us to compensate with words for what we lack in the biological realm alone. Through the symbolic constructions of language, humans act economically to reduce the chaos of material flux to relatively stable categories of meaning.

Technologies of linguistic artifice are a constitutive aspect of any society's material survival. Language constructs are also central to what Karl Marx called the mode of production—the organization of species survival in keeping with historically specific forms of restrictive economic exchange. Social constructions of meaning and value are crucial to this task. As Marx declares in *The Eighteenth Brumaire of Louis Bonaparte* (1852/1972), humans

> make their own history, but they do not make it just as they please; they do not make it under circumstances chosen by themselves, but under circumstances directly encountered, given and transmitted from the past. The tradition of all the dead generations weigh on the brain of the living. . . . In like manner a beginner who has learnt a new language always translates it back into his mother tongue, but he has assimilated the spirit of the new language and can freely express himself in it only when he finds his way in it without recalling the old and forgets his native tongue in the use of the new. (p. 97)

Just as figurative social constructions help shape the mode of production, the way in which society organizes economic survival also constrains the forms of meaning available to its members. The reciprocal interplay between linguistic technologies and the mode of production is a key determinant of the scope of reality articulated by a given society. The location of individuals and groups within a regimen of production also shapes the standpoint from which people make meaning of things. People subordinated by a given economic order typically construct meanings about that order that put them at a distance from those whom this order privileges. As such, standpoint must be taken into account when attempting to discern how specific social constructions illuminate (or obscure) reality. Antagonism typically walks a thin blue line between one standpoint and another.

Species survival and a society's dominant mode of production are crucial to understanding the natural history and scope of reality implicated in the labor of social construction. Also influential is what Georges Bataille (1988) refers to as the realm of *general economy*. Bataille extends Marx's theoretical framework by refusing to limit the analysis of economic matters to the *restrictive economy*—an economy organized in terms of useful or instrumental human production. Unlike Marx, Bataille does not view human animal existence as governed exclusively by contests over the control of productive labor. Although essential to human survival, restrictive economic practices and the social constructions that accompany them are not in themselves the essence of human life. Productive labor is but one aspect of our being. Equally important is the *general economy*— a realm in which boundaries surrounding what is distinctively human yield to the vibrant movement of living energetic matter. In the general economy, reality extends beyond words, pulsating in radiant, web-like connections in excess of language. Here, instrumental productivity is subordinated to the more expansive realities of cosmic material interconnectedness.

The restrictive productivity of an effective social construction is purchased, then, not only at the expense of subordinated classes of humans but also by our temporary exile from open-ended participation in the infi-nite variety of the general economy. This is to acknowledge that there is more to reality than survival-oriented economic production. Human existence comes into being first and foremost as a gift of nature. Nature is the source of life, or mother, the web of energetic materiality from which we come and to which we return. Nature is the matrix within which human animals are nourished and to which we owe our breath, our flesh, and our blood. Thus, despite the dominant social constructions of nature produced by our society, we humans are never really outside of nature looking down. We are, instead, dynamically situated within the relational fluxes of living matter, an immanent aspect of nature's own energetic history. We are participants in nature's dynamic evolution, just as we productively carve out a time and place for ourselves by the material linguistic technologies of social construction.

The social constructions we produce about nature and our relations with one another are parasites. They feed on a living energetic host that is always infinitely more complex and more real than the scope of reality offered by even the most expansive of social constructions. As such, reflexive attunement to the general economic realm facilitates discernment of the scope of reality implicated by a specific social construction. Social constructions are real. But their reality is also limited. Social constructions are never as real or far-reaching in scope as the general economy from which they draw their energy. Nor are social constructions ever really separate from the world they claim to represent. Social constructions are, at once, representations of the real world and a dynamic aspect of the world's natural history.

When we act in the world on the basis of the social constructions by which we picture the world, the effects are material and sometimes long lasting. Social constructions may alert us to problems that, although real, may have never been put into words. Feminism, for instance, today provides names and narrative constructions for a reality that, although sensed and suffered by women, had long eluded the realm of words. At other times, the material effects of social construction can be more catastrophic. An example involves dominant U.S. constructions about what constitutes an acceptable source of energy. Constructions guiding major U.S. energy-consuming institutions continue to barter off the future by legitimating unsustainable carbon-based technologies of industry, consumption, and war. These technologies, and the social constructions that justify their excessive use, are literally killing the planet. Here, socially constructed reality rubs tragically against the reality of the general economy.

Sometimes the reality of the world pushes back against the grain of our social constructions. This creates anxiety, particularly for those who mistake the restrictive economy of social constructions for what is real (in the general economic sense of the word). Do you believe in global warming as a social construct? Regardless of what you believe, the world of living energetic matter appears to be communicating the truth of the matter, independent of how we think and act. This we need to remember when attempting to discern the scope of the reality of both the social constructions we analyze and those we use as tools of analysis. Attunement to the movement of the general economy—being in touch with the web of living energetic matter in which we participate—can also prove a canny resource in the process of power-reflexive analytic discernment. I return to this matter in the closing section of this chapter.

The Psychic Subjectivity of Social Construction

A second vector of influence on the reality of social construction involves the subject position of those engaged in the labor of construction. In *The Alchemy of Race and Rights*, Patricia Williams, an African American law professor and critical legal theorist,

writes, "Since subject position is everything in my analysis of the law, you deserve to know that it's a bad morning. I am very depressed" (1991, p. 3). Williams alerts her readers to constructed historical matters that bear on her depression. She is preparing a lecture on laws pertaining to redhibitory vice—"a defect in merchandise which, if existing at the time of purchase, gives rise to a claim allowing the buyer to return the thing and to get back part or all of the purchase price" (p. 3). Williams's lecture analyzes an 1835 court decision from Louisiana. The redhibitory vice in question concerns the alleged "craziness" of a slave named Kate. Kate had been purchased for $500. But after judging his slave insane, Kate's master wants his money back. Dominant social constructions concerning the meaning of property and racialized ideas about who counts as a human come together in this case. The brutal associations between these two realms haunt Williams's tale. "I would like to write," she declares, "in ways that reveal the intersubjectivity of legal constructions, that forces the reader to participate in the construction of meaning and to be conscious of that process" (p. 7).

Dominant social constructions at the time of Kate's enslavement viewed her as a unit of property, not a human being with unequivocal rights. Thus, after being "satisfied that the slave in question was wholly, and perhaps worse than useless," the Louisiana court ruled in favor of the plaintiff, stating that he had a right to get his money back. With this as background, it is hardly surprising that Williams is "very depressed." But "on this bad morning," in foregrounding the psychic social position from which she reads (and rereads) the 1835 case, Williams also invites her readers to consider the relation between her subject position and theirs. "It always takes a while to sort out what's wrong," suggests Williams, "but it usually starts with some kind of perfectly irrational thought such as: I *hate* being a lawyer" (1991, p. 3).

Effective social constructions pave the way for meaningful action in history. Yet, as

Marx points out, although people make history, they never do so just as they please or under circumstances entirely chosen by themselves. Thus, although it is a crucial component of social construction, subject position is never truly the beginning or end of socially constructed reality. Berger and Luckmann (1966) make a related point. Although social constructions are produced by subjective efforts to classify the world (externalization), they can also take on a life of their own, limiting the intelligibility of experience and restricting the future actions of their creators (objectification). An analogous distinction is made in the social psychoanalytic teachings of Jacques Lacan (1977). For Lacan, social psychic constructions of the world are simultaneously real, imaginary, and symbolic.

For Lacan, psychic constructions are real because the subjects that create them are part of the realm of living energetic matter. What Lacan calls "the real" is irreducible to either the realm of projective imaginary identifications or the objectifying symbolic confines of language. The imaginary realm is constituted by phantasmic identifications that misrecognize the complexities of reality, reducing reality to the restrictive psychic economy of the Ego. Lacan pictured the dominant phantasms at play in contemporary Western (or Northwestern) society as resulting in a narcissistic imagination of oneself as if autonomous of the actual material dependencies and social interconnections that shape our existence. Psychic misrecognition institutes a "gap" between imagined subjective existence and what is real. This begins with a refusal of the debt we owe to our mothers, a debt to the living energetic matters from which we come and to which we return. This is Egoism—a form of subjectivity that mistakes a self-enclosed mirror image of itself for the actuality of one's (natural historical) relations to others. Lacan suggested that the psychic social misrecognitions beget by Egoism were most acute in the United States. Nevertheless, and despite its perceptual derangements, there is no getting around the

Imaginary. As human animals we neither passively receive nor simply perceive the world. We, instead, actively hallucinate or project an ordered place for ourselves, substituting an imaginary point of view for what is complexly real and reciprocally dynamic.

It is important to reckon with the constitutive force of the imagination when thinking about the reality of social constructions. While providing us with an image of ourselves, the imaginary realm also generates the phantasm of being separate from and even on top of the world. This is an aggressive gesture of psychic departure from what is real. In this, the world to which we belong is judged from the standpoint of the "I" and projected as an object to be assessed at an eye's distance. Yet, despite its illusory quality, we can never entirely exit the imaginary realm. This is a constitutive aspect of our psychic social subjectivity. We are fated, however, to repeatedly double back in language on our phantasmic misrecognitions, replaying narcissistic projections in the key of collectively orchestrated words.

As subjects of language, we exist in the field of what Lacan, following structuralist anthropologist Claude Lévi-Strauss (1963), calls the Symbolic Order—the objectifying realm of normative linguistic constraint. In the Symbolic Order the phantasmic desires and fears we experience are never ours alone. They are hooked up to a network of sliding cultural and linguistic signifiers. Within this network we are pushed and pulled by forceful constructed loops of meaning but also by what the network excludes or keeps from consciousness. As such, when we communicate with one another, we never speak entirely person-to-person or in the here and now. Whenever we speak to each other we are also addressing the Other of our culture's dominant linguistic system. This is a socially constructed Other—an abstract Other standing between us and toward whom we direct even our most intimate thoughts.

The Imaginary and Symbolic realms forever interact, dynamically contributing to the shape of our subject positions in history. Sometimes interaction balances one realm with the other. At other times, the effect is to suppress one realm or repress the other. But regardless of outcome, each realm is steeped in artifice. In the Imaginary, artifice is projective and phantasmic. In the Symbolic Order, what is socially constructed appears almost "second nature" and governed by laws. But narcissistic or normative pretense aside, neither the Imaginary nor the Symbolic realm is truly real. In Lacanian thought, the Real assumes a paradoxical status, akin in many ways to Georges Bataille's notion of the general economy. And, just as the general economy provides an energetic material context for restrictive economic actions, so does the brute materiality of the Real provide a foundation for all that is subjectively imagined and linguistically symbolized. The Real is an aspect of all subjective constructions of reality, even as attempts to imagine and symbolize it fall short of capturing its complexity and fullness of being. As such, from the vantage point forged by psychic social constructions, what is real is always at least partially unconscious.

This distinguishes Lacan's Freudian phenomenology of social construction from Berger and Luckmann's. Some portion of the real is repressed every time it is imaginarily or symbolically represented. Although repressed, the Real, however, is never actually rendered void by the psychic work of social construction. The opposite is true. What is real forever haunts psychic social constructions of reality, if in unconscious ways. For this reason, grappling with unconscious tensions between the Real and the reality of social construction is crucial for critical analyses of socially constructed reality. In Lacanian theory, this analytic imperative accords not only with Freudian notions about the inevitably repressive character of representational systems but also with Baruch Spinoza's (1985) imagination of thought and extension as complementary attributes of human nature itself.

With thought, humans make constructs of the natural world to which we belong. But thoughts, representations, and social constructs, although rooted in the human body, are never equal to the material complexities of nature, of which human subjective life is but an extension. Spinoza refused philosophical distinctions between mind and body, thought and material reality, social constructions and the realm of being, declaring each an aspect of the other. At the same time, Spinoza contended that the realm of thought was more limited than the realm of nature that thought extends (Lloyd, 1996). As such, he advocated what today might be called a reflexive epistemological approach to the inevitable limits of conscious thought or constructed ideas. As a young student, Jacques Lacan papered his bedroom wall with diagrams depicting Spinoza's *Ethics*.

Lacan's discussion of unconscious dimensions of socially constructed reality also resembles key aspects of Emile Durkheim's study of "totemic" social constructions, or collective representations. In *The Elementary Forms of Religious Life*, Durkheim (1995) conceptualized the representational power of the totem—a "primitive" linguistic signifier—as a ritual social substitution of a word, emblem, iconic image, or figure of speech for the otherwise undifferentiated metamorphosis of material reality-in-flux. Like Lacan, Durkheim (1993, p. 81) was deeply influenced by Spinoza, hailing Spinoza as a pioneer in the theoretical study of the unconscious (Nielsen, 1999, pp. 32–37). When discussing the dual character of totemic representations (the prototype of all social constructions), Durkheim declared that human reality is double (*Homo duplex*). This repeats, in a sociological register, Spinoza's distinction between thought and extension as complementary attributes of a singular underlying state of being.

For Durkheim, representational reality participates in, but is never equivalent to, the physical reality from which it derives its energy (1995, p. 15). In discussing the dual character of representational constructs, Durkheim likens socially constructed reality to delirious hallucinations or delusions, insisting that linguistic artifice inevitably reduces or deforms the nature of reality. But Durkheim is equally insistent that representational artifice (social construction) is itself never entirely outside reality (1995, pp. 74–75). Although they distort or screen reality, representations also participate in reality. As such, they always bear traces of what is real, if in unconscious ways. According to Durkheim, artificiality enters into collective social representations as "constructed concepts." Nevertheless, the "artifice" that "enters . . . constructed concepts . . . is artifice that closely follows nature" (p. 17). This is the case, suggests Durkheim, because socially constructed representations are "part of the natural realm" and it is impossible that nature . . . should be radically different from itself" (p. 17). In this sense, "the social realm" is viewed by Durkheim as "a natural realm, which differs from the others only in its greater complexity" (p. 17).

Although close to the natural reality they artificially distort, representations also "repress the original state into the unconscious and . . . replace it with other states through which the original one is sometimes not easy to detect" (Durkheim, 1995, p. 17). In this way, unconscious aspects of social construction play a constitutive role in the social dynamics of psychic subjectivity. Following William James, Durkheim depicts "psychic experience" as "a continual stream of representations that blend into each other so that no one can say where one begins and another ends" (1974, p. 12). Yet, when caught up in a particular stream of social constructs, "our judgments are influenced at every moment by unconscious judgments; we see only what our prejudices permit us to see and yet we are unaware of them" (Durkheim, 1974, p. 12). Moreover, in language closely resembling Sigmund Freud's, Durkheim suggests that unconscious psychic aspects of representational life manifest themselves through such "signs of mental ac-

tivity" as "hesitation, tentativeness, and the adjustment of movement to a [repressed but] preconceived idea" (1974, p. 20). The connection between unconscious psychic activity and representational constructs is amplified in the work of Jacques Lacan. Lacan (1981) acknowledges an intellectual debt to the Durkheimian tradition of thought on these matters, stating that "the unconscious is structured like a language" and "what organizes this field" and "inscribes its initial lines of force" represents the "truth of the totemic function"—"the primary classificatory function" (p. 20).

Spinoza's, Lacan's, and Durkheim's thinking about psychic social subjectivity is complex and provocative. But when linking questions about the reality of social construction to the subject positions from which constructions arise, several key lessons may be drawn from this general tradition of thought. First, all constructions involve imaginary or phantasmic projections that forge a gap between the artifice of psychic existence and what is real. Second, all constructions, no matter how subjective or imaginary, are also mediated by social conventions that govern a given Symbolic Order or system of language. Third, all constructions—imaginary and symbolic—are unconsciously haunted by a real order of natural historical relations, repressed in the social constitution of psychic subjectivity itself. These lessons are given a decidedly political twist in the writings of critical social theorists Louis Althusser and Teresa Brennan.

Althusser (1971) pairs Lacan with Marx, describing how psychic subjectivity is socially "hailed" or "interpellated" into existence in the ritual materiality of linguistic performance. This clothes the subject from the inside out in a garb of ideology, substituting normatively sanctioned "imaginary relations" for "the real conditions of social existence" (pp. 162–165). In this process, artificial social constructions take on the accent of naturalized reality. In Teresa Brennan's reconfiguration of *History After*

Lacan (1993), the work of Melanie Klein and feminist social thought are added to the mix. Brennan extends Lacan's story of the aggression involved in substituting imaginary social relations for real relations by theorizing the historical emergence in the modern Northwest of an "era of the ego" (p. 3). The era of the Ego is characterized by a collective "social psychosis" (p. 3) that imagines, first, our actual mothers, then the wider realm of energetic nature as a whole, not as the source of life but as dependent on the controlling will of an intensely masculine form of psychic subjectivity. In denying its debt to others and nature as a whole, this historically specific form of subjectivity objectifies everything that moves.

The collective social psychosis described by Brennan began to take shape in the seventeenth century. Analyzing a wide range of historical data, Brennan identifies social forces enabling the realization of a long-standing "foundational fantasy" about matter (and mothers) as destined to be exploited as "natural resources" by men, "denying any notion of indebtedness or connection to origin" (1993, p. 167). Forces that facilitate the social construction of this aggressive fantasy include the ascendance of profit-driven capitalist logic and new technologies of measurement, manufacture, and transportation. Together these forces permit an increased objectification and appropriation of earth's energies. In this, "fantasy is made into reality, as commodities are constructed to serve their human masters, to wait upon them, at the expense of the natural world. These commodities are objects to be controlled: they are nature transformed into a form in which it cannot reproduce itself, nature directed toward human ends" (Brennan, 2000, p. 9).

Brennan (1993) describes the psychic subjectivity privileged by the "era of the ego" as psychotic because it is literally out of touch with material actuality. The technological realization of this subject's foundational fantasy also begets a haunting collective feeling of paranoia—a repressed awareness of the vi-

olence enacted by modern men of power in the name of economic and scientific progress. This paranoia leads to defensiveness—fear that the objectified "other" of modernity will retaliate in kind—and to further cycles of aggressive cultural projections and action aimed at domination, locking the modern Northwest into a self-enclosed death culture of masculine and imperial violence. Although it is hardly the only form of psychic subjectivity associated with the social constructions of modernity, Brennan may be correct in positing a fateful correspondence between this deranged subject position and dominant forms of modern social power. This leads to a consideration of power as the third significant vector affecting the reality of social construction.

The Power of Social Construction

A third vector that affects the reality of social construction involves the field of power. From the early 20th century until the present, sociology's most consistent understanding of power is derived from Max Weber. Weber (1964, p. 152) defined power as the ability of one set of social actors to exert influence over others, despite the resistance of others. This definition has proved useful in underscoring inequalities in the ability to influence social actions that are derived from the hierarchical organization of social resources.

Weber's perspective on power has long been a feature of social constructionist approaches to the shaping of reality. This is particularly the case for research on matters pertaining to deviance, crime, and social problems, in which power is typically viewed as a tool in the construction and application of labels separating what is normative from what is problematic. But this is also a limited imagination of power and one that assumes that power is itself a resource that can be owned or controlled by persons or groups who wield it as a weapon against others. In what follows, I supplement Weber's instrumental approach to power in several ways: first, by conceiving power as a constitutive field of overlapping social forces, rather than simply a resource or possession of the powerful; second, by distinguishing between hegemonic and coercive forms of power; and third, by situating contemporary forms of power—including all economic, gendered, and racialized fields of power—as also mediated by what might be called a *global coloniality of power.*

Power is a term that has undergone significant transformations in recent social theory. The word *power* is derived from the Latin verb *potere,* meaning "to be able." A dynamic characteristic of all productive human relations, power is the ability to make things happen. Power enables and constrains. It permits us to act toward each other in socially patterned ways, influencing what we are attracted to or repulsed by. Power opens the door for effective social constructions that make sense of the world while closing the door on others. This is what gives power its transformative social force. Functioning as a dynamic and historically contingent field of forces, power gives our knowledge of the world its socially constructed form. This is to imagine power as a complex "network of relations" in dynamic tension with each other (Foucault, 1979, pp. 26–27). Sometimes relations of power converge and amplify the force of one another. At other times, power relations contest and resist one another.

This vision of power and its relation to socially constructed knowledge finds its roots in the philosophy of Friedrich Nietzsche. Nietzsche's ideas about power might be described as a kind of social physics. For Nietzsche, power is not something that someone or some group could possess. Power is, instead, pictured as a constitutive field of forces or "dynamic quanta" affecting everything we do. This field of forces, "in a relation of tension" to all other forces, conditions human historical actions and socially constructed truths (Nietzsche, 1968, p. 339). It burns memories and forgetfulness into

the flesh of people ensnarled in social institutions and provokes lines of flight and resistance (Nietzsche, 1967, p. 61). In this sense, as a field of forces—some dominant and others dominated—power sets the scene for social action and the interpretive construction of human meaning and morals. Power is also reshaped by the effective history of action at every moment in time. The influence of Nietzsche's conception of power is particularly evident in the writings of Michel Foucault. Following Nietzsche, Foucault (1977b) pursued a genealogy of socially constructed discourses pertaining to madness (1965), medicine (1973), penal practices (1979), sexuality (1980), and the figure of Man in modern European science and culture (1970). Each was portrayed as emerging out of and feeding back upon fields of historically specific power. The goal, declared Foucault, was to create a "common history of power relations and object relations" (1979, p. 24).

As Mark Taylor (2001) observes, Foucault made use of Nietzsche's approach to culture and power "to develop a sophisticated analysis of the construction of knowledge and construction of social and culture codes. . . . [Moreover], since the constitution of the knowing subject and known object occurs in a field of fluctuating powers, subjects, objects and their interrelation are always changing and thus ever incomplete" (pp. 57–58). Key to Foucault's approach to social construction involved the power of what he called "discursive practices." Although articulated by flesh-and-blood human beings, discursive practices are never simply the product of creative human agents alone. Neither do discourses act mechanistically as causes of human action from the outside. As interactive networks or fields of power, discursive practices are ritually "embodied in technical processes, institutions, in patterns for general behavior, in forms for transmission and diffusion, and in pedagogical forms which, at once, impose and maintain them" (Foucault, 1977a, p. 200).

Foucault likened discourses to both micropolitical "technologies of the flesh" and "techniques of the self" (1979, 1985). Like fields of power in general, discourses are viewed as simultaneously depending on and partially autonomous of the human actors who ritually enact them. Discourses productively mobilize a wide range of material and psychic habits and sensibilities, fascinations and fears, desires, imaginings, and bodily dispositions. At the same time, discourses are recurrently transformed by the everyday actions of people in history. In addition to Foucault, Nietzsche's social physics of power aligns in important ways with the constructionist thought of theorists as diverse as Donna Haraway (1991), Pierre Bourdieu (1977), Patricia Williams (1991), Patricia Hill Collins (2000), Avery Gordon (1997), Paul Gilroy (1993), and Judith Butler (1997).

Power sets into place and continually replaces the fields of force in which we are constructively positioned alongside or against others. As a "multiplicity of force relations" immanent to the social fields in which we are situated, "power is everywhere; not because it embraces everything, but because it comes from everywhere" (Foucault, 1980, pp. 92–93). An omnipresent feature of social life, power is also structured differently in various times and places. Moreover, although it is possible to imagine relatively equal or reciprocal forms of power, such forms seem far from our historical present. As such, power is a contradictory (and often unequal) feature of everyday life, an aspect of our ritual relations to others that transforms fluid open-ended possibilities into things that appear timeless, fixed, and objective. Power works through, upon, and between our bodies, ceaselessly constructing and reconstructing the boundaries and limits of what we experience as real. But just as it works in this fashion, power also provokes resistance, compelling those it subordinates to push back against the fields of force in which power circulates (Foucault, 1980, pp. 95–96; Weedon, 1997, pp. 104–131).

Power assumes both *coercive* and *hegemonic* forms. Coercive fields of power are brutal. Whether deployed by authoritarian religious forces, gangs of thugs, bloodthirsty conquerors, or supposed democratic governments, such as the United States in such places as Abu Ghraib or Guantánamo Bay, coercive power propagates certain socially constructed worldviews while smashing others apart. Violence, the threat of violence, terror, and torture—these are all weapons in the arsenal of coercive power. Hegemonic forms of power, on the other hand, involve the seduction or social engineering of consent.

As developed in the prison writings of Antonio Gramsci (1971), hegemony refers to the ritual production of what passes for social consensus or common sense. Hegemony also always involves social struggle. Sometimes this takes the form of direct political contestation aimed at seizing control. At other times hegemonic struggle is more indirect and involves jockeying for position. In either case, hegemony results in a contested equilibrium among those who are divided by power's unequal blessings but united by a common sense about particular social constructions (Hall, Lumley, & McLennan, 1977). Why do people who are oppressed or damaged by hierarchical fields of power sometimes embrace social constructions that constrain them? Inquiry into this matter is crucial for critical analyses of the place of reality in constructionist thought.

Coercion and hegemony bend or distort reality. So does what Peruvian sociologist Aníbal Quijano (2000) calls the "coloniality of power." Quijano contends that no aspect of contemporary culture or economy is ever entirely free of the continuing shadows of colonial domination. In this sense, the legacies of colonial formations of power have an impact on all other social processes—from definitions of success and pleasure to ideas about value, cost-effectiveness, preemptive warfare, and pain. As Ramón Grosfoguel states:

> Quijano uses the notion of "coloniality" as opposed to "colonialism" in order to call attention to the historical continuities between colonial and so-called "post-colonial" times. . . . One implication of the notion of "coloniality of power" is that the world has not fully decolonized. The first decolonization was incomplete. It was limited to the juridical–political "independence" from the European imperial states. The "second decolonization" will have to address heterarchies of entangled racial, ethnic, sexual, gender and economic relations that the "first decolonization" left untouched. . . . A key component of Quijano's "coloniality of power" is his critique of Eurocentric forms of knowledge. According to Quijano, the privileging of Eurocentric forms of knowledge is simultaneous with the entangled process of core–periphery relations and racial/ethnic hierarchies. . . . Subaltern knowledges were excluded, omitted, silenced and/or ignored. This is not a call for a fundamentalist or essentialist rescue mission for authenticity. The point here is to put the colonial difference . . . at the center of knowledge production. (2006, pp. 495–497)

As a constitutive field of transformative social relationships, power—in both its coercive and hegemonic modes—functions as an energetic material terrain in which forceful social constructions are produced, impose themselves, and are resisted. Understanding the complexities of power is critical for efforts aimed at grasping the reality of a given regime of social constructions. What realities are fostered by a given regime? Which remain in excess of the commonsensical constructions that dominate our perceptions and thoughts? Related questions are posed by the coloniality of power, as it casts long shadows upon the knowledge of reality produced by world historical institutions and people in everyday life. This brings us to a fourth vector of influence affecting the reality of social construction—the realm of knowledge.

The Knowledge of Social Construction

Power and knowledge are reciprocal. Each shapes the form and content of the other. As Michel Foucault points out, "there is no power relation without the correlative constitution of a field of knowledge, or any knowledge that does not presuppose and constitute at the same time power relations" (1979, p. 27). And, just as multiple forms of power influence the reality of social construction, so do multiple forms of knowledge. To know something is to apprehend, perceive, or understand the reality of a given phenomenon. For the most part, however, analytic discussions of social construction picture knowledge in cognitive or categorical terms. The social construction of terrorism is a case in point. What are terrorism's defining characteristics? Although this is a contested matter in today's "global war against terrorism," cognitive constructions of terrorism typically refer to something such as the creation and use of terror (intense states of fear) as a political weapon aimed at intimidating or subjugating an opponent. Other social constructions of terrorism are more limited, restricting it to categories of warfare that violate lawful "rules of engagement," such as deliberate attacks on civilians.

Although important by themselves, cognitive approaches fail to do justice to the multiple dimensions of knowledge evoked by powerful social constructions. In this sense, restricting the study of social construction to the realm of cognition limits our analytic appreciation of the complex operations of knowledge by which effective constructions wield their power. For this reason, I ask you to consider other modalities of socially constructed knowledge that supplement the dynamics of cognitive apprehension. These include narrative, emotional, bodily, moral, aesthetic, sacrificial, and haunted dimensions of knowledge. In combination with cognition, these additional ways of knowing provide a more holistic sense of the reality and power of socially constructed frameworks of meaning. Sometimes these multiple forms work in concert, strengthening the force of a particular social construction. At other times, they may be at odds with each other, weakening a construction's overall power.

In order to gain a more nuanced understanding of the role of knowledge in shaping the reality of social construction, I briefly discuss each of these supplemental forms of knowledge. I also illustrate the analytic value of these multiple forms by connecting aspects of each to social constructions of terrorism. Many other examples could be selected as well. Indeed, social constructions of marriage, AIDS, global climate change, normal business practices, and the origin of the species today all represent contested constructions that mobilize multiple levels of knowledge. Terrorism is selected simply because so much of social life today—from the meaning of international law to definitions of privacy, patriotism, and torture—are affected by powerful constructions associated with the current "war on terrorism."

In addition to framing constructs in cognitive terms, social constructions typically cast the meaning of things in the form of a story or narrative (Polkinghorne, 1988; Riessman, 1993). As the sociologist and dissident surrealist writer Georges Bataille (1978) once observed, "To a greater or lesser extent, everyone depends on stories . . . to discover the manifold truths of life. Only such stories, read sometimes in a trance, have the power to confront a person with [her or] his fate" (p. 153). Narrative forms of knowledge inform us about why things are the way we categorically apprehend them. Why, for instance, do those "we" know as terrorists defy the conventions of international law and attack civilian populations? In keeping with social constructions of terrorism that are hegemonic in the United States today, the story goes something like this: Terrorists attack civilians in countries such as ours because they hate freedom and have no respect for human life.

This simplistic narrative about terrorism, told repeatedly by top U.S. officials in the Bush administration, renders null and void a great many other interpretations as to why militants might possibly wage war against the United States and those America considers its allies. In addition, for those who buy into it, another powerful story may block American soldiers from being perceived as terrorists, even when U.S. troops deliberately target civilians. This is that Americans are said to love freedom and respect human life. In this way, narrative forms of knowledge may overwhelm what is merely cognitive, reshaping categorical perceptions of factual matters to fit a story that is commonly accepted. Thus, when American troops attack civilians, it must be by accident. If not, then a few aberrant individuals must be responsible, because surely it can be taken for granted that—unlike "real" terrorists—freedom-loving U.S. soldiers respect the sanctity of civilian life.

Emotional forms of knowledge are also at play in powerful social constructions (Brennan, 2004; Katz, 1999). For instance, when critics of the current war offer narratives that contest the dominant story about how terrorists attack us because they hate freedom, such counter-hegemonic stories are often met with a dramatic outpouring of angry affect. To suggest, for instance, that the actions of militants who conduct operations against the West have something to do with the contradictions of global capitalist domination or a continuing coloniality of power is to open oneself to the emotional wrath of those believe the dominant story. For many patriotic Americans, counter-hegemonic stories about the war on terrorism may be literally experienced as an assault on a heartfelt truth. As such, effective social constructions of terrorism typically combine cognitive and narrative understandings with strong emotional doses of fear.

Emotional apprehension is an important dimension of socially constructed knowledge. The same holds for bodily ways of knowing. As a material vector of power in history, knowledge sometimes enters the flesh in ways that defy words (Grosz, 1994; Mellor & Shilling, 1997). In particular, recent feminist scholarship encourages us to attend to the "body's innate capacity for knowledge" (Brooks, 2006, p. 50), for complexly sensuous understanding and communication (Jaggar & Bordo, 1989; Longino, 2000). As such, constructionist theories must take people at their word when they say that simply seeing a picture of a reputed terrorist, such as Osama bin Laden, makes them sick. When most powerful, social constructions of terrorism assume the form of carnal knowledge, stiffening one's back, creating a pain in the neck, arousing states of nervousness or irritability. Even one's eyesight may be shaped by powerful social constructions, leading social control agents or frightened American civilians to literally see signs of potential terrorism in people they perceive as South Asian or Middle Eastern (but not Israeli).

Moral and aesthetic dimensions of knowledge are also aspects of the reality of social construction. When social constructions draw boundaries around specific classes of people, action, and things, they inevitably shade what they frame with moral strictures and tones (Pfohl, 1994, p. 411). Sometimes the strictures are explicit. The war against terrorism, it is said, is a war between good and evil. At other times the moral meanings of social constructions may be less direct. In politically polarized America, when conservatives decry an opponent as liberal, this social construction is likely to carry significant moral tones, suggesting, for instance, that a particular person or group is soft on matters of security or acting in ways that support terrorism. But whether explicitly or implicitly, all effective social constructions mobilize an edge of moral judgment, rendering what falls inside the construct as either good or bad, something to be supported or something to be opposed.

The halo of morality may, however, be an obstacle to the reflexive recognition of the historically contingent and artificial character of socially constructed realities. By bestowing certain objects and social practices with an aura of sanctity and goodness, the moral boundaries help naturalize or normalize the taken-for-granted character of certain ways of doing things to the exclusion or subordination of others. This is why Friedrich Nietzsche criticizes unreflexive submission to dominant forms of morality as reactive, utilitarian, and laced with resentment (Nietzsche, 1969). The ritual construction of moral boundaries between what a society values and what it condemns is also a key aspect of Emile Durkheim's theorization of the social functions of crime (Durkheim, 1964) and George Herbert Mead's "psychology of criminal justice" (Mead, 1918). For both Durkheim and Mead, moral revulsion contributes to collective social solidarity while reinforcing dominant forms of social knowledge.

Aesthetic judgment operates in a related way. Some social constructions attract us, fitting beautifully into forms that command our respect. Others strike us as repulsive and even ugly. Aesthetic judgment, which often operates at an unconscious level, is another realm in which power interacts with knowledge (Berger, 1972; hooks, 1992). In the throes of the current war against terrorism, multiple levels of hegemonic knowledge may converge in blurring the aesthetics of Islam and terror. As such, whereas traditional Islamic garb, language, and song may strike people in many regions of the world as beautiful, caught up in a hegemonic force field of fearful social constructions, many Americans today ridicule traditional forms of Muslim apparel. Others may find the sound and rhythmic structure of Arabic verse repugnant or difficult to listen to. This is further evidence of the complex power of social construction as it bends and shapes what is experienced as real.

Because all social constructions are selective, it is important to attend to what is sacrificed by particular constellations of power and knowledge when drawing boundaries around specific regimes of cognition, narrative, affect, bodily feeling, morality, and aesthetics. This is to suggest that what is sacrificed by a given social construction invariably contributes to the experience of that construction itself. This is certainly true in the current war against terrorism. It may be difficult, for instance, for people under the spell of shadowy Northwestern constructions of "Islamic terrorism" to recognize the spiritual complexities of the Muslim world. Nevertheless, what is sacrificed or repressed by a dominant order of social construction does not cease to exist. The opposite is true. What is repressed commonly returns to haunt those same constructions. This can disturb or subvert the seeming "naturalness" of the constructions in question. As Avery Gordon (1997) suggests, "haunting describes how that which appears to be not there is often a *seething presence*, acting on and often meddling with taken-for-granted realities" (p. 8). As such, to faithfully discern the reality of social construction, in addition to the other modes of knowledge discussed in this chapter, it is vital to consider the sacrifices and hauntings brought about by the ritual labor of construction itself.

Power-Reflexive Attunement to the Reality of Social Construction

Produced at the ritual crossroads of natural historical materiality, psychic social subjectivity, and complex fields of both power and knowledge, social constructions participate in what is real. At the same time, ritual constructions reduce the experience of reality to binding figurations graced with energy and a halo of belief. By repetitively enacting ritual constructions of the world, we sacrificially transform what is real into a kind of virtual reality—a "second nature" managed by the social constructions we invent. In this sense, rituals of social construction produce the appearance of an objectified world that

those enchanted by these rituals misrecognize as reality itself (Bell, 1992). Ritual removes things from the natural historical context in which they are socially constructed and provides them with the aura of being timelessly real. If the terms I am using to describe the power of social constructions—terms such as *ritual, crossroads, sacrifice, grace, halo, aura,* and *belief*—carry religious connotations, this is no accident. When most effective, social constructions supernaturalize the worlds they symbolize, blessing social realms of artifice with the strictures of common sense and a taken-for-granted character.

The term *ritual* also underscores the performative dimension of social construction. Social constructions are, after all, socially enacted artifice. To be effective they require the "ritualized repetition" of coded symbolic interactions and a captivating suspension of disbelief (Butler, 1993, p. x). But artifice performed at the ritual juncture of the vectors of force discussed in the previous section is not artifice produced by human agents alone. Each field of force actively shapes and is shaped by the others. The material and psychic effects—although often unevenly distributed—are reciprocal. Each feeds off and back into the constitution of the other. In this exchange, the wide-awake reality of conscious human action is important, but not king of the hill. Indeed, even the innermost realms of our psyches are touched by what Judith Butler (1997) calls "the psychic life of power"—a doubled space in which interior subjectivity simultaneously comes into being and is ritually subjugated by spellbinding forces that enter the self from the outside.

Critical analyses of social construction endeavor to deconstruct this process, returning the labor of reality construction to the fragile exigencies of everyday life. This demands more than showing the supposed relativity of social constructions. As suggested at the outset of this chapter, relativism—being nowhere, while claiming to be everywhere—is not a viable option. Recognizing that sociological constructions are also ritual social constructions, the challenge is to engage the labor of social construction in ways that foreground the socially situated work of the analyst her- or himself. This invites readers to enter a dialogue about the advantages and limitations of one's methods and conclusions. It also situates the reality of social analysis by displaying its material and psychic links to history and the subject positions of those who perform this work. This helps optimize the objectivity of our theory and research. With this in mind, I conclude this chapter by briefly discussing several *power-reflexive* methods aimed at situating the objectivity of the constructions we produce and are partially produced by.

To be power-reflexive is to engage critically with the circuits of power and knowledge in which we are located in history (Pfohl, 1994, pp. 7–9, 470–475; Pfohl, 2005, pp. 584–588). Power-reflexive analytic attunement is forever partial and provisional. It endeavors to fold back on the psychic social and natural historical terrains in which power and knowledge are shaped and forever reshaped. Power-reflexive attunement is vigilant in recognizing socially constructed knowledge as an active intervention within the world. It views knowledge as participating in the world's real constitution and never a mere description of the world's reality. Power-reflexive forms of knowledge aim to materially transform—rather than idealistically transcend—existing global matrices of domination. To accomplish this, it is necessary to understand the ritual labor of social construction in holistic geopolitical and ecological terms. This is to partially reverse the disembodied flight of knowledge enacted by leading professional sectors of contemporary social science. By contrast, power-reflexive knowledge imperfectly mirrors back on the ways in which our analytic constructions of the world are situated within historical knots of power.

Power-reflexive approaches to social construction entail *attunement* to the energetic material effects of both natural history and psychic subjectivity. In so doing, they act as a supplement to the rigors of other forms of critical social inquiry. How are we as analysts attracted or repulsed by multilevel assemblages of knowledge and power in which we are employed? How might we tune into the impact on knowledge production of the vast global institutional and interpersonal networks into which we are hailed or interpellated? Although power-reflexive methods are often more sensuous than the abstractions that guide mainstream sociology, in reckoning with the effects and exclusions of hegemonic forms of social construction, they seek to augment, rather than entirely replace, more traditional forms of analytic work.

Power-reflexive strategies resemble, in part, what Avery Gordon, in homage to Walter Benjamin, calls *profane illumination*:

> These illuminations can be frightening and threatening; they are profane but nonetheless charged with the spirit that made them. Sometimes you feel they are grabbing you by the throat, sometimes you feel they are making you disappear, sometimes you are willing to talk to them. . . . Whether it appears unexpectedly or whether you cultivate and invite its arrival, the profane illumination is a discerning moment. It describes a mode of apprehension distinct from critique or commentary when . . . "thought presses close to its object, as if through touching, smelling, tasting, it wanted to transform itself." (1997, pp. 204–205)

Gordon connects profane illumination and another component of critical sociological inquiry—a willingness to reckon with figurative ghosts, whose *seething presence* haunts all regimes of reality construction. In power-reflexive terms, reckoning with what haunts us widens the expanse of reality grappled with by sociology. It also changes the sociologist. "To be haunted and write from that location . . . is about making a contact that changes you and refashions the social relations in which you are located" (p. 22).

Donna Haraway's discussion of "situated objectivity" also inspires a power-reflexive approach. Haraway argues for a "practice of objectivity that privileges contestation, passionate construction, webbed connections, and hope for transformations of systems of knowledge and ways of seeing" (1991, pp. 191–192). Haraway recognizes that we are never "immediately present to ourselves" and calls for strategies of "mobile positioning" and passionate "attunement" to the resonances of power. Guided by historical specificity and "loving care" for the viewpoints of others—especially for those subjugated by dominant forms of power—Haraway invites a "power-sensitive conversation" with the world, including the natural world (1991, pp. 192, 196). This is to converse with the world through which we are diffracted, the real world that we name nature but that we are never in charge of.

Power-reflexive attunement widens the scope of reality reckoned with by constructionist theory and research. It recognizes that power and knowledge feed back into one another at the ritual crossroads of natural historical materiality and psychic social subjectivity. Despite its ritual repetition, the reality that is constructed at these crossroads is never entirely objective. Constructed reality never fully transcends or stands free of the world in which it is situated. At the same time, even when it is most imaginary, constructed reality is never entirely subjective. The reason is that the psychic subjectivity of those involved in the labor of construction is affected by its ritual position in a system of language and by what is real, but which escapes the confines of language. These complex processes are all aspects of the reality of social construction. The challenge, then, for power-reflexive analysis is to enter analytically into conversation with the world, while simultaneously meditating on the nature and effects of this communicative engagement.

In concluding, I leave you with a short list of modest methodological suggestions. There is nothing exclusive about this list. It is intended to supplement, not entirely replace, the technologies of inquiry deployed by more conventional forms of sociology. Nor is this short list exhaustive. Maybe it will inspire you to add a few methodological offerings of your own to the conversation. The strategies I have in mind include historical specificity, (dis)autobiographical analysis, and subreal ethnography.

Historical Specificity

It is important to locate the constructions we work with in historical terms. This demands attention to how even the most insightful performances of sociological construction are restricted by a continuing coloniality of power and by sociologists' professional complicities with complex global matrices of economic, gendered, and racialized dominations. History is an ally of critical constructionist analysis. More challenging yet is grappling with how our work is affected by our location within entangled historical webs of both restrictive and general economic power. At the present moment in time we face another challenge as well. This concerns how to understand social construction within a historical context increasingly structured by what Jean Baudrillard (1983) calls *hyperreality*. Hyperreality is media-engineered reality—an ultramodern form of social construction set in motion by high-speed communicative feedback loops between humans and machines and by the fascinations and fears of being immersed in a wash of electronic imagery and cybernetic information systems of all sorts.

In the hyperreal world, social constructions are based less on the reductive copying of reality than on virtual realities generated from technologically powered stereotypical schemas. Here, world-changing models of reality precede socially constructed representations. Rather than copying the real world, hyperreal constructions copy a prefabricated model—a preprogrammed double of the real—its abstracted code. Constructions based on simulations engage in ceaseless interaction with the world they code. In so doing, what is imaginarily modeled in simulation materially alters the world and what is experienced as real about the world. In this way, what is fascinating or fearful at emotional or aesthetic levels of knowledge often eclipses the reality and restrictions of cognition. This, suggests Baudrillard (1983), is to travel a slippery "slope of a hyperrealist sociality, where the real is confused with the model" (p. 53) and in which "hyperreality and simulation are deterrents of every principle [of reality] and every objective" (p. 43). At the same time, hyperreal society routinely covers over traces of the transformations in reality it induces. Baudrillard cites Disneyland as an example, stating:

> Disneyland is there to conceal the fact that it is the "real" country, all of the "real" America, which *is* Disneyland (just as prisons are there to conceal the fact that it is the social in its entirety, in its banal omnipresence, which is carceral). Disneyland is presented as imaginary in order to make us believe that the rest is real, when in fact all of Los Angeles and the America surrounding it are no longer real. It is no longer a question of a false representation (ideology), but of concealing the fact that the real is no longer real. (p. 25)

The so-called global war on terrorism provides, perhaps, an even more disturbing example. Following the attacks on the World Trade Center and the Pentagon on September 11, 2001, the social construction of the "war on terror" orchestrated by the Bush administration resulted in a highly aestheticized and flexible simulation of terrorism. This deceptive simulation has proved capable of absorbing cognitive dissonance generated by counterfactual evidence and other inconvenient truths. Dominant constructions of the "war on terror" may be thought of as simulations because the claims they make about reality are based not on observations that can be verified or disconfirmed but on predetermined, abstract, stereotypical, and generally erroneous models of what constitutes terrorism. As mentioned previously, these simulated constructions picture terrorism as the jealous actions of "uncivilized" groups said to hate freedom and to care little for the value of human life.

When most effective, these simulations appear capable of bypassing cognitive dissonance almost entirely, appealing, instead, to emotional modalities of knowledge, fueled by fear and the fascinations of (orientalized) evil. Within the United States, for the most part, this has insulated the U.S. military from accusations of acting in a terrorist manner itself, even when it targets predominantly civilian populations. Simulations of terrorism were key weapons in the arsenal of mass persuasion deployed by the Bush administration in making its case for war against Iraq. In one speech or orchestrated media performance after another, the constructed reality of terrorism produced by such simulations blurred Iraq with al Qaeda and the horrors of 9/11 with the need for preemptive war. Under the spell of such simulations, much of the American public appeared unable to differentiate social phantasm from fact. Saddam Hussein became virtually equivalent to Osama bin Laden, and most of the public was convinced that Iraq possessed weapons of mass destruction (WMD) and on the verge of unleashing them against the United States.

The reality constructed by of all this showed up in polls. But by feeding the public statistical images of its own simulation-based construction of reality, polls only furthered hyperreal aspects of the march to war. Shortly thereafter, "59 percent of Americans were in favor of the war, 90 percent believed that Hussein was developing WMD, and 81 percent thought that Iraq was a threat to the United States" (Berman, 2006, p. 207). Moreover, despite being falsified by the actual events of the war, the reality effects of the simulated constructions of reality used to justify the invasion and occupation of Iraq were slow to fade:

> A poll taken by the Washington Post just before the second anniversary of 9/11 revealed that 70 percent [of Americans] thought that

Saddam Hussein had been directly involved in the attacks, and that the 9/11 hijackers were Iraqis, and that Hussein had used chemical weapons against our troops. Another poll, taken in June 2003, indicated that 41 percent believed that WMD had been found (or they weren't sure), and 75 percent thought Bush showed strong leadership on Iraq. (Berman, 2006, p. 212)

Although the results of these polls accord with Baudrillard's (1993) analysis of historical changes in the nature and scope of constructed reality, as journalist Ron Suskind notes, not everyone was as clueless about the process as the public at large. When interviewing a Bush aide about communication strategies guiding the war on terror, Suskind reports the following exchange:

> The aide said that guys like me were "in what we call the reality-based community," which he defined as people who "believe that solutions emerge from your judicious study of discernable reality." I nodded and murmured something about enlightenment principles and empiricism. He cut me off. "That's not the way the world really works anymore," he continued. "We're an empire now, and when we act, we create our own reality. And while you're studying that reality—judiciously, as you will—we'll act again, creating other new realities, which you can study too." (2004, p. 51)

Despite the admonitions of the Bush aide, it is hard to imagine a better reason to couple the study of social constructions with the exigencies of history. In an age of media-driven simulations, it is also important to pay reflexive attention to the multiple forms of knowledge in which the reality of things reveal themselves. Even when seeming to nullify cognitive dissonance, simulations remain haunted by realities they exclude. This is a reason to engage with forms of knowledge that exceed cognitive logic.

(Dis)autobiographical Analysis

As a second strategy of power-reflexive discernment, *(dis)autobiographical analysis* reck-

ons with the ways our subject position in history shades what we know. The goal of (dis)autobiographical work is not to tell a solipsistic or narcissistic story about oneself as a sociologist. Moreover, although it is attentive to the singularity of the analyst's subject position, unlike autoethnography and other recent experiments with first-person writing, (dis)autobiographical analysis does not tell sociological stories from a strictly subjective viewpoint. Although autoethnography fosters a valuable "emotional exposure" of sociologists' positions within "local institutional sites" of knowledge production, it typically falls short of situating the labor of sociology within complex global histories of power (Clough, 2000, pp. 180–181). (Dis)autobiographical analysis, on the other hand, aims to double back on the imaginary and symbolic frameworks and vectors of power guiding social science viewpoints on what is real.

In addition to examining how "the knowing subject" is embedded in "intersubjective relations of knowledge production" and "face to face communities" of inquiry, (dis)autobiographical analysis also explores what Patricia Clough refers to as our "embeddedness in environments of 'knowledge objects,'" where agency and reflexivity refer as much to an 'interobjectivity' or 'the sociality of objects' as it does to intersubjectivity" (2000, p. 154). This is no easy matter, particularly when confronting self-knowledge that has become commonsensical, taken for granted, or unconscious. Working reflexively with multiple levels of power and knowledge is a beginning. Indeed, we often learn more about the constructions we inhabit by being mindful of our emotions and bodily sensations than we do by attending to cognitions alone.

One method used to facilitate (dis)autobiographical analysis involves techniques of collage/montage writing. Rooted in the disruptions of Dada and surrealism (and incorporated today into all kinds of popular culture forms, including advertising and prime-time TV shows), collage can be one performative strategy for telling more than one story at a time, bringing together on the same textual surface—and outside . . . common sense or sensations of linear time—pieces of history, fiction, ethnography, dream, and autobiography in a noticeably constructed, suggestively *surreal* evocation of social realities. (Orr, 2006, p. 29)

When most effective, collage writing may reveal the artificial character of social identities and the cultural constructs we take to be most real (Pfohl, 1992, pp. 97–101). As Jackie Orr suggests, "performing sociology" in this way "is not simply a strategy to foreground how the borders between science and literature, fact and fiction, evidence and affect, social reality and psychic fantasy are far more permeable that 'normal' science wants to recognize"; it is "also and most immediately about critical, creative responses to struggles over what gets to count as, and who gets to make, public knowledge and collective memory" (2006, p. 27).

Subreal Ethnography

As a power-reflexive strategy, *subreal ethnography* is energetically inspired by surrealism. Although commonly misunderstood as a "modern art movement," surrealism is better imagined as a radical assemblage of social criticism and poetic agitation. In the words of Robin Kelley, "surrealism is about making a new life" (2002, p. 158). Kelley connects the "freedom dreams" of surrealism to radical African diasporic thought and poetics, showing how surrealism was "animated" as much by the "revolts of the colonial world and its struggles for cultural autonomy" as by "reading Freud or Marx" (p. 160). Surrealism dreams of ways of knowing that exceed the limits of commonsensical realism:

Surrealism finds realism deficient in its estimate of reality. Ignoring dreams and the unconscious . . . realism inevitably bows to the accomplished fact. . . . Surrealism introduces . . .

an expanded awareness of reality. It demonstrates not only the continuity between internal and external reality but their essential unity. . . . Surrealism, a unitary project of total revolution, is above all a method of knowledge and a way of life . . . an unparalleled means of pursuing the fervent quest for freedom and true life beyond the veil of ideology. (Rosemont, 1978, pp. 24, 25)

Like surrealism, subrealism represents an inquiry into the intersection between wide-awake consciousness and the dream world. Advertising and the allures of popular culture already cull this terrain in manipulative and profit-driven ways. But, taking its cue from surrealism and other social movements aimed at culture subversion, subrealism seeks, instead, to uproot constructed realities based on modern, Eurocentric, masculine, and instrumental forms of rationality. Like surrealism, subrealism celebrates the marvelous, the poetic, and erotic. With imagination and laughter it artfully engages with matters of pleasure and terror. Yet, unlike surrealism, subrealism does not attempt to transcend the boundaries between wide-awake reality and the reality of dreams. It strives, instead, to maintain provocative tension and dialogue between these distinct realms. In this sense, subreal ethnography displaces the data-driven desires of a realist epistemology by performing social science fiction. In the words of the Black Madonna Durkheim:

Subreal ethnography conjures up a spiraling dance with monsters, phantoms, and ghosts. These uncanny creatures weave their way between what's real and what is culturally abstracted from the real. This involves a magical play of passion and mirrors, enabling the subreal ethnographer to take flight from the force field of dominant social constructions, expanding the reality of social construction from the outside in. (2006, p. 2)

Energized by critical historical inquiry, (dis)autobiograhical analysis, and subreal ethnography, power-reflexive methods direct attention to how the labor of social construction at once illuminates and conceals the nature and scope of reality. This suggests a different aesthetic for social science storytelling from that which governs the professional mainstream. The challenge is not simply to discover better ways to account for the social construction of reality but to enable a more attentive conversation with the real world itself. "Accounts of a 'real' world do not, then depend on a logic of 'discovery,' but on a power-charged social relation of conversation. . . . Objectivity is not about dis-engagement, but about mutual and usually unequal structuring, about taking risks in a world where 'we' are permanently mortal, that is, not in 'final' control" (Haraway, 1991, pp. 198, 201).

● References

Althusser, L. (1971). Ideology and ideological state apparatuses. In *Lenin and philosophy and other essays* (B. Brewster, Trans., pp. 127–186). New York: Monthly Review Press.

Bataille, G. (1978). *The blue of noon* (H. Mathews, Trans.). New York: Urizen Books.

Bataille, G. (1988). *The accursed share: An essay on general economy* (R. Hurley, Trans.). New York: Zone Books. (Original work published 1967)

Baudrillard, J. (1983). *Simulations*. (P. Foss, P. Patton, & P. Beitchman, Trans.). New York: Semiotext(e).

Bell, C. (1992). *Ritual theory, ritual practice*. New York: Oxford University Press.

Berger, J. (1972). *Ways of seeing*. New York: Penguin Books.

Berger, P. L., & Luckmann, T. (1966). *The social construction of reality: A treatise in the sociology of knowledge*. New York: Anchor Books.

Berman, M. (2006). *Dark ages America*. New York: Norton.

Bourdieu, P. (1977). *Outline of a theory of practice*. Cambridge, UK: Cambridge University Press.

Brennan, T. (1993). *History after Lacan*. New York: Routledge.

Brennan, T. (2000). *Exhausting modernity*. New York: Routledge.

Brennan, T. (2004). *The transmission of affect*. Ithaca, NY: Cornell University Press.

Brooks, A. (2006). "Under the knife and proud of it": An analysis of the normalization of cosmetic surgery. In S. Pfohl, A. Van Wagenen, P. Arend, A. Brooks, & D. Leckenby (Eds.), *Culture, power, and history: Studies in critical sociology* (pp. 23–58). Leiden, The Netherlands: Brill.

Butler, J. (1993). *Bodies that matter*. New York: Routledge.

Butler, J. (1997). *The psychic life of power: Theories in subjection*. Stanford, CA: Stanford University Press.

Clough, P. T. (2000). *Autoaffection: Unconscious thought in the age of teletechnology*. Minneapolis: University of Minnesota Press.

Durkheim, B. M. (2006). A genealogy of subreal methods. In S. Pfohl (Ed.), *Black Madonna Durkheim: Selected writings* (pp. 2–22). Brookline, MA: Parasite Café Imaginary Press.

Durkheim, E. (1964). *The rules of the sociological method* (S. A. Soovay & J. H. Miller, Trans.). New York: Macmillan.

Durkheim, E. (1974). Individual and collective representations. In *Sociology and philosophy* (D. F. Peacock, Trans., pp. 1–34). New York: Free Press.

Durkheim, E. (1993). *Ethics and the sociology of morals* (R. T. Hall, Trans.). Buffalo, NY: Prometheus Books. (Original work published 1887)

Durkheim, E. (1995). *The elementary forms of religious life*. (K. E. Fields, Trans.). New York: Free Press. (Original work published 1912)

Foucault, M. (1965). *Madness and civilization* (A. Sheridan, Trans.). New York: Pantheon.

Foucault, M. (1970). *The order of things* (A. Sheridan, Trans.). New York: Pantheon.

Foucault, M. (1973). *The birth of the clinic* (A. Sheridan, Trans.). New York: Pantheon.

Foucault, M. (1977a). History of systems of thought. In D. F. Bouchard (Ed.), *Language, counter-memory, practice: Selected essays and interviews* (pp. 199–204). Ithaca, NY: Cornell University Press.

Foucault, M. (1977b). Nietzsche, genealogy and history. In D. F. Bouchard (Ed.), *Language, counter-memory, practice: Selected essays and interviews* (pp. 139–164). Ithaca, NY: Cornell University Press.

Foucault, M. (1979). *Discipline and punish: The birth of the prison* (A. Sheridan, Trans.). New York: Vintage Books.

Foucault, M. (1980). *The history of sexuality* (Vol. 1, A. Sheridan, Trans.). New York: Vintage Books.

Foucault, M. (1985). *The uses of pleasure: The history of sexuality* (Vol. 2). New York: Random House.

Gilroy, P. (1993). *The black Atlantic: Modernity and double consciousness*. Cambridge, MA: Harvard University Press.

Gordon, A. (1997). *Ghostly matters: Haunting and the sociological imagination*. Minneapolis: University of Minnesota Press.

Gramsci, A. (1971). *Selections from the prison notebooks* (Q. Hoare & G. N. Smith, Eds. & Trans.). New York: International.

Grosfoguel, R. (2006). Geopolitics of knowledge and the coloniality of power: Thinking Puerto Rico and Puerto Ricans from the colonial difference. In S.

Pfohl, A. Van Wagenen, P. Arend, A. Brooks, & D. Leckenby (Eds.), *Culture, power, and history: Studies in critical sociology* (pp. 479–506). Leiden, The Netherlands: Brill.

Grosz, E. (1994). *Volatile bodies: Towards a corporeal feminism*. New York: Routledge.

Hall, S., Lumley, B., & McLennan, G. (1977). Politics and ideology: Gramsci. In Centre for Contemporary Culture Studies (Ed.), *On ideology* (pp. 45–75). London: Hutchinson.

Haraway, D. (1991). Situated knowledges: The science question in feminism and the privilege of partial perspective. In D. Haraway, *Simians, cyborgs, and women: The reinvention of nature* (pp. 183–201). New York: Routledge.

Hill Collins, P. (2000). *Black feminist thought: Knowledge, consciousness, and the politics of empowerment* (2nd ed.). New York: Routledge.

hooks, b. (1992). *Black looks: Race and representation.* Boston: South End Press.

Jaggar, A. M., & Bordo, S. R. (Eds.). (1989). *Gender/body/knowledge: Feminist reconstructions of being and knowing.* New Brunswick, NJ: Rutgers University Press.

Katz, J. (1999). *How emotions work.* Chicago: University of Chicago Press.

Kelley, R. D. G. (2002). Keepin' it (sur)real: Dreams of the marvelous. In R. D. G. Kelley, *Freedom dreams: The black radical imagination* (pp. 157–198). Boston: Beacon Press.

Lacan, L. (1977). *Écrits: A selection* (A. Sheridan, Trans.). New York: Norton.

Lacan, L. (1981). *The four fundamental concepts of psycho-analysis* (A. Sheridan, Trans.). New York: Norton.

Lévi-Strauss, C. (1963). *Structural anthropology* (C. Jacobson & B. G. Schoepf, Trans.). New York: Basic Books.

Lloyd, G. (1996). *Spinoza and the ethics.* New York: Routledge.

Longino, H. (2000). Foreword. In M. M. Lay, L. Guark, C. Gravon, & C. Myniti (Eds.), *Body talk: Rhetoric, technology, reproduction.* Madison: University of Wisconsin Press.

Marx, K. (1972). *The eighteenth brumaire of Louis Bonaparte.* In *Selected works* (Vol. 1, pp. 97–185). New York: International. (Original work published 1852)

Mead, G. H. (1918). The psychology of punitive justice. *American Journal of Sociology, 23,* 577–602.

Mellor, P. A., & Shilling, C. (1997). *Re-forming the body:*
Religion, community and modernity. Thousand Oaks, CA: Sage.

Nielsen, D. A. (1999). *Three faces of God: Society, religion, and the categories of totality in the philosophy of Emile Durkheim.* Albany: State University of New York Press.

Nietzsche, F. (1967). *On the genealogy of morals* (W. Kaufmann, Trans.). New York: Random House.

Nietzsche, F. (1968). The will to power. (W. Kaufmann & R. J. Hollingdale, Trans.). New York: Vintage Books.

Orr, J. (2006). *Panic diaries: A genealogy of panic disorder.* Durham, NC: Duke University Press.

Pfohl, S. (1992). *Death at the Parasite Café: Social science (fictions) and the postmodern.* New York: St. Martin's Press.

Pfohl, S. (1994). *Images of deviance and social control: A sociological history* (2nd ed.). New York: McGraw-Hill.

Pfohl, S. (2005). New global technologies of power: Cybernetic capitalism and social inequality. In M. Romero & E. Margolis (Eds.), *The Blackwell companion to social inequalities* (pp. 546–592). Cambridge, MA: Blackwell.

Polkinghorne, D. E. (1988). *Narrative knowing and the human sciences.* Albany: State University of New York Press.

Quijano, A. (2000). Coloniality of power, ethnocentrism, and Latin America. *NEPANTLA, 1*(2), 533–580.

Riessman, C. K. (1993). *Narrative analysis.* Newbury Park, CA: Sage.

Rosemont, F. (1978). Introduction. In A. Breton (Ed.), *What is surrealism?: Selected writings* (pp. 1–139). New York: Pathfinder Press.

Schutz, A. (1970). *On phenomenology and social relations: Selected writings.* Chicago: University of Chicago Press.

Spinoza, B. (1985). *Complete works* (Vol. 1, E. Curley, Trans.). Princeton, NJ: Princeton University Press.

Suskind, R. (2004, October 17). Faith, certainty and the presidency of George W. Bush. *New York Times Magazine,* pp. 44–51, 64, 102, 106.

Taylor, M. C. (2001). *The moment of complexity: Emerging network culture.* Chicago: University of Chicago Press.

Weber, M. (1964). *The theory of social and economic organizations.* New York: Free Press.

Weedon, C. (1997). *Feminist practice and poststructuralist theory* (2nd ed.). Cambridge, MA: Blackwell.

Williams, P. (1991). *The alchemy of race and rights.* Cambridge, MA: Harvard University Press.

CHAPTER 34

Can Constructionism Be Critical?

● **Dian Marie Hosking**

M y purpose in this chapter is to set out a number of interrelated lines of distinction that together create a critical constructionist discourse (Deetz, 1996b). In this context, I am using the term *discourse* to refer to a metalevel framework of premises that is wider than a theory, less monolithic than a paradigm, and more modest than a worldview. One implication of this is that what I have to say about critical relational constructionism is not directly comparable with theories[1] framed within a postpositivist approach to science. It is not my intention to claim that critical relational constructionism is superior to other discourses or theories—only to claim that it is different, that these differences open up new possibilities for action, and that they should, therefore, be given serious attention.

I begin by drawing on literatures that declare and center a *critical orientation*—for ex-
ample, to studies of management and organization or to research methodology. This allows me to overview previously established meanings of the term *critical* and to link them with relational constructionism. In so doing, I discuss the special role and significance of processes and language, the focus on relational realities, and the view of relational processes and realities as local in both a cultural and a historical sense. I return to these critical themes and further develop them in each of the remaining parts of the chapter. In the second part, I develop the theme of relational processes as the ongoing and simultaneous coming together of multiple acts or texts. It is in these relational processes that the construction and reconstruction of self and other and relations goes on, so to speak. In other words, the relational realities of persons and worlds emerge in processes, and they are always emerging.

The third part of the chapter further develops the theme of self–other relations as constructed realities. It does so by contrasting the "hard" differentiation of self and other as subject and object with the more rare construction of "soft" self–other differentiation (Berman, 1990). The former involves ways of relating that construct self and other as singular, stable, bounded, and independent existences (entities) interacting in instrumental relations; elsewhere I have referred to this is as an "entitative" style of thinking (Hosking & Morley, 1991). In contrast, practices that are open to otherness—including other selves—construct what I call *soft self–other differentiation*.

The discussion of self–other relations lays the groundwork for the fourth part, in which I examine different forms of relating. In particular, I compare processes dominated by visual forms and seeing with processes in which sound, hearing, and listening are more prominent. I focus on the very particular role and significance of listening in relation to soft differentiation and stress its links with openness and appreciation. I finish with a brief discussion of how this critical relational constructionism and the associated possibility of soft self–other differentiation together open up new possibilities for inquiry and intervention.

Going Critical

A common construction of the term *critical* is that it implies *critique*, usually negative, of positions that differ from one's own. Critique involves generalizing one's own standards, applying them to other discourses, and finding those other discourses deficient. The discovered weaknesses of other positions can then be claimed as evidence of the superiority of one's own position. However, a critical relational constructionism does not provide the grounds for critique in this sense. The reason is that a *critical* constructionism does not center the assumption of one transhistorical and transcontextual

reality. Instead, it centers the assumption that constructions of persons and worlds and their relations—including constructions of knowledge, truth, and ethics, and including constructions of science—are *local relational realities*. By this I mean something similar to what Wittgenstein spoke of as "language games," which he saw as part of an activity, or a "form of life" (Wittgenstein, 1953). Such activities involve their own local forms and interests and their own rules; these "games" are neither true nor false and, indeed, may create their own facts (Chan, 2000; Falzon, 1998)

The critical themes that make up the present discourse come from many different literatures and different areas of professional practice. These include: the history of ideas, epistemology, feminist critiques of science, cognitive and social psychology, interactionism, cognitive and phenomenological sociology, radical family therapy, critical social anthropology, continental philosophy and some expressions of "postmodernism" and poststructuralism (Berman, 1981, 1990; Corradi Fiumara, 1990; Dachler & Hosking, 1995; Danziger, 1997; Fine, 1994; Foucault, 1977/1980; Gergen, 1994; Harding, 1986; Hermans, Kempen, & Van Loon, 1992; Latour, 1987; Pearce, 1992; Schroder, 2005; Stenner & Eccleston, 1994; Toulmin, 1990; Woolgar, 1996). I bring these critical themes together to make a very distinctive discourse of critical relational constructionism. This culminates in a particular emphasis on appreciation and openness—viewed as vital to the construction of soft self–other differentiation: "openness is key to a genuine encounter with other . . . other possible selves, other humans . . . the world . . . and dialogue is crucial for this[2]" (Falzon, 1998, p. 38).

Powers, Interests, and Possibilities

The present focus on relational realities as local "language games" and "forms of life" sets our critical constructionist discourse apart from constructivist theories. The latter usually center individuals and individual mind operations as they construct some linguistic representation of reality (Hosking, 2006). In other words, construction is theorized as a cognitive operation,[3] knowledge is the product of construction, and knowledge is separate from action. Constructivist theories (implicitly) embrace metatheoretical assumptions that center a singular real-world reality (the assumption of ontology) and sharply distinguish this real-world reality from knowledge about it (the assumption of epistemology).

The metatheoretical assumptions of the present discourse differ from those just described. Construction is viewed as ongoing in relational processes that make and remake local language games and their related forms of life. Unlike constructivist theories and investigations, a critical relational constructionism includes its own activities within the scope of its discourse of construction. Thus it treats the activities of theorizing and empirical work as processes of construction. In addition, and just like any other discourse, critical relational constructionism provides a position from which to reflect on the local particularities of other theories and metatheoretical standpoints.

A critical relational constructionism may turn its gaze, for example, to deconstructing writings in organizational behavior and in management and organization studies. Some writings may seem to imply a "managerialist" standpoint (Hosking & Morley, 1991). Others, such as early versions of "critical theory," might explicitly espouse a Marxist ideology, speak of "false consciousness," and be oriented toward an interest in revolutionary change. Reading on, some feminist approaches might speak of a "critical" interest in liberating women and other oppressed minorities (see, e.g., Denzin & Lincoln, 1994). Furthermore, postpositive science (Alvesson & Deetz, 2000; Gergen, 1994) might be represented as taking a "critical" view of the possibility of objective knowledge,[4] and so on. However, the present discourse is not critical in any of these ways. Rather, it is critical in the sense that it is suspicious about any claim to know what is and what is best for another. So, for example, to assume that the Other needs "liberating" is to assume a superior position from which one can know the Other. This assumption reproduces the subject–object construction of relations that characterizes constructivist theories and postpositivist science, and so, in the present view, it cannot be critical.

Explicitly critical orientations often focus on power and inequalities of the status quo. For example, Marxist versions of critical theory assume a managerial elite with its own particular interests that dominate labor and its (different) interests. Again, I think that a critical relational constructionism can do something rather different. For a start, it is *not* characterized by the assumption that any particular form of life possesses power over other groups and certainly does *not* assume that power is one way and uncontested. Rather than constructing a particular form of life as a stable entity with properties and possessions, a critical constructionism theorizes power as a relational process. Power is an ongoing, relational construction, able both to open up and to close down possibilities. So all acts (texts) "act into" processes that are already ongoing (contexts) and so may contribute to the ongoing (re)production of power relations.

This line of talk about acting into ongoing power relations also applies to relational constructionist writings and related practices—viewed as a particular local form of life. One of the many ways in which a critical relational constructionism is critical is that it invites reflexive recognition of its own constructive potential and participation in power relations (Foucault, 1977/1980). It assumes that the human scientist, who acts to observe the Other, is necessarily acting into some already ongoing processes and relations and is, in this sense, intervening. This reconstructs the (post) positivist science account of research design and procedures: Research processes now are storied as power-full processes of social construction.

To summarize, a critical relational constructionism (1) cannot rest on any claim to know how things *really* are, (2) is not defined in terms of an interest in challenging closure or dominance relations, and (3) does not limit itself to talk of knowledge independently of power relations. A critical relational constructionism collapses the process–product binary and views the process as itself the product[5] (e.g., Brown & Hosking, 1986). Relations become significant not as the instrumental means to achieving some rational ends but for their moment-by-moment openness to and appreciation of other possible selves and worlds (e.g., Harding, 1986).

A Critical Anomaly

I have defined a critical relational constructionism as one that does *not* embrace the metatheoretical premises of a postpositivist paradigm (Guba & Lincoln, 1994). In this sense it could be called an anomalous discourse of construction—in that it cannot be located on a map whose coordinates are realist–relativist (ontology) and objective–subjective (epistemology). A critical relational constructionist discourse does not center some assumed "real" reality, does not center an individual knower, and is not about the world as the subjective creation of mind. For these same reasons it is also very different from the "constructivist" paradigm[6] referred to by Guba and Lincoln (1994).

In contrast to the (post) positivist and constructivist paradigms as defined by Guba and Lincoln, a critical relational constructionism collapses dualist oppositions such as those between fact and value, description and explanation, theoretical and empirical. Furthermore, it collapses the traditional distinction between the "context of discovery" (assumed to the province of empirical science) and the "context of justification" (assumed to be the province of philosophy). In this respect, it shares some of the themes of an epistemology that wishes either to "naturalize the mind"—by linking individual psychology and epistemology[7]—or to "socialize the mind"[8]—by linking epistemology and social psychology (Bem & Looren de Jong, 2006; Morley & Hunt, 2006). However, and as will become clear, the present discourse moves a long way away from the particular "form of life" that is analytic philosophy, together with its language games that distinguish the individual from the social, speak of mind, and center an interest in knowledge and truth. As Falzon said of Foucault's line of talk about self, other, and relations, the present discourse *is not* about objective and subjective knowledge (see Falzon, 1998, p. 38) of a singular, "real" reality. Rather, it is about relational processes as they construct local relational realities.

Centering Construction Processes

The present discourse is characterized by a focus on the "how" rather than the "what" of construction; however, the "how" is theorized in a very special (some might say "postmodern"[9]) way. Processes are theorized as the ever-moving construction site in which the relational realities of persons and worlds are continuously (re)produced. This means that person and world, self and other (including other people) are viewed as reciprocal co-constructions that are always in the process of becoming. This view is very different from most other (some might say "modernist") conceptions that treat person and world as ontologically prior to processes and theorize the latter as receiving inputs from persons and from the world.

The present discourse of processes contrasts with what I earlier referred to as an "entitative" discourse (Hosking & Morley, 1991). The latter centers persons, organizations, cultures, and so forth as relatively stable, unitary, and bounded states of existence. Processes go on, so to speak, within and between (the assumed-to-be stable) entities. As a result, processes can only express entity characteristics and are limited (by entity boundaries) to subject–object relations (Hosking & Morley, 1991). In contrast, a critical relational discourse centers processes and tries to say something about how persons, cultures, and the like emerge, in relational processes. Self–other boundaries can then be seen as constructions—constructions that may be relatively firm and stable (i.e., hard) or variable and permeable (i.e., soft), so to speak. So, unlike (post) positivism and constructivism, a critical relational constructionist discourse views stability as an ongoing construction[10] and opens up the possibility of transformative change, that is, of self becoming other.

Constructing Self–Other Relations and the Possibility of Soft Differentiation

By discoursing self and other as work in progress, so to speak, I am centering an "ontology of becoming" rather than the more usual "ontology of being" (Chia, 1995). This means that I view self–other differentiation as made in ongoing relational processes, rather than dictated and fixed by the assumption of independent, knowing, and acting beings (Hosking, 2004). This critical move opens up radically changed possibilities for self, other, and relations by allowing that hard differentiation is a construction and by adding the possibility of soft or minimal differentiation. Attention can now be directed to *how* differentiation—whether hard or soft—can be constructed. This is an important theme in this chapter. In order to develop it, I need first to say something about language, its role in relational processes, and how this constitutes a critical departure from (post) positivist and constructivist paradigms.

Language as a Relational Process

The present discourse gives an important role to language—a role that reflects the critical themes I have already outlined. In sum, language plays an important part in the relational processes that construct a particular form of life. Language is key to the processes in which self, other, and relations are con-

structed and reconstructed as relational ontologies. Emphasis shifts from language to relational processes, and the latter are theorized broadly to include not just conceptual language as it is written and spoken but also the simultaneously embodied, aesthetic and sensual, local–cultural, and local–historical aspects of relating.

The present discourse contrasts with the more usual construction of language as a vehicle for representing reality. The representational view is outlined in the following account of language in relation to "objectivism": "language is needed to express concepts mapped onto objects, properties and relations *in a literal, unequivocal, context-independent fashion*" (Hermans et al., 1992, p. 25, italics added).

In the objectivist discourse, people are storied as language users who are more or less capable of correctly "mapping" what exists in the world (including themselves) through language. The scientist is presented as a language user capable of correct reasoning, that is, is assumed to be able to use language to describe what she or he discovers about an already existing and independent reality. In other words, objectivism discourses language in relation to the assumption of a realist ontology and a (more or less) representational epistemology. This objectivist view provides part of the metatheoretical context of constructivist theories; it has no part in the present discourse of relational processes.

The Particularities of Relational Processes

It is time to say more about how relational processes may be theorized in ways that reflect our critical themes and, therefore, in ways that distinguish the present discourse from related but noncritical alternatives.

Interacting Intertextuality

Constructionist writings use various language tools to discuss relational processes.

Often-used terms include *storytelling, conversation, narrative,* and *discourse*—often to center written and spoken language. Sometimes the term *performance* is used, partly to give more emphasis to nonverbal actions and partly to suggest an ontological (rather than epistemological) discourse of construction (Newman & Holzman, 1977). Terms such as *act–supplement* and *text–context* also have been used in attempts to open up the relational qualities of processes (Hosking, Dachler, & Gergen, 1995). Bruno Latour (1987) employs the term *actant* and, by writing of networks of relations between actants, seems neatly to avoid limiting talk of interaction to face-to-face or verbal relations between fully fledged persons.[11] He defines an actant as "whoever and whatever is represented" (Latour, 1987, p. 104), including people, objects, statements, facts, events, and so forth, and further writes of relations as processes of enrolling and controlling that construct and stabilize reality.[12]

In my view, a truly critical relational constructionism requires a broad definition of acts that goes beyond the usual focus on written and spoken language and gives attention to the body, both as a "tool" of construction (e.g., Foucault stresses that action requires embodiment) and as a "result."[13] Furthermore, this broad definition should give space to widely distributed constructions, such as, for example, constructions of "personhood," of what counts as knowledge, and of changing patterns and means of communication (Berman, 1981; Foucault, 1977/ 1980; Ong, 1967). In sum, talk of inter-acting here refers to (1) performances (2) that involve the coming together (3) of "whoever and whatever" (Latour, 1987) to (re)construct person–world relations as (4) relational realities. Of course, whenever people are involved in "coming together," then conceptual language is often implicated—even if only in unvocalized talk (thinking).[14] The present discourse of inter-acting is both distinctive and critical in a number of important ways. First, it centers both humans and nonhumans as actants that participate in, and are products of, construction processes. Second, relational realities are storied as always-in-construction in relations between actants and not as the ahistorical product of individual action. Third, talk about the "textuality" of inter-acting refers to *all* inter-acts and not just to written and spoken texts (Stenner & Eccleston, 1994).

Multiple, Simultaneous Inter-acts

I have proposed that a critical relational constructionist discourse assumes that many simultaneously related inter-acts contribute to ongoing constructions of reality. This is very different from an empiricist approach that (1) focuses on simple behavioral acts that are performed in sequence and are objectively definable; (2) sharply distinguishes between human actors, natural and man-made objects, and language; and (3) centers objective knowledge of an independently existing Other.

To illustrate this difference, I invite you to consider Magritte's painting *Ceci n'est pas une pipe.* An entitative discourse treats the painter, the painting, the viewer, and other possibly relevant actants (con-texts) as independent entities. From the present standpoint, it turns complex, ongoing, relational processes into an interest in a seemingly singular and stable "it" (e.g., the painting) in relation to the Aristotelian logic of either–or (e.g., *either* it is a pipe *or* it is not). In contrast, a critical relational constructionism attempts to open up the "black box" of relating (Latour, 1987) by centering multiple, simultaneous intertextualities (rather than a singular object), by centering the "how" of ongoing processes (rather than the "what" of inputs and outputs), and by staying open to the possibility of otherness—for example, multiple and changing constructions of what "it" can be.

So returning to *Ceci n'est pas une pipe,* our critical relational constructionist discourse assumes that multiple texts are simultaneously interrelated. Construction processes could relate: the visual symbol (which many would say was a picture of a pipe) with the written text below it (which says *Ceci n'est pas une pipe*– in English, "this is not a pipe"); the written text with the French language; the written text with some other language. Contexts could also include narratives of earlier viewings and/or of smoking a pipe, of what others have said about the painting, of what counts as a painting, of what is appropriately called a pipe, and so on.

Power-Full Processes

Still staying with Magritte's painting, the question "what is it?" (text) could invite many equally correct answers (con-texts), depending on which of all the multiple possible texts are interrelated: "it's a pipe," "it's a painting of a pipe," "it's a paradox," "it is a work of art," and so on.[15] This suggests that an interest in asking "what is it" questions goes together with an interest in "knowledge that" while at the same time muting and marginalizing the powerful qualities of relating. For example, which particular set of the multiple possible intertextual relations is defined as producing the (one and only) right answer, by whom, and in relation to rules and standards provided by which "form of life"?

Continuing this theme of questioning and its relations with knowledge and power, the practice of asking "what is it" questions ignores, or rejects as wrong, any answer that does not fit with the questioner's own local–cultural discourses.[16] And yet, as we have seen, a critical relational constructionist discourse proposes that relating *constructs* stabilized effects or patterned inter-acts and accepts that not all acts are stabilized but some go unheard, unseen, and unnoticed. In this view, the fate of any claim depends on whether or not it is socially certified (Hosking & Morley, 1991; Weick, 1979), that is, on whether or not it is warranted as "real and good" (Gergen, 1994). As Latour (1987) has said, the fate of a statement depends on others who have to read it, take it up and

use it; others have to be "enrolled" and they have to be "controlled" (Latour, 1987, p. 104). In sum, in the current view, constructions–for example, of identity, knowledge and truth, good and bad–are made and are stabilized and changed in power-full processes.

A critical discourse of construction suggests that relational processes and the forms of life they reflect and construct necessarily involve what Foucault called the "power/knowledge" nexus (e.g., Falzon, 1998). But some forms of life are able to enroll and control on a larger scale than others and may appear, for example, to be supported by more powerful Gods or to have better methods for producing objective knowledge. Once particular constructions become stabilized– such as what counts as science, such as white supremacy, such as masculine norms–other possibilities become less probable or, if articulated, find it harder to achieve warrant. Closure of this sort is especially likely when a (post) positivist discourse with related assumptions of right and wrong is already stabilized and widely distributed (Deetz, 1996a). A critical discourse of construction centers power[17] as ongoing in *all* relational processes and realities.[18]

Local–Cultural, Local–Historical Processes

As I have already suggested, the present discourse talks about multiple relational realities and views them as local in both the cultural and historical senses. The assumption of *multiple* local realities contrasts with the more usual assumption of a singular "real" reality about which generalizable, transhistorical knowledge can be produced. The assumption of multiple *local–cultural* realities emphasizes that what is validated or discredited as (not) real and (not) good is local to the ongoing practices that (re)construct a particular form of life. However, and as I also have noted, inter-acts vary in the scale of their interconnections. This means that my reference to "local" could apply to forms of life as general as "Western" or "scientific."

Those who participate as locals may take it for granted that their particular constructions are universal facts about the world as it really is, so to speak. However, the present discourse emphasizes the artfulness of stabilized effects (scientific methodology, bureaucratic organization, social structures) and draws attention to the multiple, more or less local scale of the inter-acts that make and remake them.

A critical discourse of construction also discourses relational processes and realities as *local–historical*. But a critical relational constructionist discourse provides a very special context for the meaning of "historical." For example, it does not refer to temporary truths when permanent truths are potentially available, and it is not intended to imply a linear process in which the present is a moment between (the now finished) past and the (yet to come) future. Such a view of history (some would call it "modernist") goes together with the separation of means and ends, process and content, "tool and result" (Newman & Holzman, 1977) and reproduces a very particular construction of time.

Relational processes have a historical quality in that acts both supplement previous acts and have implications for how the process will go on. The ongoing present reproduces some past structurings—for example, the convention of shaking hands—and acts in relation to possible and probable futures—for example, that a greeting will be performed successfully. All acts (texts) supplement other acts (con-texts) and are available for possible supplementation and possible (dis)crediting. Interacts, and particularly regularly repeated ones, "make history," so to speak (Falzon, 1998; Foucault, 1977/1980) and history is constantly being remade (Hermans et al., 1992). I now turn to history making as the construction of self and other and their relations. I argue that hard self–other differentiation is a relational construction that could be otherwise and that a critical relational discourse adds the additional possi-

bility of soft differentiation and a changed relational aesthetic.

Differentiating Self from Other

> We should ask: under what conditions and through what forms can an entity like the subject appear in the order of discourse; what positions does it occupy; what functions does it exhibit; and what rules does it follow in each type of discourse? (Foucault, 1977/1980, pp. 137–138)

The present discourse has positioned relational processes as the ongoing production site of self and other and their relations and has noted that forms of life can differ in their particular lines and degrees of differentiation. So, for example, empiricism and the "received view of science" (Woolgar, 1996) often have been claimed to be characterized by hard differentiation in the form of "subject–object" relations (Dachler & Hosking, 1995). Similarly, many theories that focus on particular aspects of organizational life embrace subject–object constructions—for example, of relations between leaders and subordinates, of relations between organizations and their environment, and of markets and hierarchies.

Differentiating Subject and Object

An active–passive binary characterizes the subject–object discourse of relations. It is reflected in distinctions between a responsible agent or subject (e.g., a leader, manager, or scientist) who is or should be active in relation to some ready-to-be-acted-upon Other whom they treat as a passive object (e.g., subordinates, an organization, research objects). The subject is assumed to be active in two main ways: in building knowledge about the Other and in mobilizing their knowledge as the (rational) basis for achieving power over the Other. For example, the "received view of science" presents the scientist as the knowing subject acting in relation to the knowable objects of his or her research, stories scientific knowledge as technical or neutral, and assumes that such knowledge provides the rational basis for action and influence.

A subject–object construction reduces relations to the one-way production of "knowledge that" and "power over" (Gergen, 1995), knowledge and power that is presented as instrumental—for the subject. Of course, the latter is presumed to be acting in terms of technical, rational, neutral interests, and this is supposed to warrant Other's rational compliance. So, for example, a scientist or manager should produce value-free knowledge about the world "in its so being" and, in so doing, provide the rational basis for action, for example, in pursuit of societal improvement or organizational goals.

The assumption of subject–object relations presumes stability and makes change problematic. Change, by being located in the context of subject–object relations, can only be discoursed in relation to "knowledge that" and "power over" other as an object. So, for example, it is quite common to read of both leaders and organizations as relatively stable things with characteristics. This means that change must be understood as movement from one stable state to another. Subjects (leaders, change agents) are portrayed as those who can and/or should know about and achieve influence over the Other. Their knowledge forms the basis for changes that they construct as "real and good" for the organization. Should their claims fail to achieve sufficient rhetorical force, then they can try to achieve influence through tactics such as persuasion, bargaining, and negotiating (Carnall, 1990; Dachler & Hosking, 1995).

Subject–object practices privilege some constructions and silence others. The subject constructs "resistance to change" as the irrational response of Other—one that requires more "power over." This means that patterns of relating are likely to reproduce more of the same—more facts, more rational arguments, more persuasion. In a subject–object construction, politics is a dirty word,

so to speak. Politics is viewed as an unnecessary and regrettable practice, one that reflects the play of local, partisan interests when neutral, nonpartisan interests are at stake. Change can only be theorized and practiced in relations in which some entitative construction of self (other) achieves "power over" an independently existing other (self). Changed constructions of change require a shift from hard to soft constructions of self–other relations (Hosking, 2004).

Soft Differentiation

I have said that an entitative discourse treats self and other as independent, although interacting, existences. Of course, not all discourses are quite so "hard" in their lines of differentiation. For example, post-positivist science and constructivist discourses blur the boundaries between subject and object, but the blurring mostly concerns what the self can know of other (epistemology), and not the assumption that they are separate existences (ontology) (Hosking, 2006). A discourse of relational processes allows for the possibility of soft or minimal self–other differentiation; opening up to these possibilities constitutes another critical dimension to relational constructionism. In exploring these possibilities, I begin by reconstructing subject–object themes.[19]

First, relational constructionism does not assume that there is a stable active–passive binary between self and other. Rather, relating is viewed as an active and ongoing process that constructs and reconstructs self/other and relations of soft or hard differentiation. Second, there is no assumption of a knowing subject who relates to the other as a knowable object to construct "outsider" knowledge of an external reality. In soft self–other differentiation, there is no position (for God or Man) from which the characteristics of one "real" reality could be known. Rather, relational processes are assumed to construct multiple relational realities, as local ontologies.[20]

Relational realities can only be multiple and softly differentiated when "power over" does not dominate. This brings us to our third theme. In a critical relational view, power is constructed in always ongoing, relational processes, that is, in ongoing relations between acts as texts. This means that power is a quality of intertextuality rather than being inherent in entities and individual acts. Power is critical to the production and reconstruction of local realities and relations between them. "Power to" can be theorized as the power to act (Foucault, 1977/1980), and "power with" can be theorized as practices that allow the construction of different but equal forms of life (Gergen, 1995; Hosking, 1995). Appreciation of and openness to other possible selves and relations and to other forms of life, enables, supports, and reconstructs soft differentiation.[21]

Last, processes in which soft differentiation is (re)constructed are not characterized by competition over who will be subject in subject–object relations and do not construct Other as potentially instrumental for self. By not centering "knowledge that" and mind operations, relational processes are constructed as embodied[22]; not centering language as representation makes space for nonconceptual ways of relating; not centering cognitive operations and universal rationality makes more space for the sensual and aesthetic qualities of relating. In the absence of a singular and stable self who may know and influence Other, there is more space for otherness and for appreciation of the continuing present[23] (the here and now). I now turn to an exploration of how embodied, conceptual and nonconceptual, sensual ways of relating could be theorized in relation to soft differentiation, appreciation, and openness to otherness.[24]

Re-sounding Relations: A Changed Aesthetic

I begin by discussing different relational forms (sounds, music, visual artifacts, etc.),

the senses (particularly seeing, hearing, and listening), and historical–cultural shifts in their roles and relations. Important in this discussion are the links that some make between the organization of "the sensorium" (the relative emphasis on different senses and sensual forms), local–cultural practices, and self–other differentiation. For example, writers have suggested that the dominance of visual media and seeing, seems to go together with *hard* self–other differentiation. A stronger participation in sound and listening, together with a greater "democracy of the senses" (Berendt, 1992, p. 28), seems to go together with *soft* self–other differentiation (Berendt, 1992; Berman, 1990; Levin, 1989; Ong, 1967). The latter could provide a "changed aesthetic" that could help transformative change work as a critical alternative to finding out about, emancipating, or liberating others.

Changes in the Sensorium: The Increasing Dominance of Vision

Many have written about changing patterns and forms of relating, commenting on developments such as the creation of an alphabet and written script[25]; creation of the means mechanically to reproduce texts; and the emergence, reproduction, and increased use of maps, together with technologies that allowed greater physical exploration of the world (e.g., ships and navigational equipment). Writers suggest that the (relatively recent) development of written language and visual inscriptions, together with an emphasis on appearances and on observation, gradually came to dominate (shall we say, Western) constructions of self and other and relations (Ong, 1967).

These changing constructions included freeing persons from the will of the gods and reconstructing them as autonomous beings or agents able to act in their own right. Science became established as the way of knowing most likely to produce the best of knowable truths about an independently existing Other. Western philosophy became increasingly dominated by a focus on epistemology and the speaking aspect of communications (Corradi Fiumara, 1990). A person's relationship to time, to space, and to event-fullness also changed. For example, cultures of alphabet and print give a more permanent sense of existence to visualized words—words frozen in space, words made seemingly timeless by being stripped from the progression of sound. According to Ong (1967), visualized words gain "a quiescence and fixity which is unrealisable in actual sound," and this Ong further associated with a change in self–other relations such that the former felt an increased "sense of order and control" over other (Ong, 1967, p. 45).

The increasing visualization of words also gave rise to the possibility of "literal" meaning—that is, meaning "according to the letter."[26] Knowledge become increasingly associated with the written word and books, with the individual mind and individual property. The increasing dominance of vision made it possible for Locke to write of the mind as a *camera obscura* that receives "external visual resemblances or ideas of things" and for Kant to refer to knowledge as phenomena, from the Greek *phainomenon*, meaning "appearance," "to show," to "expose to sight" (Ong, 1967, p. 74). Observation—something for the eyes—came increasingly to dominate a person's relationship to the self and to the (by then "outside") world.

The increasing dominance of vision in all its many aspects has been linked with what Ong (1967) called a transformation of "the sensorium." In other words, minimal or "soft" differentiation of self and other gave way to "hard differentiation," sharply separating and opposing self and other in subject–object relation.

> The view of nature which predominated in the West down to the eve of the Scientific Revolution was that of an enchanted world. Rock, trees, rivers and clouds were all seen as wondrous, alive, and human beings felt at home in

this environment. The cosmos, in short, was a place of belonging. (Berman, 1981, p. 16)

The relational reality of a live and enchanted world was replaced by a dead secularized and denatured universe. Mechanical philosophy and materialist science produced dead texts of representation. The world became a "neutralized, devocalized physical world," and man "a kind of stranger, a spectator and manipulator" (Ong, 1967). Self–other relations were "disenchanted" and "participating consciousness" largely lost (Reason, 1994). With their newly constructed, nonparticipating knowledge, men could become "masters and possessors of nature" (Descartes, 1637, quoted in Berman, 1981, p. 25).

One obvious implication is that a critical constructionism must be sensitive to different relational forms, to the possible dominance of vision and visual actants, and to their possible relations with self–other differentiation. So, for example, many constructionist writings theorize language as action, and yet research practices typically turn live talk into visualized and frozen words—into dead interview transcripts that can be analyzed. Perhaps we need to amplify our sensitivity to live sound, to live processes, and to time if we wish to open up possibilities for soft differentiation and transformative change work.

Some Sound Qualities of Relational Processes

Bergson (1934; as cited in Schroder, 2005, p. 107) argued that the lived experience of time involves an interweaving of past, present, and future in an "elan vital" that encompasses everything that lives; he called this lived experience of time *durée*. For example, in sound cultures, the past is made present in what people say and do, in the performances of epic singers, storytellers, and poets, in the arts of oratory and rhetoric—in performances that join play, celebration, and community with learning. For Ong, "*being in* is what we experience in a world of sound"[27] (1967, p. 130, italics added). This seems rather different from the visualized, spatialized and bounded, linear and sequential construction of time associated with clocks and timetables, entitative conceptions of processes, science and modernity.

To participate in sound is to participate in action in a way that is rather different from looking at visual (dead) texts (Berendt, 1992; Ong, 1967). For example, in sound cultures, the word is clearly "a vocalization, a happening . . . an event," and it is experienced as "contact with actuality" (Ong, 1967, p. 33). And sound "situates man in the middle of actuality" (Ong, 1967, p. 128) as he relates to sounds in front, behind, above, below . . . all these things simultaneously . . . I not only can but must hear all the sounds around me at once. Sound thus situates me in the midst of the world" (Ong, 1967, p. 129). Furthermore, in sound processes, knowing is clearly a live event rather than a dead possession; a relational process and not an individual act; and is from within inter-action rather than the product of an outside observer's distant gaze.[28] Relational processes of this sort have been linked with soft self–other differentiation (Berman, 1981, 1990; Ong, 1967).

In Ong's view, "the word, and particularly *the spoken word, is curiously reciprocating*" (Ong, 1967, p. 125, italics added). For example, and as I noted earlier, the past and the present "come together" in the sense that every action echoes and develops what has gone before. Sounds echo and resonate, and rhythms synchronize. Inside and outside come together not in the sense of inside and outside some singular and bounded Self (as in subject–object relations) but in the sense of interiors "manifesting themselves"—such as a cave when a wolf howls or the body of a violin when a string is bowed or plucked (see Ong, 1967, p. 117). So relating is achieved in variable reciprocations[29] that allow sounds, multiple overtones, multiple voices to be heard. This seems very relevant to our critical interest in soft differentiation, as "relational responsiveness" (McNamee & Gergen, 1999) is impossible when one voice dominates. A sound metaphor seems to open up new possibilities for listening and for "going on" in ways that are open to and appreciative of otherness.

A Sound Discourse of Listening

Earlier I described subject–object relations as constructing an active subject who is largely closed to Other,[30] where "other" includes other possible selves, one's own body (as a possession, as separate from one's knowing mind), and other people and things viewed as independently existing objects. In subject–object ways of relating, the subject acts to construct knowledge about other as an object and acts (on the basis of that knowledge) to form, mold, or structure the other. Self is understood to possess a private interiority that is closed to other—to "not-self."[31] And closed subjects already know what they want to know and what they want to do with that knowledge. Closed subjects relate to other in ways that are self-interested, that speak for and about other, and in ways that are largely closed to other possible self–world relations.

The assumption of subject–object relations seriously limits the way listening can be understood. Listening becomes something that someone does in order to know other as a separately existing entity (ontology). Listening becomes more or less instrumental in the production of propositional knowledge and is evaluated in relation to issues of accuracy and truth (epistemology). Silence implies no-thingness—nothing to listen to; silence is a void to be avoided (Berman, 1990).

To reconstruct listening in relation to *soft* self–other differentiation will require letting go of overly sharp distinctions between the senses, between the senses and the mind, between the mind and the body, between inside and outside self, and between self and other. In the absence of these hard differentiations, and in the presence of our discourse of relational processes and sound participation, listening is shifted out of the "self-contained individual" (Sampson, 1995) and into embodied participation in local–cultural, local–historical processes. Our discussion of sound spoke of processes of coming together of processes that allow sounds, overtones, and multiple voices to be heard. This brings me to the "other side of language," that is, to the listening side, rather than the more commonly emphasized talking and world structuring in subject–object relations (Corradi Fiumara, 1990).

Corradi Fiumara (1990, p. 2) reflected on Western philosophy's one-sided attention to "the moulding ordering sense of 'saying'," which she called *logos*. She argued that attention to *logos* constitutes attention to "saying without listening" and so to "a generalized form of domination and control" (Heidegger, 1975, as cited in Corradi Fiumara, 1990, p. 2). She continued by making use of Heidegger's exploration of the relatively neglected verb form of *logos*, that is, *legein*. Heidegger's *Early Greek Thinking* (1975) provided a key text in which we find an emphasis that helps us with the possible relevance of "sound constructions" of relational processes.

For Heidegger, listening as *legein* includes "gathering," "heeding," or "hearkening." "But gathering is more than mere amassing. To gathering belongs a collecting which brings under shelter"—an action performed with a view to "safekeeping" (Heidegger, 1975, as cited in Corradi Fiumara, 1990, p. 4). He continued by connecting gathering with laying: "Laying brings to lie, in that it lets things lie together before us" and "whatever lies before us involves us and therefore concerns us." "Laying is the letting-lie-before—which is gathered into itself—of that which comes together into presence" (Heidegger, 1975, as cited in Corradi Fiumara, 1990, p. 5). Given our earlier discussion of visual and auditory actants, it is perhaps surprising that Heidegger's language, or at least someone's translation of it from German to English, seems so dominated by visual imagery. Perhaps "gathering" and "letting lie" that which involves

requires sound metaphors, such as the reciprocal allowing and appreciation of overtones, of multiple voices, of otherness.

Heidegger's discussion of *legein* resonates with our earlier discussion of the ontological[32] significance of relational processes. His discussion seems to imply that soft differentiation is constructed in processes characterized by listening in the sense of gathering and letting lie, giving space to otherness. Sound processes and listening as *legein* may provide opportunities for "the patient labours of co-existence"—labors that seem to need a "modesty and mildness of language that can exorcise the risk that it (i.e., language) becomes an end in itself" (Corradi Fiumara, 1990, p. 40).

For example, management and organization studies could expand their limited focus on the forming–ordering–molding–structuring aspects of language (*logos*), on "power over" Other—that is, achieving closure. Such expansion could include exploration of communications and language as sound processes, listening as *legein*, and power as "power to" (Hosking, 1995)—power to be open to Other, that is, to soft self–other differentiation. Work of this kind would constitute a radically changed orientation to ecological issues and to notions such as "servant leadership," "empowering," "green management," "flat organizations," and so on. Work of this kind would radically reconstruct the present range of "holistic" approaches, such as cybernetics, chaos theory, and complexity theory. So, for example, these approaches can now become embodied and enchanted, live and sensuous, can embrace somatic life, emptiness, reflexivity, and openness (cf. Berman, 1990, p. 307). But, as I have argued, these possibilities become available only through a critical relational constructionist discourse. I conclude with a brief reconstruction of inquiry and intervention in relation to (1) a critical relational constructionist discourse and (2) a soft self–other differentiation—reconstructions that offer a changed aesthetic for inquiry and intervention.

A Changed Aesthetic for Inquiry and Intervention

Discourses of inquiry as an activity that is separate from intervention make sense in relation to relatively hard differentiations between self, other, and relations. For example, scientific inquiry requires separation of self (e.g., as scientist) from other (as the object to be known) for the proper production of objective knowledge. Intervention would simply be an act of dominance without the legitimizing discourse of being "rationally" grounded in scientific observation, neutrality, and facts. However, the distinction between inquiry and intervention is no longer quite so plausible when all actions are seen to have the potential for changing how processes go on and influencing the realities that are made.

In addition, critical sensitivity to power and to construction means that any claim to have observed that this is how things really or probably are (as in inquiry) now must be viewed as a claim that (1) reflects a particular local "form of life" and (2) has the potential to *influence* how others define reality. As we have seen, a critical constructionist orientation directs attention to inter-acts, to the forms of life they invite, support, or suppress, and to how they do so, paying special attention to multiplicity (or its absence) and to relations (different but equal, or dominance). So the interest(s) pursued by a critical orientation must differ from those of, for example, the received view of science.

In the present view, *critical interests* include (1) opening up rather than closing down possibilities and (2) transformation within soft self–other differentiation rather than intervention through subject–object relations. When all processes are viewed as ongoing, multiple, and simultaneous joinings of texts, it becomes possible to view all relational processes as both inquiry and intervention, to view both inquiry and intervention as relational processes, and, reflexively, to study them in

that way (Van der Haar & Hosking, 2004). So, returning to our interest in ways of relating that only softly differentiate self and other, we can imagine and view as legitimate forms of inquiry and forms of organizational and community intervention that would otherwise be unimaginable or just plain wrong. Furthermore, we gain a very particular understanding of practices such as participative action research and appreciative inquiry[33] (Hosking, 2004)—practices that do not sharply separate inquiry and intervention. The following constitute some core themes of such critical practices.

Processes of Knowing and Influencing

Recognition and significance is given to the influence potential of all acts—asking questions, voice tone, words used, posture, and so forth—including artifacts such as interview findings, percentage summaries, diagnostic classifications, and so forth. Any and all of these have the potential to contribute to the social construction of reality.[34] All acts now are theorized as having the potential to change[35] how processes go on, and change agency is located in ongoing processes and not in someone referred to as a "change agent."

Making Space for Multiple Local Realities

Attempts are made to give space to and to work with multiplicity rather than to suppress or homogenize, through the application of statistical procedures or management drives, to consensus. In general terms, polyphony may be constructed in nonhierarchical ways that recognize and support difference and that construct *power to* rather than what I earlier called *power over*. In principle, this means creating space for voices from all local forms of life in intertextual relation with some issue. However, the point of such participation is not to increase the likelihood of acceptance of someone else's decision,[36] nor to increase the quality of a (consensus) solution. Rather, it is a way of including and enabling multiple local realities in different-but-equal relation.

Centering Possibilities and Appreciation

The view that relational processes construct realities has major implications for all inquiry and change work. For many (though not all) it means working with possibilities, rather than with closed recipes, and with what is positively valued rather than problems and critiques grounded in a particular form of life. For many (though not all) it means working "appreciatively" (Cooperrider & Srivastva, 1987). The shift to possibilities invites, for example, change work that helps participants learn how better to improvise and to imagine new ways of going on together. Evaluation work is also reconstructed to be a multivoiced, appreciative, and reflexive quality of ongoing change work (Van der Haar & Hosking, 2004). The shift to appreciation is a way of recognizing the participation of multiple forms of life and their differing constructions of knowledge. It is a way of working in power-full processes—working in ways that might facilitate "power to" and "power with" rather than "power over." The shift to appreciation is a way of recognizing that we are always already in the middle of relational realities and therefore without secure grounds either for claiming self as superior (e.g., more knowing) or for critique of Other.

Both Inquiry and Intervention

Because relational processes construct realities, there is no requirement (although, of course, one could) to narrate activities as *either* inquiry *or* intervention; rather, a *both–and* approach is enabled. Participative action research is clearly a move in this direction, as are coinquiry and collaborative inquiry, although they are more usually framed in relation to a humanistic discourse rather than a discourse of critical relational constructionism. Change work shifts from

intervention—suggestive of "power over"—to "transformation"—suggestive of ways of relating that (re)construct "power with" and "power to." Large-scale change methodologies such as Future Search are (re)constructed as future making in the here and now; appreciative inquiry becomes a way of making self–other relations in an ongoing present. Care-full questioning and care-full listening are reconstructed as ways of doing different-but-equal relations.

Questioning and Listening Form Relations and Realities

The present interest in soft self–other differentiation gives a changed role and significance to asking questions, to how they are asked, why, and by whom. For example, rather than seeing questioning as finding out about some preexisting reality, it now can be theorized as *formative* of relational realities. Good questions are theorized as those that help to enlarge possible worlds and possible ways of being in relationship (see Harding, 1998). Careful attention to listening to Other is centered, as it is in many approaches that aim to facilitate dialogue rather than debate, such as the public conversations project and the MIT dialogue project (Isaacs, 1993). But given our present critical orientation and interest, the importance of listening lies, so to speak, in its relational message and in its role in openness and appreciation. To listen in ways that are more open to Other(ness), to multiple voices, and to possibilities involves listening in ways that are both "not knowing" (Anderson, 1997) and not self-centered. Listening that is open and appreciative seems crucial in relation to "power with" and "power to."

Constructing in Conceptual and Nonconceptual Performances

Of course, relating is much more than conceptual language; listening has a wider context in sound processes and oral/aural cultures. Many change practitioners work with *how* people talk. For example, they might explore the dominant metaphors (e.g., "business is war"). Equally, they might explore who talks the most, who interrupts, who claims authority and expertise and on what basis, and so forth. Similarly, practitioners might work with and through less conceptual performances, such as acting, dance, and other kinds of body work, collective sculpture making, or singing. Learning how to learn, getting "unstuck," and constructing "power to" are central to such approaches. Performative change work, whatever its form, achieves a radically changed significance in the context of a critical relational constructionist discourse that collapses hard distinctions, such those between mind and body, knowing and action, rational and irrational. Indeed, nonconceptual forms of relating may be especially helpful in avoiding the subject–object constructions built in to most current, natural languages.

A Deep Ecological Approach

When self and other are theorized as co-constructed, care of the other is also care of the (moral) self. Discourses of care no longer have to be understood in relation to "soft" humanist narratives and opposed to a "hard" (factual) world of, for example, economic realities and relations that are (rationally) instrumentalized, secularized, and disembodied (see Hosking, 2000). In the present thought style, Einstein's question, Is the universe friendly?, seems less relevant and less urgent than the critical question, How can self and other relate in ways that allow and support interdependent, different-but-equal relations?

• Notes

1. For example, constructivist *theories*.
2. Even though we actively "organize" other in relation to our own discourses—just as Other organizes us.
3. More or less attention will be given to social influences, and some theorists use the language of social constructionism to emphasize the role of other persons and cultural factors.

4. So the language of "critical realism" is offered as a replacement for "naive realism" (Guba & Lincoln, 1994).

5. The more common distinction between means and ends, processes and outcomes is here collapsed; the path is the goal, so to speak (e.g., Brown & Hosking, 1986).

6. Guba and Lincoln (1994) are in good company; many writers characterize constructionism or constructivism as "mental constructions" and as idealist and relativist (e.g., Bem & Looren de Jong, 2006).

7. e.g., Locke, Hume, and Kant; Piaget and Popper (see Morley & Hunt, 2006).

8. Morley and Hunt make reference to, for example, the works of "the late" Wittgenstein (1953), some feminist philosophers of science, and Continental philosophers involved in hermeneutics (the meaning of texts).

9. See, for example, Chia (1995).

10. Not as a given—as "how things really are."

11. By which I mean to refer to the entitative view in which persons are "always already" theorized with their own ontology—with their entity characteristics—such that understandings of processes are limited by metatheoretical assumptions about ontology and epistemology.

12. In Latour's view, cultures (we could also say "forms of life") differ in how they do this and differ in the extent to which they are able to enroll and control reality constructions. Science is different from other cultures by being able to act on a bigger scale.

13. The language of "tool" and "result" is taken from Newman and Holtzman (1977).

14. I presume that constructionist theorists' common reference to "language-*based*" interactions (Gergen, 1994) is intended to refer to the ubiquitous involvement of conceptual language.

15. Which some may take as good reason for not getting too involved in games that focus on the question "what is it?" Perhaps Lewis Carroll (2001) was playing with this idea in *Alice's Adventures in Wonderland*. In that book, the mouse was telling a story in which he declared that various named characters " 'found it advisable'—'found *what*?' said the Duck. 'Found it,' the mouse replied rather crossly: 'of course you know what it means' " (p. 31).

16. Here viewed as reconstructed stabilities characteristic of a particular "form of life."

17. More usually I have used the language of politics to speak of these aspects of relational processes.

18. As I have said, this includes the processes that some form of life might call "research."

19. Of course, this discourse is itself a local–historical construction that discourses my reflections on both hard and soft differentiation; only having experience of the latter would produce a very different discourse, and in an "insider voice."

20. Different forms of life may differently construct what is (locally) viewed as knowledge. For example, engineering may value numeric calculations and precision up to and beyond three decimal places, while management may value "ballpark" estimates and trust.

21. The possible meanings of *appreciation* and *openness* are seriously limited by assumptions of one real world and knowledge of the same.

22. Not restricted to mind operations and rational acts.

23. Without the linear construction of history.

24. There is a view that openness is the "natural" way for humans to be and that out of openness and space self and other are created; that we create closure. I do not explore these views here.

25. "The modern age was thus much more the child of typography than it has commonly been made out to be" (Ong, 1967, p. 9).

26. Unlike complex and polysemous utterances.

27. "To hear = to be" and "being is only oneness" (Berendt, 1992, p. 48).

28. Again we see that vision and subject–object relations go together (see Ong, 1967, pp. 219–231).

29. And does not have to refer to a relatively fixed boundary between self and other.

30. Open only to instrumental relations in which they can (1) know and (2) achieve power over other.

31. Interestingly, Julian Jaynes (1976) In *The Origin of Consciousness in the Breakdown of the Bicameral Mind* wrote about the mind of early Greek man as *open* to the gods—open for them to speak to him and tell him what to do. So the gradual construction of the bounded, possessive individual involved shifting the locus of agency away from the gods and placing it in the knowing individual. Perhaps this is also connected with the story of Adam and Eve, who, once they became knowing, could no longer remain in the enchanted world, the Garden of Eden.

32. Rather than epistemological.

33. Of course, these practices are often discoursed in relation to humanistic constructions of persons and relations; it is not my intention to suggest that a particular form of inquiry *is* this or *is* that.

34. This is very different from mainstream approaches that differentiate data gathering, analysis, intervention design, and implementation. In the latter case, activities are understood as *either* to "find out"/seek to know about *or* to attempt to influence the other.

35. Only the "potential," as it depends on how they are supplemented and whether or not they are warranted as "real and good."

36. As in participative management and common forms of industrial democracy and worker participation.

• References

Alvesson, M., & Deetz, S. (2000). *Doing critical management research*. London: Sage.

Anderson, H. (1997). *Conversation, language, and possibilities: A postmodern approach to therapy*. New York: Harper Collins.

Bem, S., & Looren de Jong, H. (2006). *Theoretical issues in psychology* (2nd ed.). London: Sage.

Berendt, J. E. (1992). *The third ear*. New York: Holt.

Berman, M. (1981). *The re-enchantment of the world*. Ithaca, NY: Cornell University Press.

Berman, M. (1990). *Coming to our senses*. New York: Bantam Books.

Brown, H., & Hosking, D. M. (1986). Distributed leadership and skilled performance as successful organization in social movements. *Human Relations, 39*(1), 65–79.

Carnall, C. A. (1990). *Managing change in organizations*. New York: Prentice Hall.

Carroll, L. (2001). *the annotated Alice* (M. Gardner, Ed.). London: Penguin Books.

Chan, A. (2000). *Critically constituting organisation*. Amsterdam: Benjamins.

Chia, R. (1995). From modern to postmodern organizational analysis. *Organization Studies, 16*(4), 579–604.

Cooperrider, D. L., & Srivastva, S. (1987). Appreciative inquiry into organization life. In R. W. Woodman & W. A. Pasmore (Eds.), *Research into organizational change and development* (pp. 129–169). Amsterdam: Elsevier B.V.

Corradi Fiumara, G. (1990). *The other side of language: A philosophy of listening*. London: Routledge.

Dachler, H. P., & Hosking, D. M. (1995). The primacy of relations in socially constructing organizational realities. In D. M. Hosking, H. P. Dachler, & K. J. Gergen (Eds.), *Management and organization: Relational alternatives to individualism* (pp. 1–29). Aldershot, UK: Avebury.

Danziger, K. (1997). The varieties of social construction: Essay review. *Theory and Psychology, 7*(3), 399–416.

Deetz, S. (1996a). Describing differences in approaches to organization science. In P. Frost, R. Lewin, & D. Daft (Eds.), *Talking about organization science* (pp. 123–152). Thousand Oaks, CA: Sage.

Deetz, S. (1996b). Describing differences in approaches to organization science: Rethinking Burrell and Morgan and their legacy. *Organization Science, 7*(2), 191–207.

Denzin, N. K., & Lincoln, Y. S. (Eds.). (1994). *Handbook of qualitative research*. London: Sage.

Falzon, C. (1998). *Foucault and social dialogue: Beyond fragmentation*. London: Routledge.

Fine, M. (1994). Working the hyphens: Reinventing self and other in qualitative research. In N. K. Denzin & Y. S. Lincoln (Eds.), *Handbook of qualitative research* (pp. 70–82). London: Sage.

Foucault, M. (1980). *Power/knowledge: Selected Interviews and Other Writings*. New York: Pantheon Books. (Original work published 1977)

Gergen, K. J. (1994). *Realities and relationships: Soundings in social construction*. Cambridge, MA: Harvard University Press.

Gergen, K. J. (1995). Relational theory and the discourses of power. In D. M. Hosking, H. P. Dachler, & K. J. Gergen (Eds.), *Management and organization: Relational alternatives to individualism* (pp. 29–51). Aldershot, UK: Avebury.

Guba, E. G., & Lincoln, Y. S. (1994). Competing paradigms in qualitative research. In N. K. Denzin & Y. S. Lincoln (Eds.), *Handbook of qualitative research* (pp. 105–117). London: Sage.

Harding, S. (1986). *The science question in feminism*. Milton Keynes, UK: Oxford University Press.

Harding, S. (1998). *Is science multicultural?* Bloomington: Indiana University Press.

Heidegger, M. (1975). *Early Greek thinking* (D. F. Krell & F. A. Capuzzi, Trans.). New York: Harper & Row.

Hermans, H. J., Kempen, H. J., & Van Loon, R. J. (1992). The dialogical self: Beyond individualism and rationalism. *American Psychologist, 47*(1), 23–33.

Hosking, D. M. (1995). Constructing power: Entitative and relational approaches. In D. M. Hosking, H. P. Dachler, & K. J. Gergen (Eds.), *Management and organization: Relational alternatives to individualism* (pp. 51–71). Aldershot, UK: Avebury.

Hosking, D. M. (2000). Ecology in mind, mindful practices. *European Journal for Work and Organizational Psychology, 9*(2), 147–158.

Hosking, D. M. (2004). Change works: A critical construction. In J. Boonstra (Ed.), *Dynamics of organizational change and learning* (pp. 259–278). Chichester, UK: Wiley.

Hosking, D. M. (2006). Bounded entities, constructivist revisions and radical re-constructions. *Cognitie, Creier, Comportament [Cognition, Brain, Behavior], 9*(4), 609–622.

Hosking, D. M., Dachler, H. P., & Gergen, K. J. (Eds.). (1995). *Management and organization: Relational alternatives to individualism*. Aldershot, UK: Avebury.

Hosking, D. M., & Morley, I. E. (1991). *A social psychology of organising*. Chichester, UK: Harvester Wheatsheaf.

Isaacs, W. M. (1993). Taking flight: Dialogue, collective thinking and organizational learning. *Organizational Dynamics, 22*(2), 24–39.

Jaynes, J. (1976). *The origin of consciousness in the breakdown of the bicameral mind*. London: Penguin Books.

Latour, B. (1987). *Science in action*. Milton Keynes, UK: Open University Press.

Levin, D. M. (1989). *The listening self*. London: Routledge.

McNamee, S., & Gergen, K. J. (Eds.). (1999). *Relational responsibility: Resources for sustainable dialogue*. Thousands Oaks, CA: Sage.

Morley, I. E., & Hunt, G. M. K. (2006). *Philosophy and psychology: The design and implementation of theories*. Unpublished manuscript.

Newman, F., & Holzman, L. (1977). *The end of knowing*. London: Routledge.

Ong, W. J. (1967). *The presence of the word*. London: Yale University Press.

Pearce, W. B. (1992). A "camper's" guide to constructionisms. *Human Systems: The Journal of Systemic Consultation and Management, 3*, 139–161.

Reason, P. (1994). *Participation in human inquiry*. London: Sage.

Sampson, E. E. (1995). *Celebrating the other*. London: Harvester Wheatsheaf.

Schroder, W. R. (2005). *Continental philosophy: A critical approach*. Oxford, UK: Blackwell.

Stenner, P., & Eccleston, C. (1994). On the textuality of being. *Theory and Psychology, 4*(1), 85–103.

Toulmin, S. (1990). *Cosmopolis: The hidden agenda of modernity*. Chicago: University of Chicago Press.

Van der Haar, D., & Hosking, D. M. (2004). Evaluating appreciative inquiry: A relational constructionist perspective. *Human Relations, 57*(8), 1017–1036.

Weick, K. (1979). *The social psychology of organizing* (2nd ed.). Reading, MA: Addison Wesley.

Wittgenstein, L. (1953). *Philosophical investigations* (G. E. M. Anscombe, Trans.). Oxford, UK: Blackwell.

Woolgar, S. (1996). Psychology, qualitative methods and the ideas of science. In J. T. E. Richardson (Ed.), *Handbook of qualitative research methods for psychology and the social sciences* (pp. 11–25). Leicester, UK: BPS Books.

CHAPTER 35

Feminism and Constructionism

● **Barbara L. Marshall**

There is likely no area in which social constructionism has had more lasting and critical impact than in feminist work on gender. As a counter to biological essentialism, a constructionist stance gave impetus to second-wave feminism. Gender, as differentiated from biological sex, was understood by feminists as socially constructed, historically and culturally variable, and subject to de- or reconstruction through conscious social and political action (see Lorber, Chapter 27, this volume). Gender as a social construction is the focus that continues to define the feminist project, both theoretically and politically. Seyla Benhabib (1989, p. 368) calls it the "problem horizon" of feminism; Evelyn Nakano Glenn suggests that it is "the closest thing to a unifying concept in feminist studies" (Glenn, 2000, p. 5).

At the same time, the very term *gender* has functioned as a lighting rod for a number of theoretical and political debates, from both feminist and nonfeminist perspectives.

This chapter reviews the relationship between feminism and social construction. It outlines a number of key issues of contention and considers how constructionism figures in the vexed relationship of theoretical to political feminisms, as well in a series of nonfeminist critiques of feminist constructionism that emerged in the 1990s. In conclusion, I outline some emergent directions in feminist theory and suggest that "constructionist feminism" is not only possible but necessary, but that constructionist feminists need to attend more carefully to what is being constructed and how.

Feminism and the Social Construction of Gender

Reviewing the relationship between feminism and constructionism is complicated by the various understandings of each term in the relationship. *Feminism* and *constructionism* each encompasses a wide range of perspectives. As many of the contributions to this *Handbook* demonstrate, there are a variety of theoretical and methodological strategies that might be included in this rhetoric. Michael Lynch suggests that "as social constructionism has become diffused throughout the social sciences and humanities, it has become increasingly *diffuse*, and one may question whether there can be a coherent discussion of the subject" (2001, p. 242). Although constructionism is often associated with postmodern forms of discourse analysis, earlier sociological variants—such as symbolic interactionism, phenomenology, and ethnomethodology—all understood social worlds as constructed via the meaning-making practices of human actors, and these have been important resources for feminists.[1]

All varieties of feminism are constructionist on some level, as none would accept that extant gender arrangements are either natural or unchangeable. Ian Hacking (1999) notes in *The Social Construction of What?* that social constructionism is, by definition, critical of the status quo. Whatever it is that is presumed to be socially constructed is "not determined by the nature of things, is not determined to be inevitable" (p. 6).[2] And, as he notes, most social constructionists also go on to assert that the present order of things, in addition to not being inevitable, is bad and should be changed. Feminists would surely agree with this regarding the prevailing gender order. Without embracing the basic constructionist principle that social relations and processes forge our identities and what we experience as social "reality," there would be little grounds for either feminist theory or feminist politics. The normative, *interested* nature of feminism, however, means that we do not see our definition of the situation as just one of any number of possible interpretations. Thus some feminists fear that a dangerous relativism might follow from a fully constructionist position. Avery Gordon, for example, argues that some forms of nonfeminist constructionism represent a "quiet and polite assault on feminist and other explicitly 'interested' social and cultural studies" (1993, p. 311). They do this by seeing different accounts of social problems as equally competing constructions and failing to see their own construction of the situation as a political position—a stance that Gordon quite rightly associates with liberal individualism. One of the ongoing debates within feminist theory is how to reconcile a constructionist perspective with normative political commitments, and I return to this issue later in the chapter.

Feminist theory, as it has developed over the past several decades, provides a diverse body of literature united by its concern with explicating the social construction of gender. As Terry Lovell has summarized it: "Feminist social theory has an object: the social construction of gender in its effects in determining the social position of women" (1996, p. 310). Feminist engagements with the contemporary social world identify the many ways in which gender difference—usually manifested as inequality—is produced, experienced, regulated, and resisted and suggest how prevailing modes of gender organization might be transformed. Feminist work has also been concerned with the sociohistorical conditions that permit particular ways of thinking about gender. The questions that concern, and the very conditions that permit, feminist inquiry are shaped by such sociohistorical changes as the widespread entry of women into paid work and the creation of spaces for feminist work in the academy. Feminist analysts have also continually reconstructed their vocabulary—sex, gender, sex roles, gender roles, sex/gender system, patriarchy, gender identity, gender order, gender trouble—and reinvented their conceptual frameworks as the limitations of previous conceptual apparatuses became apparent. The influence of feminist social constructionism has also extended beyond the academy. "Natural" differences of sex once thought to be beyond the purview of the social have been denaturalized and politicized, and academic concepts and explanatory frameworks (such as "socialization") have become part of the stock of common knowledge that people use to make sense of their experience. Anthony Giddens refers to this as the "double hermeneutic," whereby "the concepts and theories invented by social scientists . . . circulate in and out of the social world they are coined to analyse" (1987, p. 19).

Feminists are constructionist in more than one sense. Certainly the basic distinction of *gender* from *sex* grounds the idea that masculinity and femininity are social constructions. This has been a premise of feminist work from its earliest inception, as the study of "sex roles" as social constructs. But feminists are also concerned with demonstrating the construction of gender as a hierarchy, not just a categorical division of persons. This draws attention to the construction of gender as a property of "the social" itself—something above and beyond the individuals who enact gender as a personal quality or an identity. Knowledge itself is viewed as constructed in and through a gendered social. In one of the earliest formulations of this line of critique, Dorothy Smith (1974) criticized sociology's claims to objectivity from the standpoint of women. Political philosopher Mary O'Brien (1981) coined the term *malestream thought*, which gained wide circulation among feminists to describe the (masculine) gendered character of the taken-for-granted knowledges of the disciplines. As one review of disciplinary history put it, there has been a shift from the "sociology of women" to the "gendering of knowledge" (Franklin, 1996, p. ix). Across a range of disciplines, feminist theorists such as Sandra Harding, Nancy Hartsock, Hilary Rose, Donna Haraway, and Patricia Hill Collins exposed the ways in which knowledge (and presumptions of objectivity) were constructed in and through social hierarchies of gender, race, and class (see, e.g., the contributions collected in Harding, 2004).

Feminist Theory: From "Weak" to "Strong" Constructionism

The development of feminist theory over the past several decades might be seen as a development toward increasingly "strong" forms of constructionism. That is, rather than seeing any form of feminist theory as nonconstructionist, we might see theories on a continuum from "weak" to "strong" versions. The development of feminist constructionism in the 1960s and 1970s, with the differentiation of *sex* from *gender* and the focus on the latter as a social construction via concepts such as "gender roles," might be seen as a "weak" form of constructionism. As R. W. Connell (1987) summarizes it, it was this weak form of constructionism that characterized the two dominant modes of theorizing gender in mainstream sociology—role theory and categorical theory. Whereas role theory was criticized for its underlying functionalism, its inability to grasp the dynamics of change, and its focus on individual behaviors rather than social institutions and power structures, categorical theories were criticized for unproblematically associating interests with specific categories (e.g., men and women) and for focusing on "the category as a unit, rather than on the processes by which the category is constituted" (Connell, 1987, p. 54). Neither sort of theory is really adequate to an analysis that goes much beyond treating gender as a variable.

By the 1980s, feminist theory was becoming more diverse, and a number of shifts were apparent. In one important line of critique, the manner in which the social construction of gender was originally taken up by white Western feminists was challenged as more diverse voices entered the conversation. Chroniclers of shifts in feminist theory such as Linda Nicholson and Nancy Fraser (1990) locate the growing feminist interest in postmodern[3] modes of analysis as coincidental with feminist debates about difference and diversity, arguing that "as the class, sexual, racial and ethnic awareness of the movement has altered, so has the preferred conception of theory" (p. 33). Others, however, would argue that concern for co-constructions of gender with race, class, and sexuality within feminism long predates the interventions of postmodernism and that postmodern feminist theory itself tends to be exclusionary of "others" once they have served their purpose in discrediting earlier formulations.[4] In any case, there was a distinct shift in feminist theory from "things to words" (Barrett, 1992, p. 201) or from the social to the cultural, denoting a move from the social sciences to the humanities in the development of feminist constructionism (see also Adkins, 2002; Rahman & Witz, 2003).

As feminist theory developed through the 1980s and 1990s, two key axes of debate emerged. One comprised a set of debates about whether or not we have been too constructionist or not constructionist enough; the other is concerned with how a constructionist stance informs "feminism" as a distinctive analytic frame or political position. Those who argued that extant feminist approaches were not constructionist enough took the very distinction between sex and gender as their starting point, arguing that it reified sexual dimorphism, and urged feminists to be constructivist "all the way down." Part of the problem with the sex–gender split that grounded much of the early feminist social constructionism was that it construed sex (biology) as relatively fixed and stable, whereas gender (culture) was viewed as variable, malleable, and open to conscious reconstruction. This is a problematic assumption in a number of respects. First of all, biology turns out to be much less fixed than we once presumed it to be. As Myra Hird (2004, p. 25) puts it, "this binary depends on the idea that biology itself consistently distinguishes between females and males." Instead, she argues, "nature . . . offers shades of difference and similarity much more often than clear opposites"

(p. 25). Furthermore, cultural constructions of gender might be construed as far more obdurate and determining than anything that is "socially constructed" ought to be.

Judith Butler's *Gender Trouble* (1990) provides one of the most influential critiques of the sex–gender distinction. As she writes: "gender is not to culture as sex is to nature; gender is also the discursive/cultural means by which . . . 'natural sex' is produced and established as 'prediscursive,' prior to culture, a politically neutral surface on which culture acts" (p. 7). She goes on to raise some trenchant criticisms of feminist social constructionism that takes the sex–gender distinction as its premise, concluding that "on some accounts, the notion that gender is constructed suggests a certain determinism of gender meanings inscribed on anatomically differentiated bodies, where those bodies are understood as passive recipients of inexorable cultural law. . . . In such a case, not biology, but culture, becomes destiny" (p. 8). As taken up across a number of disciplines, the "turn to culture" emphasized gender as a discursive construction, sedimented through performance, with no determinate relationship to sex. We can contrast this "strong" form of constructionism, with its rejection of stable sex or gender categories and its emphasis on contingency, indeterminacy, and language, with the "weaker" forms of constructionism outlined earlier. It is the stronger version that has since become almost synonymous with "feminist constructionism," and it is this particular form of cultural constructionism, associated with feminist postmodernism and poststructuralism, that has been the target of internal feminist critique.

Feminist Critiques of Postmodern and Poststructuralist Constructionism

Two important forms of feminist critiques of postmodern/poststructuralist constructionism might be termed the "radical" feminist and "materialist" feminist critiques.

The radical feminist critique charges that postmodern feminism has unfairly characterized radical feminism as "essentialist." As those who claim the label "radical feminist" without apology point out, "essentialism" and "biological determinism" have been unduly conflated, and radical feminists have been unfairly branded as biological determinists (see, e.g., Bell & Klein, 1996). Thus, in a defense of radical feminism, Diane Richardson (1996) asserts that "it is abundantly clear that sexual and gender difference is understood to be socially constructed, not biologically determined, and that, contrary to what many seem to want to believe, radical feminists have consistently challenged essentialist conceptions of sexuality and women" (pp. 144–145). The increasing influence of postmodernism, she argues, has unfairly renewed perceptions of radical feminism as essentialist and determinist. The real difference between radical and postmodern feminism, according to Richardson, is not one of essentialism versus constructionism but one of how understand the subject of feminism. Although "within postmodernism women are in danger of being deconstructed out of existence," radical feminists "continue to argue that, however diverse and varied our experiences may be, women exist as a political and as a socially constructed category whose lives are materially shaped by belonging to that category" (Richardson, 1996, p. 146). That is, radical feminists see postmodern feminism as too strong a form of constructionism.

Part of the radical feminist critique of "gender" as it has been deployed as a socially constructed category is that it has shifted attention away from women *qua* women. Other feminists argue that it has not gone far enough in this respect—that "gender" still tends to signal the spots in the text where women appear, leaving the rest a supposedly gender-free zone. This has the effect of directing attention away from the ways that masculinity operates as a form of power in society even when women are not immediately present. Materialist feminists are thus concerned with developing a materially grounded relational understanding of gender that exceeds a focus on "woman" as an identity or category of analysis.

Dorothy Smith, for example, criticizes poststructuralist feminism for failing to recognize "discourse as an organization of social relations among people, the text as material as well as meaning, its materiality inserting new properties of organization into social relations" (1993, p. 186). Stevi Jackson, in several publications, has worked to distinguish a materialist social constructionism from poststructuralism, charging the latter with being "not very social at all" (2001, p. 289). Whereas Jackson sees poststructuralism as focusing on "women as a cultural category, in terms of their culturally defined difference from men," she conceptualizes gender as "a *social, hierarchical* division" (p. 270). As she elaborates: "Yes, it's also a cultural distinction, yes it's also an identity, but its basis is a social relation between two socially constituted groups" (p. 270). Thus the materialist feminist project, as she conceptualizes it, is not to eliminate the *binary* of constructed gender categories, permitting a multiplicity and fluidity of genders, but to eliminate the *hierarchy*, which will do away with gender. Jackson uses the analogy of class: "doing away with gender is synonymous with doing away with inequality between women and men—just as in Marxist terms, the abolition of class inequality entails the abolition of class itself" (Jackson & Hird, 2001, p. 270).

In a particularly insightful review, Momin Rahman and Anne Witz (2003) outline the trajectory of the concept of the "material" in feminist thought, arguing that feminists have long deployed it within a "relentlessly sociological" constructionist frame, expanding it in attempts to capture an increasingly broad range of social practices. At the same time, they worry that expecting such a concept to cover all aspects of the "social" bequeathed a series of lacunae within feminist analysis "that are ripe for colonization by post-structuralism—most significantly, that which comes to be termed cultural" (p. 250). Likewise, Lisa Adkins (2002) suggests that the division is between those who "insist that gender and sexuality are best understood as primarily social in character, and in particular as socio-structural" and those who "foreground their cultural constitution, especially analyses which foreground issues of linguistic and discursive practice" (p. 9). That is, what is at stake is the relative weight of the social and the cultural in the accounts of the construction of gender and sexuality.[5]

Seyla Benhabib (1996) worries about the shift in paradigms from "standpoint feminisms" to "postmodernist feminisms" in which research agendas have "shifted away from analyzing women's position within the sexual division of labour . . . to the analysis of identity; its constitution and construction" (p. 32). Similarly, Nancy Fraser has worried that an effect of this shift has been "to subordinate social struggles to cultural struggles" (Fraser & Naples, 2004, p. 1111). Although much has been gained in terms of opening up to analysis and critique issues hitherto obscured, there have also been losses, a key concern being the loss of "the female subject" for feminism, with the resulting normative lacunae left in the wake of its deconstruction. Feminist theory has been generally unwilling to accept the wholesale deconstruction of "woman" as the very subject of feminism. There were good reasons, of course, for troubling previous constructions of womanhood within feminism. For one thing, feminists wished to emphasize the contingent and historically constructed nature of femininity. For another, it was recognized that overly homogenous constructions of "woman" did little to take into account the internal diversity of the category. But many feminists worry that the postmodern deconstruction of 'woman' will leave us no firm political ground to stand on. Linda Alcoff (1988) articulated this concern in her now-classic juxtaposition of essentialism and nominalism: "if gender is simply a social construct, the need and even the possibility of a feminist politics becomes immediately problematic. What can we demand in the name of 'women' if 'women' do not exist and demands in their name simply reinforce the myth that they do?" (pp. 420–421).

Antifeminism and the Critiques of Constructionism

Clearly many feminist theorists have been critical of a presumed takeover of feminist constructionism by a postmodern/poststructuralist sensibility. However, there has been another series of debates about the poststructuralist–feminist alliance—and constructionism more generally. This is the critique of constructionism more closely associated with cultural conservatives.

The idea of "social constructionism" was central to the "culture wars" that implicated feminism, alongside a range of other theoretical tropes, as part of a wholesale assault on rationality. It also figured as part of the intellectual takeover of "special interests" in the academy, which has supposedly replaced systematic and cumulative knowledge acquisition with the "mantra" of "race, gender and ethnicity" (Horowitz, 1993, p. 17). Paul Gross and Norman Levitt (1994), for example, grouped together feminism, anticolonialism, environmentalism, queer theory, postmodernism, and other forms of "cultural constructivism" in their scathing critique of the "academic left," a potent force that has supposedly undermined the legitimation of natural science as the most privileged form of knowledge. In their account, feminism is charged with wanting, not just equality for women, but "a complete overthrow of traditional gender categories, with all their conscious and unconscious postulates" (p. 3). The worry for those who see social contructionism as political correctness gone amok is that "experiences of gender, race, sexual orientation, and cultural difference" will be "permitted to rearrange our notions of family, marriage, political decision making [and] education" (Darby & Emberley, 1996, p. 239). (Well, feminists would hope so!)

The critique of the social construction of gender—and of the very concept of gender—has functioned in antifeminist critiques in two distinct ways. One line of critique is that of the explicitly conservative, antifeminist forces associated with religious, fundamentalist "profamily" moral projects. This line of critique gained a good deal of steam in the preparations leading up to and the activities at the United Nations Fourth World Conference on Women, held in Beijing in the fall of 1995, where the very presence of "gender" in the draft platform for action acted as a flashpoint. "How" asked one critic, "could the United Nations organizers have possibly been unaware of the origin and implications of this controversial concept?" (de Casco, 1995, p. 16). The origin, she notes, citing feminist theorists such as Judith Butler, was to "dispute the biology-is-destiny formulation." Well, so far no argument. But de Casco goes on to assert that this means the "stark rejection of all our assumptions about what it means to be human (that men and women are not defined by their sex, but by culturally imposed norms)" and that the result can only be "a new and sexless world," "the elimination of the biological family," and the destruction of "the legal moral financial and social support all societies have always given to the institutions of marriage and the family" (de Casco, 1995, pp. 14–16). Catholic conservative Dale O'Leary (1995) also reviews feminist theory to mount a widely circulated critique of "gender" as a social construction. She energetically attacks the social constructionism that underlies the concept of gender, suggesting that it does not advance the "real" interests of women, as it denies them their "nature." Once we loosen the link between sex and gender, hell is but a short handcart ride away—the family will lie in tatters, one would be able to change one's sexual identity at will, the population will fail to replace itself. Feminism's "war against 'socially constructed' roles is a war against the natural relationships between women and their children, between women and men, and between women and

their own feminine nature" (O'Leary, 1995, p. 28). The fundamentalist critique of feminism is, at heart, a critique of social constructionism.

Another sort of antifeminist critique has emerged from a liberal individualist perspective, which critiques what it calls "gender feminism." Christina Hoff Sommers (1994) coined the term *gender feminism* in opposition to *equity feminism*. "Gender feminism" (bad feminism) believes "that our society is best described as a patriarchy, a male hegemony, a sex-gender system, in which the dominant gender works to keep women cowering and submissive" (p. 16). "Equity feminism" (good feminism) eschews the concept of gender and asks for nothing more than formal legal equality of individuals before the law. Politicizing gender as a social construction is an affront to liberal individualism. The very concept of "gender" becomes a "codeword" or "mantra," which, along with "race," is central to the aims of feminist social engineers. Academic feminism is charged with violating all standards of "reasonableness": manipulating evidence, lacking in conceptual rigor, ideologically driven. Thus Sommers confidently predicts that "once their ideology becomes unfashionable, many a gender feminist will quietly divest herself of the sex/gender lens through which she now views social reality and join the equity feminist mainstream" (p. 275).

Both religious fundamentalist conservatives and political liberal individualists take aim at the feminist emphasis on gender as a socially constructed category within a defense of individualism. The religious fundamentalist critique is premised on a defense of natural individual difference based on biological sex. The concept of gender as socially constructed poses a threat to individualism because it challenges this concept of natural difference. This conception of individualism is implicit in the continual conflation of "gender" and "family" in the fundamentalist analysis. Deconstructing gender is equivalent to destroying the family—the latter defined as the nuclear, heteropatriarchal family. The very idea that gender is socially constructed is viewed as a futile attempt to "redefine human nature" (Joseph, 1995, p. 94). If women abdicate their "natural" role, as defined by the patriarchal family, "society will deteriorate into anarchy" (O'Leary, 1995, p. 22).

Whereas for the conservatives the insistence on social construction has underemphasized what are seen as divinely ordered "natural" differences of sex, the liberal individualist critique charges feminism with privileging group membership over the individual. The politicization of gender and sexuality is criticized on the grounds that feminism has overly polarized men and women, *creating* difference through the insistence on social construction. John Fekete (1994), for example, charges feminism with creating a "panic culture of group antagonisms" (p. 336) and a "backlash against heterosexual pleasure" (p. 56). Daphne Patai (1998) even invents a new word to describe this supposed overpoliticization: *heterophobia*. Furthermore, the feminist insistence on the social construction of gender is charged with emasculating men. Camille Paglia, for example, tells us: "I have intensely disliked the tendency of many feminists to want men to be remade in a kind of shy, sensitive form to become, in essence, new kinds of women, contemporary eunuchs which is less inconvenient to women" (Paglia, 1994, p. 15). That the critique of gender hierarchies is conflated with an attack on men and heterosexuality is not coincidental. As Oakley has noted: "Antifeminist attacks on gender continually conflate sex and gender, particularly in their critiques of male-bashing; critiques of masculinity on the level of gender are presumed to be an attack on sex itself" (1997, p. 37).

I think that the political critiques of the social construction of gender by both religious fundamentalists and liberal individualists crystallize a number of important issues for feminism. First, both lines of critique bring into sharp relief the heterosexual matrix of gender and hence the feared threat to normalized heterosexuality that a deconstruction of gender poses. Second, their discomfort with the manner in which the social construction of gender disrupts the notion of some stable, essential masculinity reinforces the importance of insisting on gender as a relational concept, not just a descriptor of the construction of discrete categories of people. Third, the manner in which "gender" and "race" and/or "ethnicity" are linked together, particularly in the liberal individualist critique, is instructive. Framed as a "mantra," standing in for all differences that threaten some idealized universality of good academics or good citizens, this should act as a clear signal of the importance of linking the construction and politicization of gender with other axes of difference. Finally, I'm just enough of a cynic to think that if antifeminists and conservatives are that exercised about social constructionism, then feminists are on the right track. What *sort* of social constructionism we need and clarity on *what* exactly is being constructed are outstanding issues.

Feminism and Social Constructionism: Toward Reconstruction

The urgency of the feminist constructionist project is underscored by the political debates just reviewed. For critics such as Christina Hoff Sommers, the location of feminism's ultimate truth in its classical liberal moment, asking only for a "fair field and no favors" (1994, p. 51), allows only an individualist understanding of gender. Given a "fair playing field," presumably achieved through the removal of formal legal barriers to equality, differences in outcomes—the empirically observable differences in the status of men and women in our society—must then be attributed to primarily individual factors. The latter might be conceived of as failure (lack of motivation, laziness, inability to overcome sexist socialization), choice (rationally weighing the options and "choosing" motherhood, dependence, typically female occupations, etc.), or as the result of natural difference (biological predispositions). Each of these conceptions hypostatizes gender as essentially presocial and fails to grasp the manner in which both gender-as-difference and gender-as-inequality are continually produced in different ways and in different contexts—a project that is axiomatic for feminist constructionism.

Far from being a relic of less enlightened times, gender difference and inequality are constantly constructed, reconstructed, and given varying degrees of political significance, and not always in predictable ways. As Sylvia Walby (1997) asserts, patterns of inequality between men and women have changed, "but in complex ways, not simply for better or worse" (p. 1). That complexity appears, on the surface, paradoxical in that there seem to be patterns indicating a simultaneous convergence and polarization. Donna Haraway (1991, p. 167) has termed it a simultaneous intensification and erosion of gender; for Wendy Brown, it is the simultaneous "radical instability" and "relentless power" of gender (2003, p. 365). But it appears paradoxical only to the extent that we hold gender to be a relatively static and homogenous categorization. Gender does not just signify ready-made difference but is *productive* of difference.

Clearly, gender cannot be treated in the manner of a Durkheimian "social fact," with the acquisition of gender seen as the "acquisition of a social identity that is already there" (Barrett, 1988, p. 268). Yet neither is gender "constructed anew in every encounter" (p. 268). The effectiveness of a feminist social constructionism rests not on finding some middle ground between these two poles but on grasping both poles simultaneously. Historicity and contingency do not infer unintelligibility—we can observe how gender is taken up, regularized, institutionalized, policed, resisted, contested, and transformed. To do so requires that we are willing to work with gender as a construct ex-

isting at varying levels of abstraction, always understanding that we are freezing a complex and fluid set of social relationships through its usage. In the remainder of this chapter, I revisit some of the feminist debates about epistemology and ontology as these relate to the constructionist project and sketch some emergent directions in feminist theory that are actively grappling with the issues at stake.[6]

One of the epistemological debates that continues to inflect feminist theory is that between relativism, a position associated with postmodern constructionism that denies any secure, objective foundations for knowledge, and varieties of realism, which seek to retain, however minimally, some anchor for making claims about the empirical world. Whereas relativism suggests that the "real world" exists only in our interpretation and representation of experience, realism asserts that are things that exist independent of our experience of them. Although most feminists agree that the old modernist notion of the "truth" setting us free is an untenable one (and feminists have been some of the key contributors to exposing the fiction of extant "truths"), few are willing to travel to the end of the relativist line, where political strategies are cleanly severed from ontological and epistemological grounds.

Some feminists have argued that relativism is not only troublesome for feminist theory but might actively work against it. Rosalind Gill (1995), for example, worries that an unintended consequence of constructionist relativism is to institute a form of "epistemological correctness"[7] that may act to "silence feminist (and other critical) voices" (p. 173). Alexa Hepburn (2000) disagrees, arguing that relativism primarily means skepticism about objectivist foundations for knowledge and that this does not disallow feminists to engage in interested, politically committed research. On the contrary, she asserts that "without the relativism of a strong constructionist position, as a researcher you are left with the difficult job of arguing for, and providing evidence of, nonconstructionist realities" (pp. 101–102). There is a clear dilemma here in which, on the one hand, constructionism is hailed as crucial to feminism's project of dismantling naturalized hierarchies but, on the other hand, is seen as antithetical to feminist politics because of its association with relativism (Speer, 2000, p. 519).

As some commentators have pointed out (Gill, 1996; Gordon, 1993), a constructionism that is afraid to take sides bears an uncanny resemblance to a liberal pluralist utopia, or perhaps Jürgen Habermas's idealized "public sphere," in which "all have communicative rights and the opportunity to question received truths" (Gill, 1996, p. 352). As Gill continues:

> We need to ask *why* particular readings hold such sway and others disappear without a trace. The answer lies not in some formal property of the interpretation that makes it "better," but in the capacity of actors to make interpretations stick. This capacity is not evenly distributed. We do not live in a semiotic democracy. (1996, p. 352)

This highlights the importance for feminists of locating constructionism within an understanding of power and the manner in which it constrains and/or enables particular forms of practice. To poach one of Marx's more enduring insights, we do not construct (or deconstruct) things entirely under conditions of our own choosing. Feminists tackle the social construction of sex and gender as more than just a theoretical puzzle—inquiry is rooted in the political project of identifying and analyzing sites of the production and reproduction of sex–gender divisions and inequalities.

As reviewed earlier, one of the primary objections to the dissolution of identity categories implied by a thorough constructionism has been the fear that once we have deconstructed gender, we will have done away with "women" as a category, and hence there will be no secure grounds for political action. Without a clearly articulated subject, whither feminist politics? But "the dissolu-tion of the category 'woman' as an epistemological referent is not the same as arguing that gender is not a category of oppression" (Ashendon, 1997, p. 55).

Grasping both the discursive and material aspects of our analytic categories is essential to any transformative politics, such as feminism. Gender categories, like those of sexuality and race, are formed and reformed in different contexts and through processes of struggle over meaning, recognition, and distribution. As Jan Jindy Pettman (1991) argues, they are both discursive and systematic—that is, they exist in and through languages, images and ideological practices, but at the same time they produce and reproduce unequally structured social relations that have material consequences for living, breathing persons. As Pettman's analysis suggests, the use of such categories for analytic or political purposes invokes different strategies: "Some may seek to deconstruct and demystify categories, to reveal the politics behind their makings and remakings. Others, *or else the same people in different contexts*, may seek to use the category as a resource" (p. 192, italics added).

If "gender" is to have any theoretical or political purchase for feminists, then the tendency to conceptualize it categorically—as having some fixable referent—rather than as the process of constructing categories must be resisted. To simultaneously recognize the fiction of gender while treating it as concrete is not, as one critic of feminism has charged, "epistemological schizophrenia" (Fekete, 1994, p. 334).[8] It is, as Denise Riley (1988) so famously put it, a strategy of accepting that " 'women' don't exist—while maintaining a politics of 'as if they existed'—since the world behaves as if they unambiguously did" (p. 112). Jeffrey Weeks (1995) has outlined a similar tack in conceptualizing sexual identities as "necessary fictions." Feminist theorists have developed a range of mediating concepts such as situated knowledges (Haraway, 1991), strategic essentialism (Spivak, 1988), ironic coalitions (Ferguson, 1993), and gender-as-seriality

(Young, 1994), all of which admit to the tension between sex and gender categories as constructed and the virtual reality of those categories as they are experienced. And for feminists, it is the social relations that hold such potentially paradoxical terms together that are of interest.

Some of the most exciting developments in feminist theory are occurring in moves to reconsider the "material" or "materiality" within a constructionist feminist framework. As this "new materialism" inflects the development of feminist theory, it invokes the social construction not only of gender but also of science, the body, sexuality, and race. And, as other chapters in this volume outline, feminist work has been, and continues to be, central to the development of constructionist perspectives on these topics.

There are two senses in which a "new materialism" has been suggested as the way forward for constructionist feminism. One emerges from feminist science studies, in which there is a new enthusiasm for understanding the construction of the biological material that supposedly underpins the "sex–gender" distinction. Here, feminists such as Celia Roberts (2002), Donna Haraway (1997), Anne Fausto-Sterling (2000), Karen Barad (2003), and Vicki Kirby (1999) are developing trenchant analyses of such entities as hormones, genes, chromosomes, and neurons as produced through the interaction of both "culture" and "nature" and, in doing so, are "contesting previous paradigms which posited a changeable culture against a stable and inert nature" (Hird, 2004, p. 146). As they invoke the term, *materialization* refers to the ways in which science as a social practice brings into being the very material that it purports to study. Such analyses bring feminist work on embodiment into a creative and productive interface with constructionist studies of science and technology to open up new questions about the "material" by which gender and sexuality are constructed and regulated.

The second sense in which a new materialism is being invoked is in attempts to rethink and rework the concept of the "social" in relation to the "cultural" as the matter of social construction. Rahman and Witz (2003) argue that emergent terminologies of materiality and materialization "do not simply signal the displacement of the concept of the material by the cultural . . . but can induce feminist constructionism to work with a sociologically more adequate reconceptualization of the social as a more fully integrated realm of symbolic and material practices" (Rahman & Witz, 2003, pp. 253–254). Thus they, alongside other theorists such as Lisa Adkins (2002), reject a sharp division between the social and the cultural. Perhaps a rapprochement between cultural and social constructionism is best achieved not just by rejecting the cultural–social distinction but by pursuing a more fully *sociological* form of constructionism that is concerned not only with meaning making and discourse but also with sedimented structures of power and inequality that constrain and/or enable various ways of making meaning. New directions in feminist theory indicate that the challenges are being actively taken up—through, for example, research being conducted under the general rubric of "intersectionality" (Glenn, 2000; McCall, 2005; Stasiulis, 1999) and the development of more sociologically grounded frameworks for analyzing cultural constructions—for example, recent work that draws on Pierre Bourdieu (e.g., Adkins & Skeggs, 2004).

In conclusion, I think the future of the relationship between feminism and social constructionism will be shaped not so much by academic debates as by political exigencies. Feminist constructionists are now increasingly challenged by new sources of essentialism. On one hand, biological essentialism has gained new influence via evolutionary psychology and other deterministic explanations of difference.[9] On the other hand, accounts of gender that appear to have captured the popular imagination are those that see gender differences as being rather static and immutable, whether "socially constructed" or not.[10] Thus the clearest challenge to feminist constructionism will surely be to keep opening up the "black boxes"[11] of gender and sexual difference against renewed attempts to nail the lid down.

◦ Notes

1. See, for example, Stevi Jackson (1999), who argues that "sociologists have long been aware... that there is no essential pre-social self, that language is not a transparent medium of communication, that meanings shift as they are contested and re-negotiated, that knowledge is a social construct rather than a revelation of absolute truth" (2.2).

2. Hacking (1999, p. 7) suggests that the most influential doctrines of social constructionism have had to do with gender and takes Simone de Beauvoir's *The Second Sex*, with its assertion that "one is not born, but becomes a woman" (1961, p. 249), as a canonical text.

3. Although I believe that postmodernism and poststructuralism should be distinguished, this task is made difficult by their frequent conflation in the literature (often by the hybrid term *postmodernism/poststructuralism*. Because my concern here is to focus on the ways that postmodern and poststructuralist themes have been taken up and/or criticized, I use the terms used by the authors that I am discussing.

4. See Marshall (2000) for a review of these debates.

5. An exchange between Judith Butler and Nancy Fraser in *New Left Review* has been widely cited as crystallizing some of the issues regarding the material and the cultural in feminist theory. Responding to Fraser's (1997) outline of what she calls the "recognition–redistribution" dilemma, in which she identified different political struggles as primarily about either cultural/symbolic change (recognition) or social/economic change (redistribution), Butler (1998) challenges the stability of the very distinction between the material and the cultural.

6. For a lengthier review of some of these debates as they have played out in critical studies of technology, see Marshall (2003).

7. She attributes this phrase to Christine Hine.

8. As he describes it, feminism is objectivist about identity but constructivist about its prospects.

9. See, for example, Geary (1998) or Rhoads (2004). Mainstream media have been particularly enthusiastic about promoting "new" scientific findings about "natural" sexual difference.

10. Here, I am thinking not only of the continuing popularity of the "men are from Mars, women are from Venus" line of thought made popular by John Gray (1992) but also of even more academic versions, such as Deborah Tannen's (1990) work on gendered communication styles, which urges us to recognize and accept obdurate differences between men and women and work toward "cross-cultural" communication as a route to gender harmony.

11. The term *black-boxing* has its origin in the literature on the social construction of technology, in which it refers to the tendency for technologies to become stabilized in such a way as to obscure other possible constructions. Thus they appear to be naturalized and/or immune to political critique.

◦ References

Adkins, L. (2002). *Revisions: Gender and sexuality in late modernity*. Buckingham, UK: Open University Press.

Adkins, L., & Skeggs, B. (Eds.). (2004). *Feminism after Bourdieu*. Oxford, UK: Blackwell.

Alcoff, L. (1988). Cultural feminism vs. poststructuralism: The identity crisis in feminist theory. *Signs, 13*(3), 405–436.

Ashendon, S. (1997). Feminism, postmodernism and the sociology of gender. In D. Owen (Ed.), *Sociology after postmodernism* (pp. 40–64). Thousand Oaks, CA: Sage.

Barad, K. (2003). Posthumanist performativity: Toward an understanding of how matter comes to matter. *Signs, 28*(3), 801–831.

Barrett, M. (1988). Comment on a paper by Christine Delphy. In C. Nelson & L. Grossberg (Eds.), *Marxism and the interpretation of culture* (pp. 268–269). Chicago: University of Illinois Press.

Barrett, M. (1992). Words and things: Materialism and method in contemporary feminist analysis. In M. Barrett & A. Phillips (Eds.), *Destabilizing theory* (pp. 201–219). Cambridge, UK: Polity Press.

Bell, D., & Klein, R. (Eds.). (1996). *Radically speaking: Feminism reclaimed*. London: Zed Books.

Benhabib, S. (1989). On contemporary feminist theory. *Dissent, 36*, 366–370.

Benhabib, S. (1996). From identity politics to social feminism. In D. Trend (Ed.), *Radical democracy* (pp. 27–41). London: Routledge.

Brown, W. (2003). Gender in counterpoint. *Feminist Theory, 4*(3), 365–368.

Butler, J. (1990). *Gender trouble: Feminism and the subversion of identity.* New York: Routledge.

Butler, J. (1998). Merely cultural. *New Left Review, 227,* 33–44.

Connell, R. (1987). *Gender and power.* Cambridge, UK: Polity Press.

Darby, T., & Emberley, P. C. (1996). "Political correctness" and the constitution. In A. A. Peacock (Ed.), *Rethinking the constitution: Perspectives on Canadian constitutional reform* (pp. 233–248). Toronto, Ontario, Canada: Oxford University Press.

de Beauvoir, S. (1961). *The second sex.* New York: Bantam Books.

de Casco, M. L. (1995). The battle at Beijing. In M. Cook (Ed.), *Empowering women: Critical views on the Beijing conference* (pp. 13–17). Crows Nest, New South Wales, Australia: Little Hills Press.

Fausto-Sterling, A. (2000). *Sexing the body: Gender politics and the construction of sexuality.* Toronto, Ontario: HarperCollins Canada.

Fekete, J. (1994). *Moral panic: Biopolitics rising.* Montreal, Quebec, Canada: Davies.

Ferguson, K. (1993). *The man question: Visions of subjectivity in feminist theory.* Berkeley: University of California Press.

Franklin, S. (1996). Introduction. In S. Franklin (Ed.), *The sociology of gender* (pp. ix–xivii). Brookfield, VT: Elgar.

Fraser, N. (1997). *Justice interruptus: Critical reflections on the "postsocialist" condition.* New York: Routledge.

Fraser, N., & Naples, N. A. (2004). To interpret the world and to change it: An interview with Nancy Fraser. *Signs, 29*(4), 1103–1124.

Geary, D. C. (1998). *Male, female: The evolution of sex differences.* Washington, DC: American Psychological Association.

Giddens, A. (1987). *Social theory and modern sociology.* Cambridge, UK: Polity Press.

Gill, R. (1995). Relativism, reflexivity and politics: Interrogating discourse analysis from a feminist perspective. In S. Wilkinson & C. Kitzinger (Eds.), *Feminism and discourse: Psychological perspectives* (pp. 165–186). London: Sage.

Gill, R. (1996). Power, social transformation and the new determinism: A comment on Grint and Woolgar. *Science, Technology and Human Values, 21*(3), 347–353.

Glenn, E. N. (2000). The social construction of gender and race: An integrative framework. In M. M. Feree, J. Lorber, & B. B. Hess (Eds.), *Revisioning gender* (pp. 3–43). Walnut Creek, CA: AltaMira Press.

Gordon, A. (1993). Twenty-two theses on social constructionism: A feminist response to Ibarra and Kitsuse's "Proposal for the study of social problems." In J. A. Holstein & G. Miller (Eds.), *Reconsidering social constructionism* (pp. 301–326). New York: Aldine de Gruyter.

Gray, J. (1992). *Men are from Mars, women are from Venus.* New York: HarperCollins.

Gross, P., & Levitt, N. (1994). *Higher superstitions: The academic left and its quarrels with science.* Baltimore: Johns Hopkins University Press.

Hacking, I. (1999). *The social construction of what?* Cambridge, MA: Harvard University Press.

Haraway, D. (1991). *Simians, cyborgs and women.* London: Routledge.

Haraway, D. (1997). *Modest_Witness@Second_Millennium: FemaleMan_Meets_Oncomouse.* New York: Routledge.

Harding, S. (Ed.). (2004). *The feminist standpoint theory reader: Intellectual and political controversies.* New York: Routledge.

Hepburn, A. (2000). On the alleged incompatibility between relativism and feminist psychology. *Feminism and Psychology, 10*(1), 91–106.

Hird, M. (2004). *Sex, gender and science.* New York: Palgrave MacMillan.

Horowitz, I. (1993). *The decomposition of sociology.* Oxford, UK: Oxford University Press.

Jackson, S. (1999). Feminist sociology and sociological feminism: recovering the social in feminist thought. *Sociological Research Online, 4*(3). Retrieved April 30, 2007, from *www.socresonline.org.uk/socresonline/4/3/jackson.html*

Jackson, S. (2001). Why a materialist feminism is (still) possible—and necessary. *Women's Studies International Forum, 24*(3/4), 283–293.

Jackson, S., & Hird, M. (2001). Theorizing the end of gender: A conversation with Stevi Jackson. *International Feminist Journal of Politics, 3*(2), 263–274.

Joseph, R. (1995). Beijing's blueprint for revolution: An experiment in social engineering. In M. Cook (Ed.), *Empowering women: Critical views on the Beijing conference* (pp. 81–104). Crows Nest, New South Wales, Australia: Little Hills Press.

Kirby, V. (1999). *Telling flesh: The substance of the corporeal.* New York: Routledge.

Lovell, T. (1996). Feminist social theory. In B. Turner (Ed.), *The Blackwell companion to social theory* (pp. 307–339). Oxford, UK: Blackwell.

Lynch, M. (2001). The contingencies of social constructionism [Review]. *Economy and Society, 30*(2), 240–254.

Marshall, B. L. (2000). *Configuring gender: Explorations in theory and politics.* Peterborough, Ontario, Canada: Broadview Press.

Marshall, B. L. (2003). Feminist theory, critical theory and technology studies. In P. Brey, A. Feenberg, T. Misa, & A. Rip (Eds.), *Technology and modernity* (pp. 105–135). Cambridge, MA: MIT Press.

McCall, L. (2005). The complexity of intersectionality. *Signs, 30*(3), 1771–1800.

Nicholson, L., & Fraser, N. (1990). Social criticism without philosophy: An encounter between feminism and postmodernism. In L. Nicholson (Ed.), *Feminism/postmodernism* (pp. 19–38). New York: Routledge.

Oakley, A. (1997). A brief history of gender. In A. Oakley & J. Mitchell (Eds.), *Who's afraid of feminism?: Seeing through the backlash* (pp. 29–55). London: Hamish Hamilton.

O'Brien, M. (1981). *The politics of reproduction.* Boston: Routledge & Kegan Paul.

O'Leary, D. (1995). *Gender: The deconstruction of women.* Unpublished manuscript.

Paglia, C. (1994). *Vamps and tramps.* New York: Vintage.

Patai, D. (1998). *Heterophobia: Sexual harassment and the future of feminism.* New York: Rowman & Littlefield.

Pettman, J. J. (1991). Racism, sexism and sociology. In G. Bottomley, M. de Lepervanche, & J. Martin (Eds.), *Intersexions: Gender/class/culture/ethnicity* (pp. 187–202). Sydney, Australia: Allen & Unwin.

Rahman, M., & Witz, A. (2003). What really matters? The elusive quality of the material in feminist thought. *Feminist Theory, 4*(3), 243–261.

Rhoads, S. E. (2004). *Taking sex differences seriously.* New York: Encounter Books.

Richardson, D. (1996). "Misguided, dangerous and wrong": On the maligning of radical feminism. In D. Bell & R. Klein (Eds.), *Radically speaking: Feminism reclaimed* (pp. 143–154). London: Zed Books.

Riley, D. (1988). *Am I that name?: Feminism and the category of "woman" in history.* Minneapolis: University of Minnesota Press.

Roberts, C. (2002). "A matter of embodied fact": Sex hormones and the history of bodies. *Feminist Theory, 3*(1), 7–26.

Smith, D. (1974). Women's perspective as a radical critique of sociology. *Sociological Inquiry, 44,* 7–13.

Smith, D. (1993). High noon in textland: A critique of Clough. *Sociological Quarterly, 34*(1), 183–192.

Sommers, C. H. (1994). *Who stole feminism? How women have betrayed women.* New York: Simon & Schuster.

Speer, S. A. (2000). Let's get real?: Feminism, constructionism and the realism/relativism debate. *Feminism and Psychology, 10*(4), 519–530.

Spivak, G. C. (1988). Subaltern studies: Deconstructing historiography. In R. Guha & G. C. Spivak (Eds.), *Selected subaltern studies* (pp. 3–32). Oxford, UK: Oxford University Press.

Stasiulis, D. (1999). Feminist intersectional theorizing. In P. Li (Ed.), *Race and ethnic relations in Canada* (2nd ed., pp. 269–305). Toronto, Ontario, Canada: Oxford University Press.

Tannen, D. (1990). *You just don't understand: Women and men in conversation.* New York: Morrow.

Walby, S. (1997). *Gender transformations.* New York: Routledge.

Weeks, J. (1995). *Invented moralities: Sexual values in an age of uncertainty.* New York: Columbia University Press.

Young, I. M. (1994). Gender as seriality: Thinking about women as a social collective. *Signs, 19*(3), 713–738.

CHAPTER 36

Institutional Ethnography and Constructionism

● Liza McCoy

The aim of the sociology we call "institutional ethnography" is to *re-organize the social relations of knowledge of the social* so that people can take that knowledge up as an extension of our ordinary knowledge of the local actualities of our lives. It is a method of inquiry into the social that proposes to enlarge the scope of what becomes visible from that site, mapping the relations that connect one local site to others.

—D. E. SMITH (2005, p. 29; original emphasis)

The actualities of our lives are intricately shaped by social relations of coordination and control that are not wholly knowable from within the scope of local experience. This is a fundamental, taken-for-granted feature of everyday life in contemporary society. We have names for the extra-local determinants that figure so powerfully in our lives: government, economy, media, capitalism, and science, to name a few. In institutional ethnography these are viewed not as abstract entities but as social relations: as the doings of people organized into extended, translocal chains of action that bring about similar forms of practice and subjectivity in multiple settings while also generating characteristic forms of inequality. What commonly mediate these chains of action, carrying them from one setting to another, are forms of language, technologies of representation and communication, and text-based, objectified modes of knowledge through which local particularities are interpreted or rendered actionable in abstract, translocal terms. All of this can be empirically investigated in a way that makes visible how it occurs through what people do. Such knowledge is continuous with the way we know our own actualities, and it has the potential to inform practical projects of advocacy and reform.

The project of institutional ethnography was initially proposed by Canadian sociologist Dorothy Smith (1987, 1991a, 1991b, 1999, 2005). She relates it to the discoveries of the feminist movement of the 1960s and 1970s, when women explored the ruptures between their everyday experience and the dominant forms of knowledge which, although seemingly neutral and general, concealed a standpoint in particular experiences of gender, race, and class. Combining the power of this consciousness-raising project with her reading of Marx's materialist method (Marx & Engels, 1981), Smith sought a form of inquiry that would begin with people in the grounded fullness of their embodied, everyday lives. She wanted a way to do research that would not objectify people and their activities, subsuming them as instances of theoretical categories. Instead of studying designated social groups in order to explain their behavior, their culture, or their meanings, research would investigate the social forms of knowledge, coordination, and control that shape our and others' lives and in which we participate; such research would extend rather than replace our everyday knowledge of the world. Smith describes institutional ethnography as an alternative, feminist "sociology for people." This is not sociology in a narrow disciplinary sense: Institutional ethnography has been taken up by researchers working in education, social work, nursing, and other health sciences, as well as sociology. An expanding network of researchers continues to develop institutional ethnography as an empirical project of inquiry.[1]

It is the assigned task of this chapter to position institutional ethnography in relation to constructionist research. Given the breadth of the field of constructionism, whose many variations are presented in this *Handbook*, it could be argued that institutional ethnography is just one more variant.

It shares a similar ontology and some of the same intellectual antecedents as constructionist research, and there are frequent points at which the empirical interests and analytic strategies of institutional ethnography converge with those self-labeled "constructionist." On the other hand, institutional ethnographers do not commonly locate their research under the umbrella of constructionism. By not affiliating with constructionism as a category label, institutional ethnography has been free to join the constructionist conversation on its own terms. This independent positioning is an important element in a project of inquiry that means to begin not in theoretical topics or schools but in the actualities of people's lives. In this chapter I provide an introduction to institutional ethnography that emphasizes its core ontology, key terms, and conceptual framework; I describe some of the ways institutional ethnographic studies are conducted and pull those elements together in an extended discussion of one example of institutional ethnographic analysis. Then I briefly discuss institutional ethnography in relation to constructionism(s), arguing that institutional ethnography is a broader project than constructionism, albeit similar in parts.

The Social Happens

An explicit social ontology grounds institutional ethnography and is expressed in a careful conceptual framework that orients the researcher (look here!) without imposing a determined theoretical content. For institutional ethnographers, the social consists in the ongoing, moment-by-moment concerting of people's activities. The starting place is people. "Individuals are there; they are in their bodies; they are active; and what they're doing is coordinated with the doings of others" (D. E. Smith, 2005, p. 59). The research goal is to investigate and explain how—in particular times and places—

people's activities, including the activities we call consciousness, are coordinated with each other. The analytic focus is on mapping distinct social forms of coordination, not explaining individuals or social groups; yet active individuals in their bodies should never disappear from the analysis. The goal is to explain how what happens happens in what people do, even when—especially when—that happening involves extended, translocal courses of action that pass through multiple settings and generate sometimes unintended outcomes.

In contemporary society the dominant form of coordination is a historically distinctive type of social relation, which Dorothy Smith (1987) calls "ruling relations": a mode of knowledge that involves the "continual transcription of the local and particular activities of our lives into abstracted and generalized forms . . . and the creation of a world in texts as a site of action" (p. 3). In institutional ethnography, "text" orients the researcher to forms of representation, whether verbal, visual, numerical, or digital, on paper or film or in computers, that have a materiality separate from embodied consciousness, thereby providing a mediating link between people across time and place and making it possible to generate knowledge separate from knowers. Modern technologies create textual forms that are easily reproduced and widely circulated, such that multiple copies of the "same" text can show up in different places at the same time. This is a feature of everyday life that we take for granted, yet it is one of the main ways that similar practices are evoked in diverse sites, and local settings connected one to the other. Modern governance and large-scale coordination occur through generalized, and generalizing, text-based forms of knowledge. It is through texts that "[t]he ruling relations [generate] forms of consciousness and organization that are objectified in the sense that they are constituted externally to particular people and places" (D. E. Smith, 2005, p. 13). But to discover the coordinative work of texts, they

must be studied "in action"—as they are produced and used and oriented to by particular people in ongoing, institutional courses of action.

As used in institutional ethnography, *institution* refers to the way clusters of ruling relations interconnect around a specific function, such as health care, child protection, or television news. This sense of institution cuts across domains that are traditionally marked for separate kinds of study. When you start with people and what they are doing and trace out the interconnections, you find extended relations and work processes that traverse organizational or subdisciplinary boundaries. For example, starting with the experience of people involved in training programs in the steel industry, what comes into view is an institutional complex occurring through and coordinating the interconnected activities of public- and private-sector educational organizations, human resources departments that commission training programs for their staff, industry councils that work with educational institutes to develop industry-relevant training, government offices that establish policy and fund training, employment counselors and employment centers that provide information and advice to individuals looking for work or a better job, and universities where theories and models of adult education and employment counseling are produced. Also involved are the equipment manufacturers whose products create a need for different skills or new combinations of skills, along with evolving business practices whose implementation demands new forms of knowledge and new subjectivities in managers and staff, thereby occasioning the need for training in so-called soft skills. All of these relational strands of action turn out to be somehow involved in shaping the experience of the people involved in training programs in the steel industry. Institutions cannot, of course, be identified and mapped in their entirety, and such is not the analytic goal. But segments of institutional complexes can be explored; and what people know about the parts where they are active can be supplemented with descriptions of the parts where other people are active. In this way, crucial linkages become visible and navigable.

The liberatory or reform intent embedded in this project will be clear. Why else should it matter what knowledge "people" have? Why is it important to "enlarge the scope" of what people can see and know from their/our location in everyday actualities? Why the care to produce a knowledge of the social that is continuous with ordinary, everyday knowledge? There is an implicit, sometimes explicit, orientation to activist projects of advocacy, intervention, and social change. You have to know how things work in order to know how to fix or change them. For institutional ethnography, "knowing how things work" means knowing how they happen in what people do, as these doings are evoked and linked across multiple sites and as they shape the possibilities and constraints people encounter in their everyday lives. This is the kind of knowledge that extends but does not replace people's ordinary, practical knowledge and that can inform, in sometimes quite small but not unimportant ways, projects of advocacy and reform.

Starting with People in Local Actualities

Many institutional ethnographers find the starting place for their investigations in their own experience. For example, Dorothy Smith (1987) has written about how the initial idea for what later came to be known as institutional ethnography arose from a disjuncture she experienced between the forms of consciousness generated in her daily work as the single parent of young children and the kind of thinking and knowing she did as a sociologist; she set about exploring how that conceptual disjuncture was produced. Other researchers began from situations they knew as activists, for example, in the women's movement (Walker, 1990), the gay liberation movement (G. W. Smith, 1988), and the environmental movement (Eastwood, 2005), or through their professional work as, for example, educators (Andre-Bechely, 2005), social workers (de Montigny, 1995), and occupational therapists (Townsend, 1998). These are common routes into institutional ethnography; researchers are often drawn to this analytic project precisely because it offers a way to investigate the institutional organization of the everyday life circumstances that perplex or concern them. But it is just as possible to start from settings and activities in which the researcher is not already a participant, such as my research into the management of college restructuring (McCoy, 1998) or Eric Mykhalovskiy's (2003) research into the social organization of knowledge transfer aimed at physicians. What is important is that the research has a clear starting place in some setting where people are active from which the investigation can begin tracing out translocal relations of coordination and control, with a focus on the text-mediated practices of knowledge that organize those relations.

It is also important for researchers to begin, as much as possible, outside of academic theories, professional discourse, or administrative categories. Because all of these may become objects of analysis (to the extent that they are found to be at work in the conceptual and coordinative practices of the setting), the researcher tries to avoid adopting them at the outset to frame the research interest or provide the categories through which the world can be knowable; to do so effectively renders them invisible as distinct practices of knowledge. This is where institutional ethnography's orienting concepts are particularly useful. No one can do research without some conceptual framework to direct attention or talk about what is learned, so the idea is to use a small set of carefully chosen concepts that are consistent with the core ontology and that offer an alternative to standard institutional or theoretical categories.[2]

How do institutional ethnographers go about "starting in local actualities"? First, let me clarify that in institutional ethnography, *actuality* is an empty term that refers the researcher to a world of things, activity and experience that includes but is not coterminous with texts and language. It is a way of referencing what is going on without committing at the outset to any particular definition, naming, or interpretation, so that these can become visible. Verbal descriptions and visual depictions, whether art or science or everyday talk, can never represent an actuality in its totality, and they are always shaped within an interpretive schema that emphasizes some features over others. This includes, of course, research writing, as well, but deconstructing one's own attempt at description is not institutional ethnography's analytic goal; what institutional ethnography generally focuses on are the ways actualities are worked up as knowable, in actionable terms, within institutional spheres where consequential decisions are made or in which the work processes at stake have immediate relevance for people's everyday lives.

To learn about specific actualities in which people are active, institutional ethnographers rely on people's ordinary ability to describe or show what they do and, as much as is visible to them within their sphere of movement, explain how their doings are coordinated with those of other people. The focus is on their work knowledge and experience, two more empty concepts that serve to orient the researcher. What we can know and say about our experience is, of course, heavily shaped by—requires—the language, discourse, and interpretive frameworks that are given to us and in which we participate. It is also shaped by what is happening in and to our bodies, what is going on around us, and what we can see and smell and hear from our bodily location, as well by the material conditions and urgencies of our lives. Experience is not some kind of prelinguistic or discourse-free zone, but, like actualities, where experience takes shape, it is not com-

pletely subsumed by them, either. (The extent to which people feel frustration as they try to speak an experience for which they do not yet have a language is testament to this.) Experience is a starting place and a resource in institutional ethnography; it is not the final analytic object. Institutional ethnographers are particularly alert to disjunctures between the knowledge that arises for people in their everyday experience and the objectified knowledge that mediates institutional relations; this "line of fault" (D. E. Smith, 1987, p. 49) provides an investigative entry point into the institutional order.

"Work" orients the researcher to what people do that involves some conscious intent and acquired skill; it includes emotional or thought work as well as physical labor or communicative action.[3] It does not mean occupational employment in a narrow sense. An institutional ethnographer might be as interested in the work of feeding a family (DeVault, 1991) or living with HIV infection (Mykhalovskiy & McCoy, 2002) as in the work performed by teachers (Manicom, 1995) or security guards (Walby, 2005). This notion of work helps the researcher to recognize, for example, that institutional courses of action, such as health care and education, recruit and depend on the work of patients, clients, and family members to fit themselves and their families into the professional work process and carry the institutional relevancies into their homes. (See, for example, Debra Brown's [2006] description of how the work mothers do is central to the success of risk reduction strategies set in motion by child protection workers, although not recognized as such in the case files that constitute the mothers as objects of case workers' scrutiny.) Work is an important orienting concept in institutional ethnography because it keeps the focus on what people do and what they know how to do. This is where coordination happens, as people's activities are concerted (sometimes, of course, in conflictual ways—the notion of coordination does not assume a comfortable complementarity of purpose). The goal is to discover how coordination happens within and across settings; focusing on the everyday forms of work people engage in and their ordinary working knowledge provides the best access. Indeed, institutional ethnography largely proceeds through gathering up accounts of work and work knowledge from people differently located within translocal relations in order to generate an analytic map that shows how their work is interconnected. "Finding [people], exploring what they do and how they are organized to do it is how an institutional ethnographer discovers ruling" (Rankin & Campbell, 2006, p. 17).

Pursuing an Investigation

Institutional ethnography is a determinedly empirical project that can be pursued in different ways. Ethnography is here used in its broadest sense to signal a commitment to empirical exploration of the way things happen through people's describable activities. It should not be understood as a call for participant observation or any other method as the primary means of generating data. Institutional ethnographers use interviews, observation, reflection on their own experience, photographs, text analysis, and the examination of naturally occurring language, fitting the method to the practicality of the research setting as well as the relations to be explored, also taking into consideration the analytic tastes and skills of the researcher. Although most institutional ethnographies investigate present-day institutional processes, some researchers examine discourses and institutional processes of the past, using a combination of oral history interviews and archival research (e.g., Kinsman, 2000; Luken & Vaughan, 2006). Just as there is no prescribed method of data generation, there is no template or recipe for conducting a study. Some institutional ethnographies unfold in unexpected ways as the researcher follows an emergent process of discovery; others involve more deliberate

planning (often in response to the requirements of supervisory committees, funding bodies, and research ethics boards). Nonetheless, certain strategies have evolved that many institutional ethnographers deploy because they work well, and I describe some of them here not with prescriptive intent but to provide a sense of what this kind of research might involve.

Institutional ethnographies often progress across two or more stages. In the first stage, some local actuality is explored in a way that generates the puzzle or problem to be investigated; initial research brings into view how people's work is articulated to the work of other people, both in the setting and in other settings, and begins to make visible, as much as is possible at this stage, the hooks to discourse and translocal relations of ruling. Interviews or focus groups are often done at this initial stage because they bring people in as the subjects of knowledge from the very beginning. (For an extensive discussion of different "shapes" of research and the practice of interviewing in institutional ethnography, see DeVault & McCoy, 2002.) Some researchers also do observations, if the local actuality they are starting from lends itself to observation, such as workplace settings or other kinds of gatherings (e.g., Diamond, 1992; Olsen, 1995). But because so much of people's working knowledge is not available simply through observation, institutional ethnographers rarely rely on observations alone. The combination of observation and interviews, however, is powerful because the researcher gets to see things happen, rather than just hearing about them; the participants can fill in with explanations about the parts that are not visible. This is crucial in institutional ethnography because it is in this knowledge, in people's interpretive practices, that the institutional linkages may be occurring. In fact, many text-based processes work in this way. The observer will not see people consulting or filling in a text, yet when they describe what they are doing, it turns out that they were orienting to some written policy or preparing to fill out a report at a later time, and this interpretive work shaped what they were able to see and say.

The next stages or levels of research follow coordinative processes and ruling discourses beyond what can be seen in the starting place. If the research has started from the experience of people who are at the receiving or less powerful ends of ruling relations, which is often the case, the investigation will usually move into the settings and modes of knowledge where decisions are made, working conditions established, or access to resources determined. For example, Debra Brown (2006) began by talking with mothers involved in a risk reduction program. She then moved her inquiry into the social service agency that ran the program, interviewing case workers and examining the assessment tools and case records that rendered the women and their circumstances knowable in institutional terms. Institutional chains of action can be traced in the other direction as well. I started by interviewing college managers about their efforts to reposition their college as a "business" (McCoy, 1998). As I heard from them about a project to introduce program costing, I began tracing that process down the administrative hierarchy into the further reaches of the college, interviewing deans and department heads and teachers about the way this new form of visibility entered their work.

In these later stages of research, interviews continue to be an important method of inquiry, and people's everyday working knowledge and ability to tell their experience and explain what they do continue to be essential resources. Here, however, the researcher is likely to be interviewing service providers, professionals, policymakers, or managers about specific segments of an institutional process that they know something about. Observations can be very useful when studying institutional work processes, especially when combined with interviews or informal opportunities to ask questions. Some researchers have made audio recordings of meetings or other settings where in-

stitutional work proceeds in talk, which allow for close analysis of the way forms of language operate, for example, to recast or exclude alternative experiences within the work processes of the institution. Susan Turner (1995), in a study of municipal land use planning, audiotaped a city council meeting in which a developer's request for rezoning, which was opposed by local residents, was considered and approved by the councilors. Her analysis examines how the documents that represented the physical location proposed for development, including a contour map of the area, were taken up by the participants in ways that shifted the focus of the decision making away from the residents' concerns.

At this stage of the research, institutional ethnographers commonly explore specific texts and textual processes. The researcher will have heard about them from people interviewed (and will, indeed, have asked the kinds of questions that make texts visible). Or the researcher might have entered the research already interested in certain texts she knew to be doing important work in the setting. For example, Lauri Grace (2006), who worked in Australia's highly centralized vocational training sector, started her research with an interest in exploring the disjuncture between the outcomes-based language in the texts of standardized training packages and the difficulties trainers and trainees had fitting that language to the actualities of their work as they knew it.

What do researchers look at when they examine texts and textual processes? Recall that the overall focus is on discovering how settings and individual people are hooked into translocal relations of coordination and control. Text-based modes of knowledge are the usual means for doing this in contemporary institutional relations, so the research aims at discovering and mapping how they occur through and coordinate people's activities. Some of these activities involve representing the local and particular in the abstract and general terms that render it institutionally actionable or accountable.

For example, nurses chart their patients' conditions and their own work, social workers write up case notes about their clients, and intake staff members fill out forms that collect the particulars of an individual's life in terms that intend some rationalized process of decision making. Further into the institutional processes, individuals may work solely within the virtual world of texts, interpreting and making decisions about other individuals and situations on the basis of their textual presence; this is largely what managers and policymakers do. Outside of specific agencies or institutional workplaces, there are broad text-mediated public discourses and the interpretive frameworks they circulate, which are activated by people in ways that produce local actualities as instances of the discursive category. (See, e.g., Alison Griffith and Dorothy Smith's [2004] description of the way some mothers drew on a child development discourse to organize and talk about their parenting vis-à-vis their child's schooling.) Other researchers focus high up in what Smith (2005) calls the intertextual hierarchy, examining the development of policy texts and other framing documents or tracing the ways a sequence of subsidiary documents carry policies and administrative priorities into various local settings, hooking them into a loop of accountability (see, e.g., Lauren Eastwood's [2005] work on international forestry policy).

Text-based forms of knowledge are so widespread that it is not possible to characterize here all the different types of text and textual process that institutional ethnographers might study. What kinds of textual practices are in operation in any given setting is always an empirical question. Institutional ethnographers do not impose a schematized typology of texts, and, indeed, there is no requirement that researchers study texts and textual processes. However, when the analytic interest is directed toward investigating institutional, ruling processes that link different settings and coordinate the activities of people across time and place, texts of some sort do turn out to be

there. What is important is that texts not be abstracted for scrutiny from the settings in which they work. An institutional ethnographer may do a close analysis of specific texts, examining how they represent the local in abstract categories, for example, or how they recruit the reader into a subject position as agent of the text. But the analysis will also focus on the work that people do to produce such texts or to activate them within particular courses of action. The ethnographic commitment—to explore "the social relations individuals bring into being in and through their actual practices" (D. E. Smith, 1987, p. 161)—remains.

An Example: *Managing to Nurse*

In their book, Janet Rankin and Marie Campbell (2006) examine managerial processes in Canadian health care reform from a standpoint in the experience of nurses at work in Canadian hospitals, drawing on a series of related institutional ethnographic studies they have carried out, separately and together, over a period of 20 years. Their research is grounded in their own experiences (both are former nurses) and in observations in hospital units, as well as interviews with nurses, nurse managers, and hospital administrators. Narrated episodes from their observations are used in the book to present the puzzle or situation whose institutional organization will be traced out in the analysis that follows. For example, one episode concerns a routine morning on a postsurgical unit when Linda, a unit nurse, assisted by Janet Rankin, the participant observer, discharges a patient who is still feeling pain and nausea, sending her off with a disposable basin in case she needs to vomit in the car on the way home.

> We use these observations as an entry point to explore how Linda and Janet's nursing work— not optimal nursing care—happened as it did. We now ask, How it is that two competent and experienced nurses would make these choices

about nursing care? . . . If Linda and Janet's practice is *not* organized by or oriented to professional codes and nursing standards, what *is* its organizing principle or focus? (Rankin & Campbell, 2006, pp. 48–47)

Opening up this entry point leads to an examination of the hospital's computer-based technology of knowledge that tracks patients and assigns them to beds in ways that intend maximum efficient utilization of hospital resources. Rankin and Campbell (2006) describe the new forms of visibility this creates and how it restructures the ways hospital personnel can think and know about their work, as well as the pressures and disjunctures that arise for nurses working at the interface between the virtual hospital in which beds are assigned and actual units filled with real patients. The analysis traces the information produced by this patient-tracking system in another direction as well: Data are sent beyond the hospital to a centralized agency that collects similar information from other hospitals, which is then used both to establish standard reporting categories and to compare hospitals in terms of their resource use. This sets up relations of accountability (linked to funding) that orient managers to textual measures of hospital efficiency. Their managerial work then attempts to establish information and management practices that will show up in the texts as increased efficiency. Rankin and Campbell focus in subtle detail on the standardized forms of knowledge and representation that carry this work, as well as on the ways they are deployed by people in actual situations.

Rankin and Campbell (2006) also show how nursing discourses are aligning with managerial discourses, thereby coordinating nurses' consciousness in new ways. For example, in an analysis of professional and scholarly nursing texts, they explore how certain key concepts are coming to work in a double-sided way. Terms such as *efficiency* and *quality of care* have long been used in professional nursing discourses to describe

embodied aspects of nursing work under the nurse's control and assessed with reference to nursing standards (e.g., "efficient" nurses do not make two trips to the linen cart when one would do). Now they operate in managerial discourses, where they refer to managerial objects created in texts: "efficiency" is found in commensurable measures of resource allocation, and "quality of care" is discovered through measures of the numbers of patients readmitted after discharge and the results of patient-satisfaction surveys (which Rankin and Campbell also examine). Current nursing texts teach student nurses to take up these managerial relevances as their own professional nursing standards. "Nurses . . . are learning to take seriously their own responsibility to act in ways that accommodate and advance a hospital's cost savings" (p. 149).

In their conclusion Rankin and Campbell (2006) argue that "[i]nformation is a social product and how it does or does not conform to what it purports to represent can and must be examined" (p. 182)—especially in an arena such as health care where work processes with serious, life-or-death consequences are powerfully coordinated through technologies of knowledge. They call for more research into the social organization of information in health care and attention to the (often unintended) ways "such textual products may accomplish . . . ruling purposes but otherwise fail people and, moreover, obscure that failure" (p. 182). They encourage nurses to speak out from their experiential knowledge of what they see happening in the places where they work.

In a brief summary I cannot do justice to Rankin and Campbell's wide-ranging, complex, and many-layered analysis, but I have tried to highlight some of its methodological and analytic features that are distinctive of institutional ethnography. There is a clear starting place in the embodied work of hospital nurses, and the research takes their standpoint, studying not them but the translocal relations that organize the conditions of their work and, consequently, the care they can give their patients. Rankin and Campbell (2006) conduct their investigations using observation, interviews, and the examination of texts and textual processes; they also draw on their own experiences of participation in the health care system. Their analysis focuses on socially organized forms of knowledge and is highly attentive to language and discourse. It does not blame managers or impute some kind of vague "managerial ideology"; rather, Rankin and Campbell examine the relations of accountability that managers work in, which pull them into national processes of standardization, comparison, and control. They focus on the break between text-based managerial knowledge of hospital activities and the kind of experiential knowledge that arises for people—patients, nurses, and other staff—in the world of lived illness, bodies, and material beds. They are urgently concerned about health care and present their research as showing the kinds of things that need to be examined in order to reform health care in more humane ways.

Institutional Ethnography and Constructionist Research

If constructionism is considered as a broad collection of varied research approaches that share a nonpositivist epistemology and a keen interest in social practices of knowledge, meaning, and representation, it might seem clear that institutional ethnography belongs somewhere in that set. Institutional ethnography studies the forms of knowledge through which people and situations are represented (constituted) in ways that render them institutionally actionable. What could be more constructionist than that? Yet institutional ethnography is not formulated, either by Dorothy Smith or by other institutional ethnographers, as a type of social constructionism. Some institutional ethnographers do incorporate constructionist language into their analyses (e.g., Griffith,

2006; Kinsman, 2000), but institutional ethnographers describe their overall projects as examining the social *organization* of X rather than the social *construction* of X (e.g., Campbell & Manicom, 1995; DeVault, 1991; Eastwood, 2005; Weigt, 2006). The notion of social organization[4] better reflects the core ontological focus on coordination, the ongoing, routine processes in which people are active, and the actualities where their experience takes shape. It includes what the notion of construction makes visible (how things are made knowable and speakable), but it throws a wider analytic light (what happens in people's lives when the knowable/speakable is constructed in this way). Institutional ethnography is a broader project than (most) social constructionism.

It is not an accidental development that institutional ethnography avoids claiming affiliation with the category label of constructionism. From the beginning, Dorothy Smith has positioned institutional ethnography as independent of allegiance to any specific school or approach: "Once we are free from the constraints of belonging to and subordinating our investigation to the dictates of one of [sociology's] 'schools' and governing what can be found by its conventions, we can draw on what comes to hand in our cartography" (2002, p. 22). In developing institutional ethnography, Smith drew appreciatively but selectively from Marx, as already mentioned, but also from George Herbert Mead (1962), Alfred Schutz (1964), Maurice Merleau-Ponty (1962), Harold Garfinkel (1967), Michel Foucault (1972), V. N. Voloshinov (1973), and Mikhail M. Bakhtin (1981, 1986), among others. Like an Independent member of the legislature whose shifting alliances are rooted in the concerns of her constituency, Smith's approach to other theorists and schools is grounded in her commitment to inquiry that starts with actual people in the actualities of their lives. What needs to be explored, from that standpoint, should not be limited to whatever segment or type of activity a particular school or approach knows how to make visible. Rather, inquiry starts from what is happening that is a puzzle or problem to people and then draws on whatever theoretical or analytic strategies are (or can be made) ontologically compatible and that help the researcher to trace out and map the social relations that are producing what is happening. Thus calling institutional ethnography a variant of social constructionism would obscure institutional ethnography's distinctive features. It starts in a different place and aims at a different analytic goal from most constructionist research, although the two share many empirical interests and analytic strategies.

Let me give some examples of these convergences and divergences by considering institutional ethnography in relation to the stream of constructionist research that studies social problems and public claims-making activities. Research in this stream analyzes the way social movements, media coverage, professional discourses, and policy processes work to establish the existence and nature of a particular social problem as a warrant for action. (For some recent examples, see Herda-Rapp, 2003; Parnaby, 2003; Robinson, 2002.) Institutional ethnography as a project of inquiry studies much more than the construction of social problems, as earlier examples will have shown; however, many studies do bring into view institutional relations in which public advocacy and claimsmaking are going on. These may become focal in the analysis, as in Gillian Walker's (1990) study of the conceptual practices through which the feminist activist issue of "women battering" was introduced into public discourse and then reworked into the policy and service object of "family violence." A frequent topic in institutional ethnography is the way certain people and their circumstances come to be viewable as some kind of problem from within the relevancies of ruling, although in this case the analytic focus is usually on the documents and practices that carry the concept of the "problem" into local settings. As Dorothy Smith (1993) argues, "social problem" is best

viewed as a coordinative device that "articulates expression of local experience to public text-mediated discourse, creating standardized interpretive practices applying across multiple settings" (p. 343). For example, Alison Griffith (2006) examines the concept of the "single-parent family" as it organizes the relationship of single parents with their children's schools. Her analysis looks at the way the concept is pursued in scholarly research and media discourse; she also draws on interviews with teachers and school administrators to explore how they use the concept to talk about and work with particular local children and families in ways that locate them as instances of a general phenomenon. What makes Griffith's analysis characteristic of institutional ethnography is the starting place in the standpoint of single parents, whose experience of being defined as different and defective generates the situation to be explained, and the focus not just on how teachers take up the concept of "single parents" at the level of the local school but also on the ways the concept is used in text-mediated administrative work processes, such as those that allocate funding to schools on the basis of standardized types of students.

When it comes to the treatment of social and advocacy movements, there are noticeable differences between institutional ethnography and constructionist research. Constructionist research would typically focus on the way advocacy organizations frame issues and make public claims (e.g., Einwohner & Spencer, 2005; McMullan & Eyles, 1999); it would be positioned as contributing to the sociological study of social movements or claimsmaking activities. Institutional ethnographers have different analytic goals. Some institutional ethnographers pursue their research as participants in social movements or advocacy organizations; their goal is not to study the social movement but to inform advocacy efforts by producing detailed descriptions of institutional processes that are shaping the circumstances the advocacy addresses. The work of

George Smith (1990) offers strong examples of the deployment of institutional ethnography within political activism. For example, in response to a series of police raids of gay bathhouses in the early 1980s, Smith (1988) studied the process through which undercover police established the grounds for the raids as legitimate police business. Later, working as an AIDS activist, Smith (1995) studied the routine organization of the government process for granting expedited access to experimental drugs. Both of these investigations took the standpoint of people in marginalized positions: gay men arrested and publicly "outed"; people dying of AIDS who could not get quick access to experimental drugs. Smith's research sought to extend the knowledge that activists had of the text-mediated institutional processes that produced the situations of trouble their work addressed, so that they could decide where to focus their advocacy efforts in order to be more effective in bringing about change. Analyses of claimsmaking strategies can be useful to activists, of course, but it is also crucial to understand how behind-the-scenes institutional processes work, as this is usually where change needs to happen. (For other institutional ethnographies that seek to extend rather than study the knowledge of activists and advocacy groups, see Eastwood, 2005; Pence, 2002; Turner, 1995, 2006.)

Conclusion

This introduction to institutional ethnography is necessarily brief and selective. Its purpose has been to explain enough about institutional ethnography to make clear why institutional ethnography belongs in this section of the *Handbook*: It is not constructionism but has a strong family resemblance in parts; it is critical of the limitations of constructionist research but shares many empirical interests. Institutional ethnography is a distinct project, an alternative "sociology for people," as Dorothy Smith calls it.

It offers a method of inquiry for investigating relations of coordination and control from a standpoint in people's everyday actualities. It seeks to extend the scope of people's working knowledge, with the potential to inform projects of advocacy and social change. The goal is to explicate the social organization of everyday actualities in a way that makes visible the linkages across settings as these occur through text and language and in what people do. As a project of inquiry, institutional ethnography includes attention to the social construction of knowledge, especially in modes of ruling, but it goes beyond studying the "what" and "how" of construction to map the way particular practices of knowledge organize the translocal relations that shape the actualities of our lives. In so doing, it seeks to "reorganize the social relations of knowledge of the social" (D. E. Smith, 2005, p. 29)—in other words, to change the way we investigate our world, so we can change our world.

● Notes

1. See Campbell and Manicom (1995), Campbell and Gregor (2002), DeVault (2006), DeVault and McCoy (2002), G. W. Smith (1990), and a recent collection on the practice of doing institutional ethnography edited by D. E. Smith (2006). Four journals have produced special issues highlighting institutional ethnographic research (*Social Problems*, 43(3), 2006; *Journal of Sociology and Social Welfare*, 30(1), 2003; *Studies in Cultures, Organizations and Society*, 7(2), 2001; and *Human Studies*, 21, 1998). There is an Institutional Ethnography Division in the Society for the Study of Social Problems, a U.S.-based association of researchers that meets annually. Current and back issues of the division newsletter are available on the SSSP website (*www.sssp1.org*).

2. Reflexive forms of research frequently invite researchers to engage in self-scrutiny to discover the biases stemming from their personal history and to recognize how their positioning within relations of gender, race, and class shapes their perceptions. Institutional ethnographers, although not unsympathetic to this kind of awareness, are usually more concerned about recogniz-

ing the ways they might be relying on conceptual frameworks that import managerial or administrative relevances into their research; see McCoy, 2006.

3. Dorothy Smith (1987) explains that her "generous" notion of work was originally inspired by feminist campaigns in the 1960s and 1970s to raise awareness that all the unpaid work women do in the home is actually a critical element sustaining modern relations of capital. I also see a parallel to Alfred Schutz's (1964) notion of "the everyday world of working" in which we are located, in our bodies, and which we "gear into" through our purposive actions (1964, pp. 226–227).

4. The term *social organization* is, of course, not unique to institutional ethnography; almost all of institutional ethnography's orienting concepts are drawn from existing sociological vocabularies but used in distinctive ways. In Bakhtin's (1981) terms, they take on a new "taste" (p. 292) when spoken by institutional ethnographers.

● References

Andre-Bechely, L. (2005). *Could it be otherwise? Parents and the inequalities of public school choice*. New York: Routledge.

Bakhtin, M. M. (1981). *The dialogic imagination* (M. Holquist, Ed., C. Emerson & M. Holquist, Trans.). Austin, TX: University of Texas Press.

Bakhtin, M. M. (1986). *Speech genres and other late essays* (C. Emerson & M. Holquist, Eds., V. W. McGee, Trans.). Austin, TX: University of Texas Press.

Brown, D. (2006). Working the system: Re-thinking the role of mothers and the reduction of "risk" in child protection work. *Social Problems, 53*, 352–370.

Campbell, M., & Gregor, F. (2002). *Mapping social relations: A primer in doing institutional ethnography*. Aurora, Ontario, Canada: Garamond.

Campbell, M., & Manicom, A. (Eds.). (1995). *Knowledge, experience and ruling relations: Studies in the social organization of knowledge*. Toronto, Ontario, Canada: University of Toronto Press.

De Montigny, G. A. J. (1995). *Social working: An ethnography of front-line practice*. Toronto, Ontario, Canada: University of Toronto Press.

DeVault, M. L. (1991). *Feeding the family: The social organization of caring as gendered work*. Chicago: University of Chicago Press.

DeVault, M. L. (2006). Introduction: What is institutional ethnography? *Social Problems, 53*, 294–298.

DeVault, M. L., & McCoy, L. (2002). Institutional ethnography: Using interviews to investigate ruling relations. In J. F. Gubrium & J. A. Holstein (Eds.), *Hand-*

book of interview research: Context and method (pp. 751–776). Thousand Oaks, CA: Sage.

Diamond, T. (1992). *Making gray gold: Narratives of nursing home care*. Chicago: Chicago University Press.

Eastwood, L. (2005). *The social organization of policy: An institutional ethnography of UN forest deliberations*. New York: Routledge.

Einwohner, R., & Spencer, J. W. (2005). "That's how we do things here": Local culture and the construction of sweatshops and anti-sweatshop activism in two campus communities. *Sociological Inquiry, 75*, 249–272.

Foucault, M. (1972). *The archeology of knowledge* (A. M. Sheridan Smith, Trans.). New York: Pantheon.

Garfinkel, H. (1967). *Studies in ethnomethodology*. Cambridge, UK: Polity Press.

Grace, L. (2006). *Language, power and ruling relations in vocational education and training*. Unpublished doctoral thesis, Deakin University, Australia.

Griffith, A. I. (2006). Constructing single-parent families for schooling: Discovering an institutional discourse. In D. E. Smith (Ed.), *Institutional ethnography as practice* (pp. 127–138). Lanham, MD: Rowman & Littlefield.

Griffith, A. I., & Smith, D. E. (2004). *Mothering for schooling*. New York: Routledge Falmer.

Herda-Rapp, A. (2003). The social construction of local school violence threats by the news media and professional organizations. *Sociological Inquiry, 73*, 545–574.

Kinsman, G. (2000). Constructing gay men and lesbians as national security risks, 1950–1970. In G. Kinsman, D. Buse, & M. Steedman (Eds.), *Whose national security? Canadian state surveillance and the creation of enemies* (pp. 143–153). Toronto, Ontario, Canada: Between the Lines Press.

Luken, P. C., & Vaughan, S. (2006). Standardizing childrearing through housing. *Social Problems, 53*, 299–331.

Manicom, A. (1995). What's class got to do with it? Class, gender, and teachers' work. In M. Campbell & A. Manicom (Eds.), *Knowledge, experience, and ruling relations: Studies in the social organization of knowledge* (pp. 135–148). Toronto, Ontario, Canada: University of Toronto Press.

Marx, K., & Engels, F. (1981). *The German ideology* (C. J. Arthur, Ed.). New York: International.

McCoy, L. (1998). Producing "what the deans know": Textual practices of cost accounting and the restructuring of post-secondary education. *Human Studies, 21*, 395–418.

McCoy, L. (2006). Keeping the institution in view: Working with interview accounts of everyday experience. In D. E. Smith (Ed.), *Institutional ethnography as practice* (pp. 109–126). Lanham, MD: Rowman & Littlefield.

McMullan, J., & Eyles, C. (1999). Risky business: An analysis of claimsmaking in the development of an

Ontario drinking water objective for tritium. *Social Problems, 46*, 294–311.

Mead, G. H. (1962). *Mind, self and society: From the standpoint of a social behaviorist* (C. W. Morris, Ed.). Chicago: University of Chicago Press.

Merleau-Ponty, M. (1962). *Phenomenology of perception.* (C. Smith, Trans.). London: Routledge & Kegan Paul.

Mykhalovskiy, E. (2003). Evidence-based medicine: Ambivalent reading and clinical recontextualization of science. *Health, 7*, 331–352.

Mykhalovskiy, E., & McCoy, L. (2002). Troubling ruling discourses of health: Using institutional ethnography in community-based research. *Critical Public Health, 12*, 17–37.

Olsen, L. (1995). Record keeping practices: Consequences of accounting demands in a public clinic. *Qualitative Sociology, 18*, 45–70.

Parnaby, P. (2003). Disaster through dirty windshields: Law, order and Toronto's squeegee kids. *Canadian Journal of Sociology, 28*(3), 281–307.

Pence, P. (2001). Safety for battered women in a textually mediated legal system. *Studies in Cultures, Organizations, and Societies, 7*(2), 199–229.

Rankin, J. M., & Campbell, M. L. (2006). *Managing to nurse: Inside Canada's health care reform.* Toronto, Ontario, Canada: University of Toronto Press.

Robinson, E. E. (2002). Community frame analysis in Love Canal: Understanding messages in a contaminated community. *Sociological Spectrum, 22*, 139–169.

Schutz, A. (1964). *Collected papers: II. Studies in social theory* (A. Brodersen, Ed.). The Hague, The Netherlands: Martinus Nijhoff.

Smith, D. E. (1987). *The everyday world as problematic: A sociology for women.* Toronto, Ontario, Canada: University of Toronto Press.

Smith, D. E. (1991a). *The conceptual practices of power: A feminist sociology of knowledge.* Toronto, Ontario, Canada: University of Toronto Press.

Smith, D. E. (1991b). *Texts, facts and femininity: Exploring the relations of ruling.* London: Routledge.

Smith, D. E. (1993). Literacy and business: "Social problems" as social organization. In J. A. Holstein & G. Miller (Eds.), *Reconsidering social constructionism: Debates in social problems theory* (pp. 327–346). New York: Aldine de Gruyter.

Smith, D. E. (1999). *Writing the social: Critique, theory, and investigations.* Toronto, Ontario, Canada: University of Toronto Press.

Smith, D. E. (2002). Institutional ethnography. In T. May (Ed.), *Qualitative research in action* (pp. 17–52). London: Sage.

Smith, D. E. (2005). *Institutional ethnography: A sociology for people.* Lanham, MD: Altamira Press.

Smith, D. E. (Ed.). (2006). *Institutional ethnography as practice.* Lanham, MD: Altamira Press.

Smith, G. W. (1988). Policing the gay community: An inquiry into textually mediated relations. *International Journal of Sociology and the Law, 16*, 163–183.

Smith, G. W. (1990). Political activist as ethnographer. *Social Problems, 37*, 629–648.

Smith, G. W. (1995). Accessing treatments: Managing the AIDS epidemic in Ontario. In M. Campbell & A. Manicom (Eds.), *Knowledge, experience, and ruling relations: Studies in the social organization of knowledge* (pp. 18–34). Toronto, Ontario, Canada: University of Toronto Press.

Townsend, E. (1998). *Good intentions overruled: A critique of empowerment in the routine organization of mental health services.* Toronto, Ontario, Canada: University of Toronto Press.

Turner, S. M. (1995). Rendering the site developable: Texts and local government decision making in land use planning. In M. Campbell & A. Manicom (Eds.), *Knowledge, experience, and ruling relations: Studies in the social organization of knowledge* (pp. 234–248). Toronto, Ontario, Canada: University of Toronto Press.

Turner, S. M. (2006). Mapping institutions as work and texts. In D. E. Smith (Ed.), *Institutional ethnography as practice* (pp. 139–161). Lanham, MD: Rowman & Littlefield.

Voloshinov, V. N. (1973). *Marxism and the philosophy of language* (L. Matejka & I. R. Titunik, Trans.). Cambridge, MA: Harvard University Press.

Walby, K. (2005). How closed-circuit television surveillance organizes the social: An institutional ethnography. *Canadian Journal of Sociology, 30*, 189–214.

Walker, G. A. (1990). *Family violence and the women's movement: The conceptual politics of struggle.* Toronto, Ontario, Canada: University of Toronto Press.

Weigt, J. (2006). Compromises to carework: The social organization of mothers' experiences in the low-wage labour market after welfare reform. *Social Problems, 53*, 332–351.

CHAPTER 37

Ethnomethodology as a Provocation to Constructionism

● **Michael Lynch**

James Holstein and Jaber Gubrium, in their introduction to this *Handbook*, describe constructionism as a "mosaic"—suggesting a composition made up of discontinuous but systematically placed elements. To this I would add that the mosaic shows signs of wear and tear: cracks, missing tiles, and faded outlines, as well as patches and other traces of a history of repair. Repaired sections not only attempt to restore the original but also express ambitions to improve on outmoded designs and themes. Considered along these lines, ethnomethodology is something less than a mosaic: the patchwork dominates, borders are indistinct, and large sections have never been completed. To compare the two and discuss their relationship is a hopeless task, especially if we consider the job to be a matter of surveying two well-defined fields in an effort

to identify boundaries and overlapping territories. Instead of a survey, I offer a provocation. Ethnomethodology is sometimes considered to be a constructionist approach, given the repeated emphasis in research throughout the field on the local *production* of order and the *practical achievement* of social structures. However, I believe that for present purposes, an understanding of ethnomethodology (my understanding, though certainly not mine alone) can serve as leverage for identifying a deep and continuing challenge to constructionism. This challenge is, or at least should be, familiar by now, but it is often ignored, summarily dismissed, or passed over. The challenge sometimes rides under the banner of reflexivity,[1] but it is broader than the sometimes hyperintellectualized debates about reflexivity would suggest. Insisting that it should

715

be addressed can provoke frustration, and even anger, possibly signaling that proponents of constructionism have never met the challenge and perhaps will never meet it in a convincing or effective way.

Ethnomethodology is a research program that investigates practical actions and language use in ordinary and professional settings (some approaches to ordinary language analysis, semiotics, and discourse analysis also do so). Of particular interest for ethnomethodologists is how professional (including academic) methods of reasoning, argumentation, and explanation relate to ordinary "common sense" methods. When examining that relationship, ethnomethodologists suspend judgment on the supposed superiority of professional methods over their vulgar counterparts, and they attempt to show how, in any given case, such methods constitute social orders. The orientation toward professional (including scientific) methods is one of indifference rather than skepticism or rivalry.

Constructionism is a way of thinking, or a form of argument and explanation, that appears in numerous social science and humanities fields. Sometimes prefaced by the words *social* or *cultural*, constructionism has taken hold in an array of social science and humanities fields, and there are numerous variants of it. A common, if not universal, feature of constructionism is skepticism—sometimes outright hostility—toward established facts, events, policies, or doctrines that are widely held as objective, rational, or immutable. Constructionist analysis, or deconstruction, often attempts to elucidate (or "unmask") contingent origins, sources of fallibility, and potential alternatives that are hidden by the sense of inevitability associated with the subject of investigation.

The provocation I discuss arises from identification of constructionist language and argument as an ethnomethodological phenomenon; as a recurrent form of situated language use that has a constitutive role in many ordinary and professional settings. Rather than aligning with constructionist arguments, ethnomethodologists locate such arguments within everyday and professional circumstances of action. This particular way of reframing constructionist arguments identifies a conundrum for academic researchers who adopt constructionism as a general interpretative perspective. The conundrum arises from the ease with which the general perspective can be confused with particular socially located arguments, and it also implicates efforts to use constructionist arguments as rhetorical leverage for political causes.

Construction Is a Word

C. Wright Mills (1940) pointed out in an early article that *motive* is a word. At the time, *motive* was a key conceptual term in sociology and social psychology, but, as Mills observed, it had a familiar place in legal and in ordinary language use long before being included in the sociological glossary. Mills's observation was so obvious as to be (almost) beneath mention, but it had important consequences for considering the way social scientists deploy *motive* as an explanatory term (see also Winch, 1958). Mills argued that social scientists' analytic usage of *motive* is readily confused with familiar, often highly partisan, discursive practices of casting blame, making excuses, or justifying problematic conduct. Rather than seeking to establish a concept of *motive* as a neutral explanatory term that remains uncontaminated by vulgar usage, he recommended a shift in sociological perspective to examining how vocabularies of motive come into play in recurrent situations of human conduct.

A similar point can be made about variants of the word *construction*, such as *made* or *manufactured*. Such words are, of course, central to constructionist approaches that have taken hold in the past 40 years in numerous social science and humanities fields. Constructionism might even be called a social movement, though one that is largely confined to academic communities. Constructionist research is not all of one piece, but in many cases the burden taken up is to show that something that initially seems firmly established, natural, and real, indifferent to cultural context and political machination, actually is the product of prior and/ or ongoing "construction." Moreover, it is often suggested that, having been constructed, the thing in question can be reconstructed or re-formed (Hacking, 1999). Though the term is sometimes endowed with arcane significance in academic research, *construction* also is an ordinary word. In many situations, its use is uncontroversial: to say that a building, concrete sidewalk, or jet engine is constructed is merely to point out that it is an artifact, owing its existence to human design and manufacture. When *construction* is turned into an academic concept and scholarly banner (an *ism*), it remains shadowed by ordinary language use. Ian Hacking (1999) points out that, in order to provoke interest, a constructionist argument must show that *what* was constructed or *how* it was constructed is somehow nonobvious. Perhaps one reason that constructionism has turned out to be such a provocative theme in the sociology of scientific knowledge is that scientific facts, theoretical laws, and entities such as microbes, gravity waves, and quarks are widely held to be objective. Once they are established, natural scientific facts, laws, and entities are assumed to be independent of the techniques, instruments, calculations, and theoretical inferences that disclose, analyze, and demonstrate their existence. Scientists and mathematicians explicitly speak of the construction of proofs, theories, models, experiments, and cell lines, and they recognize that inadvertent constructions (research artifacts, akin to noise in electronic data) frequently confound laboratory research; but for a sociologist of science to assert that things that are presumed to be objective are actually "constructed" is to provoke argument, and even hostility and indignation, from scientists and others who subscribe to their existence. In the common idioms of the laboratory, to say that something presumed to be objective is really constructed is to question the technical competence, or even the honesty, of the researchers who subscribe to its objectivity. To say that all scientific results are constructed might seem to spare specific results from particularistic doubt, but it also can be heard to impugn all of science. A series of hostile exchanges in the 1990s about the (alleged) construction of scientific knowledge was commonly called the "science wars," and although the publicity such "wars" drew to social and cultural studies of science was often highly negative, it also may have enhanced the profile of the field (in terms of the "all publicity is good publicity" maxim). Proponents of social and cultural studies repeatedly insisted that they were not arguing or insinuating that scientific results are false or dubious, but such qualifications were often dismissed as a matter of waffling or shifting between stronger and weaker claims depending on the audience.[2]

Arguments about the construction of technological artifacts and built environments initially would seem to be nonstarters: Who would think otherwise than that bicycles, automobiles, refrigerators, computers, plastic materials, and interstate highway systems are "constructed"? However, as Wiebe Bijker, Thomas P. Hughes, and Trevor Pinch (1987) established, the issue was not *that* such things are constructed but that their construction does not necessarily progress along lines of rational efficiency. The adoption of a novel design, a choice between alternative models, and the automation of what had been a manual human task does not simply yield to inherent laws of efficiency; it expresses political, cultural, and other networks of association, market demands, and hierarchical powers. It became popular to argue that technology is politics by other means or that technology itself *is* political (Latour, 1987; Winner, 1986). Again, however, such arguments are readily confused with particularistic claims and counterclaims made by engineers, media analysts, and popular critics of specific technologies and technological systems. It is common for engineers whose designs fail to be implemented to ascribe the failure to "politics" or for critics of entities such as the U.S. Food and Drug Administration to complain that economic interests influence the approval of drugs that offer no inherent advantage over competitive products and that may also have potentially harmful side effects (Angell & Relman, 2002). Such criticisms are part of the give-and-take of public controversies about science and technology; controversies that go on with or without input from constructionist science and technology studies (STS). Nevertheless, the vocabularies and modes of argumentation used by participants in such controversies are readily confused with the analytic positions espoused by constructionist sociologists.

Readers familiar with long-standing arguments in the social problems and sociology of mental illness fields should recognize a family resemblance between constructionist arguments in STS and various arguments associated with antipsychiatry and with labeling and societal reaction theories of deviance. Such arguments were precursors for current lines of research on the construction of social problems and of disease categories. Once again, analytic arguments and terms were readily confused with debates within the fields under analysis. In some instances the arguments were explicitly directed against established medical doctrines and social control institutions. For example, Thomas Szasz (1974) and Herbert Fingarette (1988) explicitly disputed the validity of entire medical domains ("mental illness") and particular disease categories ("alcoholism"), calling them "myths." Szasz's arguments gave rise to fierce debate, both within and about psychiatry. His arguments and examples seemed to resonate with those in sociological theories of deviance—the so-called "labeling" and "societal reaction" perspectives espoused by Howard Becker (1963) and Thomas Scheff (1963). However, Szasz's arguments rested on medical realist

assumptions: He asserted that disease categories such as "hysteria" are pseudoconditions that only mimic genuine diseases involving insults to the body, infections, toxins, tumors, and the like. Far from treating all disease categories as sociohistorical constructs, he presumed the validity of established illness categories while questioning their "mental" counterparts. More recent sociological arguments about the construction of disease categories such as "conduct disorder" and "ego-dystonic homosexuality" (Kirk & Kutchins, 1992), ADHD (Conrad & Potter, 2000), and "female sexual dysfunction" (Fishman, 2004) bring other elements into play, such as the influence of third-party insurance coverage and pharmaceutical company marketing, but they also call some, but not all, disease categories into question. Although constructionist positions often gesture toward antirealist philosophy, arguments about the construction of specific disorders are readily assimilated into realist arguments that dispute the authentic medical basis for the particular disease categories in question. The edginess of constructionist analysis thus depends on its resemblance to ordinary lines of criticism within the fields studied while at the same time remaining somewhat aloof from the professional battlefields in which particularistic disputes take place.

The banal observation that *construction* and its analytic cognates are *words* and that such words have common use in various contexts of professional and nonprofessional conduct and dispute invites a shift in perspective akin to the one Mills recommends in his discussion of *motive*. Mills, of course, was not an ethnomethodologist, nor was Peter Winch (1958). However, their arguments in favor of shifting from using ordinary language concepts as names for explanatory variables in causal models to examining pragmatic uses of such concepts in everyday situations of conduct has strong affinity with ethnomethodology (Coulter, 1973; Sharrock & Watson, 1984). Ethnomethodology also has some affinity with a particular approach to discourse analysis that stresses the situated, rhetorical uses of knowledge claims (Gilbert & Mulkay, 1984; Mulkay, Potter, & Yearley, 1983; Potter, 1996), and, indeed, discourse analysis owes some debt to ethnomethodology.

Ethnomethodology, discourse analysis, and other orientations to situated action are often placed under the constructionist umbrella. The fit is unremarkable when constructionism is defined as a research program that looks into the way concerted actions produce stable intersubjective orders. The relationship with ethnomethodology— and with some lines of discourse analysis— becomes more contentious when constructionism is treated as a general theory of knowledge, or even an ontology. Rather than deploying the argumentative tropes associated with *construction* and its cognates to vanquish real and imagined realists, positivists, or objectivists, ethnomethodologists and discourse analysts treat constructionist arguments as what G. Nigel Gilbert and Michael Mulkay (1984) call a "repertoire" that is used occasionally and circumstantially. In STS and social problems research, questions about the uses of such discourse have been addressed in critical arguments and exchanges about "reflexivity" (Pollner, 1974; Woolgar, 1988; Woolgar & Pawluch, 1985). Reflexivity is itself a problematic concept, and it is used tendentiously to advocate or criticize a wide variety of sociological positions (Ashmore, 1989; Lynch, 2000).

Constructionism as a Constitutive Discourse

The circularity signaled by the term *reflexivity* recalls the *tu quoque* refutation that is so often leveled against relativism in philosophy and social studies of science. Simply stated, that argument asserts that epistemological relativism refutes itself because any general assertion of the position contradicts the premise that all positions are relative to particular situations and standpoints. A variant

in sociology of science is that a relativist analysis of natural science cannot simultaneously hold, without contradiction, that it is grounded in (social) science. Because constructionism is often affiliated with relativism about natural scientific "beliefs" (indicated by the substitution of the term *scientific belief* for *scientific knowledge* and/or by the plural term *knowledges*), the reflexive conundrum for constructionists is how to assert their position without begging the question of why anyone would take that position rather than another, equally (in)valid, one.

In the social problems literature, a critical discussion of societal reaction theories of deviance by Melvin Pollner (1974) and a later critique of the "construction of social problems" perspective by Steve Woolgar and Dorothy Pawluch (1985) both point to what appears to be a contradiction. In the former case, Pollner targets a fourfold typology developed by Howard Becker (1963, p. 20).

	Obedient Behavior	Rule-Breaking Behavior
Perceived as Deviant	FALSELY ACCUSED	PURE DEVIANT
Not Perceived as Deviant	NORMAL	SECRET DEVIANT

The contradiction Pollner identifies is between the antirealist, nominalist conception of deviance in labeling or societal reaction theory and the realist way it is articulated. Labeling theorists propose that deviance is in the eyes of the (collective) beholder rather than being inherent in particular acts. Accordingly, as a public matter, there is no practical difference between the status of a "secret deviant" and that of a "normal" member. However, as Becker's fourfold table illustrates, the sociologist distinguishes the nominal (and moral) status of a person's or group's *actual* behavior (as obedient or rule breaking) from the status assigned to that behavior by relevant social control authorities (the "perception" of the behavior as deviant or not). Such a distinction is not, on the face of it, problematic. We routinely make such judgments when we assert, for example, that O. J. Simpson got away with murder or that a Guantanamo Bay detainee was falsely accused of terrorist activity (or, worse, wrongly incarcerated without being accused). However, the clarity of the typology begins to dissolve when we consider the burden of establishing, independently of any extant forum for adjudicating such matters, whether or not a given accusation was false or that a significant moral or legal rule was violated without a mitigating excuse. Similarly, placement of an action or person into the "normal" category presumes that possibilities for detecting "secret deviance" have been exhausted for that case. If a sociologist were to apply the same skepticism to her own judgments about deviance that she applies to judgments made by police officers, judges, and psychiatrists, she might find that she is in the same boat with them. Or, worse, she might find that she lacks the resources to call witnesses and compel them to testify, and her judgments may seem even more ad hoc and unchecked than the established procedures of a tribunal. The point is not that a sociologist cannot support inferences about actual behavior (or rates of behavior) with independent and reliable evidence but that the labeling theorist's judgment takes the same general form as the deviance-conferring judgments of police, courts, psychiatrists, and ordinary citizens. In other words, the labeling theorist *virtually* participates in the very social process the theory would describe, but instead of describing that constitutive process, the articulation of the theory reiterates it.

Ethnomethodology's focus on constitutive actions would take in the deviance-conferring acts identified by the labeling theorist, but it also would include the labeling theorist's virtual reiteration of such acts, though the latter is likely to be less consequential for establishing what counts as crime, mental disorder, or normality. However, ethnomethodological indifference toward the correct or incorrect status of a given allegation, whether made by an official tribunal or on the basis of sociological study, comes at a heavy cost. The cost is the apparent inability to use a preconception of real conformity or rule breaking to describe and critique extant institutional processes through which persons and actions are categorized as deviant.

Although given new legs by arguments about constructionism, the apparent "problem" of reflexivity and efforts to contend with it have had a long history in the sociology of knowledge. Various efforts to avoid self-contradiction have been tried in the sociology of knowledge, starting with Karl Mannheim's (1936, p. 79) effort to provide a relatively neutral institutional vantage point for a "nonevaluative general total conception of ideology." More recent, and perhaps more convincing, arguments were put forward in the 1980s and 1990s in favor of a sociology of scientific knowledge (Collins, 1985; Collins & Yearley, 1992). Harry Collins recommended a distinction between what he called "empirical" or "methodological" relativism and the philosophical variety, so that the assumption that relativism is total and pervasive would no longer be in play (to some extent, this parallels Mannheim's effort to distinguish "relationism" from "relativism"). The idea is that relativism is a methodological device used for the empirical purpose of investigating a target belief—for example, arguments made by physicists for or against the validity of experimental results purporting to show evidence for the existence of gravity waves. A sociologist who examines the sometimes heated disputes about such results would try to maintain a relativist position, treating both sides equivalently while refraining from judgments about which side is right (as recommended by David Bloor, 1976). The relativism would be circumscribed, however, as it would concern a limited set of questions, such as "Did Joseph Weber's critics definitively disprove his claim to have found experimental evidence for gravity waves?" The relativizing impulse would not extend to the sociologist's characterizations of the scientists involved, the organization of the scientific field, the historical background of the research, and so forth. The validity of such sociological characterizations would be presumed, or in some cases empirically documented. Collins (1985) recognizes that partisans in a controversy produce conflicting "social" characterizations (e.g., judgments about which groups of scientists in the field are competent, honest, central, or marginal), as well as conflicting claims about the "natural" phenomena in question. However, he explicitly allows the sociologist to have a privileged view of these matters by drawing on the expertise that arises from sociological training and empirical research.

The "problem" of reflexivity and its affiliation with relativism and refutations of relativism is most acute when one assumes that reflexivity undermines, destabilizes, or deconstructs tacit agreements and taken-for-granted presumptions about reality. But, as Mannheim (1936) struggled to establish, the idea that a given belief arises from and is sustained by specific ideological and existential conditions does not necessarily imply that the belief is false or even doubtful. Indeed, reflexivity is sometimes treated less as an invitation to fall into an epistemological abyss or travel a vicious circle, and more as a source of insight or even objectivity. Akin to the classic philosophical virtue of self-reflection, reflexivity can be upheld as a situated capacity or methodological skill that enables an academic analyst to make explicit what participants in a social setting take for granted, presume, or systematically hide from themselves and others. In an inversion of the classic identification of truth with elevated hierarchical standing,[3] standpoint theories—best known in the feminist writings of Dorothy Smith (1992) and Sandra Harding (1996)—identify specific reflexive possibilities with membership in oppressed social groupings. Marx's valorization of the proletariat's position is respecified in terms of cultural asymmetries between, for example, the self-avowed objectivity of a dominant (gendered) discourse and the "subjective" life worlds of women and members of minority groups. Harding identifies the subordinate standpoints with a "strong objectivity"—a socially ordered capacity to see (often through suffering the effects of) how the presumed objectivity of elite knowledge is related to particular social interests and agendas.

Both Collins's methodological relativism and the inverted objectivity claimed by standpoint theorists have been criticized for being intellectual exercises that circumvent or truncate reflexivity in a way that is all too advantageous for the theorists in question (Ashmore, 1989; Grint & Woolgar, 1995; Pels, 1996). Woolgar and Pawluch (1985) also made a similar argument about the construction of social problems perspective (Spector & Kitsuse, 1977). The expression "ontological gerrymandering" denotes how focal arguments about the construction of one or another social problem (an alleged crime wave, drug epidemic, or threat to the "nature" of marriage) are set off against a field of realist presumptions about society, culture, and the specific agents involved in defining or promoting the problem. The boundaries between realist presumption and constructivist unpacking tend to shift in a way that bolsters a particular argument, resulting in the contortions signaled by the analogy with a gerrymandered political district.[4] Woolgar and Pawluch's arguments challenged proponents of constructionism to maintain a consistent position. For interlocutors who associate constructionism with a novel, bold, intellectually sophisticated, relativist position and realism with a naive trust in appearances that fails to reflect critically on its assumptions, the challenge was both irresistible and a source of angst (see the debates in Holstein & Miller, 1993). The angst arose from the difficulty of squaring global disavowals of realism with arguments or insinuations that a *constructed* social problem is somehow less real than social control agents and other interested parties make it out to be. But, then, if one assumes that all social problems are constructed, the critical edge gets lost in a discussion of a particular problem. Hacking (1999)—a rare philosopher who has waded into these arguments—addresses the problem by stating that it is impossible (or meaningless) to assume that everything is constructed and that it is necessary to distinguish between socially constructed kinds (for example, culturally or historically bound disease categories such as ADHD or hysteria) and indifferent kinds (categories that remain stable in the face of changing medical fashion and popular interest).[5] He gives schizophrenia as an example of the latter, though that category was one of the primary targets of antipsychiatric and societal reaction theories. Avowed social constructionists often are less forthright than Hacking in specifying what they are willing to hold as real or constructed, and they are liable to accusations of harboring *realism under denial.* However, both in social studies of science and social problems circles, it became common to complain that extreme demands for reflexivity would lead to navel gazing and endless academic arguments that would deflect attention from substantive social problems and processes.

Though an unyielding focus on reflexivity has been criticized for creating an untenable situation in which any attempt to pursue substantive sociological research inevitably collapses into endless internecine debate about the possibilities of knowing anything at all, an alternative research program is in the offing that recalls Mills's recommendation to treat "motive" not as a sociological concept or variable but as a word in a pragmatic discursive *vocabulary* that has constitutive significance in historical and socially located situations of conduct. In other words, to borrow a distinction deployed by ethnomethodologists (Garfinkel & Sacks, 1970; Zimmerman & Pollner, 1970) and later adopted by discourse analysts (Gilbert & Mulkay, 1984), Mills recommended that the pragmatic and situated uses of "motive" accounts should be treated as a sociological *topic,* rather than as a conceptual *resource* for sociological explanations. Accordingly, the

very idea of "objectivity," together with situated efforts to claim, bolster, or undermine the credibility of one or another "standpoint," can be turned into a topic of historical research on the changing meaning of "objectivity" (Daston & Galison, 1992; Porter, 1995), or of ethnographic research on the situated claims, maneuvers, and allegiances that give rise to and stabilize objective discourse. However, unlike constructionist ethnographies, which take up the challenge to unpack the "construction" of facts and to reveal the "artifactual" nature of laboratory objects (Knorr Cetina, 1981; Latour & Woolgar, 1986), ethnomethodological ethnographies treat critical inquiries about facts and accounts of artifact as themselves constitutive features of laboratory practices (Lynch, 1985).

Ethnomethodology

The word *ethnomethodology* was coined by Harold Garfinkel nearly a half-century ago, and yet, as Garfinkel (2002, p. 91) observes, the question What is ethnomethodology? continues to be asked, and answers to that question still tend to be greeted with head scratching. It is less difficult to understand other terms in the *ethno* family, such as *ethnobotany* and *ethnomusicology,* both of which are names for the systematic study of, respectively, indigenous botanical classification systems and culturally specific musical arts and instruments. *Ethnomethodology* may seem more elusive because the term *methodology* is all encompassing. In the case of ethnobotany, Linnaean taxonomies sometimes provide a background matrix for casting into relief the distinctive features of a given "folk" taxonomy. However, there is no comparably stable, authoritative, or detailed notation system that would provide a backdrop for elucidating characteristics of a given "folk" methodology. Moreover, many ordinary methods have no scientific counterpart, and an analyst can be charged with making a category mistake when insisting, for example, that the (ir)rationality of a religious ritual should be exposed through comparison with an (idealized) experimental testing procedure (Winch, 1970). Considered broadly, ethnomethodology encompasses the entire domain of practical actions in a given social system. In contrast to a general theory of social action, it is a program of open-ended investigation of actions in all of their situated varieties, and not a one-size-fits-all scheme of means and ends (Heritage, 1984).

Not surprisingly, ethnomethodology is often identified with the constructionist movement. Garfinkel's *Studies in Ethnomethodology* (1967) was published within a year of Peter Berger and Thomas Luckmann's *Social Construction of Reality* (1966). Both texts explicitly used Alfred Schutz's sociology of the life world to supplement and counteract then-dominant Weberian/Parsonian theories of social action and structure. Both emphasized the constitutive role of concerted actions in the formation and stabilization of recurrent social activities and institutions. However, there also has been significant tension and disagreement between constructionists and ethnomethodologists as those programs developed and transmuted themselves over the past 40 years. Berger and Luckmann's theory of institutionalization followed the classic sociological tradition by distinguishing the objectivity of social institutions from that of physical phenomena. They were content to assume that natural things are independent of human consciousness, and they were more concerned with showing how social institutions begin as subjective realities that depend on human actions to sustain them, but later develop into forms that constrain actions and are encountered as objective facts of life. Rather than undercutting objectivity, Berger and Luckmann defended and articulated the objectivity of social realities.[6] Later lines of constructionist research challenged the objectivity of natural phenomena, such as disease categories and even subatomic particles, arguing that such "natural" kinds could be otherwise and that their factual status depended on social alignments that sustained

the view that they could not be otherwise. Ethnomethodologists expressed little sympathy for a view of construction that would undermine (or, in ethnomethodological terms, *ironicize*) presumed objective facts. In an interview with Norbert Wiley, Garfinkel expressed a preference for "production" over "construction" (Wiley & Garfinkel, 1980), saying that the latter term too often connoted a skeptical aim to unmask the phenomena under investigation. The nominal difference may seem slight, but the exemplary research exhibits a fairly marked programmatic difference: to show how a social phenomenon is produced or achieved does not necessarily threaten its ontological status by showing that it is other than it seems (Button & Sharrock, 1993; Lynch, 1993).

Garfinkel occasionally speaks of "constructive analysis" as a widespread practice in the social sciences. Though he never directly says so, it is clear that he is not referring to the perspective of "constructionism." In fact, constructive analysis is the sort of analytic social science that constructionism often takes as its target and antithesis. Constructive analysis includes any of a variety of research methods in the social and administrative sciences through which a system of indicators, a literary record, or other "signed object" stands proxy for a real-worldly social domain. Analysis of the signed object produces data and findings that are then assigned (with all due qualifications and expressions of modesty) to the real-worldly domain and the actions of its inhabitants. Examples include the coding of interview data or organizational records to render them analytically tractable, the use of fixed-choice questionnaire items and interview protocols to solicit analyzable responses, the use of structured games as methodological proxies for actions in an indefinite range of social settings, and the use of a set of transcription conventions to render audio- or videotape recordings analyzable. By placing such methodic strategies under the rubric of constructive analysis, Garfinkel explicitly disavows any interest in undermining them or improving on their validity. Instead, he proposes a shift from, for example, coding open-ended interview responses as a preliminary analytic procedure to examining *the work* of coding as a constitutive phenomenon in its own right. In such a case, ethnomethodological investigation is paired with constructive analysis; instead of using coded data for methodological purposes, the investigation examines the contingent production of coding. We can note further that constructive analysis is not limited to academic sociology; it is ubiquitous in the organization and maintenance of administrated orders. Garfinkel's stance toward constructive analysis is akin to constructionist or deconstructionist investigations of, for example, how criminal codes are administered by prosecutors and police, how disease categories are deployed in psychiatric evaluations, or how the literary products of inscription devices are analyzed and disseminated in laboratory research. However, he does not suggest that the categories and products of constructive analysis are mythical or otherwise doubtful.[7]

Garfinkel speaks of constructive analysis as an array of sociological practices for rendering a field of phenomena tractable. His focus on sociology owes in part to Garfinkel's background as a research sociologist. As a trained sociologist, he has firsthand familiarity with research in that professional discipline, as well as access to forums and audiences with an interest in sociological methods. However, he also makes clear that constructive analysis is not limited to professional sociology, as variants of it can be found in other academic social sciences and in many administrative programs for registering, tracking, and evaluating individuals, aggregate populations, and systems of activity. (As Michel Foucault's dark explications of administrative disciplines made clear, far from being ineffectual, social engineering has been remarkably successful in constituting the modern world, only it has done so not as applied sociology but as programs of discipline administered in hospitals, asylums, prisons, military organiza-tions, and education and reeducation institutes.)

Constructionist research tends to stir controversy—either deliberately or as a byproduct—by opposing another view that, depending on the case, attributes factual status, objectivity, rationality, or immutability to a phenomenon. The opposing view is sometimes an entire philosophy, such as Platonism about mathematical entities, positivism about physical facts, or technical determinism in the history of technology. At other times a more particular belief or presumption is called to account. The belief in question sometimes is assigned to a diffuse common sense and at other times to established orthodoxies in a specific profession or other social group. Often such orthodoxies became established after a protracted controversy, and in some instances a marginalized opposition continues to press for controversy. Constructionist research may seem to aid the cause of the marginal opposition by suggesting that the orthodox view has a less firm hold on reality than its proponents claim. Analytic translations of "facts" to "beliefs" or "claims" suggest the possibility of continued opposition and dispute. Consequently, constructionist analysis dovetails with campaigns against orthodoxy. There is a large difference, however. Activists and other engaged participants in a controversy not only seek to undermine the factual claims of their opponents, but they also tend to press the case for an alternative set of factual claims. Constructionist researchers, in some respects like journalists, try to treat both sets of factual claims equivalently without subscribing to their inherent truth. Such evenhanded treatment can itself be a source of complaint, and it can be exploited for partisan purposes. However, even the proponents of a marginalized view sometimes express dissatisfaction at how constructionist arguments do not go all the way to endorse their claims. I return to this issue later, in a discussion of the politics of construction.

Ethnomethodological investigations of the production of social order are less readily assimilated within extant efforts to promote controversy. Ethnomethodology has been the subject of heated controversy within sociology, mainly because reflexive ethnomethodological studies of social science methods suggest (or at least seem to suggest) that sociological findings rest on a shaky foundation of commonsense assumptions about the world, combined with ad hoc practices for infusing data with worldly significance. However, such lessons constitute criticisms only when one assumes that sociological methods could somehow get direct access to the world as it is. Garfinkel's assertion that ethnomethodology is *alternate* to constructive analysis can be misunderstood to imply that it is a naturalistic *alternative* that avoids, evades, or transcends the necessity to construct data as a precondition for analysis (Garfinkel & Wieder, 1992). But, as Garfinkel makes clear, it does not set itself up as a competitor; instead, ethnomethodology examines the locally organized work of constructive analysis while being indifferent to the validity and significance of the outcomes of such analysis. The locally situated performance of constructive analysis furnishes ethnomethodology with its subject matter; without constructive analysis, there would be no job for the ethnomethodologist. That job, however, is not competitive with the constructive analyst's effort; instead, it is a matter of describing the practices of constructive analysis in fine detail. Of course, many activities are outfitted with practical literatures, ranging from how-to manuals to highly elaborate methodological treatises. But, again, the ethnomethodologist's job is not to formulate a better how-to manual but to observe and describe the way extant instructions are paired with the moment-to-moment, singular, situationally specific practical actions. At this point, the question may arise: "Well, how does the ethnomethodologist do *that*?" We would face a regress if we were to suppose that what the ethnomethodologist aims to do is to correct a deficiency, or overcome an insufficiency, with extant practical literatures.

The sense in which ethnomethodology is an alternate, but not necessarily an alternative, to constructive analysis is sometimes obscured in sociology because of rivalries between ethnomethodologists and other sociologists. However, the theme of constructive analysis also can be used to describe natural science practices, and without any sense of rivalry. So, for example, laboratory practices can be described as a matter of disciplining specimen materials to render them analyzable—observable, measurable, stable, countable, comparable (Lynch, 1985). For example, in cytology, chromosome counting depends on practices such as squash preparation and karyotyping that separate entangled and overlapping entities, preserve and enhance integral borders, purge fields of junk, and align pairs of chromosomes in rows and columns (Martin, 2005). Such preparatory work is preanalytic and protosemiotic in the sense that it provides a material platform on which number use, naming, classification, and visual imaging depends. To point this out, and to describe it in detail, does not rival or undermine the practices. For academic perspectives that embrace the constructionist banner, confusion can arise, or controversy can be deliberately provoked, from a homology between the general terms of (constructionist) analysis and particular arguments in the field being analyzed over the natural or constructed status of a phenomenon.

The topics of ethnomethodological research are often uncontroversial. For example, the large body of ethnomethodologically informed research on the sequential organization of conversation delves into the regular ways in which participants coordinate their discourse through systematic practices of turn taking, sequentially organized utterances (e.g., greetings and return greetings; sequences of questions and answers), and "repairing" mistakes and infelicities (Sacks, Schegloff, & Jefferson, 1974). Similarly, many of the studies of workplace activities inspired by ethnomethodology examine uncontroversial matters such as the coordination of software code writing (Button & Scharrock, 1998), practices for following instructions (Lynch & Jordan, 1995), and situated performances of observations, experiments, and proofs (Garfinkel, Lynch, & Livingston, 1981; Goodwin, 1995; Livingston, 2006). Controversy sometimes is generated by pitching such studies against established academic theories, some of which have a stronghold in the domains of practice studied. For example, Lucy Suchman's (1987) research on the situated actions of machine users confronts the orthodox tendency in artificial intelligence to stress the causal role of rules, algorithms, and plans over the contingencies of practical use and social interaction. The alternative view in ethnomethodology is that the practical use of rules and related formal resources is not brought about through a mechanical cause-and-effect process; instead, it is organized through contingent actions in which formal structures become embedded in sequences of action in which unformulated knowledge and emergent orders of interaction have a crucial role.

The Politics of Construction

Because of the way social constructionist arguments often seem akin to discourse within a controversy, constructionist research is, or can seem to be, inherently political. However, if constructionism is political, the politics are not necessarily consistent or predictable. As noted earlier, constructive analysis of "orthodox" or "objective" positions partially jibes with opponents' efforts to undermine those positions. It is not surprising, then, that active participants in public controversies sometimes entertain the hope that constructionist research will support their positions with evidence, refined arguments, and academic authority. And, also not surprisingly, many academic analysts have been willing to lend enthusiastic support to activist causes.

Engagement in controversy might seem to require that a researcher must backtrack on some of the supposed tenets of constructionist research. This is most clear in the sociology of scientific knowledge, with its doctrines of symmetry and impartiality, initially formulated by David Bloor (1976) in programmatic statements about the "Strong Programme" in the sociology of knowledge.[8] The "strength" of this program rests in its claim to treat all knowledge—including the most stable parts of science and mathematics—as subjects of social explanation. Explanations would, of course, be attentive to the peculiar mix of persons, groups, doctrines, assumptions, incentives, and interests operating in any given case, but it would not be necessary for a sociologist to establish whether a given item of knowledge was subject to doubt or error before exploring the existential conditions under which it was accepted and used. Following such a research policy, sociologists would give the same basic form of explanation for belief in neo-Darwinian theory among members of some social groups and regional communities as they would for belief in creationist doctrines by others. Authority, influence, socialization, and other aspects of the sociocultural milieu would be available to explain the actions of parties on both sides of the dispute. But, once again, there is a problem with the homology between participants' discourse within a controversy and the form of a social explanation of that controversy. As Gilbert and Mulkay (1984) elucidate in an ethnomethodologically informed analysis of a controversy among biochemists about a proposed mechanism of ion transfer, parties to the dispute discredit their opponents' claims by citing vested interests, authority, blind tradition, experimental contingencies that confound experiments, and other "social" matters, the same parties deploy naturalistic and objectivistic tropes when presenting and justifying the positions with which they agree. To propose that one could then step back from the fray and explain the overall controversy in "social" terms requires a redeployment of partisan discourse that, somehow, neutralizes the skepticism that is (or at least seems to be) implied when a sociologist of science describes participants' just-so statements as "claims" or delves into the conflicting interests and gang-like alignments among members of rival laboratories.

Unlike a "weak" sociology of knowledge that reserves constructionist explanations for disease categories, alleged causal effects, or claims about material entities and facts that are doubtful and contestable, a "strong" sociology of knowledge proposes that *anything* can be shown to be constructed. And so disease categories such as cholera should be no less available for constructionist analysis than more ambiguous and contested disorders such as ADHD; the photoelectric effect should be no less describable as a construction than a psychokinetic effect; an established phenomenon such as "hot" fusion should be no less a construction than "cold" fusion; and the "beliefs" of nuclear physicists would be held equivalent, for analytic purposes, to those of flying saucer cult members. As mentioned earlier, during the 1990s, a controversy—popularly called the "science wars"—broke out when self-proclaimed defenders of Science, Truth, and Reason attacked the "academic left," accusing constructionist science studies of promoting antiscientific views (Gross & Levitt, 1994; Gross, Levitt, & Lewis, 1996). A prime target of criticism was symmetry, which was (mis)understood as a general philosophical position that called all established science into doubt and at the same time assigned equal credibility to the most marginal and dubious beliefs. A common rebuttal to the charge was that a constructionist explanation does not necessarily imply that the thing explained is somehow less (or more) stable or credible than it had been; instead, it gives an account of how the thing became stable and credible. The science wars eventually lost steam, but a more serious political controversy about science emerged in their wake.

The new "science war" is about government and interest group attempts to create the appearance of scientific controversy for political purposes. It includes some of the same defenders of Science and Reason who took part in the earlier fracas, but their opponents are now for the most part identified with the nonacademic right. A capsule summary of what is at stake is presented in a *Doonesbury* cartoon in which "Stevie," a teenager doing a homework assignment, complains, "Drat! These pesky scientific facts won't line up behind my beliefs!" Enter Dr. Nathan Null, White House Situational Science Advisor, who advises Stevie that evolution, global warming, and the effects of tobacco smoke, mercury, and dioxin are all matters of "controversy" and that, as "situational science" teaches us, we should respect both sides of these scientific arguments, "not just the one supported by facts!"[9] Not only was this a dig at the G.W. Bush administration, which was under criticism by the Union of Concerned Scientists and many environmental groups for suppressing, doctoring, or "spinning" science advisory reports that did not support its policies, but it also lambasted the relativistic tendency (usually associated with the cultural left) to translate scientific "facts" into "situated knowledges."

Unlike the science wars of the 1990s, the new science war is not simply an academic dispute between spokespersons for two philosophies of science, realism versus social constructionism. Instead, the defenders of scientific realism (some of whom weighed in during the earlier science wars) are objecting to a *performative* version of constructionism strategically situated within the most powerful government in the world. "Situational science" has itself been situated, and with political effects, but not the effects constructionist sociologists of science had in mind (Latour, 2004). This peculiar condition can be dubbed "ethnomethodological politics," meaning that a version of a general theoretical position (in this case, constructionism) has been turned into a vulgar political tool.

Given what I have said about ethnomethodology, its approach to science, technology, and social problems would seem rather ineffectual as a source of leverage for political critiques and reformist actions. Constructionism might seem more attractive for supporting emancipatory politics because of its homology with arguments that seek to destabilize an opponent's assertions about what is natural, objective, rational, or inevitable. Moreover, the careful documentation and refinement of argument associated with the best constructionist scholarship should offer strong critical resources for activists who hope to promote progressive reforms. However, when treating "construction" as a reflexive ethnomethodological phenomenon, we get a different picture of the politics of construction. As illustrated by the new science wars, constructionist arguments are contingently embedded in courtrooms and other organizational circumstances. Their political effects are not intrinsic to the arguments but relative to audiences and situated machinations. Though associated with the academic left, constructionist arguments can also be used to promote corporate "emancipation" from environmental regulations or to deconstruct "establishment" findings suggesting that smoking causes cancer. In any case, the proponents of a general "school" are well advised to avoid becoming "captives of controversy" (Scott, Richards, & Martin, 1990), and to choose their controversies wisely (cf. Lambert, 2006; Lynch, 2006).

Conclusion

Ethnomethodology challenges constructionism to show how its vocabulary and arguments are more general, credible, and stable than the sort of commonplace argument that disputes the validity of a particular assertion of fact. One possible response to the challenge is to try to transcend it—to operate on a different epistemic plane by making use of special evidence and interpretive procedures or to attempt to gain a severe degree of analytic detachment. There have been

many such efforts in the past, and no doubt there will be more. Another response is to circumscribe it—to limit constructionist analysis to cases that can be shown to be uncertain, retrograde, or possibly harmful. Laborious scholarship would then be used to demonstrate and document just how a given phenomenon can be said to be doubtful, problematic, or unacceptable. Such research, however excellent and convincing it might be, would be part and parcel of the activities or controversies analyzed.

It is doubtful that a single political leaning can be ascribed to ethnomethodology. If anything, the politics associated with it are antiadministrative. By this I do not mean that ethnomethodologists necessarily are hostile to administrators. Instead, the idea is that no amount of foresight or planning will ever be sufficient to guarantee the effective realization of administrative schemes. This lesson applies to reformists no less than to reactionaries. Though it might seem to encourage cynicism and defeatism, that is not necessarily the implication. One implication is that an academic perspective and the studies that give it empirical specificity provide a thin and specialized basis for concerted social actions and political reforms. Social actions and movements call on much broader constituencies and deeper reservoirs of judgment and practice—reservoirs that no social science has plumbed to much depth. The authority of "schools" and academic "perspectives" is not necessarily vacuous but thin; any value they provide is embedded in larger, and largely unfathomed, forms of life.

• Notes

1. The term *reflexivity* enjoys (or, perhaps, suffers) several different uses in academic discussions, some of which contradict others (Lynch, 2000). Harold Garfinkel (1967) was among the first sociologists to use the term systematically, but as he later confesses, with tongue in cheek, "[m]any academic lives were lost or were cut off as cases of arrested development by careful at-

tempts to provide for reflexivity as the name for a general phenomenon" (Garfinkel, 2002, p. 203). He goes on to elaborate a version of reflexivity that, on the face of it, seems mundane, as it would describe, for example, how a particular instruction is embedded within, and an accountable part of, the actions that refer to it and attempt to follow it. A different sense of reflexivity became established as a problem—or, in Steve Woolgar's (1988) terms, a "methodological horror"—in constructionist science studies. This sense of reflexivity was related to the familiar *tu quoque* refutation of relativism: the relativist's general assertions—for example, "all knowledge is relative"—become paradoxical when applied to themselves. The reflexive challenge for constructionism would thus be to account for the "construction" of its own analytic posture without negating it.

2. The "science wars" gave rise to a flurry of books and articles and a huge volume of Internet traffic starting in the early 1990s. Interest abruptly fell off after 2000, as the debates became exhausted and the partisans moved on to other matters. The most notorious publications were Gross and Levitt (1994), Sokal (1996), and Ross (1996). For a conciliatory effort, see Labinger and Collins (2001).

3. Steven Shapin (1994) explicates the social logic through which early modern gentlemen were presumed (especially by themselves) to be trustworthy witnesses. Truth telling and trustworthiness were paramount; so much so that accusing a gentleman of lying was tantamount to challenging him to a duel. In his analysis of Robert Boyle's writings on civility, as well as his experiments, Shapin chronicles how the form of life of gentlemanly society became interwoven with the conduct of experiment. The credibility of an experimental result (especially a surprising result, or one that disturbed orthodoxy) hinged on the credibility of the experimental witness. According to Shapin, Boyle—a relatively *nouveau* gentleman who perhaps exaggerated the virtues associated with the gentlemanly life—devised a "technology of virtual witnessing" that displaced the virtues of modest witnessing into the form of the experimental report.

4. The word *gerrymander* is a satirical term referring to the salamander-like shape of political districts whose lines have been redrawn to the advantage of the political party in charge of the redistricting effort. It is named after Eldridge

Gerry, a late-18th–early-19th-century American politician and U.S. vice president, who apparently achieved such a salamander-like effect in an early redistricting project. The editors of this *Handbook* alerted me to a further pun that circulated in the 1970s: *jerrymathering*—referring to a person who had disappeared from public sight—invoking the name of Jerry Mathers, the child actor who played the lead role in the popular 1950s TV series *Leave it to Beaver* and later faded into deep obscurity.

5. Hacking's position differs from the aforementioned effort by Collins to combine realist sociology with methodological relativism about the natural science subject matter.

6. Also see John Searle's (1995) more recent account of constructed social realities, which apparently was written without knowledge of Berger and Luckmann's earlier, and similarly titled, book.

7. In a more recent analysis of survey interviewing, Maynard, Houtkoop, Schaeffer, and Vander Zouwen (2002) underscore the nonironic stance of ethnomethodology toward a constructive analytic project, and they go so far as to suggest that a close analysis to the interactional technology of interviewing should be able to yield practical benefit for the undertaking. Despite his disclaimers, however, Garfinkel's accounts of constructive analysis in sociology have a critical edge, and there is no mistaking the uneasy, and sometimes openly hostile, relation that he had to professional sociology.

8. Bruno Latour (1993) compounds (as well as confounds) the notion of symmetry by adding another axis to Bloor's proposal to give the same form of explanation to true and false knowledge. An implication of Bloor's symmetry is that the same form of explanation should be given for natural and social facts. Taking another metaphysical step, Latour eschews the ontological distinction between natural and cultural objects: Not only are naturally accountable entities reconceptualized as cultural objects (as proposed by Garfinkel et al., 1981), but also the actions of a watch are placed on the same plane as the actions of a watchmaker (whether blind or not). The political implications of this move are disconcerting, if what one wants is an account of what is *really* real (or natural) in order to expose the naturalized constructions that mask their social origins while selectively privileging powerful groups. Nevertheless, as Latour has argued, the leveling

strategy—all mechanisms become actions; all entities become actors—enables the actor–network theorist to tease out the way naturalization and technicization, and the forms of expertise that go along with and speak for natural and technological imperatives, themselves become potent forms of power.

9. The cartoon, by Garry Trudeau, was dated March 5, 2006, and is available on several websites, including *www.oilcrisis.com/junkScience/doonesbury20060305v.jpg*.

• References

Angell, M., & Relman, A. (2002). Patents, profits and American medicine: Conflicts of interest in the testing and marketing of new drugs. *Daedalus, 131*(2), 102–111.

Ashmore, M. (1989). *The reflexive thesis: Wrighting the sociology of scientific knowledge.* Chicago: University of Chicago Press.

Becker, H. (1963). *Outsiders: Studies in the sociology of deviance.* New York: Free Press.

Berger, P., & Luckmann, T. (1966). *The social construction of reality.* New York: Doubleday.

Bijker, W. E., Hughes, T. P., & Pinch, T. J. (Eds.). (1987). *The social construction of technological systems: New directions in the sociology and history of technology.* Cambridge, MA: MIT Press.

Bloor, D. (1976). *Knowledge and social imagery.* London: Routledge & Kegan Paul.

Button, G., & Sharrock, W. (1993). A disagreement over agreement and consensus in constructionist sociology. *Journal for the Theory of Social Behaviour, 23,* 1–25.

Button, G., & Sharrock, W. (1998). The organizational accountability of technological work. *Social Studies of Science, 28,* 73–102.

Collins, H. M. (1985). *Changing order: Replication and induction in scientific practice.* London: Sage.

Collins, H. M., & Yearley, S. (1992). Epistemological chicken. In A. Pickering (Ed.), *Science as practice and culture* (pp. 301–326). Chicago: University of Chicago Press.

Conrad, P., & Potter, D. (2000). From hyperactive children to ADHD adults: Observations on the expansion of medical categories. *Social Problems, 47*(4), 559–582.

Coulter, J. (1973). *Approaches to insanity: A philosophical and sociological study.* London: Robertson.

Daston, L., & Galison, P. (1992). The image of objectivity. *Representations, 40,* 81–128.

Fingarette, H. (1988). *Heavy drinking: The myth of alcoholism as a disease.* Berkeley: University of California Press.

Fishman, J. (2004). Manufacturing desire: The commodification of female sexual dysfunction. *Social Studies of Science, 34,* 187–218.

Garfinkel, H. (1967). *Studies in ethnomethodology.* Englewood Cliffs, NJ: Prentice Hall.

Garfinkel, H. (2002). *Ethnomethodology's program: Working out Durkheim's aphorism.* Lanham, MD: Rowman & Littlefield.

Garfinkel, H., Lynch, M., & Livingston, E. (1981). The work of a discovering science construed with materials from the optically discovered pulsar. *Philosophy of the Social Sciences, 11,* 131–158.

Garfinkel, H., & Sacks, H. (1970). On formal structures of practical actions. In J. C. McKinney & E. A. Tiryakian (Eds.), *Theoretical sociology: Perspectives and development* (pp. 337–366). New York: Appleton-Century-Crofts.

Garfinkel, H., & Wieder, D. L. (1992). Two incommensurable, asymmetrically alternate technologies of social analysis. In G. Watson & R. M. Seiler (Eds.), *Text in context: Contributions to ethnomethodology* (pp. 175–206). London: Sage.

Gilbert, G. N., & Mulkay, M. (1984). *Opening Pandora's box: An analysis of scientists' discourse.* Cambridge, UK: Cambridge University Press.

Goodwin, C. (1995). Seeing in depth. *Social Studies of Science, 25,* 237–274.

Grint, K., & Woolgar, S. (1995). On some failures of nerve in constructivist and feminist analysis of technology. *Science, Technology and Human Values, 20,* 286–310.

Gross, P., & Levitt, N. (1994). *Higher superstition.* Baltimore: Johns Hopkins University Press.

Gross, P. R., Levitt, N., & Lewis, M. W. (Eds.). (1996). *The flight from science and reason.* New York: New York Academy of Sciences.

Hacking, I. (1999). *The social construction of what?* Cambridge, MA: Harvard University Press.

Harding, S. (1996). Standpoint epistemology (a feminist version): How social disadvantage creates epistemic advantage. In S. Turner (Ed.), *Social theory and sociology: The classics and beyond* (pp. 146–160). Oxford, UK: Blackwell.

Heritage, J. (1984). *Garfinkel and ethnomethodology.* London: Polity Press.

Holstein, J. A., & Miller, G. (Eds.). (1993). *Reconsidering social constructionism: Debates in social problems theory.* New York: Aldine de Gruyter.

Kirk, S., & Kutchins, H. (1992). *The selling of DSM.* New York: Aldine de Gruyter.

Knorr Cetina, K. (1981). *The manufacture of knowledge.* Oxford, UK: Pergamon Press.

Labinger, J. A., & Collins, H. M. (Eds.). (2001). *The one culture? A conversation about science.* Chicago: University of Chicago Press.

Lambert, K. (2006). Fuller's folly, Kuhnian paradigms, and intelligent design. *Social Studies of Science, 36*(6), 835–842.

Latour, B. (1987). *Science in action.* Cambridge, MA: Harvard University Press.

Latour, B. (1993). *We have never been modern* (C. Porter, Trans.). London: Harverster Wheatsheaf.

Latour, B. (2004). Why has critique run out of steam?: From matters of fact to matters of concern. *Critical Inquiry, 30*(2), 225–248.

Latour, B., & Woolgar, S. (1986). *Laboratory life: The construction of scientific facts.* Princeton, NJ: Princeton University Press.

Livingston, E. (2006). The context of proving. *Social Studies of Science, 36,* 39–68.

Lynch, M. (1985). *Art and artifact in laboratory science.* London: Routledge & Kegan Paul.

Lynch, M. (1993). *Scientific practice and ordinary action: Ethnomethodology and social studies of science.* New York: Cambridge University Press.

Lynch, M. (2000). Against reflexivity as an academic virtue and source of privileged knowledge. *Theory, Culture, and Society, 17*(3), 27–56.

Lynch, M. (2006). From ruse to farce. *Social Studies of Science, 36*(6), 819–826.

Lynch, M., & Jordan, K. (1995). Instructed actions in, of, and as molecular biology. *Human Studies, 18,* 227–244.

Mannheim, K. (1936). *Ideology and utopia.* New York: Harvest Books.

Martin, A. (2005). Can't any body count?: Counting as an epistemic theme in the history of human chromosomes. *Social Studies of Science, 34,* 923–948.

Maynard, D. W., Houtkoop, H., Schaeffer, N. C., & vander Zouwen, H. (Eds.). (2002). *Standardization and tacit knowledge: Interaction and practice in the survey interview.* New York: Wiley.

Mills, C. W. (1940). Situated actions and vocabularies of motive. *American Sociological Review, 5,* 904–913.

Mulkay, M., Potter, J., & Yearley, S. (1983). Why an analysis of scientific discourse is needed. In K. Knorr-Cetina & M. Mulkay (Eds.), *Science observed: Perspectives on the social study of science* (pp. 171–203). London: Sage.

Pels, D. (1996). The politics of symmetry. *Social Studies of Science, 26,* 277–304.

Pollner, M. (1974). Sociological and common-sense models of the labeling process. In R. Turner (Ed.), *Ethnomethodology* (pp. 27–40). Harmondsworth, UK: Penguin.

Porter, T. M. (1995). *Trust in numbers: The pursuit of objectivity in science and public life.* Princeton, NJ: Princeton University Press.

Potter, J. (1996). Discourse analysis and constructionist approaches: Theoretical background. In J. E. Richardson (Ed.), *Handbook of qualitative research methods for psychology and the social sciences* (pp. 125–140). Leicester, UK: British Psychological Society.

Ross, A. (Ed.). (1996). *Science wars.* Durham, NC: Duke University Press.

Sacks, H., Schegloff, E. A., & Jefferson, G. (1974). A simplest systematics for the organization of turn-taking in conversation. *Language, 50*(4), 696–735.

Scheff, T. (1963). The role of the mentally ill and the dynamics of mental disorder: A research framework. *Sociometry, 26,* 436–453.

Scott, P., Richards, E., & Martin, B. (1990). Captives of controversy: The myth of the neutral social researcher in contemporary scientific controversies. *Science, Technology and Human Values, 15,* 474–494.

Searle, J. (1995). *The construction of social reality.* London: Penguin.

Shapin, S. (1994). *A social history of truth: Civility and science in seventeenth-century England.* Chicago: University of Chicago Press.

Sharrock, W. W., & Watson, D. R. (1984). What's the point of "rescuing motives"? *British Journal of Sociology, 34*(3), 435–451.

Smith, D. (1992). Sociology from women's experience: A reaffirmation. *Sociological Theory, 10,* 88–98.

Sokal, A. D. (1996). Transgressing the boundaries: Toward a transformative hermeneutics of quantum gravity. *Social Text, 14,* 217–252.

Spector, M., & Kitsuse, J. I. (1977). *Constructing social problems.* New York: Aldine.

Suchman, L. (1987). *Plans and situated actions.* Cambridge, UK: Cambridge University Press.

Szasz, T. (1974). The myth of mental illness. *American Psychologist, 15,* 113–118.

Wiley, N., & Garfinkel, H. (1980). *Discussion: (1) The case of Agnes; (2) Why do ethnomethodologists prefer to talk about "production" instead of "reality construction"?* Unpublished manuscript, University of Illinois, Department of Sociology.

Winch, P. (1958). *The idea of a social science and its relation to philosophy.* London: Routledge & Kegan Paul.

Winch, P. (1970). Understanding a primitive society. In B. Wilson (Ed.), *Rationality* (pp. 78–111). Oxford, UK: Blackwell.

Winner, L. (1986). *The whale and the reactor: A search for limits in an age of high technology.* Chicago: University of Chicago Press.

Woolgar, S. (Ed.). (1988). *Knowledge and reflexivity: New frontiers in the sociology of knowledge.* London: Sage.

Woolgar, S., & Pawluch, D. (1985). Ontological gerrymandering: The anatomy of social problems explanations. *Social Problems, 32,* 214–227.

Zimmerman, D. H., & Pollner, M. (1970). The everyday world as a phenomenon. In J. D. Douglas (Ed.), *Understanding everyday life: Toward the reconstruction of sociological knowledge* (pp. 80–103). Chicago: Aldine.

CHAPTER 38

Saving Social Construction
CONTRIBUTIONS FROM CULTURAL STUDIES

● **Joseph Schneider**

In a recent essay titled "Saving Sociology," Michal McCall (2005) argues that Patricia Clough has contributed to the discipline in a way that helped keep it open to thought and questions that always seemed at its horizons, if not beyond them. By asking and pursuing feminist, psychoanalytic, poststructural, and cultural studies/critical theory questions, as a "card-carrying" sociologist, McCall says that Clough helped keep the discipline exciting and alive. I want to take a page from McCall to argue that certain recurrent themes in cultural studies analysis and criticism—as a political, academic, and intellectual project that long has borne a "family resemblance" to disciplinary sociology—have, in effect, "saved" social constructionist analysis from becoming mundane, banal, and naive as an analytic form.[1]

Toward that end, I first set down what I take "social construction" to be, then de-scribe my own involvement in a branch of that work and say why I think it needed (still needs?) saving. Then I characterize cultural studies and its relevant themes. Drawing on various authors who write cultural studies of technoscience, I identify those particular contributions that I think have made social construction both much more complicated than we first thought and also much more intellectually provocative.

Social Construction and Social Problems Theory in U.S. Sociology

Social construction in U.S. sociology before the mid-1970s typically drew on Peter Berger and Thomas Luckmann's 1966 book, *The Social Construction of Reality: A Treatise in the Sociology of Knowledge*.[2] Seeking to correct an overemphasis on structure in sociological accounts of social life, Berger and Luckmann put forward the acting and interacting human(ist) being as the primary agent in the constitution, maintenance, and change—the "social construction"—of society. They defended social construction as rooted firmly in classical theory (e.g., it was "mainstream") and also fully behavioral (not "idealist"). The following questions are at the heart of their social constructionist analysis: What does a collection of people located at a particular time and in a particular place take to be real, and how is this way of seeing/knowing—this "construction"—to be understood as something they do? How are these conceptions linked to relevant social and historical contexts? How are differences in social realities and worlds across different local collections of people understood as implicating those varying contexts? The very existence of different social realities, they argued, underwrites the study of the social—and symbolic interactional—processes through and by which these differences have come about and are maintained and changed. They insisted that the sociology of knowledge "must concern itself with whatever passes for 'knowledge' in a society, regardless of the ultimate validity or invalidity (by whatever criteria) of such 'knowledge' " (Berger & Luckmann, 1966, p. 3). This requires the sociologist–analyst to take up a "disinterested" or neutral position—effecting a phenomenological bracketing—with regard to the epistemological and moral status of the claims studied. The social constructionist here is not interested in adjudicating the factual or ethical status of the knowledge claims under study—those being made by the people studied—by invoking a discourse of professional, scientific expertise. Presumably, however, this disinterested stance is not encouraged toward their own factual and analytic claims, and matters of "settled" scientific knowledge were not seen as subject to such analysis.

Language in use here coordinates and loosely integrates the diverse lines of situated symbolic (which is to say meaning-making) interaction. Although the paramount or everyday realities thus constructed are mostly taken for granted by those who produce them, Berger and Luckmann (1966, pp. 106, 116) insist that "every symbolic universe is incipiently problematic" and routinely requires conscious "maintenance work" by embodied individuals who make them up. "What remains . . . essential," they write, "is the recognition that all symbolic universes and all legitimations are human products; their existence has its base in the lives of concrete individuals, and has no empirical status apart from these lives" (Berger & Luckmann, 1966, p. 128).

"Social construction" became the focus of new attention in sociology roughly a decade later in John Kitsuse and Malcolm Spector's work on social problems theory. In a series of papers culminating in their book, *Constructing Social Problems*, Spector and Kitsuse (1977/2001) drew directly on the symbolic interactionist tradition that had emerged at the University of Chicago in the 1930s writing of George Herbert Mead as influenced by American pragmatism and carried forward (and westward) by Herbert Blumer, among others. Kitsuse's earlier contributions to the "labeling" and "societal reaction" theories of deviance, along with the work of Howard Becker, were foundational for the arguments Spector and Kitsuse made. A flavor of early ethnomethodology in this work is traceable to Kitsuse's prior collaboration with Aaron Cicourel (see, e.g., Cicourel & Kitsuse, 1963).

Kitsuse and Spector were concerned to provide a theoretically cogent and empirically focused set of definitions and directions for how to think about the object "social problem" as constituted in symbolic interactional, processual, and situated terms. Equally important was to offer a clear guide for empirical research consistent with that thinking. Although they easily could have cited Berger and Luckmann as intellectual ancestors, they did not. Perhaps that work seemed to them all too "grand" (and compromised) as a theoretical base for research, compared with their own quite focused interests in social problems as directly accessible activity.

In what would become a signature move in social constructionist writing—and one that Berger and Luckmann had made regarding "knowledge"—Spector and Kitsuse (1977/2001) rewrote an "objective condition"—a social problem—as a situated process of meaning-infused interaction. Social problems, they wrote, are "the activities of individuals or groups making assertions of grievances and claims with respect to some putative conditions" (p. 75). The job of their social constructionist "is to account for the emergence, nature, and maintenance of claims-making and responding activities" (p. 76). Because social problems here were to be understood as constituted in and by those activities and not due to context or structure or history (although there later would be argument over this point among those who took up Spector and Kitsuse's work[3]), research attention focused precisely on those definitional activities and not on questions of what allegedly prior "social factors" had caused them.

I became involved in this work in the late 1970s, when Peter Conrad and I were writing on the medicalization of deviance (Conrad & Schneider, 1980/1992). We drew on Spector and Kitsuse's work in that project, and I continued collaboration with them both in writing social constructionist social problems theory (Kitsuse & Schneider, 1989; Schneider & Kitsuse, 1984). I found their deconstruction—although they did not use that word, nor did they allude to Jacques Derrida—of the sociological discourse of nonconstructionist writing about social and moral problems to be provocative and very powerful. This struck me as a telling critique of the realist epistemology and ontology that I had learned and relied on from conventional social science practice. Spector and Kitsuse showed how their realist colleagues who wrote about social problems as undesirable conditions took a variety of ontological, as well as moral and ethical,

positions as foundations, treating these tacit understandings as un(re)marked resources for the arguments they themselves made. In this they shined a bright analytic light on how conventional scientific argument is done, allowing us to see our colleagues as, indeed, engaging precisely in "claims-making and responding activities" in their scholarly work on social problems.[4]

Spector and Kitsuse saw this accomplished quality of objects/conditions so clearly when it came to conventional social problems arguments. But they did not include their own argument and their "sacred" theoretical objects as fitting topics for the resource that their analysis offered. Perhaps this should not surprise, given their and our aims and uncritical positioning within conventional realist epistemology. After all, we wanted to "get somewhere" in these arguments from this new social problems theory as measured, especially, by the stimulation of theoretically directed and consistent, empirical research. And this is precisely what was happening, quite robustly so, in no small part through publications of research reports in the journal *Social Problems*, the official journal of the Society for the Study of Social Problems.[5]

Other readers and writers beyond the disciplinary confines of social problems theory in sociology also were interested in getting somewhere, but it was to a place other than the uncritical embrace of this particular kind of analysis. Beyond the Marxist critics of Spector and Kitsuse's social constructionist argument, who saw in it an all-too-familiar reiteration of the liberalism of labeling theory (see, e.g., Piven, 1981), the most telling and decentering criticism came from two sociologists familiar with similar but more broadly based constructionist work in the interdisciplinary field of the social studies of science. Steve Woolgar and Dorothy Pawluch's 1985 article charging the Spector and Kitsuse argument with "ontological gerrymandering," or selective relativism, drew on both ethnomethodology and continental thought to do what those of us writing this argument could or had not. They made the social constructionist argument itself the topic for an even more thoroughgoing, if not radical, constructionist criticism. They showed how it made problematic the reality of members' claims and definitions while taking the reality of its own factual claims about "other people's" claims and putative conditions as given, all in the service of making a critical argument about those (other) members' claims. Our colleagues who made factual and evaluative claims about what we called a "putative condition" became *members*, a term used in early ethnomethodology to mark those being studied; we constructionists were analysts, positioned to speak about data, research, and findings, without the ascribed and distancing putativity (see Schneider, 1993).

Woolgar and Pawluch (1985) told us, in effect, to take our constructionist argument more seriously, radically, than we had; to see and say that the done-and-carried nature of claimsmaking and responding activities includes the professional work that we were doing. Although it is a bit glib to say so, they urged us to see that "it's *all* constructed," or, as it is sometimes put with regard to the social and cultural, "it's elephants on top of elephants on top of elephants, all the way down." Woolgar and Pawluch were not offering a better explanation of the social construction of social problems but rather were showing how the argument itself was made and what had to be ignored for it to be successful. Ours was, indeed, a "gerrymander" that called out to be critically noticed. Our rather egregious not noticing—"innocent" and/or "ignorant" as it was—coupled with the growing popularity of the Spector and Kitsuse formulation made the Woolgar and Pawluch criticism a turning point in constructionist analysis in sociology.[6]

As Melvin Pollner (1987, 1991) has pointed out, in both scientific work and mundane practice, ontological and epistemological claims-about-some-thing typically take the thing about which claims are made to exist independent of the claims made.

And as Woolgar (1988, pp. 30–38) insisted in a later work, all representation is supported by an ideology that is effaced by the discourse of scientific realism, which protects the vulnerability of all attempts to represent the world from the hopeless ambiguity between language and that to which language seemingly refers. We can never be sure, he notes, that the mark or representative of the absent object believed to exist "out there" and that we take to stand in for that object, "here," represents it in a *valid, true* way. The connection in meaning that representation makes between mark and object, between signifier and signified, is always haunted by the question: What is the warrant for the link proposed? How do you know that *this* gets at what *that*, truly, essentially, is? And such questions themselves, of course, reinforce the assumption that the valid and the true are attainable in the familiar senses of those terms.

Woolgar (1988) says that questions such as these raise "methodological horrors" that have devastating implications for conventional notions of epistemology and ontology.[7] If we cannot be sure of the validity of these representatives of objects in the world, then the very notion of certain knowledge of that world (those objects) is troubled. Moreover, if certain knowledge is thus decentered, the very notion of the stable world itself—what is—begins also to move and multiply. And, whether we draw on symbolic interactionism, Freud, or feminist poststructuralism, this latter point opens up onto the dissolution or destabilization of the semi-sovereign, whole, and integrated self that has been such a staple of Enlightenment humanist thought, not to mention the prime agent in conventional social constructionist argument.

Subjectivity, language, writing, and reality become hopelessly entwined and fluid, and Woolgar insists that there is no getting around or "seeing through" language or discourse in order to grasp an unmediated nature or world; no Archimedean or God's-eye position from which a supposedly centered subject can see "the way things really are" separate from the technology used to see and to inscribe.[8] Given this, Woolgar (1988) urges an interrogation of how this practice of making and knowing worlds both constitutes what we know and grounds the prime agent of this knowledge, the humanist self.

These questions stem from the emergence, after the mid-20th century, of a collection of critical and oppositional movements and developments in academic, intellectual, and political work and life in Western Europe, Great Britain, and the United States—in "Western" thought, at least—that have been elaborated in various lines of work that go by different names. Professional, disciplinary sociology in the United States was relatively slow to register an interest in these developments in feminism, cultural Marxism, psychoanalytic criticism, deconstruction, poststructuralism, antiracism, queer theory, and postcolonial studies variously found in writings by Michel Foucault, Derrida, Jacques Lacan, Edward Said, Judith Butler, Gayatri Spivak, and Eve Sedgwick, among others.[9] "Cultural studies," arguably, marks a heterogeneous intellectual space that more easily overlapped disciplinary sociology and in which some of the effects of such critical discourses first began to be felt. Woolgar and Pawluch's (1985) article and Woolgar's other critical work in science studies (1988) reflect the influence of these ideas.

Cultural Studies: Some Disturbing Themes

Authoritative intellectual and political histories of the emergence and flowering of cultural studies in Britain—at the Birmingham Centre, beginning in 1964, in particular—have been written (see Hall, 1992; Turner, 1990), and provocative reflections on that emergence and subsequent writing are drawn together in a then-definitive collection of papers from a 1990 conference at the University of Illinois, Urbana–Champaign

(Grossberg, Nelson, & Treichler, 1992). Douglas Kellner (1995), in a somewhat different mix, draws together British cultural studies and critical theory influenced by the Frankfurt School toward a postmodern critical theory. Interdisciplinary or even antidisciplinary in its approach to the study of culture-and-society or culture-and-practice, cultural studies draws on a broad array of humanities and social science disciplines and interdisciplines and aspires to critical and engaged scholarship that aims to "make a difference" in the particular worlds studied. It is theoretically and methodologically catholic as a matter of principle and open to any content defensible as "culture."

Early in the introduction to his overview of British cultural studies, which I privilege here, Graeme Turner (1990, p. 2) quotes Paul Willis on the importance of giving academic attention to popular culture, or culture and the everyday—something Willis, of course, notably did in his widely cited *Learning to Labor: How Working Class Kids Get Working Class Jobs* (1977/1981)—as at the very heart of the social and cultural. Willis writes:

> it is one of the fundamental paradoxes of our social life that when we are at our most natural, our most *everyday*, we are also at our most cultural; that when we are in roles that look the most obvious and given, we are actually in roles that are constructed, learned and far from inevitable. (Willis, as cited in Turner, 1990, p. 2)

Most provocative here, Turner says, is Willis's claim that that which is most taken for granted—which the very notion of "mundane" and "everyday" would seem to mark—and seen as "natural" and "just there" in our lives is indeed not: "how our everyday lives are *constructed*, how culture forms its subjects" and how these practices and subjects are, as Willis puts it, "far from inevitable" (Turner, 1990, p. 2; original emphasis). If that is the case, Willis continued, the popular and everyday deserve to be central both to academic study—which they had not been (perhaps especially, but not only so, in the "Oxbridge" system in Britain)—and to a more complex understanding of the political as well. Willis here implies that the very notions and particular forms of that social-cultural–political themselves have complex histories that can be studied; that are themselves "sites of struggle" that could have been (and might still be), as Foucault was then putting it in his emerging work, otherwise. The natural is thus rewritten as an achievement of representational practice, as historically particular and contingent, and as having genealogies of power relations that may have been and may be imagined and enacted differently. That cultural studies emerged at the Birmingham Centre from a program in adult education that served a diverse population of students not readily found in the ranks of elite British schools adds a particular sociohistorical grounding to such ideas.

Although Willis's work is not the most typical of what would become British cultural studies—Stuart Hall's work is a clearer choice (see Gilroy, Grossberg, & McRobbie, 2000) or even that of Raymond Williams and Richard Hoggart[10]—the points that Willis makes, that the details of everyday life as lived should be seen as constructed in language and practice rather than (somehow) immanent and that these questions should become compelling topics for academic analysis, remain at the heart of cultural studies. Willis also insisted that such construction is never random nor innocent but operates rather more in service of some lives and ways of life than others and that an awareness of this differential is not distributed equally across the society.

Although the word *constructed* was not and is not always elaborated theoretically or methodologically in this work (as well, arguably, as in most other work), it at least served to focus analytic and critical attention on how sociocultural objects and practices that had been untheorized and unnoticed by scholars might now be seen as emergent, contingent, and differentially supportive of various groups' and individuals' interests and lives. One substantive focus of this early Birmingham work was popular media and television and the ways they propose a political consensus—spoken as the "public," the "people," "we," "civil society"—that might be seen more productively as, in fact, serving dominant interests. A key theoretical resource used in *Policing the Crisis: Mugging, the State, and Law and Order* (Hall, Critcher, Jefferson, Clarke, & Roberts, 1978)—offered up by many as a representative Birmingham text—is that of the "moral panic" (see Cohen, 2002). This concept reads as quite congenial to much (but not all) of the interactionist-labeling analysis of deviance that was going forward at about the same time in the United States. And such a reading draws it similarly close to the constructionist argument of Spector and Kitsuse.

Although cultural studies has no theoretical orthodoxy, its long and fraught but still lively relationship to Marxism (Hall, 1992) has meant that as an intellectual practice and positioning, it aims always to produce (1) a critique of and an implied intervention in the current political, economic, and cultural arrangements studied and (2) that such critique is offered explicitly as a strategic resource for change. That, certainly, was not part of the most widely cited interactionist writing and research on deviance and social problems in the United States.

This Marxist connection helped keep a critical eye on the nature and operation of structures of economic inequality, especially as shaped by capital production, but it was a so-called cultural or critical Marxism from Europe—shaped especially in the writings of Louis Althusser (1971) and Antonio Gramsci (1978)—that has been more important as a theoretical resource (and see Kellner, 2005). Here, attention shifts to ideology and the dominations it frames and directs rather than remaining focused primarily on the operation of economic exploitation and domination of a "working class" by a "ruling class" through the extraction of profit and the social relations of production that make this happen. Beyond Althusser, and especially in Gramsci's notion of hegemony as carried forward in Hall's writing, ideology in cultural studies work becomes not the origin of false consciousness as found in Marx but rather a consideration of how any dominant or conventional "consciousness" or, more to the point, system of meanings-in-practice foregrounds some objects and questions as important and backgrounds or erases others as unimportant or nonexistent. In this view, there is, indeed, no end, ever, to ideology. And there is also no end to the theoretical and empirical questions about how ideology, writ large, is taken up and used to order, make sense of, open up, close down, support, and change worlds and the objects that constitute them. These are, at heart, constructionist questions.

Gramsci's notion of hegemony underlines the consent and participation of those who embrace and embody the ideas and practices that simultaneously dominate them, adding complication to the understandings of power and domination consistent with those offered by Foucault—as always interactional or relational, always local, and always negotiated, in which notions of agency are complex and dispersed. Finally, Althusser's (1971) characterization of how ideology shapes the very possibilities for being, for appearing as a recognizable subject in the worlds in question, freed cultural studies from the individualism that has been such a powerful heritage of humanism and Marxism.

Rather than agency emerging only from the essential and distinctive core of the rational human actor or "self," subjectivity was rewritten here as itself profoundly cultural and discursive. The rational and fully-present-to-himself individual person is supplanted by subjects shaped importantly by the complex dynamism of culture—and, especially, by language and discourse—to fit more and/or less productively the dominant social and cultural formations. This shaping, however, is seen as far from complete, and subsequent cultural studies scholars would argue that the same cultural formations that urged consensus and extended domination could be read by their consumers to serve resistant projects (see McGuigan, 2005).

The Birmingham Centre also shaped cultural studies with a decidedly feminist flavor that carried it beyond an orthodox Marxism and even beyond Gramsci's vision toward a more mobile and relational understanding of ideology, power, and domination. Hall (1992, pp. 282–283) calls the entrance of feminist criticism and colleagues against the sex/gender-blind writing, thought, and practice being done there an "interruption"; action that was "ruptural" and that "reorganized the field in quite concrete ways."[11] From "the personal as political" to an understanding of power as at the heart of the private—effectively undermining the previously untheorized public–private dualism— to a clear-eyed view of sex/gender as itself an arena of power to a reopening of a productive conduit between social theory and psychoanalysis in questions of subjectivity, Hall insists that feminism made enormous contributions to the theoretical and critical power of cultural studies. He also makes it clear that these contributions were not, initially, welcomed by the (mostly) male figures leading Centre work, including himself: "As the thief in the night, [feminism] . . . broke in; interrupted, made an unseemly noise, seized the time, crapped on the dinner table of cultural studies" (Hall, 1992, p. 282). As a political movement "outside" cultural studies, feminism—in what was to become good cultural studies form—derailed that early masculinist train onto different and far more productive tracks.

Cultural studies at Birmingham and after inherited more from continental thought than a cultural Marxism. Of equal and signature importance is the tradition of structuralism or structural linguistics begun most famously in the writing of Ferdinand de Saussure (1972/1983). This work made the use of language as a system of differential signs and associated meanings central to cultural studies analysis. Turner (1990, pp. 12–16; see also Hall, 1992, pp. 283–284) describes this importance both in terms of its view of culture as a *system* of interconnected elements—that language and meaning are constituted as/in a structure, making the analysis of an entity taken out of this context impossible to understand—and that such meanings are always differential rather than referential. That is, words mean what they mean not because they point to objects that exist in the world independent of them that (somehow) contain those meanings (a.k.a. realism), but rather because the meanings linked to these words, as well as the signs themselves, are different from those for other words. The sign and the associated meaning here have no necessary relationship beyond those that convention installs and maintains.

The very notion of objects existing in the-world-for-us separate from language thus is disallowed, such that *what* we see and *how* we see are for all time inseparable. Although cultural studies would eschew the determining rigidity of structuralist formulations and embrace much more what came to be called poststructuralism, the deconstruction of realism that Saussure's work offered is at the heart of its vision. And through that deconstructive move we can see how meanings and practices, ways of seeing and thinking, acting and speaking—indeed, of being itself—are, constitutively, "put together" not merely as determined by a rigid subtending or overarching "structure"—including culture itself—but by and through the ongoing and always open intersection of embodied human beings in a real-time local, messy, often contradictory language-and-discourse-saturated set of very material practices.

Finally, Hall (1992, pp. 280–281) credits Gramsci with bringing cultural studies something more: raising specifically the question of the responsibility of those who do such scholarship to become what he called "organic intellectuals." Here the intellectual or academic (and Hall, after Gramsci, notes that these are not synonyms), as such, be-

comes a recognizable figure in the political movement of the day; intellectual work becomes political work as intellectual work. Hall argues that for the organic intellectual, and for the emerging cultural studies scholar, it was not enough to be "at the very forefront of [critical,] intellectual theoretical work," although that was indeed essential. Of course, one had to "know more," and more deeply, than conventional scholarship required. But there was the added responsibility of seeing that the results of this work—the "knowledges" produced—are conveyed beyond the "intellectual class," as Hall puts it, working to make them explicitly relevant to politics inside but especially outside conventional academic institutions. For cultural studies, Hall (1992, p. 281) insists, this legacy requires that "intellectual and theoretical work" itself become "a political practice." The two tasks that Gramsci set for those wishing to become more organic were (1) "to challenge modern ideologies 'in their most refined form,' and … " (2) "to enter into the task of popular education" (Hall, 1991, p. 46). Cultural studies scholarship has inherited and retained this standard.

This schematic vision of cultural studies, even in this brief and truncated form, underlines both its difference from and parallels to the social constructionist views of Spector and Kitsuse and of Berger and Luckmann before them. Partly, this is a result of its interdisciplinarity, drawing together as it does literary, linguistic, and philosophical studies and criticism with elements of the social sciences. It also, of course, results from the distinctly political and critical nature of cultural studies, including the whole question of the intellectual's responsibility as critic of dominant social and cultural life. This positioning is explicitly rejected in the social problems theory that Spector and Kitsuse wrote. The parallels, arguably, turn more on an insistence that any study of culture and society must keep an unwavering empirical focus on what embodied beings are doing together in particular times and places. Inflecting this latter in the previously described social constructionist direction, this veers close to one of Howard Becker's (1986) many homely but insightful phrases (and in this case a title of one of his books) describing essential features of social life, "doing things together." But seasoning that characterization with a more cultural studies flavor, the question of who or what is doing what "together," how, and for or with whom becomes an invitation to complexity in thinking the social and cultural that very likely would offend our interactionist and sociological forebears, as well as many contemporary colleagues who describe themselves in those terms.

This offense and decentering is precisely what I think the criticisms by Woolgar and Pawluch and Woolgar that I have described earlier achieved. As noted, those criticisms were enabled by the same influences that helped to shape the cultural studies themes just described. In the balance of this chapter, I follow the cultural studies critique of social construction as it emerged in certain corners of technoscience and technology studies. The aim is to see what these criticisms add to our sense of what it could mean to say "construct" with regard to the social and cultural.

Reflexivity, Diffraction, Dispersed Agency, and Affect

Today, just how "social construction" might story social and cultural life has become considerably more complicated than in the Kitsuse and Spector or Berger and Luckmann versions first offered some 35 and more years ago. An important part of this complication has come from criticism and social theory that have been at the center of cultural studies writing, particularly in its poststructural themes dealing with subjectivity. And again feminist theory and criticism, especially that friendly to poststructuralism, also have pressured social constructionist argument to declare its moral and ethical positions as to what sorts

of constructions/worlds might be imagined as desirable.

Like the critique of Spector and Kitsuse's formulation by Woolgar and Pawluch (1985), two of the more important recent critics of social construction themselves embraced the term in their earlier writing. French sociologist Bruno Latour, with Woolgar, authored one of the most important early books using a social constructionist argument, their 1979 *Laboratory Life: The Social Construction of Scientific Facts*. Seven years later, when the book was reissued with a new postscript, Latour was sufficiently unhappy with the phrase *social construction* that he insisted on dropping the *social* from the subtitle, leaving it *The Construction of Scientific Facts* (Latour & Woolgar, 1986). And feminist science studies scholar Donna Haraway, who had given *Laboratory Life* a strongly positive review when it was published (Haraway, 1980) and who had drawn on social construction to shape her famous critical analysis of primatology (see, for instance, Haraway, 1989, pp. 1–9), now avoids the phrase as overused to the point that it means almost nothing because it is used to mean so much (see Haraway's comment in Schneider, 2005a, p. 155). She also has considered and then rejected Woolgar's proposal in his critique of the Spector and Kitsuse formulation, that is, the ongoing reflexive interrogation of the humanist subject of representation, the prime "social constructor." And she has chided Latour's *Science in Action* (1987), the book that founded the actor–network theory (ANT) in science studies, for the agonistic and heroic—which she calls *masculinist*—vision of social construction that it offers (Haraway, 1997, p. 34). I take up Haraway's criticisms of social construction first.

Whereas Haraway appreciates the power of Woolgar's move to deconstruct the ideology of representation and its agent with a radical self-reflexivity—that is, she clearly grasps the ontological, epistemological, and political weight of this critical strategy (and uses it herself)—Haraway has insisted, paradoxically, that it does not go far enough in trying to understand and contribute to how worlds and realities are put together in real time so that one's work might "make a difference" in those very worlds, in what they might become. It is Woolgar, Haraway says, in effect, who suffers a "failure of nerve" in this work and not his feminist critics, as he has claimed (see Grint & Woolgar, 1995). The radical relativism that such reflexivity effects, Haraway argues, leaves us in the same place that dominant forms of scientific realism—what Sharon Traweek (1988) aptly called the "culture of no culture"—long have done. Both are dominating discourses that erase complexity, multiplicity, and difference, insisting on closure (Haraway, 1997, pp. 23–39; but see Smith, 2005, pp. 23–25).

Those moves also erase questions of who benefits differentially from which constructions of what sorts of particular worlds that are pursued and protected. Although Haraway draws such questions from her socialist and feminist commitments, they are precisely congenial with the cultural studies requirement, noted earlier, that the work of the scholar/intellectual aims to affect social and political realities framed in terms of the suffering or flourishing of living beings. The fact that all arguments and realities are vulnerable to deconstruction, which is to say that they all can be shown to be made up—"constructed"—with particular interests in mind (or perhaps in mind but not at its front) does not help us enough, she insists, in our attempts to know and speak productively about how we and others do live and might live our lives. Using the metaphor of hypertext, in which all choices in a given net are in principle available (and they all are also deconstructable), which ones will you make? How will you decide? What do you love? What are your desires in the work that you do? What are your fears? For what kinds of worlds do you hope and strive in that work? And who will benefit differently and how? For Haraway, there are no "innocent," neutral, guaranteed "correct," detached places to stand where one can avoid implication in

the collective and always morally freighted work of constructing and living in worlds.

Importantly, taking Haraway's critical constructionist questions seriously does not mean giving up on careful, even rigorous empirical work typically linked to science; nor does it mean that there are no truths or realities. Doing good (and constructed) scientific work—although, of course, she has a particular vision of what that is—remains a requirement. It becomes, rather, a matter of asking ourselves—always seen as part of a collective—*why* such work should be taken up and pursued, requiring a re-vision of what objective knowledge and truth (without the distancing quotes) can mean. Here, human constructors must "own" and indeed struggle for the constructions they contribute to, chosen through an inextricable collective weave of partially (and sometimes uneasily) shared interests, hope, love, and careful attention to always constructed and thus always mobile matters of fact. There are here no guarantees from "method" that the constructions you, together with others, make will turn out—even temporarily—to be "right" or to be repudiated. Instead of multiple mirrors that reflect endless and always deconstructable attempts to represent (a discourse that dissolves all and insists that you be subject to it), Haraway offers the metaphor of diffraction, as when rays of light pass through a prism and their directions and angles are changed unmistakably by that passage. The scholarly and political work that she encourages contributes to and is a version of that diffraction.

Haraway's criticism of Latour's vision of the collective in *Science in Action* is not only that it is all too familiar but that it sees things from a very predictably—and particular—gendered place. She argues that his view of science (and of society) is all about would-be heroic struggle and conflict; of vanquishing opponents, of battles, strategies, and overcoming opposition; of "enrolling" so much and so many behind one's own proposals that it becomes virtually impossible and/or too costly for actors seeking to tell different stories to sustain their views and visions (1997, p. 34). It is not that Haraway is allergic to conflict, but rather that she invites a more complex and diverse vision of how knowledge and the social and cultural can be done, made, and seen, with more possibilities for collaboration, openness, and change. Instead of these agonistic frames as her metaphors of choice, she offers that of cat's cradle, the string-on-fingers game that requires close attention to the others with whom one plays and that rewards game-specific collaboration that has more limited and focused aims (Haraway, 1994). "Winning" may remain important as a shared aim, but the very playing–being in play, relationally–is as important as who takes what home at game's end; and zero-sum thought is nowhere in sight. I want to see Haraway's critique as an attempt to imagine social construction as more about the experience and process of the making-in-relationality than about the permanence of what is made by a heroic being and action.

And Haraway has made another enormously important contribution to thinking about social construction differently from versions common in social science and literary studies and in cultural studies, as well. Simultaneous with but independent of similar arguments by Latour, especially in his concept of the "actant" and in the central place given to laboratory "inscription devices," Haraway has seen the cast of active constructors in all the worlds she has studied as much larger, more diverse, and more linked or connected than what social construction in sociology, social science, and elsewhere has allowed. The messy richness of her vision of who or what is doing what to and with what/ whom, moving what where and how, opening up and closing off options for what movement, with what collaborators (fully "willing" or not), offers an appreciation of "construction" and "agency" that makes clear the overimportance given to the humanist "member" or "participant" or "self" in other versions of social construction (see,

e.g., Haraway, 1997, p. 129). The story that "social" construction has thus far told is all too simple and does not begin to reflect the dispersed yet networked agency involved in making up and sustaining, not to mention changing, worlds.

In her object, "material–semiotic entities," Haraway follows Foucault's "discursive practices" in yoking together the insights from poststructuralism's appreciation of the power of discourse and language–the ever-tropic figurative and metaphoric–in constituting worlds (it "speaks us into existence"), on the one hand, with the grounded and local, embodied, and "fleshly" doings and dynamisms that living beings–human and nonhuman–as well as machines pursue. Her list, beyond the famous cyborg (Haraway, 1985), here includes "the chip, the gene, the fetus, the bomb, the genome, the database" (Haraway, 1997) and, most recently, the relationality of "companion species" in the dog–human join (Haraway, 2003). Haraway insists that many of her metaphors are organic and material in the sense that the what and how of actual biological organisms become her "theory" for understanding not only how knowledge comes about but also how worlds–always complex and relational–are made and sustained (or not).

Haraway is famous for transgressing boundaries that conventional disciplinary thought does not violate in order to tell stories of networks of machines and living beings (e.g., her cyborg), of connections between primates and humans, of the force of constructed "nature" and "culture." The word *construction*, arguably, can be used to describe what is happening, and perhaps it is even *social* (she is not as averse to the word as is Latour), but it certainly is not under the control of nor only or even primarily the accomplishment of any human(ist) beings. For both Haraway and Latour, this is all about the place of agency in construction, but their visions offer views of considerably more widely dispersed actants across mobile networks than disciplinary sociology ever imagines.

A similarly expansive view of agency as always distributed and embodied is found in the work of N. Katherine Hayles (1999), a feminist literary theorist and critic who writes on technoscience. Against the mind-privileged individualism of what some have called the "brain in a vat" view of knowledge and information—which is to say, a privileged brain within an inconsequential holding-tank body—Hayles insists that information be seen as always having a body that is part of a diverse network of distinct and material other bodies with associated computational processes and that this embodiment always matters. Taken together, these entities constitute a "cognitive system." Similar to Haraway and Latour, Hayles here sees the human mind or thinker as only one of a number of dynamic entities acting more or less in concert with other entities, not all of which/whom are human or alive, and over which that human mind does not have control but with which/whom it is implicated.

Hayles (1999, pp. 288–289) illustrates with a critique of philosopher John Searle's famous Chinese room experiment, which Searle offered to counter the claim that machines can think. Searle imagined himself—a person knowing no Chinese language—inside a closed room containing baskets of Chinese characters and a rule book for how to link those characters together meaningfully. In response to Chinese texts slid under the door, Searle said he might be able to send out strings of characters in response, and that those texts might then be read by others outside as "clever" and knowing "responses." But he insists that from this alone he could not be said to "know Chinese" or to be "thinking," as he, like a machine, would not comprehend what the strings of characters, coming in and going out, possibly could *mean*.

Hayles urges us, however, to pause to consider that the terms *thinking* and *knowing*—and I want to include *constructing*—can be used to characterize Searle's Chinese room itself as a "sociocultural cognitive system," even if they may not accurately describe any single element of that system, including Searle himself. She notes that many of us live our lives in circumstances similar to Searle's: "for every day we participate in systems whose total cognitive capacity exceeds our individual knowledge," such as the countless machines and electronic systems with which we interact (Hayles, 1999, p. 290; see also Hutchins, 2000). This recommendation is less about the disappearance of the body than the emergence of what she calls a "certain kind of subjectivity" (Hayles, 1999, p. 193), one that is certainly not humanist.

Hayles suggests that we can appreciate this emergent subject by thinking about the intersection of "the body" as a cultural construction on the one hand and the "experiences of embodiment" that humans speak as feelings and observations on the other. She urges us to notice the "inscription" or the normative writing/encoding on/in "the body" by culture on the one hand and the "incorporation" or incorporating practices that are always local, embedded in context, performative, and intensely physical on the other. In this, Hayles proposes that the body itself, its materiality, must be appreciated as an important source of agency or constructing and not simply under the control of a mind or consciousness, an argument that she shares with Latour and Haraway. Quoting the neuroscientist Francisco Varela and his colleagues, Hayles (1999, p. 201) writes: "The closer one comes to the flux of embodiment . . . the more one is aware that the coherent self is a fiction invented out of panic and fear."

I want to continue this line of thought about embodiment and the material and their relevance to thinking construction more broadly—and conclude this chapter—with two brief comments: one in reference to Latour's recent prescription for saving constructionism and then a description of what sociologist Patricia Clough recently has called "the affective turn" in critical studies and social theory.

Latour (2003), almost apoplectically opposed (and I think incorrectly) to poststruc-

turalism and deconstruction as indeed destructive of what he hopes the promise of
constructivism—his preferred term—might be,
has reiterated his argument that constructionist analysis must be alive to and inclusive
of the importance of the material, the *matter*,
involved in the process of making to which
construction refers. Sounding as though he
has considered Haraway's critique of his
earlier agonistic vision, Latour describes a
constructivism worth saving:

> there is no maker, no master, no creator that
> could be said to dominate materials, or, at the
> very least, [there is] a new *uncertainty* . . . intro-
> duced as to what is to be built as well as to who
> is responsible for the emergence of the virtual-
> ities of the materials at hand. To use the word
> constructivism and to forget this uncertainty
> so constitutive of the very act of building is
> nonsense. (2003, p. 32; original emphasis).

Not only has the concept of "the builder"
been grossly misunderstood, Latour says,
but even worse is the picture usually given of
the matter at the center of this building. In
short, the "stuff" *with which the building is
done*—and the preposition and passivity of
the verb form here both are themselves
fundamentally wrong, he insists—has faired
poorly in constructionist writing as we know
it. Things, as told in that story, can take only
three roles: (1) to be an "obstinate blind
force"; (2) to be there "as the mere support
for human fanciful ingenuity"; (3) or simply
"to offer some 'resistance' to human action"
(Latour, 2003, p. 32). The first is a mirror image of an all-powerful creator; the second
disallows matter any agency in view of the
wonder-ful agency of the human; in the
third, matter is something for the human to
push against (and he notes that this creator
has to be a "he"). If there is any hope for constructionist analysis, he says, it is in leading
us to an appreciation of agencies in things.

Clough has made significant contributions to cultural studies and critical theory in
sociology and beyond with a collection of
work in feminist, psychoanalytic, and post-

structural criticism, writing texts that bridge
the discipline and a variety of interdisciplinary projects, including technology and
science studies (Clough, 1994, 1998, 2000).
She has been a virtual "lone voice" in the discipline in underlining the force of what
might be called "psychic construction" in social life, especially involving what she takes
from Derrida as "the technical substrates of
unconscious memory" and the working of
psychic trauma—topics that typical constructionist analyses do not consider.

In *Autoaffection*, Clough (2000, p. 14) critically reviews "feminist theory, Marxist cultural studies, queer theory, and postcolonial
theory," along with the discursive construction of authority in science, to examine how
they do or do not consider bodily materialities as relevant to understanding the dynamisms of the social and cultural. An important theme in this work has been to
highlight a view of human subjectivity as
fragmented, dispersed, and linked in complex networks including machines and nonhuman life, themes already familiar here.
Adding insights from feminist film theory,
Clough follows Derrida's lead to focus our
attention on the ways that material technologies connect to human bodies (e.g., the technical apparatus of film and film production,
but, then, of television, of computers, and so
on) to enable both "seeing" and "being" that
(1) is in no sense determined by the hu-
man(ist) self and (2) is also in no sense a diminution of human capacities or productive
possibilities (and see Johnston, 1999). From
this, she argues, we may see the relations of
"being and technicity . . . nature and technology, body and machine, the virtual and
the real, and the living and the inert" not as
oppositional but as "différantial"; as always
already "inextricably implicated, always already interlaced" (Clough, 2000, p. 11).

Most recently, Clough has drawn attention to and extended the writing of a collection of scholars who have taken up the topic
of affect or affectivity to give more attention
to the place of the "sub-individual" and molecular qualities of bodies (Clough, 2004,

2007, in press; Clough & Halley, 2007). She argues that cultural studies and critical theory have been unable, in their exclusive attention to *meaningful* action or dynamism centered in the humanist individual, to open productive interrogation of how such subindividual and molecular bodily materialities help to shape—and, I argue, construct—that which we call the social (see Taylor, 2001). Moreover, she notes that global capital, state war machines, and other elements of what Gilles Deleuze called "control societies" (beyond the disciplinary), along with developments in technoscience, not only have recalibrated their visions to focus on these molecular (and nonorganic) elements of bodies worldwide but also have already drawn them deeply into their operations. Clough is convinced that critical social theory, including cultural studies, lags behind in noticing and theorizing this, in no small part due to their preferred focus on meaning and its authorizing subject.

The "affect" to which Clough (2007, pp. 1–2) and others refer does not mean emotion, but rather "a substrate of potential bodily responses, often autonomic responses, which are in excess of consciousness. . . . [A]ffect refers generally to bodily capacities to affect and be affected or [to] the augmentation or diminution of a body's capacity to act, to engage, to connect." Emotion and desire are here seen as objects *narrated from*—as is subjectivity itself—this substrate of affect. Not seen as "pre-social," this understanding and even si(gh)ting of affect have been enabled by the use of recent technologies such that the technical is itself bound up with the "felt vitality" that affect names.[12] Clough underlines that whereas "matter" here is central, it is a matter more complicated than past theory has considered, if it has been considered at all:

> Drawing on discourses of political economy, philosophy, psychology, sociology and literary studies as well as biotechnology, information theory, complexity theory, genetics, neuroscience and physics, the affective turn expresses a new configuration of the body, technology and matter. . . . [It] is a shift from the *social construction or discursive construction* of the body or bodily matter explored in the critical theory of the late twentieth century. Affect . . . is not a conscious matter; it is not even unconscious in the psychoanalytic sense. (p. 2; emphasis added)

Here, bodily matter and materiality become much more important as "constructors" in their own right, so to speak, as sources of movement that connect to what might be called the social and cultural but that also exist independently—and consequentially—of them. Long kept at arm's length in most cultural studies and critical cultural theory, bodily matter and the material must be taken into account, although of course not as determinative or prior. And on this point, Clough cites Peng Cheah's (1996) friendly critique of Judith Butler's (1993) vision of (bodies that) matter. That is, this sense of the material reflects the insights of psychoanalysis and poststructuralism while reworking elements of both (see, e.g., Massumi, 2002). The challenge is to take dynamic matter into account in critical cultural theory—that is, of course, in discourse—in a way that does not reduce it to culture's and language's impoverished "other," needing to be "given meaning" by the human(ist) subject in order to become significant. What must emerge, then, when meaning is ultimately made must not be seen as "constructed" by a sovereign subject or "master builder" who controls the material but rather more as a joint "invention" (Massumi, 2002, p. 12), a co-evolutionary emergence that did/does not begin to exist before the *co-* commences.

But Is It Worth Saving, after All?

Having spent this much of my effort and your good will as a reader to claim that interdisciplinary work from cultural studies has "saved" social constructionist argument, I must admit that I can appreciate the perhaps still nagging question of whether or not it deserves to be kept alive at all. Some, including more than a few of us who have written quite a lot in its name, may conclude, understandably, that if social construction has come to signify so much, if it includes so many diverse moves of theory and so many would-be empirical examples or illustrations, it hardly brings us any insights as a theoretical and empirical project in its own right.

It is not a new criticism of social constructionist work to say that it often takes the form of glib and superficial overarching assertions that this or that social and cultural formation or object is "socially constructed," with little empirical support or elaboration offered. In her review of Latour and Woolgar's 1979 publication of *Laboratory Life: The Social Construction of Scientific Facts*, Haraway (1980) praises the authors for the extent to which they avoid this kind of casually drawn claim. Rather, she calls attention to the empirical detail they provide in showing just how, to draw a verb from Latour's (2003) own recent brief for constructivism, scientific facts are indeed *built*. And to use this verb is of course to say that such facts are not simply "there to be found." This kind of claim—that the apparently given is better understood both to have a history and to have been "done" with unmistakable intentions—was seemingly foundational to the criticism by both Berger and Luckmann and by Spector and Kitsuse of the structural–functional, normative, and realist–"objective" arguments and analyses that were then privileged in the sociological study of knowledge, on the one hand, and of social problems, on the other. This claim that some thing is "socially constructed," followed by an empirically detailed analysis that sets forth just how, where, when, and by what/whom the entity in question has been and is being "put together," *qua* entity, strikes me as one of the most important if not the most important contributions these authors—especially Spector and Kitsuse—made. This remains clearly relevant today as a premise of critical inquiry into all that is social and cultural.

Surely, one of the insights of my selected sample of cultural studies work from the past 40 years is that the moral and the given (or the "natural" or the "real") in knowledge and practice typically are entwined. That which is thought to be real is also often that which is thought to be right. And the long-lived relationship between untheorized realist ontology and epistemology, despite Foucault and Derrida, despite Haraway and Butler, is hardly gasping its last breath as I write. Presumption and ideology, myriad forms of domination—not to mention a common sense that endorses uncritically that which is thought to be "natural"—all these and more are easily found in popular and professional thought and practice. In the face of this, writing the social and cultural to involve "claims-making and responding activities" and "discursive practices" carried by very "interested" human (and even humanist) beings—all of which are directly accessible to inquiry—is no small achievement of the formulation of social construction that Spector and Kitsuse set out. Their and our myopia was in not turning that analysis fully on ourselves as we constructed social constructionism. The selection of work from cultural studies cited here has made that occluded vision much less possible or likely today.

As is apparent, I think the criticisms and contributions by Haraway and Latour and by Hayles and Clough that (1) insist on a detailed account of construction as "building"; (2) widen the range of "actants" or "entities" that are given what Karen Barad (1999) has called "agential realism" beyond human(ist) beings and to include inanimate as well as living-but-nonhuman "players"; and (3) see the first two items in terms of constitutive relationality and connectivity—that it is *in the building or construction*, with all of the potential "subroutines" involved, that the entities are constituted as such—are of central importance for the "saved" version of this kind of criticism and analysis. And, of course, the particular insights having to do with the operation of power and domination that have been and remain central to what I have marked as the "core" of the cultural studies tradition, including what Haraway has called "making a difference in the world" through one's scholarly work, can only help enliven constructionism and its promise.

Finally, borrowing again from Haraway, I suggest that giving up the notion of construction—and I agree with Latour that losing the "social" is probably a gain—because of its glib and casual use or because it has come to mean so much that it ends up meaning so little is to give up too much. In her work, Haraway repeatedly refuses to jettison such words as *truth, objectivity, fact, nature, culture*, and *science*—all of which she considers seriously polluted *and* constructed *and* important—because they help her see things in ways that other terms do not. She, in effect, struggles over the meaning of these terms because of their value to her ways of seeing, arguing that there are in any case no "innocent" terms or positionings to be found. I think construction is just such a metaphor and thus has become more rather than less useful at the hands of its friendly critics. In its nondisciplinary flavor, it goes well beyond the humanist theoretical resources on which Berger and Luckmann and Spector and Kitsuse drew: "Construction" is not owned by any human science discipline; its very openness or ambiguity is also its promise. And at the hands of those in science and technology studies who have perhaps used it most famously, it also goes beyond the contributions of the Birmingham tradition of cultural studies. In both of these latter traditions, the drama and action of the stories told always center on the human(ist) "stars" of the show. To the extent that constructionist analysis can bring forward insights on the breathtaking complexity of how things can be built without any single builder in charge—human or not—but to serve quite particular ends in always differential ways, it deserves our ongoing attention as a resource for critical thought.

• Notes

1. I do not mean that particular empirical studies using a social constructionist frame should be so described. Rather, I want to focus on the nature of the argument or "theory" itself. And David Morley (2000, pp. 246–247), in a tribute to Stuart Hall, suggests that cultural studies has done the same saving work for sociology more generally.

2. This discussion of Berger and Luckmann is adapted from Schneider (2005b).

3. This was framed in terms of the "strict" versus "contextual" constructionist arguments. See Kitsuse and Schneider (1989) and Best (1993).

4. Science studies at the University of Edinburgh was developing what would come to be known as the sociology of scientific knowledge (SSK) in the work of Barry Barnes and Steven Shapin (1979) and David Bloor (1976), among others, and was referred to as the "strong program" of such study. What distinguished this approach to the study of science from earlier work is that the very production of, the doing of, scientific knowledge and argument themselves—rather than only the social structure of science, its hierarchies, reward and recruitment mechanisms, norms, culture, and history—was the prime object of study and analysis. In this, sociologists positioned themselves as anthropologists might relative to social worlds and practices that were foreign if not alien to them in order to see and understand how scientific facts, research findings, and theories are made and made good, so to speak.

5. Kitsuse was president of this society in 1978–1979, as Becker had been before him (1965–1966). His symbolic interactionist, feminist colleague at Northwestern, Arlene Daniels, had been editor of *Social Problems* from 1975 to 1978 and published work sympathetic to social constructionist argument. Spector subsequently became editor (1981–1984), and I myself served in that post from 1987 to 1990. Later editors of the journal, especially Joel Best (1996–1999) and Jim Holstein (2002–2005), published similar work. It is fair to say that these positions helped make social constructionist analysis in the Spector and Kitsuse mode more available to the journal's readers.

6. Woolgar and Pawluch's article was not, of course, the only criticism of the social constructionist argument as set out by Spector and Kitsuse. For a collection of more or less friendly criticism, see Holstein and Miller (1993).

7. These are, he says, *indexicality*, that multiple readings/representations of allegedly the same event/object imply multiple events/objects; *inconcludability*, that we can always ask for further definition, clarification, and specification of terms; and *reflexivity*, that each half of the representational couple elaborates, refers back to, what the other means or is. The account and the object are thus inseparable (Woolgar, 1988, pp. 32–33).

8. See the paper by Macy Conferences on Cybernetics participants, Lettvin, Maturana, McCulloch, and Pitts (1959), that makes this point—much earlier—in an unmistakably material way, in which mediation has everything to do with biophysiology rather than language, and that anticipates the complications for "construction" described later. See also Hayles's (1999, pp. 131–159) discussion of the implications of this and related work for what I am here calling *construction*.

9. See, for instance, Foucault (1971, 1978, 1979); Derrida (1998); Lacan (1977); Said (1979); Butler (1990, 1993); Spivak (1988, 1999); and Sedgwick (1990, 1993).

10. Works by Hoggart (1957) and Williams (1958, 1961) are often cited as Birmingham Centre founding texts rooted in a tradition of English literary criticism that focused on textual form and its social relevance (see Turner, 1990, p. 12). Turner (1990, pp. 75–76) suggests that the collaborative book *Policing the Crisis: Mugging, the State, and Law and Order* (Hall, Critcher, Jefferson, Clarke, & Roberts, 1978) could stand as a virtual paradigm case of the kind of analysis the Centre encouraged under Hall.

11. Hall (1992, p. 282) writes: "The title of the volume in which this dawn-raid was first accomplished" is *Women Take Issue: Aspects of Women's Subordination* (Women's Studies Group, 1978).

12. Mark Hansen's (2004b) discussion of video artist Bill Viola's use of slowed digital imaging of human faces helps one see affect as the bodily, molecular dynamism out of which the culturally shaped emotions are storied and felt. And see Hansen (2004a).

• References

Althusser, L. (1971). On ideology and ideological state apparatuses. In *Lenin and philosophy, and other essays* (B. Brewster, Trans.). London: New Left Books.

Barad, K. (1999). Agential realism: Feminist perspectives in understanding scientific practices. In M. Biagioli (Ed.), *The science studies reader* (pp. 1–11). New York: Routledge.

Barnes, B., & Shapin, S. (Eds.). (1979). *Natural order: Historical studies of scientific culture*. London: Sage.

Becker, H. S. (1986). *Doing things together: Selected papers*. Evanston, IL: Northwestern University Press.

Berger, P., & Luckmann, T. (1966). *The social construction of reality: A treatise in the sociology of knowledge*. New York: Doubleday.

Best, J. (1993). But seriously folks: The limitations of the strict constructionist interpretation of social problems. In J. A. Holstein & G. Miller (Eds.), *Reconsidering social constructionism: Debates in social problems theory* (pp. 129–147). New York: Aldine de Gruyter.

Bloor, D. (1976). *Knowledge and social imagery*. London: Routledge & Kegan Paul.

Butler, J. (1990). *Gender trouble: Feminism and the subversion of identity*. New York: Routledge.

Butler, J. (1993). *Bodies that matter: On the discursive limits of sex*. New York: Routledge.

Cheah, P. (1996). Mattering. *Diacritics, 26*, 108–139.

Cicourel, A. V., & Kitsuse, J. I. (1963). *The educational decision-makers*. Indianapolis, IN: Bobbs-Merrill.

Clough, P. T. (1994). *Feminist thought: Desire, power, and academic discourse*. New York: Blackwell.

Clough, P. T. (1998). *The end(s) of ethnography: From realism to social criticism*. New York: Lang.

Clough, P. T. (2000). *Autoaffection: Unconscious thought in the age of teletechnology*. Minneapolis: University of Minnesota Press.

Clough, P. T. (2004). Future matters: Technoscience, global politics, and cultural criticism. *Social Text, 80*, 1–23.

Clough, P. T. (2007). Introduction. In P. T. Clough & J. Halley (Eds.), *The affective turn* (pp. 1–33). Durham, NC: Duke University Press.

Clough, P. T. (in press). The affective turn: political economy, biomedia, and bodies. *Theory, Culture and Society*.

Clough, P. T., & Halley, J. (Eds.). (2007). *The affective turn*. Durham, NC: Duke University Press.

Cohen, S. (2002). *Folk devils and moral panics*. New York: Routledge. (Original work published 1972)

Conrad, P., & Schneider, J. W. (1992). *Deviance and medicalization: From badness to sickness*. Philadelphia: Temple University Press. (Original work published 1980)

Derrida, J. (1998). *Of grammatology* (G. C. Spivak, Trans.). Baltimore: Johns Hopkins University Press.

Foucault, M. (1971). *The order of things: An archeology of the human sciences*. New York: Pantheon.

Foucault, M. (1978). *The history of sexuality: Volume 1. An introduction* (R. Hurley, Trans.). New York: Random House.

Foucault, M. (1979). *Discipline and punish: The birth of the prison* (A. Sheridan, Trans.). New York: Vintage.

Gilroy, P., Grossberg, L., & McRobbie, A. (Eds.). (2000). *Without guarantees: In honour of Stuart Hall*. New York: Verso.

Gramsci, A. (1978). *Selections from the prison notebooks of Antonio Gramsci* (Q. Hoare & G. N. Smith, Trans.). London: Lawrence & Wishart.

Grint, K., & Woolgar, S. (1995). On some failures of nerve in constructivist and feminist analyses of technology. *Science, Technology, and Human Values, 20*, 286–310.

Grossberg, L., Nelson, C., & Treichler, P. (1992). *Cultural studies*. New York: Routledge.

Hall, S. (1991). Cultural studies and the Centre: Some problematics and problems. In S. Hall, D. Hobson, A. Lowe, & P. Willis (Eds.), *Culture, media, language: Working papers in cultural studies, 1972–1979* (pp. 15–47). London: Routledge.

Hall, S. (1992). Cultural studies and its theoretical legacies. In L. Grossberg, C. Nelson, & P. Treichler (Eds.), *Cultural studies* (pp. 277–286). New York: Routledge.

Hall, S., Critcher, C., Jefferson, T., Clarke, J., & Roberts, B. (1978). *Policing the crisis: Mugging, the state, and law and order*. New York: Holmes & Meier.

Hansen, M. B. N. (2004a). *New philosophy for new media*. Cambridge, MA: MIT Press.

Hansen, M. B. N. (2004b). The time of affect, or bearing witness to life. *Critical Inquiry, 30*, 584–626.

Haraway, D. J. (1980). Laboratory life: The social construction of scientific facts. *Isis, 71*, 488–489.

Haraway, D. J. (1985). Manifesto for cyborgs: Science, technology, and socialist feminism in the 1980s. *Socialist Review, 80*, 65–108.

Haraway, D. J. (1989). *Primate visions: Gender, race, and nature in the world of modern science*. New York: Routledge.

Haraway, D. J. (1994). A game of cat's cradle: Science studies, feminist theory, cultural studies. *Configurations, 2*, 59–71.

Haraway, D. J. (1997). *Modest_witness@second_millennium. FemaleMan[c]_meets_Oncomouse*(tm). *Feminism and technoscience*. New York: Routledge.

Haraway, D. J. (2003). *The companion species manifesto: Dogs, people, and significant otherness*. Chicago: Prickly Paradigm Press.

Hayles, N. K. (1999). *How we became posthuman: Virtual bodies in cybernetics, literature, and informatics*. Chicago: University of Chicago Press.

Hoggart, R. (1957). *The uses of literacy: Changing patterns in English mass culture*. Boston: Beacon.

Holstein, J. A., & Miller, G. (Eds.). (1993). *Reconsidering social constructionism: Debates in social problems theory*. New York: Aldine de Gruyter.

Hutchins, E. (2000). *Cognition in the wild*. Cambridge, MA: MIT Press.

Johnston, J. (1999). Machinic vision. *Critical Inquiry, 26*, 27–48.

Kellner, D. (1995). *Media culture: Cultural studies, identity politics between the modern and the postmodern*. New York: Routledge.

Kellner, D. (2005). Cultural Marxism and British cultural studies. In G. Ritzer (Ed.), *Encyclopedia of social theory* (pp. 171–177). Thousand Oaks, CA: Sage.

Kitsuse, J. I., & Schneider, J. W. (1989). Preface. In J. Best (Ed.), *Images of issues: Typifying contemporary social problems* (pp. xi–xiii). New York: Aldine de Gruyter.

Lacan, J. (1977). *Écrits: A selection*. New York: Norton.

Latour, B. (1987). *Science in action: How to follow scientists and engineers through society*. Cambridge, MA: Harvard University Press.

Latour, B. (2003). The promises of constructivism. In D. Ihde & E. Selinger (Eds.), *Chasing technoscience: Matrix for materiality* (pp. 27–46). Bloomington, IN: Indiana University Press.

Latour, B., & Woolgar, S. (1986). *Laboratory life: The construction of scientific facts*. Princeton, NJ: Princeton University Press. (Original work published 1979)

Lettvin, J. Y., Maturana, H. R., McCulloch, W. S., & Pitts, W. H. (1959). What the frog's eye tells the frog's brain. *Proceedings of the Institute of Radio Engineers, 47*, pp. 1940–1951.

Massumi, B. (2002). *Parables for the virtual: Movement, affect, sensation*. Durham, NC: Duke University Press.

McCall, M. (2005, May). *Saving sociology*. Paper presented at the International Conference on Qualitative Inquiry, University of Illinois, Urbana.

McGuigan, J. (2005). Cultural studies and the new populism. In G. Ritzer (Ed.), *Encyclopedia of social theory* (pp. 177–181). Thousand Oaks, CA: Sage.

Morley, D. (2000). Cultural studies and common sense: Unresolved questions. In P. Gilroy, L. Grossberg, & A. McRobbie (Eds.), *Without guarantees: In honour of Stuart Hall* (pp. 245–253). New York: Verso.

Piven, F. F. (1981). Deviant behavior and the remaking of the world. *Social Problems, 28*, 489–508.

Pollner, M. (1987). *Mundane reason: Reality in everyday and sociological discourse*. New York: Cambridge University Press.

Pollner, M. (1991). Left of ethnomethodology: The rise and decline of radical reflexivity. *American Sociological Review, 56*, 370–380.

Said, E. (1979). *Orientalism*. New York: Vintage.

Saussure, F. D. (1983). *Course in general linguistics*. Peru, IL: Open Court. (Original work published 1972)

Schneider, J. (1993). Members only: Reading the constructionist text. In J. A. Holstein & G. Miller (Eds.), *Reconsidering social constructionism: Debates in social problems theory* (pp. 103–116). New York: Aldine de Gruyter.

Schneider, J. (2005a). *Donna Haraway: Live theory*. London: Continuum.

Schneider, J. (2005b). Social constructionism. In G. Ritzer (Ed.), *Encyclopedia of social theory* (pp. 724–729). Thousand Oaks, CA: Sage.

Schneider, J. W., & Kitsuse, J. I. (Eds.). (1984). *Advances in the sociology of social problems*. Norwood, NJ: Ablex.

Sedgwick, E. K. (1990). *Epistemology of the closet*. Berkeley: University of California Press.

Sedgwick, E. K. (1993). *Tendencies*. Durham, NC: Duke University Press.

Smith, B. H. (2005). *Scandalous knowledge: Science, truth and the human*. Durham, NC: Duke University Press.

Spector, M., & Kitsuse, J. (2001). *Constructing social problems*. New Brunswick, NJ: Transaction. (Original work published 1977)

Spivak, G. C. (1988). *In other worlds: Essays in cultural politics*. London: Routledge.

Spivak, G. C. (1999). *A critique of postcolonial reason: To-ward a history of the vanishing present*. Cambridge, MA: Harvard University Press.

Taylor, M. C. (2001). *The moment of complexity: Emerging network culture*. Chicago: University of Chicago Press.

Traweek, S. (1988). *Beamtimes and lifetimes*. Cambridge, MA: Harvard University Press.

Turner, G. (1990). *British cultural studies: An introduction*. London: Unwin Hyman.

Williams, R. (1958). *Culture and society, 1780–1950*. Harmondsworth, UK: Penguin.

Williams, R. (1961). *The long revolution*. Harmondsworth, UK: Penguin.

Willis, P. (1981). *Learning to labor: How working class kids get working class jobs*. New York: Columbia University Press. (Original work published 1977)

Women's Study Group, Centre for Contemporary Cultural Studies. (1978). *Women take issue: Aspects of women's subordination*. London: Hutchinson.

Woolgar, S. (1988). *Science! The very idea*. London: Tavistock.

Woolgar, S., & Pawluch, D. (1985). Ontological gerrymandering: The anatomy of social problems explanations. *Social Problems, 32*, 214–227.

CHAPTER 39

Writing Culture, Holism, and the Partialities of Ethnographic Inquiry

● **Vered Amit**

I n a recent article, Douglas Holmes and George Marcus outlined their efforts to reimagine

the norms and design of ethnography, especially as it has developed in the design of anthropology, under the changed contemporary circumstances in which it is practiced. We are very much guided by the strategy and tropes of the influential 1980s so-called Writing Culture critique of ethnography, but now fully extended to the conditions of fieldwork as well and in terms of a different mise-en-scène, so to speak, for the practice of ethnography in which objects of study are often diffuse, fragmented and multi-sited. (2005, p. 246)

Holmes and Marcus are not alone in their effort to "reimagine" ethnography, for there has been a significant flurry of recent publications and conferences focusing attention on anthropological fieldwork (Amit, 2000a; Gupta & Ferguson, 1997; Robbins & Bamford, 1997). But is this recent focus on fieldwork modalities indeed the next stage in a paradigmatic shift launched by James Clifford and George Marcus's highly influential book, *Writing Culture* (1986)? Or should it be?

I ask these questions in the context of the continuing challenges of locating the delineation and representation of ethnographic fields, especially as these challenges relate to the constructionist issues raised in this *Handbook*. This chapter argues that anthropologists (and ethnographers more generally) must take responsibility for the constructed and selective nature of their field of investigation and consequent representations. However, I also argue that in doing so, they should not apologize for the particularity of their analytic "voice" but assert it as a necessary aspect of forwarding investigation and analysis. This necessity is not new, but it is further highlighted by the complex problems of locating the field in times of increasing personal disjunction. The chapter's aim is twofold: to present the implications of the continuing holistic impulses of anthropological analyses and to address empirically contemporary forms of disjunctive complexity by using examples from my current research on international student travel.

How New Are the Challenges of *Writing Culture*?

For Matti Bunzl, *Writing Culture* and other texts of the 1980s, although extremely influential, obscured their own historicity under claims of unique newness (Bunzl, 2005, pp. 187–188). The paradigmatic shift in which they participated was, according to Bunzl, actually launched in the 1960s, precipitated by the postcolonial predicaments of the period, which were brought to a head by the publication of Bronislaw Malinowski's field diaries in 1967. Similarly, in the early 1990s, Richard Fox noted that the demands of some anthropologists— whom he identified somewhat apologetically as postmodernists or reflexivists—for a radical break compressed the entire history of anthropology into one horizon of "realist ethnography," which was then dismissed as being incapable of addressing the changed circumstances of the present:

> These anthropologists do not recognize the works on complex society from the 1950s or the calls for reinvention from the 1970s, which I mentioned earlier, as progressive, or even separate, stages of anthropology's development. Indeed such development seems possible to them only in the present: anthropology has to be worked up almost from scratch; the *present condition* of the world both compels and enables radically novel works. (Fox, 1991, p. 5; emphasis added)

To a certain extent, this emphasis on the compelling imperatives occasioned by historical shifts in the "condition of the world" is also echoed in some of the recent reconsideration of fieldwork methods. In critically reevaluating the idea, practice, and location of fieldwork in anthropological research, Akhil Gupta and James Ferguson (1997) noted that one of the imperatives for this reappraisal is a concern about the lack of fit between the changing circumstances of a mobile, globalizing world and ethnographic field methods originally developed to study small-scale societies (p. 3). Similarly, a special issue of the journal *Anthropology and Humanism* published in the same year was devoted to a consideration of the effect of globalization on the situation of fieldwork (Robbins & Bamford, 1997, p. 3). According to the issue's editors, these changing conditions were "unmaking" the distinction between home and away, raising new ethical dilemmas, and necessitating the development of new methods (Robbins & Bamford, 1997, p. 4).

But the particular brand of presentism that is so often vested in recent calls for a reconsideration of fieldwork is much more likely to be modulated by an appreciation of the historical trajectory of this methodology, noting continuities as well as shifts. Thus Gupta and Ferguson's (1997) critique took account of the historical genealogy of the territorialization of the "field." More recently, in a keynote presentation, James Ferguson[1] cautioned skepticism about claims of historical novelty in current considerations of fieldwork practice and urged a primary focus on the study of relations and interconnections rather than objects, an emphasis that he argued was as relevant to Malinowski's study of the Trobrianders as it was for contemporary studies of transnational relationships. Similarly, Marcus (1998), while locating the development of multisited ethnography as a response to "empirical changes in the world and therefore to transformed locations of cultural production" (p. 80), has also argued that ethnographic fieldwork "as traditionally perceived and practiced is already itself potentially multi-sited" (p. 83). In short, the demand for a radical break with past practice that Fox noted as a feature of some 1980s critiques is much less likely to occur in current reevaluations of fieldwork.

But other aspects of the critique of *Writing Culture* and Clifford's later, more explicit call in *The Predicament of Culture* (1988) do linger on in various efforts at reimagining ethnographic fieldwork practice. Principal among them have been repeated calls for a collaborative approach to ethnographic practice, one in which "informants" are reconceived as coauthors and partners rather than as objects of study. Even Marcus, who noted that Clifford's call for polyphony was less a radical break from previous ethnographic practice than a problematic rereading that "preserves the idea of the representation of a bounded culture" (Marcus, 1998, p. 113), has recently called, with Holmes, for "a more active and explicit practice of collaboration in ethnography" (Holmes & Marcus, 2005, p. 249). Holmes and Marcus (2005) made this latter call in the context of their study of cultures of expertise, characterizing their effort as an attempt to assimilate the domains of representation and practice used by these experts in tracking the global (p. 248).

Leaving aside for the moment the question of whether elite American bankers are likely to be interested in a collaborative partnership with anthropologists, I want to argue that the ideal of collaboration obfuscates some of the most productive aspects of the connections and disjunctions that are rightfully highlighted in so many of the recent reconsiderations of ethnographic fieldwork.

Productive Selectivity and Holistic Impulses

In his introduction to *Writing Culture*, James Clifford (1986) characterizes ethnographic representations as fictions that are inher-

ently partial. According to Clifford, traditionally, this partiality resided in the deliberate exclusions and rhetorical contrivances of ethnographic accounts, which obscured the situated relations of production through which these texts are constructed. This partiality cannot be "filled in," but it can be more explicitly addressed by enlisting "informants" as coauthors. Clifford argued that the resulting dialogical or polyphonic accounts thus more explicitly and critically reveal the negotiated, intersubjective, and hierarchical nature of ethnographic representations.

I argue instead for a rather different, if equally deliberate, partiality, one that cannot be resolved through a collaborative ideal and that is ultimately inspired by the holistic impulse of anthropological inquiry, challenging *Writing Culture*'s version of partiality. *Holism* has become something of a dirty word in anthropology, with analysts of rather different convictions nonetheless equally rushing to reassure their audience that, whatever approach they may propose, it is definitely not an argument for holism. Holism acquired this negative connotation because it was identified with a kind of "island" approach involving distorted representations of speciously bounded and uniform cultural isolates. In other words, depiction of life "in the round" was achieved at the expense of leaving out crucial information, with Evans-Pritchard's omission of the colonization of the Nuer and his own official status often cited as a classic example of this kind of misrepresentation. But one kind of portrait—and most certainly not an unnecessarily simplified one—need not determine the onus toward holism in anthropology. Quite to the contrary, at its most productive, holism is driven by a concern with fleshing out context and, in a world of infinite connections, is a committed search for context in an effort to apprehend complexity. As Marilyn Strathern has noted:

> If at the end of the 20th century, one were to invent a method of inquiry by which to grasp

the complexity of social life, one might wish to invent something like the social anthropologist's ethnographic practice. (Strathern, as cited in Sykes, 2003, p. 164)

But the very scope of the complexity we are striving to grasp always necessitates some measure of analytic selectivity. So, a sincere onus toward holism always involves an admission of the basis of that selection, that is, the analytic questions we are addressing and the strategy we as analysts have selected to engage them. A search for context, therefore, not only admits absences or partiality but also positively enjoins them as the necessary condition that permits analysis.

The history of anthropology is therefore one of successive debates about and orientations toward appropriate strategies of contextualization and their necessarily accompanying selectivity. One of these, as I have already noted, is the "island" approach, which has been so heavily castigated over the past 20 years or so. But it has hardly been the only one. Another example was Ely Devons and Max Gluckman's (1964) assertion of the necessity to simplify, to circumscribe, and to be self-consciously naive in order to forward social science analysis (p. 259). Yet another is the multisited strategy that has been most systematically articulated by Marcus (1998).

But this search for context need not be, as in Clifford's version of partiality, an effort at representation. Rather, as Karen Sykes (2003) has noted in reviewing Roy Wagner and Bruno Latour's work, it can be an effort to model reality rather than to represent it, "thereby creating the means to describe the world without creating a false sense of difference between the researcher and the field" (p. 163). A model is concerned with postulating possible associations rather than a "native" point of view, the "how" rather than the "what" of the processes under examination (Sykes, 2003). But, as such, its selective framing and focus is inescapably the responsibility of its designer and has to be judged in respect to its interrogative effectiveness. To posit other "voices" as in a dialogical eth-

nography is beside the point if they are addressing other questions. The issue is not the veracity or value of one set of issues versus another but that they are likely to be oriented toward different purposes.

But here we reach the nub of a set of issues that has bedeviled anthropology virtually from the outset, that is, the degree of convergence or affinity that can or should arise between the purposes of the anthropologist and the people he or she is studying. Given the long history and density of these debates, I can do little more here than signpost some of the key epistemological, methodological, and ethical grounds on which presumptions of various forms of convergence have historically been mounted. In major part, the question of convergence has arisen from the inductive nature of anthropology, in which generalizations are presumed to arise from the comparison of particular cases rather than from the prior formulation of general hypotheses. As a means of pursuing this form of inquiry, ethnography was traditionally supposed to furnish an open-ended mode of inquiry, with the process of immersion through participant observation often likened to that of a child learning cultural mores and social practices from his or her "native" teachers. Although subsequent cross-cultural comparison involved a different and more independent mode of abstraction, it still supposedly drew on materials originally generated and imparted by local interlocutors. A second basis of convergence was generally presumed to arise from the affinities ideally achieved through long-term participant observation. As a principal mode of fieldwork, participant observation is distinctive in its aspiration toward the cultivation of intimacy between researcher and "informants." In turn, that familiarity and closeness has posed long-standing ethical dilemmas for anthropologists; can one treat as simple data the insights and information one has gained from people who have become intimates rather than distanced research objects? When these kinds of ethical quandaries are combined with significant socioeconomic disparities between researcher and local interlocutors, including accusations—both from within and beyond the discipline—of historical complicity variously with colonial regimes and intelligence or military agencies, then the stage is set for repeated agonizing over and efforts to transcend the exploitative potential of participant observation. From advocacy to collaboration, there have thus been repeated calls within the discipline for a deliberate convergence between the purposes of the anthropologist and the people he or she is studying.

At the same time, however, from the venerable distinctions between emic–etic and native–outsider to the "rigorous partialities" of the *Writing Culture* critique, there has been an equally long history of deliberations over the inescapable and necessary divergence between the perspectives and interests of researcher and research subjects. Thus a significant aspect of recent debates about the "crisis of representation" and, more recently, the "crisis of fieldwork" has concerned efforts to address a central conundrum—namely, that anthropology has developed a mode of inquiry grounded in the pursuit of a convergence between the perspectives of researcher and researched at the same time that anthropologists have also repeatedly argued that this distinction is never entirely bridgeable. Therefore, to raise the possibility of an epistemological stance that, by design rather than resigned regret, seeks to assert the utility of an autonomous anthropological "voice" is truly to open up a can of worms.

But without raising this possibility, it is difficult to know how anthropologists are going to enlarge the range and scope of circumstances they are willing to investigate. If we are unwilling from the outset to construct fields of investigation that may differ from—even while overlapping—the parameters constructed by our ethnographic interlocutors, we will be increasingly confined to a range of very limited research questions. Without asserting the autonomy of the ana-

lyst's questions, there is a risk that the development of anthropological investigations is going to be the hostage of the most limiting aspects of its methodological traditions rather than its beneficiary.

Discontinuities

One of the most apparent effects of this epistemological trap has been the continued reluctance of many anthropologists to construct their investigations around the discontinuities as much as the multiple connections of contemporary life. Discontinuities in various forms are often viewed as potentially imperiling one aspect or another of familiar media for seeking convergence between anthropologist and "informant." A focus on persons who are not directly linked to one another may make participant observation difficult or ineffective. A focus on disjunctions between situations, networks, and systems, for example, may mean that the questions posed by the researcher cannot be addressed by primarily following the train of concerns held by a particular set of people. It may also mean that the interfaces of primary concern for the anthropologist may be of relatively little import or interest to some or even many of the persons with whom he or she is engaging. Thus, in spite of proliferating invocations of disjuncture and fragmentation in so much contemporary anthropological literature, fieldwork strategies are still more often designed to mitigate the effect of these discontinuities than to adapt to them the better to engage them. In outlining the interview-based nature of her fieldwork with the dispersed members of her former high school class, Sherry Ortner (2003) explained, that although they were now scattered across numerous and diverse sites, she drew "enormous ethnographic benefit" from the fact that these individuals had once been part of a face-to-face community (p. 16). Indeed, although she recognized the increasing prevalence of "delocalized" anthropological fieldwork (Ortner, 1997,

2003), Ortner still argued that "social linkages between informants" constitute a crucial condition for ethnographic research:

> While not all researchers doing delocalized fieldwork can expect to work with a historically connected group like this, the point is that some kind of social linkages between informants, whether of kinship, institutional connections, or shared projects—the possibilities are open to much creative construction—seem crucial in order to avoid the problem of unrelated talking heads, that is, the production of highly individualized, socially decontextualized talk. (2003, p. 16)

Even a researcher such as Marcus, who has been so identified with the development of a "mobile ethnography" that takes "unexpected trajectories" across multiple sites of activity, has still asserted the importance of an affinity between ethnographer and subject stemming from a shared anxiety and uncertainty about the effects of a shadowy elsewhere (1998, p. 119) or collaboration with counterpart "experts" (Holmes & Marcus, 2005). But sometimes the most provocative aspects of the multisited situations increasingly being investigated by anthropologists arise in the breaks between the concerns, claims, and involvements of the various subjects they involve. What research subjects may shrug off or even be unaware of may, in some circumstances, be as reasonably compelling to the investigator as what excites or worries them.

Student Travel

I turn now to an examination of some of the quandaries raised by my current research on international student travel, a set of activities characterized as much by its disjunctions as by its association with an expansive discursive construction that insistently conjoins varying forms of travel.

> Today's university students will be our future leaders, and they will need to work and live in a global society. We must find ways to equip them with the international experiences and understanding that they will need—providing more Canadian students with the opportunity to participate in international exchanges, co-op and work experience programs and encouraging top-flight international students to study in Canada. (Association of Universities and Colleges of Canada [AUCC], 2004)

It was the proliferation of statements such as these in and around us that served as the catalyst for a study of international student mobility on which Noel Dyck and I are currently collaborating with the support of several postgraduate students and with which I am concerned in this chapter.[2]

Across a variety of Canadian sectors and institutions, including government, tourism, and academia, an increasingly expansive set of rhetorical claims portray international student and youth mobility as a crucial tool of training that will impart a competitive edge to individual careers and, by extension, will make the national economies in which they are citizens more globally competitive. And these claims feature an increasing tendency to reframe discursively almost any extended stay abroad by youths as a useful form of credential and training in a globalizing world, quite apart from the particular purpose to which a specific type of sojourn may be ostensibly dedicated.

This kind of reframing—which in Canada is promoted by a wide range of agencies such as the federal Department of Foreign Affairs and International Trade, the Student Work Abroad Program (administered by the Canadian Federation of Students), the Youth Tourism Consortium of Canada, the AUCC, the Canadian Bureau of International Education, and many others— deliberately blurs the boundaries between work, education, and leisure and tourism. Thus the Department of Foreign Affairs and International Trade Canada (2007) claims that the various working holiday and co-op educational programs made possible by the reciprocal agreements it has negotiated with

20 other countries allow young Canadians between the ages of 18 and 30 years to "gain valuable global experience and skills that are sought after by employers both in Canada and around the world." Not only can a student work or study while he or she tours, but also supposedly all of these different impetuses for international travel can serve as career signposts, inculcating and denoting the kind of cosmopolitan capacity and "entrepreneurial spirit"[3] demanded in a global economy. So even the seemingly carefree grounds of a summer spent working in a London pub or a semester in an Australian university supposedly carries with it the imminent potential for competitive nation building.

At the same time, within the university sector in Canada and other affluent, industrial countries, there appears to be some degree of bureaucratic diversification around the notion of internationalization generally, as well as student mobility more specifically. There is now an entire occupational sector of "international educators" with institutional offices, career paths, national and regional associations, annual meetings, and journals. And if you attend the exhibition hall at the annual meeting of one of the largest of these associations, NAFSA,[4] you will quickly become aware of the various government agencies and an even larger number of private businesses, consortiums, and companies, from insurance providers to tour operators, that also operate in this sector.

A diversifying range of governmental and legal regimes of working holidaymaker and student visas, regulations, and reciprocal agreements now administer the movement of students and youths across state borders, and there are a significant and increasing number of young adults traveling across these borders. Indeed, globally, youth travel appears to have increased by 20–25% each year throughout the 1990s and now constitutes the fastest growing segment of the travel market, accounting for over 20% of tourism worldwide (d'Anjou, 2004, p. 1),

with working holidays featuring an especially strong expansion.

And yet, in spite of the seemingly wide-ranging nature of these regimes and the regularity with which certain kinds of rhetorical claims feature in so much of this global talk of student travel, the discontinuities between the different sectors and participants that may be implicated in this form of movement are never far from view. For example, officials who administer university exchanges may have little contact with associates in their own institutions who are dealing with international students, and even less so with faculty advisors who are responsible for evaluating and approving academic equivalences of courses completed abroad or senior administrators who actually decide policy on internationalization, let alone with their counterparts in other universities. Some of these officials are not able to and others only intermittently attend the conferences sponsored by "international education" associations; they are unlikely to have contacts with government officials who administer related visa programs or intergovernmental agreements and even less so with the politicians who have had a hand in determining regional or national policies governing student mobility. As a result, the official who is actually running a university exchange program may have little experience or substantive knowledge of the political, bureaucratic, network, and interpersonal dynamics shaping decisions about the procedures they are administering. Officials who process students for exchange programs are unlikely to have actually visited the institutions their clients are attending, and they often have little contact with these students while they are studying abroad or even after they return. They are therefore unlikely to have much direct knowledge as to what actually happens to students on their stays abroad. It is very unlikely that these officials will have any means of tracking the effects of a stay abroad on the student's remaining studies and even less so of the effects on subsequent career prospects.

The kind of gaps I have outlined regarding the development and administration of university exchanges could easily be paralleled in many other sectors of student mobility and travel, such as working holidaymaker programs, internships, and so on. Furthermore, the organizers, policymakers, and administrators engaged in these different sectors of student travel are unlikely to have much, if any, contact with each other or with the other parties whose patronage is either valorized or assumed. Thus, although parents are often the financial sponsors for various forms of student travel, most of the officials we have so far spoken to expect them to remain in the background, and they greet the occasional more direct parental intervention with some bemusement. The employers who are assumed to be eager recruiters of youths with "international experience" remain almost entirely anonymous; evidence of their actual motivations and reactions is rarely, if ever, sought or produced. But the frequency and extent of these disjunctures do not seem to do much to diminish the rhetorical expansiveness of the various institutional claims that are often made about student mobility.

Programs

Within the available Canadian promotional literature on student stays abroad, terms such as *program* and *opportunity* are ubiquitous. Opportunities are "created" or "offered" by the respective association or institution. Programs set out goals and objectives or list "projects." The resulting impression is of standing transnational structures organized by and mutually agreed on by participating institutions with students as clients following already established protocols. But the youthful movement across borders, organizations, educational systems, labor markets, and immigration systems is rarely so well mapped or integrated. Instead, as they bump up against the contradictions and incomprehension between different institu-

tional, local, and national systems, young travelers often find that they have to carve out their own ad hoc, ingenious paths in and around these fractures.

One student, Melissa, went to Paris for a semester's study on an "official university exchange." When she arrived, she had little idea about which courses she would be able to take or the difference between the French system of postsecondary education and the Quebec system, in which she was normally enrolled. She was a student in a communications program but did not realize that the French university she was visiting did not have a comparable program. She ended up taking art history courses. On a visit back to Quebec between completing her semester abroad and traveling in Europe over the summer, she visited her home university and showed her handwritten French transcript to the administrator responsible for organizing international exchanges.

> She [the administrator] said, "No, you have to get something that's official." So I went back. Thank God, I came back to Canada. So when I went back to France I went into the international exchange office and I said I need an official transcript and they said, "we don't do official transcripts." Because they write everything, nothing gets on computers. It's the most frustrating thing. I could have had it with me and I should show it to you, it's hysterical. Anyway, I *made my own* transcript. I do graphic design, I made my own transcript and I went to the international exchange office in Paris. I said, "Can you sign this and stamp it?" She . . . [says], "No problem."

Her home university then accepted Melissa's new handmade transcript as properly official.

Rather than slotting into a well-developed set of prior bureaucratic arrangements that had been carefully negotiated through agreements between universities, government departments, student travel agencies, employers, or housing agencies, these student sojourners more often worked out their own improvised arrangements, for which they then sought some form of official imprimatur: a visa, university credit, and so on. In other words, although there is indeed a linkage between the individual arrangements made by student travelers and the various agencies that claim them as clients, it is often mutually opportunistic rather than systematically integrated. It is easier for students to move for extended periods across international borders and between organizations if they assert official status in a "program," and institutions can claim fairly rough-and-ready individual arrangements as part of their "program" numbers.

Making Futures

When students wonder "where's the beef?" in an international exchange, Peter, a manager in the international office of a Canadian university, argued that they should think of it as "value added," a feature that, although barely marked out in their university transcripts, would still, he maintained, make their degree distinctive from that of anyone else. Similarly, Martin, a manager in a student travel agency, characterized the work-abroad experience as "resumé enhancing":

> Because it's true, right? But what our challenge is there is to get across to them that its all jolly well and good if one can get overseas experience in what one deems to be their field of study, right? However, we also have to try to convince folks that nowadays fields of study tend to vary over one's career, right? A lot of people are in two, three careers even in this day and age and it's probably going to stay that way for some time. But more importantly, we try to get across to them that, look, it doesn't matter what the overseas work experience is, it's the fact that you've done it. And that we've had untold examples of people telling us, you know, that when they returned back to Canada and had that big interview with IBM, or whatever, that the interview board seemed more interested in the fact that they worked for six months in a pub called the Frog and Night-

gown than, you know, in their internship in Kitchener [Ontario] working with some database, kind of thing, right?

Yet, in a 1998 report for the Canadian Bureau of International Education, David Wilson found that a survey of senior persons in private and public sector corporations and institutions evoked the worth of "intercultural skills" among employees but did not apparently evaluate study abroad, extensive travel, or international contacts as very important. And given a Canadian federal immigration policy that has recently emphasized the recruitment of highly educated immigrants in spite of the well-recognized difficulty these newcomers have faced from Canadian employers and professional associations in achieving recognition of their foreign credentials, there are reasonable grounds to doubt the certainty of ubiquitous assurances to young travelers that even the most tangential of international experiences will proffer career advantages.

Mark, a Montreal engineering student, didn't think that his experience working in a London coffee bar would be relevant to his future job applications. And anyway, he noted, that was not why he had gone. He went because he wanted to travel. Although the student sojourners we spoke to varied widely in their views as to whether or not a stay abroad would be a "résumé enhancer," the vast majority were clear that their primary motivation in traveling was touristic, an escape from, rather than a transformation of, the usual routines and pathways of school and career. Many were at a point of transition in their lives when they were uncertain about their next step, whether to continue with further studies or venture out to work and, if so, in what or where. Going away provided a pause, a diversion from these issues with little at risk in taking this step. If a stint of work abroad was not enjoyable, they could always just go home. With a pass–fail system, there was little scholastically at stake in a semester abroad. But with relatively little at stake, the future was also not likely to be significantly transformed by this experience.

Convenient Disjunctures

What, then, are we to make of this apparent divergence between, on the one hand, an increasingly pervasive institutional construction of student and youth stays abroad as part of systematic efforts at training "global citizens" for "new economies" and, on the other hand, young sojourners' own tendency to represent their travel as less (rather than more) consequential tourist interludes? If it is not evident whether or how international experience imbues youths with the capacities to perform competitively in a global economy, it is rather more apparent that whatever the effects on young travelers themselves, their movement across international borders is creating significant global markets. An economic model developed by members of the Youth Tourism Consortium of Canada (YTCA)[5] estimates that "total youth travel expenditures in Canada in 2002 were approximately C$12.3 billion," representing close to 23% of total travel and tourism expenditures in Canada that year (d'Anjou, 2004, p. 14). And this is a field of global competition that is expanding and intensifying, with countries such as Brazil, Taiwan, and Costa Rica aggressively targeting the world young traveler market (d'Anjou, 2004, p. 18). Competition is similarly escalating for the world market in international students. With the reduction of state support for postsecondary education in countries such as Australia, Canada, and the United Kingdom, the income provided by higher international student fees has become a ever more critical source of revenue. Thus not only does the cross-border movement of students and youths constitute an increasingly lucrative and competitive global marketplace, but its expansion is also increasingly drawing on a convergence between sectors of tourism, education, and labor and an overlap in the roles of these young travelers as both consumers and workers.

But the structural changes in these particular sectors are discursively deflected to the individual futures of these youthful protagonists so that personal prospects, sectoral realignments, and national economies are represented as thoroughly integrated. As educational establishments become increasingly corporatized and "alternative" tourism becomes big business, it is all apparently in the service of producing a new entrepreneurial, flexible agent who will lead his or her national economy to global competitiveness. And yet, ironically, changes in and the expansion of these sectors often seem to rely on the relatively limited expectations of their youthful clients, who seem largely unaware of or concerned about the expansive claims made on their behalf. In other words, for all the talk of programmatic integration, many of these systemic changes have in some respects depended on discontinuities that are rhetorically elided. Indeed, if student travelers actually believed that their future expectations would be significantly transformed by their periods of work and study abroad or that they were entering a well-developed set of transnational protocols for inculcating new forms of cosmopolitanism, then their demands and/or dissatisfaction might well make the lives and routines of their institutional patrons far more challenging.

Constructing Contexts

The kind of systemic gaps between political policy, bureaucratic structures, and individual experiences that I have briefly sketched herein are hardly unusual or unique to the sectors with which I have been concerned. At the very least, most of us encounter them regularly in our daily lives, but pursuing them ethnographically is no easier for all their ubiquity. The very nebulousness of a diffuse rhetoric about "global citizens" and "student mobility" makes tracking its implications hardly a matter of self-evident contextualization. However, to follow Sherry Ortner's prescription of searching out, as a point of investigative departure, socially linked "informants" would have been to circumvent some of the most critical questions raised by this discourse—namely, *are there* actual links between the various people, organizations, experiences, skills, and prospects identified with student mobility, and, if so, what is their scope and nature? Asking questions about *possible* connections—as opposed to asserting connections as a precondition for inquiry—necessarily assumes the possibility of discovering discontinuities.

Nor does participant observation, as opposed to conducting interviews, necessarily resolve the question of social context. Our project has involved participant observation in dispersed sites combined with interviews, e-mail communication, Internet searches, and documentary reviews. But the people we have contacted both in the same locale and between locales often did not know each other, or even *of* each other. Canadian students encountered in Australia or Scotland while temporarily participating in an academic exchange or working abroad were still far from their families, partners, friends, employers, or teachers. In such a diffuse range of activities and relationships, every presence draws attention to what is absent, to what might also be connected.

At the end of the day, the contacts we are pursuing respond to a context that has been demarcated by our questions rather than by an intrinsic linkage between our interlocutors.

Yet in a world of infinite interconnections and overlapping contexts, the ethnographic field cannot simply exist, awaiting discovery. It has to be laboriously constructed, prised apart from all the other possibilities for contextualization to which its constituent relationships and connections could also be referred. (Amit, 2000b, p. 6)

But having constructed that field, we cannot, nor should we want to, evade accountability for doing so. Our analyses can be judged in terms of the effectiveness of our questions, our strategies for pursuing them, and the empirical material they have yielded. Life goes on without us, but our investigations of it are a matter of selective contextualization. So, in answer to the question that I raised at the start of this chapter—should recent efforts by anthropologists to reevaluate, or "reimagine," to use Holmes and Marcus's term, be addressed as the next stage of the *Writing Culture* critique of the 1980s?—I would have to answer that the version of partiality it offered was more likely to narrow rather than expand the range of questions that anthropologists could pursue. Instead, I have argued for a version of epistemological partiality that continues a long-standing anthropological onus toward holistic aspirations that necessarily entail selective contextualization. I have also argued that anthropologists should explicitly claim authorship of their efforts at constructing the field of their inquiry rather than either naturalizing their accounts or obscuring their authorship in claims of partnership with people who may reasonably wish to pursue other objectives or agendas. James Clifford was correct in observing that "anthropology no longer [did it ever?] speaks with automatic authority for others defined as unable to speak for themselves" (1986, p. 10). But the flip side of this assertion is not to bury the anthropological voice and vision but rather to declare and exercise it boldly and thus lay it open to interrogation.

• Notes

1. An account of this keynote presentation was provided by Finkelstein and Zeiderman in *Anthropology News* (September 2006, p. 23).

2. This project has been made possible by a grant from the Social Sciences and Humanities

Research Council of Canada. Research on this project commenced in 2004, and interviews with students, organizers, and administrators in Canada are still ongoing. In addition, Heather Barnick conducted fieldwork and interviews in Australia, principally in Melbourne but also in Sydney and Perth, focusing on exchange students. Vered Amit conducted interviews with officials and administrators in Australia. Meghan Gilgunn conducted fieldwork with Canadian students on athletic scholarships in Boston, and Noel Dyck conducted interviews with university athletic officials in Boston. Kathleen Rice has conducted fieldwork in Edinburgh with students and youths on working holidaymaker visas. Vered Amit has conducted interviews with organizers in the United Kingdom. Heather Barnick, Jennifer Smith, and Isabelle Goulet have provided some assistance with previous interviews in Canada.

For the purposes of this chapter, I focus only on those sections of our project with which I have been most closely involved, that is, the work and exchange aspects of our project.

In order to preserve the confidentiality of people who participated in our study, pseudonyms have been used in place of their real names.

3. Citing a report by Goldfarb Consultants, the AUCC argued that study abroad "greatly improves students' adaptability skills, creating in them an 'If I can do this I can do anything!' attitude. In the new economy, it is crucial to cultivate such an entrepreneurial spirit" (AUCC, 2002).

4. The National Association of Foreign Student Advisers, or NAFSA, was initially founded in 1948 as the professional association of American university and college officials advising foreign students studying in the United States. Its scope subsequently expanded to include the wider range of officials, such as English-language specialists or admissions personnel, who were also involved in "acclimating" these foreign students. Accordingly, in 1964, the name of NAFSA was changed to the National Association for Foreign Students Affairs. Subsequently, NAFSA expanded to include those organizers and officials who were involved in handling students moving in the opposite direction, that is, those American students studying abroad for short periods (while still enrolled in an American institution), participating in university exchange programs, or studying foreign areas and languages. Hence in May

1990, while retaining the acronym as a reminder of the past, the association was renamed NAFSA: Association of International Educators (NAFSA, 2006). But the NAFSA annual conference has also become a major international venue in itself, drawing administrators from universities and colleges across the world, who attend workshops on mobility programs and procedures, promote their respective institutions, negotiate exchange agreements with partner establishments, and so on. Indeed, the 2006 NAFSA conference was held outside the United States, in Montreal.

5. Joel Marier, national executive director of Hostelling International—Canada and the current chair of the Youth Tourism Consortium of Canada (YTCC), and Michael Palmer, executive director of the Student Youth Travel Association, developed the model.

• References

Amit, V. (Ed.). (2000a). *Constructing the field: Ethnographic fieldwork in the contemporary world*. London: Routledge.

Amit, V. (2000b). Introduction: Constructing the field. In V. Amit (Ed.), *Constructing the field: Ethnographic fieldwork in the contemporary world* (pp. 1–18). London: Routledge

Association of Universities and Colleges of Canada. (2002). *Study abroad*. Retrieved May 7, 2007, *www.aucc.ca/_pdf/english/reports/2002/innovation/study_abroad_e.PDF*

Association of Universities and Colleges of Canada. (2004). *Building Canada's international influence: Election 2004*. Retrieved May 7, 2007, from *www.aucc.ca/_pdf/english/reports/2004/international_e.pdf*

Bunzl, M. (2005). Anthropology beyond crisis: Toward an intellectual history of the extended present. *Anthropology and Humanism, 30*(2), 187–195.

Clifford, J. (1986). Introduction: Partial truths. In J. Clifford & G. E. Marcus (Eds.), *Writing culture: The poetics and politics of ethnography* (pp. 1–26). Berkeley: University of California Press.

Clifford, J. (1988). *The predicament of culture: Twentieth-century ethnography, literature, and art*. Cambridge, MA: Harvard University Press.

Clifford,, J. & Marcus, G. (Eds.). (1986). *Writing culture: The poetics and politics of ethnography*. Berkeley: University of California Press.

d'Anjou, A. (2004). *Youth tourism in Canada: A situational analysis of an overlooked market*. Ottawa, Ontario: Youth Tourism Consortium of Canada.

Devons, E., & Gluckman, M. (1964). Conclusion: Modes

and consequences of limiting a field of study. In M. Gluckman (Ed.), *Closed systems and open minds: The limits of naïvety in social anthropology* (pp. 158–261). Chicago: Aldine.

Finklestein, M., & Zeiderman, A. (2006). The practice and politics of global fieldwork. *Anthropology News*, 23–24.

Foreign Affairs and International Trade Canada. (2007). *International youth programs (travel and work abroad): How our programs work.* Retrieved May 7, 2007, from *www.international.gc.ca/ 123go/works-en.asp*

Fox, R. (1991). Introduction: Working in the present. In R. Fix (Ed.), *Recapturing anthropology: Working in the present* (pp. 1–16). Santa Fe, NM: School of American Research Press.

Gupta, A., & Ferguson, J. (Eds.). (1997). *Anthropological locations: Boundaries and grounds of a field science*. London: University of California Press.

Holmes, D. R., & Marcus, G. (2005). Cultures of expertise and the management of globalization: Toward the re-functioning of ethnography. In A. Ong & S. J. Collier (Eds.), *Global assemblages: Technology, politics and ethics as anthropological problems* (pp. 235–252). Malden, MA: Blackwell.

Marcus, G. (1998). *Ethnography through thick and thin.* Princeton, NJ: Princeton University Press.

NAFSA. (2007). *The history of NAFSA: Association of International Educators.* Retrieved May 7, 2007, from *www.nafsa.org/about.sec/history*

Ortner, S. B. (2003). *New Jersey dreaming: Capital, culture and the class of '58.* Durham: Duke University Press.

Orner, S. B. (1997). Fieldwork in the postcommunity. *Anthropology and Humanism, 22*(1), 61–80.

Robbins, J., & Bamford, S. (Eds.). (1997). Fieldwork revisited: Changing contexts of ethnographic practice in the era of globalization [Special issue]. *Anthropology and Humanism, 22*(1).

Sykes, K. (2003). My aim is true: Postnostalgic reflections on the future of anthropological science. *American Ethnologist, 30*(1), 156–168.

Wilson, D. N. (1998). *Defining international competencies for the new millennium* (CBIE Research, No. 12). Ottawa, Ontario: Canadian Bureau for International Education.

CHAPTER 40

Constructionist Research and Globalization

● **Pertti Alasuutari**

After reading Justin Rosenberg's (2005) and Ray Kiely's (2005) critical but well-grounded reviews of globalization theory, one could ask whether there is any point any more in discussing the relationship between constructionism and globalization studies. According to Rosenberg, the "age of globalization" is over. In the mid-1990s it was still believed that the term *globalization* identified a social change of epochal dimensions and that because of it globalization theory would revolutionize social theory by spatializing it (Featherstone & Lash, 1995). However, the problem with globalization theory was that it entailed an inversion of the designation of *explanans* and *explanandum*: Instead of giving sociological explanations for spatiotemporal phenomena, it tried to transform a spatiotemporal process into a causal force that explains social change. However, the enormous subjective plausibility of the idea was never matched by an equivalent theoretical potential for orienting coherent social analysis.

Similarly, Kiely (2005) argues that the main weakness of globalization literature is the tendency to give causal significance to globalization where none exists. As a case example, Kiely examines the claim, made, for instance, by the World Bank, that in recent years there has been a reduction in poverty in the global order and that this development is a product of nation-states adopting good, "globalization-friendly" policies. According to him, these claims are doubtful because the methods used to measure poverty are questionable. Instead, evidence suggests that there is a bias toward a downward trend over time. In addition, Kiely argues that even if there has been a reduction in poverty, this has not been caused by "pro-globalization" policies. Kiely also shows that there is the same tendency in general globalization literature to utilize globalization as a determining variable, which results in fallacious explanations. Although globalization theorists do not necessarily consciously promote neoliberal policies, according to Kiely the overlap between globalization theory and neoliberalism becomes an effective apology for neoliberalism.

According to Rosenberg (2005), toward the end of the 1990s the age of globalization was over. The beliefs that the world was opening up to a new form of interconnectedness and that a multilayered, multilateral system of global governance would emerge were shattered, and at the same time it became increasingly obvious that globalization theory had failed to produce any empirical results. It became obvious that *globalization* was just a catchy referent to the rapid changes people had experienced in recent years:

> Worldwide social changes were indeed occurring during the 1990s; and these changes do indeed . . . explain the rise of the idea of "globalization." But the reverse never applied. The idea of "globalization" could not in turn explain the changes. It was a *Zeitgeist*, not a proto-scientific concept. And the attempt to turn it into the latter, however understandable, could only generate confusion and equivocation, in short, "follies." (Rosenberg, 2005, p. 15)

However, although Rosenberg has already performed a postmortem on globalization theory, judged by the prevalent use of the term, the announcement of the death of globalization may be premature. For instance, near the end of the first decade of the 21st century, the number of journal articles and books published each year containing the term *globalization* in their titles still seems to be rising.

Besides, even if enthusiasm about globalization as a theoretical concept and as a notion will eventually wear out, it is not a problem for constructionist research. On the contrary, no matter how seriously scientists take a concept, the archetype constructionist take on it is to ask how it constructs reality rather than simply reflecting it. In that light, a doubtful concept can be seen as a particularly suitable target for constructionist analysis, because the constructive role of concepts that are regarded as truthful and self-evident is much more difficult to tackle.

Because of the tremendous popularity of the concept, one would expect to find a lot of literature in which globalization is approached from a constructionist perspective. However, that is not quite the case. There is plenty of research in which different aspects or assumed effects of globalization are scrutinized, which in that way contribute to our understanding of the phenomenon, but relatively little has been done so far to study the uses of the notion itself.

In this chapter I discuss the different perspectives from which globalization can be approached in constructionist research. First, I discuss the most common usage of the term, in which researchers place their own objects of research within a larger social and historical framework by making a reference to globalization. Second, I deal with theories of, and studies about, cultural dimensions of globalization. The third section deals with constructionist analyses of the notion of globalization.

Globalization as a Context

Typically, constructionist researchers do not build structural theories about societies they study. Instead, constructionism looks at the reality of everyday life from the viewpoint of the actors: how they make sense of that reality by using the constructs available to the common sense of the ordinary members of society (Berger & Luckmann, 1967, p. 19). Constructionism does not deny the existence of objective reality of human societies, but because constructionist research is concerned with analyzing how that reality becomes socially constructed, it avoids taking part in that ongoing activity. Building constructs is left for others, because notions about society form the object of research for constructionist studies.

As neat and convenient as such a division of labor between constructionist researchers and structural theorists is in many respects, it is also problematic. One cannot do entirely without using knowledge of the object of research as a resource of inquiry, as well as a topic.[1] When researchers contextualize their object of research, for instance a particular society or institution, and in that way motivate the interest in studying how reality is constructed in that particular site or situation, they normally refer to previous research and theories about the object in question. Even if the study itself may end up questioning previous knowledge about the institution under scrutiny, one cannot bracket everything at once.[2] Besides, typically, constructionist researchers are concerned with the bearings of particular historical situations in a society on the way in which people conceive of their lives and construct their identities.

That is the reason that references to globalization are often used as a way of contextualizing a constructionist study. It is particularly common to refer to a reflexive process of identity construction in today's globalizing world. For instance, Dannie Kjeldgaard (2003) frames his analysis of young people's identity discourses in Denmark and Greenland by arguing that globalization is creating an explosion of products and images from which young consumers may choose. By making a reference to social theorists such as Ulrich Beck, Fuat Firat, Anthony Giddens, and Steven Miles, Kjeldgaard also writes:

> As globalization is creating an explosion of products and images from which young consumers may choose, one is left with questions of how young consumers construct meaning-

ful identities and how strategies of identity may be evoked as lifestyles and subcultures fragment. Contemporary theories of identity in late modernity suggest that the project of identity has become a reflexive process in which the self is negotiated in terms of choice among a plurality of lifestyle options. These options are made available by the materialization of the global market in local contexts. (p. 287)

On the basis of such a framing, Kjeldgaard introduces his research question, which is "how young consumers construct meaningful identities and how strategies of identity may be evoked as lifestyles and subcultures fragment."

Jan Blommaert, James Collins, and Stef Slembrouck's (2005) study of language use and multilingualism in an immigrant neighborhood in Ghent, Belgium, is another example. The empirical part of the article consists of descriptions of how languages and cultures coexist and interact in the densely mixed neighborhood, in which "the reality is that the child from Brugse Poort in all likelihood enters one of the local primary schools, takes Qu'an classes in the local mosque, buys bread in the local bakery and plays soccer on the local car park inside the compound of the *Vieze Gasten*" (Blommaert et al., 2005, p. 230). The authors relate these ethnographic accounts to "issues of globalization, and more particularly with the question of the production of locality under conditions of globalization" (p. 207). By that they refer to the challenge "to explore the 'implosion' of the world into a neighborhood; put otherwise, to describe and analyse an everyday tangibleness that has global dimensions" (p. 222).

In some studies, globalization literature is not used so much as a context by which to justify the research in question but rather as a resource at the conclusion to show that the case being studied represents a more general, global trend. Greg Gow's (2004) article dealing with the media culture of the

Oromo, an ethnonational, stateless group within Ethiopia, is a good example. His empirical analysis comprises case examples of the ways in which the advocates of Oromo nationalism construct the nation as a translocal community by means of cultural products, such as music, films, or images. The article concludes that the media resources of globalization have enabled the Oromo to creatively respond to the adversity of statelessness. "Their experience says something about the fate of diaspora nationalism(s) in the 21st century: the contradiction that nationalisms seem on the rise everywhere while globalization has severely eroded the sovereignty of the nation-state" (p. 317).

When globalization is used as a broader context for one's own research in that way, previous literature on globalization is seldom radically criticized or questioned. For one thing, globalization as an assumed international developmental trend cannot easily be challenged on the basis of the case-study approach that is typical of these constructionist inquiries. Second, the whole idea is to give one's own case a broader framework, and for that reason shaking the credibility of the key concept would be unwise. However, these studies can make a contribution to the discussion about globalization by showing what the global phenomenon means at the grassroots level and by critically assessing whether the theorizing aligns with the local reality. For instance, in discussing his findings, Kjeldgaard returns to the theories of globalization and late modernity and says that identities in non-Western cultural settings are not necessarily nonmodern, "but rather emerge as the result of localities' relations to the global cultural economy intersecting with local sociohistorical developments" (Kjeldgaard, 2003, p. 301). In a similar vein, Blommaert and colleagues (2005) emphasize that their project of studying neighborhoods challenges neat theoretical classifications and points out that "macro-processes have their feet on the ground, so to speak" (p. 230).

Cultural Dimensions of Globalization

The relationship between globalization literature and constructionist studies works both ways. Constructionist researchers use references to globalization to contextualize their studies, and those studies are raw material for theory building about globalization. Because researchers have been interested in the cultural consequences and aspects of globalization, there is a strand of social theory that deals with globalization of culture (Anderson, 2001; Appadurai, 1996; Cvetkovich & Kellner, 1997; Tomlinson, 1999).

Theorizing about the cultural dimension of globalization typically starts from the idea according to which globalization depicts the rapidly developing and ever-densening network of interconnections and interdependencies that characterize the contemporary global world. This opens the question of what it means for the everyday life, lived experience, meaning making, and identity construction of people who live in different parts of the globe, in which time and space are becoming less important or limiting, or at least where there are growing cultural flows between local lifeworlds.

In this instance, many researchers and theorists refer to Arjun Appadurai's (1996, pp. 33–37) list of five dimensions of flows, which are (1) ethnoscapes, (2) mediascapes, (3) technoscapes, (4) financescapes, and (5) ideoscapes. With the suffix -scape Appadurai wants to emphasize the fluid, irregular shapes of these landscapes. The terms also indicate that they are not objectively given relations that look the same from every perspective. Rather, they are "deeply perspectival constructs, inflected by the historical, linguistic, and political situatedness of different sorts of actors: nation-states, multinationals, diasporic communities, as well as subnational groupings and movements (whether religious, political, or economic), and even intimate face-to-face groups, such as villages, neighborhoods, and families" (Appadurai, 1996, p. 33). These landscapes are navigated by agents who both experience and constitute larger formations, in part from their own sense of what these landscapes offer.

By *ethnoscape*, Appadurai means the landscape of persons who constitute the shifting world in which we live: tourists, immigrants, refugees, exiles, guest workers, and so forth. According to him, such moving groups and individuals constitute an essential feature of the world and appear to affect the politics of (and between) nations to a hitherto unprecedented degree. Similarly, by *technoscape* he means the global configuration of technology and the fact that technology now moves at high speeds across various kinds of previously impervious boundaries. According to Appadurai (1996), the complicated technoscapes contribute to very complex fiscal and investment flows that link economies of different countries through a global grid of currency speculation and capital transfer. That is the reason he deems it useful to speak about *financescapes*. That term refers to the disposition of global capital, "which is now a more mysterious, rapid, and difficult landscape to follow than ever before." According to him, currency markets, national stock exchanges, and commodity speculations move huge amounts of money through national turnstiles at blinding speed, with vast, absolute implications for small differences in percentage points and time units. The global relationship among these aforementioned three scapes is disjunctive and unpredictable because each of these landscapes is subject to its own constraints and incentives, at the same time as each acts as a constraint and a parameter for movements in the others.

What is more, according to Appadurai (1996), these disjunctures are further refracted by *mediascapes* and *ideoscapes*. *Mediascapes* refer both to the distribution of the electronic capabilities to produce and disseminate information, which are now available to a growing number of private and public interests throughout the world, and to the images of the world created by these media. Finally, *ideoscapes* are also concatenations of images, but they are often directly political and frequently have to do with the ideologies of states and the counterideologies of movements explicitly oriented to capturing state power or a piece of it. According to Appadurai, these ideoscapes are composed of elements of the Enlightenment worldview. However, "the diaspora of these terms and images across the world, especially since the nineteenth century, has loosened the internal coherence that held them together in a Euro-American master narrative and provided instead a loosely structured synopticon of politics, in which different nationstates, as part of their evolution, have organized their political cultures" (Appadurai, 1996, p. 37).

Under the current global conditions, characterized by increasing cross-border and cross-cultural flows and by a fluidity of time and space, theories and research dealing with the cultural dimensions of globalization typically address the tension between cultural homogenization and cultural heterogenization.

On the one hand, there is a vast array of literature that supports the homogenization argument, and much of it comes from critical theory media studies. The homogenization thesis is partly a rejuvenation of the older thesis about cultural imperialism and Americanization (see Holton, 1998, pp. 166–172). According to the arguments presented from that viewpoint, American companies have a predominant role in the ownership of "the cultural industry" (Cvetkovich & Kellner, 1997). The United States also has been claimed to hold a role in constructing a regulatory framework within culture and information industries that favors the United States' interests. Moreover, it is argued that there is a more deep-running diffusion of (American-originated) cultural practices and social institutions throughout the world, referred to as "McDonaldization" by George Ritzer (1996, 1998). All this is claimed to contribute to a thorough homogenization of world cultures (e.g., Thussu, 1998), with the United States as the model.

The discourse about homogenization is employed to address the worries and embedded political interests people have in regard to global capitalism, such as a loss of "national identity" in the face of increasing flows of capital, culture, and people across borders. On the other hand, those who hope that cultural globalization leads into a "global culture" believe that multiculturalism erases prejudices and racism, which are associated with strong national(ist) cultures.

The homogenization thesis has also been criticized. For instance, it is argued that it is capitalism rather than American culture that is becoming globalized. Although many aspects of capitalism, such as Taylorist scientific management, may be seen as originating in the United States, not nearly all social innovations have an American origin. Besides, it is pointed out, the global field is multicentered rather than dominated by a single center. This also goes for the cultural domain. As Appadurai points out, "it is worth noticing that for the people of Irian Jaya, Indonesianization may be more worrisome than Americanization, as Japanization may be for Koreans, Indianization for Sri Lankans, Vietnamization for the Cambodians, Russianization for the people of Soviet Armenia and the Baltic Republics" (Appadurai, 1996, p. 295). Similarly, Ien Ang and Jon Stratton (1996) argue that Australia is "Asianing." It has also been noted that, instead of homogenization, the world is facing a process of polarization. For Benjamin Barber (1996), one of the adherents of this theory, the polarization is between McWorld and *jihad*, between global consumer capitalism and retribalization, often linked with religious fundamentalism. For Samuel Huntington (2002), the polarization is between civilizations, especially between the West and an emergent Islamic–Confucian axis. The polarization theory brings to the homogenization discussion the point that there is no conformity in the face of homogenizing forces; rather, the perceived threats of "cultural imperialism" give cause for resistance.

However, although the polarization theory at first sight seems to be markedly different from the homogenization thesis, it nonetheless implies that there are only a few "cultural camps" on the globe. Besides, the assumed clash of those camps suggests that they are discursively defined in relation to each other. For instance, as Anthony Giddens (1994, p. 100) has pointed out, fundamentalism, as an "assertion of formulaic truth," can be seen as a reaction to the difficulties of living in a world of radical doubt. In that sense Roland Robertson's (1992, p. 6) formulation of the idea of "the compression of the world into a 'single place'" comes close to the polarization thesis. For him, the argument about a trend toward the unicity of the world does not imply a simplistic uniformity but rather a complex social and phenomenological condition in which different orders of human life—from the level of the individual all the way to humankind—are brought into articulation with one another. For Robertson, globalization is the increasing interaction between these orders. Therefore, for him, "the world as a single place" implies the transformation of these forms of life as they are increasingly positioned against, and forced to take account of, each other (for a discussion of Robertson, see Tomlinson, 1999, pp. 11–12).

These theories about the cultural dimension of globalization entail a constructionist perspective in the sense that, according to them, people's lifeworlds and ways of making sense of their world have an increasingly global context. The homogenization and polarization theories have also served as hypotheses to be tested, but empirical constructionist research has probably contributed the most to counterarguments leveled against the homogenization thesis. The proponents of a thesis of cultural heterogenization have, for instance, pointed out that the same (imported) cultural products or adopted practices are interpreted differently in different cultural contexts. This emphasis is partly a response to the thesis about cultural imperialism. Thus, although the hegemony of the cultural industry seems to inevitably lead into the adoption of the dominant Western culture throughout the world, empirical research shows that the intermingling of local culture and external influences leads into active defense of "traditional" culture, to resistance of foreign influences, and to hybrid identities. This point, also influenced by cultural media studies and reception research, has led to the theory of hybridization. Unlike many other areas of the globalization discussion, there is ample empirical research on hybridization. Inspired by writers such as Homi Bhabha (2001), Ulf Hannerz (1987, 1996), Robert Young (1995), and Stuart Hall (1992), many researchers have analyzed how, along with migration, different cultural influences intermingle with each other to create hybrid cultural forms (e.g., Appadurai, 1996, pp. 89–113; Dolby, 1999; Qureshi & Moores, 1999; Stoddard & Cornwell, 1999).

To take just one example, consider Johanna Schmidt's (2003) study of the changing attitude toward Samoan *fa'afafine*, individuals who are biologically males but who express feminine gender identities. According to her study, the apparent cultural acceptance and very real social marginalization of *fa'afafine* is a consequence of a combination of "traditional" Samoan culture and the impact of globalization on indigenous constructions, representations, and understandings of gender and sexuality. According to Schmidt, although *fa'afafine* blend into Samoan society without drawing attention to themselves, it is the more recent emphasis on sexuality, especially what is understood as "deviant" sexuality, that most Samoans object to. Samoan disapproval of the newly sexualized, Western-influenced femininity of *fa'afafine* may be seen to emerge

from an already existent cultural tendency to devalue sexuality in general and women as sexual beings in particular. Schmidt emphasizes that the recent pressure on *fa'afafine* to alter their sexual habits is more complex than a simply misplaced homophobia originating in missionary values targeted at a traditionally accepted group:

> The lived experience of, and Samoan attitudes to, contemporary fa'afafine can be seen as a complex reaction to a complicated set of circumstances, which include the impact of globalization on the Samoan political economy, shifts in how Samoan gender in general is enacted, considerable changes in the construction and expression of fa'afafine identities, and the globalization of sexual discourses, together with the continued existence of "traditional" (although modified) attitudes about gender and sexuality and understandings of the self. For increasingly sexual and feminine fa'afafine who are, however, actually "men," an already existent cultural devaluing of feminine sexuality has intersected with the relatively recent disapproval of homosexuality, so that fa'afafine are in some sense damned as women and as men. (2003, p. 428)

As a corollary and a theoretical contribution of her study, Schmidt argues that these processes of change in Samoa support George Marcus's (1992, p. 321) observation that although the globe is becoming more integrated, "this paradoxically is not leading to an easily comprehensible totality, but to an increasing diversity of connections among phenomena once thought disparate and worlds apart."

By taking "exotic" examples in which obviously Western cultural influences intermingle with more "traditional" or "local" traditions, these studies seem to celebrate hybridity. However, at a more theoretical level, these studies show that hybridization is and always has been "the ongoing condition of all cultures" (Rosaldo, 1995, p. xv, as cited in Tomlinson, 1999, p. 143). By emphasizing that there is no purity in cultural forms, studies of hybridization enable researchers from humanities and social sciences to enter the discussion by bringing in their contribution. In other words, globalization is a Trojan horse by which cultural researchers bring their own bravura to the agenda.

To reiterate what has been said in this section, for researchers approaching people's lifeworlds from a constructionist viewpoint, globalization studies have not only provided a global and theoretical context for their case studies, but they have also made a considerable contribution to the discussion, bringing to the fore points that were largely and unduly neglected in the social sciences, especially in the economics and political science in which globalization theory originated. Researchers interested in the cultural dimension of globalization have also been quite careful not to treat globalization as a causal force in its own right. Rather, to use Justin Rosenberg's useful distinction between globalization theory and theory of globalization (Rosenberg, 2005, p. 42), they have primarily made observations about the cultural impacts of the process and left the question about the original reason behind it untouched. For them, globalization has served as a new term by which to refer to the developments that have been discussed within the social sciences at least since the time of Karl Marx.

Yet the literature on the tension between cultural homogenization and cultural heterogenization published under the rubric of globalization has not brought much new to the discussion. For instance, if all historical cultures have always been hybrid, then what is new? one has to ask (Tomlinson, 1999, p. 144). There is also the problem that the concept of hybridization itself evokes the myth of pure indigenous cultural forms, which are then supposed to be "hybridized" along with globalization (Tomlinson, 1999, pp. 141–149). In that sense the concept of hybridization is not a very effective way of making the point it wants to make. Ulf Hannerz's (1987) term *creolization*, which he introduced before the globalization discus-

sion, is better in that sense. According to Hannerz, the term *creole*, previously used only by linguists to refer to the mixing of languages, is a good root metaphor to be extended into cultural theory:

> As I see it myself, creole cultures like creole languages are those which draw in some way on two or more historical sources, often originally widely different. They have had some time to develop and integrate, and to become elaborate and pervasive. People are formed from birth by these systems of meaning and largely live their lives in contexts shaped by them. There is that sense of a continuous spectrum of interacting forms, in which the various contributing sources of the culture are differentially visible and active. And, in relation to this, there is a built-in political economy of culture, as social power and material resources are matched with the spectrum of cultural forms. (p. 552)

One problem with the discussion about the cultural dimension of globalization is that the discourse has been essentially framed by the general globalization theory. Whereas the globalization discussion has been concerned with the increasing flows of capital, commodities, and people across borders, the discussion about the cultural dimension has been engrossed with the effects of flows of culture, such as hybrid worldviews and identities. Although social scientists and economists have also been interested in global governance and in the processes that it triggers in individual nation-states, the cultural aspects of global governance have been unduly neglected. When constructionist research on globalization primarily concentrates on the end result of foreign influences, often hastily emphasizing that a simplistic cultural homogenization thesis does not hold, it indirectly reinforces the assumption that globalization is not only a term referring to certain events and developments but a real causal force and an inevitable evolutionary process. In that way, the politics of globalization, the fact that much of the developments labeled as globalization are based on conscious political decisions, is overlooked.

Globalization as a Construct

As the key idea in constructionist theory is to bracket concepts that we tend to take for granted in natural attitudes and to analyze how they are used as social constructs, it is interesting that much of the discussion about globalization as a social construct comes from outside the circle of scholars who identify themselves with social constructionism. For instance, Justin Rosenberg's (2005) Marxism-influenced "postmortem" calls globalization the *Zeitgeist* of the 1990s. According to him, it helped to legitimate the filling of the geopolitical and socioeconomic vacuum left after the collapse of Soviet Union.

> Meanwhile, the ideological vacuum was temporarily filled by an unstable mixture of three sets of ideas, each of which had a powerful temporary correspondence to these processes: multilateralism, democratization and human rights, and of course "globalization." Briefly, multilateralism provided an institutional framework for orchestrating the new order without the appearance (or burdens) of a dictated peace—useful cover for Cold War victors and vanquished alike. Democratization and human rights gave it a practical as well as rhetorical language of legitimacy. And "globalization" was the magic word which simultaneously naturalized and dramatized this tiger-leap of capitalist expansion, representing it as the unstoppable, uncontrollable climax of a universal human destiny. (p. 42)

In other words, Rosenberg points out that by picturing the political and economic development of the 1990s as an inevitable evolutionary process, globalization as a social construct served to justify the actions of the political actors involved as a necessary adaptation to the global condition.

> And for this reason the idea was taken up by a huge variety of actors pursuing a wide variety of purposes: corporate executives and neoliberal governments, functionaries of International Organizations, some international lawyers and supportive legislators, and a multiplying host of activist NGOs—pro-human rights, anti-capitalist, pro-indigenous, anti-big business and many others. All of these actors sensed a momentum to the times, which they could harness to their different causes by capturing the definition of the Zeitgeist. And why not? All of them were certainly right to believe that moments of sudden opening up and political change do create opportunities to be grasped. (p. 59)

Similarly, Kiely (2005) argues that the conflation of process and outcome in globalization theory is utilized by the World Bank and other international institutions to promote neoliberal policies. He points out that in its role as a theory that legitimates current policy, globalization theory is a neoliberal version of earlier modernization theory, which was also used to justify the policy of the Western countries.

In their attempt to show the faultiness and the political uses of globalization theory, Rosenberg and Kiely are hardly the first ones. As Philip F. Kelly (1999) points out, the representation of globalization as an interconnected set of economic and cultural processes operating at the global scale with an inevitable, inexorable, and ultimately benign logic has been widely criticized and often dismissed as "globethink," "globaloney," or "globabble" (p. 383). For example, Robert Spich (1995, pp. 10–11) argues that globalization "is a mind set, an idea set, an ideal visualization, a popular metaphor and, finally, a stylized way of thinking about complex international developments." Similarly, David Steingard and Dale Fitzgibbons (1995, p. 35) argue that behind globalization is the academic business community's sycophantic allegiance to spreading the gospel of globalization: "Those who foresee a happy, multicoloured, and economically equitable global culture are peddling ideology, not reality."

It is characteristic of these critiques of globalization, deemed as a justifying ideology of neoliberalism, to construct an opposition between myth and reality. In other words, because the critics show that globalization theory is erroneous as a scientific theory, its existence and popularity can be explained by its ideological role. However, although these critics consider globalization as unreal, or as an ideological construction, they attribute very material consequences to it. For instance, Steingard and Fitzgibbons (1995) argue that globalization leads to homogenization of world cultures, to accumulation of wealth and poverty, and to increasing use of child labor.

The explanation for the contradiction of denying the reality of globalization on the one hand and attributing real consequences to it on the other can be found in the way in which social reality is understood. For many critics of globalization who come from outside social constructionism, material reality is conceived to consist of law-like mechanisms that have causal effects on economy and society. Thus, because assigning any (mechanical) causality to globalization is shown to be problematic (Kiely, 2005; Rosenberg, 2005), it is not considered a true description of a mechanism of social change. However, in this theoretical framework, one also recognizes another set of causes of change: political decisions, made consciously or fooled by false ideologies. Thus the diagnosis of these critics of globalization is that globalization theory is false but that as an ideology it serves the interests of global capital. Moreover, it has real material consequences insofar as economists, policymakers, and the general public accept it as an objective description of current conditions and act accordingly.

In numerous national contexts it is easy to find examples of the ideological uses of globalization. For instance, in Canada, Prime Minister Jean Chrétien has pronounced: "in-

ternational finance knows no borders . . . we cannot stop globalization, we need to adjust to it. . . . Globalization is imposing a healthy discipline that will result in healthier economies in the long run" (cited in Kelly, 1999, p. 383). Similarly, before assuming power, British Prime Minister Tony Blair noted that "the determining context of economic policy is the new global market. That imposes huge limitations of a practical nature—quite apart from reasons of principle—on macroeconomic policies" (as cited in Saul, 1995, p. 19). In the Philippines, President Fidel Ramos has argued that "there is a new reality that underscores our national life. We are part of a new global economy—in which every nation must compete, if it is to prosper. . . . [We must] imbibe and expand the culture of globalization . . . [or] be left behind in the march toward progress and prosperity for all" (as cited in Kelly, 1999, pp. 383–384). As it is quite clear that the beliefs about the effects of globalization have already led to policy changes in national states and other major actors, thus affecting others' conditions of action, it is obvious that the theoretical framework discussed earlier is in trouble.

Several authors deal with this problem by saying that globalization must be seen both as a social construction and as a real process. As Kelly (1999) emphasizes, although the representations of globalization might be used for national political purposes, they are more than just rhetoric. They are "rooted in material power relations of contemporary capitalism and geopolitics," and "there are real political repercussions tied up in the globalization debate as the caricature of a global end-state is deployed prescriptively" (Kelly, 1999, p. 384).

Considering how much discussion has occurred about globalization as a representation or as a social construct, there is fairly little literature that discusses how globalization works as a social construction. For instance, how does the globalization discourse produce the factuality of globalization as a process, or how are demarcations made about phenomena that are counted as part of, as opposed to outside, globalization? Many of these questions still await constructionist analysis.

Thomas Olesen's (2005) analysis of the uses and misuses of globalization in the study of social movements addresses some of those questions. To avoid reification of globalization as a force at work outside the reach of social actors, Olesen applies the theory of framing (Snow & Benford, 1988; Snow, Rochford, Worden, & Benford, 1986) to scrutinize transnational mobilization of social movements. The social constructionist framing perspective emphasizes that the formation of social movements is inextricably linked to the social construction of shared understandings in a context of specific grievances and social conditions. In this instance, Olesen talks about frames as facilitative conditions, by which he stresses that frames must not be seen as explanatory variables but rather as characteristics of actors' understandings of the situation that are useful in explaining the "how" of transnational mobilization. According to him, there are four conditions that facilitate transnational framing processes: global consciousness, neoliberalism, democracy, and the Internet (Olesen, 2005, p. 53).

As to global consciousness as a facilitative condition for transnational mobilization, Olesen stresses that there is a dialectical relationship between them. Transnational framing usually draws on a global consciousness, but it also produces it. From this perspective, a global consciousness is not something given or stable. It is constantly produced and reproduced by social actors and considerably affected by social theories that treat the globe as one "planetary society." Olesen also emphasizes that the presence of global consciousness in transnational frames does not preclude the presence of a local or national consciousness. In fact, this is more often the case than not. Empirical frames invoking a global consciousness will typically be attempts by a social movement to frame a local or national problem in such a way as to make it relevant to an audience outside the con-

crete physical territory. This is the case, for instance, when repression and persecution in Guatemala are framed in terms of universal human rights or when forest degradation in the Amazon is framed as a threat to our common human heritage (Olesen, 2005, pp. 54–55).

Neoliberalism, according to Olesen, is a facilitative condition for transnational mobilization because it works as an injustice frame, and, according to the framing theory, a successful frame must define a specific problem and substantiate a possible amelioration. In transnational mobilization, the process of neoliberal restructuring since the 1970s and 1980s is used extensively as the axis of transnational injustice frames. Constructing transnational injustice frames thus presupposes a degree of global consciousness of the consequences and nature of neoliberalism. On the other hand, this consciousness is also produced and constructed through transnational framing (Olesen, 2005, pp. 55–56).

Democracy functions as a master frame in transnational mobilization. It is often closely related to the injustice frame of neoliberalism. The reason is that the opposition to neoliberalism is often formulated in a radical democratic terminology. To its critics, neoliberalism is considered undemocratic because of social inequalities created by neoliberalism and because of a democratic deficit that it creates, as more and more decisions are made by unelected technocrats in international institutions (Olesen, 2005, pp. 56–57).

Finally, according to Olesen (2005), the Internet forms a facilitative condition for transnational mobilization. The reason is that the transnational framing process is highly dependent on the availability of means of communication in that it is a communicative process taking place across considerable physical, social, and cultural distance. Olesen stresses that the availability of the Internet makes it easier for distant actors to share everyday experiences and thus to verify empirical credibility and construct experiential commensurability. The role of the Internet is also related to global consciousness (Olesen, 2005, pp. 57–58).

Olesen's (2005) discussion of the conditions and corresponding frames is an attempt to explain why transnational mobilization has taken place in social movements, but the elements that he points out also help to explain the great overall interest in the notion of globalization since the 1990s. However, in order for them to work as explanations of the overall interest in the notion of globalization, I suggest we need to add one crucial frame: the evolutionary predestination perspective. By that I refer to the way in which globalization as a notion continues the tradition of thinking in terms of which the development of world societies is assumed to have an inevitable direction. Within this tradition, started by the Enlightenment philosophers, it is assumed that social development follows its natural course, dictated by mechanical, law-like processes. According to Enlightenment thinkers, the task of social science was to detect the natural laws of society in order to facilitate them so that development leads toward increasing rationality. In present-day social science, the tradition of evolutionary predestination can be seen in arguments about present and future evolutionary trends, based on analyses about the current condition in "advanced" societies.

Modernization theory is a prime example. With the Cold War and the U.S. government's interest in the economic, political, and social development of third-world societies in the background, Talcott Parsons and his followers developed the ideal types of traditional and modern societies into real stages in an evolutionary course and into criteria by which to assess the relative "modernity" of a society in question (Parsons, 1951, 1966; Shils, 1963). According to Jeffrey Alexander (1995), by the end of the 1960s modernization theory died, but in a broader sense the modernization discourse and the historicist method that invigorate the world

historical narrative imagination are alive and well. After the heyday of Parsonian modernization theory, concepts such as postindustrial society (Bell, 1973), postmodernity (Lyotard, 1984), post-Fordism (Harvey, 1989), high or late modernity (Giddens, 1990, 1991), and reflexive modernization (Beck, Bonss, & Lau, 2003; Beck, Giddens, & Lash, 1994) have been used to capture the spirit of the time and to present more or less universalizing claims about historical turns. In discussing recent social and cultural trends, the participants revisit the motifs of older modernization literature. Globalization (see, e.g., Featherstone, 1990; Held, McGrew, Goldblatt, & Perraton, 1999) is one of the concepts that continues this tradition.

By representing globalization as an inevitable process determined by the mechanical dynamics of global social change, its advocates depoliticize their prediction and their recommendations about how to adapt to the change. The change itself is reified as a causal force, whereas all the acts by the actors involved are described as reactions and necessary adaptive measures. However, the notion of globalization as an inevitable, law-like process is also utilized by those who do not support the neoliberalist policy, justified by globalization. First, as was discussed in previous sections, researchers from several disciplines have used globalization to make their fields of research seem more up-to-date and relevant, thus adding new elements to the list of effects or dimensions of globalization. Second, critics of neoliberalism have proposed a "semiotic guerrilla war": Simply because globalization has been used discursively for political ends to justify neoliberalist policy, one does not have to accept it as its only possible use; its discursive construction is open to alternatives (Kelly, 1999). Finally, also, several critics are partly caught in the underlying assumption that history is directed by causal forces, for instance by the laws of capitalism. That is the reason that, to show that capitalism is the real causal force, these critics want to deny the causal force of globalization, thus arguing that it does not really exist. As Rosenberg puts it:

> One can readily see how and why such an idea rose to the level of a *Zeitgeist*. Yet as a causal process in its own right, "globalization" had no momentum of its own. In fact, if the conjunctural analysis developed in this article is broadly correct, "globalization" did not even exist. (2005, p. 65)

According to this line of thought, because globalization does not exist as a real historical trend, the true reason for its existence as a "folly" is ideological: It is a tool of global capital and neoliberalism. This position thus wants to reveal the true nature of globalization and oppose it as a capitalist, neoliberalist conspiratory political program that, if not resisted, will have harmful consequences. Thus, for this variant of the globalization discourse, globalization represents the enemy and therefore helps in forming a social movement that opposes it.

Future Challenges: The Dynamics of Global Change

The discussion of globalization has shown a plethora of uses for the concept. Researchers have used it to give a global historical framework to their own studies, or they have added new elements to the list of phenomena that are seen as aspects or effects of globalization. As a concept, it has been useful because it seemed to speak to the lived experience of many people in the 1990s. For instance, as a framework it resonated with people's growing global consciousness during the age of the Internet, thus also strengthening it. Besides, the globalization discussion allowed people to readdress the question of democracy at the global scale, especially because the rise and spread of neoliberalist economic policy was an essential part of the globalization discourse. As to

the nature of globalization as a phenomenon, there has been a tension between two positions. On the one hand, by making use of the Enlightenment tradition of explaining social change by evolutionary predestination, globalization has been pictured as a mechanical, law-like process that inevitably changes world societies. Contrary to this reified notion, the other position could be characterized as personification; according to it, globalization is only an ideological concept and political program, which can be opposed by forming an antiglobalization movement. Those with a constructionist inclination have avoided treating globalization as a causal force and used it as a name that simply refers to a process of change, while hastening to add that globalization is both a real process and a social construct.

Because of its incredible breadth, the globalization discussion has been quite useful in addressing various questions related to recent social change in a global perspective and in problematizing the relationship between local and global. However, the globalization discourse has not only been enabling but it has also directed and structured the discussion and ruled certain questions outside the field.

If we treat globalization as a concept that characterizes the changes in world societies from the 1980s onward, the problem is that it does not explain that much. In a way the concept is both too broad and too narrow. It is too broad in that within that concept discussants have talked about a great variety of phenomena, which are hardly related to a single process in any other ways than that they are simultaneous. On the other hand, the concept is too narrow in that all significant recent phenomena can hardly be seen as outcomes of the process of increasing interdependencies. In other words, globalization does not really provide an explanation for recent profound changes in world societies. As has been pointed out, it is often used simply as a name to refer to poorly understood developments. There is basically nothing wrong with that kind of use, but the problem is that using a single, descriptive word in that way implies that all the events referred to as the effects or aspects of globalization actually form a single process. Yet it is obvious that there can never be found a single process that accounts for everything that is going on during a particular period. Certainly, human interaction in complex societies produces law-like processes that are relatively independent from the will of individual actors, but all manner of simultaneous changes can be related to each other only to the extent that they are articulated with each other in a hegemonic discourse that guides people's action.

At a more theoretical level, the discussion about globalization touches on the question about the dynamics of social change. However, perhaps because of the way the globalization discourse has framed the discussion, this question has not received the attention it deserves. For instance, if we take seriously the argument made repeatedly in the globalization discussion that the world is increasingly becoming a single place, it would be logical to study how it works: how the same or similar practices are implemented in separate regions or countries. Or to put it differently, if we want to challenge the assumption that social change follows a law-like predestined process at the global scale, it would be logical to test it by trying to form a theory about global change. Which are the actors involved? What is the role of international governmental organizations (IGOs) such as the Organization for Economic Cooperation and Development (OECD) as think tanks and as consultants in guiding the national governments and other actors? How do global-level pressures or policy recommendations turn into local-level policy changes in the private and public sector? What is the role of definitions of the situation and notions such as globalization in these processes? It was not until the late 1990s that these questions attracted more attention. Besides, an interest in analyzing

processes of global social development has often arisen outside or despite the globalization discussion.

For instance, these questions have been addressed in studies that deal with "policy convergence" among advanced industrial states, a strand of studies that predates the globalization discussion. Yet the critical discussion about policy convergence studies is directly relevant to researchers interested in globalization from a social constructionist perspective. For instance, Colin Bennett (1991) argues that studies of policy convergence among advanced industrial states are often based on an overly deterministic logic, a static conception of convergence, and an unclear specification of the aspects of policy that are supposed to be converging. In a similar vein, Lisa Martin and Beth Simmons (1998) criticize previous research for focusing on proving that institutions matter without sufficient attention to constructing well-delineated causal mechanisms or explaining variation in institutional effects. The critics recommend that more attention be paid to domestic politics rather than treating the state as a unit. The reason is that, if IGOs affect global social change, they do it by influencing social and political developments and decision making in national states, and there need to be mechanisms for such influence. On the other hand, the policies that the IGOs expect or recommend the national states to implement do not come from out of the blue; the issues on the agenda are brought there by representatives of nation-states. The totality is a dense network of social relations and material conditions, coupled with conflicting and converging definitions of the situation.

The concept of governmentality, coined by Michel Foucault, is relevant from this viewpoint (Dean, 1999; Foucault, 1991; Rose & Miller, 1992), and, partly related to the globalization discussion, there is growing international interest in the governmentality framework. Foucault's theories and research, which emphasize the productive role of power relations, have particularly inspired studies that analyze the way in which individuals are constructed as subjects and how their mentalities are formed in various institutions of territorialized polities. Foucault himself studied the clinic, the prison, the asylum, and the formation of the discourses of sexuality (Foucault, 1973, 1976, 1977, 1980, 1985, 1986), and scholars inspired by his approach have studied, for instance, alcoholism (Alasuutari, 1992), the museum (Bennett, 1995) and the "psy" disciplines (Rose, 1996). There is relatively little research that applies Foucault's governmentality framework to the study of global social change, but previous research shows that it is well suited to analyzing global governance. James Keeley (1990) argues that Foucault's work gives us analytic devices to better understand the formation and change of international regimes. In a similar vein, Michael Merlingen (2003) argues that the governmentality framework is particularly suitable for studying IGOs because it brings into focus the microdomain of power relations, thereby highlighting what mainline IGO studies fail to thematize. According to him, they exercise a molecular form of power that evades and undermines the material, juridical, and diplomatic limitations on their influence: "Our understanding of IGOs remains incomplete if we do not pay attention to the effects of domination generated by their everyday governance tasks and projects of improvement" (Merlingen, 2003, p. 377).

To conclude, because of its incredible popularity as a concept, globalization should be of great interest for constructionist researchers who want to analyze the role of social constructs in society. On the other hand, its actual uses also illustrate the uneasy relationship between social constructionist research and theories of contemporary societies. We cannot bracket everything at the same time, but if we uncritically adopt others' concepts to our own analytic language, we may miss an essential aspect of social reality.

● Acknowledgments

This work was supported by a grant from the Academy of Finland for the research project *Knowledge Production, Power, and Global Social Change: The Interplay between the OECD and Nation States* (Grant No. 208094).

● Notes

1. On the distinction between topic and resource, see Garfinkel (1967) and Wieder (1988).

2. For a discussion about analytic bracketing, see Holstein and Gubrium (2000, pp. 97–100).

● References

Alasuutari, P. (1992). *Desire and craving: A cultural theory of alcoholism*. Albany: State University of New York Press.

Alexander, J. C. (1995). Modern, anti, post and neo. *New Left Review, 210*), 63–101.

Anderson, A. B. (2001). The complexity of ethnic identities: A postmodern reevaluation. *Identity, 1*(3), 209.

Ang, I., & Stratton, J. (1996). Asianing Australia: Notes toward a critical transnationalism in cultural studies. *Cultural Studies, 10*(1), 16–36.

Appadurai, A. (1996). *Modernity at large: Cultural dimensions of globalization*: Vol. 1. *Public worlds* (D. Goankar & B. Lee, Eds.). Minneapolis: University of Minnesota Press.

Barber, B. R. (1996). *Jihad vs. McWorld*. New York: Ballantine Books.

Beck, U., Bonss, W., & Lau, C. (2003). The theory of reflexive modernization. *Theory, Culture and Society, 20*(2), 1–33.

Beck, U., Giddens, A., & Lash, S. (1994). *Reflexive modernization: Politics, tradition and aesthetics in the modern social order*. Cambridge, UK: Polity Press.

Bell, D. (1973). *The coming of post-industrial society: A venture in social forecasting*. New York: Basic Books.

Bennett, C. J. (1991). What is policy convergence and what causes it? *British Journal of Political Science, 21*(2), 215–233.

Bennett, T. (1995). *The birth of the museum: History, theory, politics*. London: Routledge.

Berger, P. L., & Luckmann, T. (1967). *The social construction of reality: A treatise in the sociology of knowledge*. New York: Doubleday.

Bhabha, H. K. (2001). *The location of culture*. London: Routledge.

Blommaert, J., Collins, J., & Slembrouck, S. (2005).

Polycentricity and interactional regimes in "global neighborhoods." *Ethnography, 6*(2), 205–235.

Cvetkovich, A., & Kellner, D. (Eds.). (1997). *Articulating the global and the local: Globalization and cultural studies: Vol. 5. Politics and culture.* Boulder, CO: Westview Press.

Dean, M. (1999). *Governmentality: Power and rule in modern society.* London: Sage.

Dolby, N. (1999). Youth and the global popular: The politics and practices of race in South Africa. *European Journal of Cultural Studies, 2*(3), 291–309.

Featherstone, M. (Ed.). (1990). *Global culture: Nationalism, globalization and modernity.* London: Sage.

Featherstone, M., & Lash, S. (1995). Globalization, modernity and the spatialization of social theory: An introduction. In M. Featherstone, S. Lash, & R. Robertson (Eds.), *Global modernities* (pp. 1–24). London: Sage.

Foucault, M. (1973). *Madness and civilization: A history of insanity in the age of reason.* New York: Vintage Books.

Foucault, M. (1976). *The birth of the clinic: An archeology of medical perception.* London: Tavistock.

Foucault, M. (1977). *Discipline and punish: The birth of the prison.* London: Penguin Books.

Foucault, M. (1980). *The history of sexuality: Vol. 1. An introduction.* New York: Vintage Books.

Foucault, M. (1985). *The history of sexuality: Vol. 2. The use of pleasure.* Harmondsworth, UK: Viking.

Foucault, M. (1986). *The history of sexuality: Vol. 3. The care of the self.* New York: Pantheon Books.

Foucault, M. (1991). Governmentality. In G. Burchell, C. Gordon, & P. Miller (Eds.), *The Foucault effect: Studies in governmentality* (pp. 87–104) Chicago: University of Chicago Press.

Garfinkel, H. (1967). *Studies in ethnomethodology.* Englewood Cliffs, NJ: Prentice Hall.

Giddens, A. (1990). *The consequences of modernity.* Cambridge, UK: Polity Press.

Giddens, A. (1991). *Modernity and self-identity: Self and society in the late modern age.* Cambridge, MA: Polity Press.

Giddens, A. (1994). Living in a post-traditional society. In U. Beck, A. Giddens, & S. Lash (Eds.), *Reflexive modernization: Politics, tradition and aesthetics in the modern Social Order* (pp. 56–109) Stanford, CA: Stanford University Press.

Gow, G. (2004). Translocations of affirmation: Mediascapes and cultural flows among the stateless Oromo. *International Journal of Cultural Studies, 7*(3), 301–319.

Hall, S. (1992). The question of cultural identity. In S. Hall, D. Held, & T. McGrew (Eds.), *Modernity and its futures* (pp. 273–325) Cambridge, UK: Polity Press.

Hannerz, U. (1987). The world in creolization. *Africa, 57*(4), 546.

Hannerz, U. (1996). *Transnational connections: Culture, people, places.* London: Routledge.

Harvey, D. (1989). *The condition of postmodernity: An enquiry into the origins of cultural change.* Oxford, UK: Blackwell.

Held, D., McGrew, A., Goldblatt, D., & Perraton, J. (1999). *Global transformations: Politics, economics and culture.* Stanford, CA: Stanford University Press.

Holstein, J. A., & Gubrium, J. F. (2000). *The self we live by: Narrative identity in a postmodern world.* New York: Oxford University Press.

Holton, R. J. (1998). *Globalization and the nation-state.* Basingstoke, UK: Macmillan Press.

Huntington, S. P. (2002). *The clash of civilizations and the remaking of world order.* London: Free Press.

Keeley, J. F. (1990). Toward a Foucauldian analysis of international regimes. *International Organization, 44*(1), 83–105.

Kelly, P. F. (1999). The geographies and politics of globalization. *Progress in Human Geography, 23*(3), 379–400.

Kiely, R. (2005). Globalization and poverty, and the poverty of globalization theory. *Current Sociology, 53*(6), 895.

Kjeldgaard, D. (2003). Youth identities in the global cultural economy: Central and peripheral consumer culture in Denmark and Greenland. *European Journal of Cultural Studies, 6*(3), 285–304.

Lyotard, J. F. (1984). *The postmodern condition: A report on knowledge.* Minneapolis: University of Minnesota Press.

Marcus, G. E. (1992). Past, present and emergent identities: Requirements for ethnographies of late twentieth century modernity worldwide. In S. Lash & J. Friedman (Eds.), *Modernity and identity* (pp. 309–330) Oxford, UK: Blackwell.

Martin, L. L., & Simmons, B., A. (1998). Theories and empirical studies of international institutions. *International Organization, 52*(4), 729–757.

Merlingen, M. (2003). Governmentality: Towards a Foucauldian framework for the study of IGOs. *Cooperation and Conflict, 38*(4), 361–384.

Olesen, T. (2005). The uses and misuses of globalization in the study of social movements. *Social Movement Studies, 4*(1), 49–63.

Parsons, T. (1951). *The social system.* Glencoe, IL: Free Press.

Parsons, T. (1966). *Societies: Evolutionary and comparative perspectives.* Englewood Cliffs, NJ: Prentice Hall.

Qureshi, K., & Moores, S. (1999). Identity remix: Tradition and translation in the lives of young Pakistani Scots. *European Journal of Cultural Studies, 2*(3), 311–330.

Ritzer, G. (1996). *The McDonaldization of society: An investigation into the changing character of contemporary social life.* Thousand Oaks, CA: Pine Forge Press.

Ritzer, G. (1998). *The McDonaldization thesis: Explorations and extensions.* London: Sage.

Robertson, R. (1992). *Globalization: Social theory and global culture.* London: Sage.

Rose, N. (1996). *Inventing our selves: Psychology, power,*

and personhood. Cambridge, UK: Cambridge University Press.

Rose, N., & Miller, P. (1992). Political power beyond the state: Problematics of government. *British Journal of Sociology, 43*(2), 173–205.

Rosenberg, J. (2005). Globalization theory: A post mortem. *International Politics, 42*(1), 2–74.

Saul, J. R. (1995). *The unconscious civilization*. Concord, Ontario, Canada: House of Anansi Press.

Schmidt, J. (2003). Paradise lost?: Social change and *Fa'afafine* in Samoa. *Current Sociology, 51*(3–4), 417–432.

Shils, E. (1963). The contemplation of society in America. In A. M. Schlesinger & M. G. White (Eds.), *Paths of American thought* (pp. 392–410) Boston: Houghton Mifflin.

Snow, D. A., & Benford, R., D. (1988). Ideology, frame resonance, and participant mobilization. In B. Klandermans, H. Kriesi, & S. Tarrow (Eds.), *From structure to action: Comparing social movement research across cultures* (pp. 197–217). Greenwich, CT: JAI Press.

Snow, D. A., Rochford, E. B. J., Worden, S. K., & Benford, R. D. (1986). Frame alignment processes, micromobilization, and movement participation. *American Sociological Review, 51*(4), 464–481.

Spich, R. S. (1995). Globalization folklore: Problems of myth and ideology in the discourse on globalization. *Journal of Organizational Change Management, 8*(4), 6–29.

Steingard, D. S., & Fitzgibbons, D. E. (1995). Challenging the juggernaut of globalization: A manifesto for academic praxis. *Journal of Organizational Change Management, 8*(4), 30–54.

Stoddard, E., & Cornwell, G. H. (1999). Cosmopolitan or mongrel?: Creolite, hybridity and "Douglarisation" in Trinidad. *European Journal of Cultural Studies, 2*(3), 331–353.

Thussu, D. K. (1998). *Electronic empires: Global media and local resistance*. London: Arnold.

Tomlinson, J. (1999). *Globalization and culture*. Chicago: University of Chicago Press.

Wieder, D. L. (1988). From resource to topic: Some aims of conversation analysis. In J. A. Anderson (Ed.), *Communication yearbook 11* (pp. 444–454) Beverly Hills, CA: Sage.

Young, R. (1995). *Colonial desire: Hybridity in theory, culture, and race*. London: Routledge.

Author Index

Subject Index

Page numbers followed by *f* indicate figure; *n*, note; and *t*, table.

About the Editors

James A. Holstein (PhD, University of Michigan) is Professor of Sociology in the Department of Social and Cultural Sciences at Marquette University. His research and writing projects have addressed social problems, deviance and social control, family, and the self—all approached from an ethnomethodologically informed, constructionist perspective. Dr. Holstein's books include *Court-Ordered Insanity: Interpretive Practice and Involuntary Commitment* (1993, Aldine de Gruyter) and, with Gale Miller, *Reconsidering Social Constructionism: Debates in Social Problems Theory* (1993, Aldine de Gruyter), *Dispute Domains and Welfare Claims: Conflict and Law in Public Bureaucracies* (1996, JAI Press), and *Challenges and Choices: Constructionist Perspectives on Social Problems* (2003, Aldine de Gruyter).

Jaber F. Gubrium (PhD, Wayne State University) is Professor and Chair of Sociology at the University of Missouri–Columbia. He has had a long-standing program of research on the social organization of care in human services institutions and pioneered in the reconceptualization of qualitative methods and the development of narrative analysis. Dr. Gubrium's publications include *Living and Dying at Murray Manor* (1997, University Press of Virginia), *Speaking of Life: Horizons of Meaning for Nursing Home Residents* (1993, Aldine de Gruyter), and *Out of Control: Family Therapy and Domestic Disorder* (1992, Sage). He has also published numerous articles on aging, the life course, medicalization, and representational practice in therapeutic context.

As collaborators for 20 years, Drs. Holstein and Gubrium have developed a distinctive constructionist approach to everyday life in a variety of projects, including *What is Family?* (1990, Mayfield), *Constructing the Life Course* (2000, Rowman & Littlefield), *The Self We Live By* (2000, Oxford University Press), *Institutional Selves* (2001, Oxford University Press), and *Inner Lives and Social Worlds* (2003, Oxford University Press). They have outlined the conceptual, theoretical, and methodological implications of their approach in several other texts, including *The New Language of Qualitative Method* (1997, Oxford University Press), *The Active Interview* (1995, Sage), and *The Handbook of Interview Research* (2002, Sage). Their most recent work brings a new perspective to narrative studies in *Analyzing Narrative Reality* (forthcoming).

Contributors

Pertti Alasuutari, PhD, is Professor of Sociology and Director of the International School of Social Sciences at the University of Tampere, in Finland. He is editor of the *European Journal of Cultural Studies* and has published widely in the areas of cultural and media studies and qualitative methods. Dr. Alasuutari's books include *Desire and Craving: A Cultural Theory of Alcoholism* (1992, State University of New York Press), *Researching Culture: Qualitative Method and Cultural Studies* (1995, Sage), *An Invitation to Social Research* (1998, Sage), *Rethinking the Media Audience* (1999, Sage), and *Social Theory and Human Reality* (2004, Sage).

Vered Amit, PhD, is Professor of Anthropology at Concordia University. She is the author or editor of 10 books, including, most recently, *Going First Class?: New Approaches to Privileged Travel and Movement* (2006, Berghahn Books). Dr. Amit has done fieldwork in London (United Kingdom), Montreal, and Vancouver, as well as the Cayman Islands, and her research has focused on such areas as youth cultures, occupational itinerancy, expatriacy, citizenship, ethnic lobbying, and mobilization. She is currently conducting a study of international student travel as a contemporary rite of passage.

Paul Atkinson, PhD, is Distinguished Research Professor of Sociology at Cardiff University, where he is Co-Director of the ESRC Centre for Economic and Social Aspects of Genomics. His research interests include qualitative methods, biomedical knowledge, and cultural production. Dr. Atkinson's recent books include *Everyday Arias: An Operatic Ethnography* (2006, AltaMira Press) and *Risky Relations* (with Katie Featherstone, Aditya Bharadwaj, and Angus Clarke; 2006, Berg). He is an Academician of the Academy of Social Sciences.

Mitch Berbrier, PhD, is Associate Professor and Chair of the Department of Sociology at the University of Alabama in Huntsville. His research has addressed the intersecting terrain of ethnicity and race, deviance and normality, and social activism and agency. Dr. Berbrier has authored numerous articles in general sociology journals. Currently, he is using the 90-year history of the Cleveland Cultural Gardens in Cleveland, Ohio, to explore the construction of ethnicity and race. He is Chair of the Theory Division of the Society for the Study of Social Problems.

Joel Best, PhD, is Professor of Sociology and Criminal Justice at the University of Delaware. Much of his work concerns the social construction of social problems. Dr. Best's most recent books are *Flavor of the Month: Why Smart People Fall for Fads* (2006, University of California Press) and *Social Problems* (2008, Norton).

Arthur P. Bochner, PhD, is Professor of Communication at the University of South Florida and Vice-President of the National Communication Association. He is coeditor of the Left Coast Press series *Writing Lives: Ethnographic Narratives* and is currently working on a book for the series, *Researchers as Storytellers: The Narrative Turn in Social Science*. Dr. Bochner has published numerous monographs, articles, and book chapters on interpretive social science, narrative, autoethnography, close interpersonal relationships, and social construction.

K. L. Broad, PhD, is Associate Professor in the Department of Sociology and the Center for Women's Studies and Gender Research at the University of Florida. Her research interests are sexualities, social movements, identities, and feminist/qualitative methodology. Dr. Broad's articles about various aspects of interpretive and identity work in the current lesbian, gay, bisexual, and transgender (LGBT) movement in the United States have been published in such journals as *Sociological Quarterly*, *Sociological Perspectives*, *Research in Political Sociology*, and *Journal of Contemporary Ethnography*.

Kathy Charmaz, PhD, is Professor of Sociology and Coordinator of the Faculty Writing Program at Sonoma State University. Her current research and writing projects are in social psychology, qualitative methods, and the sociology of health and illness. Dr. Charmaz's books include *Good Days, Bad Days: The Self in Chronic Illness and Time* (1991, Rutgers University Press) and *Constructing Grounded Theory* (2006, Sage), as well as the forthcoming coedited *Handbook of Grounded Theory* (Sage).

Sara L. Crawley, PhD, is Assistant Professor in the Department of Women's Studies at the University of South Florida. Her research interests are sexualities, gender and queer theories, and feminist/qualitative methodologies. Dr. Crawley's articles center around aspects of interpretive and identity work among LGBT people and performances of the gendered body have been published in such journals as *Sociological Quarterly*, *Gender & Society*, *Hypatia*, and *Journal of Contemporary Ethnography*. Her book *Gendering Bodies* (with Lara J. Foley and Constance L. Shehan; Rowman & Littlefield) is forthcoming.

Jennifer Croissant, PhD, is Associate Professor of Women's Studies at the University of Arizona. She is coauthor of *Science, Technology, and Society: A Sociological Approach* (with Wenda K. Bauchspies and Sal Restivo; 2006, Blackwell) and coeditor of *Degrees of Compromise: Industrial Interests and Academic Values* (with Sal Restivo; 2001, State University of New York Press), and author of many essays in science studies. Dr. Croissant's teaching and research interests are grounded in science, technology, and society, with a focus on body projects, feminist science studies, and social theory. Her current work, on values and epistemology in technology-intensive education, is supported by the National Science Foundation.

Laura L. Ellingson, PhD, is Associate Professor of Communication at Santa Clara University. Her research focuses on feminist theory and gender studies, qualitative methodology, and communication in health care organizations, including interdisciplinary communication, teamwork, and provider–patient communication. Dr. Ellingson is the author of *Communicating in the Clinic: Negotiating Frontstage and Backstage Teamwork* (2005, Hampton Press) and has published articles in several journals. Currently, she is conducting an ethnography of communication in a dialysis clinic and a qualitative study of communication between aunts and their nieces/nephews.

Carolyn Ellis, PhD, is Professor of Communication and Sociology at the University of South Florida. She is interested in interpretive and artistic representations of qualitative research, in particular, autoethnographic narratives. Two of Dr. Ellis's books are *Final Negotiations: A Story of Love, Loss, and Chronic Illness* (1995, Temple University Press) and *The Ethnographic I: A Methodological Novel about Autoethnography* (2004, AltaMira Press).

James D. Faubion, PhD, is Professor and Chair of Anthropology at Rice University. His publications include *The Shadows and Lights of Waco: Millennialism Today* (2001, Princeton University Press) and *Modern Greek Lessons: A Primer in Historical Constructivism* (1993, Princeton University Press). Dr. Faubion is also the editor of the second and third volumes of *Essential Works of Michel Foucault, 1954–1984* (1997–2000, New Press) and of *The Ethics of Kinship: Ethnographic Inquiries* (2001, Rowman & Littlefield).

Elissa Foster, PhD, is Assistant Professor in the Department of Communication Studies at San José State University. Her research integrates topics in interpersonal relationships and health communication. Dr. Foster's principal area of research is relationships at the end of life, particularly in hospice care, and the application of narrative ethnographic methods to this context. She has published in a number of journals and has written a book, *Communicating at the End of Life: Finding Magic in the Mundane* (2007, Erlbaum).

Kenneth J. Gergen, PhD, is Senior Research Professor in the Department of Psychology at Swarthmore College and the President of the Board of the Taos Institute, a virtual organization dedicated to the sharing of social constructionist ideas in diverse fields of practice. His primary interests lie in the development of a relational account of human action, the implications for issues of moral relativism, and transformative dialogue. Dr. Gergen's work at the Taos Institute focuses on the extension of social constructionist theory to societal practices. Among his major writings are *Realities and Relationships: Soundings in Social Construction* (1994, Harvard University Press), *The Saturated Self: Dilemmas of Identity in Contemporary Life* (1991, Basic Books), and *An Invitation to Social Construction* (1999, Sage).

Mary M. Gergen, PhD, is Professor Emerita at Penn State University–Delaware County. She has taught in the Department of Psychology and continues to do so in Women's Studies. Dr. Gergen's research interests are at the crossroads of feminist theory and social constructionism. Her most recent book is *Feminist Reconstructions in Psychology: Narrative, Gender, and Performance* (2001, Sage). Dr. Gergen is also a founder and board member of the Taos Institute.

Maggie Gregory, PhD, is a research fellow in the Centre for Economic and Social Aspects of Genomics at Cardiff University, where she is working on a project, funded by the Wellcome Trust, on transgenerational communications about genetic disorders. Her research interests include family narratives, everyday life and the home, qualitative research methods, and the social theory of time and risk.

Jaber F. Gubrium, PhD (see "About the Editors").

Scott R. Harris, PhD, is Associate Professor of Sociology at Saint Louis University. His interests include constructionist theory, interpretive approaches to inequality, and family. Dr. Harris's research has appeared in journals such as *Human Studies* and *Symbolic Interaction*, and in his book *The Meanings of Marital Equality* (2006, State University of

New York Press). He has also edited a special issue of the *Journal of Contemporary Ethnography* on "Social Constructionism and Social Inequality."

Alexa Hepburn, PhD, is Senior Lecturer in Social Psychology in the Social Sciences Department at Loughborough University. She has studied school bullying, issues of gender, violence against children, and interaction on child protection helplines, as well as writing about the relations of the philosophy of Derrida to the theory and practice of social psychology. Dr. Hepburn has two recent books: *An Introduction to Critical Social Psychology* (2003, Sage) and *Discursive Research in Practice: New Approaches to Psychology and Interaction* (with Sally Wiggins; 2007, Cambridge University Press). She has also recently coedited a special issue of *Discourse & Society* on developments in discursive psychology.

James A. Holstein, PhD (see "About the Editors").

Dian Marie Hosking, PhD, is Professor in Relational Processes at Utrecht University School of Governance, The Netherlands. Her research interests include social constructionism and its implications for organizational and community development, theories of organizing, leadership processes, and approaches to inquiry. Dr. Hosking's publications include *A Social Psychology of Organizing: People, Processes, and Contexts* (with Ian E. Morley; 1991, Harvester Wheatsheaf) and *Management and Organization: Relational Alternatives to Individualism* (edited with H. Peter Dachler and Kenneth J. Gergen; 1995, Avebury).

Peter R. Ibarra, PhD, is Associate Professor in the Department of Sociology at Syracuse University. He has written about social problems theory, popular culture, deviance, qualitative research methods, technology and domestic violence, and the internal social dynamics of urban neighborhoods. Dr. Ibarra's most recent articles appear in *British Journal of Criminology*; *Sociology of Crime, Law, and Deviance*; and *Behavioral Sciences and the Law*. His current writing projects include a coauthored urban ethnography of neighborhoods in Hollywood, California.

Helen Ingram, PhD, is Warmington Chair of Social Ecology at the University of California, Irvine, where she holds joint appointments in three departments: Planning, Policy, and Design; Political Science; and Criminology Law and Society. She specializes in public policy theory, and has authored many books and articles on social constructions and public policy. Dr. Ingram's other major area of interest is environmental policy, especially as related to water resources.

Kara Jackson, PhD, is a Research Associate in the Department of Teaching and Learning at the Peabody College of Education at Vanderbilt University. Her research interests include understanding individuals' learning of mathematics as constituted, in part, by processes of socialization and social identification within and across in- and out-of-school contexts.

Mirka Koro-Ljungberg, PhD, is Associate Professor in the Department of Educational Psychology at the University of Florida. Prior to joining the faculty at the University of Florida, she spent 3 years as a visiting scholar at the University of Georgia. Currently, Dr. Koro-Ljungberg's research interests focus on the conceptual and theoretical foundations of qualitative inquiry as well as on the implementation of qualitative methods in various empirical settings. Her recent publications appear in *International Journal of Qualitative Studies in Education, Qualitative Inquiry, Social Science and Medicine*, and *Qualitative Research*, among others.

Margarethe Kusenbach, PhD, is Assistant Professor of Sociology at the University of South Florida. Her research interests lie in the areas of urban and community sociology, the sociology of emotions, and qualitative methodology. Her current research focuses on community resources and disaster resilience in Florida mobile home parks. She has published papers in *Symbolic Interaction, Studies in Symbolic Interaction*, and *Ethnography*. A coauthored book reporting on a team study of urban neighborhoods in Los Angeles is in progress.

Joanna Latimer, PhD, is Reader at the School of Social Sciences at Cardiff University, where she teaches the social study of medicine, anthropology, and social theory. As well as many articles in medical sociology, culture, and social theory, she has published monographs on the clinic (*The Conduct of Care: Understanding Nursing Practice* [2000, Blackwell]), the family (*Women in Transition* [2003, Policy Press]), and methodology (*Advanced Qualitative Research for Nursing* [2003, Blackwell]). Dr. Latimer is a member of the Economic and Social Research Council's Centre for the Economic and Social Aspects of Genomics at Cardiff and Lancaster Universities (CESAGen), Faculty Fellow of Manchester University's School of Health and Medicine, Chair of the Cardiff University Medicine and Society Research Interest Group (MASRIG), and on the editorial boards of *Sociological Review* and *Gender, Work, and Organisation*.

Annulla Linders, PhD, is Associate Professor of Sociology at the University of Cincinnati. Her research interests include comparative–historical sociology, social movements, social problems, moral politics, and culture. Dr. Linders's Publications include "Victory and Beyond: A Historical Comparative Analysis of the Outcomes of the Abortion Movements in Sweden and the United States," published in *Sociological Forum* (2004), and "The Execution Spectacle and State Legitimacy: The Changing Nature of the American Execution Audience, 1833–1937," published in *Law and Society Review* (2002).

Judith Lorber, PhD, is Professor Emerita of Sociology and Women's Studies at Brooklyn College and the Graduate Center, City University of New York. Her areas of work focus on gender issues and feminism. Dr. Lorber is the author of *Breaking the Bowls: Degendering and Feminist Change* (2005, Norton), *Gender Inequality: Feminist Theories and Politics* (3rd ed., 2005, Oxford University Press), and *Paradoxes of Gender* (1994, Yale University Press) and coauthor (with Lisa Jean Moore) of *Gendered Bodies: Feminist Perspectives* (2007, Oxford University Press) and *Gender and the Social Construction of Illness* (2nd ed., 2002, Rowman & Littlefield). She is also coeditor of the *Handbook of Gender and Women's Studies* (with Kathy Davis and Mary Evans; 2006, Sage) and *Revisioning Gender* (with Myra Marx Ferree and Beth B. Hess; 1999, Sage). She is also founding editor of the journal *Gender & Society*.

Donileen R. Loseke, PhD, is Professor and Graduate Director in the Department of Sociology at the University of South Florida. Her research interests include the construction of social problems, identity, and emotion. Dr. Loseke's books include *The Battered Woman and Shelters: The Social Construction of Wife Abuse* (1992, State University of New York Press), *Thinking about Social Problems: An Introduction to Constructionist Perspectives* (2003, Aldine de Gruyter), *Current Controversies on Family Violence* (with Richard J. Gelles and Mary M. Cavanaugh; 2005, Sage), and *Social Problems: Constructionist Readings* (with Joel Best; 2003, Aldine de Gruyter).

Kathleen S. Lowney, PhD, is Professor of Sociology and Graduate Coordinator at Valdosta State University. Her research interests include analyzing the intersections of professional wrestling and daytime soap operas; the study of new religious movements, especially Satanism; how the media construct social problems such as stalking; and narratives about multiple personality disorder/dissociative identity disorder. Dr. Lowney's most recent book is *Baring Our Souls: TV Talk Shows and the Religion of Recovery* (1999, Aldine de Gruyter).

Michael Lynch, PhD, is Professor and Director of Graduate Studies in the Department of Science and Technology Studies at Cornell University. His books and articles take an ethnomethodological approach to discourse and practical actions in research laboratories, clinical case conferences, criminal courts, and government tribunals. Dr. Lynch's current research examines the interplay between law and science in criminal cases involving DNA evidence, and is the basis for the forthcoming book (with Simon Cole, Ruth McNally, and Kathleen Jordan) *Truth Machine: The Contentious History of DNA Profiling*. He is editor of the journal *Social Studies of Science*, and president of the Society for Social Studies of Science.

George E. Marcus, PhD, was for 25 years Chair of the Department of Anthropology at Rice University. During that period, he coedited (with James Clifford) *Writing Culture* (1986, University of California Press), coauthored (with Michael Fischer) *Anthropology as Cultural Critique* (1999, University of Chicago Press), inaugurated the journal *Cultural Anthropology*, published *Ethnography Through Thick and Thin* (1998, Princeton University Press), and, through the 1990s, created and edited a *fin-de-siècle* series of annuals, *Late Editions*. Dr. Marcus's most recent book (with Fernando Mascarenhas) is *Ocasião: The Marquis and the Anthropologist, a Collaboration* (2005, AltaMira Press). In 2005, he moved to the University of California, Irvine, as Chancellor's Professor, and founded the Center for Ethnography, dedicated to examining the vulnerabilities and possibilities of this venerable technology of knowledge making.

Barbara L. Marshall, PhD, is Professor of Sociology at Trent University in Peterborough, Ontario, Canada. Her research interests include feminist and sociological theory, gender, sexuality, the body, and biomedical technologies. Dr. Marshall's books include *Engendering Modernity: Feminism, Social Theory, and Social Change* (1994, Northeastern University Press), *Configuring Gender: Explorations in Theory and Politics* (2000, Broadview Press), *Engendering the Social: Feminist Encounters with Sociological Theory* (edited with Anne Witz; 2004, Open University Press), and the *Encyclopedia of Social Theory* (edited with Austin Harrington and Hans-Peter Müller; 2006, Routledge).

Amir Marvasti, PhD, is Assistant Professor of Sociology at Penn State University–Altoona. His research focuses on the social construction of deviant identities in everyday life. He is the author of *Being Homeless: Textual and Narrative Constructions* (2003, Lexington Books), *Qualitative Research in Sociology* (2004, Sage), and *Middle Eastern Lives in America* (with Karyn D. McKinney; 2004, Rowman & Littlefield). Dr. Marvasti's articles have been published in the *Journal of Contemporary Ethnography*, *Qualitative Inquiry*, and *Symbolic Interaction*.

Liza McCoy, PhD, is Assistant Professor in the Department of Sociology at the University of Calgary. Her broad area of specialization is the social organization of knowledge, which she has explored through institutional ethnographic studies in the fields of health, public-sector restructuring, and immigration.

Gale Miller, PhD, is Professor of Sociology and Research Professor of Social and Cultural Sciences at Marquette University. His scholarly interests include interpretive sociologies, qualitative methods, language use in human service organizations, and the sociology of coping. Dr. Miller's publications include *Becoming Miracle Workers: Language and Meaning in Brief Therapy* (1997, Aldine de Gruyter), *Enforcing the Work Ethic: Rhetoric and Everyday Life in a Work Incentive Program* (1991, State University of New York Press), and *Constructionist Controversies: Issues in Social Problems Theory* (with James A. Holstein; 1993, Aldine de Gruyter).

Leslie Miller, PhD, is Associate Professor of Sociology at the University of Calgary. Her areas of interest are feminist theory, the sociology of the body, gender relations, and the sociology of families, employing a discursive–analytic approach. Publications include "The Poverty of Truth-Seeking: Postmodernism, Discourse Analysis and Critical Feminism" (in *Theory and Psychology*) and "Claims-Making from the Underside: Marginalization and Social Problems Analysis" (in *Challenges and Choices: Constructionist Perspectives on Social Problems* [edited by James A. Holstein & Gale Miller]; 2003, Aldine de Gruyter).

Pirjo Nikander, PhD, is Assistant Professor in the Department of Sociology and Social Psychology at the University of Tampere, in Finland. Her research interests include the analysis of institutional interaction, decision making in the workplace, age identities and ageism, and moral discourse.

Stephen Pfohl, PhD, is Professor of Sociology at Boston College, where he teaches courses on social theory; postmodern culture; crime, deviance, and social control; images and power; and sociology and psychoanalysis. He is the author of numerous books and articles, including *Death at the Parasite Café: Social Science (Fictions) and the Postmodern* (1992, St. Martin's Press) and *Images of Deviance and Social Control: A Sociological History* (2nd ed., 1994, McGraw-Hill). Dr. Pfohl is also coeditor of *Culture, Power, and History: Studies in Critical Sociology* (with Aimee Van Wagenen, Patricia Arend, Abigail Brooks, and Denise Leckenby; 2006, Brill). He is a past president of the Society for the Study of Social Problems and a founding member of Sit-Com International, a Boston-area collective of activists and artists.

Jonathan Potter, PhD, is Professor of Discourse Analysis in the Department of Social Sciences at Loughborough University. He has written on constructionism, discourse analysis and discursive psychology, cognitivism, psychology and institutions, child protection, relativism, racism, science, method, and reality. Recent books include *Representing Reality: Discourse, Rhetoric and Social Construction* (1996, Sage), *Focus Group Practice* (with Claudia Puchta; 2004, Sage), and *Conversation and Cognition* (with Hedwig te Molder; 2005, Cambridge University Press).

Sal Restivo, PhD, is Professor of Sociology, Science Studies, and Information Technology in the Department of Science and Technology Studies and the IT Program at Rensselaer Polytechnic Institute, and Special Professor at Nottingham University (United Kingdom). He has written and lectured on the sociology and anthropology of science, math, and mind for more than 40 years. Dr. Restivo is most recently the editor-in-chief of *Science, Technology, and Society: An Encyclopedia* (2005, Oxford University Press) and coauthor of *Science, Technology, and Society: A Sociological Approach* (with Wenda K. Bauchspies and Jennifer Croissant; 2006, Blackwell).

Dalvir Samra-Fredericks, PhD, teaches in the Department of Human Resource Management at Nottingham Trent University. Her areas of research include organizational theory and organization behavior, particularly discourse, talk, and interaction in organizations.

Anne L. Schneider, PhD, is Professor of Justice and Social Inquiry at Arizona State University. Her primary interests are in public policy's role in solving (or exacerbating) public problems, particularly questions of the role of policy in enhancing social justice and quality of life. With Helen Ingram, Dr. Schneider is the author of *Policy Design for Democracy* (1997, University Press of Kansas) and *Deserving and Entitled: Social Constructions and Public Policy* (2005, State University of New York Press). She is also the author of *Deterrence and Juvenile Crime: Results of a National Policy Experiment* (1990, Springer-Verlag) as well as journal articles focusing on social constructions, public policy, policy change, and democracy.

Joseph Schneider, PhD, is the Ellis and Nelle Levitt Professor of Sociology in the Department for the Study of Culture and Society at Drake University. He has written on the medicalization of deviance, the experience of illness, constructionist theory, family caregiving in China, postmodern ethnography, and feminist science studies. Dr. Schneider's books include, among others, *Deviance and Medicalization: From Badness to Sickness* (with Peter Conrad; 1992, Temple University Press), *Giving Care, Writing Self: A New Ethnography* (with Wang Laihua; 2000, Peter Lang), and *Donna Haraway: Live Theory* (2005, Continuum).

Brett Smith, PhD, is a Lecturer in Qualitative Research in the School of Sport and Health Sciences, University of Exeter. His research interests include disability and the body, the storied construction of embodied depression, and narrative theory. Dr. Smith has published in a variety of journals, such as *Time and Society* and *Qualitative Research*. This work has spanned the genres of autoethnography, realist tales, fiction, poetic representations, and scientific tales.

Andrew C. Sparkes, PhD, is Professor of Social Theory and Director of the Qualitative Research Unit in the School of Sport and Health Sciences, University of Exeter. His research interests include performing bodies, identities, and selves; interrupted body projects and the narrative reconstruction of self; sporting auto/biographies; and the lives of marginalized individuals and groups. Dr. Sparkes is drawn toward qualitative methodologies as a way of exploring these interests and seeks to represent his findings using multiple genres. His books include *Telling Tales in Sport and Physical Activity: A Qualitative Journey* (2002, Human Kinetics).

Bo Stråth, PhD, is Academy of Finland Distinguished Professor of Nordic, European, and World History at Helsinki University. He was Professor of Contemporary History at the European University Institute in Florence from 1997 to 2007 and Professor of History at Gothenburg University from 1990 until 1996. Dr. Stråth's research focus is on the modernity of Europe in global comparison, and he has published widely in this area. His works include *Europe and the Other and Europe as the Other* (with James Kaye; 2000, Peter Lang), *Myth and Memory in the Construction of Community: Historical Patterns in Europe and Beyond* (2000, Peter Lang), and *Reflections on Europe: Defining a Political Order in Time and Space* (with Hans-Ake Persson; 2007, Peter Lang).

Tom Strong, PhD, teaches for the Division of Applied Psychology at the University of Calgary and Massey University's Post-Graduate Program in Discursive Therapies. His